Children's
Literature
Review

Guide to Gale Literary Criticism Series

For criticism on	Consult these Gale series
Authors now living or who died after December 31, 1959	*CONTEMPORARY LITERARY CRITICISM (CLC)*
Authors who died between 1900 and 1959	*TWENTIETH-CENTURY LITERARY CRITICISM (TCLC)*
Authors who died between 1800 and 1899	*NINETEENTH-CENTURY LITERATURE CRITICISM (NCLC)*
Authors who died between 1400 and 1799	*LITERATURE CRITICISM FROM 1400 TO 1800 (LC)* *SHAKESPEAREAN CRITICISM (SC)*
Authors who died before 1400	*CLASSICAL AND MEDIEVAL LITERATURE CRITICISM (CMLC)*
Authors of books for children and young adults	*CHILDREN'S LITERATURE REVIEW (CLR)*
Dramatists	*DRAMA CRITICISM (DC)*
Poets	*POETRY CRITICISM (PC)*
Short story writers	*SHORT STORY CRITICISM (SSC)*
Black writers of the past two hundred years	*BLACK LITERATURE CRITICISM (BLC)*
Hispanic writers of the late nineteenth and twentieth centuries	*HISPANIC LITERATURE CRITICISM (HLC)*
Native North American writers and orators of the eighteenth, nineteenth, and twentieth centuries	*NATIVE NORTH AMERICAN LITERATURE (NNAL)*
Major authors from the Renaissance to the present	*WORLD LITERATURE CRITICISM, 1500 TO THE PRESENT (WLC)*

ISSN 0362-4145

volume 48

Children's Literature Review

Excerpts from Reviews,
Criticism, and Commentary
on Books for Children
and Young People

Alan Hedblad
Thomas McMahon
Editors

DETROIT • NEW YORK • LONDON

STAFF

Alan Hedblad, Thomas McMahon, *Editors*

Deron Albright, Linda R. Andres, Cindy Buck, Sheryl Ciccarelli, Melissa Hill, Motoko Fujishiro
Huthwaite, Paul Loeber, Carolyn C. March, Bonnie Reidinger, Gerard J. Senick, Stephen Thor Tschirhart,
Crystal A. Towns, Martha Urbiel, Kathleen L. Witman, *Contributing Editors*

Joyce Nakamura, *Managing Editor*

Susan M. Trosky, *Permissions Manager*
Maria L. Franklin, *Permissions Specialist*
Michele M. Lonoconus, *Permissions Associate*
Andrea D. Grady, *Permissions Assistant*

Victoria B. Cariappa, *Research Manager*
Norma Sawaya, *Project Coordinator*
Tamara C. Nott, Tracie A. Richardson, Cheryl L. Warnock,
Robert Whaley, *Research Associates*

Mary Beth Trimper, *Production Director*
Deborah Milliken, *Production Assistant*

Gary Leach, *Desktop Publisher*
Randy Bassett, *Image Database Supervisor*
Robert Duncan, Michael Logusz, *Scanner Operator*
Pamela A. Reed, *Photography Coordinator*

The paper used in this publication meets the minimum requirements of American National Standard for Information Sciences—Permanence Paper for Printed Library Materials, ANSI Z39.48-1984.

Library of Congress Catalog Card Number 76-643301
ISBN 0-7876-2025-4
ISSN 0362-4145
Printed in the United States of America

10 9 8 7 6 5 4 3 2 1

Contents

Preface   vii
Acknowledgments   xi

Lloyd Alexander 1924- 1
American author of fiction and nonfiction; major works include The High King *(1968)*
and The Fortune-Tellers *(1992)*.

Pat Cummings 1950- 31
American author and illustrator of fiction and picture books; major works include
C.L.O.U.D.S. *(1986) and* Carousel *(1994)*.

Lensey Namioka 1929- 58
Chinese American author of fiction; major works include The Samurai and the Long-
Nosed Devils *(1976) and* Yang the Youngest and His Terrible Ear *(1992)*.

Doris Orgel 1929- 70
Viennese-born American author and translator of fiction and verse; major works include
The Devil in Vienna *(1978) and* Ariadne, Awake! *(1994)*.

Dav Pilkey 1966- 99
American author and illustrator of picture books; major works include When Cats Dream
(1992) and The Paperboy *(1996)*.

Marilyn Singer 1948- 115
American author of fiction, nonfiction, poetry, and picture books; major works include
It Can't Hurt Forever *(1978) and* Turtle in July *(1989)*.

Cynthia Voigt 1942- 148
American author of fiction and picture books; major works include Dicey's Song *(1982)*
and When She Hollers *(1994)*.

Barbara Williams 1925- 187
American author of fiction, nonfiction, and plays; major works include Albert's Toothache
(1974) and Chester Chipmunk's Thanksgiving *(1978)*.

Cumulative Index to Authors   211
Cumulative Index to Nationalities   227
Cumulative Index to Titles   233

Preface

Literature for children and young adults has evolved into both a respected branch of creative writing and a successful industry. Currently, books for young readers are considered among the most popular segments of publishing. Criticism of juvenile literature is instrumental in recording the literary or artistic development of the creators of children's books as well as the trends and controversies that result from changing values or attitudes about young people and their literature. Designed to provide a permanent, accessible record of this ongoing scholarship, *Children's Literature Review (CLR)* presents parents, teachers, and librarians—those responsible for bringing children and books together—with the opportunity to make informed choices when selecting reading materials for the young. In addition, *CLR* provides researchers of children's literature with easy access to a wide variety of critical information from English-language sources in the field. Users will find balanced overviews of the careers of the authors and illustrators of the books that children and young adults are reading; these entries, which contain excerpts from published criticism in books and periodicals, assist users by sparking ideas for papers and assignments and suggesting supplementary and classroom reading. Ann L. Kalkhoff, president and editor of *Children's Book Review Service Inc.,* writes that "*CLR* has filled a gap in the field of children's books, and it is one series that will never lose its validity or importance."

Scope of the Series

Each volume of *CLR* profiles the careers of a selection of authors and illustrators of books for children and young adults from preschool through high school. Author lists in each volume reflect:

- an international scope.

- representation of authors of all eras.

- the variety of genres covered by children's and/or YA literature: picture books, fiction, nonfiction, poetry, folklore, and drama.

Although the focus of the series is on authors new to *CLR*, entries will be updated as the need arises.

Organization of This Book

An entry consists of the following elements: author heading, author portrait, author introduction, excerpts of criticism (each preceded by a bibliographical citation), and illustrations, when available.

- The **Author Heading** consists of the author's name followed by birth and death dates. The portion of the name outside the parentheses denotes the form under which the author is most frequently published. If the majority of the author's works for children were written under a pseudonym, the pseudonym will be listed in the author heading and the real name given on the first line of the author introduction. Also located at the beginning of the introduction are any other pseudonyms used by the author in writing for children and any name variations, including transliterated forms for authors whose languages use nonroman alphabets. Uncertainty as to a birth or death date is indicated by question marks.

- An **Author Portrait** is included when available.

- The **Author Introduction** contains information designed to introduce an author to *CLR* users by presenting an overview of the author's themes and styles, biographical facts that relate to the author's literary career or critical responses to the author's works, and information about major awards and prizes the author has received. The introduction begins by identifying the nationality of the author and by listing the genres in which s/he has written for children and young adults. Introductions also list a group of representative titles for which the author or illustrator being profiled is best known; this section, which begins with the words "major works include," follows the genre line of the introduction. For seminal figures, a listing of major works about the author follows when appropriate, highlighting important biographies about the author or illustrator that are not excerpted in the entry. The centered heading "Introduction" announces the body of the text.

- **Criticism** is located in three sections: **Author's Commentary** (when available), **General Commentary** (when available), and **Title Commentary** (commentary on specific titles).

  - The **Author's Commentary** presents background material written by the author or by an interviewer. This commentary may cover a specific work or several works. Author's commentary on more than one work appears after the author introduction, while commentary on an individual book follows the title entry heading.

  - The **General Commentary** consists of critical excerpts that consider more than one work by the author or illustrator being profiled. General commentary is preceded by the critic's name in boldface type or, in the case of unsigned criticism, by the title of the journal. *CLR* also features entries that emphasize general criticism on the oeuvre of an author or illustrator. When appropriate, a selection of reviews is included to supplement the general commentary.

  - The **Title Commentary** begins with the title entry headings, which precede the criticism on a title and cite publication information on the work being reviewed. Title headings list the title of the work as it appeared in its first English-language edition. The first English-language publication date of each work (unless otherwise noted) is listed in parentheses following the title. Differing U.S. and British titles follow the publication date within the parentheses. When a work is written by an individual other than the one being profiled, as is the case when illustrators are featured, the parenthetical material following the title cites the author of the work before listing its publication date.

    Entries in each title commentary section consist of critical excerpts on the author's individual works, arranged chronologically by publication date. The entries generally contain two to seven reviews per title, depending on the stature of the book and the amount of criticism it has generated. The editors select titles that reflect the entire scope of the author's literary contribution, covering each genre and subject. An effort is made to reprint criticism that represents the full range of each title's reception, from the year of its initial publication to current assessments. Thus, the reader is provided with a record of the author's critical history. Publication information (such as publisher names and book prices) and parenthetical numerical references (such as footnotes or page and line references to specific editions of works) have been deleted at the discretion of the editors to provide smoother reading of the text.

- Centered headings introduce each section, in which criticism is arranged chronologically; beginning with Volume 35, each excerpt is preceded by a boldface source heading for easier access by readers. Within the text, titles by authors being profiled are also highlighted in boldface type.

- Selected excerpts are preceded by **Explanatory Annotations,** which provide information on the critic or work of criticism to enhance the reader's understanding of the excerpt.

- A complete **Bibliographical Citation** designed to facilitate the location of the original book or article precedes each piece of criticism.

- Numerous **Illustrations** are featured in *CLR*. For entries on illustrators, an effort has been made to include illustrations that reflect the characteristics discussed in the criticism. Entries on authors who do not illustrate their own works may also include photographs and other illustrative material pertinent to their careers.

Special Features: Entries on Illustrators

Entries on authors who are also illustrators will occasionally feature commentary on selected works illustrated but not written by the author being profiled. These works are strongly associated with the illustrator and have received critical acclaim for their art. By including critical comment on works of this type, the editors wish to provide a more complete representation of the artist's career. Criticism on these works has been chosen to stress artistic, rather than literary, contributions. Title entry headings for works illustrated by the author being profiled are arranged chronologically within the entry by date of publication and include notes identifying the author of the illustrated work. In order to provide easier access for users, all titles illustrated by the subject of the entry are boldfaced.

CLR also includes entries on prominent illustrators who have contributed to the field of children's literature. These entries are designed to represent the development of the illustrator as an artist rather than as a literary stylist. The illustrator's section is organized like that of an author, with two exceptions: the introduction presents an overview of the illustrator's styles and techniques rather than outlining his or her literary background, and the commentary written by the illustrator on his or her works is called "illustrator's commentary" rather than "author's commentary." All titles of books containing illustrations by the artist being profiled are highlighted in boldface type.

Other Features: Acknowledgments, Indexes

- The **Acknowledgments** section, which immediately follows the preface, lists the sources from which material has been reprinted in the volume. It does not, however, list every book or periodical consulted for the volume.

- The **Cumulative Index to Authors** lists all of the authors who have appeared in *CLR* with cross-references to the biographical, autobiographical, and literary criticism series published by Gale Research. A full listing of the series titles appears before the first page of the indexes of this volume.

- The **Cumulative Index to Nationalities** lists authors alphabetically under their respective nationalities. Author names are followed by the volume number(s) in which they appear.

- The **Cumulative Index to Titles** lists titles covered in *CLR* followed by the volume and page number where criticism begins.

A Note to the Reader

CLR is one of several critical references sources in the Literature Criticism Series published by Gale Research. When writing papers, students who quote directly from any volume in the Literature Criticism Series may use the following general forms to footnote reprinted criticism. The first example pertains to material drawn from periodicals, the second to material reprinted from books.

[1]T. S. Eliot, "John Donne," *The Nation and the Athenaeum,* 33 (9 June 1923), 321-32; excerpted and reprinted in *Literature Criticism from 1400 to 1800,* Vol. 10, ed. James E. Person, Jr. (Detroit: Gale Research, 1989), pp. 28-9.

[1]Henry Brooke, *Leslie Brooke and Johnny Crow* (Frederick Warne, 1982); excerpted and reprinted in *Children's Literature Review,* Vol. 20, ed. Gerard J. Senick (Detroit: Gale Research, 1990), p. 47.

Suggestions Are Welcome

In response to various suggestions, several features have been added to *CLR* since the beginning of the series, including author entries on retellers of traditional literature as well as those who have been the first to record oral tales and other folklore; entries on prominent illustrators featuring commentary on their styles and techniques; entries on authors whose works are considered controversial; occasional entries devoted to criticism on a single work or a series of works; sections in author introductions that list major works by and about the author or illustrator being profiled; explanatory notes that provide information on the critic or work of criticism to enhance the usefulness of the excerpt; more extensive illustrative material, such as holographs of manuscript pages and photographs of people and places pertinent to the careers of the authors and artists; a cumulative nationality index for easy access to authors by nationality; and occasional guest essays written specifically for *CLR* by prominent critics on subjects of their choice.

Readers who wish to suggest authors to appear in future volumes, or who have other suggestions, are cordially in-vited to contact the editor. By mail: Editor, *Children's Literature Review,* Gale Research, 835 Penobscot Bldg., 645 Griswold St., Detroit, MI 48226-4094; by telephone: (800) 347-GALE; by fax: (313) 961-6599.

Acknowledgments

The editors wish to thank the copyright holders of the excerpted criticism included in this volume and the permissions managers of many book and magazine publishing companies for assisting us in securing reproduction rights. We are also grateful to the staffs of the Detroit Public Library, the Library of Congress, the University of Detroit Mercy Library, Wayne State University Purdy/Kresge Library Complex, and the University of Michigan Libraries for making their resources available to us. Following is a list of the copyright holders who have granted us permission to reproduce material in this volume of *CLR*. Every effort has been made to trace copyright, but if omissions have been made, please let us know.

COPYRIGHTED EXCERPTS IN *CLR*, VOLUME 48, WERE REPRODUCED FROM THE FOLLOWING PERIODICALS:

The ALAN Review, v. 12, Fall, 1984; v. 19, Fall, 1991. All reproduced by permission. —*Appraisal: Children's Science Books,* v. 9, Fall, 1976; v. 13, Winter, 1980; v. 24, Autumn, 1991. Copyright © 1976, 1980, 1991 by the Children's Science Book Review Committee. All reproduced by permission. —*Archaeology,* v. 34, July-August, 1981. Reproduced by permission. —*Best Sellers,* v. 36, November, 1976; v. 41, June, 1981; v. 41, February, 1982; v. 46, June, 1986. Copyright 1976, 1981, 1982, 1986 by the University of Scranton. All reproduced by permission. —*Booklist,* v. 72, May 1, 1976; v. 72, July 1, 1976; v. 73, January 1, 1977; v. 74, September 15, 1977; v. 74, October 15, 1977; v. 74, February 1, 1978; v. 74, June 15, 1978 ; v. 75, October 15, 1978; v. 75, November 15, 1978; v. 75, December 1, 1978; v. 76, September 15, 1979; v. 76, April 15, 1980; v. 77, November 1, 1980; v. 77, November 15, 1980; v. 77, June 1, 1981; v. 78, November 15, 1981; v. 78, June 1, 1982; v. 79, November 1, 1982; v. 79, September 15, 1982; v. 79, October 1, 1982; v. 79, March 15, 1983; v. 79, May 15, 1983; v. 80, June 15, 1984; v. 80, July, 1984; v. 81, November 1, 1984; v. 81, April 15, 1985; v. 81, June 1, 1985; v. 81, July, 1985; v. 82, September 15, 1985; v. 82, March 15, 1986; v. 82, April 1, 1986; v. 82, June 15, 1986; v. 82, August, 1986; v. 83, February 1, 1987; v. 83, April 1, 1987; v. 84, November 15, 1987; v. 84, February 1, 1988; v. 84, May 1, 1988; v. 85, September 15, 1988; v. 85, December 1, 1988; v. 85, March 15, 1989; v. 85, April 15, 1989; v. 85, May 1, 1989; v. 85, May 15, 1989; v. 85, June 1, 1989; v. 86, October 1, 1989; v. 86, October 15, 1989; v. 86, December 15, 1989; v. 86, January 15, 1990; v. 86, February 15, 1990; v. 86, August, 1990; v. 87, January 1, 1991; v. 87, February 1, 1991; v. 87, February 15, 1991; v. 87, April 1, 1991; v. 87, May 15, 1991; v. 87, July, 1991; v. 88, September 1, 1991; v. 88, February 1, 1992; v. 88, March 1, 1992; v. 88, May 1, 1992; v. 88, July, 1992; v. 88, August, 1992; v. 89, October 15, 1992; v. 89, December 1, 1992; v. 89, March 1, 1993; v. 90, September 1, 1993; v. 90, September 15, 1993; v. 90, December 1, 1993; v. 90, February 1, 1994; v. 90, February 15, 1994; v. 90, March 1, 1994; v. 90, May 1, 1994; v. 90, July, 1994; v. 91, September 1, 1994; v. 91, September 15, 1994 ; v. 91, October 15, 1994; v. 91, January 1, 1995; v. 91, February 1, 1995; v. 91, April 15, 1995; v. 91, May 1, 1995; v. 91, May 15, 1995; v. 91, July, 1995; v. 92, October 1, 1995; v. 92, September 15, 1995; v. 92, February 1, 1996; v. 92, March 1, 1996; v. 92, April 1, 1996; v. 93, October 1, 1996; v. 93, January 1, 1997. Copyright © 1976, 1977, 1978, 1979, 1980, 1981, 1982, 1983, 1984, 1985, 1986, 1987, 1988, 1989, 1990, 1991, 1992, 1993, 1994, 1995, 1996, 1997 by the American Library Association. All reproduced by permission. —*The Booklist,* v. 67, April 15, 1971; v. 69, June 1, 1973; v. 71, September 15, 1974. Copyright © 1971, 1973, 1974 by the American Library Association. All reproduced by permission. —*Books for Keeps,* n. 66, January, 1991. © School Bookshop Association 1991. Reproduced by permission. —*Bulletin of the Center for Children's Books,* v. XVII, November, 1963. Copyright © 1963, renewed 1991 by The University of Chicago. / v. 20, May, 1967; v. 23, December, 1969; v. 23, January, 1970; v. 24, November, 1970; v. 24, December, 1970; v. 24, April, 1971; v. 25, January, 1972; v. 26, January, 1973; v. 28, January, 1975; v. 29, November, 1975; v. 30, January, 1977; v. 32, November, 1978; v. 32, January, 1979; v. 32, July-August, 1979; v. 33, October, 1979; v. 33, February, 1980; v. 34, January, 1981; v. 34, March, 1981; v. 34, April, 1981; v. 36, October, 1982; v. 36, September, 1982; v. 36, January, 1983; v. 36, May, 1983; v. 37, July-August, 1984; v. 37, July-August, 1984; v. 37, May, 1984; v. 38, February, 1985; v. 38, April, 1985; v. 39, October, 1985; v. 39, April, 1986; v. 39, June, 1986; v. 39, July-August, 1986; v. 40, September, 1986; v. 40, October, 1986; v. 40, March, 1987; v. 40, June, 1987; v. 40, July-August, 1987; v. 41, December, 1987; v. 41, June, 1988; v. 42, April, 1989; v. 42, June, 1989; v. 42, July-August, 1989; v. 43, September, 1989; v. 43, March, 1990; v. 43, May, 1990; v. 43, July-August, 1990; v. 44, July-August, 1991; v. 45, November, 1991; v. 45, April, 1992; v. 45, June, 1992; v. 46, September, 1992; v. 46, October, 1992; v. 46, November, 1992; v. 46, February, 1993; v. 46, May, 1993; v. 46, June, 1993; v. 47, September, 1993; v. 47, January, 1994; v. 47, June, 1994; v. 48, July-August, 1995; v. 48, March, 1995; v. 48, May, 1995; v. 49, September, 1995; v. 49, October, 1995; v. 49, December, 1995; v. 49, February, 1996; v. 49, March, 1996; v. 49, April, 1996; v. 50, July-August, 1997; v. 51, December, 1997. Copyright © 1967, 1969, 1970, 1971, 1972, 1973, 1975, 1977, 1978, 1979, 1980, 1981, 1982, 1983, 1984, 1985, 1986, 1987, 1988, 1989, 1990, 1991, 1992, 1994, 1995, 1996, 1997 by The Board of Trustees of the University of Illinois. All reproduced by permission. —*Catholic Library World,* v. 58, July-August, 1986 for "Lloyd Alexander: 1986 Regina Medal Recipient" by Lloyd Alexander. Reproduced by permission of the author. —*Children's Book Review Service, Inc,* v. 25, July, 1997. Reproduced by permission. —*Children's Literature Association Quarterly,* v. 10, Spring, 1985; v. 10, Winter, 1986. Both reproduced by permission. —*Children's Literature in Education,* v. 21, December, 1990 for "Fantasy at Its Best:

Children's
Literature
Review

Lloyd Alexander

1924-

American author of fiction and nonfiction.

Major works include *The High King* (1968), *The Beggar Queen* (1984), *The Jedera Adventure* (1989), *The Remarkable Journey of Prince Jen* (1991), *The Fortune-Tellers* (1992), *The Iron Ring* (1997).

INTRODUCTION

An acknowledged master of twentieth-century fantasy celebrated for his contributions to children's literature, Alexander is best known as the author of series-based high adventure stories that are often rooted in historical fact and legend and explore such universal themes as the opposition of good and evil and the search for self-identity. Among his most acclaimed works are three series of novels published between 1964 and 1990. In the five-book Prydain Chronicles, Alexander relied on the *Mabinogion*—a compilation of Welsh tales that dates to the Middle Ages and is revered as a literary classic—as his main source. Recounting the trials of a young hero named Taran who is tested repeatedly by the forces of evil, the series culminates with *The High King,* which earned Alexander the prestigious Newbery Medal in 1969. Alexander's subsequent series—The Westmark Trilogy, which examines ethical issues related to war while detailing the grand exploits of its hero, Theo, and the Vesper Holly Adventures, featuring the endeavors of a bright, bold teenage heroine—also garnered much praise and a wide readership. Alexander is particularly commended for his ability to craft a tightly woven story—complete with imaginative plot twists, suspenseful situations, and comic characters—while exploring such destructive institutions as war and revealing what is both noble and corrupt within the human spirit. *Horn Book* critic Mary M. Burns has praised Alexander for "his strong sense of story, controlled but not dominated by a substantial theme, and his ability to meld the actual and the imagined into a plausible reality." For Alexander, who has received numerous awards for his novels for young people, the motivation to write fantasy lies in the similarities he sees between imagined worlds and our own. "At heart, the issues raised in a work of fantasy are those we face in real life," he remarked in his Newbery Award acceptance speech published in *Horn Book.* "In whatever guise—our own daily nightmares of war, intolerance, inhumanity; or the struggles of an Assistant Pig-Keeper against the Lord of Death—the problems are agonizingly familiar. An openness to compassion, love, and mercy is as essential to us here and now as it is to any inhabitant of an imaginary kingdom."

Biographical Information

Alexander was born in Philadelphia, Pennsylvania, in 1924.

Because money was scarce during his childhood, his parents having been forced into bankruptcy by the Stock Market Crash of 1929, Alexander turned to books for entertainment, becoming an avid reader of a wide spectrum of authors, including Charles Dickens, and genres, including Greek and Celtic mythology and Welsh tales and legends. At age fifteen, Alexander decided to become a poet, but his father was concerned that he would not be able to earn a sufficient living. A compromise was then reached: Alexander could embark on a writing career as long as he was earning a regular paycheck from a more stable occupation. After high school he accepted a position as a bank messenger to earn money for college tuition; however, when he subsequently enrolled in a local college, he quickly became disenchanted with the quality of his writing courses and discontinued his studies. In search of adventure and writing fodder, Alexander enlisted in the U.S. Army in 1943. He was assigned to military intelligence and traveled with his unit to Wales for combat training. The language, culture, and history of Wales intrigued Alexander, and he would later use that country as the setting for several of his books. After serving for a period as a military interpreter/translator in Paris, he resumed his education, having received a scholarship from the French Foreign Ministry that allowed him to attend the Sorbonne. In 1945 Alexander met Janine Denni, a Parisian, and they married the following year. It was important to Alexander to return to his roots while pursuing a writing career, so the couple soon moved to the United States—to an old farmhouse in Drexel Hill, just outside of Philadelphia. The early 1950s brought little success for Alexander; he wrote three novels, all of which were rejected by publishers, and supported his family by working in various artistic and editorial capacities. In 1955, when Alexander was tempted to give up his writing dreams, his novel *And Let the Credit Go* was accepted for publication. This initial success was followed by other books for adults, each overtly autobiographical, and, in 1963, Alexander's first children's book, *Time Cat: The Remarkable Journeys of Jason and Gareth,* a fantasy that captured his love of ancient Welsh history and mythology. Over the next three decades of his illustrious writing career, Alexander went on to produce an impressive and varied body of works, most notably his acclaimed series the Prydain Chronicles, the Westmark Trilogy, and the Vesper Holly Adventures, as well as other fantasies for children and humorous books for adults.

Major Works

In "The Westmark Trilogy"—comprised of *Westmark* (1981), *The Kestrel* (1982), and *The Beggar Queen*—Alexander explores the political evolution of an imaginary land called Westmark, which bears similarity to both colonial America and feudal Europe. Invoking themes concerning the horrors of revolution, corrupt leadership, and tyranny, these works trace the adventures of Theo, a printer's apprentice who escapes prosecution for the accidental killing of a royal officer and eventually joins a revolutionary group, and Mickle, a young woman from the streets whom Theo befriends and later comes to love. Alexander's final installment in the series, *The Beggar Queen,* reveals that Mickle is Westmark's missing princess, and Theo, in his efforts to restore her to her queenship, becomes embroiled in a war with a neighboring country and is forced to confront issues of loyalty, duty, and the ravages of war. In his "Vesper Holly" series, set in the 1870s, Alexander stages each of five "adventures" in a different locale. His heroine, the savvy, spirited, sixteen-year-old Holly, travels with her guardian, Professor "Brinnie" Garrett, to exotic lands, becoming immersed in situations of mystery and intrigue. The fourth installment, entitled *The Jedera Adventure,* features the advanced vocabulary and sophisticated sentence structure that has become a trademark of Alexander's writing style, while showcasing Holly's resourcefulness and charm in Jedera, North Africa, as she once again outsmarts the evil Dr. Helvitius, the villain of previous novels.

In *The Remarkable Journey of Prince Jen,* Alexander portrays another young hero whose adventures parallel his inner journey from innocence to experience. Drawing from the popular novels of the Ming and Ch'ing

Dynasties and the vernacular literature of the Sung Dynasty, the story is set in China during the Tang Dynasty, and follows Prince Jen—heir to the Dragon Throne—as he sets off to find T'ien-kuo, the utopian kingdom described to him by a wandering stranger. On his quest Jen learns the harshest of life's lessons, losing all he has—his retinue of soldiers, his possessions, his friends, his dreams, and his very identity, ultimately finding himself a criminal in his own kingdom. Alexander lightens his tone somewhat in his fantasy *The Fortune-Tellers.* Set in Cameroon, West Africa, this story about a carpenter who visits a fortune-teller also features a trickster, the mysterious demise of an old man, and the cautionary message that misfortune comes as readily as good fortune. In *The Iron Ring,* Alexander returns to the fantasy-quest genre, this time inventing an epic adventure based in part on the myths and legends of India. After losing a dice game to King Jaya, a young Indian king named Tamar embarks on a journey to his rival's kingdom to repay the debt—his own life—and, as in many of Alexander's books, what happens to him on the way becomes more important than the destination. It is Tamar's honorable conduct on his quest that earns him a loyal retinue of talking animals as well as the love of a young maiden, but what adds interest and dimension in this work is Alexander's emphasis on Tamar's spiritual and psychological growth.

Awards

The Black Cauldron was named a Newbery Honor Book in 1966, and Alexander earned a Newbery Medal and a National Book Award nomination in 1969 and an American Book Award nomination in 1980 for *The High King.* Alexander also received a National Book Award for *The Marvelous Misadventures of Sebastian* in 1971, an American Book Award for *Westmark* in 1982, and Honor Book selections from *Boston Globe-Horn Book* for *The Cat Who Wished to Be a Man* in 1973 and *The Fortune-Tellers* in 1993. *The Iron Ring* was named to *Voice of Youth Advocate*'s list of "Books in the Middle" as an outstanding title of 1997. For his body of work, Alexander has received the Drexel Award in 1972 and 1976, the 1984 Golden Cat Award, the 1986 Regina Medal from the Catholic Library Association, a Lifetime Achievement Award from Pennsylvania Center for The Book in Philadelphia in 1991, and a Golden Kite Award in 1992.

AUTHOR'S COMMENTARY

M. Jean Greenlaw

SOURCE: "Profile: Lloyd Alexander," in *Language Arts,* No. 4, April, 1984, pp. 406-13.

This interview is the result of a project conducted by this

writer in a fifth grade class in Brandenburg Elementary School, Irving, Texas. The teacher, Mrs. Gay Westmoreland and I introduced the works of Lloyd Alexander to the class. Students read his books, viewed a filmstrip interview, and listened to *The Marvelous Misadventures of Sebastian* read aloud to them. They then constructed questions for me to use in an interview with Alexander as a means to satisfy their curiosity about this author of books they enjoyed.

Profile: Can you explain what it feels like to be an author?

Alexander: That is the hardest question on that list. I don't think it feels any different than being anybody else. But sometimes it feels terrible. Sometimes it feels so horrid, so miserable; it's so tiring.

Profile: Sitting up in that room all alone?

Alexander: No, it's not being alone that's the worst of it—it's the terrible, hard work and the frustrations when you're trying to do the best that you can and sometimes you have difficulty doing it. You know, Jean, everybody goes through the same thing. It doesn't feel any different. As a matter of fact I suppose everybody, no matter what they do, probably feels the same way. We're all people and I think that the sensations are all equal.

Profile: Do you have an author you look up to as a model?

Alexander: Oh, I have so many. I'll forget half of them. All right, let's say for a start Shakespeare, Dickens, Mark Twain, Lewis Carroll. I can think of a dozen.

Profile: Do you have an absolute favorite?

Alexander: An absolute favorite? No, I don't, because they are all my favorites. They all speak to different parts of me that respond to them. So, no, I cannot single one out and say this is my absolute favorite.

Profile: I remember an article you wrote recently for the Children's Book Council.

Alexander: Yes, that was for the *Calendar*. They caught me in that terrible question "What is your favorite author and your favorite book?" What is my favorite book? Well if I name Shakespeare, I'm going to offend Mark Twain; I'm going to offend Charles Dickens. The only solution I saw that was quite truthful was to say that my favorite book in my childhood was the dictionary. It is the one single book that includes all books that have ever been written and ever will be written. All the words are there, it's just a question of how you put them together.

Profile: I've never understood why people don't love dictionaries. They feel that looking words up is a chore.

Alexander: Oh, I love dictionaries. I can spend hours just roaming through the dictionary. One word leads you to another—and it's one of the greatest things you can do.

I read the dictionary for sheer pleasure. Using the dictionary should be as much an adventure as anything else and for me it always has been. I dearly love it and not a day passes that I don't learn something that I didn't know before.

Profile: Where do you get the ideas for your characters?

Alexander: All the characters are parts of people whom I have met, certainly large parts of myself. Everybody that any author sees in some way, possibly ends up as a character in some part or another. You take a face from one and a voice from another, an idea from somebody else, and to a large part your own personality because we aren't just one personality. I think within ourselves we have an infinite number of personalities, which is where the characters come from.

Profile: All right, then I have to ask you two other questions. Are you Fflewdur Fflam?

Alexander: All right, the first quick answer is yes. No question about that. But I am a great many of the others too, to a certain extent. Not any of the great heroic characters, because they're sort of—I'll never quite make it to that type of heroism. I'm too scared—too much of a natural-born coward for that. But let's say the ordinary characters who make mistakes and get into trouble. Yes, I'm all of them. The good guys and the bad guys too, because within ourselves we have as many dark shadowy parts of our nature as we have bright and good parts. This includes the villains as well as the heros. But certainly Fflewdur Fflam was quite a large part of my personality. I can't deny it—it's obvious.

Profile: Are you also Sebastian, the fiddle player?

Alexander: Yes indeed. No question about that. But, see this is the interesting thing, Jean, to a large extent I've used my own character and personality plus some aspects that are better than I am, that I wish I could be. Because this is the secret. You don't always write about what you are; you write about what you hope you could be or try to become. Even though you may never succeed in changing, it's maybe what you could be. So, yes indeed, Sebastian's very close to me. The only thing I have to admit is that I don't think I could be as brave as he was. I think if some of those things happened to me, I would tend to go to my room and close the door. But, that's the way I would like to be; I would like to be as courageous as Sebastian.

Profile: Where do you get the ideas that go into your books? I know you're asked that a thousand times, but it's because people really want to know.

Alexander: I never come up with an easy answer to that. There are only two places that ideas can come from. One is from the outside and the other is from the inside. The outside part, or I would call it "input or raw material," is everything that happens to you, everything you see or do. The other part, the inside part of it, is your own personality and the way you as an individual react to certain things, your own emotions, your own feelings about things. When these two sides start working together, ideas begin coming from there. The ideas come from the things that concern me most deeply, which is very simple to say. The hard part is finding out what those things are. That's not as easy as you might think because there are a great many things that concern me deeply and right at the moment I can name them—a thousand different things. All you have to do is read the newspapers and you can be very concerned about any number of things. All right this is true, this is fine, but there are certain things that concern you so deeply at a certain point, that move you to create something about them. And this is what is hard—to feel your way into what you really want to say now.

Profile: Is this why you chose fantasy as the form in which you write?

Alexander: I think it must be; it has to be one of the factors. Fantasy somehow makes it easier. At a given time you can somehow sense or understand what you want to say and you don't need to confine yourself to the reality of what's happening in your daily life at the moment or last year or whenever, but you can deal with it in very imaginary terms. Now you can deal with it as a fable, as an allegory, as an image and this is very attractive to me. It suddenly occurs to me, I realized as we were talking; the things that I have written about looked beneath the surface of the story to see what ideas are being talked about and what the feelings are below the actual story. I could not, even as I sit here, think of a way I could express those ideas except in fantasies. I can't think of another form in which I could deal with those questions the way I was able to deal with them through the form of fantasy. I can't imagine how I could do it.

Profile: Your new book *Westmark* is a slightly different kind of book for you. Talk about why you are moving into this realm now.

Alexander: Again, it's funny because it's not a conscious decision. It wasn't that I deliberately, cold-bloodedly sat down and said, "Well, now let's see what I've done so far. . . . I've done this, this, and this, therefore, I decide, well now I'm going to do something else." Perhaps it's a book that is not a fantasy or maybe it is or maybe it isn't. It was a question of trying to find out how I really feel about the world, about my own life, about my own emotions, about what's happening. How I feel about that now at this point in my life and how I can best express it. What kind of a story will allow me to use these emotions that I have? It's a question of what is the natural way to do this? What is almost the inevitable way I've got to do it that makes any kind of sense to me? The only way I could manage to express myself was through that particular kind of story which oddly enough turned out not to be a fantasy in the sense that there is no magic in it, there's no enchantment, there's no magical spells, there's no magical fiddles . . . there's nothing like that. The interesting question—is it a fantasy or isn't it—I don't know. It's quite different from my others.

Profile: It still has that element though of high fantasy, of good and evil.

Alexander: Yes, indeed it does. It's a fantasy to the extent that it never happened. It takes place somewhere that never existed in a world that's never existed. It's a fantasy to that extent and some of the things that happened are fantastic. But, it could happen in real life, presumably.

Profile: As I was reading *Westmark,* right towards the end I thought, "Lloyd's done it again; he got me into one where he's not going to finish." *Westmark* is complete on one level, but you know that another book is coming.

Alexander: True, I haven't said my last words by any means. I knew when I came to the last page of *Westmark* that I hadn't finished. Indeed, I started on *The Kestrel* immediately. Now that book is complete.

Profile: Since this is going to be a series, are you looking forward to going on to a third book?

Alexander: Yes, but as we discussed earlier it is very hard work. I'm still working on the third book and I don't know how it is going to end. I don't even know how it is going to begin.

Profile: Who do you go to when you are stuck? Is there anyone who can help you?

Alexander: Well, first, unfortunately there is no one who can help me. And secondly, that doesn't make any difference, I will go to anybody for help. I'll ask the cashier at the supermarket counter, "Do you have an idea what I can do about this?" or have a long conversation with my barber—he's not going to help me either, or Janine or anybody who is willing to listen. Unfortunately, all my friends have become very tired of having their ears beaten with "What am I going to do?" So they've given up and now I'm afraid the only one who can help me is myself.

Profile: When you're stuck, do you still go upstairs everyday to write? Sit yourself down there and . . .

Alexander: Indeed I do. I get up, dress as I normally would, I go there and sit and think and I cry, and I scream, and I complain and just behave in a terrible way. Sometimes something works and sometimes it doesn't. But I'm there; I'm ready for anything that happens because this is part of the thing too. If you aren't there to be available when something comes along that you are able to write about, then you'll miss it. So I'm there, I'm waiting, I'm working, I'm hoping. I'm open for any ideas. Otherwise, you won't get any ideas at all.

Profile: Do you still go through the actual physical process of writing or are you sitting there thinking?

Alexander: I will sit, and I will think, and I will try to make notes on what I'm thinking about. If a little bit of an idea somehow comes up for a scene of some kind or for something that catches my interest I make a note of it. I won't know what to do with it, for example, but at least I've written it down and that will keep me from forgetting it later. This is what I do, and what I hope is sooner or later over the course of time, something is going to come out.

Profile: Since it's such hard work, why did you decide to write?

Alexander: Ahh . . . good question. I didn't decide to write. This is the interesting thing. I've thought about this and it's not a question, as far as I'm concerned that at a certain point I said, "O.K. I have now decided to be a writer." I don't think it works that way. I think maybe you can decide on going into real estate or decide I'm going to do this or I'm going to do that. I think when it comes to the arts, whether it's writing, painting, music, or what have you, I'm not sure you decide. I think you find out. I think you discover it or realize it, because I don't think there was ever a day that I consciously decided I was a writer. I think I just realized it and then decided— "Well yes, I'm going to have to work and do something about it"—and that's a little different. I think it was a question of discovering what I wanted to do or what I really was supposed to do rather than cold-bloodedly sitting down and saying what can I do? This is a different thing, if this makes any kind of sense.

Profile: But I know you had other kinds of jobs. When was it that you decided you could make it as a writer and that this is what you had to do all the time?

Alexander: Well, here is a case where you can say "decide," because I had always made the decision that whatever else I have to do I am going to keep on writing no matter how hard it is. And I worked for twenty-five years at regular daytime jobs, you know from 8:30 to 5:00 in the afternoon, at all kinds of different things, and wrote when I got home at night or early in the morning. As I say, I did that for twenty-five years and it was only a couple of years ago that I stopped doing it for the simple reason the last job I was working at was on a magazine and the magazine shut down. There I had a decision; should I look for another job or should I take a chance and stay home and see how things work out? There I deliberately decided, "Oh, I'm going to try staying home," and indeed things worked out that I was able to stay home and write and didn't have to keep going in to work during the day. But as far as deciding to work at writing, I had decided to do that from the very beginning.

Profile: Did you write when you were very young?

Alexander: I wanted to write since the time I was thirteen or twelve or ten or whatever. That's a little different than really, seriously doing something about it. Sure, I'd say from thirteen on I was writing some poems and stories and things like that. But this is not quite the same as really, finally deciding this is what you are going to do all the time—it's a little bit different because it's a serious thing to do. You don't realize just how much work is involved until you really try to do it.

Profile: Many beginning writers expect their work to be perfect the first time.

Alexander: Very few people that I know of, and I believe that includes the greatest writers who have ever lived, ever got it right the first time. And I think the secret is, as you know and every writer knows, the hardest part is not writing, it's rewriting. That is where the work truly begins, and once you've caught on to that you will have understood a great deal. Here again, talking about writing, it took me many years before I realized that. Sure, as a thirteen year old I would write a poem, I would write a story, "Oh this is the greatest thing that has ever been done; don't dare change a word of it; this is absolutely perfect," which of course it wasn't. It was terrible. And even into my twenties it never occurred to me that anything I wrote could possibly be improved until I found out that, indeed, it could be vastly improved.

Profile: Do you think your editor, Ann Durell, helps you in any way with the rewriting part?

Alexander: Oh, enormously, for the simple reason that if you are writing, it is a very lonely, personal occupation. There is nobody there with you, there is nobody there telling you what to do. You are locked into what you're doing. You are almost too close to it at the end really to see what you've done. Now you get very nearsighted when you write. You believe you are saying things and putting things on paper that are in your head and really you aren't. And because you know what's in your mind, you just haven't bothered to write it down. You are too close to it. You can't see your mistakes; you can't see the good things that you've done; you can't see the bad things that you've done. It's the same way that you can look in the mirror and say, "Yeah I'm looking pretty good there; I'm looking pretty bad." This is a very subjective, very personal view, and the great thing that an editor can do is look at it from the outside and point out to you things that you never realized, like "Hey, why did you do this? This is terrible." It never occurred to you because you are too close to it.

Profile: Has Ann Durell ever told you anything was really terrible?

Alexander: Oh, many times, many times. How long has it been? Going on almost twenty years now. And she still does.

Profile: Do you sulk when she does that?

Alexander: No, I can truthfully say I got past that long before Ann Durell and I started working together. No, I got past that reasonably quickly. When I came back from the Army and seriously started to write and began working during the day but writing nevertheless, it took me seven years before I had one book published. In the course of those seven years I had written about three long novels that every publisher in New York thought were terrible, the worst things that they had ever seen. Now this hurt my feelings. Oh, this broke me up something awful, seriously. And no, I didn't sulk; I just cried and screamed and had fits. And having gone through that for seven years of truly constant rejection, I suddenly realized that, O.K., this is a hard thing to go through, but I wouldn't have traded those years for anything in the world because that is how you learn that you cannot be that sensitive to honest criticism. It's a very hard lesson to learn because writing is a very personal thing and when somebody says—you didn't do this well—in effect they are saying you yourself failed to do something right.

Profile: That is very personal.

Alexander: It's the most personal thing anyone can say to you, and somehow you have to grow up enough to realize that this kind of criticism is really for the good of the work. And the only important thing is the work, not your tender feelings or whether this upsets you or whether you go off and sulk or what have you. The work is more important than the person who writes it. This sounds like a very simple thing to say, but if you can realize that this is the truth of it then you have made enormous strides in understanding what art is about. It's as simple as that, and the art is greater than the artist. If you really understand that in the marrow of your bones, then you have made quite a step forward. Unfortunately, the number of steps are infinite so that if you make one step forward there are still an infinite number of steps that you still have to make. But that is one of the most important—if you don't take that step you are going to be so locked into your own ego that you will never create as you should.

Profile: I have one last question for you. What tips do you have for those who would like to become writers?

Alexander: Ahhh. . . . Well, now that finally is an easy question. It's much easier than it might seem. It is a very simple answer that everyone will give. There are really only four things you can do. The first is that you've got to read everything that you possibly can. And I mean everything—good, bad, indifferent, great classics, paperback junk—anything you can think of. Read everything. As much as you can, at all times, forever. And indeed I do. Secondly, you've got to write as much as you can. It doesn't matter what you write. Keep writing, whether it's poetry, short stories, anything. It's the same as when a musician will do finger exercises or a ballet dancer will do warm-up exercises. And the younger the better. You're not going to write the world's greatest novel or the greatest poem or anything right off. You've got to learn to do that. This is part of the learning process. You learn to write by writing. Simple as that. And you keep on doing it forever. The third thing, again very simple, is to live as much as you can. Be as open to experience and to life as you possibly can. Keep your eyes open, your ears, look at things. There's an enormous difference between looking at something and seeing something, and that's all you can do. I guess the fourth thing is just to have patience, which is hardest of all.

Lloyd Alexander

SOURCE: "Future Conditional," in *Children's Literature Association Quarterly,* Vol. 10, No. 4, Winter, 1986, pp. 164-66.

One great law of nature, if I understand it correctly, is that matter can be neither created nor destroyed. The best we can do is shuffle the DNA. If we come up with something different, it was already implied in the data; much as a windmill is implied in a box of Tinker Toys, or a space ship, automobile, or dinosaur is implicit in those transformers which young people currently find so fascinating.

This is true in the natural world: the objective, real world, here and now; the material world complete with grocery bills, dental problems, lurking nuclear disasters, and other cultural embellishments. We recognize this world as our immediate reality. At least, I hope we do. I, for one, would feel uncomfortable if, say, an airline pilot seriously believed in Peter Pan and Tinker Bell.

What of the artificial worlds? The worlds we devise by artifice, by artfulness; that is, the worlds of literature? Here, it would seem that writers are in total command of their material, ultimate authorities in their own creations; self-appointed demiurges, omnipotent, omniscient—as close to divinity as any human being is likely to get.

Nevertheless, I believe the same principle applies to the worlds of art as much as it does to the world of nature. First, as everyone lurching into middle age unhappily realizes, we are physical organisms. This includes writers, though we may like to pretend otherwise. We are subject to the laws of physiology, biology, gravity, and similar encumbrances.

No matter how amazing our inventions, no matter how inspired our conceptions, they are not zapped onto us from somewhere in outer space. Writers are often asked where their ideas come from. The ultimate answer is: they come from only one place: inside our heads. The divine afflatus, or whatever we choose to call it, can only operate through material structures: neural synapses, electrochemical processes. Mysterious—but not mystical. I don't find this demeaning to the human spirit. On the contrary, I think it's quite marvelous.

Even in literary creation, nothing comes from nothing. There is no output without input. We may seemingly create out of whole cloth, but our cloth is woven from a variety of threads; from all the experiences and information we have absorbed, consciously or otherwise, in the course of our lives.

These raw materials are all we have to work with. But they are susceptible to infinite restructuring and recombination. What we call creativity may have less to do with creation in the absolute sense than with finding unexpected connections and making new syntheses.

In some instances, this may be self-evident. Let me very briefly talk about the fictional modes that match our present topic, dimensions in children's literature—and that apply, as well, to adult literature.

The past: this would encompass the form of the historical novel. It may be the result of the most painstaking research, scrupulous accuracy, the greatest effort to reproduce the past as it was—or as we believe it to have been. Or it may be the type of novel that uses history as an occasional dab of color: as Pooh-Bah says, "Merely corroborative detail intended to give artistic verisimilitude to a bald and unconvincing narrative." We can recognize one type of pseudo-historical novel by the frequent occurrence of the words "Avaunt!" and "Forsooth!" In the trade, this is known as a "bodice-ripper."

Even so, good or bad, to one degree or another, the historical novel obviously relies on, or evokes, reference points from real history.

The present: to oversimplify, let me call it the societal novel, the work of social realism, the novel of manners; or, to echo Anthony Trollope, "the way we live now." In this, the reference points are all around us; the main question, how the writer chooses to see them and how to express that vision.

The future: the world which has not yet come into being is, most fittingly, the realm of science fiction. The mechanism at work in most science fiction is: extrapolation. The reference points come from genuine science, extended to its furthest and most imaginative limits. The characters are essentially human beings, perhaps extended to their furthest limits, but human nonetheless. Science fiction takes the phrase "Nothing human is alien to me" and adds, "everything alien is also human." I don't believe the human mind can conceive something truly and qualitatively alien to it.

Indeed, why should we want to? Our concerns—at least in the foreseeable future—are not with aliens but with each other. As for those good old bug-eyed monsters, one way or another a staple of much science fiction, known affectionately in the profession as BEM's—I maintain that they are, in essence, very large New York City cockroaches.

In short, our imagination transforms what it already contains: sometimes brilliantly, sometimes badly; convincingly or unconvincingly; but it is there to begin with.

As for other times, not included in—or perhaps including—all of the above: the mode is fantasy; the locale, a world that never existed and never could exist. What Tolkien calls the "secondary world." The Land of Oz, Middle Earth, Narnia, Lilliput, and so many others we love dearly; and which I often find more sensible than our own in its present condition.

The type of fantasy that offers a completely invented, self-contained world might seem completely detached from all but its own reality. Even so, I think the principle applies: no matter how fantastic a fantasy world may be,

there are, at one level or another, sometimes obviously, sometimes heavily disguised, resonances of our primary world.

In Tolkien's Middle Earth, one of the most thoroughly conceived of all fantasy universes, we glimpse a more familiar world. The Shire, as its name implies, evokes a sort of good old British yeomanry, disguised as humble Hobbits. Beyond the Shire, the ambiance is that of heroic romance, of Norse, Celtic, and half a dozen other mythologies.

Another couple of quick examples. Forgive me if I use my own work as cases in point. It's the only work I'm in any way competent to analyze—and sometimes I wonder about that.

In the Prydain Chronicles, the world stems, to a degree, from Welsh mythology. Not, I should add, in any scholarly sense. Following the time-honored tradition of storytellers, I felt free to use what bits and pieces suited my purposes, without violating the essential spirit of the myth. There are, too, certain historical underpinnings. Prydain, to a certain extent, draws on Fifth Century Britain. That is, there is none of the full body armor of a later age, no anachronistic weaponry or costume. The magical elements are, in effect, consistent with those of that folkloric era.

In *The First Two Lives of Lukas-Kasha,* the kingdoms of Abbadan and Bishangar exist on no map, in no history book. But the flavor is Fifteenth Century Persian. As for magical elements, there is only one: the device that takes Lukas to those kingdoms in the first place.

In the Westmark Trilogy, there is no magical device whatever. If I call it a fantasy world it is only because no such world ever existed. Still, as I suggest, everything comes from something. While it would be misleading to suggest parallels with real history, behind the imagined characters and settings are vague shadows of actual people and events: Europe before the French Revolution; shades of the notorious humbug, Cagliostro; of the young Bonaparte; images of Goya's etchings. Certainly, in *The Kestrel* and *The Beggar Queen,* I relied on my own experiences and observations of some forty years ago.

In addition to raw material drawn from the primary world, the secondary world of fantasy operates according to the same principles found in any work of literature. I don't mean to offer a do-it-yourself kit for building a fantasy world. There isn't any; unfortunately, there's no book of instructions for creating anything. As Somerset Maugham said, there are three rules for writing a novel—but nobody knows what they are.

But if there is one guideline to observe in fantasy—even more than in other genres—I think it is, paradoxical though it may seem: logic. Logic gives the solid support every fantasy must have.

I'm thinking of one of the Offenbach operas—a marvelously comic scene where hero and heroine are locked in an absolutely escape-proof dungeon. All hope is lost, there's nothing they can do. Then, all of a sudden, the wall opens and a little old man arrives to lead them to safety. He warns them: "Never, never tell anybody how you got out."

This is a wonderful send-up of all such melodramatic situations. Unfortunately, we can't do likewise in creating a fantasy world. What we do must be plausible, more so than in real life. Once we set our ground rules, we must abide by them. Especially when magic is involved. For example, if an enchanter can do such-and-such, why not so-and-so? If a spell works here, why doesn't it work there? In other words, we must create a rationale for the non-rational.

I won't venture further into the murky waters of literary technics. My point here is simply to suggest an underlying unity in all these genres, and repeat what I've said elsewhere and often: that all forms of literature are, in a large sense, fantasy—they are words on a page, not the actual objects themselves. They may reflect reality, and give us valid insights into it; but even the most convincing depiction of reality only seems to be real. The material is selected, manipulated, enhanced. In other words, it is a work of art. I see no essential conflict between the most exacting realism and the most inventive science fiction or fantasy.

They come from the same source, they share the same goals: to help us discover who we are and what we are. If I dare quote myself: realism is fantasy pretending to be true; fantasy is truth pretending to be a dream.

In addition to the four dimensions of this conference's theme, there is a fifth, one that unifies them all: the human dimension. This dimension, I believe, is central to every work of art, central to the nature of art itself.

Whether for children or adults, literature is concerned with the human dimension. Literature that strives for any level of excellence engages the question: how do we perceive ourselves as human beings?

Is the human role merely that of docile consumer of packaged goods and packaged ideas? Shall we see ourselves only as overgrown infants, obedient to self-appointed guardians of our virtue, with no questions asked? We already have too many examples, past and present, of human beings perceived as nothing more than bodies to be kept voiceless, prisoned, tormented, or made to disappear altogether.

Do we see ourselves as angels or devils, builders or destroyers, or simultaneously all of the above? We are clever enough to find ways we can all die together. Are we also wise enough to find ways we can all live together? If the extraterrestrials of science fiction visited our planet, would the equivalent of Captain Kirk transmit the message: "Beam us up, Scottie. There's no intelligent life here"?

These questions are not new. They have come up, in one form or another, throughout most of our history. Literature has always tried to deal with them, to show us the value of the personal above the impersonal. Literature is, surely, one of the durable human connectives. Our great books are voices linking the past with the present.

As for the future: I don't fear the future. What I fear is the past; that is, the long chain of events that has led us to where we are and may possibly determine what happens next. Still, the best thing about the future is that it doesn't exist yet. The past has already happened, the present is transitory. The future is what we can help to create.

But the future is indeed conditional. Let me claim the time-honored privilege of authors to read their own words—especially to a captive audience.

In the last chapter of *The High King,* the old enchanter, Dallben, speaks to Taran about *The Book of Three:*

> The book is thus called because it tells all three parts of our lives: the past, the present, and the future. But it could as well be called a book of 'if.' *If* you had failed at your tasks; *if* you had followed an evil path; *if* you had been slain; *if* you had not chosen as you did—a thousand 'ifs,' my boy, and many times a thousand. *The Book of Three* can say no more than 'if' until the end, of all things that might have been, one alone becomes what really is. For the deeds of a man, not the words of a prophecy, are what shape his destiny . . . Until now, my boy, you were always a great 'perhaps.'

If our future is conditional, it is conditioned by what we do in the present, through our work as writers, teachers, parents. But we are not simply the custodians of young people. We are their stewards. Ultimately, we have to answer to them for what we've done.

The young have a right to demand answers from us, as we did from our own elders. They may not get the answers they want or like, but they have a right to demand them. The duty of the young has always been to clear up the mess the older generation made—so as to make room for their own.

I don't pretend that we can make young people happy. Except in the most superficial way, we can't *make* children happy any more than we can *make* them kind, honorable, or generous. Perhaps we can do something even better.

> As Dallben himself learned, the pages of *The Book of Three* told not only of death, but of birth as well; how the earth turns in its own time and in its own way gives back what is given to it; how things lost may be found again; and how one day ends for another to begin . . . that the lives of men are short and filled with pain, yet each one a priceless treasure, whether it be that of a prince or a pig-keeper.
>
> And, at the last, the book taught him that while nothing was certain, all was possible.

So, it may be that the best we can offer young people is the one gift that encompasses all others: the gift of the possible; the means of creating their own possibility for the future. After all, it's their future, not ours.

Beyond that, if we must answer to the young, we should be able to answer that we tried our best. They can ask no more of us; and we can give them no less.

Lloyd Alexander

SOURCE: "Lloyd Alexander 1986 Regina Medal Recipient," in *Catholic Library World,* Vol. 58, No. 1, July-August, 1986, pp. 14-15.

[The following is Alexander's acceptance speech, given April 1, 1986, for the Regina Medal of the Catholic Library Association. The medal is awarded for "continued distinguished contribution to children's literature."]

Telling a friend the identity of this year's Regina Medalist, I had to admit I was more than joyfully bedazzled. I was, in fact, overawed; and keenly aware of the merits of my predecessors. This time, I said, I was afraid that a great honor had been given to a great sinner. "No," he assured me, "you're not a great sinner. You're only a small one, like all the rest of us."

We should, I suppose, be modest about our faults as we should be modest about our virtues. Chances are, we're not as terrible as we sometimes imagine. By the same token, it's quite sure that we're never as good as we hope to be. Perhaps we can only remind ourselves: *"Domine, non sum dignus."* And get on about our day's work as best we can.

Yet, each of us strives for excellence in that work. The nature of our vocation demands no less from us. The nature of our vocation also requires a permanent state of dissatisfaction. It comes with the territory. Happily so. It's a built-in protection against complacency. If what we do seems too easy, we probably aren't doing it right.
Along those lines, I have a certain amount of rueful experience. Forty years ago, I came home from Paris, France, where I had been living since the end of the war. This was by no means the return of the prodigal son. I brought back more than I had when I left: namely, a wife and small daughter.

My parents took us in stride. Also lodging with them were my sister, her husband, and their infant son; one elderly aunt; two dogs; and three canary birds—a population from time to time enhanced by the transient presence of an uncle who made his living selling tombstones but seldom found customers to buy them. The addition of only three more inhabitants caused barely a ripple.

We were installed in the west wing—of the attic, where a remarkable arrangement of curtains operated by pulleys gave an effect of private cubicles. The central feature was a kerosene stove emitting, like Mount Vesuvius, a constant plume of smoke: an ever-present reminder that our quarters could become, at any moment, a latter-day Pompeii.

Even so, my time was my own; my days free, unhampered by gainful employment. It seemed the propitious moment to begin a literary career.

Accordingly, I salvaged an early model typewriter from the cellar, invested in a large quantity of paper, and started working. The kerosene stove finally did erupt and had to be retired, leaving a veneer of soot as a memento of the occasion.

I continued unperturbed, my thoughts on higher considerations: fame; fortune; immortality; even someday a bathroom in the attic. After long labor—a full six weeks, good things can't be rushed—I finished what I instantly recognized as the world's greatest novel. Anyone who appreciates fine literature can imagine my shock and disbelief when I found no one to share my opinion; though many publishers did agree the manuscript was, in a way, altogether unique.

As often as I've told this story, no matter how I try to embellish it, I can't make that novel better than it was. It suffices to say the publishers clung stubbornly to their evaluation; until, finally, I realized they might actually have some basis for their attitude.

If I have to smile at my grandiose ambition, I can't reproach myself for it. The young need their dreams; their elders need them even more. It took some years before I had an inkling of what I should have known from the first: Our work does not serve our purpose; our purpose is to serve the work.

These past years, I've met a good number of young people. Talking about a favorite book, they remember the story but sometimes forget the author's name. This no longer distresses me. Books are more important than authors; and readers more than writers.

Though impermanence is one condition of mortality, writers hope their work will outlast them. So do librarians, educators, and parents. In the process of human development, whatever is valuable becomes valuable only when passed on to others.

By a remarkable coincidence, one of our distinguished speakers just happens to be a long-time friend. I'm sure Myra Cohn Livingston won't object if I quote a few of her words: "Poetry," she says, "is a way of growing, of coming to grips with the self and its relationship to the external world, of communication with all the other selves who are also striving to grow and communicate the meaning of their lives. . . ." (*The Child as Poet,* p. 309. Horn Book, Boston 1984.)

Here we may be close to this year's convention theme. In the large sense, I think mission and ministries take many forms: the form of librarianship or literature, the form of a poem, the form of a prayer. Implicit in all is the goal of serving others more than ourselves. Salman Rushdie, the novelist, observes: "Takers eat better. Givers sleep better."

Celebration, another of the convention's themes, is one I don't want to overlook. I won't spoil celebration by long discourse. Still, I can't resist the opportunity to recognize another distinguished speaker, Mimi Kayden; and my admired colleagues—who just also happen to be Philadelphians—Sister Mary Arthur and Carolyn Field. And to send greetings to my editor, Ann Durell. I'll spare her the polite formalities; we've known each other too long to worry about them.

Expressions of appreciation are not improved by length. If they were, I'd gladly keep on for quite a while. There is, in addition, a law of literature known to every writer—to this one, in any case: The more we wish to be eloquent, the less we succeed in doing so. Language may be a writer's friend, but it is a fickle one. When needed most, it is usually out to lunch. In those circumstances, brevity must take the place of gratitude.

The Catholic Library Association has given me a highest, happiest honor. I accept it with great pride, with great joy; and, in exchange, offer all my whole-hearted and full-hearted thanks.

GENERAL COMMENTARY

Jill P. May

SOURCE: "Lloyd Alexander's Truthful Harp," in *Children's Literature Association Quarterly,* Vol. 10, No. 1, Spring, 1985, p. 37-8.

Lloyd Alexander's talent as a children's author lies in his ability to use the personal experiences which have shaped his own understanding of human values in his fantasy stories. Alexander wants to show young readers how the individual can rise above the society he lives in and work toward the creation of a better, more just world. Although he often uses the typical quest structure in his stories, his characters are not large scale heroes. Each is an "everyman" who becomes involved in a drama, who returns home happy to have been involved, but who is equally eager to stay put and resume his old lifestyle. Alexander himself has suggested that his writing

> presents the world as it should be. . . . Sometimes heartbreaking, but never hopeless, the fantasy world as it "should be" is one in which good is ultimately stronger than evil, where courage, justice, love and mercy actually function. Thus, it may appear quite different from our own. In the long run, perhaps not ("The Flat-Heeled Muse," *Horn Book,* April, 1965). . . .

In his books for children, Alexander has created a three dimensional world in which good and evil are contrasted. Many of his heroes are not handsome young fellows, nor are they adventuresome characters setting forth with high expectations. In even the darkest of Alexander's tales, however, a mood of hope and a perpetual faith in the intrinsic goodness of mankind is evident.

Typical of his heroes is Coll, a minor character in the Prydain series whose earlier heroism is explored in *Coll and His White Pig.* Coll, once a warrior, has now grown middle aged, and is a farmer. His magical pet, the pig Hen Wen, is stolen by the warriors of Death, so that this stoutly built farmer is forced upon the road of adventure in order to save the pig from evil. It is not his war-like manner that saves the pig, but his kindness to various forest animals: in return for his assistance they help Coll. Alexander's middle aged hero is not a man of strength, not attractive or muscular. He is "everyman," forced to fight for his possessions.

While Alexander's tales are based upon Welsh legend, they clearly reflect his modern attitudes. His heroes realize their own shortcomings, and learn to live with them. Their growth comes when they realize that their life can be pleasant and purposeful if they accept themselves as they are. In some cases, their failings can even be viewed as assets. In *The Truthful Harp,* for instance Alexander's hero Fflewddur resorts to stretching the truth in order to paint a more exciting scene. "But facts are so gray and dreary," he says, "I can't help adding a little color. Poor things, they need it so badly."

Alexander's hero is admitting that while he wants to have an honest real world, he likes to imagine one that is more clearly defined and more heroic. And like Fflewddur, Alexander himself creates stories based not upon the daily activities of real people, but upon the noble activities of journeying heroes. But these stories nevertheless show their heroes searching for peace and tranquility. Usually they are busy helping those around them, rather than fighting duels.

According to Alexander,

> The fantasy hero is not only a doer of deeds, but he also operates within a framework of morality. His compassion is as great as his courage—greater, in fact. We might even consider that his humane qualities, more than any others, are what the hero is really all about ("High Fantasy and Heroic Romance," *Horn Book,* December, 1971, p. 583).

Alexander has also said, "At the end, like all of us in our commonplace world, [t]he [hero] must accept death" ("Identifications and Identities," *Wilson Library Bulletin,* October, 1979, p. 147). His stories, then, reflect not only the joys of youth and the bitter-sweet experiences of maturity but also the ultimate change brought to all people with the passing of generations and civilizations.

Those who have met Lloyd Alexander comment that he looks like a character from his fantasies come alive; some have likened him to Hans Christian Andersen. This slight, gentle man with expressive eyes and craggy features has more in common with the acknowledged inventor of the literary fairy tale than physical appearance. Like Andersen, Alexander began his stories using an already established body of legends and gradually changed these tales until the messages of the earlier stories were lost and a new meaning—his own—evolved. Like Andersen, Alexander is content to write for children, knowing full well that adults will read the stories and will gain insight concerning civilization which children might never see. And like Andersen's, a group of Alexander's fantasy stories are sad, cautionary lessons about the evils found within his existing country.

Unlike Andersen, however, Lloyd Alexander has created realistic characters within humorous stories that are neither overly dramatic nor tragic. Lloyd Alexander has brought to American fantasy both a world of hope and a voice of warning. His truthful harp reflects the realities of the twentieth century within the imagined adventures of some very realistically drawn fantasy heroes.

Michael O. Tunnell and James S. Jacobs

SOURCE: "Fantasy at Its Best: Alexander's Chronicles of Prydain," in *Children's Literature in Education,* Vol. 21, No. 4, December, 1990, pp. 229-36.

Just over twenty years ago, Holt published Lloyd Alexander's *The High King,* the last in a five-book fantasy series set in mythical Prydain, an ancient country with a geography similar to Wales. This Newbery Medal-winning novel completed the story of Taran, an impetuous Assistant Pig-Keeper turned hero who searches for his destiny while engaging in a cosmic battle against the ultimate powers of evil. The five books (*The Book of Three, The Black Cauldron, The Castle of Llyr, Taran Wanderer,* and *The High King*), known as the Chronicles of Prydain, sprang from Alexander's fascination with the *Mabinogion,* an ancient book of Welsh mythology, and fashion a dazzling tale of adventure, magic, the struggle between good and evil, and the eventual triumph of the human spirit. With the release of its first volume, *The Book of Three,* over a quarter century ago, the Prydain series was an immediate hit and has maintained a great measure of its popularity to this day.

Prydain's place on the list of enduring children's books is partially confirmed by its strong sales record, which indicates continued readership. Maintaining readers over the years is not always the case with winners of the Newbery Medal. George Nicholson, editor at Dell, where the Prydain paperbacks are published, reported (in a 1987 telephone interview) that sales figures have held steady these twenty years, which he calls "amazing—particularly in this day and age." The balance sheet simply reflects what readers have long known: The Chronicles of Prydain are cut from a lasting kind of cloth.

What is it about Prydain which endures? Pinpointing what makes a particular story stand the test of time is a problem. A yardstick to measure literary excellence simply does not exist. No formula for creating power in print has been developed.

Yet a closer look at the Chronicles of Prydain reveals four characteristics that may help explain why the five titles still find so many readers: (1) credibility, (2) tension, (3) humor, and (4) hope. Alexander's attention to these elements is certainly one reason that critics and young people find the Prydain books so appealing that they receive serious attention as literature while also reaching across age lines to be publishing successes in two formats: one for elementary children and another which is sold to adolescents.

While we know that fiction is a manipulation of truth, we nevertheless desire to be caught up in Coleridge's "willing suspension of disbelief," treating the story as if it were real. We want to know how things turn out and fault the work when it violates logic or reason, thereby reminding us of its illusion. The characters must be real personalities and must behave consistently. The action must be sensible. The setting should offer all the earmarks of actually existing. Through fiction, we humans try on others' lives, and the fit must not droop or show wrinkles.

The credibility in Prydain is due in large part to Alexander's ability to breathe life into his characters. He does this two ways: creating unique personalities and showing the range of a character. The people of Prydain are not stereotypes. While the depth of no character is completely plumbed, each has a distinct personality which is believable and readily recognizable to the reader. Alexander reveals this individuality largely through trademark speech patterns. Eilonwy, Prydain's headstrong heroine, is given to speaking in comparisons. When Taran finds his lost charge, the oracular pig Hen Wen, Eilonwy says, "It's always nice to see two friends meet again. It's like waking up with the sun shining." And when the irritable dwarf, Doli, can't make himself turn invisible, the princess counsels that "It's silly . . . to worry because you can't do something you simply can't do. That's worse than trying to make yourself taller by standing on your head."

Gurgi, the half-man, half-beast with a somewhat cowering personality, interjects his speech with rhyming pairs of words. After Gurgi meets Taran and a companion, he says, "The two strengthful heroes will give Gurgi something to eat? Oh, joyous crunchings and munchings!" Nearly a hundred different pairs occur through the story: "smackings and whackings," "lotions and potions," "sighings and dyings," and so on.

Even characters who do not share center stage sport individual speech. Rhun, the bumbling but lovable Prince of Mona, greets everyone with "Hullo! Hullo!" Fflewddur Fflam, the energetic king turned bard, laces his speech with obvious exaggerations. And Doli replies in brusque and curt sentences.

While these characters are unique and provide ways for the reader to identify them quickly, it is in showing the complex range of a personality where Alexander really shines. Ellidyr, a bitter and selfish prince from a small kingdom, develops enough concern and courage to destroy the Black Cauldron by literally sacrificing his life, thus nullifying its curse. The whimpering Gurgi is able to rally and provide moments of honest courage in the face of frightening opposition.

However, through no one does Alexander reveal the intricate workings of the human soul as much as through Taran. During the course of the story, he goes from being an impulsive, thrill-seeking boy to an adult who knows his place in life as well as his strengths and limitations. Alexander lets the reader see these changes gradually, as such changes generally occur in life. The changes begin when readers hear Taran complaining bitterly to his guardian, the enchanter Dallben: "I think there is a destiny laid on me that I am not to know anything interesting, go anywhere interesting, or do anything interesting. I'm certainly not to *be* anything!" He finds it almost impossible to accept that life is worth living without the "glories" of battle and adventure. Then he meets his idol, the war leader Prince Gwydion, only to discover that he is only a man—and a man who despises war. Taran also finds out that another less-than-spectacular fellow, the farmer Coll, was a former war hero. ("But . . . he's so bald!") At this point, his foot is set upon the path to understanding that indeed "there is more honor in a field well-plowed than in a field steeped in blood."

The seemingly mundane events in Taran's life often lead him to the deepest understandings of himself. In fact, his greatest moment of truth comes at just such a time. During his long and lonely search for his parentage which takes most of the fourth book, *Taran Wanderer,* Taran fervently hopes his background proves to be noble so he may feel worthy to ask Eilonwy's hand in marriage. But then an old shepherd named Craddoc claims to be his father. Discouraged and disappointed with his peasant past, Taran nevertheless stays on with Craddoc to fulfill a son's obligation, even though this choice means his days are filled only with monotony.

One day Craddoc falls into an icy gorge, his body flat and still on a ledge halfway down. Taran initially is stunned—and then flooded with a sudden, wild sense of freedom. The man is far down in the crack where sense dictates he is lost. He is not moving; perhaps he is already dead. No one would blame Taran for not risking a rescue that might claim other lives. At this moment Taran faces himself as never before:

> It was not despair that filled him, but terror, black terror at the thoughts whispering in his mind. Was there the slimmest hope of saving the stricken herdsman? If not, even Prince Gwydion would not reproach Taran's decision. Nor would any man. Instead, they would grieve with him at his loss. Free of his burden, free of the valley, the door of his cage opened wide, and all his life awaited him; Eilonwy, Caer Dallben. He seemed to hear his own voice speak these words, and he listened in shame and horror.

> Then, as if his heart burst with it, he cried out in a terrible rage, "What man am I?"

No longer does Taran speak with the impatient tongue of a boy—the surety of untested youth. He now knows even the best human heart has a dark side as well as a side of light, and the person does the choosing.

Other elements beyond the carefully chronicled personalities lend credibility to the story: the precise geography of Prydain; the intricate plot, which remains consistent in the smallest detail; and the powerful magic, which is still less powerful than the decisions made by humans. But perhaps none is as strong as the masterful picture of believable and real people.

Without conflict, no story exists. Stories must not only create but maintain tension. At the center of reader interest is how the problem defined in the tale will be resolved. By what ways and means will the characters be able to conquer? Readers of Prydain find themselves rushing in pursuit of answers to plaguing questions. The end of the struggle is always in the forefront: Who is Taran and from where did he come? What will happen to him? To him and Eilonwy together? To the evil which has threatened the land—can it be erased even if those behind it are gone? And so on.

To add further fuel to central issues, Alexander deliberately ends chapters with cliffhangers. Readers are unable to mark their places and turn out the light when coming to the end of Chapter 10 in *The High King.* Pryderi finally arrives at the Caer Dathyl, bringing reinforcements that will guarantee the stronghold's security in the face of the Death-Lord's attack. But events turn swiftly and unexpectedly with words Pryderi speaks to conclude the chapter: "You summoned me, Prince of Don,' Pryderi answered in a hard voice. 'I am here. To join you? No. To demand your surrender.'"

Alexander also adds puzzles and riddles: What is the significance of the indecipherable runes on the magical sword Dyrnwyn? How can a river burn with frozen fire and night turn to noon—and yet prophecy says both must happen before evil can be vanquished. The Cauldron-Born warriors are reconstructed from corpses and cannot die. How can these formidable warriors be stopped? And Alexander asks questions in one book which are not answered until the reader gets to another volume.

Another technique Alexander uses for creating tension is to make the stakes high. The loss of the final battle to Arawn Death-Lord will forever end the chance for happiness in the entire land. The people have already lost to Arawn their helpful tools and knowledge of many crafts, as well as a great portion of their freedoms. And their leaders seem unable to pit themselves evenly against the necromancy of the master of evil. Some spells cannot be undone without supreme sacrifice, including the voluntary offering of one's own life. Who can rise to the occasion? If the hero does, the story is over. Yet the others seem incapable.

In addition to scenarios which cause the mind to wonder and the heart to race, Alexander incorporates subtle, almost unnoticed elements calculated to create tension in the reader. Alexander purposely does not describe the Death-Lord nor his kingdom in detail. For instance, he never tells what symbols are on Arawn's banner, only that it is black. Never do readers get a decent look at the Lord of the Death. The element of mystery and horror are better preserved in one's imagination, the author explained in a personal interview in 1985:

> I think, particularly when you're dealing with terrible villains, . . . the less description specifically, the better. Once you've described something you can have its measure. . . . If there is some way you can express or suggest to the imagination awful things, [that's] much stronger.

With the future of the world at stake, humor is not at the forefront of anyone's mind. Yet Alexander knows that a reader has difficulty holding up under serious assault without relief. Alexander's well-developed sense of humor serves not only to add dimension to his characters, but also as an element of style; it sets apart his high-fantasy writings. Most of the great names in high fantasy—including Tolkien, Garner, Cooper, and Lewis—seldom combine humor with something as serious as the eternal battle of good against evil. Alexander does it effectively, providing welcome moments of relief in the building tension. Memorable are Gurgi's "crunchings and munchings" and "smackings and whackings," Fflewddur's mighty exaggerations (quickly corrected as his harp senses a deviation from truth and prepares to snap yet another string), and Doli's sincere attempt to refine his magic and turn invisible by holding his breath, which results only in headaches.

Alexander's humor is not a focal point of the books, nor does it attempt to be. Yet, it is a spice sprinkled sparingly which improves the flavor without drawing attention to itself. Breathing room through humor is provided a number of ways. King Eiddileg of the Fair Folk is blustery and curt, perhaps even formidable. He tries to appear unyielding and uncompassionate when he refuses to return Hen Wen to Taran and his companions. "Finders keepers," the Dwarf King snaps. But even he can drop his front, giving in when Taran mentions that this is a matter of honor and honesty. When Eilonwy kisses his head and tells him he is a "perfectly lovely king," Eiddileg explodes, "Out! Out!" as he throws her from his chamber. Just before the door closes, however, Taran sees the small king "fondling his head and beaming happily."

King Smoit's humor is in his language. Not a man to mince words, he calls them as he sees them. The bard Fflewddur Fflam to him is a "butter-headed harp scraper." The calculating Morgant, later proven a traitor, is an "icicle." And when Gwydion solicits support for destroying the Black Cauldron, Smoit shouts, "Any whey-blooded pudding guts who fears to stand with you will have to deal with me."

Lord Gast's humor comes in his self-deception. Believing he is the perfect host—he even calls himself "Gast the Generous"—Gast invites his visitors to eat to their hearts' content:

> "Eat your fill," cried Gast to Taran and Gurgi, pushing a small hunch of gravy-spotted bread toward them and keeping the rest for himself. "Gast the Generous is ever openhanded! A sad fault that may turn me into a pauper, but it's my nature to be free with all my goods; I can't fight against it!"

His guests never have their plates or drinking horns more than partially filled during the meal, as Gast continues to urge all to fill their stomachs.

Even Eilonwy and Taran are good for a smile or two. Once, when ordered to stay within the walls of the stronghold during a siege, the princess suddenly appears on the battlefield, rushing forward on her steed with her plaited hair tucked under a leather helmet and a lance in her grasp. "Go back!" Taran shouts. "Have you lost your wits?" But Eilonwy only smiles and retorts, "I understand you're upset, but that's no cause to be rude."

One of four values Alexander identifies as being inherent in strong fantasy literature is hope. He calls it perhaps the most precious of the values offered readers: "Whatever the hardships of the journey, the days of despair, fantasy implicitly promises to lead us through them."

Prydain fosters hope that the better side of human nature will prevail, as occurs with a haunted, despairing Ellidyr, who eventually atones for his misdeeds. There exists hope that good will prevail over evil, for not only is Arawn destroyed but also those mortals who succumb to his promises of power. And there is hope for love realized, as evidenced by the union of an Assistant Pig-Keeper and a princess.

Yet the most powerful message of hope within the Chronicles of Prydain is linked to Taran's longing for fulfillment, which he hopes to achieve by adventure and valor on the battlefield. Instead, Taran discovers that life's meaning is found in the small, quiet moments most often overlooked, that all of us can become something worthwhile. At the end of the series Taran speaks of this to Dallben:

> "Long ago I yearned to be a hero without knowing, in truth, what a hero was. Now, perhaps, I understand it a little better. A grower of turnips or a shaper of clay, a Commot farmer or a king—every man is a hero if he strives more for others than for himself alone. Once," he added, "you told me that the seeking counts more than the finding. So, too, must the striving count more than the gain."

This sort of personal fulfillment in the quiet moments Alexander himself derived from the writing of the Prydain Chronicles. He said of his Chronicles, "Certainly no work has given me greater joy in the doing." It was his most satisfying creative experience—an extremely personal experience. Friends believe they recognize Alexander in his characters, particularly the garrulous Fflewd-dur Fflam, and are convinced that they hear the real Lloyd Alexander in the voices of Gwydion; Adaon, a bard of great wisdom; or Dallben. The wisdom of these characters mirrors what Lloyd Alexander understands of life and of mankind's noblest aspirations. Note Dallben's gentle words to Eilonwy in time of great stress. "Child, child, do you not see? For each of us comes a time when we must be more than what we are."

Perhaps, finally, this is the missing piece. Prydain has endured simply because it makes us nobler for the reading. It gives us hope that we, too, can become more than what we are.

TITLE COMMENTARY

THE BEGGAR QUEEN (1984)

Trev Jones

SOURCE: A review of *The Beggar Queen*, in *School Library Journal*, Vol. 30, No. 7, March, 1984, p. 168.

Fans of *Westmark* and *The Kestrel* will revel in Alexander's magnificent conclusion to his trilogy, but the enormous cast of characters and the complexity of the preceding adventures will make this one incomprehensible to newcomers. Although he does refer to events and characters from the earlier volumes, this background information about these adventures set in an undesignated distant past is too sketchy for a full understanding. As the story continues, Cabbarus and his forces have taken over Westmark. Queen Augusta has gone into hiding, along with Florian, Theo and Keller. With the aid of townspeople, they begin their struggle to topple Cabbarus' regime and institute a democratic government. But plans go astray—and the leaders become the followers of the people. Cabbarus dies, Theo and Mickle are relieved of their ruling responsibilities and (sigh) are finally able to marry. The rich characterization of lovable rogues, evil assassins, unwilling rulers, sympathetic townspeople, spies, traitors and con-men is deftly interwoven in this exciting adventure that is told with tongue-in-cheek humor and eloquent language. With a minimum of adjectives and a maximum of action verbs, Alexander conveys the noise, confusion, despair and hope as the people fight against Cabbarus.

Zena Sutherland

SOURCE: A review of *The Beggar Queen*, in *Bulletin of the Center for Children's Books*, Vol. 37, No. 9, May, 1984, p. 159.

Third in the trilogy that included *Westmark* and *The Kestrel*, this is just as fine a piece of craftsmanship as the first two books, and just as exciting a story. Alexander is deft at

incorporating references to the past, so the book is linked to—and continues from—its predecessors, but it also stands nicely as a literary entity. Here the young queen of Westmark and her advisors learn that their arch enemy Cabbarus is planning to take over the country; he does, and the beggar queen must fight to retrieve it and to decide whether she will wed the commoner Theo (the Kestrel) and give up her throne after victory is won. Theo is the hero of the story, a character who grows and develops, but he is only one of many vivid characters in a story that has pace, polished style, and suspense.

Publishers Weekly

SOURCE: A review of *The Beggar Queen*, in *Publishers Weekly*, Vol. 225, No. 19, May 11, 1984, p. 273.

Closing the trilogy begun in *Westmark* and *The Kestrel*, Alexander relates developments after the end of the war with Westmark's neighboring realm, Regia, where the traitor Cabbarus has fled. The beggar maid Mickle, now Queen Alexandra, hopes for an end to strife in Westmark. Her valiant betrothed Theo and their friends, Florian and Justin, are by the queen's side, helping her to rule. But opposing factions stir up dissension, abetted by conspirators in Regia. Cabbarus persuades Duke Conrad to assassinate his nephew, young King Constantine, and crown himself king, thrusting Regian forces on the march to seize control of Westmark. The author's resolution to the conflict is surprising and touching when one realizes the implications of Queen Alexandra's *beau geste* and Florian's secret. In retrospect, however, one sees that the splendid tale had to end as it did.

Mary M. Burns

SOURCE: A review of *The Beggar Queen*, in *Horn Book Magazine*, Vol. LX, No. 4, August, 1984, p. 472.

The concluding volume of the Westmark trilogy resolves the fates of the characters through a surprising, carefully wrought climax. Although references to earlier events are smoothly integrated into the text, they cannot fully convey the skill of the author's complicated, fully realized characterizations. Emphasis on action and dialogue rather than explanation heightens tension and intensifies the final drama of Westmark's political evolution but would perhaps confuse those unacquainted with its earlier history. As the story opens, the king of Regia has recognized the government of Westmark under Mickle, the beggar waif acknowledged to be the missing heir to the throne. Officially, hostilities have ended, but disaffected factions among the courtiers and the military, incensed by populist reforms, join with the schemer Cabbarus to establish a more favorable regime. Meanwhile, the former comrades-in-arms, Theo, Florian, and Justin, now consuls to the queen, find themselves ideologically opposed to one another. When a skillfully engineered coup places Cabbarus in power, the three must somehow resolve their differences if their old enemy is to be eliminated. Despite the conflicting theories of the leaders, the fate of Westmark is ultimately determined by its citizens—not by ideologues. Justin dies in battle; Florian survives to become part of the new country; but, ironically, Mickle and Theo, for the common good, must choose exile. Yet, as Mickle sagaciously observes, they have each other and "all the rest of the world"—a reassuring conclusion to a panoramic, romantic adventure story of epic proportions. In creating a country of the mind the author offers a commentary on the dynamics of revolution and insight into the tragic flaws of leaders like Justin whose concentration on the attainment of an ideal overrides a concern for humanity—represented in all its facets by a varied and memorable cast of heroes, rogues, charlatans, and scholars. Some are larger than life; others quite ordinary; but each character is unique and important.

Wendy Bell

SOURCE: A review of *The Beggar Queen,* in *The Alan Review,* Vol. 13, No. 1, Fall, 1984, p. 19.

Readers of the first two books in the Westmark trilogy will perhaps be eager to learn what has happened to Mickle and her companions, Theo, Florian and Justin, who, in this final volume, continue to fight for freedom against their old enemy, Cabbarus. The elements for an exciting story are here—appealing characters, intrigue, and a noble cause—but *The Beggar Queen* doesn't pull it off. The characters are superficial, and Alexander describes them too much for us rather than letting them reveal themselves. He also moves back and forth so rapidly in time and space that his focus is blurred. It is difficult to know what is important, the present cause for which Mickle is fighting, or her past relationship with her companions. However, the author's wordy style does lend itself to description; the crowd scenes and other areas of Marianstat are vividly painted. In a trilogy, each book should stand solidly on its own merit making us eager to read the other two. *The Beggar Queen* is not substantial enough in thought and style to hold the attention of readers, young or old.

Diane G. Yates

SOURCE: A review of *The Beggar Queen,* in *Voice of Youth Advocates,* Vol. 7, No. 4, October, 1984, p. 204.

As the third book of the Westmark trilogy begins, Mickle has been established as Queen Augusta, with Theo one of her consuls. However, the evil Cabbarus quickly accomplishes the overthrow of the government, forcing Theo and Mickle into hiding in the thieves' dens of the city of Marianstat. From there they plot to save Westmark once again from Cabbarus.

The former comrades in arms, Florian and Justin, disagree on whether a monarchy or a republic is the best form of government for Westmark, and Justin's intense fanaticism almost destroys their solidarity. Theo senses that his actions are moving in a circle and although he

abhors the killer he was as Kestral, he fears what he is becoming as he tries to take the city and hold it until Florian and his troops arrive.

Alexander is a master at building suspense by giving his characters many narrow escapes. In addition to the fast-paced adventure, however, he provides food for the thoughtful reader. Who should govern; what is worth fighting and dying for; is killing ever justified? The language is simple enough for a fourth grader, the ideas complex enough to interest teens and adults. Sure to be on the Best Books List; a candidate for the Newbery award.

THE ILLYRIAN ADVENTURE (1986)

Zena Sutherland

SOURCE: A review of *The Illyrian Adventure,* in *Bulletin of the Center for Children's Books,* Vol. 39, No. 8, April, 1986, p. 142.

A gentleman scholar goes to collect his sixteen-year-old ward, Vesper, and straighten out her estate, but instead finds himself embroiled in an adventure halfway around the world. The time is 1872, and the place a small, autocratic kingdom in the Mediterranean, where Illyrian guerillas are carrying on skirmishes against their traditional enemies, the king (not a bad fellow) and his advisor (a very bad fellow). Vesper has stumbled over a secret in her deceased father's research, which eventually leads to the reconciliation of the warring factions, but not before a harrowing series of escapades—all revealed by the stuffy narrator, whose slowness to catch on adds calculably to the reader's suspense and high estimation of Vesper's cleverness. Alexander's archeological mystery has intricate plotting and witty wording—a romp of a read-aloud for Raiders of the Lost Ark fans. And doesn't the ending hint at more enterprises to come?

Denise M. Wilms

SOURCE: A review of *The Illyrian Adventure,* in *Booklist,* Vol. 82, No. 15, April 1, 1986, pp. 1137-38.

"Miss Vesper Holly has the digestive talents of a goat and the mind of a chess master." That grabbing first line gets this vintage Alexander adventure off to a lively start; the pace never flags as readers are transported to the intrigue-ridden kingdom of Illyria, where Vesper plans to continue the archaeological investigation begun by her late father. Dr. Holly's studies centered on his theory that an army of magical warriors, once said to have fought in Illyria, were actually real. His papers on the subject had made him a laughingstock in his field, but Vesper, in possession of her father's final writings; is sure he was onto something and plans to continue his research. In Illyria things take a sinister twist. The political situation is a tinderbox because the native Illyrians are oppressed by their powerful conquerors. A smooth-talking grand vizier obviously holds no love for Vesper's planned investigations, and after receiving a naive king's enthusiastic approval for their project, Vesper and her guardian Brinnie encounter one obstacle after another, not to mention getting unavoidably caught up in the area's civil unrest. As one might expect in this *Westmark*-like tale, all is not what it seems; the delightfully quick-thinking Vesper manages—unlike Brinnie (the story's narrator and her companion)—to keep them one step ahead of disaster most of the time. A lively yarn from this veteran teller of robust tales.

Kirkus Reviews

SOURCE: A review of *The Illyrian Adventure,* in *Kirkus Reviews,* Vol. LIV, No. 7, April 1, 1986, p. 543.

Award-winning Alexander's stories have often taken inspiration from Welsh mythology. This time, an imaginary epic is the pivot for an adventure set in a not-quite-possible kingdom on the Adriatic 100 years ago.

Vesper Holly, 16, orphaned by the death of her scholar father, welcomes his lifelong friends, Professor Brinton Garrett (Brinnie) and his wife, who come to Philadelphia to provide for her future life. But Vesper is determined to go with him to Illyria to fulfill her father's dream of proving that the *Illyriad,* an epic poem presenting the country's mythology, is rooted in history. Brinnie soon is provisioning an expedition to Illyria. Nothing is an obstacle to Vesper, a brilliant, fearless and determined young woman. It quickly becomes apparent that the wars between the Illyrians and the Zentans, both indigenous ethnic groups, are as alive in 1872 as they were in mythological times. It is also clear that the two warring kings of long ago had intended to make peace and that a treasure was involved. When Vesper and Brinnie explore the ruins of King Vartan's castle, they find the treasure that would have been the token of peace. Vesper makes peace by showing the two leaders in her own time that their ancestors would have settled their wars had it not been for deception and unwillingness on both sides to be the first to forgive and give up the quarrel.

A truly exciting story, it carries the reader along to a triumphant conclusion and the hope that Vesper may have another adventure before she settles down—perhaps in Illyria, where she seems to have left her heart.

Sara Miller

SOURCE: A review of *The Illyrian Adventure,* in *School Library Journal,* Vol. 32, No. 9, May, 1986, pp. 99-100.

Vesper Holly at 16 is an intrepid heroine too candid for 19th-Century comfort and more than a match for the villains she meets in this charming fantasy adventure. Whisking her staid guardian Brinnie off to Illyria—a tiny kingdom on the Adriatic—to investigate one of her late father's theories, she involves them both in a search for treasure, an attempted revolution and a conspiracy to murder Illyria's

King Osman. With the help of the rebel leader Vartan and in spite of Brinnie's habit of trusting the villains, Vesper solves an ancient puzzle and shows rebels and proud King how to make peace. A touch of romance adds the finishing touch. Narrated by loyal, rather naive Brinnie, the story moves briskly from one crisis to another until the final, quite satisfying resolution. The language holds hints of 19th-Century expression without being overdone, and the contrast between Brinnie's formal habits of speech and Vesper's directness adds humor. Each character is sketched briefly but clearly, and the relationship between guardian and ward is developed nicely throughout their adventures, each showing a growing regard for the other. Young readers may find it hard to relate to middle-aged Brinnie's voice, but none will complain of lack of action.

Publishers Weekly

SOURCE: A review of *The Illyrian Adventure,* in *Publishers Weekly,* Vol. 229, No. 22, May 30, 1986, pp. 67-8.

With this new novel, Alexander adds another delightful adventure to his many popular and award-winning books. . . . This time, the intrepid protagonist is 16-year-old Vesper Holly. She's a precocious orphan from Philadelphia who sets out to prove her scholarly father's theories about the national legend of Illyria, a small Adriatic nation. It is 1872 and Illyria's ethnic conflict is brewing into a revolution. Vesper is caught up in the intrigue, and proves a shrewd and valiant ally. She reconciles the king and the rebel leader, thereby preventing a war, and in the bargain finds the historical evidence she seeks. The appealing characters and the nice blend of challenges—intellectual and moral as well as physical—are matched by lively storytelling.

Michael J. Shanahan

SOURCE: A review of *The Illyrian Adventure,* in *Best Sellers,* Vol. 46, No. 3, June, 1986, p. 115.

Lloyd Alexander's latest novel is a winner. ***The Illyrian Adventure*** has everything a young person looks for in a book: mystery, excitement and, most of all, a child who solves the problem. Professor Brinton Garrett, the narrator, also a main character, is a soft-hearted friend of the family who becomes the guardian of Vesper, the young heroine, after her father's untimely death. He soon finds his hands full as his young ward becomes bound and determined to solve the mystery her father was trying to uncover when he died. The heroine, Vesper, is a high-strung cross between Nancy Drew and [Pippi] Longstocking, who works her way into the hearts of everyone she meets, readers included, and has an uncanny knack for trouble. When one combines these two characters with lost treasure and a country in revolt, you can just imagine the consequences.

Lloyd Alexander seems to be on the right track if he plans to start a series of adventures with these two characters. With his imagination the possibilities seem endless.

Mary M. Burns

SOURCE: A review of *The Illyrian Adventure,* in *Horn Book Magazine,* Vol. LXII, No. 4, July-August, 1986, pp. 447-48.

Lloyd Alexander has a positive genius for creating imaginary kingdoms which seem as real as the lands documented in atlases. Some of the ingredients for his success are easily recognized: skill in delineating setting, facility for developing unusual characters, and distinctive use of language. What makes his work truly excellent, rather than simply very good, is his strong sense of story, controlled but not dominated by a substantial theme, and his ability to meld the actual and the imagined into a plausible reality. Although quite different in locale, subject, and persona than his previous books, *The Illyrian Adventure,* set in 1872, is vintage Lloyd Alexander. The central character, sixteen-year-old Vesper Holly, is a red-haired original with "the digestive talents of a goat and the mind of a chess master." Orphaned by the sudden death of her archaeologist father, she is placed under the guardianship of his two old friends, Professor and Mrs. Brinton Garrett. But the relationship is not that found in the usual orphan story, for Vesper "does not appear to require consolation." Indeed, she assumes command of the situation and controls her own destiny, with Brinnie cast in the role of a well-meaning, somewhat bumbling Dr. Watson. Consequently, much against his better judgment, he suddenly finds himself accompanying her to the small country of Illyria in southeastern Europe, where she hopes to continue her father's investigations into the historical basis for a twelfth-century epic. This great literary classic incorporated references to a lost treasure and an army of magical warriors into descriptions of the legendary deeds of a dashing king. But an ordinary archaeological expedition is quickly transformed into high adventure as Vesper and Brinnie find themselves caught between opposing factions in Illyria's internal political struggles. As they proceed into the country's interior, conspiracy, danger, and intrigue seem to be the three constants. An engrossing tale of derring-do, laced with marvelous touches of comic relief, the story moves at a brisk pace to a smashing conclusion as Vesper unravels the legend, finds the treasure, outwits her would-be assassins, and reconciles the disparate political factions before returning in triumph. The ending hints at a sequel.

THE EL DORADO ADVENTURE (1987)

Kirkus Reviews

SOURCE: A review of *The El Dorado Adventure,* in *Kirkus Reviews,* Vol. LV, No. 5, March 3, 1987, pp. 369-70.

The heroine of last year's *Illyrian Adventure* returns for another series of hair-breadth escapes. Vesper Holly seems to be children's literature's answer to Indiana Jones: as such, she succeeds pretty well.

Vesper and her amiable but bumbling narrator-guardian, Professor Brinton Garrett (Brinnie), receive a summons to the Central American country of El Dorado to see some territory, including a volcano, which turns out to belong to Vesper. They are welcomed but then imprisoned by de Rochefort, who is attempting to build a Panama-like canal (it's 1870), first exterminating the indigenous Chiricas. Escaping, Vesper and Brinnie fall in with the Chiricas, discovering that their chief, Acharro, is half Irish and Cambridge-educated. Illyria's arch-villain, Helvetius, turns up as the mastermind of the canal scheme and plays an extended game of cat-and-mouse, the irrepressible Vesper engineering escapes with the intelligence and cool confidence of a Houdini, till the volcano erupts and provides an unexpected resolution.

Though this is chiefly a saga of derring-do, Alexander is too good a writer not to incorporate both thoughtful and subtle touches. He's firmly on the side of the Chiricas, and also of the Chirica women who have been doing all the tribe's labor; they get the vote as well as some help from their men. Brinnie's posturing and incompetence are still funny, though they begin to be tedious. Vesper is refreshingly vigorous and omniscient. Lightweight, compared to Alexander's *Westmark* series, but should entertain adventure fans.

Denise M. Wilms

SOURCE: A review of *The El Dorado Adventure,* in *Booklist,* Vol. 83, No. 15, April 1, 1987, p. 1202.

The intrepid Vesper Holly, who braved intrigue and adventure in a mythical Middle Eastern kingdom in *The Illyrian Adventure,* is off on another mystery-laden journey, this one to a tiny Central American country where, it turns out, her late archaeologist father acquired a chunk of valuable property. Events get under way when a letter invites her and her guardian, Brinnie, on an expense-paid trek south to the republic of El Dorado. There, an unctuous Frenchman, Alain de Rochefort, presents his plan of buying out Vesper's land so that he might construct a canal through the territory. The only problem is, Vesper has already spoken to some less-moneyed El Doradans, who have explained that the canal plan will result in exterminating the last tribe of the Chirica Indians who dwell in the region. Vesper's sympathies lie with the Indians, of course, but as she plots to aid them, she is kidnapped by de Rochefort and his forces, who turn out to be under the thumb of the archvillain Dr. Helvitius from *The Illyrian Adventure.* An action-packed finale sees Vesper and her Indian allies out of danger but the diabolical Helvitius out of their clutches as well—leaving room for further adventures. This tale is marked by the same wit and rapid-fire storytelling that made its companion so entertaining. Though not in the same class as Alexander's more probing and philosophical *Westmark* trilogy, these Vesper Holly stories are intelligent and entertaining—a rare combination in today's children's book market.

Susan Harding

SOURCE: A review of *The El Dorado Adventure*, in *School Library Journal*, Vol. 33, No. 8, May, 1987, p. 105.

The indomitable Vesper Holly returns in this sequel to *The Illyrian Adventure.* This escapade begins when Vesper learns that she has inherited a large amount of land, including a volcano, in the wilds of Central America. She and her faithful guardian Brinnie journey to El Dorado to investigate, only to become involved in the struggle of a tribe of Indians to protect their homeland from unscrupulous developers who want to build a canal across the isthmus. As always, Brinnie naively accepts things at face value, while Vesper sees through to the truth. The charming Alain de Rochefort turns out to be a henchman of the evil Dr. Helvitius; the disreputable Captain O'Hara and his scurvy crew are staunch freedom fighters and become Vesper's loyal allies; and the savage chief of the Chiricas has been educated at Cambridge and has brought to his people such civilizing influences as the game of cricket. This book is even more enjoyable than the first; there is a light-hearted sense of fun entwined throughout the plot. There is also plenty of action and a number of cliff-hangers that create an episodic quality reminiscent of old Saturday matinée serials. All of the characters, even those who appear only briefly, are well fleshed-out, and there is a great deal of affection between Vesper and Brinnie.

Ethel R. Twichell

SOURCE: A review of *The El Dorado Adventure*, in *Horn Book Magazine*, Vol. LXIII, No. 3, May-June, 1987, pp. 344-45.

Once again the intrepid Vesper's derring-do sweeps aside Brinton Garrett, her cautious guardian, and his derring-don'ts in an exuberant adventure which leads them to the small Central American country of El Dorado. That the devices which initiate the story are a tad shaky is of no import. It is enough to enjoy Vesper's aptitude for danger and delight in her encounters with a seamy set of characters who cheat, connive, brag, and greatly enliven the jungle scene. Who but Lloyd Alexander could create the likes of the suave Alain de Rochefort; the garrulous Captain O'Hara and his infamous parrot, Adelita; the Cambridge-educated Chirican chieftain; and the oily and devious Dr. Helvitius, the daemon of *The Illyrian Adventure*? The imperturbable Vesper can quite convincingly repair a balky boat engine, devise a way to simulate a volcano, engineer impossible escapes, and survive recapture and an earthquake to save the tiny El Dorado from the unwanted exploitation of Helvitius's scheme for a canal. That the author has a soft spot for the lively Vesper and her prim but loyal Brinnie is quite evident, as is his pleasure in contriving their outrageous predicaments. Writing in his usual fast-paced yet carefully crafted style, the author again displays his mastery of the nasty surprise at chapter endings and delivers a rollicking adventure, well stocked with humor.

Susan Isaacs

SOURCE: A review of *The El Dorado Adventure*, in *The New York Times Book Review*, June 7, 1987, p. 29.

Seventeen-year-old Vesper Holly is everything a heroine of a Victorian-style adventure story should be: brave, intelligent, rich, willful and energetic. And *The El Dorado Adventure* is the perfect vehicle for her: an old-fashioned tale filled with shining heroes, nasty villains and a great deal of derring-do.

It is precisely this old-fashioned quality that is both the novel's strength and its weakness. Vesper, an orphan and the sole heir of a wealthy and charmingly eccentric family, is living on her estate near Philadelphia, "where she has begun experiments in fractionating hydrocarbons," when she receives an invitation to visit the Central American country of El Dorado. As it turns out, along with her other holdings, Vesper owns a healthy chunk of El Dorado. She accepts the offer with alacrity and, accompanied by her guardian, Professor Brinton (Brinnie) Garrett, she sets sail.

Throughout the novel, Vesper is unfailingly strong and competent. When the engine of a steamship is stalled, she merely rolls up her sleeves and gets to work. And when she is not busy in the boiler room, she repeatedly engineers escapes from the clutches of the evil Dr. Helvitius—and still manages to find time to give the women of the Chirica Indian tribe a fast but effective course in assertiveness training.

Like H. Rider Haggard and Jules Verne, Lloyd Alexander, the author of *The High King* among other books, gives his adventure the proper exotic atmosphere. Not only are there near-impenetrable jungles and alligator-infested rivers, there is a tall, handsome tribal chief, Acharro, who has a Cambridge University education, to say nothing of a volume of Euclid's geometry and a complete set of Rousseau's writings in his hut.

Vesper wins over Acharro with her intellect; it is a potent weapon. Like other fictional adventurers, she uses neither brute force nor sly tricks, but rather her own considerable intelligence to foil the forces of evil.

So in many ways, *The El Dorado Adventure* is a good, solid, traditional adventure yarn. But it is simply not adventurous enough. Vesper may be a feminist's dream, but as a character she is flat and undeveloped. The reader never gets any sense of how she became so brilliant and strong and valiant; she simply is. And because Vesper is always in such complete control, there is no sense of real excitement or danger in the novel. Even Wonder Woman had a bad moment now and then, but no matter how horrible the trap Dr. Helvitius sets, it is a foregone conclusion that Vesper will think her way out.

The El Dorado Adventure is weakened not only by the predictability of its plot, but by the staleness of its characters. Vesper, like Frodo the Hobbit and Sherlock

Holmes, has a doting and somewhat bumbling companion, the ever-amiable Brinnie. Her adversary, the seemingly omnipotent Helvitius, is also a stock character the reader has met before; J. R. R. Tolkien's Dark Lord and Arthur Conan Doyle's Professor Moriarty are memorable examples. But Lloyd Alexander's prose lacks the texture and the power to breathe new life into these familiar types.

Still, *The El Dorado Adventure* is engaging enough that the reader can't help but root for the smart, cool, courageous Vesper as she fights to save the Chirica Indians and their land from the villain's base designs. She may not be a woman of substance, but at least she is a woman of valor.

Brooke Dillon

SOURCE: A review of *The El Dorado Adventure,* in *Voice of Youth Advocates,* Vol. 10, No. 6, February, 1988, p. 285.

Indomitable, intelligent, and unbeatable, young Vesper Holly triumphs once again over evil in this second book of the Vesper Holly series. She and her guardian, Professor Brinton Garrett, set off for the tiny Central American republic of El Dorado to see for themselves the volcano and land holding which Vesper inherited upon the untimely death of her father. Almost immediately, they are kidnaped by the unsavory and ill-intentioned Alain de Rochefort, from whom they manage to escape, only later to fall into the diabolical clutches of Dr. Helvitius, the villain from the previous novel and mastermind of the plot to lure Vesper to El Dorado. Only Vesper's quick thinking saves her and "Brinnie" from certain death, although Dr. Helvitius manages to escape, leading the reader to assume that the Vesper Holly series will continue.

An Indiana Jones-type plot keeps the action moving swiftly, albeit not always totally believably (the volcano erupts and an earthquake occurs, both timed coincidentally for Vesper's short stay in El Dorado). Nonetheless, the book is entertaining; if offers some low-key history lessons concerning Central America, Simon Bolivar, and the oppression of native tribes; and it is beautifully written with wry humor and a vocabulary much more challenging than the average adolescent novel, a fact which should appeal to both teachers and parents. *The El Dorado Adventure* is, in fact, probably best-suited to the avid or gifted junior-high reader or to the high school fantasy fan. Alexander triumphs again!

THE DRACKENBERG ADVENTURE (1988)

Kirkus Reviews

SOURCE: A review of *The Drackenberg Adventure,* in *Kirkus Reviews,* Vol. LVI, No. 7, April 1, 1988, pp. 533-34.

In her third adventure, Vesper Holly engages her adversaries, with her usual flamboyant Amazonian style, in a small Balkan country. As before, the story is narrated by the bemused and confused Brinnie Garrett, Vesper's guardian.

When Brinnie and his wife Mary accept an invitation to the Duchess of Drackenberg's Diamond Jubilee, they are plunged into a plot involving a takeover attempt from neighboring Carpatia. In short order, the Garretts and Vesper find themselves mixed up with Gypsies, a kidnapping, and the discovery of an unknown Leonardo portrait of a 15th-century member of the ruling family who bears an uncanny resemblance to Vesper. Helvitius, Vesper's former antagonist, is again the villain; and, once again, Vesper saves the day while Brinnie bumbles through— and Helvitius escapes, to reappear (no doubt) in the future adventures promised at the conclusion.

Alexander has set up an entertaining formula, and he follows it effectively. Readers will find familiar elements— Brinnie's unconscious humor is especially welcome. Followers of the *Westmark* series may also find comic echoes of its sober political themes. A happy addition to the Alexander *oeuvre.*

Ilene Cooper

SOURCE: A review of *The Drackenberg Adventure,* in *Booklist,* Vol. 84, No. 17, May 1, 1988, p. 1514.

Vesper Holly returns in her third adventure, once again matching wits with the evil genius, Dr. Helvitius. It's off to Drackenberg for Vesper, her loyal guardian Brinnie, and his dear wife Mary when they receive an invitation to the Grand Duchess' diamond jubilee. But things are not well in Drackenberg; the country is poor and on the verge of being annexed by neighboring Carpatia. The Grand Duchess would like to help her citizens, if only she knew how. Vesper has some ideas she's willing to share, but once Dr. Helvitius shows up, she has her hands full— especially after he kidnaps Mary. Once again, Alexander offers a story that moves at break-neck speed and is filled with delicious details. Vesper's sojourn with the Gypsies and her saving of a never-before-seen da Vinci painting are the high points of the exciting tale. As usual, Alexander is to be commended for his elegant writing, astute characterizations, and his presentation of an intelligent heroine. There are hints in the book that another sequel is forthcoming, which should please Vesper's many fans.

Zena Sutherland

SOURCE: A review of *The Drackenberg Adventure,* in *Bulletin of the Center for Children's Books,* Vol. 41, No. 10, June, 1988, p. 197.

Ruritania lives again, as Alexander's atypical, picaresque heroine Vesper Holly (*The Illyrian Adventure, The El Dorado Adventure*) meets new challenges and once more outwits the nefarious Dr. Helvitius. Again the story is told by seventeen-year-old Vesper's guardian, an incorrigibly pompous Philadelphian (whose complacent parochialism, while still amusing, does get a bit repetitious). He blunders along as Vesper deals with villains, Gypsies, heads of state, etc. with successful impunity when attending the diamond jubilee celebration of Her Most Serene Highness, Maria-Sophia of Drackenberg. Adventures galore, humor as usual, colorful (if not wholly convincing) characters, and the appeal of a series book are combined in a story written with typical Alexandrian gusto and aplomb.

Ethel L. Heins

SOURCE: A review of *The Drackenberg Adventure,* in *Horn Book Magazine,* Vol. LXIV, No. 4, July-August, 1988, p. 499.

Returning to central Europe as the setting for another of his fictitious countries, Lloyd Alexander sends his dauntless seventeen-year-old heroine Vesper Holly, accompanied by her conscientious guardians Brinnie and Mary Garrett, to Drackenberg, a tiny impoverished duchy that has fallen "between the cracks of history." Propelled by Vesper's determination, they leave Philadelphia and sail away to attend the diamond jubilee celebration of the grand duchess, "Her Most Serene Highness Maria-Sophia." Predictably, the festivities prove to be only a prelude to another series of breathless escapades combining high comedy and suspense. At a resplendent party Brinnie and Vesper run into their old archenemy, the diabolical Dr. Helvitius, who has discovered priceless treasures in Drackenberg and is working, for his own selfish purposes, to deliver the country into the hands of a greedy neighboring monarch. Helvitius promptly tries to murder the three Americans, so Brinnie, Mary, and Vesper are given refuge in the palace—for the shrewd, crusty, but kindly Maria-Sophia is attracted to the percipient, strong-willed girl. The story has all the ingredients of a rousing comic opera: a beautiful heroine, picturesque scenery and costumes, frustrated villains, disguises, hairbreadth escapes, and outrageous situations—all the action rushing headlong to a grand finale. With its wonderfully exaggerated characters, tantalizing chapter endings, literate style, and witty repartee, the book—probably the best of the trilogy—must have been almost as much fun to write as it is to read.

Susan H. Williamson

SOURCE: A review of *The Drackenberg Adventure,* in *Voice of Youth Advocates,* Vol. II, No. 4, October, 1988, p. 190.

Vesper Holly (*The Illyrian Adventure* and *The El Dorado Adventure*) fans will not be disappointed in her latest adventure. Vesper and her guardians are guests at The Grand Duchess of Drackenberg's diamond jubilee celebration when they once again tangle with the evil Dr. Helvitius. With the help of Gypsies, they foil Helvitius' attempts to promote the annexation of Drackenberg, and Vesper finds a way to ease the small country's financial problems. Despite the 19th century setting, Vesper is a wonderful heroine; she is independent, intelligent, and charming. Told in the first person by Brinnie, Vesper's guardian, snappy prose and a fast pace will insure the book's popularity.

THE JEDERA ADVENTURE (1989)

Janice L. Del Negro

SOURCE: A review of *The Jedera Adventure,* in *School Library Journal,* Vol. 35, No. 9, May, 1989, p. 124.

Number four in the Vesper Holly adventures, this time our always-intrepid heroine must return an overdue library book—a rare, valuable, very overdue library book—to the famed library at Bel-Saaba, in the North African country of Jedera. There's something here for everyone: a mysterious desert chieftain, a forbidden love, even an early flying machine. Following his formula in his own pleasant way, Alexander sees Vesper and her guardian Brinnie through encounters with slave traders, desert wars, and the evil Dr. Helvitius, Vesper's arch rival. As in the previous titles, Alexander does a nice job in giving a sense of reality to foreign (and fantastic) locations, filling them with "local" color. Light-hearted and breezy (although for more sophisticated readers because of the high reading level), this is easy to booktalk and sure to be popular with fans of the earlier Vesper Holly escapades.

Betsy Hearne

SOURCE: A review of *The Jedera Adventure,* in *Bulletin of the Center for Children's Books,* Vol. 42, No. 10, June, 1989, p. 242.

Like Vesper Holly's *Illyrian, El Dorado,* and *Drackenberg* adventures, this one is a swashbuckling affair in which the narrator, Vesper's guardian Brinnie, relates their dangerous but always triumphant travels during the 1870s. Vesper is a superhero, and here she has met her equal in a chieftain (there's even a hint of romance between them) who helps her cross a desert, free the walled city Bel-Saaba from its despotic ruler, and save a street magician who has eloped with a sheik's favorite daughter. This, and more, is all done by way of returning a rare old library book that Vesper's father had borrowed, before his death, from a scholar in Bel-Saaba. Arch villain Dr. Helvitius proves, of course, to be the power behind the despot, and his scheme to build a flying machine that will drop explosives and so win him the world is foiled only by Vesper's instant grasp of aeronautic principles. Alexander's fictional worlds are always inventively imagined and his stylistic capsules easy to swallow ("He was the sort of fellow who should be a governor-general and seldom is"). The whole series is valuable in that it bestows elegant writing on unsuspecting young readers looking to gallop through books with familiar characters and lots of action.

Denise Wilms

SOURCE: A review of *The Jedera Adventure,* in *Booklist,* Vol. 85, No. 19, June 1, 1989, p. 1718.

When Vesper Holly discovers an old and valuable library book borrowed by her late father she decides it must be returned immediately—a seemingly simple task. The book, however, comes from the renowned Bel-Saaba library in Jedera (a mythical kingdom somewhere in North Africa). With her guardian, Brinnie, in tow, Vesper turns what should be an uncomplicated errand into one of intrigue, adventure, and down-and-dirty trouble, fueled yet again by her old nemesis, Dr. Helvitius. This latest Vesper Holly adventure runs true to form: Vesper is suitably larger than life, and her friends and enemies are more virtuous and more diabolical, respectively, than the average person. Alexander's clever style helps to assuage the feeling that this series, while enticing, approaches the formulaic; his considerable charm is sufficient to smooth over occasional plotting or character exaggerations. Fans of the other escapades will find this newest just as entertaining as its predecessors.

Brooke Dillon

SOURCE: A review of *The Jedera Adventure,* in *Voice of Youth Advocates,* Vol. 12, No. 3, August, 1989, p. 162.

Once again, young Vesper Holly triumphs over evil in this fourth book of the Vesper Holly series. Her guardian, Professor Brinton ("Brinnie") Garrett, and she determine that an ancient and valuable book about medicinal herbs, borrowed 15 years earlier by Vesper's deceased father, must be returned to the Bel-Saaba library in Jedera, North Africa. With the help of the street magician Maleesh; the mysterious blue-skinned stranger, An-Jalil; and the identical twins Smiler and Slider, last seen in *The El Dorado Adventure,* Vesper and Brinnie venture across the desert, surmounting a series of misadventures, only to once again fall into the diabolical clutches of Dr. Helvitius, the villain from the previous novels. Vesper's quick-wittedness and the help of her new friends protect her and "Brinnie" from certain death. Dr. Helvitius once again manages to escape, leaving open the prospect of a later adventure for Vesper and Brinnie.

Swift action, monumental coincidences, Brinnie's tongue-in-cheek observations, and an always-twisting story line result in a book both entertaining and humorous. The high level of vocabulary and sophisticated sentence construction will appeal to both teachers and parents, and make the book a very effective one for reading aloud. *The Jedera Adventure* is another delightful Alexander creation.

Ethel L. Heins

SOURCE: A review of *The Jedera Adventure,* in *Horn Book Magazine,* Vol. LXV, No. 5, September-October, 1989, p. 624.

Having previously subjected his beauteous heroine and her faithful guardian to outrageous adventures in imaginary places in Europe and in Central America, Lloyd Alexander plunges Vesper Holly and Professor Brinton Garrett, known as Brinnie, into a series of daunting escapades in North Africa. This time the delightfully absurd excuse is Vesper's desire to return a long-overdue book—an eight-hundred-year-old scholarly treatise borrowed years ago by her late father from the legendary library of the remote ancient city Bel-Saaba. Arriving at a North African port, Vesper and Brinnie start to organize a caravan for their journey, which will take them over precipitous mountains and a barren desert, and immediately become entangled in a web of conspiracy and danger. Kidnaped, the two narrowly escape being sold into slavery and then are caught in the crossfire of fiercely feuding tribes. After surviving further perils and the malevolent terrain, they finally reach their destination, only to fall into the clutches of more scoundrels—including the ingenious archfiend, Dr. Helvitius. Once again the novel is dominated by the incomparable intelligence, idealism, courage, and charm of the protagonist, and, as before, the hyperbolic aspects of the story are counterbalanced by the elegant, witty, beautifully paced writing.

THE PHILADELPHIA ADVENTURE (1990)

Kathryn Pierson

SOURCE: A review of *The Philadelphia Adventure,* in *Bulletin of the Center for Children's Books,* Vol. 43, No. 7, March, 1990, p. 152.

Philadelphia is the setting for the fifth book about the intrepid nineteenth-century heroine Vesper Holly. Scheming to control Brazil's natural resources, arch-villain Helvitius is also intent on destroying Vesper, her guardian, Brinnie, and anyone else nearby. An amazingly resourceful young man, Toby ("The Weed") Passavant, has been added to the cast of characters as an innocent love interest for Vesper; bumbling Brinnie is characteristically jealous. Alexander has thoroughly researched the events and personalities surrounding the 1876 World's Fair. The combination of historical fact, non-stop danger and intrigue, and masterful writing style adds up to another energetic predicament for Vesper Holly.

Christine Behrmann

SOURCE: A review of *The Philadelphia Adventure,* in *School Library Journal,* Vol. 36, No. 3, March, 1990, p. 215.

This fifth Vesper Holly adventure is set during the 1876 Philadelphia Centennial Exhibition. Once again Alexander successfully combines ingredients familiar to the series' readers—eccentrically entertaining characterizations, seamless plotting, and breakneck pace. Narrated as usual by Brinnie, Vesper's guardian and friend, the events are set in motion by an appeal from President Grant when the emperor of Brazil's grandchildren are kidnapped by none other than Vesper's nemesis, Dr. Helvitius. Vesper, who must deliver a ransom at Helvitius' demand, suspects her old enemy has a larger scheme in mind, as indeed he does. As usual, events pile on top of events and each chapter ends with a cliff-hanger, speeding readers to the exciting conclusion. Fans will welcome back friends from previous adventures, especially Tobias Wistar Passavant, "The Weed," who is coming into his own here as hero and as budding love interest for Vesper. Brinnie's narration is the accustomed diverting counterpoint to the action, enriched with amusing asides. In sum, this is a treat for followers of this series; indeed for anyone who enjoys a well-told adventure story.

Kirkus Reviews

SOURCE: A review of *The Philadelphia Adventure,* in *Kirkus Reviews,* Vol. LVIII, No. 6, March 15, 1990, p. 420.

Still narrated in hilariously flowery style by Brinnie—her dim, sentimental old guardian—the adventures of marmalade-haired superperson Vesper Holly continue in this fifth, but apparently not last, in the series. This time the evil mastermind, Dr. Helvetius, invades her native turf, where President Grant ("Sam," to Vesper) and the Brazilian emperor have met to open the 1876 Centennial Exposition. A lively series of kidnappings, escapes, and battles of both wit and vigorous slapstick ensues before Vesper realizes just what fiendish plot the villain is trying to hatch and how to avert it. The contrast between Brinnie's good-hearted bombast and Vesper's forthright common sense is as funny as ever. Alexander provides a note to distinguish historical fact from his clever fictions. Vastly entertaining.

Brooke Dillon

SOURCE: A review of *The Philadelphia Adventure,* in *Voice of Youth Advocates,* Vol. 13, No. 1, April, 1990, p. 36.

This fifth Vesper Holly book is another engaging adventure of the intellectual and spirited young woman and her dear friend and guardian, Dr. Brinton Garrett. Set in Philadelphia, the book opens with the surprise visit of President Ulysses Grant to Vesper's mansion. He requests Vesper's help in finding two kidnapped young Brazilian children who have come to Philadelphia with Don Pedro and Empress Theresa to attend the Centennial Exposition of 1876. Not surprisingly, Vesper learns that the evil Dr. Helvitius has masterminded the dastardly plot, and she plunges headlong to return the children and to save Brazil and the entire Western Hemisphere from Helvitius's clutches. That she is able to do so, while escaping several near-death episodes, is no surprise to loyal readers of this series.

Once again, as with the other books in the series, the reader will encounter a swift and entertaining plot loosely based on historical events, along with Alexander's tongue-in-cheek humor, his use of challenging vocabulary, and

his complex sentence structure. A pleasure for students and a delight for book-talks. *The Philadelphia Adventure* should be added to the ever-growing shelf of Alexander gems.

THE REMARKABLE JOURNEY OF PRINCE JEN (1991)

Kirkus Reviews

SOURCE: A review of *The Remarkable Journey of Prince Jen,* in *Kirkus Reviews,* Vol. LIX, No. 18, September 15, 1991, p. 1219.

Recounting the adventures of the son of an imaginary Chinese emperor, a master storyteller once again weaves a compelling tale.

Prince Jen and his sharp-tongued servant, Mafoo, volunteer to journey to the kingdom of T'ien-kuo to discover the secrets of governing from the king of that unusually happy and prosperous land. They set out bearing six gifts, but lose them all along the way; they also encounter a rich array of characters, including an evil bandit, a thief with a rigid code of conduct, a little girl who learns to fly, and an older one with whom Jen falls in love. Stories concerning the gifts are smoothly woven into the adventurous journey, which ends happily in the Prince's own kingdom.

There are familiar Alexander types here—the plucky but naive hero; the sarcastic, often wrong-headed sidekick; the girl who's smarter than either—but the characterizations get a fresh twist in a setting depicted with the abundant detail of a carefully woven tapestry, while the reader is hypnotically drawn into the lively story.

Kathryn P. Jennings

SOURCE: A review of *The Remarkable Journey of Prince Jen,* in *Bulletin of the Center for Children's Books,* Vol. 45, No. 3, November, 1991, p. 55.

Young lord Prince Jen of T'ang leaves his elderly father to seek T'ien-kuo, a kingdom that is legendary for its contented subjects. In order to gain an audience with the king of T'ien-kuo, Jen is advised to bring along six magic gifts. Jen is distracted from his destination by a series of disasters, first forfeiting the magic saddle and then being robbed of the magic sword. As he searches for the friends he has found and lost again on his journey, Jen gives the rest of the gifts to the people he meets who need them most. True to folklore tradition, Jen's friends reappear to help him with the gifts when he gets into trouble. Alexander's masterful prose works beautifully in the Chinese setting, in passages that are both witty ("The Nose of Thoughtful Inhalations sniffed it instantly") and serious ("Somewhere in his mind, a little frightened animal began to scurry back and forth. Its name was panic"). As usual, Alexander's characters are lively, funny, and eccentric, adding depth to the fast-moving story. Unfortunately, readers will be momentarily distracted at the end of each chapter by arch authorial comments encouraging them to continue reading (" . . . How reliable is Master Shu? These questions require time to find their answers, so it will be necessary to go on to the next chapter"). Unnecessary—one can't help but follow Jen on his journey as he changes from pampered prince to outlaw and beggar, a journey that teaches him how to be a man and a king.

Margaret A. Chang

SOURCE: A review of *The Remarkable Journey of Prince Jen,* in *School Library Journal,* Vol. 37, No. 12, December, 1991, p. 113.

From deep in the cauldron of world story comes a rich fantasy about a young man's journey from innocence to experience. In China during the Tang Dynasty, young Prince Jen, heir to the Dragon Throne, sets off to find T'ien-kuo, or Heavenly Kingdom, the utopia described by a mysterious wandering scholar. Accompanied by a large retinue of soldiers and his practical, plain-spoken servant, the idealistic, sheltered prince bears six gifts for the ruler of T'ien-kuo. As his journey progresses, he loses everything: his retinue, his possessions, his identity, his illusions, his friends, until at last, in one of Alexander's most moving passages, he finds himself a common criminal, wandering the roads of his own kingdom, wearing the wooden collar of punishment. Although experience is a harsh teacher, Jen never loses his common humanity, nor his faith in the bondmaid he loves. Alexander borrows form and content from the popular novels of the Ming and Ch'ing Dynasties, particularly Shi Nai'an's *Outlaws of the Marsh,* and is influenced, as are the Ming-Ch'ing novels, by the vernacular literature of the Sung Dynasty. Yet Jen's story transcends all boundaries, mixing Alexander's familiar cast—the impulsive, good-hearted boy; the clever, independent young woman; the assortment of eccentric, loyal companions—with flavors of European folklore; Hans Christian Andersen; admiring Chinoiserie, Buddhist and Taoist ideas; Arabian Nights extravagance, Alexander satisfies the taste for excitement, but his vivid characters and the food for thought he offers will nourish long after the last page is turned.

Ann A. Flowers

SOURCE: A review of *The Remarkable Journey of Prince Jen,* in *Horn Book Magazine,* Vol. LXVIII, No. 2, March-April, 1992, pp. 200-01.

Young Prince Jen, heir to the kingdom of T'ang, sets out on a journey to the legendary kingdom of T'ien-kuo to learn from King Yuan-ming the methods of governing a happy, harmonious realm. He is accompanied on his quest by his guards and his devoted servant, Mafoo. Jen is carrying six valuable gifts for Yuan-ming. Almost immediately things begin to go wrong. Owing to an act of kindheartedness, Jen loses his guards and one of his gifts. Event follows event, with the prince's fortunes swaying from good to bad and back again. Jen is joined by a peasant girl, Voyaging Moon, whose common sense is frequently the salvation of the party, and a robber, Moxa, whose career is blighted by his ethical principles; however, Jen is separated from his companions and subjected to a terrible form of punishment. Eventually Jen's generosity and his slow advance to maturity bring about a happy ending. Alexander's forte is the coming-of-age novel, and he skillfully uses symbolism and humor to reinforce his theme. Sometimes one feels too strong a resemblance between the characters in this book and those in Alexander's famous Prydain books. However, the circuitous plot is clever; the Chinese setting is purely imaginary; and the writing style is amusingly embellished with exaggeration and flowery language.

📖 *THE FORTUNE-TELLERS* (1992)

Lloyd Alexander

SOURCE: "The Fortune-Tellers," in *Horn Book Magazine,* Vol. LXX, No. 1, January-February, 1994, pp. 46-7.

[The following is Alexander's acceptance speech for the Boston Globe-Horn Book *Award, which was awarded to him and illustrator Trina Schart Hyman for* The Fortune-tellers *in 1993.]*

This is a rare instance when plain truth is so astonishing that even I, known to exaggerate a little from time to time, can find no way to embroider it. The report is accurate. My wife, Janine, decided to clear out the old junk from the attic to make room for new junk—and insisted on my attendance. I was unwilling. I do not like the attic. Hornets live there; so do bats. I always hit my head on the rafters; dust flies up my nose. I told Janine that my physical presence was not required; she had full authority to toss out everything, no exceptions, simple as that. But no, I was subpoenaed to take an active part in the exhumation of old newspapers, cocktail napkins, miniature vodka bottles, and all such artifacts of my profligate younger days. I even unearthed my correspondence files from 1947: two manila folders, one marked "Personal"; the other, "Editorial." In "Personal" was a letter from a friend; in "Editorial," nothing.

Since I wanted to get out of the attic as soon as possible, I began to jettison this motley accumulation with great rapidity. I did pause a moment when I turned up a ragged brown envelope. Out of idle curiosity, I opened it. And there was the completed text of something called ***The Fortune-tellers.*** This is a little like finding an old snapshot of yourself, say, at the Waukesha Natural Bridge. It's you, undeniably. How you got there, what you were doing, and why—long forgotten. I finally did recall writing it. I had put it aside temporarily; something else had caught me up. And, by the same process that causes paper clips to reproduce and multiply, the manuscript had made its way to the farthest reaches of the attic and had sat there patiently for fifteen years.

Purely for her amusement, with no expectations whatever, I sent it to Ann Durell, my editor at Dutton. She phoned soon after, convinced it would make a splendid picture book. Best yet, Trina Schart Hyman might be induced to illustrate it. Trina and I had been promising each other that we'd do a picture book together. Maybe this was the moment. It was. End of story. My part, at any rate.

I'm still dazzled by the turn of events. But my purpose today is not to speculate on the nature of luck, of loss and recovery, the mysterious workings of coincidence, or the whirligig of time. Actually, I have two purposes.

Since Trina is not given to praising herself, one of my purposes is to do it for her. Through sheer force of genius, or magical power unique unto herself, she has transmuted a few words into a whole world of beauty, exuberant humanity, and delicious wit constantly discovered and rediscovered. Thank you, Trina. You have worked wonders.

My other purpose—my main purpose—is directed to the judges of the Boston Globe-Horn Book Award, to fond friends and colleagues. The young man who wrote that small parable sends you his delight and gratitude. The much older man, here substituting for him, adds the same. Both of them have been honored even beyond their combined imaginations. And both offer their heartfelt and most affectionate thanks.

Publishers Weekly

SOURCE: A review of *The Fortune-Tellers,* in *Publishers Weekly,* Vol. 239, No. 28, June 22, 1992, p. 61.

The hands of fate deftly propel this original folktale. A seedy fortune-teller profits from gullible and sometimes desperate villagers who seek predictions for a rosier future. One unhappy carpenter takes to heart the seer's hardly helpful advice . . . and looks forward to a prosperous life. Most surprising to the craftsman, he ends up in the right place at the right time and the prediction comes true. Alexander's chipper text has a jaunty and infectious "just so" tone. Amazing coincidences fuse the plot elements, but the story's logic remains intact, successfully suspending the reader's disbelief. Hyman's acrylic, ink and crayon illustrations capture the landscape and people of West Africa in vivid detail. Indigenous plants and animals—including comically placed lizards—dot each scene, and the villagers' lushly textured apparel is spectacular. Especially opulent are spreads featuring the fortune-teller's cluttered quarters and the market stalls with their baskets and pottery.

Hazel Rochman

SOURCE: A review of *The Fortune-Tellers,* in *Booklist,* Vol. 88, No. 21, July, 1992, p. 1938.

Alexander's rags-to-riches story combines universal ele-

ments of the trickster character and the cumulative disaster tale. Hyman's pictures set it all in a vibrant community in Cameroon, West Africa. An old fortune-teller assures a young carpenter he'll be rich (if he earns large sums of money), he'll be famous (once he becomes well known), etc. Then the old man disappears; the people think he's been transformed into the carpenter, who quickly takes on the fortune-teller's role, learns the portentous babble, and becomes rich, famous, and happy. Meanwhile, we discover what really happened to the old man: he fell out of the window, had a series of accidents, and disappeared without a trace.

The energetic, brilliantly colored paintings are packed with people and objects that swirl around the main characters. Bathed in golden light, the carpenter's dreams of wealth, power, and romance look pale beside the magical daily life of the community. You can look and look at these pictures and see ever more detail of patterns and textures in foods, creatures, carvings, basketware, and, above all, the woven patterned cloths worn by everyone in gorgeous combinations. For the last part of the story—the bad fortune that happens as easily as the good—the packed pictures empty out to a view of wide savanna and the old man falling from the sky like Icarus, lost without a trace. With its ups and downs, this is a funny, playful story that evokes the irony of the human condition.

Kirkus Reviews

SOURCE: A review of *The Fortune-Tellers,* in *Kirkus Reviews,* Vol. LX, No. 15, August 1, 1992, p. 985.

When the poor, hard-working young carpenter seeks comfort from a fortuneteller, the old man hoodwinks him with double talk: "Rich you will surely be . . . [if] you earn large sums of money." But fate has a more benign trick in store. The cheating seer mysteriously vanishes; his cloth-merchant landlords, supposing that he has transformed himself into this fine young man, spread word of his predictive powers, and the youth is off to a prosperous new career. Meanwhile, the old man has been as unlucky as his successor is fortunate. Alexander narrates his original tale with folkloric verve and his own mellow brand of irony; Hyman realizes the African setting in broad double spreads rich with the lovely patterns and subtle, warm tones of the fabrics of Cameroon. There are also fine touches of humor in these splendid illustrations, and intriguing characterizations—especially of the carpenter, who enjoys his luck without being overearnest about it, and the beautifully individualized figures in the many crowd scenes. A winning tale, superlatively presented.

Betsy Hearne

SOURCE: A review of *The Fortune-Tellers,* in *Bulletin of the Center for Children's Books,* Vol. 46, No. 1, September, 1992, pp. 4-5.

The problem with this book is that there's so much to

look at you won't want to put it down. If you're lucky, somebody will read it to you so that you can listen to the resounding story while you look; if you're clever, in fact, you'll *make* someone read it to you while you look (slowly, look again, read it one more time); and if you're generous, you'll give kids the same experience. The title page opens on a vivid market scene in Cameroon, where a carpenter sets out for his day's work. "Will I be hammering and sawing the rest of my days?" he asks himself. No, says a fortune-teller whom he consults. "Rich you will surely be . . . on one condition: that you earn large sums of money. . . . You shall wed your true love . . . if you find her and she agrees. And you shall be happy as any in the world if you can avoid being miserable." We should all have such prophesies—and turn them into the same satisfying life as the carpenter's. As for the fortune-teller? Ask the runaway ox, the lion, the hornets, and the giant eagle, all of whom affect his fate beyond the wildest possibilities of prediction, an irony that should not escape sharp observers old or young. The trickster's hand is hidden here; it is the author's, and a clever tale he has turned, proving as adept at a picture book text as he is at complex fantasy series. What lends the words special significance is the contemporary West African setting that Trina Schart Hyman has peopled with a witty cast of individualized men, women, and children. Each double spread bursts with action in the form of physical posture and facial expression. Hyman's linework has always been powerful, but the colors, patterns, and textures here seem freshly energetic and profoundly warm-hearted. The sceneric detail is rich without becoming cluttered; equatorial chameleons, it turns out, are just as entertaining as European fairies. In the form of a funny story, this offers children a vital new world through which to wander.

Linda Boyles

SOURCE: A review of *The Fortune-Tellers,* in *School Library Journal,* Vol. 38, No. 9, September, 1992, p. 196.

A young carpenter, tired of hammering and sawing, seeks out a fortune-teller to see what his future holds. The cagey old prophet promises him a rosy future—well, maybe. "'Rich you will surely be,'" says the fortune-teller, if "'you earn large sums of money.'" Moreover, "'You shall wed your true love . . . if you find her and she agrees. And you shall be happy as any in the world if you can avoid being miserable.'" Pleased with these promising, if ambiguous, predictions, the carpenter leaves, only to get halfway home and decide he has more questions to ask. But the fortune-teller has mysteriously vanished, leaving the carpenter in the quirky hand of fate where, in typical Alexander fashion, his life takes a surprising and humorous turn. The story's warm and witty tone is reinforced by Hyman's masterful illustrations. Expressive figures are dynamically placed against a West African landscape, in colors so rich and clear that they invite readers to touch the fabrics and breathe the air. Visual details— carved wooden stools, traditional cloth patterns, signs in French—add an authenticity to the story (which is actually set in Cameroon), while touches of humor in postures

and expressions underscore Alexander's gentle wit. These illustrations are obviously a labor of love. Vibrant with life and good humor, this is a supremely satisfying creation.

Ellen Fader

SOURCE: A review of *The Fortune-Tellers,* in *Horn Book Magazine,* Vol. LXVIII, No. 5, September-October, 1992, pp. 570-71.

An unhappy carpenter seeks the advice of a fortuneteller, from whom he hears only what he wants to hear: he will be rich, if he earns a lot of money; he will become famous, after he becomes well-known; and he will marry his true love, if he can find her and she will agree. When he returns to ask the man more questions, he discovers his room empty except for his cap and crystal ball. The landlady mistakenly assumes that the old man has used his powers to change himself into an attractive young man and invites him to stay rent free in exchange for telling the family's fortunes. His predictions for them and the townspeople are modeled after those he himself received, and, finding his new trade easier than his old, he quickly becomes rich and famous and marries the woman of his dreams. Alexander's explanation of what happened to the real fortuneteller provides the perfect conclusion to this light-hearted romp: a series of misfortunes in the savanna cause him to be carried off by a giant eagle, and he is never heard from again. The book jacket indicates that the story takes place in Cameroon; Hyman's rendering of scenes in this central-African country delights the eye—there are bustling street markets, lengths of gloriously patterned cloth, and plenty of creepy claws, roots, and bones decorating the seer's room. Through the felicitous use of color, the multitude of patterns harmonize instead of fight for attention, providing a visual feast. A book that begs to be read aloud and pulses with life and good humor.

M. Jean Greenlaw

SOURCE: A review of *The Fortune-Tellers,* in *The New Advocate,* Vol. 6, No. 1, Winter, 1993, p. 74.

Oh, the delicious wit of Alexander is in full flourish here! A young carpenter seeks his fortune to be told that he will be rich "On one condition: that you earn large sums of money." He will be famous, once he becomes well known. The logic is inescapable, but when the carpenter returns to have more questions answered, the fortune-teller is gone. Assuming his mantle, the carpenter/fortune-teller does become rich, famous, and happy, having caught the drift of telling accurate fortunes. What a great read-aloud, suitable for young listeners as well as older students who will enjoy the satire. Hyman has set the tale in Cameroon, West Africa. The richness of the fabrics and the beauty of the people and setting are perfect subjects for her detailed paintings that emphasize humor and portraiture.

📖   *THE ARKADIANS* (1995)

Cheri Estes

SOURCE: A review of *The Arkadians,* in *School Library Journal,* Vol. 41, No. 5, May, 1995, p. 104.

An expertly developed cast of characters rounds out this witty epic that's filled with romance and adventure. Lucian, the archetypal hero, knows more than he should about the king's nefarious soothsayers and must escape the palace or be killed. He takes with him Fronto, a poet whose folly has turned him into a donkey. Guided by Joy-in-the-Dance, a pythoness oracle who serves the Lady of Wild Things, they seek the Lady on an Oz-like journey for answers to their problems, joined on the way by Ops, a chief who was cast out of his village. The travelers do not get what they had hoped for from the Lady, but Lucian does learn why her followers and his Bear Clan are enemies. The seekers are then sent on another journey that completes the heroic cycle. On one level, this is a rousing adventure complete with cliffhangers and do-or-die situations. On another, readers familiar with Greek mythology will find clever hints at the myths' purpose and genesis. The Arkadians have experiences and listen to tales that resemble the stories of Narcissus, the Wooden Horse of Troy, Odysseus, and Theseus and the Minotaur, among others. The women are the wise ones in this novel and play their own heroic roles. On a deeper level, this tale is about love and peace, symbolized by the marriage of Lucian and Joy-in-the-Dance and the subsequent uniting of the Bear Clan and the Followers of the Lady. Thus, Arkadia becomes the mythical Arcadia, which poets lauded as a utopia. The plot has many twists and turns, but is not hard to follow, and Alexander's style is eminently readable.

Ilene Cooper

SOURCE: A review of *The Arkadians,* in *Booklist,* Vol. 91, No. 17, May 1, 1995, p. 1561.

Part Greek myth, part *Canterbury Tales,* part *Wizard of Oz,* Alexander's latest is also a story with a feminist sheen. Lucian, the castle bean counter who uncovers a scandal, is forced to flee when he mistakenly confides in the wrong people. So begins an extraordinary journey through Arkadia for Lucian and Fronto (once a poet, now a talking jackass) as they try to find the goddess figure who can help them out of their predicament. Along the way, they are joined by a remarkable band of characters, including a village chief turned village scape-goat, a goat boy, a disguised king, and Joy-in-the-Dance, a spirited young wise woman who takes more than a passing interest in Lucian. Done in epic style, the book almost brims over with tales, twists, and trouble. Occasionally, a character gets lost, and readers might wish that more attention be paid to the burgeoning romance between Lucian and Joy-in-the-Dance. But Alexander is as good as anyone when it comes to creating strong women characters, and one of the most interesting things about this book is his focus on the goddess culture and its role in both history and myth.

Kirkus Reviews

SOURCE: A review of *The Arkadians,* in *Kirkus Reviews,* Vol. LXIII, No. 9, May 1, 1995, p. 630.

When Lucian, a young bean counter in the palace of King Bromios of Arkadia, discovers that the royal soothsayers are fleecing the treasury, he is forced to run for his life. Out in the countryside, he discovers that Bromios, at the advice of the wicked soothsayers, has ordered the destruction of the temples and oracles of the Woman-Who-Talks-to-Snakes, and the hunting down of all the wise women and priestesses. He soon encounters Fronto, a poet turned into a donkey; Joy-in-the-Dance, a mysterious girl with strange powers; and many other strange and wonderful characters, and embarks on a quest to restore Fronto to his human state.

Based on a variety of Greek myths and legends, this wild and woolly adventure covers territory both geographical and literary. Master storyteller Alexander (**The Fortune-Tellers,** 1992, etc.), known for rollicking fantasy and mystery adventures, keeps the action brisk, packs the text with a riveting collection of weird characters, fantastic settings, plot twists, derring-do, heroes, villains, magic, prophesies, humor, shipwrecks, fires—what more could readers ask for?

Publishers Weekly

SOURCE: A review of *The Arkadians,* in *Publishers Weekly,* Vol. 242, No. 24, June 12, 1995, p. 62.

Lucian flees corrupt palace officials in pre-classical Greece, his flight becoming a quest to discover his role in life. Soon, he's trying to help a second-rate poet turned donkey regain human form. Roaming the land, he also gets caught up in the great conflict between followers of the mother goddess and believers in the Olympian pantheon. Fortunately, he has the help of Joy-in-the-Dance, a young prophetess, in a relationship strikingly similar to that of Taran and Eilonwy in Alexander's five-volume Prydain Chronicles. And like the Prydain novels, this adventure draws heavily on a great body of myths and legends. Perhaps to accommodate the constraints of a single volume, Alexander relays many myths in comic, de-bunked forms—he shows poets transforming a clan of horse-riders into centaurs, a skilled mariner separated from his barmaid love into the epic hero Odysseus. Even with much of the raw material developed only minimally, the result is a good, involving story. Readers already acquainted with Greek literature and legend will enjoy picking out familiar threads.

Elizabeth Bush

SOURCE: A review of *The Arkadians,* in *Bulletin of the Center for Children's Books,* Vol. 48, No. 11, July-August, 1995, p. 375.

Lucian, a bean-counter for the king, is on the lam from

the crooked ministers he's discovered with their hands in the treasury; Fronto, a pompous poet transformed into a jackass, is on the hoof from a cruel owner; Joy-in-the-Dance, a displaced oracle whose sanctuary was ransacked by a warring tribe, is on her way home to mother. Banding together in a sort of Crosby-Hope-Lamour team on the road to Metara, the trio share adventure and hear tales that are, in fact, twists on classical myths and epics. The entire odyssey seems little more than a *raison d'être* for Alexander's clever spoofs on the Trojan Horse, Narcissus, the Minotaur, and a particularly shady Jason; however, these tales are never directly named, so readers must hone their Homer and be up on their Olympians to catch the references. Fronto's wisecracking, Joy-in-the-Dance's condescension, and Lucian's bumbling chauvinism wear thin quickly, and the poets-are-really-jackasses theme limps with overuse. Although a happy ending sees Lucian united with Joy-in-the-Dance, Fronto returned to human form, and a host of hangers-on basking in bliss, little character development has occurred over the nearly three hundred pages to justify the felicitous conclusion.

Kathleen Beck

SOURCE: A review of *The Arkadians,* in *Voice of Youth Advocates,* Vol. 18, No. 5, December, 1995, p. 312.

Lucian's boring life as a bean counter in the royal palace of Arkadia is interrupted when he stumbles onto a fraud perpetrated by the king's closest advisors. Fleeing for his life, Lucian finds himself collecting unexpected companions: a poet who has been turned into an ass; a beautiful girl named Joy-in-the-Dance, who, as the oracle pythoness, had pronounced an unwelcome prophecy to King Bromios; a goat boy; a wandering seafarer; a horseman so swift he seems at one with his mount; and last, but not least, a scapegoat. All of them seek the Lady of the Wild, whose divine intervention alone can save Arkadia.

Alexander has cleverly larded his adventurous tale with elements from Greek poetry and mythology. Alert readers will recognize many of the characters and stories, slightly mangled in the telling. We meet Odysseus, hear the true account of what happened at Troy, encounter Jason on his way to the fleece (not such a hero after all) and navigate with Lucian the labyrinth of Mynos. One might accuse the author of a degree of self-indulgence, being smart at readers' expense. It is true that most of these references will slip by the average reader, but those well-informed will feel justifiably smug while others will enjoy a good adventure. The book's appeal is not dependent on deciphering all the clues. This has more in common with Alexander's lighter works such as *The Marvelous Misadventures of Sebastian* or *The First Two Lives of Lukas-Kasha* than with the more thoughtful *Prydain* or *Westmark* series. Challenging literature it's not, but those looking for a pleasant way to spend an afternoon could do worse than to wander in Arkadia.

Maurice Saxby

SOURCE: A review of *The Arkadians,* in *Magpies,* Vol. 11, No. 1, March, 1996, p. 31.

There are two ways of reading this text. It can be taken as a somewhat loose and rambling picaresque adventure involving three main characters—Lucian, a rather earnest young bean counter who runs foul of two dastardly soothsayers; Fronto, a poet who has been turned into a donkey; and Joy-in-the-Dance, a volatile female of marvels and mysteries. As the trio pursue their peripatetic course through Arkadia (remember that Arcadia was a tranquil mountainous district of Greece in the Peloponnesus, and the map in the front of the book is very much Greece!) they meet a host of bizarre characters with names like Woman-Three-Women, Think-Too-Late and Hope-Never-Lost. (Reminiscent of Ruth Manley's Japanese fantasies!) The plot consists of a string of stories told to the travellers by the strange personalities they meet or the stories they themselves relate. At one point Fronto, in exasperation, bids Ops—one of the narrators—to get on with it. No need to string it out, we understand the situation. There, Lucian, is an example of bad storytelling. Ops, for the sake of mercy and my patience, come to the point. Exactly! If readers approach *The Arkadians* expecting a fast-moving fantasy in the Kelleher style they will be disappointed. If, however, they are conversant with Greek mythology (in fact with world mythology) they may well rise to the challenge of 'deconstructing' the text by spotting the references to a host of myth elements: a parody of the Narcissus story; a variation of Pandora's Box; reference to Jason's early life and his father's sandals (that is when Ops infuriates Fronto); Sigurd, the Daughters of the Hesperides; Atalanta's race with role reversal (she drops the apples); a tangled thread of the Theseus legend; and even an off-beat Tiddalik! Plus many more motifs and patterns from mythology: spells and enchantments, amulets, sacrifice, transmutation and transmogrification. All is done light-heartedly, with irony and even parody. Good fun for the reader steeped in myth and perhaps entertaining for devotees of fantasy. But don't expect the High Fantasy of Tolkien, Le Guin or even the author's own Prydain series. By comparison, this is a lightweight frolic.

THE HOUSE GOBBALEEN (1995)

Hazel Rochman

SOURCE: A review of *The House Gobbaleen,* in *Booklist,* Vol. 91, No. 21, July, 1995, p. 1882.

Tooley is always grumbling about his bad luck. His wise cat, Gladsake, tries to set him straight ("Which would you rather have? A roof with a leak or a leak without a roof?"), but Tooley won't listen. He invites a fat, little monster man into the house, sure that he will bring good luck, but eventually the cat has to trick the monster out of the house and prove to Tooley that he can make his own luck. It all goes on too long: too many scenes of the monster bawling and grabbing and demanding food and service, too many tricks to get rid of him. But the storytelling is droll; the fool, the monster, and the trickster are gloriously exaggerated characters, whose roles are sometimes reversed. [Diane] Goode's bright, slapstick pictures, full of curls and points and dislocation, are as good natured and silly as the story. The monster has drumstick arms, a lumpy nose, and what the cat calls "a lopsided, squinny-eyed look": he's like everything else in this story, somewhere between clown and gargoyle.

Publishers Weekly

SOURCE: A review of *The House Gobbaleen,* in *Publishers Weekly,* Vol. 242, No. 29, July 17, 1995, p. 230.

Newbery Medalist Alexander, storyteller par excellence, effortlessly whips up a confection featuring a feckless fellow named Tooley, his clever cat Gladsake, and Hooks, a no-good member of the Friendly Folk. Hoping for his luck to change, Tooley invites Hooks into his home. But Hooks is bent only on sponging off his host, not rewarding his hospitality, and he soon has Tooley running to do his bidding. The little man (who grows rotunder by the day) guzzles Tooley's cider, cleans out his larder, sleeps in the best bed and appropriates the best chair. Meanwhile, Tooley's fortunes show no sign of improving. Realizing he's been hoodwinked, Tooley bemoans his new fate until his savvy cat takes charge and routs the intruder with tales of none other than himself, the House Gobbaleen. It's an utterly delicious tale, and Alexander and Goode are an unbeatable combination. Goode's beguilingly tattered backdrops can hardly contain the droll, frisky action she depicts in such warm colors, and her artwork's elfin charm matches Alexander's sprightly originality. Readers will hope for another collaboration from these two, and soon.

Donna L. Scanlon

SOURCE: A review of *The House Gobbaleen,* in *School Library Journal,* Vol. 41, No. 9, September, 1995, p. 167.

In this original fairy tale, Tooley is convinced that he suffers from bad luck—his roof leaks, his potatoes are too small, and his pig keeps breaking out of her sty. Nonsense, says his sensible cat Gladsake, but the man is determined to attract one of the Fair Folk and change his lot. When a round little figure named Hooks shows up at the door, Tooley is elated, until he finds himself spending his days serving and feeding him. Tooley catches on finally, but it is Gladsake who saves the day with a wily scheme worthy of Brer Rabbit. Alexander's rolling, lilting language is a joy to read aloud, and the seamlessly written story with its wry undertone will engage both young listeners and older readers. Tooley is a good-natured and appealing character, if a bit slow to grasp his situation, and Gladsake is not only clever and sensible, but also extraordinarily patient. Goode's bright, cheery paintings and distinctive style capture the spirit of the tale

and carry it to its triumphant conclusion. She maintains a sense of motion with abrupt shifts in angle and perspective and through repeated images that move across one page to the next. The scenes are packed with detail: Tooley's cramped cottage, chock-full of chipped crockery, conveys an air of shabby gentility. Hooks is a marvel of cherubic malevolence, while Tooley's gangly arms and legs and long face with its endearing, if goofy, expression illustrates his eagerness to please. A delightful treat from beginning to end.

Betsy Hearne

SOURCE: A review of *The House of Gobbaleen,* in *Bulletin of the Center for Children's Books,* Vol. 49, No. 4, December, 1995, pp. 118-19.

A perfect story-hour companion to Margot Zemach's picture-book version of the old Jewish tale *It Could Always Be Worse,* this plays on the same theme: when things seem bad, just invite trouble into the house and things will soon seem so terrible that the old days will look terrific. The setting here, though, is distinctly Irish. Tooley grumbles about his small potatoes, leaking roof, and rebellious pig. His wise cat, Gladsake, asks whether Tooley would prefer "a roof with a leak or a leak without a roof," but Tooley insists on seeking better luck through a leprechaun-like visitor who commandeers Tooley's food, tobacco, and bed. (Surely Tooley should take a hint from those suspicious scowls dominating all the ancestral portraits on his wall.) It's Gladsake who finally gets rid of the creature by fabricating an even more malevolent presence (the Gobbaleen), leaving Tooley to count his blessings instead of complaining. Goode's mellifluous colors and textures are sharpened by the grotesque expressions and poses of her bug-eyed characters. The artistic action is fast-paced, but the liveliest figure is gingery Gladsake, whose fur matches—but whose brain far outweighs—his master's.

Mary M. Burns

SOURCE: A review of *The House Gobbaleen,* in *Horn Book Magazine,* Vol. LXXII, No. 1, January-February, 1996, p. 58.

An original story with echoes of an Irish *shanachie*'s style in its phrasing draws on a familiar folkloric motif—that of wit triumphant. But other motifs are cleverly used as well in this captivating tale about luck. There are three pivotal characters: the feckless, over-eager Tooley' his sensible (and more intelligent) cat Gladsake; and a small rotund man named Hooks who is an unregenerate con artist. Convinced that this last is one of the Friendly Folk and a purveyor of good fortune, Tooley invites him to share hearth and home with hopes of having a change in his luck which the guest never really promises. The resulting events are a series of comic turns as the hapless Tooley becomes the slave of a demanding master. "'It's luck I wanted,' he moaned to the cat, 'and luck I got. All of it bad!'" But Gladsake comes up with a plan to evict their nemesis by convincing him that he will be attacked by the Gobbaleen, a most unfriendly spirit. The ruse works; Hooks is vanquished; and Tooley learns that he has to make his own luck. Diane Goode has captured the action in spirited illustrations with a sly touch of caricature to underscore the characterizations. Look for the changing expressions in Tooley's ancestral portraits for an added fillip.

THE IRON RING (1997)

Publishers Weekly

SOURCE: A review of *The Iron Ring,* in *Publishers Weekly,* Vol. 244, No. 15, April, 14, 1997, pp. 76-7.

A master storyteller draws loosely on the great myths and literature of India in this semi-mystical epic adventure. It begins with a riveting scene: bound by the principles of dharma (the code of honor), the young king Tamar receives a disagreeable guest, King Jaya, who insists on playing a high-stakes game of dice; after winning round after round, Tamar is obliged to gamble on his very life— and loses. He pledges to travel to King Jaya's palace to make good on his debt, although it may well mean his death. The next morning, however, Tamar's courtiers have no recollection of Jaya's visit and are sure that Tamar has simply dreamed it. But a ring on Tamar's finger convinces him that, dream or not, he is honor-bound to undertake the journey. The journey proves more important than the destination, and along the way Tamar's conduct earns him a retinue that includes various talking animals as well as the cowherd Mirri, a typically self-possessed Alexander heroine. Once they have fallen in love, the quest involves them in the downfall of both an evil king and a rapacious demon seeking a gem with the power to determine life and death. Alexander's emphasis on Tamar's psychological/spiritual growth adds a personal note to the epic material, but lessens the sweep of such climactic scenes as the defeat of the evil king with the help of monkeys and forest elephants and tends to flatten the cliffhangers that close almost every chapter. In balance, however, the imaginative scope of the story and its philosophical complexities will make this an exciting journey for the reader as well.

Cindy R. Larson

SOURCE: A review of *The Iron Ring,* in *Children's Book Review Service, Inc,* Vol. 25, No. 13, July, 1997, p. 153.

When Tamar, King of Sundari, loses a dice game, he not only loses his kingdom and all its riches to the mysterious King Java, but he also loses his life as a free person. To Tamar, born a noble warrior, honor is everything. He sets out on his journey to make good his debt. Along the way he befriends a monkey who has a gift for finding trouble. Tamar saves the monkey's life and in return Hasket promises to see Tamar to Java's palace. On the way, they encounter a variety of magical characters you will fall in

love with. There are heartbreaking and hilarious moments, but the story always keeps the reader wanting more.

Amy E. Brandt

SOURCE: A review of *The Iron Ring,* in *Bulletin of the Center for Children's Books,* Vol. 50, No. 11, July-August, 1997, p. 386.

Tamar, the young and inexperienced king of Sundari, wagers his life on a game of dice, and he loses the game. Honor-driven to pay his debt, he embarks on a journey to find the mysterious king who challenged him, despite the possibility that the game was only a dream. *The Iron Ring* is a complex, episodic tale told in the tradition of great Indian epics such as the *Mahabharata* and *Ramayana.* Set in a mythical India, Tamar's quest is a karmic one; his stubborn insistence on following a strict *kshatriya's dharma,* or warrior's code of ethics, has far-reaching consequences for the fates of friend and foe alike. While the conclusion seems overly constructed, the abundance of character-driven subplots does require closure, and Tamar's maturation is satisfyingly evident as he becomes a wiser and more compassionate king. Filled with swordplay, enchantment, and enough endearing human and animal characters to warrant an oft-consulted cast list, this may be a reader advisory wish-come-true. Have philosophically savvy, *Redwall*-weary readers contemplate this one for awhile.

Rebecca Barnhouse

SOURCE: A review of *The Iron Ring,* in *Voice of Youth Advocates,* Vol. 20, No. 4, October, 1997, p. 250.

One step forward, two steps back. That is about as fast as young King Tamar goes on his journey to the mysterious King Jaya of Mahapura. And who can blame him? At the end of his journey, only death awaits: In a game of dice with Jaya, Tamar has gambled away his life. On his path through ancient India, Tamar befriends the king of the monkeys, a talking elephant, a meditating bear, and other marvelous creatures. He falls in love with Mirri, a wise *gopi,* or cow-girl, and offers his sword and army to help another king. Before he leaves his sheltered, peaceful kingdom, Tamar is a hasty youth, quick to anger. By journey's end, he has learned the difference between honor and arrogance, has fought and suffered, and has come to understand much more of the world.

Folktale elements fill the novel: a perilous journey to a place that might not even exist; a wise old companion; unexpected help along the way; a beautiful maiden. Alexander uses the mythology and folktales of India to create a lush, enchanting world while teaching readers concepts such as *dharma* and *karma.* (A list of characters and places and a glossary help untangle the unfamiliar names and large cast of characters.) Tamar's path to Mahapura leads inevitably to self-knowledge—by way of visits to peaceful *ashramas* and gory battlefields, loss of honor and honor regained, and tales told by fellow travelers. Readers will want to leap astride their horses to accompany Tamar and his companions on this trek through a rich landscape of wonder and excitement.

Additional coverage of Alexander's life and career is contained in the following sources published by Gale Research: *Authors and Artists for Young Adults,* Vol. 1; *Contemporary Authors New Revision Series,* Vol. 55; *Dictionary of Literary Biography,* Vol. 52; *Junior DISCovering Authors (CD-ROM); Major Authors and Illustrators for Children and Young Adults; Something about the Author,* Vols. 3, 49, 81; and *Something about the Author Autobiography Series,* Vol. 19.

Pat Cummings

1950-

American author and illustrator of fiction and picture books.

Major works include *Jimmy Lee Did It* (1985), *C.L.O.U.D.S.* (1986), *Clean Your Room, Harvey Moon!* (1991), *Carousel* (1994).

INTRODUCTION

Cummings is a children's author and illustrator whose works feature people of various races taking positive, constructive approaches to everyday problems. Known for her keen sense of humor and vivid imagination, she developed an interest in cultural diversity while spending her childhood living in Germany and Japan and in various regions of the United States, as her father's career in the U.S. Army involved moving to a new base every two or three years. Being immersed in different cultures as a child sensitized Cummings to the importance of including people of all races in her work as an adult. "I've chosen at times not to illustrate stories that contained what seemed to be negative stereotypes," Cummings affirmed in an essay for *Something about the Author Autobiography Series*. "When the vast majority of books published for children still reflects a primarily white, middle-class reality, I've always felt it was essential to show the spectrum of skin tones that truly make up the planet. I want any child to be able to pick up one of my books and find something of value in it, even if only a laugh. The stories have truly universal themes: a jittery first day of school, the arrival of a new baby, attacking a messy room." Cummings combats negative stereotyping in her own books by presenting young African American protagonists in stories featuring strong family relationships that are often modeled on the author's personal experience. *Clean Your Room, Harvey Moon!,* for instance, is based in part on Cummings's fond recollection of things found in her brother's childhood bedroom. Cummings's illustrations, both for her own books and those of other authors, have garnered praise from commentators citing favorably the artist's bold designs, vivid use of color, and warm, emotionally expressive character portrayals. In the *Sixth Book of Junior Authors and Illustrators,* Cummings remarked: "I want children to be able to see positive reflections of themselves in my books and hopefully to find, as I always have, a little magic and mystery between the covers."

Biographical Information

Born in 1950 in Chicago, Illinois, Cummings was the second of four children. Her brother and sisters were her clos-

est friends while she was growing up, mainly because moving so often made it difficult to develop lasting friendships. She had already moved to Virginia and back to Chicago by the age of five, when she first left American soil to live in Germany. One memorable event happened in Germany that proved to have a lasting effect on Cummings's life and career. While out one day with Linda, her older sister, Cummings decided to hop on board a school bus—uninvited—with other girls after Linda had left her alone for a moment. The bus traveled deep into Germany's Black Forest and stopped at a ballet school. Cummings got out with the other girls, pretending to belong, and spent an enchanting afternoon practicing ballet. When she finally returned home, she discovered that her distraught mother had alerted the police. She was grounded for a long time after that incident. "As it turned out, I found myself with quite a bit of time on my hands to practice drawing," she recollected. "[I] began drawing ballerinas. They all had pinpoint waists and enormous skirts. . . . As I perfected my ballerinas, I found that my classmates would pay me for them. I got a nickel for a basic ballerina, a dime for the more elaborate ones. If they had glitter, or were special requests (hearts on Valentine's Day or monsters for Halloween, for example), I might even get some M & Ms or Twinkies as payment. Candy was as good as money in those days. So, at a very early age, I made a connection between artwork being thoroughly enjoyable and good business as well."

Cummings went on creating ballerinas and other works of art throughout her school years. Although many of her school experiences were positive—she used her artistic talents to help out with school projects and meet new friends—one incident at a Virginia elementary school taught her some of the harsh realities of life. "At recess I ran to the playground and hopped on a merry-go-round," she recalled. "One of the nuns hastily came and led me away from the slides and see-saws, jungle gyms and sand-box I had my sights on next. She took me over to a dirt lot where there was a lone basketball hoop. My sister Linda was there. The nun told me that this was 'my' playground. . . . We were black and we couldn't play with the white kids we sat next to in the classroom. That wasn't clear to me then, even looking around at the other black children that had been steered to the dirt lot. It took me several years and more of such encounters to make any connection. . . . That non-inclusion puzzled me, trou-bled me, and finally, as I was growing up, led me to an awareness of America's deeply rooted racism." This ex-perience laid the foundation for Cummings's professional goal of creating works that appeal to people of all races.

After graduating from high school in 1968, Cummings decided to attend Pratt Institute in New York City. She majored in fashion because illustration was not offered as a major at that time. Although she dropped out of Pratt, worked for a year, and traveled to Georgia to attend Spelman College and Atlanta School of Art, Cummings eventually returned to Pratt to earn her degree in fine arts in 1974. During her last year of school she began work-ing as a freelance commercial artist. Cummings's break into book illustration came after some of her artwork was featured in the *Bulletin* published by the Council on In-terracial Books for Children. Without any experience il-lustrating books, Cummings was offered the chance to draw the pictures for Eloise Greenfield's *Good News.*

Major Works

The success of Cummings's picture-book artwork has led her to illustrate many other stories, among them several of her own: *Jimmy Lee Did It, C.L.O.U.D.S., Clean Your Room, Harvey Moon!,* and *Carousel.* Each of these imag-inative and often humorous tales has strong ties to Cum-mings's family. The inspiration for *Jimmy Lee Did It* came from her brother Artie, who during childhood had an imaginary friend who was conveniently assigned the blame when trouble occurred. Cummings got the idea for *C.L.O.U.D.S.* after sitting on the porch in Virginia with her mother and applauding a stunning sunset. The story's main character, Chuku—the name of Cummings's hus-band—is a cloud designer for Creative Lights, Opticals, and Unusual Designs in the Sky who finds himself in

trouble after spelling out "Hello Down There" over New York City. A tale of the unusual things a boy keeps in his room, *Clean Your Room, Harvey Moon!* is also based on Artie's childhood and was produced while Cummings stayed with her younger sister Barbara in Jamaica. *Car-ousel* describes a little girl's feelings of disappointment and frustration when her father is not home as promised for her birthday celebration. A dreamscape sequence fea-turing a miniature carousel the girl received as a birthday present enhances what a *Kirkus Reviews* commentator called "a likable, deceptively simple story that provides a fine model of forbearance and clemency strengthening an already loving relationship." Cummings has also written and illustrated *Peter Moroni's Camp Runamok Diary,* her 1992 story about food disappearances at summer camp.

Whether working on her own books or illustrating for others, Cummings maintains her philosophy that children's books ought to encourage optimistic, constructive ap-proaches to life: "There is a responsibility attached to making books for young readers," she stated. "A lot of stories focus on the children's emotions and scratching up those feelings is pointless unless there is a positive reso-lution by the book's end. I feel the best stories allow a child to discover a solution or approach to their own sit-uation."

Awards

Cummings received the Coretta Scott King Illustrator Award from the American Library Association in 1984 for *My Mama Needs Me,* written by Mildred Pitts Walter, and earned honorable mention consideration for the same award in 1987 for *C.L.O.U.D.S.* and in 1989 for *Storm in the Night,* written by Mary Stolz. Cummings also received a *Boston Globe-Horn Book* Award for Nonfiction in 1992 and an Honor Book designation from the Orbis Pictus Award for Outstanding Nonfiction for Children from the National Council of Teachers of English in 1993 for *Talking With Artists.*

AUTHOR'S COMMENTARY

Pat Cummings with Jim Roginski

SOURCE: in an interview in *Behind the Covers, Vol. II,* Libraries Unlimited, 1989, pp. 81-92.

Pat Cummings, once tied to the do-it-ten-minutes-ago world of advertising and editorial illustration, finds chil-dren's books a welcome relief and a chance, in her words, to get "into the art." Increasingly involved in book devel-opment, she finds the business of publishing endlessly fascinating for its operations and the exposure she is re-ceiving. She is savvy; she is effervescent; she is articu-late; but, most of all, she is in the midst of carving out a demanding career.

She and her husband, Chuku Lee, a real estate appraiser and entrepreneur, live in a loft studio in Brooklyn, New York overlooking the East River and the Statue of Liberty. The light is ample, filling her artist's needs; her home is spacious and frequently filled with friends and family.

Born in Chicago, Illinois in 1950, she received her Bachelor of Fine Arts degree from Pratt Institute in 1974. She is a member of the Graphic Artists Guild, the Society of Children's Book Writers, and the Children's Book Illustrators' Group.

Although not raised in New York City, most people would think otherwise, since she exudes the city's attitudes. Her kinetic style of talking (scattershot mixed with a healthy laugh), her broad mannerisms, with a great deal of hand and shoulder punctuation, and a deeply felt interest in perfecting her work and craft, make for circuitous twists and turns in a conversation of any length. A dialogue with Pat is easy, simply because she loves to talk. When it's about her work and craft, she loves to talk even more. Sometimes, she doesn't even mind if a willing listener takes her away from her work—especially when a deadline is near, though there will be a momentary pause for the requisite *angst!*

[Jim Roginski]: Pat, before you entered children's book illustration, you were known for your advertising and editorial work. Why don't you talk about your beginnings?

[Pat Cummings]: I was walking home from art school with my portfolio one day when a man literally stopped me on the street and said, "Are you an artist? Would you like a job?" I said, "Sure!" and jumped into his car. That was my second year in New York City. I certainly wouldn't advise anyone else to do that!

He took me to the Billie Holiday Children's Theater in Brooklyn. The woman running the theater needed posters and flyers. I learned some about the technical side of graphics and production from that job. That was also my introduction to work for children.

Then I started working professionally for magazines and newspapers, spots for "Letters to the Editor," "Reviews," and things like that. You're not told what to draw, although some magazines can be pretty precise. Usually the better paying magazines are because they have a firmer idea of what they want. The majority of magazines let you come in with your sketches and run them. Advertising agencies tell you exactly what they want.

I thought in advertising you need to come up with the ideas for them.

You go in and show them six sketches for one piece and they'll tell you, "I like this one, I don't like that one, go in this direction." On rare occasion, some places will tell you to come back only with the finished artwork, so you don't know until you bring it in if they're going to like it or not. But it's not really a gamble financially. The "concept" is subject to change, but you get paid once it's accepted.

That's all done on speculation? You don't get paid unless they buy it?

No, no. It's never done on spec[ulation]. When you go in, you have the job and you get paid.

What I'm saying is that the rules change from job to job. When I worked for *Women's Wear Daily,* there were no rules. They would give me the topic to illustrate a concept to attract advertisers of shoes or summer fabrics, for example. They'd tell me, "We're going to be advertising for winter knits, do something. Whatever you do is fine, just bring it in."

So I'd go home, beat my brains out and do something I knew would be okay. Generally, there was no guidance whatsoever. All you do is reach into your little bag of tricks and ask what do I feel like drawing today? One time I asked a friend to pose because I wanted to do her portrait and asked her to pose for summer knits or something. I was able to do two things at once!

Sometimes you get a manuscript to work from. You have to bring in a sketch. You decide what you think about the story and how you want to interpret it. It's fairly open. It's a little bit like children's books, but it's a lot quicker. And it pays well.

It's pretty much a high pressure environment, right?

Very much pressure. I've had Madison Avenue art directors come to my loft, stand over my shoulder and grab a piece of art as soon as it was finished.

It was too much pressure for me. It's the difference between being treated as a functionary rather than as a professional. In advertising, you're a supplier and you're treated like one. "Where is it? When is it coming in? Change this, change that."

Children's books are such a haven in comparison. I'm glad I made the change when I did.

What brought you to make that change?

The IRS! In the winter of 1984, I got a letter from them saying I had to pay $32.44 for back taxes. I knew I had paid it. It was one of those amounts that stay in your head.

I ended up spending two weeks going through every piece of paper I had in storage looking for proof that I had paid that amount. I found the check, but what I really saw was thousands of pieces of artwork. For every last one of them I had to run into an office, pick up the manuscript, go back with sketches, go back with finishes, possibly go back with changes, and wait a month or two to get paid.

What else I saw was this massive amount of work that really didn't amount to anything much but a bunch of portfolios full of art in the loft. I didn't "live" with them.

I had done a few books by then and decided that's what I really liked. I liked the long-haul projects and I liked having a solid object in my hands at the end of it. I liked the concept that you could do something that might keep earning you money. I hadn't heard of "passive income" yet! That's when I decided to make my body of book work grow.

If my husband hadn't been so supportive of that move, I probably wouldn't have been able to do it. His attitude was that I was investing in myself. The only way to have publishing work for you, is to have a volume of books under your belt—and in print!

Very true. You don't enter children's books for the money.

No, you can't look at it strictly for money. It's not a business you get into for the sake of money. It doesn't pay extremely well, so I can't go out and get a Jaguar yet. I took at least a thirty percent drop in income when I decided to spend the majority of my time on books.

You can make a living, and some people make a good living. You do it because you enjoy it. That's why I don't rush through things. I like what I'm doing and I like spending time on my projects. If I want to noodle it to death and get in there and get all down into the fold of a dress, I can do it. That's where the enjoyment is for me.

Once you realized the drop in income, what made you continue?

It's a decision you make. When I was in my twenties I liked running around. I liked the excitement of doing advertising, their crazy next-day deadlines, the pressure and the money. I was getting as much money for a small black and white ad as I did for a whole thirty-two page book! It depends on what you enjoy. I like the drawing and I like spending the time with the art.

Since your income is directly tied into how fast you produce, do you find yourself trying to maintain the pressured schedule you had in advertising?

In advertising and editorial work, that stuff can't be late. It's different in book publishing. Newspapers go to press every day and won't have a blank space where a piece of art was supposed to be. You can have a gaping bullet hole in your forehead, but make sure that artwork is in on time. They're sorry about the bullet hole, they do feel for you, but, "Where is the art?"

Books are so much different. One thing I really admire about publishing is they really let you do what it is you do. They try to create this environment to do it in. From my end I feel gently handled. I appreciate it.

My editors, for example, might not send me a copy of a negative review. I think I can distinguish between constructive criticism, which is good and might affect me,

and criticism which tells me more about the reviewer than the work. I don't care about negative criticism based on a reviewer's value judgments. See how nicely that works out?

Are you pretty good about meeting your deadlines?

You agree to finish the book. You try to get it on time. And you come as close as you possibly can. Editors will call you when it's time.

I had a book due on something like December 15. On Christmas Eve day the phone rang. I told my mother, "If it's my editor, tell her I died of overwork." My mother told me, "Your editor is not thinking of you on Christmas Eve. She has her own life and her own family to think about." I picked up the phone and it was the editor! So I asked her why she was calling because my mother said she wouldn't do that. And, yes, she was calling about the book. She had a half day at work and was just calling to see how it was going.

There's the difference. I think of it in terms that editors and I have a tacit understanding that I'm thinking of them around deadline time. They're in my thoughts. I try to make the deadline. If I haven't made the deadline, they can see in the work what is taking up the time. I haven't broken relationships with anybody over a deadline. Also, I keep in constant touch.

I tend to go in almost every ten pages. That way, if there are going to be some changes I'll know right away. Then I try and have any problems resolved when I come in with the next batch of pages.

At least that way everyone is aware of what's going on— or at least being developed—so there are no real "surprises" at the end.

My whole reference point is a "Peanuts" cartoon where Charlie Brown didn't have his book report done. He sat in class sweating bullets that the teacher was going to call on him. The teacher doesn't and he's out of the room, heading for the playground. Lucy says, "Why don't you go home and do your work?" He says "What for, what for, the night is young." That's how I feel.

When I've finished a book, hey! I tell everybody this will never happen again. I honestly feel the next deadline is a piece of cake. My mother goes, "Uh-huh." Now, when your mother won't buy it, it's ugly.

I know you have closely-held feelings about black characters in children's books.

When I was a kid I didn't see many black kids in children's books. And now I want to make sure all kids do. I think it's important. I don't think black characters in books excludes any child from enjoying them.

Having a black character in books includes black readers; they can see themselves in it. They just don't see white, blue-eyed blonde haired kids.

Generally I do black characters because I genuinely like to make sure there are black characters in books out there. There aren't very many. I don't want to see a quota system, though, where a book is published because a publisher needs a "black" book on that season's list. If ten good black stories come in or ten good Chinese or Hispanic ones, ideally they should be published. I've *never* seen an abundance of minority books on one list.

Do you honestly think children realize the difference of one type of character over another?

Yes. I have had black kids coming up and asking why I do predominantly black kids in a book, so they notice that's unusual. I tell them because I think there should be more books with black kids in them. That if I don't do them I can't be sure somebody else is doing them and because I'm black and I want to see us represented, I do them.

What about reviewers? They will make a point of saying a book has "black characters" in it as opposed to not saying a book has "white characters" in it.

Reviewers will often, and I will say over fifty percent of the time, say a book has black characters in it. My reaction depends on the context in which it's stated. I don't mind it so much when it reads as an afterthought "and it has black characters" so if black parents read the review and want to get a book with black characters in it, fine.

But they're not reading *School Library Journal* and the other review magazines. Teachers and librarians who want to buy books that have black characters in them for a black readership do.

It's like when an actor is being reviewed in a movie for his looks instead of how he acts. When I read a review for my book which shows a distinct slant on the part of the reviewer of what she thinks black life should be about, I'm offended.

For example?

I had a review about **Just Us Women** that said my art was cloyingly sweet because I was depicting black and female life as a warm, wonderful thing. I thought, "Well, what's wrong with that?" **Just Us Women** is a warm and wonderful story about a young black girl and her favorite aunt on a car trip. What the reviewer had problems with was that to be black and a woman was a good thing. That was a slant. If the aunt had been alcoholic and crashed all over the highway, then perhaps it would have been "realistic" for the reviewer.

The same thing happened with **Good News** when it first came out. One review said it was "too tame domestically." "Too tame domestically!" Mom was cooking dinner at five o'clock because she had to go to her night job. Dad isn't home yet. The parents are working in shifts, but it was "too tame domestically." The reviewer probably thought there should have been rats and roaches crawling around or the family should have lived in the ghetto; something rougher should have been going on in the house than just a two-job family living together. That was a slanted review.

Is there an audience for black character books?

I'm sure there is. I don't think that it's as broad as it could be.

When I'm told by teachers and librarians that they don't order certain books because "we don't have any black kids in our school," that tells me a lot of things. I've also been told by people who work in the publishing business that if a book has a black face on the cover, sales could be limited. I'm sure having black characters in books affects sales because this is what librarians and teachers—and publishers—are telling me. It must happen with parents, too. I've had it reinforced too often in too many ways to know that those attitudes don't exist.

It's unfortunate and irrational, but I've come to realize that exists. I've had librarians come up to me, with broad smiles on their faces, and they'll say after I've finished talking to a group of kids that they've never thought of buying my books because of the black characters in them. They're saying this in a very pleasant, affable way. They're surprised to learn that these books may be enjoyed by all kids. I've never, never had a child say to me, "I wouldn't read this book because there's a black character in it."

What's the problem then?

There's a tendency to not let a book be a slice of life or just your art. There's a tendency to let it stand for a lot more. I don't necessarily view it as a form of censorship because I've never run into any extremes like I did in textbooks. And I don't view it as censorship because I've never been told there's been anything I have to take out of a picture book to make it more appealing.

When I worked in textbook publishing, which is the most maniacal form of publishing to work for, there were these guidelines fifty pages long telling how you could and could not portray various ethnic and age groups. They were based on demands from previous lobby groups—blacks, native Americans, Hispanics, Jews—everybody had a lobby so they had to be portrayed a certain way. Everything everybody said they had to have was in there. You couldn't have mothers wearing aprons; you couldn't show girls in pink dresses; you couldn't show black girls with braids; you couldn't show Indians with braids. The list is endless. When I was told to take udders off a cow I said you guys have gone too far. I'm thinking there's some child somewhere who's looking at this cow without udders and saying, "Mom, there's something wrong with this cow!"

That's all edited that way to—publishers hope—induce sales. What about self-editing on the part of authors and illustrators. That is, not putting something in a book, whether it belongs there or not, because it may adversely affect sales?

There is some of that. Because I'm in New York City, I have to remember that what we see here, other people may not. The urban setting is not necessarily the norm.

It's also a question of what you show a kid. Everybody edits to an extent of what they think a kid should or shouldn't see. When Maurice Sendak had a bare-bottomed boy in *In the Night Kitchen,* a lot of people were upset. That to me is bizarre. That's the kind of thing I think is so innocuous.

You edit yourself to a certain extent, based upon what you anticipate for the book, but I can't think of really wanting to do something and having a picture book editor tell me I couldn't do it because it would affect sales.

But for me, it's more a matter of focus. Sometimes I have to be pulled in by the editors because I've wandered off with the art! At the very inception of a book, I think about kids and their view of things. With *Storm In the Night, Springtime Bears, Jimmy Lee Did It,* I tried to look around a kid's room. What would you find in it? What are things they'd relate to? I try to think on their level, get down to their size, look around at things from their angle. I try to think of a kid's perspective and then change things around so their interest is maintained. That's why I like aerial views so much. You don't see those too often. Also, when I was a kid, I spent time with book illustrations. I spent time looking at them and seeing a lot of things in them before going to the next page. So I like to put in little details that kids like to pick up on.

How do the editors "focus" you?

I can get carried away, because I can do whatever I want. There was a book about lunchboxes I was working on, *I Need a Lunchbox,* by Jeannette Caines. I got all carried away with lunchboxes!

There is one scene where the boy dreams of different types of lunchboxes every night of the week. In one scene, I saw everything in red; I wanted a strawberry lunchbox with a whole circus with a red theme. As it turned out, the editor said a boy is not going to want to carry a strawberry lunchbox! Because I'm thinking from a visual point of view and what's going to be fun to draw, the editor focuses me by saying a strawberry lunchbox is not necessarily something other boys will relate to!

When I wrote *Jimmy Lee,* I put in all my nine dollar college words and labored over every one to get the book to rhyme. I really had this thing going! I had to learn to keep the text light and simple. The editor had to help me sift out the frills because what I put in was too chewy for early readers.

Do you have a tendency to work on more than one project at a time?

I've got about forty stories started! I have the endings for about twenty-five, but no middles. I tend to have the conclusion first, then the beginning. I build the shell; stuffing it is the difficult part for me. My problem is that I try to force it into a form. I like rhyming.

I have a tendency to smash my stories into a rhyme and that doesn't always work. One of my editors prefers I don't pursue this angle much further! I tell myself he lacks vision. That's what I say to him when he quietly slides the manuscript back to me across his desks.

I don't work on more than one book at a time when doing the art, though. If my desk is set up for pastels and I'm doing a particular style, I won't switch to another medium or try and do both. It's too jarring.

You vary your art styles from book to book. Why?

For the lunchbox book, the editor wanted me to experiment with new forms, so that was fine. I got rubber stamps and started stamping everything. If it had been left to me I probably would have covered the page and you wouldn't have been able to find the type in all of it. I had seventy different stamps I wanted to use. I tend to get involved in my work.

How involved?

I don't work fast. I don't do little line drawings or washes that can be done quickly. A lot of times I work from models and have to set them up. That takes a lot of time. One of my editors has a tendency to want me to work with new mediums, so each time it's starting brand-new, instead of doing the same medium I did before. That means ten pages in the trash before I can get the first page done in the new style.

You also have a tendency to put unusual combinations of color together such as purple and yellow side by side in Fred's First Day.

I love those colors together! I used to be intimidated by color. I started off working in just black and white, because color scared me.

I love it now. I had an art director tell me once, "There is no such color as this one that you brought in. What is this color? We can't even print it because it doesn't exist." It's simply a combination of colors reading as one.

When I was travelling in Italy, looking at those wonderful old statues, I felt the sculptors were compulsive. They loved those statues to death. They got into every nook and cranny and the fold was never deep enough or soft enough or the angle of the hand was never gentle enough, you know? They just loved those statues to death.

At the same time I love that type of rapport with the work, I'm also horrified by it because I can see where other people get obsessed by it and it'll turn me off. When

I'm sitting in front of a piece of paper, I get carried away. I have to have someone tap me on the shoulder and say, "Go on to the next piece."

I'm as obsessive about colors as those sculptors were about their statues. That's where my tendency for "making" new colors comes from. I'll start with a pink underneath and I'll see the need for a little bit of orange on top and maybe a shot of magenta on the bottom. My colors have three or four layers of color to them. And printers sometimes can't reproduce that.

My problem is I don't see where there's anything optional about it. I sit down and whatever is supposed to happen, happens. I put down a little patch of olive green and then it demands red. I think, "Of course, red!"

I've had one of my editors say to me, "Why don't you bring your work in before you're finished with it? Let's look at it before you think you're finished with it." I don't know if that happens with other people.

It's very hard for me to know when a piece is finished because I always see something else I can do. If I'm enjoying it, I want to keep playing with it. That's what probably makes some of my books take a year.

That's a long time for one picture book.

Actually, most take about six months. A long time! First of all, I have to make the dummy, sometimes photograph models, lay the poses out, and if portions of the book change, do more sketches.

When I first get the manuscript, I'll start speculating how the pages will look. I read it over a few times and discuss possible sizes with the publisher.

Publishers give me a sheet of possible sizes that the book could be. I choose from that sheet the size of book that feels comfortable for me. I have to then think of the book in terms of vertical or horizontal.

When I first started out, I designed the whole book, choosing typefaces and colors, the whole thing. Now I just decide on the shape of the book, then start breaking up the story into pages, and figuring out how much I'm taking for front matter. Then I have to decide how much

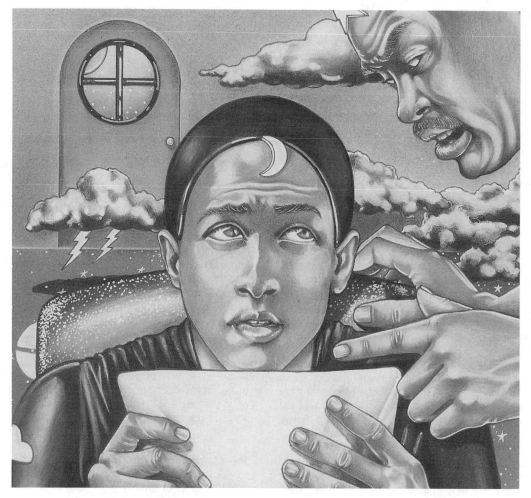

From C.L.O.U.D.S., *written and illustrated by Pat Cummings.*

type will appear on each page and where the story will turn.

After it's broken down, I start doing sketches of how the pages will look. Initially, I tend to go way out there and cram all kinds of things into the pictures. Things calm down as the editor and I talk about each page.

After everything is approved and I know which way I'm going, I tend to spend two or three days on a page. A day to set it up and do the underpainting and two days for detailing the drawing and finishing it up. By this time, the dummy is usually done so I'm just taking the dummy and transferring it onto the page.

Just getting the image on paper can take a day. I've spent twenty-four hours working on eyes or the corner of a mouth. It makes you crazy! I'll work until five or six in the morning, which I prefer, when I'm really caught up in an image.

When I get frustrated, I walk away, come back, get a coffee, come back, and that mouth is still not right. It hasn't corrected itself while I was gone for some strange reason. Plus, you need to step away because things do look so much differently when you come back.

Can you give an example here?

When I was doing *C.L.O.U.D.S.*, there was one page where "Chuku," the main character—he's also my husband—was sitting up in the corner of a building with his notepad, looking down at the city. The model for "Chuku" was a friend and the model for "Chuku's" boss was Chuku. You figure it out.

In one scene, "Chuku" is sitting on a building. There's a huge gray cloud over the building. I needed a break, and went to get a cup of coffee. From across the room I could see this drawing on my desk—what it looked like was a huge nude woman's torso! I hadn't seen it at the desk because I was sitting right on top of it. So of course that image was changed!

I never know what's going to happen in a book until I sit down in front of the piece of paper. I see it in my head, but it doesn't always make it to paper. When you go into something, you want each page to be everything you wanted it to be. You don't want anything less. It's a terrible feeling to know you have a page in there that is not what you wanted, but it leaves room for the next time.

Ideally I would do a book every four months. The problem is I like to enjoy it and have a good time with it. I don't like to work at a fast pace. I don't like the feeling that you have this page done, so it's on to the next and the next and the next. I do other things in between to break things up, things that will take two or three days.

Each drawing takes as long as it takes. There will always be a page or two that I'm not satisfied with. Maybe there was something I saw that I could not get down on paper. But that is what carries you on to the next book and the

next. If I ever did one perfect book, I would probably have to stop.

Describe your usual working condition.

It seems I have three stages per book. I'll get my panicky beginning, the "white paper syndrome" where I don't know what I'm going to do, how to handle a new media; then I get to a stage where I'm a little more confident, the style is falling into place; and then I get to the fanatical every-little-detail-popping-out stage.

I never think if something doesn't work that I'll never work in this town again. I used to. But it's never that bad. It's just growth. When I started to think of my art in growth terms, as part of the process as always on the way to something, that it's not finite or carved in stone, it made more sense.

People talk about their "body of work." Well, bodies are growing things. You keep adding to it and expanding it.

But don't you tire of starting from scratch each time?

No, no. I like the change. I live with a project for at least five months. That's my minimum. When I finish a project I love to clean my desk of all the evidence of it. Everything is put away, filed, it's over, and I can go onto the next project. The scary part is looking at the white paper and saying, "Okay, now. . . ."

But as I'm finishing up one book, my head starts to turn to the new one coming up. And I'll continue to think about it until I get started on it.

When I'm finishing up a book, my head is somewhere else, because I'm only working the last little details. All the real work has been done. It's almost like blacking out while you're working on it so you can think about other things.

I lose all concept of time when I do this. I'll look up and it's dawn. When I was younger, I used to think that if you stayed up all night to work on something, that meant you finished something—when the sun comes up, you must be through because you worked all night. I don't know what happened to that theory. All I know is there is something grossly unfair about working all night, seeing the sun come up and knowing you're not finished with whatever it is you're working on!

Do you ever take time to relax before starting a new project?

Sometimes, but you're talking to somebody who's always up against a deadline. Usually by the time I get to the end of something I feel like I can join the company of man and walk in the sun—until that night!

Pat Cummings with Rudine Sims Bishop

SOURCE: in an interview in *Language Arts,* Vol. 30, No. 1, January, 1993, pp. 52-9.

In *C.L.O.U.D.S.*, Pat Cummings offers a kind of artist's heaven, as well as an illustration of the way one artist took a proverbial lemon and turned it into lemonade. New York is not a desirable assignment for a C.L.O.U.D.S. artist. "Nobody ever looks up!" But one day, bored with weeks of "Classic Sunny Day Blue" mixed with a few clouds and relieved by some mandatory rain, Chuku discovers that one person *is* looking up and paying close attention. It's all he needs to inspire spectacular skies painted with colors such as Oh So Turquoise, Peacock's Tail Blue, Cloud-Lining Silver, Unbelievably Brilliant Gold, and Awfully Pretty Rose. His beautiful skies earn him a transfer to a very attractive assignment in the tropics, but Chuku has made New York his, and he doesn't want to leave it or his special sky-watching fan. Chuku finds a creative way to solve his problem.

Pat Cummings knows what it is to be, like Chuku, the "new kid." When she was a child, her father was a career military man, and the family moved every 3 years. Until 11th grade, she did not attend the same school for 2 consecutive years, so her art became the vehicle for making friends. In each new school, Cummings would join the art club or volunteer to do posters for school projects, effectively creating a role for herself and bringing herself into contact with others who shared her interest.

Apparently, even as a preschooler, Cummings also shared with Chuku an intolerance for boredom and the will and wit to do something about it. In her recent book, *Talking with Artists,* she relates an incident that occurred when she was about 5 years old and living in Kaiserslauten, Germany. One day, left outdoors alone by her older sister with instructions to watch over their toys "for a minute," Cummings became bored when the minute stretched into more time than seemed reasonable. When a bus stopped at the corner, Cummings simply "ran straight across the grass and hopped on!" When the bus arrived at its destination, she followed the passengers, all of whom were young girls, into a building where, it turns out, the girls were taking ballet lessons. Unable to speak German, Cummings watched the girls and tried to imitate their movements. The teacher was not favorably impressed with her dancing and sent her back home on the bus with a note pinned to her blouse: "Please don't send her back until she's at least eight." Cummings was "grounded" for some time, but that gave her a chance to practice drawing her new favorite subject—ballerinas. She continued drawing ballerinas even after she started school, where she found that other children liked them so much they would offer a nickel, or dime, or some M&M's, or Twinkies for their own personal Pat Cummings original. She became a professional artist at an early age.

Her career as a picture book artist began in 1977 when she created the illustrations for a new edition of what had been Eloise Greenfield's first book, *Bubbles,* retitled *Good News.* Since then, she has illustrated more than a dozen picture books, including four for which she also wrote the text. Cummings was awarded the Coretta Scott King award for her illustrations for *My Mama Needs Me* by Mildred Pitts Walter. Her most recently published book at this writing is *Talking with Artists,* a collection of profiles of 14 artists, including Cummings herself. Created for children, it includes an autobiographical sketch by each artist and their lively answers to the questions Cummings is asked most frequently on school visits.

Cummings is married to Chuku Lee, who not only lent his name to the main character in *C.L.O.U.D.S.* but also has been known to pose for his wife, the artist, at 2:30 in the morning. They have one cat, Cash, who can be seen in the drawings for Mary Stolz's *Storm in the Night.* Although they have no children, Cummings says they have discussed the possibilities of finding "a 12-year-old who likes to do the dishes." They live in Brooklyn, New York.

Cummings attended the annual convention of the American Library Association in San Francisco in June of 1992, where we had the conversation that follows.

[Rudine Sims Bishop]: You've said you cannot remember a time when you didn't draw. When you were in grade school and high school, did your teachers nurture the artist in you?

[Pat Cummings]: I had a good experience with teachers for the most part. I remember a fifth-grade teacher in Okinawa. It wasn't so much that he encouraged us to draw, but he was an artist himself. That made a real impression. Art was something that was legitimate, something that people did even when they were adults.

Did you go to art school?

I went to Pratt Institute in Brooklyn, New York. At 18, I thought it would be interesting, even though my father warned me that New York *eats* 18-year-old girls. After living on army bases all my life, I didn't have a clue what civilian life was like. The first year I lived in the dorm. Then I dropped out, thinking I was going to join "the revolution." We had 10 non-negotiable demands that we sat down to negotiate the minute they asked us to. We were trying to get black and Latino professors and a study center at Pratt. It was not well organized; it was just the mood of the times. This was the late '60s, around the time of the Kent State incident. After I dropped out, I worked in Boston for a year. My father kept introducing me as "my daughter, the dropout," so I took the hint and went back to school at Spelman in Atlanta. I stayed a year at Spelman, long enough to realize that nobody knew that the art department existed. It was on the fifth floor of a building where the elevator stopped at four. I transferred to the Atlanta School of Art, which was a little like Pratt. For a year everybody there kept asking me why I had left Pratt, so I decided to go back to Pratt.

Painting was a way you entertained yourself as a child. Were you also a reader?

Oh, yes. Actually, my oldest sister was the one who read voraciously. I thought it was unbelievable that she could devour a book a day. I liked to read an awful lot, but not that intensely. I enjoyed fairy tales and fantasies.

I keep insisting that children, particularly minority children who have been excluded for so long, need to see themselves when they hold up the mirror of literature. Do you remember consciously seeking reflections of yourself in your books?

No, and I don't think most children do. I think children respond to stories viscerally. When I was reading those fairy tales as a child, I identified with the princess. If the dragon was after her, I felt we were both in danger. Today when I visit all-white schools, I find that the children don't notice that the characters in my books are black until a teacher or librarian or parent points it out to them. The children relate to the content; they think it's a story about a boy and his younger sister, or the first day of school. On the other hand, I do think children might feel excluded if they don't see themselves represented in books. Seeing themselves offers a subtle reinforcement. They know they're part of the group.

What are your thoughts about this current push toward multiculturalism? Do you think it will be sustained?

It has to be. It's a logical and long overdue recognition of the way the world is. Now that we've entered that reality, I don't see how we can come back out. It's like trying to forget how to ride a bicycle. Some people are threatened by multiculturalism because they're insecure about what it means, but people who respect information and respect the truth realize that including a variety of cultures enhances the picture. Can you imagine living in a world where there was just scrambled eggs and bacon to eat every day? It wouldn't be very appealing. Not only is multiculturalism necessary, but it also has to be cultivated.

Even though the overall percentage is still small, there are a growing number of African American writers and artists. How do we nurture that and get more writers and artists from other parallel cultures?

This is an aside, but about 5 years ago I realized that I could call—at home—about 90% of all the black children's book writers and illustrators in the business. That's much too small a group.

When I go out and speak on multicultural panels all around the country, I keep seeing the same writers and artists over and over again. One of the questions that keeps coming from audiences is, "Where are the the Korean illustrators, Filipino writers, Hispanic illustrators . . . ? So a group of us decided to get together to see what we can do. Initially, we called ourselves the Traveling Multiculturals since we always seemed to be on the road together, bumping into each other. One thing we started to talk about was finding and mentoring new talent.

For example, I met a Hispanic artist whose portfolio was informed by a Puerto Rican sensibility. I knew that one of my publishers needed an illustrator for a manuscript about a Puerto Rican folkloric character. I put this artist in touch with them, and he's going to do the book. His work will have something about it that a Chinese illustrator might not bring to it. Culturally, there are things that an artist can bring to the work.

The group that's come together is going to help identify and mentor writers and illustrators. Publishers are trying to do the right thing, and we hope to be able to facilitate their search for writers and artists from the various cultural groups. We don't want publishers to be able to say any longer that they can't find them. (Note: The newly formed group, called the Center for Multicultural Children's Literature, can be contacted through HarperCollins Children's Books.)

Do you think an African American manuscript has to be illustrated by an African American or a Puerto Rican manuscript by a Puerto Rican artist, and so on?

It has been my experience that if you write something from your own perspective, it will ring true. But I am not a person who feels that an African American manuscript has to be illustrated by an African American because then the reverse would have to be true as well, and it all becomes too restrictive. I illustrated Mary Stolz's book *Storm in the Night.* The story focuses on the relationship between a grandfather and his grandson. The author is white, but there was nothing in the text that said the characters had to be black or white or Chinese. As far as I know, she wanted the characters to be black. I feel that that was legitimate, just as I feel I can draw kimonos. I can draw something from all around the world. Artists can avail themselves of a virtual smorgasbord. It's important to find the best artist for a book, one who can really bring life to a manuscript.

Some writers and artists say, "I am a writer who just happens to be black." Then there are others who say, "I do this because I feel that black children need x, y, or z, and I feel a special responsibility to them." Do you fall into one of those categories?

I feel both ways. It's not one or the other. I want to do books with black characters from my own experience. I did not grow up in a black community *per se;* I grew up in the army, in a multicultural environment. I want to bring what I know to the stories because not only does that make it more personal and enjoyable, but it also shares with kids one way of seeing the world. When I was living in Okinawa, I remember seeing Buddha ash trays. Now you would never see an ashtray made out of Christ on the cross. That is a culturally offensive thing that only happened because people were not aware that the Buddha is somebody else's deity. In my books I want to share with kids some of what I've seen, growing up.

I also happened to have had a very happy childhood. I'm extremely close to my family, and I love them dearly. I feel very fortunate, but I don't think that all kids have a happy environment, and I'd like them to feel included in the one between the pages of my books.

Primarily, I do want the black kids who are out there, who have been underrepresented, to feel that they are represented in the books. I remember going to talk to a group in Portland, Oregon. There were all white kids, except one little black boy way in the back of the huge auditorium. When I walked in, he did a double take. He hadn't realized I was going to be black, and his eyes just lit up. He had felt all alone. I know it has an impact on kids to feel that they are different. It doesn't matter if it's color or whatever it is; kids don't like to feel that there's something odd about them or that they're different. They want to be included, and that's what I feel is the most important aspect of the books—that everybody feels successful.

Let's talk about your work. You said earlier that you had done magazines, free-lance work. Are you now doing books full time?

I'm doing books full time. It wasn't that I didn't enjoy free-lance work; I loved magazines and advertising. That's all I did. I really thought children's books were something you did on the side, for fun. The first editor I worked with took me into his office and explained that I should not try to make a living doing children's books. He showed me a map of the United States with pins all over it and said, "These are the bookstores that we deal with all over the country." He pointed to the South and said, "You can see there are very few bookstores down there." He was telling me black people don't read and that my books were not going to sell. That's how I interpreted it, so I thought you illustrated books for the art of it, and then you went back and did the real work. The real work for me was advertising, which is godless and soulless and heartless. It pays well. They buy your soul, but they pay you nicely for it. In my 20s, it was lovely. In my 30s, it was fun. And then I hit about 35 and started to think I didn't want to do that for the rest of my life.

How did you get into doing children's books?

I was coming home from one of the classes at Pratt carrying a huge portfolio, and a man in a car stopped me and asked if I was an artist. He told me he had a job for me at the Billie Holiday Theatre for Little Folk if I was interested. I actually went with him in his car, which is exactly what my mother warned me against doing in the big city. He did take me directly to the theatre, however, and I started doing children's theatre posters, which was a lot of fun. So my portfolio became full of art for children. I wanted to do children's books, but I had no idea how to go about it. At that time publishers would sit down with artists and give feedback on their work. I was getting a lot of feedback, but no manuscripts. I had also put a piece on the back page of the *Bulletin* of the Council on Interracial Books for Children, where they spotlighted photographers and artists. I received a call from a publisher who had seen that piece. Ironically, it was a publishing house I had visited previously with no success. The editor said they had a manuscript they wanted me to do. She didn't even ask to see the portfolio. I floated over there with my head in the clouds. She handed me

a manuscript and asked if I knew what I was doing. I said, "Sure. No problem." Then I went home and called Tom Feelings for help because that's when I realized I didn't have a clue.

What book was that?

It's called **Good News.** It's by Eloise Greenfield.

What kinds of things do you do when you visit schools? Do you do workshops with the children?

I do presentations for the most part. I've done a few workshops, but they're not very productive because I have only about an hour, and that's not very much time. Basically what I want them to come away with is the sense that books are made by real people and that this is something they can grow up and do. It's a profession; it's not some inaccessible thing out there. That's how **Talking with Artists** came to be. I wanted them to see the kinds of drawings I did when I was little because that's accessible. I also want them to see the mistakes. I found they love to see how you messed up on a page. They want to hear that because that's what they can relate to. They do a drawing and they don't feel it's perfect, so they want to know how to get it just right. I also want to show them something about the process. I'll get the kids to volunteer ideas for a story, usually an animal story, and show them how that would get put together and how, as an illustrator, I would choose which scene is important to illustrate.

Talk about what happens once you receive a manuscript, someone else's text. What kinds of things do you look for? How does the process work for you?

The manuscript is offered to me, and generally I decide whether I'm going to take it, based on whether or not it's going to be fun to draw. Or else it's just a story that I love, period. What happens is the same thing that happens when anybody reads a text without pictures. I start to envision scenes in my head. Based on my first feeling about what might be fun to draw, I start blocking it out. I also have to take into account how many pages there are, where the pages are going to turn, things like that. I will mathematically divide the story up by 27 pages because most picture books are 32 pages, and you lose about 5 for all the front matter. So I divide the total number of lines by 27, and that gives me a rough sense of how many lines might appear on a page if it were broken down that way. Then I start pacing through and figuring out what scenes I want to pull out. I tend to like the ones that have some tension in them or action—something dynamic needs to be happening.

Your pictures are full of action—and humor.

You should see the ones that don't get published. There's one with the cat flipping in **Clean Your Room, Harvey Moon!** I had the cat upside down with his tongue hanging out of his mouth. I loved it. My editor has a different relationship with her cat than I have with mine.

What determines your medium?

It just suggests itself. I'm getting ready to work on a Spanish fairy tale, and I want it to be in oil because I want it to be lush. It's called *The Blue Lake.*

This is my new theory, my new concept: I want to live inside the book. I want to be there, to direct it more. When I did *Talking with Artists,* I noticed a pattern. Most of us illustrators are thrilled and excited when we get our first book. With the second, we're delighted to have the chance to do it again. By the third or fourth, we start to make commitments to books that may not really excite us, but we're thrilled to be working in the business. Eventually, we find we have five or six contracts, which could be three or four years of commitments, and for a while that feels like job security. Then one day it feels like pressure, almost like being an indentured servant. By the time we get to those last books, our feelings about them may have changed.

Based on that, I'm starting to feel that I want each book to be more personal. This Spanish fairy tale came from Augusta Baker. I heard her tell a story and asked her about doing a picture book. She referred me to some collections she had done, and I selected one of the stories. It's set in Spain, and my editor and I thought that Moorish Spain would be ideal. So my husband and my mother and I went to Spain and walked around in castles because castles figure heavily in the story. I really want to smell the environment, and taste the environment, and get into the culture a little bit more, and live within the book. Each book is something of a capsule. Ideally, I want to record what captures my interest. For example, I'm really interested in Bali—the art and fabrics and things like that. I'm thinking that instead of just investigating what I'm interested in anyway, I can record it, make it a story, and share it with somebody else.

I've noticed that a lot of artists move from illustrating other people's texts to being both artist and writer. Is this part of that process you're describing?

Yes. You realize that nobody is going to write the story you feel like illustrating. If there's an image playing itself in your head, you may as well write the story that goes with it because otherwise you might be waiting indefinitely.

Who or what are some of the important influences on your work?

I think the fairy tales in my upbringing influenced me a lot. Fantasy has always appealed to me so strongly that sometimes, even if the story doesn't call for fantasy, I'll put it in. I like aerial views, because I have flying dreams. As I've gotten older, I've gotten more practical in my dreams, so that I even convince myself I can fly. Then I wake up. It's so bitterly disappointing that I find if I draw aerial views, it brings me back to that sensation.

Then there are other artists. I think my first book looked like a tribute to Tom Feelings. Work by other artists, like the ones in *Talking with Artists,* could immobilize me with awe, but I try to let it inspire me. I look at other people's work all the time. There will be some element, maybe the combination of colors or the way they use shadow or something like that, that will strike me.

Are most of those influences unconscious, then? There are people whose work you like, and some element they use just appears in your work?

I think some are surprisingly conscious. If there's someone whose palette I like, I might clip out something and put it on my drawing table. Perhaps I like the way they had brown next to olive next to red or something like that. Or it could be their use of line in a particular piece. I might surround my desk with things like that, but it's not a literal lift.

On to the future. At the exhibits I saw an advance copy of your new book, **Petey Moroni's Camp Runamok Diary.** *Where did that idea come from?*

A girlfriend of mine went camping, and she told me that while she was asleep, raccoons got her Cheese Doodles and Ring Ding Juniors. I don't go camping, so I thought that raccoons were out there eating nuts and berries. I thought she had to be kidding, but when I ran across another reference to raccoons stealing food, *Petey Moroni's Camp Runamok Diary* just came to me. I liked the title, so I thought maybe I'd do a story with a raccoon loose at camp to go with the name. One thing I liked about Petey Moroni is he's got this Italian last name. People might not expect him to be black, but I've got black friends whose last names are Cohen or Giovanni. It's presumptuous to assume that all blacks have had a southern upbringing or a ghetto upbringing. Those stereotypes don't apply. What I also liked about this camp was the possibility for it to be totally multicultural. I like, too, that Petey's the recorder; he's the one with the overview.

What else is coming up?

In addition to *The Blue Lake,* I'm working on a book about carousels. I like the way carousels look. Then, because I'm going to Ghana in the fall, and I've never done an African folk tale, I want to do a Ghanaian folk tale. I've also got a manuscript coming up from Nikki Grimes, and I love it. It's an alphabet book, a poem. It will be my first alphabet book, and it excites me no end. I have a lot of projects in different stages.

Any advice to teachers about nurturing young artists?

One thing. It's not a criticism because I think it's a natural tendency. I grew up with art teachers who would put an apple on a table and then have everybody draw the apple. It becomes evident very quickly who is the "class artist" because his or her apple looks most like the apple on the table. That effectively destroys a whole room full of potential. In every school I go to, everybody knows who the class artist is, and I wonder what that means. For example, I visited a school, and after my presentation the principal took me down the hall to show me a display of masks that the children had done. They were fantastic papier mache masks made by second and third graders. I wanted to buy them and put them on the wall at home. The children were lined up in the hall for lunch, and I was trying to make a point of pausing at all of the masks. But the principal was saying, "Don't look at those, come down here." She wanted to show me the one that was the most realistic, that looked most like a face. She had bypassed all the colorful ones, the ones with the imaginative shapes and the unique textures. The kids were conscious that all those had been passed over, and that unless their work was photographic, it wasn't being considered art.

But look at some of the styles that are in books now. Picture books are a haven for artists because they can use practically any kind of style, and children are open to it. So what I would say to teachers is just to inform themselves that art is more than their definition might be. Let kids have some free loose running space, and try to encourage the ones who want to stick to it. A child can be complimented on her use of color, or her use of texture, or on her imagination. Expose them to different materials and sit back. Art is not the sort of thing that necessarily gets taught; it gets indulged.

TITLE COMMENTARY

📖 *GOOD NEWS* (written by Eloise Greenfield, 1977; originally published as *Bubbles*, 1972)

Kirkus Reviews

SOURCE: A review of *Good News,* in *Kirkus Reviews,* Vol. XLV, No. 11, June 1, 1977, p. 573.

James Edwards is excited because he has learned to read some words, and he runs home from school to tell Mama. But she only says, "That's nice, James Edward," and, instead of listening to him read, asks him to amuse baby Deedee so she can fix dinner before she goes to work. Coming out of his own funk when Deedee starts to feel neglected, James Edward tells *her* his news— and "even though she didn't know what it meant" she laughs with him. The deflating "That's nice" from a busy mother will win James Edward sympathetic allies, and the black family and working mother will score with librarians on the lookout for that extra recognition. There's not much to it, however, beyond the cathartic model, and though Cummings' decoratively framed drawings are full of motion, they too suggest the tame domestic content. Still, as Greenfield avoids manipulation and false solutions, it's a creditable example of its limited genre.

Wendie Old

SOURCE: A review of *Good News,* in *School Library Journal,* Vol. 24, No. 4, December, 1977, p. 44.

Having learned to read three words, James Edward is all smiles, but Mother is too tired and busy to listen. Finally, he whispers them to his baby sister. Greenfield does convey the boy's quiet joy of accomplishment, but there is little more plot than that and this lacks the appeal of *Olaf Reads* by Lexau and Cohen's *When Will I Read?* The expressive black, white, and turquoise illustrations capture the mood but the attempt to show movement (the course of a bouncing ball, of a jump rope, etc.) by picturing the same object in different poses may confuse a young audience.

📖 *BEYOND DREAMTIME: THE LIFE AND LORE OF THE ABORIGINAL AUSTRALIAN* (written by Trudie MacDougall, 1978)

Kirkus Reviews

SOURCE: A review of *Beyond Dreamtime: The Life and Lore of the Aboriginal Australian,* in *Kirkus Reviews,* Vol. XLVI, No. 18, September 15, 1978, p. 1019.

A brief history of Aboriginal settlement plus, in stodgy social-studies supplement fashion, "stories and myths that tell about the life and adventures of Aboriginals in three different parts of Australia before the Europeans came." Traditional myths and stories concocted by the author to illustrate Aboriginal folkways are virtually indistinguishable; both tend to be episodes rather than dramatic narratives with character or plot interest; and MacDougall's deliberate, painstakingly informative telling hardly catches the reader up. She does, however, convey a sense of the rigors and pleasures of life in the different regions—the difficulty of hunting kangaroo, for instance, and the euphoria of celebrating a kill—along with more routine, but not mundane particulars (like the technique of bark painting). Some of the pictures verge on the gross (notably, the transformation of babies into bees) but overall they are lifelike if not particularly appealing. With a few optimistic words on the situation of the Aboriginals today in conclusion, this will do for want of better.

Jeannette Small

SOURCE: A review of *Beyond Dreamtime: The Life & Lore of the Aboriginal Australian,* in *Social Education,* Vol. 43, No. 4, April, 1979, p. 300.

The fascinating history of the Aboriginals who settled in Australia some 30,000 years ago. It is an intimate exploration of the culture, tradition, and folklore of a unique people and of the white man's influence on their way of life. Distinctive sepia illustrations give vital substance to the text.

From Carousel, *written and illustrated by Pat Cummings.*

THE SECRET OF THE ROYAL MOUNDS: HENRY LAYARD AND THE FIRST CITIES OF ASSYRIA (written by Cynthia Jameson, 1980)

Judith Goldberger

SOURCE: A review of *The Secret of the Royal Mounds: Henry Layard and the First Cities of Assyria,* in *Booklist,* Vol. 77, No. 6, November 15, 1980, pp. 459-60.

In the mid-1800s, the Englishman Austen Henry Layard began to unearth what he thought were the ruins of Nineveh. Salaried as a spy for the British government during a bitter time of war between the Turks and the Arabs, Layard struggled with a French competitor, a ruthless pasha, and crumbling alabaster that dissolved when it met air. The author brings to life Layard's story—an important one, for his work was the foundation for modern theories on the birthplace of Western civilization and for much biblical study. Jameson's style is formal and her hero not quite three-dimensional, but the value of the book is as evident as the discoveries are vivid. With dramatic, if somewhat stiff, black-and-white drawings. A brief annotated list of people and places involved and a selective bibliography are appended.

Zena Sutherland

SOURCE: A review of *The Secret of the Royal Mounds: Henry Layard and the First Cities of Assyria,* in *Bulletin of the Center for Children's Books,* Vol. 34, No. 5, January, 1981, p. 96.

An account of the archeological explorations and discoveries of Henry Layard in what is present-day Iraq has, save for an "as he looked back, remembering" opening, a chronological arrangement and a modicum of fictionalization. (It is doubtful that a well-born English gentleman of the mid-nineteenth century would have said, "We shall meet up in India.") Although the writing style is not impressive, the material is adequately organized and inherently dramatic, for Layard was a romantic figure and his discoveries were of tremendous importance in themselves and for the future discoveries they inspired. The illustrations are heavy-handed black and white drawings, more satisfying at a distance than close at hand.

Ruby G. Campbell

SOURCE: A review of *The Secret of the Royal Mounds: Henry Layard and the First Cities of Assyria,* in *School Library Journal,* Vol. 27, No. 7, March, 1981, p. 146.

A very readable book about Layard, who not only unearthed biblical Ninevah and the Babylonian records in cuneiform that changed the thinking of scholars concerning the birthplace of Western civilization, but also raised the level of archaeology from mere treasure hunting to a science. At the age of 22, Layard left his uncle's London law firm on horseback, bound for India in search of a position with the British Colonial Government. A year later, when he reached Mesopotamia, he felt compelled to remain there, and thus begins the fascinating tale of Layard's dangerous adventures as an archaeologist and a spy amid jealous competitors, a scheming pasha and many other hardships. Jameson's use of dialogue and personal thoughts serve to recreate the incidents as they may have occurred. The square (8 ¼") format has chapters, and the black-and-white illustrations do their share to help set the mood and bring the pages to life.

📖 *JUST US WOMEN* (written by Jeanette Caines, 1982)

Kirkus Reviews

SOURCE: A review of *Just Us Women,* in *Kirkus Reviews,* Vol. L, No. 14, July 15, 1982, pp. 793-94.

Smiling confidently from the heavily drawn cover illustration are a young black woman at the wheel of a convertible and a little-girl passenger of nine or ten—suggesting, as does the title, that this will be a glowing evocation of sisterhood. And so it proves. The little girl and her Aunt Martha are about to depart for North Carolina (presumably from New York, judging by the states they go through), and this is the little girl's future-tense anticipation of their unhurried stops . . . to shop at roadside markets, walk in the rain, pick mushrooms ("but we have to be careful not to pick the poisonous ones"), and so on. The pictures are similarly idealized, to the point where there is no life in the proceedings. Cummings is good at translating vague expectations to concrete scenes, but these scenes are all coated over with her cloying affirmation that being black and female together is a warming and wonderful thing. For that message, the book is sure to be praised and listed. But the message is imposed at the expense of a shared experience.

Zena Sutherland

SOURCE: A review of *Just Us Women,* in *Bulletin of the Center for Children's Books,* Vol. 36, No. 1, September, 1982, pp. 4-5.

In soft two-color illustrations, the joys of a leisurely motor trip with the narrator's aunt are depicted. This has only incidental action, as the small black girl who tells the story of what they'll do on their trip to North Carolina anticipates the freedom and companionship they'll enjoy. Nobody to hurry them, time to stop at roadside stands and have picnics, or to go to fancy restaurants, or even just stop to walk in the rain. The text has a warm, happy tone; it's written in a free, casual style and concludes with the response to the North Carolina relatives who might ask, "What took you so long?" "We'll just tell them we had a lot of girl talk to do between the two of us. No boys and no men—just us women."

Hazel Rochman

SOURCE: A review of *Just Us Women,* in *School Library Journal,* Vol. 29, No. 1, September, 1982, p. 105.

Warm, cheerful pictures in three colors illustrate this story of a Black little girl planning a long car trip with her favorite aunt. Enjoying being together, "no boys and no men, just us women," they pack carefully and buy two road maps (because last year Aunt Martha forgot their lunch and the map on the kitchen table). But the special delight of the trip is the escape from fixed routes, timetables and routine, and from those who see no reason to "mosey down the back roads" and walk in the rain. The magic of "We'll turn the day around and have our breakfast at night" is caught in a double-page illustration of the earth's tilting around them as they eat. The text's unhurried rhythm reinforces the sense of their relaxed, companionable journey.

Denise M. Wilms

SOURCE: A review of *Just Us Women,* in *Booklist,* Vol. 79, No. 2, September 15, 1982, p. 109.

A young black girl relishes the car trip she's about to take with her Aunt Martha. "No boys and no men, just us women," says Aunt Martha. They'll stop at all the roadside markets and buy all the junk they like. They'll mosey down the back roads, take pictures, picnic, and later stop at a fancy restaurant. And when they get home and everyone says, "What took you so long?" they'll just say, "We had a lot of girl talk to do between the two of us." The pleasure of that trip and the warm relationship it represents shine through in realistic, sometimes photograph-like pictures. The two-color drawings have airbrush-effect shadings and occasional deco details. Aunt Martha, a polished-looking young woman, and her pretty niece look like their day of fun is something worth sharing.

📖 *MY MAMA NEEDS ME* (written by Mildred Pitts Walter, 1983)

Geraldine L. Wilson

SOURCE: A review of *My Mama Needs Me,* in *Interracial Books for Children,* Vol. 14, No. 5, 1983, pp. 26-7.

My Mama Needs Me deals nicely with important themes. One is the welcome of a new baby by a sister or brother and the older child's subsequent adjustment to the new baby. A second theme is the help and concern young children can learn to express for the new baby in a positive family setting. This straightforward, uncomplicated text conveys Jason's welcome and concern for a new sister, as well as his concern for his mother. We see the worry Jason feels when he's away from home for even a brief while. What Jason really needs is reassurance that he can get a hug from his Mama when he needs it in spite of the presence of the new baby. And that's what he gets.

The illustrations are interesting and convey a fine sense of design. Combinations of pastel colors are set off occasionally by two or three bright colors. There are some beautiful close-ups of Jason, who is Black, and his friends and the supportive adult neighbors. It is through the illustrations that we know that Jason's family is in a neighborhood where both Black and white people live.

Ilene Cooper

SOURCE: A review of *My Mama Needs Me,* in *Booklist,* Vol. 79, No. 14, March 15, 1983, p. 974.

A warm portrayal of a young black child's reaction to the arrival of his baby sister. Jason is invited out to play with friends, go over to a neighbor's for cookies, and feed the ducks in the pond. And while he reluctantly participates in some of these activities, Jason's overriding concern is to be home in case his mama needs him. Still, the baby sleeps most of the time and there doesn't seem to be much for him to do. When Mama asks, "Why don't you go and find your friends?" Jason answers, because she needs him—doesn't she? "Of course I need you. I need a big hug from you right now." At last Jason knows what he has been waiting to do. The perceptive story is bolstered by artwork with an unusual mix of bold shapes and pastel colors. Cummings uses bird's-eye views and interesting perspectives that will keep readers' attention. Those with their own new siblings will relate to the familiar sights of bathing and breast feeding as well as to Jason's unspoken emotions.

Ann A. Flowers

SOURCE: A review of *My Mama Needs Me,* in *The Horn Book Magazine,* Vol. LIX, No. 4, August, 1983, p. 437.

Jason is both thrilled and apprehensive when his new sister arrives home from the hospital. He hopes to be helpful in caring for her, but she seems to sleep all the time, and his mother only wants to rest, too. Jason receives several alluring invitations, but each time he anxiously hurries home just in case his mama needs him. Finally, Jason is allowed to hold the baby but realizes that what he really needs is a big hug. The decorative illustrations show a warm family situation, and at the end one sees a cheerful view of Jason in a multi-racial neighborhood. An encouraging book, especially for the child who is a trifle uncertain about the arrival of a new sibling.

FRED'S FIRST DAY (written by Cathy Warren, 1984)

Zena Sutherland

SOURCE: A review of *Fred's First Day,* in *Bulletin of the Center for Children's Books,* Vol. 37, No. 11, July-August, 1984, p. 215.

As in so many books about a first school experience, a child learns to adjust and finds that it helps to think of others when you are having difficulty. Being a middle child, Fred finds it gratifying when his younger brother is envious. Simply written, the story lacks any quality of momentum or spontaneity, but it's useful as another reas-

suring book about starting school. The illustrations show Fred as one of a moon-faced black family, not unattractive but rather stiff; the children in Fred's classroom all look (as does Fred) too old for a play school.

Ilene Cooper

SOURCE: A review of *Fred's First Day,* in *Booklist,* Vol. 81, No. 5, November 1, 1984, p. 376.

Fred is too old to play with his baby brother and too young to play with his older brother. His mother decides that school will be a good place for Fred, but he is unsure if he wants to go. Will he like it? What will he do there? Will he have friends? At first, the experience is not a positive one, he is lonesome and tentative. Fortunately, by the end of the day Fred has made some friends and is eager to return. The text is flat and has some problems; a continually crying child, for instance, is a disturbing element. But these deficiences are offset by the sturdy, colorful drawings executed in watercolor, color pencil, and airbrush and by the unstereotyped black protagonist and his family.

JIMMY LEE DID IT (1985)

Zena Sutherland

SOURCE: A review of *Jimmy Lee Did It,* in *Bulletin of the Center for Children's Books,* Vol. 39, No. 2, October, 1985, p. 25.

Even those children who haven't already invented their own imaginary culprit-friend will recognize the usefulness of the device. The anecdotal versifying is of variable quality, with more attention to rhyme than scansion. "Jimmy Lee did it," is mischievious little Artie's explanation of domestic damage, as described by his sister Angel. This is Cumming's first attempt at writing and it's adequate rather than impressive; primarily an illustrator, she shows, in bright if sometimes overcrowded realistic paintings, two attractive black children.

V. M. Sykes

SOURCE: A review of *Jimmy Lee Did It,* in *School Library Journal,* Vol. 32, No. 3, November, 1985, p. 67.

A story told in rhyme that has a jazzy beat and will make a great read-aloud. The narrator, a young black girl, tells of her brother, Artie, who always blames mischievous happenings on Jimmy Lee. Of course, Jimmy Lee is only there when Artie is, and, of course, no one but Artie ever sees him. Frustrated, Angel dresses up as Sherlock Holmes and sets out to solve the mystery. The illustrations, done in warmly glowing watercolors and gouache with pencil, capture the story's playful mood and the activities of the children. The total package of the rhyme, mystery and vivid colors makes this a special book for young listeners and readers, who are likely to catch on to Jimmy Lee's identity much faster than Angel.

Emily Leinster

SOURCE: A review of *Jimmy Lee Did It,* in *Interracial Books for Children,* Vol. 17, No. 1, 1986, p. 8.

Jimmy Lee Did It is a fun story featuring African American children as the main characters.

The story is told in rhyme by Angel. Her brother Artie would, under normal circumstances, be in lots of trouble because of all the mishaps that occur around the house, but he has a great excuse for everything that happens— "Jimmy Lee did it." Little sister finally decides to track this illusive Jimmy Lee down; she sets various traps but Jimmy Lee evades them all. Most youngsters will already have figured out the solution, but they—like most adults— will identify with this storyline because we all wish we had a Jimmy Lee from time to time.

Pat Cummings' illustrations, using gouache, watercolor and pencil, work very well with the lively mood of the story and the text.

C.L.O.U.D.S. (1986)

Kirkus Reviews

SOURCE: A review of *C.L.O.U.D.S.,* in *Kirkus Reviews,* Vol. LIV, No. 2, January 15, 1986, p. 130.

Cummings' brilliantly hued pictures delight the eye in this enjoyable fantasy of how those weird and wonderful cloud shapes, sunsets and sunrises are created.

Chuku, a new C.L.O.U.D.S. (Creative Lights, Opticals and Unusual Designs in the Sky) employee, is given New York City's sky as his first assignment. It's called a "less demanding area," which he discovers is true because "no one ever looks up." Chuku is inspired to his most original cloud formations when he notices a girl named Chrissy watching the plain blue sky one day in the park. From then on, Chuku entertains her, using colors like "Oh So Turquoise" and "Cloud Lining Silver" in a daily private show. As a result, Chuku's supervisor offers to transfer him to the tropics to reward his creativity. But Chuku wants to stay in New York to continue his work for Chrissy, so he breaks the rules. Chuku and his sky designs will undoubtedly enchant young readers.

Publishers Weekly

SOURCE: A review of *C.L.O.U.D.S.,* in *Publishers Weekly,* Vol. 229, No. 26, June 27, 1986, p. 86.

Chuku has a new job as a junior artist with Creative Lights, Opticals, and Unusual Designs in the Sky, or

C. L. O. U. D. S. His first assignment, considered safe but dull for a beginner, is to create skies over New York City where it's raining and smoggy, and people don't look up. He starts slowly, but when a little girl in the park notices his sky, Chuku is inspired to greater works. He's so good that he gets promoted, right out of the city. On his last day, he uses letters to tell the girl, Chrissy, "Hello down there." Of course, using letters is strictly forbidden, and Chuku loses the promotion, to his delight. Cummings's artwork is fantastic and futuristic, in pinks, purples and blues, but the story is encumbered by a lot of unnecessary text. And Chuku's lot is ambiguous: do we admire someone who is content to stay in one place, or has he bucked the system out of an act of love?

Betsy Hearne

SOURCE: A review of *C.L.O.U.D.S.,* in *Bulletin of the Center for Children's Books,* Vol. 40, No. 1, September, 1986, pp. 4-5.

A fantasy tailored to the New York City picture book audience, this follows young Chuku on his first assignment for the department of Creative Lights, Opticals, and Unusual Designs in the Sky. At first Chuku sticks to the manual and does a lot of Classic Sunny-Day Blue, with some rainy gray and sunset colors occasionally thrown in. Then a playful child who cloud-watches in Central Park inspires him to fantastic effects that lead to a promotion that in turn leads him to use forbidden letters ("Hello Down There"). Chuku's transfer to the tropics is cancelled, and he settles happily back into the job he's learned to make creative. The strong colors and futuristic tone of the art, with its (sometimes cluttered) designer-style comment on the subject of graphic design, turn this into a spoof on several levels. Young listeners will miss the jabs at corporate bureaucracy but probably enjoy the story level, which, like the art, is fairly sophisticated in itself.

CHILLY STOMACH (written by Jeanette Caines, 1986)

Kirkus Reviews

SOURCE: A review of *Chilly Stomach,* in *Kirkus Reviews,* Vol. LIV, No. 12, June 15, 1986, p. 936.

When Sandy's Uncle Jim tickles and kisses her, she gets what she calls a chilly stomach—she wants to avoid him, but doesn't know how.

In this simple picture-book treatment of a common trouble, Sandy easily differentiates between Uncle Jim's unwelcome attention and the more appropriate affection of her parents, which makes her feel "nice and happy and cuddly." Her friend Jill urges Sandy to tell her parents; Sandy is reluctant, lest they be angry or not believe her, and the book stops as she is trying to decide what to do. This leaves the way open for good discussion, which will be aided by the story's well-chosen details: Jill, too, has an

Uncle, loving and trustworthy; the straightforwardly realistic illustrations accentuate the open friendliness in both families, Sandy's distress, and the fact that her oblivious parents are too busy to notice what's going on.

A healthy, non-threatening approach to the difficult problem of child molesting.

Zena Sutherland

SOURCE: A review of *Chilly Stomach,* in *Bulletin of the Center for Children's Books,* Vol. 39, No. 11, July-August, 1986, p. 203.

Sandy is not comfortable around her Uncle Jim: "Sometime he hugs me and kisses me on the lips, and I get a chilly stomach." Jim never does anything overt, nothing Sandy's parents would see as being amiss; nevertheless, "When Uncle Jim tickles me, I don't like it." While this picture book gets high marks for its consistently childlike perspective, there are serious problems with its resolution. During a sleepover at best friend Jill's house (Sandy always tries to go there when Uncle Jim stays over), Sandy confides her secret fears. Jill says she is going to tell her mother, and that Sandy should tell her parents, too. Sandy is afraid to tell: "Maybe Mommy and Daddy won't like me anymore." Last page: "But I want them to know." The picture shows a fearful Sandy, Dad waving goodbye to Jim, and Mom picking up the phone. The implication, one supposes, is that Jill's mother is calling, but this is too subtle for young children. More of a problem is that Sandy's fears—that her parents won't believe her or love her—are not resolved. The author's message may be that it doesn't matter how scared you are, *tell someone,* but the abrupt finish will only lead readers to think that a page is missing. Cummings' illustrations are better than the text: intensely bright colors and a dramatic use of space make each page a vivid tableau.

Karen K. Radtke

SOURCE: A review of *Chilly Stomach,* in *School Library Journal,* Vol. 32, No. 10, August, 1986, p. 79.

A chilly stomach is what Sandy feels when her uncle tickles or hugs her or kisses her on the lips. Her friend Jill suggests to Sandy that she tell her parents, but Sandy is afraid that her parents won't believe her or that they won't like her anymore. At the end, she is sitting in a chair, looking very alone, hoping that Jill's parents will tell her parents. Cummings' impressionistic chalk pictures provide a comfortable background for an uncomfortable subject. She places both black and white families in casually middle-class surroundings, full of flowery wallpaper backgrounds and plump, overstuffed chairs. The book is bibliotherapy rather than story, and the open ending that raises Sandy's concerns but does not alleviate them makes the book one that demands discussion between adult and child. This book should not be dumped in the picture book section; it belongs in parents' or teachers' collections. Linda W. Girard's *My Body Is Private* is also very good and informative but is more encompassing and for older children.

STORM IN THE NIGHT (written by Mary Stolz, 1988)

Kirkus Reviews

SOURCE: A review of *Storm in the Night,* in *Kirkus Reviews,* Vol. LVI, No. 2, January 15, 1988, p. 129.

As in Grifalconi's *Darkness and the Butterfly,* a black child learns to face a fear with the help of an older person.

A thunderstorm has left Thomas and his grandfather without TV or light to read by, but they are not without resources. Grandfather knows some good stories: "Thomas hadn't heard all of them yet, because he kept asking for repeats." Thomas can't believe that Grandfather was ever a boy like him, but then—after Grandfather tells about hiding under the bed with his dog, Melvin, during storms, till the day he bravely set forth to rescue Melvin, who had been left out in a sudden storm—Thomas admits his own trepidation and perhaps realizes that Grandfather was once young, too.

Stolz can be counted on for a thoughtful story, gracefully told, and she does not disappoint here. Though her text is quiet and perhaps overlong for its subject, the dark, vibrant page-and-a-half paintings by Cummings (Coretta Scott King Award for *My Mama Needs Me*) should hold attention. White highlights on the cat; the delicate, wind-blown curtains; and the old man's beard—plus creative use of blues and greens—effectively evoke the stormy night world. Thomas looks a bit old (both in his proportions and size), but perhaps that will extend the use of the book to independent reading by older children.

Ilene Cooper

SOURCE: A review of *Storm in the Night,* in *Booklist,* Vol. 84, No. 11, February 1, 1988, p. 937.

Thomas, a young black child, and his grandfather are alone one dark, stormy night when the lights go off. Thomas says he is not afraid, as he hugs his cat, Ringo. But when he asks for a story, Grandfather tells about a time during his own boyhood when he was very scared indeed. As a boy, Grandfather didn't like storms; thunder and lightning always drove him and his dog Melvin under the bed. When a storm comes up one night without warning, Grandfather realizes that Melvin is out in the storm. Love overcomes fear, and Grandfather is reunited with his dog, but not without a lecture from the man who has found Melvin. The story gives Thomas several things to think about—not only the nature of fear but human nature as well. Perhaps if the lights don't come on for a long,

long time, he might be a little frightened too, Thomas admits. After a while they do blink on, but the two comfortably turn them off when they go to sleep. The words are as mesmerizing as the art in this finely crafted story-within-a-story. Stolz' crisp dialogue rings with authenticity, and she uses inflection to get across very complex ideas. When, for instance, Thomas says he's not afraid of anything, Grandfather remarks not many people can say that—then adds, "Well, I suppose anyone could *say* it," thus raising the issue of truthfulness to oneself. Cummings' striking artwork develops the mood as nighttime colors of heavy purples and deep blues overlay the pictures. When showing Grandfather's tale, she carefully keeps an inset of child and man in the corner, maintaining the structure of the story. In sum, a wonderful book, fully realized, capturing both the sensibilities and experiences of two special characters.

Ethel L. Heins

SOURCE: A review of *Storm in the Night,* in *The Horn Book Magazine,* Vol. LXIV, No. 4, July-August, 1988, p. 486.

A poetic quality flows back and forth between words and pictures in a book that serenely celebrates the unique bond that can link a child with a grandparent. During a nighttime storm of thunder, lightning, and "rain streaming down the windows, babbling in the downspouts," the electricity is cut off; and Thomas, Grandfather, and Ringo, the cat, are left in the dark. With no possibility of their reading or watching television, the old man surprises Thomas by saying that he'll have to tell his grandson a tale of his own boyhood. "Because Grandfather said so, Thomas believed that long, long ago, probably at the beginning of the world, his grandfather had been a boy. . . . A grandfather could be a boy, if he went back in his memory far enough; but a boy could not be a grandfather." In the darkness the wind-torn trees and the rain-drenched garden make Thomas newly sensitive to intriguing scents and sounds, which elicit a barrage of eager questions and boastful observations until Grandfather's storytelling becomes an honest revelation of a long-remembered experience of another boy on a frightening stormy night. Presenting a glorified portrayal of a white cat, a beautiful black child, and a gentle old man, the dark, shadowy paintings are made luminous by "the carrot-colored flames in the wood stove" or by lightning slashing across the navy-blue sky; every illustration is imbued with the boy's sensory awareness during a night of wonder and discovery.

I NEED A LUNCH BOX (written by Jeanette Caines, 1988)

Kirkus Reviews

SOURCE: A review of *I Need a Lunch Box,* in *Kirkus Reviews,* Vol. LVI, No. 14, July 15, 1988, p. 1057.

A straight forward story about a rite of passage to which

preschoolers universally look forward. Sister Doris, getting ready for first grade, has just gotten her first lunch box; but the narrator—although he has new sneakers and a coloring book—has been told by Mommy that he must wait for his own lunch box till he's ready for school. He imagines what he could keep in a lunch box if only he had one, and even dreams a splendidly illustrated dream in which he has a different colored and shaped box for each day of the week. Cummings (1984 Coretta Scott King award winner for *My Mama Needs Me*) has depicted sturdy, healthy-looking children who almost push out of the pages' bounds; they are happy and attractive, although rather older-looking than stated in the text. Dad does come up with a lunch box after all, and this seems to be the sort of happy family in which his undermining Mommy's authority won't cause trouble. A useful here-and-now story.

Denise M. Wilms

SOURCE: A review of *I Need a Lunch Box,* in *Booklist,* Vol. 85, No. 2, September 15, 1988, p. 156.

A little boy's big sister has just gotten a lunch box, and he wants one too. Mama says no, because unlike his sister, he isn't about to start school. Still, the boy covets one, thinking about what he could keep in it—his crayons, marbles, bug collection, or toy animals—and dreaming of a different model for each day of the week. All that wishing pays off, because on the morning his sister begins first grade, Daddy surprises the boy with the lunch box he so dearly wants. The family portrayed here is black, but their experience is universal. Cummings' pictures are exuberant paintings that don't stint on strident displays of strong color. The faces of her characters are slightly stiff, a weakness barely noticed in the jangling color and offbeat page design; the book's strength is its portrayal of the yearnings that siblings often feel when they're excluded from the realm of their elder brothers or sisters.

Leda Schubert

SOURCE: A review of *I Need a Lunch Box,* in *School Library Journal,* Vol. 35, No. 4, December, 1988, p. 83.

A black girl is beginning first grade and getting all sorts of goodies, in particular a lunch box for which her little brother yearns with a single-minded passion. However, his mother says that he must wait until he starts school. This rather slim plot is fleshed out through a sequence in which the narrator dreams of a brightly-colored, imaginatively-shaped lunch box for each weekday. At last, on his sister's first day of school, their father surprises the boy with a spaceship lunch box of his own. Brightly patterned objects such as shoes, school supplies, marbles, animals, and of course decorated lunch boxes float through the vividly-colored pages. The simple text makes the story suitable for preschoolers. The drama of family relationships is honestly portrayed, although the issue of whether the father has contradicted the mother, which may bother some parents, is buried in the happy ending.

WILLIE'S NOT THE HUGGING KIND (written by Joyce Durham Barrett, 1989)

Barbara S. McGinn

SOURCE: A review of *Willie's Not the Hugging Kind,* in *School Library Journal,* Vol. 35, No. 14, October, 1989, p. 74.

Because his best friend teases him about it, Willie decides that he doesn't want to be hugged anymore. He tells his older sister, who hugs everyone including her worn teddy bear, that hugging is silly; and he backs off when his mother, father, or teacher try to hug him. Secretly though, Willie misses the hugs and "how safe and happy he always felt with his daddy's strong arms around him." He tries to hug things—a towel, a tree, even his bike—but he soon realizes that he wants to hug some*one*, not some*thing*. The ending is nicely crafted, and Willie even saves face with the friend who teased him. The realistic tempera illustrations are colorful and complement the story line, although the use of almost all bright colors sometimes jars the eye. On the whole, children will welcome this well-written story about a small black boy with a universal theme.

Ilene Cooper

SOURCE: A review of *Willie's Not the Hugging Kind,* in *Booklist,* Vol. 86, No. 3, October 1, 1989, pp. 343-44.

Willie, a young Afro-American boy, used to get hugs from the other members of his family and wishes he still did. But no one has hugged him in a while. His Asian pal, Jo-Jo, has convinced him that hugging is for babies, so now Willie's reputation is that he's "not the hugging kind." In a rather drawn-out scenario, Willie is shown vacillating between Jo-Jo's point of view and his own need for affection. Happily, Willie is able to throw over Jo-Jo's values and get some of the hugging he so desperately craves. Though the message is overstated, it is a good one, especially for boys who think they're above all that mushy stuff. Cummings' full-color art occasionally looks stiff, but the warm family life she portrays carries as much weight as the words.

TWO AND TOO MUCH (written by Mildred Pitts Walter, 1990)

Publishers Weekly

SOURCE: A review of *Two and Too Much,* in *Publishers Weekly,* Vol. 237, No. 8, February 23, 1990, pp. 216-17.

Walter and Cummings, winners of Coretta Scott King Awards for fiction and illustration, respectively, both bring considerable talent to this gentle story of a seven-year-old boy and his mischievous two-year-old sister. Brandon agrees to take care of Gina while Mama cleans the house for company. In no time at all, he begins to wish he had decided to go out and play with his friends instead. Gina answers "no" to all his suggestions, gets into Mama's makeup, makes a mess of Brandon's room and pours milk into the jelly jar at lunch. Finally, to Brandon's horror, Gina disappears altogether. With Mama's help, he discovers his sister on her bedroom floor—sleeping like an angel. With its vibrant paintings and reassuringly realistic text, this is a book that will appeal to several age groups: younger children will find Gina's antics most amusing, while those closer to Brandon's age who must put up with younger siblings will identify with his frustrations.

Christine Behrmann

SOURCE: A review of *Two and Too Much,* in *School Library Journal,* Vol. 36, No. 4, April, 1990, p. 100.

Walter and Cummings use precise characterization and sharp attention to detail to bring freshness to the familiar situation of a young black boy who has to deal with a younger sister in the throes of the terrible twos. Brandon agrees to help his mother by watching Gina, although he'd rather do anything else—even vacuum. It's truly a tough job—she runs off to try on her mother's make-up, knocks over his toy garage, and spills her milk. After lunch, he can't find her. His anger dissipates into fear as he and his mother search the house and, when they find her napping on the floor beside her bed, his relief helps him to put his problems with Gina into perspective. What lifts this depiction of an everyday situation out of the commonplace is the immediacy with which Walter and Cummings convey Brandon's many conflicting emotions—pride, selfishness, reluctant amusement, anger, worry, love—in both language and image. Walter allows Brandon's feelings to flow out of each situation, expressing them with concrete accuracy. Cummings' full-page close-ups of the faces of mother, brother, and sister are done in warm watercolors, capturing Brandon and Gina's many moods. Gina, especially, scrambles across the pages with lively mischief, although she looks a little older than a two year old. It's a conventional predicament, one that many children will recognize, and Cummings and Walter skillfully portray its many dimensions.

Roger Sutton

SOURCE: A review of *Two and Too Much,* in *Bulletin of the Center for Children's Books,* Vol. 43, No. 9, May, 1990, p. 229.

Seven-year-old Brandon rapidly regrets his generous offer to look after two-year-old Gina so that their mother can prepare for a party. Gina, whose favorite word is "no," gets into Mama's makeup ("I pretty?"), knocks down Brandon's toy garage, and pours milk into the jelly. All this appealing mayhem is brightly captured in Cummings' day-glowing, firmly lined illustrations that give graphic weight to the fuzz exploding from the vacuum cleaner, pink powder liberally scattered, and other assorted solids and liquids that fly through the air. Both pictures and text capture family devotion as well as disaster. Although this isn't a new story, it's an ever-appealing one, and kids will find this black family a pleasure to know.

CLEAN YOUR ROOM, HARVEY MOON! (1991)

Kirkus Reviews

SOURCE: A review of *Clean Your Room, Harvey Moon!*, in *Kirkus Reviews,* Vol. LIX, No. 3, February 1, 1991, pp. 181-82.

Harvey's unwilling, but Mom is firm: no more TV until he picks up! Bemoaning the passing hours and missed Saturday programs, he tackles a truly monumental mess (succinctly described in verse), stuffing most of it under his rug. Mom's not so easily fooled, but she does have a sense of humor: after lunch, we'll "get started on lump number one!" Cummings's bold, sculptural forms and unusual perspectives add to the humor. An entertaining exaggeration of a familiar situation, by a Coretta Scott King Award winner.

Publishers Weekly

SOURCE: A review of *Clean Your Room, Harvey Moon!*, in *Publishers Weekly,* Vol. 238, No. 8, February 8, 1991, p. 56.

Harvey's Saturday cartoon viewing is disrupted by "the voice of DOOM" (his mother): "Today, young man, . . . Is the day you clean your room!" Spurred on by the hope of getting back to the TV, Harvey reluctantly begins the difficult task of sorting out the monumental mess that he has accumulated. He hurriedly puts away T-shirts and sneakers, marbles and a toothbrush. But during Harvey's travails, mysterious lumps begin to form on his bed. Harvey's "hide-it" method of housekeeping may be neat, but it's not clever enough to fool Mom. Many children will empathize with Harvey and his sloppiness, and recognize the familiar items that lurk under beds and in closets. Cummings's art is a boisterous clutter of color, providing just the right mood for her bouncy, rhyming text. The facial expressions of Harvey and his cat are particularly amusing.

Deborah Abbott

SOURCE: A review of *Clean Your Room, Harvey Moon!*, in *Booklist,* Vol. 87, No. 12, February 15, 1991, p. 1201.

Thinking about his Saturday-morning television programs, Harvey Moon is interrupted by a command from his mother that would make any army private jump. As Harvey sorts through the clothes and toys, finding lost trinkets and furry, damp, unrecognizable leftovers, even (yes!) forgotten library books, time disappears along with his favorite shows. Finally, just when Harvey thinks the job is done—having shoved everything underneath his rug in clumps—his Mom announces that after lunch they can work together on "lump number one!" The text, in singsong rhymes, comes alive in the perky, color drawings, filled with details that youngsters will savor. A read-aloud winner in which the scenes of bedroom chaos will tickle children and get an all-knowing nod from adults.

Anna DeWind

SOURCE: A review of *Clean Your Room, Harvey Moon!*, in *School Library Journal,* Vol. 37, No. 4, April, 1991, p. 94.

Harvey Moon is just settling in to watch his favorite Saturday morning cartoon when his mother tells him to clean his room. Absolutely stricken, he moans about the television shows he'll miss, but grudgingly proceeds to bring some order to his messy bedroom. Dirty jeans; wet swim trunks; and warm, gray, unrecognizable lumps are just some of the items he discovers during his marathon chore. The bright illustrations in crayon-box hues are lively and humorous, depicting a middle-class African-American child and his wealth of worldly possessions. The rhyming story line, although slight, will appeal to anyone who has ever faced the inevitability of chores when more enjoyable possibilities beckon.

GO FISH (written by Mary Stolz, 1991)

Ruth Semrau

SOURCE: A review of *Go Fish,* in *School Library Journal,* Vol. 37, No. 5, May, 1991, p. 84.

Grandfather and Thomas, who appeared in Stolz's picture book, ***Storm in the Night,*** return in a liberally illustrated beginning chapter book. Cummings confines herself to watercolors in shades of gray on white. On almost every page are depictions of the actions or ornamental motifs. Grandfather and Thomas are a family of two, "semi-poor" and dependent on food that they catch or produce themselves, plus their cat, Ringo. They begin the day by fishing for trout, and finish it with a game of cards (Go fish, of course) and a story. The before-you-were-born hurricane, the grandfather as a small boy himself listening to the stories of his own grandfather, the line of ancestors leading back to ancient African cities, the fossils preserved in the limestone of long dried-up seas—all these are the elements of a single summer day. Colorful details of life at the seashore abound: hummingbirds in the bougainvillea, the seawall rocks at low tide, blowfish and flounder, sea oats and sand spurs, coquinas and herons. Stolz evokes the spirit of childhood with graceful description and metaphor. At day's end, Thomas glimpses his own future, recalling this present day as a past golden-time, telling tales to an as yet unborn child.

Ilene Cooper

SOURCE: A review of *Go Fish,* in *Booklist,* Vol. 87, No. 15, May 15, 1991, p. 1800.

Thomas and his grandfather, first introduced in the well-received picture book **Storm in the Night,** spend some poignant, special moments together in this beginning chapter book. Once again, Stolz, aided by Cummings' artistry, portrays a warm relationship shaded by everyday events. Thomas and his grandfather go fishing, share stories, and hold intense conversations. It is grandfather's sage advice ("The ideal is to tell nothing but the truth. But perfect honesty at times comes out to perfect rudeness. . . . Our problem is to know which is which") as well as Thomas' probing questions ("Why did there have to be cockroaches?") that elevates the story. Though Cummings' gray-wash pictures do not pack quite the same punch as the last book's intensely colored art, they are certainly successful. A quiet, thoughtful book that can be used as a discussion piece for second- and third-graders.

Maeve Visser Knoth

SOURCE: A review of *Go Fish,* in *The Horn Book Magazine,* Vol. LXVII, No. 4, July-August, 1991, pp. 454-55.

Thomas and his grandfather, who first appeared in Stolz's **Storm in the Night,** spend a summer day fishing, playing cards, and talking. In the morning, Thomas, restless and impatient, tries one distraction after another until he finally succeeds in interrupting his grandfather's reading. They get their fishing equipment together and walk down to the edge of the Gulf of Mexico. After much conversation and a successful fishing trip, they cook dinner, talk some more, and finish off the evening with a game of "Go Fish." Thomas goes to sleep imagining himself as a grandfather sharing stories with his own grandchild. The strength of this quiet story lies in the characters; Stolz draws detailed portraits of Thomas and his grandfather through their conversation, using precise, poetic language. Thomas's mind jumps from one topic to another, absorbing information from his grandfather and the world around them. With his grandfather's help, he learns to define himself in terms of his family, back to his "great-great-great-and-one-more-great-grandfather" in Africa. Stolz seamlessly weaves together themes involving friendship and family heritage, creating characters who immerse themselves in life and appreciate minute aspects of it. Cummings's soft black-and-white illustrations match the mood of the text and often flow across the page, as uncontained as Thomas's thoughts. Young readers will appreciate the attractive format of this chapter book; every page is illustrated, and white space is used generously. A graceful, quiet story that celebrates the richness of human relationships.

📖 *TALKING WITH ARTISTS* (compiled and edited by Pat Cummings, 1992)

Betsy Hearne

SOURCE: A review of *Talking with Artists,* in *Bulletin of the Center for Children's Books,* Vol. 45, No. 8, April, 1992, p. 202.

The fourteen artists here have already said a good deal to children through their illustrations, but Cummings' set of candidly child-like questions ("Where do you get your ideas?") brings out telling background patterns. Almost all of the interviewees drew compulsively from a young age—most of them astonishingly well, if the samples of their childhood art are indicative. They speak of art supplies with sensuous reverence and recall persons whose encouragement or direction was crucial to their development. Few have children living with them, and all work compulsively. The photographs of each artist as child and adult, along with reproductions of their early and recent work, combine with an easygoing text for the impression of—well, maybe not a fireside chat, but at least a classroom visit, something many schools find increasingly hard to afford. As inspiration for budding artists or information for reports, this will make a natural companion to picture books by the award-winning subjects, who are arranged alphabetically from Victoria Chess to David Wiesner and who represent a range of styles and interests.

Stephanie Zvirin

SOURCE: A review of *Talking with Artists,* in *Booklist,* Vol. 88, No. 7, May 1, 1992, p. 1598.

While the 14 children's book illustrators profiled here may not be picture-lady material like Claude Monet or Andrew Wyeth, their work is known and loved by many children, and several have been recipients of the Caldecott Medal. Editor Cummings (who justly includes herself in the roundup) offers encouragement to young artists before introducing her assemblage, which includes such stellar figures as David Wiesner, Jerry Pinkney, Leo and Diane Dillon, and Lisa Campbell Ernst. The group represents a variety of artistic styles—from Stephen Kellogg's signature crew of smiling, cherubic children to Lois Ehlert's colorful collage. With the exception of Lane Smith's freewheeling illustrated comments, the artists' brief, informal personal profiles are similarly structured, often including a childhood anecdote or a bit about how the person became a children's book illustrator. Each résumé is followed by eight questions (e.g., Where do you work? Do you have pets or children?) that children commonly ask. Cummings attends further to children's insatiable curiosity by including a recent photo of each artist, a sampling of his or her work, and the artist's signature. But what kids will love best is the picture of each artist as a child and the sampling of childhood artwork. The sunny dust jacket invites kids to sample the book's friendly, forthright conversations, while the full-color re-

B is for butcher or
breakfast with bagels
or block-party bands
out on hot summer nights.

C is for city or
cabbies named Clarence
or cool cats who chat
under boulevard lights.

From C is for City, *written by Nikki Gimes. Illustrated by Pat Cummings.*

productions will carry them right on through. A delight for aspiring artists, the book will also attract teachers. A glossary and a listing of some of each artist's favorite book projects are appended.

Karen Nelson Hoyle

SOURCE: A review of *Talking with Artists,* in *The Five Owls,* Vol. VI, No. 5, May-June, 1992, pp. 62-3.

Among the many biographies and autobiographies about authors and illustrators of children's books, Cummings's compilation proves the most accessible. Along with photographs from both childhood and adulthood, the book shows the artist's signature and gives his or her birthday. Minority, girl, and economically deprived readers can find role models among the fourteen artists, who include Victoria Chess, Pat Cummings, Leo and Diane Dillon, Richard Egielski, Lois Ehlert, Lisa Campbell Ernst, Tom Feelings, Steven Kellogg, Jerry Pinkney, Amy Schwartz, Lane Smith, Chris Van Allsburg, and David Wiesner.

Each illustrator recalls his or her childhood experiences with art and then art training in the "My Story" section. Lois Ehlert comments on the card table reserved for her exclusive use. Jerry Pinkney competed for a scholarship at the Philadelphia Museum College of Art. Steven Kellogg's own Great Dane puppy became the Pinkerton of his books.

The questions posed to each of the artists seem child-generated. They range from the origin of ideas to family life to what they like to draw. Pat Cummings recalls her dreams. David Wiesner married a surgeon. Lisa Campbell Ernst loves to draw her dog and rabbit along with other animals. Curiosity about when and where artists work is satisfied, too. Chris Van Allsburg works eight or nine hours each day, incorporating tennis to offset the soli-

tude. Richard Egielski and his wife work in an attic studio with skylights.

A drawing made by each artist as a child receives equal billing with the reproduction of an illustration from a published book. Leo Dillon was nine when he created his watercolor entitled "Desert with Mountains."

In the back of the book is a glossary of art and publishing terms and a section in which each artist has listed his or her own favorite works. Definitions of art media and the description of professionals in the publishing business can be understood by a child. In this business a "dummy" is "a model of a book" and an "agent" is "a person who shows your work to clients to find work for you." The glossary would be enhanced with pronunciation assistance for words such as *gouache.*

For children who like to draw, this book can make a significant contribution to their appreciation of backgrounds of artists and to their own career goals. It's next best to having a mentor. Libraries will want to order in multiple copies to assure that one copy is kept on the reference shelf while others circulate. Full-color printing justifies the price.

Mary M. Burns

SOURCE: A review of *Talking with Artists,* in *The Horn Book Magazine,* Vol. LXVIII, No. 4, July-August, 1992, pp. 465-66.

In an innovative approach to informational books, fourteen well-known children's book illustrators respond to questions about their lives and work in a lively interchange of ideas which will have direct appeal to young—and not-so-young—audiences. Each of the segments is preceded by an autobiographical essay with photographs of the subject as a child and as he or she looks today. A sampling of early artistic efforts is also included, accompanied by a pithy statement of advice to the reader such as Amy Schwartz's comment that "art improves with practice. A loving familiarity with books and stories will help you think like an illustrator" or Tom Feelings's suggestion to "carry a sketchbook wherever you go because it's a record of what you're seeing and feeling." The questions posed to each respondent are identical, thus suggesting wonderful opportunities for comparison and contrast in tracing the evolution of the creative impulse. Well-reproduced samplings of illustrations for each contributor add to the book's handsome appearance and inviting format. No effort has been spared to make this a substantial, but not formidable, reference: even the childhood artworks are accorded the same respect given those produced as adults, with information appended about the medium used, size of the original, and title. In addition to the two artists mentioned, the other subjects of this splendid compilation are Victoria Chess, Pat Cummings, Leo and Diane Dillon, Richard Egielski, Lois Ehlert, Lisa Campbell Ernst, Steven Kellogg, Jerry Pinkney, Lane Smith, Chris Van Allsburg, and David Wiesner. An inspired concept, executed with class!

📖 *PETEY MORONI'S CAMP RUNAMOK DIARY* (1992)

Kirkus Reviews

SOURCE: A review of *Petey Moroni's Camp Runamok Diary,* in *Kirkus Reviews,* Vol. LX, No. 14, July 15, 1992, p. 919.

The title sets the tone for this lighthearted look at a bunch of normally ebullient kids outwitted by a crafty raccoon who snitches most of the snacks they've brought to camp, despite their increasingly ingenious hiding places. In Cummings's crisp, bold illustrations, the diarist is an earnest, owl-eyed African-American; the other kids are thoroughly multicultural; and the raccoon, though not seen by the campers, will be gleefully noted by readers who can observe him, up to his tall-tale tricks, in every picture: this wily bandit blows bubble gum and squeezes mustard on his hot dog. When the kids leave on Day 14, the overstuffed thief gets the last grin. Good summer fun.

Deborah Stevenson

SOURCE: A review of *Petey Moroni's Camp Runamok Diary,* in *Bulletin of the Center for Children's Books,* Vol. 46, No. 2, October, 1992, p. 41.

Petey Moroni's diary of his two weeks at camp focuses on two things: comics ("Samurai Surfer meets Bonzai Dave for only the second time, and this time on earth") and food, especially the disappearing act every camper's edible treasures are performing ("Nancy Patanky *knew* she had three boxes of individually wrapped fruit-flavored Puff n' Stuff Pastries she bought from home, but two whole boxes were missing"). Even after a raccoon is identified as the culprit, the kids' ingenuity is no match for that

of the raccoon, who has clearly won this summer's round ("Ollie found nothing but a hole where he put his Caramel Crunchies"). The illustrations are slickly and robustly goofy, if occasionally somewhat luridly colored, with boys and girls in all shapes and colors remaining oblivious to the raccoon's constant peeking; the critter itself has a strongly human attitude as it lies sleepily among the snack food wrappers and then dons a camp T-shirt. Since no introductions are provided, it may take young readers a bit to figure out which kid is Petey Maroni, but it's always clear what's going on. Cummings uses some nicely humorous specificity, such as the strategic employment of food brand names and comic book heroes. You won't learn much about camp activities here, but both the protagonists and the readers should find Runamok an entertaining camp experience.

Rachel Fox

SOURCE: A review of *Petey Moroni's Camp Runamok Diary,* in *School Library Journal,* Vol. 38, No. 12, December, 1992, pp. 78, 80.

While at sleep-away camp, many children have treats stolen, and it takes them quite some time to figure out who the culprit is. Finally, the thief is identified as a raccoon but the youngsters still can't come up with a way to get it to stop eating their food. Each double-page spread contains a daily diary entry by camper Peter Moroni informing readers of which child has had what taken. Every page shows either glimpses or full views of the animal for readers to locate. The full-color, graphic illustrations are quite enjoyable and add to the humor of the campers' plight.

📖 *CAROUSEL* (1994)

Publishers Weekly

SOURCE: A review of *Carousel,* in *Publishers Weekly,* Vol. 241, No. 12, March 21, 1994, p. 72.

"Off went the sneakers. On went the bows. Off went the jeans. On came the frills." Alex's mother and aunts have made a birthday dinner, but the African American girl is *not* pleased: her father, en route home from a trip, still hasn't arrived. Alex's grumpiness gets the best of her when her mother gives her the present her father has picked out—a miniature carousel—and the child realizes that he definitely won't make it home. Sent to bed without cake, Alex snaps the tiny zebra off the carousel. After falling asleep, she "awakens" to see it and the other carousel animals fly out the window—and magically grow. She follows, and is treated to a ride through the night sky on the festively painted creatures' backs. Her father is there when she wakes up in the morning, and after exchanging apologies (he for missing her birthday; she for breaking his gift), all ends happily. Though its message will reassure children dealing with anger, the story never takes wing, and the dream sequence seems gratuitous. The book's strong point is Cummings's (*Clean Your Room, Harvey Moon!*) affecting, vividly hued art, which depicts the realistic and the fanciful scenes with equal vibrancy.

Kirkus Reviews

SOURCE: A review of *Carousel,* in *Kirkus Reviews,* Vol. LXII, No. 7, April 1, 1994, p. 478.

Since Daddy's not back, Alex is too upset to enjoy dressing up for her birthday, or even to appreciate the present he's left. Seizing the delicate toy carousel, she flounces off to bed, carelessly breaking off a zebra. Later, she "wakes" to see the carousel animals jumping out her window; following, she finds them waiting to give her a joyous series of rides. Come morning, the carousel is empty but Daddy's there to explain how angry he felt when his plane was late (but only because he was so happy to be coming home) and to help put the animals back. Cummings's depiction of the disappointed child being rude to the aunts who have come to help celebrate is refreshingly true to life, while the nuances of her emotions are also warmheartedly portrayed in the Coretta Scott King Award winner's vibrant realistic art. At the end, Daddy and morning arrive like the restorative breeze blowing in Alex's window. A likable, deceptively simple story that provides a fine model of forbearance and clemency strengthening an already loving relationship.

Deborah Abbott

SOURCE: A review of *Carousel,* in *Booklist,* Vol. 90, No. 21, July, 1994, p. 1953.

Upset that her father is not home for her birthday celebration as he promised. Alex pouts throughout the meal and the opening of presents. Although she appreciates her father's gift of a little carousel, she utters one last angry remark, and her mother sends her to bed without her cake. Not paying attention to where she placed the carousel, she jumps into bed and bumps it, breaking off the zebra. She falls asleep and dreams she follows the carousel animals out the window. They become life-size, and she happily rides them around the night sky, even apologizing to the zebra. When she awakes in the morning, her father is home, explaining that he felt as angry about not being with her as she did about his not being home. Although there is a slight stiffness in the writing. Cummings' vibrant double-page-spread illustrations depict the moods accurately and sensitively. The joyfulness in the dream scenes has instant child appeal. There are many ups and downs to birthday celebrations, and this book captures one beautifully.

Jane Marino

SOURCE: A review of *Carousel,* in *School Library Journal,* Vol. 40, No. 8, August, 1994, pp. 127-28.

Cummings has ably demonstrated her propensity for fan-

tasy in *C.L.O.U.D.S.* and for reality in *Petey Moroni's Camp Runamok Diary.* Here, she combines elements of both. Alex's disappointment at her father's failure to arrive home from a business trip in time for her birthday party overshadows all of her mother and aunts' attempts to provide fun and festivity. Finally, the child's bad temper leads to bad manners; roughly clutching the music-box carousel that is her father's gift to her, she storms off to her room. When she falls asleep, the animals come to life and she rides them through the night. She awakens to find her father, who is glad to be home and sorry to have missed her birthday. Alex, too, is sorry at having spoiled the party and broken the carousel, but is glad that her Dad is back. Cummings's brightly hued illustrations effectively portray both the real and dream worlds; bright pinks, blues, and greens dominate her palette. The African-American characters' faces evoke just the right emotions, while the carousel creatures populate the dreamscape convincingly. A family story that's perfect for sharing.

TALKING WITH ARTISTS, VOLUME TWO (compiled and edited by Pat Cummings, 1995)

Kirkus Reviews

SOURCE: A review of *Talking with Artists: Vol. II,* in *Kirkus Reviews,* Vol. LXIII, No. 17, September 1, 1995, p. 1279.

Cummings delights with a lively, intimate look at the working lives of 13 diverse artists. From Thomas Allen's realistic pastels to Kevin Henkes's simple, powerful lines to Brian Pinkney's trademark scratchboard drawings and David Wisniewski's intricate cut-paper illustrations, each artist's approach to the work of making picture books is unique. As varied as these artists are (among them, Floyd Cooper, Maira Kalman, Julie Downing, and William Joyce) common threads run through their stories.

Following the format set in the first volume, each entry begins with a two-page essay entitled "My Story," accompanied by photos (mostly full-color) of the artist, past and present. Then Cummings asks a series of eight questions perfectly geared to children's own interests, such as "Where do you work?" "Do you have any children?" and "What is a normal day like for you?" Readers see examples of one childhood effort, a present-day piece, and new to this volume, a photograph of the artist's workspace. Cummings finishes up with a secret technique from each person and brief bibliographies. Great inspiration for young artists, good for researching author projects, or fun just to browse.

Stephanie Zvirin

SOURCE: A review of *Talking with Artists, Vol. 2,* in *Booklist,* Vol. 92, No. 2, September 15, 1995, pp. 157-58.

Cummings once again addresses kids' curiosity about the people behind the picture books they love. The look of this book is slightly different from her 1992 volume: type-faces have been changed, photos of the artists are now in color, and the jacket colors have been softened. The "My Story" section that introduced each profile in the first book remains a wonderful feature here, giving artists an opportunity to tell about themselves in a vivid, personal way; the general questions posed are the same as those in volume one; and there's still a fascinating glimpse of the artists' work as children. There are also some great, new features. Instead of a glossary of art terms, this book includes a simple, technical tip from each artist and a photo of the artist's workspace. Cummings' selection of artists is especially good this time, demonstrating a great diversity in artistic style and choice of media. Kevin Henkes, Floyd Cooper, Denise Fleming, and Vera B. Williams are among the 13 included. A special treat for budding artists and wonderful for teachers.

Roger Sutton

SOURCE: A review of *Talking with Artists: Volume Two,* in *Bulletin of the Center for Children's Books,* Vol. 49, No. 2, October, 1995, p. 50.

In this companion to **Talking with Artists,** thirteen more picture-book illustrators answer Cummings questions, which aim to get at what kids really want to know: "Where do you get your ideas from?" "Do you ever put people you know in your pictures?" "What do you use to make your pictures?" The answers (from, among others, Denise Fleming, Kevin Henkes, and Brian Pinkney) are direct and unpatronizing, and a goodly assortment of photographs and reproductions from each subject's childhood art and picture-book work gives the book an inviting browsability. New to this volume is a "secret techniques" section, where Julie Downing shows how to draw clothes on a clothesline so that they're dancing in the wind and David Wisniewski tells how to layer paper for a bas-relief effect.

Carol Schene

SOURCE: A review of *Talking with Artists, Vol. 2,* in *School Library Journal,* Vol. 41, No. 10, October, 1995, p. 145.

Using the same eight questions that she used in the first volume of **Talking with Artists,** e.g., What is a normal day like for you? What do you enjoy drawing the most? What do you use to make your pictures?, Cummings probes the minds and hearts of 13 illustrators—Thomas B. Allen, Mary Jane Begin, Floyd Cooper, Julie Downing, Denise Fleming, Sheila Hamanaka, Kevin Henkes, William Joyce, Maira Kalman, Deborah Nourse Lattimore, Brian Pinkney, Vera B. Williams, and David Wisniewski. The tone of each interview is casual. These conversations are as humorous, insightful, and as original as the artists themselves. Although the author has kept the format the same as in the first volume, instead of a glossary of art terms, here she includes a section in which each artist describes a special technique that students may want to try. Excel-lent, full-color photos of the illustrators, their studios, and their work are also included. Full of insight and inspiration, this is an entertaining resource that young people, teachers, and librarians will enjoy. Cummings has another hit on her hands.

Mary M. Burns

SOURCE: A review of *Talking with Artists: Volume Two,* in *The Horn Book Magazine,* Vol. LXXI, No. 6, November-December, 1995, pp. 755-56.

Illustrated with photographs and reproductions of artwork by various artists. A baker's dozen of contemporary illustrators for children are included in the handsomely produced sequel to Cummings's initial volume of conversations with artists. The format is similar: a succinct autobiographical sketch followed by a series of questions and answers that address topics such as sources of inspiration, working habits and environs, comments on family and pets, art techniques, favorite subjects, and the story leading to the acceptance of that all-important first book. However, there are subtle changes as well as similarities: the photographs—one of the artist as a child, a second as an adult—are larger; a section of each artist's "Secret Techniques" replaces the glossary in Volume One; and a view of the artist's studio has been included. As always, the comments are revealing, from the iconoclastic observation of Maira Kalman that she begins her day by reading "the obituaries to remind myself that I am still alive" to Vera Williams's description of her encounter, at age eight, with Eleanor Roosevelt. As in the earlier volume, two samplings of the artist's work are included for each entry—one from a published book, the other a piece of artwork from younger days. In addition to the two artists mentioned, eleven equally fascinating and provocative studies are included of Thomas B. Allen, Mary Jane Begin, Brian Pinkney, Floyd Cooper, Julie Downing, Denise Fleming, Sheila Hamanaka, Kevin Henkes, William Joyce, Deborah Nourse Lattimore, and David Wisniewski. With a selective bibliography of works by each artist.

📖 *C IS FOR CITY* (written by Nikki Grimes, 1995)

Julie Yates Walton

SOURCE: A review of *C Is for City,* in *Booklist,* Vol. 92, No. 3, October 1, 1995, p. 322.

City is the operative word in this hustling, bustling, urban ABC book. It begins, "A is for arcade or ads for Apartments / on short streets with alleys alive with stray pets. / A is for Afghans named after their owners / who drive them to art shows in silver Corvettes." Cummings' lively cartoonish illustrations depict all of these *a* words, plus countless more tucked in for the keen-eyed reader. (A key in the back of the book lists all illustrated objects.) The rhymes themselves are quite clever and packed with vocabulary-expanding images.

Each illustration is a hearty slice of urban life, with all its intersecting dramas and scenes within scenes. At a diner, for instance, four different dramas play out, including a doorman jumping double-Dutch and a teen flirting with the waitress. Certainly city children will identify with the book, but any child should find in its busy illustrations much worth discussing or poring over alone.

Sally R. Dow

SOURCE: A review of *C Is for City,* in *School Library Journal,* Vol. 41, No. 11, November, 1995, p. 71.

In this rhyming alphabet book, each letter represents different New York City experiences—e.g., "A is for arcade or ads for apartments . . . / B is for butcher or/ breakfast with bagels / or block-party bands / out on hot summer nights. C is for city / or cabbies named Clarence / or cool cats who chat / under boulevard lights." Many of the arresting images reflect the ethnic, religious, and economic diversity of urban life. From a sleek sports car with a bejeweled Afghan to tawdry fortune tellers and other entertainers, a wide range of people and neighborhoods are depicted. The rhythm of the verses is also varied, but it is always interesting and right on target for the audience. Illustrations in vivid, neon colors suggest the electricity and brashness of a loud city with its hard edges as well as the teeming population. In addition to the letter-specific items mentioned, others are incorporated into the pictures for sharpeyed viewers to find. An entertaining selection along the lines of "A my name is Alice," set in the Big Apple.

Additional coverage of Cummings's life and career is contained in the following sources published by Gale Research: *Contemporary Authors New Revision Series,* Vol. 44; *Major Authors and Illustrators for Children and Young Adults; Something about the Author,* Vols. 42, 71; and *Something about the Author Autobiography Series,* Vol. 13.

Lensey Namioka

1929-

Chinese American author of fiction.

Major works include *The Samurai and the Long-Nosed Devils* (1976), *Valley of the Broken Cherry Trees* (1980), *Village of the Vampire Cat* (1981), *Island of Ogres* (1989), *Yang the Youngest and His Terrible Ear* (1992), *April and the Dragon Lady* (1994).

INTRODUCTION

Namioka is best known as the author of a series of adventure and mystery novels set in sixteenth-century feudal Japan. Centering on the exploits of two samurai warriors, her engrossing tales of bravado have acquired a loyal audience of teenage readers and a reputation for addressing difficult social issues—from political corruption to racial prejudice, family violence, and rape. Namioka has also gained favorable notice for her children's books with a contemporary setting. Related with an authenticity born of personal experience, two such works, *Yang the Youngest and His Terrible Ear* and its sequel, *Yang the Third and Her Impossible Family,* describe the comical misadventures of a family of Chinese musicians who have just immigrated to Seattle. In these works, according to Nancy Vasilakis of *Horn Book,* Namioka "explores issues of diversity, self-realization, friendship, and duty with sensitivity and a great deal of humor."

Biographical Information

Namioka was born in China in 1929 to Yuen Ren, a linguist, and Buwei Yang Chao, a working mother who pursued dual careers as a physician and writer. Namioka came to the United States to attend college, graduating from Radcliffe in 1949 and earning a master's degree from the University of California at Berkeley in 1951. She married a Japanese mathematician, Isaac Namioka, in 1957, helping to enhance a knowledge of Japanese history that had been imparted to Lensey by her mother, a one-time resident of Japan.

Also a mathematician, Namioka began her career as an instructor, first at Wells College and then at Cornell. Translation work for the American Mathematical Society followed; Namioka also translated her mother's book *How to Order and Eat in Chinese* (1974). In 1976 she began her writing career with the publication of her first novel, *The Samurai and the Long-Nosed Devils,* initiating a series of books about the young samurai warriors Zenta and Matsuzo. Many of Namioka's books published in the 1990s have focused on the experiences of Chinese immigrants in the United States. She has also written plays and contributed humor and travel pieces to magazines and newspapers.

Major Works

The Samurai and the Long-Nosed Devils introduces two characters at the center of seven Namioka novels: Konishi Zenta and Ishihara Matsuzo, sixteenth-century samurai warriors, or *ronin,* whose lords have been ousted and who must therefore wander to find work. When they gain employment as bodyguards for Portuguese missionaries in the capital city of Miyako, they find themselves enmeshed in a murder mystery and a web of political intrigue. Another mystery—as well as man-eating carp, six-foot amazons with swords, and the ghost of a white serpent—greets Zenta and Matsuzo in *White Serpent Castle,* considered by some commentators the most tautly constructed of Namioka's historical adventures. *Valley of the Broken Cherry Trees* received similar accolades, along with plaudits for pacing and characterization. In this novel, Zenta and Matsuzo go to a beautiful valley to visit a friend and are shocked to see the mutilation of its cherry trees. Drawn into yet another of the many power struggles that plagued feudal Japan, the two young men solve the mystery of the "broken" cherry trees with courage and loyalty, both to each other and to the samurai code.

In *Village of the Vampire Cat,* Zenta and Matsuzo encounter a particularly troubling mystery: a "Vampire Cat" is killing young women. Once again coming to the aid of the powerless, the popular protagonists investigate, uncovering a human rather than supernatural source for the tragedies. Namioka illuminates the Japanese tea ceremony, the practice of hara-kiri, and New Year's celebration in this work, while again garnering praise for deft plotting and well-handled suspense. Both *Island of Ogres* and *The Coming of the Bear* take place on islands. In the former, Matsuzo must help Zenta, who is hiding on an island recovering from a wound. Kajiro, a dissipated samurai sent to the syame island with the last-chance assignment of spying on the commander, is mistakenly identified as Zenta—just one intriguing element in a plot that more than one reviewer called byzantine. The complications and counterplots accumulate, the style is elliptical, and perspective can change abruptly, but readers are rewarded for their efforts with another satisfying Namioka adventure. In *The Coming of the Bear,* both Zenta and Matsuzo are taken prisoner by the Ainu (a race of round-eyed people) but somehow manage to solve the mystery of the killer bear and stop a war between the Ainu and the Japanese.

Namioka began writing contemporary fiction with *Who's Hu?,* which chronicles the struggles of Emma, a Chinese teenager who must decide whether to follow Chinese ways or those of the Americans she meets in her new home in Massachusetts. Emma is led to believe that appearances and fitting in are more important in American culture than academic excellence. Similarly, *April and the Dragon Lady,* told in the first person, concerns a young woman striving to balance her commitment to her heritage with contemporary American expectations. April Chen has been forced by the death of her mother and by Chinese cultural expectation into the role of caretaker for her grandmother, the "dragon lady," whose behavior has become increasingly erratic and domineering. April respects her family and its traditions, but she has also been inspired by the American cultural imperative to pursue independence and her own dreams. When her grandmother tries to drive away her boyfriend, Steve, connives to arrange a second marriage for her father, and even threatens April's college plans, April must take a stand.

Yang the Youngest and His Terrible Ear is the first of two humorous novels about a family of Chinese musicians who have immigrated to Seattle. *Yang the Youngest* focuses on the tone-deaf youngest member of the family, Yang Yingtao. The nine-year-old's contributions to the family quartet are hardly felicitous. Yingtao is not untalented, however; he is a star on the baseball field. His coach is his best friend Matthew's father, who expects great things of his son; unfortunately, Matthew would rather play the violin. The novel brings a light touch to themes of family expectations, self-realization, cultural adjustment, and friendship. A sequel, *Yang the Third and Her Impossible Family,* features Yingtao's sister Yingmei, or Mary, who must gradually come to terms with the embarrassment of awkward cross-cultural differences between her family and their new community.

Awards

Namioka received Washington State Governor's Awards for *White Serpent Castle* in 1976 and *April and the Dragon Lady* in 1996. She also garnered a Certificate of Merit in 1994 from *Parents'* magazine for *The Coming of the Bear,* and Parents' Choice recognition for *Yang the Third and Her Impossible Family* in 1995.

AUTHOR'S COMMENTARY

Suzanne Rahn

SOURCE: "An Interview with Lensey Namioka," in *The Lion and the Unicorn,* Vol. 13, No. 1, 1989, pp. 74-81.

In the dining room of her [Lensey Namioka's] Seattle home, two striking pictures hang side by side. One is a finely-detailed brass rubbing of a knight and lady that she made herself in a Cotswold church, "crouching for hours over a cold stone sarcophagus." The other is a stone rubbing of a Chinese sculpture'—two jolly-looking, round-bellied men, chuckling together at some ancient joke'; this she bought on a visit to China. As we talked, the two pictures began to reflect in their own way what Lensey

Namioka was telling me about a storytelling tradition, both heroic and humorous, that spans time and space, and of which she feels herself a part.

[Suzanne Rahn]: Let me start by asking you why you began writing historical novels.

[Lensey Namioka]: I write historical novels because I read them. I just love history, and I have an insatiable appetite for historical novels. I think that was about the earliest western book that I can remember reading. Of course, Chinese literature is just full of historical novels. There is a whole genre of Chinese swashbucklers, usually about outlaw bands deep in the mountains battling injustice, and they're usually set back in historical times. I used to read these by the ton. Not only did I read them, my whole family did. My mother, whenever she relaxed, would have a pile of these pop novels. They're universally read in China by intellectuals, by people in the streets, everybody.

*I remember in **Who's Hu?** the father is addicted to them.*

Well, that father's addiction reflects my mother's addiction to them. But we all read them. So, I loved this type of thing from as far back as I can remember. When I first came across these translations from the French, *The Three Musketeers,* oh, that was wonderful. I couldn't stop reading them. And then after I came to this country and started reading in English, I read all of the King Arthur stories, the Song of Roland and all those. So from a very early age I liked the heroic, epic tales—and then the Trojan War in all its various translations. I guess my love for historical fiction goes back to my very earliest childhood.

It encompasses several cultures too.

I think that's one thing about historical fiction; people who like it usually like different periods of history. Any historical far away and long ago thing appeals to me, and that includes things like "Star Wars," the science fiction far away and long ago. All this heroic fiction is really related. It has the larger than life hero, his henchman and fair ladies—and sometimes the ladies get pretty feisty too—and a few grotesque characters for humor.

When you started writing, though, it's a little surprising that instead of using a Chinese setting you went to Japan.

There's a reason for that. When I started writing, it was just at the end of the Cultural Revolution in China, and things went very badly for many of my relatives. So I didn't want to write about China. In fact, my relatives had to play down their connections with people abroad, because anybody who was known to have relatives living in the West was immediately suspect. So I didn't want to do anything that would make trouble. And since I'm married to a Japanese, and had lived in Japan, I decided to write about Japan. My first published book, ***The Samurai and the Long-Nosed Devils,*** is about some Portuguese arriving in Japan in the sixteenth century. But the book that I first started writing is ***White Serpent Castle,*** and I started that because I was visiting my husband's home town, which has one of the most beautiful castles in Japan. So I visited the castle, and my father-in-law was very helpful in arousing my interest in feudal times. He was a real nut about historical fiction too, and helped me a lot with the background of Japanese feudal history. And every Sunday night from eight to nine o'clock on Japanese public television, there's a historical drama we used to watch. It's a serial that lasts precisely one year, from January 1st to December 31st, and it's always set in some period in Japanese history. So when we lived there we always tuned in. Whatever we were doing, we dropped it.

All year long?

Yes, all year. It builds up tremendous audience loyalty. Even when you're traveling and staying at an inn, you find that all of the television sets go click to this drama. So that also helped. And, of course, I go to a lot of Japanese samurai movies, the movies made in the fifties by Kurosawa and his colleagues. They've helped a lot in providing background details, costumes. But lately the samurai movies have been terribly bloody. They are really very gory. I don't like them as much.

Why did you decide to write for young people rather than adults?

Well, I didn't really. I decided to write a mystery story set in feudal Japan, taking place in this castle. And when it came out, it just seemed like a young adult book. I didn't put in large amounts of sex—in fact, I didn't put in any sex, I guess—a little love interest, but not real sex. And when the publishers looked at it they said, "Well, it's obviously a juvenile book. It's not something that would interest adult readers." So I went along with that.

Then you weren't conscious at first of writing specifically for a young audience.

No. It's just that I like to read the stuff young people like to read. So I write what I read.

One thing that I have enjoyed about your historical novels is that they have such a strong sense of the culture of Japan, and of China in Phantom of Tiger Mountain.

I am imitating the historical novels that I've read myself, and I've tried to learn what makes those novels work. For instance, there are the books of Mary Renault, *The King Must Die* and all her others. I've tried to analyze what makes her books so powerful and sets the scene so well, the details she uses—the foods, the smells, the sounds. And I will try to do the same with feudal Japan, or thirteenth-century China, or whatever.

Why did you decide to have two protagonists—Zenta and Matsuzo—in the samurai series?

Sherlock Holmes and Dr. Watson. Again, it's a matter of imitation. One person is the clever one and the other feeds him the lines. The junior partner is always slightly comical; he's the one that gets into the scrapes. He's the one who asks all of the leading questions, while the senior partner, Holmes, does all the detecting.

Do you think that there are certain qualities that are especially important in a hero for young people?

No, I don't. The two heroes in the samurai books turned out one way. But in the book set in China, **Phantom of Tiger Mountain,** the heroes are quite different. Little Li is slightly naive, but he promises to mature. I have been hoping to write sequels to this book in which he does mature and eventually assumes leadership of the outlaw band. So he is different from the heroes in the other books. In my latest book in the samurai series, **Island of Ogres,** Zenta and Matsuzo appear, but they have relatively peripheral roles, whereas the main character is another ronin who stumbles into the plot. And he is very different. He's a reforming alcoholic, and he's acting as a spy and hates himself for doing that, but because of circumstances he's forced to take whatever job he can get. So he's very different from the others.

So you like to have a variety of heroes.

Yes. That's why I'd like to write books other than the samurai series, just so that I can take on some other character. It's too late to change Zenta and Matsuzo, but I can write other books without them.

How do young people respond to your protagonists?

I get letters mostly from boys, which isn't surprising, because this kind of adventure fiction is more appealing to boys, I suppose, than to girls. They like the action. They don't say much about the protagonists. They say that they like the suspense, they like the action, they like the mystery, and they like the fact that the good guys come out on top. But they never really go into what they like about the character, except that they like heroes to be brave. But I don't think they analyze characters much.

I suppose that Zenta and Matsuzo exemplify the samurai code of heroism.

They're idealized. Whether the real samurai were like that or not is another question. According to the official bushido code, you are supposed to protect the weak, and correct injustice, and be loyal to your superiors, which in the case of Zenta and Matsuzo is difficult because they are ronin; they don't have a master. But once they decide to enlist with a certain side, they feel that they should be absolutely loyal to that side. This question comes up in **Valley of the Broken Cherry Trees,** where they're not sure their sympathies are actually with that side, but having committed themselves to it, they have to stick with it. So loyalty is certainly very important. And honor—namely, once you've given your word, you must absolutely keep your word. And truth. I think those are the most important elements.

It seems to me that there might be something attractive to an American teenager about two young men who are trying to live up to a heroic code like this.

I think so. I think that's why young people also enjoy those science fiction stories where you're in a totally different culture and you've a different code. But still the protagonists are struggling to live up to whatever code exists there. Maybe young people like codes and want something to hang on to, to live up to. With the samurai code, its very harshness sometimes appeals to young people, because they feel that if they can live up to a really harsh code, they can accomplish more than if they choose something easier.

*You also suggest, though, at the end of **Village of the Vampire Cat,** that this code has its limitations as a way of life. It doesn't give a complete pattern for living.*

It's been said many times that the samurai is really a parasite. He doesn't produce. All he does is maintain the status of his lord. That's his chief duty.

*Perhaps that is one reason you shift in **Phantom of Tiger Mountain** to a different kind of ethos, where Little Li decides at the end not to take up a warrior's life but to build a community.*

That's right. There it's not a matter of dying heroically according to the warrior's code, but simply surviving, so that the Chinese civilization, as they know it, will survive the invasion by the Mongols which ultimately engulfed China.

Is there a difference between Japanese and Chinese heroes?

I think that the feeling of absolute loyalty to your immediate feudal lord may be stronger in Japan. China has been centralized longer, at least in theory, and there is a feeling of loyalty to the central figure, the emperor, who is in turn responsible to the people because of his mandate from Heaven. But in Japan, at least in the period that I'm describing, which is the civil war period when the country was divided, the loyalty just goes to your immediate superior. Even if it means dividing up the country and prolonging the civil wars, your first loyalty is to your lord.

I've heard that it's often difficult for a historical novelist to stay true to the period and still give women strong roles. But the female characters in your samurai stories seem to share some of the same heroic qualities as the men.

At that particular period of Japanese history the women were pretty strong and independent, and there were a number of women warriors trained to fight with a particular weapon, a long spear with a broad blade. So women were pretty feisty in those days, but later, beginning in the seventeenth century, the Confucian code was more or less imposed, and women were supposed to be kept very much in the background. But I suspect that in the home

Japanese wives have quite a bit of power, because they control the finances. They plan the budget, and they control the education of the children quite a bit. But officially they are supposed to be meek and submissive, they bow, they walk a few paces behind. The stereotypical Japanese woman is a very retiring kind of person. But in the period that I'm talking about, the second half of the sixteenth century, women were a lot more independent than they were to become later. So it's not too inaccurate to have the women fighting, talking and speaking out the way that they do.

Do you find in picturing the past that you stress or omit certain aspects of it?

Yes. When I wrote my first book, **White Serpent Castle,** I did a huge amount of research and was helped by my father-in-law, and I also read all the books that I could get hold of. I had all these wonderful facts about seventeenth-century Japan, and I wanted to put them all into the book. You know, after you've sweated for it, you certainly don't want to throw anything away. I thought that it would make a rich-looking tapestry to have all of these details. But, of course, what that did was to slow up the story, and, in fact, much of the time it wasn't really relevant either. So in the course of time, with the help of friends and editors, I took a lot of it out. Even now I find it's hard to throw away something that I've worked on. But you have to do it, because you can't load the story down with details that don't push it forward. I want my books to be fast moving; they are suspense stories, and they have to have lots of action.

Are there things that you leave out because you are writing for young people? Sex? Violence?

In the samurai books there isn't all that much sex, because women were unimportant and you had sex more or less to relieve yourself. Between men and women there is sex, but that is for physical reasons. The true, deep, meaningful friendships are between man and man. Now in this day and age, if you write such a thing, people will immediately think that the characters are homosexuals. But it may have been just that it was the only friendship that was acceptable. If a man cherished deep friendship for a woman, he would be considered strange.

What about gruesome or really unpleasant things?

Well, I haven't left out too much gore. In fact, if anything, the complaints from some parents have been that there's too much gore in my books, especially the **Vampire Cat** book. You can't write about that particular age or these particular people without some gore. But I don't think kids want real gruesomeness; at least normal kids don't, and I think normal readers don't want it either.

Another thing that leavens the grimness of the eras that you are writing about is the humor in your stories.

I think that humor is absolutely essential. And I think that the best historical novels are humorous. Certainly the books of Alexandre Dumas are full of humor—*The Three Musketeers* for instance. Sir Walter Scott and Robert Louis Stevenson are marvelous humorists.

How do you design your plots?

I think that my books are stronger on plot than they are on characterization, because plotting is more important to me. I like a good puzzle, so I want to present a good puzzle to the reader. So I do plot very carefully. I usually start with the end of a book; that is, I have to know what the solution is. Then I work backwards, so that I have everything point to the end. If I work from the beginning, then it sounds as if the story's made up as I went along. So I always start with a solution—why a particular thing happened, who did it, why he did it—and then start planting my clues along the way. I have a strong instinct for thrift, which comes from my mathematical days, namely, that everything in the hypothesis has to be used to the fullest, so there isn't going to be a clue planted without its being important in some way. Nothing is thrown in just to make a book longer.

I think that's very satisfying to the reader.

It certainly satisfies me when I read a good mystery and everything clicks into place. So my secret is to start with a solution. This is also good in preventing writer's block. Sometimes you don't know what to write about, but if you know where you're headed, then it's much easier to keep on writing because your destination is right there in front of you.

It's as if something is pulling you.

Exactly. It pulls me toward a solution.

TITLE COMMENTARY

📖 *THE SAMURAI AND THE LONG-NOSED DEVILS* (1976)

Kirkus Reviews

SOURCE: A review of *The Samurai and the Long-Nosed Devils,* in *Kirkus Reviews,* Vol. LXIV, No. 15, August 1, 1976, p. 848.

Namioka's conscientious research is obtrusive at first when Zenta and Matsuzo, itinerant 16th-century samurai, sometimes sound like lecturers on Japanese culture. Then the pair is hired to guard two Portuguese missionaries, Zenta finds himself forced to turn detective in order to clear his masters of a murder charge, and subtle details of costume, swordsmanship, and manners are transformed into clues. The motive for the crime is hidden behind a stolen gun and layers of political intrigue and, ultimately and startlingly, hinges partly on Zenta's own unbending sense of honor. Zenta conducts himself soberly without resort to fancy dress prose, and when he himself becomes a fugitive by virtue of his own successful solution the plucky, ingenious doings take a philosophical turn—can one be literally too good for this world? After a so-so beginning, a neatly turned entertainment.

📖 *WHITE SERPENT CASTLE* (1976)

Booklist

SOURCE: A review of *White Serpent Castle,* in *Booklist,* Vol. 73, No. 9, January 1, 1977, p. 661.

Zenta and Matsuzo, the two young unemployed samurai of *The Samurai and the Long-Nosed Devils,* embark on another adventure when they approach a warlord's castle where the nine-year-old heir is endangered by power-seeking rivals and where the White Serpent Ghost—said to emerge when crisis threatens—has been seen prowling the battlements. Since Zenta's reputation has preceded him, each of the warring factions tries to enlist his aid, but once again the clever samurai cuts through sham to solve the mystery and set things right. As in the first story, a sense of fun as well as excitement and action is important to the plot. Suggested for younger teenagers.

📖 *VALLEY OF THE BROKEN CHERRY TREES* (1980)

Booklist

SOURCE: A review of *Valley of the Broken Cherry Trees,* in *Booklist,* Vol. 76, No. 16, April 15, 1980, p. 1195.

Fans of the stalwart Zenta and his companion Matsuzo will welcome the return of the young samurai turned ronin (samurai without masters) in a third adventure—following *White Serpent Castle.* In their wanderings the pair come to a valley noted for its beautiful cherry blossoms and are soon exposed to danger engendered by the power struggle between two warlords, but once more Zenta astutely sorts out a tricky situation and justice prevails. With a lively flair, Namioka again combines humor, suspense, and a sense of the period.

Catherine Harper

SOURCE: A review of *Valley of the Broken Cherry Trees,* in *Voice of Youth Advocates,* August, 1980, p. 34.

Set in medieval Japan, this adventure story centers around two young unemployed samurai—Zenta, an expert swordsman and all-round hero type, and his comical yet brave and honorable side-kick, Matsuzo. Arriving in a valley renowned for its beautiful cherry trees, they become embroiled in a multi-faceted intrigue involving the mysterious mutilation of several of the sacred cherry trees and a plot to kill the feudal overlord of the region, Lord Kawai.

Using subterfuge themselves, they manage to foil the assassination attempt and restore order.

Adventure fans who like solving puzzles will enjoy the intricate plot, while those looking for action will quite possibly find it too sedate. The latter type of reader is unlikely to be attracted to the book anyway, though, because its title and cover art are anything but violent. Recommended as a good choice in historical fiction for 6th to 9th graders; it is not meaty enough for older readers, who will find the treatment of Japanese customs superficial and the main characters too boyish.

Kirkus Reviews

SOURCE: A review of *Valley of the Broken Cherry Trees,* in *Kirkus Reviews,* September 15, 1980, p. 1236.

Konishi Zenta, the 16th-century samurai and astute detective first met in *The Samurai and the Long-Nosed Devils* and *White Serpent Castle* (both 1976), and his junior partner Ishihara Matsuzo thread their way deftly through another complex, ethically nuanced adventure. Returning penniless to an inn where Zenta once distinguished himself, they are horrified by the mutilation of some of the celebrated local cherry trees and puzzled by the truculent, ungainly youth, obviously well-born, who lurks about unoccupied and unattended. Why does Lord Ohmori's shifty son warn them against concerning themselves with the boy? Why does icy Lady Sayo, wife of Ohmori's overlord Kawai, warn them against concerning themselves with the cherry trees? Why is the boy, Torazo, who asks Zenta for lessons in swordsmanship, so inept, so misinstructed? Mysteries abound—pointing first to a plot to set up the unhappy, ill-favored boy, Lord Kawai's son and heir, as the tree-mutilator. Before it is unraveled, Zenta and Matsuzo will have caused a comic shambles (and escaped death) and a cherry-viewing party, Matsuzo and Lord Kawai will have performed incognito (and indelibly) in a Noh play, the two unemployed samurai will have turned down one after another lucrative offer . . . and of course proved Torazo's worth to his father and uncovered the cherry-tree mutilator (a real surprise). That the many, many characters have distinct personalities and motives, that the whole imbroglio accurately reflects the internal turmoil of the period, adds substance and continuous interest to what is also spanking entertainment.

📖 *VILLAGE OF THE VAMPIRE CAT* (1981)

Stanley Swanson

SOURCE: A review of *Village of the Vampire Cat,* in *Best Sellers,* Vol. 41, No. 3, June, 1981, p. 119.

Zenta, a young ronin or unemployed samurai, returns with his companion to the village of his former teacher. They discover that the villagers are being robbed by a gang of fraudulent pill makers and being terrorized by a vampire cat. Solving and righting these schemes and terrors be-

comes a thrilling and chilling task. There is the heart-stopping meow of the cat, the unaccountable biting of Zenta by a dog every time he encounters him, the robbers and their schemes with fake medicines which are supposed to ward off attacks by the cat.

Mrs. Namioka, with two characters from a previous novel, *White Serpent Castle,* once again writes of feudal Japan and the ronin. The reader reads racingly trying to keep up with the action as Zenta pursues the cat. One learns along the way about sword fighting, costumes, New Year's festivities, marriage customs, family relationships.

Taut action, exotic locale, good characterization all combine to make this a fine novel for teenagers. Scenes are done with remarkable vividness: the defense of the house, the cooks and maids armed with knives, poles, rakes, pots; the splendidly spine tingling approach of the cat to a victim in an old abandoned house; the merriment and festivities of the New Year's parade; the fatal confrontation of Zenta and the cat, alone with just their swords in the large fencing room.

Surely these novels will continue in a series of the further adventures of Zenta and his sidekick. Buy them and the readers will love you.

Ann A. Flowers

SOURCE: A review of *Village of the Vampire Cat,* in *The Horn Book Magazine,* August, 1981, pp. 434-35.

An unusual adventure story set in medieval Japan concerns the experiences of Zenta and his friend Matsuzo, two *ronin,* or unemployed samurai. They are making a visit to Zenta's old teacher Ikken, whom Zenta has not seen in many years, and they are distressed to see the village looking shabby and poverty-stricken. On the way to Ikken's house Zenta and Matsuzo have an unsettling encounter with a strange attacker who makes a thin, high, mewing sound and is able from a distance to inflict raking wounds. Ikken himself is distracted and almost unwelcoming, and the two friends discover that the whole village is terrified by the mysterious murders of four girls—murders that have been popularly attributed to a vampire cat. Zenta and Matsuzo eventually solve the mystery, but in doing so they become involved with a siege, several bloodthirsty sword fights, and even a ritual harakiri. The unfamiliar setting of the book and the samurai code of behavior are as interesting as the plot, original though it is. The well-drawn characters—especially the thoughtful, self-controlled Zenta and the carefree Matsuzo—and the touches of humor liven up a fine mystery story.

Kirkus Reviews

SOURCE: A review of *Village of the Vampire Cat,* in *Kirkus Reviews,* Vol. XLIX, No. 16, August 15, 1981, p. 1011.

Earlier adventures of unattached samurai, or *ronin,* Zenta

and Matsuzo (*The Samurai and the Long-Nosed Devils, White Serpent Castle, Valley of the Broken Cherry Trees*) have been intricate and textured; so it's a disappointment to find that this could be classified simply as a samurai mystery. On a nostalgic visit to Ikken, Zenta's one-time mentor, the two find his village terrorized by a "Vampire Cat," a dark-garbed, mewing creature brutally slaying young women. Chief beneficiaries are a band of medicine peddlers, who've been extorting money from the villagers for alleged anti-Cat potions. But they are mere accomplices, Zenta learns from the chief of the band; and the crazed "Cat" is not only after blood—he wants to get the money that Ikken's niece, Asa, will inherit from her rich merchant-grandfather. But why does Asa's canine protector Kongomaru keep going after *Zenta*? Except for some samurai/merchant class frictions, the unraveling is just a matter of incidental swordplay and eliminating suspects—including of course Zenta. The culprit turns out to be Ikken's sword-master son, *not* killed three years back but hideously disfigured . . . and not only nursing a grievance against the villagers but loco about Asa, to whom he'd been engaged. In the wind-up, Ikken and son Shunken both commit hara-kiri, freeing Zenta and Matsuzo—more one-dimensional than in previous episodes—to go on to new challenges. Readers who've been caught up by the pair will probably go along for the action, but it's a thin whodunit overall.

WHO'S HU? (1981)

Stephanie Zvirin

SOURCE: A review of *Who's Hu?*, in *Booklist*, Vol. 77, No. 19, June 1, 1981, p. 1296.

Written as a retrospective narrative, Namioka's novel conveys the conflicts faced by Chinese-American Emma Hu as she tries to find a niche for herself in a special segment of American teenage life in the 1950s. Emma's efforts to get a date for the prom and to reconcile her aptitude for math with the "American" concept of being female and her concern about her older brother's inability to adjust to their adopted country are the strands that constitute the plot. Though as a novel, Namioka's story lacks depth and dramatic impact, its wonderfully dry wit (sometimes verging on slapstick comedy), eccentric characters, and interfusion of information about Chinese culture, experience, and adjustment are redemptive enough to keep readers well entertained.

ISLAND OF OGRES (1989)

Publishers Weekly

SOURCE: A review of *Island of Ogres,* in *Publishers Weekly,* Vol. 235, No. 17, April 28, 1989, p. 82.

When Kajiro first arrives on the tiny island he is mistaken for Zenta, the famous samurai warrior. The islanders are sure that he has come to save them from the ogres that have begun to lurk outside their homes, stealing chickens and killing dogs. Kajiro's real job is to keep an eye on the commander of the island's garrison, so posing as Zenta gives him a good excuse for his own investigations. And he doesn't mind that his false identity seems to have impressed Lady Yuri, the commander's bedraggled yet appealing sister-in-law. In the course of this rambling novel, the truth about the ogres unfolds, the real Zenta appears, the commander's mettle is tested, several romances are hinted at and a rebellion against the young Daimyo is foiled. The story is related by a bewildering number of narrators, and while some elements of the mystery seem almost intentionally transparent, others are impossible for readers to deduce. Despite these structural problems, the author succeeds in depicting an exotic world.

Kirkus Reviews

SOURCE: A review of *Island of Ogres,* in *Kirkus Reviews,* Vol. LVII, No. 9, May 1, 1989, p. 695.

Another in the series of mystery-adventures about two independent ronin—Zenta and Matsuzo—who try to defend the right in feudal Japan. A third young ronin, Kajiro, takes center stage here, having been sent as a spy to an island fortress. Out of condition from too little exercise and too much drink, Kajiro finds himself mistaken for the famous Zenta and expected to clear the island of the "ogres" who have been terrorizing the people there. He also becomes the defender of young Lady Yuri, whose cat leads her into several dangerous escapades. While Kajiro's health and reflexes improve, Zenta himself is recovering in the castle and trying to discover who is behind an attempt to rescue the mad Lord being held there. Sixteenth-century politics mix with lively dialogue, an intriguing setting, swordplay, and several romances. A good light read for mystery lovers.

Hazel Rochman

SOURCE: A review of *Island of Ogres,* in *Booklist,* Vol. 85, No. 18, May 15, 1989, pp. 1638-39.

In another of Namioka's mystery-adventures set in feudal Japan, Kajiro, an unemployed young samurai, down-and-out and alcoholic, finds self-respect and romance when he helps thwart a rebel invasion of a small island. The dialogue is wooden and the action is diffuse, split between several scattered groups. But there's genuine surprise in the identity of the main conspirator, and characters and plot undermine formula. Not only is Kajiro seedy and bumbling, but Zenta, a famous warrior, also messes up and accidentally causes the death of the ruler he's defending. In fact, much of the plotting, fighting, and killing comes to nothing, and the loyalists' cause is no more noble than that of the rebels. The women are the liveliest characters—bossy Lady Sada and her tomboyish teenage sister, Yuri (whom Kajiro loves). Yuri's fat, fierce cat is the most stalwart fighter.

Mary M. Burns

SOURCE: A review of *Island of Ogres,* in *The Horn Book Magazine,* September-October, 1989, pp. 647-48.

Against the backdrop of sixteenth-century Japan, the author blends intrigue and romance into the fast-moving tale of an unemployed samurai who successfully foils a political conspiracy and wins the affection of an independent, stubborn young noblewoman. An unusual mystery-adventure for the more demanding lovers of the genre.

THE COMING OF THE BEAR (1992)

Kirkus Reviews

SOURCE: A review of *The Coming of the Bear,* in *Kirkus Reviews,* Vol. LX, No. 9, May 1, 1992, p. 615.

In the newest entry in this action-packed series, Namioka's two wandering samurai are shipwrecked on the northern island of Ezo (modern Hokkaido) and find themselves trying to avert a battle between a new Japanese settlement and the indigenous Ainu. As in their previous adventures, Zenta and Matsuzo have a mystery to solve: a bear has been attacking the Japanese, and it soon becomes evident that it has been trained to do so. By whom? There are suspects on both sides. The two *ronin* are given complex character traits—young Matsuzo's optimistic enthusiasm plays off Zenta's moodiness and experience, often to comic effect—and the author throws up a few red herrings to complicate the otherwise simple, quickly paced plot. There is some violence—the culprits and several bears die—but it's emphasized less than the theme of working toward peace.

YANG THE YOUNGEST AND HIS TERRIBLE EAR (1992)

Publishers Weekly

SOURCE: A review of *Yang the Youngest and His Terrible Ear,* in *Publishers Weekly,* Vol. 239, No. 23, May 18, 1992, pp. 70-1.

Newly transplanted to Seattle from his native China, nine-year-old Yingtao is a tone-deaf thorn among musical roses. His parents—professional musicians both—assume the problem is lack of practice and chide him for playing baseball (he's a natural) when he could be rehearsing with his virtuoso siblings for an upcoming family recital. When Yingtao hooks up with a new friend from school, a boy as talented musically as Yingtao is athletically and whose parents have put him in an opposite predicament—the boys scheme a "lip-syncing" violin switch for the recital quartet that finally opens the eyes of both families. Peppered with wry commentary on the often baffling experience of adapting to a new country and a new language, Beijing-born Namioka's fresh and funny novel serves up a slice of modern, multicultural American life. Her comic timing and deadpan delivery are reminiscent of Betsy Byars, and her book will leave readers begging for more. [Kees] de Kiefte's keenly observed black-and-white sketches evoke a maximum of expression with a minimum of intrusion.

Kirkus Reviews

SOURCE: A review of *Yang the Youngest and His Terrible Ear,* in *Kirkus Reviews,* Vol. LX, No. 11, June 1, 1992, p. 722.

Youngest of four in a musically gifted family, Yingtao is miserable because he's tone-deaf—a fact denied by his father, who obtusely persists in trying to teach him the violin. The family has recently immigrated to Seattle from Shanghai and is struggling financially; Father hopes that if his children play a quartet creditably at a recital it'll bring him more students. Meanwhile, Yingtao makes friends with Matthew, who *does* play the violin well—but *his* father thinks Matthew should concentrate on baseball, in which Yingtao now begins to excel. In the nicest moment here, Yingtao's Third Sister unmasks their scheme to have Matthew play from behind a screen while Yingtao fakes it during the recital—with the result that both fathers begin to see the light.

Along with the theme of overcoming parents' unrealistic expectations, Namioka (author of several Japanese historical adventures, depicts in some detail the problems of adjusting to a new country and countering stereotypical thinking. The message, however, overwhelms the rather slight story, while Yingtao's portrayal seems inconsistent: He knows too much English to be so unfamiliar with American slang and customs. Adequate but simplistic and overextended. [Kees] de Kiefte's frequent impressionistic drawings are a plus.

Susan Stan

SOURCE: A review of *Yang the Youngest and His Terrible Ear,* in *The Five Owls,* Vol. 7, No. 1, September-October, 1992, pp. 16-17.

Yingtao Yang is the fourth child in a family of musicians. His father, formerly with the Shanghai Philharmonic Orchestra, is now an alternate violinist with the Seattle Symphony Orchestra, his mother is a pianist, and his three older siblings are all accomplished string players. At his birth, his parents delighted at the string quartet they now had, but they didn't count on Fourth Son's tin ear. They find it hard to accept that his screechy playing does not stem from lack of practice.

Yingtao's unique situation in his family parallels his family's status in their new country. Each family member adjusts to the new life differently: Yang's father, who hopes to increase the family income by teaching violin lessons, focuses all his energy on finding private students and is counting on the quartet to perform well in an upcoming recital to further that goal; Eldest Brother and Second Sister keep to themselves, while Third Sister immediately makes friends at school and even takes on an American name. Yingtao is happy when he makes a friend, Matthew, who sits next to him in the school orchestra.

While Yingtao's father is continually reminding him to practice the violin, Yingtao's own thoughts run toward baseball, which Matthew has introduced him to. Matthew, on the other hand, has a natural talent for the violin, but his father wishes that he would spend more time on baseball and less time on the violin. How the two fathers come to understand and accept their sons' special talents is played out in the events of the last half of the book.

Namioka laces her story with amusing incidents and conversational mistakes common when two cultures mix. Yingtao's feelings ring true, and many of the situations could easily have been experienced by the author, who immigrated to the U.S. from Beijing. Black-and-white sketches done in pencil [by Kees de Kiefte] decorate the chapter openings and illustrate high points in the story.

Hazel Rochman

SOURCE: A review of *Yang the Youngest and His Terrible Ear,* in *Booklist,* December 1, 1992, p. 661.

Though the hero, Yingtao, is only nine years old, readers will identify with this warm, funny immigrant story that extends the meaning of outsider and home. The light-hearted first-person narrative captures the bewilderment of the new immigrant, the confusion about customs and language, and also the longing for home in China and the sting of prejudice here.

APRIL AND THE DRAGON LADY (1994)

Merri Monks

SOURCE: A review of *April and the Dragon Lady,* in *Booklist,* Vol. 90, No. 13, March 1, 1994, p. 1253.

April Chen, a Chinese American high-school junior, lives in Seattle with her widowed father; her brother, Harry; and her Grandma, the "Dragon Lady." Harry, the first-born son, is very much favored by Grandma, but as Grandma's health begins to fail, it is April who must relinquish important activities, one by one, to care for the elderly woman. April's story, rich in authentic detail, tells of a young woman's journey from one culture to another as she simultaneously travels from childhood to adulthood. The conflict between April and her grandmother, interwoven with several subplots, forms a complex but very readable novel. April must contend with her family's disapproval of her Caucasian boyfriend. She also struggles with the constraints of her traditional female role, enviously watching her indulged brother's total freedom. April's surprise ally is her father, Grandma's elder, but not favored, son, who falls in love with Ellen, also a Mandarin-speaking Chinese, but a divorced college professor and not liked by Grandma. As both April and her father escape Grandma, leaving Harry to contend with the source of his lifelong pampering and adoration, April receives a jade bracelet from Grandma, a symbol of love and the beginning of change.

Publishers Weekly

SOURCE: A review of *April and the Dragon Lady,* in *Publishers Weekly,* Vol. 241, No. 14, April 4, 1994, p. 81.

April Chen, a 16-year-old Chinese American, has a problem: her grandmother. A "dragon lady" of the old school, Grandma belongs to an entirely different world, both culturally and generationally, and her ideas about a woman's place clash with April's more Westernized views. She openly disapproves of April's Caucasian boyfriend and attempts to undermine her plans to go away to college—as a sure token of the author's skill, Grandma comes across as both manipulative and sympathetic; the reader will share April's affection and even her respect for the cunning old woman. Namioka, an altogether accomplished novelist, deftly weaves narrator April's compelling account of her quest for her own path with a well-developed subplot involving the girl's widowed father and his own struggle for independence. Her characterizations are particularly strong: the Chen family members, and especially the feisty, likable April, are thoroughly believable, and her sensitive handling of April's dilemma and eventual solution sheds light on the Chinese American culture in a manner that at times recalls Amy Tan's *The Joy Luck Club.*

Kirkus Reviews

SOURCE: A review of *April and the Dragon Lady,* in *Kirkus Reviews,* Vol. LXII, No. 11, June 1, 1994, p. 778.

April Chen is a typical American teenager. Her flute playing is of solo quality; she's interested in geology and hopes to go to the Colorado School of Mines; she has a red-haired boyfriend, Steve, who agreeably accommodates to the demands of her Chinese-American family. As embodied in her widowed father's mother, these are difficult and, by US standards, unreasonable; indulged older brother Harry declares himself unavailable on the flimsiest of pretexts, so April must give up field trips and rehearsals to stay with Grandma, who has taken to vague wanderings. April finds her family's assumption that, as a girl, Grandma's care is her responsibility unfair but hard to challenge; in time, she also becomes aware that Grandma, far less helpless than she pretends, deliberately manipulates her. Namioka's accessible narrative verges on simplistic; supportive Steve is a stock character, and only April and Grandma are realized with any depth. Still, the questions of responsibilities within families and of the division of competences and powers between men and women are effectively addressed, illuminating both Chinese tradition and issues that transcend any particular culture. Grandma finally overreaches herself and gets a fair, but not unkind, comeuppance that frees both April and her dad: a cultural hybrid of a conclusion that's certainly satisfying and probably within the realm of possibility.

📖 YANG THE THIRD AND HER IMPOSSIBLE FAMILY (1995)

Roger Sutton

SOURCE: A review of *Yang the Third and Her Impossible Family,* in *Bulletin of the Center for Children's Books,* Vol. 48, No. 9, May, 1995, p. 318.

Unlike her younger brother (see *Yang the Youngest and His Terrible Ear*), Yingmei (Mary) is a talented musician; her problem is that she wants desperately to become friends with Holly, a pretty, popular girl in the school orchestra. Holly doesn't seem all that interested until it appears that Yingmei will be able to take a kitten, forbidden by Holly's parents, off her hands. The kitten is forbidden by Yingmei's parents as well, and although the subplot about Yingmei and Fourth Brother hiding the kitten in their basement is clichéd and formulaic, it provides light relief to the more serious story about Yingmei's attempts to fit into American culture—not an easy task, considering her "impossible" family. Her father sometimes mispronounces English to embarrassing effect ("lice" for "rice," for example) and her mother continually if unknowingly thwarts Yingmei's friendship with Holly by alienating Holly's mother with inappropriate questions and compliments ("Why, you're not skinny at all, Mrs. Hanson. You're actually quite fat!") that were considered polite back in China, but aren't in America, where the Yang family has lived for just over a year. Yingmei learns her lessons (including the fact that Holly isn't worth it), makes a good friend elsewhere, and finds a home for the kitten, all of which is predictable but satisfying, and her bouncy narration is a refreshing contrast to the more sober "multicultural" fare we've been seeing. Occasional line drawings [by Kees de Kiefte] are witty and graceful.

Joyce Yen

SOURCE: A review of *Yang the Third and Her Impossible Family,* in *Voice of Youth Advocates,* Vol. 18, No. 2, June, 1995, pp. 97-8.

Mary Ying-Mei Yang and her family have just recently moved to the United States from China. Mary is so excited to be in America and cannot wait to learn all the American customs. Mary also desperately wants to befriend the popular Holly Hanson. In an attempt to win Holly's favor, Mary agrees to adopt one of Holly's new kittens. Everything seems to be great except for one small problem: Mary's parents will not allow any pets in their home because their family owns a lot of musical instruments. Mary decides to keep the kitten a secret from her parents although it is not easy to hide a curious kitten.

In addition to keeping the kitten out of trouble, Mary finds herself always having to explain the comments her parents make. Chinese compliments are very different from American compliments. During Thanksgiving dinner Holly's mother claims she cannot have dessert because she has already gained two pounds. Mary's mother does not understand Mrs. Hanson's concern and compliments her on being quite fat. Mary is extremely embarrassed. Later she explains to Holly that the Chinese consider being fat good because it symbolizes good fortune. Mary is disappointed that her parents do not put forth a big enough effort to become Americans.

Mary has a lot of different issues to which the reader can relate and from which the reader can learn. Mary, like most children, wants to fit in. She wants to be friends with the most popular girl in school. As she tries to establish a friendship with Holly, she learns a lot about herself and about the meaning of friendship.

Through Mary's adventures, the reader gets to experience some Chinese traditions and life as part of a Chinese family. The reader sees how difficult it is to adapt to a new culture with new customs while still maintaining your cultural identity. Mary learns to be both Chinese and American.

Yang the Third and Her Impossible Family is a delightful book suitable for lower middle school students. The book makes its readers aware of the issues new Americans sometimes face as well as provides entertaining reading.

Carla Kozak

SOURCE: A review of *Yang the Third and Her Impossible Family,* in *School Library Journal,* Vol. 41, No. 8, August, 1995, p. 144.

Yingmei (a.k.a. Mary) Yang, the third of four children, tries to communicate the dichotomous feelings of a young Chinese girl, newly immigrated to the U.S., who is working hard to fit in, but whose efforts seem to be held back by the mannerisms and traditions of her family, the musical Yangs. Torn by her feelings of both pride and embarrassment for them, and yearning to win the friendship of a popular blonde schoolmate, Mary agrees to take one of Holly's cat's kittens, although she knows her family does not want pets because they fear animals would damage their expensive instruments. She and her younger brother cook up an elaborate and increasingly ridiculous scheme to hide the kitten in their basement. In this book, which is not as successful as *Yang the Youngest and His Terrible Ear,* Namioka has resorted to many clichés, such as the substitution of "l" for "r" in the Chinese pronunciation of English, along with a few pat, hearty "we are all ethnic" conversations. The lack of subtlety reflects poorly on both the newcomers and their American neighbors. While the foundations of some of the situations, and Mary's reactions to them, ring true, their broad expression seems to promote stereotypes more than to show greater truths and understanding among people of different cultural backgrounds.

Suzanne Li

SOURCE: A review of *Yang the Third and Her Impossible Family,* in *MultiCultural Review,* Vol. 4, No. 4, December, 1995, p. 92.

Namioka explores with humor and sympathy again what it means to become a Chinese American from the perspective of a spunky little girl, Yingmei Yang, who was so supportive of her younger brother, Yingtao, the narrator of *Yang the Youngest and His Terrible Ear.* She presents her slant on life with the same disarming honesty as her brother but with some differences that girl readers especially will appreciate.

Although Yingtao admired Yingmei for adjusting so smoothly to their new life in Seattle, here she admits her acculturation techniques, such as using the name Mary in school, don't always protect her from making mistakes. At first Yingmei is willing to give up any vestige of her old life in Shanghai that might interfere with becoming best friends with a popular classmate. She is also embarrassed that her family members maintain so many Chinese standards of polite behavior inappropriate in their new community, and exasperated that they don't seem to be trying as hard as she to fit in. Gradually, though, she is able to regain her pride in them and feels remorse for her harsh judgment. She finally sees that newcomers can retain their cultural identity and still be accepted by the established community and, moreover, other people's opinions don't matter when people are content with themselves.

Although Namioka used funnier anecdotes more effectively in *Yang the Youngest,* this sequel positively addresses the mixed feelings of new arrivals in ways that both newcomers and longtime resident should appreciate.

📖 *THE LOYAL CAT* (1995)

Kirkus Reviews

SOURCE: A review of *The Loyal Cat,* in *Kirkus Reviews,* Vol. LXIV, No. 16, August, 15, 1995, p. 1192.

The learned priest Tetsuzan is poor, so poor that even the mice leave his temple. Only his cat Huku remains, loyal because the priest once saved his life. When the lord of the nearby castle dies, the priest is too humble to think his prayers will be wanted, but the practical, magical Huku sees an opportunity to make Tetsuzan famous, the temple rich, and his own life more comfortable.

In a quiet, unobtrusive narrative, Namioka gives this Japanese legend of how the Cat Temple got its name a satisfying twist that is true to the spirit of the unusual hero. [Aki] Sogabe's serenely picturesque cut-paper illustrations are a consummate complement to a traditional story, dem-

onstrating a wide range of perspectives and deft use of color.

Susan Dove Lempke

SOURCE: A review of *The Loyal Cat,* in *Booklist,* Vol. 92, No. 2, September 15, 1995, pp. 175-76.

A priest in Japan lives simply, speaks softly, and knows "thousands of prayers by heart," but his plain temple doesn't attract important visitors and their gifts. The kitten he has rescued has magical powers, and when the two companions almost starve, the clever cat uses magic to draw attention to his owner's piety. The cat is chagrined, however, when the modest priest only asks for three pieces of gold and then returns to his quiet life. The slow pace and solemn tone of the story may lose a few listeners, but Namioka's retelling is smooth, and children will surely delight in the cat's levitation of a coffin that even warriors and wrestlers are unable to bring down. Be sure to point out [Aki] Sogabe's authentic Japanese paper-cut illustrations: colored rice papers show through the outlines of cut black paper for a stained-glass effect.

Susan Middleton

SOURCE: A review of *The Loyal Cat,* in *School Library Journal,* Vol. 41, No. 10, October, 1995, p. 110.

In this retelling of a family tale, a cat is rescued and cared for by Tetsuzan, a priest at Hukuzo-ji, a mountain temple in the north of Japan. Tetsuzan is content with his simple life of prayer and work. As he becomes poorer and poorer, he must even beg for food for Huku, the cat. Huku, wanting a more comfortable life for himself, as well as for the good priest, decides to use his magic powers to gain both recognition and funds. The determined and clever feline is successful, but at first disappointed when Tetsuzan is content with just enough gold to repair the temple and live simply. Huku, ever loyal, adjusts, although he occasionally thinks about the luxuries they could have had. The magic adds suspense and humor to the tale, and the pictures, [by Aki Sogabe] stunning in design and exceptional in detail, are a visual delight, adding greatly to the impact. The technique, Japanese paper cutting, is done by placing intricately cut black paper over papers that have been airbrushed or painted with watercolors. The resulting art has a depth that draws viewers into the scenes. Children who are fond of animal stories will keep this title in continuous circulation.

Elizabeth Bush

SOURCE: A review of *The Loyal Cat,* in *Bulletin of the Center for Children's Books,* Vol. 49, No. 3, November, 1995, pp. 100-01.

Too humble and modest to attract rich and important visitors to his temple, priest Tetsuzan sadly watches his temple fall into disrepair and his cat Huku go hungry. However, the funeral of a powerful lord inspires Huku with an idea that will raise his self-effacing master to a position of respect: the magical cat secretly causes the lord's coffin to levitate, and he doesn't release it until Tetsuzan is summoned to "pray" it back down. The priest claims a reward just large enough to refurbish the temple, which became known as Hukuzo-ji (Cat Temple), a site "you can visit . . . in northern Japan." Listeners will find Tetsuzan endearingly naïve, Huku charmingly devilish, and the episode of the flying coffin a delightful twist to a tale that begins so gently and piously. Intricate black paper cuttings which overlay tinted rice papers are displayed to advantage on spacious white pages and invite close examination. Source notes, unfortunately, are relegated to the jacket cover, so readers might overlook the fact that the tale comes from "a priest at the real 'cat temple' in Japan."

Joanne Schott

SOURCE: "Pigs & Prairies," in *Quill and Quire,* Vol. 61, No. 11, November, 1995, p. 47.

Tetsuzan, a holy and humble priest, has lived a life of such simplicity that he attracts little attention. Few gifts come to his temple. It grows too poor to support the monks, and soon the priest's only companion is the cat Huku, whom he rescued as a kitten.

When the old lord of the castle dies, Huku plots a way to bring Tetsuzan's holiness to the attention of important mourners, who might bring gifts so both priest and cat can have enough to eat. Huku has magical powers and uses them in a remarkable way at the funeral. Things do not turn out exactly as he intends, but the temple does become prosperous enough for both monks and mice to return.

Chinese-born writer Namioka heard this story from her husband's uncle, a priest at what is still called the "cat temple" in northern Japan. She tells it with simplicity, grace and the slightest edge of humour, characterizing and contrasting priest and cat with economy and precision. The lovely illustrations [by Aki Sogabe] in traditional Japanese style are of black cut paper over painted rice paper. Their sharp clarity matches the text to create a perfectly integrated, fresh and attractive book.

Maria B. Salvadore

SOURCE: A review of *The Loyal Cat,* in *The Horn Book Magazine,* Vol. LXXII, No. 1, January, 1996, p. 68.

Using crisp, straightforward language, Namioka tells the story of how Hukuzo-ji, a small temple in the mountains of northern Japan, came to be known as the Cat Temple. Tetsuzan, a kind and humble priest, saves a treed kitten from cruel monkeys. The cat, Huku, remains at the temple as Tetsuzan's loyal friend and one day discovers that he has magical powers. Huku can elevate objects and keep them in the air, but, as cats will, Huku remains silent about his strange power until it is needed to help his impoverished friend. When the old lord of the castle dies, his son arranges for an elaborate funeral to prove his own greatness. To the amazement of the young lord and his elegant court, the old lord's coffin is suddenly raised fifteen feet in the air, and even the most famous priests, the strongest warriors, and undefeated wrestlers cannot get the coffin down. Only Tetsuzan's earnest prayer combined with the anonymous help of his feline friend succeeds. To Huku's chagrin, Tetsuzan accepts only a small reward, but one large enough to repair and refurbish the small, remote temple. On the final page Namioka writes, "Today, you can visit the Cat Temple in northern Japan," but no further documentation is given. Black cut paper placed over rice papers that have been colored by watercolor or airbrush produce illustrations with strong line and interesting texture. Each framed picture augments the mood of the tale and creates a strong sense of place in this handsomely designed book.

Additional coverage of Namioka's life and career is contained in the following sources published by Gale Research: *Contemporary Authors New Revision Series,* Vol. 52; *Something about the Author,* Vols. 27, 89; and *Something about the Author Autobiography Series,* Vol. 24.

Doris Orgel

1929-

(Born Doris Adelberg) Viennese-born American author and translator of fiction and verse.

Major works include *Dwarf Long-Nose* (translation of the story by Wilhelm Hauff, 1960), *The Devil in Vienna* (1978), *Risking Love* (1984), *Ariadne, Awake!* (1994), *The Princess and the God* (1996).

INTRODUCTION

Best known initially as an accomplished translator who brought the fairy tales of her native Austria to an American audience, Orgel is now recognized as a leading author and reteller of fiction for young people. Her work has delighted children since her translation of Wilhelm Hauff's *Dwarf Long-Nose* was published with illustrations by Maurice Sendak in 1960. Along with her translated books, however, Orgel has published retellings, including adaptations of E. T. A. Hoffman's *The Child from Far Away* and Theodor Storm's *Little John,* and whimsical original stories, such as her popular *Merry, Rose, and Christmas-Tree June.* Although perhaps best known as an author of books for middle graders, Orgel has also written several respected works for young adults, including *The Devil in Vienna,* a thought-provoking novel based on Orgel's childhood during Hitler's occupation of Austria. Her books for teenage readers often feature humorous, sensitive stories in which contemporary urban youths face problems involving busy parents, divorce, death, and first sexual relationships. Advocating the female perspective, Orgel often presents young women struggling to discover their voices and make them heard. While her settings have varied greatly, ranging from Nazi-occupied Vienna to a New York walk-up apartment, Orgel's principal focus has been on human relationships and the trials of everyday life. John D. Stahl writes that Orgel has created "a legacy of historical awareness, humor, and shared humanity through children's literature."

Biographical Information

Orgel was born in Vienna in 1929 to Jewish parents, Ernest and Erna Adelberg. Her father managed a small textile company, and her mother was well educated, having studied law at the University level. Orgel's childhood was spent principally in the company of her mother, her sister Lotte, and her upstairs neighbor, Kitty. She began writing stories almost as soon as she learned the alphabet, filling the pages of a blank book she received from her mother. Hitler's annexation of Austria in 1938 marked a major turning point in Orgel's life; by August of that year her family had emigrated to Zagreb, Croatia. After seven months there, the Adelbergs moved to England, where

they were placed in a small town in Hertfordshire. Orgel and her sister attended boarding school, and the family eventually settled in a small cottage in the hamlet of Barwick. Orgel continued her studies and was promoted to the "Upper A" level, where she began learning Latin, Shakespeare, and algebra. Late in 1939 the Adelbergs received permission to enter the United States, and arrived in New York City by boat in January, 1940. Despite being the age of a typical fifth-grader, Orgel was placed in a ninth-grade classroom, where she struggled to fit in with the more mature students. Her family relocated again in the fall of 1940, moving to live with relatives in St. Louis, but returned a year later, disheartened by the racism that reminded them too much of Hitler's Germany. This time Orgel was placed in eighth grade and was encouraged to pursue a career as a writer. In 1946 she enrolled at Radcliffe College in Cambridge, Massachusetts, where she studied German authors and met her future husband, Shelly Orgel. She returned with him to New York City, transferring to Barnard College in 1949. Upon graduation in 1950, Orgel began work in publishing, primarily as a reader for Viking Press. Between 1957 and 1959, Orgel and her husband had three children, Paul, Laura, and Jeremy. In 1960 she launched her literary career with her highly regarded translation of Wilhelm Hauff's fairy tale *Dwarf Long-Nose.*

Major Works

Orgel has translated many of the favorite stories of her youth into English language versions. These tales include *Dwarf Long-Nose,* which concerns a young boy who, bewitched as a hideous dwarf, becomes a master chef, and *The Tale of Gockel, Hinkel, and Gackeliah* (1961), a story by poet Clemens Brentano. Martha Bennett King called the former translation "a gift beyond price" to American children. The majority of Orgel's work, however, comprises fiction for middle-graders. In *Merry, Rose, and Christmas-Tree June,* illustrated by Edward Gorey, Jane goes to visit her great aunt and misses her beloved dolls Merry and Rose. Given the chance to select a new one at a doll shop, Jane chooses an old doll that was first put up for sale several Christmases ago. The shop owner tells Jane that the newer dolls can do mechanical things, such as walk a few steps or cry a few tears. Even so, Jane chooses the old doll who can't do any mechanical things but can dance and sing and eat and play and do everything Jane wants her to—via pretend, as all well-loved dolls can do. According to a reviewer in the *Bulletin of the Center for Children's Books,* Orgel "strikes a blow for imaginative play." Orgel introduces seven-year-old Becky in *My War with Mrs. Galloway.* Becky dislikes Mrs. Galloway, her family's new sitter and housekeeper, from the start. Mrs. Galloway is strict, takes precious time away from Becky's mother, and does not seem to respect Becky's beloved, pregnant cat, Whiskers. Becky finds ways to show her discontent—she draws an unkind picture of the woman and uses vanishing cream to try to make her disappear. She remains hostile to Mrs. Galloway until the woman helps Whiskers with the birth of her kittens and accepts one of the three for herself. In Becky, Charlotte W. Draper averred in *Horn Book,* "Orgel has created another unmistakably contemporary child." Becky appeared in subsequent adventures in *Whiskers, Once and Always, Midnight Soup and a Witch's Hat,* and *Starring Becky Suslow.*

Among Orgel's most notable books are two for older readers, *The Devil in Vienna* and *Risking Love.* In the former work, which earned a Sydney Taylor Book Award in 1979, Orgel recalls her life in Nazi Austria. Inge, the narrator and protagonist of *The Devil in Vienna,* is a combination of Orgel and her older sister. The book is written in the form of entries in a young girl's diary. Inge begins her story in 1938 when Hitler and his troops arrive in Austria and the Jews there face degradation and persecution. Inge has one non-Jewish person she can count on—Lieselotte, her best friend. Although Lieselotte's father is a Nazi, she remains loyal to Inge. The girls maintain their forbidden friendship, even after Inge is sent to a school for Jews and Lieselotte moves to Germany. Stahl calls the work "a major achievement, and a book of considerable significance for children's literature in the 20th century." *Risking Love* profiles Dinah, a young woman who has just completed a year of college and contem-

plates leaving school for the man she loves. The narrative is uniquely couched almost entirely in her self-discovery through psychoanalytic therapy sessions.

In addition to writing original stories and novels, Orgel continues to retell traditional and ancient tales. Instead of just revisiting the usual versions of these stories, Orgel makes neglected characters come to life with their own personalities, desires, and concerns. *The Princess and the God,* for instance, takes up the story of Cupid and Psyche from the perspective of Psyche. Similarly, in *Ariadne, Awake!,* Orgel takes a character heretofore marginal to the tale of Theseus and the Minotaur—Ariadne, the Minotaur's half-sister and Theseus's lover—and transforms her into the heroine of her own story. Horn Book reviewer Mary M. Burns writes that the story's "style is contemporary in feeling, reinforcing the concept that ancient tales have universal applications."

Awards

Orgel has won awards for both her translated and original work. *Dwarf Long-Nose* won the 1960 Lewis Carroll Shelf Award, and *Sarah's Room* was named one of the year's best 100 books by the *New York Times* in 1963. *A Certain Magic* (1975) was named a Notable Book by the American Library Association. *The Devil in Vienna* received the Wel-met Children's Book Award from the Child Study Association of America and Honor Book designation from Golden Kite and from the American Library Association in 1978, and the Sydney Taylor Book Award from the Association of Jewish Libraries in 1979. Orgel's translation of Elke Heidenreich's *Nero Corleone: A Cat's Story* was named a Mildred L. Batchelder Award Honor Book in 1997.

TITLE COMMENTARY

📖   *DWARF LONG-NOSE* (translated by Orgel from the story by Wilhelm Hauff, 1960)

Martha Bennett King

SOURCE: "Heirloom Tales from America, Europe, and the Ancient Mid-East," in *Chicago Sunday Tribune Magazine of Books,* November 6, 1960, p. 18.

Doris Orgel has given American children a gift beyond price, translating a tale she loved as a child in Vienna, a tale rich as a steaming plum pudding prepared by Dwarf Long-Nose himself for a king's royal dinner.

For more than a century, children in Germany "have linked Wilhelm Hauff's name with that of Hans Andersen as a spinner of magical adventures," Phyllis McGinley says in a charming preface. Hauff's stories were original, yet they have the rooted-in-earth quality of tales told beside household fires thru the ages.

This tale concerns a boy stolen by an old crone, turned into a dwarf with a ludicrous nose, and taught the secrets of fine cooking. He becomes a great chef and, at long last, discovers the herb which can restore him to human shape. The happy ending, aided by magic, is justified by the dwarf's own efforts and courage. [Maurice] Sendak's synthetically humorous illustrations are classic, calling on a tradition of European masters.

New York Herald Tribune Book Review

SOURCE: "Miracles, Magic, Elves, Dwarfs, and a Bogle or Two," in *New York Herald Tribune Book Review*, No. 15, November 13, 1960, p. 36.

The literary fairy tale, as distinct from the folk tales garnered from the lips of old grandmothers who in turn had heard them from their grandmothers, flourished in Germany, France and England after the collections of great fairy tales, Grimm and Perrault, were published. They often had folk themes but were neither as simple nor as full of the wisdom of the race as the shorter stories which had been cut and polished by innumerable retellings. In 1957 some of these from Germany, by various authors were retold by Gertrude C. Schwebell in "Where Magic Reigns" (Stephen Daye), among them the famous "Undine," and two by Wilhelm Hauff.

Now we have another long story by William Hauff (a young author of the nineteenth century who died at the age of twenty-five) translated by Doris Orgel, in which a poor boy is kidnaped by a witch, transformed into a hideous dwarf with a long nose and taught to be a very clever cook.

His sufferings are great until he is aided by a goose, really the bewitched daughter of a magician, who helps him find the magic herb that will let him regain his lost shape. It is the kind of tale that will appeal to children more than most of the elaborate literary confections, and it has been given a beautiful format. The theme is perfectly suited to Mr. Sendak's special gift of humorous portraiture combined with mock medieval scenes—turreted castles, gabled houses and other quaint trappings used decoratively.

Elizabeth Enright

SOURCE: A review of *Dwarf Long-Nose*, in *New York Times Book Review*, November 13, 1960, pp. 48, 50.

[The preface to *Dwarf Long-Nose*], by Phyllis McGinley, tells us that the author, Wilhelm Hauff, lived in Germany in the early nineteenth century. "Younger than Keats when he died he left as his legacy to European children dozens of strange and wonderful stories."

Dwarf Long-Nose is in the tradition of the Brothers Grimm: full of vengeance and magic, of baiting of the deformed and ill-treatment of the innocent, of final vindication and stout material reward.

The narrative is couched in the language of the classic fairy-tale: rather comfortably portentous. "In one of Germany's big cities, many years ago, there lived a righteous, modest shoemaker and his wife," the story begins. And "these good people had a handsome son, pleasant of visage, well formed, and rather tall for his 12 years." It is this boy, Jacob, who is heir to the ills and blessings: enslavement to a witch, a spell of ugliness, escape and ridicule, hard, meritorious work, the rescue of an enchanted goose who subsequently rescues him, and the final deliverance for both. Children who love the old fairy-tales will love this one.

There is one novelty: at the conclusion of the story Jacob, freed from his dwarfdom, and the magician's daughter, freed from her goosedom, fail to marry or fall in love. Instead, Jacob returns to his parents with enough riches to buy himself a store and live sensibly and profitably ever after. Maurice Sendak's illustrations are appropriately, Teutonic and grotesque.

Margery Fisher

SOURCE: A review of *Dwarf Long-Nose*, in *Growing Point*, Vol. 18, No. 1, May, 1979, p. 3510.

Doris Orgel's translation of the long German tale of *Dwarf Long-Nose*, first published in America in 1960, is somewhat more stately and inverted in style than Anthea Bell's (in Abelard-Schuman's collection of Hauff's Fairy tales) but it communicates readily the feeling of humanity through the image of a grotesque being restored to normality, of pathos turned to triumph. The melancholy and mystery of the tale is expressed in homely terms but with the kitchen settings coloured by the presence of enchanted animals— the squirrels and guinea-pigs who serve the witch, the girl imprisoned in goose-form. Maurice Sendak's brown and buff wash pictures are immensely varied and brilliantly pertinent. They may be marginal glosses on the text, punctuating it with minute and precise representations of domestic objects, or linear sequences moving round the text to a focal point. His loving attention to detail shows in facial expression and postures and through the chunky, childlike characters he plots the visual course of a sharply individual tale.

Marcus Crouch

SOURCE: A review of *Dwarf Long-Nose*, in *The Junior Bookshelf*, Vol. 43, No. 4, August, 1979, p. 195.

Hauff's fairy-tales belong with Andersen's rather than Grimm's. He uses folk materials but dresses them up with many literary sophistications. *Dwarf Long-nose* is a good example of his manner. A young lad is bewitched, in punishment for what is after all a very small offence, and acquires a very long nose and dwarfish stature. In this guise he is disowned by his parents, but makes up for it by developing phenomenal skills as a cook. In his position as chef to the Duke he wins fame and prestige, until a minor error brings him into disgrace. At this crisis, kindness brings its reward. Long-nose has been kind to a goose, also bewitched, and she not only solves his cookery problem but helps him to escape the tyrannical Duke.

Sendak illustrated this long tale in 1960, just after his edition of Andersen and in the same manner. Here too are the lively marginal drawings and the architectural settings, but the humour, appropriately enough, is broader and the draughtsmanship less delicate. Here surely the master is at his most amiable. The whole design of the book is very pleasing, from the bold typography to the good-humoured end-papers.

📖 THE TALE OF GOCKEL, HINKEL AND GACKELIAH (retold and translated by Orgel from the story by Clemens Brentano, 1961)

Virginia Kirkus' Service

SOURCE: A review of *The Tale of Gockel, Hinkel and Gackeliah*, in *Virginia Kirkus' Service*, Vol. XXIX, No. 12, June 15, 1961, p. 504.

A German legend hundreds of years old has been translated for folk tale fanciers by Doris Orgel. It concerns the fortunes and misfortunes of Gockel, Hinkel and their daughter Gackeliah as well as a host of animal characters who "people" their lives. Poor and discouraged, the family of three are transformed into a wealthy and noble group after killing the wise old rooster, Alektryo. The ring of Solomon encased originally in the rooster's throat is responsible for this change of fate as well as for a number of subsequent miraculous acts. The story is written in language suitable for teenagers, though a few younger children may be able to listen to it with comprehension, despite the formal terminology, scattered verse and some difficult concepts.

Spencer Shaw

SOURCE: A review of *The Tale of Gockel, Hinkel and Gackeliah*, in *Library Journal*, July, 1961, p. 2532.

German fantasy of a banished nobleman Gockel, his wife, daughter, and two fowls: Gallina and Alektyro. Grieved yet blessed by the latter's death, Gockel prospers but loses all by his daughter's thoughtlessness. However, kindness brings unexpected rewards. Filled with good and wicked characters, talking animals and humans, the tale embodies humor and folklore motifs and settings. Occasionally, the prose style, sprinkled liberally with varied-length verse, smothers the plot. For the more advanced, discriminating reader who delights in involved fantasy.

Elizabeth Enright

SOURCE: A review of *The Tale of Gockel, Hinkel and Gackeliah*, in *New York Times Book Review*, November 12, 1961, p. 35.

Last year another fairy-tale, *Dwarf Long-Nose*, introduced us to Clemens Brentano, well-known to the children of German-speaking countries for more than a century. Like its predecessor, the present book could only have been written by a German in the early nineteenth century, in a place and time which proved most fertile soil for fairy tales.

All the proper ingredients are here: Gothic setting, trials and dangers, magic and treachery, loyal animals who know how to talk. The characters are nicely drawn: Gockel, the righteous and long-suffering father; Hinkel, the fallible but loving mother; and Gackeliah, their willful but goodhearted child. Also important to the tale are two extremely human mice and one self-sacrificing rooster.

As in all satisfying fairy stories, acts of piety and acts of vengeance are comfortably balanced. The villains, presumably with the Lord's blessing, are finally turned into donkeys, while the reader is left in no doubt as to the rewards bestowed on the deserving—renewed youth, wealth, castles, hams, sausages, wine and scores of servants, including "one stuffer of capons." A very satisfying book.

Virginia Haviland

SOURCE: A review of *The Tale of Gockel, Hinkel, and Gackeliah*, in *The Horn Book Magazine*, Vol. XXXVIII, No. 1, February, 1962, pp. 49-50.

An early nineteenth-century fairy tale created in Germany by a storyteller who delighted in complex magic, allegorical implications, and puns on names (alluding here to poultry and eggs; e.g., "Hinkel," a pet name for hen, and "Gockel," for rooster). In spite of its length and unbridled fancies, this has something of folklore flavor in its following of the changing fortunes of Gackeliah and her parents, whose luck depended upon securing a magic ring long in the possession of the cock Alektryo. Most children will skip over the interpolated passages of spiritless poetry, but those who love make-believe will be glad for the fullness of the story. [Maurice] Sendak's drawings are perfect in picturing the folk figures and the animals and birds who are important in the action.

📖 SCHOOLMASTER WHACKWELL'S WONDERFUL SONS (retold and translated by Orgel from the story by Clemens Brentano, 1962)

Marguerite A. Dodson

SOURCE: A review of *Schoolmaster Whackwell's Wonderful Sons*, in *School Library Journal*, Vol. 9, No. 4, December, 1962, p. 42.

Because the family is destitute, Schoolmaster Whackwell sends his five sons out into the world to follow their callings. From what they learn, they are able to rescue a beautiful princess, and the family is justly rewarded. Less involved and allegorical than the earlier *Tale of Gockel, Hinkel and Gackeliah,* this also has the advantage of being retold as well as translated, making it more palatable to American children. As a result, the prose is more concise but retains the folk and fairy tale flavor, humor, puns, and lyricism associated with Brentano's stories for children. Illustrations [by Maurice Sendak] complement the text perfectly. Excellent for reading aloud. Recommended for any library where children like their fairy tales with a slightly different approach.

Virginia Haviland

SOURCE: A review of *Schoolmaster Whackwell's Wonderful Sons,* in *The Horn Book Magazine,* Vol. XXXIX, No. 1, February, 1963, p. 58.

Maurice Sendak's properly Gothic pictures make companions of this and the retellings of Wilhelm Hauff's *Dwarf Long-Nose* and Brentano's *The Tale of Gockel, Hinkel and Gackeliah.* Here now is a tale of five impoverished sons sent out into the world by their father to fend for themselves, each to follow a calling which he will come to know because of his name. These names, evolved as part of the story's structure, are odd enough: Gripsgrabs for the one who learns thievery; Piffpaff for him who becomes a marksman (every arrow goes *piff paff*); Pinkiepank for an apothecary; Splishsplosh, a boatman; and Tiraling for the modest young lad who learns to trill like the birds. Their rescue of Princess Ringlejing, each doing the thing in which he excels, follows a folk-tale pattern, but the story is unlike true folklore in elaborateness of style and exaggerated somberness of characters.

SARAH'S ROOM (1963)

Dorothy M. Johnson

SOURCE: "A Ham in Babe's Clothing," in *Book Week—The Sunday Herald Tribune,* No. 4, October 6, 1963, p. 18.

This short story in verse with characteristic and touching little scenes in pen and ink, tinted blue and yellow, by Maurice Sendak, could well have been called "The Ballad of the Younger Sister." In true ballad fashion (similar meter and rhyme scheme but with capitals at the beginning of sentences rather than of verses), it tells of a tiny sister's longing for a room like her older sister's.

"Of all the rooms in all the world the best is Sarah's room"—wallpaper on the walls, glass animals on the shelf and a dolls' house. Jen's, though, is very plain. "When Jen was small she marked the wall with smudges and with smears. Wallpaper would be wasted there, that is what mother fears." Jen had done worse. She had made a frightful mess in Sarah's room—"that's why they put the latch up high on Sarah's door." This story of how Jen grows up should delight all small sisters, although the

more lively among them may think at one point that Jen becomes just a trace too good.

Zena Sutherland

SOURCE: A review of *Sarah's Room,* in *Bulletin of the Center for Children's Books,* Vol. XVII, No. 3, November, 1963, pp. 47-8.

A small book, with old-fashioned illustrations that are right for the precise rhyming story that has an old-fashioned "moral tale" flavor. Jenny has been banned from her older sister's room because she made a mess there; one night she dreams about going in and playing with Sarah's dolls, who have come alive. The next morning Jenny goes into Sarah's room; Sarah finds and begins to scold her—then realizes that the room is in impeccable order. Jenny is given freedom of the premises, and is told by mother that she is now big enough for flowered wallpaper like the paper in Sarah's room. Slight but satisfying; the story is a bit static but all small girls will find attractive the thought of girl-size living dolls.

B. Clark

SOURCE: A review of *Sarah's Room,* in *The Junior Bookshelf,* Vol. 36, No. 3, June, 1972, p. 156.

A charming little tale in rhyme of the naughty little girl Jen and her very good little sister, and the difference between the ways in which they look after their own bedrooms. It takes a vivid dream of Jenny's to make her realise that her sister Sarah's way is better and so she earns the right to "use, as she may choose, her own or Sarah's room". Maurice Sendak's drawings give it a period flavour which suits the story ideally, and form a complete contrast to his recent large picture books.

THE HEART OF STONE (retold and translated by Orgel from the story by Wilhelm Hauff, 1964)

Joan H. Bodger

SOURCE: A review of *The Heart of Stone,* in *New York Times Book Review,* November 1, 1964, p. 46.

Peter Munk, a poor charcoal burner, wants to impress his neighbors at the local tavern. The little glassman grants him his wish and grants him a second one, too—ownership of a prosperous glass factory. But because Peter does not know enough to wish for common sense he so sorely needs, the glassman keeps the third wish in abeyance. A good thing, too, for Peter falls into the clutches of Hollander Mike, the evil-spirited lumberjack, and exchanges his bothersome beating heart for a marble substitute.

This is not a true folktale, but an original fairy tale written in Germany at a time when the Brothers Grimm were collecting their famous *Housmärchen* and when Hans Christian Andersen, in Denmark, was beginning to seek publication of his own unique stories. Wilhelm Hauff was born in 1802 and died in 1827. Although his works partake of the Romanticism extant during his short lifetime, they are also remarkable for their universality and practicality. He makes of Peter a real and complex character. Doris Orgel gives a sprightly translation to a much-loved story which, in some collections, is known as "The Little Glassman."

The stylized pen and ink drawings [by David Levine] that grace the margins of this edition have something of the haunting quality that characterizes Tenniel's famous illustrations for "Alice in Wonderland." Some children may be put off by them, but few will forget their crabbed humor.

Priscilla L. Moulton

SOURCE: A review of *The Heart of Stone*, in *The Horn Book Magazine*, Vol. XL, No. 6, December, 1964, p. 610.

Peter Munk makes charcoal in a section of the Black Forest where glassblowing and lumberjacking are the respected occupations. Foolish, dissatisfied, and poor, the boy's joy is unbounded when given three wishes by the little forest spirit, Glassman. Now rich, but still foolish and dissatisfied, Peter is persuaded by the evil giant, Hollander Mike, to exchange his true heart for one of stone so that he may live unencumbered by feelings. It is many adventures later before Peter realizes that riches and comfort do not bring conte tment. Regardless of the level on which the tale is read, the triumph of sense over stupidity, charity over greed, and good over evil brings satisfaction. Action and dialogue have forthright simplicity, embodying customs and values of the Black Forest people. Green border designs and pictures at the bottoms of the pages [by David Levine] give an appearance of quaint, ornate woodcarving.

📖 *CINDY'S SNOWDROPS* (1966)

Kirkus Reviews

SOURCE: A review of *Cindy's Snowdrops*, in *Kirkus Reviews*, Vol. XXXIV, No. 21, October 15, 1966, p. 1101.

"Let's go to the nursery and buy some bulbs," said Cindy's father one September day. Cindy knew what kind of nursery. Not the one for little people. The one for little plants. And she knew what kinds of bulbs. Not the bulbs you put in lamps to make light. Bulbs you put in the ground to make flowers. Cindy picks out three snowdrop bulbs to plant all by herself. The nurseryman tells her that they will come up in March "I'll be six in March," says Cindy. Winter comes and winter stays; it is only February when Cindy sees "a very green something beside the gray rock . . . was it, could it be —?" It *is*, and the first blos-

soms appear just on time, on the day Cindy eats birthday cake for breakfast. With Atti Forburg's ephemeral illustrations, this might have been a pleasant harbinger of spring for threes and fours, but it's just a drop in the snow for the sevens and eights who'll be able to read it alone.

Mary Silva Cosgave

SOURCE: A review of *Cindy's Snowdrops*, in *The Horn Book Magazine*, Vol. XLIII, No. 1, February, 1967, p. 62.

In September Cindy planted seven tiny snowdrop bulbs, six for her next birthday and one to grow on. Through the long winter she waited and watched, hoping they would come up in time for her birthday in March. They did, right on the dot. Cindy also did a bit of growing herself, and so will her contemporaries as they "read alone" and share Cindy's pride and joy in a first do-it-yourself experience with nature. It is a pity that there should be even this one jarring sentence: "The garden still looked like Cindy had imagined it. . . . " The illustrations [by Ati Forberg] in black, spring green, and frosty white are so appealing that there will probably be a bumper crop of snowdrops next season.

Elsie T. Dobbins

SOURCE: A review of *Cindy's Snowdrops*, in *Library Journal*, Vol. 92, No. 4, February 15, 1967, p. 874.

It is early fall and everyone in Cindy's family is buying bulbs to plant. Cindy finds some tiny ones which the nursery-man says are snowdrops. She decides to buy six because she will be six years old in March. After planting them, she pastes a picture of the flowers next to her bed where she admires it all winter, and on her birthday she is rewarded with three snowdrops in full bloom and four more in bud. A pleasant, but not unusual, nature story of fall, winter, and spring. Easy enough for second- and third-graders to read for themselves. Black-and-white with green wash illustrations [by Ati Forberg] complement the text nicely.

📖 *THE GOOD-BYES OF MAGNUS MARMA-LADE* (1966)

Library Journal

SOURCE: A review of *The Good-Byes of Magnus Marmalade*, in *Library Journal*, Vol. 91, No. 22, December 15, 1966, p. 6195.

"Oh, shady weedy pond, how nice / You were to wade in! Now you're ice, / And I with grief would be undone— / If skating weren't also fun." In this little book of four-line verses, there are too few (two or three) that have child appeal or are good enough to warrant purchase by libraries.

Zena Sutherland

SOURCE: A review of *The Good-Byes of Magnus Marmalade,* in *Bulletin of the Center for Children's Books,* Vol. 20, No. 9, May, 1967, p. 144.

Illustrated with engaging black and white drawings [by Erik Blegvad], a charming book of light verse in which a small boy bids farewell to a school principal, a raincoat, a television announcer, poison ivy, et cetera. Sample: a farewell to his dentist. "You filled my tooth with gentle care, And yet I leave your dental chair With such great joy, it must be true: It's not your drill I hate, it's you!" The last few pages diverge: Magnus is described as going off somewhere, leaving his mother for the first time, then coming home. This seems to add little to the book, but doesn't detract much either. The poems are also nice to read aloud to smaller fry.

IN A FORGOTTEN PLACE (1967)

Kirkus Reviews

SOURCE: A review of *In a Forgotten Place,* in *Kirkus Reviews,* Vol. XXXV, No. 6, March 15, 1967, p. 342.

"Memento meminisse"—remember to remember—cautions the wizard Memini before granting an unlimited number of wishes. Son of a Roman peasant and a Roman god, he spends five hundred years in each place and by now has a mind so full of a quillion memories that he reads it rather than the mind of others. Mary, a bright, independent New England girl, finds him by chance in a forgotten place, where Indians used to visit him with their requests. She is afraid of him but brings her best friend Andrew to meet him, starting a series of misunderstandings between them. Mary's research into the origin of their town's disturbing name, Pagantown, and Andrew's troubles with his senile fourth-grade teacher Miss Ingledinger complement the unobtrusive fantasy. Five hundred years are up on the last day of school which is coincidentally Memini's fifteen-hundredth birthday; with no time left to grant Andrew's wish for Mary's renewed friendship, he gives him instead the gift of memory for little things, like pumping up the bike tires or taking his homework to school. Memory helps Andrew to win Mary over *and* enjoy school better. Despite the uncommon dependence of Andrew on Mary, this is light, pleasant fantasy, quick to read and leaving behind a faint wildflower fragrance.

Elinor Cullen

SOURCE: A review of *In a Forgotten Place,* in *Library Journal,* Vol. 92, No. 12, June 15, 1967, p. 2454.

The part of this story that recounts the history of the 1500-year-old wizard Memini is an airy excursion into fantasy, but the rest of the tale is a thudding flop, a weak combination of irrelevant components. In his later appearances even Memini seems doddering. The boy Andrew, who visits Memini, appears remarkably unimaginative for a daydreamer, and his wishes are prosaic. His best friend Mary's interest in a research project to free respectable Pagantown from the connotations of its name is overworked, and the accompanying lectures on library behavior and use of reference materials are dull and intrusive. Andrew's despised teacher Miss Ingledinger is a crude slapstick caricature of a type of teacher seldom encountered today.

Aileen Pippett

SOURCE: A review of *In a Forgotten Place,* in *New York Times Book Review,* July 9, 1967, p. 34.

The people of Pagantown dislike the name of their town but don't know what else to call it until two fourth graders and a wizard get together. After absent-minded Andrew stumbles on the wizard's hiding place and shares the secret with Mary, queer things begin to happen—a bicycle turns into a horse and spells are cast. Just the same Mary is determined to solve the town's problem and with the wizard pointing the way slogs through a learned library book about Indians and finds out that Pagan was an old Indian pronunciation of pecan. So Pagantown is renamed at a glorious picnic. Only the wizard isn't there to be thanked; he takes off in a whirlwind before the fun begins.

The author has ingeniously combined inexplicable and ordinary events. She leaves one with the suggestion that dictionaries are necessary but so is the magic of memory in finding a way through bewilderment to understanding. James McMullan's illustrations heighten the engaging oddity of this unusual fantasy.

CINDY'S SAD AND HAPPY TREE (1967)

Publishers Weekly

SOURCE: A review of *Cindy's Sad and Happy Tree,* in *Publishers Weekly,* October 30, 1967, p. 50.

Illustrations [by Ati Forberg] so oriental in mood that they would harmonize happily with *haiku* reflect here the story of a little girl who wept over the death of an elm tree and rejoiced over the arrival of a weeping cheery (cherry) tree. The mudcolored paper used for the book makes the sad part of the title more believable than the happy part.

Barbara Gibson

SOURCE: A review of *Cindy's Sad and Happy Tree,* in *School Library Journal,* January, 1968, p. 64.

An elm dies in Cindy's yard and her family wants to plant another in its place. Because Cindy loved the old elm, her father gives her the responsibility of choosing a replacement. Cindy decides that the new tree "has to be a sad sort of tree because of the elm. But it has to be sort of happy, too" to cheer her up. Ultimately, she solves the problem by choosing a weeping cherry tree or, as she says, a "weeping cheery tree." An imaginative format (brown, black and white drawings on brown pages), challenging vocabulary, and sensitive depiction of a child's identification with nature combine to make this better than the usual easy reader.

 ## *WHOSE TURTLE?* (1968)

Kirkus Reviews

SOURCE: A review of *Whose Turtle?*, in *Kirkus Reviews,* Vol. XXXVI, No. 10, May 15, 1968, p. 547.

Frankly speaking, it's Wally's turtle (Buddy) but he gives him to sister Rachel (who renames him Quertz) when she breaks her arm. Rachel decides having a cast is like . . . having a shell, but as the weeks drag on even Quertz' companionship cannot ease her restlessness, and she counts the days to the end of her confinement. Arm freed, she realizes that Quertz' shell is a part of him, that living in a bowl is his disability, comparable to her jail dream the night before; Rachel celebrates her freedom by giving Quertz his. Martha Alexander's pencil-and-wash drawings soft-focus on a summery scene, but the extended parallel between girl and turtle never opens up into anything.

Gertrude B. Herman

SOURCE: A review of *Whose Turtle?*, in *Library Journal,* Vol. 93, No. 13, July, 1968, p. 2730.

Two ideas provide the structure for this story: the care of a pet found in the woods and the tedium of waiting for a broken arm to heal. The pet is a box turtle found by Wally but coveted by his sister Rachel. The broken arm is what befalls Rachel and prompts Wally to give her the turtle. For Rachel the irksome days in a cast are lightened by the joy of observing Quertz (the turtle). But when the day of liberation from her cast comes, Rachel realizes that Quertz has been imprisoned, too, and she returns him to the freedom of nature. A gentle moral tale illustrated with very feminine pencil-and-wash drawings [by Martha Alexander], this is a somewhat wordy but easily read book which will interest little girls.

ON THE SAND DUNE (1968)

Kirkus Reviews

SOURCE: A review of *On the Sand Dune,* in *Kirkus Reviews,* Vol. XXXVI, No. 13, July 1, 1968, p. 688.

The sand dune that older sister Joan and her friends scale easily is as precipitous as Everest to Annie; she can't get up it, envies them their elevated make-believe. But she

has, it seems, the best-balanced (plastid) sea horse of the four and Peter asks to borrow it. "She wants you to help her climb up the dune," tattles Joan. Did Peter hear before he grabbed the sea horse? In any case, he comes down from playing Arab tribesmen on the dune to include her as a prisoner and shows her how to inch her way up; later in the day she does it again by herself. On a black-and-bisque beach, the plight of the younger child struggling to keep up is intertwined with some rather mundane imaginings; it also depends on a dune that seems to get steeper every time you look at it. Nothing special to look at, nothing special to sweat about.

Mary Ann Wentroth

SOURCE: A review of *On the Sand Dune,* in *School Library Journal,* Vol. 15, No. 2, October, 1968, p. 144.

Text and pictures sensitively depict the concentration of older children in their imaginative play and the frustrations of the smallest child as she tries to keep up with them. Young Annie's dogged but good-humored determination to climb the steep dune ends in success, and her achievement is hailed by the other children as she joins them in their play on the top. Leonard Weisgard's sand dunes are as beautiful as they are challenging to climb, and his children are appealing without being sweet. Only a sand color is added to the black, gray and white drawings, but that is enough to produce a visually satisfying, well designed book. The story is told almost entirely as conversation among the children, and the characterizations are remarkably cohesive and three-dimensional for a picture book.

THE ENCHANTED DRUM (translated by Orgel from the story by Walter Grieder, 1969)

Kirkus Reviews

SOURCE: A review of *The Enchanted Drum,* in *Kirkus Reviews,* Vol. XXXVII, No. 10, May 15, 1969, p. 556.

If youngsters can be borne along by the high spirits of an impending celebration and the fear of Bitgi that, not having practiced on his drum, he'll be left out, then perhaps the oversights in this oversized book won't matter—namely that the colors don't match from page to page (making it hard to identify the children), that the Baslers' celebration, *Morgenstreich,* is never explained. At their best, the illustrations have the cocky wit of Tomi Ungerer; at their worst, the host of colorful forms cancel each other out. Altogether an uproar, okay if you can make it out.

Ann D. Schweibish

SOURCE: A review of *The Enchanted Drum,* in *School Library Journal,* Vol. 16, No. 1, September, 1969, p. 101.

Story line and characterizations are weak—and of minor

importance—in this visual, carnival extravaganza. It's almost time for the Morgenstreich celebration in Basel, Switzerland, and the children in the normally placid city—with the exception of lazy Bitzgi—are excitedly practicing their fife and drum marches. Though given the drum of a great, deceased drummer, Bitzgi still can't make himself practice; finally, he has a dream in which every living thing in the city flies away while drumming merrily. A desolate Bitzgi is left alone on the ground, taunted by nightmarish creatures who shriek "No lazybones allowed!" at him. Repentant, Bitzgi vows to practice in the future and meanwhile is able to march successfully as his singularly inspired, independent drum plays of its own accord. Fantastical, poster-like, full-page illustrations in the oversized (9¼" X 13¼") book are vividly colored and lively, making this a likely choice to show at story hours.

PHOEBE AND THE PRINCE (1969)

Kirkus Reviews

SOURCE: A review of *Phoebe and the Prince*, in *Kirkus Reviews*, Vol. XXXVII, No. 16, August 15, 1969, p. 852.

A tiny book with a wisp of a plot set in a seven-or-eight-year-old frame of reference is at best a stocking stuffer, here today and forgotten tomorrow. With little loss accept some passing cleverness in the doleful ballad of a flea with royal blood in his veins who now sucks on commoner fare. Anemic.

Eleanor Glaser

SOURCE: A review of *Phoebe and the Prince*, in *School Library Journal*, Vol. 16, No. 4, December, 1969, p. 43.

A very thin, fanciful tale is awkwardly spun around a long poem that begins: "Once upon a time, a flea / Lived on a good old German king / Who loved him very tenderly, / And gave his fav'rite everything / From leather boots to feathered hat / Befitting an aristocrat—." Phoebe finds this princely flea in her pet Prince Deardog's ear. His fortunes have changed and he tells her the sad tale in sophisticated vocabulary befitting a regal flea but not young listeners or readers. The small detailed line drawings in this tiny (6¾" X 4 ½") book match the text in dry wit that is also too advanced and not likely to reach the intended audience.

Zena Sutherland

SOURCE: A review of *Phoebe and the Prince*, in *Bulletin of the Center for Children's Books*, Vol. 23, No. 5, January, 1970, p. 86.

Sometimes Phoebe called her dog "Deardog" and sometimes she called him "Prince." A disappointed voice said one day, when Deardog had yipped with pain, "Oh. I thought you were speaking to me." Thus enters into Phoe-

be's life a flea with an exceptionally distinguished background. He admits it himself, as he describes (in verse) the past glories of his career at court, testily rebuking Phoebe when she interrupts. As suddenly as he hopped into her life, Phoebe's new friend departs with a blithe, "Auf wiedersehn." Brisk, silly, and spiced with sense, this is a small portion of sophisticated writing that can be enjoyed by any reader but that has nuances that can be an additional attraction for the unusual reader. The illustrations are also sophisticated, small-scale and witty: [Erik] Blegvad at his best.

MERRY, ROSE, AND CHRISTMAS-TREE JUNE (1969)

Publishers Weekly

SOURCE: A review of *Merry, Rose, and Christmas-Tree June*, in *Publishers Weekly*, Vol. 196, No. 9, September 1, 1969, p. 52.

Not technically a Christmas story, but truly a Christmas present to all book-sellers who asked, "Do you have a new story about dolls?" Doris Orgel has given them a new, delectable story about dolls. And to make the present perfect, Edward Gorey has illustrated it. Merry Christmas!

Marilyn Singer

SOURCE: "Inside the Vacuum of Reverence," in *School Library Journal*, Vol. 16, No. 2, October, 1969, p. 169.

Doris Orgel's **Merry, Rose, and Christmas-Tree June** is in a much lighter, more natural vein [than Elizabeth Goudge's *I Saw Three Ships*]. Combined with Edward Gorey's drawings (much gayer than his usually are), it ought to delight the doll set. The book is actually more about dolls than Christmas but is felicitous enough to apply under Trina Schart Hyman's principle of Christmas. Jane loves the two very undistinguished dolls she received for Christmas because she can wash them, feed them, and pretend with them, etc. Unhappily, she forgets to take them with her when she visits her rich great-aunt, and so is taken to I. Greedy's Distinguished Dollarama where there are only expensive, complicated dolls that each do one thing—talk, dance, etc. She accidentally breaks a few, rejects the rest, but finally discovers a forgotten plain old doll that she loves because simple dolls that do nothing are really the ones that can do the most.

Zena Sutherland

SOURCE: A review of *Merry, Rose and Christmas-Tree June*, in *Bulletin of the Center for Children's Books*, Vol. 23, No. 4, December, 1969, pp. 62-3.

A deftly written story that mingles the real and the fanciful with aplomb; the style is smooth and forthright, with a hint of satire that is reflected in the [Edward] Gorey illustrations. In championing the plain old-fashioned doll with no mechanics and no gimmicks, the author strikes a blow for imaginative play, and her depiction of a small girl's make-believe is neither patronizing nor sugary. Jane, who has received two dolls for Christmas, is devoted to Merry and Rose, and mourns their absence when she spends a night, doll-less, with Great Aunt Beulah. Promised another doll, Jane spurns all the marvelous creations that I. Greedy's Distinguished Dollarama sells, and chooses the one old doll left from many Christmases ago. "But she can't do *anything*," says Mr. Greedy, while Jane—who has examined the limited, repetitive performances of the newer dolls—thinks happily that Christmas-Tree June will be able to do *everything*.

NEXT DOOR TO XANADU (1969)

Ethel L. Heins

SOURCE: A review of *Next Door to Xanadu,* in *The Horn Book Magazine,* Vol. XLVI, No. 1, February, 1970, p. 42.

Worries, fears, problems, and superstitions are all part of growing up—even for a child cushioned by the warm security of a happy home. Ten-year-old Patricia is a city child; she has a lovable baby sister and understanding, sensitive parents. But Patricia has been ineffectual at making friends at school; overly plump and self-consciously lonely, she is fast becoming a compulsive eater. She longs to be willowy and slender; still more she dreams of having a special, particular friend. When Dorothy comes to live in the next-door apartment, Patricia realizes that her secret wishes and even her Halloween incantation have been productive. But Dorothy's sojourn is all too brief. Patricia is again threatened by loneliness; but now, having had a friend, she has learned to be one. The old prejudice against first-person narrative has apparently disappeared: With spontaneity and conviction, Patricia tells her own story.

Amy Kellman

SOURCE: A review of *Next Door to Xanadu,* in *Grade Teacher,* Vol. 88, No. 1, September, 1970, p. 162.

Next Door to Xanadu handles the problem . . . [of a young girl finding her way to maturity through her increased understanding of other people] directly and seriously. More than anything, Patricia wanted a girlfriend next door to help her face the world, especially that part of it that held two unpleasant boys. Dorothy moves in and life becomes like Coleridge's Xanadu. The boys are tamed, a pet is acquired, and Patricia begins to cope with her weight problem. When Dorothy has to move away, Patricia is crushed, but finds she has learned to handle her life more effectively. The book scores because of the author's quiet, sincere style of writing that creates true people and makes the situation real to the reader.

Zena Sutherland

SOURCE: A review of *Next Door to Xanadu,* in *Bulletin of the Center for Children's Books,* Vol. 24, No. 3, November, 1970, pp. 46-7.

Patricia admits it: she's fat. The boys call her "fatsy Patsy," and she has no close friends. What she wants more than anything in the world is a bosom pal. And along comes Dorothy Rappaport, just her age, and right across the hall! The progress of their friendship is rapid, and Patricia is smitten with anguish when she learns that Dorothy is going to move away. But friendship has brought a measure of self-confidence; Patricia pulls herself together and makes their last days cheerful. There is no major action in the story, but the realistic and perceptive events and relationships are touched with humor and told in a style that is convincingly that of a girl of ten.

THE UPROAR (1970)

Kirkus Reviews

SOURCE: A review of *The Uproar,* in *Kirkus Reviews,* Vol. XXXVIII, No. 13, July 1, 1970, p. 678.

Fleeting, phantomlike dreams spun on a thin thread of misconception: Saul Laurence thinks his mother and father are going to see *Madame Butterfly* in an "uproar." Partly to escape from baby-sitter Mrs. Onion (she peels off layers of clothing), and her offensive rendition of "Now I lay me down to sleep," he dreams up a fairy godmother Madame Butterfly who wafts him to a Lincoln Centric opera house where a transformed Mrs. Onion performs like a duck, a stage villain calls down lightning and thunder, and various large and small noises combine in "a wonderful uproar." After making his own medley, Saul Laurence tries for the sound of a triangle . . . and hears it in his mother's 'little ting-a-ling laugh.' Mrs. Onion is mercifully gone and "'It was a wonderful opera.'" One can begin to 'queery' this almost anywhere—with his parents' also saying Mrs. Onion, for instance, or his conception of the "uproar house" as indeed an opera house. Anyhow overall it's as delicate bordering on preciousness as that little ting-a-ling laugh.

Sada Fretz

SOURCE: A review of *The Uproar,* in *School Library Journal,* Vol. 17, No. 1, September, 1970, p. 95.

"Saul Laurence's mother had a soft, wispy dress on," begins this soft, wispy-to-flimsy story based on a small boy's confusion over the words "opera" and "uproar." After his parents leave for the opera to see *Madame Butterfly,* Saul Laurence dreams that Madame Butterfly (looking like a fairy princess) flies into his room and takes him to the "uproar" house where he participates in an elaborate, fantastic uproar with all the other people there. Anita Lobel's attractive pictures, grey and white highlighted in blue and/or yellow, echo the gentle tone and fantastical nature of the slight story which will, however, be further weakened by the probable need to explain the two words to young readers or listeners in the first place.

Zena Sutherland

SOURCE: A review of *The Uproar,* in *Bulletin of the Center for Children's Books,* December, 1970, p. 64.

A picture book that combines a small boy's imaginative dreams and the mild humor of a situation based on a misunderstood word. When Saul Laurence's mother kissed him goodnight, she said she was going to the opera house to see Madame Butterfly. "Uproar" house, he thought she said, and then (after an anti-babysitter incident) he dreams of Madame Butterfly flying him to the Uproar House, where he is the star performer at noises. His dream ends with the return of his parents, who report that it was a wonderful opera. The illustrations [by Anita Lobel] have some humor and vigor but are bland in color and, on some pages, busy with detail. The story line is slight, its embroideries tenuous.

Diane Farrell

SOURCE: A review of *The Uproar,* in *The Horn Book Magazine,* Vol. XLVI, No. 6, December, 1970, pp. 606-07.

Saul Laurence's parents go to hear *Madame Butterfly,* and Saul wonders why they wanted to go to an "uproar." "[A]t home they were almost always quiet, they hardly made any noises." Saul Laurence goes to bed, and Madame Butterfly (a beautiful lady the color of moonlight with shimmering butterfly wings) comes in through the window. She flies away into the night with Saul Laurence to center stage in the tall "uproar" house where everyone, including Saul Laurence, participates in a thrilling cacophony of sound—quacks, rumbles, clicks, thwoks, stomps, wuffs, whirs, gurgles, plops, chirps, crunches, and roars. The small children who will enjoy the book probably will not understand the joke; but they will like the fantasy, taking it literally and seriously, especially appreciating all the solemn importance of the moment when Saul Laurence makes the noise of a snowflake falling. The black-and-white drawings [by Anita Lobel] are highlighted by dreamlike, swirling pastels. A wonderful uproar.

THE GRANDMA IN THE APPLE TREE
(translated by Orgel from the story by Mira Lobe, 1970)

Zena Sutherland

SOURCE: A review of *The Grandma in the Apple Tree,* in *Bulletin of the Center for Children's Books,* Vol. 24, No. 8, April, 1971, p. 126.

First published in 1965 under the title *Die Omama im*

Apfelbaum, the story of a small boy who feels underprivileged. Everybody else has a grandmother, and grandmothers take you to the merry-go-round or buy toys or knit caps just for you. So Andi invents one. His parents remonstrate gently when he talks of their joint adventures, and his older brother and sister tease him. Then a gentle, affectionate old woman moves next door, and she confesses that she yearns for her grandchildren in Canada. So she and Andi make a pact: she will be his everyday grandmother, and when he's in the apple tree he will go on having magical adventures with his other grandma. The sequences in which Andi has imaginary adventures are almost slapstick, but most of the story has a quiet, ingenuous quality; the writing style is smooth, the translation competent, and the family scenes realistic.

Sheryl B. Andrews

SOURCE: A review of *The Grandma in the Apple Tree,* in *The Horn Book Magazine,* Vol. XLVII, No. 2, April, 1971, pp. 163-64.

A modest tale by an award-winning Austrian writer, who explores in a quietly uncomplicated way a child's desire for the companionship of an older person. "All the kids on the street had a grandmother. Some even had two. Only Andi had none, and that made him sad." So Andi invented a wildly improbable grandmother, complete with flowered hat, carpet bag, and lace bloomers, and together they sailed the seven seas, roped wild horses, and started off on a tiger hunt to India—all from the base of the apple tree in the front lawn. How Andi acquired a real "grandma" who needed a little eight-year-old boy to love completes the unaffectedly childlike story.

Ruth P. Bull

SOURCE: A review of *The Grandma in the Apple Tree,* in *The Booklist,* Vol. 67, No. 16, April 15, 1971, p. 703.

Sitting in his favorite thinking spot in the apple tree, eight-year-old Andi, the only child on his street without a grandmother, is suddenly joined by an imaginary, adventure-loving grandma who takes him on tiger hunts and journeys to pirate-infested seas. She becomes his Sunday-grandma, however, when his new neighbor, old Mrs. Finch, shows him the simpler pleasures that a real everyday grandma can bring. A lightly told, enjoyable fantasy, illustrated with black-and-white drawings [by Judith Gwyn Brown], some of which reflect the humor in the story.

THE MULBERRY MUSIC (1971)

Kirkus Reviews

SOURCE: A review of *The Mulberry Music,* in *Kirkus Reviews,* Vol. XXXIX, No. 20, October 15, 1971, p. 1122.

Disappointed when her Grandma Liza's cold interferes

with their weekly swimming date, 11-year-old Libby becomes more distraught as the cold turns to pneumonia, Grandma is hospitalized, and Mother refuses to take Libby on her daily visits to the sickbed. The everyday distractions that fill the waiting time—exciting rides at Danbury Fair, a dress-up parade when her best friend "sleeps over"—proceed under the growing oppression of Grandma's illness, and Libby's uncertainties and resentments are conveyed with fidelity and restraint. Finally, Libby *must* see Grandma Liza, and one Sunday morning she leaves the house against orders, takes a taxi to the hospital, and talks her way into Grandma's room—there to confront a rasping, dying woman with unseeing eyes and liquid dripping through a tube into her arm. Her parents, to Libby's surprise, are sympathetic about her outbursts and her escapades, and in the end Mother, a concert pianist, plays Libby's and Grandma's "mulberry music" (from Mozart's *Jupiter* symphony) at an appropriate home funeral that Libby has proposed for her non-churchgoing grandmother. (Though Libby is "not musical," the story, too, has a musical background.) A subject that could be sticky is nicely muted and perceptively attuned to the sensibilities of real girls like Libby.

Rose S. Bender

SOURCE: A review of *The Mulberry Music*, in *School Library Journal*, Vol. 18, No. 3, November, 1971, p. 117.

A sixth grader's first encounter with death is the subject of this slow-moving story in which the events take place in less than a fortnight. At first disbelieving the report of Grandmother Liza's illness, Libby runs away to her house. There, she discovers from neighbors that her grandmother has been hospitalized. Contrary to hospital rules, she gains entrance to her grandmother's room and is terrified at the sight of the woman encased in tubes and bottles and struggling to breathe. She flees, is brought home by a policeman, and then hears the final news of her grandmother's death. Libby's memories of her adored Grandmother Liza—the woman's understanding nature, the trips the two took together, the music they shared—and the touching funeral service that concludes the book are believably handled. However, there's insufficient action and Libby's overstated misery is likely to cause reader interest to wane.

Zena Sutherland

SOURCE: A review of *The Mulberry Music*, in *Bulletin of the Center for Children's Books*, Vol. 25, No. 5, January, 1972, pp. 77-8.

A most moving story about a child's love for her grandmother and her adjustment to Grandma Liza's death. Grandma had always done whatever she pleased. If she wanted to wear a mulberry-colored sweatsuit ("Nobody wears that color," Mom said when her mother appeared in a home-dyed mulberry blouse and skirt) she did. Grandma Liza lived graciously, and Libby was terrified at the thought of losing her. The story is told in convincing fashion, bittersweet, with a home memorial service during which Libby realizes that the music played at her suggestion, Grandma's favorite—will stay with her always, just as will the memory of Grandma Liza.

Virginia Haviland

SOURCE: A review of *The Mulberry Music*, in *The Horn Book Magazine*, Vol. XLVIII, No. 2, April, 1972, p. 147.

The compatibility of eleven-year-old Libby and her grandmother, and the consequent pain to Libby because of her beloved Grandma Liza's critical illness are poignantly portrayed in this contemporary suburban-Connecticut family story. Libby's feelings about her dual background—Lutheran and Jewish—and about the slight family ties with either faith are also important in the vividly detailed domestic picture. Grandma, an independent spirit who had dyed her sweat suit mulberry, loved to play a piano arrangement of Mozart's *Jupiter Symphony*, which Libby called "the mulberry music." After her grandmother's death, Libby suggested that this music be played at the funeral service. The author is successful in handling important personal relationships.

LITTLE JOHN (retold and translated by Orgel from the story by Theodor Storm, 1972)

Publishers Weekly

SOURCE: A review of *Little John*, in *Publishers Weekly*, Vol. 201, No. 10, March 6, 1972, p. 63.

Theodor Storm's *Der Kleine Häwelmann*, the story of the nighttime escapades of Little John in his trundle bed, has as much charm and enchantment for contemporary children as when it was first written in 1849. Little John begins his imaginative voyage by the light of the moon and ends it in a bright dawn; but not before his trundle bed has taken him through the city, into the woods and right up into the sky with the stars. Anita Lobel has appropriately illustrated the book in gray, black and white, with a bright burst of yellow and orange for the moon and sun. A real charmer, perfect for bedtime reading.

Kirkus Reviews

SOURCE: A review of *Little John*, in *Kirkus Reviews*, Vol. XL, No. 6, March 15, 1972, pp. 322-23.

Though more successful than ***The Uproar*** (1970), this is another Orgel-Lobel collaboration whose substance never lives up to the dreamlike and billowy pictures. Based on a 19th-century German tale, it relates the night voyage of Little John who ties his nightgown to his toe for a sail, then trundles himself in his trundle bed around his room, through the town, into the woods and right up to the moon, only to tumble out of bed and into the sea with the emergence of the sun (whose face, like an angry oriental mask, would waken any dreamer). But Little John neither wakens in his room nor meets the fate of Icarus. Instead, "What happened? Don't you remember? You and I came along just in time, and took Little John in our boat with us, and rowed him safely to shore." Though Storm's fantasy of flight is an accessible starting point, the coy conclusion (whether Storm's or Orgel's) is all the more of a let-down.

Mary M. Burns

SOURCE: A review of *Little John,* in *The Horn Book Magazine,* Vol. XLVIII, No. 4, August, 1972, pp. 365-66.

Trundle beds and nightshirts are no longer familiar childhood accouterments, but the bedtime demands and dream fantasies of small children have not changed remarkably since 1849, when the story was first told of Little John who "couldn't get enough of trundling." When his exhausted mother no longer responded to his insatiable "Trundle me more!" the ingenious youngster transformed his nightshirt into a sail; and blowing "like the wind," he trundled himself around the room, onto a moonbeam, out of the house, through the town, and finally into the sky, where he trundled wildly until dawn brought his escapade to an abrupt end. Retaining the cosy narrative style of nineteenth-century nursery tales, complete with references to the "dear stars" and "the good old moon," the text suggests the romanticists' emphasis on the emotional and the intuitive—qualities emphasized by the sensuous lines of the illustrations [by Anita Lobel], which build up to the crescendo appearance of a flaming Teutonic sun. By evoking the fragmented, half-remembered erotic fancies of childhood dreams, the book emerges as a nineteenth-century version of Sendak's *In the Night Kitchen.* And if the beautifully executed illustrations seem at first glance overly sophisticated in relation to the surface simplicity of the narrative, one should recall the influence of Freudian theory on textual interpretation. Each generation, it has been observed, rewrites history in terms of its own experience; the same comment might well be applied to twentieth-century reassessments of childhood.

Zena Sutherland

SOURCE: A review of *Little John,* in *Bulletin of the Center for Children's Books,* Vol. 26, No. 5, January, 1973, p. 82.

Little John thinks of a way to trundle himself when his exhausted mother has fallen asleep; he hoists his nightshirt (this was written in 1849) for a sail, and puffs up a wind. Helped by the amused moon, he trundles through the keyhole and off into the sky. With the coming of dawn, the indignant sun evicts the intruder, and Little John falls out of bed and into the sea. "And then what happened?" The story ends, "Don't you remember? You and I came along just in time and took Little John in our boat with us, and rowed him safely to shore." The ending is anticlimactic, the story imaginative but tenuous. The illustrations [by Anita Lobel] are appropriately dreamy, with soft pictures in black and white relieved only by the pale lemon-yellow of the smiling moon and the vivid pink and orange of the sun's large, irate face.

A CERTAIN MAGIC (1976)

Matilda Kornfeld

SOURCE: A review of *A Certain Magic,* in *School Library Journal,* Vol. 22, No. 9, May, 1976, pp. 62-3.

Without her aunt's knowledge, 11-year old Jenny reads the diary that Trudl, then Jenny's age, kept during that unhappy time in the late 1930's when she stayed with a family in England waiting for word from Austria that she and her parents could emigrate to the U.S. Homesick and resentful of being teased by the English children, Pam and Mark, Trudl used what she believed to be the evil magic of her emerald ring to win Pam's doll and cause their goldfish's death. When the goldfish actually died, guilt-ridden Trudl hid the ring. On a trip to England with her parents, Jenny feels compelled to visit the village where Trudl stayed as a refugee. Following clues from the diary Jenny finds Pam, now Mrs. Harwood, and takes home to Trudl the doll that Pam had once promised her and the emerald which Trudl had hidden in it so long ago. The book keeps a nice pace as it moves from present to past in Trudl's diary, building suspense along the way. The characters—Jenny's artist mother and lawyer father; Trudl, a successful translator now in her 50's—are individual and believable. But most interesting are the themes of guilt and evil that motivate the story in terms that children can well understand.

Mary M. Burns

SOURCE: A review of *A Certain Magic,* in *The Horn Book Magazine,* Vol. LII, No. 4, August, 1976, p. 400.

Shortly before the long-awaited trip from New York City to London with her artist-mother and lawyer-father, eleven-year-old Jenny Ehrenteil discovers a dusty copybook in her Aunt Trudl's apartment. Written when Trudl was also eleven, the journal recorded her experiences as a Jewish refugee living with an English family during the months preceding the German annexation of the Sudetenland and Austria's capitulation to the Nazis. For homesick, bewildered Trudl, the impressions of the months spent waiting for her parents were a blend of childlike fears and loneliness as she attempted to counter the teasing of the English children with whom she lived by summoning up imaginary magical powers for an heirloom emerald ring her parents had given her. Jenny is compelled to read beyond the ominous warning that the emerald has *"eevil powers"* and is fascinated by the possibilities of exploring further that long-forgotten part of Aunt Trudl's life; but she is ashamed to confess that she has read the copybook. Piecing together the clues leading to the resolution of the mystery is the key element in a suspenseful, contemporary story which explores in childlike terms the unity of past and present as well as the notion of evil—real or imagined.

Susan Terris

SOURCE: A review of *A Certain Magic,* in *New York Times Book Review,* September 26, 1976, p. 14.

Although the past few years have produced a number of fine novels about the young Anne Franks who survived the horrors of World War II—such as Johanna Reiss's *The Upstairs Room,* Judith Kerr's *When Hitler Stole Pink Rabbit* and Marilyn Sachs's *A Pocket Full of Seeds*— Doris Orgel's new book approaches memories of this bitter era from a different angle. Here it is the contemporary, American-born niece of an Austrian Jewish refugee girl. Jenny Ehrenteil, who uses an accidentally discovered (and secretly read) journal of 1938: to learn about the long-ago but still partially unresolved sufferings of her beloved Aunt Trudl.

Like many refugees from that period Trudl, as she became Americanized, locked those old memories inside herself. It is Jenny who succeeds in beginning to release them when she uses a vacation trip to England to search back into her aunt's past. Jenny finds her clues in Twiford, the small English town where Trudl lived temporarily after having been evacuated from Austria on one of the "children's trains" that took youngsters to safety in the last hectic months when Jews were still able to flee from Hitler and the Nazis. The clues, such as an antique doll that has swallowed an emerald with "evil powers," lead to an emotional reunion in New York where Jenny and Trudl—each a bit wiser—meet again.

In *A Certain Magic,* as in earlier Orgel works, the subject matter tends to be sentimentalized and the plot depends rather heavily on superstition and on not-quite-credible coincidences. However, for anyone willing to suspend disbelief, the book does have strong, sympathetic characters who make the reader care—and sometimes cry too.

Mrs. John Gray

SOURCE: A review of *A Certain Magic,* in *Best Sellers,* Vol. 36, No. 8, November, 1976, p. 271.

Vicarious living holds a fascination for young and old, and a special charm for the shy reader who can come alive disguised as someone else. The book's heroine, eleven-year-old Jenny, discovers her aunt's old copybook and reads herself back to the days of child-evacuation from Nazi Germany to safer England.

A string of coincidences and incredibly indulgent parents let Jenny return to the very town where Aunt Trudl had lived and to the people with whom she was staying. Jenny sets old grudges straight. A family heirloom, an emerald ring, seemed to have some magical powers. Trudl, in fear

and desperation, had hid the ring in a doll. After all this time, the doll is relocated, Jenny solves the "where-abouts" mystery, returns the ring to Aunt Trudl, and all ends well!

Please don't read Miss Orgel's book for historical information, personality revelations, or excitement; they're absent. Don't look for romance, humor, or jolting action either. Then, what? *Involvement,* relating to a favorite relative or friend, putting yourself in someone else's shoes, is the only story offered. Deceivingly relaxed, the theme probes deeply, yielding a good reading selection for the 10-14 year-old girl.

MERRY MERRY FIBRUARY (1977)

Kirkus Reviews

SOURCE: A review of *Merry Merry FIBruary,* in *Kirkus Reviews,* Vol. XLV, No. 17, September 1, 1977, p. 929.

Orgel's little pun hardly seems capable of supporting 30 four-line verses consisting of nonsensical untruths about what happened during the silly month of February—and indeed, with divisions into weeks and pictured calendars in between, the extended gimmick does show occasional signs of wearing thin. But the bouncing silliness of the rhymes doesn't lag, whether it's in the form of backwards-day humor ("Every Fibruary Zoo Day, / All the animals must wear / Shoes and socks and pants and dresses— / You and me, though, we go bare"), violations of the laws of nature (or of adage: "In dromedary Fibruary, / Though we heard a camel call, / 'This needle's eye is far too narrow,' / He got through it—hump and all!"), or just more puns (as when the leopard changes his spots to pussy willows and tiger lilies). You have to see [Arnold] Lobel's camel—and in fact the whole performance gets a saving boost from his quietly clever accompaniment.

Publishers Weekly

SOURCE: A review of *Merry Merry FIBruary,* in *Publishers Weekly,* Vol. 212, No. 13, September 26, 1977, p. 137.

Orgel has had as much fun as her little readers are bound to, making up impossibilities to go with the nonmonth, FIBruary. The oddities are all delivered in energetic verses: "In FIBruary, old MacDonald / Had an egg called Speckled Jen. / Ee-Ii-yO—it laid a little / Hen upon hen upon hen." Other rhymes sing of the leopard who changes his spots, Uncle Harry who grows down to babyhood, a canary who sings "Aida" at the Met, etc. [Arnold] Lobel's fanciful paintings are perfectly in tune with all the nonsense.

Barbara Elleman

SOURCE: A review of *Merry Merry FIBruary,* in *Booklist,* Vol. 74, No. 4, October 15, 1977, pp. 379-80.

"In the month of FIBruary, / Fairest month in all the year,

/ Streets are paved with peanut brittle, / Rainbows bend from ear to ear"—and from here on it's delightful nonsense as Orgel liltingly introduces readers to a newly concocted month for the year. Twenty-eight verses, one for each day—referred to varyingly as "Toothday," "Wind's Day," and "Thirstday"—relate occurrences such as babies delivered via rockets, mountains made of ice cream, a camel sliding through a needle's eye, a centipede with only 99 galoshes, a paisley-colored leopard, and a zoo where animals must wear clothing. [Arnold] Lobel expands the humor with illustrations that are rich in hue and subtle in tone. At the end of each week, a calendar recaps the days with a distinctive motif from each verse. A monthful of silly patter.

Jane Langton

SOURCE: A review of *Merry Merry FIBruary,* in *New York Times Book Review,* January 29, 1978, p. 26.

> On the first of FIBruary,
> Setting out from Hackensack,
> My Aunt Selma, in a seashell,
> Sailed to Samarkand and back.

I, for one, have always wanted to go to Samarkand, and I'll bet you have, too. The way to get there is certainly in Arnold Lobel's pink seashell, buoyantly tossing on a charming blue sea. There's a nice word for these pictures: winning. And I was also completely won over by Doris Orgel's delicious nonsense verses, as they romp through the month of FIBruary, telling funny white lies on every page.

> Every FIBruary Zoo Day,
> All the animals must wear
> Shoes and socks and pants and dresses—
> You and me, though, we go bare.

Even this unseemly overturning of convention is delicately handled by the impeccable Lobel. This is a swell Lobel and Orgel orgy.

Ethel L. Heins

SOURCE: A review of *Merry Merry FIBruary,* in *The Horn Book Magazine,* Vol. LIV, No. 1, February, 1978, p. 62.

With cunning and punning and plenty of outlandish humor in words and illustrations, the traditional calendar is augmented by an entirely original extra month—FIBruary. After a rhymed introduction twenty-eight verses are arranged in four weekly groups, each one separated by a calendar page which pictorially sums up the madcap proceedings of the previous seven days. The buffoonery is undeniably childlike: "Every FIBruary Zoo Day, / All the

animals must wear / Shoes and socks and pants and dresses—You and me, though, we go bare." Other quatrains deal with such incongruities as a centipede with only ninety-nine galoshes, a leopard with flowery spots, and an agile nonagenarian who turns cartwheels on his window sill. Soft-hued watercolor illustrations [by Arnold Lobel] expand the preposterous nonsense in every verse; author and artist—both nimble-witted—have produced a work in the tradition of Edward Lear.

THE DEVIL IN VIENNA (1978)

Matilda Kornfeld

SOURCE: A review of *The Devil in Vienna,* in *School Library Journal,* Vol. 25, No. 3, November, 1978, p. 66.

Told in diary form, this is another account of a young Jewish girl's brush with Nazism and eventual escape. With mounting suspense, Orgel skillfully juxtaposes the daily concerns of 13-year-old Inge Dornenwald with the Anschluss and the Nazis' increasingly harsh treatment of Viennese Jews. Throughout the horrifying events of that spring, Inge's longtime friendship with Lieselotte, whose father is a Nazi, surreptitiously continues and sustains them both, even though Lieselotte wears the uniform of the Jungmadel and Inge must go to a "Jew school." Eventually their friendship provides the means for the Dornenwalds' escape, for it is Lieselotte's uncle, Father Ludwig, who helps them cross the border to Yugoslavia. A variety of reactions—those of Inge's parents and their friends, her grandparents, servants, schoolmates, and teachers— are part of the story that Inge records, and they make the evil of the period comprehensible on a preadolescent level.

Kirkus Reviews

SOURCE: A review of *The Devil in Vienna,* in *Kirkus Reviews,* Vol. XLVI, No. 22, November 15, 1978, p. 1254.

Through the "secret journal" of a 13-year-old Jewish girl and letters from her Aryan best friend who has moved to Munich, Orgel manages a readable, revealing glimpse of the crucial months between November 1937 and March 1938 which marked the end of a free Austria and the arrival of ***The Devil*** (the one with a brush mustache) ***in Vienna.*** In rapid succession, Inge is expelled from her gymnasium, Vati's business is taken over by the Nazis, Muti gets fired from her publishing job, beloved Opa (Grandpa) Oscar emigrates to America, and a once-trusted family servant tries to blackmail the Dornenwalds (which precipitates their sudden and lucky exodus to Yugoslavia). Of all the traumas, however, the hardest for Inge is her separation from Lieselotte whose Papa is now a bigwig in the SA and who is not only forced to join the "Jungmadel" but also forbidden to "befriend a Jewess." The business about the star-crossed friends gets a bit thick at times what with code phone calls and secret rendezvous upon Lieselotte's return to Vienna. And Orgel's attention to this dual Jewish-Gentile perspective is sometimes at the expense of the action: too often key scenes are not seen but reported (even Inge's sneak visit to Lieselotte's priest-uncle is barely mentioned although it ultimately provides the avenue for the Dornenwalds' escape). Still, there is an affecting sense of authenticity to this diary, and Orgel's likable heroine, forced to do a lot of growing up fast, understands and relates events with disarming astuteness.

Virginia Haviland

SOURCE: A review of *The Devil in Vienna,* in *The Horn Book Magazine,* Vol. LV, No. 1, February, 1979, p. 70.

Two strong and tightly related elements direct the action of the autobiographical story. An unshakable friendship exists between Jewish Inge, who reports the story in her journal, and Catholic Lieselotte, daughter of a Nazi officer. The account begins in 1938 with a graphic documentary picture of the intrusion of Nazism into Vienna and of the following years of harassment and brutality. The girls' loyalty survived many obstacles, the greatest of which was their separation when Lieselotte had to move to Munich. Her regularly written letters came to Inge only after the war was over. In a naturally exuberant, girlish style Inge describes the little celebrations of her happy home life as well as her fears and losses; and with quotations from songs she pictures the cruel fervor of the Anschluss. There is also a moving revelation of the compassion of Lieselotte's priest, who fabricated birth and baptismal dates for the visas of Jews.

Maggie Lewis

SOURCE: Childhood's End," in *The Christian Science Monitor,* No. 137, June 11, 1979, p. B4.

The Devil in Vienna is the story of a best-friendship between two girls told during their 13th year, mostly through the journal of Inge Dornenwald and sometimes by letters from Lieselotte Vesseley. Their 13th year happens to be the year Austria is annexed to Germany by Hitler, Inge happens to be Jewish, and Lieselotte is Catholic, the daughter of a Nazi soldier.

Doris Orgel, drawing from her own experiences as a Jewish girl in Austria at the time, portrays the historical events compellingly but gives equal time to other important aspects of being 13 and best friends. Even as things take terrifying turns—a plebiscite to decide if Austria should remain independent or be annexed to Germany is cancelled, Inge's father's business is taken over by the Nazis, Lieselotte is beaten by her father for writing to Inge—the girls stay themselves, refreshingly smart-alecky.

About National Socialist Ideology, which Lieselotte must take in school when her family moves to Germany, she writes to Inge: "It's about the force of history and the invisible bonds that unite all Germans through Hitler and the destiny of the Aryan race—stuff which I already have up to here."

Inge is also discerning but is the more naïve of the two. For a while she has a daydream that Hitler will meet her and be so charmed that he'll change his mind about the Jews. Her father is only slightly more realistic. He puts off getting papers for the family to leave the country with a carelessness that becomes agonizing as Hitler moves in. Orgel tells only a few of the indignities Inge's parents and friends must suffer, but they give the reader a feeling of the menace growing all around them. By the time the Dornenwalds finally plan their escape, there is great suspense.

What is most compelling is Orgel's portrait of a friendship which survives great odds. Inge's father tells her that if she goes on seeing Lieselotte her father will have the Dornenwalds arrested. But they go on. An account of one of history's blackest hours is told in Inge's wisecracking eighth grade style, and it works. It's lit by the chatty, confidential tone of two 13-year-olds somehow having a good time. Far from being frivolous, it seems heroic that the girls go to an amusement park on the eve of the Dornenwalds' departure, take all the rides, and let balloons go from the top of the Ferris wheel, hanging onto their childhood until the last minute.

The Devil in Vienna won the 36th annual Children's Book Award for "dealing honestly with problems that confront young people today." I assume the problem it deals with in a prize-winning manner is racial prejudice. There is an episode at the beginning where a local derelict exposes himself to Inge. Neither graphic nor particularly threatening, the passage is annoying because it seems to have been tacked on in an effort to be relevant.

Colin Richmond

SOURCE: "In Search of the Authentic," in *Times Literary Supplement,* No. 4769, September 2, 1994, p. 8.

All writing ought to subvert repose; to stumble disoriented and disquietened from the library should be every reader's ambition. Historical novels tend to be reassuring where science fiction is not: 1349 has happened; 2001 is coming soon. It is true that all novels are historical because they deal with last year not this year, yesterday not today, and it is equally the case that getting the "personal life of the spirit" into fiction is the obsession of every novelist. To do so is most difficult for the historical novelist. But is it so difficult that it is impossible? Not quite. Not if it is set in the recent, culturally accessible past and has personal recollection at its narrative core. Because, as Proust also taught us, the recollections of childhood are the most powerful, a historical novel based on them may be compelling. Such is the case with Doris Orgel's *The Devil in Vienna,* set in that city in 1938. It is an episodic account of the friendship of two adolescents, Inge, who is Jewish, and Lieselotte, who has a Nazi father, and is based on the author's own experience. Readers are entertained and instructed, and perhaps enraged. We are far from romance, far from fantasy; for we are made to confront a historical truth, that those intent on "making history" are the barbarians and they stalk the past, the present and the future.

RISKING LOVE (1984)

Marilyn Kaye

SOURCE: A review of *Risking Love,* in *New York Times Book Review,* October 14, 1984, p. 16.

Dinah Moskowitz does not want to be sitting in a psychiatrist's office at 4:30 on an April afternoon. She's only there because she promised her father she'd get a professional opinion regarding a plan she has. She wants to take a year off when she completes her freshman year at Barnard College and spend that year in the Florida Everglades with her boyfriend, Gray, who's going to be a park ranger.

She faces the elderly, female Dr. Schneck reluctantly, even cynically. ("The smile seems friendly. As well it should, at sixty-five dollars for fifty minutes. How much does that come to per smile?")

But there's more to Dinah Moskowitz than meets the eye, and there's more on her mind than she cares to admit She claims, "It's not that complicated!" But, of course, it is. Slowly, gently, Dr. Schneck asks the questions enabling Dinah to cull from her memory the moments that shed light on her current state of mind. They go back to her parents' divorce, when she was 10, at which time Dinah was offered the choice of which parent she would live with. In the course of the therapy, the submerged guilts associated with her decision rise to the surface. She also begins to realize how manipulated she felt and she confronts some questions: did she reject her mother, or did her mother, in some subtle way, reject her? Does the love of one person demand the abandonment of another? And how is her deeply rooted confusion affecting her relationship with Gray? Is she capable of loving without the fear of losing?

Dinah's condition is not particularly neurotic, nor is she in desperate need of psychiatric care. But therapy helps her to embrace feelings, to move toward a level of emotional comfort she might not have achieved otherwise. The reader is placed in a remarkable position. The first-person, present-tense narrative by Dinah lends an immediacy and intimacy that pull the reader inside her feelings, while at the same time the reader listens, with the doctor, to the gradual uncovering of a mind.

But the story is not so deeply mired in the psychological that it neglects the lighter side of Dinah's life. Here is all the breath-taking euphoria of a new, young love, with its romance, uncertainties, awkward sexual gropings and humor. And as in all her relationships—with parents, with friends—Dinah encounters the absurdities, the demands and the rewards that puzzle her, that keep her from feeling comfortable with herself.

Doris Orgel is an accomplished writer. *Risking Love* is no paean to the wonders of therapy, nor is the therapist portrayed as a miracle worker. It's a warm, honest expression of one person's experiences, within which are recognizable elements common to therapies—Dinah's conversations, with irrelevancies wrapped around insights; her relationship with Dr. Schneck, moving from hostility to dependency to the ultimate pain of separation; and always, the questions, which lead to no sudden dramatic revelations or fast-acting panacea, only to the beginning of understanding.

Rita S. Padden

SOURCE: A review of *Risking Love,* in *School Library Journal,* Vol. 31, No. 4, December, 1984, p. 93.

Dinah Moskowitz, a Barnard freshman, meets Gray Dawson, a college senior and biology major. Their first rendezvous at a Chock Full o' Nuts, where Gray brings her a pale pink rose, leads to romance and Dinah's first (and at first disappointing) sexual relationship. When Dinah reveals her plans to leave college at the end of the year to follow Gray to Florida, her father suggests therapy. Throughout the therapy sessions with Dr. Schneck, which comprise the major portion of the story, readers see into Dinah's psyche: her guilt, disappointments, insecurities and fears. Dinah's rambling dialogue and the techniques used in the psychotherapy sessions ring true, but readers will become impatient with some of the pretentious and verbose conversations throughout the book. "In your psychiatric training, did you have a course on how to look inscrutable in perpetuity?" The conclusion is extended beyond effectiveness, with an ending weakened by coincidence and mawkishness. Gray arrives from Florida while Dinah is again sitting in Chock Full o' Nuts and presents her with a deep red rose. Orgel has succeeded with a younger audience in a way she does not here.

Zena Sutherland

SOURCE: A review of *Risking Love,* in *Bulletin of the Center for Children's Books,* February, 1985, p. 114.

Dinah, eighteen, tells her story almost entirely through the therapy sessions she's agreed to just to pacify her father, who worries about her decision to leave Barnard in order to be with Gray, the man she loves. Dinah feels that she's perfectly happy and knows her own mind, but as her sessions with Dr. Schneck go on, Dinah discovers her fears about losing love, fears engendered by her parents' divorce years ago. Orgel creates the atmosphere of the consulting room: the initial resentment, the growth of trust, the increasing ability to face oneself and maintain perspective. Characters and relationships are strong, and the story has good pace and momentum. Moving and positive, this is an impressive novel.

Nancy C. Hammond

SOURCE: A review of *Risking Love*, in *The Horn Book Magazine,* Vol. LXI, No. 2, March-April, 1985, p. 187.

As a concession to her father, Dinah Moskowitz, a Barnard college freshman, agrees to talk with a psychiatrist about her decision to take a year off from school and accompany her lover, a handsome senior, on his job in the Everglades. While asserting, "'We need to be together,'" to Dr. Schenk, Dinah hears an inner voice spontaneously cry, "If I'm not with him, I lose him!" With the therapist's support, Dinah begins to listen to herself and to admit she gets "'pretty blue. Even when things are going fine. Especially then.'" Picking her way through the past, she retraces her exultant romance and her disappointment with sex; until, focusing on the period of her parents' divorce when she was ten, she recognizes that divorce "'lets in the idea that love stops. Not just the idea, the reality.'" But she also discovers that to fearfully deny love is even costlier. The epilogue discloses her subsequent decisions. Although anchored by the prologue and epilogue, the story is told chiefly through the psychiatric sessions; yet it bears a strong sense of immediacy. Weaving seamlessly between past and present, Dinah's first-person narrative eschews psychological jargon and still effectively reveals the common issues in a therapeutic relationship. The pair are standard romantic characters; the final scene is unnecessary and slick; but the girl comes alive through her psychological vulnerability.

Carole A. Barham

SOURCE: A review of *Risking Love*, in *Voice of Youth Advocates,* Vol. 8, No. 3, August, 1985, p. 188.

When 18-year-old Dinah Moskowitz announces her decision to leave college to follow boyfriend Gray Dawson to Florida, her father asks her to see a psychiatrist. For most of the novel, we sit in with Dinah during her therapy sessions with Dr. Schneck as Dinah reveals her guilts, insecurities, hurts, and fears. Although Dinah chose to live with her father after her parents' divorce, she harbors much resentment and anger toward her mother. Also revealed during the sessions is her deepening relationship with Gray; the romance which eventually leads to first sexual experiences, and Dinah's confrontation with her past and the beginnings of her journey into the future. At the end of the therapy, Dinah understands that she must accept the risks and possible consequences of her decisions, and *we* understand that she has done a lot of growing up—and that the future is full of hope.

An insightful, realistic, and thoroughly believable story, it is weakened somewhat by an ending that is a bit too pat and that comes together a little too quickly. However, YAs will be held by the sympathetic and well-drawn characters and the convincing honesty of Orgel's latest.

MY WAR WITH MRS. GALLOWAY (1985)

Zena Sutherland

SOURCE: A review of *My War with Mrs. Galloway,* in *Bulletin of the Center for Children's Books,* Vol. 38, No. 8, April, 1985, pp. 153-54.

Rebecca, the narrator, is an only child whose mother is a doctor, whose father lives on the opposite side of the country, whose current enemy is Mrs. Galloway, the babysitter. Rebecca's complaints: Mrs. G. is unkind to the family cat, she scolds when creative play results in a messy room, and—worst of all—she won't let Rebecca crawl under the bed to watch the cat having her kittens. What changes Rebecca's mind is the discovery that Mrs. G. is protecting the cat (Mom agrees that the animal is best left alone) and that she really is understanding, just not as infinitely tolerant as a child would prefer her to be. This is a nice vignette exploring a change in relationships, but it's slight as a book; the light humor and controlled writing make pleasant reading, but the plot and its development may leave readers feeling unsatisfied.

Kirkus Reviews

SOURCE: A review of *My War with Mrs. Galloway,* in *Kirkus Reviews,* May 15, 1985, p. J-35.

There will probably be takers for Orgel's slight, soft story of an eight-year-old's rapprochement with her sitter, but it is one of the author's lesser, more facile efforts.

Rebecca, who tells her own story, is one of those glibly affectionate fictional children who dotes on "our private time" with her M.D. ("Mom Doc") mother and responds on the phone to her divorced Dad's "I miss you, Becky-Boo" with "Ditto, ditto, Dad-O!" She is destined to cozy up to Mrs. Galloway as well, but first they seem, in Rebecca's words, to be "fighting a war."

Rebecca hoards complaints against the sitter, and she is especially outraged by what she views as Mrs. Galloway's rough handling of Whiskers the cat. But when Rebecca starts worrying about the disposal of Whiskers' expected kittens, it is all too predictably clear that Mrs. Galloway will prove a cat lover and take one. En route to this end, the Rebecca-Galloway relationship goes through requisite ups and downs, culminating in a showdown during the kittens' birth—when it is Mrs. Galloway who protects Whiskers from Rebecca's too-close curiosity.

Orgel fills out the Rebecca-Galloway story with some amusing scenes of Rebecca and her friend Michael at play. These help make the story a workmanlike model of its kind, but it never breaks that mold.

Charlotte W. Draper

SOURCE: A review of *My War with Mrs. Galloway,* in

The Horn Book Magazine, Vol. LXI, No. 3, May-June, 1985, pp. 312-13.

Becca, almost eight years old, declares war on her new sitter from the moment she whisks Becca's cat off the top of the refrigerator. Mrs. Galloway is stricter than Becca's previous sitters, and she insinuates herself into the all-too-brief private time Becca shares with her mother, a busy physician. But Mrs. Galloway's attitude toward cats is particularly galling to Becca, especially now that Whiskers is expecting kittens. Becca is surprised, however, when the older woman seems to know all about how cats give birth and is prepared to protect Whiskers from noise and confusion—even from Becca herself. Becca's appreciation of Mrs. Galloway's ministrations eases the girl's resentment. And when the sitter agrees to take one of the kittens, the armistice yields to peace. In Becca, Orgel has created another unmistakably contemporary child. Though the first-person account is told with economy, a picture emerges of the concerns and pastimes of an urban, middle-class child of divorce. Becca's imaginative games include "Subway" and "Divorce." Yet her identification with Whiskers and her concern about Whiskers' homeless kittens provide themes which link Becca's experience to those of generations of children.

Louise L. Sherman

SOURCE: A review of *My War with Mrs. Galloway,* in *School Library Journal,* September, 1985, p. 138.

Becca has resented Mrs. Galloway, the new housekeeper/babysitter, from the moment she first entered the apartment and brushed Becca's cat Whiskers off the refrigerator top. The "war," however, is more of a border skirmish. After a few mild encounters—Becca uses Mrs. Galloway's galoshes as flotation devices, draws an uncomplimentary picture of her and attempts to make her disappear with vanishing cream—the two become sufficiently friendly for Becca to give her one of Whisker's three kittens. The story hovers between humor and poignancy but never really achieves either. Although the enmity a child may feel for a caretaker is a subject which is timely, this story is too slight to really deal with this problem. Becca, the narrator, is a seven year old who sounds like she is nine or ten. The timely topic, catchy title and jacket art, brevity, large print and illustrations may win this book an audience, but the story will not live up to expectations.

GODFATHER CAT AND MOUSIE (retold and translated by Orgel from the story by Jakob and Wilhelm Grimm, 1986)

Ilene Cooper

SOURCE: A review of *Godfather Cat and Mousie,* in *Booklist,* Vol. 82, No. 14, March 15, 1986, p. 1086.

Orgel offers a new version of this Grimm story about the cat and mouse who decide to set up housekeeping. Here, the cat is a dignified fellow in top hat, dashing scarf, and cloak, while the mouse is an innocent female. As in the original tale, they decide to buy a pot of cream and hide it away until winter when food is scarce. But Cat cannot restrain himself and goes back to the stash three times until finally the cream is gone. When Mousie, who's had her vague suspicions, finally says it's time to drink the cream, she gets a rude surprise. Cat tells her it's gone, and according to the Grimm version (repeated here), he is ready to make her his next meal. Orgel also provides a happier alternative ending in which the mouse runs into a hole and feasts with her family, much to the cat's frustration. The neatly bordered watercolors [by Ann Schweninger] have a soft, appealing glow to them. The depiction of the mouse as a trusting, naive female seems somewhat sexist even if the female is a rodent.

Liza Bliss

SOURCE: A review of *Godfather Cat and Mousie,* in *School Library Journal,* Vol. 32, No. 9, May, 1986, p. 83.

A retelling of the Grimm Brothers' tale, in which cat and mouse save some food for the winter months ahead. Before those months arrive, the cat periodically visits the church where they hid their food and eats it. Orgel has lessened the harshness of the Grimm's style. She presents their ending, in which the cat eats the mouse after her discovery of his scam, as an opinion held by some people. "But here's what *I* say happened, and maybe you'll agree": Mousie escapes and rejoins her large, loving family outside the cat's reach. Another difference between the Grimm and Orgel outlooks is reflected in **Godfather Cat's** implication that the cat is the bad guy and the mouse, the good guy: Whereas the Grimms accept the relationship as "the way of the world" and state no judgment, Orgel hints at a little more malice on the cat's part, even adding a coda suggesting that the cat could have died of shame. Illustrations [by Ann Schweninger] in soft watercolor tones and pencil, are pleasant. Like the story, they have an overall look of prettiness and innocence, but contain something beneath the surface—often found in the cat's eyes—which hints at danger. Tone of retelling and illustrations are sufficiently different from those in Ruth Hurlimann's *Cat and Mouse Who Shared a House* (1974) that the two books could supplement each other.

Publishers Weekly

SOURCE: A review of *Godfather Cat and Mousie,* in *Publishers Weekly,* Vol. 229, No. 22, May 30, 1986, p. 65.

A large gray gentleman cat meets a lady mouse; the unlikely pair take up residence together in the cat's elegant townhouse. So they won't go hungry in winter months, the two purchase a pot of cream and hide it beneath the church altar. When the cupboards are empty, the sly feline slips away to indulge in the cream, telling mouse he must visit a succession of curiously named godchildren: Topoff, Halfup and Allup. Poor mouse becomes so famished that she nibbles at the wall. When cat returns with a full belly, mouse accuses him of deceit. The author has created an unexpected choice of endings, giving the traditional finish and then a new twist to this Brothers Grimm tale.

Bulletin of the Center for Children's Books

SOURCE: A review of *Godfather Cat and Mousie,* in *Bulletin of the Center for Children's Books,* Vol. 39, No. 10, June, 1986, p. 185.

This has always been a troubling tale, with its stark warning of what happens to gullible mice who are foolish enough to set up housekeeping with a cat. However, that's its power as well. Orgel has offered an alternative to the mouse's being peremptorilly gobbled up, a sort of choose-your-own-ending ("*some* people say . . . " but "*I* say . . . "). Mousie escapes through a hole she has gnawed in hunger to find a new home with her rodent relatives, and the cat is left forever watching shamefaced beside that mousehole. To this end, the story itself has been slightly altered to foreshadow the escape, but otherwise, the abridgment does maintain close ties to the Grimms' version. [Ann] Schweninger's earthtone colors are subtly blended with simply defined linework, graceful shapes, and artfully framed compositions. There's a real world established in this art, serene on the surface, slightly menacing underneath, but ultimately orderly. A carefully—but nonetheless strategically—reshaped version, more attractive to most parents, less forceful as folklore.

WHISKERS, ONCE AND ALWAYS (1986)

Kirkus Reviews

SOURCE: A review of *Whiskers, Once and Always,* in *Kirkus Reviews,* Vol. LIV, No. 18, September 15, 1986, p. 1451.

This brief story is packed with feelings and thoughts familiar to children who have experienced the death of a cherished pet.

Rebecca Suslow, heroine of *My War with Mrs. Galloway,* returns to tell what happens when her cat Whiskers falls and is fatally injured. Becca's mother, Dr. Suslow, helps make Whiskers comfortable, since the cat seems only to have hurt her leg, but by the next evening Whiskers is going into shock. Rushed to the vet, she dies of internal injuries. Afterward, Becca feels not only sad but angry and confused. She punches Jason, a boy who asks her a touchy question, and when she won't explain why, she is sent to the principal to tell him her story. Mr. Bruzzo helps Becca to understand her feelings, paving the way toward acceptance of Whiskers' death.

This touching, well-plotted story has two flaws. Despite Dr. Suslow's excuse, it is unbelievable that Whiskers is not taken to the vet sooner. And the implications of Jason's remark and Mr. Bruzzo's "between-the-lines" expla-

nation of Becca's reaction to it will escape most young readers. Nevertheless, they will sympathize with Becca and feel better when she comes to terms with the death and is able to create a very personal memorial to Whiskers.

Betsy Hearne

SOURCE: A review of *Whiskers, Once and Always,* in *Bulletin of the Center for Children's Books,* Vol. 40, No. 2, October, 1986, p. 34.

In a sequel to Orgel's *My War with Mrs. Galloway,* Becky has to deal with the death of Whiskers, her pet cat, and the anger and guilt she feels afterwards. It doesn't help that her mother is dating a veterinarian, whom Becky resents for intruding and for not saving her cat's life. She misses her own father, and it is only the art supplies he sends her, along with a talk from a supportive school principal, that enables her to resolve her conflicts in a picture she draws for herself and her mother. The plot is well focused without being insistent, the writing is easy-going, the characters well drawn. With the built-in animal appeal, this is a real find for "in-between" readers just ready for a first novel.

Ginny McKee

SOURCE: A review of *Whiskers, Once and Always,* in *School Library Journal,* December, 1986, p. 107.

In this sequel to *My War with Mrs. Galloway* (1985), Orgel looks at Becky's relationship with her pet cat and her feelings when Whiskers dies after a fall. Told in flashback after an opening description of Becky's punching Jason in the nose when he interrupts a conversation about the cat's death, the story acknowledges Becky's anger. Becky's hostility is partially directed toward her mother's boyfriend Pete, a vet who could not heal her beloved cat. It is the sensitive principal who is able to get Becky to discuss her true feelings. Orgel is a skillful writer, and this story moves quickly. Descriptions create mental pictures that make the characters come alive.

Karen Jameyson

SOURCE: A review of *Whiskers, Once and Always,* in *The Horn Book Magazine,* Vol. LXIII, No. 1, January-February, 1987, pp. 56-7.

Becky Suslow, who determinedly fought one battle in *My War with Mrs. Galloway,* now finds herself wrestling with a new set of difficulties, triggered by the death of a cherished cat. Struggling with her grief, Becky misbehaves at school, pulls away from her mother, and bitterly blames her mother's boyfriend—the vet who could not save Whiskers—for the animal's death. How Becky comes to terms with her sadness and begins to channel her reactions is the focus of a sensitive, quiet book. While the story is not extraordinary, the author's handling of the subject for young intermediate readers is quite perceptive. Solid, believable characters and well-drawn relationships in combination with attractive full-page pencil illustrations [by Carol Newsom] make the book one that will serve as a comfortable stepping stone for readers just advancing to chapter books.

📖 *MIDNIGHT SOUP AND A WITCH'S HAT* (1987)

Zena Sutherland

SOURCE: A review of *Midnight Soup and a Witch's Hat,* in *Bulletin of the Center for Children's Books,* Vol. 40, No. 11, July-August, 1987, p. 216.

In a third story about Becky Suslow, she is thrilled when her father (divorced) funds a trip from Brooklyn to Portland, Oregon. Thrilled by the travel and by the prospect of a week with Dad, Becky is taken aback when she realizes that the six-year-old daughter of Dad's resident lover (also divorced, also time-sharing an only child) is ensconced. This is a well-written story about adaptability and acceptance, as Becky adjusts to sharing her Dad's time and even grows to like pesty little Hope as she understands her problems. Orgel has a light touch and a smooth narrative flow in her writing, and her story is economically structured; the weaknesses of the book are the uneven pace and the unflagging precocity of Hope.

Kirkus Reviews

SOURCE: A review of *Midnight Soup and a Witch's Hat,* in *Kirkus Reviews,* August 15, 1987, p. 1243.

A third book about Becky Suslow, eight, last seen in *Whiskers, Once and Always* (1986); this time she travels across the country for a week-long visit to her artist father at his new home in Oregon.

The many adults in Becky's life are all loving and comfortingly predictable. Mom sends Becky off cheerfully; the reunion with Dad is warm, but marred by the discovery that his new friend, Rosellen, lives in—and he hadn't wanted to tell Becky that over the phone. Still, Rosellen is nice, and it doesn't take Becky long to make friends with the obstreperous dog. Rosellen's daughter, Hope (six), is more of a problem. Unexpectedly present because her new stepmother is in labor with a dangerously premature baby, she proves to be a total pest; moreover, Becky's Dad has amused her by cooking "midnight soup," which Becky thinks of as her own private shared experience with him. But as the week goes on, Becky does get some quality time with Dad, and as she comes to understand Hope's worries she is well on the way to making friends with her.

For young readers ready for chapter books, these make a fine alternative to the Haywoods: Orgel presents realistic, contemporary concerns and experiences with understanding, humor, and affection.

Katharine Bruner

SOURCE: A review of *Midnight Soup and a Witch's Hat,* in *School Library Journal,* October, 1987, p. 128.

Becky Suslow, who appeared in *My War with Mrs. Galloway* (1985) and *Whiskers, Once and Always* (1986), is now nearly nine and at long last going on a visit from Brooklyn to her Dad's home in Oregon. She knows his friend, Rosellen, lives with him, but no one has told her that Rosellen's six-year-old daughter Hope is there also. Becky's dreams of having her adored Dad all to herself are dashed when Hope firmly plants herself between them and succeeds in upsetting everything. In exasperation, Becky tells her off. Then she begins to feel sorry for her—Hope too has unfulfilled dreams and divorced parents. Becky's persistence in making amends brings about the realization of Hope's secret wish that Becky will be her friend. The story is narrated by Becky in an intelligent third grader's style. She handles the commonplace circumstances of split families with a blend of understanding, confusion, and acceptance. The plot's resolution, aided by demonstrably caring adults, should leave readers satisfied and hopeful.

Publishers Weekly

SOURCE: A review of *Midnight Soup and a Witch's Hat,* in *Publishers Weekly,* November 13, 1987, p. 71.

Becky, the inquisitive, artistic heroine of *My War with Mrs. Galloway* and *Whiskers, Once and Always,* is still involved in the aftermath of her parents' divorce. Her father sends airplane tickets to her so she can visit him in Oregon. Becky has braced herself to meet Rosellen, her father's live-in girlfriend, but she isn't prepared for Hope, Rosellen's daughter, who is staying with them temporarily. Hope is younger and clamors for attention, usurping time Becky would like to spend alone with her father. She even knows about Midnight Soup, which Becky considers a family secret. Orgel subtly observes the small but significant pressures that are an integral part of such families as Becky's. The previous two books centered on more involving problems, but this one has its own strengths: a gently probing style and Becky's spirited methods for working out things herself.

Phillis Wilson

SOURCE: A review of *Midnight Soup and a Witch's Hat,* in *Booklist,* Vol. 84, No. 6, November 15, 1987, p. 572.

Becky Suslow flies from Brooklyn to Portland, Oregon, for a long-promised visit with her dad. Her parents are divorced, and in an economic flip-flop her mother is a doctor and her dad, an artist, is in much more of a financial crunch. Becky discovers that Dad's live-in girlfriend and her six-year-old daughter, Hope, are also there. With a sibling relationship suddenly thrust upon her, Becky's plans for lots of time alone with Dad go awry. In a classic tug-of-war Hope vies for Mr. Suslow's attention while trying in vain to win acceptance from Becky. Amid the tribulations of dealing with the pesky Hope, Becky finds out that Hope was allowed to make the cherished midnight soup recipe with Dad, a major intrusion into Becky's personal territory. However, Dad is unusually good at picking up the vibes of Becky's emotional pain, and their talks give Becky the insight she seeks. The domino effect of today's blended families becomes apparent when Becky's father's live-in girlfriend's daughter's stepmom's new baby becomes ill, and one and all are concerned. While Orgel's depiction of Dad is almost too good to be true, he comes through with strength in helping Becky deal with some very real eight-year-old anger and emotion. An engaging sequel to Orgel's two earlier books about Becky, most recently *Whiskers, Once and Always.*

STARRING BECKY SUSLOW (1989)

Kirkus Reviews

SOURCE: A review of *Starring Becky Suslow,* in *Kirkus Reviews,* Vol. LVII, No. 20, October 15, 1989, p. 1533.

Fans of the four earlier books about Becky will be delighted with this sequel in which she and her best friends, Kyra and Mel, make a quartet with the addition of Rainbow Rothstein—a self-assured newcomer to their fourth grade in Brooklyn's Park Slope, who has appeared in several commercials and whose mother is a talent scout.

Like a comfortable visit with old friends, this starts with a roundup of news. The pace quickens when Mrs. Rothstein wants Becky—who hopes to be an artist like her dad—to audition for a crayon commercial. The first audition, when the crayons are make-believe, is a success, but it leaves Becky out of sorts with her old friends. The callback is a disaster—Becky fails to disguise her disgust with the shoddy project she's trying to demonstrate—but its aftermath is a reconciliation that is far more important to Becky than her disappointment.

As before, Orgel has a sure grasp of Becky's concerns, not only her friendships but her place in a family in which the parents are amiably divorced; her glimpse of the vicissitudes of the talent market is also fair and realistic. A pleasant story, sure to engage its audience.

Carrol McCarthy

SOURCE: A review of *Starring Becky Suslow,* in *School Library Journal,* Vol. 35, No. 16, December, 1989, p. 102.

Becky Suslow and her two best friends, Kyra and Melanie, are happily anticipating entering fourth grade. Through Rainbow Rothstein, a new student in their class, Becky

has a chance to audition for a TV commercial; this opportunity puts a strain on the relationship between Becky, Kyra, and Melanie. In the end the girls reaffirm their special friendship, and agree to include Rainbow as a friend. The background glamour of TV will appeal to upper-elementary age girls, but the young age of the characters may limit the range of readers. Each girl is developed as an individual, with a unique personality, problems, and expectations. The main adult characters are also shown in a human way: Becky's mother is impatient but caring; the housekeeper loves Becky and extends her help, despite a certain callousness on Becky's part. The dialogue is simplistic and choppy, but its uncomplicated conversational style may appeal to reluctant readers. The plot is somewhat splintered, with many side issues introduced but not developed—divorce, working parents, boy-girl relationships, etc. These unresolved problems reflect reality, but are intrusive because there are so many of them that briefly surface, and then just disappear. The relationship between the girls is the strength of this slight story.

Denise Wilms

SOURCE: A review of *Starring Becky Suslow,* in *Booklist,* Vol. 86, No. 8, December 15, 1989, pp. 834-35.

For Becky Suslow, having two best friends is great. She's proud of the way she, Kyra, and Melanie look out for each other, and when grumpy Mrs. Galloway, Becky's babysitter, says it won't last, Becky's retort is "That's baloney." But trouble quickly follows when glamorous Rainbow Rothstein arrives at school. She's friendly and nice, but when her mother, a talent agent, taps Becky for a commercial audition, Becky is unsure of how to handle her good fortune, and ruffled feelings result. Things work out for the best, and by the story's end, it's one for all and all for one once more—with everyone liking Rainbow to boot. Simply written, this story handles the dynamics between the girls convincingly. Characters are well drawn, and the story's point that three can be as good as two is well taken. A solid popular read for the lower end of the middle-grade spectrum.

CRACK IN THE HEART (1989)

Publishers Weekly

SOURCE: A review of *Crack in the Heart,* in *Publishers Weekly,* Vol. 236, No. 20, November 24, 1989, p. 73.

After her father's death, Zanna moves to New York City with her mother. There, Zanna slowly comes to terms with the loss of her father. A brief but vivid involvement with a glamorous older boy adds spice to Zanna's life. Unfortunately, the author was apparently not satisfied with creating a moving chronicle of the grieving process, and chose to tackle an additional, more fashionable issue: drug abuse. Grafted onto the main body of the novel and impossible to ignore, this unwieldy subplot drains the life and believability from the novel. The real story, Zanna's delicately constructed predicament, is lost in a tangled thicket of just-say-no hysteria. What's more, the inaccurate descriptions of intoxication and drug use detract from the author's authority and may alienate even the most naïve teen readers. A disappointing effort from an author whose excellent earlier novels (*The Devil in Vienna* and *Risking Love*) have led her audience to expect much more.

Hazel Rochman

SOURCE: A review of *Crack in the Heart,* in *Booklist,* Vol. 86, No. 10, January 15, 1990, p. 991.

There's far too much going on here for one little glossy YA paperback: high school senior Zanna copes with her father's death, her subsequent tension with her mother, and their move to New York City, where she's nearly ostracized at her fancy girls' prep school, makes some bad mistakes with drugs, and has a love affair with a teacher's son. Yet Orgel does manage to give her characters some ambiguity. The charismatic college boy who seduces Zanna is pretentious and inadequate, but he's also exciting and tender, and it hurts when he leaves. In love and friendship and in family relationships, Zanna finds that people do change and heal, though it takes a long time.

Rosemary Moran

SOURCE: A review of *Crack in the Heart,* in *Voice of Youth Advocates,* Vol. 13, No. 1, April, 1990, pp. 32-3.

When 17 year old Zanna Dobbs's father is killed in a traffic accident, Zanna and her mother move to New York City to start a new life. Mrs. Dobbs is the nurse at an exclusive school where Zanna will be a student. At the school, Zanna is miserable and makes few friends among the rich and spoiled girls who are students there. While babysitting a teacher's nine year old daughter, Zanna meets older son Jeff, a college student who's into music, creativity, inspiration and, it turns out, drugs. Zanna has a couple of drug-related experiences, as do some of her friends, but drugs never become a big problem for her.

This novel suffers from uneven character development, as some characters are very well developed and believable, and others are not. Zanna is sometimes mature and level-headed, but at other times is selfish and immature. Her mother, suffering the pain of recent widowhood, is withdrawn and uninvolved in Zanna's day-to-day life. Jeff is portrayed as intense, creative, and flighty. Coincidence plays a big part in the plot. The mysterious sax player Zanna sees on her first visit to the school turns out to be Jeff whom she meets later in the book. A pin she loses early on eventually turns up in the possession of a new friend whose brother found it in the car of one of his college friends, a boy Zanna had met once.

Orgel is a well-known author of YA books, and this one

is certainly acceptable. The blurb leads the reader to think this is about teens and drugs, but it's really more about a hurt and lonely teenage girl trying to adjust to a new life.

NOBODIES AND SOMEBODIES (1991)

Kirkus Reviews

SOURCE: A review of *Nobodies and Somebodies,* in *Kirkus Reviews,* Vol. LIX, No. 12, June 15, 1991, p. 792.

Suddenly finding herself in a new school at midyear because of her dad's transfer, Laura's hopes of making friends are thwarted by her new fifth grade's competing cliques. She's just getting to know nice Janet when she hurts Janet's feelings by courting the "Supes," a rich, talented, snobbish-seeming trio: Beth has famous parents, Liz dances, and Vero "used to swim with dolphins." When a second club forms around Janet, Laura finds herself excluded from both. Two events cause all the girls to reassess what's going on: a sensible teacher requires Janet and Beth to list their real similarities and differences; Vero's mother and stepfather, in all innocence, throw her a surprise swimming party—not realizing that a traumatic boating accident with Jencks, the perpetual-adolescent father with whom Vero lived until a few months ago, has left her terrified of her favorite sport.

Orgel, whose best-known book is *The Devil in Vienna* (1978), raises this above formula with her carefully selected incidents and perceptive characterizations. The alternated narrations of Laura, Janet, and Vero reveal that there are no villains here, just normal children—some with loving families and others who have effectively been neglected, some with new situations to contend with but all both fallible and trying to do the best they can. Easily read, but not simplistic; a satisfying, carefully crafted story.

Leone McDermott

SOURCE: A review of *Nobodies and Somebodies,* in *Booklist,* Vol. 87, No. 21, July, 1991, pp. 2045-46.

Orgel brings a new approach to the perennial subject of school-yard cliques. The "somebodies" in this case are the Supes, a trio of the best-dressed and richest girls at Ludcomb Middle School. Their struggle with the "nobodies" is chronicled from three different viewpoints. First, there's Laura, who's new in town, desperate for friends, and torn between her desire for the genuine friendship offered by Janet and her fruitless but powerful yearning to win acceptance into the clique. Janet, still hurting from the way the Supes used and rejected her, is another voice; despite their behavior, she feels bound by her promise to keep their secrets. Finally, there's Vero, who gained admission to the Supes by lying about her accomplishments and is fearful of being exposed. Eventually, the "nobodies" start their own clique, and then the skirmishes begin. Orgel is perceptive about the irrational power cliques possess and how family problems can lead to an increased need for peer approval. The triple narrative structure, though, may throw less able readers. When the narrative changes, the new speaker's name appears once at the top of the page and is easy to overlook; since all three narratives have a similar tone, one can lose track of who's talking. However, the school-yard power plays, manipulations, and crushing exclusions will be instantly recognizable to young readers.

Phyllis G. Sidorsky

SOURCE: A review of *Nobodies and Somebodies,* in *School Library Journal,* Vol. 37, No. 7, July, 1991, p. 74.

Arriving midterm at her new school, Laura is drawn to three girls who obviously are best friends and have formed an exclusive club. The story is told in succeeding chapters from the viewpoints of Laura; Janet, another excluded girl; and Vero, a recent arrival in town who has been accepted by the group because she seems to have the necessary attributes. In the end, all the problems are sorted out and both the nobodies and somebodies have an opportunity to join an open, environmentally sound club. The arrangement of the chapters is not entirely successful because the resulting flashbacks and overlapping versions create an untidy and somewhat confusing progression. Vero's account is almost a complete story in itself without the issue of clubs. While the book will find an audience, the unhappiness caused by cliques deserves a more serious treatment and a less contrived conclusion.

Roger Sutton

SOURCE: A review of *Nobodies and Somebodies,* in *Bulletin of the Center for Children's Books,* Vol. 44, No. 11, July-August, 1991, p. 270.

Liz is In. So is Beth, and so is Vero. Janet was In briefly, but now she's Out and so is the new girl, Laura. The "Supes," as Janet sarcastically refers to them, have the school's most exclusive club, whose dramas and downfalls are chronicled in turn by Janet, Vero, and Laura. The revolving narration is a little confusing: first, because the three girls sound too much alike; and second, because the ins-and-outs of secret clubs are just like that, thriving on their own perplexities. Despite some structural awkwardness, the writing is clipped and telling, as when Janet recalls the time she and the others all planned to wear blue to school on the same day. "The three of them wore green from head to toe . . . I decided I would hate that color till the day I died." Orgel is also aware of the ironies of inclusion: "We discussed who we'd have. Whoever wanted to join. As long as they were in fifth grade, and as long as we all liked them." A thoughtful entry in a popular genre.

Margaret A. Bush

SOURCE: A review of *Nobodies and Somebodies,* in *The*

Horn Book Magazine, Vol. LXVII, No. 6, November-December, 1991, pp. 737-38.

"The first thing I saw when I walked into Room 309 were three girls sitting on the windowsill, looking like they owned the place. They were a club—*the* club." Laura Hoffman's plight as a fifth-grade newcomer is common enough; in an effort to join the ranks of the exclusive club, she botches an early attempt at friendship with another classmate, putting herself in the lonely position of outsider. Doris Orgel uses a scheme of three alternating narrators to explore the issues of friendship and belonging. Laura's perspective is the most frequent focus; other voices belong to Janet, almost allowed into the club earlier and cruelly dropped in favor of a new girl, Vero; and Vero herself, seen by the other girls as glamorous and special because of her claim that she has swum with dolphins. As the narrators each add details to their versions of events, their personal stories unfold. The peer dynamics and family styles are realistic and interesting, and Orgel smoothly meshes the intersecting views. All three of the girls eventually feel more like "somebodies" as friendships emerge. Janet's moment of personal insight is most touching, and Vero's trauma and self-deception bring moments of drama to the story. With economy and precise choice of detail, the author conveys the essential characteristics of a wide cast of contemporary parents and children and organizes their individual concerns into a coherent, compelling story.

NEXT TIME I WILL: AN OLD ENGLISH TALE (1993)

Gale W. Sherman

SOURCE: A review of *Next Time I Will: An Old English Tale,* in *School Library Journal,* Vol. 39, No. 8, August, 1993, p. 160.

Bumbling Bill's lack of common sense causes him problems in this retelling of the British "Lazy Jack" folktale. Unfortunately, both the ordinary text and the unappealing, static watercolors are below average. Even the humor in Bill's following the right directions at the wrong time is missing. Consider other versions of this story such as the one in Jane Yolen's *Favorite Folktales from around the World* (1986) or Malcom Carrick's beginning reader, *Happy Jack* (1979).

Hazel Rochman

SOURCE: A review of *Next Time I Will: An Old English Tale,* in *Booklist,* Vol. 90, No. 7, December 1, 1993, p. 702.

For the child getting ready to read, this retelling of an old English folktale makes a funny read-aloud. It's the story of the good-hearted foolish boy who means well but gets in trouble by applying his mother's advice too literally. The farce of his mistakes—as he carries milk in his pocket, smelly goat cheese on his head, and a donkey on his shoulders—will make new readers feel wonderfully superior. True to storytelling style, Orgel's version is simple and direct without being stilted, and [Betsy] Day's bright, clear watercolor and line illustrations express the cheery slapstick of the story.

THE FLOWER OF SHEBA (with Ellen Schecter, 1994)

Carolyn Phelan

SOURCE: A review of *The Flower of Sheba*, in *Booklist*, Vol. 90, No. 11, February 1, 1994, p. 1012.

Spurred by tales of the wisdom of King Solomon, the wise Queen of Sheba visits him in order to test his knowledge and increase her own. First she asks him riddles, then she challenges him to find the one real flower among a thousand blooms made of silk, paper, and glass. Confounded by the scented, artificial garden, Solomon opens a window and lets in a bee, which leads him to the real white rose growing amid the "permanent flowers." The African queen leaves Solomon enriched by the knowledge that "to the wise, even small creatures can be great teachers." Colorful illustrations [by Laura Kelly] add to the book's appeal. While the tale is charming, well told, and evidently traditional, the story demands source notes and the book does not supply them. Still, this Bank Street Ready-to-Read book is an unusual and worthwhile choice for young readers.

Kirkus Reviews

SOURCE: A review of *The Flower of Sheba*, in *Kirkus Reviews*, Vol. LXII, No. 3, February 1, 1994, p. 148.

The great queen visits King Solomon to "prove him with hard questions," as the Bible says. Here, the questions are riddles, plus a challenge from traditional lore: to pick the one real flower from a mass of artificial ones, which Solomon achieves with the help of a bee, demonstrating that "to the wise, even small creatures can be great teachers." [Laura] Kelly's art isn't distinguished, but she captures the opulence of the court and the monarchs' retinues and the beauty of the black queen in glowing colors. The text is more accomplished, with a dignity and economy honoring the biblical original while telling a story that will make a diverting change of pace for beginning readers. One lack: a historical source note to enrich the experience for children and adults "reading together," as intended for this *Bank Street Ready-to-Read* book.

Gale W. Sherman

SOURCE: A review of *The Flower of Sheba*, in *School Library Journal*, Vol. 40, No. 5, May, 1994, p. 109.

A solid retelling of the Old Testament story of the Queen of Sheba's visit to Solomon to see just how wise he was.

The rich, vibrant, full-color illustrations [by Laura Kelly] with pen detail are filled with flowers, the focus of the third riddle that King Solomon must solve. A good series entry for beginning readers.

ARIADNE, AWAKE! (1994)

Kirkus Reviews

SOURCE: A review of *Ariadne, Awake!*, in *Kirkus Reviews*, Vol. LXI, No. 8, April 15, 1994, pp. 561-62.

A novella-length adaptation of the myth in a large, handsome format that's much enhanced by the arresting perspectives and pellucid Grecian light in [Barry] Moser's elegantly crafted watercolor portraits. Ariadne describes her role in vanquishing the Minotaur, Theseus's abandoning her on Naxos, and her union with Dionysus. Orgel selects details skillfully, shaping the narrative to a dignity appropriate to the myth. She also gives it emotional coherence by providing Ariadne with compelling reasons to betray her father and her half-brother the Minotaur, and by suggesting that Theseus's inconstancy—which he tells Ariadne is because "the gods are jealous of our love"— also has to do with an Athenian girl. On the other hand, though she details the remarkable means by which the Minotaur was conceived, Orgel evades some of the implications of Ariadne's "wedding." She's neither priestess nor debauchee here; she and Dionysus simply have "many children together [and teach] people the arts of cultivating grapes and making wine." A note exploring sources and the author's philosophy in creating her version would have been a real plus. Still, a dramatic introduction to a fascinating myth.

Hazel Rochman

SOURCE: A review of *Ariadne, Awake!*, in *Booklist*, Vol. 90, No. 17, May 1, 1994, p. 1599.

Ariadne is the young princess who helps Theseus defeat the Minotaur; it's her thread that guides him back through the twists and treachery of the labyrinth. The myth has always focused on Theseus as hero; in fact (except for those familiar with Strauss' opera *Ariadne aux Naxos*), most of us can't remember who Ariadne is. Now Orgel puts Ariadne center stage and lets her tell the story from the beginning. Always a rebel, she hates her cruel father, King Minos of Crete, who keeps the Minotaur imprisoned in the labyrinth and feeds him on human flesh. Then Theseus arrives, one of the 14 Athenians who are the required annual tribute to the monster. Dazzled by Theseus' beauty, power, and attention, Ariadne loves him and helps him; she leaves home and sails away with him— and then wakes up to find that he has abandoned her on an island. Ariadne tells her story with simple drama, and the book design is spacious and beautiful. [Barry] Moser's watercolors, however, are sunlit and idyllic, with little sense of the darkness and terror that are also part of the story. His full-front view of the Minotaur is a mistake, maybe because it jars our own images; it's not nearly as compelling as his woodcuts for *Frankenstein* (1984), which kept the monster mysterious and distanced. What is heartrending is the view of Ariadne on the shore, searching the horizon for a sail, waiting for Theseus to return. This version of the story shakes you up. Theseus is undoubtedly a hero who sacrifices himself for others; does he deliberately mislead Ariadne? The treachery is a shock, but just as astonishing is the way that Ariadne recovers from her pain and finds love and joy with the god Dionysus. Orgel shows that the young woman's perilous journey is also a personal one of leaving home and transforming herself.

Betsy Hearne

SOURCE: A review of *Ariadne, Awake!*, in *Bulletin of the Center for Children's Books,* Vol. 47, No. 10, June, 1994, p. 330.

Orgel's version of the Theseus myth is related by Ariadne and begins—after a brief prologue describing Pasiphae's passion for a sacred bull, and the Minotaur that's born as a result—with Ariadne's early memory of trying to find and comfort her bestial half-brother in the Labyrinth. She's almost killed in the process and is punished by her tyrannical father, so when Theseus appears and wakes her own passion, she determines to save his life in defiance of her King Minos. Her appeal to Daedalus for help, the golden thread he gives her, Theseus' killing the Minotaur, and their escape from the guards all lead to Theseus' abandoning Ariadne on the Isle of Naxos, where she's saved by a satyr and wedded to Dionysus. Like Nancy Willard's *Beauty and the Beast,* also illustrated by Barry Moser, this is a tale that's been fictionalized far beyond its usual length but not quite to the full development of a novel. Gracefully written and cannily illustrated with vivid portraits (though Minos looks more like a Viking raider than a king of Crete) or scenes playing on unexpected perspectives, the book will especially appeal to readers who think they've outgrown picture-book editions of myth but aren't ready for dense historical fiction such as H. M. Hoover's *The Dawn Palace: The Story of Medea.*

Patricia Dooley

SOURCE: A review of *Ariadne, Awake!*, in *School Library Journal,* Vol. 40, No. 6, June, 1994, p. 152.

A prologue sets the stage for readers: King Minos angered the god Poseidon and as punishment saw his wife enamoured of a bull. She died at the birth of the product of that union: the Minotaur, now immured and fed an annual sacrifice of Athenian youth. This fictionalized, first-person narrative begins with 10-year-old Ariadne as she tries to approach her monstrous half-brother, only to learn a brutal lesson about his—and her father's—nature. The core story begins five years later, as Ariadne watches the Greek prince Theseus arrive to be sacrificed—and instantly falls in love with him. In quick order she helps him es-

cape, is abandoned on Naxos, and is rescued from despair by a satyr who introduces her to Dionysus (who in turn introduces her to wine). The god marries her on the spot, just after spelling out the lesson of the tale: "Even love that ends in pain and grief is precious as a stop along the way toward greater love." Who could quarrel with this consoling moral, even if Ariadne's rebound is rather precipitous? The prolific [Barry] Moser gets better and better, though his bull-headed Minotaur is more pathetic than terrifying. Minos looks like a Viking, but Theseus and Dionysus clearly represent opposing male types. Ariadne, with her button-nose and straggling red locks, doesn't look much like a Cretan or a princess, but perhaps the idea is that the young teenage target audience will identify with the face above the flowing robes. The emotional heroine, and the romantic and sexual themes, may make this myth material more than palatable to middle-school readers.

Mary M. Burns

SOURCE: A review of *Ariadne, Awake!*, in *The Horn Book Magazine,* Vol. LXX, No. 5, September-October, 1994, pp. 589-90.

In conventional retellings of the ancient story of the Minotaur, the Greek hero Theseus is at the center, celebrated for his cleverness in securing the assistance of the Cretan princess Ariadne to escape from the labyrinth in which the creature is confined. In this work of fiction based on the Greek legend, Doris Orgel has chosen to turn the spotlight on Ariadne, exploring her motivation for aiding and abetting the enemy, her reaction to being abandoned on Naxos, and her final triumph as the wife of the god Dionysus. The result is a romantic—but not saccharine—tale which traces the development of a headstrong preadolescent into a determined young woman. The expansion of the legend adds dimension to Ariadne's character and immediacy to the story. The style is contemporary in feeling, reinforcing the concept that ancient tales have universal applications. Barry Moser's luminous watercolors capture the essence of Ariadne's longing in a series of dramatic tableaux, emphasizing her personality rather than the terror of the conflict with the Minotaur.

📖 *SHE'LL BE COMING AROUND THE MOUNTAIN* (with Emily Coplon and Ellen Schecter, 1994)

Daniel Menaker

SOURCE: A review of *She'll Be Coming Around the Mountain,* in *New Yorker,* Vol. LXX, No. 41, December 12, 1994, p. 122.

[It's] a relief to turn to the unmitigated, inspired silliness of *'She'll Be Coming Around the Mountain,'* a Bank Street Ready-to-Read book, by Emily Coplon, Doris Orgel, and Ellen Schecter, illustrated by Rowan Barnes-Murphy. These loony extensions of the traditional song lyric—"We'll wear rhinestones and pajamas like our papas and our mamas"—will delight two-to-six-year-olds through many rereadings, and the cartoon pictures are bursting with high spirits and celebration.

Sharon McElmeel

SOURCE: A review of *She'll Be Coming Around the Mountain,* in *School Library Journal,* Vol. 41, No. 2, February, 1995, p. 90.

As a parody of the popular folk song, this version presents a boisterous family celebration that is a little too overzealous for emerging readers to comprehend. Few will be able to handle vocabulary such as "do-si-do," "rhinestones," "razzle-dazzle," "Hallelujah," "piccalilli," or "cavorting." The print, however, is large and well suited to early readers. Barnes-Murphy's illustrations are delightful in their zany depiction of the people and animals. All of the characters look jubilant and somewhat silly. But in terms of the text itself, Robert Quackenbush's *She'll Be Comin' 'Round the Mountain* (1973) or Tom and Debbie Birdseye's *She'll Be Coming 'Round the Mountain* (1994) make more satisfying readalouds.

BUTTON SOUP (1994)

Sharon McElmeel

SOURCE: A review of *Button Soup,* in *School Library Journal,* Vol. 41, No. 2, February, 1995, pp. 78-9.

Children familiar with Marcia Brown's *Stone Soup* (1979) or Harve Zemach's *Nail Soup* (1964) will appreciate this modern version of the classic story. When Rag-Tag Meg approaches a young girl and her grandfather for food, she is turned away. Shortly thereafter, Mandy spots Meg strolling past their house. She goes out to greet the woman, who proceeds to find a button, a pot, and a wooden spoon—all the necessities for creating button soup over an outdoor fire. Urban characters crowd around and contribute parsley, onions, noodles, soup bones, greens, beans, and a carrot. Finally, Mandy retrieves a chicken from her house and brings her grandpa out to join in the fun. Overall, this predictable tale, told in the first person by Mandy, will delight beginning readers. [Pau] Estrada's full-color illustrations are just right for the story—they depict people of many ethnic groups and both genders. A satisfying choice.

THE SPAGHETTI PARTY (1995)

Hazel Rochman

SOURCE: A review of *The Spaghetti Party,* in *Booklist,* Vol. 91, No. 9, January 1, 1995, p. 828.

In this Bank Street Ready-to-Read book, Orgel tells a cheerful friendship story. Annie calls up Keesha to ask her over to play. Keesha says she's a mess. "Just come as you are!" says Annie. On the way to Annie's house, Keesha picks up all their friends in various stages of play-acting and disarray, "spotted and spattered, sopping and dusty." Keesha says to everyone, "Come as you are," and they end up at Annie's house for a great spaghetti party. The playfulness and the diversity are picked up in the line-and-watercolor illustrations that show the kids doing their own thing in a vital neighborhood.

TWO CROWS COUNTING (1995)

April Judge

SOURCE: A review of *Two Crows Counting,* in *Booklist,* Vol. 92, No. 3, October 1, 1995, p. 329.

As they fly through the sky, Big Crow and Little Crow see and count a wide variety of objects, people, and animals on the ground below. The easy-to-read rhyming text is delightfully illustrated [by Judith Moffatt] with brightly colored cut-paper collages. Youngsters will learn to count from 1 to 10 and back again as they join the crows on their lighthearted flight.

Marilyn Taniguchi

SOURCE: A review of *Two Crows Counting,* in *School Library Journal,* Vol. 42, No. 2, February, 1996, p. 88.

This slight, easy-to-read counting tale follows two crows, from sunrise to sundown, as they count up to 10 and down again. Their day begins with "1 ONE sun rising," and ends with "1 ONE sun glowing." There is much repetition, the type is large, and phrases are kept simple with the needs of prereaders in mind. Each scene is observed twice: as they fly, the crows observe "9 NINE farmers haying/10 TEN children playing." Then, as they return home, they see "10 TEN children snoozing/9 NINE farmers snoring." The appealing, textured cut-paper illustrations [by Judith Moffatt] add depth and vibrancy to the pastoral scenes. Moffatt also uses darker silhouettes to depict objects seen against the rising or setting sun. An attractive addition.

THE PRINCESS AND THE GOD (1996)

Kirkus Reviews

SOURCE: A review of *The Princess and the God,* in *Kirkus Reviews,* Vol. XLIV, No. 2, January 15, 1996, p. 140.

The Greek myth of Cupid and Psyche, retold in novel form: Psyche is a princess so beautiful that she is said to rival Venus, who sends her son Cupid to punish Psyche. Cupid falls in love with her instead, and takes her to his palace as his wife. When she breaks her promise never to try to look at him during his nightly visits, Psyche is subjected to impossible labors by the ever-jealous Venus.

With a naked couple making love on the cover and passages that are clearly, though not graphically, sexual, teenagers will snatch this from the YA shelves (if they find it there; the reading level is actually accessible to a middle-grade audience and the publisher pegged the book for "11-up"). In fact, if the jacket art and implicit sensuality of the book don't get past the censors, readers will miss one of Orgel's most lyrical, compelling works, with an epic love story at its center and adventure running through it like a stream.

Betsy Hearne

SOURCE: A review of *The Princess and the God*, in *Bulletin of the Center for Children's Books*, Vol. 49, No. 6, February, 1996, p. 199.

As she did in *Ariadne, Awake*, Orgel here elaborates a romantic Greek myth into a novella that will have appeal for teenage reluctant readers (who may be drawn in by the sexy cover) as well as for junior high students who have outgrown—but still secretly enjoy—fairy tales. Told primarily by Psyche, the story occasionally lapses into an omniscient voice (italicized) describing behind-the-scenes action by Cupid/Amor, his mother Venus, and various other gods whose behavior is all too human. Unlike many revisionist retellings of folklore, this presents no twist on the traditional point of view, but simply personalizes the story. Psyche's youthful beauty arouses the jealousy of Venus, who commands Cupid to shoot her with an arrow that will make her fall in love with a fool. Instead, he falls in love with her himself, abducts her from a mountaintop to a magic palace, and comes to her by night until she tries, at her sisters' urging, to look at him by the light of a lamp. The lamp oil burns him, he flies away, and Psyche must undergo trials before she recovers her love and becomes immortal herself. This is a complex tale, and readers might benefit from hearing an unembroidered version of the myth before reading Orgel's on their own, but the style is plain and the emotional situation of intense interest to girls in the throes of first love.

Hazel Rochman

SOURCE: A review of *The Princess and the God*, in *Booklist*, Vol. 92, No. 11, February 1, 1996, p. 926.

The archetypal love story of Cupid and Psyche is told here with dramatic immediacy. Psyche is the princess so beautiful that the goddess Venus is jealous and sends her son, Cupid, to make Psyche love a monster. Instead, Cupid is entranced by her beauty, and they make passionate love in the darkness, night after night. Then the princess loses the great god of love and must undertake harsh, punishing labors to win him back. Psyche's personal narrative voice is direct, but some of the intensity is lost when her story is interwoven with other viewpoints and with a whole panorama of Greek mythology as she wanders Earth, Hades, and Heaven in search of her love. In Orgel's *Ariadne, Awake!* (1994), Moser's illustrations were often

overwhelming; this time, there are no pictures (just Peter Catalanotto's sweeping cover of the embracing lovers in a vital universe)—it's the words that paint powerful scenes. Teens will be stirred by the story. They'll recognize the motifs of fairy tale, especially *Beauty and the Beast*, with the jealous sisters, the dragon lover, and the brave young woman on a quest. Orgel makes it clear that this is a story about growing up and leaving home. Above all, it's about the transforming power of love.

Cheri Estes

SOURCE: A review of *The Princess and the God*, in *School Library Journal*, Vol. 42, No. 4, April, 1996, p. 157.

A mature retelling of the Cupid and Psyche myth. Psyche tells of the problems created by her extraordinary beauty, her love affair with Cupid, and the trials she must go through to appease Venus, his angry mother. Other chapters, written in the third person, relate Venus's point of view as well as that of other gods. Psyche's character is the best developed; readers see into her soul as her love for Cupid and the child she carries grows, and as she journeys to Mount Aroanius and the Underworld to complete her tasks. Cupid, whom Psyche renames Amor, remains a somewhat immature character, even after he stands up to his mother and battles a Stygian sleep to save his beloved. Orgel emphasizes the physical as well as romantic relationship. Psyche describes the nights she spends with her "dragon bridegroom," whom she cannot look upon. At times, the prose reads like a bad romance novel, with passages like "Each night he awakened new joys in me. If he paused, I would whisper, 'Love me again in darkness,' and he would resume ever more tenderly." Myths and folklore were originally told for adults, but it is hard to determine the intended audience for this book. Its length and format belie the level of the vocabulary and theme, but may attract reluctant readers. There's nothing shocking here for the right reader, and Psyche's quest is grippingly related.

David Sacks

SOURCE: A review of *The Princess and the God*, in *New York Times Book Review*, June 16, 1996, p. 33.

How do you bring young readers to an ancient, mystical fable about the ennobling power of sexual love? That's the challenge tackled in two very different ways by a pair of fine books, both of which retell the Greco-Roman legend of Cupid and Psyche.

In *The Princess and the God,* the veteran children's writer Doris Orgel handles the sexual element tastefully and appropriately, keying it to adolescents' own anticipations and concerns. In *Cupid and Psyche,* the first-time author Marie Charlotte Craft and her mother, the award-winning illustrator Kinuko Y. Craft, circumvent sex in favor of less specific romance: their book uses gorgeous oil-over-watercolor paintings to capture the magic of the legend.

The charming Cupid and Psyche story—which has echoes in the "Beauty and the Beast" tale—comes down to us from an extant Latin novel, usually known as *The Golden Ass,* written around A.D. 170 by a Roman scholar named Apuleius and based on a Greek myth. Psyche (the name means "soul" in Greek) is a virgin princess whose beauty provokes the jealousy of Venus, goddess of love.

In obedience to an oracle, Psyche's father abandons her on a mountaintop for an unearthly wedding to an un-named creature. Psyche is borne on a wind to a luxurious palace, where invisible servants wait on her and where nightly she is visited and made love to by her mysterious, adoring new husband. He stays invisible in the darkness and departs before each dawn, asking that she never try to learn his identity. Yet the child-like girl cannot keep this trust. She discovers he is Venus' son Cupid, the boy god whose arrows inspire desire and who, defying his mother, has himself fallen for Psyche. Wounded by Psyche's betrayal, he flies away.

The legend's second half describes the pregnant Psyche's wanderings and supernatural ordeals—part penance, part education—until the lovers can reunite. The Psyche of this section is less passive, more resourceful, braving even a treacherous visit to the underworld. Significantly, Cupid, too, is matured by events. From a mischievous boy (god of infatuation), he becomes a steadfast husband and father (god of devoted love).

Apuleius' tale is meant as an allegory for religious enlightenment. Ms. Orgel reshapes it as 16-year-old Psyche's coming-of-age story, told mainly in the first person. Writing for preteen-agers and young adolescents, Ms. Orgel—whose many books include *Ariadne, Awake!* and *The Devil in Vienna*—describes with dignity Psyche's experience of marriage: "Each night he awakened new joys in me. If he paused, I would whisper, 'Love me in darkness,' and he would resume ever more tenderly." Although the writing rarely brings out the full grandeur or humor of the legend's supernatural scenes, *The Princess and the God* succeeds because it interprets Psyche's heart.

DON'T CALL ME SLOB-O (1996)

Blair Christolon

SOURCE: A review of *Don't Call Me Slob-o,* in *School Library Journal,* Vol. 42, No. 7, July, 1996, pp. 85-6.

Filomeno Pazzalini laments the fact that he is constantly being called Shrimp because of his small stature. When Slobodan Vladic moves into town from the former Yugoslavia, there is a new kid to pick on—one who is too tall, gawky, speaks with an accent, and wears clothes that don't fit. Shrimp finds himself torn between wanting to make fun of Slob-o in order to be one of the group and understanding how the boy feels. Readers will relate to Shrimp's ambivalence, yet will be comforted to find that he does have a conscience and becomes Slob-o's friend. Realistic black-and-white sketches [by Bob Dorsey] appear throughout. Readers will be satisfied with this short, upbeat story featuring a boy from a country that is frequently mentioned in the news. This is the second book in the series, but it stands on its own.

Shelley Townsend Hudson

SOURCE: A review of *Don't Call Me Slob-o,* in *Booklist,* Vol. 93, Nos. 9-10, January 1, 1997, p. 860.

Filomeno Pazzalini, an Italian American boy living in an inner city, wants to be included in neighborhood pickup basketball games, but the other guys think he's too short to play. They've dubbed him Shrimp and won't even give him a chance. Things change when a new boy, Slobodan Vladic (Slob-o) moves into the neighborhood and becomes the target of the jokes. Although the pressure is off Shrimp, he is sensitive and clearheaded enough to know how bad put-downs feel. He also recognizes that the strange boy, who came from what was once Yugoslavia, is not much different from Shrimp himself. Orgel deftly develops the theme and convincingly portrays Shrimp's evolving character in this installment in the West Side Kids chapter-book series.

Additional coverage of Orgel's life and career is contained in the following sources published by Gale Research: *Contemporary Authors New Revision Series,* Vol. 2; *Something about the Author,* Vols. 7, 85; and *Something about the Author Autobiography Series,* Vol. 19.

Dav Pilkey

1966-

(First name pronounced "Dave") American author and illustrator of picture books.

Major works include *Dragon's Merry Christmas* (1991), *When Cats Dream* (1992), *The Dumb Bunnies* (written by Sue Denim, 1993), *The Hallo-Wiener* (1995), *The Paperboy* (1996).

INTRODUCTION

Pilkey is best known for his popular "Dragon" series for young children, which features a daft but lovable anthropomorphic hero who both amuses and endears himself to readers. Influenced by such children's book authors and illustrators as Arnold Lobel, Cynthia Rylant, James Marshall, and Harry Allard, Pilkey has developed a unique artistic sensibility, crafting illustrations that have been praised as vibrant, often whimsical, and always appropriate to the story, which generally contains large doses of Pilkey's wry humor. Besides his "Dragon" books, Pilkey has a number of other well-received stories to his credit, including his self-illustrated works *'Twas the Night Before Thanksgiving* (1990), *When Cats Dream*, and *The Paperboy*, the latter a Caldecott Honor Book. He has also created illustrations for the "Dumb Bunnies" series, written by Sue Denim; observing the phonic similarity of the author's name to the word "pseudonym," one critic suggested Pilkey himself wrote the books. Despite having received the supreme compliment of favorable comparison to impressionist painter Marc Chagall, Pilkey remains grounded about his accomplishments and cites the artwork of children as one of his main sources of inspiration. "Children often send me pictures that they've drawn, and I'm always amazed at the way they present shape and color," he once commented. "Children are natural impressionists. They're not afraid to make their trees purple and yellow, and it's okay if the sky is green with red stripes.... Of course, you know that one day an art teacher is going to grab hold of these kids and turn them all into accountants, but while they are still fresh and naive, children can create some of the liveliest and most beautiful art there is."

Biographical Information

Pilkey was born on March 4, 1966, in Cleveland, Ohio, the son of David and Barbara Pilkey, a sales manager and an organist. Pilkey's elementary school years were spent in a strict parochial school where he was a self-described class clown, often in trouble with his teachers. By second grade he had spent so much time standing in the hall outside his classroom for poor behavior that his teacher moved a desk there for him. "I was the only kid in the

whole school with my own personal desk out in the hall, and I made good use of it," he once remarked. "I kept the desk stocked with pencils, paper, magic markers, and crayons. For the next four years (my hallway desk followed me through the end of fifth grade) I spent so much time drawing out in the hall that I became an artist."

Pilkey's first experiences with writing were also accompanied by some notoriety; in grade school, he wrote and illustrated comic books that his classmates loved but his teachers criticized as distasteful and a waste of time. When Pilkey became serious about wanting to write and illustrate children's books, he read such classics as Anita Lobel's *Frog and Toad*, Cynthia Rylant's *Henry and Mudge*, James Marshall's *George and Martha*, and Harry Allard's *The Stupids* over and over again to pick up rhythms and identify patterns. He also attended Kent State University, where he graduated with a degree in art.

Major Works

Pilkey's "Dragon" series—which includes the titles *A Friend for Dragon* (1991), *Dragon Gets By* (1991), *Drag-*

on's *Merry Christmas, Dragon's Fat Cat* (1992), and *Dragon's Halloween* (1993)—features a lovable but dim-witted dragon whose antics and adventures are intended to amuse and delight young readers. In *Dragon's Merry Christmas,* comprised of four separate stories, Dragon: finds a Christmas tree in a forest that he thinks is too perfect to chop down so he decorates it on the spot; succumbs to his cravings to eat the chocolates on his candy wreath; and attempts to avoid losing his mittens by attaching them to his coat—which he promptly loses. In the fourth story, Pilkey celebrates themes about giving and the true spirit of Christmas, his illustrations in the last pages recalling van Gogh's *Starry Night. When Cats Dream,* another story written and illustrated by Pilkey, offers an original take on the dream world of cats: in contrast to the drab black-and-white setting of their waking world, in which their food and toys are always in the same place, cats dream with great freedom and imagination—they change shape, wear shoes and ties, lose their socks in the sea, and generally move about in a technicolor universe. Geared toward four- to seven-year-olds and featuring artwork that has drawn comparison to the paintings of Marc Chagall, Pilkey's whimsical book centers on the importance of dreams and has been praised for its effective blending of text and illustration.

Another series of stories that Pilkey illustrated—written by "Sue Denim"—depicts a family of pink bunnies who act silly and look befuddled most of the time. In *The Dumb Bunnies,* Pilkey's humorous illustrations complement the deadpan text as a character called Little Red Goldilocks makes herself comfortable in the home of the bunnies, who have left their porridge on the table and gone to town. *The Hallo-Wiener* (1995), which Pilkey both wrote and illustrated, combines many of the elements that have made his other books for young children so appealing: a seasonal setting, a lovable but somehow flawed animal character, frequent puns and jokes, and vibrant, cartoon-style illustrations. In this story, a sympathetic daschund named Oscar, whose odd shape—"half-a-dog tall and one-and-a-half-dogs long"—makes him the target of many Halloween jokes when his mother sews him a hot-dog costume complete with mustard. Yet Oscar becomes the hero of the story when he rescues his friends, earning their appreciation and, at last, some self-respect. Pilkey offers an intriguing perspective on a somewhat familiar pre-dawn occupation with *The Paperboy,* which portrays a young African American child and his faithful canine companion on the boy's newspaper delivery route. Mary M. Burns called *The Paperboy* "a meditative evocation of the extraordinary aspects of ordinary living," noting that Pilkey's "palette is rich and inviting, and the situations are exotic for children whose days begin in light, not darkness." Citing the "mystical allure" of the book's "hushed moonlight setting," Roger Sutton asserted: "Pilkey paints a night at once ordinary and enchanted."

Awards

Pilkey received a Caldecott Honor Book citation in 1997 for *The Paperboy.*

TITLE COMMENTARY

WORLD WAR WON (1987)

Susan Scheps

SOURCE: A review of *World War Won,* in *School Library Journal,* Vol. 34, No. 7, March, 1988, p. 174.

A charming group of deftly drawn cartoon animals outshine the poetic text in this tale of two (animal) kings and their fight for power. The tongue-in-cheek result of their weapon stockpiling is a "nuclear freeze" in which both piles of weapons are sprayed with water and left at the ever-frozen Icicle Springs forever. The moral, of course, is that peace comes only through understanding and cooperation. A major flaw is Pilkey's effort to relate the story in poetic form. His attempt to rhyme and mete each couplet has resulted in excessive wordiness and overuse of colloquialisms. Nineteen-year-old Pilkey's full-page colored pencil cartoons are of professional caliber. Background coloring and detail on the largest illustrations are especialy nice. Minor flaws include palm trees in a country whose temperature reaches to 20° below zero. *World War Won* is the winner of a national writing and illustrating competition for teenagers. While Dr. Seuss' *The Butter Battle Book* is a far better parody of the nuclear arms situation, Pilkey's book provides a model for other hopeful young authors.

'TWAS THE NIGHT BEFORE THANKSGIVING (1990)

Kirkus Reviews

SOURCE: A review of *'Twas the Night Before Thanksgiving,* in *Kirkus Reviews,* July 1, 1990, p. 934.

This parody of [Clement] Moore's Christmas poem, stuffed with eclectic references, attempts to be both farce and vegetarian tract but succeeds in none of its over-diverse intentions.

A pointedly integrated group of eight kids visits jolly old Farmer Mack Nuggett, where a joyful meeting with his "cockerels" is followed by a grim discovery: " ' Tonight,' said Mack Nuggett, / 'These feathery / beasts / Will be chopped up and roasted / For Thanksgiving feasts.'" While Nuggett goes for water to quell the kids' ensuing tears, they hide the turkeys under their clothes; next day, the birds are guests of honor at their homes—at Thanksgiving dinners featuring "veggies," jelly, and toast. All this is reported in not-very-clever doggerel forced into Moore's mold, accompanied by lively but garish illustrations that include pointless takeoffs of Grant Wood and van Gogh.

The attempted wordplay here suggests humor—until Santa-like Mack Nugget's abrupt transformation into an ax-wielding butcher. If it's supposed to be a genuine plea for the turkeys, the book lacks dignity. Good grief.

Denise Wilms

SOURCE: A review of *'Twas the Night Before Thanksgiving,* in *Booklist,* Vol. 86, No. 22, August, 1990, p. 2179.

As you might guess from the title, this is a takeoff on [Clement] Moore's *The Night Before Christmas.* Pilkey takes that holiday staple and recasts it as a Thanksgiving tale about a busload of schoolchildren who feel sorry for a friendly batch of turkeys and save them from the farmer's ax. What might surprise you is that this wacky recasting really is funny. " / And then in a twinkling / They heard in the straw / The prancing and pawing / Of each little claw. / More rapid than chickens / His cockerels they came. / He whistled and shouted / And called them by name: / 'Now Ollie, now Stanley, now Larry and Moe, / On Wally, on Beaver, on Shemp and Groucho! '" The robust, cartoon-style art has van Goghesque sky vistas popping up from time to time and a manic energy that spills off the page. Loud and brassy on the surface, this also has an underlying softness that will appeal to kids.

Publishers Weekly

SOURCE: A review of *'Twas the Night Before Thanksgiving,* in *Publishers Weekly,* Vol. 237, No. 52, August 10, 1990, p. 443.

Patterned as a parody of the celebrated Clement Moore poem, this story of eight baby turkeys unfolds with joyous abandon and crackling vitality, as eight children embark on a Thanksgiving field trip that will change their lives forever. They are breathless as they catch sight of Farmer Mack Nuggett for the first time: "He was dressed all in denim, / From his head to his toe, / With a pinch of polyester / And a dash of Velcro." The exuberant turkeys—Ollie, Stanley, Larry, Moe, Wally, Beaver and Groucho—catch the children up in raucous barnyard antics until the merriment is quelled by the sight of the ax. Deeply touched by the turkeys' plight, the children—who have grown mysteriously fatter and have feathers sticking out from under their clothes—board the bus to go back to the city. The next night, family silhouettes can be seen—each with a grateful turkey guest—as "They feasted on veggies / With jelly and toast." This humorous, light-hearted story, adorned with bold, bright illustrations, convey a sense of wacky high-spiritedness that is sometimes lacking in traditional holiday fare.

Kathy Piehl

SOURCE: A review of *'Twas the Night Before Thanksgiving,* in *School Library Journal,* Vol. 36, No. 9, September, 1990, p. 208.

Pilkey has adapted Clement Moore's classic poem for another holiday. The day before Thanksgiving finds eight boys and girls of various races taking a field trip to a turkey farm. Although Farmer Mack Nuggett seems kind at first, the children eventually discover his horrible plan to kill the turkeys for Thanksgiving dinners. Smuggling the turkeys home with them, the children save the birds, who join eight families for vegetarian dinners. The weakest part of this slapstick offering is the verse, in part because the story isn't at all parallel to Moore's and in part because of the stretches in rhyme to accommodate a pre-existing pattern. Some of the word play will escape children. Similarly, visual humor such as the placement of Farmer Nuggett and the teacher in an "American Gothic" pose will remain unappreciated by those too young for Grant Wood. The cartoon illustrations reinforce the story's general silliness but are unremarkable in themselves. Those seeking Thanksgiving humor will better served by Marc Brown's *Arthur's Thanksgiving,* while those looking for a human-turkey relationship should dust off Lorna Balian's *Sometimes It's Turkey, Sometimes It's Feathers.*

A FRIEND FOR DRAGON; DRAGON GETS BY (1991)

Publishers Weekly

SOURCE: A review of *A Friend for Dragon; Dragon Gets By,* in *Publishers Weekly,* Vol. 237, No. 51, December 21, 1990, p. 56.

In the first title of this new series, *A Friend for Dragon,* a snake plays a joke on gentle Dragon that is carried too far. Tricked into believing that an apple is his new friend, Dragon is brokenhearted when a hungry walrus eats it. He buries the apple core, and eventually the seeds sprout and grow into a tree that bears a new apple. *Dragon Gets By* is a lighter, comical tale in which the beguiling blue creature wakes up groggy and does everything wrong. "First he read an egg and fried the morning newspaper." He sweeps his dirt floor so diligently that he accidentally digs himself a basement, then he has a zany adventure at the grocery store. Children will laugh at Dragon's antics while enjoying Pilkey's *('Twas the Night Before Thanksgiving)* bright, inviting illustrations. Each episode constitutes a chapter; beginning readers will take pride in being able to read a chapter book independently. With his excellent vocabulary choices and crafty characterizations—small squiggles carry large meanings—Pilkey has created a positively precious prehistoric prototype.

Carolyn Phelan

SOURCE: A review of *Dragon Gets By* and *A Friend for Dragon* in *Booklist,* Vol. 87, No. 15, April 1, 1991, p. 1578.

Pilkey, the author of *'Twas the Night Before Thanksgiving,* offers two episodic books about Dragon, a good-hearted if rather dimwitted protagonist. In the first, Dragon's the butt of a practical joke, but in his innocence, he emerges the winner. The second book details the mishaps of a day in the life of Dragon. While his solutions to problems often seem a bit silly, the silliness is right on target for tickling young readers' funny bones. They'll enjoy the logical nonsense Dragon shows in the grocery store, where "he bought food only from the five basic food groups: He bought cheese curls from the dairy group. He bought doughnuts from the bread group. He bought catsup from the fruits and vegetables group. He bought pork rinds from the meat group. And he bought fudge pops from the chocolate group." Contrasting with the deadpan simplicity of the text, Pilkey's lively illustrations brighten the pages with a profusion of colors and patterns. An appealing choice for beginning readers.

Lori A. Janick

SOURCE: A review of *Dragon Gets By* and *A Friend for Dragon* in *School Library Journal,* Vol. 37, No. 6, June, 1991, p. 88.

An endearing blue dragon is the star of this series for beginning readers. In ***Dragon Gets By,*** groggy Dragon has a mixed-up day. He reads an egg, fries his morning paper, and sweeps his dirt floor until it becomes a basement. Finally, exhausted, he goes to sleep, but only after watering his bed and curling up on his plants. In *A Friend for Dragon,* the lonely fellow, encouraged by an unseen mischievous snake, adopts an apple for a friend. Once the snake is gone, the apple's conversation is limited, but Dragon finds many good qualities in his new pal—it is a good listener and it is always willing to share. Unfortunately, the apple is left unattended and is devoured by a hungry walrus. A heartbroken Dragon buries his friend but his loneliness is short-lived. An apple falls on his head and Dragon looks up to see a treeful of round, red friends. The gentle humor of these stories is accentuated by Pilkey's simple but engaging cartoons. Swirls and dots bejewel the skies, giving the pictures a colorful, childlike appeal. Dragon's good-natured naïvete should win him many new friends.

📖 *DRAGON'S MERRY CHRISTMAS* (1991)

Carolyn Phelan

SOURCE: A review of *Dragon's Merry Christmas,* in *Booklist,* Vol. 87, No. 21, July, 1991, p. 2048.

In these four episodes, Dragon expresses the Christmas spirit in his own daft, lovable way, familiar to those who have read ***Dragon Gets By*** and ***A Friend for Dragon.*** After searching the forest, he finds the perfect Christmas tree, *too* perfect to chop down, so he decorates it on the spot and, with the help of many extension cords, enjoys it long distance. Next, his doomed attempt *not* to eat the chocolates on his candy wreath sets up a tale that's a worthy successor to Frog and Toad's classic trial by cookies. In "Mittens," Dragon logically solves the problem of lost mittens by attaching them to his coat; then he loses his coat. In the last story, Pilkey downplays the daffiness, delivering a message of Christmas giving that's true to the season and to his big-hearted character, too. Throughout, brightly colored, highly patterned illustrations por-

tray characters and action in lively fashion. In the final scenes, Pilkey pays a visual tribute to Van Gogh's *Starry Night.* Recommended for beginning readers as well as for teachers and librarians seeking short, seasonal read-aloud tales.

Kirkus Reviews

SOURCE: A review of *Dragon's Merry Christmas,* in *Kirkus Reviews,* Vol. 59, No. 14, July 15, 1991, pp. 939-40.

An appealing blue creature, first introduced in 1990, displays his independent thinking and good humor in four episodes appropriate to the season. Dragon decides to decorate his tree where he finds it growing, without cutting it; he's proud of the candy wreath he makes, but it's too tasty to last long; he gives away the presents he's bought for himself to needier animals. Not exceptional, but genuinely warmhearted; the art, drawn with assurance and verve, is vibrantly colored.

School Library Journal

SOURCE: A review of *Dragon's Merry Christmas,* in *School Library Journal,* Vol. 37, No. 10, October, 1991, p. 32.

Four short, easy-to-read stories about a likable dragon. All have recognizable, easy-to-digest morals about such topics as the value of a tree in its natural state; the irresistible temptation of a chocolate wreath; the importance of not losing things—like coats and mittens; and the spirit of sharing with those less fortunate. These are lessons young readers could be taught during any season of the year; Pilkey has just chosen to hang Christmas on them. Illustrated in simple, serviceable, cartoon watercolors, this will appeal to fans of Pilkey's first two dragon books.

📖 *DRAGON'S FAT CAT* (1992)

Kirkus Reviews

SOURCE: A review of *Dragon's Fat Cat,* in *Kirkus Reviews,* Vol. 60, No. 1, January 1, 1992, p. 56.

Pilkey's series about a little blue dragon who keeps house (***Dragon's Merry Christmas,*** 1991) gets stronger with each entry. Here, Dragon takes in a cat on a snowy day, then has trouble teaching her the things she needs to know: a sign reading "roll over" means nothing to her, and her "yellow puddles" are "smelly" (there's a particularly funny picture of the obliging cat peering out of the toilet she's trying to use). The mailmouse suggests a litter box, but roadside litter proves to be even smellier. A trip to the pet shop helps to straighten Dragon out; then Cat produces kittens, with still more amusing results. Never a dull moment here; the amiable Dragon's misapprehensions are as much fun as his quirky problem-solving, while the light-hearted illustrations display an unusual sensitivity to color and design in their artless-seeming background detail.

Carolyn Phelan

SOURCE: A review of *Dragon's Fat Cat,* in *Booklist,* Vol. 88, No. 11, February 1, 1992, p. 1029.

In his fourth appearance, Dragon adopts a stray cat and learns by trial and error how to care for it. Once again, our hero (as innocent of the mechanics of pet care as he is of everything else) makes a number of mistakes and experiences a range of emotions along the way, and as before, his good heart is rewarded in the end. Pilkey, whose first book was *'Twas the Night before Thanksgiving,* has a distinctive style of illustration based on broad lines that express a world of emotion with the droop of a whisker or the tilt of a head. Playful and original in his use of color, he vitalizes the scenes with bold patterns and vibrant hues that sometimes shift from page to page. The interplay of pictures and words is vital to the broad humor that ensures the book's success, whether read aloud or read alone. The Dragon series is fast moving toward that pantheon of children's reading reserved for books that make kids laugh out loud. Since nothing is actually *easy* for a beginner to read, what more could we ask for newcomers than the intrinsic reward of a genuinely funny book? Again and again, Pilkey delivers.

Nancy Vasilakis

SOURCE: A review of *Dragon's Fat Cat,* in *The Horn Book Magazine,* March-April, 1992, p. 197.

This fourth book of tales about Dragon assigns to the guileless beast the responsibilities of pet ownership. Dragon scoops a stray cat out of the snow and takes the stiff, frozen animal indoors. Before long he is fussing over sleeping arrangements—though the cat prefers Dragon's bed to the soft basket he has carefully prepared for her—and the smelly puddles that Cat creates. A trip to the pet store is in order, and there Dragon receives some good advice from the sales pig, plus all the necessary supplies—but leaves his cat behind. Searching for Cat later, he finds her at last huddled inside an old crate with five little kittens. Proud Dragon takes the new family home, and in a fitting dénouement that harks back to the beginning, he makes up beds for the newcomers—all of whom, after careful thought, he has named "Kitty"—only to discover them sleeping on *his* bed, just like their mother. The ridiculous humor in the story will appeal to beginning readers who enjoy the insouciant literal-mindedness of Amelia Bedelia. The unselfconscious childlike quality of the artwork, with green and purple snow, orange moon, and blue dragon, provides a perky setting for the amusing antics."

Rachel Fox

SOURCE: A review of *Dragon's Fat Cat,* in *School Library Journal,* Vol. 38, No. 4, April, 1992, p. 98.

The loveable blue dragon stars in his fourth book for

beginning readers. This time, he rescues a fat gray cat from freezing in the snow, decides to keep it, and quite logically names it "Cat." The only problem is that Dragon knows nothing about caring for pets, or the smelly puddles they leave. When he finally gets to the pet store for advice, he leaves with all the things Cat will need to live comfortably, but forgets Cat. When Dragon finally finds his new companion, he is in for quite a surprise. The simple cartoon illustrations in vibrant watercolor and pencil enhance the gentle humor of the story and the characters as well. A book that will be loved by Dragon's fans, and one that's sure to win him many new friends.

Roger Sutton

SOURCE: A review of *Dragon's Fat Cat: Dragon's Fourth Tale,* in *Bulletin of the Center for Children's Books,* Vol. 45, No. 10, June, 1992, pp. 273-74.

Dragon (blue and bulbous) finds Cat (fat, gray and frozen) in his snowy yard one day, and a friendship—among other things—is born. Dragon tries to take good care of Cat, and even his mistakes stem from affection; feeding Cat ice cream and catsup, for example. Pilkey's text is simple and straight-ahead; most of the humor is delivered visually in the luridly colored, loony but loving illustrations. Both Dragon's tender stewardship and his mistakes (trying to put Cat on the toilet!) are childlike; kids will want to take both creatures home with them.

WHEN CATS DREAM (1992)

Ann A. Flowers

SOURCE: A review of *When Cats Dream,* in *The Horn Book Magazine,* Vol. LXVIII, No. 2, March, 1992, p. 200.

An exuberant frolic describing what cats dream about—the ability to swim with fish, be unafraid of dogs, romp in the jungle, be tickled on their paw pads—is more arresting for the art than for the text. Starting with a picture of a monochromatic cat about to fall asleep on the "soft-warm" lap of Whistler's mother, the book features a group of colorful cats who gambol and frisk energetically through the cat's dreams. They have been executed in a series of artistic styles that resemble those of Picasso, Rousseau, and Chagall. The cat ends up, awake again, in the lap of a monochromatic Mona Lisa. The liveliness will no doubt be enjoyable to young readers, but the artistic references will probably appeal more to those with some knowledge of painting. Interesting, unusual, and humorous.

Kirkus Reviews

SOURCE: A review of *When Cats Dream,* in *Kirkus Reviews,* Vol. 60, No. 13, July 1, 1992, p. 853.

An imaginative exploration of the world of dream. "When cats are awake, all the world is the same"—predictable

From When Cats Dream, *written and illustrated by Dav Pilkey.*

and, in neatly framed black and white, realistic. When puss goes to sleep (in Whistler's mother's lap), the illustrations bloom into full color and expand to fill pages of surreal activity echoing the fantasies of such great voyagers in the dream world as Henri Rousseau and (Pilkey's apparent favorite) Chagall. After waking for a quick snack, it's off to sleep again in another lap—Mona Lisa's. Pilkey's simple text suggests the dream adventures' liberating quality, splendidly realized in his glowing, beautifully designed paintings; handsome in themselves, they also make a unique introduction to modern art's ideas and images.

Karen Hutt

SOURCE: A review of *When Cats Dream,* in *Booklist,* Vol. 88, No. 22, August, 1992, p. 2019.

"When cats are awake, all the world is the same. . . . But when cats go to sleep, everything begins to change." Pilkey's wide-awake cat lives in a black-and-white world, dependable but dull: the food is always in the same corner, the ball is always under the rocker, and there's always a lap (albeit Whistler's mother's) in which to nestle. But dreaming cats live in a colorful, topsy-turvy world: the fishbowl is an ocean to dive in, the back door is always open, and there's a jungle for stalking and swinging from vines. As Pilkey's cat begins to awaken, it returns to its black-and-white world—though now the lap it snuggles in belongs to Mona Lisa. Young audiences will know for sure when the cat is dreaming: the bordered, formal black-and-white illustrations give way to brightly colored, surrealistic drawings filled with activity and expression. Even the typeface changes. A book sure to delight cat lovers and dreamers everywhere.

Roger Sutton

SOURCE: A review of *When Cats Dream,* in *Bulletin of the Center for Children's Books,* Vol. 46, No. 1, September, 1992, pp. 20-1.

This visually exuberant homage to Chagall (with prominent nods to Whistler, Rousseau, Picasso and Miro) demonstrates some of the best and liveliest picture book art this year (proving, like [Tomie] DePaola's *Bonjour, Mr. Satie,* that the highest form of imitation can be inspiration). Pilkey's cats dream and dance and pounce in a wildly colored dream world where a fishbowl becomes an ocean, the dog is always asleep, and the cats "can eat up the sun and swallow the stars." Unfortunately, like Lane Smith's *The Big Pets,* and like many other dream books, there is no plot here, just a free-floating series of images, occasionally too whimsical, of what cats dream about. Maybe, though, it doesn't matter: a rear view of a large purple cat, outfitted in necktie and cowboy boots, ponderously sailing through the sunlight, seems a story all its own.

James Howe

SOURCE: "Purrchance to Dream," in *The New York Times Book Review,* November 8, 1992, p. 57.

I love "When Cats Dream" for a lot of reasons, not the least of which is the relief it provides. Ever since the most recent cat entered my life, a year ago, I'd been worrying that there was something wrong with him because he slept so much. Then I read that cats sleep an average of 18 hours a day. This awareness only heightened my anxiety.

"What a boring life," I thought. "What deprivation."

Now, thanks to Dav Pilkey, I know that cats' lives are not boring at all. In Mr. Pilkey's world, when cats dream, their bodies and spirits take flight. They change shape. They wear shoes and ties, and they lose their socks in the sea. And all in glorious Technicolor.

"Nothing is the same when cats dream," the author-illustrator informs us. "The moonbeams come in the window, swish, swish. . . . The fishbowl is now an ocean, and cats can dive in."

Best of all, "When cats dream, someone always has left the back door open, and no cat is afraid."

I asked my 5-year-old why she liked this book. "Because," she replied without hesitation, "it's true about cats." I like it for that reason, too, but there's something more. I like it because it's about dreams.

When Mr. Pilkey takes us from the drab black-and-white waking world of his cats, where "the food is always in the same corner" and "the ball is always under the wooden chair," to their color-explosive dream world, he is revealing more than the inner life of cats. He is speaking as well of the need for dreams in the life of those other domesticated animals: you and me.

Dreams, whether they transport us in our sleeping hours or when we're awake, put the feathers in our fedoras, the wings on our wing-tipped shoes. Fortunately, children don't need to be told to dream, but as the world tries to make children more literal, it's not such a bad thing to remind them that "dream" is just another way of saying "imagine." Not a bad reminder for the grown-up whose lap they occupy either.

Another reason I love this book: it's a perfect blend of text and art. It isn't just the words that give us the message. It's the Chagall-like paintings that fly off in every direction. I imagine a physical impossibility as I look at them: I see the artist dancing while he paints. There's more than vibrancy here; there's humor, and it will have both you and your child laughing. For instance, the first "softwarm" lap our wakeful cat encounters turns out to belong to Whistler's mother. When that cat begins to dream, however, Whistler's mom loses her dour expression, kicks off her shoes and dons shades. You may want to save this for the 10th or 12th reading, but "When Cats Dream" provides a great opportunity for discussing art and comparing artists in a way that's guaranteed to be fun and nonthreatening.

One nice touch in the illustrations is the child's stick-figure rendering of a cat that keeps popping up. In a book that is, among other things, a homage to artists, here's recognition that children are artists too.

Dav Pilkey is also the author and illustrator of *'T was the Night Before Thanksgiving* and, I have discovered, a series of early readers featuring a lovable, dopey dragon named Dragon. That series had my daughter chortling with delight. If it's been a while since you've heard a 5-year-old chortle, you owe it to yourself to think of Dav Pilkey when gift giving time rolls around. And that's another reason I love this book: it has introduced me to a big new talent. I look forward to the dreams he will awaken in me and in those children lucky enough to know him in the years to come.

JULIUS (written by Angela Johnson, 1993)

Kirkus Reviews

SOURCE: A review of *Julius,* in *Kirkus Reviews,* Vol. 61, No. 3, February 1, 1993, p. 148.

The author of *When I Am Old With You* (1990) and other celebrations of loving companionship teams up with the mad colorist of *When Cats Dream* (1992) for a tale of a black family that finds itself saddled with a huge, exuberant pet. Maya has always wanted a horse or an older brother, but her traveling Grandaddy brings her an Alaskan pig instead ("Something that will teach you fun and sharing"). Like a teenager from hell, Julius romps through the house munching on junk food, dropping crumbs, listening to loud music, and staying up till the wee hours. He and Maya are inseparable; and as he teaches her how to dance to jazz records and eat peanut butter right from the jar, she firmly teaches *him* table manners and cleaner habits. Using ink, paint, fabric swatches, and even coffee spatters, Pilkey creates a riotous sequence in which Maya's happy face contrasts comically with her parents' glowers while her adored pink friend floats with bulbous grace.

Joy Fleishhacker

SOURCE: A review of *Julius,* in *School Library Journal,* Vol. 39, No. 3, March, 1993, p. 179.

When Maya's Granddaddy brings home a big crate from Alaska, she hopes for a horse or an older brother, but is happy to welcome a huge, pink, Alaskan pig named Julius. Maya's parents aren't thrilled by the pig's behavior: he makes a mess of the newspapers, leaves crumbs on the sheets, and plays records too loudly. However, she knows a different Julius who sneaks into stores and tries on clothes, spends hours at the playground, and protects her from scary night things. Johnson tells this tale through simple language and great humor. Using watercolors, fabrics, crayons, ink, and even instant coffee, Pilkey captures the spirit of the story with brightly colored paintings filled with energy and ebullience. Pieces of patterned and floral fabric are featured throughout—on the walls, on

Maya's dresses, or as a frame for an illustration—giving the drawings a comfortable, folk-art appearance. Whether Julius is sporting white underwear with hearts, joyfully swinging Maya around to a jazz tune, or unhappily submitting to a bath, his love for his friend shines as brightly as his glossy pink skin. A warm-hearted, yet quirky tale of friendship, sharing, and affection.

Ilene Cooper

SOURCE: A review of *Julius,* in *Booklist,* Vol. 89, No. 13, March 1, 1993, p. 1236.

Maya's grandfather, back from wintering in Alaska, brings a gift for Maya. She hopes it's a horse or an older brother, but it's a pig. Julius is no ordinary pig; he's an Alaskan pig, who can do polar bear imitations. Much to Maya's parents' dismay, he also rolls himself in flour when he wants homebaked cookies, leaves crumbs on the sheets, and doesn't pick up his towels. However, Maya knows another Julius, the one who'll swing for hours on the playground and protect Maya from scary things in the night. There's no real story here—this is more a string of one-liners—but Maya and Julius are such engaging characters and their relationship is so silly and strong that they transcend the absence of plot. Much of the characters' charm comes from Pilkey's eye-catching illustrations, which mix fabric and watercolors into collage-style art bursting with fun. Maya and her family are African Americans, but this is just the sort of book where the race of the characters is incidental to the story. The dustjacket—which shows Julius, sporting sunglasses, listening to an old-fashioned phonograph, with Maya on his back—has instant appeal.

Ellen Fader

SOURCE: A review of *Julius,* in *The Horn Book Magazine,* Vol. LXIX, No. 2, March-April, 1993, pp. 196-97.

Young Maya receives a gift from her grandfather—"'something for my special you'"—which he believes will help her learn about fun and sharing. The present is an always playful, sometimes sloppy and inconsiderate, pig named Julius. As Maya's grandfather predicts, the pig and his owner do share many adventures together, often to the chagrin of Maya's parents. On some of their outings they would try on hats. "Maya liked red felt. Julius liked straw—it tasted better." While this tale of friendship discovered and developed trails off at the end, the vibrant illustrations more than compensate for the lack of suspense or tension in the plot. The illustrator's multimedia collages, created with acrylic, watercolor, fabric, instant coffee, crayon, and India ink, constitute an evolution from his more modest efforts in such books as ***Dragon's Fat Cat.*** The pictures—which alternate between paintings that extend to the edges of each page and smaller paintings framed with a heavy black line or quiltlike border—contain many artistic references, including a Mondrian canvas that decorates the wall of Maya's home. At times

recalling the fabric work of Faith Ringgold in *Tar Beach* or the naiveté of Marc Chagall's flying figures, Pilkey's constructions feature large areas of bright color or pattern, juxtaposed to create a visually dazzling, childlike vision of the world. An exuberant, joyful collaboration.

Betsy Hearne

SOURCE: A review of *Julius,* in *Bulletin of the Center for Children's Books,* Vol. 46, No. 9, May, 1993, p. 284.

This gleeful celebration of silliness starts out with just the right hint of what's coming: "Maya's granddaddy lived in Alabama, but wintered in Alaska." So when he brings her "something for my special you" and it turns out to be even better than a horse or an older brother ("She'd always wanted one or the other"), Maya is thrilled to meet Julius, an Alaskan pig ("a big pig"). Julius climbs out of the box doing a polar bear imitation, wreaks havoc in the house, keeps Maya company in multiple endeavors (e.g., "peanut butter from the jar, without getting any on the ceiling"), and in turn learns some things from Maya (how not "to act like he lived in a barn"). Maya's parents are less than thrilled, but of course that's the main attraction of the situation, which steadily veers out of control in all the ways children love—noise, mess, late TV, sneaking into stores to try on clothes ("Julius liked anything blue and stretchy"), and generally transforming order into chaos. The fact that these characters are black—except for Julius, of course, who is pink when not rolling in flour—makes this an exceptionally refreshing break from the folklore and nostalgic childhood memories that have dominated African-American picture books lately. Pilkey's paintings are a major factor in the hilarity. He translates a keen sense of the ridiculous into vivacious hues and wildly varied patterns without ever getting cluttered. The picture of the family at breakfast, for instance, features flowered wallpaper framed in patchwork—a very pretty sight except for the coffee dribbling down the page from one of Julius' many spills. These are not idealized parents either; their expressions range from critical disapproval to desperate disapproval. It's the kids who have all the fun, and they do it with an abandon reminiscent of Sendak's free spirits. Despite the vast artistic differences, readers will recognize a tone common to both: wheeeee!

📖 *DOGZILLA; KAT KONG* (1993)

Sonja Bolle and Susan Salter Reynolds

SOURCE: A review of *Dogzilla,* in *Los Angeles Times Book Review,* June 20, 1993, p. 3.

The quiet, law-abiding citizens of Mousopolis are preparing for their First Annual Barbecue Cook-Off. The smells awaken the dreaded, the terrible, the super-ugly Dogzilla from his slumber in a nearby volcano. Brave troops led by the Big Cheese implement a plan masterminded by Professor O'Hairy to run the mutt out of town. The stars of this show are the author's pets: Flash, Rabies and

Dwayne (the mice), and Leia (Dogzilla). The illustrations are beautiful, campy, colorful collages of photos and drawings.

Suzanne Curley

SOURCE: A review of *Kat Kong,* in *Los Angeles Times Book Review,* June 20, 1993, p. 7.

Dogzilla stars Flash, Rabies and Dwayne appear again in this new thriller, *Kat Kong,* introducing Blueberry the cat as you-know-who. Doctor Vincent Varmint, his beautiful assistant Rosie Rodent and Captain Charles Limburger discover the hideous monster on an uncharted island and bring it back to Mousopolis in the name of science. But Kat Kong escapes, taking Rosie with him straight up to the top of the Romano Inn. Once again, mouse ingenuity triumphs over brute strength. What finally kills Kat Kong? Curiosity, of course!

Kirkus Reviews

SOURCE: A review of *Kat Kong,* in *Kirkus Reviews,* Vol. LXI, No. 16, August 15, 1993, p. 1078.

The irrepressible Pilkey strikes again with a spoof of the famous film, enacted by a real cat and some mice ("Flash as Professor Vincent Varmint, Rabies as Rosie Rodent," etc.) in color photo images imposed on background paintings. Puns and parody abound—the voyaging mice find natives "offering up a sacrificial can of tuna" while chanting, "'Heeeer, Ki-tee Ki-tee!'"; they trap the cat in a bag (being careful not to let him out), and attempt to display him back home, but he escapes, captures Rosie, climbs tall "Romano Inn," and falls: "Curiosity killed the cat!" Artfully designed, colorful, and funny—especially for those who know *King Kong.* In the same vein: *Dogzilla,* starring the same intrepid mice and a pleasant looking corgi.

Publishers Weekly

SOURCE: A review of *Dogzilla* and *Kat Kong* in *Publishers Weekly,* Vol. 240, No. 33, August 16, 1993, p. 101.

In a bold departure for Pilkey (*When Cats Dream*), these two brazenly funny picture books spoof Godzilla and King Kong as they launch the mice inhabitants of Mousopolis against, respectively, a killer cat and dog. Touched-up photographs of the author's pets are set against fluorescent cityscapes and luminous skylines. The texts ripple with corny but kid-pleasing puns ("The Big Cheese tried to catch up to the hot dog with all the relish he could muster") and shameless gags ("'What are you, men or mice?' 'Mice,' they squeaked"), while the pictures are packed with sly allusions (the mice give Kat Kong passage on the U.S.S. *Ignatz*). *Dogzilla* is the more successful volume, for it works within its own simple framework—giant dog steals cookout food, mice win a playful

revenge—and even delivers a surprise ending. The more hard-hearted *Kat Kong* jestingly raises serious issues (Does morality have a position in science?) without acknowledging their validity. Pilkey's irreverent exuberance is irresistible nonetheless. These inventive books may lack the elegance and soul of William Wegman's work, but they are infinitely more fun.

Stephanie Zvirin

SOURCE: A review of *Dogzilla* and *Kat Kong* in *Booklist,* Vol. 90, No. 1, September 1, 1993, pp. 69-70.

"Written and directed by Dav Pilkey" and starring the author's own pets (a dog, a cat, and an assortment of mice), these two charmers, larded with puns and pop-culture references, combine boldly painted backgrounds and photographs to give the slavering monsters of movie classics fresh, funny faces. Pilkey's cat Blueberry assumes the monster role in *Kat Kong,* the less successful of the two books, both in terms of story and artwork. Jokes are plentiful and the story is recognizable as it follows the terrible, terrorizing villain from the jungles of a strange "uncharted island" to the top of Mousopolis' Romano Inn. Unfortunately, the lack of variety in the superimposed shots of the beast (and one fuzzy, magnified head shot is especially hard to discern) deflates the tale. "Dreadful Dogzilla," with "doggy breath" enough to send the Mousopolis population scattering, seems a much more photogenic and expressive fiend, and Pilkey dresses up his mouse-filled escapades with an ending that cannot fail to get a laugh. The jokes will make more sense if readers are familiar with the originals, but the pictures are still plenty goofy and the puns outrageous enough to attract uninitiated kids—along with a sizable audience of adults.

John Peters

SOURCE: A review of *Dogzilla* and *Kat Kong,* in *School Library Journal,* Vol. 39, No. 12, December, 1993, p. 92.

The furry residents of Mousopolis are twice terrorized by overgrown house pets in these daffy picturebooks "Written and directed" by the author of *When Cats Dream.* Dogzilla rises from a volcano to break up the First Annual Mousopolis Barbecue Cook-Off, and scatter the Big Cheese's troops with her fearsome doggy breath—but the threat of a bath sends her scurrying back to her mountain. On the other hand, or paw, Dr. Vincent Varmint and his lovely assistant Rosie Rodent capture giant Kat Kong on an uncharted island and return to civilization, only to have the ferocious feline escape, create chaos in the streets, climb the tall Romano Inn, and take that long fall. Illustrations are painted in bright acrylics around cleverly trimmed and placed photographs of Pilkey's pet mice, cat, and corgi, for a wonderfully silly look, appropriately accompanied by a pun-laden text. Less elaborate, but much funnier and more creative than William Wegman's *Cinderella.*

📖 *DRAGON'S HALLOWEEN: DRAGON'S FIFTH TALE* (1993)

Carolyn Phelan

SOURCE: A review of *Dragon's Halloween: Dragon's Fifth Tale,* in *Booklist,* Vol. 90, No. 2, September 15, 1993, p. 163.

The latest bewitching book in a popular series puts Dragon into three Halloween predicaments and lets him bumble his way out. In the first tale, he goes to the pumpkin patch with visions of scary jack-o'-lanterns, but the six little pumpkins left don't seem to have much potential for wreaking terror. In the next, his scary Halloween costume gets soggy as he walks through the rain to a party. In these tales, Dragon may be the butt of his friends' jokes, but he has the last laugh. The third story concerns a walk through the woods at night, when Dragon unexpectedly frightens himself. As expressive as the wild and unexpected colors in the artwork, the cartoonlike drawings carry much of the humor. Art and text work together for laughs as well as for the sense of love and loneliness that make Dragon such a beguiling hero.

Publishers Weekly

SOURCE: A review of *Dragon's Halloween,* in *Publishers Weekly,* Vol. 240, No. 38, September 20, 1993, p. 30.

Bright blue Dragon never disappoints; Pilkey's series hero is affability incarnate. In one episode here, Dragon arrives at the pumpkin patch too late to find any pumpkins large enough for a truly imposing jack-o'-lantern, so he carves up six small pumpkins. The jack-o'-lanterns look so dopey that Fox and Crocodile roll on the floor with laughter. Then Dragon piles up the pumpkins, like components of a snowman, into a figure that terrifies Fox and Crocodile—and Dragon. Elsewhere Dragon dreams of very scary Halloween disguises, inspiring some of Pilkey's funniest pictures (Dragon posing before a mirror in rubber nose and witch's cap; Dragon "wrapping himself up just like a mummy" in unsightly strips of toilet paper). "Endearing" doesn't begin to do Dragon justice.

Roger Sutton

SOURCE: A review of *Dragon's Halloween: Dragon's Fifth Tale,* in *Bulletin of the Center for Children's Books,* Vol. 47, No. 2, October, 1993, p. 54.

Few easy-reader heroes are as endearingly hapless as Pilkey's big blue Dragon, who here finds out that six small jack-o'-lanterns can be even scarier than the one big one he really wanted. That's the first of three Halloween adventures; the others feature Dragon's attempt at a costume (he goes to a party as a witch, vampire, *and* mummy) and his scary walk home through the woods. The eccentrically colored pencil-and-watercolor paintings provide some zippy punchlines and a spooky/silly evoca-

tion of the Halloween mood, as in a picture of the blue beast yelping for help under a huge lemon-lime moon.

Gale W. Sherman

SOURCE: A review of *Dragon's Halloween,* in *School Library Journal,* Vol. 39, No. 10, October, 1993, p. 107.

This fifth book about Dragon is just right for beginning readers who want to be scared, but not too scared. In three episodes, Dragon cleverly turns six small, unimposing pumpkins into a tall, frightening jack-o-lantern; accidentally wears the most fearsome costume at a Halloween party; and is frightened by his own moaning and groaning hungry stomach as he walks home through a dark forest. Pilkey's bright, bold watercolors complement and visually enhance the text. Young readers will laugh out loud as they enjoy this scary Halloween from a safe vantage point.

📖 *THE DUMB BUNNIES* (written by Sue Denim; 1994)

Publishers Weekly

SOURCE: A review of *The Dumb Bunnies,* in *Publishers Weekly,* Vol. 240, No. 47, November 22, 1993, p. 62.

Denim and Pilkey parody a parody in this supremely silly effort. The jacket art, placing the title characters in the room featured in *Goodnight Moon,* loudly proclaims the author and artist's dependence on allusions; their book, dedicated to James Marshall, is clearly indebted to Marshall and Henry Allard's Stupids books, with a dose of Marshall's version of *Goldilocks* thrown in for good measure. Here, three roly-poly, bucktoothed pink bunnies grin goofily as they leave their porridge on the table and head to town. Poppa Bunny wears polka-dotted Y-front briefs and scratches his head in befuddlement, Baby Bunny picks his nose and puts ketchup on his watermelon, and Momma Bunny wears obnoxious harlequin glasses and a baseball cap marked "Duh." Meanwhile, back at their "log cabin made out of bricks," Little Red Goldilocks (who has skin "as white as snow") makes herself comfortable. Denim's deadpan narration complements the all-out corniness of Pilkey's colorful illustrations, but it doesn't capture the amiability of the Stupids (or, for that matter, of Pilkey's beatifically bemused Dragon).

Roger Sutton

SOURCE: A review of *The Dumb Bunnies,* in *Bulletin of the Center for Children's Books,* Vol. 47, No. 5, January, 1994, p. 150.

Let's hope the book's dedication to the late James Marshall means that author "Sue Denim" and illustrator Pilkey (a team à la Edward and James Marshall, perhaps?) intend it as an hommage rather than a rip-off; the Dumb Bunnies are the Stupids in pink fur. With prose that mimics Harry Allard's cadences for the Stupids, and pictures that resemble Marshall's more than they do anything else Pilkey has illustrated, this is the story of the Bunny family, who are really stupid, I mean, dumb: "Momma Bunny's porridge was too cold, so she blew on it. Poppa Bunny's porridge was too hot, so he put it in the oven. But Baby Bunny's porridge was just right, so he poured it down his pants." Kids will love the dumb jokes, but the silliness is more forced than inspired, and the Bunnies' encounter with Little Red Goldilocks is shamelessly inane: "Poppa Bunny loved her so much, he danced a merry dance. Momma Bunny loved her so much, she sang a merry song. And Baby Bunny loved her so much . . . he flushed her down the merry toilet." "Toilet" will always get you a laugh, of course, that's easy. What's hard is what Allard and Marshall managed that this book does not: they made us laugh at and love the Stupids in equal measure.

Kirkus Reviews

SOURCE: A review of *The Dumb Bunnies,* in *Kirkus Reviews,* Vol. LXII, No. 1, January 1, 1994, p. 65.

This labored effort is obviously meant to be funny, but it's more in the goofball style of Beavis and Butthead than an entry in the ranks of fractured fairy tales by such masters as Scieszka/Lane or James Marshall. Dedicated to the latter, this is a sort of "The Stupids Meet Goldilocks," illustrated with Marshallesque settings and characters. The Dumb Bunnies (Momma, in bra-top and skirt, is "really dumb"; Poppa, in polka dot briefs, "even dumber"; Baby Bunny is "the dumbest bunny of all") leave their wrong-temperature porridge for an outing that includes a picnic inside a working carwash and bowling in the public library while a librarian glares. They come home to flush "Little Red Goldilocks" down the toilet. One problem here is that these bunnies aren't out of step in a well-ordered universe; their world is occupied by similarly witless souls. A sign advertising a spelling bee is misspelled; when Momma Bunny notes that someone has been eating her bed, someone *has.* The lava lamps in a jacket send-up of the *Good Night Moon* room will be funny to adults, as will several of the other props (some may even notice the pun in lieu of the author's real name). But let's not elevate this by calling it wit—at best, it's harmless silliness.

Eunice Weech

SOURCE: A review of *The Dumb Bunnies,* in *School Library Journal,* Vol. 40, No. 3, March, 1994, p. 197.

A cross between Harry Allard's "The Stupids" and a fractured fairy tale. A moronic rabbit family lives in a "log cabin made out of bricks," bowls a game of baseball at the public library, and has lunch in a car wash. While they are out, their home is invaded by Little Red Goldilocks. Poppa Bunny wears red polka-dotted jockey shorts and Momma wears a short skirt and bra. Poppa, Momma, and Baby Bunny all have very prominent overbites. Many

of the jokes require a degree of sophistication beyond that of average primary graders: the Bunnies drive a Yugo, Baby Bunny uses a pimple cream called Zit-B-Gone, and Momma sings "Feelings" and wears butterfly wing glasses. Book titles at the library include *The Condo that Jack Subleased, Pair 'O Dice Lost, The Second to the Last of the Mohicans,* and *Moby Richard.* Some of the slapstick humor will appeal to youngsters, e.g., pouring porridge down pants and on heads, ice skating on the bottom of an unfrozen lake, letting Baby Bunny drive the car, and flushing Little Red Goldilocks down the toilet. The most appreciative audience for this title, however, will be older students who grew up with the Stupids and now have the experience to appreciate the more subtle visual humor.

DOG BREATH: THE HORRIBLE TROUBLE WITH HALLY TOSIS (1994)

Publishers Weekly

SOURCE: A review of *Dog Breath: The Horrible Trouble with Hally Tosis,* in *Publishers Weekly,* Vol. 241, No. 37, September 12, 1994, p. 90.

It could be said that Pilkey (*Kat Kong,* the Dragon books) never let a good story go unPUNished. From its openmouthed mutt to its put-upon family to its climactic burglary scene, this latest entry might have been modeled on Susan Meddaugh's *Martha Speaks.* But Pilkey's silly tales forage unabashedly for lowbrow laughs, and his aim is usually accurate, even if adults more than kids will catch these halitosis jokes. Here, "a dog named Hally, who lived with the Tosis family," emits green puffs of breath so toxic they knock Grandma Tosis out of her chair. When the Tosis parents put their putrid pet up for adoption, the Tosis kids try to save Hally: they bring her to a site with a "breathtaking view"; to a movie (starring "Perry O'Donnel and Giner Vitus") said to leave audiences "breathless"; and to a roller coaster so fast it makes riders lose their breath—to no avail. Yet a glimpse of a headline on a newspaper (called *The Daily Foreshadow*) and a wanted poster showing two robbers presage a happy ending: the villains visit the Tosis home and suffer the odiferous consequences. Pilkey's punchy art, characterized by heavy black outlines and bold colors, matches the clowning quality of the text (the copyright page, tellingly, lists Pilkey's preferred media as "acrylics, watercolors, pencils, magic markers, and Dijon mustard"). Guaranteed to ward off smellancholy.

Stephanie Zvirin

SOURCE: A review of *Dog Breath: The Horrible Trouble with Hally Tosis,* in *Booklist,* Vol. 91, No. 2, September 15, 1994, p. 144.

Wordplay at a basic level is at the heart of this sweet, funny picture book, much as it was in *Dogzilla.* Here, however, the plot is totally original, and the canine featured is Pilkey's artistic creation, not his real-life dog.

Good-natured Hally, who belongs to the Tosis family, has bad breath. Fearing the loss of their loving pet, the Tosis children search for a cure, but not even a "breathtaking" mountain view seems to help. When Hally knocks two burglars cold with slurpy, smelly kisses, the Tosises decide to opt for clothespins on their noses "because life without Hally Tosis just wouldn't make any *scents.*" Clouds of green breath wafting through the pictures create a scenario that's sure to appeal to a child's goofier side—especially if there's a pooch in the family. And the bright colors Pilkey uses add a marvelous effervescence to the zany goings-on.

Nancy Seiner

SOURCE: A review of *Dog Breath: The Horrible Trouble with Hally Tosis,* in *School Library Journal,* Vol. 41, No. 1, January, 1995, p. 92.

Corny jokes, plays on words, and garishly colored illustrations are Pilkey's stock-in-trade. This outrageous book continues the tradition. Hally is a fine, loving dog with horrible breath. Even skunks avoid her. When Mr. and Mrs. Tosis decide to give her away, their children try to cure the problem, but nothing works. Her days as the family pet are numbered—until she licks the faces of two burglars. They pass out cold on the living-room floor, and Hally becomes a heroine. With clothespins on their noses, the family concludes that " . . . life without Hally Tosis wouldn't make any *scents.*" Two levels of humor coexist in this book, neither of them subtle. Children will laugh at pictures of people reeling from Hally's breath, while adults will groan over some of the more sophisticated puns. The simplified cartoon drawings in comic-book colors will attract many browsers. While this is a one-joke story, many children should find it funny.

THE DUMB BUNNIES' EASTER (written by Sue Denim; 1995)

Christine Heppermann

SOURCE: A review of *The Dumb Bunnies' Easter,* in *The Horn Book Guide,* January-June, 1995, p. 262.

This time the Dumb Bunnies prove their stupidity by mangling and lumping together customs from Christmas, Thanksgiving, Valentine's Day, and Halloween in an attempt to celebrate Easter on December 24th. Text and illustrations create an unsubtle, off-the-wall comedy that is *so* dumb, fans of the genre will find it hysterical, but others won't even crack a smile.

Christine A. Moesch

SOURCE: A review of *The Dumb Bunnies' Easter,* in *School Library Journal,* Vol. 41, No. 2, February, 1995, p. 72.

The Dumb Bunnies get ready on December 24th to celebrate Easter by hanging a Merry Halloween sign with shamrocks on it, buying an Easter tree, spray-painting fried eggs, and waiting for Santa, who arrives in a red minivan pulled by eight flying pilgrims. Such goofiness makes for a fun read, and that's why Harry Allard and James Marshall were so successful with the Stupids. There is absolutely nothing new here, however, except that the characters are rabbits. The style of art is much like Marshall's; even the page outlines and type are the same. At first glance, one would swear this is another installment of *Space Case.* For Marshall's many fans, it may be a welcome story; however, be forewarned that it falls short of the inspired silliness of the Stupids.

Mary Harris Veeder

SOURCE: A review of *The Dumb Bunnies' Easter,* in *Booklist,* Vol. 91, No. 11, February 1, 1995, p. 1009.

The Bunny family is a worthy successor to those all-time favorites the Stupids. Here, the bunnies have some holiday problems. For example, they expect the Easter Bunny to come in a "shiny red minivan pulled by eight flying pilgrims." Their glorious ability to get every single thing wrong will leave preschoolers in stitches. The illustrations—done by an artist who describes his medium as "watercolors, India ink, acrylics, and Hamburger Helper"—match the story perfectly: pink, buck-toothed, and round in the middle, the bunnies are goofy indeed. This is dumbness supreme and a real treat.

THE MOONGLOW ROLL-O-RAMA (1995)

Publishers Weekly

SOURCE: A review of *The Moonglow Roll-O-Rama,* in *Publishers Weekly,* Vol. 242, No. 1, January 2, 1995, p. 76.

In this inventive nocturnal romp, Pilkey's (*When Cats Dream;* the Dragon books) delectable poetry sweeps readers into a fun-filled world where animals can be found "skating in moonlight / And drifting in breezes, / Rolling in starshine / And dancing in treeses." From its anticipatory opening query ("Have you ever wondered / Where animals go, / At night when the light / Of the moon is aglow?") the excitement gradually mounts, as myriad assorted species can be seen converging from great distances on the eponymous rink— "It's open all night!" Through shadowy forests and across moonlit rivers the animals trek, finally skating by the glow of Christmas tree lights in a rush of color and movement. Pilkey's generally dark-toned illustrations, both impressionistic and primitive, resemble his work in *When Cats Dream.* Here, giant moons in changing hues illumine several spreads (the final page, in fact, makes a nod to [Steven] Spielberg's *E.T.*), filling the book with all the mystery and magic of the night.

Carolyn Phelan

SOURCE: A review of *The Moonglow Roll-O-Rama*, in *Booklist*, Vol. 91, No. 11, February 1, 1995, p. 1011.

"Have you ever wondered / Where animals go, / At night when the light / Of the moon is aglow?" In a moonlit, Chagall-like scene, a little dog leaves his home and joins a varied crew of animals wending their way to the Moonglow Roll-o-Rama. They don roller skates and take to the outdoor rink, then fly through the sky, enchanted by the moonlight's magic. Slowly they return to earth, skating together "paw-in-paw, hoof-in-claw," until dawn breaks and they return to their houses, yards, and zoos. A *pourquoi* tale in rhyme, the book explains why we see animals sleeping during the day. An updated "peaceable kingdom," it fantasizes the tiger and the cow (if not the lion and the lamb) getting along just fine. As a picture book, it lilts along in rhymed couplets illustrated by large, striking scenes of animals making their way across brilliantly colored landscapes and skies lit by an enormous moon. The watercolor paintings, stronger than the text, convey an unabashed celebration of color and a convincing depiction of the fantasy. Good for bedtime reading, this picture book shows night in a positive light, without diminishing its mystery.

Roger Sutton

SOURCE: A review of *The Moonglow Roll-O-Rama*, in *Bulletin of the Center for Children's Books*, Vol. 48, No. 7, March, 1995, p. 245.

There's some sumptuously expansive painting for this story-in-verse about where the animals go at night. Furred and feathered alike leave their houses and zoos to roller-skate in the moonlight until "the magic sweeps all of them / Over the sky, / To moonglow enchanted / Where animals fly." It's a pretty fancy, and an even prettier moon, shifting from blue to ivory to yellow to a mysterious pink as it lights the festivities and dances the animals into the sky. The versifying, however, has little such beguiling mystery, with verses that sound more than they mean ("There's magic in moonlight— / The creatures detect it. / It finds them each night / For they merely expect it") and sacrifice grammar for scansion ("They say it gets darkest / Just before dawn, / The clouds rolling in / And the moonlight is gone"). The painting demonstrates a fetching talent; the words need work.

Joy Fleishhacker

SOURCE: A review of *The Moonglow Roll-O-Rama*, in *School Library Journal*, March, 1995, pp. 185-86.

If you've ever wondered "Where animals go, / At night when the light / Of the moon is aglow," here is one imaginative possibility. Zoo creatures escape from their cages, farm animals creep past sleeping towns, and pets leave

From The Paperboy, *written and illustrated by Dav Pilkey.*

behind collars and leashes, as they all head for the Moonglow Roll-O-Rama. Surrounded by shadowy evergreens decorated with colorful lights, the animals put on their red "rollin' shoes" and skate around the shiny wooden rink. As the moon works its special magic, they fly up into the "star-riddled" sky to skate "celestial ballets." When the enchantment wears off at dawn, the tired beasts hurry back to their everyday lives, to sleep all day and dream of the Moonglow. The rhyming text has a fast-paced rhythm that moves the story along quickly, despite some awkward sounding pairings. The vibrant watercolor-and-pencil illustrations grab the imagination and set the tone. Deep shades of pink, blue, and green wrap the story in magic and mystery. The full moon glows and flickers in almost every spread: bubblegum pink on the cover, peach against a red sky, and bright yellow over the roller rink. A beautifully colored moon, shrouded in dark green clouds, provides an enchanted backdrop for the animal silhouettes that skate across the sky.

📖   *THE HALLO-WIENER* (1995)

Kirkus Reviews

SOURCE: A review of *The Hallo-Wiener,* in *Kirkus Reviews,* Vol. LXIV, No. 15, August 1, 1995, p. 1116.

Oscar (last name: Myers) is a sweet, sensitive dachshund who is troubled by his unique appearance ("half-a-dog tall and one-and-a-half dogs long"). He looks like a hot dog and his friends never let him forget it, until Oscar's unusual physique saves the day.

Raising this story above cliché and bringing it poignancy is Oscar's goodness, which shines almost perpetually. When his mother makes a Halloween costume in the shape of a frankfurter, he bravely wears it even though he knows it means ridicule. He doesn't give up on his friends; in fact, this nice guy finishes first. In paintings steeped in autumn colors, puns abound and so do loony visual jokes, but the telling is simple, comical, and fast. Pilkey demonstrates his kinship to both Rosemary Wells and James Marshall with a book that has moments of high comedy, lowbrow humor, and good old-fashioned heroics.

Mary Harris Veeder

SOURCE: A review of *The Hallo-Wiener,* in *Booklist,* Vol. 92, No. 2, September 15, 1995, p. 172.

Oscar the dachshund is a dog with a problem: it's hard to win doggy respect when your mother calls you "my little Vienna Sausage." Mom's idea of a Halloween costume is a bun with mustard, but Oscar makes the most of the outfit, defeating a monstrous pair of masquerading cats to get his nickname changed from Wiener Dog to Hero Sandwich. Pilkey's wacky humor comes out in both story and pictures—a recalcitrant pupil

at school writes on the chalkboard, "I will not sniff my neighbor." Set against a series of vivid, clearly painted skies, the pictures promise a world in which menace is only artificial and underdogs can become wonderdogs.

Roger Sutton

SOURCE: A review of *The Hallo-Wiener,* in *Bulletin of the Center for Children's Books,* Vol. 49, No. 2, October, 1995, p. 65.

A little dachshund named—what else?—Oscar is constantly teased by the other canines who call him "wiener dog," and Halloween only makes things worse when Oscar's mother decides to dress him up as a hot dog. It's a dumb little joke, not quite enough to stretch into a story, but it's more than enough to provide in Oscar an object of both pity and empathy. When the dogs are threatened by a marauding "pumpkin-monster," Oscar, in true underdog fashion, gets the disguised cats out of the bag and finally gains the respect of his friends. The harmless and not-too-scary story is punctuated with some wit that may be more enjoyed by the adult reader-aloud than by young listeners themselves, but the paintings are undeniably pup-pleasing, placing cartooned canines in a mysterious Halloween atmosphere reminiscent of the artist's *The Moonglow Roll-O-Rama.*

Vanessa Elder

SOURCE: A review of *The Hallo-Wiener,* in *School Library Journal,* Vol. 41, No. 10, October, 1995, p 113.

Oscar is a dachshund who is " . . . half-a-dog tall and one-and-a-half dogs long." All the other neighborhood dogs—a motley crew of meanies—make fun of him. His mother doesn't help matters any, showering him publicly with endearments that refer invariably to sausage. What Oscar wants more than anything is to be something scary for Halloween, but when he rushes home from obedience school his mother surprises him with a costume that's exactly the opposite of what he had in mind—" . . . a giant hot-dog bun, complete with mustard." He gives his mom a kiss, but the look on his face is pure pain. Poor Oscar! Slowed down by his silly costume, he trails behind his pack of greedy peers, who snarf up all the treats at each house before he has a chance to grab any. But Oscar is truly a good dog—when two cats disguised as a monster chase his pals into the lake, he swims to their rescue and finally earns their appreciation. Pilkey's vibrant, cartoonstyle illustrations include tons of hilarious touches—Oscar's mother has crazy human lipstick lips painted on her muzzle; his teacher has a milkbone on his desk instead of an apple (and the lesson of the day is SIT—STAY); and the two ornery felines can often be seen laughing at the canines from their unique vantage point. This may be the funniest Halloween story ever written, and it's definitely got the most lovable hero.

📖   *MAKE WAY FOR DUMB BUNNIES* (written by Sue Denim; 1996)

Stephanie Zvirin

SOURCE: A review of *Make Way for Dumb Bunnies,* in *Booklist,* Vol. 92, No. 11, February 1, 1996, p. 937.

The spirit of James Marshall's Stupids is here, with words and robust visuals carefully calculated to produce the jokes. But this slapstick tale, in which the eccentric rabbit family visits the beach, then causes havoc in town, isn't as successful as *Dumb Bunnies' Easter.* Sometimes the humor hits the mark just right, but at other times it seems more calculated to grown-ups than children (movie posters outside a theater promote "Citizen Candy Kane"). Kids accustomed to taking things literally may find the book's quirky surprises a delicious change, but adults should still be prepared to do some explaining.

📖   *THE PAPERBOY* (1996)

Roger Sutton

SOURCE: A review of *The Paperboy,* in *Bulletin of the Center for Children's Books,* March, 1996, p. 239.

A young African-American boy gets ready for his paper route, makes his deliveries (followed closely by his dog), and gets back to bed just as the rest of the world is waking. This is a slender concept rather than a story; while not enough happens to interest those of actual paper-delivery age, the hushed moonlit setting as conveyed in the illustrations has a mystical allure. Pilkey paints a night at once ordinary and enchanted, with the strong, safe beam of the paperboy's bicycle headlight a beacon among mysteries of dark-green hills and shifting shades of sky. The tone is quiet—in fact, while this book closes with the arrival of dawn, it might find a more comfortable place at bedtime.

Wendy Lukehart

SOURCE: A review of *The Paperboy,* in *School Library Journal,* Vol. 42, No. 3, March, 1996, pp. 180-81.

A quiet mood piece that depicts the bond between a paperboy and his dog. Human and canine both struggle to rouse themselves, eat breakfast from bowls, and have an intimate knowledge of their route. Pilkey paints their shared experiences with a graceful economy of language. Morning is the third character in the story— " . . . this is the time when they are the happiest." Deep, sumptuous acrylics portray the initial darkness, the gradual lightening, and the riotous magenta and orange sunrise. The artist has cleverly designed parallel, yet contrasting, opening and closing scenes of the African American child in bed, feet covered by his dog, room framed by a sloping roof. In the first spread, the still starry morning surrounds the house and "enters" it through the uncurtained window.

When the duo return and crawl back into bed, the shade is pulled against the brilliance, the room darkened—a scene clinching their camaraderie. A totally satisfying story for small groups or individuals.

Carolyn Phelan

SOURCE: A review of *The Paperboy,* in *Booklist,* Vol. 92, No. 13, March 1, 1996, p. 1179.

In the quiet hour before dawn, a boy and his dog get out of their warm bed, eat their breakfasts, and deliver the newspapers. Riding his bike along the delivery route, the boy thinks about "Big Things. And small things. And sometimes he is thinking about nothing at all." Meanwhile, his dog travels the same route in his own way: "He knows which trees are for sniffing. He knows which birdbaths are for drinking, which squirrels are for chasing, and which cats are for growling at." Happy together before the rest of the world awakes, they finish the job and head back home to bed, where they dream of flying across the night sky. The story tells the details of a paperboy's morning in a matter-of-fact way, and young children will find those details fascinating: the wordless pages that show how the papers arrive at the boy's house; the paperboy snapping the green rubber bands around the rolled newspapers; and the empty red bag flapping behind the boy as he pedals home. The dual story of boy and dog adds dimension throughout and leads to a satisfying conclusion, but just as important is the sense of time passing within the story and the artwork. Using simplified shapes and muted colors shot with light, the acrylic paintings include beautifully composed landscapes and interiors, ending with a Chagall-like dream scene on the last page. An evocative mood piece, this captures the elusive feeling of being outside before dawn.

Mary M. Burns

SOURCE: A review of *The Paperboy,* in *The Horn Book Magazine,* Vol. LXXII, No. 4, July-August, 1996, p. 453.

Like many of today's movies or television shows, Pilkey introduces his story with title and credits before the central characters appear, as a full-page painting followed by two wordless double-page spreads focus on a newspaper truck making its delivery to a young paper carrier's home. What then follows is a lyrical combination of text and pictures describing the pre-dawn routine of a paperboy and his dog as they force themselves from bed, make their rounds, and return at break of day for a well-deserved nap and a chance to dream—for it is Saturday. The words are carefully chosen to explain but not overwhelm the illustrations, and the print never obscures pictorial content. The emphasis is on balance and geometric form, giving solidity to this celebration of routine (so dear to the heart of preschoolers). Yet this interpretation is never boring, for the palette is rich and inviting, and the situations are exotic for children whose days begin in light, not darkness. A meditative evocation of the extraordinary aspects of ordinary living.

📖 *GOD BLESS THE GARGOYLES* (1996)

Kirkus Reviews

SOURCE: A review of *God Bless the Gargoyles,* in *Kirkus Reviews,* Vol. LXIV, No. 18, September 15, 1996, p. 1406.

Pilkey joins the medieval fray with a bucolic approach to the journey of gargoyles from the cathedrals of the Middle Ages to modern cityscapes.

The half-comic, half-grotesque, goblin-like animals and monsters from medieval religious art, once representing evil and temptation from a dragon-infested underworld, here become contemporary symbols of the misunderstood, in contrast to the spooky black-and-white gargoyles in Eve Bunting and David Wiesner's *Night of the Gargoyles* (1994). In rhyming pairs of couplets, Pilkey tells of the lonely, the lost, the left behind, all in lowercase type: "god bless the ones who sing everything wrong / god bless the ones who do not belong." Blue angels rescue shadowy gargoyles and wing their way amidst cathedrals and stained glass windows, above skyscrapers, across a deep blue-and-purple night. Pilkey infuses his skies with much of the same fantasy inventiveness as Chagall; however, the solitary spread that pinpoints a specific setting creates for readers a visual pun of sorts—gargoyles hover as witnesses to angels who land in the well-known Edward Hopper painting of a diner, *Night Hawks.* Perhaps the quintessential American image of loneliness and isolation, the scene proves "that the souls of the lost weren't *really* alone." The constrained cadences are more statement than story, weighing down the lilting paintings with their hopeful but heavy message. Still, readers will find solace in this modern-day answer to existentialism.

Susan Dove Lempke

SOURCE: A review of *God Bless the Gargoyles,* in *Booklist,* Vol. 93, No. 3, October 1, 1996, p. 336.

Pilkey spins a rhyming tale of gargoyles, which were originally set in place on cathedrals to keep away evil spirits, and which then become scorned as "'grotesque!' and 'horrid!' / 'those beasts don't belong on the house of the lord!'" The gargoyles' grief is assuaged by angels, who not only comfort them but also take them on flights as they sing songs over the world: "god bless the rain, and the stormclouds that bring it. / god bless the music, and the voices that sing it. / god bless the ones who sing everything wrong. / god bless all creatures who do not belong." The verse in the first half of the book is strained and a tad maudlin (and the convergence of two trendy subjects, gargoyles and angels, seems facile as well), but the second half, with the song of the angels, is exquisitely moving. Pilkey's illustrations in dark purples, blues, and greens are moody and compelling, showing protective angels walking alongside homeless people and even one sitting by a lonely patron in a diner (an obvious homage to the famous Edward Hopper painting). The darkness of the pictures is relieved by large stained glass windows, many depicting musicians; the comically endearing gargoyles also offset the somber mood. By using the popular gargoyles as his messengers, Pilkey will catch the attention of many children who otherwise might be oblivious to the pain of the outcast.

Publishers Weekly

SOURCE: A review of *God Bless the Gargoyles,* in *Publishers Weekly,* Vol. 243, No. 42, October 14, 1996, p. 82.

Pilkey's (the Dragon books; *The Hallo-Weiner*) exuberant artwork takes on a mystical tone in this inspirational story about the presence of angels. As his occasionally labored rhyming verse posits, gargoyles were originally intended to guard churches against evil spirits, but over the years they came to be seen as "grotesque" and, in response, became "crumbled and broken." Yet, in Pilkey's vision, all was not lost. Passing angels befriended the unhappy statues, and now angels and gargoyles take evening flights together. Velveteen night scenes surpass the text in invoking a magical cosmology. Soft shadows brush turquoise and violet skies, bathing them in moonlight. On nearly every page, vivid stained glass windows interrupt the darkness with lapidary flashes of color. Pilkey imbues these dreamy vistas with electricity, the skin-prickling feeling of witnessing a special event. His angels, chunky females with flowing hair and feathered wings, are shadowy messengers the color of the sky. Under their care, ungainly gargoyles become limber and soar with them through the night. In imagining this incongruous camaraderie, Pilkey draws attention, too, to the human struggle for existence: his angels scatter "songs of rebirth" upon those who wrestle with loneliness, homelessness and grief. His optimistic message is easy to embrace."

Additional coverage of Pilkey's life and career is contained in the following sources published by Gale Research: *Contemporary Authors,* Vol. 136; and *Something about the Author,* Vol. 68.

Marilyn Singer

1948-

American author of fiction, nonfiction, poetry, and picture books; editor.

Major works include *It Can't Hurt Forever* (1978), *The First Few Friends* (1981), *Tarantulas on the Brain* (1982), *Several Kinds of Silence* (1988), *Turtle in July* (1989).

INTRODUCTION

A prolific and popular author whose works encompass a variety of genres and subjects, Singer is praised as a skillful and perceptive writer whose works appeal greatly to young people and reflect her understanding and appreciation of them. Lauded for her smooth, lively prose style as well as for the believability of her characterizations and dialogue, Singer, who directs her books to readers in the early primary grades through high school, is the creator of humorous stories, realistic fiction, fantasies, mysteries, bibliotherapy, poetry, picture books, original folktales, and works that blend both realism and fantasy. Her genre books such as mysteries, love stories, and ghost stories are often considered superior to others of their type, and critics often celebrate the author for providing distinctive treatments of familiar topics and themes. Singer's works, which range from simple picture books to complex fantasies and young adult fiction with deeper subtexts, are often autobiographical or semiautobiographical and reflect personal interests such as nature and Eastern philosophy. Singer is perhaps best known as the author of two mystery series for primary graders: a comic parody of detective stories featuring canine sleuth Samantha Spayed and middle grade fiction about twin brothers Sam and Dave Bean, who solve mysteries at their school and in their local community. Singer is also well known for her two humorous stories about the charmingly obsessive middle-grader Lizzie Silver as well as for her poetry on such subjects as animals, family relationships, and the sky. In addition to her books for children and young adults, Singer has written teacher's guides, catalogs, and program notes on films and filmstrips and has been a scriptwriter for the television program *The Electric Company*. She has also contributed short stories to books and poems to periodicals and is the editor of both a history of avant-garde cinema and a volume on American filmmakers.

Biographical Information

Born in New York City, Singer spent the first five years of her life in the Bronx in an apartment owned by her maternal grandmother, Frieda Lax. Singer has written, "I don't think I ever would have become a writer if it hadn't been for Grandma Frieda." Her grandmother told nightly

bedtime stories to Singer, often ghost stories or reminiscences about her homeland, Rumania. Singer later wrote that her grandmother "made me feel that the world is magical, beautiful, always interesting, always unique. Because of her stories, I could not wait to learn how to read. If my grandma's stories were so good, how many more stories were out there for me to enjoy?" Singer's father and mother, Abraham and Shirley, read to her and bought her Little Golden Books and collections of fairy tales. "All that reading, all those stories," she wrote, "stirred up something in me. It made me want to create my own stories and pass them on for others to enjoy." In 1953, Singer's sister Sandi was born and the family moved to suburban Long Island, where Marilyn first began writing and sending her work to magazines. Her earliest concentration was poetry, which, she says, "is still my favorite thing to write today." In 1956, Singer underwent heart surgery to repair a defect; however, she was not told by either the doctor or her parents what was wrong, a decision that left her feeling, she says, "betrayed and abandoned. It took many years to sort out and deal with these feelings. In fact, it took writing a book—*It Can't Hurt Forever*." Considering herself unpopular throughout junior high and high school, the author took solace in her reading and writing, becoming especially interested in the work of William Shakespeare, to whom she often refers in her books for children.

At Queens College in New York City, Singer majored in English and minored in education and began making friends with other students with literary and artistic interests. Spending her junior year abroad, Singer attended Reading University in England, where her popularity, she says, "which had been so low in high school, reached a zenith." Returning to New York, she began student teaching during the day and hanging out with rock musicians at night. After graduation, she moved to Manhattan and pursued a master's degree in media ecology from New York University; she also worked as an editor at a literary agency and a magazine and became more committed to the social issues of the late 1960s. After receiving her degree, Singer taught English and speech in New York City public schools for five years. Encouraged by her husband Steve Aronson, she became a full-time writer in 1974. Aronson, who at the time worked as the director of the director of the film department of the American Federation of Arts (AFA), hired Singer to write film program notes, catalogues, and teaching guides on films. She wrote guides for Jacob Bronowski's *The Ascent of Man,* David Attenborough's *The Tribal Eye,* and several films in the *Nova* series of public television programs. In 1980, she became the curator of *SuperFilm-Show!,* a traveling exhibition of avant-garde films for children put on by the AFA. Singer studied screenwriting with the prominent scriptwriter and novelist Terry Southern and continued to send her articles and poetry to magazines. However, she was unsatisfied with the type of writing she was doing until one day, while sitting in the Brooklyn Botanical Garden, she wrote a story featuring talking insect characters that she had first made up at the age of eight; these characters would later become a feature of her book *The Lightey Club* (1987). Singer sent the stories to publishers and joined a writing workshop at Manhattan's Bank Street College before deciding to make a career of creating books for children.

Singer has written that when people ask her "why I write books for children and young adults, rather than grown-ups, I've given them a lot of answers such as 1) Kids are interesting to write about and for; 2) If you understand the child in yourself, you can understand the grown-up better. I want to understand myself better; 3) There's nothing else I know how to do. All of these answers are basically true. But now I think the truest, most honest answer I can give is that I write books for children and young adults because I like to."

Major Works

Singer's first published contribution to juvenile literature is *The Dog Who Insisted He Wasn't* (1976), a story for primary graders about Konrad, a German shepherd that thinks he is a person. Konrad's young owner Abigail convinces her family to treat him as a human until the other dogs in the neighborhood decide that they want the same treatment; in the end, Konrad agrees to pretend that he is a dog. Singer, who based her story on the pet that she shared with Steve Aronson, was praised for writing an amusing, appealing tale. *School Library Journal* reviewer Carol Chatfield notes, "Konrad is a canine with a winning personality, and Singer's text has enough vitality and action to make it a good choice for reading aloud. . . ." A critic in *Bulletin for the Center for Children's Books* concurs, claiming that the author "handles the animal-human dialogue deftly, and the adult-child relationships are exemplary." With *It Can't Hurt Forever,* Singer is acknowledged for turning her childhood medical experience into successful middle grade fiction that does not minimize either the severity of the situation or the pain of the operation. In this story, Ellie Simon, who has entered the hospital for corrective heart surgery, is afraid of the procedure and of dying until she meets an African-American girl with sickle cell anemia. Writing in *School Library Journal,* Karen Harris says that Singer "has written an interesting and very useful book." A critic in *Kirkus Reviews* concludes that *It Can't Hurt Forever* is "sharp, fast, funny, genuinely serious, and helpfully informative—a tonic for older kids as potent as Curious George's confinement for small fry." Singer's next book, the semiautobiographical young adult novel *The First Few Friends,* is set in 1968 and describes Nina Ritter's return to New York City from her junior year in England. Through her involvement with the rock scene and the student protest movement, Nina gains maturity and a sense of social responsibility; the novel also includes some profanity and instances of casual sex and drug use. "Singer renders the political, moral, and sexual flux of that era with precision and authenticity," writes Stephanie Zvirin in *Booklist,* who concludes that although the novel is pushed "almost into the adult sphere . . . , her re-creation of the crazy stunts, late night gab sessions, and frank talks about sex and love ring true." *School Library Journal* reviewer Kay Webb O'Connell notes that while the events in *The First Few Friends* "are history, the issues of war, media hype and the price of individuality are still with us. Well worth reading."

Singer's books about Lizzie Silver, *Tarantulas on the Brain* and *Lizzie Silver of Sherwood Forest* (1986), are humorous, fast-paced stories that feature a spunky, science-minded ten-year-old. In the first book, Lizzie, who badly wants to buy a tarantula, works for a magician to earn money while she's supposed to be studying at the library. When a classmate tattles on her, Lizzie runs away. However, her family is surprisingly sympathetic, and she eventually gets her wish. In the second story, Lizzie is passionately interested in Robin Hood and dreams about becoming a member of his band; she also tries to learn to play the harp in six weeks so that she can join her best friend at a prestigious music school. *Voice of Youth Advocates (VOYA)* reviewer Kim Sands writes of the second book, "*Lizzie Silver* will be a favorite of 5th and 6th graders and should be an especially good read-aloud. . . ." In *The Course of True Love Never Did Run Smooth* (1983), a contemporary young adult novel with dialogue from and references to *A Midsummer Night's Dream,* Singer describes how the romantic lives of four high school students parallel those of the characters in Shakespeare's comic play. *Booklist* reviewer Sally Estes describes the book as a "sprightly, funny junior novel that, while making observations about the verities as well as varieties of love and infatuation, leaves the reader with a pleasantly satisfied feeling that all's well that ends well," while Janet R. Mura of *VOYA* predicts, "This one will not be a shelf-sitter." Another of Singer's well-received works for young adults, *Several Kinds of Silence,* has prejudice as its theme. Singer calls this work "the hardest of all of my books to write. It forced me to dig up all sorts of thoughts and feelings and memories I did not want to examine. It made me wonder if I really wanted to be a writer." The novel outlines how sixteen-year-old Franny Yeager, whose father dislikes the Japanese for their effect on the U. S. economy, among other reasons, falls in love with Ren, a Japanese-American boy she meets in the florist shop where she works. Franny is afraid to tell her parents about her relationship because of their bigotry; however, after an intense conversation with Ren, she decides to open up to her family. Writing in *School Library Journal,* Cindy Darling Codell says, "Singer's characterization is masterful, with clear psychological motivation carefully layered and subtly revealed. . . . This book can be appreciated as an entertaining love story, or upon further study as an excellent thematic examination."

With the "Samantha Spayed" books—*The Fido Frame-Up* (1983); *A Nose for Trouble* (1985); and *Where There's a Will, There's a Wag* (1986)—Singer spoofs the private eye genre by featuring narrator Sam, the clever canine who actually solves the cases of her master, the obtuse private detective Philip Barlowe. Fashioned as parodies of writers such as Dashiell Hammett and Raymond Chandler, the stories alternate clues with surprises and feature Sam's sardonic commentary. The multivolume "Sam and Dave" series is considered an action-packed, easy to read collection of mysteries about the twin gumshoes. Writing in *Booklist* about *A Clue in Code* (1985), a story in which the boys come to the aid of the school bully, who has been accused of stealing money set aside for a class trip, Linda Callaghan notes, "Singer's ability to subtly incorporate the necessary facts of the case into the narrative demonstrates her respect for young readers eager for satisfying mysteries they can solve on their own." In 1989, Singer published her first book of poetry for young readers, *Turtle in July.* Nature poems directed to the early primary grades and illustrated by Jerry Pinkney, *Turtle in July* pairs animals with the months or times of year associated with them, such as a bear emerging from hibernation in March or Canadian geese taking flight in October, and expresses the voice of that animal in verse. "Nothing," wrote Singer, "was as pleasurable as [this] collection of poems. . . . Of all of my books, I think this one was the most pleasant to write." *Bulletin of the Center for Children's Books* reviewer Betsy Hearne claims, "Both writer and artist have captured the essence of the fish, fowl, and mammals featured here," while Ilene Cooper of *Booklist* concludes, "Singer and Pinkney join their considerable talents to create a book that is both fresh and

engaging. . . . An excellent source for both poetry and nature units." Since the publication of *Turtle in July,* Singer has published several more volumes of poetry and continues to write realistic fiction for middle graders and young adults as well as stories that combine the realistic and the supernatural. She is also the author of picture books; fantasies, science fiction, and stories in the folktale tradition; and informational books on exotic birds and vegetables in the onion family.

Awards

It Can't Hurt Forever received the Maud Hart Lovelace Award in 1983. Singer received "Best Books for Young Adults" citations from the American Library Association for *The Course of True Love Never Did Run Smooth* in 1983 and *Several Kinds of Silence* in 1988. In 1989, *Turtle in July* received citations from the *New York Times* as best illustrated children's book and from *Time* magazine as a best children's book. In 1990, this work was also named a notable trade book in the language arts by the National Council of Teachers of English. Singer has also received several parent- and child-selected awards for her writings.

AUTHOR'S COMMENTARY

Marilyn Singer with Jim Roginski

SOURCE: An interview in *Behind the Covers,* Libraries Unlimited, 1985, pp. 187-93.

[Jim Roginski:] *As it happens, you, like so many writers, have a background in working with youth. You left a secure situation to join the ranks of the insecure. Want to fill in the details?*

[Marilyn Singer:] Oh, I was an English teacher in the New York City school system. The department got a new head, we took one look at each other and it was, immediately, *bad news.*

We got into a political discussion, somehow, and she told me about a teacher who wore a black armband on Moratorium Day [a nationwide protest held in 1969 to demand an end to American involvement in Viet Nam].

I thought it was a great idea. She didn't. She said, "I can see his point of view but I don't think that politics and teaching have anything to do with each other." And I said, "You teach what you are. And whatever your views are affect what you do."

So we started off on the wrong foot and stayed on the wrong foot for three years. Although she couldn't fire me she made my life very unhappy. She observed me frequently, she wrote up lousy reports on me. Finally she gave me an "unsatisfactory" rating that the principal supported, and that I appealed. It was a real Catch-22 situation because when you appeal it's to a committee of other principals. It was a big hassle situation.

So I decided to quit teaching to write. I did some substitute teaching just to pay the bills. And I came up with a few ideas for proposals, which I sent around.

Had you written anything for publication up to then?

No. Just poetry for myself.

Had you published?

No.

Did you have any kind of income?

No, but my husband did hire me to do some program notes for a film, you know those inserts to tell teachers how to use a film with kids.

I liked doing them and saw new possibilities for a career with them. So I started contacting film companies like Phoenix Films and Time-Life.

Eventually I got quite a bit of work from Time-Life, including doing all the study guides for *The Ascent of Man.* That was thirteen full booklets! And I didn't have a background in science, which made that project interesting for me. Luckily, I am a very good researcher and I did a lot of research for those booklets.

Time-Life gave me a lot of work because they really liked my writing. When the man who'd hired me left, I worked for his replacement until she left. Then I pretty much stopped writing for them altogether. By then I was tired of that and wanted to make some money from the books I'd started writing.

How did you start writing children's books?

I got a job doing both notes and catalogs for a bunch of films from the British Arts Council that the American Federation of Arts wanted distributed in this country. So I went to England for a month in 1974. I had some problems there not related to the work. I came home rather agoraphobic. To help deal with my problems, I started to write fiction.

I don't think it was a conscious decision.

One day I just sat down and started writing stories. I drew on characters I made up when I was eight years old. Talking insects!

Nothing came of it but I loved writing about those insects. It was like getting in touch with that little child part of myself, you know. I wrote a bunch of stories and kept reading them to my husband. He encouraged me to continue.

Then I signed up for a writing class that was going to take a year, but it got cancelled. The instructor mentioned a free workshop at Bank Street College. This was in 1974 or 1975. So I sent Betty Boegehold [an author and organizer of the Bank Street workshops] some samples. She called me up and said, "You know, you may be a talent."

I went to the workshop and Betty really encouraged me, too.

I want to add a lovely piece of irony here. The insect stories didn't sell when I wrote them, over ten years ago. But recently, my husband, who, as you can tell, has probably been more instrumental in my career than almost anybody, suggested I show them to Meredith Charpentier at Macmillan. He knows her and felt she would know how to turn the stories into a book. He was right. She will be publishing *The Lightey Stories* as a book!

Were you doing any other types of writing in the mid-seventies?

I was still writing teacher's guides, program notes, and catalogs. Later on, I did some filmstrips for a company that had to teach me how to do it.

They taught me mainly about form. I'd turn in something and then they would tell me to rewrite. They hired me because they looked at my resume and said, "You've written everything else so you might as well learn to write this." Really!

I've been writing full-time since 1976.

Are you a difficult author?

No. In fact, I've been told I'm good to work with. I do changes very quickly and I usually don't have any problems with the changes the editors want.

I feel that editors should be tough if they know their business. If they tell me to do something there's a reason for it, and nine times out of ten they're right. So I really respect them.

In some ways writing is a partnership between an author and an editor. I like it. I like somebody going over my work with a fine-toothed comb—as long as what she or he does is subject to my approval. I really mean that. Editors are there to help make the book better. Not necessarily more saleable, but better.

In *The Course of True Love,* for example, Liz Gordon [publisher of children's books at Harper & Row] said about the last chapter, which has a bit of sex in it, "I'm not going to tell you whether to take it out or not. I just want you to think about it and decide what you want." She said the book would probably be more saleable without it but if it was artistically important to leave it in to do so. It stayed in.

How do you handle rejection?

I just do.

I figure there are editors who want books to be perfect so they don't have to do much editing. They turn down imperfect ones. Mine are rarely perfect at the beginning. Others will see something in a book and are willing to work with it until it's right.

I did a book set in a hospital once and the editor wrote back, "This is too much of a downer. People don't want to read about hospitals, number one. And number two, your character doesn't learn as she goes along."

I thought, "Uh-huh. That's your opinion." Then I gave it to another publisher who read it and said, "This is good, but it needs some work."

This is not quite the same thing you asked but when someone sends a manuscript for me to criticize I ask if they want me to say if I like it or don't like it or if they really want me to criticize. Let me tell you, it's tough. Actually, though, I find most people want to be criticized.

If *I'm* going to be rejected, I prefer rejection with criticism accompanying it.

As a professional writer what is, to your thinking, a mandatory prerequisite?

Professional conduct.

It has to do with being prepared and disciplined. It has to do with listening to other people's ideas and meeting deadlines. If you say you're going to do something, you do it.

There are a lot of professional writers without professional conduct. Both parties must respect each other. That's why I have such a good relationship with one of my publishers, Harper & Row—mutual respect. Their attitude toward me is you are a talent and you're going to get better. Their attitude is, "We're going to nurture you."

For example, Liz called me up one day in between books and said, "What are you doing these days? I haven't seen anything from you. Come in and let's talk. I want to hear what's on your mind." And I think, "What a difference that makes."

My feeling is to give them things they want to publish. I want to be a professional. I want to do the work. I don't want to get into ridiculous unnecessary arguments. I don't like getting on a high horse. That's nonsense. There's no such thing as something that can't be worked out. That's absurd.

Let's back up for a minute. I'm unclear on one point. Did you start publishing books because of the Bank Street workshop?

Actually, yes. In that workshop, I read a story about a dog who thought he was a person. The group liked it. So

I sent it around. I didn't even know enough then to send it to one publisher at a time. So I sent it to three and I got a letter from Ann Durell, [publisher of children's books at E. P. Dutton] who took it.

She took another two of my books very quickly including my first novel, *No Applause, Please,* which is one of those semi-autobiographical things about growing up on Long Island.

So I sent her another one. And she didn't want it. I sent it to Harper. I had met Liz at an SCBW [Society of Children's Book Writers] conference at Bank Street. I really liked her a lot so I just walked up and introduced myself. She turned the book down, too, but said, "If you have anything else, just send it to me." So I sent her *It Can't Hurt Forever,* which I think has probably been my most successful novel to date.

So much for loyalty to a publisher?

Oooo, that's a tricky question. Yeah, I think loyalty is a good thing. But. . . .

I know, I know. It's also an unfair question. Let's get safe. Go through your day.

I get up very late because I go to sleep very late. It depends how many projects I'm working on. I usually don't start writing until three or four o'clock in the afternoon and then I write for two, three hours. I get a lot done in those hours. I spend so much time thinking before I sit down to write it, the idea is in good shape. Also, I find after writing for two or three hours I'm absolutely bonkers. It's invigorating to write but if I do it too long I don't do it as well.

When I write, I write linearly—first chapter, second chapter, et cetera. I go straight through. I never used to outline because frankly I hate to. I prefer watching the story unfold before me along the way. But lately I've been selling books before I write them. What I mean is, I guess I'm well known enough so that if I give a publisher a proposal and sample chapter, the publisher will give me a contract without having to see the finished work. So, sometimes I now outline.

As you are writing, how aware are you of trends and topics?

I think a lot of books have a proper timing. Sometimes I'll write a book because there seems to be something in the air that tells me to. It fits right. If the book comes out too much later, it misses the timing. If it comes out too early, readers may not be ready for it. But to be just early enough is to be on the vanguard.

When I wrote *The First Few Friends,* which is about growing up in New York in the turbulent late '60s, I was on the vanguard. There weren't many '60s books around. But I suspected there soon would be. And, in fact, several showed up after mine came out.

But the book didn't sell well. I don't know exactly why. I got good reviews on it and even some fan mail. But now I wonder if I wasn't too early after all. Or maybe it's the present "moral" climate in this country that accounted for the poor sales. The book has some rough language in it, which was appropriate to the '60s, but that seems to bother a lot of people now. It also has sex, drugs, and rock and roll. Basically, it's a borderline young adult-adult book, and that may have had something to do with its inability to find a niche.

But was it successful?

Financially, no. Artistically, yes.

How?

Because it was genuinely exhilarating to write. And because when I pick it up even now I still feel a sense of wonder that I managed to get all that stuff down on paper.

TITLE COMMENTARY

📖 *THE DOG WHO INSISTED HE WASN'T* (1976)

Publishers Weekly

SOURCE: A review of *The Dog Who Insisted He Wasn't,* in *Publishers Weekly,* December 13, 1976, p. 61.

The author has produced scripts for the popular TV program, "The Electric Company," and proves again that she knows how to appeal to the young with this gently amusing story about Konrad who truly believes he is a person, not a dog. [Kelly] Oechsli's cartoons are expert and a necessary part of the fun here as a little girl, Abigail, persuades her parents to accept Konrad's humanness. Konrad even goes to school with Abigail, which is OK until all the other children's dogs insist that they, too, are people and invade the classroom. Clearly, the situation is out of hand. Thanks to Abigail's ingenuity, Konrad is persuaded to stay home, when the other dogs are expelled, and to compromise by pretending to be a dog.

Zena Sutherland

SOURCE: A review of *The Dog Who Insisted He Wasn't,* in *Bulletin of the Center for Children's Books,* Vol. 30, No. 5, January, 1977, p. 82.

Oechsli's illustrations catch just the right note of sly ingenuousness that makes the text such pleasant nonsense. Konrad, convinced he isn't really a dog, finally finds a girl who sympathizes with his problem and who convinces her parents to go along. So Konrad sits at the dining table and goes to school with Abigail. Then the other dogs in the neighborhood begin insisting they aren't dogs either, which results in a tumultuous classroom; the dilemma is ingeniously solved by Abigail's teacher. Konrad agrees with Abigail to pretend he's a dog, "And as far as I know, he's still pretending," the story ends. Singer handles the animal-human dialogue deftly, and the adult-child relationships are exemplary.

Carol Chatfield

SOURCE: A review of *The Dog Who Insisted He Wasn't,* in *School Library Journal,* February, 1977, p. 58.

Canine Konrad, who disdains a dog's life, is fortunate enough to find a family that allows him to live out his fantasy of personhood. Pandemonium results when all the neighborhood dogs, envious of Konrad's freedom, decide to follow suit and accompany their masters to school. Treated as people, they now must eat oatmeal for breakfast, take bubble baths, and do math assignments. In the end, all opt for a return to doghood with Konrad graciously deciding to pretend to be a dog. Although an animal imagining himself to be human has been dealt with before in picture books, Konrad is a canine with a winning personality, and Singer's text has enough vitality and action to make it a good choice for reading aloud to one or two children.

📖 *NO APPLAUSE, PLEASE* (1977)

Idelle S. Wood

SOURCE: A review of *No Applause, Please,* in *School Library Journal,* Vol. 23, No. 9, May, 1977, p. 72.

Fourteen-year-old Ruthie Zeiler exuberantly shares with readers the frustrations of adolescence. Younger than everyone in her class and a self-styled outsider, Ruthie enjoys a brief moment in the limelight when she and her friend Laurie are first runners up in a school talent show. The girls' friendship becomes stormy, however, because of a shady agent who turns down the duo in favor of Laurie's solo act. Ruthie's concerns and the situations she finds herself in are typical—smoking in the school john; pot at a party—and, although her grandmother, with her old world stories and her Jewish cooking, does not seem to be the great font of wisdom as Singer tries to present her, this is brisk and believable and will be applauded by Ruthie's contemporaries.

Kirkus Reviews

SOURCE: A review of *No Applause, Please,* in *Kirkus Reviews,* Vol. XLV, No. 9, May 1, 1977, p. 493.

Essentially a story about friendship, and the need—as Ruthie's favorite teacher and her old-country grandmother keep reminding her—to stick by a friend even though she might be less than loyal. It's a lot to ask considering that Ruthie has always been the first to make up after fights with Laurie, and especially considering that Laurie and her silly, ambitious mother don't hesistate to drop Ruthie when the agent who auditions the girls as a winning high school duo decides he wants to handle only Laurie. Ruthie doesn't care about a performing career, only about her friend's treachery, but when it turns out that the agent has been taking Laurie and her mother for an expensive ride, even a nice new boyfriend doesn't keep Ruthie from running to her side. Certainly the theme applies widely at this level and the daydream of being a teenage duo appeals. (So, incidentally, will Ruthie's bold putdowns of Laurie's mother.) But Laurie hardly seems worth it-and though that might be part of the point, her shallowness sets the tone.

Denise M. Wilms

SOURCE: A review of *No Applause, Please,* in *Booklist,* Vol. 74, No. 2, September 15, 1977, p. 199.

The earthy brand of city-suburban cheek exhibited by Ruthie will score points with her audience; certainly some of her targets—a pretentious classmate whose pseudo-chic affectations are off-putting, or Sylvia, the pushy stage mama engineering best friend Laurie's singing career at the cost of the two girls' friendship—are made to seem deserving. The story's action turns on the hot-and-cold swings between Ruthie and Laurie. Laurie's cut about Ruthie being unnecessary to their singing duo hurts. The wound is deepened when Sylvia pushes Laurie solo into an agent's hands after the girls have auditioned together. When the agent turns out to be unscrupulous and Laurie is left in the lurch, it's up to Ruthie to be big about it and allow a renewal of the friendship on sadder, if wiser, grounds. The dialogue flows easily and another story thread, a budding romance between Ruthie and a classmate, nicely rounds out the plot development. Ephemerally satisfying for those inclined to a light, contemporary junior novel.

IT CAN'T HURT FOREVER (1978)

Karen Harris

SOURCE: A review of *It Can't Hurt Forever,* in *School Library Journal,* Vol. 25, No. 1, September, 1978, p. 149.

Ellie Simon enters the hospital for corrective heart surgery. Despite her parents' intelligent efforts to comfort her, she is afraid of the pain she anticipates and also of dying. She does find support from some of the nurses and from other young patients, but others exacerbate her fears either through lack of sensitivity or, in one instance, deliberately. The author provides an honest and thorough look at pre- and post-operative care and at the concerns of a girl facing a major trauma. She does not gloss over the suffering involved nor does she dismiss her heroine's worries that she may not survive the operation. Despite

some stilted dialogue, Singer has written an interesting and very useful book.

Kirkus Reviews

SOURCE: A review of *It Can't Hurt Forever,* in *Kirkus Reviews,* Vol. XLVI, No. 20, October 15, 1978, p. 1140.

She won't die, Ellie Simon's mother has promised her. Just what's wrong with her *patent ductus arteriosus,* she knows. But even with the finest preparation, the sanest, most sympathetic parents, being in the hospital for heart surgery is tough—and a sense of humor is the best defense. "'Urine analysis,' a jolly voice said" . . . and Ellie launches into an account of the embarrassment of bedpans (especially when "nothing happens"), the awfulness of some kids' mothers (*boy* roommate Kevin's "gets nervous," he says, "if she doesn't have anything to be concerned about"), the pluses and minuses of various doctors, and such side issues as race (to bouncy fellow-patient Sonia, who questions Ellie's disbelief in God: "Being Jewish is more like being black than like being Baptist"). She rebels at the prospect of a catheterization that she wasn't warned about and can't escape depression at the constant talk of death. Thinking about her scar-to-be, she's sorry for herself; then ashamed because Theresa, who has sickle cell anemia, "won't live until she's eighty," scar or not: "And she knows it." It's sharp, fast, funny, genuinely serious, and helpfully informative—a tonic for older kids as potent as Curious George's confinement for smaller fry.

Denise M. Wilms

SOURCE: A review of *It Can't Hurt Forever,* in *Booklist,* Vol. 75, No. 7, December 1, 1978, p. 620.

Ellie Simon's first-person, day-by-day account of her hospital stay and heart operation is strictly bibliotherapy but interesting enough nonetheless. Personality types are instantly recognizable—nice doctors, nurses, patients, and parents are offset by their mean or problematic counterparts. Emotional seesawing is correctly sketched, and the problems of befriended fellow patients introduce holding secondary story lines. Medical information generously sandwiched between story lines is interesting in its own right but will be especially relevant to youngsters themselves facing surgery for Ellie's "pretty common" *patent ductus arteriosus.* Effectively supportive.

Zena Sutherland

SOURCE: A review of *It Can't Hurt Forever,* in *Bulletin of the Center for Children's Books,* Vol. 32, No. 5, January, 1979, p. 88.

Ellie describes her experiences as a heart surgery patient in a story that is often weakened by being obtrusively informative, but that can nevertheless hold reader interest because of the hospital setting, the competent style and dialogue, and some of the well-defined characters Singer introduces. Ellie is frightened almost as much by the prospect of cardiac catheterization as by the operation itself; she does not have open heart surgery, but has a congenital defect that interferes with proper flow of blood. Singer doesn't minimize the pain and is candid about all medical details, although her Ellie is occasionally coy in dialogue (She gets a shot in her "you-know-what.") A black girl becomes her friend, she learns that other patients range from attention-getters to comforters and she observes the differences in parental attitudes toward other children who are patients.

WILL YOU TAKE ME TO TOWN ON STRAW-BERRY DAY? (1981)

Publishers Weekly

SOURCE: A review of *Will You Take Me to Town on Strawberry Day?,* in *Publishers Weekly,* Vol. 220, No. 10, September 4, 1981, p. 60.

Singer's verses resound with the glad excitement of an old-time country fair, the variety of entertainments celebrated by a pretty miss singing to her swain. [Trina Hakes] Noble imbues the bucolic scenes with life and loveliness in watercolor paintings that delight the eye on each page. They picture each development as the girl sings, "Will you take me to town / on Strawberry Day? / Hey nonny nonny nonny O! / In my raspberry dress / on a cart full of hay?/ And that'll be something to see O!" It is indeed. So is everything that goes on as the young couple feast, play games, wave at the queen passing by, dance an energetic reel and so on until they finally end their festive day. Singer appends an easily playable and singable musical arrangement to the book.

Kirkus Reviews

SOURCE: A review of *Will You Take Me to Town on Strawberry Day?,* in *Kirkus Reviews,* Vol. XLIX, No. 20, October 15, 1981, p. 1294.

An imitation folk rhyme, complete with music and a "Hey nonny nonny nonny O" in every verse, in which a girl reminds her boyfriend of the expected pleasures of an upcoming country fair. But instead of conjuring up the charms of the old-time occasion, Singer only ticks off conventional associations: the pair will, unimaginatively, "buy me a tart," drink "rosy-hip tea," "feast us on goose, on custard, on cream," and "dance us a reel." And instead of tripping along, her lines jog by on square wheels of contrivance: "Will we see Johnny Slack turn cartwheels-a-few?"; "Will we twine in our hair bright garlands so gay?" Noble has the pair disporting as called for among thatched roofs and canopied stalls, but these are just standard props for a flat performance.

Carolyn K. Jenks

SOURCE: A review of *Will You Take Me to Town on Strawberry Day?,* in *School Library Journal,* Vol. 28, No. 3, November, 1981, p. 82.

"Will you take me to town / on Strawberry Day? / Hey nonny nonny nonny O! / In my raspberry dress / on a cart full of hay? / And that'll be something to see O!" Twelve of these bucolic-nostalgic stanzas comprise this picture book, nicely illustrated in three colors. The score to this text is found at the end of the book; it flows more smoothly as a song than as a poem. Reminiscent of a simple, pleasant folk song, it could be used with a group as a light, if slight, June festivity activity.

THE FIRST FEW FRIENDS (1981)

Kay Webb O'Connell

SOURCE: A review of *The First Few Friends,* in *School Library Journal,* Vol. 28, No. 3, November, 1981, p. 111.

The vivid efflorescence of the late 60s seems now like the last fling for American youth. Singer lived it. Her warts-and-all depiction is humorous and engrossing. Nina Ritter, returning from her J.Y.A. in England in 1968, finds everything different and disturbing. Students at Queens College are uptight, her lover is back in England, and her closest girlhood friends (the Whole Sick Crew) are pulling in different directions. Aviva, for instance, is a rock vocalist, and her band, the Rabbit's Foot, is raunchy. In fact, all of Nina's crowd is acting out their new-found sex obsessions. Singer moves Nina, her alter ego, from a pseudo-intellectual kvetch to a socially responsible woman. The juxtaposition of college, which used to be safe and snug and where Nina is working toward a secure future in teaching, with the rock scene impels Nina forward to a new identity and involvement with student protest and antiwar demonstrations. Until Nina's senior year she'd never faced deep personal loss nor social inequity. In that one year she's betrayed by her first lover, is witness to her friends' deepening drug dependence and finds herself reaching out unexpectedly to a crippled veteran and a militant Black. The characterizations are true to life. While the events are history, the issues of war, media hype and the price of individuality are still with us. Well worth reading.

Stephanie Zvirin

SOURCE: A review of *The First Few Friends,* in *Booklist,* Vol. 78, No. 6, November 15, 1981, pp. 435-36.

Drawing on her own memories as a "child of the '60s," Singer renders the political, moral, and sexual flux of that era with precision and authenticity. When Nina Ritter returns to New York in 1968 after a year of study abroad and a serious romance with a poetic and passionate Welshman, she finds much changed. Youthful enthusiasm for motorcycles and leather jackets has given way to a reverence for rock music and an acceptance and widespread use of drugs. The Black Panthers have launched a bid for student support, the civil rights movement is gaining momentum, and the Vietnam War has become a highly volatile campus issue. Even Nina's old Queen's College buddies—the "Whole Sick Crew" as they christened themselves—have changed, especially Aviva, now a struggling rock singer whose brashness and uninhibited energy still hold the group together, but whose self-indulgence and promiscuous behavior leave Nina frankly appalled. But it is easier for Nina to follow Aviva into the bizarre world of rock music, engulf herself in a romantic haze of memory, and write erotic poetry to Gwyn than commit herself to new people or to the emotionally charged issues that surround her. Even the shock of Gwyn's arrival in New York with a wife is not quite enough to shake her entirely from her complacency. It takes betrayal from Aviva, police brutalization of a black activist to whom Nina is attracted both sexually and intellectually, and the drafting of a college friend to force her to rethink her attitudes toward friendship, love, independence, and obligation, and to put Aviva, the "Crew," and what they once signified in her life into proper perspective. While the wide spectrum of 1960s concerns and the plethora of characters dealt with (some very vividly drawn) burden and fragment the plot, and Singer's calculated reliance on bawdy humor, sexual explicitness, and rough language to convey character and drama push the novel almost into the adult sphere and put it out of reach of some teenage readers, her re-creation of the crazy stunts, late night gab sessions, and frank talks about sex and love ring true. Even more potent is Singer's portrayal of Nina's character—a rich, sensitive combination of romance and self-discovery that compels, involves, and gives cause for remembrance and reflection.

Tony Bednarczyk

SOURCE: A review of *The First Few Friends,* in *Best Sellers,* Vol. 41, No. 11, February, 1982, pp. 443-44.

At the opening Nina Ritter is returning to New York in 1968 after a year of study in England. She is a romantic, a poet, and wonders how she will readjust to America while pining over the separation from her Welsh boyfriend/lover, Gwyn. The transition is helped along by her three closest friends, Aviva, Dorrie and Nancy (a.k.a. The Whole Sick Crew) who immediately involve her in their new-found lives and interests, summarized by the great youth motto of the Sixties, "Drugs, sex and rock-and-roll." Interwoven with this are the growing civil unrest over Vietnam and the unsettling social changes fomented by militant and politically aware students.

At first Nina is confused and frightened, but as she realizes the inevitability of her evolving environment, she seeks to reevaluate her philosophy and values as they express themselves in relationships with various men. Nina finally establishes her identity by aligning herself romantically and politically with an activist in the Black Panthers.

I am very offended and not a little incensed that this should be offered to the public as a novel for young people (ages 12 and up). The language is certainly realistic and the instances of casual sex and even more casual experimentation with drugs are true to the times and temperament of some young adults during that time. Also, many teenagers would probably find little in Singer's work either shocking, distasteful, or particularly out of the ordinary. Nevertheless, I see absolutely no reason to legitimize and in some cases lionize what were and are still common, if less than appropriate, practices and propagate them in the guise of young people's literature. Furthermore, any value this book may have had in exploring one person's search for self definition is lost by placing it in a unique historical period which no adolescent could adequately comprehend. As adult fiction *The First Few Friends* might be a moderate success; as a Young People's title, it is a consummate failure.

THE FANATIC'S ECSTATIC, AROMATIC GUIDE TO ONIONS, GARLIC, SHALLOTS, AND LEEKS (1981)

Carolyn K. Jenks

SOURCE: A review of *The Fanatic's Ecstatic Aromatic Guide to Onions, Garlic, Shallots and Leeks,* in *School Library Journal,* Vol. 28, No. 7, March, 1982, p. 160.

"There's more to an allium than meets the nose." This statement, combined with the title, tells a lot about the content, style and tone of the book. The history, superstitions, botany, literature, chemistry, medicinal uses and many recipes are included. . . . The author certainly likes her subject, and has done much research; but the cluttered organization of her ideas gives the impression that she is overflowing with bits of information that she must give immediately, all at once. It is a humorous, self-indulgent book that an adult might dip into for some lighthearted reading.

TARANTULAS ON THE BRAIN (1982)

Zena Sutherland

SOURCE: A review of *Tarantulas on the Brain,* in *Bulletin of the Center for Children's Books,* Vol. 36, No. 1, September, 1982, p. 20.

Her older sister thinks Lizzie is peculiar because she's not interested in anything but science, and Lizzie is in despair because her mother is allergic to animals. The one thing in the world she really wants is a tarantula—Lizzie thinks they're beautiful—and when she finds one in a pet store she makes complicated arrangements to earn money to buy and keep it. She plans to sneak it into the house in a tank and keep it under her bed. Earning money by having a junk sale and caring for a magician's animals leads to appearing as the magician's assistant, a fact kept secret from her parents. After several abrasive experiences, Lizzie gets what she wanted: appreciation from her parents and sister, plaudits from her classmates, and even—after she's given up hope—the beautiful tarantula she's yearned for. The protagonist is appealing, although her intense focus is not quite believable; the writing style is lively, but the characterization is uneven and at times exaggerated (for example, the magician and his innamorata, other minor characters) although some of the relationships, particularly the friendship between Lizzie and her best friend in the fifth grade, have warmth and substance.

Ilene Cooper

SOURCE: A review of *Tarantulas on the Brain*, in *Booklist*, Vol. 79, No. 3, October 1, 1982, p. 250.

Lizzie is an animal lover and spider aficionado; her troubles begin when she decides that a tarantula would be the perfect pet. Her schemes to raise enough money to buy Ariadne, currently living at Noah's Ark Pet Shop, get her enmeshed in all sorts of catastrophes and involved with some quirky characters, including Buster, whose nickname leads him to dress as the various famous Busters in history. The humor is broad and the incidents are just this side of plausible, but Lizzy is a spunky character who manages to center a convoluted story that otherwise might have spun off in all directions.

Kirkus Reviews

SOURCE: A review of *Tarantulas on the Brain*, in *Kirkus Reviews*, Vol. L, No. 20, October 15, 1982, p. 1156.

Effortful, shopworn funny-business. The assumption here is not only that it's freakish to be interested in science, like ten-year-old narrator Lizzie, but that "science" means "trying to find out if mold grew faster on a hot dog or a hamburger," and other idiotic such. Virtually the whole book is on that burlesque level. Lizzie, fixated on tarantulas, locates one at a pet shop that will cost her, with supplies, $40.68. She has $5.57. Thanks to best-friend Tessa's weird uncle Buster—who dresses up as various characters (supposedly because he, like Lizzie, has an inferiority complex)—she gets a job taking care of a magician's menagerie. When the magician's girlfriend defects, she fills in—all this unbeknownst to her parents (from whom she's also concealing the fact that she may have sold her mother's engagement ring at a flea market). The scheme unravels because a nasty classmate squeals. But Lizzie does, true to form, get recognition, vengeance, and the tarantula. Even years back, though, this would have been pretty dreadful.

Susan I. Matisoff

SOURCE: A review of *Tarantulas on the Brain*, in

School Library Journal, Vol. 29, No. 4, December, 1982, pp. 68-9.

Unappreciated by family and school, Lizzie's interest in science turns into an obsession to own a pet tarantula. A small down payment, her best friend's moral support and a lot of gumption set Lizzie on a series of secret schemes to earn enough money to buy the tarantula. A junk sale that backfires and a stint as magician's assistant in a nightclub set the stage for eventual discovery and admiration by family and schoolmates. Much like Ruthie in Singer's *No Applause, Please,* Lizzie is intense and abrasive; secondary persons are one-dimensional caricatures. The exaggerated characterization will tickle some, leave others cold. Nevertheless, *Tarantulas on the Brain* is a lively plot which untangles an increasingly complicated web of dishonesty, secrecy and misunderstanding. The reader may very well identify with Lizzie's best friend Tessa, who observes the exuberance with sympathy and awe and participates in Lizzie's schemes with measured restraint.

THE COURSE OF TRUE LOVE NEVER DID RUN SMOOTH (1983)

Kirkus Reviews

SOURCE: A review of *The Course of True Love Never Did Run Smooth*, in *Kirkus Reviews*, Vol. LI, No. 8, April 15, 1983, p. 463.

Another high school cast plays musical boy-and-girlfriends while rehearsing a Shakespeare play. Singer's entry is lighter than Cohen's *Henry IV* workout in *Fat Jack*, less frivolous than Krensky's *The Wilder Plot*, which, like this one, was hung on *A Midsummer Night's Dream*. The outcome is obvious even without the jacket-flap giveaway, but the getting-there is likable enough. The first-person focus is on Becky, who plays Helena, and on her long-time friendship with fellow-junior Nemi, a talented actor who tries for Bottom but gets Puck, a role to stretch and challenge. Like most of the girls, Becky is gaga over handsome newcomer Blake, who'll do the lighting; and when Blake's knockout sister Leila, a senior, wows them all with her Titania, Nemi becomes her foremost victim. Soon Becky and Nemi are plotting to lure Blake and Leila by making a film that will feature the four of them. Leila is game, hoping the film will further her acting career, and soon the plot succeeds. But why does Becky feel so strange when Nemi comes out of the shower in just a towel? And why do Blake's kisses leave her cold? While Becky and Nemi are fleeing, then facing, the knowledge that they belong together, two other cast members are falling in love but having trouble with the girl's strict father; and, for a contemporary touch, a gay couple is also happily together except for difficulties with one boy's family. The kids are all infected with "the Quoting Disease," applying apt lines from the play to their own affairs, which gives the story that seductive atmosphere of group cohesion as well as the borrowed resonance of the parallels and Shakespeare's phrasing.

Zena Sutherland

SOURCE: A review of *The Course of True Love Never Did Run Smooth*, in *Bulletin of the Center for Children's Books*, Vol. 36, No. 9, May, 1983, p. 179.

This isn't the first book in which a boy and girl who've been childhood friends fall in love, nor is it the first in which the characters are involved in putting on a high school play—but it's better than most. Becky and Nemi are infatuated with the handsome brother and sister Blake and Leila; Becky suggests that Nemi, who's a film buff, create a movie so that he can give Blake and Leila parts. It works, but familiarity breeds awareness if not contempt: both protagonists find that physical attraction is not, after all, as strong as love. Not an unusual plot, but unusual treatment makes this a strong novel; the minor characters are sharply defined, the familial relationships are strongly drawn, with perceptive treatment of the dynamics of the acting group and especially of its gay members; the writing style has a smooth flow, natural dialogue, and good pace.

Sally Estes

SOURCE: A review of *The Course of True Love Never Did Run Smooth*, in *Booklist*, May 15, 1983, p. 1197.

Narrator Becky Weiss and Nehemiah (Nemi) Barish, a pair of 16-year-olds who have been best friends since third grade, get leading roles in the high school production of *A Midsummer Night's Dream*. Not long after Becky becomes enamored of new student Blake Harris, a veritable Adonis, Nemi falls for Blake's gorgeous sister, Leila, a talented senior playing the part of Titania, and the two friends launch a complicated scheme to win Blake and Leila. But when Blake responds to her, Becky finds herself confused not only by her lack of feeling for him but also by her jealousy over the apparently blossoming romance between Nemi and Leila. Incorporating plenty of dialogue from and references to the play (both in and out of rehearsal scenes), Singer neatly uses Shakespeare's comedic mix-up as a foil for the tangled web woven by her teenage protagonists. Though the vicissitudinous relationship between Becky and Nemi is at the center, other characters—peers and adults—are fleshed out enough to give all-around substance to a sprightly, funny junior novel that, while making observations about the verities as well as varieties of love and infatuation, leaves the reader with a pleasantly satisfied feeling that all's well that ends well. A note of warning however; those who are unfamiliar with the plot of Shakespeare's *Midsummer Night's Dream* may find this tough going.

Joan McGrath

SOURCE: A review of *The Course of True Love Never Did Run Smooth*, in *School Library Journal*, Vol. 29, No. 10, August, 1983, p. 80.

Becky Weiss is experiencing the usual adolescent turmoil of discovering herself and her true feelings, especially regarding the opposite sex. She has an unusually warm and supportive relationship with Nemi Barish, her friend since childhood. Just as she suffers pangs of unrequited love for blond and attractive Blake Harris, so Nemi languishes over Blake's gorgeous sister. The youngsters, and most of their friends, are deeply committed to the upcoming school production of *A Midsummer Night's Dream*. The complexities of the play, with its teasingly appropriate exposition of love vs. infatuation, offer an interesting counterpoint to the story of two young people discovering that they love one another, not the glamorous strangers over whom they have been mooning and scheming. There is much suggestive sexual banter, and a sympathetic treatment of the difficulties encountered by a gay couple who are "coming out" amidst the theatrical confusion; but readers will enjoy this good-humored and sensible story of a trying time in everyone's life.

THE FIDO FRAME-UP (1983)

Publishers Weekly

SOURCE: A review of *The Fido Frame-Up*, in *Publishers Weekly*, Vol. 224, No. 14, September 30, 1983, p. 116.

[Andrew] Glass's shaded-gray drawings spoof the menace in Singer's takeoff of revered private eyes, a frolic that kids will appreciate even if they have to be told who Sam Spade et al. are. Samantha (Sam) Spayed is Detective Philip Barlowe's shrewd dog and she gives readers the inside dope on how she has solved cases that have made him famous. Thanks to Sam, the affair of the Maltese Maltese is chalked up to Barlowe and the crook Derek Dangerfield is behind bars when the sleuth gets a new assignment. Lady Binghamton-Nugget hires him to find her priceless cameo, stolen by the Black Feather gang, Spayed suspects. Sniffing around, the cunning dog unearths clues that her master misses and brings the thieves to justice while earning more kudos for the rather feckless sleuth.

Nancy C. Hammond

SOURCE: A review of *The Fido Frame-Up*, in *The Horn Book Magazine*, Vol. LIX, No. 6, December, 1983, p. 712.

Reading like a spoof of the novels of Raymond Chandler and Dashiell Hammett, an amusing mystery story seems to mimic their sleuths, their sardonic style, and their staccato sentences. Enter the dog Sam (Samantha) Spayed and her human companion Philip Barlowe. Sam tells the story of their latest case: They were sitting around waiting for the phone to ring ("Barlowe was itching for a job and I was tired of sitting around scratching my fleas") when a call came from Lady Binghampton-Nuggets. Her cameo was stolen by the clever Black Feather Gang, and that meant trouble. But Sam marshaled clues; she kept her nose to the ground, used her "tail-wagging, tongue-licking" pooch act to deflect suspicion, and employed a canine informer. Then, steering Barlowe, who "has as much subtlety as a Saint

Bernard landing in a two-foot-deep puddle of water," she chased down the gang and retrieved the cameo. Nimbly alternating clues with surprises, the story sets a good pace and creates an appealing character—sardonic, supercilious Sam.

School Library Journal

SOURCE: A review of *The Fido Frame-Up*, in *School Library Journal*, Vol. 30, No. 4, December, 1983, p. 83.

In the tradition of Mary Blount Christian's canine sleuth Sebastian comes Singer's equally clever and resourceful four-legged sidekick Sam (short for Samantha) Spayed. Her master is detective Philip Barlowe but, like her canine counterpart Sebastian, it is really Sam who solves the cases. It all starts with the theft of Lady Binghampton-Nuggets' cameo. A feather left at the scene of the crime points the finger at the notorious Black Feather Gang. But proving it and capturing the crooks is no easy matter, especially when not even the gang members themselves know the name of the real boss. Barlowe dutifully follows up all the confusing leads and clues but it is Sam who guides him to the right conclusions by getting important information from other dogs. A trip to the pound and a madcap chase through a railroad station is in store for Sam before the identity of the "Boss" is revealed and a happy ending insured. *The Fido Frame-Up* may rely on the gimmick of being a detective spoof to get started but the plot itself is quite interesting. Lots of action and humor plus Glass' lumpy pencil drawings will have readers hoping that Sam gets off her leash again.

📖 THE CASE OF THE SABOTAGED SCHOOL PLAY (1984); *LEROY IS MISSING* (1984)

Zena Sutherland

SOURCE: A review of *The Case of the Sabotaged School Play*, in *Bulletin of the Center for Children's Books*, Vol. 37, No. 9, May, 1984, p. 174.

[In *The Case of the Sabotaged School Play*, two] brothers, Sam and Dave, are the detectives who solve the mystery of who is causing accidents and creating problems for the cast and crew of a school play. Like many other plays the Drama Club has put on, this one has been written by Mary Ellen, who also has a small part in the play *The Merry Pirates*. When somebody tampers with the light board, Sam thinks of a way to catch the culprit. This has action and some humor, but the characters are superficially drawn, the plot has a measure of contrivance, and the writing style is not Singer at her best.

School Library Journal

SOURCE: A review of *The Case of the Sabotaged School*

Play and *Leroy Is Missing,* in *School Library Journal*, Vol. 30, No. 9, May, 1984, p. 102.

The first two mysteries in a new series starring twins Sam and Dave. In *The Case of the Sabotaged School Play*, the better of the two, the boys are able to discover the saboteur of the school play, someone who wasn't suspect. In *Leroy Is Missing*, the twins set out to help Rita O'Toole find her missing brother. In the process they first uncover a bookie joint operating out of the basement of Tony's Pizzeria. Although there is nothing particularly special to set these books apart from other mysteries written for this age group, they do offer agreeable plots and characters packaged in an unintimidating format. Reluctant reader potential is an added bonus.

Publishers Weekly

SOURCE: A review of *The Case of the Sabotaged School Play*, in *Publishers Weekly*, Vol. 225, No. 22, June 1, 1984, p. 65.

Launching the Sam and Dave Mysteries, Singer tells a fast, twisty tale [*The Case of the Sabotaged School Play*] with [Judy] Glasser's nifty caricatures increasing the jollity and suspense. Ms. Kirby insists that the school drama club produce yet another turkey by Mary Ellen Moseby, *The Merry Pirates*. Sam and Dave Bean groan with others in the cast, begging to put on a real play, but Ms. Kirby is bent on encouraging her student's original scripts. During rehearsals and on opening night, a saboteur plants a snake near the timid leading actress, drops a chandelier on stage and commits other crimes, determined to wreck the performance. And so Sam and Dave investigate their first case, nabbing the culprit whose identity will amaze readers trying to outguess the author. The second series title, also a humdinger, is *Leroy Is Missing*.

Ilene Cooper

SOURCE: A review of *The Case of the Sabotaged School Play*, in *Booklist*, Vol. 80, No. 20, June 15, 1984, p. 1486.

[In *The Case of the Sabotaged School Play*,] Sam and Dave, the Bean brothers, are both taking part in a school play written by one of their classmates. The consensus is that the play, *The Merry Pirates*, is not very good, but it soon becomes apparent that someone thinks the play is so bad that it should not be produced at all. A snake appears in the leading lady's desk, the scripts are ruined, a chandelier falls (almost hurting one of the cast members), and a hidden stink bomb is the final straw. Singer carefully plots her mystery so that at one time or another any of the cast or crew might be the culprit. It is only through the clever sleuthing of Sam and Dave that the perpetrator is finally caught. This has much going for it—fast pacing, a breezy style, touches of humor, and enough red herrings to do Agatha Christie proud. A cut above most mysteries for this age group. Look for more from this deductive duo.

Zena Sutherland

SOURCE: A review of *Leroy Is Missing,* in *Bulletin of the Center for Children's Books,* Vol. 37, No. 11, July-August, 1984, pp. 212-13.

[In *Leroy Is Missing,* twins] Sam and Dave help their classmate Rita O'Toole in her hunt for Leroy, her eight-year-old brother who has not come back after being sent on some errands. The three friends trace Leroy's path, alarmed when they learn he's in the company of a man referred to as "Uncle Doug." They follow false clues and encounter danger in a story that is heavily dependent on coincidence and contrivance, and in which Leroy turns up with "Uncle Doug" quite on his own. There is plenty of action, but the plot isn't convincing enough to create suspense.

ARCHER ARMADILLO'S SECRET ROOM (1985)

Publishers Weekly

SOURCE: A review of *Archer Armadillo's Secret Room,* in *Publishers Weekly,* Vol. 227, No. 8, February 22, 1985, p. 158.

Singer's touching and quietly amusing story is bound to keep her audience involved in the problems of Archer, in misery at the prospect of losing his dear home. It's the best burrow in Texas, Archer declares, fine for exploring passages that have led him to his own private room. Old Paw (the armadillo's grandfather) is the only one in the family who agrees with Archer. His brother and parents are delighted with their new burrow, the uncomfortable dwelling that Archer slips away from while they are all asleep. Back in his den, the lonely one has second thoughts, especially when Old Paw joins him and announces that he, too, is running away. The author encompasses information on armadillo diets, etc., in her lyrical story, enhanced by Beth Lee Weiner's excellent, color-washed drawings.

Laura Bacher

SOURCE: A review of *Archer Armadillo's Secret Room,* in *School Library Journal,* Vol. 32, No. 4, December, 1985, pp. 82-3.

For any child who's had to move, the experience of leaving behind familiar faces and secure places can be devastating. *Archer Armadillo's Secret Room* is a gentle account of just such an experience. Archer loves his burrow: it was his grandfather's burrow before it became home to Archer, his 12 brothers and their Mom and Dad; there's plenty to explore and discover and, best of all, there's a special room where Archer can be all alone. When his father moves the family to a new burrow, Archer is not happy. In desperation and anger, he runs away, back to the old burrow. He soon realizes that its not the same any longer; however, it is the appearance of Old

Paw, also running away, that helps Archer deal with his confusion and loss. The black-and-white illustrations with touches of gold and green are as soothing as the story. A welcome book for both children and parents who are dealing with this difficult situation.

A NOSE FOR TROUBLE (1985)

Karen Stang Hanley

SOURCE: A review of *A Nose for Trouble,* in *Booklist,* Vol. 81, No. 16, April 15, 1985, p. 1200.

Sam (Samantha) Spayed, introduced in *The Fido Frame-up* as the canine helpmeet of detective Philip Barlowe, has resolved to let Barlowe crack his next case on his own. But when the genial gumshoe is called on to investigate the pirating of La Maison de Beauté's secret cosmetics formulas, only Sam understands that clues supplied by a stray amnesiac spaniel are the key to exposing the instances of industrial espionage. As before, Sam's terse narration parodies detective novel stereotypes. Witness the book's first sentence: "She was small, blonde, and very confused." (Not until five pages later do readers learn that the blonde is a dog.) Most of the humor, however, and all of the action will be enjoyed by fans of Blount's Sebastian series and younger mystery lovers in general.

THE CASE OF THE CACKLING CAR (1985); A CLUE IN CODE (1985)

School Library Journal

SOURCE: A review of *The Case of the Cackling Car* and *A Clue in Code,* in *School Library Journal,* Vol. 31, No. 9, May, 1985, p. 110.

These two mysteries star identical twins. Better than the twins' first two adventures, *The Case of the Sabotaged School Play* and *Leroy Is Missing,* these stories feature short but interesting plots with well-placed clues, giving young detectives plenty of chances to do their stuff. In the first mystery, the boys are visiting their aunt in Texas when they crack a case that involves smuggling pet birds into the country from Mexico. In the second, Sam and Dave come to the aid of the school bully before he is framed for stealing money saved for the class trip. A good choice for readers ready to tackle books more difficult than Adler's Cam Jansen series.

Kirkus Reviews

SOURCE: A review of *The Case of the Cackling Car* and *A Clue in Code* in *Kirkus Reviews,* Vol. LIII, Nos. 5-10, May 15, 1985, p. J-36.

One of many easy mystery series that readers tell apart chiefly by their identifying gimmicks, Singer's is the one with the twin brother sleuths. But if Singer's writing is typically mechanical, Judy Glasser's oblique, atmospheric pictures provide some offbeat charm and style.

Of this season's two entries, *A Clue in Code* poses a standard kids'-mystery problem—who stole the class trip money—and duly scatters suspicion among several of Sam and Dave's classmates. In the course of the twins' investigation, a coded message hits Sam on the head (it is written on a paper airplane) and a valuable comic-book collection gets mixed up with the missing money. For the genre, the solution is sufficiently well prepared and unexpected.

The second story is farther fetched. *The Case of the Cackling Car* takes the twins to Papagayo, Texas; lays on some poster-paint local color with fiesta floats and a string of Spanish-named characters; stirs things up with a kidnapping; and has Sam himself tied up in a car trunk with the kidnapped child before Dave and the twins' aunt, following in her car, catch up with the culprit—a parrot smuggler who snatched the kids when they discovered the cackling contraband in his car. This one is strictly for puzzle-story addicts who don't ask for credible motivation or for characters of even two dimensions.

Denise M. Wilms

SOURCE: A review of *The Case of the Cackling Car,* in *Booklist,* Vol. 81, No. 21, July, 1985, p. 1560.

[In *The Case of the Cackling Car,]* Sam and Dave are off to visit their aunt in Papagayo, a small Texas border town where they encounter several colorful characters and a kidnapping; little Cielita, daughter of an acquaintance of their aunt, has disappeared. The only real clue is the cryptic description, "cackling green Chevy," given them by a taciturn local named Nelson. In the course of the investigation, Sam disappears as well; it turns out that he, like Cielita, heard noises coming from a car that was being used for parrot smuggling by a town salesman named Hotshot. The story unfolds smoothly. . . . A good pick for readers new to full-length books.

Linda Callaghan

SOURCE: A review of *A Clue in Code,* in *Booklist,* Vol. 82, No. 2, September 15, 1985, p. 140.

[In *a Clue in Code,* the] detective twins, Sam and Dave Bean, are back on the crime trail when the class trip money disappears from Mrs. Corfein's classroom and Willie Landers, the custodian's son, is presumed guilty. When Sam and Dave catch Willie sneaking into the school, Willie insists someone stole his comic book collection and planted the money in his locker to frame him. Eager to solve the mystery, the twins begin to gather clues with the aid of Rita O'Toole. Sam finds a paper airplane with a strange message in green ink but, before Rita can decipher the message, someone knocks her down and steals the paper.

The simply structured tale has enough red herrings and possible suspects to keep readers sifting through the clues until the culprit is identified, the motivation revealed, and Sam and Dave have engineered the return of the money. Singer's ability to subtly incorporate the necessary facts of the case into the narrative demonstrates her respect for young readers eager for satisfying mysteries they can solve on their own.

HORSEMASTER (1985)

Denise M. Wilms

SOURCE: A review of *Horsemaster,* in *Booklist,* Vol. 81, No. 19, June 1, 1985, p. 1406.

Fantasy and adventure blend in this ambitious story of a 14-year-old girl who is pulled into another world, where she becomes a pivotal figure in a royal struggle between good and evil. A horse is the connecting fantasy link; Jessica first encounters him in powerful dreams, during which she flies on his back through the sky. The horse is related to a tapestry she discovers while exploring an abandoned house with her boyfriend. Possession of the tapestry thrusts her into a world where a benevolent king is in retreat from his sinister queen. From an ancient magus, or magician, named Ashtar, Jessica learns that she is to be the protector of this tapestry, which has great power. Its pictured horse is none other than Godrun, the horse-god Kadi's son, without which no one who calls himself Horsemaster can rule. Jessica believes she must deliver the tapestry safely to the absent King Tarkesh. Inhibiting her is the queen, who plots against Jessica so that she and her corrupt son might rule; aiding Jessica is the princess Noura, who is too weak to guard the tapestry as her father has asked, and who is held suspended in time by Ashtar. As Noura watches Jessica and communicates support, Noura gains strength and eventually is revealed as the new Horsemaster. Singer's plot is complicated and leaves a few questions dangling, but it's also brisk, intriguing, and laced with a bit of romance. Some may find the story's dramatic conclusion a little overwrought; others will relish its excitement. In any case, fantasy buffs will find it quite consumable.

Paul M. Lloyd

SOURCE: "Good Flying Horse Tale," in *Fantasy Review,* Vol. 8, No. 8, August, 1985, pp. 27-8.

Like most tales of fantasy, this one tells of the wanderings of mortals in the "perilous realm" of Faerie. In this case the wanderers are two troubled teenagers from Wisconsin. Jessica's father abandoned his family years ago and Jessica finds her mother more and more critical of her conduct as she grows up, to the point that she believes that her mother doesn't love her. Her only friend is Jack, a harum-scarum boy on equally bad terms with his parents who finally decide that they must send their wayward son to a military school. He is not really a bad boy, and both he and Jessica each find the other to be the only one who can understand how they really feel. Jessica also has strange dreams of riding a flying horse.

One day, out riding on a motorcycle without permission, they find an old farm house in which is a dusty tapestry depicting a beautiful horse. The tapestry turns out to be a gate leading to another world and the horse appears when Jessica calls him. Jessica and Jack decide to run away from home and make a life for themselves in the west, but are chased by the cops until Jack is injured and somehow they find themselves in the alternate universe to which the horse belongs. It is a sort of Middle Eastern (but not Islamic) kind of world. In this world Jessica turns out to be a royal princess involved in complicated intrigues in a civil war between two brothers contending for royal power. Opposed to the forces of good is the queen, mother of the princess and her brothers, formerly a good woman who has become addicted to black magic.

Books like this depend for their effect on how convincingly the authors make us believe in the story they tell us, and Singer does an exceptional job. Jessica and Jack are believable adolescents with genuine problems and their adventures in the fantasy world are close reflections of their troubles in the primary world. Their personalities and lives are depicted with great skill. This book is highly recommended.

Debra Loop Maier

SOURCE: A review of *Horsemaster,* in *Voice of Youth Advocates,* Vol. 8, No. 3, August, 1985, p. 194.

Fourteen-year-old Jessica is rebellious and has as a best friend the town's worst kid, Jack. When family tensions grow too taut, the pair decide to run away. Taking refuge in an old house, Jessica is given a horse tapestry to guard. Jack is kidnapped by the Red Lady, an evil Queen, who pulls him into her own world. The price of his release is the tapestry. Jessica follows her love into this oriental world and learns that the pictured horse is really Godrun, a demigod and whoever holds him has immense powers. The Princess Noura is supposed to guard the tapestry, but she is unable to stand up to her mother, the Red Lady, once she turns to black magic. Noura is transported to a place out of time for her own safety and Jessica is given the responsibility of guarding Godrun. Jessica goes through many adventures in this strange land and at the climax of her experiences a bloody war between the Queen and her husband threatens to destroy the land. At this point, Noura accepts her position to Horsemaster and peacebringer and Jessica is free to take Jack and return home. During her travels, Jessica finds out much about herself and her family. She accepts the fact that her father has deserted them and respects the pressure her mother withstands. Her time away has turned her from a child into an adult.

There is action, adventure, and love in this work. Jessica is a gutsy heroine with strong beliefs. The weak links are the characterizations of adults. Most are weak, shallow, or misguided. Jessica is no angel and argues and swears. Although she is innocent sexually, hints of activity around her are made. There are many books that interweave modern life with the fantastic. Although *Horsemaster* will never be a classic like *Wizard of Oz,* or works by L'Engle, and C. S. Lewis, it is a satisfying read.

Barbara Hutcheson

SOURCE: A review of *Horsemaster,* in *School Library Journal,* Vol. 32, No. 1, September, 1985, p. 149.

Teenage Jessica has been having strange dreams about a flying horse. When she and local bad boy Jack run away from home to escape family troubles, they hide in an abandoned farmhouse. Inside is a tapestry portrait of the dream horse. This becomes the key to another world and time, a desert kingdom where Jessica and Jack are caught up in a murderous struggle for power. At first, Jessica is an unwilling participant, but gradually her faith in herself and strength grow, and she begins to assume the role demanded of her. Magical her adventures may be, but when she and Jack return to their own place and time, it is clear that their lives have been changed forever. The language is colorful, occasionally poetic, with some interesting imagery. Careful reading is required to avoid confusion as time and characters shift, and narrative changes from third to first person and back again. The balance of the real and the fantastic is sustained, but there is no plausible explanation as to how the tapestry got into the farmhouse in the first place. The Thanksgiving Day reunion of Jessica with her mother is far too pat, and the one real disappointment of the novel. Overall, a successful fantasy with some minor flaws.

LIZZIE SILVER OF SHERWOOD FOREST (1986)

Zena Sutherland

SOURCE: A review of *Lizzie Silver of Sherwood Forest,* in *Bulletin of the Center for Children's Books,* Vol. 39, No. 8, April, 1986, p. 158.

The protagonist of *Tarantulas on the Brain* is the narrator of another funny but not wholly convincing story. It combines two themes: one is Lizzie's passionate interest in Robin Hood and her fantisizing about being one of his band. The other is her attempt to enter the music school where her best friend has just won admittance. Lizzie's conviction, when she meets an actor playing Robin Hood at a medieval festival, that he needs her help, is not credible, nor is her belief that she can learn, in six weeks, to play the harp well enough to get accepted by a very selective music school. However, the story has brisk pace, humor, and a lively style and should therefore be appealing to readers.

Kim Sands

SOURCE: A review of *Lizzie Silver of Sherwood Forest,* in *Voice of Youth Advocates,* June, 1986, p. 83.

Ten-year-old Lizzie Silver's "newest obsession" (as her mother calls it) is Robin Hood. Her best friend Tessa's poetic Uncle Buster feeds Lizzie's imagination with books and shared fantasies and even a trip to Sherwood Forest (New York) where Lizzie forgets she's watching rehearsed scenes and attempts to rescue Robin Hood. Despite the fun and frolics, Lizzie has a most serious task at hand as she tries to become talented enough musically to accompany Tessa to Pemborough, an elite music school to which Tessa has earned a scholarship. After determining she has an aptitude for the harp (a la Allan-a-Dale), Lizzie diligently (however woefully) applies herself to becoming a virtuoso in six weeks' time. At one point in Lizzie's identity showdown, she and Buster agree they like science because it's about what's real and what's imagined. Buster tells Lizzie, "The best scientists have feet in both worlds" to which Lizzie replies, "I think one of my feet slipped."

Lizzie eventually completes her summer with an unexpected job, an unexpected new friend, and an unexpected new obsession, leaving the reader eager for a third Lizzie Silver story (this being the sequel to *Tarantulas on the Brain,* but standing well on its own). *Lizzie Silver* will be a favorite of 5th and 6th graders and should be an especially good read-aloud at 6th grade.

Ilene Cooper

SOURCE: A review of *Lizzie Silver of Sherwood Forest,* in *Booklist,* Vol. 82, No. 20, June 15, 1986, p. 1544.

Lizzie Silver, the spider-obsessed middle-grader who was introduced in *Tarantulas on the Brain,* has two new interests—Robin Hood and mastering the harp so she can follow her best friend, Tessa, to a world-renowned music conservatory. Plunging into these avocations with her usual intensity, Lizzie soon finds her exuberance causing some difficulties. She comes to realize that she will never play an instrument as well as Tessa; at the same time, her overactive imagination leads to a run-in with an actor who is playing Robin Hood at a medieval "faire." It's difficult to believe that the ultrasensible Tessa and the act-first, think-later Lizzie are the same age, much less best friends. However, readers who can get past that disparity will enjoy the story's fast pacing and many humorous moments.

Patricia Manning

SOURCE: A review of *Lizzie Silver of Sherwood For-*

est, in *School Library Journal,* Vol. 33, No. 2, October, 1986, p. 183.

Lizzie Silver, ten, first encountered in *Tarantulas on the Brain* is back with a new obsession—Robin Hood! No Maid Marian she, but a Merry Man, and her fantasizing rushes her to Robin's aid at a Medieval Faire, to the disgruntlement of the actors, and a rude awakening to reality for herself. Lizzie has more on her mind than the workings of her tenacious imagination—best friend Tessa has won a scholarship to a prestigious, though far-away, music school, and Lizzie, determined to accompany her, attempts to master the harp (of all things) in a desperate six-week struggle. Just when all seems lost, a new friend appears and teaches her to be a one-girl band. No accolades from the music world, to be sure, but balm to a battered self-esteem. Exaggerated, of course, and a tad improbable, but light, fluffy, and fast.

📖 **WHERE THERE'S A WILL, THERE'S A WAG (1986)**

Publishers Weekly

SOURCE: A review of *Where There's a Will, There's a Wag,* in *Publishers Weekly,* June 27, 1986, p. 92.

According to Samantha Spayed, percipient dog detective, "When it comes to books there's sometimes more between the covers than just the pages." As usual, Sam is right. From the double pun of its title to its irresistible end, this new Sam Spayed title is a cleverly conceived, delightful spoof. Sam not only tells the story of the search for a missing will, she solves the crime. (Her human partner Barlowe is too dim-witted to follow a clue.) The mystery could easily stand on its own, but [Andrew] Glass's shadowy black-and-white drawings add just the right touch of affection and grit.

Denise M. Wilms

SOURCE: A review of *Where There's a Will, There's a Wag,* in *Booklist,* Vol. 82, No. 22, August, 1986, p. 1694.

Singer's tongue-in-cheek, dog-detective series continues in this witty third installment. Samantha Spayed, canine partner and real brains behind the fumbling but famous detective Philip Barlowe, narrates the story of how she and Barlowe figure out just what Miss Carlotta Bucks intended when she left her millions to her cat Snoogums. Carlotta's will is being contested by her nephew, who hires Barlowe. As Sam and Barlowe search for a more logical and alternative will, they uncover a fraudulent scheme involving some of Carlotta's associates; they also discover that Carlotta was no fool and enjoyed a good mystery herself—hence, the strange plot she evolved before her death ensuring that her money went where she really wanted it to go. The comic mystery is deftly handled; Sam's arch narrative is brisk and entertaining and the action never flags. This is good fun.

Katharine Bruner

SOURCE: A review of *Where There's a Will, There's a Wag,* in *School Library Journal,* Vol. 32, No. 10, August, 1986, p. 97.

Samantha Spayed, the brainy canine sidekick of private detective Philip Barlowe, returns for her third case in this verbally appealing woof-spoof. The casting is pure TV cardboard; the plot, dog-gone serial; but the style is zippy and chock full of word play. Carlotta Bucks, wealthy manufacturer of Peaceable Kingdom All-Vegetarian Pet Food, has died and willed her fortune to her cat, Snoogums. The gambler, Hy Stakes, convinced that his aunt should have left him more than just a box of old books, hires Barlowe—and Sam Spayed—to sniff out the real will. After following several leads with bumbling Barlowe, Sam solves the case on her own, finding that Carlotta Bucks has actually left her dough to "the greatest detective in the world" (that's Sam) and named Philip Barlowe trustee. Like the Howes' *Bunnicula,* Singer's tale will please young readers who have developed an ear for farcical take-off. Alone, the mystery is light but likable.

📖 THE LIGHTEY CLUB (1987)

Kirkus Reviews

SOURCE: A review of *The Lightey Club,* in *Kirkus Reviews,* Vol. LV, No. 7, April 1, 1987, p. 562.

Three young sisters—Henny, Alex, and Celia Rubin—are sent to stay with their grandparents for six weeks one summer. They are not looking forward to it—Grandfather is silent and hard to talk to, and Grandmother plans every moment of every day with various "enriching activities." To fight their boredom, they form the Lightey Club, at which Henny, the eldest sister, tells stories about Lightey the lightning bug and his friends, all of whom, the girls are sure, live in the lush garden behind their grandparents' house. The story of the girls' summer is interspersed with stories about Lightey and his world. Unfortunately, the bug tales are far less appealing than the growth and changes that the girls experience as they come to understand their grandparents. In the last half, as the action picks up, the bug stories appear more often and become more intrusive.

Although Lightey's adventures reflect the feelings and activities of the girls, the two worlds have not been successfully linked. A gentle story, but slow-moving and fragmented.

Publishers Weekly

SOURCE: A review of *The Lightey Club,* in *Publishers Weekly,* Vol. 231, No. 16, April 24, 1987, p. 71.

When Henny and her sisters are sentenced to their grandparents' house for six weeks while their parents are away, Grandma determines to fill the girls' days with organized activities. Chafing under this well-meant but boring supervision, Henny invents an ongoing fantasy about the bugs in the garden. Henny's inventions about the talking bugs read like a bright fifth grader's writing efforts, and the stolen moments the girls spend in the garden are realistic. However, these stories fail to sustain interest; they mirror the sisters' feelings, but the transition to bugdom just does not work. A potentially interesting character, a long-lost cousin, is introduced and then jarringly dispatched in one chapter. But readers may easily identify with Henny and her attempts to entertain.

Katharine Bruner

SOURCE: A review of *The Lightey Club,* in *School Library Journal,* Vol. 33, No. 8, May, 1987, p. 104.

Three young sisters dread being sent to their grandparents for six summer weeks, where Grandmother always enforces a strict regime of activities. Trying to enliven the dull summer, Henny begins telling her younger sisters imaginative tales about Lightey, a lightning bug who lives in the garden, and his insect friends. The result is a dull book. The two story lines, one real, one make-believe, are not drawn out in neatly converging rays but, in glowworm fashion, only seen briefly here and there without much sense of continuity. Characterizations are minimal. Singer has done her entomological homework and makes some attempt at illuminating human behavior through insect antics. But readership may be limited to the special young person who, like Henny, is beginning to create a fantasy world and share it with special friends.

Betsy Hearne

SOURCE: A review of *The Lightey Club,* in *Bulletin of the Center for Children's Books,* Vol. 40, No. 10, June, 1987, p. 197.

Three sisters, "stuck" with their grandparents while their parents are digging artifacts in Mexico, suffer through Grandma's rigid scheduling by escaping into the oldest girl's stories about garden insects. A lightning bug named Lightey is the main character in these ventures, all of which reflect episodes in the girls' daily lives, but there is a large cast including Drusilla the Fruitfly, Twinky the Monarch Butterfly, Ms. Mantis, Millicent Ladybug, Morris the jolly earthworm, George the centipede poet, etc. Unfortunately, both the bugs and the people are flattened to one or two characteristics, the former tending toward cuteness and the latter to stereotype. The style is awkward, too, both in the narrative ("But when they got to the farm, Grandma told them to work quickly and not eat any berries because they had to fill a lot of pints so the Do-Our-Part Club (which she was running for president of) could make strawberry shortcake for the senior citizens at the Autumn Age Center") and in the child's stories ("And, sure enough, the graceful and gorgeous butterfly fluttered up to them. 'Gee, everyone's awake. That jay is causing quite a stir,' she said, unruffled"). The structure of a tale within a tale is somewhat distracting, with fantasy and realism alternately pulling at a reader's attention. Overall, this is the kind of game that is delightful (and revealing) to overhear children playing but that is hard to translate into fiction without expert, objective crafting.

GHOST HOST (1987)

Randy Brough

SOURCE: A review of *Ghost Host,* in *Voice of Youth Advocates,* Vol. 10, No. 2, June, 1987, p. 83.

Bart Hawkins has it all—he is dark, handsome, the star quarterback of the high school football team, and he dates Lisa, the cute, vivacious captain of the cheerleading squad. Bart also loves to read, but fear of being branded a nerd causes him to keep his passion for books a secret. When Bart discovers that a poltergeist by the name of Stryker inhabits his home, his life is thrown into a turmoil. Enlisting the help of Millie, a friendly ghost, and Arvie, the class egghead, Bart strives to find a way to pacify the mischievous spectre before Stryker ruins him.

Ghost Host is above all else fun to read. Singer's deft introduction of the supernatural into the world of a high school junior, his family, and friends creates headaches for everyone, ghosts included. Bart Hawkins is a fully realized protagonist, sympathetic in his struggle to balance his desire for popularity with his intellectual inclinations. The supporting characters, ghosts and humans alike, are interestingly developed as well. The novel advocates reading and libraries in an understated yet convincing fashion. *Ghost Host* is a quirky, spirited book which should appeal to a broad YA audience.

Kirkus Reviews

SOURCE: A review of *Ghost Host,* in *Kirkus Reviews,* Vol. LV, No. 13, July 15, 1987, p. 1076.

When Bart Hawkins moved to Sprocketsville, he left behind one identity, Bart the Bookworm, and arrived with a new one, Bart the Big Man. He soon became star quarterback of his high-school team, but two years later he still likes to read (secretly), and his cover is about to be blown. Furniture begins rearranging itself, china breaks and messes appear—and then the spirit of young Millicent appears and tells Bart he's living among a houseful of ghosts, all friendly except for Stryker, the poltergeist. Bart's problem is to rid the house of Stryker without ridding it of Millicent and the others. He begins reading up on ghosts and haunted houses, and is soon striking deals with spirits, teaming up with the school nerd, neglecting his football, putting himself in danger of once again becoming Bart the Bookworm.

This deftly turned novel is more than just another ghost story; with plenty of action and humor, it is also about a young boy coming to grips with who he is, relationships and understanding. The characters, including the ghosts, are believable and likable. Pleasantly unpredictable and entertaining.

Michael Cart

SOURCE: A review of *Ghost Host,* in *School Library Journal,* Vol. 34, No. 1, September, 1987, pp. 182-83.

Bart and Lisa are a match made in heaven—or in *Seventeen* magazine, at least. He's the darkly good-looking quarterback of the Dr. Kelley DeForest High School football team. Lisa is captain of the cheerleading squad and vice president of the junior class. Everything should be perfect. But wait! There's trouble in paradise. Bart has a dark secret: he's a closet bookworm who would rather read *Macbeth* than score a touchdown. Could anything possibly be worse? Yep. Bart discovers the old house his family has moved into on Hexum Road is haunted. For reasons which Singer never clarifies, Bart must keep this as dark a secret as his literary proclivities. This becomes increasingly taxing when the friendly ghosts are joined by a rambunctious poltergeist whom Bart must exorcise—but without harming the more salutory spirits who have, after all, promised to help him win the big football game. Bart, an engaging and sympathetic character, will probably score as many points with readers as he does on the football field. But even he can't redeem the predictable plot, the cardboard characters, and the leaden style which—like poltergeists—plague Singer's latest.

SEVERAL KINDS OF SILENCE (1988)

Cindy Darling Codell

SOURCE: A review of *Several Kinds of Silence,* in *School Library Journal,* Vol. 35, No. 2, October, 1988, p. 164.

Singer vividly portrays a family in crisis. Angered by what he perceives to be his failure to support his family adequately, Mr. Yeager suppresses his discomfort by venomously attacking the Japanese for dislocating the economy and his own family for whatever small faults he can uncover or imagine. Each member of the family has developed an indvidual survival response. Mrs. Yeager desperately tries to run the perfect household. Rebellious Lainie exhibits behavior designed to provoke her father. Quiet 16-year-old Franny submerges her distress with silent, controlled behavior, and finally gains a measure of escape in her work with a kind florist. Pressure mounts on Franny as her beloved grandmother becomes ill, her new Japanese boyfriend demands to meet her family, and her sister hints at exposing her cross-cultural romance. Singer's characterization is masterful, with clear psychological motivation carefully layered and subtly revealed. Excellent foreshadowing makes the plot twists seem quite natural. This book can be appreciated as an entertaining love story, or upon further study as an excellent thematic examination. Singer has written movingly about silence, or the failure to communicate, and all the noise that people use to hide it.

Denise M. Wilms

SOURCE: A review of *Several Kinds of Silence*, in *Booklist*, Vol. 85, No. 7, December 1, 1988, p. 640.

Franny finds relief from her tension-riddled family not only in learning Japanese flower arranging and dabbling in Zen, but also in Ren, short for Renfrew Tanazaki, the gorgeous Japanese-American grandson of the florist who employs her. But her enjoyment of both flowers and Ren begins to fade as troubles build at home. Her beloved grandmother loses part of her leg to diabetes; her father loses his job; and Franny's younger sister, Lainie, becomes ever more contentious and rebellious. Worst of all, however, is Franny's belief that she can't tell her family about Ren lest she be forbidden to see him. Her father is very vocal about his dislike of the Japanese, who, he believes, are responsible for his losing his auto-parts job. Franny responds by withdrawing from everyone until a battle royal with her sister and a cathartic meeting with Ren put her back in touch with her emotions and give her the courage to deal with her parents' prejudices. Singer's picture of a working-class family under strain is credible, and Franny's romance with Ren (who is almost too good to be true) will have great appeal. Worthwhile popular reading that Singer's fans will welcome for its diversions.

Eugene La Faille

SOURCE: A review of *Several Kinds of Silence*, in *Voice of Youth Advocates*, Vol. 11, No. 6, February, 1989, p. 290.

Franny Yeager is a 16 year old girl whose role of "Miss Perfect" in a troubled family often causes her anguish. Franny's younger sister Lainie is bold and sassy beyond her years, her father's job at an auto parts plant is precarious and he hates anything Japanese, her mother is excessively submissive, and her grandmother is diabetic. When Franny gets a job at a florist shop where she can learn Japanese flower arranging and falls in love with a young Japanese man who is the grandson of the florist, her father loses his job and her grandmother has surgery. All these difficulties are more than she can handle.

Too many plot elements are contrived in this novel, such as the father's hatred of Japanese; Franny's desire to learn Japanese flower arranging; her surprise at being hired by a florist who can teach her this skill; the coincidence that she falls in love with Ren who is the grandson of the owner of the florist shop; and the juxtaposition of the amputation of her grandmother's leg, Franny's inability to tell her secret about Ren to her family, and her father losing his job. Much of the dialogue is breathless and melodramatic in tone, with few of the characters showing the necessary maturity for a book which has been nominated as a 1988 BBYA.

Ai-Ling Louie

SOURCE: "Growing Up Asian American: A Look at Some Recent Young Adult Novels," in *Journal of Youth Services in Libraries*, Vol. 6, No. 2, Winter, 1993, pp. 115-27.

Franny Yeager falls for a boy she sees only briefly. All she knows is that he has a red dragon emblazoned on his black jacket. The boy turns out to be Ren Tanazaki, the romantic hero of *Several Kinds of Silence* by Marilyn Singer. Franny cannot bring Ren home to meet her folks because her father spouts racist epithets against the Japanese, who he thinks are ruining the U.S. auto industry, in which he works.

The author does not seem to have a deep understanding of what it means to be Japanese American. When Franny greets Ren for the first time with "Ohayo," which she thinks means "Hello" in Japanese, Ren laughs it off by saying he doesn't come from Ohio. Franny, in her assumption that Ren should be greeted this way, is showing how ignorant she is about Asian Americans. Ren doesn't even speak Japanese. I know it makes me angry when people come up to me and try to speak Chinese. It shows they perceive me, a third-generation American, as first and foremost a foreigner.

Franny is studying ikebana, Japanese flower arranging, and is interested in Zen. She's "into" Japanese things, and it seems it is Ren's "Japaneseness" that Franny finds most attractive. Ren is only half-Japanese, but Franny's fantasies about him always have him wearing a black silk kimono with silver fans embroidered on it. And Ren isn't the only one wearing a kimono in her fantasies:

> The doorway led to a white-tiled room. Franny followed him into it. There was a big raised bath in the center, the kind Franny'd seen in movies about Japan. . . . She stood before him wearing her butterfly kimono.

Ren seems to be a male Suzy Wong. He is described as having "looks, brains, talent, taste, and a beautiful butt." He's handsome and sexy and seems very Japanese to Franny, and that's what she seems to like best about him. Of course, he isn't very Japanese—he plays and sings in a rock band, wants to fly a plane, and, other than owning a kimono, doesn't exhibit any ties to his grandfather's homeland. Franny has fallen in love with her stereotypical image of Ren, not his substance.

📖 *MINNIE'S YOM KIPPUR BIRTHDAY* (1989)

Kirkus Reviews

SOURCE: A review of *Minnie's Yom Kippur Birthday*, in *Kirkus Reviews*, Vol. LVII, No. 7, April 1, 1989, p. 554.

Minnie was born on Rosh Hashanah, the Jewish New Year—but this year her birthday falls on Yom Kippur, the Day of Atonement. She knows that because her fifth birthday falls on the holiest day of the year it will be "different"; but since she hasn't much idea of what Yom Kippur is, she doesn't know what to expect. Dressing in her nicest clothes and rushing downstairs, she is surprised to find her parents and older brother fasting rather than eating breakfast. Later, she and her younger sister are left with a babysitter while the others go to Temple. But in the late afternoon, the entire family attends services; and, after the congregation breaks their fast, the Rabbi announces "something we've never done before": a birthday celebration for Minnie, complete with cake.

This pleasant little story could serve as a young child's introduction to Yom Kippur, though the Temple service is seen through Minnie's eyes, leaving much for an adult to elucidate. . . . Not outstanding, but certainly useful.

Ellen Mandel

SOURCE: A review of *Minnie's Yom Kippur Birthday,* in *Booklist,* Vol. 85, No. 17, May 1, 1989, p. 1554.

When her birthday falls on Yom Kippur, her religion's most solemn observance, young Minnie is miffed. Instead of a special birthday breakfast, there are only cornflakes (Yom Kippur is a fast day for adults), and instead of friends coming over for a party, there is only the babysitter—her parents and brother are off to worship. Minnie's frustration dissipates near day's end when she enters the sanctuary for the first time, hears the shofar, responds to the call to self-improvement, and shares a surprise birthday cake when the entire congregation breaks their fast. Singer's unusual approach makes the holiday's themes and symbols accessible to all who can identify with Minnie's distress over a spoiled birthday. At the same time, [Ruth] Rosner's wispy watercolors convey the new experiences and torrent of emotions flooding Minnie's memorable celebration.

Micki S. Nevett

SOURCE: A review of *Minnie's Yom Kippur Birthday,* in *School Library Journal,* Vol. 35, No. 12, August, 1989, p. 132.

Minnie's fifth birthday falls on Yom Kippur, the most solemn of Jewish holidays. She is disappointed at how different this birthday is: no fuss is made over her, and the grownups go to temple and fast. Then, at the end of the day, the entire congregation has a huge birthday cake in honor of her birthday at a break-the-fast celebration. Watercolors are lively and capture Minnie's wonderful expressions. Singer does an excellent job of incorporating all of the rituals and beliefs of Yom Kippur into the story. However, while the device of making this Minnie's first visit to a temple works well in terms of providing explanations, it is difficult to believe that a five year old has never been to services previously. This book is obviously geared toward a liberal Jewish community, as more observant Jews will find a female Cantor offensive.

THE CASE OF THE FIXED ELECTION (1989); THE HOAX ON YOU (1989)

Elaine E. Knight

SOURCE: A review of *The Case of the Fixed Election* and *The Hoax on You,* in *School Library Journal,* Vol. 35, No. 10, June, 1989, p. 109.

Twins Sam and Dave, the Bean Brother detectives, return in two new adventures. In *Fixed Election,* Dave's run for Student Council president is marred by a campaign filled with rumors and dirty tricks attempting to discredit him and the other candidates. Dave and Sam are accused of stuffing the ballot box to assure Dave's election and must clear their names by discovering which candidate is responsible for the scandals. *Hoax on You* finds the brothers preparing to enter a magazine contest for the best hoax. Their plans are complicated by Dave's crush on a new exchange student, Dardanella, and by a practical joker friend. Sam suspects that Dardanella may not be what she seems, but when she becomes the suspect in a series of jewel thefts, the detectives set a trap to catch the real crook. Clues and red herrings are scattered liberally through the stories, and middle-grade mystery fans will have fun trying to outguess the Bean Brothers.

Phillis Wilson

SOURCE: A review of *The Case of the Fixed Election* and *The Hoax on You,* in *Booklist,* Vol. 85, No. 19, June 1, 1989, p. 1727.

Two more in the action-packed mystery series featuring the Bean brothers, Sam and Dave. In *Fixed Election* the private eyes are up to their ears in dirty politics. Dave is running for student council president with Sam as his campaign manager. In a series of incidents involving stuffed ballot boxes and stolen toys, suspicions and counter suspicions fly until the real culprit is uncovered. *Hoax* features a hoax within a hoax. Dardanella, a foreign exchange student, is enchanting everyone (including Dave); Sam seems to be the only one making the connection between her and jewelry that turns up missing. Can Sam cast suspicion on the lovely Dardanella? Will Dave help him catch the thief? Is Dardanella even who she claims to be? Singer keeps the tantalizing suspense going right up to the last page. Well-delineated characterizations and brisk pacing add to the fun.

Zena Sutherland

SOURCE: A review of *The Case of the Fixed Election,* in *Bulletin of the Center for Children's Books,* Vol. 42, No. 11, July-August, 1989, p. 284.

There are three candidates for student council president [in *The Case of the Fixed Election,*] and as the campaign progresses, there is increasing evidence of dirty tricks. One of the candidates is Dave Bean, who—with his twin brother, Sam—does some detective work to ferret out who did or said what and for what reason; their investigations reveal the power-hungry classmate who is the culprit. The story loses suspense as the clues to labored incidents emerge; it seems an overextended treatment (although it is not really a long story) that is unleavened by humor or drama and that lacks any interesting characterization.

📖 *STORM RISING* (1989)

Publishers Weekly

SOURCE: A review of *Storm Rising,* in *Publishers Weekly,* Vol. 236, No. 8, August 25, 1989, p. 65.

This love story of a 17-year-old pianist, Storm, and a 28-year-old psychic, Jocelyn, is told from the boy's point of view. Storm is one of the walking wounded—his absent father is an alcoholic, his mother is a floozy, and his girlfriend has just left him. At first Storm is disturbed by Jocelyn, who hires him to help remodel her house, especially after he discovers her talent for healing, but he grows to love her. Their 11-year age difference, however, makes their relationship impossible in their small town. Jocelyn leaves town, and Storm begins counting down the days until his 18th birthday, when he can begin searching for her. Storm's story is handled well—his relationship with Jocelyn is presented tastefully and responsibly. Secondary characters are drawn skillfully, and Storm seems a believable person tottering between naïveté and maturity. Readers will be left curious as to the happy ending promised by Storm's premonition.

Jack Forman

SOURCE: A review of *Storm Rising,* in *School Library Journal,* Vol. 35, No. 14, October, 1989, p. 137.

Seventeen-year-old Storm Ryder lives with his undependable mother, Sunny, and her boorish boyfriend, Boyce, who belittles and mocks Storm. So alienated from them is Storm that when his usually witty and breezy first-person narration concerns Boyce, Storm lapses into a cold and heavy third-person narration. Storm is infatuated physically with Vicki, but loses interest in her when he meets mysterious, 28-year-old Jocelyn Sayers, an electrician who hires him to work on her house. As his alienation from his family grows, his friendship with his new employer, whom he soon discovers has extrasensory powers, mushrooms into love. When Storm moves in with Jocelyn, Boyce tries to sabotage the electrician's work but instead almost kills Storm. Jocelyn uses her healing powers to save her lover, and then turns her magic against Boyce. In a too-abrupt ending, Jocelyn bids a hasty farewell to Storm, who seems to have emerged from his experience a more confident and wiser person. Singer has loaded the story with literary devices—characters' metaphorical names, the title's multilayered meaning, Storm's occasional third-person narration, the use of electricity to symbolize emotion, etc. Jocelyn and Storm are the only fully developed characters; others seem to be developed just to fit into the lovers' romance. There is, however, heartfelt and crackling emotion that bubbles up from these two wounded and sensitive young people, and many teen readers will be caught up in the strange and poignant relationship that links them to each other.

Kirkus Reviews

SOURCE: A review of *Storm Rising,* in *Kirkus Reviews,* Vol. LVII, No. 19, October 1, 1989, p. 1481.

Storm Ryder, 17, lives with his mother, who spends her time watching TV—and who expects Storm to do all the housework and to absent himself when Boyce, her obnoxious boyfriend, is around; Storm, who detests Boyce's heckling, is glad to oblige. With his girlfriend two-timing him and his best friend chronically on the prowl for more girls than Storm wants to be involved with, Storm's ripe for something different. Enter Jocelyn: petite electrician, near 30, who needs help fixing up her house and can repair the synthesizer that Storm hopes will earn him money for college. After some hesitation on both sides because of their ages, they fall in love, and into bed, in that order. So far, a well-deserved idyll for a nice kid. Then Storm discovers that Jocelyn has powers: they can be used for healing, but when roused to righteous wrath (as she is at the climax, by Boyce) she can be dangerous. Jocelyn disappears, conscientiously hoping to tame her gift; Storm can take comfort in Boyce finally moving out, Mom getting a job, and the possibility of an eventual reunion with Jocelyn.

Singer's plotting isn't particularly original, but it's sure to have popular appeal. Her strengths here are a style that is not only engagingly facile but also intelligent and literate; and characters of real individuality and some depth—even such minor figures as Storm's boss, whose profanity is both original and funny. Good, lightweight stuff.

📖 *TURTLE IN JULY* (1989)

Betsy Hearne

SOURCE: A review of *Turtle in July,* in *Bulletin of the Center for Children's Books,* Vol. 43, No. 1, September, 1989, pp. 20-1.

The great joy of these fifteen nature poems is the pattern of verbal rhythms that reflect the character of each subject creature. The befuddled bear emerging from hibernation in March asks "Who I? / Where I? / When I now? / No matter / Need water / Few berries / Fresh ants / Not so hungry / Or am I?" The timber rattlesnake sibilantly describes summer and winter with long coiling sounds. The beavers in November hurry here and there with the refrain, "This stick here/ That stick there/ Mud, more mud, add mud, good mud. . . . " The joy of the art is [Jerry] Pinkney's venture into new effects without sacrificing his characteristic style. While his human figures are sometimes studied, these animal drawings are anatomically spontaneous. The settings are lusciously simple, with spacious color and sharply focused compositions. Both writer and artist have captured the essence of the fish, fowl, and mammals featured here. Perfect to share in classrooms or story hours emphasizing themes of nature study and seasonal change.

Ilene Cooper

SOURCE: A review of *Turtle in July,* in *Booklist,* Vol. 86, No. 4, October 15, 1989, p. 464.

Singer and Pinkney join their considerable talents to create a book that is both fresh and engaging. The animal poems, framed by the seasons of the year, are sharply evocative: "I am a January deer, / so swift and light / the hard-packed snow does not even / crunch / beneath my hooves." Mice, a barn owl, rattlesnakes, and assorted insects are among the first-person speakers describing their thoughts about the various months. Illustrating each poem are Pinkney's glorious full-page, richly layered watercolors, which pulse with life. An excellent source for both poetry and nature units.

Marilyn Iarusso

SOURCE: A review of *Turtle in July,* in *School Library Journal,* Vol. 35, No. 15, November, 1989, p. 99.

A picture-book collection of 16 poems in which various creatures speak of their thoughts in relation to the month or season represented. The poems convey the state of mind, preoccupations, and the character of each animal: the alertness of the deer; the silence and concentration of the barn owl as it hunts prey; the staccato of the tense, busy deer mouse; the befuddled bear awakening after hibernation. The bullhead fish appears in each season; while it is certainly *not* the most interesting of the animals featured, and its seasonal activities lack much variety, its poems provide a sort of steadying, calming unity to the collection. Interestingly, it is the most gorgeously portrayed in Pinkney's graceful, fluid watercolors. The colors move from warm browns and wintery blues to the greens of spring, golds of summer, and back to browns of autumn, but there is overall unity in this well-designed book. The paintings of the animals are strong, compelling, and vivid, especially the methodical and determined beaver who gazes directly into readers' eyes. A beautifully illustrated picture book for children to enjoy on their own and for reading aloud to primary grades.

Nancy Vasilakis

SOURCE: A review of *Turtle in July,* in *The Horn Book Magazine,* January-February, 1990, pp. 82-3.

A bullhead catfish lying in the sediment at the bottom of a pond sets down the underlying rhythm of the changing seasons in this symphony of verses that features an animal for each month of the year. The variety of wildlife and the corresponding changes in meter and tone, combined with Jerry Pinkney's lush, full-page illustrations in full color, create a vivid picture book that is visually as well as auditorily pleasing. By using the first person throughout, Singer captures the essence of each animal: the slow, ponderous sonority of the March bear awakening from its long hibernation; the giddy spirit of a terrier in April as it charges through the park. A subtle humor underscores the beaver's two-beat rhythmic chant as it fortifies its dam in November: "Mud, more mud, add mud, good mud / You pat / I gnaw / I pile / You store." The refrain of the timber rattlesnake, in contrast—"Warm bones / Warm blood / Strike I still can / Yes"—evokes a macabre fascination. While Pinkney's pictures are more static portrait than true illustration, the combination of text and art creates a striking effect that will draw the attention of younger readers.

TWENTY WAYS TO LOSE YOUR BEST FRIEND (1990)

Publishers Weekly

SOURCE: A review of *Twenty Ways to Lose Your Best Friend,* in *Publishers Weekly,* Vol. 237, No. 15, April 13, 1990, p. 64.

Fourth-grader Emma has a big problem—she's followed her mother's advice about choosing the best person for a job and has ended up losing her best friend. It's school play time, and Emma votes for the snooty-but-talented Marguerite rather than her friend Sandy. When Sandy discovers this, the two friends' reconciliation and Emma's realizations about relationships make this a perceptive book for the younger middle-school, Beverly Cleary crowd. While not delving deep, Singer's essentially humorous, first-person novel contains strong characterizations and a sympathetic heroine.

Kirkus Reviews

SOURCE: A review of *Twenty Ways to Lose Your Best Friend,* in *Kirkus Reviews,* April 15, 1990, p. 585.

Breezy writing and interesting characterizations enliven a predictable tale. As Emma tells it, it's the President's fault: taking her mother's advice, which is inspired by Election Day, she votes for the most qualified person to star in her fourth-grade class play. Unfortunately, that person is *not* best friend Sandy, who immediately cools—an estrangement that extends to the girls' mothers. Things go from bad to worse when Emma retaliates by befriending her choice, Marguerite, whom she actually finds hard to take. Finally, after a blow-up with Marguerite, Emma finds a way to rekindle her friendship with Sandy—one she suggests to her mother as well.

The matching short fuses of mother and daughter, plus

Emma's spirited narration, animate an otherwise routine middle-grade story.

Sally T. Margolis

SOURCE: A review of *Twenty Ways to Lose Your Best Friend,* in *School Library Journal,* Vol. 36, No. 6, June, 1990, p. 126.

There's principle at stake here. Emma's outspoken mother has declared that people who vote for someone they like rather than the right person for the job have "small minds." Under this influence, Emma has no choice but to vote for the snooty Marguerite for the lead in the play instead of her best friend, Sandy. Sandy finds out and it's major trauma time, sixth-grade variety. Along the way to resolution, there are other betrayals on both sides, but true friendship wins out. The girls finally get together through list-making, the same device that initially clinched their friendship. This listing ploy is not new with Singer, who has highlighted it in other books for this age with a friendship theme, such as *Lizzie Silver of Sherwood Forest. Twenty Ways . . .* is fast, glib, and predictable—a comfortable story for preadolescents. While it lacks the genuine feel for young friendship found in Judy Blume's *Just as Long as We're Together,* it's bound to be popular.

CHARMED (1990)

Publishers Weekly

SOURCE: A review of *Charmed,* in *Publishers Weekly,* Vol. 237, No. 41, October 12, 1990, pp. 64-5.

At 12, Miranda has been told often enough that she has an active imagination. Yet when she is yanked out of her bedroom one evening in the company of a snake-goddess named Naja and a human-size feline named Bastable, she knows this is no ordinary fantasy. Miranda and her companions, including a boy, a rat and the angelic Bennu, have to defeat the dreaded Charmer, an evil creature who will use any means he can to enslave the universe. Dealing with each character's separate world, the Charmer employs insidious forms of mind control and addiction. True to form, good overcomes evil, but Singer interweaves a convincing—if unexpected—anti-drug message into her exciting narrative. Fans of fantasy will welcome this addition to the genre.

Kirkus Reviews

SOURCE: A review of *Charmed,* in *Kirkus Reviews,* Vol. LVIII, No. 21, November 1, 1990, p. 1536.

The evil Charmer threatens many worlds; only a small group of companions with the "Correct Combination" of traits can stand against him.

Amanda, 12, has always been saddled with a vivid imag-

ination, but that doesn't prepare her for being snatched through an ancient snake-charmer's basket into other worlds, or for being cast into a desperate struggle with an apparently invulnerable soul-stealer. Surviving several narrow squeaks, Amanda and five new friends confront the Charmer in near-future Los Angeles, where—after a rather ritualized battle—they send him packing.

The evil here is a creature who can convince whole populations that drugs and mind-control gadgets create real peace and happiness; he is defeated by Amanda's ability to imagine a universe without him. The characters making up the Correct Combination of traits are particularly appealing, especially the nonhumans; an uneasy truce between Rattus, a rat with a wry sense of humor, and proud, catlike Bastable provides comic relief amid the grave goings-on. Winning, well-wrought fantasy.

Susan L. Rogers

SOURCE: A review of *Charmed,* in *School Library Journal,* Vol. 36, No. 12, December, 1990, pp. 111-12.

Typical quest fantasy combines with a science-fiction vision of worlds controlled by an omnipotent, evil genius on a possible and quite believable future Earth. Miranda, 12, has often been faulted for her overactive imagination, and no one knows if Bastable, an invisible catlike creature with whom she often converses, is just an imaginary friend, or actually a deposed king, as he claims. The gift of a snake charmer's basket from Miranda's Uncle Gerald draws Miranda and Bastable into a series of dangerous adventures in various worlds. With a cobra-goddess, a clever rodent, a primitive humanoid, and an immortal bird, they form the Correct Combination—the only entity with any hope of fighting and conquering the Charmer, an evil being who has used a different identity in each of their worlds to enslave the minds and bodies of its inhabitants. Singer seems less comfortable in these genres than in her many novels with contemporary, realistic settings; phrases like the Correct Combination and the Charmer do not have the music or power of high fantasy, and while the characters are interesting, the plot jumps awkwardly rather than flowing seamlessly to its somewhat surprising and quite satisfying conclusion. Dedicated fantasy and science-fiction fans will find much to ponder and enjoy in this novel, but readers new or indifferent to the genres may be put off.

Sally Estes

SOURCE: A review of *Charmed,* in *Booklist,* Vol. 87, No. 9, January 1, 1991, p. 922.

"Forget your rabbit hole, Alice. The heck with fairy dust and Peter Pan, Wendy. And as for you, Dorothy, your tornado has nothing on this. We're off to fight the Charmer, the terrible Charmer of . . . everywhere." And with this, 12-year-old Miranda and Bastable, her invisible catlike friend from another world, travel through time and space with the telepathic cobra goddess, Naja the Ever-Changing, in search of the other beings they need as part of the team that can defeat the evil Charmer, who is threatening the universe. The action is fast paced and exciting as the team is rounded up, despite the efforts of the Charmer, and as the final battle ensues. Though the Charmer is the stereotypical evil doer, other characters are developed well as individuals—Miranda, possessed of a vivid imagination, who starts the adventure with normal fears and misgivings and later gains self-confidence; the irascible Bastable; wise Naja; the quick-witted rat, Rattus; and Iron Dog, a human from an alternate world—and the various worlds created by Singer are fascinating. A story that is sure to please fantasy fans.

EXOTIC BIRDS (1991)

Leone McDermott

SOURCE: A review of *Exotic Birds,* in *Booklist,* Vol. 87, No. 11, February 1, 1991, pp. 1126-27.

Gorgeous watercolor illustrations [by James Needham] and a clear, simple organization of material mark this volume. A fact-filled but readable introduction explains the distinctive characteristics of birds, such as feathers, egg laying, and nest building, and presents the range of differences between bird species. Then 18 diverse environments are described and illustrated along with a number of the birds that inhabit them. Mount Everest, the Everglades, and the Antarctic are among the locations included, as are rain forests from three different countries. In general, each environment receives a double-page spread, with the text in columns along the edges and the central space filled with brilliantly colored and detailed pictures. The book's generous format (each double-page spread runs 12 by 20 inches) permits some striking illustrations: the picture of the great argus pheasant stretches about 18 inches across and 9 inches high and draws the reader in by size alone. The text includes information on the birds' behavior, diet, nests, plumage, and any interesting idiosyncrasies. The endpapers present a global map marked with the locations discussed in the book, plus a picture of a bird from each area. Though the book will probably see its widest use at report time, some will read it just for pleasure.

Ellen Dibner

SOURCE: A review of *Exotic Birds,* in *School Library Journal,* Vol. 37, No. 6, June, 1991, p. 120.

More than 75 birds from rain forests, deserts, mountains, islands, and oceans are illustrated in ample-sized drawings, creating a rainbow of color on every double-page spread. A personable introduction covers distinctive characteristics and habits including beaks, feet, voices, feathers, eggs, and migration. The rest of this large, slim volume takes readers to 18 regions of the world. A map appears on both the front and back endpapers. Brief dis-

courses point to the uniqueness of each species. Print size is generous, and text is framed on every page, minimally distracting from the colorful opulence of the scenes. Researching individual birds is somewhat cumbersome because the species are indexed rather than specifically identified birds, e.g., the Andean condor is listed under "Vulture"; the macaw is located under "Parrots." Otherwise, this is a most satisfying book for browsing, general information, and exotic-bird watching.

Gwyneth E. Loud

SOURCE: A review of *Exotic Birds,* in *Appraisal: Science Books for Young People,* Vol. 24, No. 4, Autumn, 1991, p. 57.

This beautiful and informative book will appeal to young ornithologists as well as to readers who are fascinated by "bizarre" animal behavior. The introductory chapter gives basic and clearly explained information about birds' anatomy and behavior, from beaks and feathers to migration and nest-building. This is followed by eighteen one or two-page chapters describing unusual birds in various parts of the world. For example, the chapter on "The Serengeti Plains" discusses the Lesser flamingo, Ostrich, Greater Honeyguide, Masked weaver, and Pin-tailed whydah. The first paragraph describes the savanna habitat and subsequent paragraphs describe the unusual behavior or appearance of each bird, i.e. why it is included in the book. Some chapters, such as those on the Everglades of the Amazonian rainforest, include sentences about human activities which threaten the habitat and therefore, the birds. All the birds are shown in superb color illustrations. Each bird is clearly labeled and the pictures also give a feeling for the place and habitat. Inside the front and back covers, a world map shows the eighteen places where the birds in the book can be found, from the Pribiloff Islands to New Zealand. There is an index and throughout the book the names of birds and special vocabulary (e.g. "preening", "migration") are italicized.

Barbara C. Scotto

SOURCE: A review of *Exotic Birds,* in *Appraisal: Science Books for Young People,* Vol. 24, No. 4, Autumn, 1991, p. 57.

The deep-purple cover of *Exotic Birds* is a perfect foil for the brightly plumed creatures that spread across it. Opening the book to the lavender and blue title page graced by the beautiful Paradise whydah continues the drama. Singer opens the text less spectacularly by presenting some general information about birds. She follows this with eighteen short chapters, most occupying a double-page spread, about unusual birds found in various locations, ranging from the Pribilof Islands in the Bering Sea to a Rain Forest in Papua, New Guinea. In each chapter, she describes several birds. The descriptions tend to be brief and focus on unusual behaviors exhibited by that particular species. Although generally good, the text occasionally raises questions. For example, on the remote Galapagos Islands one wonders where the Galapagos mockingbird finds some of its "treats," such as butter and vinegar.

The real highlight of this work is the art. The birds are beautiful, drawn with enough realistic detail so that the pictures could serve as a guide to identification. The habitats of the birds are indicated but never become the focus of the picture. One looks at the beautiful creatures instead.

NINE O'CLOCK LULLABY (1991)

Publishers Weekly

SOURCE: A review of *Nine O'Clock Lullaby,* in *Publishers Weekly,* Vol. 238, No. 11, March 1, 1991, pp. 72-3.

A series of bright vignettes provides an ingenious response to children's curiosity about what youngsters in other parts of the world are doing while they themselves are going to bed. Armchair travelers can espy their counterparts dancing at a late-night party in Puerto Rico, raiding the pantry in the wee hours in London, dreaming by the Congo and drawing water from the village well at dawn in India. By the book's end, the scenarios come full circle to 9 p.m., "sleepytime" in Brooklyn, N.Y. Enhanced by [Frané] Lessac's primitive paintings, Singer's text ably suits the various locales—a bicycling aunt in China "pedals quickly, flying like a dragon"; a serene Japanese grandfather "floats a tulip so the fish can greet the spring." Though simple in concept, text and design, the book works on several levels—as a primer on time and the time zones, as an introduction to foreign cultures and as a rhythmic, pleasing lullaby.

Kay Weisman

SOURCE: A review of *Nine O'Clock Lullaby,* in *Booklist,* Vol. 87, No. 18, May 15, 1991, p. 1806.

As a mother reads a quiet bedtime story to her child (9 p.m. in Brooklyn), readers are transported around the world to view a series of 16 simultaneous happenings on six continents. In Puerto Rico (10 p.m.), some children have been allowed to stay up late at a special party; in China (10 a.m.), a young girl pedals her bicycle near some shops; and in Australia (12 noon), a kookaburra steals sausages at a backyard barbecue. Most of these events involve children; all emphasize the sights, sounds, and animals of faraway places. Lessac's vibrant naive paintings complement the rhythmic text and include many cultural details. Reminiscent of Anno's *All in a Day* this will make a perfect introduction to the concept of time zones and cultural similarities. It should also find a niche at bedtime story hours and serve as a good title for linking stories from other lands. Appended with a note for parents on time zones.

Patricia Dooley

SOURCE: A review of *Nine O'Clock Lullaby,* in *School Library Journal,* Vol. 37, No. 7, July, 1991, p. 64.

Beginning (and ending) in Brooklyn at bedtime, this picture book jumps a step east around the world, where the same moment becomes a different hour in 15 different time zones. Singer's brief narrative contains cultural and auditory cues, humor, and some interesting connections. Lessac's paintings are lively and detailed, in her familiar naïve style. It would be hard to imagine her work without its vibrant colors, but here they work against the grain. Uniformly gay pages and flat light sacrifice part of the sense-experience of difference. Although half the book occurs at dusk or night, when "all cats are gray," Lessac's glowing palette remains constant. Switzerland and Zaire at 3 a.m. are just as colorfully bright as Sydney at noon. Nor are the essential props, a globe and clock, incorporated into the work. In any case, the concept of time zones may be beyond the grasp of the intended audience. What this title does convey is the connectedness of the inhabitants of our global village.

THE GOLDEN HEART OF WINTER (1991)

Kirkus Reviews

SOURCE: A review of *The Golden Heart of Winter,* in *Kirkus Reviews,* Vol. LIX, No. 13, July 1, 1991, p. 861.

A new story in a traditional mode: a blacksmith sends his three sons on an heir-deciding quest for "something of value." En route, the first two scorn a trapped raven; the third, Half[wit], frees her and is rewarded with the story of a magical heart: Life has buried it, but Death would like to find it in order to create eternal winter. The raven gives Half a riddle that he shares with his brothers; finding the heart, the two quarrel, invoking Death and a cruel cold. Back at his father's forge, Half thaws the heart and even offers his own in exchange if only spring will come—thus defeating Death and winning his father's contest.

The quickly moving story is different enough from its sources to hold attention, while the powerful images are well realized in [Robert] Rayevsky's vigorous, finely detailed art. Death looks chillingly like one of the Apocalyptic horsemen; other figures are tellingly caricatured. Some of the symbolism seems a bit muddled (why would Spring's lifeblood be restored by fire?); still, an interesting venture from this versatile author.

Publishers Weekly

SOURCE: A review of *The Golden Heart of Winter,* in *Publishers Weekly,* Vol. 238, No. 30, July 12, 1991, p. 66.

An elderly smithy sends his three sons on a quest, promising to name as his heir whoever brings back the most valuable object. Wasting no time, the sons—two loutish older ones and a dreamy younger one named "Half" by his brothers—set out. The "something of value" they seek turns out to be the Golden Heart of Winter—symbol of rebirth—buried long ago in a pact between Life and Death. The older brothers rip it from the earth and, in their ensuing fight, plunge the world into bitter winter. Half rescues it, of course, restoring spring, proving his own worth and uniting his family. Singer's formal, fluid style dovetails neatly with the story's mythlike elements, and the result is an original fairy tale in the grand tradition. Rayevsky has given his singular, sharply etched illustrations a vaguely medieval setting that helps foster a mystical mood.

Barbara Hutcheson

SOURCE: A review of *The Golden Heart of Winter,* in *School Library Journal,* Vol. 37, No. 12, December, 1991, p. 102.

An original folktale that includes many familiar elements. Three sons of an aging blacksmith are sent off by their father to bring back the prize of greatest value so he can choose his successor. Predictably, the two selfish older sons miss the opportunities presented to them, while the noodle third son Half (as in wit) responds with kindness when called upon. A talking raven whom he frees from imprisonment tells him of the golden heart that returns spring to the Earth each year. Half will save the heart from the power of Death if he can solve a riddle posed by the raven. However, the brothers find the heart first, and the boy must protect it from Death and from his brothers' greed. Rayevsky uses color effectively to reflect the warmth of the heart and the seasons, both in watercolor washes underlying pages of text and in his oddly elongated, angular figures. The settings are generic medieval Europe. The language is appropriately folkloric with occasional slips ("Shut up, foul creature"), but the story line stumbles in two key areas. Death vanishes from the story without explanation, and astute readers may guess the heart is the prize needed to fulfill the quest, but Singer never says so, thus failing to close the circle of the plot. The theme does tie in with exploration of environmental themes or discussions of good and evil, but younger children may find the illustrations of death disturbing.

📖 *IN MY TENT* (1992)

Kirkus Reviews

SOURCE: A review of *In My Tent,* in *Kirkus Reviews,* Vol. LX, No. 18, September 15, 1992, p. 1194.

A cycle of poetic vignettes centering on the young narrator's tent ("what I like best is the color / suddenly orange / like an oriole landing / in the emerald woods / quietly saying, I'm here"), promised her during a snowfall "On the day the twins were born." Most of the episodes occur during a summer camping trip: Dad's affectionately teasing wake-up call; getting a little lost in the woods; finding out that even baked beans are delicious here; regretfully taking down a spider's web with the tent. In the last scene, the narrator and her friend are building a tent-like igloo on the twins' first birthday. Subtly, in economical, gracefully phrased descriptions, Singer conveys a great deal about this unique, not-quite-perfect family. [Emily Arnold] McCully's impressionistic watercolors nicely reflect the quiet mood and warm interaction.

Virginia E. Jeschelnig

SOURCE: A review of *In My Tent,* in *School Library Journal,* Vol. 39, No. 1, January, 1993, p. 84.

One wintry day just before the birth of her twin sisters, a little girl receives the promise of a wonderful gift—her very own tent. That following summer, the bright orange dome becomes her special haven when the family spends time camping in the woods. She savors the sensory beauty of nature all around her as they enjoy canoeing, hiking, swimming, the campfire. Each experience is expanded through poetry filled with sensitive detail. There is an air of reverence in the descriptions. There are no flashy antics, no humorous episodes—simply quiet examinations of the child's observations paired with soft watercolor images. That is the difficulty. The challenging text calls for more sophisticated illustrations to engage better readers. As it is, few children will be drawn into this book.

📖 *CHESTER THE OUT-OF-WORK DOG* (1992)

Publishers Weekly

SOURCE: A review of *Chester the Out-of-Work Dog,* in *Publishers Weekly,* October 12, 1992, p. 78.

A working sheepdog becomes a fish out of water when he moves from the farm to the city. Chester loved spending his days rounding up sheep on the Wippenhoopers' farm, and the calm quiet of country evenings there. But when the Wippenhoopers trade their rural existence for an urban apartment life, Chester feels lost—"his paws hurt too much from the concrete," and he hates being unemployed. The resourceful canine finds surrogate flocks to herd—pigeons, squirrels, delivery men—much to the family's chagrin. As a last resort, Chester decides to flee back to the country when he spies an odd bunch of sheep (school children in costume) desperately in need of direction. Singer's slightly daffy but heartfelt story runs the gamut of emotions; Chester's feelings of anxiety and uselessness are easy to identify with, [Cat Bowman Smith's] loose, bubbly watercolors convey wackiness and warmth. Her portraits of the toothy Wippenhooper clan and the ovine-outfitted kids are particularly memorable.

Ilene Cooper

SOURCE: A review of *Chester, the Out-of-Work Dog,* in *Booklist,* Vol. 89, No. 4, October 15, 1992, p. 425.

Chester is all border collie, and though a sheep might be just a sheep to others, to Chester each one is an individual. When he and his human family, the Wippenhoopers, move from their farm to the city, he's out of work. Oh, he tries to pursue his former career: he herds a squirrel into a mailbox, a pair of pigeons into the post office, four garbage collectors (with garbage) into the fanciest restaurant in town. But none of the herdees are very happy about being pushed around. "What are we going to do with him?" the Wippenhoopers ask. Overhearing that remark, a defeated Chester tries to head back to the country, only to find a busload of sheep who need herding to Chester A. Arthur Elementary School. True, these are two-legged sheep, actually kids in costume, but all Chester sees are woollies who need to get to a specific destination. This picture book has it all—slapstick comedy, a touch of pathos, and an actual story with a beginning, a middle, and an end (a small detail that's missing in a lot of today's offerings). Smith's art is full of action and fun, and her characters are particularly memorable: the goofy-looking Wippenhoopers, the kids/sheep (on their way to perform their play, *Woolly Bully*), and, of course, Chester—forthright, determined, and a darn good herder.

Kirkus Reviews

SOURCE: A review of *Chester the Out-of-Work Dog,* in *Kirkus Reviews,* October 15, 1992, p. 1316.

Busy caring for the sheep, Chester is happy on the farm; but then his family moves to a city apartment. The frustrated Chester starts rounding up people: he forces four garbage collectors into a restaurant, five firemen into a fountain, and so on; herding a girls' softball team into the boys' bathroom is the last straw. Chester, predictably, redeems himself: dolefully setting out for his old home, he happens on a lost class of children (in sheep costumes, yet) and shepherds them back to school, winning himself a new job as crossing guard. Contrived but briskly told, and the human analog may provide some insights in these hard times. Smith's lively, comical illustrations effectively convey the characters' feelings, especially the appealing dog's.

Cynthia K. Richey

SOURCE: A review of *Chester the Out-of-Work Dog,* in *School Library Journal,* November, 1992, p. 78.

When the Wippenhoopers sell their farm and move to the city, Chester, their sheep-herding Border collie, finds himself out of work. He dislikes the city: the concrete hurts his feet; the noise hurts his ears; and he's bored and restless. At last he decides to herd something besides sheep. For a week he rounds up, among other things, firemen into a fountain, a squirrel into a mailbox, and a girl's softball team into a boy's bathroom. Ostracized by his family, he decides to leave the city for his old home. At a nearby field, he encounters a group of children in sheep costumes who are looking for the city school to put on a play. After herding them there, Chester is given a job as a school crossing guard. The story progresses quickly, employing simple, direct text and much humor. Witty ink-and-watercolor cartoon drawings enhance the text; the faces of the characters are particularly expressive. Earth tones and quiet colors are used until the encounter in the field. There, in a double-page spread, the tones become brighter and more pastels are used, as if to indicate Chester's new, happier life. Children are sure to flock to this satisfying story.

CALIFORNIA DEMON (1992)

Janice Del Negro

SOURCE: A review of *California Demon,* in *Booklist,* Vol. 89, No. 7, December 1, 1992, p. 671.

When Rosy Rodriguez opens the wrong bottle in her mother's Vermont magic shop, she releases an "impus mischevious," all revved up and looking for trouble. The imp stows away in a Christmas present headed for California, where, in the guise of "Mr. Ed" the genie, he disrupts the lives of Danny and Laura Pauling. Back in Vermont, Rosy and her mother, a practitioner of "the craft" of white magic, are desperately trying to locate the imp before he causes serious trouble. All ends well, with the imp being sent where he belongs, Danny and Laura's estranged parents talking about reconciling, and Rosy happily learning "the craft" and anticipating the possibility of two boyfriends. Singer's breezy style suits the light-hearted chase, and her easygoing, enjoyable characters move along at an easygoing, enjoyable pace.

Kathryn Jennings

SOURCE: A review of *California Demon,* in *Bulletin of the Center for Children's Books,* Vol. 46, No. 6, February, 1993, p. 191.

In a world where magic lies close to the surface of everyday life, Rosie Rivera accidentally lets a demon (more properly, *"impus mischievous"*) out of a bottle where it has been safely trapped since 1928. The demon disappears by climbing into the purchases of a customer of the Riveras' Vermont magic shop and reappears again in California, having been shipped with the presents to the customer's children. Danny, twelve, and his sister Laura, ten, think the imp is a genie who will obey their every command. The demon pretends to be submissive, for a while, but soon his inherent evil nature takes over. The fulfillment of Danny and Laura's wishes takes on a sinister side they don't intend, and soon they realize that the demon was never under their control, but instead they are helplessly under his. Rosie and her mom, Lydia, feel responsible for releasing the demon, so they track him down. The final confrontation takes place on a California mountainside, with Rosie and Lydia's witchcraft matched against the imp's powers. Although the plot has many elements similar to Mahy's *The Changeover* (the book is even mentioned as Rosie's favorite), Rosie's initiation as a witch does not seem as desperate, nor do Danny and Laura seem to be in as much mortal danger as do Mahy's characters. The demon, with his wild hair and electric blue eyes, is a comical bad guy, especially when he is scolded by his mother, The Queen of the Genies, Ammomgib ("Big momma" spelled backwards). The humor keeps the story buoyant, magic gives it sparkle.

📖 IT'S HARD TO READ A MAP WITH A BEAGLE ON YOUR LAP (1993)

Deborah Stevenson

SOURCE: A review of *It's Hard to Read a Map with a Beagle on Your Lap,* in *Bulletin of the Center for Children's Books,* Vol. 46, No. 10, June, 1993, p. 330.

This is a collection of twenty-six silly dog poems ranging in length and format from the title couplet to longer poems about particular breeds or canine habits ("Dogs . . . like to sleep on sofas / Instead of on the floor / They like to crawl in bed with you / And then they like to snore"), plus a few lickety-split paeans to "Ears," "Tails," and "Fur." The poems are entertaining, although most of them seem driven by rhyme rather than a guiding idea, and the rhythm is sometimes forced. [Clément] Oubrerie's scratchy lines and mixed-media art emphasizes the variety in both dogs and poetry by depicting the protagonists sometimes in cartoonish exaggeration and sometimes in highly detailed realism, ranging from full-page bleeds—or, in the case of the dachshund, four full pages—to a tiny Mexican Hairless adrift in white space. The effect, coupled with interestingly varied type arrangements (circles, snakes, and so on) and a continuing rhyme that unfolds in the upper-right-hand corner throughout the book, can be visually overwhelming, although it's always energetic. Kids won't exactly take these up as chants, but the tilted investigation of the doggy world has a giggle-provoking appeal.

Publishers Weekly

SOURCE: A review of *It's Hard to Read a Map with a Beagle on Your Lap,* in *Publishers Weekly,* Vol. 240, No. 24, June 14, 1993, pp. 70-1.

This unfocused volume celebrates dogs of all shapes and sizes with limericks, rhyming couplets and other sing-song verses. The title phrase, which constitutes an entire poem (and the sole reference to a beagle), serves as the jumping-off point for mini-odes to such breeds as the "Mexican hairless" ("The time you save not cleaning hair / Will let you knit her underwear"). Singer's over-abundant, frivolous rhymes, unified only by their doggy theme, neither follow a story line nor stand as solid components of a collection. Oubrerie's pen-and-ink sketches of recognizable but soulless canine types coexist with exaggerated, crocodile-mouthed cartoon dogs; his highly colored illustrations suffer from the same disjointedness that afflicts Singer's refrains. Although the authors show a willingness to experiment, their fluctuating styles—paralleled by varying typefaces—produce little more than cacophony.

Kathleen Whalin

SOURCE: A review of *It's Hard to Read a Map with a Beagle on Your Lap,* in *School Library Journal,* Vol. 39, No. 7, July, 1993, p. 93.

Singer follows her wonderful *Turtle in July* with a joyous romp through the canine world. In limericks ("There once was a young weimaraner / Who frequently ate at a diner"), verse ("Dogs like to stop at hydrants / They like to stop at trees / They like to lean out windows / And catch a little breeze"), and rhythmic combinations (on ears: "Floppy / Sloppy / Standing High"), the essence of dogdom is celebrated. The author's humor is matched by Oubrerie's playful, stylized drawings. Poems run in circles, stretch across pages, and appear in inserts. This is a rare book of poetry, one in which the subject matter is interpreted perfectly in text, art, and design. A book to chase down, leash, and own.

📖 BIG WHEEL (1993)

Publishers Weekly

SOURCE: A review of *Big Wheel,* in *Publishers Weekly,* Vol. 240, No. 46, November 15, 1993, p. 79.

Wheel and his friends are going to host the best Fourth of July carnival ever—if they don't kill each other first. Wheel demands that everyone practice difficult tasks constantly, even in the hot summer sun. Desite his best friend Tag's warnings, Wheel pushes the gang even harder. Then Topper, the new kid in town, offers Wheel's friends ice cream, an old attic to explore and a large, cool swimming pool. A lonely Wheel soon realizes he's pitted against Topper. Eventually both boys realize they have a lot to learn about friendship. Neither character, however, is especially appealing. Humorous metaphors spring up throughout the text ("My mouth feels like sunrise on the Sahara. My heart's taking off like a pigeon at a cat show"), but because they do not sound like a boy's words, they distract from the narrative. Still, a surprise twist and an energetic ending wind up the book on a positive note.

Kirkus Reviews

SOURCE: A review of *Big Wheel,* in *Kirkus Reviews,* Vol. LXI, No. 23, December 1, 1993, p. 1529.

Big Wheel Wiggins is the undisputed leader of his gang—an affable and diverse clutch of boys and a few girls who acquired local notoriety with high-jinks like conducting a bowling tournament with plastic flamingos, toadstools, and elves on a vacationing family's lawn. Then slick Topper Smith juggles his way into Marietta and challenges Wheel's position. One by one, members of Wheel's gang defect to explore Topper's old house, swim in his pool, and raid his well-stocked refrigerator. The erosion of Wheel's power base is giving him a massive case of executive stress. When he follows his know-it-all grandfather's crack-down advice, he alienates the last loyal holdout, life-long best friend Tag. After one act of sweet revenge, Wheel is forced to revise his Big Wheel code of ethics: he has to make room for two leaders of the gang, stroke his stray troops, and apologize to Tag. A smart, funny story, with a rollicking pace, smart-alecky dialogue, and snappy similes (when Wheel meets his radio deejay idol, Wild Willie, his heart is "taking off like a pigeon at a cat show"). Wheel's meteorologist father's disastrous foray into TV weather-forecasting makes an interesting backdrop. A surefire story from a popular author.

Susan W. Hunter

SOURCE: A review of *Big Wheel,* in *School Library Journal,* Vol. 40, No. 1, January, 1994, p. 116.

Proudly nicknamed "Big Wheel" by his competitive grandfather, Gordon Wiggins craves attention. As the leader of his friends, he is planning a stupendous Fourth of July celebration in order to win a contest sponsored by Wild Willie, the funniest, hottest deejay on a local radio station. Wheel sweet-talks his multicultural clique into staging a carnival, but makes the mistake of excluding a clever new kid, Topper Smith, who turns out to be a master at juggling while riding a unicycle. Wheel pushes his friends so hard to rehearse their acts that he loses them to Topper, who is planning his own extravaganza. Meanwhile, Wheel's father, a mild, bookish meteorologist, is offered a position as a TV weatherman, and Gramps is pushing him to accept it. The fall to humility is predictable for Wheel and Gramps alike; both are cocky, insensitive, and manipulative. Further dismay awaits the boy when he learns too late that Topper's father is the great Wild Willie himself, something readers will suspect early on. Although the opening chapter is attention-grabbing, the first-person narrative has a corny, self-consciously adult tone that does nothing for this contrived, heavy-handed tale.

SKY WORDS (1994)

Kirkus Reviews

SOURCE: A review of *Sky Words,* in *Kirkus Reviews,* Vol. LXII, No. 3, February 1, 1994, p. 150.

Fifteen poems about the sky, its changing moods and weathers and the things to be seen in it—skywriting or fireworks, the moon and stars, "Monarchs Migrating," birds. In irregular lines with rhymes sometimes cropping up in unexpected places, Singer puts a unique slant on familiar sights—"At the Fair": " . . . the scariest ride / at the fair / Red and gold in the air / . . . like a giant's hammer / covered with jewels"; "Twilight": "In the hour of the bat / when the world fades like a photo / left lying in a drawer . . . "; or, "Fog": "The fog is / a river with no direction / a dream with no doors . . . " [Deborah Kogan] Ray's mixed-media illustrations range from jagged slashes that convey the fair's perpetual motion and garish lights to the subtlest of washes for "Fog" and myriad shades of gray for "Twilight." A good collection for use in thematic teaching units as well as in the poetry section.

Julie Corsaro

SOURCE: A review of *Sky Words,* in *Booklist,* Vol. 90, No. 12, February 15, 1994, p. 1086.

This picture-book poetry collection is worth noting because of the high quality of the 15 evocative poems and the vibrantly colored illustrations. While the "sky" theme is somewhat forced, Singer demonstrates the value of a fresh image when she describes a meteor ("This rock / as heavy as five thousand smashed cars"), the twilight ("when the sky turns the color / of an old man's hair"), and the fog ("All footsteps belong to strangers / even your own"). While the mixed-media illustrations are generally soft and suggestive, they range from the haunting, Whistler-like seascape, with its almost undefined space, for "Fog," to the bold strokes of color used to hint at the "scariest ride at the fair." A wonderful source for introducing lyrical verse to primary-grade students.

Susan Scheps

SOURCE: A review of *Sky Words,* in *School Library Journal,* Vol. 40, No. 5, May, 1994, p. 127.

Singer's facility with language is evident in this collection of 15 poems. Her verses are about the natural world (the movement of the stars, a swarm of monarch butterflies, twilight) and human nature (arguing about cloud names as a thunderstorm approaches, being frightened during a tornado, swinging skyward on the scariest ride at the fair). Her ability to evoke certain images with wordplay allows attentive readers to experience the situations she describes. About the fog, she writes: "No one is your friend / in the fog / The sky is a liar / The ground is a sneak / All footsteps belong to strangers / even your own." Ray's mixed-medium artwork ranges from the soft, gray-green watercolor of fog; to a striking, orange-and-black marker rendering of monarchs against a pale blue penciled sky; to a batiklike, neon blur of fairground lights in oil pastel; to a soft, charcoal twilight scene. Each picture is a mirror of the poem beside it. An appealing collection for pleasure reading or for classroom use.

Nancy Vasilakis

SOURCE: A review of *Sky Words,* in *The Horn Book Magazine,* Vol. LXX, No. 3, May-June, 1994, p. 330.

The poet finds boundless inspiration in the sky as she creates poems about skywriting and tornadoes, about the world at twilight ("in the hour of the bat / when the sky turns the color / of an old man's hair"), about clouds and fog and monarch butterflies filling the air like orange leaves. Singer varies the rhythm and length of lines within each poem and employs subtle internal and end rhyme schemes and rich imagery to create a sumptuous flow of words. The fifteen poems run the gamut of moods, from humor to excitement to a dreamlike spookiness in the poem "Fog," where "all footsteps belong to strangers / even your own." The illustrations vary in tone to reflect the text, ranging from an abstract expressionistic style that conveys the excitement and glitter of flashing lights at a fair to the almost geometric purity of line in "Moon-dog." A notable achievement by both poet and artist.

THE PAINTED FAN (1994)

Kirkus Reviews

SOURCE: A review of *The Painted Fan,* in *Kirkus Reviews,* Vol. LXI, No. 8, April 15, 1994, p. 564.

Set in long-ago China, a tale of a greedy lord who hopes to evade his fate and the courageous girl who brings it to pass. After hearing that the Painted Fan will be his undoing, Lord Shang commands that all fans be destroyed; still, Bright Willow, a poor farmer's daughter, brings along an heirloom fan after Lord Shang selects her as his unwilling bride. When she's caught talking with a young groom, Shang agrees to waive her punishment if she can fetch a huge pearl that's guarded by a terrible demon. The fan's magic is instrumental in her success and the subsequent destruction of the wicked lord; the young people, revealed as heirs to the warring houses Lord Shang supplanted, are happily united. Singer knits together several folkloric motifs to create an original tale with satisfying strands of adventure and romance. The Chinese-born illustrator [Wenhai Ma], now a professor at Duke University, makes a fine picture-book debut with dramatically posed scenes of realistically depicted figures in impressionistic settings that effectively enhance the mood.

Publishers Weekly

SOURCE: A review of *The Painted Fan,* in *Publishers Weekly,* Vol. 241, No. 16, April 18, 1994, p. 62.

"When the imperial houses of Li and Chen would not stop fighting," begins this exquisitely told tale, "it was easy for Lord Shang to march in and set himself up as ruler." When cruel Lord Shang discovers that his bride-to-be, the peasant girl Bright Willow, loves not him but

his groom, Seahorse, he angrily sentences Seahorse to death and Bright Willow to prison—unless she can bring him the Great Pearl. Her enchanted fan shields her from the powers of Red Fang (the pearl's demon guardian), and the fan's painted words, changing to suit the occasion, banish both Red Fang and Lord Shang forever. But Seahorse and Bright Willow are not the peasants they seem, and when they marry they hang above their bed the fan, which now reads, "The houses of Li and Chen are reunited at last." In his first children's book, Ma contributes watercolors of unusual delicacy, but his penchant for expressionless faces may frustrate readers. Nonetheless, this polished story is utterly satisfying in its journey from chaos and confusion to order and harmony.

Carolyn Phelan

SOURCE: A review of *The Painted Fan,* in *Booklist,* Vol. 90, No. 17, May 1, 1994, p. 1609.

Set in ancient China, this tale tells of cruel Lord Shang, who conquers a land long fought over by two imperial houses, the Li and the Chen. Shang oppresses the people and soon has everything he wants except the heart of Bright Willow, a goat girl who takes his fancy. Seahorse, a stable boy, also loves Bright Willow, and when Shang learns of their friendship, he sentences them to death. To save her life and that of her friend, Bright Willow agrees to brave a demon and bring the enormous pearl it guards to Shang. Shang's greed and cruelty prove his undoing, and in the end, the houses of Li and Chen are reunited with the marriage of the goat girl and the stable lad. Told with simplicity and dignity, the story builds to a crescendo as the heroine takes control of the demon and uses him to conquer her arrogant oppressor. The text usually appears on the left-hand page within a framework of open-worked borders, while on the facing pages and on some two-page spreads, the illustrations dramatize the action. . . . A satisfying fairy tale well suited to classroom or bedtime reading.

FAMILY REUNION (1994)

Publishers Weekly

SOURCE: A review of *Family Reunion,* in *Publishers Weekly,* Vol. 241, No. 35, August 24, 1994, p. 78.

In a series of jaunty poems, Singer sets forth the idiosyncrasies and cheerful activities that characterize the large family reunion held in Small Park. Like the musicians in Aunt Dena's "family band," the child narrator's relatives are "perfectly out-of-tune / and perfectly in harmony." The book has no conventional plot, but the escapades of various aunts and uncles and cousins form discrete poem-chapters that will sustain the interest of even the youngest readers. While "patrolling the pond" in faded blue pedal boats, for example, the children mourn what they think is a dead beaver—until Uncle Bill fishes it out, a water-logged wig. Quarrelsome Cousin George gets his comeuppance when Max drops a bug down his back. Although the verses are filled with apt images and telling details, they are more like prose sentences, with line breaks and indentations in place of the usual commas and periods: "*Chucka chucka ding* / goes Peter / running his teeth up and down the cob / like an old-fashioned typewriter carriage / flying across the page." [R.W.] Alley's lively illustrations combine the pleasing, cartoony figures and action of Lynn Munsinger with the busyness of Richard Scarry, lending a complex visual counterpart to the extended family's exploits. Readers will agree that this reunion stars "quite a family!"

Julie Corsaro

SOURCE: A review of *Family Reunion*, in *Booklist*, Vol. 91, No. 1, September 1, 1994, pp. 46-7.

Anyone who has ever been to a summertime family reunion will recognize the people, events, tastes, and smells captured in this lively collection of 14 poems. Lyrical, sometimes funny verse and snappy watercolors tell a tale that begins the night before with the weather report and ends the morning after Labor Day when "even Dad is sad" until "the photographs come in the mail." In between, there's a wide range of humanity that includes proper Aunt Alicia in her blue silk dress ("I wish someday she'd startle us in sneakers") and wheelchair cowboy Uncle Nicholas who transforms the baseball diamond into a "rich green prairie / where rabbits run for cover / and buffalo still roam." Children should enjoy picking out the scruffy young narrator in the delightfully detailed cartoons that come in as many shapes and sizes as the members of the large, affectionate clan.

Lynn Cockett

SOURCE: A review of *Family Reunion*, in *School Library Journal*, Vol. 40, No. 11, November, 1994, p. 101.

Read in sequence, this collection of 14 free-verse poems tells the story of a great day at a family reunion. Read alone, each selection stands on its own. Outrageous, silly fun is the theme; and this gathering is full of gregarious, entertaining types. Singer's writing—filled with visual imagery—introduces young people to poetry in an unconventional style. In "Slow-Motion Spring," Uncle Steve, long-bearded and round-bellied, proclaims that the slowest runner will win the race so Cousin Jeff won't win yet another contest. Other highlights include "Aunt Alicia," a character sketch of the only family member who comes to the park each year in a silk dress and sips papaya juice from a silver thermos. Alley's watercolor and pen illustrations help to reinforce the free-spirited mood of the day. Children frolic, grownups laugh, everyone smiles. Details are meticulous, right down to the way the twins eat corn on the cob. Family love and humor make this book a winner to share with children. A delightful romp!

PLEASE DON'T SQUEEZE YOUR BOA, NOAH (1995)

Publishers Weekly

SOURCE: A review of *Please Don't Squeeze Your Boa, Noah!*, in *Publishers Weekly*, Vol. 242, No. 12, March 20, 1995, p. 61.

Singer and [Clément] Oubrerie pour a litter of animal rhymes and pictures—some catchy, some otherwise—into this volume. The entries commence with the eponymous poem ("Be fonder of your anaconda / That's what you must do / Please don't squeeze your boa, Noah / Or he just might squeeze you"), then continue with similarly lightweight odes to other creatures; the rhymes here are for the sake of rhyming, rather than to convey meaningful information. Some lack polish ("Tricky treat / my parakeet / mimics noises from the street"). Oubrerie's fine-line drawings, dominated by drab browns and greens, are equally silly but often more fun, e.g., a spider named Mary sports blond curls and ruby slippers.

Lauren Peterson

SOURCE: A review of *Please Don't Squeeze Your Boa, Noah!*, in *Booklist*, April 15, 1995, p. 1504.

Animal lovers will delight in this humorous collection of poetry featuring a widely diverse group of pets. Dogs and cats top the list as the most frequent subjects, but some of the best selections consider less common pets, such as ants and toads. The poems vary in length, with some just a few lines, and the colorful, cartoon illustrations are sometimes postage stamp sized (with many on a page) and sometimes elaborate scenes that fill an entire double-page spread. The popularity of the subject matter and the witty treatment Singer gives it should ensure a brisk checkout record.

Martha Topol

SOURCE: A review of *Please Don't Squeeze Your Boa, Noah!*, in *School Library Journal*, Vol. 41, No. 5, May, 1995, pp. 102-03.

An eclectic collection of poems about pets. From the ordinary to the exotic, a variety of animals from cats and birds to camels and ants are represented. The verses, while inventive in places, are not particularly engaging; having read them once, there's no real incentive to read them again. Oubrerie's heavy, full-page illustrations often overpower the poetry. In their effort to be hip and meaningful, showing undertones of George Booth, they are simply crude and unattractive. The mix of text and pictures works best when the poems are broken up line by line and illustrated with small, individual drawings printed against a white page. Here the illustrator's raw humor does shine through. This title shows some promise, but not enough to justify purchase.

📖 *THE MAIDEN ON THE MOOR* (1995)

Donna L. Scanlon

SOURCE: A review of *The Maiden on the Moor,* in *School Library Journal,* Vol. 41, No. 4, April, 1995, p. 146.

Singer weaves a haunting, poetic tale from an anonymous medieval verse. Two shepherd brothers find a maiden lying on the snowy moor. Fearing enchantment, the elder man flees to his comfortable house, but the younger one takes her home, where he and his three dogs tend to her for a week. The lonely young man begs her to awaken and be his companion; when she does not respond, he sinks into a grief-stricken sleep. Only then does she stir. She takes the smallest dog with her to the moor where, as a flock of snow geese flies overhead, she asks it to kill her. As she dies, she returns to her original form of a snow goose and the dog turns into a young woman who gladly becomes the shepherd's companion. As a poet, Singer knows how to distill words into images, and she conveys the bleak beauty of the setting with clarity and precision. While more literal-minded readers might puzzle over how the maiden got on the moor in the first place, the tale is sure to spark imaginations as it transcends ordinary fairy-tale conventions. The story is romantic without being sentimental, and the resolution is satisfying. [Troy] Howell's colored-pencil illustrations, many of which are double-page spreads full of texture and detail, capture the mood, employing mostly icy tones that bring alive the winter atmosphere. Text is set in boxes decorated with either a tiny illustration, a border with Celtic knotwork designs, or other motifs reminiscent of medieval tapestries. A unique contribution to any folklore collection.

Publishers Weekly

SOURCE: A review of *The Maiden on the Moor,* in *Publishers Weekly,* Vol. 242, No. 16, April 17, 1995, p. 60.

Embroidering upon a medieval English verse, Singer turns out a finely wrought fairy tale. Two shepherd brothers, the elder married and prosperous, the younger alone and poor, find a dark-haired maiden lying unconscious on the moor in the dead of winter. The elder shuns her, but the younger takes her to his cottage and, for seven days and nights, takes care of her. On the last night, while the younger brother sleeps, the maiden finally awakens and sets in motion various plans to ensure that each brother will receive his just deserts. And then she slips away, assuming the form of a snow goose. Howell's misty colored-pencil drawings of the bleak moor, the young shepherd's rustic cottage and the maiden's surprising transformation are suitably romantic but lack sufficient momentum to convey the full drama of this story.

📖 *IN THE PALACE OF THE OCEAN KING* (1995)

Publishers Weekly

SOURCE: A review of *In the Palace of the Ocean King,* in *Publishers Weekly,* Vol. 242, No. 16, April 17, 1995, p. 59.

A versatile and prolific author of picture books as well as fantasy novels, Singer meshes elements of these two genres in this overly elaborate tale. Bold, clever Mariana, the daughter of a lord, fears nothing but the ocean. When her father brings her to the seaside castle of a duke, she is spellbound by his son Sylvain's story of a merman punished by the Ocean King and saved by a brave youth (who turns out to be Sylvain himself). The tale, only half-told, fills her with dread, and soon enough she realizes that she has a role to play in determining its conclusion: in love with Sylvain, she is called upon to rescue him when he is taken captive and condemned to an eternity of "moving in the circles of a slow and endless waltz" with the other prisoners in the Ocean King's underwater palace. Rendered in ink, bamboo pen and acrylics, [Ted] Rand's dreamlike paintings handsomely serve the fanciful setting. The text is reproduced on scroll-like panels that stand out against the eerie blend of blues, greens and aqua shades used to convey the shadowy underwater world. Though rich in imagery, Singer's ultimately thin narrative lacks that magical spark found in enduring fairy tales.

Hazel Rochman

SOURCE: A review of *In the Palace of the Ocean King,* in *Booklist,* Vol. 91, No. 21, July, 1995, p. 1884.

In this original fairy tale for the 1990s, the traditional roles are reversed: this time it's the young prince who is passive and immobilized, a prisoner of the evil Ocean King. Brave, young Mariana loves the prince, and she must dive deep into the ocean to set him free. . . . The fantasy goes on too long, especially the details of the underwater action. What will hold kids is the romance between the shy prince and the dazzling blond woman who overcomes her own fear of the ocean to rescue her beloved.

Cheri Estes

SOURCE: A review of *In the Palace of the Ocean King,* in *School Library Journal,* Vol. 41, No. 8, August, 1995, pp. 128-29.

In this original fairy tale, Singer tells the romantic tale of love conquering fear. One evening in his castle by the sea, Sylvain tells Mariana the story of how he saved a merman who had angered the Ocean King. That night, Mariana, who is afraid of the ocean, dreams that she will have to save Sylvain from the Ocean King. When his ship sinks offshore at the beginning of a journey, she knows what she must do. With the help of the merman, she overcomes her fear and cleverly outsmarts the Ocean King. In an unfortunate plot twist, after Mariana goes through such trials to save Sylvain, it is Sylvain, "with a burst of strength born of love," who wakes up from his trance and actually gets them out of the water. The tale gets a little saccharine at the end, but overall has the tone of a traditional story. Singer uses the right language and syntax for a proper fairy tale, yet it is not as complex as some and could be used in preschool story time.

Additional coverage of Singer's life and career is contained in the following sources published by Gale Research: *Contemporary Authors New Revision Series,* Vol. 39; *Junior DISCovering Authors (CD-ROM); Major Authors and Illustrators for Children and Young Adults; Something about the Author,* Vols. 48, 80; and *Something about the Author Autobiography Series,* Vol. 13.

Cynthia Voigt

1942-

American author of fiction and picture books.

Major works include *Dicey's Song* (1982), *The Runner* (1985), *Izzy, Willy-Nilly* (1986), *The Wings of a Falcon* (1993), *When She Hollers* (1994).

Major works about the author include *Presenting Cynthia Voigt* by Suzanne Elizabeth Reid (1995).

For information on Voigt's career prior to 1987, see *CLR*, Vol. 13.

INTRODUCTION

One of the most highly respected writers of contemporary juvenile literature, Voigt is recognized as an especially gifted creator of books for young adults and middle graders, several of which explore serious and often controversial issues. Praised for her range and versatility, Voigt, who sets her works in both current and historical periods, has written realistic fiction, fantasy, romance, and mystery in addition to a picture book for younger readers. She is perhaps best known for her "Tillerman" series, seven novels for adolescents that revolve around the lives and personal growth of the Tillerman children, four siblings who have been abandoned by their father, a shiftless merchant seaman, and their mother, who is mentally ill. The series also includes individual novels about the children's uncle, who died in Vietnam; the boyfriend of the eldest sister, Dicey; and an African-American girl introduced in the second book of the series, *Dicey's Song.* Voigt is also well known as the creator of the "Kingdom" books, three heroic fantasies set in an imaginary medieval time that blend epic adventures with political themes. Lauded for her understanding of both young people and human nature in general, Voigt is considered an eloquent writer who is celebrated for her strong characterizations and authentic evocation of place and community. She is also acknowledged for the scope and uncompromising nature of her books, which are usually regarded as demanding yet satisfying, challenging yet entertaining. Often drawing on archetypes from myths, folktales, and fairy tales, most notably the metaphor of the orphan who goes on a quest to find his or her identity, Voigt addresses highly charged subjects and themes, such as abandonment, incest, child abuse, racism, the nature of power, the impact of war, and coping with amputation. In these works she often uses the viewpoint of her young male and female protagonists to reveal the pomposity and duplicity of adults. She also invests her books with a profound sense of the importance of family and the healing quality of family relationships as well as a more subtle thread of feminism. Most frequently, Voigt writes coming of age stories: through their adventures and experiences, the boys

and girls in her books learn to develop self-sufficiency, courage, and emotional strength while learning to trust and value others. Stressing personality development, story, themes, and ideas, Voigt often relies on dialogue to establish her narratives. Although some reviewers find her works too long, ponderous, and unfocused, most appreciate her skill as a storyteller, her wisdom, her compelling topics, and her ability to delineate character. A critic writing in *Kirkus Reviews* says, "Voigt is a master of pure story; her enthralling narratives are seamlessly interwoven with telling perception of human nature," while a *Publishers Weekly* reviewer notes that the author "just gets better and better." Writing in *School Librarian,* Mary Hoffman calls Voigt "one of the most stimulating writers for older readers today," while *Books for Keeps* reviewer David Bennett concludes, "Few other contemporary authors portray character with such insight."

Biographical Information

In an interview with Roger Sutton in *School Library Journal,* Voigt stated that her most famous character, Dicey Tillerman, "is the kind of thirteen-year-old I would have liked to have been . . . instead of being a sort of mashed potato, lumpish sort of person." Born in Boston as the second of five children, Voigt spent her childhood in a small town in southern Connecticut and in Pittsburgh, Pennsylvania. She has noted that, in contrast to the Tillerman family, she and her two sisters and twin brothers "were not neglected children" but instead grew up in a secure environment. Voigt became an avid reader and has stated that perhaps her most influential book from childhood is Frances Hodgson Burnett's *The Secret Garden.* Discovering the story in the library of her grandmother's house in Connecticut, Voigt relates that she "pulled *The Secret Garden* off one of her shelves and read it. This was the first book I found entirely for myself and I cherished it." Among her other favorite books were the "Nancy Drew" and "Cherry Ames" series as well as the animal stories of Walter Farley and Albert Payson Terhune; she was also strongly attracted to fairy tales and mythology and read Shakespeare, Tolstoy, Camus, and other classics as a youngster. Voigt began to write at fourteen while a student at Dana Hall, a boarding school in Wellesley, Massachusetts that later provided her with material for her book *Tell Me if the Lovers are Losers* (1982). While attending Smith College, she wrote novels, short stories, and poems and took classes in creative writing; however, Voigt has commented that she never received a great deal of encouragement for her efforts. After graduating from Smith in 1963, Voigt moved to New York City, where she worked for the J. Walter Thompson advertising agency. The next year, Voigt married and moved to Santa Fe, New Mexico, where her husband was a student at St. John's University. Wanting to write, Voigt claims that she "backed into a teaching career" when the school certification official in Santa Fe noticed her degree from Smith and signed her up for accreditation courses; six months later, she was a teacher.

In her teaching career, which spanned nearly twenty-five years, Voigt taught elementary, middle, and high school, both public and private. During her first marriage, she concentrated on teaching and on raising her daughter, not on writing. Divorced and living in Maryland, Voigt was inspired to write books for children when she was teaching middle graders at the Key School in Annapolis. After assigning book reports to her fifth graders, she went through the alphabet of her local library, checking out twenty to thirty books at a time. Especially impressed by such works as Louise Fitzhugh's *Harriet the Spy,* Russell Hoban's *The Mouse and His Child,* and the books of Lloyd Alexander, Voigt noted, "It was then that I realized one could tell stories which had the shape of real books—novels—for kids the age of my students. I began to get ideas for young adult novels and juvenile books. . . . I felt I had suddenly discovered and was exploring a new country." Remarrying in 1974, Voigt reduced her teaching schedule to part-time after the birth of her son three years later and began writing in earnest. Voigt stopped teaching in 1988 to pursue writing full-time; before retiring from teaching, she served for sixteen years as the chairperson of the English department at the Key School. After her retirement, Voigt and her family moved to Maine, the setting for several of her works.

While she was writing *Tell Me if the Lovers are Losers,* a chance encounter inspired Voigt to create her "Tillerman" books. "I went to the market," she says, "and saw a car full of kids left to wait alone in the parking lot. As the electric supermarket doors whooshed open, I asked myself, 'What would happen if nobody ever came back for those kids?' I made some jottings in my notebook and let them 'stew' for a year, the way most of my ideas do. When I set down to write the story that grew from my question (and this is typical of my process) I made a list of character names. Then I tried them to see if they fit. I knew Dicey was the main character, but was not sure precisely *who* she was. The more I wrote about her, the more real she became to me. I'd planned a book about half the size of *Homecoming.* But a few chapters into the novel, the grandmother became central and I began to see that there was a lot more going on that would fit in one book."

Major Works

With *Homecoming* (1981), Voigt begins the saga of the Tillerman children, whose stories are continued in *Dicey's Song, Sons from Afar* (1987), and *Seventeen against the Dealer* (1989). The author takes Dicey, Maybeth, James, and Sammy, who are ages six to thirteen when they are abandoned, into young adulthood and, in Dicey's case, adulthood. After their mother departs in *Homecoming* with the words "Listen to Dicey," the siblings embark on a journey to find a home, eventually leaving Massachusetts to settle with their grandmother in Crisfield, a small town on the eastern shore of Maryland. The second novel in the series, the Newbery Award-winning *Dicey's Song,* describes Dicey's acceptance of herself, her grandmother, and her new situation. Relinquishing control of her siblings to Gram, who herself must learn to accept the children, Dicey allows herself to become friends with her schoolmate Mina Smiths, a young black girl with whom she shares much in common; Voigt tells Mina's story in *Come a Stranger* (1986), describing her growth as both a young woman and an African American. At the end of *Dicey's Song,* Dicey and Gram go to Boston to be with the children's mother, who is dying in a catatonic state at a Boston mental hospital; however, the messages of the book—the importance of letting go and holding on as well as the joys of music and daily family life—suggest the survival of the children. In *Sons from Afar,* Voigt focuses on fifteen-year-old James and twelve-year-old Sammy, who search for Francis Verricker, the father they never knew. Through their quest, which leads them into a bar fight on the Baltimore waterfront with a man whom Verricker had swindled, the boys discover that although they may have inherited some of their father's qualities, each of them is stronger ethically; in addition, the brothers realize how much they complement and depend on one another. In *Seventeen against the Dealer,* Dicey, now twenty-one, again demonstrates the strength of character that she showed in the earlier books. Determined to create a successful boatyard business, she makes serious errors and lets herself be duped by a con artist, who turns out to be her father. Embarking on a spiritual journey, Dicey realizes the sustaining power of her family and friends, most notably her faithful boyfriend Jeff Greene, whose story Voigt tells in *A Solitary Blue (1983)*. In this work, Jeff comes to terms with abandonment by his philanthropist mother, learns to accept his taciturn father, and finds solace in music. One of Voigt's most highly regarded "Tillerman" books is *The Runner (1985)*, the story of Samuel "Bullet" Tillerman, a champion cross-country runner who learns to overcome his prejudice against African Americans before dying in Vietnam at the age of eighteen.

In her trio of "Kingdom" stories, Voigt balances exciting narratives with strong personal and sociopolitical themes such as the horrors of slavery, the nature of heroism, and the consequences of selfishness; critics note the richness and totality of the imaginary world that she has created. *Jackaroo* (1985) is the first and perhaps most popular "Kingdom" volume. Filled with medieval details, high adventure, and romance, the fantasy describes how Gwyn, the teenage daughter of the local innkeeper, assumes the role of the legendary Jackaroo, a masked rider, to help the poor and oppressed; in the process, Gwyn uses courage and cunning to save both her people and herself. In *On Fortune's Wheel* (1990), Gwyn's granddaughter, fourteen-year-old Birle, embarks on an adventure with Orien, the runaway earl of the kingdom. After being shipwrecked, captured by pirates, and sold into slavery, they return home, where Orien abdicates rule to his stern but fair younger brother in order to share life with Birle. A critic writing in *Kirkus Reviews* calls *On Fortune's Wheel* a "satisfying love story, a grand adventure, and a rich mix of ideas and action," while Hazel Rochman of *Booklist* concludes that "*Jackaroo*'s many fans will willingly suspend disbelief and follow the intrepid Birle as Fortune's Wheel swings. . . ." *The Wings of a Falcon* outlines how teenagers Oriel and Griff escape from an island stronghold of slave boys to journey to the Kingdom; they end up on the farm of Beryl, a puppeteer and herbalist who is the granddaughter of Orien and Birle of *On Fortune's Wheel*. Oriel and Beryl become lovers; when the brave Oriel is killed after becoming earl, Griff, who has proven himself both thoughtful and resilient, takes over as ruler and marries Beryl, who is carrying Oriel's child. A *Publishers Weekly* contributor calls *The Wings of a Falcon* "an episodic tale certain to entrance readers. . . . A model for the genre," while a *Kirkus Reviews* critic notes that Voigt "skillfully sustains a heroic tone while challenging heroic models at every turn."

Voigt has written a number of well-received individual titles that were published in the late 1980s and 1990s. *Tree by Leaf* (1988), for example, is a historical novel set on a remote Maine peninsula just after World War I. The story describes how twelve-year-old Clothilde Speer finds stability in a confusing world; Clothilde, who resents both God and her family after her father returns from the war with a facial disfigurement and she discovers that her home may be sold, learns to find peace with her situation after communicating with "the Voice," an omniscient presence and higher power that allows her to see the interdependence of all living things. In her review in the *Horn Book Magazine,* Ethel L. Heins notes that *Tree by Leaf* "will speak to the child who, like Clothilde, is puzzling out life alone. . . ," while Dulcie Leimbach of the *New York Times Book Review* notes that Clothilde "is as complex and strong-willed as Dicey. . . . Here the author distinguishes herself from other young adult novels of the 'coping' genre." *David and Jonathan* (1992), a young adult novel set on Cape Cod in the 1950s, explores both coming of age and the results of war, especially the effects of the Holocaust. In this work, Voigt describes how the close friendship of two bright, literate teenagers—Henry, a Protestant, and Jonathan, a Jew—is changed by the intrusion of Jonathan's older cousin, David. An orphaned Holocaust survivor who has come to live with Jonathan's family in a final effort to alleviate his depression, David, who has spent the last six years in an institution, is intent on suicide. Henry finds himself locked into a struggle for Jonathan with the cruel and manipulative David; at the end of the novel, David, who has ruined the friendship between Jon and Henry and has awakened the latter's latent homosexuality, kills himself. In a framing episode set in Vietnam in 1967, Henry, who has become a doctor, again meets Jon, who has been tortured as a POW, and saves his eyesight. Writing in *Booklist,* Hazel Rochman says, "For once in a YA story the hell of the Holocaust is not overcome by individual goodness. And for once, here are YA characters for whom *brilliant* is more than a designer label."

Throughout her career, Voigt has been acknowledged as a writer unafraid to tackle difficult subjects. With *When She Hollers,* she created her most controversial novel to date. In an interview with Elizabeth Deveraux in *Publishers Weekly,* Voigt said that she was prompted to write this book when she "ran into sexual abuse in a way that made me feel it, from the inside out." The novel outlines a day in the life of seventeen-year-old Tish, a girl who has been raped by her stepfather Tonnie since she was a young child. At a breaking point, Tish decides to be a survivor rather than a victim: she confronts Tonnie with a knife at the breakfast table and, jolted by the suicide of a classmate who was pregnant due to incest, writes down what has happened to her and gives the document to a lawyer. At the end of the day, she returns home with the knife in her boot, empowered by the realization that Tonnie's power over her is limited. Carolyn Polese of *School Library Journal* writes, "Nowhere in children's literature is the link between abuse and violence . . . so clearly delineated, nor the mind-bending defenses so accurately portrayed," while *Horn Book* reviewer Patty Campbell calls *When She Hollers* "a small literary masterpiece." Writing in *Junior Bookshelf,* Marcus Crouch notes, "It argues much for Ms. Voigt's skill and understanding that a story which consists largely of the inner thoughts of an inarticulate girl should be so tensely exciting as well as so deeply moving. . . . A master craftsman is at work here." Voigt's more recent book is *Bad Girls* (1996), a novel for middle graders that depicts the unholy alliance of two fifth grade pranksters. Motivated by anger and loneliness, Margalo and Michelle ("Mikey") are a pair of new students whose paybacks to their classmates mask their need to be accepted; finally, after experiencing both trust and betrayal, the girls realize that they are each other's best friend. A contributor to *Kirkus Reviews* comments, "A distinguished writer is at the top of her form in a sharp, sassy tale. . . . [This] pair of unlikable but admirably capable mavericks outmatch even Barbara Robinson's Herdman family for sheer sand," while *School Library Journal* critic Mary Jo Drungil says, "Rarely does a novel set in elementary school celebrate the fierce joy that 'troublemakers' derive from successfully manipulating the personalities and situations around them." Lois Metzger of the *New York Times Book Review* concludes that with *Bad Girls* Voigt "becomes a kind of Margaret Mead of the fifth grade." Other recent works by the author include *The Vandemark Mummy* (1991), a contemporary mystery story for young adults that involves a brother and sister in a search for the vandals that disturbed the mummy of a young Egyptian girl, and *Orfe* (1992), a YA novel based on the Greek myth of Orpheus and Eurydice that portrays a talented young musician who falls in love with a recovering drug addict. Voigt is also the author of a pic-ture book, *Stories about Rosie* (1986), vignettes about the Voigt family dog told from the dog's perspective, and an adult novel, *Glass Mountain* (1991); in addition, she served as the compiler of *Shore Writers' Sampler II* (1988), a collection of stories and poems edited with David Berman.

Awards

Homecoming was nominated for the American Book Award in 1982. In 1983, *Dicey's Song* received the Newbery Medal and was named a *Boston Globe-Horn Book* honor book. *A Solitary Blue* was named a Newbery honor book and a *Boston Globe-Horn Book* honor book in 1984; *The Callender Papers* won the Edgar Allan Poe Award in the same year. In 1989, *The Runner* won the Silver Pencil Award from the Netherlands and the Deutscher Jugendliteratur Preis from Germany, while *Tree by Leaf* was given the Sugarman Children's Book Award. In the same year, Voigt received the ALAN Award for achievement in young adult literature. She was also the recipient of the Margaret A. Edwards Award in 1995, presented to her by the American Library Association Young Adult Library Association/*School Library Journal* for outstanding contributions to young adult literature. In addition, Voigt has received several citations from the ALA as well as other adult- and child-selected awards for her works.

AUTHOR'S COMMENTARY

Cynthia Voigt with Hazel Rochman

SOURCE: An interview in *Booklist,* Vol. 85, No. 16, April 15, 1989, pp. 1452-53.

BKL: Why do you think the Tillerman books are popular? They're long and dense, with complex feelings and ideas, not what's generally thought of as popular with young people.

VOIGT: I think we underestimate kids. I know from my work as a teacher that students are curious about ideas and about themselves. I teach *Crime and Punishment,* and it never fails to excite high school seniors. On the other hand, Judith Krantz is a remarkable writer: she says what she's going to do, and then she does it well. Books can be read and enjoyed and thought about at a whole lot of different levels.

One of the things that's true of the Tillermans that's not supposed to be popular is that they're very strong characters. They often slip over into arrogance, and I'm always delighted that people welcome that in them. Especially in young people, the call for the lowest common denominator bothers me.

BKL: To be liked at all costs?

VOIGT: And to be told by the adult world that it all comes down to compromises and not coming down too firmly on one side or the other. There's a kind of anti-character that society welcomes.

BKL: It's not only arrogance. The YA writer Margaret Mahy says that she admires ***The Runner*** because you make us care for the not very likable protagonist, Bullet, who's solitary, angry, bigoted. Now in your new book you take your star, Dicey, and you make her quite unsympathetic at times, driven and self-obsessed. Is that risky?

VOIGT: I can't worry about that. I think Bullet is wonderful (he's the one character I really hated having to kill off). And I think Dicey's terrific. She's doing things wrong, but they are exactly the same things that in ***Homecoming*** had gotten her what she needed. This time she doesn't get there just because circumstances are different, but there's no way for her to know that, except by learning it. I think she's doing exactly what she would do and doing it the way she would do it. I guess I always like people who make unhedged bets. It's inevitable that she should fail at what she's doing. It's important to fail and learn whatever there is to learn from the experience.

BKL: It's interesting that you've written a book about failure. You break the formula. Determination and hard work don't overcome all obstacles.

VOIGT: And she's got to start again and she knows she's going to fail many more times. In that respect, it's a very personal book. There's been a lot of failure in my life, things I wanted for one reason or another that didn't fall into my lap.

BKL: Is the focus on work in the latest book also personal?

VOIGT: It certainly was in my mind while I was writing the book. My attitude toward work is Dicey's—if you've got work you like to do, you're lucky. I love teaching, and it seems to be work worth doing. I've done it fulltime, and then when my son was born, I went part-time. He was in the back of the classroom in a playpen, and we did *Crime and Punishment* together. He's the one who later thought I'd won the "Blueberry" Medal.

BKL: There are classroom scenes in just about every book, and you don't hesitate to have some bad teachers.

VOIGT: There are some good ones, too, like the one in *The Runner.* My editor is very careful not to let the teacher in me get control. It's not that she cuts back on the classroom discussion, but more that she keeps reminding me when I have a brickbat in my hand of one kind or another. In *Tell Me If the Lovers Are Losers,* I had complete instructions for how to write a good paper, and we did take that out—it wasn't exactly the kind of thing you could work *naturally* into dialogue.

BKL: And Dicey's building a boat and failing at it relates to making anything. It could be writing a paper, or any work or dream.

VOIGT: Yes. I hope so. Because I wouldn't know how to build a boat.

BKL: You wouldn't? What about the landscape? You write so vividly about the Chesapeake Bay area; the shore, the waves and wind. You do like sailing?

VOIGT: Well, I don't know. I guess I like it. It's a landscape in which I'm comfortable. I'm clearly not a city person. I like having the physical landscape in general, but I don't look at it carefully. I think it has to do with not having a visual imagination. I don't see things clearly, and I don't remember them visually, and I don't hold them in my memory.

BKL: So you have to work hard to be accurate about what she's doing with all those boats?

VOIGT: Yes, and things like the appearance and placement of her shop. I had to sit down and draw it, because otherwise I'd always have the doors and windows in the wrong place.

BKL: Maybe that's why there's so much internal life in your books, as if the landscape flashes together with feeling and memory. What about all your simple *w* words— *wind, water, waves,* and then *wood, work, walk, worry*— and *word?* Sometimes several in one paragraph.

VOIGT: Oh, I like that. No, I didn't know I did that. Isn't that interesting? When I'm writing a book, I have to know that I'm not the only reader, and I'm probably not the best reader. What I see in it is not necessarily what people read in it. The writer Robin McKinley lives near me here in Maine, and we got into a good quarrel about truth in fiction. I believe that fiction is a lie and people who deal in it ought to remember that they're lying. It's designed to tell the truth, but it isn't itself the truth. My own reality

isn't the one in my books. I don't want to consider myself a person who utters truths. I want to be taken seriously but not unquestioningly. I don't want that kind of authority or responsibility. As Camus said, if there's going to be a judgment, I don't want to be the judge, I want to be the joker sitting under the table.

BKL: That sounds like something your character Frank Verricker (or "Cisco") would say.

VOIGT: Yes, maybe that's where he comes from.

BKL: You seem to like him.

VOIGT: My editor wants to marry him. He is amusing, but, no, he's one I really don't like. He shouldn't do that to his kids.

BKL: It's great that you leave things uncertain about him in the last book. You don't spell out that the charming drifter "Cisco" who defrauds Dicey is really the father, Frank Verricker, who deserted the family years ago.

VOIGT: My husband suggested that I have Dicey discover his wallet with his Social Security number or something as proof.

BKL: Why didn't you? Because it would smash her?

VOIGT: Because it wasn't relevant to her. He's like Jeff's mother in *A Solitary Blue.* Both parents carry their own limitations with them, and they never know it; that's part of the pity of the whole thing.

BKL: Dicey's stronger. Is Dicey like you at all? Do you know someone like her?

VOIGT: I wish I did. Dicey's the kind of kid I would like to have been. Gram's the kind of old lady I'd like to be. And I'm not going to make either one of them. The thing is they're all larger than life. I can't tell even if they're idealized visions. I like Dicey's mistakes much better than my own. They're much more interesting and ambitious. That's because of who she is.

BKL: Did you know when you wrote the first book about Dicey that it was going to be a series? *Homecoming* seems to contain all the Tillerman books right there, including some well-developed characters, like Bullet, that become central in later books?

VOIGT: No. Well, sometimes I think I didn't know anything about it. I work with outlines and I had this thing blocked out in outline for *Homecoming,* and then somehow the character of Gram sprang into my mind, full-blown, so the book became twice as long. Then I knew I had to write *Dicey's Song* and that completes the mother's story. And Jeff came into the second book, and I knew I had to write his story next, though everyone was telling me the story they thought I should be writing. And then I always knew Bullet's story: *The Runner* strikes me as the core of the whole series. My working plan for the last one was always that it was going to be Dicey and Jeff, and that was where I thought I wanted it to end.

BKL: Are you sure this is the end?

VOIGT: I'm never sure. However, I've felt this way for a few years. I think there's a danger with a series that you take your own characters for granted and don't do as well by them, and I don't want that to happen.

Cynthia Voigt

SOURCE: "Cynthia Voigt," in an interview with Elizabeth Devereaux in *Publishers Weekly,* Vol. 241, No. 29, July 18, 1994, pp. 225-26.

Cynthia Voigt has full confidence in her newest YA novel, *When She Hollers.* "I know it's as true as I can make it," she states. All the same, she adds, "I was fully prepared to have Scholastic [her publisher] say, 'We're not comfortable with this.' My mother would say, 'Don't do this.' And there are other publishers who would say, 'Don't do this.' But Scholastic is bold. They're willing to take chances with their authors."

At first glance there seems nothing risky about publishing Voigt. Since the appearance of her first novel in 1981, she has produced 20 books, including a novel for adults. All of her titles are in print; they have earned such honors as a Newbery Medal and an American Book Award nomination, and they uniformly draw high praise.

But whatever accolades *When She Hollers* may receive, it's almost sure to be controversial. As the book begins, its teenage heroine is at the breakfast table, pointing a knife at her stepfather: "You come near me and—I'll cut your hands off, I'll . . . cut your heart out." He pretends not to understand, but the reader knows—he has been molesting Tish, and Tish is determined to stop him at all costs. There's no tidy resolution in this novel, no happy ending, and none of the stock optimism that underlies much YA fiction.

"I don't want to be a formula writer," Voigt says in a recent phone interview from her home in Maine. "I would like to feel that readers can't predict me, but that the surprises may well be interesting."

Indeed, about the only thing that Voigt's admirers can count on is her refusal to repeat herself. She switches genres with uncanny dexterity. When, for example, we met with her for the first time last fall, she was fresh from the publication of *The Wings of a Falcon,* an epic adventure set in a quasi-Renaissance fantasy realm, a novel as grandly inventive as *When She Hollers* is gritty and raw. She has written mysteries, rewritten myths, dreamed up a romantic comedy fit for Fred Astaire and Ginger Rogers. She has peopled her novels with, variously, cheerleaders, Holocaust survivors and abandoned children.

As far-flung as these subjects may seem, they all arise out of a sense of urgency. Voigt began to write *When She Hollers,* she says, because "I ran into sexual abuse in a way that made me feel it, from the inside out," a statement she declines to explain further.

"I was in a grocery store," she continues, "and I had the image of the opening scene and the first line. I was supposed to meet up with my husband—we were 35 miles from home, and we were supposed to have dinner with some friends. So there I was with my list in my hand, and a sentence in my head, and I bought myself a writing pad. I finished the grocery shopping and I was about half an hour early for the dinner. So I went into a restaurant and ordered a cup of coffee, and I wrote. I never write by hand, and I never write in a public place.

"Once I hooked into this story, I simply wrote the whole thing by hand, wherever I was," she says, noting that the first draft took three or four months. "I figured my hand would tell me if it wanted to type," she says with easy good humor. "It's one of the things I do as a writer: I attempt to hook in, and then I relax and let the rest of me tell me what to do—sort of like those mad scientist's hands that get attached to the innocent person's body."

Interestingly, another shopping trip inspired Voigt's first published novel, *Homecoming.* "I saw some kids in a car outside a grocery store. I, of course, would never leave my children alone like that"—Voigt has a daughter and a son—"but these kids were in the car. They weren't even doing anything outrageous, but for some reason, when I walked into the store to do my shopping, I thought, What if nobody comes back for those kids?

"And then I thought, What a good idea for a story. With children's novels, one of the problems is, how do you get rid of the adult world and empower the children, because they have got to be the actors." Thus began the story of the Tillerman family, which would occupy seven novels before Voigt—to the dismay of many of her readers—concluded the series in 1989. "The Tillermans and I had nothing more to say to one another."

As instinctive as the writing process appears, it has not always been easy for Voigt, who first began to write when she was 14 and a student at Dana Hall, the Wellesley, Mass., prep school. While a student at Smith College, she wrote "a couple of novels," short stories, poems. She took some courses, but her teachers "did not think I was as good as I hoped I was. They of course had experience and wisdom on their side, but I still wanted to write."

In 1964, a year after she'd graduated, Voigt married, and left the East Coast for New Mexico, where her husband was a student at St. John's. "There were two things I knew about myself," she says. "One, I wanted to be a writer. And the other thing was, I never wanted to teach." But, needing money for tuition and housing, Voigt found herself toying with the prospect of teaching—"the way I was also toying with the idea of being a spy or a detective." Before she knew it, she was "backed into a teaching career" when the school certification official noticed her degree from Smith; luckily, "I walked into the class-room the first day of teaching, and I knew I was in the right place."

As her husband transferred to St. John's Annapolis campus and later entered the Navy, Voigt taught high school, elementary school and middle school, public and private. During the seven years of that first marriage, she wrote "maybe one story."

"All through the failure years of my young womanhood—at the same time, by the way, I was succeeding at many other things, like teaching, which was a great gift, so it's not like I see myself as a little worm—I wanted this [writing] and I couldn't get it. One of the things I would flagellate myself with was this image of a middle-aged, frumpy lady, probably with a permanent, characterless, going out for lunch and saying, 'You know, I could have done this if I'd wanted to, and . . .' I was so ashamed of her, because she didn't have the good sense to say, 'I know I don't have the ability. Bam! Close the door on it.' She lacked dignity and pride, not to mention charm and wit and all the other virtues."

And then Voigt rounded a corner. "I remember turning 30, and everyone around me was palpitating at 30 and feeling that they were terribly old. I had just successfully evicted my first husband, and I had a daughter of a year, with whom I had fallen in love, and I had my teaching profession. I didn't feel like I was entering old age, I felt like I was ripe, and I said to myself, You know, maybe it doesn't matter if you never get published. Maybe you just do it because you want to do it, because it makes your life richer and keeps you sane. The question of whether I was going to fail or not became almost entirely irrelevant, and all that mattered was, I wanted to be telling stories."

By that point, Voigt was teaching middle school, and, in preparing reading lists for her students, she undertook extensive visits to the children's shelves at the library. She found "some real knockouts"—Louise Fitzhugh's *Harriet the Spy* ("It's another *Charlotte's Web* as far as I'm concerned"), Lloyd Alexander's books, Russell and Lillian Hoban's *The Mouse and His Child* ("seriously excellent"). "Because I was reading in that vein," she explains, "stories in that field just came into my head."

She recalls two or three projects from that period, including a picture book that she submitted to Ursula Nordstrom at Harper & Row. Although the manuscript was rejected, Nordstrom's letter emboldened Voigt: "I had no idea who she was, no idea of the quality of the person who had rejected me, but she somehow conveyed to me the sense that I shouldn't go put my head in a hole. She didn't say, 'Keep writing, I'm sure it will work out,' but something about the way she did it was enabling rather than inhibiting."

Voigt remarried in 1974; in 1977 she had her second child and reduced her teaching schedule to part-time. "And spent half the day writing," she remembers. "Which is when I started writing books that were published." (Much as she loved teaching, Voigt gave it up in 1988, when she and her family moved to Maine. "I never went looking for work, and nobody came to me and said, 'Please teach a senior English course.' And I love owning my entire day.")

When success came, it was rapid. Atheneum not only took *Homecoming,* which she'd sent over the transom, but quickly signed up two of Voigt's earlier efforts, *Tell Me If the Lovers Are Losers* and *The Callender Papers.* Atheneum continued to publish Voigt's juvenile titles until 1992, when she moved to Scholastic. . . .

In between, however, she had turned out her first adult novel, *Glass Mountain,* without a doubt her lightest, most comedic book. "I think adults don't like things serious. I think adolescents have a taste for tragedy, but adults are troubled by it. Probably because they've seen it more often.

"One of my basic understandings of the difference between children and adults is that children expect themselves to learn. They have that kind of open curiosity. They understand themselves as creatures who are still learning. They plan to learn, and they plan to get ahead by it. Adults seem to expect themselves to know the answers. And this means, as a readership, we all want to be amused and delighted, but the leeway adults grant to what they're reading, or watching on television or at the movies, is a little different. I find that adults are less comfortable with the unfamiliar."

But the unfamiliar seems irresistible to Voigt herself. Referring to her Kingdom sequence—the three linked fantasies *Jackaroo, On Fortune's Wheel* and *The Wings of a Falcon*—she says, "I was making up a whole world. It was something I'd never done before, and I wanted to try it." The books, she says, are more political than most of her other writing ("I had to work out what power is, and what you do with it or what can be done with it"), but at the same time they represent incursions into different genres. "*Jackaroo* is a Zorro book, full of masked people and gallivanting; *On Fortune's Wheel* is a romance; and *Wings* is a hero quest."

At the moment Voigt is hard at work, but she's not sure what her next book will be. "I know what I'm going to be writing, but I have no idea if anyone is going to want to publish it.

"When I'm writing, I feel as if I have a responsibility to the story, and the story tells me if I'm doing it wrong. The story is my touchstone, not anything else. Which assumes, of course, that the story has, in some Platonic universe, already been written. And we all know it hasn't. Or so we think. It's almost an odd way of disclaiming responsibility. But I know I'm doing something wrong if I find myself thinking not about the story, but about whether this is acceptable, what will be said, whether anybody will want to read it, what if nobody wants to read it . . . that kind of thing."

She does concede that another Kingdom book "is on the back burner. I have to write one, because of a man who reviewed *Wings* and said it was the last book in a trilogy," she says with a good laugh.

It seems, however, that Voigt counts on surprising herself as well as her readers. She is waiting for the Kingdom story, like all of her others, to come to her: "You should always avoid writing sequels, unless there's an urgency in some way to them, unless they fit in some way into some master plan. If the time comes for me to write it, I'll know it. It'll rise up unavoidably. It'll just get in my way and I won't be able to get it out of my way, I'll *have* to write it."

Cynthia Voigt

SOURCE: "Authorgraph No. 66: Cynthia Voigt," in an interview with David Bennett in *Books for Keeps,* No. 66, January, 1991, pp. 12-13.

'I don't think of myself as a creative person and I really think that's true. You notice something and you wonder, "what if?" It's as simple as that.'

So, says Cynthia Voigt, highly successful author of the Tillerman series, who once saw a bunch of kids waiting in a station wagon and wondered what would happen if the person for whom they were waiting just never came back. How long would they wait? What would make a person not come back?

Her wonderings have culminated in an acclaimed series of books, one of which, *Dicey's Song,* was a Newbery Medal winner. There will be no more. Their creator feels that she stopped at the right time—'series can go on too long and then you lose it . . . I felt that I stopped at the right time . . . I knew it was right.' Even so, this is not a series in the conventional sense. The reader should feel that each of the six is entirely different—'they tasted, when I was writing them, entirely separate . . . I see them more like a mosaic that tessellates. I conceived of them in that fashion.'

Her own secure family life was not a bit like that of the troubled Tillermans. She is one of three girls, added to by twin boys when she was twelve. The family was raised in Connecticut, later moving to Pittsburgh. Certainly her parents did well by their children, unlike some, especially fathers, who appear in the novels. Cynthia freely admits, 'If I were the parents of the person who wrote *Tree By Leaf* I'd be upset.' Frank Verricker, the absent father in *Sons from Afar,* is probably best remaining that way and poor Brann in *Building Blocks* is left feeling 'doomed to be the kind of kid who felt ashamed by his old man.' To be fair, not all of them are rotten enough to ruin the life of everyone, but many attract a fair amount of reader hostility.

For herself Cynthia professes to have strong maternal instincts and obviously admires her own son and daughter, who live with their parents in Maryland making them 'East Coast Middle-of-the-roaders.'

She was educated in the fifties in Massachusetts, first at a girl's boarding school and then at a women's college, which later proved source material for one of the early books, *Tell Me If the Lovers Are Losers.* Here Hildy, the tragic character from North Dakota, is deliberately portrayed as alien to the world that she finds herself in and to that of most readers. Her puritan, moral, religious and social values, curiously highlighted by her appalling eyesight, contrast strikingly with those of Niki, the Californian girl, world-wise and steeped in more contemporary values.

These two characters have become the hallmark of Cynthia Voigt's work. Few other contemporary authors portray character with such insight. Individuals fascinate her. She claims she'd love to grow up like the remarkable Gram in the Tillerman series—'I would like myself if I could be like her.' She also has an affection for Bullet from *The Runner.* When her editor asked, 'Who is this sullen creep?', his originator retorted, 'This is an heroic type . . . what do you mean sullen?' She confesses now, 'I think he's absolutely wonderful. I would've loved to have had him in class. I don't think he'd've liked me a bit. I would've loved to have hit my head up against his.' Like the editor, not everyone professes Bullet to be the most endearing character, but Ms Voigt likes difficult people. In her years of teaching she has always got along with the difficult students and now she tends to write about the kinds of people that she freely acknowledges she used automatically to write off when she was younger.

'Teaching taught me to recognise that everyone has his or her own life and they tend to try to do well by it, and to sit there and write them off is no way to see what is true.'

Her admiration of Bullet occasioned the only time so far that she has got into trouble with her characters. She liked him so much that she couldn't bring herself to kill him off—'I thought of a way to do it without belying anything I'd done before, and I thought "I can save his life." Then I realised that it just wasn't honest and he wouldn't have tolerated it and my reasons for not wanting to kill him off,' so Bullet died in the Vietnam war. . . .

Such hard concentration on character has its traps of which Cynthia Voigt is well aware. Over the years she has become more interested in her characters at the expense of plot and she has gone further and further into their heads and away from what they're doing.

'The Tillermans seemed to be much more about character. I used to worry about that, then I thought these things have their own shape and your job is at most a little pruning, maybe. You can belie the shape and really do a bad job by the story.'

The Callender Papers, her traditional Gothic Novel, is the most revised for this very reason—she needed to attend to the plotting. Likewise, *Jackaroo,* which she sets in an imaginary place that she calls 'The Kingdom.' This is the same setting for an imminently due novel, *On Fortune's Wheel,* which she confesses was hard work to plot, but with which she is immensely pleased. The two are her 'Zorro Novels.'

As a teenager who longed to write, the young Cynthia was hugely enamoured of the heroic adventure story. Calling cards bore 'Zorro' as her middle name and the mat outside her dormitory door was a Zorro bathmat. The romantic notion of somebody galloping around putting Z's on things and leading an heroic, secret life translated itself into Gwyn, the innkeeper's daughter in *Jackaroo,* who was, she realised,

> More at ease when she wandered about the countryside as Jackaroo than at any other time. It was odd that dressed up as Jackaroo she felt much more like herself. And in the disguise, she was free to do what she really wanted to do, much freer than was Gwyn, the innkeeper's daughter.

Real disguises, smokescreens, masks, tangible or otherwise, are a common motif and an often used image (which Cynthia finds rewarding to explore) in many of the novels. Masks that her characters show on the outside belie what's going on inside, separating the public face from the private one. 'I like kids to recognise that they are wearing costumes, not to draw any moral conclusions, just to be able to say, "Yes this is a costume," it lightens everything up and they'll be freer to move in and out of roles.'

For her own part Cynthia confesses that she'd like a more unusual or glamorous persona, maybe like the blonde cheerleader Izzy in *Izzy, Willy-Nilly,* the type that as a girl she both envied and despised. Since Izzy ends up in a wheelchair, this book gets sold as an anti drink-driving book, but its author reveals, 'I think all of us look like Izzy. It's just that most of it is invisible. We're all tottering around at the end wondering whether we're going to fall down or not. We're all marked and that's why I think it works.'

Cynthia Voigt seldom comes close to revealing how much of herself goes into her novels. She doesn't like to contemplate that, because to do so might trigger too much self-control and 'I'd get stiff and start stumbling and trip. Like in the classroom, if you become too conscious of how much of yourself you are revealing to your students, that's not good.'

She has been out of the classroom for two years, but her lively conversation is often illustrated by teaching analogies, She loved the job, but admits that essentially she prefers to stay at home and write and is delighted to find herself doing it. Yet she doesn't consider herself a professional—'a word that's not entirely clean in my vocabulary.'

'I write, I think, in a novel rhythm. I'd love to turn out good sonnets. That's like cutting a diamond just right. . . I write because I write and the way I write is because it's the way it interests me to write . . . You have an idea and the idea has its own natural size and you can abort it or stretch it out, but the ideas I have been having are novel ideas . . . I will try anything in my closet with my typewriter, but I don't come out very often.'

On a good day a couple of hours of genuine work is considered profitable, a first draft often taking six to nine months. Cynthia is only happy when a couple of ideas are in the melting pot, but even then many end up in drawers because they haven't worked. 'I feel deeply about things and occasionally a professional thought occurs—The more successful I am, the less confident I am—which I think is probably good.'

She is skeptical about any strong political motivation in her work and then, on reflection, decides she is a humanist and, if there's any feminism, it's because she feels that women and girls need to be careful about believing what they are told about themselves. Dicey believes that she can make a success as a boat builder in *Seventeen Against the Dealer* despite the odds. . . .

Similarly with racism in the Tillerman books, where settings are meticulously authentic. Prejudice in these novels had to be met head on, especially in *Come a Stranger.* 'These are American books and it's part of American life. I raised a few questions about it. What do we really think? What would we really do?'

About future plans the author is cagey. She doesn't talk about her ideas in public because—'I don't know until I'm through with them how I'm going to do them and they're so fragile. I want to make what I'm going to make out of them and then anything can happen and that's o.k.—but I want them left alone to do my part in them.'

Long may the author who professes to 'like hard thinking and daydreaming' ask 'what if?' and produce such excellent fiction enjoyed by an extraordinarily wide range of admiring readers.

Cynthia Voigt with Roger Sutton

SOURCE: An interview in *School Library Journal,* Vol. 41, No. 6, June, 1995, pp. 28-32.

[The following excerpt is from an interview by Roger Sutton that was conducted in response to Voigt winning the Margaret A. Edwards Award in 1995.]

[Roger Sutton:] When you look at the other people who've won this award, they all began in the late '60s and early '70s. Your first book, *Homecoming,* wasn't published until '81. I think of you as part of a second wave. Did you have any sense of YA lit when you started to write?

Voigt: I didn't even know it was there until I taught fifth grade in 1966 and put together a reading list. My feeling was that if the kids were going to write book reports for me, I wanted to have read the books they were writing about. So I went to the library and started at A. There were all these books there in the kid's section and I didn't differentiate [between] children's and YA—they were just books that were not adult books. I read through from A to Z, I'd take 20 or 30 books home at a time. The ones I liked I put on my list and the ones I didn't like I just stopped reading after a chapter or so. I remember one that kept me up until 3:00 in the morning (which was really unusual because I used to pass out at 11:00 regularly and exhausted): *The Great and Terrible Quest* by Margaret Lovett. It's a fantasy adventure about a boy and his grandfather. The grandfather's cruel and mean, and the boy's pretending to be sort of mentally defective. The kingdom is in a shambles, and the boy is, of course, the lost Prince. It's really high adventure, it's romance, it's a whopping good tale. I couldn't find nearly as many adult books that I had such a good time reading or had thought so hard over. As far as YA goes, M. E. Kerr and K. M. Peyton were the first I ran into.

[Sutton:] Although *Homecoming* was the first book you published, didn't you actually write *Tell Me If the Lovers Are Losers* first?

Voigt: Actually *The Callender Papers* was written first, then *Tell Me,* then *Homecoming.* Atheneum was buying backwards and I was getting anxious! Then they bought *Dicey's Song* and I felt secure again. I thought maybe I'd peaked with the first book they published and then that's it . . . and my cupboards were not that full.

[Sutton:] You've got a real span represented on this list, from *Building Blocks,* which I personally wouldn't think of as YA—

Voigt: No, neither would I; I was sort of surprised to see it on there.

[Sutton:]—to *The Runner,* which is clearly high school. It's quite a range of appeal.

Voigt: Yes, and in *kind,* too, I think. I like to think that *Jackaroo* and *Izzy* and the rest are different kinds of stories told in different kinds of ways with different kinds of characters. I like that a lot.

[Sutton:] When I look at the level of difficulty in your stories, the density of language, most of the books you've been cited for are among the most difficult that have been cited for the Edwards award. A couple of the Cormiers aside.

Voigt: Yeah, Cormier blows me out of the water on difficulty.

[Sutton:] But, his difficulty is mostly conceptual. The language isn't that complicated, the sentences aren't long, the writing isn't dense, whereas I think yours is.

Voigt: Well, sometimes. I've never understood exactly what language is difficult and what language is not difficult. I'm always pleased when I hear that *Homecoming* is being taught to a remedial reading class. Because that fulfills my sense that if you've got a good story, it'll do the work for you. The kids will try, and they will grow into the ability to read language even if it is, quote, difficult.

[Sutton:] Look at the way you start that book. Dicey and the kids are sitting in the car in the mall parking lot, and Momma says "Listen to Dicey" and then disappears. How can you stop reading?

Voigt: It's called being *seductive.* That's what a writer is supposed to do. My job, like a teacher's, is to seduce and charm and sell—and make kids better readers than when they came in. You can't do that by telling them they ought to be better at it. I like reading difficult things when they engage me. I like seeing movies that are difficult when they engage me. I like having my experiences be rich. As long as they don't make me feel like I'm stupid or scare me inordinately. So I'm always a little dubious about people saying this is difficult language, this is easy language. A good story is the kind of story that whenever you tell it, you can see people buying into it. It's almost like a magic trick in some way.

[Sutton:] Why do you think *Seventeen against the Dealer,* for example, is so much more difficult than *Homecoming?*

Voigt: Most of the Tillerman books don't really have what I would call a plot. They're slice-of-life things, where you catch somebody over a period of time, and during that period of time things happen that get them to change and grow. *A Solitary Blue,* for example, is not about how Jeff comes to terms with his mother. The end of *A Solitary Blue* is, in fact, that he hasn't finally come to a real balanced peace with his mother, but it's not nearly so important as his understanding of what he might think the nature of love is. The nature of love is not a plot point.

Seventeen against the Dealer has a rhetorical conclusion and a thematic conclusion, but it's not exactly as if the plot of that book is to have Dicey and Jeff end up getting married. That isn't the pull of it. The pull, in fact, is everybody making mistakes and dealing with them in different ways. Failure. I call that a book about failure, which is why it's dedicated to my students.

[Sutton:] I think that's a hard book for kids emotionally. Dicey's prickly all along, but there she gets pretty impossible.

Voigt: The same thing that allows Dicey to save the family in *Homecoming* gets in her way in *Seventeen against the Dealer.* It's the same quality and it just doesn't work for her in the last book. So it's not a happily-ever-after kind of ending for the series.

[Sutton:] Did you know that this six-book saga was evolving when you began?

Voigt: Not when I started *Homecoming,* which was going to be half the length it was when I'd written my first outline. But then I got to the end of *Homecoming* and I realized that until I solved the problem with Dicey's mother, that particular story was unfinished. So I think of *Dicey's Song* as *Homecoming Part III.* And then when I was writing *Dicey's Song* I discovered the character of Jeff, whom I liked very much, and wanted to write his story . . . and then I realized I was in for the long haul. Once I got to the end of *Dicey's Song,* I think I knew what I was doing. In that respect. [Laughter] I knew what I *thought* I was up to.

[Sutton:] Was it hard to leave the Tillermans behind?

Voigt: Yes, because, you see, I had this wonderful writing rhythm going where I would do something else and then I'd do a Tillerman book, and I could be fairly sure that the Tillerman book would be received at least with interest. And since so much of the thinking about who the characters were and what the world was like had already been done, I could focus. When I'm writing a book, there's a beginning stage where it's very cumbersome and clumsy because I don't really know the people I'm dealing with, and I have to sit down and make maps and birth charts and age charts. After a while with the Tillermans, it was like turning on the television set and there they were again. All of the cumbersome, clumsy parts didn't have to be dealt with each time, which gave me more energy for a lot of other stuff that I wanted to have go on.

[Sutton:] Because you had this world set out for you.

Voigt: Yes, and the people were already alive in my mind, so I didn't have to blow all of that *breath* into them. [Laughter]

[Sutton:] It certainly was an ambitious feat.

Voigt: I don't know that it's that ambitious; it was so much fun to write. Ambitious . . . I guess so.

[Sutton:] Oh, I think you're pretty ambitious. Look at all the different genres you've tried—family drama, mystery, time travel, medieval adventure. I think some books work better than others, but they're always difficult shots. You're not turning out one little well-made novel after another. You could have churned out Tillerman books for the rest of your life and people would have been happy.

Voigt: It seemed to me that I had gone as far with those books as I'd wanted to go . . . and I wanted to leave everything else open. When I came to the end of *The Runner,* I thought of a way that I didn't have to kill Bullet off . . . and I was really tempted to do it because I liked him so much. But there's a voice inside you that says no, no, no—this is an error in judgment.

[Sutton:] Bullet's death comes like a slap.

Voigt: Yep, and it must be that way. I mean, there must have been people who got phone calls like the one Gram got. And they came like a slap. There was one reviewer of *Wings of a Falcon* who said she was just *furious* . . . she was furious, all of my readers were gonna be furious about my killing the hero off. All I could think of to say was that, well, that's the way we felt when Kennedy was assassinated. You know, this shouldn't happen, this doesn't happen, it can't happen, right? But it does happen.

[Sutton:] I think that a lot of your heroes and heroines have not come up to many people's ideal of what a likeable protagonist should be. Even pretty early on, Dicey can be kind of unpleasant.

Voigt: I have a predilection for difficult people. Dicey does seem to speak to a lot of people despite her prickliness, despite the fact they probably wouldn't like to have her living next door. She knows what's important to her. I'd like to be the kind of person who knew that about herself. That I wouldn't fall to pieces in a crisis, or I wouldn't let other people take care of me badly rather than taking care of myself. That the things that were important to me were *that* important to me. Most of us don't know, beyond hypothetical dinner table conversation, if my kid or my dog were drowning, which one would I save? That kind of thing. But Dicey, in fact, actually knows.

[Sutton:] Where do you think she came from?

Voigt: She's the kind of 13-year-old I would have liked to have been . . . instead of being a sort of mashed potato, lumpish kind of person. She has something all of the Tillermans have. As somebody once said—critically—of them, they're all larger than life. So they all have got to come out of, you know, fairy tales, mythology, Nancy Drew, all the reading I did when I was a kid. In that sense they're cast in a heroic mold.

[Sutton:] You don't seem concerned with making your characters typical. I would exempt Izzy (of *Izzy, Willy-Nilly*) on this count, but I think Izzy is deliberately typical. She's actually rather dull and only becomes more interesting as the story goes on.

Voigt: Yeah, isn't that interesting? I love that book—I really am proud of that one. [Laughter] Sometimes, though, I think my books are getting into the hands of kids who should wait two or three years before they read them, like when I get a letter from a fifth grader about *Izzy.* They're not letters where they've got the book all wrong, but I think Izzy's story is one that if you're in ninth or 10th grade it's probably the perfect time for it, and to give it to somebody who's 10 instead of 15 is to give it a different reader.

[Sutton:] How do you think they might see it differently?

Voigt: Oh, when Izzy feels sort of rebellious about whether her parents will let her go to the party or not, and the way she manipulates the situation and very soon comes to the understanding that that's what she's doing. I think understanding that involves a level of self-knowledge that is not appropriate for a younger student to have. I think younger kids should still be operating within child illusions about themselves. Kids are supposed to be kids and adolescents are supposed to be adolescents—you live the life that you're old enough to live, right? Instead of acting like you're 10 or 20 years older. In the same way that *Mrs. Frisby and the Rats of NIMH* is so perfect for fifth graders, nobody else should read it at any other age. It seems to me that when you're having all the experiences you're supposed to have, and having them the way you're supposed to have them, you have a better chance of ending up a balanced adult, whatever that means.

[Sutton:] Who are the *Jackaroo* books for? To tell you the truth, had I reviewed the first one when it came out, I would have said this is too long and too leisurely and too dense for kids. They won't touch it. And then I look inside the paperback I have and it's in its 12th printing. That's a lot. Who do you expect is reading it?

Voigt: You know, I don't expect. I really don't. Some of my readers are 80. Some of them are hospitalized. I very carefully try not to think of how old my readers are. Who's reading it? I don't know. My son's friend John was asked to read *Jackaroo* in seventh grade, and he certainly had a few pungent remarks to make—not admiring remarks at all. [Laughs] The "Kingdom" books [*Jackaroo, On Fortune's Wheel, The Wings of a Falcon*] are books I would have loved in seventh and eighth grade. Because they're adventures, right? And they're romantic and rich; they have a lot of details in them. So if you want to, you can savor them as they go along. I like to think that they're richly and intricately enough made so you can discover things when you reread them. What was it someone was telling me? She was teaching *Wings of a Falcon* and said, "I always read the first chapter out loud and then I've really got 'em." I used to teach Carol Kendall's [1959 fantasy] *The Gammage Cup* to fifth graders, and I would spend a week or two on the first chapter. After which the book did all the rest of the work for me.

[Sutton:] Right, because you get them into the world; you get them used to the language.

Voigt: You show them all the things in there. All the history things and the color things and the character things . . . and you help them discover it. I think kids like those books because they're really ripping good stories. For those of us who are *romantics.*

[Sutton:] Do you miss teaching?

Voigt: I still miss being in a classroom; I don't miss the hours of work. Do I like entirely owning my own day? Yes! Yes! [Laughter] Nobody can tell me what to do—except for the dentist, right?—nobody can tell me where to go. There's a great deal of silence and solitude where I live, and I look out my window and it's beautiful.

[Sutton:] How do you think it affects your writing?

Voigt: I worry that I might have less external stimulation.

When you're teaching, you keep running into people and who they are. My pace seems to have slowed down over the last couple of years, but there have been other distractions—like my father was ill for a couple of years and then died. Maybe that's what's been slowing me down. But other than that, I don't think it's making that much difference. But who knows, slowing down and having less external stimulation, maybe *that* was the difference. [Laughter] As I become more self-involved, perhaps I won't be the person to notice it.

I went to visit a class in Germany where they said to me, "You're so . . . *jolly.*" In person, they meant. In contrast [to my books]. My word for myself is "earnest." I think I'm incorrigibly earnest in my writing and by nature, too. Well, writers have a secret, you know. The things you dare to do when you're all alone with a piece of paper are different, aren't they?

GENERAL COMMENTARY

Suzanne Reid

SOURCE: "Reaching Out, Holding on, and Letting Go: Images of Music, Wood and Sailing in Cynthia Voigt's Tillerman Series," in *The ALAN Review,* Vol. 19, No. 1, Fall, 1991, pp. 10-1.

Cynthia Voigt's series about the Tillerman family begins with the children's search for a home in *Homecoming* and ends with their entrance into the adult world in *Seventeen Against the Dealer.* In the seven novels of the series, Voigt describes how characters escape from damaged relationships by *reaching out* of themselves, *holding on* to the natural strengths of familial bonds, and finally *letting go* of ties that imprison—themes, Voigt says, which ran through her mind like a recurrent tune as she was writing the Tillerman story.

Voigt brings these themes to life with three motifs, which recur in a cyclic rhythm throughout the Tillerman saga: singing, wood, and sailing. The Tillermans and their friends learn to reach out through the music they make, hold on through some contact with wood, and let go by sailing out onto the sea. These metaphoric images appear in varying degrees in each of the Tillerman novels.

Music, especially singing, is Voigt's metaphor for reaching out of oneself. In *The Runner,* we learn that the original Tillermans, Abigail Hackett and her husband John Tillerman, are isolated on a farm with their three children, John Jr., Samuel (Bullet), and Liza. The father walls himself in further with books and ideas, becoming self-righteous and cruelly stern (*Homecoming*). Similarly the mother, Abigail, immured in a passive sense of duty that keeps her from reaching out (*Dicey's Song,*), has let her children get away from her. Her eldest son, John, has fled to California; and Bullet, buried in anger and hatred, has died in Vietnam. Only her daughter Liza reaches out and gives life through her lovely singing. Liza, however, is not strong enough to cope with the irresponsible wanderings of her husband, Francis Verricker. Unable to handle parenthood alone, she abandons her children in a parking lot and is eventually taken to a mental institution.

Although Liza is no longer capable of caring for her children, the songs she has taught them sustain their hope as they try to survive on their own. Asleep in the parking lot where their mother abandoned them, Dicey, now in charge as the oldest, wakes to the sound of her youngest sister, Maybeth, "singing softly, one of Momma's songs, about making her love a baby with no crying" (*Homecoming*). Maybeth, mentally slow like their mother but instinctively sensitive to the emotional aura of a situation, recognizes the needs of the children. Practical and earthbound, Dicey is the strength of the family who squarely faces the fact that her mother will not return. She feeds her family and starts to plan their future. But later, after their first day of walking, when life seems impossible, it is again Maybeth who comforts: "It's all right, Dicey. . . I'm going to sing." When the children seem most defeated and split apart by exhaustion and tension, singing brings them back to each other.

The words of the Tillerman's songs give clues to their story. In her [*School Library Journal*] article, "A Newbery Song for Gifted Readers," Eliza Dresang discusses the relevancy of the song-lyrics to the plot in *Dicey's Song,* and we may extend her thesis to the other novels. The folksong "Pretty Polly," which the Tillerman children also sing in *Homecoming,* tells the story of a young mother who dies after being deserted by her man. The children do not recognize this song as prophecy and merely feel content in the mutual warmth of making music. Later, however, the words of another song bring both comfort and a helpful message. Stuck on the wrong side of the Connecticut River, in sight of a bridge that is impossible to walk across, Dicey is lost in despair:

> Was this how Momma felt? Was this why Momma ran away? Because she couldn't think of anything more to do and couldn't stand any more to try to take care of her children? . . . Sitting around, her head not thinking, not worrying, . . . a melody came into her head and she sang one of Momma's old, sad songs: "The water is wide, I cannot get o'er. Neither have I wings to fly . . . Give me a boat that will carry two, and two shall row—my love and I."

As the song dispels her worry and allows her to reach out in thought to the others, Dicey becomes receptive to the musical solution of her problem. They "borrow" a rowboat and row across.

Singing is also the way the Tillermans connect to other people they meet, and each song reflects the singer's character and impact on the children's moral development. In *Homecoming,* the Tillerman children pass the time at a beach resort with a couple of vagrant teenagers,

Louis and Edie. Edie has an autoharp and plays "Pretty Peggy-O." "But this wasn't their song. This song was about William the false lover and how he tricked pretty Peggy-O into running away with him but then murdered her. Edie sang the song quick and cruel, with sharp metallic sounds from her instrument." "You're a good singer," says James, but Louis and Edie don't turn out to be good people, not innocent like Momma. After an evening of lively dancing with Maybeth, Sammy, and James, this furtive couple slips off at the first sign of a police car. Apparently Louis has induced the more innocent Edie to run off with him, suggesting that the song is prophecy. The sinister air of this couple infects the children, for at this park Sammy steals first food and then a wallet, and James exaggerates the effects of a head injury, failing to be honest to Dicey. The vagrants' singing in this seaside resort reflects a moral laxity as the children succumb to easy stolen pleasures and falsehoods. It has been a place of physical rest but also moral danger.

The children learn a contrary lesson when they meet Stewart and Windy at Yale. This time, when James steals money from Windy, rather than excusing it as justifiable as had Louis and Edie, Stewart teaches James the concept of personal integrity. Stewart produces his Dobro, a traditional folk instrument, as Maybeth agrees to sing. Though "Greensleeves" is another song about abandonment in love, the perspective now shifts from the false gaity of the murderous lover to the righteous sorrow of the one betrayed: "Alas, my love, you do me wrong, to cast me off discourteously." Then Stewart teaches Maybeth another song that will be repeated in Dicey's mind through the Tillerman books: "Oft I sing for my friends, When death's dark form I see. / When I reach my journey's end, who will sing for me?" The song affirms friendship as a bond that gives solace against the final separation of death. The time spent at Yale is beneficial for the children, and morally instructive for James (who will eventually return as a student).

During their wanderings, Dicey's goal had been Bridgeport, where she hoped to find a home for her sister and brothers with her cousin Eunice, the only relative her Momma had ever mentioned. But when they reach the house in Bridgeport, there is no singing. Prim and fearful, Cousin Eunice only superficially goes through the motions of reaching out, either because duty is all she is capable of, or because, at heart, she does not want to have the children live with her. Dicey knows that she must find another place to stay when she sees Maybeth sitting outside the circle of girls on the playground, not doing the one thing that is easy and lovely to her, singing. "It was as if Maybeth wasn't even there, not even to herself." Music is the measure of Maybeth's mental health: "She learns songs fast, music and words. She couldn't be retarded and do that, could she?" The Tillerman children leave Bridgeport, and two days later, Maybeth is humming Stewart's song, "Oft I sing for my friends," reaching out again.

Music brings Maybeth to life, and music introduces the first adult friend into the family's life. After Bridgeport, the children finally reach Crisfield and their grandmother, a fierce and independent woman who has chased her own children away. When Dicey finally convinces her to let them stay, they gradually form a family. Gram grudgingly dares to reach out to Mr. Lingerle, the music teacher, first for Maybeth's sake as she swallows her pride and accepts his offer of extra piano lessons, and then also for his sake as she recognizes his need for them. Her insight turns out to be correct, for as the novels progress, Mr. Lingerle benefits from the family's adventures, just as they benefit from his generous help in times of emergencies.

In *Dicey's Song,* Dicey tells a friend that she chooses people by their courage and their music, which, for her, signifies their ability to reach out. Indeed, she meets Jeff by listening to his music; they will eventually marry. After her initial aloofness, she joins him in song, and it is through music that Jeff is introduced into the Tillerman family. Eventually he brings his guitar to their house and gets Maybeth to sing. James and his friend Toby overcome their awkwardness by discussing the words to the songs with Jeff, and soon Dicey's new friend, Mina, comes by and adds her alto. This scene clearly illustrates the emergence from the silent, desolate Tillermans of the previous generation to the current family, who begin to connect to a network of friends and to each other. Music has helped provide the courage and the confidence to build these bridges.

Dicey's Song is the story of how Dicey reaches out beyond the small circle of her family, finally able to share the responsibility for her sister and brothers with Gram, finally sure enough of her home to reach out, first to Jeff through music, and then to Mina and others with the her own medium, writing.

Music as a symbol for reaching out is just as explicit in *A Solitary Blue,* the story of Jeff Greene before he meets Dicey and the other Tillermans. Jeff's mother, aptly named Melody, is a lovely young woman who spends her life reaching out to a succession of charitable causes but abandons her husband and six-year-old son to do so. After a hiatus of several years, mother and son are reunited when Jeff spends an enchanted summer at her homeplace in Charleston. Because she plays the guitar, Jeff decides to emulate her and spends the ensuing year struggling to learn the instrument; but the next summer he discovers that, as with most other ventures, she has abandoned music and him again for something new.

In *Sons From Afar* an older James and Sammy try to find their own identities by searching for their father, the sailor who, like Jeff's mother Melody, drifts through peoples' lives without holding on to any sure identity. Temporarily buried within themselves as they try to work out the source and solutions for their insecurities, James and Sammy are finally purged of their anger through a dangerous brawl in a bar full of sailors. The imagery in this book centers around stars, the moon, and exploring, as the boys work out their definitions of fatherhood, but music still acts as a metaphor for reaching out of oneself. When

Maybeth reaches out to her schoolmates as a member of the chorus, James is afraid to join because he thinks it would emphasize his image as a "dork." Only when he learns to accept himself and gains the courage to be himself does he decide to join the singing group. He and Sammy sing together, partly to watch over Maybeth.

The words of the songs in *Homecoming* and *Dicey's Song* tell the story of Liza, the mother of Dicey, James, Sammy, and Maybeth and the only daughter of Gram. In *Sons From Afar* "Full fathom five they father lies" is perhaps the real news about their father, either literally or figuratively: "Of his bones are coral made . . . Nothing of him but doth change." The mystery of their father's character and his whereabouts is never solved for the Tillermans. In *The Runner* he is introduced as a figure who plays music on the jukebox and gets people to have fun for a time, but he does not sing himself nor does he commit himself to others. For his children, he is forever absent.

Singing and music not only reach out, but they invite others to join in. Liza and her daughter are naturally generous; Dicey and the other children learn to join in the music and the world. Their success contrasts with those who cannot sing. Their father can make music happen, but he doesn't have the character to sing himself. Bullet, Liza's youngest brother, for whom her own youngest son Sammy is named, and who died in Vietnam, was unable to carry a tune. Too consumed by hatred for and anger at his father who built walls rather than music, Bullett would not or could not reach out of himself and was thus destroyed.

Wood is a metaphor Voigt uses for the theme of holding on. In an interview in 1983, she described the importance of wood:

> Wood is like water; it's one of those things that is so responsive to humans. It's like a living metaphor. Wood has the grain; it has the color; and it's never quite the same. It can be shaped into many things. You can touch it with your hands and it has a certain warmth to it. . . . You're in touch with something that's more real and permanent than you are—although not necessarily more true. It's like standing next to something that's contagiously good.

Just as singing is the image and the means of reaching out to dispel alienation of the self, wood is Voigt's metaphor for holding on to the verities of family, home, and fellow humanity. Wood is a natural living substance, traditionally used to symbolize that which is rooted and yet keeps growing—the family tree, the tree of knowledge that separates humanity from the animal world.

Dicey's first home was in Provincetown on the beach, nestled among the dunes, but "if you took home to mean where you rested content and never wanted to go anywhere else, Dicey had never had a home . . . the ocean made her restless" (*Homecoming*). As the children travel, occasionally they find resting places among trees, where they feel more a family than otherwise, but the image of wood does not become strong until they find their home in Crisfield. In Bridgeport the house they found does not prove to be a home. Its plastic, artificial surfaces are "shiny clean. The gray linoleum floor gleamed, the refrigerator shone, the windows looking over a tiny yard, were polished. There was a formica-topped table in the center of the room" (*Homecoming*). In contrast, their future home in Crisfield is faded white clapboard, neglected, with a wooden door. The long table is "made of wood and . . . scrubbed to a pale, smooth finish." The paperwood mulberry tree growing next to the house with its four trunks held together by strong twisted wires to keep the weight of growing branches from pulling the tree apart becomes a metaphor for their family and a resting place for their mother.

Their mother's ashes rest in a wooden box chosen by Dicey, crafted by a man whose hands have "cuts like the grains of the different woods." Dicey's hands hold the box on the long train ride south from Boston to Crisfield. She is holding on to her memories of her mother as she is holding on to her ashes in the wooden box.

The solace of wood is just as obviously described in *Come A Stranger,* the story of Mina, who has won a scholarship to a dance camp in Connecticut, where, in one wonderful summer, she learns more about music, dance, and the world outside Crisfield than she knew existed: music enables her to "reach out" of her rural Black, family-centered world. The music stops, however, when she realizes that the camp needs her only as a representative of the black race, and that "nobody . . . wants to be her roommate." Needing something to hold onto, she turns to wood: "She wanted to put her palms up against the bark of the trees, to feel how strong and solid the trees were . . . to get back in touch with those things that didn't look at her and see just the outside Mina."

Mina returns to her home in Crisfield; and, after a year of being slightly ashamed of her people and their ignorance of the white world of ballet and classical music, she begins to appreciate their variety. "The faces were all the colors of wood, seasoned and stained, oak and pecan, maple and pine." This is a world she will hold on to. She understands the image of the tree that bleeds, the punishment in Dante's Hell for those who despised their own bodies enough to kill themselves. And she returns to accepting herself as she is, holding on to what and whom she has.

The Runner tells the story of Gram's younger son, Sam, called "Bullet," who cannot hold on—whose father's stern unbending hate and the passive nonresistance of his mother forbids him from "reaching out" and keeps him from "holding on." Long ago, before he left for college, his brother Johnny had built a sailboat and a treehouse, but Bullet's anger makes him a "breaker" (*The Runner*). He smashes the barn door rather than fixing it, and he lacks the patience to sand the lovely wood boat, the fourteen-footer, that his employer and mentor, Patrice, is building.

Bullet is afraid of being boxed in by his father's stern orders, by fear, and by his feelings for his sister Liza. He cannot "reach out" and connect; he cannot "hold on" and remain in his home; but he does finally recognize how to enable his mother to survive. In blatant defiance of his father's orders, Bullet sits down at the table to eat with his mother and father. When his father protests, "the anger pouring out of [him], blowing all around him: go away, go away," Bullet sits firm and calm: "It's her table too." His father lets it go. Bullet wins the battle, holding the remains of his family together if just for an evening:

> The table they ate at was made of wood, scrubbed down to smoothness. The joints between the separate boards had been made so close that you could see just a thin pencil line where one piece ended and the next began. The table had been put together the same way that fourteen-footer had, somebody's best work. It was as old as the farmhouse.

The table reunites Bullet with his mother, Abigail, in this episode just as it unites Abigail and her grandchildren years later in *Dicey's Song*. Bullet does his best when running at the next cross-country meet, and his mother slips away from the farm to watch him, to let him know she cares more than she can say.

On his eighteenth birthday, Bullet drops out of school, enlists, and buys the fourteen-foot sailboat to give it to his mother. The boat that she has been using, the sailboat that her older son Jimmy had made long ago, is rotting, uncared for by her husband who does not sail and by herself because she lacks the strength to take it out of the water each year. Bullet then dismantles the old sails, scrapes the hull, and carefully stores it in the barn, where Dicey will discover it on her first day in Crisfield. Bullet is not able to work wood himself, "to hold on" in his own life, but he can provide the means for his mother. He cannot get her out of her own box, but he can "loosen a board or two for her."

Bullet dies in Vietnam. When his mother hears the news, she takes the phone to town and throws it through the plate glass window of the telephone company. Then she strides back to the boat:

> What was that song Liza sang? "The water is wide, cannot get o'er," the voice in her head sang, "And neither have I wings to fly. Bring me a boat—" Well she had the boat. And the wide water ran, she knew, around the whole world, ringing it around, the encircling oceans that somehow contained and connected all the lands within.

The wood that symbolizes "holding on" can be crafted into a vessel that supports the sailor as he or she "lets go" and, secure in his own humanity, connects with the adventure of humanity at large.

In *The Runner,* the oysterman, Patrice, reconstructs sailboats, lovingly restoring the beauty of the original wood just as he tries to rebuild Bullet, who is buffeted by "the old wind in the old anger" of his father and of his own racial and social prejudices. Bullet is becoming able to let go much of his former hatred and is learning to connect, when his death intervenes. Later, Dicey Tillerman tries shipbuilding as a career to combine her desire to hold on to her family with a wish to let go of old responsibilities. The sailboats she wants to build and that Patrice restores are, both metaphorically and literally, what enables those who have "held on" to the value of family to "let go" and venture out into a wider world.

Even as Dicey is holding on to her mother's ashes and the memories of her life before Crisfield, she is also letting go. Though her hands are wrapped around the wooden box that holds the ashes of her Momma, she feels "as if she were a sailboat and the sails were furled up now, the mainsail wrapped up around the boom, and she was sitting at anchor. It felt good to come to rest. . . . But a boat at anchor wasn't planted there, like a tree. Furled sails were just waiting to be raised, when the sailor chose to head out again."

For Dicey, sailing is an image of freedom. The ocean is a road that never ends, always moves (*Dicey's Song*). It is not home, and it makes Dicey restless (*Homecoming*). It never freezes, always smashing up the little ridges of ice that formed along its edges (*Dicey's Song*), and so it never traps a person. To have a sailboat or to be a sailboat is to be able to let go of responsibility and to take chances, to travel without plans which ever way life blows: "A boat could be a home. The perfect home that could move around, a home that didn't close you in or tie you down," thinks Dicey the first time she sails (*Homecoming*). After the long summer of reaching out for her family and to her family in order to hold on, "Dicey didn't feel like finding a harbor. She knew she needed one, and they needed one but she would rather sail along." She realizes, however, that "life isn't really an ocean and she wasn't really a little boat bobbling along on it. There were James and Maybeth and Sammy, . . . and for now, she was content to sit still."

When Dicey discovers the sailboat in the barn of her grandmother's farm, she decides that the boat will be her prize if they can stay, her prize for holding on until the family finds a home (*Homecoming*). When Dicey finally does put the boat into the water, it sinks; but she remains calm as she plans the next step. "Dicey doesn't mind, as long as she knows what to do about things," explains Maybeth (*Dicey's Song*). Dicey does not know enough yet to be able to let go safely; she still has a lot to learn about reaching out in order to hold on. For now, working on the boat in the barn, scraping off the old paint and sanding it, offers Dicey respite from the responsibilities of her family. She escapes to the barn and begins to relax enough to learn about reaching out.

After it is clear, in *A Solitary Blue,* that Jeff's mother has abandoned him forever, Jeff is hurt, afraid, and utterly alone in his world. In an episode where the theme of letting go and the symbol of the boat seem strongly correlated, Jeff gradually rows out to an island where, on a beach near the ocean, he spends a night finding a place of strength and peace within himself. He saves himself by letting go of his yearning for his mother. When he returns to land to go back to his father, he smashes the boat.

In *Seventeen Against the Dealer,* Dicey has tried a year at college but finds the conventional road to financial independence lacking. She wants to support herself by building sailboats. To Dicey, building sailboats is a metaphor for a balance between responsibility and independence. Before she arrived at Crisfield, Dicey had had her first experience sailing: "Boat, waves, water and wind: through the wood she felt them working for her. She was not directing, but accompanying them, turning them to her use. . . . It wasn't power she felt, guiding the tiller, but purpose" (*Homecoming*). Now she is an adult, and her sister and brothers seem safe. James is a student at Yale, Sammy and Maybeth are in high school with friends and activities of their own, and Gram seems to be getting along without her. So Dicey throws herself into developing a business, making her own paths without signs. Metaphorically, she learns the risks of sailing without a chart as she discovers the need for insurance, written contracts, and financial savvy by suffering from her mistakes. So involved does she become in the quagmire of business that she almost forgets to hold on to her family and to Jeff whom she has promised to marry.

At the end, she finds that the balance of reaching out, holding on, and letting go is never settled; "She wasn't finished learning" and she wouldn't be until, in Gram's words, she was "older than dead." Letting go is dangerous, "But never building one [a sailboat], that would be a real failure."

In *Homecoming,* Dicey learned to hold on, to keep her family together, to find a home and hold on to it. In *Dicey's Song,* Dicey and her family can afford to reach out, to learn how to trust and include others in their lives. By the time of *Seventeen Against the Dealer,* the last of the books in the Tillerman cycle, Dicey's family is strong enough to let her take the risk of letting go. Sammy keeps her from ignoring Maybeth, and Maybeth keeps Gram from succumbing to her pride and sickness. Dicey's family can now afford to give her "the chance to take a chance." And Dicey has "the eye to recognize it . . . the hand, to reach out and hold onto it. And the heart . . . or wherever courage came from." With Jeff, who first reached out to her with song, and the larch wood she has had the courage to hold on to, she has the freedom to build a sailboat. "She'd probably make mistakes, but her mistakes would tell her what she needed to learn." She can afford to do a little letting go.

In her Newbery acceptance speech, Voigt describes "A stunning book [as one which] engages the imagination, sets to work the intelligence, and fills the spirit" (*The Horn Book Magazine,* August 1983, p. 404). The Tillerman books are complicated and full of hard facts of life, but they still fill the spirit with the wisdom and courage of their characters. The metaphors of song, wood, and sailing stretch the imagination to illustrate the enigma of how courageous, wise, and complete living includes reaching out, holding on, and letting go.

Betty Greenway

SOURCE: "Every Mother's Dream: Cynthia Voigt's Orphans," in *The ALAN Review,* Vol. 19, No. 1, Fall, 1991, pp. 15-17.

Cynthia Voigt's novels have been praised for their realism, especially for their realistic characters, and indeed characterization is a strength of her novels. Young readers find themselves drawn into Voigt's books by characters very much like themselves, despite the unusual situations the novels often detail. My experience with groups of junior high school students at a series of sessions at Youngstown State University's recent English Festival showed me how compelling readers find Voigt's characters, for at first that's all they wanted to talk about. Yet characterization turned out to be a good entry into a serious consideration of larger issues.

After we had talked about the characters, I asked the students to break up into small groups and make a list of all the similarities they could find among Voigt's "Tillerman" novels (*Homecoming, Dicey's Song, A Solitary Blue, The Runner, Sons from Afar, Seventeen Against the Dealer*). One of the first similarities they discovered is that her young characters are all abandoned, in one way or another. And students were quick to find other similarly abandoned children referred to throughout the novels. This discovery led to a discussion of archetypes and the power they have to deepen a reader's response to a book.

Cynthia Voigt was a guest at that year's English Festival, and her talk to parents and teachers spoke in some way to that same issue of archetypes. She began by reporting a comment she got from a mother shortly after *Homecoming* was published. "It's every mother's dream," the mother said, to a rather astonished Voigt. The story of four children, aged six to thirteen, abandoned by their mother in a shopping mall parking lot (their father had abandoned them years before when the youngest was conceived), walking for days, hungry and tired, to their aunt's in Bridgeport, Connecticut, only to find that their aunt is dead and their cousin can't give them a home, then taking off again to find their grandmother, who, by the way, they didn't know existed and who might be crazy or violent or both—"every mother's dream"? Voigt said the more she thought about it, the less crazy it seemed. Her greatest fear as a mother, she said, was that something would happen to her, and then what would become of her children? Her dream, the more she thought about it, was that her children could survive on their own. And so we have book after book of orphans, resilient and self-sufficient—this is Cynthia Voigt's image of the child.

But, of course, Voigt is not the first author to so conceive of the child. Fairy tales are positively crammed with such

orphans, mistreated and cast out to make their own way in a hostile world.

Voigt calls our attention to the parallels early in *Homecoming.* As the Tillerman children sit in their old car in the shopping mall parking lot, waiting for their mother to return, Dicey, the oldest, orders James, ten, to tell the youngest two children, Maybeth and Sammy, a story to keep them quiet. He tells them "Hansel and Gretel." The fairy tale becomes something of a leitmotif in the book, until the end when Dicey finally meets her grandmother over a plate of spaghetti:

"You like my spaghetti?" her grandmother asked.

"No," Dicey said. "But I'm hungry. Do you like it?"

"It's easy to fix. You know what I sometimes think?" Her grandmother looked straight at her, her mouth chewing. "I sometimes think people might be good to eat. Cows and chickens eat corn and grass and turn it into good meat. People eat cows and chickens. In people, it might turn into something even better. Do you ever think that?"

Dicey shook her head.

"Especially babies," her grandmother said. She swallowed thoughtfully. "Or children. Do you have brothers and sisters?"

Voigt's orphans not only find themselves in fairy tale situations, but they have the qualities of fairy tale heroes and heroines. Therefore, Voigt's novels are reassuring in the same way fairy tales are. The small and powerless child can and does succeed through cleverness, resourcefulness, and an active innocence. Rather than waiting for the authorities to find them and put them in foster homes, probably separate ones, Dicey has them set off on foot to find the aunt she believes will take them in, with a map as her only guide. They alertly pick up stray coins careless shoppers have dropped. Dicey feeds her brothers and sisters from the day-old baked goods rack of large supermarkets, among other economies, and she stays near the ocean so they can fish and find mussels. Sammy, the youngest, even "finds" a family's picnic lunch on the beach and takes it to his family, in the same way Jack "finds" the giant's treasures and takes them down the beanstalk to his mother. When they finally get to their grandmother's, Dicey doesn't push her into the oven, but she wins her over through the ploy of the never-ending task—they make themselves useful and so give their strong and endearing personalities a chance to work on her.

So Voigt uses as one metaphor for the child the fairy tale hero, the orphan cast out from any parental security but journeying to find a mature love and life of his or her own. But Voigt also uses another metaphor for the child, one essentially similar, though, in its emphasis on the lonely journey. To get across the Chesapeake Bay to the Eastern Shore where their grandmother lives, Dicey and

James con two teenagers into sailing them over in their father's sailboat. On the trip Dicey discovers that she loves sailing and "give[s] herself entirely over to the movement of the being still." She muses:

> Maybe life was like a sea, and all the people were like boats. They were big, important yachts and little rafts and motorboats and sailboats and working boats and pleasure boats. And some really big boats like ocean liners or tankers—those would be rich or powerful people, whose lives engulfed many other lives and carried them along. Or maybe each boat was a kind of family. Then what kind of boat would the Tillermans be? A little one, bobbing about, with the mast fallen off? A grubby, worn-down workboat, with Dicey hanging onto the rudder for dear life?
>
> Everybody who was born was cast onto the sea. Winds would blow them in all directions. Tides would rise and turn, in their own rhythm. And the boats—they just went along as best they could, trying to find a harbor.

But the Tillerman's aren't a leaky boat buffeted by any strong wind that blows; Dicey takes the tiller, literally here but also metaphorically, and steers for safe harbor, a home. And *Homecoming* ends with all the Tillerman children in their grandmother's boat, after she has agreed that they can stay with her. . . .

The children, alone in the world and cast out from one home, have searched until they've found another. As James says near the end of *Homecoming,* "Whatever . . . we can take care of ourselves. Wherever."

But the fairy tale isn't over at the end of *Homecoming. Dicey's Song,* which picks up where *Homecoming* leaves off, begins:

> And they lived happily ever after.
>
> Not the Tillermans, Dicey thought. That wasn't the way things went for the Tillermans, ever.

They have found a home with their grandmother, but their journey isn't over. They children have to make their way individually as well as collectively; they have to establish their identities in school; and they have to learn to deal with their mother's death, their final abandonment. In *Dicey's Song* the mother is discovered dying in a mental hospital in Boston, and Dicey and Gram go to bring back her ashes. At the end of the book, the children accept that their mother is "gone," is not coming back to gather her brood under her wing, but now they, even the mother, are "home." The last line of the book is "So Gram began the story," the story of her children, of the Tillerman children's mother and brothers, of their family. They are all characters in the continuing human story.

But the metaphor that Voigt uses to suggest the image of the child in *Dicey's Song* is not based on the fairy tale but on the Bible and on folk music. Dicey's song, "When first unto this country a stranger came," tells the story of a man who is rejected by the girl he loves, steals, is put in jail, and has "a coat of many colors." As "Hansel and Gretel" becomes the leitmotif in *Homecoming,* the Biblical Joseph and his coat of many colors, another archetypal child cast out from one home but finding another in a new place, becomes the leitmotif in *Dicey's Song.*

Jacob has a son called Joseph, who is his favorite, and to show that he gives him a coat of many colors. When his brothers, who are jealous of Joseph, sell him into slavery to the Egyptians, they bring back the coat smeared with blood to show their father that Joseph has been killed by an animal. Ironically, Joseph eventually rises from a slave to become the Pharoah's right-hand man. God, of course, knew all this and let Joseph be sold into slavery so that he could help his family when a great famine occurs. During this famine when Joseph's family comes to the Pharoah to beg food, Jacob is overjoyed to find his son once again. Joseph forgives his brothers, and they come to live together in Egypt, in a home the Pharoah has given them.

The story has obvious parallels to the Tillerman saga. Home is not a place; it's a fluid relationship. The child, cast out like Hansel and Gretel, can find a new home in a new place. Perhaps destiny, or providence, is always working for the child, for the family: "Every mother's dream."

But the song is more complicated than that. Jeff Greene, a boy Dicey meets at school, first introduces the song to her and tries to explain it to the rest of the Tillermans when he is finally invited to share his music with her family. The song goes, "With my hands all in my pockets and my hat slung back so bold, and my coat of many colors like Jacob of old." It says Jacob, but James, Dicey's brother, remembers that in the Bible Joseph is the one with the coat of many colors. Jacob, James says, is the one with Esau, and the birthright and the blessing. Jeff suggests that the man in the song is part Jacob and part Joseph—Joseph because he comes into the land "a stranger" as Joseph was in Egypt; but Jacob because the man in the song is a thief, as Jacob who, the second-born of twins, steals his brother's birthright, his inheritance. Yet instead of punishing Jacob, God makes him the father of Israel because his brother Esau didn't really value what he had but Jacob did. This story of Jacob has important parallels in Jeff's story, which Voigt tells in her next book, *A Solitary Blue.*

A Solitary Blue begins, like *Homecoming,* with abandonment. Jeff Greene, at the start of the novel seven and a half years old, comes home from school one day to find a note from his mother saying goodbye, that she loves him but has to go where "people need her" to make the world "a better place." Melody, we discover, is another of Voigt's deficient adults, completely self-centered but hiding behind the fiction that she is saving the world with all her myriad "causes." Jeff's response to his abandonment is different from Dicey's—he withdraws over a period of years into near autism, deathly afraid that, after being abandoned by one parent, he will also be abandoned by the other, a very unexpressive father. So he becomes the perfect child, afraid of displeasing anyone. His most typical expression is "I'm sorry"—sorry for getting sick and causing his father worry, sorry for changing so much that his mother doesn't recognize him at the Charleston airport when he goes to spend a summer with her, sorry for causing his mother the pain of childbirth. He reaches his lowest point when she abandons him for the second time, leaving him in Charleston with his great-grandmother while she goes off on one more of her causes.

The second half of *A Solitary Blue* details Jeff's recovery when his father, a reserved but as it turns out a caring man, moves them to the eastern shore of Maryland, where the Tillermans live and where Jeff meets Dicey in *Dicey's Song.* There Jeff has the solitude to get to know himself, slowly, to find out that he's much stronger than he knows, and to discover that he is valued for who he is—by his father, by Dicey, and by the rest of the Tillermans. But his mother isn't out of his life yet; she returns one more time to try to get Jeff to go live with her, and he suffers at her hands yet again when he believes he has caused her terrible pain by refusing. Jeff is finally able to come to terms with himself and his mother when he discovers the real reason she tried to get him back. In a complicated turn of events, Jeff, not his mother, has inherited the estate of his great-grandmother. She wants the money. Jeff doesn't. In their last exchange, Jeff gives his mother the quite valuable diamond ring he has inherited, and his mother gives him the jade ring she has inherited, not worth much, except for its history and the great sentimental value it had for his great-grandmother. As he watches his mother walk away for the last time, he thinks, "Poor Melody . . . she never knew what the real treasures were."

The real treasures in Cynthia Voigt's books turn out to be the children. She gives us a gallery of orphans in her novels, children in one sense or another abandoned, physically or emotionally, from contemporary, fairy tale, and Biblical worlds. But despite the conditions in which her children find themselves, they aren't sad or pathetic because they're resilient. I think Voigt is suggesting that we all are brought into the world essentially alone, like boats on a sea, and that we all must go on a quest not only for a home but for our identities. These are not givens. But the allusions that resonate through her novels give assurance, as Bruno Bettelheim says fairy tales do, that we can succeed. . . . In *A Solitary Blue* Jeff reads *The Lord of the Rings,* "the story of unlikely heroes in another world, of magic and love, of battles against unremitting evil, the long arduous journey, of friendship and betrayal."

Voigt's children are all embarked on this journey. Do they live happily ever after? Well, not exactly. The Israelites don't live happily ever after in Egypt but must continue their search for a home. The search may never be over until death—the final port—as Dicey suggests when she sees carved on a tombstone "Home is the sailor home from the sea." Every mother's dream? Well, maybe.

Every child's dream? The students' responses to Voigt's novels during the English Festival seem to suggest this. And it is because Voigt speaks to our dreams and our memories, not just waking reality, that her books call up such a powerful response from readers.

Mary Hoffman

SOURCE: "The Best Is Yet to Be: The Novels of Cynthia Voigt," in *The School Librarian,* Vol. 41, No. 2, May, 1993, pp. 48-9.

Meeting Cynthia Voigt is rather like reading one of her books; she is so exactly as you imagine her. Straightforward, friendly, intelligent, very much a case of 'what you see is what you get.' But an earlier claim of hers which I had read, 'the middle of the road is my natural habitat,' certainly does her less than justice. Unless that road runs through some pretty interesting places.

Cynthia Voigt is one of the most stimulating writers for older readers today. She is widely read in the UK, where her books have gathered popularity by the sheer force of word-of-mouth recommendation and she has survived the rise—and fall—of teenage publishing. Her books are demanding and satisfying in equal measure, long and very detailed, but not particularly literary. Rather like the books she prefers to read.

'I don't go for style; I read for story and character.' That's why she likes Mary Wesley and Anita Brookner and Dick Francis, rather than Julian Barnes. And mysteries. Cynthia Voigt's first novel (though not the first to be published) was *The Callender papers,* a Gothic-influenced story of a young girl employed to sort through some old family papers, who discovers that they concern her own life and that she is not who she thought she was. It reads just as powerfully today as when it was published, and it comes as a surprise to realise that Cynthia Voigt's most successful novels have all been in a quite different genre.

It is the sequence of books about the Tillerman family, beginning with *Homecoming,* which built up Cynthia Voigt's devoted following. After seven books—'By the end of *A solitary blue* I knew what *Seventeen against the dealer* was going to be; I just didn't know how many books would come in between'—she has parted company with the Tillermans. This is much to the regret of most of her readers. 'Well, no one has *harangued* me about giving them up,' she says, with typical Voigt humour, but it is obvious that she would rather talk about her other work, that she feels she has moved on from those characters.

But what characters! Dicey, the resourceful, fiercely loving older sister, first made her appearance in *Homecoming,* where she and her three younger siblings found themselves adrift in the world without parents. She is the unquestioned heroine of the sequence, poised in the balance with another powerful female character, her grandmother. It is hard to believe that this formidable old woman, who takes on her four grandchildren, is sheer invention, but Cynthia says, 'Abigail Tillerman just jumped out of the typewriter.'

And it is not just the people but the overpowering sense of place in the Tillerman novels that make them so compelling, so eminently re-readable. I don't think I'm the only one to have a picture so clear of Gram's house on the Maryland coast that I can actually see the rooms and smell the cooking and the sea. The second book, *Dicey's song,* was the only straightforward sequel. It carries on the action of *Homecoming,* because Cynthia was interested in what happens *after* an adventure. The first book was a journey and a quest—for a permanent home. The second one is about 'how to live an ordinary life, after you have won the prize.'

Dicey's song won the Newbery Medal in 1983 and set the seal on Cynthia Voigt's reputation as a writer. It is a deeply satisfying novel. But perhaps the best written and most interesting title in the sequence is the middle one, *The runner.* It horrified fans when Collins first published it here, with its picture of a horrible-looking skinhead on the front cover. What the author had pulled off was that hardest of literary tricks, to make an unsympathetic hero someone we care about. Cynthia Voigt had gone back in time in her family saga, to the youth of Dicey's uncle, Bullet, who shaved his head because his father told him to get his long hair cut. Bullet is the runner; his running defines him. He is also an unthinking racist, a deeply unhappy rebellious teenager, with a brutal father and a mother who has made her bed of nails and is determined to lie uncomfortably on it for the rest of her life.

After the story of Bullet, which ends abruptly in Vietnam, the Tillerman novels begin to fade in power. There are other strong characters, particularly black ones, but the momentum falters and the final book, *Seventeen against the dealer,* is a let-down. By then Dicey is a young woman doing what she does best, building boats, for a living. The whole of the sequence is as dominated by water and boats as the books of Arthur Ransome. I asked Cynthia Voigt if she is an experienced sailor, knowing how much she dislikes air travel, but she said no, that the water was an opportunity for metaphor. She tells us so much about Dicey's job, I wondered if she could build a boat herself, but she laughingly admitted she couldn't—it was all research.

Dicey acquires an admirer, Jeff, in the second book (he is the hero of the third, *A solitary blue*). He is still there for her in the last one, though she never makes any concessions to him, has never done anything to attract or keep his attention. He is rich, good-looking, clever, plays the guitar, is loving, honest and faithful. Isn't he a fantasy figure? Was he invented for Dicey's benefit? Or Cynthia's? She smiles and admits that it was a conscious decision to remove all his financial problems. But then reveals that it is Bullet she really feels most attracted to, a character influenced by one of her own students in her teaching days. 'I even figured out a way for Bullet not to have to die,' she says, but her writer's honesty would not allow her that cop-out.

Standing back from the sequence, one sees that she was right to bring it to an end; her interest in the family does seem to have diminished after *The runner.* But the strong sense of family in it made me think that she must have come from a close-knit one herself. She claims it was like a family in Henry James: 'close and not close—some of my siblings are not that fond of me.' There were five children, three girls and twin boys, one of whom was deaf with a little brain damage. (One thinks of Dicey's sister Maybeth, who is a little slow but not as much as outsiders think.) Cynthia did feel very motherly to the younger children. All five have children of their own now and are 'wild about being parents.' It was a very secure childhood emotionally and economically. And it is interesting to note that her latest book is dedicated to 'all of us who have, and are, brothers and sisters.'

Cynthia Voigt has been married twice. She admitted two things to her second husband, Walter, who teaches Classics: she was a closet writer and she wanted to have a son. Both her ambitions were realised; she had Peter, now fifteen, while writing *The Callender papers.* Her older child Jessica is now a student at Bryn Mawr and Cynthia herself taught English literature for years. They are a bookish sort of family.

Cynthia only discovered the wealth of contemporary children's literature when she started teaching and found the children's books shelf. Her favourites were 'The Chronicles of Prydain' by Lloyd Alexander and the books of Russell Hoban. She is a close friend of another children's writer living in Maine, Robin McKinley.

Cynthia learned to write herself by writing *The Callender papers,* 'the hardest book to write.' But it was not the first to be published. In fact *Homecoming,* which *was* first, had a hard time finding a publisher and was turned down by four of the five she sent it to. It had to be cut by 2,000 words, which perhaps was what told Cynthia there were more books to be made out of the Tillerman story.

She now writes a first draft quite fast, then puts it on to a computer to have something smarter to present to her editor. That editor has been for a long time Gail Paris of the American publisher, Atheneum, with whom Cynthia has a relationship she describes as 'like marriage.' There will be several changes made after consultation with Gail, who doesn't waste time quarrelling with commas and is 'sweet reason itself,' but obviously has a strong influence on Cynthia's work.

That work has gone in several new directions but perhaps hasn't yet found the right voice. The most satisfactory 'non-Tillerman' novel has been *Izzy, willy-nilly,* which manages to make a real book out of the story of a girl who loses her leg in a car accident. Less successful is *Tree by leaf,* which returns to mutilation through a father whose face is badly disfigured fighting in the Great War in Europe. In *Jackaroo,* Cynthia Voigt invented her own country, the Kingdom, which is feudal and harsh, but in doing that lost the authenticity of the sense of place which has been her great strength. The other book set in the Kingdom, *On fortune's wheel,* is a wildly romantic and very powerful love story and a good read. But all these books might have been written by different hands.

As might perhaps her most ambitious to date, *David and Jonathan.* Paradoxically, this is really the story of Henry, who is Jonathan's best friend. They are almost driven apart by Jonathan's cousin David, who comes to America from Europe, a survivor of the Holocaust, in which all his other relatives have been wiped out. This is strong meat and there is more: David, although exquisitely beautiful and attractive to members of both sexes, including Henry himself, turns out to be unscrupulous, malicious, and ultimately terrifyingly evil. He has to go, but his going is the weakest part of the book. I think that Cynthia was writing for the wrong audience here and the book should have been published on an adult list. The reader is not spared the horrors as it is, but it would have freed her to follow the story the way it seems to want to go.

There is a fascination with evil in a lot of what she writes. Her very first book has Enoch Callender, a man who has killed his sister and would kill his little niece if he got the chance. He too is charming, handsome and immaculate in a white suit. In her latest book, *The Vandemark mummy,* there is another villain who attempts to kill a young girl. And yet the Tillerman children walked the highways and hidden paths of East Coast America in safety only once encountering a sinister farmer.

Yet in *Homecoming,* there is description of boiling live crabs so gorge-risingly realistic that I cut it when reading the book aloud to my children. There is no doubt that this is a tough, unsentimental writer, who is uncompromising in her material. You want the delicious taste of crab? Then you have to face what it takes to get it.

Cynthia Voigt makes no conscious change in vocabulary whether writing for seven- or eighteen-year-olds. 'I'm more concerned with what ideas they can handle. If the story and characters work then the book will be readable.' She feels we tend to underestimate the mass of readers. Of course, a lot of them will want to read nothing but Judy Blume and 'Sweet Valley High' but Cynthia thinks that is part of a need to belong. 'So many books tell the reader to be the outsider, the oddball.'

The Vandemark mummy is a return to the mystery genre and works very well. Althea and Phineas Hall are living with their father, a Classics teacher at Vandemark College while their mother is away in Oregon working for a congressman. The college receives a bequest of some Egyptian antiquities, including a mummy, and Mr Hall, in spite of being in the wrong discipline, gets the job of curator. The collection is broken into and the mummy stolen and vandalised, then Althea disappears. It's all good adventure story stuff and Cynthia Voigt handles the material like the professional she is.

Perhaps it's partly the influence of her husband's field, but Cynthia Voigt is taking up a classical theme in her next novel too. . . . *Orfe* is the Orpheus and Eurydice story with the sexes reversed. Orfe is a girl, a punk rock musician who falls in love with Eury, an exaddict. There is a third book set in the Kingdom, a very long one. . . . Cynthia Voigt is extremely fertile.

Her British publisher, Fiona Kenshole at HarperCollins, describes Cynthia Voigt as 'a recession-proof author,' and all her backlist titles are still in print. 'She holds her own,' says Fiona, 'at a time when one-off literary novels, particularly for teenagers, are hard to sell.' She is still not as well known as she deserves to be in this country. Her books are a quiet success, known to the connoisseurs, but her name is hardly a household word.

If she stopped writing tomorrow, Cynthia Voigt would have made a huge contribution to children's literature. And yet I can't help feeling her best work is still to come. She says the Tillerman books deal with 'interior events' and that I think is her real strength: the development of a character's interior world, set very firmly in a recognisable exterior one. If she could write more novels drawing on that vein, then her status would be alongside Alcott and Montgomery, those other [North] American classic chroniclers of the painful art of growing up.

TITLE COMMENTARY

📖 *SONS FROM AFAR* (1987)

Susan Schuller

SOURCE: A review of *Sons from Afar,* in *School Library Journal,* Vol. 34, No. 1, September, 1987, pp. 198-99.

In this continuation of the Tillerman saga, the focus is on brothers James and Sammy. Always the questioner, James is determined to find the father he never knew. His main objective is to see if his own character traits, especially his intelligence, which sets him apart, are inherited from this shadowy figure from the past. Reluctantly, Sammy joins in on the search, which is made more difficult because they do not confide in Gram, nor older sister Dicey, who is away at college. Readers are drawn into the hunt, hoping that the merchant seaman father is found, yet fearing what kind of man he will turn out to be. (Those familiar with Voigt's *Runner* already have an idea.) Voigt is wise to make the search inconclusive; it ends at a waterfront bar in a fight with ex-associates of their father. Yet the story itself comes to a conclusion, for James has found himself and has at least become more comfortable with his unique qualities. The theme of fatherhood is woven throughout the narrative, including Greek myths and the fathers of friends. And while the search is the main element in this story, Voigt allows her characters to pursue other interests along the way. Readers who are not familiar with the earlier Tillerman novels, such as *Homecoming* and *Dicey's Song* will have no problem finding their place in this story, as Voigt fills in enough of the background to cover any questions. However, they will no doubt be motivated to go back to the earlier episodes to become further acquainted with these characters who have remained marvelously consistent under Voigt's hand. Just as James' search drives him to the conclusion, so will readers be compelled to stay with his story from start to finish.

Betsy Bradley

SOURCE: A review of *Sons from Afar,* in *Voice of Youth Advocates,* Vol. 10, No. 4, October, 1987, pp. 208-10.

The latest story of the Tillerman family centers on the brothers, James, 15, and Sammy, 12, and their curiosity and search for information about their father. Older sister Dicey has gone off to college, and the boys still live with Gram and sister, Maybeth, on the Chesapeake Bay. The author includes an introduction for readers who have missed the other Tillerman books. The action of this story is dispersed through long introspective sections, alternating between each of the brother's point of view. The introspections are on character or lack of it. Each boy feels his faults may be inherited from the father he never knew. The father abandoned the family many years ago, before Sammy was born. The action follows the search for traces of the father's history: a talk with a grade school teacher, a high school principal, and a barroom brawl with a co-worker. You will probably want to order this book for all those patrons who have loved *Homecoming, Dicey's Song, Solitary Blue* and the others, but this book may be somewhat of a let-down compared to those excellent stories. The visual and emotional power of this book is simply not as strong as in previous books, but you will hit the mark, nevertheless, if you offer *Sons from Afar* to young adults who need a thoughtful title.

Peter Blake

SURFACE: "The Sins of the Father," in *The Times Literary Supplement,* No. 4440, May 6, 1988, p. 513.

Sons from Afar is the sixth book in which Cynthia Voigt has, in rather Trollopian fashion, given the Tillerman family parts that range from central to peripheral. Trollope's is by no means the most distinguished literary company Voigt has been invited to keep: a recent study compared the first book in the Tillerman chronicles, *Homecoming,* to the *Odyssey.* Such scholarly elucidation need not deter anyone from enjoying the book, but it does provide a useful shorthand for describing the plot of *Sons from Afar.* This is the story of a modern Telemachus. James Tillerman, an unathletic, dissatisfied schoolboy, attributes his unhappiness to his father, about whom he remembers little and is determined to find out more. So with the help of his younger brother Sammy, he sets off in search of the man described in his birth certificate as Francis Verricker, Merchant Seaman.

They begin by interviewing retired school-teachers, but they end more dramatically in a waterfront bar in Baltimore. The picture of Verricker they gather here is of a quick-witted man whose main concerns are gambling and womanizing, and who cheats in both domains. Unfortunately, their source is one of Verricker's debtors, who decides with the aid of his fists, a knife, broken bottles, and a sense of biblical tradition that the sins of the father should be visited on the sons.

The scene in the bar, tense and frightening, is the sort of thing that Voigt does extremely well. She uses the clear, sharp lens of a child's eye to reveal the duplicity, selfishness and menace of the adult world. Her stories seem not so much to ennoble children as to deflate the pompous grandeur of adults. Her good adults can occasionally seem cut from pasteboard, but her querulous, tedious or aggressive ones are full of unpleasant life. In Voigt's world, children must learn to rely not on these highly fallible beings but on themselves. So James never does find his father, nor even a father figure. Instead, in a slightly disappointing, ending, he, as the jargon has it, finds himself, and in himself the self-sufficiency that Voigt admires in both children and adults.

By using the Tillermans sparingly, Voigt has left herself with characters to be explored in later books. And we can in general look forward to these with enthusiasm. As the novels get further from the childrens' initial trek in *Homecoming,* however, they are more and more filled with detailed accounts of daily school life, while the less quotidian part of the story seems just a little thinner each time. Voigt has so far successfully kept her books and characters from atrophying into a sequence of tedious adventures of the forever young. It would be a pity if later stories became either formulaic or repetitive.

Margery Fisher

SOURCE: A review of *Sons from Afar,* in *Growing Point,* Vol. 27, No. 3, September, 1988, p. 5040

Six years before the events described in *Sons from Afar,* Dicey Tillerman had led her three siblings, after their mother had inexplicably abandoned them, on a long, hazardous journey to the shabby house in Maryland where their grandmother lived. Now the two youngest Tillerman children, James and Sammy, start on a similar journey in search of their unknown father. They know his name, they know he is a merchant seaman, and questions put to his one-time teachers give them something of a lead. The picture they are given of a financially dishonest and sponging character dismays them. After a brawl in a quayside café, where both boys are hurt defending their father's reputation among seaman he had cheated, they return home to assimilate what they have found out. This is really a tale of fraternal relations. James envies Sammy his serene self-confidence, for at school he himself is always scorned for his dreamy nature; though in their unsuccessful quest he discovers how much he depends on Sammy to keep him going, he returns home a great deal more confident in his own gifts and his newly found determination to work towards a lawyer's career. Like the earlier stories of the Tillermans, this one depends largely on a crisp, forceful dialogue through which we can see how the two boys manage their adventure and how they change as a result of it. A background of country, garden, boat and docks, a school project on mythology which teasingly echoes James's thoughts, a strong sense of place and community, make this fifth story in the sequence a worthy successor to the rest.

TREE BY LEAF (1988)

Susan M. Harding

SOURCE: A review of *Tree by Leaf,* in *School Library Journal,* Vol. 35, No. 8, May, 1988, pp. 113-14.

When 12-year-old Clothilde's father left to fight in World War I, her wealthy grandfather was so angered that he refused to support their family. With nowhere else to go, the family moved into an abandoned farmhouse on the rocky coast of Maine, which was left to Clothilde by an eccentric aunt. Now her father has come home from war, and Clothilde hopes that he will be able to solve their problems. Instead, he just adds to them. He is so scarred, both in body and soul, that he doesn't want them to see him and spends all his time alone in a small shack. Meanwhile, older brother Nathaniel is being seduced away by grandfather's wealth; their servant, Lou, is being beaten by her drunken, abusive father; and to raise enough money to survive, they may have to sell Clothilde's land. Unfortunately, the writing is not up to Voigt's usually high standard. Much as the characters are reserved with each other and hold themselves at a distance, so that readers are kept at a distance, even from Clothilde, the narrator. There is also a good deal of confusion caused by a mystical voice that speaks to Clothilde when she's in the forest. Is it God? Is it Mother Nature? Is it Clothilde's imagination? One never finds out, and it is a jarringly fantastical element in an otherwise bitterly real novel.

Elizabeth S. Watson

SOURCE: A review of *Tree by Leaf,* in *The Horn Book Magazine,* Vol. LXIV, No. 3, May-June, 1988, p. 363.

For Clothilde, age twelve, the Maine peninsula willed to her by a great aunt is the girl's stability in a perplexing world that has caused her father to become estranged, first from his own father and then—as a result of a disfiguring war injury—from his wife and children. When he enlisted in the cavalry during World War I, he incurred the wrath of Clothilde's grandfather, who insisted that if his son planned to go to war, his family must also leave the ancestral home. Clothilde's mother, who copes with the new living arrangement—a farmhouse on the remote peninsula and limited income—until her husband's return, now reverts to the role of a lady, leaving Clothilde all the chores. The frustrations of her life close in on the

girl until, in her desperate attempt to sort them out, she communes with "the Voice," representing a God figure—omniscient and omnipotent. The story is told primarily through descriptions of the setting and Clothilde's thoughts and actions, with spare use of dialogue. When dialogue is used, it is often stilted, as Clothilde feels and knows things that she has no words to express. The story has the clear ring of truth in its plot and characters and especially in its setting. The descriptions of the Maine seacoast and forest are glorious in their detail; the solid landscape forms the base above which the story drifts like fog. The book has a thread of suspense, fine writing, magnificent imagery, and an unusual mystical quality. It is, however, a demanding and difficult book that will speak to the child who, like Clothilde, is puzzling out life alone. A thoughtful and thought-provoking piece of writing for that special reader.

Dulcie Leimbach

SOURCE: A review of *Tree by Leaf,* in *The New York Times Book Review,* June 12, 1988, p. 35.

In *Tree by Leaf,* Cynthia Voigt's latest novel, the central character, Clothilde, is as complex and strong-willed as Dicey, the heroine of Mrs. Voigt's *Homecoming,* and *Dicey's Song.* . . . Like Dicey, Clothilde must contend with serious family problems. Luckily, she is able to lighten her burdens by strengthening her trust in a higher power.

The story is set on the Maine coast in the 1920's. Earlier, Clothilde's father, disinherited by his Boston Brahmin family for marrying a poor Roman Catholic, had moved his wife and children—Nate, Clothilde and Dierdre—up to Speer Point, the old family farm, and then left to fight in World War I.

When he returns his face is so badly scarred he can't bear to see anyone; he hides in the boathouse and his meals are left at the door. Clothilde's mother reacts to her husband's behavior by trying harder to become the "lady" she thinks he desires. That leaves Clothilde, not yet a teen-ager, and Lou, the servant-girl, responsible for all household chores. To make matters worse, Clothilde's brother, Nate, whom she adores, decides to live with their wealthy paternal grandfather. The beleaguered child then learns that Speer Point—a bequest to her by a great-aunt—may be sold.

At the same time that Clothilde struggles on and works harder, she builds up resentments toward everyone around her, and to God. Then she hears a "Voice," that asks her what she wants and, despite her suspicions, she answers.

Here the author distinguishes her work from other young-adult novels of the "coping" genre. The gentle, nonjudgmental way the Voice probes Clothilde's emotions allows the child to express her doubts and fears and, most important, to reach her own conclusions. Because the Voice never lectures, the wisdom Clothilde gains—which helps her to deal with her situation—is neither pietistic nor complicated but seems to be bestowed naturally. Mrs. Voigt gracefully handles the scenes in which Clothilde believes she is going crazy. The writing is detached but warm, and the thoughts are delightfully Clothilde's own: "If the Voice might be real—which she half believed, she felt her brain's shell cracking."

The narrative is straightforward without being too simple, especially when the author evokes the dramatic Maine coast and Clothilde's revelations. The dialogue between the Voice and Clothilde is mystical but not hazy, and it blends in seamlessly with the rest of the book. Once again, Cynthia Voigt has written a novel that her young adolescent audience will appreciate and remember.

Diane Manuel

SOURCE: "Special Novels for Teen-agers: Some of Year's Best and Brightest Young-Adult Titles," in *The Christian Science Monitor,* July 25, 1988, p. 22.

[*Tree by Leaf*] has the kind of believable teen-age characters and intriguing scenery that have made Newbery Medalist Cynthia Voigt such a hit with young readers.

The setting of her 13th novel is a remote Maine peninsula, circa 1920. The leading "lady" is Clothilde Speer, a 12-year-old who wishes she had a few less chores and responsibilities. The "Great War" has just ended, and Clothilde's father has returned from battle, horribly disfigured. As she tries to come to terms with her father's condition, Clothilde rebels against the perceived injustice of war and rails at a God-like figure, the "Voice."

It's not always easy to tell where Clothilde's imaginings begin and end, but Voigt fans will stick with her story to its healing conclusion. They'll also enjoy the lovely touches that the author brings to the most mundane subjects.

Anne Duchêne

SOURCE: "In the Nature of Things," in *The Times Literary Supplement,* No. 4488, April 7, 1989, p. 378.

Cynthia Voigt's reputation nowadays precedes her, of one prepared to grind her young readers fairly ruthlessly, for their own good, between the upper and the nether millstones of life. It comes as a surprise, therefore, when *Tree by Leaf* remains uncertain and blurred at its heart—very bright and exact about all physical detail, but opaque at what must be called its metaphysical centre.

It is set in 1920, on a small peninsula on the coast of Maine. Clothilde, who inherited the land from a great-aunt, and who is to bear the book's burden, has been living there with her mother, her older brother Nate and her little sister Deirdre since 1916, when her father rode away to the war on his own horse. For this, his rich and disagreeable old father disinherits him; but he had been on the brink of doing so for years, because Clothilde's

mother was such socially unacceptable things as penniless, orphaned and Catholic.

Clothilde, who is now thirteen or thereabouts, and her family live very frugally, gathering clams at low tide for chowder, and not mixing with the other inhabitants of the Point. One maidservant, Lou, aged fifteen, lives with them, because at home her father beats her. Thus far, in what is a densely plotted book, the author has managed some elegant time-shifts, and always had space as well for details of the wild flowers, or the domestic chores, and for sending the statutory feminist signals which the latter now demand.

Then, in July 1920—in a matter of days, seemingly—all this changes. Clothilde's father returns from the war, hideously disfigured, and isolates himself in the boat-house; her unconfident mother becomes distractedly detached from life; her brother Nate runs away to become his greedy grandfather's heir; and Lou's drunken father drowns, so Lou has to leave to work in the mills she dreads.

During this time, too, Clothilde hears "the Voice," and asks its help for those she loves. It has been made plain that Clothilde has been raised in (non-Catholic) piety, and that she tends to criticize God, for making what so often seem slipshod arrangements. "The Voice" is never overtly equated with God; it does allow her one single, penetrating vision, not to be recaptured, of the interdependence of all growing things, and for the rest, it expresses itself with remarkable modesty: "The design is mine, the embellishments are yours. I do not makes wars; men do," and "The leaf grows and the tree grows; it is important."

This last mesage, relating to the book's slightly cryptic title, implies that Clothilde, in invoking the help of "the Voice," has lacked humility and patience. The things she asks for are, in fact, done; but never in ways she expected or intended, and never without pain. Her understanding was imperfect; she had not yet learned that it may be best to ask nothing, for oneself or others—unless it be simply for "strength," which is all that Clothilde can finally find in her confused self to ask on Lou's behalf.

Extrapolated, this makes sense, but embedded in a vigorous narrative it fizzes and whizzes perplexingly, like an unspent fire-work. An epilogue does allow some slight measure of hope; where there has been strength, there may in the end be contentment. It seems a heavy message.

M. Hobbs

SOURCE: A review of *Tree by Leaf,* in *The Junior Bookshelf,* Vol. 53, No. 3, June, 1989, p. 142.

Tree by Leaf is a more slow-moving story than we have been accustomed to from Cynthia Voigt, probably because the Maine coastal background, brought before us in beautifully observed detail, is so important to the central character, who has inherited from a great aunt she scarcely met a promontory there. The events take place during a summer week at the end of the Great War, in which her father has fought as a cavalryman, so this is another historical recreation. We learn in flashback of his leaving her grandfather's house to fight and their subsequent hard life. He is in fact the mysterious man in the ruined boathouse below the farmstead, maimed in mind as well as body and guiltily unable to face his wife or his daughter. Clothilde, in danger of losing her land, is driven out by her anger into the woodland, where she becomes aware of a tangible Voice, the spirit of the land, which she questions. She begs four things, all apparently good. Her greedy selfish brother plans to leave them this vacation to go on a cruise—she does not want him to; she asks healing for her father (this, she thinks, is refused); and she wants their hired girl Lou free from fear of her drunken father. The answer to this last helps Clothilde see that the universal effect of such wishes, beyond the immediate world of the asker. Lou's father dies at sea, with the father of a shell-shocked simpleton left with his distressed mother. Yet in the surprise ending, we learn that as a result, the simpleton found release as a gardener from the horrors that haunted him, and Clothilde's father, though his face remained a ruin, achieved healing of mind through painting, and happiness once more with his wife. Clothilde's fourth request is to keep her land, and this the Voice refuses—she comes to see why: the land does not belong to people. For the Voice bestows on Clothilde a great gift, visibly on that first occasion, when she suddenly sees into the heart of nature: the leaf growing on the tree, the grass, the creatures. When the vision fades, she gradually discovers she retains an ability to see into people and understand their motivation. The choice of subject is interesting, but one must confess there is a certain remoteness about the narrative.

📖 **SEVENTEEN AGAINST THE DEALER (1989)**

Trev Jones

SOURCE: A review of *Seventeen against the Dealer,* in *School Library Journal,* Vol. 35, No. 6, February, 1989, pp. 103-04.

This final volume about the Tillerman family is a finely-crafted novel about goals and values and about nurturing relationships rather than taking them for granted. Dicey is now 21, and she once again exhibits the single-minded determination that served her so well in *Homecoming* and *Dicey's Song.* Here, however, it also works to her disadvantage, for at this point in her life, she is also filled with youthful arrogance, foolish independence, and naivety. She has saved enough money to start a boatyard business, and she is fiercely determined to make a go of it. She makes serious business errors and lets herself be duped by a con artist. Throughout, her blinders keep her working to the point of exhaustion and obsession, all the while missing what is happening in her family and to her relationship with her boyfriend, Jeff. Between New Year's Day and Valentine's Day, Dicey follows her spiritual quest, finally realizing that while achieving one's goals is im-

portant, so too are family, knowledge, and personal growth. As Dicey becomes more involved in her work, family members fade from the pages, and readers are as isolated from them as Dicey—until an emergency brings her back to reality. Descriptions are vivid; writing is in turn leisurely and clipped; characters spring to life, all revealing their own strengths and weaknesses. Stunning performances from all of the Tillermans.

Hazel Rochman

SOURCE: A review of *Seventeen against the Dealer,* in *Booklist,* Vol. 85, No. 14, March 15, 1989, p. 1276.

Dicey Tillerman always has things planned. At 21 she's left college to *earn* her living building boats. But drive and hard work aren't enough. Her business fails, largely through her lack of skill and experience and finally because Cisco, a charming drifter who helps her mend boats, absconds with a large check. Ashamed, she accepts responsibility not only for her mistakes, but also for the way her obsession with work has made her neglect her family, especially Gram, whose cold becomes pneumonia, and Jeff, whom Dicey loves. The whole Tillerman series is evoked here, but the first book, **Homecoming,** is the constant reference. As she worries and works, Dicey remembers how she once worried and walked to find a home for her family; it is the memory of that journey that makes her give shelter to the wanderer Cisco (who could easily be the father who deserted them years ago). There is some preachiness in relation to the family, particularly beatific Maybeth, but the characterization of dogged, passionate Dicey is superb, and her scenes with Gram and with Jeff are sharp and spare. The reader feels Dicey's thoughts: the sour unease at failure, the image that flashes landscape and past experience together with the present moment, her intense love for Jeff. Above all, this has that rarity in YA fiction, a candid, detailed celebration of work—its joy and drudgery, the sheer dailiness of "the usual"—with no easy failure-struggle-triumph formula. In a quiet climax to an acclaimed series, people let you down, there's much to learn, and work is what you do.

Roger Sutton

SOURCE: A review of *Seventeen against the Dealer,* in *Bulletin of the Center for Children's Books,* Vol. 42, No. 8, April, 1989, pp. 207-08.

Dicey is now twenty-one and proprietor of her own fledgling boat shop in this last (according to the jacket copy) installment in Voigt's series about the Tillerman family. After her workshop is robbed of all of her hard-won boat-building tools, Dicey unwillingly contracts to sand and paint thirty shoddy rowboats built by her landlord. The work is odious and long, allowing Dicey no time to design and build a dinghy, her first order. Unexpected but welcome help comes from a drifter named Cisco, who asks for nothing more than to be allowed to sleep in the shop and share Dicey's hot chocolate. Cisco is a big talker, "like constant rain, the words falling and falling," and an interesting one, describing all the places he's seen and knowledge he's gathered to an increasingly fascinated Dicey. He is also most probably Dicey's father, who abandoned the family before the first book in the series, **Homecoming,** began. While sprinkling hints throughout, Voigt doesn't name Cisco as Frank Verricker, and the relationship will probably be lost on readers unfamiliar with the previous books, particularly **Sons from Afar.** Dicey herself never realizes who Cisco really is, which makes his eventual theft of eight hundred dollars from Dicey all the more shocking, giving a dark irony to Gram's wrap-up moral that "It's not your failure. It's his. Yours would have been not to trust him." As was true in the previous books, Gram steals any scene she appears in, but here she (as well as Maybeth) has acquired a rather sentimental patina of sainthood, her dignity becoming almost picturesque. Dicey can be tryingly noble ("Days passed. Dicey worried and worked") but Voigt shows that Dicey's fortitude and stubbornness have come at the cost of other essential qualities, such as curiosity and imagination, lacks that cost her true knowledge of what she really lost when Cisco betrayed her and disappeared. A brave finale.

Hanna B. Zieger

SOURCE: A review of *Seventeen against the Dealer,* in *The Horn Book Magazine,* Vol. LXV, No. 4, July-August, 1989, pp. 492-93.

In the last of the books about the Tillerman family, the focus has come full circle back to Dicey. As in **Dicey's Song,** all of Dicey's physical and emotional energies are invested in working on a boat. At twenty-one, Dicey has left college and is working toward her dream of having her own boat-yard. Determined to succeed, she concentrates so much on the tasks she's cut out for herself that she can no longer really take the time to live. At risk of losing Jeff's love, unable to acknowledge the seriousness of Gram's illness or the needs and concerns of Maybeth, Sammy, and James, Dicey is caught in a web of her own making. Dicey's lesson in living comes from a most unexpected source—an amazingly well-read drifter who has sailed the seven seas and evolved a highly individual and amoral philosophy of life. Calling himself "Cisco" Kidd, he offers to work for Dicey in exchange for a place to stay. Throughout his nonstop conversation, Cisco—who is suggestive of the ghostly father figure in **Song from Afar**—shows a marked interest in Dicey and her family but never reveals anything of his own personal life. Ultimately Dicey has to face the fact of her total naiveté and inexperience, both in business and in human understanding: when she accepts Cisco's offer to take her money to the bank, he leaves town with all the profits from her business. Facing the shambles she has made of her life and the bankruptcy of her boat-yard dream, Dicey discovers the healing and sustaining power of her family. She is able to care for the recuperating Gram, help Maybeth study, realize Sammy's talent, appreciate James's choices, and finally accept how much Jeff means to her. With the same masterful characterization that readers have enjoyed in other books about the Tillermans, Cynthia Voigt has continued to weave the threads of each of these lives. But instead of tying up all these threads into a finished tapestry, she has left her characters on a path that will continue beyond the pages of these books and in the minds and imaginations of her readers.

Marcus Crouch

SOURCE: A review of *Seventeen against the Dealer,* in *The Junior Bookshelf,* Vol. 54, No. 5, October, 1990, p. 256.

This is the seventh (and, the publisher says, the last) of the Tillerman novels. Cynthia Voigt began her love-affair with this pleasant American family in 1981. The end—if this is really the last word—is inconclusive. These lively young men and women have still a long way to go.

The central character this time is Dicey who has dropped out of school and is determined to make a go of her boat-building business. Her assets are courage and determination. Against these must be set ignorance of basic essentials (she hasn't thought about insurance, and she can't read, let alone make, boat drawings) and an altogether too trusting nature. She accepts a commission from Mr. Hobart ('Call me Hobie' says this smoothie without meaning it) but gets no written contract. When the worldly wise and amoral Cisco drifts into her life and her workshop she accepts him at his own valuation and lives to regret it. She is much too fond of her cheque-book. When the story ends she has no money and no business. She is left with her family and Jeff.

For those coming to this book without experience of its forerunners Jeff, the man in Dicey's life, may prove hard to take. Writing of their relationships Ms Voigt's prose takes on a Mills-and-Boon tone (superior M & B but definitely of that kind). ' . . . he gathered her into his arms. The silky feel of his hair, and his strong young shoulders—the clean smell of him and the distant beating of his heart from deep inside his body . . . ' Happily this does not go on long. Dicey's family provide her with her sheet-anchor among the financial storms which beset her, and these pictures of a united family and a stable home are wholly delightful. For all that, I don't find much depth in the characterization, except perhaps in Dicey herself. These nice young people are well-drawn clichés.

ON FORTUNE'S WHEEL (1990)

Kirkus Reviews

SOURCE: A review of *On Fortune's Wheel,* in *Kirkus Reviews,* Vol. LVIII, No. 3, February 1, 1990, p. 187.

Returning to the vividly portrayed imaginary medieval world of **Jackaroo,** Voigt tells of another innkeeper's daughter, two generations later, who also struggles with her society's rigidity on her way to a self-defined, productive life.

By chance, Birle sees a stranger (Orien) taking her father's boat; in trying to retrieve it, she unexpectedly joins him on a long, adventurous trek down the river—during which they only begin to know each other: she realizes that he is of the nobility, while he is soon depending on her competence for life's necessities. Reaching the sea, they founder on a desolate rock; their "rescuers" sell them as slaves in a foreign city. There, Birle is lucky enough to learn healing herb lore, but Orien suffers the humiliation of the mines, from which he barely escapes with his life. Reunited, they agree to marry and return to their own country and to the difficult choices that still await them.

Voigt is a master of pure story; her enthralling narratives are seamlessly interwoven with telling perceptions of human nature. Here, the reader is somewhat distanced from characters who are more symbolic than those in her realistic fiction. Birle's master when she is a slave is a kind but amoral philosopher, brother to a cruel despot; in a parallel crucial to Voigt's theme, Orion abdicates rule to his younger brother, a stern but compassionate judge, choosing for himself a simpler, more creative life. A satisfying love story, a grand adventure, and a rich mix of ideas and action.

Hazel Rochman

SOURCE: A review of *On Fortune's Wheel,* in *Booklist,* Vol. 86, No. 12, February 15, 1990, p. 1156.

This is Voigt in her opulent, vaguely medieval mode, in the style of *Jackaroo.* Fourteen-year-old Birle, the innkeeper's daughter, smitten by Orien, the young, proud runaway Earl of the Kingdom, takes off with him in a series of picaresque adventures down the river to the sea, where they are shipwrecked, captured by pirates, and sold into slavery in the teeming city. She saves him, and they journey back; a stranger in his great castle, she runs away and bears his child alone, but he comes after her. The plot moves in fits and starts, as if the characters get into something and escape at the author's whim, and then they talk themselves into a final resolution. But while the story doesn't have the wit and inner conflict of Lloyd Alexander's Westmark series, its canvas is rich and crowded with types of every class: lord, scholar, upstart prince, merchant, entertainer, craftsman, slow-witted giant (no priests, though). Individual scenes are dramatic, and Voigt can hold a fleeting moment in a lovely line ("His smile stayed on his face, as if it had been forgotten there"). *Jackaroo*'s many fans will willingly suspend disbelief and follow the intrepid Birle as Fortune's wheel swings—in true saga style—from drudgery to adventure, from iron servitude to luxury, and then finally to independence.

Susan Hepler

SOURCE: A review of *On Fortune's Wheel,* in *School Library Journal,* Vol. 36, No. 3, March, 1990, pp. 240, 242.

Two generations after *Jackaroo* takes place, another inn-

keeper's daughter finds herself outside the boundaries of her society. Like Lloyd Alexander, Voigt creates a setting in no known historical past, but with many medieval echoes. Birle, 14, tries to stop a boat thief and instead becomes his passenger as he flees downriver. The thief, however, is no ordinary man but Lord Orien, the next ruler of the Kingdom who is running away because he is convinced that he will be an ineffectual leader. The two become marooned on an island, and are then sold into service. Without Orien, Birle submits to her bad fortune, works hard, and befriends others held in thrall by one master or another. It is only when she acknowledges her desires and begins to work to achieve them that she is able to rescue a nearly dead Orien. Birle is a thoughtful heroine, Orien a worthy hero, and the sudden confusion both feel over the roles assigned to them is nicely resolved. Realizing that free will, at least in part, determines their future, both separately renounce the roles society has made for them to begin a life. Readers may wonder how Orien, Birle, and their baby will manage in the fierce anarchy of the southern cities, but at least they will be making their own way, not following the ways defined by "fortune's wheel." This coming-of-age story at first moves slowly, but that makes the horror of enslavement even more dramatic. Voigt presents the horrors of slavery and despotic rule as seen through Birle's eyes, and readers are left with many powerful images of the consequences of acting dishonorably, weakly, selfishly, or thoughtlessly.

Roger Sutton

SOURCE: A review of *On Fortune's Wheel,* in *Bulletin of the Center for Children's Books,* Vol. 43, No. 11, July-August, 1990, p. 276.

Set in the same medieval Kingdom as *Jackaroo,* this companion story takes place some fifty years later. While 14-year-old Birle has no desire to marry Muir, it seems at first to be the only way out of her oppressive life at home. When an alternate escape presents itself in the form of a runaway Lord, she joins him, publicly declaring fealty and privately, instantly, falling in love: "All she knew was that his smile lit up the morning as the rising sun does." Readers may be hard put to understand the attraction, as Orien's sole positive personality trait seems to be the oft-noted "bellflower" color of his eyes. Leisurely and digressively told, this story may be appreciated for its elegant (and occasionally eloquent) writing, but the narrative is directionless and too long. Birle and Orien journey down the river to the sea, where—by virtue of Orien's stupidity—they are taken into slavery. While Birle is lucky enough to get a good master, Orien is taken to the fatal mines. She helps him escape, nurses him back to health, and takes him home to his rightful position as Earl. Dicey would have drowned him.

📖 THE VANDEMARK MUMMY (1991)

Cynthia Bishop

SOURCE: A review of *The Vandemark Mummy,* in

School Library Journal, Vol. 37, No. 9, September, 1991, p. 285.

Newly arrived in Portland, Maine, Phineas Hall, 12, and his sister Althea, almost 15, live with their father, a classics professor, while their mother pursues her own career in Portland, Oregon. Phineas concentrates on being a child, enjoying his summer, while Althea buries herself in the study of ancient Greek. The focus of their concerns shifts abruptly when a small collection of Egyptian antiquities, including a mummy, is donated to Vandemark College, and Professor Hall is chosen as curator. The collection is first threatened, and then the mummy is vandalized. It is Althea who figures out the culprit's identity; in confronting him, she risks her life and is saved only through the persistence and bravery of Phineas, who conducts a nocturnal search of the labyrinthine library basement. Pleasingly well written, this contemporary mystery is graced with a sound plot, a scary climax, and, above all, perceptive characterizations. The tone is light, deftly counterbalancing the thoughtful presentation of difficult issues concerning feminism and family. In all, it's a fine interweaving of fun and substance.

Ilene Cooper

SOURCE: A review of *The Vandemark Mummy,* in *Booklist,* Vol. 88, No. 1, September 1, 1991, p. 46.

Twelve-year-old Phineas Hall, his older sister, Althea, and their dad are in Portland, Maine, where his father has taken a job teaching college. His mother is in Portland, Oregon, working for a congressman. Though the family has made the decision to separate for the sake of the parents' careers, adjustments are not always easy. Certainly not for Mr. Hall, who finds himself the unexpected curator of a collection of Egyptian antiquities, including a mummy of a young girl. Mr. Hall is not qualified to be curator, a fact that is brought home when there is a break-in that threatens the collection. Voigt is most successful in the pure mystery parts of her story. Phineas and Althea are determined to find out who is after the mummy, and the threat to Althea's life is dramatically and effectively written. Unquestionably, the historical trappings add a luster that gilds the story just like the diamond-shaped designs decorating the mummy's shroud. But Voigt's subplot—if it can properly be called that—about women's issues, including lots of talk about career versus motherhood, stalls the action rather than adding depth to the mystery, as Voigt probably intended. She has already shown she can write about serious topics. Enjoy this one for the pure pleasure of the creepy goings-on.

Elizabeth S. Watson

SOURCE: A review of *The Vandemark Mummy,* in *The Horn Book Magazine,* Vol. LXVII, No. 6, November-December, 1991, pp. 739-40.

A move to Maine from Oregon, where their mother has remained because of her job, would have been enough for twelve-year-old Phineas Hall and his older sister, Althea, to contend with. But things become even more complicated when their father, a professor of classical languages at Vandemark College, falls heir to the curatorial chair for a collection of Egyptian antiquities recently bequeathed to the college. Unexpectedly, the historically interesting but not terribly valuable collection is threatened by mysterious thefts. Mix together a family tentatively feeling its way through a separation forced by bicoastal careers, a missing mummy, and a previously undiscovered Sappho poem; add a couple of well-developed young characters and a plausible villain; and spruce it up with a dash of the classics. What you get is a nubbly-textured mystery that sustains tension and holds the reader's interest. The resolution of the mystery is realistically drawn; just as realistically, the family situation is not resolved. But there are satisfying suggestions of a more settled future.

Marcus Crouch

SOURCE: A review of *The Vandemark Mummy,* in *The Junior Bookshelf,* Vol. 57, No. 2, April, 1993, pp. 79-80.

Fear not! The 'curse of the mummy' is raised only by a foolish young reporter and quickly dismissed. Cynthia Voigt's novel—lighter than we expect from her but by no means trivial—is concerned with weightier matters than Hammer Horrors, like academic integrity and family stability. Serious issues are under debate, but the story is exciting and highly entertaining.

Mr. Hall has made a bid for a career of his own, even if it means separation from his forceful wife. Taking Althea and Phineas with him he has moved to Vandemark College where he will teach and, by a freak of good fortune, act as curator to the Vandemark Egyptian Collection. He has no great qualifications for this job, but then the Collection is not in the first class and the pay is good. When the exhibits are unpacked Phineas, age 12, is captivated by the portrait mask of the mummy. His elder sister Althea is more interested in the mummy's wrappings which she is inclined to identify, in the face of scholarly ridicule from Dr. Simard, as Greek manuscripts. When the mummy is stolen, then abandoned in a damaged state, Mr. Hall and the police have a generous number of suspects. Althea has her own ideas which lead her into extreme danger. Phineas' instincts come to the rescue in a genuinely nail-biting climax.

This synopsis should not suggest that this book is a thriller or a detective story (although in a way it is both). It is essentially a novel, a study in personal relationships and the interplay of characters. Phineas' is a full-lengh portrait of a lively, intelligent, sensitive boy, but he is only first in a whole gallery of intriguing, sometimes horrible portraits. Not a caricature among them; even O'Meara (not, please note, Miss or even Ms O'Meara) the journalist has her depths and the college librarian her surprises. Always the reader is aware of moral and intellectual issues at work.

DAVID AND JONATHAN (1992)

Lucinda Snyder Whitehurst

SOURCE: A review of *David and Jonathan,* in *School Library Journal,* Vol. 38, No. 2, March, 1992, p. 259.

A complex novel, set in the 1950s, that explores what it was like to be Jewish in the years following World War II—the sorrow of losing one's family, the guilt of having survived when so many did not, and the religious doubt such tragedy evokes. Sixteen-year-old Henry, a New England WASP, finds that his close friendship with Jonathan is threatened when Jonathan's older cousin David, an emotionally disturbed Holocaust survivor, moves in with the Nafiche family. Having lived through the war, David is now intent on suicide. He seems to despise both boys, yet constantly demands their attention. The troubled young man's presence takes a terrible toll on all the Nafiches and changes Henry's life. Voigt's writing is intelligent and witty, but her voice is inconsistent. Both Henry and Jonathan are extremely well-read and constantly volley literary quotations and allusions back and forth. Their perspective is unconvincingly mature as they grapple with the heavy subject matter. Although they are said to be very different, it is sometimes difficult to distinguish who is speaking. The main narration is framed by short scenes of the friends in Vietnam in 1967, a device that underscores the coming-of-age and impact-of-war themes. There is a great deal more talk than action, and the questions raised are difficult ones. Dense and intense, this book will require patience from its readers, but will also give them much to consider.

Hazel Rochman

SOURCE: "Survivor Guilt," in *Booklist,* Vol. 88, No. 13, March 1, 1992, p. 1270.

Without false comfort, Voigt confronts the Holocaust and its aftermath: the cruelty, the survivor guilt, the enduring racism, and the personal questions. The core of *David and Jonathan* is compelling, but the book is too long and too talky, the story contrived, and the issues overexplained. This doesn't have the simple power of Levoy's *Alan and Naomi,* which dramatizes some of the same issues quietly. Of course, understatement has never been Voigt's style, but in her best books, like *The Runner,* her characters raise crucial issues and yet leave space for the reader's imagination.

The novel does dramatize questions about guilt and responsibility, suffering and evil, which are of intense interest to young people. With the Holocaust now a required subject in many states, classes could talk about the book (or parts of it) along with Spiegelman's graphic novels, *Maus: A Survivor's Tale* and *Maus II,* which deal with the guilt and anger between a son and his survivor father.

Voigt's story begins with friendship. Henry, 16, is a Gentile from an old Yankee family, living on Cape Cod in the 1950s. Since fifth grade, he's been close to his Jewish friend Jon, even though their families are as different as those in the movie *Annie Hall.* Then Jon's cousin David, a disturbed Holocaust survivor, now age 20, moves in with the Jewish extended family, and all their lives are darkened forever. David's parents died in the camps—only he survived. Fourteen years old at the end of the war, he weighed 66 pounds. He's been in a mental institution for six years. Henry is overwhelmed with pity, yet, at the same time, he hates David, who's hostile, crude, and manipulative (Did Voigt really have to make David brilliant as well as handsome?). David's suicidal, drowning in guilt, and determined to drag others down with him. On one level, Henry finds himself locked in a struggle with demonic David for Jon's soul.

One night, when the three young men are drinking beer on the beach in the flickering light of a campfire, David talks about the camps and the crematoria. He shocks Henry into seeing not only the harrowing physical detail of the atrocities, but also what they reveal about all of us. The questions are made personal: Could I do that to others? Could others do that to me?

For once in a YA story the hell of the Holocaust is not overcome by individual goodness. No one can save David. And for once, here are YA characters for whom *brilliant* is more than a designer label: Harvard-bound Jon and Henry talk as if they think and read. They also horse around and worry about sex. But the intensity of that beach confrontation is weakened by the overexplaining and the working out of the issues far into the future. The novel is artificially framed by a fateful meeting in a Vietnam hospital a decade later, when Henry (who's now a surgeon) saves Jon (who's barely survived months of torture). We don't need it all spelled out so exactly, "that it keeps being done." Nor do we need all Jon's ironic Talmudic parables. Henry's terror is what holds us and makes us imagine: "fear of everyone else in the world, and fear of himself, and fear for himself."

Roger Sutton

SOURCE: A review of *David and Jonathan,* in *Bulletin of the Center for Children's Books,* Vol. 45, No. 8, April, 1992, pp. 223-24.

Framed by an initially confusing and ultimately unnecessary Vietnam setting, the core of this story takes place on Cape Cod during the Korean War, although it is the events of World War II that inform the novel's greatest thematic concerns. As all this might indicate, Voigt's latest book is an ambitious effort. Henry and Jonathan, both sixteen, are best friends until Jon's cousin David, a twenty-year-old survivor of the Holocaust, comes to live with Jon's family. David, who has spent many years in a posh mental hospital, is beautiful, difficult, and cruel, shrugging off—mocking—all of Henry's efforts to "feel sorry for him." David seduces Jon's sister, sexually taunts Henry, and resists any efforts at friendship. Eventually, David kills himself, an act that seems more vengeful than despairing.

The relationship between the three boys makes a powerful triangle; unfortunately, the characters seem but to exist only for what they can reveal about history and the Holocaust. Voigt isn't didactic or preachy; in fact, she is far more daring on the subject than most writers for children or teenagers, but the novel is overintellectualized, consisting of too many Talmudic, often confusing, sometimes obscure, occasionally incomprehensible, paragraphs that take readers away from the story. "Picking up information piecemeal, that's what Henry was doing. But he didn't know what Jon was thinking. *And* he didn't know what Jon was thinking." On the other hand, there are characters (such as Jon's weepy but funny mother) and conversations (such as a desperately ironic exchange between Jon and Henry's Yankee grandmother) that further theme *and* story. As a dark contrast to such Holocaust heroics as *Number the Stars,* this is a valuable effort; unfortunately, the intensity of theme is not supported by a grounded story.

Kirkus Reviews

SOURCE: A review of *David and Jonathan,* in *Kirkus Reviews,* Vol. LX, No. 7, April 1, 1992, p. 473.

A compelling triangle: Hank, 16, child of an upper-crust Bostonian and a penniless composer; his best friend Jonathan, whose mother, a Holocaust survivor, runs a restaurant with her husband; Jonathan's cousin David, 21, who leaves a psychiatric hospital to live with Jonathan's family in a last hope of alleviating his depression. All three are gifted; in an opening episode, Hank—now a surgeon—must operate on critically wounded Jonathan (Ph.D. in linguistics) in Vietnam; David, having proven unable to face his past or his talents, is dead. Flashing back, the book develops the relationships of the boys' youth—Hank's hurt at Jonathan's apparent coldness after David arrives, David's cruel needling as he acts out his angst, Jonathan's admission to Hank that he's sticking close to David to prevent his suicide. Enlisted in the effort (which nonetheless fails), Hank does give Jonathan the courage to go on. In the concluding Vietnam episode, Jonathan survives, though he's lost an eye: again, Hank has "limited the damage."

Though these characters don't have the warmth that enthralls readers of the Dicey books, the boys' intellectual banter rings true, giving their anguished grappling with their emotions about their families, each other, and the horrors of the Holocaust special poignance. Even the rather shadowy parents are believable mixes of strengths and fallibilities, while Hank and Jonathan's vividly realized loyalties and affections carry them through the trauma of trying and failing to help David and of understanding the significance of their actions. Intelligent, thoughtful, and challenging.

Marcus Crouch

SOURCE: A review of *David and Jonathan,* in *The Junior Bookshelf,* Vol. 57, No. 1, February, 1993, p. 38.

Cynthia Voigt's long and closely argued novel is about love and friendship, sex, religion and the nature of truth. In a word, it is highly serious. It is equally highly readable, involving the reader, and not exclusively the young reader, in its tragic events.

Within the framework of the Vietnam War, represented by prologue and epilogue, we are introduced to the Nafiche family, American Jews, and their Gentile friend Henry. Henry, despite his *Mayflower* blood, is an ordinary fellow, bright but not by the standards of his great friend Jon, whose intellect sparkles out of every word he says. This in no way impairs their friendship. What immediately threatens it is the arrival of David. David is a cousin of the Nafiches, a survivor, it seems, of the death camps, and Jonathan's father, ashamed of being alive and living in comfort, offers the young man a home and a family. David is beautiful, bitter, ruthless. He imposes his will on the young people, destroying the friendship between Jon and Henry while awakening Henry's latent homosexuality. (I simplify and abridge the story intolerably.) The scene is set for tragedy, and it is a tragedy which will scar the survivors for life.

Although this is a novel of ideas, it is also, and more importantly, a novel of character. Whether or not David's story is true, his fate is controlled by his own nature. All the other characters are complex, and the action comes out of the interaction of their personalities. There are some finely drawn full-length portraits, and even minor characters (in terms of their part in the story)—Henry's superior mother, the lovely warm-hearted Mrs. Nafiche, who married her husband to escape from Nazi Germany and lived fairly happily ever after—are far more than sketches. There is keen observation here as well as deep understanding, and much wisdom in the interpretation of the dilemma in a sad, haunting story. There is much fun too. Even the grimness of the last pages is masked with laughter.

ORFE (1992)

Betsy Hearne

SOURCE: A review of *Orfe,* in *Bulletin of the Center for Children's Books,* Vol. 46, No. 3, November, 1992, p. 92.

Orfe is a flame-haired, musically talented, childhood friend of the narrator, who recounts the tragedy—with shades of Orpheus and Eurydice—of Orfe's love for a drug addict named Yuri, beautiful in all ways except for his habit. Orfe gains her first audience by vomiting onstage at every chorus of a punk rock song called "Current Events." Then she finds brief happiness with her own band, managed by the narrator, and with Yuri; but he is fed drugged icing on a cake at his and Orfe's wedding, whereupon he disappears with the evil inhabitants of his past and Orfe is killed when an ersatz performing stage collapses. Aside from melodrama, one of the basic problems here is that, while we are told repeatedly what a genius Orfe is, we never get a real sense of her music aside from her being able to throw up on cue. She mostly stands with her head bent in a too characteristic pose while her friends do a lot of talking; even the moments after Yuri's contrivedly dramatic abduction are filled with talky philosophy. When the characters are not delivering messages, they are often inarticulate ("'I think,' Orfe said, 'that love is like being alive, in this respect, or peace too. Yeah, all three of them have the quality of—you never feel as if there has been enough"). If we are to believe Yuri's frequently emphasized devotion to Orfe, and the fact that he's had the perseverance to shake his habit, it becomes unbelievable that he doesn't follow her out of the drug den when she goes in after him. The redeeming feature in all this is the narrator, Enny, a solidly realized character whose experiences as a young child, defended at school by a fierce friend, are credibly rendered and moving. Despite several time transitions that seem purposefully jarring and therefore pretentious, Enny gets the story told with some real presence.

David Sacks

SOURCE: "A Lyre of the First Magnitude," in *The New York Times Book Review*, November 8, 1992, p. 48.

Cynthia Voigt's young-adult novel *Orfe* successfully modernizes the Orpheus legend, turning it into a moralistic tale of an American folk-rock singer who loses her husband to his drug addiction. . . .

The traditional Orpheus story describes the struggle between culture and savagery. Orpheus was from Thrace, the non-Greek north Aegean coast and interior. The young man's miraculous singing and lyre playing could charm brutish Thracians, wild beasts and even trees and stones; he was said to have founded the mystical Greek religious creed called Orphism. Like Apollo or the hero Asclepius, Orpheus was imagined as someone who had brought civilizing gifts to humanity.

But art can transform humans only so far, and even Orpheus could not subdue death. After his beloved bride, Eurydice, was bitten by a snake and died, Orpheus journeyed to the underworld to plead for her release. The god Hades allowed him to lead Eurydice away, on condition that Orpheus not look back at her until they reached the upper world. The anxious husband did look back, of course, thus losing his wife forever. Eventually, the grieving Orpheus was torn to pieces by a mob of reveler who (in some versions) resented his neglect of the riotous wine god, Dionysus, The Orpheus legend has inspired works like Tennessee Williams's *Orpheus Descending* and Marcel Camus's *Black Orpheus*.

Ms. Voigt, the author of *A Solitary Blue, Dicey's Song* and other well-received young-adult novels, emphasizes music as an ennobling force. Orfe is a gifted singer-songwriter-guitarist whose music and personality have the power to inspire those around her—especially Enny, who is Orfe's manager and the novel's narrator. Enny's accomplishment as a business school student and liberated woman are due in part to Orfe's confidence-building influence back in grade school. In a fine opening chapter,

the novel introduces the mystical Orfe as a child: "Orfe would bow her head and her eyes would fill up with what she was feeling so that when she raised her face . . . whatever she was feeling was loosed, full force, out of her eyes."

The plot traces Orfe's brief career and accidental death. With her visionary songwriting and her band (it goes by the Apollonian name of Orfe and the Graces), she becomes a sensation in the unnamed city of the story and marries the ethereal dreamboat Yuri.

But then, when Yuri relapses into drug use, Orfe must follow him to a notorious house filled with Dionysian druggies, where she performs her songs and wheedles for his release. Ms. Voigt skillfully handles this climactic scene, making it atmospheric but not graphic. In this version, the failure of the rescue is Yuri's fault.

The author's equation of the drug den with the mythical House of Hades is part of a larger moral message that extends to disapproval of punk rock, heavy metal and other musical forms identified as destructive. "Three words, that's about the extent of the lyrics they knew," someone says, describing a band, not Orfe's. "The S-word, the F-word, the H-word." The H-word? "Hate." Although flawed by occasional naivete in tone and fuzziness of detail (it wouldn't have hurt for Ms. Voigt to say directly that Yuri is a crack addict), *Orfe* has much to recommend it."

Ellen Fader

SOURCE: A review of *Orfe,* in *The Horn Book Magazine,* Vol. LXVIII, No. 6, November-December, 1992, pp. 731-32.

A chance encounter reunites Orfe and Enny, grade-school best friends. Orfe's life is her music, and Enny, in spite of her own life as a full-time college student, agrees to be her manager. Orfe's band, the Graces, begins to achieve some fame; but when Orfe and Yuri, a recovering addict, decide to marry, everything changes. During what appears to be a perfect wedding, Yuri wanders off after eating a piece of cake spiked with drugs. Orfe's attempt to use her music to rescue her husband from the drug underworld of his former housemates, who had brought the cake to the wedding, fails. Some time later, when Orfe and the Graces are performing at a college gym, the bleachers collapse, and Orfe dies, leaving her friends debating whether a love story must end happily. Says Enny, "'Love stories aren't about how they end.'" This is an unusual love story, given depth by Voigt's great skill in characterization and by its parallels to the Greek myth on which it is based. Although some young readers may feel betrayed by having the most interesting character killed, there is nevertheless much to ponder. Because of its many flashbacks, the novel requires a certain sophistication; in addition, the story's content, with its glimpses into the sometimes seamy subculture of rock music and drugs, will appeal most to the mature reader.

Marcia Hupp

SOURCE: A review of *Orfe,* in *School Library Journal,* Vol. 38, No. 12, December, 1992, pp. 133-34.

Like their mythological namesakes Orpheus and Eurydice, Orfe and Yuri are lovers. Orfe, in this case the female of the pair, is a singer/songwriter (rock) of spellbinding power, Yuri a recovering addict who succumbs to his weakness on the very day of their wedding. The narrator, Enny, begins Orfe's tale by recounting their school days, when "the new girl" strides into her bleak life to become her best friend. Like Sylvia Cassedy's Polly (*M. E. and Morton*) and other heroines of the meek and the downtrodden, Orfe commands the respect of her peers by the sheer outrageousness of her behavior (most effectively, a talent for vomiting at will). As her protégé, Enny ceases to be the brunt of their classmates' cruelty. And, up to this point, the book holds promise. Then the scene shifts to the present, where a grown and confident Enny discovers her friend singing on a street corner and becomes involved in the shaping of her career. As Orfe rises to the brink of musical success (from the depths of a heavy-metal band that exploits her projectile vomiting), allusions to Yuri find their way into the narrative, though readers never actually meet him or learn his story until the tragedy of their romance has been revealed. There are lighter moments to the tale, but its overwhelming tone is one of darkness and despair. As a character, Orfe never justifies her early promise, nor, for that matter, Enny's devotion. Characterizations, in general, are disappointingly flat and unconvincing. The style is awkward and ponderous, sentence structure often clumsy, transitions often abrupt. The plot is unfocused, undirected, and, generally, uninvolving. A firmer hand might have made this more successful; a lighter touch might have made it more palatable. Voigt is more than capable of both.

Marcus Crouch

SOURCE: A review of *Orfe,* in *The Junior Bookshelf,* Vol. 57, No. 6, December, 1993, pp. 247-48.

Cynthia Voigt's new novel is rather briefer than usual but by no means trivial. Its mood is dark and brooding, its form allegorical, using an ancient myth to shed a fitful light in the dark places of the modern world.

From her first day in school Orfe's posture is characteristic, head bent, face hidden. 'The Creature from Outer Space,' Frannie calls her, and as Queen of the class Frannie tends to have her way. But Orfe has no way to have. She is content to live within herself and within the songs she writes and sings. Enny, who is her only friend in school, rediscovers Orfe when she is a student and Orfe sings for coppers in the streets. When Orfe and her colleagues form a group Enny becomes their manager, and for a time all goes well—but with always a sense of disaster impending. Orfe falls in love, and her lover, Yuri, is doomed to tragedy. When Yuri is snatched from her and taken back into the Hell of the drug-damned, Orfe

takes her guitar and follows him, like her mythological namesake, into the underworld. It is Yuri who looks back as she leads him to salvation and is lost to her. There is not much life left for Orfe, but she has the strength her lover lacks. She is free of the delusion that 'life is never going to hurt.'

A sad, bitter love-story, told with great restraint and with a quiet intensity which demands the reader's total surrender. The scene may be America and the world of drugs, the meaning is universal. Perhaps after all it is Enny's story as much as it is Orfe's. She is no passive observer of the tragedy. 'I know that Orfe and Yuri radiated a sense of loving that I can still warm my hands at, if I close my eyes and remember.'

THE WINGS OF A FALCON (1993)

Publishers Weekly

SOURCE: A review of *The Wings of a Falcon,* in *Publishers Weekly,* Vol. 240, No. 26, June 28, 1993, p. 79.

Newbery Medalist Voigt just gets better and better. While her remarkable range extends from romantic comedy (the adult novel *The Glass Mountain*) to urban tragedy (*Orfe*), she returns in this work to the fantasy sequence begun in *Jackaroo* and *On Fortune's Wheel,* spinning an episodic tale certain to entrance readers. Two boys become friends as they are raised under the complexly evil Damall's regime on an isolated island in a legendary time; they escape, embarking on a series of adventures that involve armies, fabled marauders known as Wolfers, the beautiful daughter of an earl whose hand can be won only through a death-dealing tournament, a mysteriously engraved gemstone. All the hallmarks of classic fantasy appear, transformed by Voigt's gift for storytelling and the effortless beauty of her prose—and by the superb intelligence she endows upon her characters. Each section of this novel is riveting, mined with powerful surprises. Voigt's themes reverberate beyond the fantasy world; her explorations through imaginary landscapes parallel a psychic journey through questions of identity, ethics, friendship and love. A model for the genre.

Kirkus Reviews

SOURCE: A review of *The Wings of a Falcon,* in *Kirkus Reviews,* Vol. LXI, No. 15, August 1, 1993, p. 1009.

In the mythical land of *Jackaroo,* another long tale crowded with action and driven by its themes, with well-individualized characters carefully devised to enact them. Slaves Oriel and his loyal friend Griff are reared by the brutal Damall in his island stronghold. Courageous and quick-witted, Oriel survives this vicious society's intricacies of betrayal and trust to be chosen the Damall's heir, a role he evades by fleeing. He and Griff settle near the mainland town of Selby—an oasis in an endless, bloody war of succession—where they persuade the people to give up their divisive allegiances and choose leaders to rule in concert. Then, still in their teens, the two are captured by Wolfers—lawless predators whose cruel abuse they escape to enter the Kingdom to the north, where an earldom is to be won in mortal combat. Oriel's rare gifts bear fruit when he persuades several fine contenders to support one of their number, preventing a wasteful carnage—but the outcome is not so simple. A betrayal transforms the political landscape; and power falls, surprisingly, to a wise and compassionate man who has never imagined himself a leader. Voigt skillfully sustains a heroic tone while challenging heroic models at every turn. In scene after scene, Oriel confronts the terrible choices men demand of each other with nobility and charismatic élan; but this superhero also has a true sense of justice and strives for a rule of law that is tempered, in the end, with more mercy than he has envisaged. Grand, thought-provoking entertainment.

Roger Sutton

SOURCE: A review of *The Wings of a Falcon,* in *Bulletin of the Center for Children's Books,* Vol. 47, No. 1, September, 1993, pp. 25-6.

Third and last in Voigt's Jackaroo series of medieval adventures, this lengthy entry takes Oriel and his ever-loyal friend Griff from childhood enslavement on an island of lost boys run by a sadistic master, to, eventually, a contest for the hand of the lady Merlis and the lands of her father, the King of the Kingdom. While some of the individual scenes here, such as the cruel life on the island and a later journey when the boys are captives of the ferocious Wolfers, have drama, most of the book is static, preferring belabored conversation to action, and the style is unremittingly verbose. "'I say no more,' the Innkeeper said. He said no more." (He's also no he, a complication that doesn't do anything for the novel as a whole.) Because Voigt gives each scene and occurrence the same degree of overattention, the book becomes monotonous, and it's difficult to pick out the significant events from the background. It's too bad, because Voigt casts a cool eye on some of the cliches of fantasy heroics. Oriel, for example, is often as insufferable a hero as his namesake in *On Fortune's Wheel.* But the book is far too long and nigh impossible to follow.

Susan L. Rogers

SOURCE: A review of *The Wings of a Falcon,* in *School Library Journal,* Vol. 30, No. 10, October, 1993, p. 156.

A wonderful, terrible, epic tale of heroism and cowardice, loyalty and betrayal, love and loss, joy and tragedy. Having escaped the harsh life on an island inhabited exclusively by boys abandoned or sold to the Damall, Oriel and his ever-loyal friend and follower, Griff, travel through unknown lands, followed by a three-year stay as journeymen to a saltweller. Then the Wolfers come, barbarian invaders from the north who destroy everything in their path. Oriel and Griff are taken prisoner and spend the next year on the run with them, until escape into the far mountains leads them finally to the farm of Beryl, puppeteer and herbalist (and granddaughter of Orien and Birle of *On Fortune's Wheel,* great-great-granddaughter of Burl and Gwyn of *Jackaroo.* After a season of healing, the trio devise a plan for Oriel to try his luck in a contest for the title, lands, and lady of the Earl of Sutherland. Be aware that this third novel is longer, harsher, and filled with mature themes before it reaches its satisfying conclusion. In the same way that Voigt's books about the Tillermans look at different members and generations of a family in ways that reinforce one another to form a coherent, many-volumed whole, these three books are tightly connected. Each volume stands on its own, but together they create a tapestry more complex, meaningful, and compelling than its individual parts. The story could end here, but hopefully there will be further sequels added to this fascinating saga.

Libby Bergstrom

SOURCE: A review of *The Wings of a Falcon,* in *Voice of Youth Advocates,* Vol. 16, No. 5, December, 1993, p. 314.

He doesn't know his name, but he knows how to survive, and he knows that he is meant to be a leader. He doesn't remember his life before he came to the Damall's island, but he knows that he is the best of the boys, the one most capable to be the next Damall, owner of the island and master of the boys who live there. He grows up under the sixth Damall's unrelenting cruelty, but does not become cruel himself. Rather than kill Nikol, his rival as heir, when the sixth Damall dies, the boy escapes from the island, taking with him Griff, his only friend. He also takes most of the island's treasure—gold and silver and one precious beryl stone, leaving enough to provide for the other boys. He starts his new life by choosing his own name: Oriel.

Oriel works as a journeyman to a saltweller, is captured by barbarian Wolfers, and becomes lover to Beryl, the puppeteer who lives on the edge of the kingdom. Finally, he joins the contest to become the Earl Sutherland, and is again faced with the need to kill in order to gain the title he desires. Through all of these adventures, Griff is in the background as Oriel's ever-present friend, follower, and the one who helps him make his choices. In the end, this is as much Griff's story as Oriel's, for Oriel makes a choice that thrusts Griff into a leadership role he never desired. But Griff proves that once again, Oriel's choice was the right one.

The Wings of a Falcon is third in the loosely related series which includes *Jackaroo* and *On Fortune's Wheel.* Allusions to the earlier stories are sprinkled throughout this one, but this volume easily stands on its own. Oriel's story allows Voigt to explore how people survive in the face of overwhelming cruelty and yet maintain integrity. This book can be difficult to read, with its gut-wrenching violence that will affect even those desensitized by TV and movies. It is the portrayals of Oriel's courage to choose what is right over his own desires and of Griff's wisdom that will stay with readers. This engrossing story is recommended for all fantasy and adventure readers.

WHEN SHE HOLLERS (1994)

Merri Monks

SOURCE: A review of *When She Hollers,* in *Booklist,* Vol. 91, No. 4, October 15, 1994, pp. 420-21.

Voigt's searing portrait of a teenage incest victim tells of one day in the life of 17-year-old Tish, who has been raped by her stepfather. At a breaking point, Tish threatens him with a knife at the breakfast table, screams uncontrollably in her afternoon gym class, and, finally, walks through the walls of silence and denial when she tells a lawyer, her classmate's father, the truth. The author accurately portrays both the girl's chaotic emotional life and her mental disorientation. Also well delineated is Tish's dissociation and chronic shame. As Tish makes her way through her day, she must constantly negotiate with people in her environment as well as with her own shattered and unpredictable psyche so that no one can guess her terrible secret. Yet armed with knowledge and the beginnings of trust in both herself and her lawyer, at the novel's end she faces not only her stepfather, but also the consequences of telling the truth, thus transforming herself from victim to survivor. Voigt is unsparing in depicting the ruination of a teenage girl's life. Unlike several other young adult novels about incest, this one is told in strong language from the victim's point of view. Its resulting immediacy is harrowing.

Carolyn Polese

SOURCE: A review of *When She Hollers,* in *School Library Journal,* Vol. 40, No. 11, November, 1994, p. 122.

With the first sentence of this searingly honest novel, readers are plunged into the consciousness of a teenage girl who is fighting for her life. Tish's adversary isn't disease or physical injury; instead, it is the devastation of ongoing sexual abuse. The novel spans one day, from the moment at breakfast when she warns her stepfather to stay away from her, to the realization—in the late afternoon—that she can escape his domination. In between, readers travel with Tish through her day in high school, experiencing her rage, helplessness, and blistering humor. Readers who want to go beyond the current headlines will get an accurate and unforgettable picture of domestic tyranny. Nowhere in children's literature is the link between abuse and violence (including teenage suicide) so clearly delineated, nor the mind-bending effects of dissociative defenses so accurately portrayed. Voigt wisely stays away from depictions of the abuse itself. Nonetheless, this book is strong stuff, best read by emotionally mature readers. Be sure to tell guidance counselors about this novel, which contains crucial insights into abusive relationships. The most important of these is Tish's epiphany in which she realizes that her stepfather's power, while nearly absolute at home, is limited to a relatively tiny sphere. She discovers a doorway to the rest of the world and with it her own liberation. This groundbreaking book—like its protagonist—is raw, courageous, and a winner.

Maeve Visser Knoth

SOURCE: A review of *When She Hollers,* in *The Horn Book Magazine,* Vol. LXXI, No. 1, January-February, 1995, pp. 64-5.

In an intense, powerful novel, Cynthia Voigt explores what happens when a teenage victim of sexual abuse decides to no longer be a victim. Tish is a high school student who has endured abuse from her stepfather since she was a small child. In the opening sentence of a novel in which all the action is packed into one seemingly endless day, Tish places a knife on the breakfast table in front of her stepfather and mother and declares, "'From now on . . . I'll have this knife. . . . All the time.'" Unlike the many novels in which victims of abuse find the strength to tell a sympathetic adult, Tish takes responsibility for her own survival. She confronts her stepfather, watches while her mother shuts out what is happening in her own home, and sets off for school afraid ever to return because she is sure that either she will use the knife or the abuse will continue. As the day passes, the reader learns that a schoolmate recently hanged herself when she discovered that she, another victim of incest, was pregnant. Tish's knife is in part a response to that desperate act. The novel is relentless. Voigt tells her story with short sentences and thought fragments, mirroring Tish's emotional disintegration. After a breakdown at school, during which Tish sees the ineffectuality of the adults around her, she runs away and wanders through town. Unable to go home because that would prove that her stepfather was right, that she could never change anything, Tish reluctantly visits a classmate's father, a lawyer. She will not speak to him or accuse her stepfather, but she does write down what has happened to her. With a lawyer on her side, a knife, and hope, Tish goes home. This is not an easy book to read nor an easy one to recommend to an adolescent. There is no happy ending. Instead, a young woman realizes that she "shouldn't be ashamed not to be dead" and takes the only control over the situation that she can find. Voigt's remarkable book may give some readers hope and may help others to understand why a victim of abuse might turn to violence.

Patty Campbell

SOURCE: "The Sand in the Oyster," in *The Horn Book Magazine,* Vol. LXXI, No. 1, January-February, 1995, pp. 94-8.

"She put the survival knife down on the table. It pointed across at him." These are the opening words of *When She Hollers,* Cynthia Voigt's devastating story of a young girl's desperate attempt to free herself from the trap of her stepfather's molestation. Tish has been brought to the breaking point by the suicide of Miranda, a girl pregnant by her own father, and she is tempted to take the same way out. Instead she buys a knife and works up the courage to confront her stepfather, Tonnie, with it at the breakfast table. But, appallingly, he says that he's not afraid of "'that silly knife.'" "Tish could have wept then. Because if he wasn't afraid, then she'd better be." After a violent scene, which is pointedly ignored by her mother and younger siblings, she goes off to school, knowing she must return in the evening to be the victim of his rage. The events of that day make up the novel, as her suffocating feelings of helplessness build into a turmoil that brings her to find some help at last, and to return with shaky bravery to confront the sadistic Tonnie.

Voigt's tightly controlled novel, told through the whirling images and lapses into unreality of Tish's tortured mind, is a small literary masterpiece from this already distinguished author. . . .

To evaluate the psychological and social veracity . . . , I asked two very different mental health professionals with a great deal of clinical experience in this area—psychiatrist Dr. Michael Johanek and psychological counselor Beverly Garrigues—to read *When She Hollers* and react. While they differed in their literary assessment, they agreed that the book, with the exception of one incident, was an accurate picture of the structure and dynamics of what counselors refer to as "molest cases."

Both professionals pointed out the strength of the depiction of the victim's mental state, a feature which I feel is one of its literary strong points as well. Voigt in *When She Hollers* describes Tish's sensations under duress: "She left the outside skin of herself where it was, but she detached from it," a pattern that began with her need to deny what is going on during the molestation. As Lena in [Jacqueline Woodson's] *I Hadn't Meant to Tell You This* says less elegantly, "'When my daddy's touching me, I take off, boom! and I'm gone.'" And Jen in [Chris Crutcher's] *Chinese Handcuffs* tells Dillon, "My body's there, but I perfected the art of mental evacuation long, long ago." Each day Tish comes to school with different clothes and a different attitude, so no one will know who she really is, and she protects herself fiercely from social intimacy, even with her boyfriend. Such behavior is a coping tool, says Ms. Garrigues; multiple personality disorder is an extreme form of this kind of dissociation.

More bizarrely, in the school cafeteria Tish's perceptions float to the ceiling, and she observes the tops of her friends' heads as they gossip about Miranda's suicide. The jagged rhythms of her mind are strikingly rendered by Voigt in a nightmarish passage in which Tish is running away from an imminent encounter with Tonnie at school: "Her Docs felt heavy. To lift. It seemed as if her feet stuck. To the cement walk like fly feet sticking to flypaper." She fears, with good reason, that she is going crazy. "The dissociation, emotional distance, and scattered thinking are classic," says Dr. Johanek.

The conspiracy of silence in the family is also typical,

both professionals explained. In the opening scene of *When She Hollers,* Tish slams a knife onto the breakfast table and screams threats at Tonnie, but her mother keeps on making toast, and her brothers and sister wrangle among themselves and watch television. Siblings learn to ignore "the elephant in the living room," says Ms. Garrigues. Mothers, even more so, are often committed to this silence. The typical molestation situation is "a triad, not a dyad," observes Dr. Johanek, and the mother, by lying to herself, is implicitly involved. Barbie, Tish's doll-like mother, has laid in a large supply of birth control pills, even though she is pregnant, and pretends that Tish is stealing them for liaisons with her boyfriend. The mother's complicity makes it impossible for her daughter to appeal to her for help, as Jen in *Chinese Handcuffs* learns when she tries to expose her stepfather and finds that "he had no trouble convincing my mom I was lying because she would have done anything to keep him." The daughter's need to protect her mother from the knowledge can also sustain the situation, as when Tish thinks, "If she told the truth . . . her mother would lose everything." And when she does try to tell her mother, Barbie says, "Stop it right now. . . . You can't just go around spreading lies like that, Tish." And so the molesting continues, because "that fear of spilling the secret is so ingrained," says Ms. Garrigues, a fear that is so deep that even when Tish wants desperately to tell Mr. Battle, the lawyer who is trying to help her, the words will not come out.

The offender's threats, too, are typically a powerful factor in keeping girls in the situation, says Ms. Garrigues. Jen's stepfather kills her dog to punish her for trying to tell, and threatens to extend the violence to the whole family if she persists, darkly intimating that he has done this before. Tonnie's threats to Tish are less specific but more menacing in the sinister force of his sadistic personality. His control lies in his ability to manipulate her mind: "Tonnie knew her inside and out, he knew how to make her do what he wanted. He knew what she was thinking and sometimes she even thought what he wanted." Both men are monsters, utterly inexplicable in their evil, but to society they appear to be fine upstanding fathers and husbands. As Dillon says in *Chinese Handcuffs,* "He's gotten away with this crap for so long because of the element of unbelievability; no one can *imagine* a regular, married, employed human being capable of such acts."

What psychological explanation can there be for the genesis of men like this? Dr. Johanek sees the roots of the problem in the fact that many sexual offenders have been sexually victimized and have experienced inconceivable brutality and neglect themselves as children. They are scarred with deep anger at the parent who failed to protect them—often the mother, because seventy-five per cent of molestees are abused by men. Ms. Garrigues theorizes that male sexual offenders have a rooted history of hatred for women and observes that they usually choose weak, dependent wives. They are extremely difficult to treat, she says, the rate of cure being proportionate to the degree of trauma they have suffered themselves. Most of those who are successfully treated are one-time offenders guilty only of borderline inappropriate behavior.

The one incident in **When She Hollers** that both Dr. Johanek and Ms. Garrigues identified as unlikely was the lawyer's action in sending Tish home to confront Tonnie alone, even though he knows she will probably have to try to kill him. Helping professionals—social workers, counselors, doctors, nurses, teachers—are under legal obligation to report molestations immediately by phone and within thirty-six hours in writing under the laws of many states. Chris Crutcher, himself a psychological counselor, is well aware of these laws, as can be seen when Dillon in *Chinese Handcuffs* is advised by a Child Protective Services worker that "the fine for failure to report is ten thousand dollars." A lawyer in such a situation would be obligated to call the authorities, even if it violated a client's confidences. But that is only true if the client is a minor. In **When She Hollers** Battle is careful to establish that he thinks Tish is over eighteen, and she, quickly catching on, confirms it. He armors her for the encounter by having her write down her accusations and leave them sealed with him, by extracting a promise that she will telephone him morning and evening, and by seeing that she understands that she must tell Tonnie that she has done these things.

And so off she goes to confront the monster in the house where the door bulges out with his fury behind it. She still has the knife, yes, but more important she has now the vision that Tonnie controls only a tiny piece of her world of possibilities. Clutching that knowledge like a weapon, she rings the doorbell, steps back and waits, and the door opens on one of the most heart-thumping scenes in YA literature. A scene that Voigt—infuriatingly, magnificently—has not written but has left up to us to imagine in all its possible variants of outcome.

Marcus Crouch

SOURCE: A review of *When She Hollers,* in *The Junior Bookshelf,* Vol. 59, No. 2, April, 1995, p. 83.

Like Sylvia Hall's *When You Can't Say No* the theme of Cynthia Voigt's new novel is sex-abuse, in this case the abuse of a young teenager by her stepfather. The situation in the two novels is very similar, the treatment very different. Ms Voigt takes as her starting-point a crisis in the affair, as Tish produces at the breakfast-table the knife which she has bought for her protection. It says much for the household that no one except Tish and her stepfather takes much notice. Mother has her own preoccupations, the children are wrapped up in their affairs. At school Tish meets with the same indifference. Her peculiar behaviour is met with a concern which stops short of understanding. No one wants to know. No one? Only Chrissie takes her dilemma seriously, and Chrissie is hardly even a friend. But Chrissie's father is a lawyer, and he knows how to listen. Tish engages him for a fee of one dollar. Now she can face Tonnie at the end of a long day, armed not with a knife but with a picture of the world on which Tonnie's house is one 'tiny little dot.'

It argues much for Ms Voigt's skill and understanding

that a story which consists largely of the inner thoughts of an inarticulate girl should be so tensely exciting as well as deeply moving. She allows Tish to draw her own portrait, one full of blemishes but with the strong lines of resistance dominant. Tish is maddening (one sympathises with her well-meaning and ineffectual teachers) but she is sustained by anger that Tonnie should want 'to take her whole life away from her.' She sees that 'there was more to her than what Tonnie had done.' So she rings her doorbell and runs away, not out of fear but to ensure that Tonnie must come out and face her in public. Tish is beautifully drawn, not least because she allows herself to see the element of farce in her tragedy. There are funny as well as distressing moments in her story. And Mr. Battle, solicitor extraordinary, is one of the most convincing adult characters in recent children's fiction. It would have been so easy to add some colourful caricature to his portrait, but here he is unadorned, sensible, humane, practical.

This is a compact, finely constructed narrative, one which gives a grim subject the serious treatment it demands, which wastes no words while setting the drama within a clearly seen setting of school and home. A master craftsman is at work here.

BAD GIRLS (1996)

Kirkus Reviews

SOURCE: A review of *Bad Girls,* in *Kirkus Reviews,* Vol. LXIV, No. 5, March 1, 1996, p. 381.

A distinguished writer is at the top of her form in a sharp and sassy tale of two fifth-grade troublemakers.

Thrown together by the alphabetical seating arrangement, Margalo Epps and Michelle "Mikey" Elsinger cautiously form an alliance that deepens into a stormy but firm friendship. Both are bright, tough, acerbic, and fond of stirring things up, but their differences really spark the relationship: Mikey is public and aggressive, willing to punch the class bully in the nose or dye her hair green, while Margalo prefers to start damaging rumors or slip a dead squirrel into a prissy offender's lunch. Voigt creates a set of complex, believable, still-developing characters, and parks them mostly in a brilliant, very experienced teacher's classroom to explore what makes them tick. The girls are motivated not by malice but general anger (Mikey) and loneliness (Margalo); most of their imaginative, carefully directed pranks are paybacks, less hurtful than horrifying and frequently hilarious. Unrepentant to the end, this pair of unlikable but admirably capable mavericks outmatch even Barbara Robinson's Herdman family for sheer sand.

Roger Sutton

SOURCE: A review of *Bad Girls,* in *Bulletin of the Center for Children's Books,* Vol. 49, No. 8, April, 1996, pp. 253-54.

With this book Cynthia Voigt has probably sewn up the

prize for the best come-on title of the year, and her two heroines thoroughly live up to the promise, if not in the way some readers might wish: these are *fifth-grade* bad girls.

Good girls—think of Lowry's Anastasia, Mills' Dinah, Naylor's Alice—are our friends. We watch them get into embarrassing situations, close scrapes and closer crushes, and we think, this could be me. Bad girls, though, get our attention. We don't want to be them, but we like to watch what they do. Which Sweet Valley Twin do you remember best? Not Elizabeth, forever mooning over Todd and dutifully turning in her articles for the school paper, but Jessica: mantrap, fashion plate, and saboteur. Voigt's bad girls, Margalo Epps and Mikey Elsinger, lack Jessica's chic, but they are still a dangerous, complementary pair. While feisty, hotheaded Mikey, ready to punch or kick at the slightest provocation, is don't-mess-with-me trouble, Margalo is another kind of bad girl—Machiavellian, you might say, or as Mikey puts it, "sneaky." Between them they make Mrs. Chemsky's fifth-grade classroom something akin to a war zone, with Margalo the general and Mikey the troops. They get Louis, the class clown and bully, kicked out of their class, and, with malice aforethought, get him back in ("Doesn't the expression on his face make you want to just punch him?" asks Mikey of Margalo. "'Actually,' Margalo said, 'it makes me want you to punch him'"). Margalo, unbeknownst to Mikey but in her honor, puts unpleasant surprises (such as a dead squirrel) in classmate Rhonda's lunch bag, and when Mikey finds out, she insists on sharing the blame. Sucker. This is after Margalo has betrayed Mikey by voting for someone else instead of her for class president. Mikey knows; she peeked.

Voigt is a lot harder on—and truer to—the cliques, bullies, and shifting alliances of fifth-grade society than most writers, who put the tempest in the teapot and then turn off the stove. Her story is loud, angry, and jostling—sometimes to the point of incoherence but always with the undeniable smell of fifth grade. The focus is obsessively on the school, never leaving the classroom or playground (or principal's office). Small hints, such as what the girls bring for lunch each day, give glimpses of what life is like at home for the two troublemakers, but there's no indication that Margalo and Mikey are any worse off than their classmates. Bad girls—in children's books, anyway—are more often misunderstood girls (think of Harriet the Spy), but Voigt doesn't let her girls that easily off the hook. And she gives her bad girls exactly what they want: attention. Where most books (think of any number of middle-grade stories about girls in cliques) vanquish the bully (or, more often, her bullishness) and send her to the sidelines, these girls stay at the center, unrepentant. Even in detention, where Margalo is writing lines on the blackboard and Mikey scrubbing desks, they're causing trouble. Mikey strategically cleans graffiti so it reads "you stink," and Margalo, her ever-busy brain at work, gets new inspiration from her punishment: "'Fifty-one. I will not start rumors,' but she didn't put a period. Instead, she finished the sentence, 'about Ann Tarwell going to the movies with Noah Obbink.' Then she erased back, put in

the period and wrote, 'Fifty-two. I will not start rumors,' while she thought about what other rumors she wouldn't start." We'll see about that.

Do we like these girls? Well, kids might feel a sort of rough affection for Mikey, but any reader with a brain in her head is going to be afraid of Margalo, even while sensing her loneliness and envying her power. You want to keep an eye on those sneaky ones, and we're glad Voigt is here to do it for us.

Hazel Rochman

SOURCE: A review of *Bad Girls,* in *Booklist,* Vol. 92, No. 15, April 1, 1996, p. 1366.

In her landmark YA novel **The Runner,** Voigt tells her story from the viewpoint of a proud, solitary teenage boy; here, her strong, mean outsiders are female, younger, and funny. Michelle ("Mikey") acts mean and dangerous (Why should boys be the only ones to have fistfights or play soccer or be class president?); Margalo pretends to be nice, but she's a tricky liar. When the two girls meet in Mrs. Chemsky's fifth-grade class they circle each other, slowly becoming friends, outlaws together. Voigt has written a fast-talking classroom comedy that mocks traditional gender roles. Sugar and spice are out. Being "nice" is the worst insult. Meanness is what gets you respect. Teasing keeps you on top; so does revenge, the grosser the better. The story is told almost entirely in dialogue, much like a TV movie, and set entirely at school—the classroom, playground, girls' bathroom, principal's office. It's hard at times to know whom "she" refers to, since the viewpoint keeps switching between Mikey and Margalo and, occasionally, jumps to the smart, bossy teacher; then there are the 28 other class members to keep straight: the various bullies, the Gap girls, the smart student, etc. But the talk is very funny (Mikey had leadership, "just nobody would want to follow her"); the action is nonstop; and the confrontations are dramatic, both verbal and physical. Voigt gets the querulous, jumpy, obsessive talk, the glimpses of civilization in the fifth-grade jungle, as the friends struggle for both loyalty and independence. There's so much attitude, but there's also failure, and readers will recognize the fact that meanness can be about anger and misery as well as glorious mischief.

Mary Jo Drungil

SOURCE: A review of *Bad Girls,* in *School Library Journal,* Vol. 42, No. 5, May, 1996, p. 116.

Mikey Elsinger and Margalo Epps meet in Mrs. Chemsky's fifth grade class. Both are new to Washington Street Elementary, and both have a knack for stirring up trouble. Their methods are different. Loud, aggressive Mikey will do anything to get her own way. Calm, devious Margalo enjoys starting rumors and playing mind games. Together the girls are responsible for a number of dramatic scenes, in which Mikey is always a central figure. Margalo stands up for her in front of their often-hostile classmates, but neither girl quite trusts the other, and they often argue. Then, when Margalo's sneaky pranks catch up to her, Mikey refuses to let her friend be punished alone. This act cements their bond; at last, the two are ready to expand their relationship beyond the school setting, where is has developed, to real life. But herein lies the narrative's weakness. The inference is that both girls lack attention at home. But since the action is set exclusively at school, readers never learn just what experiences have shaped them into their present selves. This frustrating lack of background information prevents youngsters from fully understanding the characters. However, it is clear that they will continue to revel in the sheer delight of being "bad girls." Rarely does a novel set in elementary school celebrate the fierce joy that "troublemakers" derive from successfully manipulating the personalities and situations around them. Readers who follow the rules in reality will find a vicarious thrill in experiencing life through Mikey and Margalo's eyes.

Lois Metzger

SOURCE: A review of *Bad Girls,* in *The New York Times Book Review,* June 30, 1996, p. 27.

Mrs. Chemsky, a teacher at Washington Street Elementary School, looks at two new girls who appear perfectly nice and perfectly ordinary—Michelle (Mikey) Elsinger, "sort of round and thick," and Margalo Epps, "sort of straight and thin"—and wonders, "How bad can two fifth-grade girls be?"

It's also the question Cynthia Voigt, well known for novels on serious, powerful issues, tackles in her funny, insightful and unusually playful *Bad Girls.* Ms. Voigt . . . sets her 21st book for young readers entirely at school, in an unnamed town, starting and ending in that brief settling-down period from early September to early October. She becomes a kind of Margaret Mead of the fifth grade—charting its intricate meanness, especially the turbulent, symbiotic teaming up of Mikey and Margalo, brought together only because of alphabetically arranged seating.

Mikey is the type who, when angry—as she is, almost always—tends to punch Louis Caselli, the class bully, in the nose. Margalo, who knows she seems like a secretary but wants to be the boss, is intuitive, manipulative. ("I have good radar," Margalo says. "I do know how to figure people out.") Cleverly, brilliantly, Margalo, without giving herself away, gets Louis Caselli transferred into another class and then reinstated—showing off to Mikey "who's really in charge."

Still, there's bad and there's bad, and Ms. Voigt carefully draws distinctions. "You're mean," Mikey tells Margalo during one of their many arguments, and Margalo replies, "But not in a mean way." Their real concern is in finding their way, and in learning about trust, betrayal and kindness as much as meanness. Only one fifth grader is mean in a mean way—the girl with the prettiest hair, Rhonda

Ransom, who talks with her hand over her heart to display sincerity. Rhonda maliciously ruins Mikey's chances to be elected class president. Not long after, Margalo places a dead squirrel in Rhonda's lunch bag and then publicly confesses to the crime. Even in the office of Mr. Delaney, the principal, Margalo is unrepentant, proudly explaining that of two run-over squirrels she'd found, she chose "the most squished." In vain Mr. Delaney tries getting Margalo to show remorse. "Rhonda does stink," Margalo says. "What she did stinks."

Mikey's right there, too, beside Margalo, insisting she was an accomplice even though she wasn't. Ms. Voigt, who allows the book to be complicated, isn't condemning or condoning, and the class, along with Mr. Delaney and Mrs. Chemsky, isn't sure whether or not to turn on Margalo and Mikey. Shy, brainy Hadrian Klenk tells them that the other kids (referred to as "go-alongs," and perfectly nice, perfectly ordinary) are afraid, deep-down afraid, "that they'll turn out to be—wrong, about everything."

But the book's grab-it-off-the-shelf title and topic compete with a leave-it-on-the-shelf length; the pivotal story about Rhonda and the roadkill takes almost 200 pages to get to. A shorter book would have produced a tighter, more focused journey to a lovely ending, when Mikey and Margalo realize who they are—each other's best friend. Mikey, said to have "a whole closetful of smiles, one for every occasion" (including a Nutrasweet smile, a snarly smile and smiles that say, "I'm one of a kind," "Eat prunes" and "Can you take the truth?"), finds herself smiling "as if Margalo was a puppy in a box" and Mikey got to take her home. As for Margalo, she smiles at Mikey "as if she had been swimming for hours from a capsized canoe, and there was the shore, she could see it, and now she knew she'd make it."

BAD, BADDER, BADDEST (1997)

Kirkus Reviews

SOURCE: A review of *Bad, Badder, Baddest,* in *Kirkus Reviews,* Vol. LXV, No. 21, November 1, 1997, p. 1650.

Fresh from their debut (**Bad Girls,** 1996), sixth-graders Mikey and Margalo cement their gloriously improbable friendship in a painful—sometimes side-splitting—effort to save Mikey's parents' marriage. It's far too late, but with the help of her spectacularly devious and manipulative friend, Mikey gives it her best; she cleans her room, goes with her mother to the mall and with her father to play miniature golf, accompanies them to a marriage counselor, and, when all that fails, runs away for a weekend. Meanwhile, she and Margalo meet their match in new classmate Gianette, who passes herself off as a New Orleans witch-in-training and turns out to be not only an expert thief and blackmailer, but part of a "child for hire" welfare fraud scheme as well. Voigt uses nearly every sentence and incident to make a point, but readers will never feel as if they're being lectured, and the complex give-and-take between Mikey and Margalo makes for plenty of funny repartee, as well as insights into themselves, other people, and life in general. A rich, entertaining episode featuring a pair of Voigt's most memorable characters since the Tillermans.

Deborah Stevenson

SOURCE: A review of *Bad, Badder, Baddest,* in *Bulletin of the Center for Children's Books,* Vol. 51, No. 4, December, 1997, p. 142.

Mikey and Margalo, heroines of ***Bad Girls*** are even badder than Dennis Rodman wants to be, and in this volume their badness gets put in a larger context as we see their lives out of school for the first time. In fact there's very little school activity at all here—we're mostly focusing on Mikey's deteriorating family life (her hard-edged, high-powered mother has had enough of Mikey's unexceptional father) and Margalo's contrastingly eccentric but sound home (her mother's on a happy third marriage, and a gaggle of stepchildren, not just from this marriage, share the house with Margalo). Mikey insists that Margalo help her keep her parents together, and the two master manipulators try everything they can (Mikey even temporarily becomes her mother's perfect daughter, and they shop for training bras at the mall) to achieve Mikey's end. The introduction of Gianette, an exotic interloper who shows signs of being criminally bad in a way Mikey and Margalo have no real interest in, provides for some interesting scenes and contrasts, but ultimately what readers want is Mikey and Margalo themselves. And there's plenty of them here, fighting, uniting, planning, self-analyzing, and pulling strings—but they're ultimately the puppets of adult whim. There's a Louise Fitzhugh flair to this installment, with its adults in a separate and often self-absorbed world, and many young readers may well consider the pair's machinations merely a form of self-defense.

Additional coverage of Voigt's life and career is contained in the following sources published by Gale Research: *Authors and Artists for Young Adults,* Vol. 3; *Contemporary Authors New Revision Series,* Vol. 40; *Junior DISCovering Authors (CD-ROM); Major Authors and Illustrators for Children and Young Adults;* and *Something about the Author,* Vols. 48, 79.

Barbara Williams

1925-

American author of fiction, nonfiction, and plays.

Major works include *Albert's Toothache* (1974), *Kevin's Grandma* (1975), *Someday, Said Mitchell* (1976), *Chester Chipmunk's Thanksgiving* (1978), *Jeremy Isn't Hungry* (1978).

INTRODUCTION

Williams is best known for her stories for primary- and middle-graders that focus on the relationships between children and other family members while exploring issues such as sibling rivalry and family misunderstandings. Williams's works have been commended for their humorous and authentic presentation of the perspectives of young people who are trying to discover their place in the family. Many of the thoughts and feelings that Williams attempts to capture in her books are based on her personal experiences with her four adopted children or on recollections from her own childhood. *Albert's Toothache,* for instance, one of Williams's best-loved books, has been praised for its exploration of the problems that can arise when parents and children have difficulty communicating.

Biographical Information

Williams was born in 1925 in Salt Lake City, Utah. Nicknamed "Bea," she was the youngest of Walter and Emily Wright's five children. Born when her parents were in their forties, Williams never knew her grandparents and says her longing for them inspired two of her most popular books, *Kevin's Grandma* and *Albert's Toothache,* both of which illustrate the importance of grandparents in the lives of children. Williams' parents and teachers encouraged her writing from an early age. Before she knew the alphabet, Williams would sit on the floor while her mother ironed, "write" in a notebook and then "read" her stories to her mother. In kindergarten, she was chosen classroom reporter for the *Salt Lake Tribune,* which published a section for children called "School News and Views." Williams says the editor of the section, Olive Woolley Burt, later became her role model. Williams wrote for the newspaper through most of grade school and was eventually elected school editor. She began appearing on Burt's weekly radio show and contributing to the *Tribune's* Sunday supplement, *Tribune Junior,* which published stories, poems and articles written by children from throughout Utah. The supplement ceased publication when Williams was twelve, but Burt selected one of Williams's stories for inclusion in the regular newspaper and Williams received a check for $1.50. Her father asked the newspaper treasurer to return the canceled check, which Williams describes as the "first tangible evidence that I might someday become a professional writer."

Writing was not Williams's only interest. Her father was a lawyer and she considered becoming a courtroom attorney. She also loved acting and planned to have a large family. After high school, Williams enrolled in the University of Utah, where she studied English and took as many theater classes as she could schedule. A job in her father's law office the summer after her freshman year convinced her that law was not the "glamorous profession" she had envisioned. In 1946, two months after graduation, she married J. D. (John Daniel) Williams, her boyfriend since junior high. They moved to Washington, D.C., where J. D. had been hired as a researcher at the Library of Congress. Williams says that as a woman, even with a college degree, her career options were restricted. She accepted a position as a clerk-typist in the Music Division of the Library of Congress and looked forward to starting a family. In 1948, J. D. enrolled in the Ph.D. program at Harvard and the couple moved to Massachusetts, where Williams continued her clerical work. By then, tests had shown the two could not have children. Frustrated in both her career and family goals, Williams became depressed. Her one distraction was a night class in creative writing. With her father's gift of $1,000, Williams applied to Boston University's graduate school and was accepted in the creative writing program. However, the couple's educational funding ran out before they could complete their degree requirements, so they returned to Washington, where J. D. resumed his job at the Library of Congress and worked on his dissertation. Williams also returned to her clerical job, but quit after the adoption of their first child. The family moved back to Salt Lake City in 1952, when J. D. was offered a teaching position at the University of Utah. The couple adopted three more children, and Williams grew more and more interested in children's books as she read aloud to her sons and daughter. Her first book, *Let's Go to an Indian Cliff Dwelling* (1965), was inspired by her son Kirk's enthusiastic reaction to a trip to the Anasazi ruins in Colorado. In 1960, Williams had begun teaching remedial English at the University of Utah and in 1966 she decided to continue her graduate studies there. While working on her degree and teaching, she wrote a composition textbook, which was later published by Charles Merrill and Company. Her creative thesis, *The Secret Name* (1972), was a middle-grade novel about the Mormon Church's Indian Placement Program, which places Native American children from reservations with white families in urban areas in an effort to enhance their educational opportunities. Shortly after graduation, Williams decided to organize a writing group, *Manuscripters.* Over the next three years, the group provided her with the push to write and publish the three books she considers her best: *Kevin's Grandma, Someday, Said Mitchell,* and *Albert's Toothache.*

Major Works

Williams's most popular stories for children involve family relationships. One of her best known books, *Albert's Toothache,* is loosely based on an experience involving her daughter Kim, who would frequently regale her mother with lists of complaints. When Kim was eleven, she told her mother she had fallen off the monkey bars at school and had broken her wrist. Williams was skeptical, but took Kim for an X-ray, which the nurse said showed no break. The next day Kim told her mother she had broken her other wrist. A second trip to the doctor revealed that both wrists were broken and that the nurse had misread the first X-ray. Williams says she wrote *Albert's Toothache* as "an act of penance." In this humorous story, Albert, a toothless turtle, tells his parents he has a toothache. While his brother and sister tease him, Albert's parents try to convince him that this is impossible, but Albert refuses to eat or get out of bed. Finally, his grandmother, obviously skilled in communicating with the very young, asks the right question: "Where do you have a toothache?" Albert replies that the toothache is in his left toe, the place a gopher bit him when he stepped in its hole. *Kevin's Grandma* also showcases the special relationship of children to grandparents. The boy who narrates the story has a traditional grandmother who drives a station wagon and gives him treats. His friend Kevin, however, says that his grandmother sky dives, rides a motorcycle, and climbs mountains. The narrator of this lively story isn't sure he believes everything Kevin says about his grandmother and ends the story with a question about her cooking: "Whoever heard of peanut-butter soup?"

Lessons about sharing are gently imparted in *Chester Chipmunk's Thanksgiving,* the story of a chipmunk with a comfortable home and plenty of food who wants to give thanks for his blessings. Chester bakes extra pecan pies and invites his neighbors and relatives to Thanksgiving dinner. His poor and sickly Cousin Archie rudely refuses the invitation and the Rabbit and Woodchuck families also decline, explaining that they are expecting relatives. Only Oswald Opossum accepts. But when Thanksgiving arrives, Archie, the Rabbits and the Woodchucks relent and arrive with their relatives and food to share. *Someday, Said Mitchell* is the story of a small boy who longs to be big so he can buy his mother a mansion and hire servants to do the housework. Mitchell's mother assures him that he is just the right size "for sitting on my lap while we smell violets and talk together." Mitchell learns to feel useful despite his size by helping his mother dust and sweep. The difficulty of learning to cope with a new baby in the house is presented in the form of a madcap dialogue between a child and his mother in *Jeremy Isn't Hungry.* Davey tries to entertain and feed his baby brother Jeremy while his mother takes a shower and gets dressed. The mother shouts instructions and Davey perseveres despite his inexperience and Jeremy's tantrums.

Awards

Albert's Toothache was designated a Children's Book Showcase title, an American Library Association Notable Book, a Junior Literary Guild selection, and one of the American Institute of Graphic Arts' 50 Books of the Year. *Chester Chipmunk's Thanksgiving* earned Williams a Christopher Award in 1979. In addition, several of Williams's works have been named Children's Choice Books by the International Reading Association and Children's Book Council (IRA-CBC).

TITLE COMMENTARY

I KNOW A POLICEMAN (1966)

Kirkus Service

SOURCE: A review of *I Know a Policeman,* in *Kirkus Reviews,* January 1, 1967, p. 6.

On a presumed visit to a classroom, Officer Glenn tells about some of the jobs of policemen in and out of uniform in various branches of the department; he also follows a rookie from training to precinct and into the station house. The style is standard reader, second grade, the tone is uplifting ("Policemen don't like to give tickets, but they must prevent accidents"), and the total effect (including the illustrations [by Charles Dougherty]) is a dullness undeserved by the subject. A supplementary source for small town and suburban schools as needed, but far too sanguine for most city children.

THE SECRET NAME (1972)

Kirkus Reviews

SOURCE: A review of *Secret Name,* in *Kirkus Reviews,* Vol. XL, No. 13, July 1, 1972, pp. 725-26.

A little muffled culture shock is experienced by the Mills family, even more by Betsy Burnsides, when the eight year-old reservation Navajo comes to live with the white family. Betsy has never had a bath or a bed or a change of clothes and her views on good luck and good manners cause a string of painful moments. But Laurie Mills, nine, is (rather improbably), patient with her new sister and Betsy is just beginning to adjust when she's called back to the reservation by her mother's serious illness. Laurie hopes Betsy will return next fall but Father still isn't sure it's right to re-program the child for an uncertain future; though the issue is never resolved Laurie is happier about it after she sends Betsy a gift via her brother's Navajo friend at college, and receives in turn the present of Betsy's secret Indian name. There's none of the depth or complexity of Neufeld's *Edgar Allan* here, no tough decisions to make despite Laurie's troubled questions about what's right for Betsy, and though the matter of Betsy's return remains open, the final exchange of gifts constitutes the kind of tidy wrap-up that makes the whole thing easy to forget. But Ms. Williams touches on a real dilemma and the details of the two girls' interaction add topical substance to the undemanding story.

Cathy S. Coyle

SOURCE: A review of *The Secret Name,* in *Library Journal,* Vol. 97, No. 18, October 15, 1972, pp. 3457-58.

Betsy, an eight-year-old Navaho Indian who comes to stay with a white, middle-class family for a school year, feels that taking a bath without a bathing suit is indecent, won't curl her hair because it might bring bad luck, and refuses to take a direct route to a friend's home for fear of leading evil spirits there. After her arrival, her new "white sister," nine-year-old Laurie, is faced with antagonism from schoolmates and the prejudice of their parents; however, she learns to cope as Betsy manages to overcome her superstitions and become a loved member of the family. When Betsy must return to her Indian family, perhaps permanently, she returns the white family's affection by revealing to Laurie her secret Indian name. Laurie is then faced with the question of where Betsy really belongs—is it better for her to become Americanized or should she remain with her people and heritage. Interesting information about Navaho art, customs and beliefs is skillfully woven into the story, and the American Indian's problems are presented simply and fairly from a child's point of view without attempting facile solutions.

Publishers Weekly

SOURCE: A review of *The Secret Name,* in *Publishers Weekly,* Vol. 203, No. 4, January 22, 1973, p. 71.

Laurie is ecstatic when her family takes an eight-year-old Navaho girl, Betsy, into her home; the white girl had always wanted a sister her own age. But adjustments for both children are difficult, and their problems are multiplied when some of their schoolmates shun Betsy and taunt Laurie with being a "squaw lover." Despite all odds, the "sisters" become real friends and both are miserable when Betsy has to return to the reservation. A happy ending of sorts is arrived at when the Indian girl tells Laurie her secret name, the most precious gift a Navaho can offer. Mrs. Williams writes sympathetically about the children of both cultures. The novel won first prize, juvenile division, in a contest sponsored by the Utah State Institute of Fine Arts.

The Times Literary Supplement

SOURCE: "Odd Ones Out," in *The Times Literary Supplement,* No. 3709, April 6, 1973, p. 382.

In Barbara Williams's **The Secret Name** essentially for

girls, the wild thing is a small Navajo Indian girl, Betsy, brought in from the reservation to live with a white family, and in particular with Laurie, who is to be her "White Sister." Here again the detail of daily life is excellent but in this case, as befits the setting, it is much more comfortable to read about. The characters both of Laurie, a pleasantly ordinary little American girl, and of Betsy, with her withdrawals, superstitions and basic dignity, are put across with much sympathy—what a pity it is that the illustrations [by Jennifer Perrott] showing these two nice characters should be so grotesque. When Betsy has to go back to look after her family, Ben Chee, a teenage Navajo boy who has stayed the difficult course of Westernization, is able to put forward his people's point of view, and Laurie, very lonely without her sister, has to go through much heart searching about the wisdom of forcing an alien way of life upon other people. The reader is given no answer to the problem, but is left with many thoughts on which to work, and they are thoughts which do not stop when the story is ended.

Booklist

SOURCE: A review of *The Secret Name,* in *Booklist,* Vol. 69, No. 19, June 1, 1973, p. 951.

In this first-person story, nine-year-old Laurie describes what happens when Betsy, a Navajo girl, comes from the reservation to live with Laurie's family in Salt Lake City. The problems of adjustment that both Betsy and Laurie have to face are presented realistically and the friendship that develops between the girls before Betsy has to return unexpectedly to the reservation is believable. No pat answers are given to the question that is raised as to whether Betsy would be better off staying on the reservation or returning to live with Laurie's family.

GARY AND THE VERY TERRIBLE MONSTER (1973)

Library Journal

SOURCE: A review of *Gary and the Very Terrible Monster,* in *Library Journal,* Vol. 98, No. 10, May 15, 1973, p. 1697.

An imaginary monster—Mr. Green Nose—whom Gary blames for his misbehavior is the star of **Gary and the Very Terrible Monster,** illustrated in color by Lois Axeman. Mr. Green Nose puts nails in the street, flies in a girl's milk, and makes burping noises. As expected, he disappears when Gary gets a puppy. The early build-up of humor soon peters out, leaving readers with a lavishly illustrated and serviceable but not outstanding story.

Margery Fisher

SOURCE: A review of *Gary and the Very Terrible Monster,* in *Growing Point,* Vol. 13, No. 6, December, 1974, p. 2540.

A very direct and somewhat coy description of a naughty

child, who blames all his mischief on a monster, visualised as an extra fantasy character, in a sequence of breaking, spilling and bashing; with the advent of a puppy the boy is diverted from trouble—in visual terms the puppy chases the monster away. The pictures [by Lois Axeman] are representational and a little over-casual in technique.

ALBERT'S TOOTHACHE (1974)

Booklist

SOURCE: A review of *Albert's Toothache,* in *Booklist,* Vol. 71, No. 2, September 15, 1974, p. 103.

An amusing tale that pokes gentle fun at the communication gap that can exist between young children and the rest of the world. A genteel family of turtles is understandably unbelieving when young Albert comes down with a toothache. Mother worries, Father rumbles about Albert's not telling the truth, and a brother and sister label his bed-stay as shirking. Grandmother solves the mystery by asking where the tooth aches: "On my left toe. . . . A gopher bit me when I stepped in his hole."

Publishers Weekly

SOURCE: A review of *Albert's Toothache,* in *Publishers Weekly,* Vol. 206, No. 13, September 23, 1974, p. 156.

This brief tale is as warm as a hug. A happy turtle home is disrupted when young Albert persists in complaining of a toothache even though his family reminds him repeatedly that turtles have no teeth. Then Grandma arrives and solves the problem in a surprisingly funny and tender way. The pictures of Albert, his parents, sister, grandmother and home spring from the talented pen of Kay Chorao. The turtles sport pinafores; knickers, middy blouses and head kerchiefs; their house and appurtenances are wrought in gentle, humorous detail.

Lillian N. Gerhardt

SOURCE: A review of *Albert's Toothache,* in *School Library Journal,* Vol. 21, No. 20, November 15, 1974, p. 3042.

The top grade in comedy is reserved for literary wit—an appreciation of the ridiculous contradictions/confusions in oral and written language which begins in the word play of early childhood. Williams gives strong support to the development of a grasp of comic communication in this story of a small turtle, toothless as are all of his kind, who takes to his bed with an announced toothache. His mother worries; his father thunders incredulous impatience; his siblings cast scorn. So it goes until grandmother investigates and discovers *where* he has a toothache: "'A gopher bit me when I stepped in his hole.'" The full-page drawings of the turtle family, dressed in Victorian-mod and domiciled in antiqued middleclass suburban comfort are as funny as the text. *Albert's Toothache* is pure gold

in support of the refinement of early childhood's levels of humor.

Zena Sutherland

SOURCE: A review of *Albert's Toothache,* in *Bulletin of the Center for Children's Books,* Vol. 28, No. 5, January, 1975, p. 88.

While the literal-minded may object to turtles standing erect or wearing boots, or even turtles that appear to have no shells, there can be no doubt of the humor in the illustrations of Albert and his family. Albert won't get up. Albert won't eat. Albert has a toothache. His father scolds, his mother worries, his brother and sister sneer, but Albert persists. Not until Grandmother Turtle comes to visit does toothless Albert reveal his source of woe, and that's because he's been asked the right question: "Where do you have a toothache?" The dialogue—and the story is told almost entirely in dialogue—is very funny indeed, but there's substance in the way it reflects relationships in human families.

Paul Heins

SOURCE: A review of *Albert's Toothache,* in *The Horn Book Magazine,* Vol. LI, No. 2, April, 1975, p. 143.

"One morning Albert Turtle complained that he had a toothache. 'That's impossible,' said his father, pointing to his own toothless mouth. 'No one in our family has ever had a toothache.'" Later, however, in the fitting finale of a picture book in which text and illustrations support and supplement each other, Albert's grandmother discovered where he did have a toothache—a gopher had bitten his left toe. The humor of the concise dialogue and of the stylized repetitions of the narrative is carefully reflected in [Kay Chorao's] sepia-line and half-tone drawings that reveal the anthropomorphically domestic life of the turtles. Although their diet consisted, on occasion, of black ants and gray spider legs, mother wore an apron, father smoked a pipe, and the family lived among beds, chairs, and tables.

Barbara Bottner

SOURCE: A review of *Albert's Toothache,* in *The New York Times Book Review,* May 4, 1975, p. 8.

Albert is a turtle with a toothache but no teeth. It hurts quite badly in any case, and this causes Albert's family to worry. He could be quite off his beam, telling tall tales, or turning into a coward. He doesn't want to learn to throw a spitball, or eat black ants; he doesn't even want to fight with Dilworth Dunlap. He just wants credibility for his dental calamity. What he also needs is some real turtle warmth from his family, which is too busy being logical to give him any sympathy. Finally, Albert's grandma enters and furnishes him with the warmth and caring his predicament requires. She also breaks through his syntactical problems by asking him a long overdue question: "WHERE do you have a toothache?" And *that* brings us to Albert's left toe. . . .

An endearing little character is Albert, in any case, and if he is not quite heroic, at least he makes this quite clear: You can have a good respectable toothache somewhere . . . anywhere . . . (And at one point or another, most of us have.)

📖 *KEVIN'S GRANDMA* (1975)

Publishers Weekly

SOURCE: A review of *Kevin's Grandma*, in *Publishers Weekly*, Vol. 207, No. 13, March 31, 1975, p. 50.

Just the thing for the doldrums on a dim day is this absurd, sprightly combination of story and pictures. The small boy narrator tells us all about his staid grandmother and the remarkably different grandmother of his friend, Kevin. "I like to sleep at my grandma's house when my parents go out of town. We play checkers and drink root beer and sometimes stay up as late as ten-thirty. Kevin likes to sleep at his grandma's house, too. They arm-wrestle and do yoga exercises and send out for pizza at midnight." Kevin's grandma drives a Honda, gives her grandson Judo lessons and *Mad Magazine* and peanut-butter soup. She is a scuba diver, a karate expert and a mountain-climber. She is some grandmother but our storyteller isn't sure he believes everything Kevin tells about her. "Whoever heard of peanut-butter soup?"

Marjorie Lewis

SOURCE: A review of *Kevin's Grandma*, in *School Library Journal*, Vol. 21, No. 9, May, 1975, p. 51.

The small narrator has a nice traditional grandma who drives a proper station wagon, brings ice cream when he's ill, lets him play checkers until 10:30 when he sleeps over, etc. *Kevin's Grandma,* according to Kevin, drives a motorcycle, makes peanut butter soup, teaches him Yoga, and sky-dives. The sly smiles on both little boys share the joke with youngest listeners. [Kay] Chorao's pen-and-ink drawings of the contrasting grandmothers—one ultra-grandmotherly and the other a slightly askew elderly hippie—and the little boys—one neat and tidy and the other with a headband around his curly mop—are winning. Fun and funny, this should arouse some good conversation among young audiences.

Ethel L. Heins

SOURCE: A review of *Kevin's Grandma*, in *The Horn Book Magazine*, Vol. LI, No. 4, August, 1975, p. 372.

Tongue-in-cheek humor pervades both the pen-and-ink

drawings and the story of small-boy braggadocio. The narrator tells his friend Kevin all about his grandmother: She gives him piano lessons, drives a station wagon, and plays bridge; she belongs to a music club and a garden club; she brings him ice cream and coloring books when he is ill. Not to be outdone, Kevin boasts about *his* grandma who used to work in the circus: She teaches him wrestling and judo and belongs to a karate club, a scuba-diving club, and a mountain-climbing club. When Kevin is sick, his grandmother arrives on her Honda bringing him "*Mad* magazine and homemade peanut-butter soup." But at last the impressive tale arouses skepticism: "I'm not sure I believe everything about Kevin's grandma. Whoever heard of peanut-butter soup?" By the author and the illustrator of *Albert's Toothache.*

Zena Sutherland

SOURCE: A review of *Kevin's Grandma,* in *Bulletin of the Center for Children's Books,* Vol. 29, No. 3, November, 1975, p. 56.

The clear message: it takes all kinds of grandmas to make children happy. The nameless speaker in this picture book compares his grandma to Kevin's: "My grandma belongs to a bridge club . . . " and "Kevin's grandma belongs to a karate club . . . " or, "I take piano lessons from my grandma . . . " and "Kevin takes judo lessons from his grandma . . . " The antiphonal catalog shows that Kevin's grandma makes peanut butter soup, rides a Honda 90, does yoga, sends out for midnight pizzas when Kevin is staying with her, mountain-climbs and scuba-dives, flies an airplane, once worked in a circus, etc. Finale: "I'm not sure I believe everything about Kevin's grandma. Who ever heard of peanut butter soup?" Blithe and bouncy, with frenetic illustrations to match, this has action, humor, variety, tall-tale appeal, and a nice quirk at the ending.

📖 *DESERT HUNTER: THE SPIDER WASP* (1975)

Margaret Bush

SOURCE: A review of *Desert Hunter: The Spider Wasp,* in *School Library Journal,* Vol. 22, No. 7, March, 1976, pp. 108-09.

Williams, author of the highly acclaimed *Albert's Toothache* and other picture books, unsuccessfully tries her hand at natural science. The predatory need of the female spider wasp to trap a tarantula on which to lay her single egg is the focus of this nonobjective account. Williams does not explain scientific terms adequately and emphasizes the drama of this process, neglecting other aspects of the life cycle of the species. The male wasp is not described at all; mating activity is omitted; and the number of times the female goes through the hunting and egg laying procedure is not mentioned (the inference is that this occurs several times). Both the language and the pen-and-ink illustrations [by Beverly Dobrin Wallace] are emotionally slanted—the tarantula "emerges from its hole like the hideous villain of a monster movie," and the insects are pictured in gigantic proportion to the landscape so that they assume a nightmarish, quality. This "scary" look of the wasp and tarantula will attract children, but field guides and other sources on insects will provide better information.

J. Richard Gorham

SOURCE: A review of *Desert Hunter: The Spider Wasp,* in *Science Books & Films,* Vol. XII, No. 2, September, 1976, p. 105.

There is no lack of wonderful creatures in the insect world to attract attention and excite curiosity. Some children may discover that world on their own, but those who need a little help will be fortunate if **Desert Hunter** falls into their hands. Here, they will find a simply stated, straightfoward account of how wasps live in the arid Southwest. At first, the many illustrations [by Beverly Dobrin Wallace] seem too crude; nevertheless they appropriately enhance the story by prompting some feeling for the harshness and aridity of the wasp's habitat and for the stranger-than-fiction quality of the wasp's economy. If the author had selected one of the several species of *Pepsis* and stuck with it throughout the story, the few minor factual errors might have been avoided. Unfortunately, a reading list was not included.

Ethanne Smith

SOURCE: A review of *Desert Hunter: The Spider Wasp,* in *Appraisal: Children's Science Books,* Vol. 9, No. 3, Fall, 1976, pp. 44-5.

The sequence of events in the life span of a *Pepsis* or spider wasp is dramatic. Flying through the desert, this solitary wasp must do what it has never seen done. It must find the proper kind of tarantula spider, paralyze it, drag it into a tunnel dug for its purpose, lay its egg on the spider's abdomen, then refill the tunnel. Though the spider offers no resistance at first, it is formidable looking. Too late does it begin to defend itself, in a viscious battle, and finally loses to the determined wasp. The next generation of the species will repeat the same process. The black-and-white illustrations are effective, and the numerous facts carefully and skillfully presented. It will hold any reader's attention.

📖 *SOMEDAY, SAID MITCHELL* (1976)

Jane Abramson

SOURCE: A review of *Someday, Said Mitchell,* in *School Library Journal,* Vol. 22, No. 8, April, 1976, p. 68.

As an ego boost for pre-schoolers who often equate being little with being useless, this is well-intentioned; otherwise, the only twist in this trifle on the shared joys of house cleaning is that Mother's devoted little helper turns out to be a boy. Mitchell, a midget Mr. Clean who assiduously dusts and sweeps, longs to "be big" so he can furnish his mom with a mansion and servants and "a vaccum cleaner that runs all by itself." Mother, however, is perfectly content with the status quo—and with Mitchell's size which, as she points out, is "just right for sitting on my lap while we smell violets and talk together." [Kay] Chorao's soft pencilled drawings not only fail to cut the sweetness of the story but are curiously expressionless (the stuffed animals strewn about have more personality than wispy-haired, moon-faced Mitchell).

Publishers Weekly

SOURCE: A review of *Someday, Said Mitchell,* in *Publishers Weekly,* Vol. 209, No. 17, April 26, 1976, p. 59.

The endearing duo who gave young readers **Kevin's Grandma** and **Albert's Toothache** have hit the bull's eye again in their story and pictures of ambitious little Mitchell. When he's big, says the boy, he will buy his mother labor-saving devices (even a mansion with servants) so she won't have to work hard and will have more time to play with him. "Fine," says mom, but adds that now, she needs someone small to help her with tasks she's too big for—such as reaching under beds for toys, dusting under chairs, etc. Best of all, she needs a little boy to go for a walk with her, pick violets and sit on her lap to help her smell the flowers. The pictures of Mitchell's fantasies are as real and appealing as those of his relationship with his mother in their actual surroundings.

Betsy Hearne

SOURCE: A review of *Someday, Said Mitchell,* in *Booklist,* Vol. 72, No. 17, May 1, 1976, p. 1273.

The successful author-artist collaborators of **Albert's Toothache** zoom in on another warm exchange between preschooler and adult, this time human instead of turtle. "Someday I will be big," says Mitchell, and proceeds to tell his mother what he will do for her. "That will be very nice," accepts Mother, but proceeds to tell Mitchell that just now she needs someone small to reach under the bed for toys, dust the chair's bottom rungs, hand her the groceries, pick violets, and sit on her lap. Chorao's soft pencil work is satisfyingly expressive and skillful; she lights up her homey details with a touch of fantasy somewhat akin to a three- or four-year-old's blend of real and imaginary. And the dialogue is straight from a mother-and-child's day that's going well.

Mary M. Burns

SOURCE: A review of *Someday, Said Mitchell,* in *The Horn Book Magazine,* Vol. LII, No. 3, June, 1976, p. 283.

A felicitous collaboration of author and artist creates a

fantasy which should evoke instant recognition in small children. The text, a series of conversational exchanges between mother and son, is extended through soft grey pencil drawings. Skillfully conveyed are both the "someday" world of Mitchell's dreams—where a self-propelled vacuum cleaner, a castle full of servants, and a "'zoomy red car'" give his mother time to play with him—and the "today" world where Mother involves Mitchell in her household chores but also finds time for picking violets. A charming mood piece, simply and joyously developed into a litany of love.

CORNZAPOPPIN'! (1976)

Kirkus Reviews

SOURCE: A review of *Cornzapoppin'!: Popcorn Recipes and Party Ideas for All Occasions,* in *Kirkus Reviews,* Vol. XLIV, No. 10, May 15, 1976, p. 599.

Popcorn—perhaps the oldest form of "our wonderful gift from the Indians"—can be grown in your own backyard, bought in almost any American supermarket, cooked (young readers are reminded) without an electric popper, and, says Williams, enjoyed through the year in a seemingly endless variety of forms. Ma Goodness! Williams serves it with chocolate fondue in January, on a cardboard log cabin for Lincoln's birthday, with maraschino cherries and marshmallows (God help us) for Washington's, with lime jello for St. Patrick's and parmesan cheese for Columbus Day . . . and so on up to the inevitable gunked up Christmas confections and decorations. There's even a local popcorn made with low-calorie salad dressing, though syrup coating is far more common here. All in all, this is just one more sad example of what we've done with all those wonderful gifts from the Indians.

Barbara Elleman

SOURCE: A review of *Cornzapoppin'! Popcorn Recipes and Party Ideas for All Occasions,* in *Booklist,* Vol. 72, No. 21, July 1, 1976, p. 1530.

Popcorn, often thought of simply as a necessary movie-viewing aid, here becomes the basis for a variety of treats, decorations, and gift items. Beginning chapters trace its early history in America and offer advice on growing, buying, storing, popping, and flavoring the tasty white morsels. Using a monthly arrangement focusing around holidays, Williams suggests such recipes as cornball fondue (New Year's), strawberry pie (Valentine's Day), and molasses cat lollipops (Halloween); decorations include flower baskets for fabric flowers (Mother's Day), cannons (Fourth of July), and cornucopias (Thanksgiving). There are lots of other ideas: blue cheese popcorn for a lemonade-stand snack, baked carmel corn as a going-away present, and a "gingerbread" house as a Christmas centerpiece. Though more illustrations of the finished product would have been helpful to children, instructions are concise and well organized, and listings of needed materials are clear and easy to locate.

Joan W. Paul

SOURCE: A review of *Cornzapoppin'!: Popcorn Recipes and Party Ideas for All Occasions,* in *School Library Journal,* Vol. 23, No. 3, November, 1976, p. 74.

Williams' enthusiasm for popcorn is truly boundless: here she has put together a compendium of tricks and treats using the crispy kernels. Staring off with traditional hot buttered popcorn for New Year's Day, she works her way through the months of the year, ending with "Midnight Popcorn Clocks" for New Year's Eve. A few recipes are simple (e.g., buttered popcorn mixed with dried beef) but some are elaborate ("Molasses Cat Lollipops" for Halloween) and quite a few are merely decorative (popcorn Easter baskets or cannons for fourth of July). All in all, this is not for beginners—the techniques involving sugared corn (hot syrup) are fairly complex—but teenagers can manage alone and they especially will enjoy making the decorations.

IF HE'S MY BROTHER (1976)

Sandra S. Ridenour

SOURCE: A review of *If He's My Brother,* in *School Library Journal,* Vol. 23, No. 1, September, 1976, p. 106.

"If He's My Brother . . . Why can't I punch him?" is the punch line to a series of questions that parents hear frequently (e.g., "If it's my room, why can't I paint it any way I want?") Illustrated with [Tomie] de Paola's characteristically gentle humor, this will be enjoyed by children, who will probably respond with an enthusiastic "Yeah. Why *can't* I?"

M. Hobbs

SOURCE: A review of *If He's My Brother,* in *The Junior Bookshelf,* Vol. 43, No. 4, August, 1979, p. 200.

A small American boy is shown frustrated in a number of funny domestic situations by the fact that ownership doesn't give the right to use the thing owned as he wishes. He is watched by his small brother, the cat and a toy bear, with shocked or bored reactions, until he attempts to punch the brother, who soon turns the tables on him. The small format is attractive, using shades of yellow, green, orange and salmon-pink as wall-backgrounds, beyond which framework obtrudes details of the figures. The text appears in large capitals on white balloons: amusing for beginner readers.

NEVER HIT A PORCUPINE (1977)

Kirkus Reviews

SOURCE: A review of *Never Hit a Porcupine,* in *Kirkus Reviews,* Vol. XLV, No. 8, April 15, 1977, p. 424.

From the moment Fletcher Fox announces "I am going off

to make my way in the world," you expect the poor kid to be, well, out-foxed by his parents. Father, a comfortably old-fashioned, sly fox lulls Fletcher with all sorts of useless, whimsical advice—"Never tease a bee . . . Never laugh at a hyena"—then hits him with a quick combination: "Take your sweater . . . don't go farther than the second chestnut tree on your right . . . and be home in time for supper." [Anne] Rockwell's illustrations of the epigrams, from the wretched goat dinner of books and clothes in "never eat a goat" to the monstrous bear hug of "never wrestle with a bear," harmonize with the general tongue-in-cheek tone. But altogether a disappointingly slim, one-shot joke.

Publishers Weekly

SOURCE: A review of *Never Hit a Porcupine,* in *Publishers Weekly,* Vol. 211, No. 19, May 9, 1977, p. 92.

The distinguished author of **Albert's Toothache** and other acclaimed stories has a real winner in this brisk, endearing story of Fletcher Fox. On his birthday (the candles on the cake prove the boy is two), he declares that he's off to make his way in the world. Mom reacts by saying her son will need a good lunch. She packs his knapsack with Fletcher's favorites while he's telling his father good-bye. Father Fox says the lad has come to the right man for advice. To outfox the world, Fletcher must never hit a porcupine, honk at a goose, tease a bee or take other long chances. Pop concludes with the warning to take a sweater and "be home in time for supper." Artist (Anne) Rockwell's lively pictures, in their decorative frames, remind us again that she is one of the most gifted workers in the field of children's literature.

Cynthia Percak Infantino

SOURCE: A review of *Never Hit a Porcupine,* in *School Library Journal,* Vol. 24, No. 3, November, 1977, p. 52.

A short catalog of common sense advice imparted by Old Fox as his little son Fletcher announces that he is leaving to make his way in the world: "never tease a bee"; "never wrestle with a bear"; "never laugh at a hyena"; etc. Of course, Fletcher is also instructed to be back home in time for his supper. Youngsters will enjoy seeing the plucky little reynard "act his way" through these imagined situations. As a visual bonus, the playful pen-and-wash drawings (by Anne Rockwell) are enhanced by active mural-style borders, alternating in red and green.

COOKIE CRAFT (with Rosemary Williams, 1977)

Publishers Weekly

SOURCE: A review of *Cookie Craft: No-Bake Designs for*

Edible Party Favors and Decorations, in *Publishers Weekly,* Vol. 212, No. 6, August 8, 1977, p. 69.

The authors' idea is a good one: to provide party decorations made from commercially packaged, already baked cookies. The text, however, is lackluster, and nothing therein suggests it is geared to young cooks. On the contrary, recipes are billed as "guaranteed to delight youngsters"—more an invitation to mothers than their offspring. The 45 recipes are certainly fanciful. Creative cooks with nimble fingers can make a haunted house from a graham cracker cube, a gumdrop garden, a marshmallow eclair Humpty-Dumpty and other equally imaginative productions. Definitely not for first-timers in the kitchen, all the recipes require patience and dexterity. Only for young people who have already exhibited some culinary expertise. Illustrated with photos.

Sharon Honig

SOURCE: A review of *Cookie Craft: No-Bake Designs for Edible Party Favors and Decorations,* in *School Library Journal,* Vol. 24, No. 4, December, 1977, p. 52.

This instruction book for transforming commercially produced cookies into edible decorations contains designs of standard interest to children (trains, windmills, boats, etc). Directions are sufficiently detailed, with many helpful black-and-white photographs. However, despite the appeal of a craft and a cookie book rolled into one, the emphasis on non-nutritious constructions and on recipe-following rather than originality prevents this from being an essential purchase.

Kirkus Reviews

SOURCE: A review of *Cookie Craft: No-Bake Designs for Edible Party Favors and Decorations,* in *Kirkus Reviews,* Vol. XLV, No. 24, December 15, 1977, p. 1324.

One hopes that most would-be crafters will be deterred by the authors' prefatory recommendation of commercial cookies—on the grounds that they are more consistent than "your own oven products," they don't get stale as fast, and (the clincher) "the completed craft items look more expensive than they really are." Others will surely be turned off by the gunky Humpty Dumpty (frosted chocolate marshmallow cookies) on his wall (frosted coconut bars) or the graham cracker cart with buttercup cookie wheels, candy cane handles, fancy iced umbrella, and cargo of artificial flowers. Perhaps some will remain to lick up the frosted fig newton luggage, ice cream cone windmill, animal cracker carousel, and other such assaults on the eye and palate. But why encourage them?

Barbara Elleman

SOURCE: A review of *Cookie Craft: No-Bake Designs for*

Edible Party Favors and Decorations, in *Booklist,* Vol. 74, No. 11, February 1, 1978, p. 929.

Parties take on a new flavor with edible decorations that have the added bonus of being tasty in the making. Using commercially packaged cookies, graham crackers, ice cream cones, and white crackers stuck together with icing, the authors concoct a wide array of party favors and decorations. Cookie flowers, graham cracker trucks, flying saucers, sailboats, parasols, circus trains, windmills, drums, a witch's hat, and a Christmas tree are among the 45 projects given step-by-step, detailed instructions. Black-and-white photographs for each completed item are included; unfortunately, some are blurred, and the inclusion of more in-process photographs would have been helpful. The projects range from easy (blocks) to difficult (Noah's Ark) and will be worthwhile for group projects, parties, and family togetherness.

📖 CHESTER CHIPMUNK'S THANKSGIVING (1978)

Publishers Weekly

SOURCE: A review of *Chester Chipmunk's Thanksgiving,* in *Publishers Weekly,* Vol. 213, No. 22, May 29, 1978, p. 51.

The new creation by Williams and [Kay] Chorao rivals their acclaimed *Kevin's Grandma* and *Albert's Toothache* in charm and meaning. Chester Chipmunk is grateful for his many blessings. As Thanksgiving Day nears, he bakes extra pecan pies and goes forth to invite relatives and friends to share his holiday dinner. But Cousin Archie claims he's too weak to venture outdoors. Mrs. Cottontail and her family, the Oswald Oppossums and the other forest creatures all have previous plans. On the holiday, however, everyone shows up at Chester's house. The guests bring their contributions to the feast and a right merry time is had by all because they have learned that sharing and caring go together.

Barbara Elleman

SOURCE: A review of *Chester Chipmunk's Thanksgiving,* in *Booklist,* Vol. 74, No. 20, June 15, 1978, p. 1620.

Chester Chipmunk's attempts to share his Thanksgiving dinner of pecan pie comes to naught when he is turned down by Cousin Archie, the Woodchuck family, and Mrs. Cottontail and her children. "My lumbago acts up when I go outside," complains Cousin Archie; "My aunt and uncle from Natchez will be here," explains Mrs. Woodchuck; "we always eat dinner with our relatives on Thanksgiving," answers Mrs. Cottontail. Only Oswald Opossum accepts the invitation, and the two settle down to begin eating. Suddenly, caught up in the holiday spirit, the others begin arriving, relatives in tow and extra food under their arms, to enjoy Thanksgiving together. . . . The giving-and-sharing theme sets well in this Thanksgiving story and offers opportunities for discussion.

Kirkus Reviews

SOURCE: A review of *Chester Chipmunk's Thanksgiving,* in *Kirkus Reviews,* Vol. XLVI, No. 11, June 15, 1978, p. 635.

Chester's Thanksgiving gets off to a slow start, as his grouchy invalid cousin Archie declines Chester's invitation to come and share his pecan pie; and though Chester then bakes another pie and invites the Woodchuck family, then makes two more pies to feed the Cottontails, everyone refuses except for Oswald Opossum who has been fishing for an invitation all along. But then the families have a change of heart; the Woodchucks show up with their crabgrass stew and the Cottontails with a carrot pudding, and even Cousin Archie arrives to share in the feasting and conviviality. Not much of a story—though no doubt Kay Chorao's soft pencil drawings and the elegant sienna-on-eggshell format will give it some seasonal appeal.

Janet French

SOURCE: A review of *Chester Chipmunk's Thanksgiving,* in *School Library Journal,* Vol. 25, No. 2, October, 1978, p. 140.

Chester Chipmunk has a cozy home and a full larder and on Thanksgiving Day he wants to share his good fortune. In his efforts to spread cheer, he bakes a spate of pecan pies and invites, in turn, his poor but irascible cousin Archie, the Woodchucks, the Rabbits, and Oswald Opossum. Only Oswald accepts, but as the two friends sit down to eat, Archie, the Woodchucks, the Rabbits and their relations arrive, having changed their minds at the last minute. The blurb indicates that the author undergoes a similar experience each year with her husband's college students. The tone is testy, as well it might be, but the same querulous air pervades the whole tale, leaving readers with a sense of something short of holiday joy.

Zena Sutherland

SOURCE: A review of *Chester Chipmunk's Thanksgiving,* in *Bulletin of the Center for Children's Books,* Vol. 32, No. 3, November, 1978, p. 56.

Having made a pecan pie for Thanksgiving, Chester thinks of poor Cousin Archie, huddling in his small burrow and suffering from assorted ailments. His invitation is turned down rudely, Archie's parting words being, " . . . think of me sitting here cold and hungry." Chester bakes more pies; save for Oswald Opossum, other invited neighbors explain that they have family guests coming. However, just as Chester and Oswald are about to tackle the (by then five) pies, the neighbors show up with their guests and their dinners, and so does Cousin Archie. The illustrations, rather repetitive pictures of semi-clad animals, are adequate but don't reflect the occasional comic note of the writing; the story is capably structured, but the style of writing, save for its humor, is bland.

📖 *BRIGHAM YOUNG AND ME, CLARISSA* (1978)

Kirkus Reviews

SOURCE: A review of *Brigham Young and Me, Clarissa,* in *Kirkus Reviews,* Vol. XLVI, No. 18, September 15, 1978, p. 1018.

This small domestic incident, involving a little girl's dishonest acquisition of a ribbon and her father's forgiveness, is narrated by Brigham Young's young daughter Clarissa in the ingenuous manner F. N. Monjo has established for the offspring of our founding fathers. But Williams lacks Monjo's humor; her telling is a shade too cute ("Would you like to know the names of Mother's [seven] children? I'll tell you who they are," says Clarissa, whose father has 55 children, "but he loves me as if I were the only one"); and where Monjo succeeds in humanizing established heroes, Williams is dealing with a figure who, if known to children at all outside of Mormon country, is more like a curiosity. Thus the historical bits Clarissa works in—"Here are two of the lies that awful Mr. Clemens tell about Father"—will be less interesting, for example, than Ellen Aroon's complaints about what the Feds call Grand Papa Jefferson or Tad Lincoln's plaintive "How could anyone want to hurt my Pa?" And it doesn't work to have eight-year-old Clarissa tell the "funny story" about Tom Thumb and Father: "General Thumb said, 'I can't figure out why you believe in polygamy.' Father looked down at him and smiled. 'That's all right,' said Father. 'I couldn't figure it out either when I was your size.'" Perhaps that's why the projection of the 60-some Youngs as one big loving family just doesn't come across despite Father's breakfast-table stories and all the housekeeping particulars—not that readers necessarily believe otherwise, but just that the whole project has a synthetic, simulated air.

Barbara Elleman

SOURCE: A review of *Brigham Young and Me, Clarissa,* in *Booklist,* Vol. 75, No. 4, October 15, 1978, p. 388.

Married to one of Brigham Young's great-grandsons, Williams bases this novel on the reminiscences of Clarissa Hamilton Young Spencer, the fifty-first child of the renowned leader of the Church of the Latter-Day Saints. Through eight-year-old Clarissa's proud family references, happy day-to-day chatter, and at times petulant self-awareness emerge a warm portrayal of Young, fascinating facts about the Mormon way of life, and a picture of a lively, irrepressible girl. Clarissa relates various incidents—being unhappily left at home when her parents take a trip, trying a ruse to get a new blue ribbon sash which she doesn't get away with, fantasizing about being an actress—as well as the wonderful stories of Mormon history her father shares over breakfast each morning. A lighthearted story that also serves as a welcome introduction for children unfamiliar with Mormon ways.

Ruth K. MacDonald

SOURCE: A review of *Brigham Young and Me, Clarissa,* in *School Library Journal,* Vol. 25, No. 3, November, 1978, p. 71.

Set in Utah in 1868, this concerns Brigham Young and his 51st child, Clarissa Hamilton Young. The book starts off with an interesting idea but quickly degenerates into an occasion for Williams to give background information about the origins of the Mormons and their way of life. Furthermore, she addresses her audience in a patronizing way. Clarissa seems to be a cute mouthpiece who does not have any real feelings about growing up in an unusual household with one father who has seven wives, 50-odd children, and who is "the living prophet of God." The book becomes travelogue rather than good historical fiction.

📖 *JEREMY ISN'T HUNGRY* (1978)

Publishers Weekly

SOURCE: A review of *Jeremy Isn't Hungry,* in *Publishers Weekly,* Vol. 214, No. 12, September 18, 1978, p. 167.

One of those days it is, in Williams's infectiously jolly story. She tells it entirely in the shouted dialogue between a put-upon small boy, Davey, and his harassed mother. Probably nobody but [Martha] Alexander could have matched the harrowing goings on as perfectly as she does with her spirited scenes. Mother is trying to shower, blow dry her hair and dress to go with Davey to a school program. Davey is trying to tend his obstreperous baby brother, Jeremy. Every move the willing little boy makes creates a crisis that propels mum out of the bath to the kitchen. Jeremy throws the kind of nonstop tantrums that every infant seems born knowing exactly how to stage at the precise wrong moments. Each page is crazy fun and the story as a whole is as suspenseful as a novel.

Kirkus Reviews

SOURCE: A review of *Jeremy Isn't Hungry,* in *Kirkus Reviews,* Vol. XLVI, No. 19, October 1, 1978, p. 1069.

A book to read to an older sibling, who will get a kick out of Davey's difficulties with baby Jeremy while Mother takes a shower, dries her hair, changes her dress (after Jeremy spills carrots on the first one), and shouts suggestions to Davey all along. As he tries to give Jeremy his baby food, Davey does his best to "smile and make him think you're playing a game": "Look, Jeremy, I'm Harold, the ice-cream store man. I'm making a malted, la-lah, la-lah. Here you go-o-o-o-o-o-O-O-OH!" There's some funny, close-to-home dialogue between Davey and Mother, and Alexander's uncooperative, wonderfully expressive baby would surely steal the show if Davey and Mother didn't hold their own so delightfully.

Carolyn K. Jenks

SOURCE: A review of *Jeremy Isn't Hungry,* in *School Library Journal,* Vol. 25, No. 3, November, 1978, p. 53.

This is not so much a story as a realistic half-hour in the life of a preschool boy, his baby brother, and his mother. The text is composed completely of dialogue between Davey, who is downstairs trying to take care of Jeremy, and Mama, who is upstairs trying to get clean and dressed to go to a program at the school of her older child. The mother is rushed and harried, but does her best to administrate Davey's inexperienced efforts in a kind and hopeful way. Davey keeps trying, but encounters one problem after another: "Come on, Jeremy, bend. What do you think you are? A bag of icicles?" And on it goes, until finally Mama is ready to go, and Jeremy is sitting happily on the kitchen floor with a lot of strained carrots. Pastel drawings, in gray and carrot, complement the text.

Booklist

SOURCE: A review of *Jeremy Isn't Hungry,* in *Booklist,* Vol. 75, No. 26, November 15, 1978, p. 551.

Mama's taking a shower and rushing to get dressed while preschooler Davey tries to help by caring for his younger brother, Jeremy. Jeremy is crying, probably from hunger, and Mama says to feed him. Davey's problems (from getting Jeremy into his chair to deciphering contents of a baby food bottle when he can't read) are hilariously understated in a running conversation between him and his mother. Alexander's soft pencil illustrations, warmly colored in yellows and browns, are integral, helping the reader or listener anticipate each potential crisis before it erupts verbally. Parents will enjoy sharing this with preschoolers who, at four and five, will readily identify with Davey's frustrations and solution.

📖 WHATEVER HAPPENED TO BEVERLY BIGLER'S BIRTHDAY? (1978)

Publishers Weekly

SOURCE: A review of *Whatever Happened to Beverly Bigler's Birthday?,* in *Publishers Weekly,* Vol. 215, No. 17, April 23, 1979, pp. 80, 82.

How could a child's big sister be so thoughtless as to get married on the little one's birthday? It is beyond poor Beverly's belief. Throughout a long day, the hoydenish girl keeps her family and the guests assembled for the wedding on tenterhooks as she persists in searching for *her* cake, presents, guests. When the happy couple finally go off on their honeymoon, Beverly gets a surprise party but it's hard to imagine her enjoying the celebration after her exhausting day. In any case, William's bubbling story is a nifty addition to the publisher's Let Me Read line and certainly enhanced by [Emily] McCully's action-filled ink drawings, sparked by the pink in the "dumb dress" Beverly has to wear.

Kirkus Reviews

SOURCE: A review of *Whatever Happened to Beverly Bigler's Birthday?,* in *Kirkus Reviews,* Vol. XLVII, No. 10, May 15, 1979, p. 574.

The answer to that silly alliterative query can be summed up in a sentence that also sums up the book: its celebration is postponed in toto until after biggest sister Lorna's wedding. But meanwhile Beverly mopes, makes a nuisance of herself, and grows more and more miserable—all because there wouldn't be any story had one of the adults said a single sensible word to Beverly (like "Wait"). It's the kind of fiction—with Beverly mistaking the wedding cake for a birthday cake, for instance—that's an insult to writing and to the reader.

Zena Sutherland

SOURCE: A review of *Whatever Happened to Beverly Bigler's Birthday?,* in *Bulletin of the Center for Children's Books,* Vol. 33, No. 2, October, 1979, pp. 39-40.

Beverly, seven, is disgruntled because all the members of her family are too busy, on the day of her sister's wedding, to notice that it's also Beverly's birthday. Grouchy, she pokes about the house. No presents. Craftily she puts her jeans on under her "dumb pink dress" and rolls the legs high. After the ceremony, she finds a birthday cake at last, but it has no candles; she finds a pile of presents, but both presents and cake are for her sister. She decides she'll run away, nobody has remembered her at all. Her father offers her a ride when he sees her leaving the hotel where the wedding reception had been held. Beverly is baffled when he drives back to the hotel and happily relieved when she walks into a room with presents, balloons, a band, and all her friends from school shouting "Surprise!" McCully's scrawly, lively line drawings are just right for the restless and resentful Beverly, and the author so consistently maintains Beverly's view of the proceedings that the story evokes the reader's sympathy even when the light treatment provokes humor.

📖 HELLO, DANDELIONS! (1979)

Kirkus Reviews

SOURCE: A review of *Hello, Dandelions!,* in *Kirkus Reviews,* Vol. XLVIII, No. 11, June 1, 1979, p. 635.

"Here's a question I bet Mother can't answer: If dandelions are pesky weeds, how come the early settlers brought dandelion seeds all the way from Europe to plant here in America?" It's also a question I bet the four-year-old in Williams' photos never asked. A better question might be why Williams chose to illustrate that one with a photo of a windmill. As the rest of the lesson continues in the same first-person voice, Williams has the little girl informing us of Europeans' uses of dandelions as food, instructing us on how to smell and see and play games with dandelions (first alone, then with a friend—hers, in the photo, is a stuffed toy animal), and warning us of people who "don't know how the sun can break up into little pieces of happiness and sprinkle itself in a meadow." There's a little more but it's no less cloyingly precious and artificial.

Zena Sutherland

SOURCE: A review of *Hello, Dandelions,* in *Bulletin of the Center for Children's Books,* Vol. 32, No. 11, July-August, 1979, p. 205.

Black and white photographs of dandelions, a small girl, and a toy bear illustrate a read-aloud text that includes some facts about dandelions as food, some about structure and reproduction but by no means all such facts, and emphasizes concepts about dandelions being decorative plants that are worth close observation. The text is weakened by the fact that it's diffuse and by the rather coy appeal to a child's sense of play: "There are lots more dandelion games . . . When you are through, you will be ready for Lesson 3, which is called *Sharing Dandelions with Someone Who Doesn't Understand Them,*" or "To some people dandelions smell like nice old sleeping bags or Fourth of July picnics. But no two people smell the same things when they smell dandelions."

Steve Matthews

SOURCE: A review of *Hello, Dandelions!,* in *School Library Journal,* Vol. 26, No. 1, September, 1979, p. 124.

Flower parts and processes are referred to only incidentally as this book is concerned with impressions, moods, and feelings rather than imparting scientific information. Yet, as an introduction to dandelions for the very young, the combination of a few selected plant facts, profuse black-and-white photographs, and simple and purposeful games such as "Do You Like Butter" or "Finding a Lucky Dandelion" is quite successful. Only "Writing to a Friend with Dandelions" which requires smashing flower heads on sidewalks to write or draw with might cause a few parental frowns. A welcome companion to Ladislav Svatos' *Dandelion* with its subtle watercolors and simple story.

Carole Cochran

SOURCE: A review of *Hello, Dandelions!,* in *Appraisal: Children's Science Books,* Vol. 13, No. 1, Winter, 1980, p. 57.

This book is a disarming public relations release on dandelions, those much maligned weeds. It is written as an instructive monologue by a young dandelion aficionado.

Tracking their development from the first "buttery heads" to the breaking away of the "downy parachutes," the narrator exhorts her readers to look closely at dandelions—to "really understand them"—remembering their noble history as an ingredient in salads, tea, wine and medicine. She then offers a few activity suggestions—wishing on silvery ones, making a chain, writing yellow pictures on sidewalks, and sharing them with the uninitiated. The book's only drawback is the black and white photographs, which are flat looking and uninspired. However, recollecting many warm, bent-stemmed specimens offered up to me at story hours, I can say that the subject matter is perfectly suited to the projected audience, and should have lots of appeal.

BREAKTHROUGH: WOMEN IN POLITICS (1979)

Booklist

SOURCE: A review of *Breakthrough: Women in Politics,* in *Booklist,* Vol. 76, No. 2, September 15, 1979, p. 114.

Williams does a creditable job of introducing seven vibrant women who have achieved success in various political spheres over the last several decades. San Jose mayor Janet Gray Hayes, Kansas senator Nancy Kassebaum, and Utah state legislator Genevieve Atwood are among the subjects whose differing stories of accomplishment Williams colorfully and admiringly reveals and whose lifestyles and backgrounds she lightly sketches. A trenchant introduction pinpoints some of the reasons political recognition of women has been slow and provides tables listing top women government officials on state and federal levels.

Zena Sutherland

SOURCE: A review of *Breakthrough: Women in Politics,* in *Bulletin of the Center for Children's Books,* Vol. 33, No. 6, February, 1980, p. 123.

Following a first chapter in which Williams surveys the participation of women in legislative, appointive, and administrative offices in the history of the United States, there are seven profiles of women who have attained positions of political importance. They are Genevieve Atwood, a state representative in Utah; Yvonne Braithwaite Burke, former U.S. representative from California; Janet Gray Hayes, mayor of San Jose; Millicent Fenwick, U.S. representative from New Jersey; Dixy Lee Ray, governor of the state of Washington; Esther Peterson, special assistant to the President for consumer affairs; and Nancy Kassebaum, U.S. senator from Kansas. In each case, the description of the subject's political career is emphasized, although personal information is provided. Candid if not probing, the writing is brisk and informal; it gives the reader insight into the obstacles women candidates encounter in a field traditionally dominated by men as well as into the vagaries of our political system, and it quite sharply defines the personalities of the seven women who are described. An index is included.

Patty Tomillo

SOURCE: A review of *Breakthrough: Women in Politics,* in *Voice of Youth Advocates,* Vol. 2, No. 6, February, 1980, p. 50.

The author has profiled seven contemporary women who have entered the political sphere at a local, state or national level. She discusses influences which encouraged them to seek office, their goals, and the opposition they have encountered. Although these women are not the best known in the political domain, the profiles offer a clear look at political duties and possible inspiration for those who may be interested in such a life. Includes an historical overview of women in the political world, photos, and index.

David A. Lindsey

SOURCE: A review of *Breakthrough: Women in Politics,* in *School Library Journal,* Vol. 27, No. 2, October, 1980, p. 160.

Intelligence and craftsmanship characterize this collection of objective profiles of seven contemporary women who have attained positions of political importance on their own and not through the tradition of allowing widows to complete the unexpired terms of their deceased husbands, or some variant of this practice. The biographies are prefaced with a short overview of the role of American women in politics. Former newswriter Williams apparently conducted interviews with at least five of her subjects who include a state legislative representative, mayor, governor, U.S. Senator, two U.S. Representatives, and special presidential assistant; this helps to give the profiles a freshness and vitality that writing from secondary sources lacks. All of Williams' subjects have shown a great deal of perseverance and determination in their private and public lives and have had to draw heavily upon those qualities in their struggles against the innate prejudices and obstacles facing women in politics. Not only will this book inform and entertain, it may even encourage some young women to seriously consider a career in politics.

📖 *BREAKTHROUGH: WOMEN IN ARCHAEOLOGY* (1980)

Sally Estes

SOURCE: A review of *Breakthrough: Women in Archaeology,* in *Booklist,* Vol. 77, No. 5, November 1, 1980, p. 398.

The author of ***Breakthrough: Women in Politics*** offers a similar treatment of six diverse, present-day women who have succeeded in the field of archaeology. The lively

profiles trace each woman's personal life and professional accomplishments, covering not only the satisfactions and fulfillments but also the challenges overcome. Williams' introduction notes the historical role of women in archaeology as well as the problems (particularly sex discrimination) and the opportunities facing today's aspiring archaeologists. Popular vocational guidance material that projects a sense of adventure and stimulation without ignoring the obstacles. Appendixes include a glossary, information on archaeological field schools, and lists of college and university departments of anthropology/archaeology and of pertinent museums (U.S. and Canada).

William O. Autry, Jr.

SOURCE: A review of *Breakthrough: Women in Archaeology,* in *Science Books & Films,* Vol. 16, No. 4, March-April, 1981, p. 216.

This short book makes an important contribution to archeological history as well as to the development of career interests in anthropology for women. The author provides stimulating career examples from various women archeologists to demonstrate hardships and opportunities for prospective women archeologists. Aside from a few questionable opinions in the author's introduction and the unexplained choice of the six women who are presented, the book is solid and useful. More diversity in the careers of the women profiled and additional insights from them would have strengthened the book. Additionally, the book would also be strengthened by adding photographs of the six women in the various tasks of archeology described in the text. I also feel, contrary to the author, that there *are* lost civilizations remaining to be found, and many civilizations remain to be elucidated. Both men and women should be encouraged to make this discipline their career, and this book is recommended as a clear statement about career development in archeology for women. It provides interesting and insightful reading both for persons considering archeological careers and for professional archeologists.

Zena Sutherland

SOURCE: A review of *Breakthrough: Women in Archaeology,* in *Bulletin of the Center for Children's Books,* Vol. 34, No. 8, April, 1981, p. 164.

Following a preface that discusses the problems women have had (and, to a lesser extent, are having) in being fully accepted as archaeologists, Williams presents the biographies of six contemporary archaeologists. These illustrate both the sex discrimination and the difficulties of working in a field in which academic posts are not easily available, unexplored cultures no longer exist, and preparation is long and demanding. The biographies also show the conflicts between the pressures of family and professional obligations, and the several areas of specialization within the profession. This is a fine example of career orientation, and it's written with vitality in a smooth, informal style; its usefulness is increased by the provision of a glossary, a list of archeological field schools (by states), a list of museum departments, and a list of departments of archeology and anthropology in colleges and universities.

Hester A. Davis

SOURCE: A review of *Breakthrough: Women in Archaeology,* in *Archaeology,* Vol. 34, No. 4, July-August, 1981, p. 75.

In the last ten years or so, the number of women training in or practicing archaeology as a profession has increased dramatically. This book profiles six women, all with their Ph.D.'s, and all working in New World archaeology. The publication is the fourth in a series of women in "nontraditional" fields, and is oriented toward high school girls thinking about career choices. This orientation, however, does not detract from the interest which many will find in reviewing the backgrounds, viewpoints, contributions and personal and professional successes of Cynthia Irwin-Williams, Leslie E. Wildeson, Ernestine Green, Jane Holden Kelley, Karen Olsen Bruhns and Mary Eubanks Dunn. The photographs leave a lot to be desired, but the appendices on available field schools, departments of anthropology/archaeology, and museums are very useful.

A VALENTINE FOR COUSIN ARCHIE (1980)

Zena Sutherland

SOURCE: A review of *A Valentine for Cousin Archie,* in *Bulletin of the Center for Children's Books,* Vol. 37, No. 7, March, 1981, p. 142.

Pink, white, and brown, the softly drawn pictures of animals [by Kay Chorao] are just a bit sweet; breezy and cozy, the text is just a bit contrived. However, the triple appeals of animals, valentines, and mishaps should appeal to the read-aloud audience. Chester Chipmunk visits Cousin Archie, and when he leaves, Archie finds a sugary message. He decides it must have come from Widow Cottontail, and sends her a valentine; she assumes her valentine has come from Oswald Opossum and sends him one, and so on. Nothing really comes of this chain of misinterpretations, since each recipient-sender is pleased. The story ends with Chester bringing Archie a hot water bottle for his lumbago and seeing the original valentine on the wall. It proves to be the torn-off half of a shopping list.

Kristi L. Thomas

SOURCE: A review of *A Valentine for Cousin Archie,* in *School Library Journal,* Vol. 27, No. 7, March, 1981, p. 138.

The plot of this heart-y story is as ornately intricate as a Victorian valentine—a tendency which the pink-tinted, lace-edged illustrations only amplify. Chester Chipmunk

invites grumpy cousin Archie on a valentine delivery jaunt and is turned down. Nevertheless, he leaves behind him a valentine message. But is it a valentine? And, for that matter, did Chester leave it? There follows a series of far-fetched misinterpretations leading from Widow Cottontail to Oswald Opossum to Mrs. Woodchuck and, eventually, back to Chester and Archie. The mystery is solved, if anyone is still following the plot, and the ending has a grumpy cheerfulness to it, but the contrivances upon which the action hinges are creaky and overcomplicated.

Kirkus Reviews

SOURCE: A review of *A Valentine for Cousin Archie,* in *Kirkus Reviews,* Vol. XLIX, No. 5, March 1, 1981, p. 282.

Just as **Chester Chipmunk's Thanksgiving** turned out the woodland community for a feast of cozy conviviality, so this merry-go-round of misunderstanding deals in good feeling and gifts of food. It begins with grouchy Uncle Archie mistaking a scrap of Chester's errand list for an anonymous Valentine. He sends an unsigned reply to widow Cottontail . . . who sends *her* reply to Oswald Opossum. . . . Somehow the chain ends with a hot pecan pie for Chester, followed by Williams' mildly ingenious explanation of the cryptic note that started it off. Like others by this pair, it's a little soft, a little contrived, but par for the occasion.

SO WHAT IF I'M A SORE LOSER? (1981)

Publishers Weekly

SOURCE: A review of *So What If I'm a Sore Loser?,* in *Publishers Weekly,* Vol. 219, No. 7, February 13, 1981, p. 93.

Blake makes it abundantly clear that he and his privileged cousin Maurice can't stand each other. Maurice lives in a dressy building with an elevator, a doorman, swimming pool and sauna. Blake lives in a crummy walk-up with a broken washing machine and Olympic-sized roaches in the basement. Visiting his snooty cousin, Blake makes no pretense of losing gracefully at swimming and other activities Maurice is good at, and Maurice jeers at Blake for being a sore loser. When Blake is the host, however, he delivers an example of how to be a sore winner, a lesson one hopes Maurice will take to heart. Williams tells her unusual story with an exuberance matched by [Linda Strauss] Edwards's energetic, droll and authentic drawings of locales in the Big Apple.

Mary B. Nickerson

SOURCE: A review of *So What If I'm a Sore Loser?,* in *School Library Journal,* Vol. 27, No. 9, May, 1981, p. 61.

Blake and Maurice are cousins and a study in seeming contrasts. Maurice lives near the park, and the doorman at his building wears gold braid and tips his hat; Blake, who is telling the story, lives across town, and his building has a super who wears T-shirts and scratches himself. Once a month, while their mothers visit, the boys are compelled to play together, and it seems to Blake that all his cousin does is lord it over him, the visits always being on Maurice's turf. One Sunday, the situation demands that Blake be the host, and he finally scores one on Maurice. The characterizations are nicely done; although Blake certainly has our sympathy, both boys are moderately obnoxious in response to a situation that is thrust upon them. The illustrations are an excellent match for the tone of the story. Fine-lined where it counts, rubbed and softened to convey well-handled textures, the contrasts in the boys' surroundings do not hide the fact that the cousins bear more than a physical resemblance. The vocabulary is simple or easy to guess, making this a versatile as well as appealing book.

Kirkus Reviews

SOURCE: A review of *So What If I'm a Sore Loser?*, in *Kirkus Reviews*, Vol. XLIX, No. 11, June 1, 1981, p. 679.

Blake, the underdog, begins this with a point-by-point comparison between his apartment building and that of his cousin Maurice who lives across town: for example, there's a doorman with gold-braided uniform at Maurice's building, a super in dirty T-shirt at Blake's; an Olympic-sized pool in the basement at Maurice's, Olympic-sized cockroaches at Blake's. Next comes an inventory of their leisure-time possessions—Maurice has an aquarium, boxing gloves, a drum set; Blake has jigsaw puzzles—and Maurice always outshines Blake when they swim or box or play at their monthly get-together's at Maurice's. Maurice is revealed in these examples as an obnoxious winner ("Oh boy oh boy oh boy oh boy! I beat you again"), Blake a grudging loser ("You only won because you practice every day"). The turn-about comes when Maurice's apartment is being painted and so the monthly visit occurs at Blake's, where he outshines Maurice in a puzzle race and Maurice realizes at last: "If there's anything in the world that's worse than a sore loser, it's a sore winner." To counter the story's predictably mechanical outline and essence, Williams' tone has a mild bite and (Linda Strauss) Edwards' pencil drawings give a wry, amusing flavor to the contrasts and the boys' interaction.

📖 MITZI AND THE TERRIBLE TYRANNOSAURUS REX (1982)

Carolyn Noah

SOURCE: A review of *Mitzi and the Terrible Tyrannosaurus Rex*, in *School Library Journal*, Vol. 28, No. 5, January, 1982, p. 82.

Mitzi, lover of motorcycles, professionally spunky, and a recently upgraded member of the Red reading group at Amelia Earhart Elementary School, would much prefer that her mom marry Mr. Ledgard, the custodian. However,

her parent, a university professor, neglects to consult Mitzi on that subject. She chooses Walter (who never speaks to Mitzi at all) instead, bringing two instant siblings into the family. One of the children believes he is a tyrannosaurus. Mitzi says, before the marriage, that she feels "lonely and awkward, a stranger in her own home." In truth, most everything seems to exclude Mitzi: her mom's plans for a five-week absence include the new brother before Mitzi is aware of the trip; the wedding itself occurs before Mitzi's mom finds time for a good talk. Overall, only Mitzi and her new brother have dimension, and despite realistic dialogue, some lively scenes and a suddenly upbeat ending, the child comes off as an unconsciously forlorn figure who is encouraged too much to "reach her potential" without getting the support she needs to do it. So much the worse, as parents' remarriage is a subject little treated for this age group, and as Mitzi's relationship with her mom and new family misses the mark.

Publishers Weekly

SOURCE: A review of *Mitzi and the Terrible Tyrannosaurus Rex*, in *Publishers Weekly*, Vol. 221, No. 22, May 28, 1982, p. 71.

Mitzi McAllister is the eight-year-old heroine of Williams's buoyant new story, engagingly illustrated by [Emily Arnold] McCully. While Mitzi struggles to get into the advanced reading group in her third grade, she meets three-year-old Darwin, who reads her hard book with aplomb. Darwin otherwise behaves atrociously in his guise as a dinosaur while he and his older brother Frederick are guests of Mitzi's mother. Darwin is impossible, Frederick is hardly easier to take with his talk of high IQs and his left-handed compliments to Mitzi on her artwork. The worst part of this visit is that it signals Mrs. McAllister's engagement to the boys' father, Walter, who is also bringing his mother to live in Mitzi's home: "making us a family," says her mother. We are on Mitzi's side all the way, and every bit as glad as she is when things start going well for her and even the terrible Darwin.

Barbara Elleman

SOURCE: A review of *Mitzi and the Terrible Tyrannosaurus Rex*, in *Booklist*, Vol. 78, No. 19, June 1, 1982, p. 1316.

Mitzi, 8, views her mother's upcoming marriage to Walter with apprehension, and when she meets his children her trepidation grows. Not only is there 11-year-old Frederick, who reminds her of a bossy school crossing guard, but there is also 3-year-old Darwin, a genius who seems to know more than she does and thinks that he is a dinosaur. The soon-to-be members of the family and the wedding plans take precedence over Mitzi's elevated status in her classroom reading groups, and she is dismayed until she acquires some independence of her own. Williams' ear for dialogue and her sensitivity to children's vulnerability is keen; by washing this with a veneer of wit and warm feelings she realizes an appealing, readable story.

Ann A. Flowers

SOURCE: A review of *Mitzi and the Terrible Tyrannosaurus Rex,* in *The Horn Book Magazine,* Vol. LVIII, No. 4, August, 1982, p. 410.

Mitzi McAllister, a third-grader, has numerous small troubles. Her divorced mother, a college professor and an archaeologist, seems to be planning to marry Walter, the rather strict father of two sons, who dislikes motorcycles—one of Mitzi's passions—and does not believe in nicknames. Mitzi must learn to get along with Walter's sons, Frederick and Darwin. Frederick is open and friendly—he's looking for an ally—and informs Mitzi that although he is gifted, three-year-old Darwin is actually a genius who already knows how to read. Mitzi finds this fact hard to believe, since practically all she ever hears him say is "'Grunch!'"—because he is obsessed with dinosaurs. Although the little boy is troublesome, Mitzi develops a knack for dealing with him and finally becomes quite reconciled to her new family. The girl has a naïve, literal point of view that is delightful, and in her efforts to get a proper share of attention and fit into the world she reminds one of Ramona Quimby. An amusing, sparkling book about a very real child.

Zena Sutherland

SOURCE: A review of *Mitzi and the Terrible Tyrannosaurus Rex,* in *Bulletin of the Center for Children's Books,* Vol. 36, No. 2, October, 1982, pp. 39-40.

Eight-year-old Mitzi did not look forward to her mother's second marriage; her stepfather-to-be never talked to her, his son Frederick was eleven and bossy, and his son Darwin, three, was an infant genius who insisted that he was a dinosaur. They were all going to move into her house, along with Walter's mother; and Mitzi's mother (an archeology professor) was going to take Frederick on a dig. Unfair! During visits from Walter and his family, Mitzi gradually learns to cope with the two boys, and by the time of the wedding, she is reassured: her mother will take her on the dig, at Walter's suggestion, and Frederick is delighted at the prospect of her company, and even the Terrible Tyrannosaurus Rex doesn't seem a problem. This is a sunny, funny, realistic story about change, adaptability, and family relationships, and it's written in a breezy style that includes well-drawn characters and convincing dialogue.

📖 *TELL THE TRUTH, MARLY DEE* (1982)

Kate M. Flanagan

SOURCE: A review of *Tell the Truth, Marly Dee,* in *The Horn Book Magazine,* Vol. LVIII, No. 5, October, 1982, p. 519.

Marly Dee Peterson, "'the toughest girl in school,'" vehe-mently protested her classmate's pronouncement that she loved the new boy in the class. The fact was, she told her mother LuDean, she hated stuck-up, know-it-all Dennis Cunningham. So the mother, "who tries so hard to be like Jesus that her soul shines right on her face," made a bargain with her daughter. If the girl would put her mind to loving Dennis Cunningham, her mother would promise to follow doctor's orders and lose forty pounds. But while LuDean plunged whole-heartedly into her diet, Marly Dee knew, even as she made the pledge, that she had "no intention of trying to love a low-life mean snake in the grass like Dennis Cunningham." The first-person narrative describes Marly Dee's hilarious confrontations with her sworn enemy as the two conduct a roundabout courtship, sixth-grade style. The author adeptly captures the tenor of preadolescent love, when a snowball in the back is a sure sign of affection and a first kiss is as formidable as it is thrilling.

Candy Bertelson

SOURCE: A review of *Tell the Truth, Marly Dee,* in *School Library Journal,* Vol. 29, No. 3, November, 1982, p. 92.

A pleasant family story set in a small town in Idaho. Marly Dee's father is a truck driver, and her mother bakes for a caterer. When her friend Jessie Fae teases her about "liking" Dennis, the new boy in sixth grade, Marly Dee goes out of her way to prove she doesn't, and a "war" develops. This disturbs Marly Dee's mother, a deeply religious woman who tries to "be like Jesus." Mama and Marly make a pact: Mama swears to lose 40 pounds, and Marly Dee must learn to love Dennis. Mama quits her baking job, only to find that Dad is out of work too, so she goes to work as a motel maid. It's not easy for any of them, but Mama says God is testing her, and that Dad won't find work until she's lost the weight. This makes Marly Dee feel guilty because she can't seem to get along with Dennis. Eventually, Marly Dee and Dennis star in the school play together and become friends, and Dennis even steals a good-night kiss. Mama loses weight, Dad gets a job, and Mama gets a scholarship to beauty school. The author has created an entertaining, involving story. She uses the popular first-person narrative, and her characterization is skillful, particularly of bright, feisty Marly Dee and her virtuous, industrious mother. The working class setting is believably portrayed. The story is contemporary, yet it also has an old-fashioned quality. The happy ending is reassuring and comforting.

Ilene Cooper

SOURCE: A review of *Tell the Truth, Marly Dee,* in *Booklist,* Vol. 79, No. 5, November 1, 1982, p. 375.

Marly Dee's nemesis is the new boy in school, Dennis Cunningham. It's bad enough that he thinks she loves him, but when he makes fun of her overweight mother, Marly Dee vows to get even. Still, Marly Dee's warm-hearted, prayer-believing Mama *is* very heavy; and when the doctor tells Mrs. Preston her weight is contributing to her high blood pressure, Marly Dee extracts from her the promise of a diet. But it's tit for tat, and Mama makes Marly Dee promise something too—she must be kind to Dennis Cunningham, an enforced kindness that turns into mutual admiration by the book's end. The story's locale, Idaho, and Marly's blue-collar parents give this first-person story an unusual perspective. But while Marly and her family seem true to life, others, such as Marly's overdressed teacher and some obnoxious classmates, are simply caricatures. This dichotomy has the book seesawing between realistic humor and a disquieting burlesque. Still, readers who are also in the throes of like/hate relationships with boys will see something of themselves here.

Zena Sutherland

SOURCE: A review of *Tell the Truth, Marly Dee,* in *Bulletin of the Center for Children's Books,* Vol. 36, No. 5, January, 1983, p. 100.

Marly Dee, the narrator, gets off to a bad start with the attractive new boy in her room when her friend Jessie Fae tells Dennis some of the nice things Marly Dee has said about him. Then Dennis makes a caustic remark about her mother's appearance (Mama *is* plump, Marly Dee admits) and boasts about his batting record—and the war is on. Mama and Marly Dee make a bargain: Mama, who has hypertension, will diet; Marly Dee will be nice to Dennis, and she'll tell Mama the truth about her behavior to him. Mama is devout, a firm believer in loving her neighbor and turning the other cheek. She's a good example of practicing what you preach, and what she preaches is admirable, but she emerges as an improbable character, and the plot that is developed on the theme of ethical values results in a plot (Mama, expectably, loses weight; Marly Dee, expectably, becomes a pal) that seems a bit overextended and a bit contrived, although it is somewhat redeemed by humor.

📖 *MITZI AND FREDERICK THE GREAT* (1984)

Zena Sutherland

SOURCE: A review of *Mitzi and Frederick the Great,* in *Bulletin of the Center for Children's Books,* Vol. 37, No. 9, May, 1984, p. 177.

In another story about the eight-year-old who has acquired two step-brothers, Mitzi goes on a dig with her archaeologist mother and Frederick, the older brother who's so knowledgeable about her mother's subject that Mitzi's nose is out of joint. She makes a small sacrifice for Frederick after he's rescued her from a rattler, and she decides he's not a bad brother after all. Low-keyed, this has a static quality although some of the episodes have movement. A pleasant but not unusual story.

Nancy C. Hammond

SOURCE: A review of *Mitzi and Frederick the Great,* in *The Horn Book Magazine,* Vol. LX, No. 3, June, 1984, p. 335.

In the third book tracing her adjustment to her new step-family, eight-year-old Mitzi leaves the confines of home; she and her eleven-year-old stepbrother Frederick accompany her mother on an archaeological dig in New Mexico. "Know-it-all" Frederick, a budding archaeologist, becomes engrossed in the dig and wins immediate acceptance from the staff and the college students. Mitzi, who finds sifting dirt tedious, chafes under the meticulous work and the relentless rules. Disgruntled at the praise heaped upon her stepbrother and at his neglect and periodic bossiness, she embarrasses him by publicly exposing his fear of water, taunting him as a "sissy." When—in a predictable scene—Frederick risks his life to save her from a rattlesnake, she reconsiders her opinion of him. Less humorous than the earlier books—in part, because eccentric three-year-old Darwin has been left at home—the story still sustains remarkably well Mitzi's point of view and feelings. And while the strength of the series clearly lies in sensibility rather than in adventure, the new book may please an audience that finds straightforward family stories less interesting.

Carolyn Phelan

SOURCE: A review of *Mitzi and Frederick the Great,* in *Booklist,* Vol. 80, No. 21, July, 1984, p. 1552.

Eight-year-old Mitzi goes on a dig at an Indian ruin with her archaeologist mother and 11-year-old brother, Frederick. Disappointed with the dig and angry with the rather pedantic Frederick, who is more interested in "dead Indians" than in playing with her, Mitzi feels like a misfit. When Frederick saves her from a rattlesnake, Mitzi recognizes his good points and grows up a little. She secretly makes a peace offering to him by burying her own find, a rare and beautiful arrowhead, where he will discover it. When he does, he offers to share the credit with her, a gesture that seems out of character. Mitzi's own personality, however, is engagingly flawed by emotions children her age will recognize: jealousy, fear, shame, anxiety, anger, and frustration. With its attractive cover and black-and-white pen drawings [by Emily Arnold McCully], this book should appeal to children who have gone beyond easy-to-read to short novels, particularly those readers who have enjoyed the two earlier Mitzi books.

Jane Agnes Furmanak

SOURCE: A review of *Mitzi and Frederick the Great,* in *School Library Journal,* Vol. 31, No. 2, October, 1984, p. 163.

The irrepressible Mitzi, whom readers will remember from ***Mitzi's Honeymoon with Nana Potts*** and ***Mitzi and the Terrible Tyrannosaurus Rex,*** is back. This time she is on a dig with her archaeologist mother and know-it-all stepbrother Frederick. Somehow, it's not as satisfying as she'd anticipated: she resents being in Frederick's charge, as she is quite confident of her ability to take care of herself. In fact, she is scornful of Frederick's ability to take care of anyone—until a run-in with a rattlesnake changes her mind. Williams has captured perfectly the frustrations of family life and the enduring affection underneath it. Mc-Cully's sketches are a combination of too-light outline drawings and too-dark cross-hatching; neither technique is particularly appealing. But this is a minor quibble, and young readers looking for chapter books about family life will find *Mitzi . . .* to be a delight: it's got humor, it's got action, and it's of manageable length.

DONNA JEAN'S DISASTER (1986)

Kirkus Reviews

SOURCE: A review of *Donna Jean's Disaster,* in *Kirkus Reviews,* Vol. LIV, No. 24, December 15, 1986, p. 1864.

An unexceptional "Concept Book" about a little girl who must learn a poem to recite at a program for parents.

Left to her own devices, Donna Jean might well have learned the poem and recited it without incident, although with some trepidation. But what with elder sister Rose-marie's taunts and put-downs, Mother's overanxious "help," and Dad's impatience, she's such a nervous wreck by curtain time that she forgets every word. Only Uncle Oscar has faith in her; and when he turns up, belatedly, she's given a second chance, does fine, and wins a standing ovation.

[Margot] Apple's soft, full-page pencil drawings contribute some humor and characterization to the competent but rather plodding text. Otherwise, each character neatly fills his or her assigned role, rather like the kids in a school play who must portray apples or pears; but they lack the dimensions of real people. An adequate, if didactic, young reader.

Denise M. Wilms

SOURCE: A review of *Donna Jean's Disaster,* in *Booklist,* Vol. 83, No. 11, February 1, 1987, p. 846.

Every child who has trembled over the prospect of delivering a solo oral presentation will identify with Donna Jean, a little girl who must prepare a poem for her school's parents' program. Though she works diligently to learn her poem, the unthinkable happens: Donna Jean forgets her lines and must leave the stage. What makes her a winner is that she has the nerve to return and deliver her poem in full—to a standing ovation. Surrounding Donna Jean in her ordeal is a funny, supportive, imperfect family who is there when it counts. The story's humorous currents are played up in Apple's pencil drawings, which display the frazzled characters with an everyday ordinariness that's appealing.

Zena Sutherland

SOURCE: A review of *Donna Jean's Disaster,* in *Bulletin of the Center for Children's Books,* Vol. 40, No. 7, March, 1987, p. 138.

Softly drawn and lightly detailed, full-page pencil sketches face each page of text in a book that focuses on a child's trepidation about performing in public. Assigned by her teacher, a poem must be learned by Donna Jean for a parents' program. Her parents and her uncle are supportive, her older sister critical. On stage, Donna Jean comes to a full, terrified stop—but she has courage enough to start over and, this time, recite the poem. Even her sister admits, "She's a disaster, but otherwise she's not too bad." This is adequately told and believable in development, but it has a flat style and sedate pace that may limit its appeal.

Nancy Menaldi-Scanlan

SOURCE: A review of *Donna Jean's Disaster,* in *School Library Journal,* Vol. 33, No. 11, August, 1987, p. 77.

Donna Jean tries to learn a poem for a school assembly, but because of her older sister's constantly disparaging remarks, she fears the outcome of her performance. Indeed, her feelings of inadequacy almost win out, until her Uncle Oscar's unshaken confidence in her ability enables her to overcome her stage fright. While the basic premise of learning to believe in oneself is laudable, there are some definite problems with Williams' text. Older sister Rosemarie is never reprimanded for her continual put-downs of her younger sister, except with a few angry looks shown in the illustrations. Then, her father tends to set a rather childish example for her when he constantly blames others, namely her teacher and her tardy uncle, for Donna Jean's initial failure. The light full-page pencil illustrations surpass the text.

BEHEADED, SURVIVED (1987)

Kirkus Reviews

SOURCE: A review of *Beheaded, Survived,* in *Kirkus Reviews,* Vol. LV, No. 18, September 15, 1987, p. 1399.

Jane, 14, and Lowell, 16, make strides toward solving their various problems during a three-week summer literary tour of England for teen-agers.

The principal narrator, Jane, is shy and quiet; she is trying to conceal the fact that she has diabetes and must follow a strict regimen. Her other problem is her flamboyant, domineering older sister, Courtney, also on the tour. Lowell's troubles are more disturbing: his mother has recently died of cancer; while Lowell cared for her, his father had an affair with Chris, with whom he is now honeymooning. Alternate chapters consist of fragments of unsent letters Lowell writes to "Jill" (his mother) and others, only gradually revealing the cause of his depression and his emergence from it. Because Jane and Lowell discover each other, they count themselves among the survivors in the mnemonic for the wives of Henry VIII quoted in the title.

Jane and Lowell are a believable pair; readers should find their romance satisfying. Other characters, especially bossy, unsympathetic Courtney, are more broadly sketched, and Lowell's recovery from his overwhelming problems is implausibly abrupt. The literary connections are authentic; Williams touches on them lightly but makes them interesting. Competent and entertaining, although reminiscent of simplistic TV drama.

Publishers Weekly

SOURCE: A review of *Beheaded, Survived,* in *Publishers Weekly,* Vol. 232, No. 15, October 9, 1987, p. 90.

Jane doesn't want anyone to know about her diabetes during the three weeks that she tours England with a group of students, and begs her sister Courtney to help her keep the secret. Courtney agrees but gets involved with a boy named Scott, while Jane is stuck with Lowell as her partner for sightseeing. Lowell has his own problems: his mother has died of leukemia, and his father married his pregnant secretary, with whom he began an affair while his wife was ill. Jane, without realizing it, gives Lowell the perspective he needs on his family. And he makes her, always the plain member of her family, feel special and pretty, introducing her to another plain, imaginative person— Jane Austen. The English countryside takes a backseat to the portraits of the two troubled teenagers. Williams's romance has a hesitancy based on misunderstandings, giving it a richness and immediacy that is compelling.

Zena Sutherland

SOURCE: A review of *Beheaded, Survived,* in *Bulletin of the Center for Children's Books,* Vol. 41, No. 4, December, 1987, p. 80.

The title alludes to a mnemonic phrase referring to the wives of Henry VIII, and it's offered by Lowell to the other teenagers who are touring historic sites in England and Wales. Lowell is moody and seldom talks to the others; Jane is nevertheless attracted to him. The story is told effectively through the separate comments of the two. It is clear that Lowell has a serious emotional problem, so that the title has a second meaning; only gradually do readers (like other characters in the story) learn what Lowell's problem is. He does, indeed, survive, and a genuine affection develops between the silent boy and Jane, who has been afraid that the others would discover she is diabetic. Natural dialogue, excellent characterization of major and minor characters, and a smooth development of plot make this an eminently readable story that is embellished but not overcome by details of cathedrals, palaces, and cultural events.

Kay E. Vandergrift

SOURCE: A review of *Beheaded, Survived,* in *School Library Journal,* Vol. 34, No. 4, December, 1987, p. 106.

Fourteen-year-old "Plain Jane Johnson, unhealthy and dull" joins her older, more attractive, sister Courtney on a student tour of Great Britain. Jane's primary concern is fitting into the group without revealing that she is diabetic. Lowell, her male counterpart as teen misfit, is obviously more seriously troubled and wants to be left alone. A buddy system throws the two together, and gradually they open up to each other. The story is told primarily through Jane's travel diary, with sporadic brief entries by Lowell. This is unfortunate, since Jane's obsession with concealing her diabetes only demonstrates that she is exactly as she has been described—dull. Lowell is the more interesting character, both as seen through Jane's eyes and through his own writing. The title comes from a mnemonic device used to remember the fates of Henry the Eighth's wives. This device, the maps tracing the tour's journey, and references to literary works from *A Proud Taste for Scarlet and Miniver* to *Murder in the Cathedral* lead readers to believe that the setting will be far more important to this story than it is. *Beheaded, Survived* survives, and readers should stay with the story to piece together the mysteries of Lowell's past, but it fails to integrate completely contemporary problems with the background of historic sites of Old England as promised.

Rosemary Anderson

SOURCE: A review of *Beheaded, Survived,* in *Voice of Youth Advocates,* Vol. 10, No. 6, February, 1988, p. 284.

This is not your typical teen romance. Lowell, 16, and Jane, 14, are together on a three-week tour of England with a group of teens and two adult leaders. The story is told through the diary entries of both Lowell and Jane. Each has major problems to face and come to terms with. Lowell's mother has just died and his father has remarried and a baby is on the way. Jane must come to grips with her diabetes. Over the course of the trip they make a start on resolving their problems by helping, somewhat reluctantly, each other.

The story is well-written with a few exceptions. The tour leader and his wife are stereotyped until almost the end of the book. And Lowell's final acceptance of his new stepmother is a little too pat. However, the rest of the book is good enough that it is possible to overlook these flaws.

The title comes from the mnemonic device Lowell uses to remember the wives of Henry VIII and is also used as a reference to Lowell and Jane and how they resolve their problems.

📖 *THE CRAZY GANG NEXT DOOR* (1990)

Connie Tyrrell Burns

SOURCE: A review of *The Crazy Gang Next Door,* in

School Library Journal, Vol. 36, No. 12, December, 1990, p. 112.

Kim Sanders, 12, and her author mother agree to watch a neighbor's house and to feed her cats and Venus flytraps while she's in New York City. To their surprise, a group of wild-looking, pipe-smoking, redheaded children called the Spikes gang claim to be relatives and immediately become ensconced in Mrs. Overfield's home. They train the cats, cut up worms for the plants, and play with Mrs. Overfield's collections, which range from Oriental art to world-class hightop sneakers. The madcap pace of this zany story never lets up as Kim and her mother try to solve the mystery of just who the Spikes are and what they might be doing next door. Slight and highly improbable, made the more so by Kim's statement that "It's one hundred percent true," but definitely humorous fare, with much of the humor coming from ineffectual adults, particularly Kim's mother.

THE AUTHOR AND SQUINTY GRITT (1990)

Ilene Cooper

SOURCE: A review of *The Author and Squinty Gritt,* in *Booklist,* Vol. 87, No. 9, January 1, 1991, p. 939.

Second-grader Truman ("Squinty") Gritt is looking forward to the school visit of author Helen Wright. Squinty's not much of a reader, but he does like to draw, and there's going to be a contest for the best poster celebrating Ms. Wright's visit. Another prize is being offered as well—a very special prize chosen by the author herself. In short chapters, Williams describes Squinty's ups and downs as he tries to win one of the prizes. Although the reading level seems slightly above that of an average second-grader, the plot, with its dollops of humor, should propel new readers along. There's a payoff, too. Squinty wins the very special prize—Ms. Wright will use his name (his real name) for the hero in her new book because, in all his efforts, Squinty has shown true grit.

Christine A. Moesch

SOURCE: A review of *The Author and Squinty Gritt,* in *School Library Journal,* Vol. 37, No. 3, March, 1991, p. 180.

When a famous author visits his school, Squinty Gritt enters a poster contest and, in the process, gains a bit of self-esteem. He wins the special prize, which he dreamed would be a ride in a red sports car or the author's limo, but instead, the author names her new character after him. The crisp writing moves along, and the characters are realistic and well developed. The charcoal illustrations [by Betsy James], while smudgy on occasion and slightly heavyhanded, for the most part help to convey the personalities of the characters and the excitement of the visit. The setting and breezy writing are appealing, and Squinty's dream of winning a special prize will strike a humorous chord with young readers.

TITANIC CROSSING (1995)

Kay Weisman

SOURCE: A review of *Titanic Crossing,* in *Booklist,* Vol. 91, No. 18, May 15, 1995, p. 1648.

Under pressure from his Grandmother Trask in Virginia, 13-year-old Albert Trask and his family are returning to the U.S. on the *Titanic.* Because his recently widowed mother is preoccupied with escaping her mother-in-law's control, and his younger sister, Ginny, is busy acting out to gain her mother's attention, Albert is free to explore the colossal ship and observe its passengers. He learns much during his four-day journey, and when the ship begins to sink (and Mother cannot be located), Albert must help Ginny and himself aboard a lifeboat. Williams includes several real passengers among her mostly fictitious characters and carefully distinguishes between the two in her afterword. The use of specific dates and times for chapter headings adds to the narrative's authentic flavor. Although Albert's mother and uncle seem one-dimensional (ensuring that few readers will mourn their demise), this is a fast-paced adventure that will appeal to history buffs as well as fans of Ballard's *Exploring the Titanic* (1988).

Gerry Larson

SOURCE: A review of *Titanic Crossing,* in *School Library Journal,* Vol. 41, No. 6, June, 1995, p. 115.

In an entertaining blend of fact and fiction, Albert Trask, 13, relates his experience aboard the opulent, ill-fated *Titanic.* He, his widowed mother, and spoiled little sister, Virginia, are returning to the U. S. from England, accompanied by domineering Uncle Claybourne. Albert's wealthy paternal grandmother in McLean, VA, is determined to oversee the lives of her daughter-in-law and grandchildren. Knowing his mother's desire for independence, Albert attempts to meet a distinguished theatrical producer who is onboard to find employment for her. His shipboard efforts fail, however, with the scrape of an iceberg. With historical accuracy, the orchestra plays on, lights are kept burning, half-full lifeboats are lowered, and passengers debate the seriousness of their situation. Albert is privy to crewmen's conversation about too much speed through the ice fields. He witnesses the desperate pleas of the ship's designer and officers to mobilize the passengers. The boy shoves his sister into a boat but is shamed into staying on deck to prove his manhood. Ultimately flung into the icy North Atlantic, he is one of the few to be plucked from the sea and taken aboard the *Carpathia.* His mother and uncle are lost, but Albert, Virginia, and Albert's friend, Emily, survive. At story's end, the young man stands up to his grandmother's overbearing demands and begins to discover that her plans for her orphaned grandchildren take their happiness into account. Readers lured more readily by fiction than nonfiction will find suspense, character development, and pathos amid the dramatic events.

Kirkus Reviews

SOURCE: A review of *Titanic Crossing*, in *Kirkus Reviews*, Vol. LXIII, No. 12, June 15, 1995, p. 865.

Williams revisits the tragic sinking of the Titanic in this engrossing historical novel. Albert, 13, and his sister Virginia, 6, are returning to America from England on the ill-fated ship with their recently widowed mother, Katherine. Also accompanying them is their Uncle Clay, sent by her late husband's wealthy mother to bring them home. Clay and his mother have heard reports that Katherine is being "defiled" by actresses and suffragists in London, and threaten to cut her off financially. Tense relationships dominate the first part of the book, as Albert tries to follow his father's order to "be the man of the family." He is given his opportunity, of course, when the ship hits an iceberg.

Williams replays the ship's last three hours in slow motion, building suspense as the passengers realize what has happened. Real-life details (those musicians playing on) add to the evocation of the tragedy. Even young children are fascinated by this tale; a cinematic cover (a life-jacketed Albert in a watery foreground, the ship sinking behind him) will ensure the book's popularity.

Publishers Weekly

SOURCE: A review of *Titanic Crossing*, in *Publishers Weekly*, Vol. 242, No. 26, June 26, 1995, p. 108.

The sinking of the *Titanic* in April 1912 provides the emotional peak of this fact-based novel. Albert Trask, 13, is thrilled to be leaving England with his widowed mother, uncle and six-year-old sister. He's had enough of private tutoring and rainy weather, and can't wait to return to the family home outside Washington, D.C. But as the journey begins, Albert overhears a passenger suggest that the vessel isn't carrying enough lifeboats—a suspicion he confirms in conversation with a crewman. Williams devotes relatively little space to the actual calamity, however, and the lengthy prelude grows tedious. The author's postscript mentions that Albert was created from a boy she discovered in her research, a 13-year-old initially prevented from boarding a lifeboat because he had attained the age of manhood. No passage in the novel itself, unfortunately, evokes the catastrophe with as much poignancy.

Roger Sutton

SOURCE: A review of *Titanic Crossing*, in *Bulletin of the Center for Children's Books*, Vol. 49, No. 1, September, 1995, pp. 33-4.

Albert is the only one in his family pleased to be leaving England for his grandmother's home in Washington. His little sister Virginia is fretful about leaving a beloved tutor behind; his widowed mother is resentful and leery of being under the thumb of her mother-in-law, who controls the purse strings and insists upon the return of the family under the watchful eye of the devious and overbearing Uncle Clay. But all Albert can excitedly think about is their passage—on the maiden voyage of the celebrated *Titanic*, no less. Considering that readers will know from the dramatic cover painting if not from popular history what the fate of that voyage was to be, there's an awful lot of superfluous foreshadowing, as when the cabin steward points out the life belts: "Nothing's going to happen what's you'll need them, of course, but I have to show you anyways." While suspenseful it isn't, the story does have grand adventure of an old-fashioned sort, with Albert and a new friend curiously combing the ship and discovering, for one thing, the paucity of lifeboats for third-class passengers, a lack that spells doom for his mother when she is caught on that deck during the accident. Both kids survive and recover nicely and with pluck, and it turns out Grandmother isn't such a bad sort after all.

H-E-L-L-L-P! THE CRAZY GANG IS BACK! (1995)

Florence H. Munat

SOURCE: A review of *H-E-L-L-L-P! The Crazy Gang Is Back*, in *Voice of Youth Advocates*, Vol. 19, No. 1, April, 1996, p. 32.

In this sequel to **The Crazy Gang Next Door**, Kim Sanders, a Salt Lake City eighth-grader, is again plagued by the red-haired Spikes siblings: Earl, DeVeda, Calvin, and Bubba Joe. This time Earl and DeVeda have transferred to Kim's school because Earl has a crush on Kim. He wants her to make the cheerleading squad so the two of them can be king and queen of the fall dance—a prospect that makes Kim ill. To achieve this end, the Spikes Gang wreak havoc on Kim's school and its students. Being befriended by the Spikes may be worse than being hated by them.

Kim has another problem: Ashlee Brinkerhoff, the quintessential nasty but popular girl, has just beaten Kim out for editor of the school paper, and is now threatening to deprive Kim of the last spot on the cheerleading roster. Enter the Spikes Gang to undermine Ashlee's attempt.

As one might expect from an author who has written fifty books, the dialogue here is realistic, funny, and contemporary; the chapter endings leave the reader with questions which keep the pages turning; the writing is economical with age-appropriate, amusing similes. Cover art is zany.

I have a problem with the basic premise of this book: that when students are tormented by this "gang of loathsome Spikes criminals," we're supposed to find it funny. Not only do the Spikes kids talk and write like the Beverly Hillbillies ("We is going to mess up Ashlys head so she can't do nothing rite"), but their antics are much more than harmless pranks. In the week during which the book takes place, one Spikes child throws a brick through a school window cutting several pupils; DeVeda blows up the science lab requiring the dispatch of a fire truck; Earl pushes Kim's friend Darci during her gymnastics routine causing her to break her leg; and DeVeda (an underage driver) steals a car and kidnaps Ashlee for the weekend so she'll fail her Monday cheerleading tryout. In the end, Bubba Joe kicks Kim in the shin, incapacitating her for her tryout. But that's okay because Kim is named newspaper editor when it is learned that Ashlee submitted a plagiarized essay for the editorship competition. If the Spikes kids are punished for any of their crimes; it doesn't happen in the book.

If you agree with the jacket blurb that such subject matter is "hilarious," then buy the book. But it's my belief that putting a humorous spin on violent behavior is poor humor indeed.

Additional coverage of Williams's life and career is contained in the following sources published by Gale Research: *Contemporary Authors New Revision Series,* Vol. 17; *Something about the Author,* Vol. 11; and *Something about the Author Autobiography Series,* Vol. 16.

CUMULATIVE INDEXES

How to Use This Index

The main reference

Baum, L(yman) Frank 1856–
1919 15
---

list all author entries in this and previous volumes of *Children's Literature Review:*

The cross-references

See also CA 103; 108; DLB 22; JRDA
MAICYA; MTCW; SATA 18; TCLC 7
---

list all author entries in the following Gale biographical and literary sources:

AAYA = *Authors & Artists for Young Adults*
AITN = *Authors in the News*
BLC = *Black Literature Criticism*
BW = *Black Writers*
CA = *Contemporary Authors*
CAAS = *Contemporary Authors Autobiography Series*
CABS = *Contemporary Authors Bibliographical Series*
CANR = *Contemporary Authors New Revision Series*
CAP = *Contemporary Authors Permanent Series*
CDALB = *Concise Dictionary of American Literary Biography*
CDBLB = *Concise Dictionary of British Literary Biography*
CLC = *Contemporary Literary Criticism*
CMLC = *Classical and Medieval Literature Criticism*
DAB = *DISCovering Authors: British*
DAC = *DISCovering Authors: Canadian*
DAM = *DISCovering Authors: Modules*
    DRAM: *Dramatists Module;* *MST*: *Most-Studied Authors Module;*
    MULT: *Multicultural Authors Module;* *NOV*: *Novelists Module;*
    POET: *Poets Module;* *POP*: *Popular Fiction and Genre Authors Module*
DC = *Drama Criticism*
DLB = *Dictionary of Literary Biography*
DLBD = *Dictionary of Literary Biography Documentary Series*
DLBY = *Dictionary of Literary Biography Yearbook*
HLC = *Hispanic Literature Criticism*
HW = *Hispanic Writers*
JRDA = *Junior DISCovering Authors*
LC = *Literature Criticism from 1400 to 1800*
MAICYA = *Major Authors and Illustrators for Children and Young Adults*
MTCW = *Major 20th-Century Writers*
NCLC = *Nineteenth-Century Literature Criticism*
NNAL = *Native North American Literature*
PC = *Poetry Criticism*
SAAS = *Something about the Author Autobiography Series*
SATA = *Something about the Author*
SSC = *Short Story Criticism*
TCLC = *Twentieth-Century Literary Criticism*
WLC = *World Literature Criticism, 1500 to the Present*
YABC = *Yesterday's Authors of Books for Children*

CUMULATIVE INDEX TO AUTHORS

Aardema, Verna 17
  See also Vugteveen, Verna Aardema
  See also MAICYA; SAAS 8; SATA 4, 68

Abbott, Sarah
  See Zolotow, Charlotte S(hapiro)

Achebe, (Albert) Chinua(lumogu) 1930- 20
  See also AAYA 15; BLC; BW 2; CA 1-4R;
  CANR 6, 26, 47; CLC 1, 3, 5, 7, 11, 26, 51,
  75; DA; DAB; DAC; DAM MST, MULT,
  NOV; DLB 117; MAICYA; MTCW; SATA
  40; SATA-Brief 38; WLC

Adams, Richard (George) 1920- 20
  See also AAYA 16; AITN 1, 2; CA 49-52;
  CANR 3, 35; CLC 4, 5, 18; DAM NOV;
  JRDA; MAICYA; MTCW; SATA 7, 69

Adelberg, Doris
  See Orgel, Doris

Adkins, Jan 1944- 7
  See also CA 33-36R; MAICYA; SAAS 19;
  SATA 8, 69

Adler, Irving 1913- 27
  See also CA 5-8R; CANR 2, 47; MAICYA;
  SAAS 15; SATA 1, 29

Adoff, Arnold 1935- 7
  See also AAYA 3; AITN 1; CA 41-44R; CANR 20,
  37; JRDA; MAICYA; SAAS 15; SATA 5, 57

Aesop 620(?)B.C.-564(?)B.C. 14
  See also MAICYA; SATA 64

Affabee, Eric
  See Stine, R(obert) L(awrence)

Ahlberg, Allan 1938- 18
  See also CA 111; 114; CANR 38; MAICYA;
  SATA 68; SATA-Brief 35

Ahlberg, Janet 1944-1994 18
  See also CA 111; 114; 147; MAICYA; SATA
  68; SATA-Brief 32; SATA-Obit 83

Aiken, Joan (Delano) 1924- 1, 19
  See also AAYA 1; CA 9-12R; CANR 4, 23, 34;
  CLC 35; DLB 161; JRDA; MAICYA;
  MTCW; SAAS 1; SATA 2, 30, 73

Akers, Floyd
  See Baum, L(yman) Frank

Alcock, Vivien 1924- 26
  See also AAYA 8; CA 110; CANR 41; JRDA;
  MAICYA; SATA 45, 76; SATA-Brief 38

Alcott, Louisa May 1832-1888 .... 1, 38
  See also AAYA 20; CDALB 1865-1917; DA;
  DAB; DAC; DAM MST, NOV; DLB 1, 42,
  79; DLBD 14; JRDA; MAICYA; NCLC 6,
  58; SSC 27; WLC; YABC 1

Alexander, Lloyd (Chudley) 1924- 1, 5, 48
  See also AAYA 1; CA 1-4R; CANR 1, 24, 38,
  55; CLC 35; DLB 52; JRDA; MAICYA;
  MTCW; SAAS 19; SATA 3, 49, 81

Aliki 9
  See also Brandenberg, Aliki Liacouras

Allan, Mabel Esther 1915- 43
  See also CA 5-8R; CANR 2, 18, 47; MAICYA;
  SAAS 11; SATA 5, 32, 75

Allen, Adam
  See Epstein, Beryl (M. Williams); Epstein,
  Samuel

Allen, Pamela 1934- 44
  See also CA 126; CANR 53; SATA 50, 81

Andersen, Hans Christian 1805-1875 6
  See also DA; DAB; DAC; DAM MST, POP;
  MAICYA; NCLC 7; SSC 6; WLC; YABC 1

Angeli, Marguerite (Lofft) de
  See de Angeli, Marguerite (Lofft)

Angell, Judie
  See Gaberman, Judie Angell

Anglund, Joan Walsh 1926- 1
  See also CA 5-8R; CANR 15; SATA 2

Anno, Mitsumasa 1926- 2, 14
  See also CA 49-52; CANR 4, 44; MAICYA;
  SATA 5, 38, 77

Anthony, John
  See Ciardi, John (Anthony)

Ardizzone, Edward (Jeffrey Irving) 1900-
  1979 3
  See also CA 5-8R; 89-92; CANR 8; DLB 160;
  MAICYA; SATA 1, 28; SATA-Obit 21

Armstrong, William H(oward) 1914- 1
  See also AAYA 18; AITN 1; CA 17-20R; CANR
  9; JRDA; MAICYA; SAAS 7; SATA 4

Arnold, Emily 1939-
  See McCully, Emily Arnold
  See also CA 109; MAICYA; SATA 50, 76

Arnosky, James Edward 1946- 15
  See also Arnosky, Jim
  See also CA 69-72; CANR 12, 32; SATA 22

Arnosky, Jim
  See Arnosky, James Edward
  See also MAICYA; SATA 70

Arrick, Fran
  See Gaberman, Judie Angell
  See also CLC 30

Aruego, Jose (Espiritu) 1932- 5
  See also CA 37-40R; CANR 42; MAICYA;
  SATA 6, 68

Arundel, Honor (Morfydd) 1919-1973 35
  See also CA 21-22; 41-44R; CAP 2; CLC 17;
  SATA 4; SATA-Obit 24

Ashabranner, Brent (Kenneth) 1921- 28
  See also AAYA 6; CA 5-8R; CANR 10, 27, 57;
  JRDA; MAICYA; SAAS 14; SATA 1, 67

Asheron, Sara
  See Moore, Lilian

Ashey, Bella
  See Breinburg, Petronella

Ashley, Bernard 1935- 4
  See also CA 93-96; CANR 25, 44; MAICYA;
  SATA 47, 79; SATA-Brief 39

Asimov, Isaac 1920-1992 12
  See also AAYA 13; BEST 90:2; CA 1-4R; 137;
  CANR 2, 19, 36, 60; CLC 1, 3, 9, 19, 26, 76,
  92; DAM POP; DLB 8; DLBY 92; INT
  CANR-19; JRDA; MAICYA; MTCW; SATA
  1, 26, 74

Atwater, Florence (Hasseltine Carroll) 1896-
  1979 19
  See also CA 135; MAICYA; SATA 16, 66

Atwater, Richard (Tupper) 1892-1948 19
  See also CA 111; 135; MAICYA; SATA 54, 66;
  SATA-Brief 27

Avi 24
  See also Wortis, Avi
  See also AAYA 10; SATA 71

Awdry, Wilbert Vere 1911-1997 23
  See also CA 103; 157; DLB 160; SATA 94

Aylesworth, Thomas G(ibbons) 1927-1995 .. 6
  See also CA 25-28R; 149; CANR 10, 26; SAAS
  17; SATA 4, 88

Ayme, Marcel (Andre) 1902-1967 25
  See also CA 89-92; CLC 11; DLB 72; SATA 91

Babbitt, Natalie (Zane Moore) 1932- 2
  See also CA 49-52; CANR 2, 19, 38; DLB 52;
  JRDA; MAICYA; SAAS 5; SATA 6, 68

Bacon, Martha Sherman 1917-1981 3
  See also CA 85-88; 104; SATA 18; SATA-Obit
  27

Bahlke, Valerie Worth 1933-1994
  See Worth, Valerie
  See also CA 41-44R; 146; CANR 15, 44; SATA
  81

Baker, Jeannie 1950- 28
  See also CA 97-100; SATA 23, 88

Bancroft, Laura
  See Baum, L(yman) Frank

Bang, Garrett
  See Bang, Molly Garrett

Bang, Molly Garrett 1943- 8
  See also CA 102; MAICYA; SATA 24, 69

Banks, Lynne Reid
  See Reid Banks, Lynne
  See also AAYA 6; CLC 23

Banner, Angela 24
  See also Maddison, Angela Mary

Bannerman, Helen (Brodie Cowan Watson)
1862(?)-1946 .... **21**
See also CA 111; 136; DLB 141; MAICYA;
SATA 19

Barklem, Jill 1951- **31**
See also CA 161

Barrie, J(ames) M(atthew) 1860-1937 ...... **16**
See also CA 104; 136; CDBLB 1890-1914;
DAB; DAM DRAM; DLB 10, 141, 156;
MAICYA; TCLC 2; YABC 1

Base, Graeme (Rowland) 1958- **22**
See also CA 134; MAICYA; SATA 67

Bashevis, Isaac
See Singer, Isaac Bashevis

Baum, L(yman) Frank 1856-1919 .... **15**
See also CA 108; 133; DLB 22; JRDA;
MAICYA; MTCW; SATA 18; TCLC 7

Baum, Louis F.
See Baum, L(yman) Frank

Baumann, Hans 1914- **35**
See also CA 5-8R; CANR 3; SATA 2

Bawden, Nina (Mary Mabey) 1925- **2**
See also Kark, Nina Mary (Mabey)
See also CA 17-20R; CANR 8, 29, 54; DAB;
DLB 14, 161; JRDA; MAICYA; SAAS 16;
SATA 72

Baylor, Byrd 1924- **3**
See also CA 81-84; MAICYA; SATA 16, 69

Beckman, Gunnel 1910- **25**
See also CA 33-36R; CANR 15; CLC 26;
MAICYA; SAAS 9; SATA 6

Bedard, Michael 1949- **35**
See also AAYA 22; CA 159; SATA 93

Belaney, Archibald Stansfeld 1888-1938
See Grey Owl
See also CA 114; SATA 24

Bellairs, John (A.) 1938-1991 .... **37**
See also CA 21-24R; 133; CANR 8, 24;
JRDA; MAICYA; SATA 2, 68; SATA-Obit
66

Bemelmans, Ludwig 1898-1962 .... **6**
See also CA 73-76; DLB 22; MAICYA; SATA
15

Benary, Margot
See Benary-Isbert, Margot

Benary-Isbert, Margot 1889-1979 .... **12**
See also CA 5-8R; 89-92; CANR 4; CLC 12;
MAICYA; SATA 2; SATA-Obit 21

Bendick, Jeanne 1919- **5**
See also CA 5-8R; CANR 2, 48; MAICYA;
SAAS 4; SATA 2, 68

Berenstain, Jan(ice) 1923- **19**
See also CA 25-28R; CANR 14, 36; MAICYA;
SAAS 20; SATA 12, 64

Berenstain, Stan(ley) 1923- **19**
See also CA 25-28R; CANR 14, 36; MAICYA;
SAAS 20; SATA 12, 64

Berger, Melvin H. 1927- **32**
See also CA 5-8R; CANR 4; CLC 12; SAAS 2;
SATA 5, 88

Berna, Paul 1910-1994 .... **19**
See also CA 73-76; 143; SATA 15; SATA-Obit 78

Berry, James 1925- **22**
See also CA 135; JRDA; SATA 67

Beskow, Elsa (Maartman) 1874-1953 .... **17**
See also CA 135; MAICYA; SATA 20

Bess, Clayton 1944- **39**
See also Locke, Robert

Bethancourt, T. Ernesto **3**
See also Paisley, Tom
See also AAYA 20; SATA 11

Bianco, Margery (Williams) 1881-1944 .... **19**
See also CA 109; 155; DLB 160; MAICYA;
SATA 15

Biegel, Paul 1925- **27**
See also CA 77-80; CANR 14, 32; SAAS 18;
SATA 16, 79

Billout, Guy (Rene) 1941- **33**
See also CA 85-88; CANR 26; SATA 10

Biro, B(alint) S(tephen) 1921-
See Biro, Val
See also CA 25-28R; CANR 11, 39; MAICYA;
SATA 67

Biro, Val **28**
See also Biro, B(alint) S(tephen)
See also SAAS 13; SATA 1

Bjoerk, Christina 1938- **22**
See also CA 135; SATA 67

Bjork, Christina
See Bjoerk, Christina

Blades, Ann (Sager) 1947- **15**
See also CA 77-80; CANR 13, 48; JRDA;
MAICYA; SATA 16, 69

Blake, Quentin (Saxby) 1932- **31**
See also CA 25-28R; CANR 11, 37; MAICYA;
SATA 9, 52

Bland, E.
See Nesbit, E(dith)

Bland, Edith Nesbit
See Nesbit, E(dith)

Bland, Fabian
See Nesbit, E(dith)

Block, Francesca (Lia) 1962- **33**
See also AAYA 13; CA 131; CANR 56; SAAS
21; SATA 80

Blos, Joan W(insor) 1928- **18**
See also CA 101; CANR 21; JRDA; MAICYA;
SAAS 11; SATA 33, 69; SATA-Brief 27

Blue, Zachary
See Stine, R(obert) L(awrence)

Blumberg, Rhoda 1917- **21**
See also CA 65-68; CANR 9, 26; MAICYA;
SATA 35, 70

Blume, Judy (Sussman) 1938- **2, 15**
See also AAYA 3; CA 29-32R; CANR 13, 37;
CLC 12, 30; DAM NOV, POP; DLB 52;
JRDA; MAICYA; MTCW; SATA 2, 31, 79

Blutig, Eduard
See Gorey, Edward (St. John)

Blyton, Enid (Mary) 1897-1968 .... **31**
See also CA 77-80; 25-28R; CANR 33; DLB
160; MAICYA; SATA 25

Bodker, Cecil 1927- **23**
See also CA 73-76; CANR 13, 44; CLC 21;
MAICYA; SATA 14

Bolton, Elizabeth
See St. John, Nicole

Bond, (Thomas) Michael 1926- **1**
See also CA 5-8R; CANR 4, 24, 49; MAICYA;
SAAS 3; SATA 6, 58

Bond, Nancy (Barbara) 1945- **11**
See also CA 65-68; CANR 9, 36; JRDA;
MAICYA; SAAS 13; SATA 22, 82

Bontemps, Arna(ud Wendell) 1902-1973 ... **6**
See also BLC; BW 1; CA 1-4R; 41-44R; CANR
4, 35; CLC 1, 18; DAM MULT, NOV,
POET; DLB 48, 51; JRDA; MAICYA;
MTCW; SATA 2, 44; SATA-Obit 24

Bookman, Charlotte
See Zolotow, Charlotte S(hapiro)

Boston, L(ucy) M(aria Wood) 1892-1990 ... **3**
See also CA 73-76; 131; CANR 58; DLB 161;
JRDA; MAICYA; SATA 19; SATA-Obit 64

Boutet de Monvel, (Louis) M(aurice) 1850(?)-
1913 .... **32**
See also SATA 30

Bova, Ben(jamin William) 1932- **3**
See also AAYA 16; CA 5-8R; CAAS 18; CANR
11, 56; CLC 45; DLBY 81; INT CANR-11;
MAICYA; MTCW; SATA 6, 68

Bowler, Jan Brett
See Brett, Jan (Churchill)

Brancato, Robin F(idler) 1936- **32**
See also AAYA 9; CA 69-72; CANR 11, 45;
CLC 35; JRDA; SAAS 9; SATA 23

Brandenberg, Aliki Liacouras 1929-
See Aliki
See also CA 1-4R; CANR 4, 12, 30; MAICYA;
SATA 2, 35, 75

Branley, Franklyn M(ansfield) 1915- **13**
See also CA 33-36R; CANR 14, 39; CLC 21;
MAICYA; SAAS 16; SATA 4, 68

Breinburg, Petronella 1927- **31**
See also CA 53-56; CANR 4; SATA 11

Brett, Jan (Churchill) 1949- **27**
See also CA 116; CANR 41; MAICYA; SATA
42, 71

Bridgers, Sue Ellen 1942- **18**
See also AAYA 8; CA 65-68; CANR 11, 36;
CLC 26; DLB 52; JRDA; MAICYA; SAAS
1; SATA 22, 90

Briggs, Raymond Redvers 1934- **10**
See also CA 73-76; MAICYA; SATA 23, 66

Brink, Carol Ryrie 1895-1981 .... **30**
See also CA 1-4R; 104; CANR 3; JRDA;
MAICYA; SATA 1, 31; SATA-Obit 27

Brinsmead, H(esba) F(ay) 1922- **47**
See also CA 21-24R; CANR 10; CLC 21;
MAICYA; SAAS 5; SATA 18, 78

Brooke, L(eonard) Leslie 1862-1940 .... **20**
See also DLB 141; MAICYA; SATA 17

Brooks, Bruce 1950-.................................... **25**
See also AAYA 8; CA 137; JRDA; MAICYA;
SATA 72; SATA-Brief 53

Brooks, George
See Baum, L(yman) Frank

Brooks, Gwendolyn 1917- **27**
See also AAYA 20; AITN 1; BLC; BW 2; CA
1-4R; CANR 1, 27, 52; CDALB 1941-1968;
CLC 1, 2, 4, 5, 15, 49; DA; DAC; DAM
MST, MULT, POET; DLB 5, 76, 165;
MTCW; PC 7; SATA 6; WLC

Brown, Marc (Tolon) 1946- **29**
See also CA 69-72; CANR 36; MAICYA;
SATA 10, 53, 80

Brown, Marcia 1918- **12**
See also CA 41-44R; CANR 46; DLB 61;
MAICYA; SATA 7, 47

Brown, Margaret Wise 1910-1952 .... **10**
See also CA 108; 136; DLB 22; MAICYA;
YABC 2

Brown, Roderick (Langmere) Haig-
See Haig-Brown, Roderick (Langmere)

Browne, Anthony (Edward Tudor) 1946- **19**
See also CA 97-100; CANR 36; MAICYA;
SATA 45, 61; SATA-Brief 44

Bruchac, Joseph III 1942- **46**
See also AAYA 19; CA 33-36R; CANR 13, 47;
DAM MULT; JRDA; NNAL; SATA 42, 89

Bruna, Dick 1927- **7**
See also CA 112; CANR 36; MAICYA; SATA
43, 76; SATA-Brief 30

Brunhoff, Jean de 1899-1937 .... **4**
See also CA 118; 137; MAICYA; SATA 24

Brunhoff, Laurent de 1925- **4**
See also CA 73-76; CANR 45; MAICYA;
SATA 24, 71

Bryan, Ashley F. 1923- **18**
See also BW 2; CA 107; CANR 26, 43;
MAICYA; SATA 31, 72

Buffie, Margaret 1945- **39**
See also CA 160; JRDA; SATA 71

Bunting, Anne Evelyn 1928-
See Bunting, Eve
See also AAYA 5; CA 53-56; CANR 5, 19, 59;
SATA 18

Bunting, Eve **28**
See also Bunting, Anne Evelyn
See also JRDA; MAICYA; SATA 64

Burnett, Frances (Eliza) Hodgson 1849-
1924 .... **24**
See also CA 108; 136; DLB 42, 141; DLBD
13, 14; JRDA; MAICYA; YABC 2

Burnford, S. D.
See Burnford, Sheila (Philip Cochrane Every)

Burnford, Sheila (Philip Cochrane Every)
1918-1984 .... **2**
See also CA 1-4R; 112; CANR 1, 49; JRDA;
MAICYA; SATA 3; SATA-Obit 38

Burningham, John (Mackintosh) 1936-...... **9**
See also CA 73-76; CANR 36; MAICYA;
SATA 16, 59

Burton, Hester (Wood-Hill) 1913-............... **1**
See also CA 9-12R; CANR 10; DLB 161;
MAICYA; SAAS 8; SATA 7, 74

Burton, Virginia Lee 1909-1968 .... **11**
See also CA 13-14; 25-28R; CAP 1; DLB 22;
MAICYA; SATA 2

Byars, Betsy (Cromer) 1928- **1, 16**
See also AAYA 19; CA 33-36R; CANR 18, 36,
57; CLC 35; DLB 52; INT CANR-18; JRDA;
MAICYA; MTCW; SAAS 1; SATA 4, 46,
80

Caines, Jeannette (Franklin) 1938- **24**
See also BW 2; CA 152; SATA 78; SATA-Brief
43

Caldecott, Randolph (J.) 1846-1886 .... **14**
See also DLB 163; MAICYA; SATA 17

Calhoun, Mary.. **42**
See also Wilkins, Mary Huiskamp
See also SATA 2

Calvert, John
See Leaf, (Wilbur) Munro

Cameron, Eleanor (Frances) 1912-1996 ..... **1**
See also CA 1-4R; 154; CANR 2, 22; DLB 52;
JRDA; MAICYA; MTCW; SAAS 10; SATA
1, 25; SATA-Obit 93

Campbell, Bruce
See Epstein, Samuel

Carigiet, Alois 1902-1985 .... **38**
See also CA 73-76; 119; SATA 24; SATA-Obit
47

Carle, Eric 1929- **10**
See also CA 25-28R; CANR 10, 25; MAICYA;
SAAS 6; SATA 4, 65

Carroll, Lewis **2, 18**
See also Dodgson, Charles Lutwidge
See also CDBLB 1832-1890; DLB 18, 163,
178; JRDA; NCLC 2, 53; PC 18; WLC

Carter, Alden R(ichardson) 1947- **22**
See also AAYA 17; CA 135; CANR 58; SAAS
18; SATA 67

Carwell, L'Ann
See McKissack, Patricia (L'Ann) C(arwell)

Cassedy, Sylvia 1930-1989 .... **26**
See also CA 105; CANR 22; JRDA; SATA 27,
77; SATA-Obit 61

Causley, Charles (Stanley) 1917-............... **30**
See also CA 9-12R; CANR 5, 35; CLC 7; DLB
27; MTCW; SATA 3, 66

Chambers, Catherine E.
See St. John, Nicole

Chambers, Kate
See St. John, Nicole

Charles, Nicholas J.
See Kuskin, Karla (Seidman)

Charlip, Remy 1929-..................................... **8**
See also CA 33-36R; CANR 44; MAICYA;
SATA 4, 68

Chase, Alice
See McHargue, Georgess

Chauncy, Nan(cen Beryl Masterman) 1900-
1970 .... **6**
See also CA 1-4R; CANR 4; MAICYA; SATA
6

Childress, Alice 1920-1994 .... **14**
See also AAYA 8; BLC; BW 2; CA 45-48;
146; CANR 3, 27, 50; CLC 12, 15, 86, 96;
DAM DRAM, MULT, NOV; DC 4; DLB
7, 38; JRDA; MAICYA; MTCW; SATA 7,
48, 81

Chimaera
See Farjeon, Eleanor

Christie, (Ann) Philippa
See Pearce, Philippa
See also CA 5-8R; CANR 4

Christopher, John **2**
See also Youd, (Christopher) Samuel
See also AAYA 22

Christopher, Matt(hew Frederick) 1917-
1997 .... **33**
See also CA 1-4R; 161; CANR 5, 36; JRDA;
MAICYA; SAAS 9; SATA 2, 47, 80

Ciardi, John (Anthony) 1916-1986 .... **19**
See also CA 5-8R; 118; CAAS 2; CANR 5, 33;
CLC 10, 40, 44; DAM POET; DLB 5; DLBY
86; INT CANR-5; MAICYA; MTCW;
SATA 1, 65; SATA-Obit 46

Clark, Ann Nolan 1896-1995 .... **16**
See also CA 5-8R; 150; CANR 2, 48; DLB 52;
MAICYA; SAAS 16; SATA 4, 82; SATA-
Obit 87

Clark, M. R.
See Clark, Mavis Thorpe

Clark, Mavis Thorpe 1909- **30**
See also CA 57-60; CANR 8, 37; CLC 12;
MAICYA; SAAS 5; SATA 8, 74

Clarke, Pauline 1921- **28**
See also CANR 45; DLB 161; MAICYA

Cleary, Beverly (Atlee Bunn) 1916- **2, 8**
See also AAYA 6; CA 1-4R; CANR 2, 19, 36;
DLB 52; INT CANR-19; JRDA; MAICYA;
MTCW; SAAS 20; SATA 2, 43, 79

Cleaver, Bill **6**
See also DLB 52; SATA 22; SATA-Obit 27

Cleaver, Elizabeth (Mrazik) 1939-1985 .... **13**
See also CA 97-100; 117; SATA 23; SATA-Obit 43

Cleaver, Vera (Allen) 1919-1992 .... **6**
See also AAYA 12; CA 73-76; 161; CANR 38; DLB 52; JRDA; MAICYA; SATA 22, 76

Clerk, N. W.
See Lewis, C(live) S(taples)

Clifton, (Thelma) Lucille 1936- **5**
See also BLC; BW 2; CA 49-52; CANR 2, 24, 42; CLC 19, 66; DAM MULT, POET; DLB 5, 41; MAICYA; MTCW; PC 17; SATA 20, 69

Coatsworth, Elizabeth (Jane) 1893-1986 .... **2**
See also CA 5-8R; 120; CANR 4; DLB 22; MAICYA; SATA 2, 56; SATA-Obit 49

Cobalt, Martin
See Mayne, William (James Carter)

Cobb, Vicki 1938- **2**
See also CA 33-36R; CANR 14; JRDA; MAICYA; SAAS 6; SATA 8, 69

Coe, Douglas
See Epstein, Beryl (M. Williams); Epstein, Samuel

Cohen, Daniel (E.) 1936- **3, 43**
See also AAYA 7; CA 45-48; CANR 1, 20, 44; JRDA; MAICYA; SAAS 4; SATA 8, 70

Cole, Brock 1938- **18**
See also AAYA 15; CA 136; JRDA; MAICYA; SATA 72

Cole, Joanna 1944- **5, 40**
See also CA 115; CANR 36, 55; MAICYA; SATA 49, 81; SATA-Brief 37

Colin, Ann
See Ure, Jean

Collier, James L(incoln) 1928- **3**
See also AAYA 13; CA 9-12R; CANR 4, 33, 60; CLC 30; DAM POP; JRDA; MAICYA; SAAS 21; SATA 8, 70

Collodi, Carlo 1826-1890 .... **5**
See also Lorenzini, Carlo
See also NCLC 54

Colt, Martin
See Epstein, Beryl (M. Williams); Epstein, Samuel

Colum, Padraic 1881-1972 .... **36**
See also CA 73-76; 33-36R; CANR 35; CLC 28; MAICYA; MTCW; SATA 15

Conford, Ellen 1942- **10**
See also AAYA 10; CA 33-36R; CANR 13, 29, 54; JRDA; MAICYA; SATA 6, 68

Conly, Robert Leslie 1918(?)-1973
See O'Brien, Robert C.
See also CA 73-76; 41-44R; MAICYA; SATA 23

Conrad, Pam 1947-1996 .... **18**
See also AAYA 18; CA 121; 151; CANR 36; JRDA; MAICYA; SAAS 19; SATA 52, 80; SATA-Brief 49; SATA-Obit 90

Cooke, Ann
See Cole, Joanna

Cooke, John Estes
See Baum, L(yman) Frank

Cooney, Barbara 1917- **23**
See also CA 5-8R; CANR 3, 37; MAICYA; SATA 6, 59

Cooper, Susan (Mary) 1935- **4**
See also AAYA 13; CA 29-32R; CANR 15, 37; DLB 161; JRDA; MAICYA; SAAS 6; SATA 4, 64

Corbett, Scott 1913- **1**
See also CA 1-4R; CANR 1, 23; JRDA; MAICYA; SAAS 2; SATA 2, 42

Corbett, W(illiam) J(esse) 1938- **19**
See also CA 137; MAICYA; SATA 50; SATA-Brief 44

Cormier, Robert (Edmund) 1925- **12**
See also AAYA 3, 19; CA 1-4R; CANR 5, 23; CDALB 1968-1988; CLC 12, 30; DA; DAB; DAC; DAM MST, NOV; DLB 52; INT CANR-23; JRDA; MAICYA; MTCW; SATA 10, 45, 83

Cowles, Kathleen
See Krull, Kathleen

Cox, Palmer 1840-1924 .... **24**
See also CA 111; DLB 42; SATA 24

Creech, Sharon 1945- **42**
See also AAYA 21; CA 159; SATA 94

Cresswell, Helen 1934- **18**
See also CA 17-20R; CANR 8, 37; DLB 161; JRDA; MAICYA; SAAS 20; SATA 1, 48, 79

Crew, Gary 1947- **42**
See also AAYA 17; CA 142; SATA 75

Crews, Donald **7**
See also CA 108; MAICYA; SATA 32, 76; SATA-Brief 30

Cross, Gillian (Clare) 1945- **28**
See also CA 111; CANR 38; DLB 161; JRDA; MAICYA; SATA 38, 71

Crossley-Holland, Kevin 1941- **47**
See also CA 41-44R; CANR 47; DLB 40, 161; MAICYA; SAAS 20; SATA 5, 74

Crutcher, Chris(topher C.) 1946- **28**
See also AAYA 9; CA 113; CANR 36; JRDA; MAICYA; SATA 52

Cummings, Pat (Marie) 1950- **48**
See also BW 2; CA 122; CANR 44; MAICYA; SAAS 13; SATA 42, 71

Curry, Jane L(ouise) 1932- **31**
See also CA 17-20R; CANR 7, 24, 44; MAICYA; SAAS 6; SATA 1, 52, 90

Dahl, Roald 1916-1990 .... **1, 7, 41**
See also AAYA 15; CA 1-4R; 133; CANR 6, 32, 37, 62; CLC 1, 6, 18, 79; DAB; DAC; DAM MST, NOV, POP; DLB 139; JRDA; MAICYA; MTCW; SATA 1, 26, 73; SATA-Obit 65

Dale, George E.
See Asimov, Isaac

Daly, Nicholas 1946- **41**
See also Daly, Niki
See also CA 111; CANR 36; MAICYA; SATA 37, 76

Daly, Niki
See Daly, Nicholas
See also SAAS 21

Dangerfield, Balfour
See McCloskey, (John) Robert

Danziger, Paula 1944- **20**
See also AAYA 4; CA 112; 115; CANR 37; CLC 21; JRDA; MAICYA; SATA 36, 63; SATA-Brief 30

Darling, Sandra
See Day, Alexandra

d'Aulaire, Edgar Parin 1898-1986 .... **21**
See also CA 49-52; 119; CANR 29; DLB 22; MAICYA; SATA 5, 66; SATA-Obit 47

d'Aulaire, Ingri (Mortenson Parin) 1904-1980 .... **21**
See also CA 49-52; 102; CANR 29; DLB 22; MAICYA; SATA 5, 66; SATA-Obit 24

Day, Alexandra **22**
See also CA 136; SAAS 19; SATA 67

de Angeli, Marguerite (Lofft) 1889-1987 .... **1**
See also AITN 2; CA 5-8R; 122; CANR 3; DLB 22; MAICYA; SATA 1, 27; SATA-Obit 51

de Brissac, Malcolm
See Dickinson, Peter (Malcolm)

de Brunhoff, Jean
See Brunhoff, Jean de

De Brunhoff, Laurent
See Brunhoff, Laurent de

DeClements, Barthe 1920- **23**
See also CA 105; CANR 22, 45; JRDA; SATA 35, 71

DeJong, Meindert 1906-1991 .... **1**
See also CA 13-16R; 134; CANR 36; DLB 52; MAICYA; SATA 2; SATA-Obit 68

de la Mare, Walter (John) 1873-1956 .... **23**
See also CDBLB 1914-1945; DAB; DAC; DAM MST, POET; DLB 162; SATA 16; SSC 14; TCLC 4, 53; WLC

Delving, Michael
See Williams, Jay

Demijohn, Thom
See Disch, Thomas M(ichael)

Denslow, W(illiam) W(allace) 1856-1915 .... **15**
See also SATA 16

dePaola, Thomas Anthony 1934-
See dePaola, Tomie
See also CA 49-52; CANR 2, 37; MAICYA; SATA 11, 59

dePaola, Tomie 4, 24
  See also dePaola, Thomas Anthony
  See also DLB 61; SAAS 15

Derry Down Derry
  See Lear, Edward

Dhondy, Farrukh 1944- 41
  See also CA 132; MAICYA; SATA 65

Dickinson, Peter (Malcolm) 1927- 29
  See also AAYA 9; CA 41-44R; CANR 31, 58;
  CLC 12, 35; DLB 87, 161; JRDA; MAICYA;
  SATA 5, 62, 95

Dillon, Diane 1933- 44
  See also MAICYA; SATA 15, 51

Dillon, Eilis 1920-1994 26
  See also CA 9-12R; 147; CAAS 3; CANR 4,
  38; CLC 17; MAICYA; SATA 2, 74; SATA-
  Obit 83

Dillon, Leo 1933- 44
  See also MAICYA; SATA 15, 51

Disch, Thomas M(ichael) 1940- 18
  See also AAYA 17; CA 21-24R; CAAS 4;
  CANR 17, 36, 54; CLC 7, 36; DLB 8;
  MAICYA; MTCW; SAAS 15; SATA 92

Disch, Tom
  See Disch, Thomas M(ichael)

Doctor X
  See Nourse, Alan E(dward)

Dodgson, Charles Lutwidge 1832-1898 2
  See also Carroll, Lewis
  See also DA; DAB; DAC; DAM MST, NOV,
  POET; MAICYA; YABC 2

Dogyear, Drew
  See Gorey, Edward (St. John)

Doherty, Berlie 1943- 21
  See also AAYA 18; CA 131; JRDA; MAICYA;
  SAAS 16; SATA 72

Domanska, Janina 1913(?)-1995 40
  See also AITN 1; CA 17-20R; 147; CANR 11,
  45; MAICYA; SAAS 18; SATA 6, 68;
  SATA-Obit 84

Donovan, John 1928-1992 3
  See also AAYA 20; CA 97-100; 137; CLC 35;
  MAICYA; SATA 72; SATA-Brief 29

Dorritt, Susan
  See Schlein, Miriam

Dorros, Arthur (M.) 1950- 42
  See also CA 146; SAAS 20; SATA 78

Dowdy, Mrs. Regera
  See Gorey, Edward (St. John)

Doyle, Brian 1935- 22
  See also AAYA 16; CA 135; CANR 55; JRDA;
  MAICYA; SAAS 16; SATA 67

Dr. A
  See Asimov, Isaac; Silverstein, Alvin

Dr. Seuss 1, 9
  See also Geisel, Theodor Seuss

Drescher, Henrik 1955- 20
  See also CA 135; MAICYA; SATA 67

Driving Hawk, Virginia
  See Sneve, Virginia Driving Hawk

Dryden, Pamela
  See St. John, Nicole

Duder, Tessa 1940- 43
  See also CA 147; SAAS 23; SATA 80

Duncan, Lois 1934- 29
  See also AAYA 4; CA 1-4R; CANR 2, 23, 36;
  CLC 26; JRDA; MAICYA; SAAS 2; SATA
  1, 36, 75

Dunne, Marie
  See Clark, Ann Nolan

Duvoisin, Roger Antoine 1904-1980 23
  See also CA 13-16R; 101; CANR 11; DLB 61;
  MAICYA; SATA 2, 30; SATA-Obit 23

Eager, Edward McMaken 1911-1964 43
  See also CA 73-76; DLB 22; MAICYA; SATA
  17

Eckert, Horst 1931-
  See Janosch
  See also CA 37-40R; CANR 38; MAICYA;
  SATA 8, 72

Edgy, Wardore
  See Gorey, Edward (St. John)

Edmund, Sean
  See Pringle, Laurence (Patrick)

Edwards, Al
  See Nourse, Alan E(dward)

Ehlert, Lois (Jane) 1934- 28
  See also CA 137; MAICYA; SATA 35, 69

Ellen, Jaye
  See Nixon, Joan Lowery

Ellis, Sarah 1952- 42
  See also CA 123; CANR 50; JRDA; SATA 68

Emberley, Barbara A(nne) 1932- 5
  See also CA 5-8R; CANR 5; MAICYA; SATA
  8, 70

Emberley, Ed(ward Randolph) 1931- 5
  See also CA 5-8R; CANR 5, 36; MAICYA;
  SATA 8, 70

Ende, Michael (Andreas Helmuth) 1929-
  1995 14
  See also CA 118; 124; 149; CANR 36; CLC
  31; DLB 75; MAICYA; SATA 61; SATA-
  Brief 42; SATA-Obit 86

Engdahl, Sylvia Louise 1933- 2
  See also CA 29-32R; CANR 14; JRDA;
  MAICYA; SAAS 5; SATA 4

Enright, Elizabeth 1909-1968 4
  See also CA 61-64; 25-28R; DLB 22;
  MAICYA; SATA 9

Epstein, Beryl (M. Williams) 1910- 26
  See also CA 5-8R; CANR 2, 18, 39; SAAS 17;
  SATA 1, 31

Epstein, Samuel 1909- 26
  See also CA 9-12R; CANR 4, 18, 39; SAAS
  17; SATA 1, 31

Estes, Eleanor 1906-1988 2
  See also CA 1-4R; 126; CANR 5, 20; DLB 22;
  JRDA; MAICYA; SATA 7, 91; SATA-Obit
  56

Estoril, Jean
  See Allan, Mabel Esther

Ets, Marie Hall 1893-1984 33
  See also CA 1-4R; CANR 4; DLB 22;
  MAICYA; SATA 2

Farjeon, Eleanor 1881-1965 34
  See also CA 11-12; CAP 1; DLB 160;
  MAICYA; SATA 2

Farmer, Penelope (Jane) 1939- 8
  See also CA 13-16R; CANR 9, 37; DLB 161;
  JRDA; MAICYA; SAAS 22; SATA 40;
  SATA-Brief 39

Feelings, Muriel (Grey) 1938- 5
  See also BW 1; CA 93-96; MAICYA; SAAS 8;
  SATA 16

Feelings, Tom 5
  See also Feelings, Thomas
  See also SAAS 19; SATA 69

Ferry, Charles 1927- 34
  See also CA 97-100; CANR 16, 57; SAAS 20;
  SATA 43, 92

Field, Rachel (Lyman) 1894-1942 21
  See also CA 109; 137; DLB 9, 22; MAICYA;
  SATA 15

Fine, Anne 1947- 25
  See also AAYA 20; CA 105; CANR 38; JRDA;
  MAICYA; SAAS 15; SATA 29, 72

Fisher, Leonard Everett 1924- 18
  See also CA 1-4R; CANR 2, 37; DLB 61;
  MAICYA; SAAS 1; SATA 4, 34, 73

Fitch, John IV
  See Cormier, Robert (Edmund)

Fitzgerald, Captain Hugh
  See Baum, L(yman) Frank

Fitzgerald, John D(ennis) 1907(?)-1988 1
  See also CA 93-96; 126; MAICYA; SATA 20;
  SATA-Obit 56

Fitzhardinge, Joan Margaret 1912-
  See Phipson, Joan
  See also CA 13-16R; CANR 6, 23, 36;
  MAICYA; SATA 2, 73

Fitzhugh, Louise 1928-1974 1
  See also AAYA 18; CA 29-32; 53-56; CANR
  34; CAP 2; DLB 52; JRDA; MAICYA;
  SATA 1, 45; SATA-Obit 24

Flack, Marjorie 1897-1958 28
  See also CA 112; 136; MAICYA; YABC 2

Fleischman, Paul 1952- 20
  See also AAYA 11; CA 113; CANR 37; JRDA;
  MAICYA; SAAS 20; SATA 39, 72; SATA-
  Brief 32

Fleischman, (Albert) Sid(ney) 1920- **1, 15**
See also CA 1-4R; CANR 5, 37; JRDA;
MAICYA; SATA 8, 59

Forbes, Esther 1891-1967 .... **27**
See also AAYA 17; CA 13-14; 25-28R; CAP
1; CLC 12; DLB 22; JRDA; MAICYA;
SATA 2

Foreman, Michael 1938- **32**
See also CA 21-24R; CANR 10, 38; MAICYA;
SAAS 21; SATA 2, 73

Foster, Genevieve Stump 1893-1979 .... **7**
See also CA 5-8R; 89-92; CANR 4; DLB 61;
MAICYA; SATA 2; SATA-Obit 23

Fox, J. N.
See Janeczko, Paul B(ryan)

Fox, Mem **23**
See also Fox, Merrion Frances
See also MAICYA

Fox, Merrion Frances 1946-
See Fox, Mem
See also CA 127; SATA 51

Fox, Paula 1923- **1, 44**
See also AAYA 3; CA 73-76; CANR 20, 36,
62; CLC 2, 8; DLB 52; JRDA; MAICYA;
MTCW; SATA 17, 60

Freedman, Russell (Bruce) 1929- **20**
See also AAYA 4; CA 17-20R; CANR 7, 23,
46; JRDA; MAICYA; SATA 16, 71

Freeman, Don 1908-1978 .... **30**
See also CA 77-80; CANR 44; MAICYA;
SATA 17

French, Fiona 1944- **37**
See also CA 29-32R; CANR 40; MAICYA;
SAAS 21; SATA 6, 75

French, Paul
See Asimov, Isaac

Fritz, Jean (Guttery) 1915- **2, 14**
See also CA 1-4R; CANR 5, 16, 37; DLB 52;
INT CANR-16; JRDA; MAICYA; SAAS 2;
SATA 1, 29, 72

Fujikawa, Gyo 1908- **25**
See also CA 113; CANR 46; MAICYA; SAAS
16; SATA 39, 76; SATA-Brief 30

Fuller, Maud
See Petersham, Maud (Sylvia Fuller)

Gaberman, Judie Angell 1937- **33**
See also AAYA 11; CA 77-80; CANR 49;
JRDA; SATA 22, 78

Gag, Wanda (Hazel) 1893-1946 .... **4**
See also CA 113; 137; DLB 22; MAICYA;
YABC 1

Galdone, Paul 1907(?)-1986 .... **16**
See also CA 73-76; 121; CANR 13; MAICYA;
SATA 17, 66; SATA-Obit 49

Gallant, Roy A(rthur) 1924- **30**
See also CA 5-8R; CANR 4, 29, 54; CLC 17;
MAICYA; SATA 4, 68

Gantos, Jack **18**
See also Gantos, John (Bryan), Jr.

Gantos, John (Bryan), Jr. 1951-
See Gantos, Jack
See also CA 65-68; CANR 15, 56; SATA 20,
81

Gardam, Jane 1928- **12**
See also CA 49-52; CANR 2, 18, 33, 54; CLC
43; DLB 14, 161; MAICYA; MTCW; SAAS
9; SATA 39, 76; SATA-Brief 28

Garfield, Leon 1921-1996 .... **21**
See also AAYA 8; CA 17-20R; 152; CANR 38,
41; CLC 12; DLB 161; JRDA; MAICYA;
SATA 1, 32, 76; SATA-Obit 90

Garner, Alan 1934- **20**
See also AAYA 18; CA 73-76; CANR 15; CLC
17; DAB; DAM POP; DLB 161; MAICYA;
MTCW; SATA 18, 69

Garnet, A. H.
See Slote, Alfred

Gay, Marie-Louise 1952- **27**
See also CA 135; SAAS 21; SATA 68

Gaze, Gillian
See Barklem, Jill

Geisel, Theodor Seuss 1904-1991
See Dr. Seuss
See also CA 13-16R; 135; CANR 13, 32; DLB
61; DLBY 91; MAICYA; MTCW; SATA 1,
28, 75; SATA-Obit 67

George, Jean Craighead 1919- **1**
See also AAYA 8; CA 5-8R; CANR 25; CLC
35; DLB 52; JRDA; MAICYA; SATA 2, 68

Gerrard, Roy 1935-1997 .... **23**
See also CA 110; 160; CANR 57; SATA 47,
90; SATA-Brief 45

Gewe, Raddory
See Gorey, Edward (St. John)

Gibbons, Gail 1944- **8**
See also CA 69-72; CANR 12; MAICYA;
SAAS 12; SATA 23, 72

Giblin, James Cross 1933- **29**
See also CA 106; CANR 24; MAICYA; SAAS
12; SATA 33, 75

Ginsburg, Mirra **45**
See also CA 17-20R; CANR 11, 28, 54; SATA
6, 92

Giovanni, Nikki 1943- **6**
See also AAYA 22; AITN 1; BLC; BW 2;
CA 29-32R; CAAS 6; CANR 18, 41, 60;
CLC 2, 4, 19, 64; DA; DAB; DAC; DAM
MST, MULT, POET; DLB 5, 41; INT
CANR-18; MAICYA; MTCW; PC 19;
SATA 24; WLCS

Glubok, Shirley (Astor) **1**
See also CA 5-8R; CANR 4, 43; MAICYA;
SAAS 7; SATA 6, 68

Goble, Paul 1933- **21**
See also CA 93-96; CANR 16; MAICYA;
SATA 25, 69

Godden, (Margaret) Rumer 1907- **20**
See also AAYA 6; CA 5-8R; CANR 4, 27, 36,
55; CLC 53; DLB 161; MAICYA; SAAS 12;
SATA 3, 36

Goffstein, (Marilyn) Brooke 1940- **3**
See also CA 21-24R; CANR 9, 28; DLB 61;
MAICYA; SATA 8, 70

Goodall, John Strickland 1908-1996 .... **25**
See also CA 33-36R; 152; MAICYA; SATA 4,
66; SATA-Obit 91

Gordon, Sheila 1927- **27**
See also CA 132; SATA 88

Gorey, Edward (St. John) 1925- **36**
See also CA 5-8R; CANR 9, 30; DLB 61; INT
CANR-30; MAICYA; SATA 29, 70; SATA-
Brief 27

Goscinny, Rene 1926-1977 .... **37**
See also CA 117; 113; SATA 47; SATA-Brief
39

Graham, Bob 1942- **31**
See also SATA 63

Graham, Lorenz (Bell) 1902-1989 .... **10**
See also BW 1; CA 9-12R; 129; CANR 25;
DLB 76; MAICYA; SAAS 5; SATA 2, 74;
SATA-Obit 63

Grahame, Kenneth 1859-1932 .... **5**
See also CA 108; 136; DAB; DLB 34, 141, 178;
MAICYA; TCLC 64; YABC 1

Gramatky, Hardie 1907-1979 .... **22**
See also AITN 1; CA 1-4R; 85-88; CANR 3;
DLB 22; MAICYA; SATA 1, 30; SATA-
Obit 23

Greenaway, Kate 1846-1901 .... **6**
See also CA 137; DLB 141; MAICYA; YABC
2

Greene, Bette 1934- **2**
See also AAYA 7; CA 53-56; CANR 4;
CLC 30; JRDA; MAICYA; SAAS 16;
SATA 8

Greenfield, Eloise 1929- **4, 38**
See also BW 2; CA 49-52; CANR 1, 19, 43;
INT CANR-19; JRDA; MAICYA; SAAS 16;
SATA 19, 61

Gregory, Jean
See Ure, Jean

Grewdead, Roy
See Gorey, Edward (St. John)

Grey Owl **32**
See also Belaney, Archibald Stansfeld
See also DLB 92

Grifalconi, Ann 1929- **35**
See also CA 5-8R; CANR 9, 35; MAICYA;
SAAS 16; SATA 2, 66

Grimes, Nikki 1950- **42**
See also CA 77-80; CANR 60; SATA 93

Gripe, Maria (Kristina) 1923- **5**
See also CA 29-32R; CANR 17, 39; MAICYA;
SATA 2, 74

Grode, Redway
See Gorey, Edward (St. John)

Gruelle, John (Barton) 1880-1938
See Gruelle, Johnny
See also CA 115; SATA 35; SATA-Brief 32

Gruelle, Johnny 34
See also Gruelle, John (Barton)
See also DLB 22

Guillot, Rene 1900-1969 22
See also CA 49-52; CANR 39; SATA 7

Guy, Rosa (Cuthbert) 1928- 13
See also AAYA 4; BW 2; CA 17-20R; CANR
14, 34; CLC 26; DLB 33; JRDA; MAICYA;
SATA 14, 62

Haar, Jaap ter 15
See also ter Haar, Jaap

Hadley, Lee 1934-1995 40
See also Irwin, Hadley
See also CA 101; 149; CANR 19, 36;
MAICYA; SATA 47, 89; SATA-Brief 38;
SATA-Obit 86

Haertling, Peter 1933-
See Hartling, Peter
See also CA 101; CANR 22, 48; DLB 75;
MAICYA; SATA 66

Hagon, Priscilla
See Allan, Mabel Esther

Haig-Brown, Roderick (Langmere) 1908-
1976 31
See also CA 5-8R; 69-72; CANR 4, 38; CLC
21; DLB 88; MAICYA; SATA 12

Haley, Gail E(inhart) 1939- 21
See also CA 21-24R; CANR 14, 35; MAICYA;
SAAS 13; SATA 43, 78; SATA-Brief 28

Hamilton, Clive
See Lewis, C(live) S(taples)

Hamilton, Virginia 1936- 1, 11, 40
See also AAYA 2, 21; BW 2; CA 25-28R;
CANR 20, 37; CLC 26; DAM MULT; DLB
33, 52; INT CANR-20; JRDA; MAICYA;
MTCW; SATA 4, 56, 79

Hamley, Dennis 1935- 47
See also CA 57-60; CANR 11, 26; SAAS 22;
SATA 39, 69

Handford, Martin (John) 1956- 22
See also CA 137; MAICYA; SATA 64

Hansen, Joyce (Viola) 1942- 21
See also BW 2; CA 105; CANR 43; JRDA;
MAICYA; SAAS 15; SATA 46; SATA-Brief
39

Hargrave, Leonie
See Disch, Thomas M(ichael)

Harris, Christie (Lucy) Irwin 1907- 47
See also CA 5-8R; CANR 6; CLC 12; DLB
88; JRDA; MAICYA; SAAS 10; SATA 6,
74

Harris, Lavinia
See St. John, Nicole

Harris, Rosemary (Jeanne) 30
See also CA 33-36R; CANR 13, 30; SAAS 7;
SATA 4, 82

Hartling, Peter 29
See also Haertling, Peter
See also DLB 75

Haskins, James S. 1941- 3, 39
See also Haskins, Jim
See also AAYA 14; BW 2; CA 33-36R; CANR
25, 48; JRDA; MAICYA; SATA 9, 69

Haskins, Jim
See Haskins, James S.
See also SAAS 4

Haugaard, Erik Christian 1923- 11
See also CA 5-8R; CANR 3, 38; JRDA;
MAICYA; SAAS 12; SATA 4, 68

Hautzig, Esther Rudomin 1930- 22
See also CA 1-4R; CANR 5, 20, 46; JRDA;
MAICYA; SAAS 15; SATA 4, 68

Hay, Timothy
See Brown, Margaret Wise

Haywood, Carolyn 1898-1990 22
See also CA 5-8R; 130; CANR 5, 20;
MAICYA; SATA 1, 29, 75; SATA-Obit 64

Heine, Helme 1941- 18
See also CA 135; MAICYA; SATA 67

Henkes, Kevin 1960- 23
See also CA 114; CANR 38; MAICYA; SATA
43, 76

Henry, Marguerite 1902- 4
See also CA 17-20R; CANR 9; DLB 22; JRDA;
MAICYA; SAAS 7; SATA 11, 69

Hentoff, Nat(han Irving) 1925- 1
See also AAYA 4; CA 1-4R; CAAS 6; CANR
5, 25; CLC 26; INT CANR-25; JRDA;
MAICYA; SATA 42, 69; SATA-Brief 27

Herge 6
See also Remi, Georges

Highwater, Jamake (Mamake) 1942(?)- ... 17
See also AAYA 7; CA 65-68; CAAS 7; CANR
10, 34; CLC 12; DLB 52; DLBY 85; JRDA;
MAICYA; SATA 32, 69; SATA-Brief 30

Hill, Eric 1927- 13
See also CA 134; MAICYA; SATA 66; SATA-
Brief 53

Hilton, Margaret Lynette 1946-
See Hilton, Nette
See also CA 136; SATA 68

Hilton, Nette 25
See also Hilton, Margaret Lynette
See also SAAS 21

Hinton, S(usan) E(loise) 1950- 3, 23
See also AAYA 2; CA 81-84; CANR 32, 62;
CLC 30; DA; DAB; DAC; DAM MST,
NOV; JRDA; MAICYA; MTCW; SATA 19,
58

Ho, Minfong 1951- 28
See also CA 77-80; SATA 15, 94

Hoban, Russell (Conwell) 1925- 3
See also CA 5-8R; CANR 23, 37; CLC 7, 25;
DAM NOV; DLB 52; MAICYA; MTCW;
SATA 1, 40, 78

Hoban, Tana 13
See also CA 93-96; CANR 23; MAICYA;
SAAS 12; SATA 22, 70

Hoberman, Mary Ann 1930- 22
See also CA 41-44R; MAICYA; SAAS 18;
SATA 5, 72

Hogrogian, Nonny 1932- 2
See also CA 45-48; CANR 2, 49; MAICYA;
SAAS 1; SATA 7, 74

Holton, Leonard
See Wibberley, Leonard (Patrick O'Connor)

Hopkins, Lee Bennett 1938- 44
See also AAYA 18; CA 25-28R; CANR 29,
55; JRDA; MAICYA; SAAS 4; SATA 3,
68

Houston, James A(rchibald) 1921- 3
See also AAYA 18; CA 65-68; CANR 38, 60;
DAC; DAM MST; JRDA; MAICYA; SAAS
17; SATA 13, 74

Howe, James 1946- 9
See also CA 105; CANR 22, 46; JRDA;
MAICYA; SATA 29, 71

Howker, Janni 1957- 14
See also AAYA 9; CA 137; JRDA; MAICYA;
SAAS 13; SATA 72; SATA-Brief 46

Hudson, Jan 1954-1990 40
See also AAYA 22; CA 136; JRDA; SATA
77

Hughes, Edward James
See Hughes, Ted
See also DAM MST, POET

Hughes, (James) Langston 1902-1967 17
See also AAYA 12; BLC; BW 1; CA 1-4R; 25-
28R; CANR 1, 34; CDALB 1929-1941; CLC
1, 5, 10, 15, 35, 44; DA; DAB; DAC; DAM
DRAM, MST, MULT, POET; DC 3; DLB
4, 7, 48, 51, 86; JRDA; MAICYA; MTCW;
PC 1; SATA 4, 33; SSC 6; WLC

Hughes, Monica (Ince) 1925- 9
See also AAYA 19; CA 77-80; CANR 23,
46; JRDA; MAICYA; SAAS 11; SATA
15, 70

Hughes, Shirley 1927- 15
See also CA 85-88; CANR 24, 47; MAICYA;
SATA 16, 70

Hughes, Ted 1930- 3
See also Hughes, Edward James
See also CA 1-4R; CANR 1, 33; CLC 2, 4, 9,
14, 37; DAB; DAC; DLB 40, 161;
MAICYA; MTCW; PC 7; SATA 49;
SATA-Brief 27

Hungerford, Pixie
See Brinsmead, H(esba) F(ay)

Hunt, Irene 1907- 1
See also AAYA 18; CA 17-20R; CANR 8, 57;
DLB 52; JRDA; MAICYA; SATA 2, 91

Hunter, Kristin (Eggleston) 1931- **3**
See also AITN 1; BW 1; CA 13-16R; CANR
13; CLC 35; DLB 33; INT CANR-13;
MAICYA; SAAS 10; SATA 12

Hunter, Mollie 1922- **25**
See also McIlwraith, Maureen Mollie Hunter
See also AAYA 13; CANR 37; CLC 21; DLB
161; JRDA; MAICYA; SAAS 7; SATA 54

Hurmence, Belinda 1921- **25**
See also AAYA 17; CA 145; JRDA; SAAS 20;
SATA 77

Hutchins, Pat 1942- **20**
See also CA 81-84; CANR 15, 32; MAICYA;
SAAS 16; SATA 15, 70

Hyde, Margaret O(ldroyd) 1917- **23**
See also CA 1-4R; CANR 1, 36; CLC 21;
JRDA; MAICYA; SAAS 8; SATA 1, 42, 76

Irving, Robert
See Adler, Irving

Irwin, Ann(abelle Bowen) 1915- **40**
See also Irwin, Hadley
See also CA 101; CANR 19, 36; MAICYA;
SATA 44, 89; SATA-Brief 38

Irwin, Hadley **40**
See also Hadley, Lee; Irwin, Ann(abelle
Bowen)
See also AAYA 13; SAAS 14

Isadora, Rachel 1953(?)- **7**
See also CA 111; 137; MAICYA; SATA 54,
79; SATA-Brief 32

Iwamatsu, Jun Atsushi 1908-1994
See Yashima, Taro
See also CA 73-76; 146; CANR 45; MAICYA;
SATA 14, 81

Iwasaki (Matsumoto), Chihiro 1918-1974 **18**

Jackson, Jesse 1908-1983 .... **28**
See also BW 1; CA 25-28R; 109; CANR 27; CLC
12; MAICYA; SATA 2, 29; SATA-Obit 48

Jacques, Brian 1939- **21**
See also AAYA 20; CA 127; JRDA; SATA 62, 95

James, Dynely
See Mayne, William (James Carter)

Janeczko, Paul B(ryan) 1945- **47**
See also AAYA 9; CA 104; CANR 22, 49;
SAAS 18; SATA 53

Janosch **26**
See also Eckert, Horst

Jansson, Tove Marika 1914- **2**
See also CA 17-20R; CANR 38; MAICYA;
SATA 3, 41

Jarrell, Randall 1914-1965 .... **6**
See also CA 5-8R; 25-28R; CABS 2; CANR 6,
34; CDALB 1941-1968; CLC 1, 2, 6, 9, 13,
49; DAM POET; DLB 48, 52; MAICYA;
MTCW; SATA 7

Jeffers, Susan 1942- **30**
See also CA 97-100; CANR 44; MAICYA;
SATA 17, 70

Jennings, Paul 1943- **40**
See also SATA 88

Johnson, Angela 1961- **33**
See also CA 138; SATA 69

Johnson, James Weldon 1871-1938 .... **32**
See also BLC; BW 1; CA 104; 125; CDALB
1917-1929; DAM MULT, POET; DLB 51;
MTCW; SATA 31; TCLC 3, 19

Johnston, Julie 1941- **41**
See also CA 146; SAAS 24; SATA 78

Johnston, Norma
See St. John, Nicole
See also AAYA 12; JRDA; SATA 29

Jonas, Ann 1932- **12**
See also CA 118; 136; MAICYA; SATA 50;
SATA-Brief 42

Jones, Diana Wynne 1934- **23**
See also AAYA 12; CA 49-52; CANR 4, 26,
56; CLC 26; DLB 161; JRDA; MAICYA;
SAAS 7; SATA 9, 70

Jones, Geraldine
See McCaughrean, Geraldine

Jones, Tim(othy) Wynne
See Wynne-Jones, Tim(othy)

Jordan, June 1936- **10**
See also AAYA 2; BW 2; CA 33-36R; CANR
25; CLC 5, 11, 23; DAM MULT, POET;
DLB 38; MAICYA; MTCW; SATA 4

Joyce, Bill
See Joyce, William

Joyce, William 1959(?)- **26**
See also CA 124; SATA 72; SATA-Brief 46

Kaestner, Erich 1899-1974 .... **4**
See also CA 73-76; 49-52; CANR 40; DLB 56;
MAICYA; SATA 14

Kalman, Maira 1949(?)- **32**
See also CA 161

Kark, Nina Mary (Mabey)
See Bawden, Nina (Mary Mabey)
See also SATA 4

Katz, Welwyn Wilton 1948- **45**
See also AAYA 19; CA 154; JRDA; SATA 62

Keats, Ezra Jack 1916-1983 .... **1, 35**
See also AITN 1; CA 77-80; 109; DLB 61;
MAICYA; SATA 14, 57; SATA-Obit 34

Keeping, Charles (William James) 1924-
1988 .... **34**
See also CA 21-24R; 125; CANR 11, 43;
MAICYA; SATA 9, 69; SATA-Obit 56

Kelleher, Victor (Michael Kitchener) 1939- **36**
See also CA 126; CANR 56; SATA 75; SATA-
Brief 52

Keller, Holly 1942- **45**
See also CA 118; SATA 76; SATA-Brief 42

Kellogg, Steven 1941- **6**
See also CA 49-52; CANR 1; DLB 61;
MAICYA; SATA 8, 57

Kemp, Gene 1926- **29**
See also CA 69-72; CANR 12; MAICYA;
SATA 25, 75

Kennedy, Joseph Charles 1929-
See Kennedy, X. J.
See also CA 1-4R; CANR 4, 30, 40; SATA 14, 86

Kennedy, X. J. **27**
See also Kennedy, Joseph Charles
See also CAAS 9; CLC 8, 42; DLB 5; SAAS 22

Kenny, Kathryn
See Krull, Kathleen

Kenny, Kevin
See Krull, Kathleen

Kerr, M. E. **29**
See also Meaker, Marijane (Agnes)
See also AAYA 2; CLC 12, 35; SAAS 1

Kerry, Lois
See Duncan, Lois

Khalsa, Dayal Kaur 1943-1989 .... **30**
See also CA 137; MAICYA; SATA 62

Kherdian, David 1931- **24**
See also CA 21-24R; CAAS 2; CANR 39; CLC
6, 9; JRDA; MAICYA; SATA 16, 74

King-Smith, Dick 1922- **40**
See also CA 105; CANR 22, 48; MAICYA;
SATA 47, 80; SATA-Brief 38

Kipling, (Joseph) Rudyard 1865-1936 ...... **39**
See also CA 105; 120; CANR 33; CDBLB
1890-1914; DA; DAB; DAC; DAM MST,
POET; DLB 19, 34, 141, 156; MAICYA;
MTCW; PC 3; SSC 5; TCLC 8, 17; WLC;
YABC 2

Klein, Norma 1938-1989 .... **2, 19**
See also AAYA 2; CA 41-44R; 128; CANR 15,
37; CLC 30; INT CANR-15; JRDA;
MAICYA; SAAS 1; SATA 7, 57

Klein, Robin 1936- **21**
See also AAYA 21; CA 116; CANR 40; JRDA;
MAICYA; SATA 55, 80; SATA-Brief 45

Knight, David C(arpenter) 1925- **38**
See also CA 73-76; SATA 14

Knight, Kathryn Lasky
See Lasky, Kathryn

Knye, Cassandra
See Disch, Thomas M(ichael)

Konigsburg, E(laine) L(obl) 1930- **1, 47**
See also AAYA 3; CA 21-24R; CANR 17, 39,
59; DLB 52; INT CANR-17; JRDA;
MAICYA; MTCW; SATA 4, 48, 94

Korinets, Iurii Iosifovich
See Korinetz, Yuri (Iosifovich)

Korinetz, Yuri (Iosifovich) 1923- **4**
See also CA 61-64; CANR 11; SATA 9

Korman, Gordon (Richard) 1963- **25**
See also AAYA 10; CA 112; CANR 34, 56;
JRDA; MAICYA; SATA 49, 81; SATA-
Brief 41

Kotzwinkle, William 1938- **6**
　　See also CA 45-48; CANR 3, 44; CLC 5, 14,
　　35; DLB 173; MAICYA; SATA 24, 70

Kovalski, Maryann 1951- **34**
　　See also SAAS 21; SATA 58

Krahn, Fernando 1935- **3**
　　See also CA 65-68; CANR 11; SATA 49;
　　SATA-Brief 31

Krauss, Ruth (Ida) 1911-1993 .... **42**
　　See also CA 1-4R; 141; CANR 1, 13, 47;
　　DLB 52; MAICYA; SATA 1, 30; SATA-
　　Obit 75

Krementz, Jill 1940- **5**
　　See also AITN 1, 2; CA 41-44R; CANR 23,
　　46; INT CANR-23; MAICYA; SAAS 8;
　　SATA 17, 71

Kruess, James 1926-
　　See Kruss, James
　　See also CA 53-56; CANR 5; MAICYA; SATA
　　8

Krull, Kathleen 1952- **44**
　　See also CA 106; SATA 52, 80; SATA-Brief
　　39

Kruss, James **9**
　　See also Kruess, James

Kuratomi, Chizuko 1939- **32**
　　See also CA 21-24R; CANR 10; SATA 12

Kurelek, William 1927-1977 .... **2**
　　See also CA 49-52; CANR 3; JRDA; MAICYA;
　　SATA 8; SATA-Obit 27

Kuskin, Karla (Seidman) 1932- **4**
　　See also CA 1-4R; CANR 4, 22, 41; MAICYA;
　　SAAS 3; SATA 2, 68

Lagerloef, Selma (Ottiliana Lovisa) 1858-1940
　　See Lagerlof, Selma (Ottiliana Lovisa)
　　See also CA 108; SATA 15; TCLC 4, 36

Lagerlof, Selma (Ottiliana Lovisa) **7**
　　See also Lagerloef, Selma (Ottiliana Lovisa)
　　See also SATA 15

Lang, T. T.
　　See Taylor, Theodore

Langstaff, John (Meredith) 1920- **3**
　　See also CA 1-4R; CANR 4, 49; MAICYA;
　　SATA 6, 68

Langton, Jane (Gillson) 1922- **33**
　　See also CA 1-4R; CANR 1, 18, 40; MAICYA;
　　SAAS 5; SATA 3, 68

Larkin, Maia
　　See Wojciechowska, Maia (Teresa)

Lasky, Kathryn 1944- **11**
　　See also AAYA 19; CA 69-72; CANR 11;
　　JRDA; MAICYA; SATA 13, 69

Latham, Mavis
　　See Clark, Mavis Thorpe

Lauber, Patricia (Grace) 1924- **16**
　　See also CA 9-12R; CANR 6, 24, 38; JRDA;
　　MAICYA; SATA 1, 33, 75

Lavine, Sigmund Arnold 1908- **35**
　　See also CA 1-4R; CANR 4, 19, 41; SATA 3,
　　82

Lawson, Robert 1892-1957 .... **2**
　　See also CA 118; 137; DLB 22; MAICYA;
　　YABC 2

Leaf, (Wilbur) Munro 1905-1976 .... **25**
　　See also CA 73-76; 69-72; CANR 29;
　　MAICYA; SATA 20

Lear, Edward 1812-1888 .... **1**
　　See also DLB 32, 163, 166; MAICYA; NCLC
　　3; SATA 18

Lee, Dennis (Beynon) 1939- **3**
　　See also CA 25-28R; CANR 11, 31, 57, 61;
　　DAC; DLB 53; MAICYA; SATA 14

Le Guin, Ursula K(roeber) 1929- **3, 28**
　　See also AAYA 9; AITN 1; CA 21-24R; CANR
　　9, 32, 52; CDALB 1968-1988; CLC 8, 13,
　　22, 45, 71; DAB; DAC; DAM MST, POP;
　　DLB 8, 52; INT CANR-32; JRDA;
　　MAICYA; MTCW; SATA 4, 52; SSC 12

L'Engle, Madeleine (Camp Franklin) 1918- **1, 14**
　　See also AAYA 1; AITN 2; CA 1-4R; CANR
　　3, 21, 39; CLC 12; DAM POP; DLB 52;
　　JRDA; MAICYA; MTCW; SAAS 15; SATA
　　1, 27, 75

Lenski, Lois 1893-1974 .... **26**
　　See also CA 13-14; 53-56; CANR 41; CAP 1;
　　DLB 22; MAICYA; SATA 1, 26

Lerner, Carol 1927- **34**
　　See also CA 102; SAAS 12; SATA 33, 86

LeShan, Eda J(oan) 1922- **6**
　　See also CA 13-16R; CANR 21; SATA 21

Lester, Julius (Bernard) 1939- **2, 41**
　　See also AAYA 12; BW 2; CA 17-20R; CANR
　　8, 23, 43; JRDA; MAICYA; SATA 12, 74

Lewin, Hugh 1939- **9**
　　See also CA 113; CANR 38; MAICYA; SATA
　　72; SATA-Brief 40

Lewis, C(live) S(taples) 1898-1963 .... **3, 27**
　　See also AAYA 3; CA 81-84; CANR 33;
　　CDBLB 1945-1960; CLC 1, 3, 6, 14, 27; DA;
　　DAB; DAC; DAM MST, NOV, POP; DLB
　　15, 100, 160; JRDA; MAICYA; MTCW;
　　SATA 13; WLC

Lindgren, Astrid (Ericsson) 1907- **1, 39**
　　See also CA 13-16R; CANR 39; MAICYA;
　　SATA 2, 38

Lindgren, Barbro 1937- **20**
　　See also CA 149; SATA 63; SATA-Brief 46

Lindsay, Norman Alfred William 1879-19698
　　See also CA 102; SATA 67

Lionni, Leo(nard) 1910- **7**
　　See also CA 53-56; CANR 38; DLB 61;
　　MAICYA; SATA 8, 72

Lipsyte, Robert (Michael) 1938- **23**
　　See also AAYA 7; CA 17-20R; CANR 8, 57;
　　CLC 21; DA; DAC; DAM MST, NOV;
　　JRDA; MAICYA; SATA 5, 68

Little, (Flora) Jean 1932- **4**
　　See also CA 21-24R; CANR 42; DAC; DAM MST;
　　JRDA; MAICYA; SAAS 17; SATA 2, 68

Lively, Penelope (Margaret) 1933- **7**
　　See also CA 41-44R; CANR 29; CLC 32, 50;
　　DAM NOV; DLB 14, 161; JRDA; MAICYA;
　　MTCW; SATA 7, 60

Livingston, Myra Cohn 1926-1996 .... **7**
　　See also CA 1-4R; 153; CANR 1, 33, 58; DLB
　　61; INT CANR-33; MAICYA; SAAS 1;
　　SATA 5, 68,; SATA-Obit 92

Lobel, Arnold (Stark) 1933-1987 .... **5**
　　See also AITN 1; CA 1-4R; 124; CANR 2, 33;
　　DLB 61; MAICYA; SATA 6, 55; SATA-
　　Obit 54

Locke, Robert 1944-
　　See Bess, Clayton
　　See also CA 129; SATA 63

Locker, Thomas 1937- **14**
　　See also CA 128; MAICYA; SATA 59

Lofting, Hugh (John) 1886-1947 .... **19**
　　See also CA 109; 137; DLB 160; MAICYA;
　　SATA 15

Lorenzini, Carlo 1826-1890
　　See Collodi, Carlo
　　See also MAICYA; SATA 29

Louisburgh, Sheila Burnford
　　See Burnford, Sheila (Philip Cochrane Every)

Lowry, Lois 1937- **6, 46**
　　See also AAYA 5; CA 69-72; CANR 13, 43;
　　DLB 52; INT CANR-13; JRDA; MAICYA;
　　SAAS 3; SATA 23, 70

Lunn, Janet (Louise Swoboda) 1928- **18**
　　See also CA 33-36R; CANR 22; JRDA;
　　MAICYA; SAAS 12; SATA 4, 68

Macaulay, David (Alexander) 1946- **3, 14**
　　See also AAYA 21; BEST 89:2; CA 53-56;
　　CANR 5, 34; DLB 61; INT CANR-34;
　　MAICYA; SATA 46, 72; SATA-Brief 27

MacDonald, Golden
　　See Brown, Margaret Wise

Mackay, Claire 1930- **43**
　　See also CA 105; CANR 22, 50; SATA 40

MacLachlan, Patricia 1938- **14**
　　See also AAYA 18; CA 118; 136; JRDA;
　　MAICYA; SATA 62; SATA-Brief 42

Maddison, Angela Mary 1923-
　　See Banner, Angela
　　See also CA 53-56; SATA 10

Maestro, Betsy C(rippen) 1944- **45**
　　See also CA 61-64; CANR 8, 23, 37; MAICYA;
　　SATA 59; SATA-Brief 30

Maestro, Giulio 1942- **45**
　　See also CA 57-60; CANR 8, 23, 37; MAICYA;
　　SATA 8, 59

Mahy, Margaret 1936- **7**
　　See also AAYA 8; CA 69-72; CANR 13, 30,
　　38; JRDA; MAICYA; SATA 14, 69

Major, Kevin (Gerald) 1949- **11**
See also AAYA 16; CA 97-100; CANR 21, 38;
CLC 26; DAC; DLB 60; INT CANR-21;
JRDA; MAICYA; SATA 32, 82

Manley, Seon 1921- **3**
See also CA 85-88; SAAS 2; SATA 15

March, Carl
See Fleischman, (Albert) Sid(ney)

Mark, Jan(et Marjorie) 1943- **11**
See also CA 93-96; CANR 17, 42; MAICYA;
SATA 22, 69

Markoosie **23**
See also Markoosie, Patsauq
See also DAM MULT; NNAL

Markoosie, Patsauq 1942-
See Markoosie
See also CA 101

Marks, J
See Highwater, Jamake (Mamake)

Marks-Highwater, J
See Highwater, Jamake (Mamake)

Marsden, John 1950- **34**
See also AAYA 20; CA 135; SAAS 22; SATA
66

Marshall, Edward
See Marshall, James (Edward)

Marshall, James (Edward) 1942-1992 ...... **21**
See also CA 41-44R; 139; CANR 38; DLB 61;
MAICYA; SATA 6, 51, 75

Martin, Ann M(atthews) 1955- **32**
See also AAYA 6; CA 111; CANR 32; INT
CANR-32; JRDA; MAICYA; SATA 44, 70;
SATA-Brief 41

Martin, Fredric
See Christopher, Matt(hew Frederick)

Maruki, Toshi 1912- **19**

Mathis, Sharon Bell 1937- **3**
See also AAYA 12; BW 2; CA 41-44R; DLB
33; JRDA; MAICYA; SAAS 3; SATA 7, 58

Mattingley, Christobel (Rosemary) 1931- **24**
See also CA 97-100; CANR 20, 47; MAICYA;
SAAS 18; SATA 37, 85

Mayer, Mercer 1943- **11**
See also CA 85-88; CANR 38; DLB 61;
MAICYA; SATA 16, 32, 73

Mayne, William (James Carter) 1928- **25**
See also AAYA 20; CA 9-12R; CANR 37; CLC
12; JRDA; MAICYA; SAAS 11; SATA 6,
68

Mazer, Harry 1925- **16**
See also AAYA 5; CA 97-100; CANR 32; INT
97-100; JRDA; MAICYA; SAAS 11; SATA
31, 67

Mazer, Norma Fox 1931- **23**
See also AAYA 5; CA 69-72; CANR 12, 32;
CLC 26; JRDA; MAICYA; SAAS 1; SATA
24, 67

McBratney, Sam 1943- **44**
See also CA 155; SATA 89

McCaughrean, Geraldine 1951- **38**
See also CA 117; CANR 52; SATA 87

McCloskey, (John) Robert 1914- **7**
See also CA 9-12R; CANR 47; DLB 22;
MAICYA; SATA 2, 39

McClung, Robert M(arshall) 1916- **11**
See also AITN 2; CA 13-16R; CANR 6, 21,
46; MAICYA; SAAS 15; SATA 2, 68

McCord, David (Thompson Watson) 1897-
1997 .... **9**
See also CA 73-76; 157; CANR 38; DLB 61;
MAICYA; SATA 18

McCulloch, Sarah
See Ure, Jean

McCully, Emily Arnold **46**
See also Arnold, Emily
See also SAAS 7; SATA 5

McDermott, Gerald 1941- **9**
See also AITN 2; CA 85-88; MAICYA; SATA
16, 74

McHargue, Georgess 1941- **2**
See also CA 25-28R; CANR 24; JRDA; SAAS
5; SATA 4, 77

McIlwraith, Maureen Mollie Hunter
See Hunter, Mollie
See also SATA 2

McKee, David (John) 1935- **38**
See also CA 137; MAICYA; SATA 70

McKinley, (Jennifer Carolyn) Robin 1952- **10**
See also AAYA 4; CA 107; CANR 31, 58; DLB 52;
JRDA; MAICYA; SATA 50, 89; SATA-Brief 32

McKissack, Patricia (L'Ann) C(arwell)
1944- **23**
See also BW 2; CA 118; CANR 38; JRDA;
MAICYA; SATA 51, 73

McMillan, Bruce 1947- **47**
See also CA 73-76; CANR 13, 35; MAICYA;
SATA 22, 70

McMillan, Naomi
See Grimes, Nikki

Meaker, Marijane (Agnes) 1927-
See Kerr, M. E.
See also CA 107; CANR 37; INT 107; JRDA;
MAICYA; MTCW; SATA 20, 61

Meltzer, Milton 1915- **13**
See also AAYA 8; CA 13-16R; CANR 38; CLC
26; DLB 61; JRDA; MAICYA; SAAS 1;
SATA 1, 50, 80

Merriam, Eve 1916-1992 .... **14**
See also CA 5-8R; 137; CANR 29; DLB 61;
MAICYA; SATA 3, 40, 73

Metcalf, Suzanne
See Baum, L(yman) Frank

Meyer, June
See Jordan, June

Milne, A(lan) A(lexander) 1882-1956 ... **1, 26**
See also CA 104; 133; DAB; DAC; DAM MST;
DLB 10, 77, 100, 160; MAICYA; MTCW;
TCLC 6; YABC 1

Milne, Lorus J. **22**
See also CA 33-36R; CANR 14; SAAS 18;
SATA 5

Milne, Margery **22**
See also CA 33-36R; CANR 14; SAAS 18;
SATA 5

Minarik, Else Holmelund 1920- **33**
See also CA 73-76; CANR 48; MAICYA;
SATA 15

Mohr, Nicholasa 1935- **22**
See also AAYA 8; CA 49-52; CANR 1, 32;
CLC 12; DAM MULT; DLB 145; HLC; HW;
JRDA; SAAS 8; SATA 8

Molin, Charles
See Mayne, William (James Carter)

Monjo, F(erdinand) N(icholas III) 1924-
1978 .... **2**
See also CA 81-84; CANR 37; MAICYA;
SATA 16

Montgomery, L(ucy) M(aud) 1874-1942 .... **8**
See also AAYA 12; CA 108; 137; DAC; DAM
MST; DLB 92; DLBD 14; JRDA; MAICYA;
TCLC 51; YABC 1

Moore, Lilian 1909- **15**
See also CA 103; CANR 38; MAICYA; SATA 52

Mowat, Farley (McGill) 1921- **20**
See also AAYA 1; CA 1-4R; CANR 4, 24, 42;
CLC 26; DAC; DAM MST; DLB 68; INT
CANAR-24; JRDA; MAICYA; MTCW;
SATA 3, 55

Mude, O.
See Gorey, Edward (St. John)

Mueller, Joerg 1942- **43**
See also CA 136; SATA 67

Mukerji, Dhan Gopal 1890-1936 .... **10**
See also CA 119; 136; MAICYA; SATA 40

Muller, Jorg
See Mueller, Joerg

Mun
See Leaf, (Wilbur) Munro

Munari, Bruno 1907- **9**
See also CA 73-76; CANR 38; MAICYA;
SATA 15

Munsch, Robert (Norman) 1945- **19**
See also CA 121; CANR 37; MAICYA; SATA
50, 83; SATA-Brief 48

Murphy, Jill (Frances) 1949- **39**
See also CA 105; CANR 44, 50; MAICYA;
SATA 37, 70

Myers, Walter Dean 1937- **4, 16, 35**
See also AAYA 4; BLC; BW 2; CA 33-36R;
CANR 20, 42; CLC 35; DAM MULT, NOV;
DLB 33; INT CANR-20; JRDA; MAICYA;
SAAS 2; SATA 41, 71; SATA-Brief 27

Myers, Walter M.
See Myers, Walter Dean

Naidoo, Beverley 1943- **29**
See also CA 160; SATA 63

Nakatani, Chiyoko 1930-1981 .... **30**
See also CA 77-80; SATA 55; SATA-Brief
40

Namioka, Lensey 1929- **48**
See also CA 69-72; CANR 11, 27, 52; SAAS
24; SATA 27, 89

Naylor, Phyllis (Reynolds) 1933- **17**
See also AAYA 4; CA 21-24R; CANR 8, 24,
59; JRDA; MAICYA; SAAS 10; SATA 12,
66

Needle, Jan 1943- **43**
See also CA 106; CANR 28; SAAS 23; SATA
30

Nesbit, E(dith) 1858-1924 .... **3**
See also CA 118; 137; DLB 141, 153, 178;
MAICYA; YABC 1

Ness, Evaline (Michelow) 1911-1986 .... **6**
See also CA 5-8R; 120; CANR 5, 37; DLB 61;
MAICYA; SAAS 1; SATA 1, 26; SATA-
Obit 49

Nielsen, Kay (Rasmus) 1886-1957 .... **16**
See also MAICYA; SATA 16

Nimmo, Jenny 1942- **44**
See also CA 108; CANR 52; SATA 87

Nixon, Joan Lowery 1927- **24**
See also AAYA 12; CA 9-12R; CANR 7, 24,
38; JRDA; MAICYA; SAAS 9; SATA 8, 44,
78

Noestlinger, Christine 1936- **12**
See also CA 115; 123; CANR 38; MAICYA;
SATA 64; SATA-Brief 37

North, Captain George
See Stevenson, Robert Louis (Balfour)

Norton, Mary 1903-1992 .... **6**
See also CA 97-100, 139; DLB 160; MAICYA;
SATA 18, 60; SATA-Obit 72

Nourse, Alan E(dward) 1928-1992 .... **33**
See also CA 1-4R; 145; CANR 3, 21, 45; DLB
8; SATA 48

Oakley, Graham 1929- **7**
See also CA 106; CANR 38, 54; MAICYA;
SATA 30, 84

O'Brien, Robert C. **2**
See also Conly, Robert Leslie
See also AAYA 6

O'Connor, Patrick
See Wibberley, Leonard (Patrick O'Connor)

O'Dell, Scott 1898-1989 .... **1, 16**
See also AAYA 3; CA 61-64; 129; CANR 12,
30; CLC 30; DLB 52; JRDA; MAICYA;
SATA 12, 60

Ofek, Uriel 1926- **28**
See also CA 101; CANR 18; SATA 36

Ogilvy, Gavin
See Barrie, J(ames) M(atthew)

O Mude
See Gorey, Edward (St. John)

Oneal, Elizabeth 1934-
See Oneal, Zibby
See also CA 106; CANR 28; MAICYA; SATA
30, 82

Oneal, Zibby **13**
See also Oneal, Elizabeth
See also AAYA 5; CLC 30; JRDA

Orgel, Doris 1929- **48**
See also AITN 1; CA 45-48; CANR 2; SAAS
19; SATA 7, 85

Orlev, Uri 1931- **30**
See also AAYA 20; CA 101; CANR 34; SAAS
19; SATA 58

Ormerod, Jan(ette Louise) 1946- **20**
See also CA 113; CANR 35; MAICYA; SATA
55, 70; SATA-Brief 44

O'Shea, (Catherine) Pat(ricia Shiels) 1931- **18**
See also CA 145; SATA 87

Ottley, Reginald Leslie 1909-1985 .... **16**
See also CA 93-96; CANR 34; MAICYA;
SATA 26

Owen, Gareth 1936- **31**
See also CA 150; SAAS 14; SATA 83

Oxenbury, Helen 1938- **22**
See also CA 25-28R; CANR 35; MAICYA;
SATA 3, 68

Paisley, Tom 1932-
See Bethancourt, T. Ernesto
See also CA 61-64; CANR 15; SATA 78

Parish, Margaret Cecile 1927-1988
See Parish, Peggy
See also CA 73-76; 127; CANR 18, 38;
MAICYA; SATA 73

Parish, Peggy **22**
See also Parish, Margaret Cecile
See also SATA 17; SATA-Obit 59

Park, Barbara 1947- **34**
See also CA 113; SATA 40, 78; SATA-Brief
35

Pascal, Francine 1938- **25**
See also AAYA 1; CA 115; 123; CANR 39,
50; JRDA; MAICYA; SATA 51, 80; SATA-
Brief 37

Patent, Dorothy Hinshaw 1940- **19**
See also CA 61-64; CANR 9, 24; MAICYA;
SAAS 13; SATA 22, 69

Paterson, Katherine (Womeldorf) 1932- **7**
See also AAYA 1; CA 21-24R; CANR 28, 59;
CLC 12, 30; DLB 52; JRDA; MAICYA;
MTCW; SATA 13, 53, 92

Paton Walsh, Gillian 1937-
See Walsh, Jill Paton
See also CANR 38; JRDA; MAICYA; SAAS
3; SATA 4, 72

Paulsen, Gary 1939- **19**
See also AAYA 2, 17; CA 73-76; CANR 30,
54; JRDA; MAICYA; SATA 22, 50, 54, 79

Pearce, Philippa **9**
See also Christie, (Ann) Philippa
See also CLC 21; DLB 161; MAICYA; SATA
1, 67

Pearson, Kit 1947- **26**
See also AAYA 19; CA 145; JRDA; SATA 77

Peck, Richard (Wayne) 1934- **15**
See also AAYA 1; CA 85-88; CANR 19, 38;
CLC 21; INT CANR-19; JRDA; MAICYA;
SAAS 2; SATA 18, 55

Peck, Robert Newton 1928- **45**
See also AAYA 3; CA 81-84; CANR 31; CLC
17; DA; DAC; DAM MST; JRDA;
MAICYA; SAAS 1; SATA 21, 62

Peet, Bill **12**
See also Peet, William Bartlett

Peet, William Bartlett 1915-
See Peet, Bill
See also CA 17-20R; CANR 38; MAICYA;
SATA 2, 41, 78

Pene du Bois, William (Sherman) 1916-1993 **1**
See also CA 5-8R; CANR 17, 41; DLB 61;
MAICYA; SATA 4, 68; SATA-Obit 74

Petersham, Maud (Sylvia Fuller) 1890-
1971 .... **24**
See also CA 73-76; 33-36R; CANR 29; DLB
22; MAICYA; SATA 17

Petersham, Miska 1888-1960 .... **24**
See also CA 73-76; CANR 29; DLB 22;
MAICYA; SATA 17

Petry, Ann (Lane) 1908-1997 .... **12**
See also BW 1; CA 5-8R; 157; CAAS 6; CANR
4, 46; CLC 1, 7, 18; DLB 76; JRDA;
MAICYA; MTCW; SATA 5; SATA-Obit 94

Peyton, K. M. **3**
See also Peyton, Kathleen Wendy
See also AAYA 20; DLB 161; SAAS 17

Peyton, Kathleen Wendy 1929-
See Peyton, K. M.
See also CA 69-72; CANR 32; JRDA;
MAICYA; SATA 15, 62

Pfeffer, Susan Beth 1948- **11**
See also AAYA 12; CA 29-32R; CANR 31, 58;
JRDA; SAAS 17; SATA 4, 83

Pfister, Marcus **42**
See also SATA 83

Phipson, Joan **5**
See also Fitzhardinge, Joan Margaret
See also AAYA 14; SAAS 3

Pienkowski, Jan (Michal) 1936- **6**
See also CA 65-68; CANR 11, 38; MAICYA;
SATA 6, 58

Pierce, Meredith Ann 1958- **20**
See also AAYA 13; CA 108; CANR 26, 48;
JRDA; MAICYA; SATA 67; SATA-Brief 48

Pig, Edward
See Gorey, Edward (St. John)

Pike, Christopher **29**
See also AAYA 13; CA 136; JRDA; SATA
68

Pilgrim, Anne
See Allan, Mabel Esther

Pilkey, Dav 1966- **48**
See also CA 136; SATA 68

Pinkney, Jerry 1939- **43**
See also MAICYA; SAAS 12; SATA 41, 71;
SATA-Brief 32

Pinkwater, Daniel Manus 1941- **4**
See also Pinkwater, Manus
See also AAYA 1; CA 29-32R; CANR 12, 38;
CLC 35; JRDA; MAICYA; SAAS 3; SATA
46, 76

Pinkwater, Manus
See Pinkwater, Daniel Manus
See also SATA 8

Polacco, Patricia 1944- **40**
See also SATA 74

Politi, Leo 1908-1996 .... **29**
See also CA 17-20R; 151; CANR 13, 47;
MAICYA; SATA 1, 47; SATA-Obit 88

Pollock, Mary
See Blyton, Enid (Mary)

Potter, (Helen) Beatrix 1866-1943 .... **1, 19**
See also CA 108; 137; DLB 141; YABC 1

Poulin, Stephane 1961- **28**

Prelutsky, Jack 1940- **13**
See also CA 93-96; CANR 38; DLB 61;
MAICYA; SATA 22, 66

Pringle, Laurence (Patrick) 1935- **4**
See also CA 29-32R; CANR 14, 60; MAICYA;
SAAS 6; SATA 4, 68

Proeysen, Alf 1914-1970 .... **24**
See also Proysen, Alf
See also CA 136

Provensen, Alice 1918- **11**
See also CA 53-56; CANR 5, 44; MAICYA;
SATA 9, 70

Provensen, Martin (Elias) 1916-1987 .... **11**
See also CA 53-56; 122; CANR 5, 44;
MAICYA; SATA 9, 70; SATA-Obit 51

Proysen, Alf
See Proeysen, Alf
See also SATA 67

Pullman, Philip (Nicholas) 1946- **20**
See also AAYA 15; CA 127; CANR 50; JRDA;
MAICYA; SAAS 17; SATA 65

Pyle, Howard 1853-1911 .... **22**
See also CA 109; 137; DLB 42; DLBD 13;
MAICYA; SATA 16

Ramal, Walter
See de la Mare, Walter (John)

Ransome, Arthur (Michell) 1884-1967 .... **8**
See also CA 73-76; DLB 160; MAICYA; SATA
22

Raskin, Ellen 1928-1984 .... **1, 12**
See also CA 21-24R; 113; CANR 37; DLB 52;
MAICYA; SATA 2, 38

Rau, Margaret 1913- **8**
See also CA 61-64; CANR 8; SATA 9

Rayner, Mary 1933- **41**
See also CA 69-72; CANR 12, 29, 52; SATA
22, 87

Reid Banks, Lynne 1929- **24**
See also Banks, Lynne Reid
See also CA 1-4R; CANR 6, 22, 38; JRDA;
MAICYA; SATA 22, 75

Reiss, Johanna (de Leeuw) 1929(?)- **19**
See also CA 85-88; JRDA; SATA 18

Remi, Georges 1907-1983
See Herge
See also CA 69-72; 109; CANR 31; SATA 13;
SATA-Obit 32

Rey, H(ans) A(ugusto) 1898-1977 .... **5**
See also CA 5-8R; 73-76; CANR 6; DLB 22;
MAICYA; SATA 1, 26, 69

Rey, Margret (Elisabeth) 1906-1996 .... **5**
See also CA 105; 155; CANR 38; MAICYA;
SATA 26, 86; SATA-Obit 93

Rhine, Richard
See Silverstein, Alvin

Rhue, Morton
See Strasser, Todd

Richler, Mordecai 1931- **17**
See also AITN 1; CA 65-68; CANR 31, 62;
CLC 3, 5, 9, 13, 18, 46, 70; DAC; DAM
MST, NOV; DLB 53; MAICYA; MTCW;
SATA 44; SATA-Brief 27

Richter, Hans Peter 1925- **21**
See also CA 45-48; CANR 2; MAICYA; SAAS
11; SATA 6

Rigg, Sharon
See Creech, Sharon

Rinaldi, Ann 1934- **46**
See also AAYA 15; CA 111; JRDA; SATA 51,
78; SATA-Brief 50

Ringgold, Faith 1930- **30**
See also AAYA 19; CA 154; SATA 71

Riq
See Atwater, Richard (Tupper)

Robert, Adrian
See St. John, Nicole

Roberts, Charles G(eorge) D(ouglas) 1860-
1943 .... **33**
See also CA 105; DLB 92; SATA 88; SATA-
Brief 29; TCLC 8

Rockwell, Thomas 1933- **6**
See also CA 29-32R; CANR 44; MAICYA;
SATA 7, 70

Rodari, Gianni 1920-1980 .... **24**

Rodda, Emily 1948(?)- **32**

Rodgers, Mary 1931- **20**
See also CA 49-52; CANR 8, 55; CLC 12; INT
CANR-8; JRDA; MAICYA; SATA 8

Rodman, Maia
See Wojciechowska, Maia (Teresa)

Rosen, Michael (Wayne) 1946- **45**
See also CANR 52; SATA 84

Roughsey, Dick 1921(?)-1985 .... **41**
See also CA 109; SATA 35

Rubinstein, Gillian (Margaret) 1942- **35**
See also AAYA 22; CA 136; SATA 68

Rudomin, Esther
See Hautzig, Esther Rudomin

Ryder, Joanne (Rose) 1946- **37**
See also CA 112; 133; MAICYA; SATA 65;
SATA-Brief 34

Rylant, Cynthia 1954- **15**
See also AAYA 10; CA 136; JRDA; MAICYA;
SAAS 13; SATA 50, 76; SATA-Brief 44

Sachar, Louis 1954- **28**
See also CA 81-84; CANR 15, 33; JRDA;
SATA 63; SATA-Brief 50

Sachs, Marilyn (Stickle) 1927- **2**
See also AAYA 2; CA 17-20R; CANR 13, 47; CLC
35; JRDA; MAICYA; SAAS 2; SATA 3, 68

Sage, Juniper
See Brown, Margaret Wise

**Saint-Exupery, Antoine (Jean Baptiste Marie
Roger) de** 1900-1944 .... **10**
See also CA 108; 132; DAM NOV; DLB 72;
MAICYA; MTCW; SATA 20; TCLC 2, 56;
WLC

St. John, Nicole **46**
See also Johnston, Norma
See also CANR 32; SAAS 7; SATA 89

Salinger, J(erome) D(avid) 1919- **18**
See also AAYA 2; CA 5-8R; CANR 39;
CDALB 1941-1968; CLC 1, 3, 8, 12, 55, 56;
DA; DAB; DAC; DAM MST, NOV, POP;
DLB 2, 102, 173; MAICYA; MTCW; SATA
67; SSC 2, 28; WLC

Sanchez, Sonia 1934- **18**
See also BLC; BW 2; CA 33-36R; CANR 24,
49; CLC 5; DAM MULT; DLB 41; DLBD
8; MAICYA; MTCW; PC 9; SATA 22

Sanchez-Silva, Jose Maria 1911- **12**
See also CA 73-76; MAICYA; SATA 16

San Souci, Robert D. 1946- **43**
See also CA 108; CANR 46; SATA 40, 81

Sasek, Miroslav 1916-1980 .... **4**
See also CA 73-76; 101; SATA 16; SATA-Obit 23

Sattler, Helen Roney 1921-1992 .... **24**
See also CA 33-36R; CANR 14, 31; SATA 4,
74

Sawyer, Ruth 1880-1970 .... **36**
See also CA 73-76; CANR 37; DLB 22;
MAICYA; SATA 17

Say, Allen 1937- **22**
See also CA 29-32R; CANR 30; JRDA;
MAICYA; SATA 28, 69

Scarlett, Susan
See Streatfeild, (Mary) Noel

Scarry, Richard (McClure) 1919-1994 .... **3, 41**
See also CA 17-20R; 145; CANR 18, 39; DLB
61; MAICYA; SATA 2, 35, 75; SATA-Obit
90

Schlein, Miriam 1926- **41**
See also CA 1-4R; CANR 2, 52; SATA 2, 87

Schmidt, Annie M. G. 1911-1995 .... **22**
See also CA 135; 152; SATA 67; SATA-Obit
91

Schwartz, Alvin 1927-1992 .... **3**
See also CA 13-16R; 137; CANR 7, 24, 49;
MAICYA; SATA 4, 56; SATA-Obit 71

Schwartz, Amy 1954- **25**
See also CA 110; CANR 29, 57; INT CANR-
29; SAAS 18; SATA 47, 83; SATA-Brief 41

Schweitzer, Byrd Baylor
See Baylor, Byrd

Scieszka, Jon 1954- **27**
See also AAYA 21; CA 135; SATA 68

Scott, Jack Denton 1915-1995 .... **20**
See also CA 108; CANR 48; MAICYA; SAAS
14; SATA 31, 83

Sebestyen, Ouida 1924- **17**
See also AAYA 8; CA 107; CANR 40; CLC
30; JRDA; MAICYA; SAAS 10; SATA 39

Sefton, Catherine
See Waddell, Martin

Selden, George **8**
See also Thompson, George Selden
See also DLB 52

Selsam, Millicent Ellis 1912-1996 .... **1**
See also CA 9-12R; 154; CANR 5, 38;
MAICYA; SATA 1, 29; SATA-Obit 92

Sendak, Maurice (Bernard) 1928- **1, 17**
See also CA 5-8R; CANR 11, 39; DLB 61; INT
CANR-11; MAICYA; MTCW; SATA 1, 27

Seredy, Kate 1899-1975 .... **10**
See also CA 5-8R; 57-60; DLB 22; MAICYA;
SATA 1; SATA-Obit 24

Serraillier, Ian (Lucien) 1912-1994 .... **2**
See also CA 1-4R; 147; CANR 1; DLB 161;
MAICYA; SAAS 3; SATA 1, 73; SATA-
Obit 83

Sewell, Anna 1820-1878 .... **17**
See also DLB 163; JRDA; MAICYA; SATA
24

Sharp, Margery 1905-1991 .... **27**
See also CA 21-24R; 134; CANR 18; DLB 161;
MAICYA; SATA 1, 29; SATA-Obit 67

Shearer, John 1947- **34**
See also CA 125; SATA 43; SATA-Brief 27

Shepard, Ernest Howard 1879-1976 .... **27**
See also CA 9-12R; 65-68; CANR 23; DLB
160; MAICYA; SATA 3, 33; SATA-Obit 24

Shippen, Katherine B(inney) 1892-1980 ... **36**
See also CA 5-8R; 93-96; SATA 1; SATA-Obit
23

Showers, Paul C. 1910- **6**
See also CA 1-4R; CANR 4, 38, 59; MAICYA;
SAAS 7; SATA 21, 92

Shulevitz, Uri 1935- **5**
See also CA 9-12R; CANR 3; DLB 61;
MAICYA; SATA 3, 50

Silverstein, Alvin 1933- **25**
See also CA 49-52; CANR 2; CLC 17; JRDA;
MAICYA; SATA 8, 69

Silverstein, Shel(by) 1932- **5**
See also CA 107; CANR 47; JRDA; MAICYA;
SATA 33, 92; SATA-Brief 27

Silverstein, Virginia B(arbara Opshelor)
1937- **25**
See also CA 49-52; CANR 2; CLC 17; JRDA;
MAICYA; SATA 8, 69

Simmonds, Posy **23**

Simon, Hilda Rita 1921- **39**
See also CA 77-80; SATA 28

Simon, Seymour 1931- **9**
See also CA 25-28R; CANR 11, 29; MAICYA;
SATA 4, 73

Singer, Isaac
See Singer, Isaac Bashevis

Singer, Isaac Bashevis 1904-1991 .... **1**
See also AITN 1, 2; CA 1-4R; 134; CANR 1,
39; CDALB 1941-1968; CLC 1, 3, 6, 9, 11,
15, 23, 38, 69; DA; DAB; DAC; DAM MST,
NOV; DLB 6, 28, 52; DLBY 91; JRDA;
MAICYA; MTCW; SATA 3, 27; SATA-Obit
68; SSC 3; WLC

Singer, Marilyn 1948- **48**
See also CA 65-68; CANR 9, 39; JRDA;
MAICYA; SAAS 13; SATA 48, 80; SATA-
Brief 38

Sis, Peter 1949- **45**
See also CA 128; SATA 67

Sleator, William (Warner III) 1945- **29**
See also AAYA 5; CA 29-32R; CANR 46;
JRDA; MAICYA; SATA 3, 68

Slote, Alfred 1926- **4**
See also JRDA; MAICYA; SAAS 21; SATA 8, 72

Smith, Dick King
See King-Smith, Dick

Smith, Lane 1959- **47**
See also AAYA 21; CA 143; SATA 76

Smucker, Barbara (Claassen) 1915- **10**
See also CA 106; CANR 23; JRDA; MAICYA;
SAAS 11; SATA 29, 76

Sneve, Virginia Driving Hawk 1933- **2**
See also CA 49-52; CANR 3; SATA 8, 95

Snyder, Zilpha Keatley 1927- **31**
See also AAYA 15; CA 9-12R; CANR 38; CLC 17;
JRDA; MAICYA; SAAS 2; SATA 1, 28, 75

Sobol, Donald J. 1924- **4**
See also CA 1-4R; CANR 1, 18, 38; JRDA;
MAICYA; SATA 1, 31, 73

Soto, Gary 1952- **38**
See also AAYA 10; CA 119; 125; CANR 50;
CLC 32, 80; DAM MULT; DLB 82; HLC;
HW; INT 125; JRDA; SATA 80

Souci, Robert D. San
See San Souci, Robert D.

Southall, Ivan (Francis) 1921- **2**
See also AAYA 22; CA 9-12R; CANR 7, 47;
JRDA; MAICYA; SAAS 3; SATA 3, 68

Speare, Elizabeth George 1908-1994 .... **8**
See also CA 1-4R; 147; JRDA; MAICYA;
SATA 5, 62; SATA-Obit 83

Spence, Eleanor (Rachel) 1928- **26**
See also CA 49-52; CANR 3; SATA 21

Spier, Peter (Edward) 1927- **5**
See also CA 5-8R; CANR 41; DLB 61;
MAICYA; SATA 4, 54

Spinelli, Jerry 1941- **26**
See also AAYA 11; CA 111; CANR 30, 45;
JRDA; MAICYA; SATA 39, 71

Spykman, E(lizabeth) C(hoate) 1896-1965 **35**
See also CA 101; SATA 10

Spyri, Johanna (Heusser) 1827-1901 .... **13**
See also CA 137; MAICYA; SATA 19

Stanley, Diane 1943- **46**
See also CA 112; CANR 32; SAAS 15; SATA
37, 80; SATA-Brief 32

Stanton, Schuyler
See Baum, L(yman) Frank

Staunton, Schuyler
See Baum, L(yman) Frank

Steig, William (H.) 1907- **2, 15**
See also AITN 1; CA 77-80; CANR 21, 44; DLB
61; INT CANR-21; MAICYA; SATA 18, 70

Steptoe, John (Lewis) 1950-1989 .... **2, 12**
See also BW 1; CA 49-52; 129; CANR 3, 26;
MAICYA; SATA 8, 63

Sterling, Dorothy 1913- **1**
See also CA 9-12R; CANR 5, 28; JRDA;
MAICYA; SAAS 2; SATA 1, 83

Stevenson, James 1929- **17**
See also CA 115; CANR 47; MAICYA; SATA
42, 71; SATA-Brief 34

Stevenson, Robert Louis (Balfour) 1850-
1894 .... **10, 11**
See also CDBLB 1890-1914; DA; DAB; DAC;
DAM MST, NOV; DLB 18, 57, 141, 156,
174; DLBD 13; JRDA; MAICYA; NCLC 5,
14, 63; SSC 11; WLC; YABC 2

Stine, Jovial Bob
See Stine, R(obert) L(awrence)

Stine, R(obert) L(awrence) 1943- **37**
See also AAYA 13; CA 105; CANR 22, 53;
JRDA; SATA 31, 76

Strasser, Todd 1950- **11**
See also AAYA 2; CA 117; 123; CANR 47;
JRDA; MAICYA; SATA 41, 45, 71

Streatfeild, (Mary) Noel 1895(?)-1986 ...... **17**
See also CA 81-84; 120; CANR 31; CLC 21; DLB
160; MAICYA; SATA 20; SATA-Obit 48

Stren, Patti 1949- **5**
See also CA 117; 124; SATA 88; SATA-Brief 41

Strong, Charles
See Epstein, Beryl (M. Williams); Epstein,
Samuel

Suhl, Yuri (Menachem) 1908-1986 .... **2**
See also CA 45-48; 121; CANR 2, 38;
MAICYA; SAAS 1; SATA 8; SATA-Obit 50

Sutcliff, Rosemary 1920-1992 .... **1, 37**
See also AAYA 10; CA 5-8R; 139; CANR 37;
CLC 26; DAB; DAC; DAM MST, POP;
JRDA; MAICYA; SATA 6, 44, 78; SATA-
Obit 73

Tarry, Ellen 1906- **26**
See also BW 1; CA 73-76; SAAS 16; SATA 16

Tate, Eleanora E(laine) 1948- **37**
See also BW 2; CA 105; CANR 25, 43; JRDA;
SATA 38, 94

Taylor, Mildred D. **9**
See also AAYA 10; BW 1; CA 85-88; CANR
25; CLC 21; DLB 52; JRDA; MAICYA;
SAAS 5; SATA 15, 70

Taylor, Theodore 1921- **30**
See also AAYA 2, 19; CA 21-24R; CANR 9,
25, 38, 50; JRDA; MAICYA; SAAS 4;
SATA 5, 54, 83

Tejima 1931- **20**

Tenniel, John 1820-1914 .... **18**
See also CA 111; MAICYA; SATA 74; SATA-
Brief 27

ter Haar, Jaap 1922-
See Haar, Jaap ter
See also CA 37-40R; SATA 6

Thiele, Colin (Milton) 1920- **27**
See also CA 29-32R; CANR 12, 28, 53; CLC
17; MAICYA; SAAS 2; SATA 14, 72

Thomas, Ianthe 1951- **8**
See also SATA-Brief 42

Thomas, Joyce Carol 1938- **19**
See also AAYA 12; BW 2; CA 113; 116; CANR
48; CLC 35; DLB 33; INT 116; JRDA;
MAICYA; MTCW; SAAS 7; SATA 40, 78

Thompson, George Selden 1929-1989
See Selden, George
See also CA 5-8R; 130; CANR 21, 37; INT
CANR-21; MAICYA; SATA 4, 73; SATA-
Obit 63

Thompson, Julian F(rancis) 1927- **24**
See also AAYA 9; CA 111; CANR 30, 56;
JRDA; MAICYA; SAAS 13; SATA 55;
SATA-Brief 40

Thompson, Kay 1912(?)- **22**
See also CA 85-88; MAICYA; SATA 16

Tobias, Tobi 1938- **4**
See also CA 29-32R; CANR 16; SATA 5, 82

Tomfool
See Farjeon, Eleanor

Totham, Mary
See Breinburg, Petronella

Townsend, John Rowe 1922- **2**
See also AAYA 11; CA 37-40R; CANR 41;
JRDA; MAICYA; SAAS 2; SATA 4, 68

Travers, P(amela) L(yndon) 1906-1996 ...... **2**
See also CA 33-36R; 152; CANR 30; DLB 160;
MAICYA; SAAS 2; SATA 4, 54; SATA-
Obit 90

Trease, (Robert) Geoffrey 1909- **42**
See also CA 5-8R; CANR 7, 22, 38; MAICYA;
SAAS 6; SATA 2, 60

Treece, Henry 1912-1966 .... **2**
See also CA 1-4R; 25-28R; CANR 6, 60; DLB
160; MAICYA; SATA 2

Tresselt, Alvin 1916- **30**
See also CA 49-52; CANR 1; MAICYA; SATA
7

Trezise, Percy (James) 1923- **41**
See also CA 132

Tudor, Tasha 1915- **13**
See also CA 81-84; MAICYA; SATA 20, 69

Tunis, Edwin (Burdett) 1897-1973 .... **2**
See also CA 5-8R; 45-48; CANR 7; MAICYA;
SATA 1, 28; SATA-Obit 24

Twohill, Maggie
See Gaberman, Judie Angell

Uchida, Yoshiko 1921-1992 .... **6**
See also AAYA 16; CA 13-16R; 139; CANR
6, 22, 47, 61; JRDA; MAICYA; MTCW;
SAAS 1; SATA 1, 53; SATA-Obit 72

Uderzo, Albert 1927- **37**

Uncle Gus
See Rey, H(ans) A(ugusto)

Uncle Shelby
See Silverstein, Shel(by)

Ungerer, Jean Thomas 1931-
See Ungerer, Tomi
See also CA 41-44R; MAICYA; SATA 5, 33

Ungerer, Tomi **3**
See also Ungerer, Jean Thomas

Unnerstad, Edith Totterman 1900- **36**
See also CA 5-8R; CANR 6; SATA 3

Ure, Jean 1943- **34**
See also CA 125; CANR 48; JRDA; MAICYA;
SAAS 14; SATA 48, 78

Usher, Margo Scegge
See McHargue, Georgess

Van Allsburg, Chris 1949- **5, 13**
See also CA 113; 117; CANR 38; DLB 61;
MAICYA; SATA 37, 53

Van Dyne, Edith
See Baum, L(yman) Frank

Ventura, Piero (Luigi) 1937- **16**
See also CA 103; CANR 39; MAICYA; SATA
61; SATA-Brief 43

Vincent, Gabrielle (a pseudonym) **13**
See also CA 126; MAICYA; SATA 61

Viorst, Judith 1931- **3**
See also BEST 90:1; CA 49-52; CANR 2, 26,
59; DAM POP; DLB 52; INT CANR-26;
MAICYA; SATA 7, 70

Voigt, Cynthia 1942- **13, 48**
See also AAYA 3; CA 106; CANR 18, 37, 40;
CLC 30; INT CANR-18; JRDA; MAICYA;
SATA 48, 79; SATA-Brief 33

Vugteveen, Verna Aardema 1911-
See Aardema, Verna
See also CA 5-8R; CANR 3, 18, 39

Waddell, Martin 1941- **31**
See also CA 113; CANR 34, 56; SAAS 15;
SATA 43, 81

Wallace, Ian 1950- **37**
See also CA 107; CANR 25, 38, 50; MAICYA;
SATA 53, 56

Walsh, Jill Paton **2**
See also Paton Walsh, Gillian
See also AAYA 11; CLC 35; DLB 161; SAAS
3

Walter, Mildred Pitts 1922- **15**
See also BW 2; CA 138; JRDA; MAICYA;
SAAS 12; SATA 69; SATA-Brief 45

Walter, Villiam Christian
See Andersen, Hans Christian

Ward, E. D.
See Gorey, Edward (St. John)

Warshofsky, Isaac
See Singer, Isaac Bashevis

Watanabe, Shigeo 1928- **8**
See also CA 112; CANR 45; MAICYA; SATA
39; SATA-Brief 32

Watson, Clyde 1947- **3**
See also CA 49-52; CANR 4, 39; MAICYA;
SATA 5, 68

Weary, Ogdred
See Gorey, Edward (St. John)

Webb, Christopher
See Wibberley, Leonard (Patrick O'Connor)

Weiss, Harvey 1922- **4**
See also CA 5-8R; CANR 6, 38; MAICYA;
SAAS 19; SATA 1, 27, 76

Weiss, Miriam
See Schlein, Miriam

Wells, Rosemary 1943- **16**
　See also AAYA 13; CA 85-88; CANR 48; CLC
　12; MAICYA; SAAS 1; SATA 18, 69

Wersba, Barbara 1932- **3**
　See also AAYA 2; CA 29-32R; CANR 16, 38;
　CLC 30; DLB 52; JRDA; MAICYA; SAAS
　2; SATA 1, 58

Westall, Robert (Atkinson) 1929-1993 ...... **13**
　See also AAYA 12; CA 69-72; 141; CANR 18;
　CLC 17; JRDA; MAICYA; SAAS 2; SATA
　23, 69; SATA-Obit 75

White, E(lwyn) B(rooks) 1899-1985 ...... **1, 21**
　See also AITN 2; CA 13-16R; 116; CANR 16,
　37; CLC 10, 34, 39; DAM POP; DLB 11,
　22; MAICYA; MTCW; SATA 2, 29; SATA-
　Obit 44

White, Robb 1909- **3**
　See also CA 1-4R; CANR 1; SAAS 1; SATA
　1, 83

Wibberley, Leonard (Patrick O'Connor) 1915-
　1983 .... **3**
　See also CA 5-8R; 111; CANR 3; SATA 2, 45;
　SATA-Obit 36

Wiesner, David 1956- **43**
　See also SATA 72

Wilder, Laura (Elizabeth) Ingalls 1867-19572
　See also CA 111; 137; DLB 22; JRDA;
　MAICYA; SATA 15, 29

Wildsmith, Brian 1930- **2**
　See also CA 85-88; CANR 35; MAICYA;
　SAAS 5; SATA 16, 69

Wilhelm, Hans 1945- **46**
　See also CA 119; CANR 48; SAAS 21; SATA 58

Wilkins, Mary Huiskamp 1926-
　See Calhoun, Mary
　See also CA 5-8R; CANR 2, 18; SATA 84

Wilkinson, Brenda 1946- **20**
　See also BW 2; CA 69-72; CANR 26, 51;
　JRDA; SATA 14, 91

Willard, Barbara (Mary) 1909-1994 .... **2**
　See also CA 81-84; 144; CANR 15; DLB 161;
　MAICYA; SAAS 5; SATA 17, 74

Willard, Nancy 1936- **5**
　See also CA 89-92; CANR 10, 39; CLC 7, 37;
　DLB 5, 52; MAICYA; MTCW; SATA 37,
　71; SATA-Brief 30

Williams, Barbara 1925- **48**
　See also CA 49-52; CANR 1, 17; SAAS 16;
　SATA 11

Williams, Beryl
　See Epstein, Beryl (M. Williams)

Williams, Charles
　See Collier, James L(incoln)

Williams, Jay 1914-1978 .... **8**
　See also CA 1-4R; 81-84; CANR 2, 39;
　MAICYA; SATA 3, 41; SATA-Obit 24

Williams, Kit 1946(?)- **4**
　See also CA 107; SATA 44

Williams, Margery
　See Bianco, Margery (Williams)

Williams, Vera B. 1927- **9**
　See also CA 123; CANR 38; MAICYA; SATA
　53; SATA-Brief 33

Williams-Garcia, Rita **36**
　See also AAYA 22; CA 159

Wodge, Dreary
　See Gorey, Edward (St. John)

Wojciechowska, Maia (Teresa) 1927- **1**
　See also AAYA 8; CA 9-12R; CANR 4, 41;
　CLC 26; JRDA; MAICYA; SAAS 1; SATA
　1, 28, 83

Wolny, P.
　See Janeczko, Paul B(ryan)

Wolny, P.
　See Janeczko, Paul B(ryan)

Wood, Audrey **26**
　See also CA 137; MAICYA; SATA 50, 81;
　SATA-Brief 44

Wood, Don 1945- **26**
　See also CA 136; MAICYA; SATA 50; SATA-
　Brief 44

Worth, Valerie **21**
　See also Bahlke, Valerie Worth
　See also MAICYA; SATA 8, 70

Wortis, Avi 1937-
　See Avi
　See also CA 69-72; CANR 12, 42; JRDA;
　MAICYA; SATA 14

Wrightson, (Alice) Patricia 1921- **4, 14**
　See also AAYA 5; CA 45-48; CANR 3, 19,
　36; JRDA; MAICYA; SAAS 4; SATA 8,
　66

Wryde, Dogear
　See Gorey, Edward (St. John)

Wynne-Jones, Tim(othy) 1948- **21**
　See also CA 105; CANR 39; SATA 67

Yaffe, Alan
　See Yorinks, Arthur

Yarbrough, Camille 1938- **29**
　See also BW 2; CA 105; 125; SATA 79

Yashima, Taro **4**
　See also Iwamatsu, Jun Atsushi

Yee, Paul (R.) 1956- **44**
　See also CA 135; JRDA; SATA 67

Yeoman, John 1934- **46**
　See also CA 106; SATA 28, 80

Yep, Laurence Michael 1948- **3, 17**
　See also AAYA 5; CA 49-52; CANR 1, 46;
　CLC 35; DLB 52; JRDA; MAICYA; SATA
　7, 69

Yolen, Jane (Hyatt) 1939- **4, 44**
　See also AAYA 4,22; CA 13-16R; CANR 11,
　29, 56; DLB 52; INT CANR-29; JRDA;
　MAICYA; SAAS 1; SATA 4, 40, 75

Yorinks, Arthur 1953- **20**
　See also CA 106; CANR 38; MAICYA; SATA
　33, 49, 85

Youd, (Christopher) Samuel 1922-
　See Christopher, John
　See also CA 77-80; CANR 37; JRDA;
　MAICYA; SATA 47; SATA-Brief 30

Young, Ed (Tse-chun) 1931- **27**
　See also CA 116; 130; MAICYA; SATA 10,
　74

Zei, Alki **6**
　See also CA 77-80; SATA 24

Zim, Herbert S(pencer) 1909-1994 .... **2**
　See also CA 13-16R; 147; CANR 17; JRDA;
　MAICYA; SAAS 2; SATA 1, 30; SATA-
　Obit 85

Zimnik, Reiner 1930- **3**
　See also CA 77-80; SATA 36

Zindel, Paul 1936- **3, 45**
　See also AAYA 2; CA 73-76; CANR 31; CLC
　6, 26; DA; DAB; DAC; DAM DRAM, MST,
　NOV; DC 5; DLB 7, 52; JRDA; MAICYA;
　MTCW; SATA 16, 58

Zolotow, Charlotte S(hapiro) 1915- **2**
　See also CA 5-8R; CANR 3, 18, 38; DLB 52;
　MAICYA; SATA 1, 35, 78

Zuromskis, Diane
　See Stanley, Diane

Zuromskis, Diane Stanley
　See Stanley, Diane

Zwerger, Lisbeth 1954- **46**
　See also MAICYA; SAAS 13; SATA 66

Author Index

CUMULATIVE INDEX TO NATIONALITIES

AMERICAN
Aardema, Verna 17
Adkins, Jan 7
Adler, Irving 27
Adoff, Arnold 7
Alcott, Louisa May 1, 38
Alexander, Lloyd (Chudley) 1, 5, 48
Aliki 9
Anglund, Joan Walsh 1
Armstrong, William H(oward) 1
Arnosky, James Edward 15
Aruego, Jose (Espiritu) 5
Ashabranner, Brent (Kenneth) 28
Asimov, Isaac 12
Atwater, Florence (Hasseltine Carroll) 19
Atwater, Richard (Tupper) 19
Avi 24
Aylesworth, Thomas G(ibbons) 6
Babbitt, Natalie (Zane Moore) 2
Bacon, Martha Sherman 3
Bang, Molly Garrett 8
Baum, L(yman) Frank 15
Baylor, Byrd 3
Bellairs, John (A.) 37
Bemelmans, Ludwig 6
Benary-Isbert, Margot 12
Bendick, Jeanne 5
Berenstain, Jan(ice) 19
Berenstain, Stan(ley) 19
Berger, Melvin H. 32
Bess, Clayton 39
Bethancourt, T. Ernesto 3
Block, Francesca (Lia) 33
Blos, Joan W(insor) 18
Blumberg, Rhoda 21
Blume, Judy (Sussman) 2, 15
Bond, Nancy (Barbara) 11
Bontemps, Arna(ud Wendell) 6
Bova, Ben(jamin William) 3
Brancato, Robin F(idler) 32

Branley, Franklyn M(ansfield) 13
Brett, Jan (Churchill) 27
Bridgers, Sue Ellen 18
Brink, Carol Ryrie 30
Brooks, Bruce 25
Brooks, Gwendolyn 27
Brown, Marcia 12
Brown, Marc (Tolon) 29
Brown, Margaret Wise 10
Bruchac, Joseph III 46
Bryan, Ashley F. 18
Bunting, Eve 28
Burnett, Frances (Eliza) Hodgson 24
Burton, Virginia Lee 11
Byars, Betsy (Cromer) 1, 16
Caines, Jeannette (Franklin) 24
Calhoun, Mary 42
Cameron, Eleanor (Frances) 1
Carle, Eric 10
Carter, Alden R(ichardson) 22
Cassedy, Sylvia 26
Charlip, Remy 8
Childress, Alice 14
Christopher, Matt(hew Frederick) 33
Ciardi, John (Anthony) 19
Clark, Ann Nolan 16
Cleary, Beverly (Atlee Bunn) 2, 8
Cleaver, Bill 6
Cleaver, Vera (Allen) 6
Clifton, (Thelma) Lucille 5
Coatsworth, Elizabeth (Jane) 2
Cobb, Vicki 2
Cohen, Daniel (E.) 3, 43
Cole, Brock 18
Cole, Joanna 5, 40
Collier, James L(incoln) 3
Colum, Padraic 36
Conford, Ellen 10
Conrad, Pam 18
Cooney, Barbara 23

Corbett, Scott 1
Cormier, Robert (Edmund) 12
Cox, Palmer 24
Creech, Sharon 42
Crews, Donald 7
Crutcher, Chris(topher C.) 28
Cummings, Pat (Marie) 48
Curry, Jane L(ouise) 31
Danziger, Paula 20
d'Aulaire, Edgar Parin 21
d'Aulaire, Ingri (Mortenson Parin) 21
Day, Alexandra 22
de Angeli, Marguerite (Lofft) 1
DeClements, Barthe 23
DeJong, Meindert 1
Denslow, W(illiam) W(allace) 15
dePaola, Tomie 4, 24
Dillon, Diane 44
Dillon, Leo 44
Disch, Thomas M(ichael) 18
Domanska, Janina 40
Donovan, John 3
Dorros, Arthur (M.) 42
Dr. Seuss 1, 9
Duncan, Lois 29
Duvoisin, Roger Antoine 23
Eager, Edward McMaken 43
Ehlert, Lois (Jane) 28
Emberley, Barbara A(nne) 5
Emberley, Ed(ward Randolph) 5
Engdahl, Sylvia Louise 2
Enright, Elizabeth 4
Epstein, Beryl (M. Williams) 26
Epstein, Samuel 26
Estes, Eleanor 2
Ets, Marie Hall 33
Feelings, Muriel (Grey) 5
Feelings, Tom 5
Ferry, Charles 34
Field, Rachel (Lyman) 21

Fisher, Leonard Everett 18
Fitzgerald, John D(ennis) 1
Fitzhugh, Louise 1
Flack, Marjorie 28
Fleischman, (Albert) Sid(ney) 1, 15
Fleischman, Paul 20
Forbes, Esther 27
Foster, Genevieve Stump 7
Fox, Paula 1, 44
Freedman, Russell (Bruce) 20
Freeman, Don 30
Fritz, Jean (Guttery) 2, 14
Fujikawa, Gyo 25
Gaberman, Judie Angell 33
Gag, Wanda (Hazel) 4
Galdone, Paul 16
Gallant, Roy A(rthur) 30
Gantos, Jack 18
George, Jean Craighead 1
Gibbons, Gail 8
Giblin, James Cross 29
Giovanni, Nikki 6
Glubok, Shirley (Astor) 1
Goble, Paul 21
Goffstein, (Marilyn) Brooke 3
Gordon, Sheila 27
Gorey, Edward (St. John) 36
Graham, Lorenz (Bell) 10
Gramatky, Hardie 22
Greene, Bette 2
Greenfield, Eloise 4, 38
Grifalconi, Ann 35
Grimes, Nikki 42
Gruelle, Johnny 34
Guy, Rosa (Cuthbert) 13
Hadley, Lee 40
Haley, Gail E(inhart) 21
Hamilton, Virginia 1, 11, 40
Hansen, Joyce (Viola) 21
Haskins, James S. 3, 39
Hautzig, Esther Rudomin 22
Haywood, Carolyn 22
Henkes, Kevin 23
Henry, Marguerite 4
Hentoff, Nat(han Irving) 1
Highwater, Jamake (Mamake) 17
Hinton, S(usan) E(loise) 3, 23
Hoban, Russell (Conwell) 3
Hoban, Tana 13
Hoberman, Mary Ann 22
Hogrogian, Nonny 2
Hopkins, Lee Bennett 44
Howe, James 9
Hughes, (James) Langston 17
Hunt, Irene 1
Hunter, Kristin (Eggleston) 3
Hurmence, Belinda 25
Hyde, Margaret O(ldroyd) 23
Irwin, Ann(abelle Bowen) 40
Isadora, Rachel 7
Jackson, Jesse 28
Janeczko, Paul B(ryan) 47
Jarrell, Randall 6
Jeffers, Susan 30
Johnson, Angela 33
Johnson, James Weldon 32
Jonas, Ann 12
Jordan, June 10
Joyce, William 26
Kalman, Maira 32
Keats, Ezra Jack 1, 35
Keller, Holly 45
Kellogg, Steven 6

Kennedy, X. J. 27
Kerr, M. E. 29
Khalsa, Dayal Kaur 30
Kherdian, David 24
Klein, Norma 2, 19
Knight, David C(arpenter) 38
Konigsburg, E(laine) L(obl) 1, 47
Kotzwinkle, William 6
Krauss, Ruth (Ida) 42
Krementz, Jill 5
Krull, Kathleen 44
Kuskin, Karla (Seidman) 4
Langstaff, John (Meredith) 3
Langton, Jane (Gillson) 33
Lasky, Kathryn 11
Lauber, Patricia (Grace) 16
Lavine, Sigmund Arnold 35
Lawson, Robert 2
Leaf, (Wilbur) Munro 25
Le Guin, Ursula K(roeber) 3, 28
L'Engle, Madeleine (Camp Franklin) 1, 14
Lenski, Lois 26
Lerner, Carol 34
LeShan, Eda J(oan) 6
Lester, Julius (Bernard) 2, 41
Lionni, Leo(nard) 7
Lipsyte, Robert (Michael) 23
Livingston, Myra Cohn 7
Lobel, Arnold (Stark) 5
Locker, Thomas 14
Lowry, Lois 6, 46
MacLachlan, Patricia 14
Maestro, Betsy C(rippen) 45
Maestro, Giulio 45
Manley, Seon 3
Marshall, James (Edward) 21
Martin, Ann M(atthews) 32
Mathis, Sharon Bell 3
Mayer, Mercer 11
Mazer, Harry 16
Mazer, Norma Fox 23
McCloskey, (John) Robert 7
McClung, Robert M(arshall) 11
McCord, David (Thompson Watson) 9
McCully, Emily Arnold 46
McDermott, Gerald 9
McHargue, Georgess 2
McKinley, (Jennifer Carolyn) Robin 10
McKissack, Patricia (L'Ann) C(arwell) 23
McMillan, Bruce 47
Meltzer, Milton 13
Merriam, Eve 14
Milne, Lorus J. 22
Milne, Margery 22
Minarik, Else Holmelund 33
Mohr, Nicholasa 22
Monjo, F(erdinand) N(icholas III) 2
Moore, Lilian 15
Mukerji, Dhan Gopal 10
Munsch, Robert (Norman) 19
Myers, Walter Dean 4, 16, 35
Namioka, Lensey 48
Naylor, Phyllis (Reynolds) 17
Ness, Evaline (Michelow) 6
Nixon, Joan Lowery 24
Nourse, Alan E(dward) 33
O'Brien, Robert C. 2
O'Dell, Scott 1, 16
Oneal, Zibby 13
Orgel, Doris 48
Parish, Peggy 22
Park, Barbara 34
Pascal, Francine 25

Patent, Dorothy Hinshaw 19
Paterson, Katherine (Womeldorf) 7
Paulsen, Gary 19
Peck, Richard (Wayne) 15
Peck, Robert Newton 45
Peet, Bill 12
Pene du Bois, William (Sherman) 1
Petersham, Maud (Sylvia Fuller) 24
Petersham, Miska 24
Petry, Ann (Lane) 12
Pfeffer, Susan Beth 11
Pierce, Meredith Ann 20
Pike, Christopher 29
Pilkey, Dav 48
Pinkney, Jerry 43
Pinkwater, Daniel Manus 4
Polacco, Patricia 40
Politi, Leo 29
Prelutsky, Jack 13
Pringle, Laurence (Patrick) 4
Provensen, Alice 11
Provensen, Martin (Elias) 11
Pyle, Howard 22
Raskin, Ellen 1, 12
Rau, Margaret 8
Reiss, Johanna (de Leeuw) 19
Rey, H(ans) A(ugusto) 5
Rey, Margret (Elisabeth) 5
Rinaldi, Ann 46
Ringgold, Faith 30
Rockwell, Thomas 6
Rodgers, Mary 20
Ryder, Joanne (Rose) 37
Rylant, Cynthia 15
Sachar, Louis 28
Sachs, Marilyn (Stickle) 2
Salinger, J(erome) D(avid) 18
Sanchez, Sonia 18
San Souci, Robert D. 43
Sattler, Helen Roney 24
Sawyer, Ruth 36
Say, Allen 22
Scarry, Richard (McClure) 3, 41
Schlein, Miriam 41
Schwartz, Alvin 3
Schwartz, Amy 25
Scieszka, Jon 27
Scott, Jack Denton 20
Sebestyen, Ouida 17
Selden, George 8
Selsam, Millicent Ellis 1
Sendak, Maurice (Bernard) 1, 17
Seredy, Kate 10
Shearer, John 34
Shippen, Katherine B(inney) 36
Showers, Paul C. 6
Silverstein, Alvin 25
Silverstein, Shel(by) 5
Silverstein, Virginia B(arbara Opshelor) 25
Simon, Hilda Rita 39
Simon, Seymour 9
Singer, Isaac Bashevis 1
Singer, Marilyn 48
Sleator, William (Warner III) 29
Slote, Alfred 4
Smith, Lane 47
Smucker, Barbara (Claassen) 10
Sneve, Virginia Driving Hawk 2
Snyder, Zilpha Keatley 31
Sobol, Donald J. 4
Soto, Gary 38
Speare, Elizabeth George 8
Spier, Peter (Edward) 5

Spinelli, Jerry **26**
Spykman, E(lizabeth) C(hoate) **35**
Stanley, Diane **46**
Steig, William (H.) **2, 15**
Steptoe, John (Lewis) **2, 12**
Sterling, Dorothy **1**
Stevenson, James **17**
Stine, R(obert) L(awrence) **37**
St. John, Nicole **46**
Strasser, Todd **11**
Suhl, Yuri (Menachem) **2**
Tarry, Ellen **26**
Tate, Eleanora E(laine) **37**
Taylor, Mildred D. **9**
Taylor, Theodore **30**
Thomas, Ianthe **8**
Thomas, Joyce Carol **19**
Thompson, Julian F(rancis) **24**
Thompson, Kay **22**
Tobias, Tobi **4**
Tresselt, Alvin **30**
Tudor, Tasha **13**
Tunis, Edwin (Burdett) **2**
Uchida, Yoshiko **6**
Van Allsburg, Chris **5, 13**
Viorst, Judith **3**
Voigt, Cynthia **13, 48**
Walter, Mildred Pitts **15**
Watson, Clyde **3**
Weiss, Harvey **4**
Wells, Rosemary **16**
Wersba, Barbara **3**
White, E(lwyn) B(rooks) **1, 21**
White, Robb **3**
Wibberley, Leonard (Patrick O'Connor) **3**
Wiesner, David **43**
Wilder, Laura (Elizabeth) Ingalls **2**
Wilkinson, Brenda **20**
Willard, Nancy **5**
Williams, Barbara **48**
Williams, Jay **8**
Williams, Vera B. **9**
Williams-Garcia, Rita **36**
Wojciechowska, Maia (Teresa) **1**
Wood, Audrey **26**
Wood, Don **26**
Worth, Valerie **21**
Yarbrough, Camille **29**
Yashima, Taro **4**
Yep, Laurence Michael **3, 17**
Yolen, Jane (Hyatt) **4, 44**
Yorinks, Arthur **20**
Young, Ed (Tse-chun) **27**
Zim, Herbert S(pencer) **2**
Zindel, Paul **3, 45**
Zolotow, Charlotte S(hapiro) **2**

AUSTRALIAN
Baker, Jeannie **28**
Base, Graeme (Rowland) **22**
Brinsmead, H(esba) F(ay) **47**
Chauncy, Nan(cen Beryl Masterman) **6**
Clark, Mavis Thorpe **30**
Crew, Gary **42**
Fox, Mem **23**
Graham, Bob **31**
Hilton, Nette **25**
Jennings, Paul **40**
Kelleher, Victor (Michael Kitchener) **36**
Klein, Robin **21**
Lindsay, Norman Alfred William **8**
Marsden, John **34**
Mattingley, Christobel (Rosemary) **24**

Ormerod, Jan(ette Louise) **20**
Ottley, Reginald Leslie **16**
Phipson, Joan **5**
Rodda, Emily **32**
Roughsey, Dick **41**
Rubinstein, Gillian (Margaret) **35**
Southall, Ivan (Francis) **2**
Spence, Eleanor (Rachel) **26**
Thiele, Colin (Milton) **27**
Travers, P(amela) L(yndon) **2**
Trezise, Percy (James) **41**
Wrightson, (Alice) Patricia **4, 14**

AUSTRIAN
Bemelmans, Ludwig **6**
Noestlinger, Christine **12**
Orgel, Doris **48**
Zwerger, Lisbeth **46**

BELGIAN
Herge **6**
Vincent, Gabrielle (a pseudonym) **13**

CANADIAN
Bedard, Michael **35**
Blades, Ann (Sager) **15**
Buffie, Margaret **39**
Burnford, Sheila (Philip Cochrane Every) **2**
Cameron, Eleanor (Frances) **1**
Cleaver, Elizabeth (Mrazik) **13**
Cox, Palmer **24**
Doyle, Brian **22**
Ellis, Sarah **42**
Gay, Marie-Louise **27**
Grey Owl **32**
Haig-Brown, Roderick (Langmere) **31**
Harris, Christie (Lucy) Irwin **47**
Houston, James A(rchibald) **3**
Hudson, Jan **40**
Hughes, Monica (Ince) **9**
Johnston, Julie **41**
Katz, Welwyn Wilton **45**
Khalsa, Dayal Kaur **30**
Korman, Gordon (Richard) **25**
Kovalski, Maryann **34**
Kurelek, William **2**
Lee, Dennis (Beynon) **3**
Little, (Flora) Jean **4**
Lunn, Janet (Louise Swoboda) **18**
Mackay, Claire **43**
Major, Kevin (Gerald) **11**
Markoosie **23**
Milne, Lorus J. **22**
Montgomery, L(ucy) M(aud) **8**
Mowat, Farley (McGill) **20**
Munsch, Robert (Norman) **19**
Pearson, Kit **26**
Poulin, Stephane **28**
Richler, Mordecai **17**
Roberts, Charles G(eorge) D(ouglas) **33**
Smucker, Barbara (Claassen) **10**
Stren, Patti **5**
Wallace, Ian **37**
Wynne-Jones, Tim(othy) **21**
Yee, Paul (R.) **44**

CHILEAN
Krahn, Fernando **3**

CHINESE
Namioka, Lensey **48**
Young, Ed (Tse-chun) **27**

CZECH
Sasek, Miroslav **4**
Sis, Peter **45**

DANISH
Andersen, Hans Christian **6**
Bodker, Cecil **23**
Drescher, Henrik **20**
Haugaard, Erik Christian **11**
Minarik, Else Holmelund **33**
Nielsen, Kay (Rasmus) **16**

DUTCH
Biegel, Paul **27**
Bruna, Dick **7**
DeJong, Meindert **1**
Haar, Jaap ter **15**
Lionni, Leo(nard) **7**
Reiss, Johanna (de Leeuw) **19**
Schmidt, Annie M. G. **22**
Spier, Peter (Edward) **5**

ENGLISH
Adams, Richard (George) **20**
Ahlberg, Allan **18**
Ahlberg, Janet **18**
Aiken, Joan (Delano) **1, 19**
Alcock, Vivien **26**
Allan, Mabel Esther **43**
Ardizzone, Edward (Jeffrey Irving) **3**
Arundel, Honor (Morfydd) **35**
Ashley, Bernard **4**
Awdry, Wilbert Vere **23**
Baker, Jeannie **28**
Banner, Angela **24**
Barklem, Jill **31**
Base, Graeme (Rowland) **22**
Bawden, Nina (Mary Mabey) **2**
Bianco, Margery (Williams) **19**
Biro, Val **28**
Blake, Quentin (Saxby) **31**
Blyton, Enid (Mary) **31**
Bond, (Thomas) Michael **1**
Boston, L(ucy) M(aria Wood) **3**
Breinburg, Petronella **31**
Briggs, Raymond Redvers **10**
Brooke, L(eonard) Leslie **20**
Browne, Anthony (Edward Tudor) **19**
Burnett, Frances (Eliza) Hodgson **24**
Burningham, John (Mackintosh) **9**
Burton, Hester (Wood-Hill) **1**
Caldecott, Randolph (J.) **14**
Carroll, Lewis **2, 18**
Causley, Charles (Stanley) **30**
Chauncy, Nan(cen Beryl Masterman) **6**
Christopher, John **2**
Clarke, Pauline **28**
Cooper, Susan (Mary) **4**
Corbett, W(illiam) J(esse) **19**
Cresswell, Helen **18**
Cross, Gillian (Clare) **28**
Crossley-Holland, Kevin **47**
Dahl, Roald **1, 7, 41**
de la Mare, Walter (John) **23**
Dhondy, Farrukh **41**
Dickinson, Peter (Malcolm) **29**
Dodgson, Charles Lutwidge **2**
Doherty, Berlie **21**
Farjeon, Eleanor **34**
Farmer, Penelope (Jane) **8**
Fine, Anne **25**
Foreman, Michael **32**
French, Fiona **37**

Nationality Index

Gardam, Jane 12
Garfield, Leon 21
Garner, Alan 20
Gerrard, Roy 23
Goble, Paul 21
Godden, (Margaret) Rumer 20
Goodall, John Strickland 25
Grahame, Kenneth 5
Greenaway, Kate 6
Grey Owl 32
Haig-Brown, Roderick (Langmere) 31
Hamley, Dennis 47
Handford, Martin (John) 22
Harris, Rosemary (Jeanne) 30
Hill, Eric 13
Howker, Janni 14
Hughes, Monica (Ince) 9
Hughes, Shirley 15
Hughes, Ted 3
Hutchins, Pat 20
Jacques, Brian 21
Jones, Diana Wynne 23
Keeping, Charles (William James) 34
Kelleher, Victor (Michael Kitchener) 36
Kemp, Gene 29
King-Smith, Dick 40
Kipling, (Joseph) Rudyard 39
Lear, Edward 1
Lewis, C(live) S(taples) 3, 27
Lively, Penelope (Margaret) 7
Lofting, Hugh (John) 19
Macaulay, David (Alexander) 3, 14
Mark, Jan(et Marjorie) 11
Mayne, William (James Carter) 25
McBratney, Sam 44
McCaughrean, Geraldine 38
McKee, David (John) 38
Milne, A(lan) A(lexander) 1, 26
Murphy, Jill (Frances) 39
Naidoo, Beverley 29
Needle, Jan 43
Nesbit, E(dith) 3
Nimmo, Jenny 44
Norton, Mary 6
Oakley, Graham 7
Ottley, Reginald Leslie 16
Owen, Gareth 31
Oxenbury, Helen 22
Pearce, Philippa 9
Peyton, K. M. 3
Pienkowski, Jan (Michal) 6
Potter, (Helen) Beatrix 1, 19
Pullman, Philip (Nicholas) 20
Ransome, Arthur (Michell) 8
Rayner, Mary 41
Reid Banks, Lynne 24
Rosen, Michael (Wayne) 45
Serraillier, Ian (Lucien) 2
Sewell, Anna 17
Sharp, Margery 27
Shepard, Ernest Howard 27
Simmonds, Posy 23
Streatfeild, (Mary) Noel 17
Sutcliff, Rosemary 1, 37
Tenniel, John 18
Townsend, John Rowe 2
Travers, P(amela) L(yndon) 2
Trease, (Robert) Geoffrey 42
Treece, Henry 2
Ure, Jean 34
Walsh, Jill Paton 2
Westall, Robert (Atkinson) 13
Wildsmith, Brian 2

Willard, Barbara (Mary) 2
Williams, Kit 4
Yeoman, John 46

FILIPINO
Aruego, Jose (Espiritu) 5

FINNISH
Jansson, Tove Marika 2
Unnerstad, Edith Totterman 36

FRENCH
Ayme, Marcel (Andre) 25
Berna, Paul 19
Billout, Guy (Rene) 33
Boutet de Monvel, (Louis) M(aurice) 32
Brunhoff, Jean de 4
Brunhoff, Laurent de 4
Goscinny, Rene 37
Guillot, Rene 22
Saint-Exupery, Antoine (Jean Baptiste Marie Roger) de 10
Uderzo, Albert 37
Ungerer, Tomi 3

GERMAN
Baumann, Hans 35
Benary-Isbert, Margot 12
d'Aulaire, Edgar Parin 21
Ende, Michael (Andreas Helmuth) 14
Hartling, Peter 29
Heine, Helme 18
Janosch 26
Kaestner, Erich 4
Kruss, James 9
Rey, H(ans) A(ugusto) 5
Rey, Margret (Elisabeth) 5
Richter, Hans Peter 21
Wilhelm, Hans 46
Zimnik, Reiner 3

GREEK
Aesop 14
Zei, Alki 6

HUNGARIAN
Biro, Val 28
Galdone, Paul 16
Seredy, Kate 10

INDIAN
Dhondy, Farrukh 41
Mukerji, Dhan Gopal 10

IRISH
Bunting, Eve 28
Colum, Padraic 36
Dillon, Eilis 26
O'Shea, (Catherine) Pat(ricia Shiels) 18

ISRAELI
Ofek, Uriel 28
Orlev, Uri 30
Shulevitz, Uri 5

ITALIAN
Collodi, Carlo 5
Munari, Bruno 9
Rodari, Gianni 24
Ventura, Piero (Luigi) 16

JAMAICAN
Berry, James 22

JAPANESE
Anno, Mitsumasa 2, 14
Iwasaki (Matsumoto), Chihiro 18
Kuratomi, Chizuko 32
Maruki, Toshi 19
Nakatani, Chiyoko 30
Say, Allen 22
Tejima 20
Watanabe, Shigeo 8
Yashima, Taro 4

MYANMARI
Rayner, Mary 41

NEW ZEALANDER
Allen, Pamela 44
Duder, Tessa 43
Mahy, Margaret 7

NIGERIAN
Achebe, (Albert) Chinua(lumogu) 20

NORTHERN IRISH
Waddell, Martin 31

NORWEGIAN
d'Aulaire, Ingri (Mortenson Parin) 21
Proeysen, Alf 24

POLISH
Domanska, Janina 40
Hautzig, Esther Rudomin 22
Janosch 26
Orlev, Uri 30
Pienkowski, Jan (Michal) 6
Shulevitz, Uri 5
Singer, Isaac Bashevis 1
Suhl, Yuri (Menachem) 2
Wojciechowska, Maia (Teresa) 1

RUSSIAN
Asimov, Isaac 12
Ginsburg, Mirra 45
Korinetz, Yuri (Iosifovich) 4

SCOTTISH
Bannerman, Helen (Brodie Cowan Watson) 21
Barrie, J(ames) M(atthew) 16
Burnford, Sheila (Philip Cochrane Every) 2
Hunter, Mollie 25
Stevenson, Robert Louis (Balfour) 10, 11

SOUTH AFRICAN
Daly, Nicholas 41
Gordon, Sheila 27
Lewin, Hugh 9
Naidoo, Beverley 29

SPANISH
Sanchez-Silva, Jose Maria 12

SWEDISH
Beckman, Gunnel 25
Beskow, Elsa (Maartman) 17
Bjoerk, Christina 22
Gripe, Maria (Kristina) 5
Lagerlof, Selma (Ottiliana Lovisa) 7
Lindgren, Astrid (Ericsson) 1, 39
Lindgren, Barbro 20
Unnerstad, Edith Totterman 36

SWISS
Carigiet, Alois 38

Duvoisin, Roger Antoine **23**
Mueller, Joerg **43**
Pfister, Marcus **42**
Spyri, Johanna (Heusser) **13**

THAI
Ho, Minfong **28**

TRINIDADIAN
Guy, Rosa (Cuthbert) **13**

WELSH
Arundel, Honor (Morfydd) **35**
Dahl, Roald **1, 7, 41**

Nationality Index

CUMULATIVE INDEX TO TITLES

1, 2, 3 (Hoban) **13**:109
1, 2, 3 to the Zoo (Carle) **10**:71
1 Is One (Tudor) **13**:195
3 and 30 Watchbirds (Leaf) **25**:127
3 X 3: A Picture Book for All Children Who Can Count to Three (Kruss) **9**:85
3rd September 1939 (Gordon) **27**:94
4-Way Stop and Other Poems (Livingston) **7**:172
10-Nin No Yukai Na Hikkoshi (Anno) **14**:40
26 Letters and 99 Cents (Hoban) **13**:112
The 35th of May; or, Conrad's Ride to the South Seas (Kaestner) **4**:123
The 60s Reader (Haskins) **39**:57
The 100-Year-Old Cactus (Lerner) **34**:130
121 Pudding Street (Fritz) **14**:110
The 379th White Elephant (Guillot) **22**:56
The 500 Hats of Bartholomew Cubbins (Seuss) **9**:172
729 Animal Allsorts (Oxenbury) **22**:141
729 Curious Creatures (Oxenbury) **22**:141
729 Merry Mix-Ups (Oxenbury) **22**:141
729 Puzzle People (Oxenbury) **22**:141
123456789 Benn (McKee) **38**:160
A and THE; or, William T. C. Baumgarten Comes to Town (Raskin) **1**:155
A Apple Pie (Greenaway) **6**:134
A, B, See! (Hoban) **13**:106
A Is for Always (Anglund) **1**:19
A Is for Annabelle (Tudor) **13**:194
A, My Name Is Ami (Mazer) **23**:231
+A Was an Angler (Domanska) **40**:54
AB to Zogg: A Lexicon for Science-Fiction and Fantasy Readers (Merriam) **14**:199
Abby (Caines) **24**:62
Abby, My Love (Irwin) **40**:111
ABC (Burningham) **9**:39
ABC (Cleaver) **13**:72
ABC (Lear) **1**:126
ABC (Munari) **9**:125

ABC (Pienkowski) **6**:233
The ABC Bunny (Gag) **4**:90
ABC of Things (Oxenbury) **22**:138
ABC Word Book (Scarry) **41**:164
ABCDEFGHIJKLMNOPQRSTUVWXYZ (Kuskin) **4**:138
The ABC's of Astronomy: An Illustrated Dictionary (Gallant) **30**:87
The ABC's of Chemistry: An Illustrated Dictionary (Gallant) **30**:88
ABC's of Ecology (Asimov) **12**:47
ABC's of Space (Asimov) **12**:45
ABC's of the Earth (Asimov) **12**:46
ABC's of the Ocean (Asimov) **12**:45
Abdul (Wells) **16**:207
Abel's Island (Steig) **15**:193
The Abominable Swamp Man (Haley) **21**:144
About David (Pfeffer) **11**:201
About Michael Jackson (Haskins) **39**:50
About the B'nai Bagels (Konigsburg) **1**:119
About the Foods You Eat (Simon) **9**:215
About the Sleeping Beauty (Travers) **2**:176
Above and Below Stairs (Goodall) **25**:53
Abraham Lincoln (d'Aulaire and d'Aulaire) **21**:43
Abraham Lincoln (Foster) **7**:94
Abraham Lincoln's World (Foster) **7**:92
Absolute Zero: Being the Second Part of the Bagthorpe Saga (Cresswell) **18**:109
Absolutely Normal Chaos (Creech) **42**:40
Abuela (Dorros) **42**:69
Ace: The Very Important Pig (King-Smith) **40**:158
The Acorn Quest (Yolen) **4**:268
Across Five Aprils (Hunt) **1**:109
Across the Sea (Goffstein) **3**:57
Across the Sea from Galway (Fisher) **18**:126
Across the Stream (Ginsburg) **45**:16
Action Replay (Rosen) **45**:146
Adam and Eve and Pinch-Me (Johnston) **41**:87

Adam and Paradise Island (Keeping) **34**:110
Adam Clayton Powell: Portrait of a Marching Black (Haskins) **3**:63
Add-a-Line Alphabet (Freeman) **30**:76
Addictions: Gambling, Smoking, Cocaine Use, and Others (Hyde) **23**:164
Adiós, Josefina! (Sanchez-Silva) **12**:232
The Adler Book of Puzzles and Riddles: Or, Sam Loyd Up to Date (Adler) **27**:17
Adler und Taube (Kruss) **9**:86
Admission to the Feast (Beckman) **25**:12
Adventure at Black Rock Cave (Lauber) **16**:113
Adventure in Granada (Myers) **16**:142
Adventures in Making: The Romance of Crafts around the World (Manley) **3**:145
The Adventures of a Puppet (Collodi)
  See *The Adventures of a Puppet*
The Adventures of Aku: Or, How It Came About That We Shall Always See Okra the Cat Lying on a Velvet Cusion, While Okraman the Dog Sleeps among the Ashes (Bryan) **18**:34
The Adventures of Andy (Bianco) **19**:52
The Adventures of Charlotte and Henry (Graham) **31**:96
The Adventures of Fathead, Smallhead, and Squarehead (Sanchez) **18**:200
The Adventures of King Midas (Reid Banks) **24**:191
The Adventures of Lester (Blake) **31**:22
The Adventures of Lowly Worm (Scarry) **41**:171
The Adventures of Odysseus and the Tale of Troy (Colum) **36**:24
The Adventures of Paddy Pork (Goodall) **25**:43
The Adventures of Peter and Lotta (Beskow) **17**:18
The Adventures of Pinocchio (Collodi)
  See *The Adventures of Pinocchio*
The Adventures of Spider: West African Folk Tales (Pinkney) **43**:155

Aesopia (Aesop)
  See *Aesop's Fables*
Aesop's Fables (Aesop) **14**:1-22
Aesop's Fables (Zwerger) **46**:198
Africa Dream (Greenfield) **4**:100
After the First Death (Cormier) **12**:143
After the Goat Man (Byars) **16**:53
After the Rain (Mazer) **23**:232
After Thursday (Ure) **34**:178
Against All Opposition: Black Explorers in America (Haskins) **39**:65
Age of Aquarius: You and Astrology (Branley) **13**:44
The Age of Giant Mammals (Cohen) **3**:37
Aging (Silverstein, Silverstein, and Silverstein) **25**:217
A-Going to the Westward (Lenski) **26**:103
The Agony of Alice (Naylor) **17**:59
Ah! Belle cité!/A Beautiful City ABC (Poulin) **28**:193
A-Haunting We Will Go: Ghostly Stories and Poems (Hopkins) **44**:89
Ah-Choo (Mayer) **11**:170
Aida (Leo and Diane Dillon) **44**:42
AIDS (Nourse) **33**:145
AIDS: Deadly Threat (Silverstein and Silverstein) **25**:223
AIDS: What Does It Mean to You? (Hyde) **23**:172
The Aimer Gate (Garner) **20**:115
Ain't Gonna Study War No More: The Story of America's Peace Seekers (Meltzer) **13**:146
Aio the Rainmaker (French) **37**:41
Air (Adler) **27**:17
Air in Fact and Fancy (Slote) **4**:199
Air Is All around You (Branley) **13**:30
The Air of Mars and Other Stories of Time and Space (Ginsburg) **45**:10
Air Raid-Pearl Harbor! The Story of December 7, 1941 (Taylor) **30**:185
AK (Dickinson) **29**:60
Akai Boshi (Anno) **14**:44
Akavak: An Eskimo Journey (Houston) **3**:84
The Alamo (Fisher) **18**:137
Alan Garner's Book of British Fairy Tales (Garner) **20**:117
Alan Garner's Fairytales of Gold (Garner) **20**:116
Alan Mendelsohn, the Boy from Mars (Pinkwater) **4**:169
The Alarm Clock (Heine) **18**:149
Alban (Lindgren) **20**:155
Albatross Two (Thiele) **27**:207
Albert's Toothache (Williams) **48**:190
Albeson and the Germans (Needle) **43**:131
Album of Dogs (Henry) **4**:112
Album of Horses (Henry) **4**:112
The Alchemists: Magic into Science (Aylesworth) **6**:50
Alcohol: Drink or Drug? (Hyde) **23**:160
Alcohol: Uses and Abuses (Hyde) **23**:175
Alcoholism (Silverstein and Silverstein) **25**:213
Alesia (Greenfield) **38**:84
Alessandra: Alex in Rome (Duder) **43**:66
Alex (Duder) **43**:64
Alex in Rome (Duder) **43**:66
Alex in Winter (Duder) **43**:65
Alexander and the Terrible, Horrible, No Good, Very Bad Day (Viorst) **3**:207
Alexander and the Wind-Up Mouse (Lionni) **7**:133
Alexander Soames: His Poems (Kuskin) **4**:137
Alexander the Gander (Tudor) **13**:190
Alexander's Great March (Baumann) **35**:50
Alexandra (O'Dell) **16**:178
Alfie and the Ferryboat (Keeping) **34**:89

Alfie Finds "The Other Side of the World" (Keeping) **34**:89
Alfie Gets In First (Hughes) **15**:128
Alfie Gives a Hand (Hughes) **15**:130
Alfie's Feet (Hughes) **15**:129
The Alfred G. Graebner Memorial High School Handbook of Rules and Regulations: A Novel (Conford) **10**:94
Alias Madame Doubtfire (Fine) **25**:21
Alice the Artist (Waddell) **31**:190
Alice's Adventures in Wonderland (Carroll) **2**:31; **18**:38-80
Alice's Adventures in Wonderland (Tenniel) **18**:201-28
Alien on the 99th Floor (Nimmo) **44**:155
All Aboard Overnight (Betsy and Giulio Maestro) **45**:85
All about Arthur (An Absolutely Absurd Ape) (Carle) **10**:78
All about Horses (Henry) **4**:114
All About Pets (Bianco) **19**:52
All about Prehistoric Cave Men (Epstein and Epstein) **26**:57
All about Sam (Lowry) **46**:37
All about the Desert (Epstein and Epstein) **26**:55
All About Whales (Patent) **19**:164
All Alone (Henkes) **23**:124
All Around You (Bendick) **5**:36
All Because I'm Older (Naylor) **17**:56
All Butterflies: An ABC (Brown) **12**:105
All Day Long: Fifty Rhymes of the Never Was and Always Is (McCord) **9**:100
All Fall Down (Oxenbury) **22**:148
All in a Day (Anno) **14**:45
All In One Piece (Murphy) **39**:173
All in the Woodland Early (Yolen) **4**:265
The All Jahdu Storybook (Hamilton) **40**:85
All Join In (Blake) **31**:28
All My Men (Ashley) **4**:15
All My Shoes Comes in Twos (Hoberman) **22**:108
All Over Town (Brink) **30**:12
All Shapes and Sizes (Hughes) **15**:132
All Sizes of Noises (Kuskin) **4**:137
All the Colors of the Race: Poems (Adoff) **7**:37
All the King's Horses (Foreman) **32**:88
All the Pretty Horses (Jeffers) **30**:130
All the Small Poems (Worth) **21**:224
All Things Bright and Beautiful: A Hymn (Politi) **29**:192
All This Wild Land (Clark) **16**:84
All Those Secrets of the World (Yolen) **44**:194
All through the Night (Field) **21**:78
All Times, All Peoples: A World History of Slavery (Meltzer) **13**:141
All Together Now (Bridgers) **18**:23
All upon a Stone (George) **1**:89
All Us Come Cross the Water (Clifton) **5**:54
All Wet! All Wet! (Stanley) **36**:134
Allan Pinkerton: America's First Private Eye (Lavine) **35**:148
Allergies (Silverstein and Silverstein) **25**:215
The Alley (Estes) **2**:73
Alligator (Scott) **20**:201
The Alligator Case (Pene du Bois) **1**:62
Alligator Pie (Lee) **3**:115
Alligator Shoes (Dorros) **42**:65
The Alligator Under the Bed (Nixon) **24**:135
Alligators All Around (Sendak) **1**:167
Alligators and Crocodiles (Zim) **2**:225
All-of-a-Sudden Susan (Coatsworth) **2**:53
Allumette: A Fable, with Due Respect to Hans Christian Andersen, the Grimm Brothers, and the Honorable Ambrose Bierce (Ungerer) **3**:199

The Almost All-White Rabbity Cat (DeJong) **1**:55
Almost Starring Skinnybones (Park) **34**:158
Alone in the Crowd (Pascal) **25**:185
Alone in the Wild Forest (Singer) **1**:173
Aloneness (Brooks) **27**:44-56
Along a Lonely Road (Waddell) **31**:202
Along Came a Dog (DeJong) **1**:56
Along Sandy Trails (Clark) **16**:83
Along This Way: The Autobiography of James Weldon Johnson (Johnson) **32**:169
Alpha Centauri: The Nearest Star (Asimov) **12**:54
Alphabeasts (King-Smith) **40**:160
Alphabet Art: Thirteen ABC's from Around the World (Fisher) **18**:127
Alphabet Soup (Yeoman) **46**:174
The Alphabet Symphone: An ABC Book (McMillan) **47**:159
The Alphabet Tree (Lionni) **7**:133
Altogether, One at a Time (Konigsburg) **1**:119
Always Reddy (Henry) **4**:110
Always Sebastian (Ure) **34**:193
Always to Remember: The Story of the Vietnam Veterans Memorial (Ashabranner) **28**:12
Am I Beautiful? (Minarik) **33**:128
Amanda and the Bear (Tudor) **13**:193
Amanda, Dreaming (Wersba) **3**:215
The Amazing and Death-Defying Diary of Eugene Dingman (Zindel) **45**:197
The Amazing Bone (Steig) **15**:193
The Amazing Egg (McClung) **11**:192
The Amazing Felix (McCully) **46**:69
Amazing Grace: The Story Behind the Song (Haskins) **39**:66
The Amazing Laser (Bova) **3**:31
Amazing Mr. Pelgrew (Schlein) **41**:180
The Amazing Mr. Prothero (Arundel) **35**:12
The Amazing Pig: An Old Hungarian Tale (Galdone) **16**:103
Amelia Bedelia (Parish) **22**:154
Amelia Bedelia and the Baby (Parish) **22**:165
Amelia Bedelia and the Surprise Shower (Parish) **22**:156
Amelia Bedelia Goes Camping (Parish) **22**:167
Amelia Bedelia Helps Out (Parish) **22**:164
Amelia Bedelia's Family Album (Parish) **22**:168
An American ABC (Petersham and Petersham) **24**:170
American Astronauts and Spacecraft: A Pictorial History from Project Mercury through Apollo 13 (Knight) **38**:110
American Astronauts and Spacecraft: A Pictorial History from Project Mercury through the Skylab Manned Missions (Knight) **38**:110
American Colonial Paper House: To Cut Out and Color (Ness) **6**:208
The American Speller: An Adaptation of Noah Webster's Blue-Backed Speller (Cooney) **23**:25
America's Endangered Birds: Programs and People Working to Save Them (McClung) **11**:191
America's Stamps: The Story of One Hundred Years of U.S. Postage Stamps (Petersham and Petersham) **24**:176
The Amethyst Ring (O'Dell) **16**:178
Amifika (Clifton) **5**:58
Amish Adventure (Smucker) **10**:191
An Amish Family (Naylor) **17**:51
Among the Dolls (Sleator) **29**:200
Amos and Boris (Steig) **2**:158
Amphigorey (Gorey) **36**:94
Amphigorey Also (Gorey) **36**:103
Amphigorey Too (Gorey) **36**:98

Amy and Laura (Sachs) **2**:131
Amy Elizabeth Explores Bloomingdale's (Konigsburg) **47**:145
Amy Moves In (Sachs) **2**:131
Amy Said (Waddell) **31**:196
Amzat and His Brothers (Fox) **44**:75
Anancy and Mr. Dry-Bone (French) **37**:52
Anancy-Spiderman (Berry) **22**:9
Anansi the Spider: A Tale from the Ashanti (McDermott) **9**:110
Anastasia, Absolutely (Lowry) **46**:49
Anastasia Again! (Lowry) **6**:195
Anastasia, Ask Your Analyst (Lowry) **46**:29
Anastasia at This Address (Lowry) **46**:41
Anastasia at Your Service (Lowry) **6**:196
Anastasia Has the Answers (Lowry) **46**:33
Anastasia Krupnik (Lowry) **6**:194
Anastasia on Her Own (Lowry) **46**:31
Anastasia's Chosen Career (Lowry) **46**:36
Anatole (Galdone) **16**:88
Anatole and the Cat (Galdone) **16**:89
Anatole and the Pied Piper (Galdone) **16**:102
Anchor Man (Jackson) **28**:139
Ancient Civilizations (Pullman) **20**:186
Ancient Egypt (Cohen) **43**:51
An Ancient Heritage: The Arab-American Minority (Ashabranner) **28**:16
Ancient Indians: The First Americans (Gallant) **30**:104
Ancient Monuments and How They Were Built (Cohen) **3**:37
The Ancient Visitors (Cohen) **3**:38
And All Between (Snyder) **31**:163
And Condors Danced (Snyder) **31**:168
And It Rained (Raskin) **1**:155
And It Was So (Tudor) **13**:196
And Maggie Makes Three (Nixon) **24**:147
And So My Garden Grows (Spier) **5**:219
And Then What Happened, Paul Revere? (Fritz) **2**:79
And This Is Laura (Conford) **10**:94
And to Think That I Saw It on Mulberry Street (Seuss) **1**:84; **9**:172
And Twelve Chinese Acrobats (Yolen) **44**:204
Andrew Carnegie and the Age of Steel (Shippen) **36**:179
Andrew Jackson (Foster) **7**:95
Andrew Young: Man with a Mission (Haskins) **39**:35
The Andrews Raid: Or, The Great Locomotive Chase, April 12, 1862 (Epstein and Epstein) **26**:54
Androcles and the Lion (Galdone) **16**:94
Andy All Year Round: A Picture Book of Four Seasons and Five Senses (Merriam) **14**:195
Andy Buckram's Tin Men (Brink) **30**:15
Andy (That's My Name) (dePaola) **4**:55
Angel and the Polar Bear (Gay) **27**:87
The Angel and the Wild Animal (Foreman) **32**:101
Angel Dust Blues: A Novel (Strasser) **11**:246
Angel Face (Klein) **19**:95
Angel Square (Doyle) **22**:32
The Angel with a Mouth Organ (Mattingley) **24**:128
Angela's Airplane (Munsch) **19**:143
Angelina and the Birds (Baumann) **35**:42
Angelo (Blake) **31**:18
Angelo, the Naughty One (Politi) **29**:185
Angels and Other Strangers: Family Christmas Stories (Paterson) **7**:237
Angel's Gate (Crew) **42**:58
Angie's First Case (Sobol) **4**:212
The Angry Moon (Sleator) **29**:199

Angus and the Cat (Flack) **28**:120
The Animal (Kherdian) **24**:114
Animal and Plant Mimicry (Patent) **19**:151
Animal Antics (Janosch) **26**:80
Animal Architects (Freedman) **20**:76
Animal Clocks and Compasses: From Animal Migration to Space Travel (Hyde) **23**:154
Animal Fact/Animal Fable (Simon) **9**:213
The Animal Fair (Provensen and Provensen) **11**:209
The Animal Family (Jarrell) **6**:162
Animal Fathers (Freedman) **20**:78
Animal Games (Freedman) **20**:78
The Animal Hedge (Fleischman) **20**:65
Animal Hospital (Berger) **32**:9
Animal Instincts (Freedman) **20**:75
The Animal Kingdom (Guillot) **22**:58
Animal Nursery Tales (Scarry) **41**:166
Animal Rights: A Handbook for Young Adults (Cohen) **43**:57
Animal Superstars (Freedman) **20**:82
Animal Superstitions (Aylesworth) **6**:56
Animal Territories (Cohen) **3**:38
The Animal, the Vegetable, and John D. Jones (Byars) **16**:58
Animal Tracks (Dorros) **42**:70
Animalia (Base) **22**:4
The Animals and the Ark (Kuskin) **4**:135
Animals and Their Babies (Carle) **10**:79
Animals and Their Niches: How Species Share Resources (Pringle) **4**:183
Animals as Parents (Selsam) **1**:159
The Animals' Carol (Causley) **30**:40
The Animals' Conference (Kaestner) **4**:125
Animals Everywhere (d'Aulaire and d'Aulaire) **21**:46
Animals for Sale (Munari) **9**:124
Animals in Field and Laboratory: Science Projects in Animal Behavior (Simon) **9**:201
Animals in Winter (Poulin) **28**:198
Animals in Your Neighborhood (Simon) **9**:211
The Animals' Lullaby (Nakatani) **30**:155
The Animals of Doctor Schweitzer (Fritz) **14**:111
Animals of the Bible (Asimov) **12**:56
Annabelle Pig and the Travellers (McKee) **38**:180
Annabelle Swift, Kindergartner (Schwartz) **25**:195
Annaluise and Anton (Kaestner) **4**:123
Anne of Avonlea (Montgomery) **8**:134
Anne of Green Gables (Montgomery) **8**:131
Anne of Ingleside (Montgomery) **8**:139
Anne of the Island (Montgomery) **8**:137
Annegret und Cara (Benary-Isbert) **12**:73
Anneli the Art Hater (Fine) **25**:21
Annerton Pit (Dickinson) **29**:46
Annie and the Wild Animals (Brett) **27**:39
Annie Pat and Eddie (Haywood) **22**:98
Anno Mitsumasa No Gashu (Anno) **14**:35
Anno's Alphabet: An Adventure in Imagination (Anno) **2**:1
Anno's Animals (Anno) **14**:34
Anno's Britain (Anno) **14**:39
Anno's Counting Book (Anno) **14**:32
Anno's Counting House (Anno) **14**:40
Anno's Flea Market (Anno) **14**:43
Anno's Hat Tricks (Anno) **14**:44
Anno's Italy (Anno) **14**:37
Anno's Journey (Anno) **14**:33
Anno's Magical ABC: An Anamorphic Alphabet (Anno) **14**:39
Anno's Medieval World (Anno) **14**:37
Anno's Mysterious Multiplying Jar (Anno) **14**:41

Anno's Three Little Pigs (Anno) **14**:44
Anno's U.S.A. (Anno) **14**:41
Ann's Alpine Adventure (Allan) **43**:5
Another Day (Ets) **33**:81
Another Fine Mess (Needle) **43**:137
Another Helping of Chips (Hughes) **15**:133
Anpao: An American Indian Odyssey (Highwater) **17**:23
Ant and Bee: An Alphabetical Story for Tiny Tots (Banner) **24**:18
Ant and Bee and Kind Dog: An Alphabetical Story (Banner) **24**:19
Ant and Bee and the ABC (Banner) **24**:19
Ant and Bee and the Doctor (Banner) **24**:19
Ant and Bee and the Secret (Banner) **24**:19
The Ant and Bee Big Buy Bag (Banner) **24**:19
Ant and Bee Go Shopping (Banner) **24**:20
Ant and Bee Time (Banner) **24**:19
Ant Cities (Dorros) **42**:65
Antarctica: The Great White Continent (Schlein) **41**:190
Anthony Burns: The Defeat and Triumph of a Fugitive Slave (Hamilton) **40**:76
The Anti-Muffins (L'Engle) **14**:153
Anton and Anne (Carigiet) **38**:74
Anton the Goatherd (Carigiet) **38**:72
The Ants Who Took Away Time (Kotzwinkle) **6**:183
Any Me I Want to Be: Poems (Kuskin) **4**:140
Anything Can Happen on the River (Brink) **30**:6
Anything for a Friend (Conford) **10**:95
Appelard and Liverwurst (Mayer) **11**:173
Appelemando's Dreams (Polacco) **40**:190
The Apple and Other Fruits (Selsam) **1**:160
Apple Bough (Streatfeild) **17**:195
The Apple Tree (Bianco) **19**:52
Apples (Hogrogian) **2**:87
Apples, How They Grow (McMillan) **47**:161
The Apprentices (Garfield) **21**:113
The Apprenticeship of Duddy Kravitz (Richler) **17**:64
April and the Dragon Lady (Namioka) **48**:66
April Fools (Krahn) **3**:103
Apt. 3 (Keats) **1**:113; **35**:137
Aquarius (Mark) **11**:152
Aquatic Insects and How They Live (McClung) **11**:186
Arabel and Mortimer (Aiken) **19**:13
Arabella (Fox) **23**:114
Arabel's Raven (Aiken) **1**:2
Arabian Frights and Other Stories (Rosen) **45**:149
Arabian Horses (Patent) **19**:157
Die Arche Noah (Benary-Isbert) **12**:70
Archer Armadillo's Secret Room (Singer) **48**:127
Archer's Goon (Jones) **23**:193
Archimedes and the Door of Science (Bendick) **5**:40
Architect of the Moon (Wynne-Jones) **21**:231
The Architects (Fisher) **18**:123
Are All the Giants Dead? (Norton) **6**:225
Are We Almost There? (Stevenson) **17**:163
Are You in the House Alone? (Peck) **15**:156
Are You My Friend Today? (Fujikawa) **25**:41
Are You There God? It's Me, Margaret (Blume) **2**:15
Ariadne Awake! (Orgel) **48**:94
Arilla Sun Down (Hamilton) **11**:76
Arithmetic Can Be Fun (Leaf) **25**:130
The Ark (Benary-Isbert) **12**:70
The Ark of Father Noah and Mother Noah (Petersham and Petersham) **24**:162
The Arkadians (Alexander) **48**:26

Arly (Peck) **45**:122

Arly's Run (Peck) **45**:124

Arm in Arm: A Collection of Connections, Endless Tales, Reiterations, and Other Echolalia (Charlip) **8**:28

The Arm of the Starfish (L'Engle) **1**:129

Armitage, Armitage, Fly Away Home (Aiken) **1**:2

Armored Animals (Zim) **2**:225

The Armourer's House (Sutcliff) **1**:183; **37**:149

Around Fred's Bed (Pinkwater) **4**:165

Around the Clock with Harriet: A Book about Telling Time (Betsy and Giulio Maestro) **45**:73

Around the World in Eighty Days (Burningham) **9**:44

Around the Year (Tudor) **13**:196

Arrow to the Sun: A Pueblo Indian Tale (McDermott) **9**:111

Art and Archaeology (Glubok) **1**:95

The Art and Industry of Sandcastles: Being an Illustrated Guide to Basic Constructions along with Divers Information Devised by One Jan Adkins, a Wily Fellow (Adkins) **7**:18

The Art Experience: Oil Painting, 15th-19th Centuries (Fisher) **18**:125

The Art Lesson (dePaola) **24**:102

The Art of America from Jackson to Lincoln (Glubok) **1**:95

The Art of America in the Gilded Age (Glubok) **1**:95

The Art of Ancient Mexico (Glubok) **1**:96

The Art of Ancient Peru (Glubok) **1**:96

The Art of China (Glubok) **1**:97

The Art of India (Glubok) **1**:97

The Art of Japan (Glubok) **1**:97

The Art of Lands in the Bible (Glubok) **1**:98

The Art of the Etruscans (Glubok) **1**:98

The Art of the New American Nation (Glubok) **1**:99

The Art of the North American Indian (Glubok) **1**:99

The Art of the Northwest Coast Indians (Glubok) **1**:99

The Art of the Spanish in the United States and Puerto Rico (Glubok) **1**:100

Art, You're Magic! (McBratney) **44**:126

Arthur, for the Very First Time (MacLachlan) **14**:181

Arthur Goes to Camp (Brown) **29**:8

Arthur Meets the President (Brown) **29**:19

Arthur Mitchell (Tobias) **4**:215

Arthur's April Fool (Brown) **29**:9

Arthur's Baby (Brown) **29**:16

Arthur's Birthday (Brown) **29**:18

Arthur's Christmas (Brown) **29**:12

Arthur's Eyes (Brown) **29**:5

Arthur's Halloween (Brown) **29**:8

Arthur's Nose (Brown) **29**:3

Arthur's Pet Business (Brown) **29**:19

Arthur's Teacher Trouble (Brown) **29**:14

Arthur's Thanksgiving (Brown) **29**:10

Arthur's Tooth (Brown) **29**:12

Arthur's Valentine (Brown) **29**:6

The Artificial Heart (Berger) **32**:38

Artificial Intelligence: A Revision of Computers That Think? (Hyde) **23**:167

Arts and Crafts You Can Eat (Cobb) **2**:64

Ash Road (Southall) **2**:147

Ashanti to Zulu: African Traditions (Leo and Diane Dillon) **44**:29

Asimov's Guide to Halley's Comet: The Awesome Story of Comets (Asimov) **12**:63

Ask Mr. Bear (Flack) **28**:120

Asking about Sex and Growing Up: A Question-And-Answer Book for Boys and Girls (Cole) **40**:22

Asleep, Asleep (Ginsburg) **45**:19

Assignment: Sports (Lipsyte) **23**:205

Astercote (Lively) **7**:151

Asterix and the Banquet (Goscinny and Uderzo) **37**:82

Asterix and the Big Fight (Goscinny and Uderzo) **37**:75

Asterix and the Chieftain's Shield (Goscinny and Uderzo) **37**:81

Asterix and the Goths (Goscinny and Uderzo) **37**:76

Asterix and the Great Crossing (Goscinny and Uderzo) **37**:81

Asterix and the Laurel Wreath (Goscinny and Uderzo) **37**:77

Asterix at the Olympic Games (Goscinny and Uderzo) **37**:76

Asterix in Britain (Goscinny and Uderzo) **37**:75

Asterix in Spain (Goscinny and Uderzo) **37**:76

Asterix the Gaul (Goscinny and Uderzo) **37**:74

The Asteroids (Nourse) **33**:139

The Astonishing Stereoscope (Langton) **33**:111

Astrology and Foretelling the Future (Aylesworth) **6**:50

Astrology: Sense or Nonsense? (Gallant) **30**:92

At Home (Hill) **13**:93

At Home: A Visit in Four Languages (Hautzig) **22**:83

At Mary Bloom's (Aliki) **9**:25

At Our House (Lenski) **26**:120

At the Beach (Tobias) **4**:217

At the Forge of Liberty (Carter) **22**:23

At the Sign of the Dog and Rocket (Mark) **11**:156

At the Stroke of Midnight: Traditional Fairy Tales Retold (Cresswell) **18**:103

Athletic Shorts: Six Short Stories (Crutcher) **28**:107

Atomic Energy (Adler) **27**:24

Atoms (Berger) **32**:3

Atoms and Molecules (Adler) **27**:20

Atoms, Molecules, and Quarks (Berger) **32**:37

Atoms Today and Tomorrow (Hyde) **23**:153

Attaboy, Sam! (Lowry) **46**:42

Attack of the Killer Fishsticks (Zindel) **45**:200

Attar of the Ice Valley (Wibberley) **3**:224

Audubon Cat (Calhoun) **42**:27

August the Fourth (Farmer) **8**:86

Augustus Caesar's World, a Story of Ideas and Events from B.C. 44 to 14 A.D. (Foster) **7**:93

Auno and Tauno: A Story of Finland (Henry) **4**:109

Aunt Bernice (Gantos) **18**:141

Aunt Green, Aunt Brown, and Aunt Lavender (Beskow) **17**:16

Auntie and Celia Jane and Miki (Petersham and Petersham) **24**:164

Das Austauschkind (Noestlinger) **12**:189

The Author and Squinty Gritt (Williams) **48**:206

Automobile Factory (Berger) **32**:18

Autumn Harvest (Tresselt) **30**:204

Autumn Story (Barklem) **31**:2

Autumn Street (Lowry) **6**:195

Avocado Baby (Burningham) **9**:50

Le Avventure di Pinocchio (Collodi) **5**:69

Away and Ago: Rhymes of the Never Was and Always Is (McCord) **9**:102

Away from Wood Street (Allan) **43**:27

Away Went the Balloons (Haywood) **22**:102

Awful Evelina (Pfeffer) **11**:200

Axe-Age, Wolf-Age: A Selection from the Norse Myths (Crossley-Holland) **47**:42

Aztec Indians (McKissack) **23**:237

B is een beer (Bruna) **7**:50

B Is for Bear: An ABC (Bruna) **7**:50

"B" Is for Betsy (Haywood) **22**:90

B, My Name Is Bunny (Mazer) **23**:231

Baaa (Macaulay) **14**:175

The Baabee Books, Series I (Khalsa) **30**:144

The Baabee Books, Series III (Khalsa) **30**:144

Babar and Father Christmas (Brunhoff) **4**:32

Babar and His Children (Brunhoff) **4**:32

Babar and the Old Lady (Brunhoff) **4**:37

Babar and the Professor (Brunhoff) **4**:34

Babar and the Wully-Wully (Brunhoff) **4**:39

Babar at Home (Brunhoff) **4**:32

Babar at the Seashore (Brunhoff) **4**:38

Babar at the Seaside (Brunhoff) **4**:38

Babar Comes to America (Brunhoff) **4**:36

Babar Goes on a Picnic (Brunhoff) **4**:38

Babar Goes Skiing (Brunhoff) **4**:38

Babar in the Snow (Brunhoff) **4**:38

Babar Loses His Crown (Brunhoff) **4**:37

Babar the Gardener (Brunhoff) **4**:38

Babar the King (Brunhoff) **4**:31

Babar Visits Another Planet (Brunhoff) **4**:38

Babar's Birthday Surprise (Brunhoff) **4**:38

Babar's Castle (Brunhoff) **4**:35

Babar's Childhood (Brunhoff) **4**:37

Babar's Coronation (Brunhoff) **4**:37

Babar's Cousin: That Rascal Arthur (Brunhoff) **4**:33

Babar's Day Out (Brunhoff) **4**:38

Babar's Fair (Brunhoff) **4**:34

Babar's French Lessons (Brunhoff) **4**:35

Babar's Mystery (Brunhoff) **4**:39

Babar's Picnic (Brunhoff) **4**:34

Babar's Trunk (Brunhoff) **4**:38

Babar's Visit to Bird Island (Brunhoff) **4**:34

Babe: The Gallant Pig (King-Smith) **40**:144; **41**:124

The Babes in the Wood (Caldecott) **14**:74

Babies! (Patent) **19**:166

Babushka Baba Yaga (Polacco) **40**:196

Babushka's Doll (Polacco) **40**:188

Babushka's Mother Goose (Polacco) **40**:200

The Baby (Burningham) **9**:46

Baby Bear Books (Hill) **13**:93

Baby Bear's Bedtime (Hill) **13**:95

Baby Bunting (Caldecott) **14**:78

Baby Dinosaurs (Sattler) **24**:219

A Baby for Max (Lasky) **11**:121

Baby Island (Brink) **30**:11

The Baby Project (Ellis) **42**:81

A Baby Sister for Frances (Hoban) **3**:75

A Baby Starts to Grow (Showers) **6**:244

The Baby, the Bed, and the Rose (Naylor) **17**:61

Baby Time: A Grownup's Handbook to Use with Baby (Brown) **29**:18

The Baby Uggs Are Watching (Prelutsky) **13**:170

The Baby Zoo (McMillan) **47**:180

The Baby's Catalogue (Ahlberg and Ahlberg) **18**:9

Baby's First Christmas (dePaola) **24**:101

The Baby-Sitter II (Stine) **37**:116

The Baby-Sitter III (Stine) **37**:123

Back Home (Pinkney) **43**:168

The Back House Ghosts (Waddell) **31**:177

Back in the Beforetime: Tales of the California Indians (Curry) **31**:86

Back to School with Betsy (Haywood) **22**:92

Backbone of the King: The Story of Paka'a and His Son Ku (Brown) **12**:102

Backstage (Isadora) **7**:104
The Backward Day (Krauss) **42**:114
The Backwoodsmen (Roberts) **33**:201
The Backyard Astronomer (Nourse) **33**:137
Backyard Bestiary (Blumberg) **21**:25
Bacteria: How They Affect Other Living Things (Patent) **19**:155
Bad, Badder, Baddest (Voigt) **48**:185
Bad Boy, Good Boy (Ets) **33**:90
Bad Girls (Voigt) **48**:183
The Bad Island (Steig) **2**:158
The Bad Little Duckhunter (Brown) **10**:54
Bad Sam! (Lindgren) **20**:157
A Bad Spell for the Worst Witch (Murphy) **39**:171
The Bad Speller (Steig) **2**:159
The Bad Times of Irma Baumlein (Brink) **30**:16
Badger on the Barge and Other Stories (Howker) **14**:127
Badger's Fate (Hamley) **47**:64
The Bad-Tempered Ladybird (Carle) **10**:81
A Bag of Moonshine (Garner) **20**:118
Bagthorpes Abroad: Being the Fifth Part of the Bagthorpe Saga (Cresswell) **18**:112
Bagthorpes Haunted: Being the Sixth Part of the Bagthorpe Saga (Cresswell) **18**:112
Bagthorpes Unlimited: Being the Third Part of the Bagthorpe Saga (Cresswell) **18**:110
Bagthorpes v. the World: Being the Fourth Part of the Bagthorpe Saga (Cresswell) **18**:110
Bailey Goes Camping (Henkes) **23**:127
Baily's Bones (Kelleher) **36**:124
The Baker and the Basilisk (McHargue) **2**:117
The Bakers: A Simple Book about the Pleasures of Baking Bread (Adkins) **7**:22
The Ballad of Aucassin and Nicolette (Causley) **30**:41
The Ballad of Benny Perhaps (Brinsmead) **47**:14
The Ballad of St. Simeon (Serraillier) **2**:135
The Ballad of the Pilgrim Cat (Wibberley) **3**:224
The Ballad of the Pirate Queens (Yolen) **44**:205
Ballet Dance for Two (Ure) **34**:170
The Ballet Family Again (Allan) **43**:12
Ballet Shoes: A Story of Three Children on the Stage (Streatfeild) **17**:185
Ballet Shoes for Anna (Streatfeild) **17**:198
The Ballet Twins (Estoril) **43**:16
Balloon Journey (Guillot) **22**:67
The Ballooning Adventures of Paddy Pork (Goodall) **25**:43
Bam! Zam! Boom! A Building Book (Merriam) **14**:197
A Band of Angels (Thompson) **24**:229
Bang Bang You're Dead (Fitzhugh) **1**:71
Banjo (Peck) **45**:117
Barbara Jordan: Speaking Out (Haskins) **39**:33
Barbara's Birthday (Stevenson) **17**:159
Bard of Avon: The Story of William Shakespeare (Stanley) **46**:146
Barefoot in the Grass (Armstrong) **1**:22
A Bargain for Frances (Hoban) **3**:75
The Barge Children (Cresswell) **18**:100
Barishnikov's Nutcracker (Klein) **19**:95
Baron Bruno; or, The Unbelieving Philosopher and Other Fairy Stories (Caldecott) **14**:72
The Barque of the Brothers: A Tale of the Days of Henry the Navigator (Baumann) **35**:40
Bartholomew and the Oobleck (Seuss) **9**:177
Baseball Flyhawk (Christopher) **33**:39
Baseball in April and Other Stories (Soto) **38**:189
Baseball Pals (Christopher) **33**:37
The Baseball Trick (Corbett) **1**:42
Basil of Baker Street (Galdone) **16**:89
The Basket Counts (Christopher) **33**:43

Basketball Sparkplug (Christopher) **33**:37
Bass and Billy Martin (Phipson) **5**:182
The Bassumtyte Treasure (Curry) **31**:82
The Bastable Children (Nesbit) **3**:161
The Bates Family (Ottley) **16**:186
Bath Time for John (Graham) **31**:92
The Bathwater Gang (Spinelli) **26**:205
Bathwater's Hot (Hughes) **15**:131
The Bat-Poet (Jarrell) **6**:158
Bats: Night Fliers (Betsy and Giulio Maestro) **45**:89
Bats: Wings in the Night (Lauber) **16**:115
Battle against the Sea: How the Dutch Made Holland (Lauber) **16**:111
The Battle for the Atlantic (Williams) **8**:223
Battle in the Arctic Seas: The Story of Convoy PQ 17 (Taylor) **30**:189
Battle in the English Channel (Taylor) **30**:192
The Battle of Bubble and Squeak (Pearce) **9**:156
The Battle of Reuben Robin and Kite Uncle John (Calhoun) **42**:19
The Battle of the Dinosaurs (Knight) **38**:126
The Battle of the Galah Trees (Mattingley) **24**:123
The Battle off Midway Island (Taylor) **30**:190
Battleground: The United States Army in World War II (Collier) **3**:44
Bayou Suzette (Lenski) **26**:106
Be Brave, Billy (Ormerod) **20**:176
Be Ready at Eight (Parish) **22**:164
Bea and Mr. Jones (Schwartz) **25**:190
Beach Ball (Sis) **45**:164
Beach Ball—Left, Right (McMillan) **47**:180
Beach Day (Oxenbury) **22**:143
A Beach for the Birds (McMillan) **47**:183
Beach House (Stine) **37**:120
Beach Party (Ryder) **37**:87
Beach Party (Stine) **37**:113
The Beachcombers (Cresswell) **18**:105
Beady Bear (Freeman) **30**:70
Beanpole (Park) **34**:155
Beans: All about Them (Silverstein and Silverstein) **25**:212
The Bear and His Brothers (Baumann) **35**:46
The Bear and the People (Zimnik) **3**:242
A Bear Called Paddington (Bond) **1**:27
Bear Circus (Pene du Bois) **1**:62
Bear Cub (Clark) **16**:82
The Bear Detectives: The Case of the Missing Pumpkins (Berenstain and Berenstain) **19**:29
A Bear for Christmas (Keller) **45**:48
Bear Goes to Town (Browne) **19**:67
Bear Hunt (Browne) **19**:63
The Bear on the Moon (Ryder) **37**:97
The Bear Scouts (Berenstain and Berenstain) **19**:25
Bear Trouble (Moore) **15**:140
The Bear Who Had No Place to Go (Stevenson) **17**:152
The Bear Who Saw the Spring (Kuskin) **4**:136
The Bear Who Wanted to Be a Bear (Mueller) **43**:118
The Bear Who Wanted to Stay a Bear (Mueller) **43**:118
Bears (Krauss) **42**:111
The Bears' Almanac: A Year in Bear Country (Berenstain and Berenstain) **19**:28
The Bear's Autumn (Tejima) **20**:202
The Bears' Christmas (Berenstain and Berenstain) **19**:26
The Bear's House (Sachs) **2**:131
Bears in the Night (Berenstain and Berenstain) **19**:27

The Bears' Nature Guide (Berenstain and Berenstain) **19**:29
The Bears of the Air (Lobel) **5**:164
Bears of the World (Patent) **19**:155
Bears on Wheels (Berenstain and Berenstain) **19**:26
The Bears' Picnic (Berenstain and Berenstain) **19**:25
Bear's Picture (Pinkwater) **4**:162
The Bears' Vacation (Berenstain and Berenstain) **19**:26
the Bear's Water Picnic (Yeoman) **46**:174
The Bears Will Get You! (Nimmo) **44**:148
The Bear's Winter House (Yeoman) **46**:174
Bearymore (Freeman) **30**:80
The Beast of Monsieur Racine (Ungerer) **3**:200
The Beast with the Magical Horn (Cameron) **1**:39
A Beastly Circus (Parish) **22**:157
Beasts and Nonsense (Ets) **33**:80
The Beasts of Never (McHargue) **2**:117
Beat of the City (Brinsmead) **47**:8
The Beat of the Drum (Waddell) **31**:194
Beat the Story-Drum, Pum-Pum (Bryan) **18**:34
Beatrice and Vanessa (Yeoman) **46**:177
Beats Me, Claude (Nixon) **24**:148
Beauty: A Retelling of the Story of Beauty and the Beast (McKinley) **10**:121
Beauty and the Beast (Brett) **27**:42
Beauty and the Beast (Harris) **30**:120
Beauty and the Beast (Pearce) **9**:154
The Beauty Queen (Pfeffer) **11**:198
The Beaver Pond (Tresselt) **30**:212
Because of a Flower (Milne and Milne) **22**:122
Because of a Tree (Milne and Milne) **22**:118
Because We Are (Walter) **15**:206
Becca Backward, Becca Frontward: A Book of Concept Pairs (McMillan) **47**:168
The Beckoning Lights (Hughes) **9**:77
Becky's Birthday (Tudor) **13**:197
Becky's Christmas (Tudor) **13**:197
Bed-knob and Broomstick (Norton) **6**:222
Bedtime for Frances (Hoban) **3**:75
The Bee Rustlers (Needle) **43**:134
The Bee Tree (Polacco) **40**:195
Bee Tree and Other Stuff (Peck) **45**:106
Been to Yesterdays: Poems of a Life (Hopkins) **44**:99
Bees Can't Fly, but They Do: Things That Are Still a Mystery to Science (Knight) **38**:119
Bees, Wasps, and Hornets, and How They Live (McClung) **11**:187
The Beethoven Medal (Peyton) **3**:171
Beetles and How They Live (Patent) **19**:151
Beetles, Lightly Toasted (Naylor) **17**:61
Beezus and Ramona (Cleary) **2**:45; **8**:47
The Befana's Toyshop: A Twelfth Night Story (Rodari) **24**:208
Before Freedom, When I Just Can Remember: Twenty-Seven Oral Histories of Former South Carolina Slaves (Hurmence) **25**:96
Before the Sun Dies: The Story of Evolution (Gallant) **30**:104
Before the War, 1908-1939: An Autobiography in Pictures (Goodall) **25**:51
Before You Came This Way (Baylor) **3**:13
Before You Were a Baby (Showers) **6**:244
The Beggar Queen (Alexander) **48**:14
Begin at the Beginning (Schwartz) **25**:191
A Beginner's Book of Vegetable Gardening (Lavine) **35**:157
Beginner's Love (Klein) **19**:94
Beginning Mobiles (Parish) **22**:165
The Beginning of the Earth (Branley) **13**:38

A Begonia for Miss Applebaum (Zindel) **45**:197

Beheaded, Survived (Williams) **48**:204

Behind the Attic Wall (Cassedy) **26**:13

Behind the Back of the Mountain: Black Folktales from Southern Africa (Aardema) **17**:4

Behind the Back of the Mountain: Black Folktales from Southern Africa (Leo and Diane Dillon) **44**:24

Behind the Bike Sheds (Needle) **43**:141

Bel the Giant and Other Stories (Clarke) **28**:75

Belinda (Allen) **44**:14

The Bell Family (Streatfeild) **17**:192

A Bell for Ursli (Carigiet) **38**:69

The Bells of Christmas (Hamilton) **40**:81

The Bells of Rome (Allan) **43**:25

Below the Root (Snyder) **31**:161

Ben Loves Anna (Hartling) **29**:103

Bend and Stretch (Ormerod) **20**:180

Beneath the Hill (Curry) **31**:70

Beneath Your Feet (Simon) **9**:211

Benjamin and the Pillow Saga (Poulin) **28**:196

Benjamin and Tulip (Wells) **16**:205

Benjamin Franklin (d'Aulaire and d'Aulaire) **21**:50

Benjamin Pig and the Apple Thieves (McKee) **38**:180

Benjamin West and His Cat Grimalkin (Henry) **4**:110

Benjamin's Barn (Jeffers) **30**:136

Ben's Baby (Foreman) **32**:101

Ben's Box (Foreman) **32**:101

Ben's Dream (Van Allsburg) **5**:240

Ben's Gingerbread Man (Daly) **41**:55

Ben's Trumpet (Isadora) **7**:104

Benson Boy (Southall) **2**:148

The Bent-Back Bridge (Crew) **42**:61

Beowulf (Crossley-Holland) **47**:39

Beowulf (Sutcliff) **1**:183; **37**:155

Beowulf the Warrior (Serraillier) **2**:135

The Berenstain Bears and the Messy Room (Berenstain and Berenstain) **19**:31

The Berenstain Bears and the Missing Dinosaur Bone (Berenstain and Berenstain) **19**:31

The Berenstain Bears and the Sitter (Berenstain and Berenstain) **19**:31

The Berenstain Bears and the Spooky Old Tree (Berenstain and Berenstain) **19**:30

The Berenstain Bears and Too Much Junk Food (Berenstain and Berenstain) **19**:32

The Berenstain Bears' Christmas Tree (Berenstain and Berenstain) **19**:31

The Berenstain Bears' Counting Book (Berenstain and Berenstain) **19**:29

The Berenstain Bears Go to the Doctor (Berenstain and Berenstain) **19**:31

The Berenstain Bears Learn about Strangers (Berenstain and Berenstain) **19**:32

The Berenstain Bears' Moving Day (Berenstain and Berenstain) **19**:31

The Berenstain Bears' Science Fair (Berenstain and Berenstain) **19**:30

The Berenstain Bears Visit the Dentist (Berenstain and Berenstain) **19**:31

The Berenstains' B Book (Berenstain and Berenstain) **19**:27

Bernard into Battle (Sharp) **27**:166

Bernard the Brave (Sharp) **27**:166

Berries in the Scoop: A Cape Cod Cranberry Story (Lenski) **26**:119

Bertie and the Bear (Allen) **44**:6

Bertie Boggin and the Ghost Again! (Waddell) **31**:191

Bertie's Escapade (Grahame) **5**:135

Bess and the Sphinx (Coatsworth) **2**:53

Best Christmas Book Ever! (Scarry) **41**:170

Best Counting Book Ever (Scarry) **41**:166

Best First Book Ever! (Scarry) **41**:168

The Best Friend (Stine) **37**:119

Best Friends (Pascal) **25**:186

Best Make-it Book Ever! (Scarry) **41**:168

The Best Mistake Ever! and Other Stories (Scarry) **41**:170

The Best New Thing (Asimov) **12**:46

The Best of Enemies (Bond) **11**:28

The Best of Michael Rosen (Rosen) **45**:150

The Best of the Bargain (Domanska) **40**:46

The Best Present (Keller) **45**:52

The Best Train Set Ever (Hutchins) **20**:149

Best True Ghost Stories of the 20th Century (Knight) **38**:129

Best Witches: Poems for Halloween (Yolen) **44**:188

Best Word Book Ever (Scarry) **41**:161

The Best-Kept Secret (Rodda) **32**:211

Der Besuch (Heine) **18**:149

Betje Big gaat naar de markt (Bruna) **7**:52

The Betrayal; The Secret (Stine) **37**:122

Betrayed (Sneve) **2**:143

Betsy and Billy (Haywood) **22**:91

Betsy and Mr. Kilpatrick (Haywood) **22**:100

Betsy and the Boys (Haywood) **22**:93

Betsy and the Circus (Haywood) **22**:96

Betsy's Busy Summer (Haywood) **22**:96

Betsy's Little Star (Haywood) **22**:94

Betsy's Play School (Haywood) **22**:103

Betsy's Winterhouse (Haywood) **22**:97

Better Than All Right (Pfeffer) **11**:197

Betty Friedan: A Voice for Women's Rights (Meltzer) **13**:149

Between Earth and Sky: Legends of Native American Sacred Places (Bruchac) **46**:21

Beware the Fish! (Korman) **25**:105

Beyond Dreamtime: The Life and Lore of the Aboriginal Australian (Cummings) **48**:43

Beyond Earth: The Search for Extraterrestrial Life (Gallant) **30**:93

Beyond the Bambassu (Guillot) **22**:63

Beyond the Burning Lands (Christopher) **2**:37

Beyond the Chocolate War (Cormier) **12**:151

Beyond the Dark River (Hughes) **9**:71

Beyond the Divide (Lasky) **11**:119

Beyond the Labyrinth (Rubinstein) **35**:211

Beyond the Ridge (Goble) **21**:137

Beyond the Tomorrow Mountains (Engdahl) **2**:69

Beyond the Weir Bridge (Burton) **1**:30

Beyond Two Rivers (Kherdian) **24**:112

The BFG (Dahl) **7**:82

A Biblical Garden (Lerner) **34**:127

The Bicycle Man (Say) **22**:210

Big and Little (Krauss) **42**:131

Big and Little (Scarry) **41**:171

Big Anthony and the Magic Ring (dePaola) **4**:62

Big Bad Bertie (Waddell) **31**:183

Big Bad Bruce (Peet) **12**:203

The Big Book of Brambly Hedge (Barklem) **31**:5

The Big Cheese (Bunting) **28**:46

The Big Cheese (Schlein) **41**:182

Big City Port (Betsy and Giulio Maestro) **45**:73

The Big Cleanup (Weiss) **4**:224

Big Dog, Little Dog (Brown) **10**:51

Big Dreams and Small Rockets: A Short History of Space Travel (Lauber) **16**:114

Big Friend, Little Friend; Daddy and I . . .; I Make Music; and My Doll, Keshia (Greenfield) **38**:92

Big Game Benn (McKee) **38**:167

Big Goof and Little Goof (Cole) **40**:27

The Big Honey Hunt (Berenstain and Berenstain) **19**:24

The Big Janosch Book of Fun and Verse (Janosch) **26**:79

The Big Joke Game (Corbett) **1**:43

Big Little Davy (Lenski) **26**:120

Big Man and the Burn-Out (Bess) **39**:4

Big Mose (Shippen) **36**:174

Big Ones, Little Ones (Hoban) **13**:104

The Big Orange Splot (Pinkwater) **4**:166

The Big Pets (Smith) **47**:199

Big Red Barn (Brown) **10**:66

The Big Red Barn (Bunting) **28**:48

Big Sister Tells Me That I'm Black (Adoff) **7**:33

The Big Six (Ransome) **8**:180

Big Sixteen (Calhoun) **42**:29

The Big Smith Snatch (Curry) **31**:87

Big Talk (Schlein) **41**:177

Big Top Benn (McKee) **38**:171

Big Tracks, Little Tracks (Branley) **13**:29

The Big Tree of Bunlahy: Stories of My Own Countryside (Colum) **36**:42

Big Wheel (Singer) **48**:142

The Big World and the Little House (Krauss) **42**:113

Bigfoot Makes a Movie (Nixon) **24**:138

The Biggest House in the World (Lionni) **7**:132

Bigmouth (Gaberman) **33**:15

The Bike Lesson (Aiken) **19**:24

Bike Trip (Betsy and Giulio Maestro) **45**:85

Bilgewater (Gardam) **12**:167

Bill and Pete (dePaola) **4**:61

Bill and Pete Go Down the Nile (dePaola) **24**:98

Bill and Stanley (Oxenbury) **22**:142

Bill Bergson and the White Rose Rescue (Lindgren) **1**:135

Bill Bergson Lives Dangerously (Lindgren) **1**:135; **39**:145

Bill Bergson, Master Detective (Lindgren) **1**:135; **39**:144

Bill Cosby: America's Most Famous Father (Haskins) **39**:56

A Billion for Boris (Rodgers) **20**:191

Billions of Bats (Schlein) **41**:192

Bill's Garage (Spier) **5**:228

Bill's New Frock (Fine) **25**:23

Bill's Service Station (Spier) **5**:228

Billy Goat and His Well-Fed Friends (Hogrogian) **2**:87

Billy Jo Jive and the Case of the Midnight Voices (Shearer) **34**:168

Billy Jo Jive and the Case of the Missing Pigeons (Shearer) **34**:167

Billy Jo Jive and the Case of the Sneaker Snatcher (Shearer) **34**:167

Billy Jo Jive and the Walkie Talkie Caper (Shearer) **34**:168

Billy Jo Jive, Super Private Eye: The Case of the Missing Ten Speed Bike (Shearer) **34**:166

Billy's Balloon Ride (Zimnik) **3**:242

Billy's Picture (Rey and Rey) **5**:196

Bimwili and the Zimwi: A Tale from Zanzibar (Aardema) **17**:7

Binary Numbers (Watson) **3**:211

Binge (Ferry) **34**:55

The Bionic Bunny Show (Brown) **29**:11

Bionics (Berger) **32**:21

Birches (Young) **27**:220

Bird and Flower Emblems of the United States (Simon) **39**:196

The Bird and the Stars (Showers) **6**:246

The Bird Began to Sing (Field) **21**:77

The Bird Smugglers (Phipson) **5**:184
Bird Watch: A Book of Poetry (Yolen) **44**:192
Birds at Home (Henry) **4**:109
A Bird's Body (Cole) **40**:4
Birds, Frogs, and Moonlight (Cassedy) **26**:12
The Birds of Summer (Snyder) **31**:165
Birds on Your Street (Simon) **9**:208
Birds: Poems (Adoff) **7**:37
Birdsong (Haley) **21**:146
Birdsong Lullaby (Stanley) **46**:135
The Birdstones (Curry) **31**:80
Birk the Berserker (Klein) **21**:164
Birkin (Phipson) **5**:180
Birth Control (Nourse) **33**:146
Birth of a Forest (Selsam) **1**:160
Birth of an Island (Selsam) **1**:160
Birth of the Firebringer (Pierce) **20**:184
Birth of the Republic (Carter) **22**:22
The Birth of the United States (Asimov) **12**:50
Birthday (Steptoe) **2**:162
The Birthday Door (Merriam) **14**:203
The Birthday Moon (Duncan) **29**:80
The Birthday Party (Krauss) **42**:122
The Birthday Party (Oxenbury) **22**:144
The Birthday Present (Munari) **9**:125
Birthday Presents (Rylant) **15**:174
The Birthday Tree (Fleischman) **20**:63
The Birthday Visitor (Uchida) **6**:257
A Birthday Wish (Emberley) **5**:100
The Birthday Wish (Iwasaki) **18**:154
Birthdays of Freedom: America's Heritage from the Ancient World (Foster) **7**:95
Birthdays of Freedom: From the Fall of Rome to July 4, 1776, Book Two (Foster) **7**:97
The Bishop and the Devil (Serraillier) **2**:136
Bitter Rivals (Pascal) **25**:186
Bizarre Crimes (Berger) **32**:32
Bizarre Murders (Berger) **32**:28
Bizou (Klein) **19**:95
The Black Americans: A History in Their Own Words, 1619-1983 (Meltzer) **13**:145
Black and Blue Magic (Snyder) **31**:154
Black and White (Brown) **10**:52
The Black BC's (Clifton) **5**:53
Black Beauty: His Grooms and Companions. The Autobiography of a Horse (Sewell) **17**:130-47
Black Beauty: His Grooms and Companions. The Uncle Tom's Cabin of the Horse (Sewell) **17**:130-47
The Black Cauldron (Alexander) **1**:11; **5**:18
Black Dance in America: A History Through Its People (Haskins) **39**:61
The Black Death, 1347-1351 (Cohen) **3**:39
Black Dog (Allen) **44**:13
Black Dog (Mattingley) **24**:125
The Black Dog Who Went into the Woods (McCully) **46**:58
Black Dolly: The Story of a Junk Cart Pony (Keeping) **34**:88
Black Duck and Water Rat (Trezise) **41**:141
Black Eagles: African Americans in Aviation (Haskins) **39**:73
Black Folktales (Lester) **2**:112
Black Forest Summer (Allan) **43**:6
Black Gold (Henry) **4**:113
Black Hearts in Battersea (Aiken) **1**:2
Black Holes, White Dwarfs, and Superstars (Branley) **13**:43
Black in America: A Fight for Freedom (Jackson and Landau) **28**:142
Black Is Brown Is Tan (Adoff) **7**:32
The Black Island (Herge) **6**:148

Black Jack (Garfield) **21**:98
Black Jack: Last of the Big Alligators (McClung) **11**:185
The Black Joke (Mowat) **20**:172
Black Magic: A Pictorial History of the Negro in American Entertainment (Meltzer) **13**:125; **17**:44
Black Misery (Hughes) **17**:45
Black Music in America: A History Through Its People (Haskins) **39**:52
The Black Pearl (O'Dell) **1**:145
The Black Pearl and the Ghost; or, One Mystery after Another (Myers) **16**:138
Black Pilgrimage (Feelings) **5**:106
Black Ships Before Troy: The Story of the Iliad (Sutcliff) **37**:183
Black Swan (Dhondy) **41**:79
Black Theater in America (Haskins) **39**:42
Blackberry Ink (Wilhelm) **46**:160
Blackberry Ink: Poems (Merriam) **14**:202
Blackbird Singing (Bunting) **28**:49
Blackbriar (Sleator) **29**:199
Blacksmith at Blueridge (Bunting) **28**:45
The Bladerunner (Nourse) **33**:138
Blair's Nightmare (Snyder) **31**:166
The Blanket (Burningham) **9**:47
The Blanket Word (Arundel) **35**:22
Blaze: The Story of a Striped Skunk (McClung) **11**:186
A Blessing in Disguise (Tate) **37**:192
Blewcoat Boy (Garfield) **21**:122
Blind Date (Stine) **37**:108
Blinded by the Light (Brancato) **32**:72
The Blonk from Beneath the Sea (Bendick) **5**:38
Blood (Zim) **2**:225
Blood Feud (Sutcliff) **37**:166
Blood Line (Hamley) **47**:62
The Bloodhound Gang in the Case of Princess Tomorrow (Fleischman) **15**:111
The Bloodhound Gang in the Case of the 264-Pound Burglar (Fleischman) **15**:111
The Bloodhound Gang in the Case of the Cackling Ghost (Fleischman) **15**:111
The Bloodhound Gang in the Case of the Flying Clock (Fleischman) **15**:111
The Bloodhound Gang in the Case of the Secret Message (Fleischman) **15**:111
The Bloody Country (Collier and Collier) **3**:44
Blossom Culp and the Sleep of Death (Peck) **15**:165
A Blossom Promise (Byars) **16**:65
The Blossoms and the Green Phantom (Byars) **16**:65
The Blossoms Meet the Vulture Lady (Byars) **16**:64
Blowfish Live in the Sea (Fox) **1**:76
Blubber (Blume) **2**:16
Blue above the Trees (Clark) **30**:57
The Blue Bird (French) **37**:35
Blue Canyon Horse (Clark) **16**:80
The Blue Day (Guillot) **22**:60
The Blue Door (Rinaldi) **46**:93
Blue Dragon Days (Allan) **43**:7
Blue Fin (Thiele) **27**:204
The Blue Hawk (Dickinson) **29**:45
The Blue Jackal (Brown) **12**:106
The Blue Misty Monsters (Waddell) **31**:184
Blue Moose (Pinkwater) **4**:163
Blue Mystery (Benary-Isbert) **12**:73
Blue Remembered Hills: A Recollection (Sutcliff) **37**:176
The Blue Sword (McKinley) **10**:123
The Blue Thing (Pinkwater) **4**:166

Blue Tights (Williams-Garcia) **36**:203
Blue Trees, Red Sky (Klein) **2**:97
Blueberries for Sal (McCloskey) **7**:205
Blueberry Corners (Lenski) **26**:105
Bluebirds Over Pit Row (Cresswell) **18**:104
A Blue-Eyed Daisy (Rylant) **15**:170
Bo the Constrictor That Couldn't (Stren) **5**:231
Boat Book (Gibbons) **8**:95
A Boat for Peppe (Politi) **29**:188
Boat Ride with Lillian Two Blossom (Polacco) **40**:184
The Boats on the River (Flack) **28**:128
Bob and Jilly (Schmidt) **22**:221
Bob and Jilly Are Friends (Schmidt) **22**:222
Bob and Jilly in Trouble (Schmidt) **22**:223
The Bobbin Girl (McCully) **46**:73
The Bodach (Hunter) **25**:78
The Bodies in the Bessledorf Hotel (Naylor) **17**:60
The Body (Nourse) **33**:134
Body Sense/Body Nonsense (Simon) **9**:217
The Body Snatchers (Cohen) **3**:39
Boek zonder woorden (Bruna) **7**:51
Bold John Henebry (Dillon) **26**:25
Bollerbam (Janosch) **26**:74
Bon Voyage, Baabee (Khalsa) **30**:144
The Bonfire Party (Clarke) **28**:80
The Bongleweed (Cresswell) **18**:105
Bonhomme and the Huge Beast (Brunhoff) **4**:39
Bonnie Bess, the Weathervane Horse (Tresselt) **30**:202
Bonnie Dundee (Sutcliff) **37**:177
Bony-Legs (Cole) **40**:5
Boo, the Boy Who Didn't Like the Dark (Leaf) **25**:130
Boo, Who Used to Be Scared of the Dark (Leaf) **25**:130
A Book about Names: In Which Custom, Tradition, Law, Myth, History, Folklore, Foolery, Legend, Fashion, Nonsense, Symbol, Taboo Help Explain How We Got Our Names and What They Mean (Meltzer) **13**:146
The Book of American Negro Poetry (Johnson) **32**:155
The Book of American Negro Spirituals (Johnson) **32**:159
A Book of Astronauts for You (Branley) **13**:31
A Book of Christmas (Tudor) **13**:201
The Book of Dragons (Nesbit) **3**:162
The Book of Eagles (Sattler) **24**:224
A Book of Flying Saucers for You (Branley) **13**:39
A Book of Goblins (Garner) **20**:108
A Book of Mars for You (Branley) **13**:34
A Book of Moon Rockets for You (Branley) **13**:28
The Book of Nursery and Mother Goose Rhymes (de Angeli) **1**:52
A Book of Outer Space for You (Branley) **13**:37
A Book of Planet Earth for You (Branley) **13**:42
A Book of Planets for You (Branley) **13**:29
A Book of Satellites for You (Branley) **13**:27
A Book of Scary Things (Showers) **6**:247
A Book of Seasons (Provensen and Provensen) **11**:212
A Book of Stars for You (Branley) **13**:33
The Book of the Goat (Scott) **20**:198
A Book of the Milky Way Galaxy for You (Branley) **13**:32
The Book of the Pig (Scott) **20**:199
The Book of Three (Alexander) **1**:12; **5**:18
A Book of Venus for You (Branley) **13**:36
Border Hawk: August Bondi (Alexander) **5**:17
Bored with Being Bored!: How to Beat The Boredom Blahs (Stine) **37**:105

Bored—Nothing to Do! (Spier) **5**:226

Boris (Haar) **15**:115

Borka: The Adventures of a Goose with No Feathers (Burningham) **9**:38

Born of the Sun (Cross) **28**:89

Born to the Land: An American Portrait (Ashabranner) **28**:12

Born to Trot (Henry) **4**:111

The Borrowers (Norton) **6**:220

The Borrowers Afield (Norton) **6**:221

The Borrowers Afloat (Norton) **6**:222

The Borrowers Aloft (Norton) **6**:223

The Borrowers Avenged (Norton) **6**:226

Boss Cat (Hunter) **3**:97

Boss of the Pool (Klein) **21**:164

Bostock and Harris: Or, the Night of the Comet (Garfield) **21**:114

The Boston Coffee Party! (McCully) **46**:61

A Bottled Cherry Angel (Ure) **34**:181

Botts, the Naughty Otter (Freeman) **30**:73

Bound for the Rio Grande: The Mexican Struggle, 1845-1850 (Meltzer) **13**:131

Bound Girl of Cobble Hill (Lenski) **26**:104

The Boundary Riders (Phipson) **5**:178

A Bouquet of Littles (Krauss) **42**:127

Bows against the Barons (Trease) **42**:173

A Box Full of Infinity (Williams) **8**:231

A Box of Nothing (Dickinson) **29**:56

The Box with Red Wheels (Petersham and Petersham) **24**:177

Boxes! Boxes! (Fisher) **18**:133

A Boy, a Dog, a Frog, and a Friend (Mayer) **11**:166

A Boy, a Dog, and a Frog (Mayer) **11**:159

Boy Alone (Ottley) **16**:183

A Boy and Fire Huskies (Guillot) **22**:59

The Boy and the Ghost (San Souci) **43**:183

The Boy and the Monkey (Garfield) **21**:100

The Boy and the Whale (Sanchez-Silva) **12**:232

The Boy Apprenticed to an Enchanter (Colum) **36**:25

Boy Blue (McBratney) **44**:118

A Boy Called Slow: The True Story of Sitting Bull (Bruchac) **46**:19

The Boy from Cumeroogunga: The Story of Sir Douglas Nicholls, Aboriginal Leader (Clark) **30**:62

A Boy Had a Mother Who Bought Him a Hat (Kuskin) **4**:141

A Boy in Eirinn (Colum) **36**:22

The Boy in the Drawer (Munsch) **19**:143

A Boy of Taché (Blades) **15**:54

The Boy Pharaoh: Tutankhamen (Streatfeild) **17**:198

Boy: Tales of Childhood (Dahl) **41**:33

The Boy Who Could Find Anything (Nixon) **24**:137

The Boy Who Didn't Believe in Spring (Clifton) **5**:54

The Boy Who Had No Heart (Petersham and Petersham) **24**:178

"*The Boy Who Lived with the Bears*" (Bruchac) **46**:21

The Boy Who Lost His Face (Sachar) **28**:204

The Boy Who Reversed Himself (Sleator) **29**:205

The Boy Who Sailed with Columbus (Foreman) **32**:107

The Boy Who Spoke Chimp (Yolen) **4**:268

The Boy Who Was Followed Home (Mahy) **7**:183

The Boy Who Wasn't There (Wilhelm) **46**:170

The Boy with the Helium Head (Naylor) **17**:57

Boy without a Name (Lively) **7**:159

The Boyfriend (Stine) **37**:115

The Boyhood of Grace Jones (Langton) **33**:113

Boys and Girls, Girls and Boys (Merriam) **14**:198

Boys at Work (Soto) **38**:207

A Boy's Will (Haugaard) **11**:110

Brady (Fritz) **2**:79

Brainbox Sorts It Out (Noestlinger) **12**:188

The Brains of Animals and Man (Freedman) **20**:76

Brainstorm (Myers) **4**:157

Brainwashing and Other Forms of Mind Control (Hyde) **23**:162

"*Brambly Hedge Books*" (Barklem) **31**:2

The Brambly Hedge Treasury (Barklem) **31**:6

A Brand-New Uncle (Seredy) **10**:181

Brats (Kennedy) **27**:101

Brave Buffalo Fighter (Waditaka Tatanka Kisisohitika) (Fitzgerald) **1**:69

The Brave Cowboy (Anglund) **1**:19

Brave Eagle's Account of the Fetterman Fight, 21 December 1866 (Goble) **21**:129

Brave Irene (Steig) **15**:201

The Brave Little Goat of Monsieur Séguin: A Picture Story from Provence (Nakatani) **30**:156

The Brave Little Toaster: A Bedtime Story for Small Appliances (Disch) **18**:114

The Brave Little Toaster Goes to Mars (Disch) **18**:116

Bravo, Ernest and Celestine! (Vincent) **13**:216

Bread and Honey (Southall) **2**:149

Bread and Jam for Frances (Hoban) **3**:76

Bread—and Roses: The Struggle of American Labor, 1865-1915 (Meltzer) **13**:124

The Breadhorse (Garner) **20**:112

The Breadwitch (Nimmo) **44**:151

Break Dancing (Haskins) **39**:51

Break for the Basket (Christopher) **33**:38

Break in the Sun (Ashley) **4**:17

Break of Dark (Westall) **13**:257

A Break with Charity: A Story about the Salem Witch Trials (Rinaldi) **46**:84

Breakaway (Yee) **44**:165

Breakfast Time, Ernest and Celestine (Vincent) **13**:219

Breaking Up (Klein) **19**:92

Breakthrough: Women in Archaeology (Williams) **48**:199

Breakthrough: Women in Politics (Williams) **48**:198

Breakthroughs in Science (Asimov) **12**:34

The Bremen Town Musicians (Domanska) **40**:49

The Bremen Town Musicians (Wilhelm) **46**:169

Brenda and Edward (Kovalski) **34**:114

Brendan the Navigator: A History Mystery about the Discovery of America (Fritz) **14**:114

Brer Rabbit and His Tricks (Gorey) **36**:92

Brer Rabbit: Stories from Uncle Remus (Brown) **10**:50

Brian Wildsmith's 1, 2, 3's (Wildsmith) **2**:211

Brian Wildsmith's ABC (Wildsmith) **2**:208

Brian Wildsmith's Birds (Wildsmith) **2**:208

Brian Wildsmith's Circus (Wildsmith) **2**:209

Brian Wildsmith's Fishes (Wildsmith) **2**:210

Brian Wildsmith's Mother Goose: A Collection of Nursery Rhymes (Wildsmith) **2**:210

Brian Wildsmith's Puzzles (Wildsmith) **2**:211

Brian Wildsmith's The Twelve Days of Christmas (Wildsmith) **2**:212

Brian Wildsmith's Wild Animals (Wildsmith) **2**:212

Brickyard Summer (Janeczko) **47**:109

The Bridge Between (St. John) **46**:99

Bridge of Friendship (Allan) **43**:26

Bridge to Terabithia (Paterson) **7**:232

Bridger: The Story of a Mountain Man (Kherdian) **24**:115

Bridges to Change: How Kids Live on a South Carolina Sea Island (Krull) **44**:109

Bridges to Cross (Janeczko) **47**:104

Bridget and William (Gardam) **12**:168

A Bridle for Pegasus (Shippen) **36**:173

Bridle the Wind (Munsch) **19**:14

Briefe an Pauline (Kruss) **9**:87

Brigham Young and Me, Clarissa (Williams) **48**:196

The Bright and Morning Star (Harris) **30**:114

The Bright Design (Shippen) **36**:170

Bright Lights Blaze Out (Owen) **31**:145

Bright Morning (Bianco) **19**:57

Bright Shadow (Avi) **24**:12

Bright Shadow (Thomas) **19**:221

Bright Stars, Red Giants, and White Dwarfs (Berger) **32**:30

Brighty of the Grand Canyon (Henry) **4**:112

Bring to a Boil and Separate (Irwin) **40**:108

Bringing the Rain to Kapiti Plain (Aardema) **17**:6

Brinsly's Dream (Breinburg) **31**:68

British Folk Tales: New Versions (Crossley-Holland) **47**:45

Broken Days (Rinaldi) **46**:91

Broken Hearts (Stine) **37**:120

The Broken Spoke (Gorey) **36**:98

Bronto's Wings (McKee) **38**:157

El Bronx Remembered: A Novella and Stories (Mohr) **22**:131

The Bronze Bow (Speare) **8**:208

The Bronze Trumpeter (Nimmo) **44**:138

Bronzeville Boys and Girls (Brooks) **27**:44-56

Brother André of Montreal (Clark) **16**:82

Brother, Can You Spare a Dime? The Great Depression, 1929-1933 (Meltzer) **13**:126

Brother Dusty-Feet (Sutcliff) **1**:184; **37**:150

Brother Eagle, Sister Sky: A Message from Chief Seattle (Jeffers) **30**:137

A Brother for Momoko (Iwasaki) **18**:153

Brother Night (Kelleher) **36**:127

Brother to the Wind (Leo and Diane Dillon) **44**:36

Brother to the Wind (Walter) **15**:207

The Brothers Grimm: Popular Folk Tales (Foreman) **32**:90

The Brothers Lionheart (Lindgren) **39**:154

Brothers of the Heart: A Story of the Old Northwest 1837-1838 (Blos) **18**:18

Brothers of the Wind (Yolen) **4**:268

Brown Angels: An Album of Pictures and Verse (Myers) **35**:204

"*The Brownie Books*" (Cox) **24**:65-83

Brumbie Dust: A Selection of Stories (Ottley) **16**:185

Bruno Munari's ABC (Munari) **9**:125

Bruno Munari's Zoo (Munari) **9**:127

Bubble, Bubble (Mayer) **11**:167

Bubbles (Cummings) **48**:43

Bubbles (Greenfield) **4**:96

Buddies (Park) **34**:156

Buddy's Adventures in the Blueberry Patch (Beskow) **17**:15

Budgerigar Blue (Mattingley) **24**:125

Buffalo Bill (d'Aulaire and d'Aulaire) **21**:51

The Buffalo Nickel Blues Band! (Gaberman) **33**:10

Buffalo: The American Bison Today (Patent) **19**:163

Buffalo Woman (Goble) **21**:134

Bufo: The Story of a Toad (McClung) **11**:179

Buford the Little Bighorn (Peet) **12**:198

The Bug That Laid the Golden Eggs (Selsam) **1**:160

Bugs for Dinner? The Eating Habits of Neighborhood Creatures (Epstein and Epstein) **26**:71

Bugs: Poems (Hoberman) **22**:112

Bugs Potter Live at Nickaninny (Korman) **25**:107

Building Blocks (Voigt) **13**:235

Building Blocks of the Universe (Asimov) **12**:32

Building Construction (Berger) **32**:21

A Building on Your Street (Simon) **9**:207

Bulbs, Corms, and Such (Selsam) **1**:161

The Bully (Needle) **43**:143

The Bumblebee Flies Anyway (Cormier) **12**:149

The Bumblebee's Secret (Schlein) **41**:181

Bummer Summer (Martin) **32**:200

The Bun: A Tale from Russia (Brown) **12**:104

The Bundle Book (Krauss) **42**:115

Bunnicula: A Rabbit-Tale of Mystery (Howe) **9**:56

Bunny, Hound, and Clown (Mukerji) **10**:135

Burglar Bill (Ahlberg and Ahlberg) **18**:4

The Burglar Next Door (Williams) **8**:235

The Buried Moon and Other Stories (Bang) **8**:19

The Burma Road (Epstein and Epstein) **26**:45

The Burning of Njal (Treece) **2**:182

The Burning Questions of Bingo Brown (Byars) **16**:66

Burt Dow, Deep-Water Man: A Tale of the Sea in the Classic Tradition (McCloskey) **7**:210

Bury Me Deep (Pike) **29**:174

The Bus under the Leaves (Mahy) **7**:182

Busiest People Ever (Scarry) **3**:183

Busy, Busy Town (Scarry) **41**:171

Busy Day: A Book of Action Words (Betsy and Giulio Maestro) **45**:68

Busy Houses (Scarry) **41**:169

Busy Monday Morning (Domanska) **40**:52

But in the Fall I'm Leaving (Rinaldi) **46**:78

But Jasper Came Instead (Noestlinger) **12**:189

The Butter Battle Book (Seuss) **9**:194

Butterfiles and Moths: How They Function (Patent) **19**:154

The Butterflies Come (Politi) **29**:190

Button Soup (Orgel) **48**:96

By Camel or by Car: A Look at Transportation (Billout) **33**:21

By the Great Horn Spoon! (Fleischman) **1**:73

By the Sandhills of Yamboorah (Ottley) **16**:183

By the Sea: An Alphabet Book (Blades) **15**:55

By the Shores of Silver Lake (Wilder) **2**:205

C Is for City (Cummings) **48**:56

C Is for City (Grimes) **42**:92

C Is for Clown: A Circus of "C" Words (Berenstain and Berenstain) **19**:28

"C" Is for Cupcake (Haywood) **22**:102

The Cabin Faced West (Fritz) **14**:110

The Caboose Who Got Loose (Peet) **12**:202

Cactus (Lerner) **34**:138

Caddie Woodlawn (Brink) **30**:7

Caddie Woodlawn: A Play (Brink) **30**:13

Cakes and Custard: Children's Rhymes (Oxenbury) **22**:139

The Caldecott Aesop (Caldecott) **14**:79

Caldicott Place (Streatfeild) **17**:197

Caleb (Crew) **42**:62

Caleb and Kate (Steig) **15**:196

The Calendar (Adler) **27**:23

Calendar Art: Thirteen Days, Weeks, Months, and Years from Around the World (Fisher) **18**:137

A Calf Is Born (Cole) **5**:64

Calico Bush (Field) **21**:76

Calico Captive (Speare) **8**:205

Calico, the Wonder Horse; or, The Saga of Stewy Slinker (Burton) **11**:45

California Demon (Singer) **48**:141

Call Me Bandicoot (Pene du Bois) **1**:63

Call Me Charley (Jackson) **28**:137

The Callender Papers (Voigt) **13**:233

The Callow Pit Coffer (Crossley-Holland) **47**:25

Camels Are Meaner Than Mules (Calhoun) **42**:18

Camilla (L'Engle) **1**:129

Camping Out: A Book of Action Words (Betsy and Giulio Maestro) **45**:74

Can Bears Predict Earthquake? Unsolved Mysteries of Animal Behavior (Freedman) **20**:82

Can I Keep Him? (Kellogg) **6**:170

Can You Catch Josephine? (Poulin) **28**:195

Can You Sue Your Parents for Malpractice? (Danziger) **20**:53

Canada Geese (Scott) **20**:195

Cancer in the Young: A Sense of Hope (Hyde) **23**:171

Cancer Lab (Berger) **32**:13

A Candle for St. Antony (Spence) **26**:198

Candy (White) **3**:220

Candy Floss (Godden) **20**:130

Cannonball Simp (Burningham) **9**:41

Can't Hear You Listening (Irwin) **40**:114

Can't You Make Them Behave, King George? (Fritz) **14**:113

Can't You Sleep, Little Bear? (Waddell) **31**:191

The Canterbury Tales (McCaughrean) **38**:137

The Canterville Ghost (Zwerger) **46**:197

The Cantilever Rainbow (Krauss) **42**:127

The Capricorn Bracelet (Sutcliff) **1**:184; **37**:164

Captain Grey (Avi) **24**:5

Captain Kidd's Cat (Lawson) **2**:109

Captain of the Planter: The Story of Robert Smalls (Sterling) **1**:177

Captain Pottle's House (Cooney) **23**:22

Captain Whiz-Bang (Stanley) **46**:138

The Captain's Watch (Garfield) **21**:106

The Captive (O'Dell) **16**:174

Capyboppy (Peet) **12**:198

The Car Trip (Oxenbury) **22**:145

Careers in an Airport (Paulsen) **19**:172

Cargo Ships (Zim) **2**:226

Carl Goes Shopping (Day) **22**:26

Carl Linneaus: The Man Who Put the World of Life in Order (Silverstein and Silverstein) **25**:203

Carl Sagan: Superstar Scientist (Cohen) **43**:47

Carlisles All (St. John) **46**:117

Carlisle's Hope (St. John) **46**:116

Carlota (O'Dell) **16**:173

Carousel (Crews) **7**:61

Carousel (Cummings) **48**:54

Carrie's War (Bawden) **2**:10

The Carrot Seed (Krauss) **42**:109

Cars and How They Go (Cole) **40**:5

Cars and Trucks and Things That Go (Scarry) **41**:166

Cars, Boats, Trains, and Planes of Today and Tomorrow (Aylesworth) **6**:52

Cart and Cwidder (Jones) **23**:184

The Cartoonist (Byars) **16**:55

A Case of Blue Murder (McBratney) **44**:126

The Case of the Cackling Car (Singer) **48**:127

The Case of the Dog-lover's Legacy (St. John) **46**:115

The Case of the Fixed Election (Singer) **48**:134

The Case of the Gone Goose (Corbett) **1**:43

The Case of the Sabotaged School Play (Singer) **48**:126

The Case of the Silver Skull (Corbett) **1**:43

Casey and the Great Idea (Nixon) **24**:140

Casey at the Bat: A Ballad of the Republic Sung in the Year 1988 (Polacco) **40**:184

Caspar and His Friends (Baumann) **35**:48

Cassie Binegar (MacLachlan) **14**:182

Castle (Macaulay) **14**:170

Castle in Spain (Guillot) **22**:71

The Castle in the Sea (O'Dell) **16**:178

The Castle Number Nine (Bemelmans) **6**:65

A Castle of Bone (Farmer) **8**:80

The Castle of Llyr (Alexander) **1**:12; **5**:19

The Castle of the Crested Bird (Guillot) **22**:70

The Castle of Yew (Boston) **3**:26

Castle on the Border (Benary-Isbert) **12**:75

Castors Away (Burton) **1**:30

Cat and Canary (Foreman) **32**:97

Cat and Dog (Minarik) **33**:125

The Cat and the Captain (Coatsworth) **2**:54

The Cat Ate My Gymsuit (Danziger) **20**:50

Cat Goes Fiddle-I-Fee (Galdone) **16**:106

Cat, Herself (Hunter) **25**:90

The Cat in the Hat (Seuss) **1**:84; **9**:182

The Cat in the Hat Beginner Book Dictionary, by the Cat Himself and P. D. Eastman (Seuss) **9**:188

The Cat in the Hat Comes Back! (Seuss) **9**:184

The Cat Who Went to Heaven (Coatsworth) **2**:54

The Cat Who Wished to Be a Man (Alexander) **1**:12; **5**:22

Catch a Little Rhyme (Merriam) **14**:194

Catch That Pass! (Christopher) **33**:44

Catch the Ball! (Carle) **10**:85

The Catcher in the Rye (Salinger) **18**:171-94

Catcher with a Glass Arm (Christopher) **33**:39

Catching the Wind (Ryder) **37**:93

Caterpillars (Sterling) **1**:178

Caterpillars and How They Live (McClung) **11**:183

The Caterpillow Fight (McBratney) **44**:132

Cathedral: The Story of Its Construction (Macaulay) **3**:140

Catrin in Wales (Allan) **43**:7

The Cats (Phipson) **5**:184

A Cat's Body (Cole) **5**:68

The Cats' Burglar (Parish) **22**:166

The Cats from Summer Island (Unnerstad) **36**:196

The Cat's Midsummer Jamboree (Kherdian) **24**:116

The Cats of Seroster (Westall) **13**:259

The Cats' Opera (Dillon) **26**:23

The Cat's Purr (Bryan) **18**:35

The Cat's Quizzer (Seuss) **9**:193

Caught in the Act (Nixon) **24**:150

A Cavalcade of Goblins (Garner) **20**:108

The Cave above Delphi (Corbett) **1**:43

The Cave Painters (Trezise) **41**:141

Cave Under the City (Mazer) **16**:133

The Caves of the Great Hunters (Baumann) **35**:36

The Cay (Taylor) **30**:176

CDB! (Steig) **2**:159

CDC? (Steig) **15**:200

Cecily G. and the Nine Monkeys (Rey) **5**:192

The Celery Stalks at Midnight (Howe) **9**:59

Cells: Building Blocks of Life (Silverstein and Silverstein) **25**:203

Cells: The Basic Structure of Life (Cobb) **2**:64

Censorship (Berger) **32**:27

Centerburg Tales (McCloskey) **7**:207

Centerfield Ballhawk (Christopher) **33**:62

Central City/Spread City: The Metropolitan Regions Where More and More of Us Spend Our Lives (Schwartz) **3**:188

The Centurion (Treece) **2**:183

Ceramics: From Clay to Kiln (Weiss) **4**:223

The Ceremony of Innocence (Highwater) **17**:30

A Certain Magic (Orgel) **48**:82

Chain Letter (Pike) **29**:171

Chain of Fire (Naidoo) **29**:166

Chains, Webs, and Pyramids: The Flow of Energy in Nature (Pringle) **4**:179

A Chair for My Mother (Williams) **9**:232

Chair Person (Jones) **23**:197

The Chalk Box Story (Freeman) **30**:81

Challenge at Second Base (Christopher) **33**:39

The Challenge of the Green Knight (Serraillier) **2**:136

Challenge of the Wolf Knight (Stine) **37**:107

Chameleons and Other Quick-Change Artists (Simon) **39**:191

Champion Dog, Prince Tom (Fritz) **14**:111

The Champion of Olympia, an Adventure (Guillot) **22**:70

Chance, Luck, and Destiny (Dickinson) **29**:44

Chancy and the Grand Rascal (Fleischman) **1**:73

Change for a Penny (Epstein and Epstein) **26**:56

The Change-Child (Curry) **31**:74

The Changeling (Snyder) **31**:157

The Changeling (Sutcliff) **37**:165

Changes, Changes (Hutchins) **20**:145

The Changing City (Mueller) **43**:115

The Changing Countryside (Mueller) **43**:115

The Changing Earth (Viorst) **3**:207

The Changing Maze (Snyder) **31**:167

Changing the Face of North America: The Challenge of the St. Lawrence Seaway (Lauber) **16**:113

The Changing Tools of Science: From Yardstick to Synchrotron (Adler) **27**:10

Chanticleer and the Fox (Cooney) **23**:22

Chanticleer, the Real Story of the Famous Rooster (Duvoisin) **23**:92

Chapters: My Growth as a Writer (Duncan) **29**:75

Chariot in the Sky: A Story of the Jubilee Singers (Bontemps) **6**:82

Charity at Home (Willard) **2**:216

Charles Darwin: The Making of a Scientist (Gallant) **30**:90

Charles Dickens: The Man Who Had Great Expectations (Stanley) **46**:149

Charles Keeping's Book of Classic Ghost Stories (Keeping) **34**:108

Charles Keeping's Classic Tales of the Macabre (Keeping) **34**:109

Charley, Charlotte and the Golden Canary (Keeping) **34**:89

Charley Starts from Scratch (Jackson) **28**:139

Charlie and the Chocolate Factory (Dahl) **1**:49; **7**:69

Charlie and the Great Glass Elevator: The Further Adventures of Charlie Bucket and Willy Wonka, Chocolate-Maker Extraordinary (Dahl) **1**:50; **7**:73

Charlie Lewis Plays for Time (Kemp) **29**:118

Charlie Moon and the Big Bonanza Bust-Up (Hughes) **15**:129

"Charlie Needs a Cloak" (dePaola) **4**:55

Charlie's House (Daly) **41**:61

Charlie's World: A Book of Poems (Hopkins) **44**:87

Charlotte and the White Horse (Krauss) **42**:121

Charlotte Sometimes (Farmer) **8**:78

Charlotte's Web (White) **1**:193

Charmed (Singer) **48**:137

Charmed Life (Jones) **23**:187

Chartbreak (Cross) **28**:92

Chartbreaker (Cross) **28**:92

Chase Me, Catch Nobody! (Haugaard) **11**:109

Chasing the Goblins Away (Tobias) **4**:216

Chaucer and His World (Serraillier) **2**:137

The Cheater (Stine) **37**:122

The Checkup (Oxenbury) **22**:145

The Cheerleader (Klein) **19**:97

Cheerleaders: The First Evil (Stine) **37**:118

Cheerleaders: The Second Evil (Stine) **37**:118

Cheerleaders: The Third Evil (Stine) **37**:119

The Chemicals of Life: Enzymes, Vitamins, Hormones (Asimov) **12**:31

The Chemicals We Eat and Drink (Silverstein and Silverstein) **25**:209

Chemistry in the Kitchen (Simon) **9**:203

Chernowitz! (Gaberman) **33**:8

Cherokee Bat and the Goat Guys (Block) **33**:32

Cherokee Run (Smucker) **10**:189

The Cherry Tree Party (Unnerstad) **36**:200

Chess-Dream in a Garden (Sutcliff) **37**:184

Chessmen of Doom (Bellairs) **37**:23

Chester Chipmunk's Thanksgiving (Williams) **48**:195

Chester Cricket's New Home (Selden) **8**:202

Chester Cricket's Pigeon Ride (Selden) **8**:201

Chester the Out-Of-Work Dog (Singer) **48**:140

Chester the Worldly Pig (Peet) **12**:196

Chester's Way (Henkes) **23**:130

The Chestnut Soldier (Nimmo) **44**:143

The Chestry Oak (Seredy) **10**:178

The Chewing-Gum Rescue and Other Stories (Mahy) **7**:186

The Chichi Hoohoo Bogeyman (Sneve) **2**:144

A Chick Hatches (Cole) **5**:64

Chicken Soup with Rice (Sendak) **1**:167

Chicken Sunday (Polacco) **40**:192

Chidwick's Chimney (Thiele) **27**:209

Chief Joseph, War Chief of the Nez Percé (Ashabranner and Davis) **28**:4

The Chief of the Herd (Mukerji) **10**:133

The Chief's Daughter (Sutcliff) **37**:160

The Child Abuse Help Book (Haskins) **39**:40

The Child in the Bamboo Grove (Harris) **30**:114

Child of Fire (O'Dell) **16**:169

Child of the Owl (Yep) **3**:235

Child O'War: The True Story of a Boy Sailor in Nelson's Navy (Garfield) **21**:105

Childern of the Maya: A Guatemalan Indian Odyssey (Ashabranner) **28**:9

The Children Come Running (Coatsworth) **2**:54

The Children Next Door (Sharp) **27**:166

Children of Christmas: Stories for the Season (Rylant) **15**:174

The Children of Green Knowe (Boston) **3**:26

The Children of Noisy Village (Lindgren) **1**:135

The Children of Odin: The Book of Northern Myths (Colum) **36**:24

The Children of Primrose Lane (Streatfeild) **17**:189

Children of the Blitz: Memories of Wartime Childhood (Westall) **13**:260

Children of the Forest (Beskow) **17**:16

The Children of the Great Lake (Trezise) **41**:144

The Children of the House (Pearce) **9**:152

Children of the Longhouse (Bruchac) **46**:23

Children of the Northlights (d'Aulaire and d'Aulaire) **21**:42

Children of the Sun (Leo and Diane Dillon) **44**:35

Children of the Wild West (Freedman) **20**:84

The Children of the Wind (Guillot) **22**:68

Children of the Wolf (Yolen) **44**:176

Children of Winter (Doherty) **21**:57

The Children on the Top Floor (Streatfeild) **17**:196

The Children on Troublemaker Street (Lindgren) **39**:151

The Children Who Followed the Piper (Colum) **36**:26

The Children's Homer (Colum) **36**:24

The Children's War (Taylor) **30**:186

A Children's Zoo (Hoban) **13**:111

A Child's Book of Poems (Fujikawa) **25**:38

A Child's First Picture Dictionary (Moore) **15**:139

A Child's Garden of Verses (Stevenson) **11**:222-43

A Child's Good Morning (Brown) **10**:62

A Child's Good Night Book (Brown) **10**:51

Childtimes: A Three-Generation Memoir (Greenfield) **4**:101

A Chill in the Lane (Allan) **43**:24

Chilly Stomach (Caines) **24**:64

Chilly Stomach (Cummings) **48**:47

Chimney Sweeps: Yesterday and Today (Giblin) **29**:87

Chin Chiang and the Dragon's Dance (Wallace) **37**:209

China Homecoming (Fritz) **14**:120

The China People (Farmer) **8**:76

Chinaman's Reef Is Ours (Southall) **2**:149

The Chinese Americans (Meltzer) **13**:142

Chinese Handcuffs (Crutcher) **28**:105

The Chinese Mirror (Ginsburg) **45**:18

Chinese Mother Goose Rhymes (Young) **27**:217

Chip Rogers, Computer Whiz (Simon) **9**:221

Chipmunk Song (Ryder) **37**:89

Chipmunks on the Doorstep (Tunis) **2**:191

Chips and Jessie (Hughes) **15**:132

The Chocolate War (Cormier) **12**:130

Choo Choo: The Story of a Little Engine Who Ran Away (Burton) **11**:44

Chris & Croc (Pfister) **42**:137

The Christ Child, as Told by Matthew and Luke (Petersham and Petersham) **24**:163

Christian Morgenstern: Lullabies, Lyrics and Gallows Songs (Zwerger) **46**:202

Christmas (Cooney) **23**:27

The Christmas Anna Angel (Sawyer) **36**:159

The Christmas Ark (San Souci) **43**:186

Christmas at Home (Brinsmead) **47**:15

Christmas at Longtime (Brinsmead) See *Christmas at Home*

The Christmas Book (Bruna) **7**:49

The Christmas Box (Merriam) **14**:202

A Christmas Carol (Ryder) **37**:95

A Christmas Carol (Zwerger) **46**:197

The Christmas Eve Mystery (Nixon) **24**:142

A Christmas Fantasy (Haywood) **22**:101

The Christmas Gift (McCully) **46**:63

Christmas in Noisy Village (Lindgren) **1**:136

Christmas in the Barn (Brown) **10**:62

Christmas in the Stable (Lindgren) **1**:136

Christmas Is a Time of Giving (Anglund) **1**:19

Christmas Manger (Rey) **5**:194

The Christmas Sky (Branley) **13**:33

The Christmas Star (Pfister) **42**:136

The Christmas Story (Keeping) **34**:90

Christmas Time (Gibbons) **8**:94

Christmas Time: Verses and Illustrations (Field) **21**:79

The Christmas Tree House (Wallace) **37**:208

The Christmas Whale (Duvoisin) **23**:92

Christmas with Tamworth Pig (Kemp) **29**:113

Christopher Columbus (Ventura) **16**:193

Chronicles of Avonlea, in Which Anne Shirley of Green Gables and Avonlea Plays Some Part (Montgomery) **8**:136

"The Chronicles of Narnia" (Lewis) **3**:126
The Chronicles of Robin Hood (Sutcliff) **37**:149
Chuggy and the Blue Caboose (Freeman) **30**:68
The Church Cat Abroad (Oakley) **7**:215
The Church Mice Adrift (Oakley) **7**:217
The Church Mice and the Moon (Oakley) **7**:216
The Church Mice at Bay (Oakley) **7**:218
The Church Mice at Christmas (Oakley) **7**:220
The Church Mice in Action (Oakley) **7**:223
The Church Mice Spread Their Wings (Oakley) **7**:217
The Church Mouse (Oakley) **7**:213
El Cid (McCaughrean) **38**:145
Les cigares du pharaon (Herge) **6**:148
The Cigars of the Pharaoh (Herge) **6**:148
Cinderella (French) **37**:48
Cinderella (Galdone) **16**:102
Cinderella (McKissack) **23**:237
Cinderella; or, The Little Glass Slipper (Brown) **12**:98
The Cinderella Show (Ahlberg and Ahlberg) **18**:12
Cindy's Sad and Happy Tree (Orgel) **48**:76
Cindy's Snowdrops (Orgel) **48**:75
Cinnabar, the One O'Clock Fox (Henry) **4**:113
Circle of Seasons (Clark) **16**:83
A Circle of Seasons (Fisher) **18**:132
A Circle of Seasons (Livingston) **7**:174
Circles, Triangles, and Squares (Hoban) **13**:103
A Circlet of Oak Leaves (Sutcliff) **37**:161
Circus (Prelutsky) **13**:164
The Circus Baby (Petersham and Petersham) **24**:177
The Circus in the Mist (Munari) **9**:128
The Circus Is Coming (Streatfeild) **17**:187
Circus Shoes (Streatfeild) **17**:187
City: A Story of Roman Planning and Construction (Macaulay) **3**:142
City and Suburb: Exploring an Ecosystem (Pringle) **4**:180
City of Birds and Beasts: Behind the Scenes at the Bronx Zoo (Scott) **20**:197
City of Darkness (Bova) **3**:32
City of Gold (French) **37**:39
The City of Gold and Lead (Christopher) **2**:38
City of Gold and Other Stories from the Old Testament (Dickinson) **29**:50
City of Gold and Other Stories from the Old Testament (Foreman) **32**:91
City Poems (Lenski) **26**:124
City Rhythms (Grifalconi) **35**:69
City Seen from A to Z (Isadora) **7**:108
City Within a City: How Kids Live in New York's Chinatown (Krull) **44**:106
The Civil Rights Movement in America from 1865 to the Present (McKissack) **23**:238
Clams Can't Sing (Stevenson) **17**:157
Clancy's Cabin (Mahy) **7**:183
Clancy's Coat (Bunting) **28**:56
Clap Hands (Oxenbury) **22**:148
Clarence Goes to Town (Lauber) **16**:112
Clarence, the TV Dog (Lauber) **16**:111
The Clarinet and Saxophone Book (Berger) **32**:14
The Clashing Rocks: The Story of Jason (Serraillier) **2**:137
Class Three and the Beanstalk (Waddell) **31**:191
Claudia and the Phantom Phone Calls (Martin) **32**:203
Claudius Bald Eagle (McBratney) **44**:122
The Clay Marble (Ho) **28**:134
Clay, Wood, and Wire: A How-To-Do-It Book of Sculpture (Weiss) **4**:220
Clean Enough (Henkes) **23**:125

Clean Your Room, Harvey Moon! (Cummings) **48**:51
Clear Skin, Healthy Skin (Nourse) **33**:141
Clementina's Cactus (Keats) **35**:143
Cleopatra (Stanley) **46**:152
Clever Cakes (Rosen) **45**:142
Climbing to Danger (Allan) **43**:19
Clippity Clop (Allen) **44**:16
The Cloak (Garfield) **21**:109
The Clock Struck Twelve (Biegel) **27**:33
The Clock Tower Ghost (Kemp) **29**:117
The Clock We Live On (Asimov) **12**:33
Clocks and How They Go (Gibbons) **8**:90
Clocks and More Clocks (Hutchins) **20**:145
Cloning and the New Genetics (Hyde) **23**:170
Close Enough to Touch (Peck) **15**:162
Close Your Eyes (Jeffers) **30**:132
The Clothes Horse and Other Stories (Ahlberg and Ahlberg) **18**:12
The Cloud Book: Words and Pictures (dePaola) **4**:57
The Cloud over Clarence (Brown) **29**:5
C.L.O.U.D.S. (Cummings) **48**:47
The Cloverdale Switch (Bunting) **28**:48
The Clown of God: An Old Story (dePaola) **4**:61
The Clown-Arounds (Cole) **40**:3
The Clown-Arounds Go on Vacation (Cole) **40**:3
Cluck Baa (Burningham) **9**:51
A Clue in Code (Singer) **48**:127
The Clue of the Black Cat (Berna) **19**:38
Clues in the Woods (Parish) **22**:156
Clunie (Peck) **45**:113
Coal (Adler) **27**:20
Coal Camp Girl (Lenski) **26**:120
The Coat-Hanger Christmas Tree (Estes) **2**:73
Cockatoos (Blake) **31**:29
Cockney Ding-Dong (Keeping) **34**:100
Cockroaches (Cole) **5**:61
Cockroaches: Here, There, and Everywhere (Pringle) **4**:176
Coded Signals (Hamley) **47**:63
C.O.L.A.R.: A Tale of Outer Space (Slote) **4**:203
A Cold Wind Blowing (Willard) **2**:216
Coll and His White Pig (Alexander) **1**:13; **5**:19
Collage and Construction (Weiss) **4**:225
Collected Poems, 1951-1975 (Causley) **30**:37
Colm of the Islands (Harris) **30**:125
Colonial Craftsmen and the Beginnings of American Industry (Tunis) **2**:192
Colonial Living (Tunis) **2**:192
Colonies in Orbit: The Coming of Age of Human Settlements in Space (Knight) **38**:120
Colonies in Revolt (Carter) **22**:22
Color Farm (Ehlert) **28**:114
Color: From Rainbow to Lasers (Branley) **13**:43
Color in Reproduction: Theory and Techniques for Artists and Designers (Simon) **39**:197
Color in Your Life (Adler) **27**:16
The Color Kittens (Brown) **10**:59
A Color of His Own (Lionni) **7**:137
The Color Wizard: Level One (Leo and Diane Dillon) **44**:38
Color Zoo (Ehlert) **28**:111
Colors (Pienkowski) **6**:230
A Colour of His Own (Lionni) **7**:137
Colours (Hughes) **15**:132
Colours (Pienkowski) **6**:230
Columbia and Beyond: The Story of the Space Shuttle (Branley) **13**:44
Columbus (d'Aulaire and d'Aulaire) **21**:51
The Columbus Story (Politi) **29**:190
Colvin and the Snake Basket (McBratney) **44**:120

Come a Stranger (Voigt) **13**:240
Come Again, Pelican (Freeman) **30**:72
Come Alive at 505 (Brancato) **32**:73
Come Away (Livingston) **7**:170
Come Away from the Water, Shirley (Burningham) **9**:47
Come Back, Amelia Bedelia (Parish) **22**:160
Come Like Shadows (Katz) **45**:37
Come Lucky April (Ure) **34**:192
Come On, Patsy (Snyder) **31**:165
Come to Mecca, and Other Stories (Dhondy) **41**:75
Com'era una volta (Ventura) **16**:197
Comet in Moominland (Jansson) **2**:93
Comets (Branley) **13**:49
Comets (Knight) **38**:107
Comets, Meteoroids and Asteroids: Mavericks of the Solar System (Branley) **13**:40
Comets, Meteors, and Asteroids (Berger) **32**:25
The Comic Adventures of Old Mother Hubbard and Her Dog (dePaola) **24**:88
The Comical Tragedy or Tragical Comedy of Punch and Judy (Brown) **10**:49
Coming Home (Waddell) **31**:201
Coming Home from the War: An Idyll (Kruss) **9**:87
The Coming of the Bear (Namioka) **48**:65
Coming-and-Going Men: Four Tales (Fleischman) **20**:67
Commander Toad in Space (Yolen) **44**:174
Commercial Fishing (Zim) **2**:226
Commodore Perry in the Land of the Shogun (Blumberg) **21**:29
Communication (Adler) **27**:22
Companions of Fortune (Guillot) **22**:54
Company's Coming (Yorinks) **20**:217
The Complete Adventures of Charlie and Mr. Willy Wonka (Dahl) **7**:77
The Complete Book of Dragons (Nesbit) **3**:162
The Complete Computer Popularity Program (Strasser) **11**:251
The Complete Story of the Three Blind Mice (Galdone) **16**:107
The Computer Nut (Byars) **16**:60
Computer Sense, Computer Nonsense (Simon) **9**:221
Computer Talk (Berger) **32**:31
Computers (Berger) **32**:8
Computers: A Question and Answer Book (Berger) **32**:35
Computers in Your Life (Berger) **32**:24
Computers That Think? The Search for Artificial Intelligence (Hyde) **23**:167
Comrades for the Charter (Trease) **42**:175
Confessions of a Teenage Baboon (Zindel) **45**:190
Confessions of a Toe-Hanger (Harris) **47**:79
Confessions of an Only Child (Klein) **2**:97
The Confidence Man (Garfield) **21**:113
The Conquest of the Atlantic (d'Aulaire and d'Aulaire) **21**:40
Conrad: The Factory-Made Boy (Noestlinger) **12**:187
The Constellations: How They Came to Be (Gallant) **30**:95
Consumer Protection Labs (Berger) **32**:14
The Contender (Lipsyte) **23**:202
Continent in the Sky (Berna) **19**:36
The Controversial Coyote: Predation, Politics, and Ecology (Pringle) **4**:182
The Conversation Club (Stanley) **46**:133
Cookie Craft (Williams) **48**:194
The Cookie Tree (Williams) **8**:229

Title Index

Cool Cooking: Sixteen Recipes without a Stove (Hautzig) **22**:84

A Cool Kid—like Me! (Wilhelm) **46**:166

The Cool Kids' Guide to Summer Camp (Stine) **37**:105

Cool Simon (Ure) **34**:188

Coot Club (Ransome) **8**:176

Copernicus: Titan of Modern Astronomy (Knight) **38**:101

Cops and Robbers (Ahlberg and Ahlberg) **18**:5

Corals (Zim) **2**:226

Corazon Aquino: Leader of the Philippines (Haskins) **39**:53

Corduroy (Freeman) **30**:75

Corduroy's Christmas (Freeman) **30**:82

Corduroy's Party (Freeman) **30**:82

Corgiville Fair (Tudor) **13**:199

The Coriander (Dillon) **26**:24

Corn Is Maize: The Gift of the Indians (Aliki) **9**:24

Cornelius (Lionni) **7**:140

Cornrows (Yarbrough) **29**:209

Cornzapoppin'! (Williams) **48**:193

Costumes for Plays and Playing (Haley) **21**:146

Costumes to Make (Parish) **22**:158

The Cottage at Crescent Beach (Blades) **15**:55

A Cottage for Betsy (Sawyer) **36**:162

Cotton in My Sack (Lenski) **26**:114

"Could Be Worse!" (Stevenson) **17**:153

Could You Stop Josephine? (Poulin) **28**:195

Count and See (Hoban) **13**:101

Count Karlstein (Pullman) **20**:187

Count on Your Fingers African Style (Pinkney) **43**:157

Count Up: Learning Sets (Burningham) **9**:50

Count Your Way Through China (Haskins) **39**:53

Count Your Way Through Germany (Haskins) **39**:62

Count Your Way Through Italy (Haskins) **39**:62

Count Your Way Through Japan (Haskins) **39**:53

Count Your Way Through Russia (Haskins) **39**:53

Count Your Way Through the Arab World (Haskins) **39**:53

The Counterfeit African (Williams) **8**:221

The Counterfeit Man: More Science Fiction Stories (Nourse) **33**:134

The Counterfeit Tackle (Christopher) **33**:40

Counting America: The Story of the United States Census (Ashabranner and Ashabranner) **28**:14

Counting Wildflowers (McMillan) **47**:166

Country, Cat, City, Cat (Kherdian) **24**:109

Country Mouse and City Mouse (McKissack) **23**:237

Country Noisy Book (Brown) **10**:49

Country of Broken Stone (Bond) **11**:28

The Country of the Heart (Wersba) **3**:215

The Country Pancake (Fine) **25**:24

A Country Tale (Stanley) **46**:135

Country Watch (King-Smith) **40**:151

The County Fair (Tudor) **13**:190

Courage, Dana (Pfeffer) **11**:203

The Course of True Love Never Did Run Smooth (Singer) **48**:124

The Court of the Stone Children (Cameron) **1**:39

The Courtship, Merry Marriage, and Feast of Cock Robin and Jenny Wren, to Which Is Added the Doleful Death of Cock Robin (Cooney) **23**:26

The Courtship of Animals (Selsam) **1**:161

The Courtship of Birds (Simon) **39**:194

Cousins (Hamilton) **40**:82

Cowardly Clyde (Peet) **12**:205

Cowboy and His Friend (Anglund) **1**:19

Cowboy Cal and the Outlaw (Calhoun) **42**:9

Cowboy Dreams (Khalsa) **30**:151

Cowboy Small (Lenski) **26**:114

Cowboys and Cattle Ranching: Yesterday and Today (Lauber) **16**:117

The Cowboy's Christmas (Anglund) **1**:20

Cowboys of the Wild West (Freedman) **20**:85

Cowboy's Secret Life (Anglund) **1**:20

Cow's Party (Ets) **33**:85

Coyote Cry (Baylor) **3**:14

Coyote in Manhattan (George) **1**:89

The Cozy Book (Hoberman) **22**:114

The Crab that Crawled Out of the Past (Milne and Milne) **22**:119

Crabs (Zim) **2**:227

Crack in the Heart (Orgel) **48**:91

Cracker Jackson (Byars) **16**:61

Crackerjack Halfback (Christopher) **33**:39

The Craft of Sail (Adkins) **7**:20

Crafty Caspar and His Good Old Granny (Janosch) **26**:78

The Crane (Zimnik) **3**:242

The Crane Maiden (Tresselt) **30**:211

Crash! Bang! Boom! (Spier) **5**:221

Crazy about German Shepherds (Ashabranner) **28**:14

A Crazy Flight and Other Poems (Livingston) **7**:169

The Crazy Gang Next Door (Williams) **48**:205

The Crazy Horse Electric Game (Crutcher) **28**:105

Crazy Weeekend (Soto) **38**:204

Creeper's Jeep (Gramatky) **22**:42

Creepy Castle (Goodall) **25**:47

The Creoles of Color of New Orleans (Haskins) **3**:63

Creta (Ventura) **16**:196

The Cricket and the Mole (Janosch) **26**:79

The Cricket in Times Square (Selden) **8**:196

Crinkleroot's Book of Animal Tracks and Wildlife Signs (Arnosky) **15**:4

Crisis on Conshelf Ten (Hughes) **9**:69

Crocodarling (Rayner) **41**:125

Crocodile Dog (Kemp) **29**:123

The Crocodile in the Tree (Duvoisin) **23**:105

Crocodile Man (Biegel) **27**:36

The Crocodile Who Wouldn't Be King (Janosch) **26**:76

A Crocodile's Tale: A Philippine Folk Tale (Aruego) **5**:30

Crocus (Duvoisin) **23**:106

Cromwell's Boy (Haugaard) **11**:108

Cromwell's Glasses (Keller) **45**:44

The Crooked Snake (Wrightson) **4**:240

Cross Your Fingers, Spit in Your Hat: Superstitions and Other Beliefs (Schwartz) **3**:188

Cross-Country Cat (Calhoun) **42**:25

The Crossing (Paulsen) **19**:176

Crossing: Australian and New Zealand Short Stories (Duder) **43**:68

Crossing the New Bridge (McCully) **46**:71

The Cross-Stitch Heart and Other Plays (Field) **21**:71

The Crotchety Crocodile (Baumann) **35**:43

Crow and Hawk (Rosen) **45**:149

Crow Boy (Yashima) **4**:251

Crowds of Creatures (Clarke) **28**:80

The Crown of Violet (Trease) **42**:182

Crow's Nest (Allan) **43**:25

The Crucible Year (St. John) **46**:107

The Cruise of the Arctic Star (O'Dell) **1**:145

The Cruise of the Santa Maria (Dillon) **26**:27

Cruising to Danger (Hagon) **43**:15

Crummy Mummy and Me (Fine) **25**:22

Crusher is Coming! (Graham) **31**:97

Crutches (Hartling) **29**:101

Cry Softly! The Story of Child Abuse (Hyde) **23**:166

Crystal (Myers) **16**:143

The Cuckoo Child (King-Smith) **40**:162

The Cuckoo Sister (Alcock) **26**:5

The Cuckoo Tree (Aiken) **1**:3

Cuckoobush Farm (King-Smith) **40**:152

The Cucumber King: A Story with a Beginning, a Middle, and an End, in which Wolfgang Hogelmann Tells the Whole Truth (Noestlinger) **12**:184

Cue for Treason (Trease) **42**:177

Cults (Cohen) **43**:58

Culture Shock (Rosen) **45**:140

The Cupboard (Burningham) **9**:47

Curious George (Rey) **5**:193

Curious George Flies a Kite (Rey and Rey) **5**:198

Curious George Gets a Medal (Rey) **5**:198

Curious George Goes to the Hospital (Rey and Rey) **5**:199

Curious George Learns the Alphabet (Rey) **5**:199

Curious George Rides a Bike (Rey) **5**:196

Curious George Takes a Job (Rey) **5**:196

The Curious Tale of Hare and Hedgehog (Janosch) **26**:80

Curlicues: The Fortunes of Two Pug Dogs (Worth) **21**:222

The Curse of Cain (Southall) **2**:150

The Curse of the Blue Figurine (Bellairs) **37**:12

The Curse of the Egyptian Mummy (Hutchins) **20**:153

The Curse of the Squirrel (Yep) **17**:208

The Curse of the Viking Grave (Mowat) **20**:172

The Curse of the Werewolf (Biegel) **27**:35

Curses, Hexes, and Spells (Cohen) **43**:37

The Curses of Third Uncle (Yee) **44**:161

Curtain Up (Streatfeild) **17**:190

Curtains (Stine) **37**:113

Cut from the Same Cloth: American Women of Myth, Legend, and Tall Tale (San Souci) **43**:190

Cutlass Island (Corbett) **1**:44

Cuts, Breaks, Bruises, and Burns: How Your Body Heals (Cole) **40**:10

The Cut-Ups (Marshall) **21**:180

The Cut-Ups Cut Loose (Marshall) **21**:184

The Cybil War (Byars) **16**:57

Cyrano the Crow (Freeman) **30**:72

Cyrus the Unsinkable Sea Serpent (Peet) **12**:203

D. H. Lawrence: The Phoenix and the Flame (Trease) **42**:189

D. W. All Wet (Brown) **29**:17

D. W. Flips! (Brown) **29**:15

Da lontano era un'isola (Munari) **9**:129

Daddles: The Story of a Plain Hound Dog (Sawyer) **36**:164

Daddy (Caines) **24**:62

Daddy Darwin's Dovecot: A Country Tale (Caldecott) **14**:82

Daddy Is a Monster...Sometimes (Steptoe) **12**:240

Dad's Back (Ormerod) **20**:177

Daedalus and Icarus (Farmer) **8**:79

Daggie Dogfoot (King-Smith) **40**:140

Daisy (Coatsworth) **2**:54

Daisy Summerfield's Style (Goffstein) **3**:58

Daisy, Tell Me! (Calhoun) **42**:17

Daisy's Christmas (Waddell) **31**:197

Dance for Two (Ure) **34**:170

Dance in the Desert (L'Engle) **1**:130

The Dancers (Myers) **16**:137

Dancers in the Garden (Ryder)   **37**:98
The Dancing Bear (Dickinson)   **29**:42
The Dancing Camel (Byars)   **1**:35
The Dancing Class (Oxenbury)   **22**:144
The Dancing Garlands (Allan)   **43**:12
Dancing Girl (Paulsen)   **19**:174
The Dancing Granny (Bryan)   **18**:34
The Dancing Kettle and Other Japanese Folk Tales (Uchida)   **6**:250
Dancing Shoes (Streatfeild)   **17**:193
Dancing Shoes (Streatfeild)
    See *Wintle's Wonders*
Dandelion (Freeman)   **30**:74
Danger from Below: Earthquakes, Past, Present, and Future (Simon)   **9**:213
Danger in Dinosaur Valley (Nixon)   **24**:136
Danger in the Old Fort (St. John)   **46**:114
Danger on the Mountain (Haar)   **15**:114
Danger Point: The Wreck of the Birkenhead (Corbett)   **1**:44
Dangerous Inheritance (Allan)   **43**:20
The Dangerous Life of the Sea Horse (Schlein)   **41**:193
Dangerous Love (Pascal)   **25**:185
Dangerous Spring (Benary-Isbert)   **12**:77
Dangleboots (Hamley)   **47**:60
Danny Dunn and the Anti-Gravity Paint (Williams and Abrashkin)   **8**:222
Danny Dunn and the Automatic House (Williams and Abrashkin)   **8**:227
Danny Dunn and the Fossil Cave (Williams and Abrashkin)   **8**:225
Danny Dunn and the Heat Ray (Williams and Abrashkin)   **8**:225
Danny Dunn and the Homework Machine (Williams and Abrashkin)   **8**:223
Danny Dunn and the Smallifying Machine (Williams and Abrashkin)   **8**:230
Danny Dunn and the Swamp Monster (Williams and Abrashkin)   **8**:232
Danny Dunn and the Universal Glue (Williams and Abrashkin)   **8**:236
Danny Dunn and the Voice from Space (Williams and Abrashkin)   **8**:229
Danny Dunn and the Weather Machine (Williams and Abrashkin)   **8**:223
Danny Dunn, Invisible Boy (Williams and Abrashkin)   **8**:233
Danny Dunn on a Desert Island (Williams and Abrashkin)   **8**:223
Danny Dunn on the Ocean Floor (Williams and Abrashkin)   **8**:224
Danny Dunn, Scientific Detective (Williams and Abrashkin)   **8**:234
Danny Dunn, Time Traveler (Williams and Abrashkin)   **8**:226
Danny Goes to the Hospital (Collier)   **3**:44
Danny: The Champion of the World (Dahl)   **7**:74
The Dare (Stine)   **37**:123
The Daring Game (Pearson)   **26**:174
The Dark (Munsch)   **19**:141
The Dark Ages (Asimov)   **12**:42
The Dark and Deadly Pool (Nixon)   **24**:150
The Dark at the Top of the Stairs (McBratney)   **44**:130
The Dark Behind the Curtain (Cross)   **28**:88
The Dark Bright Water (Wrightson)   **4**:246
The Dark Canoe (O'Dell)   **1**:146
Dark Harvest: Migrant Farmworkers in America (Ashabranner)   **28**:8
The Dark Is Rising (Cooper)   **4**:44
The Dark of the Tunnel (Naylor)   **17**:59
The Dark Secret of Weatherend (Bellairs)   **37**:16

The Dark Way: Stories from the Spirit World (Hamilton)   **40**:84
The Dark Wood of the Golden Birds (Brown)   **10**:59
The Darkangel (Pierce)   **20**:182
A Darker Magic (Bedard)   **35**:60
Darkest Hours (Carter)   **22**:22
Darkness and the Butterfly (Grifalconi)   **35**:76
Darlene (Greenfield)   **4**:103
The Date Palm: Bread of the Desert (Simon)   **39**:195
The Daughter of Don Saturnino (O'Dell)   **16**:173
Daughter of Earth: A Roman Myth (McDermott)   **9**:119
Daughters of Eve (Duncan)   **29**:73
d'Aulaire's Trolls (d'Aulaire and d'Aulaire)   **21**:53
David and Della (Zindel)   **45**:200
David and Dog (Hughes)   **15**:124
David and Jonathan (Voigt)   **48**:176
David: From the Story Told in the First Book of Samuel and the First Book of Kings (Petersham and Petersham)   **24**:169
David He No Fear (Graham)   **10**:109
David Starr, Space Ranger (Asimov)   **12**:30
David's Father (Munsch)   **19**:144
David's Little Indian: A Story (Brown)   **10**:66
David's Witch Doctor (Mahy)   **7**:184
Davy and His Dog (Lenski)   **26**:120
Davy Goes Places (Lenski)   **26**:122
Dawn (Bang)   **8**:23
Dawn (Shulevitz)   **5**:206
Dawn and Dusk: Poems of Our Time (Causley)   **30**:32
Dawn from the West: The Story of Genevieve Caulfield (Rau)   **8**:185
A Dawn in the Trees: Thomas Jefferson, the Years 1776 to 1789 (Wibberley)   **3**:224
Dawn Land (Bruchac)   **46**:12
Dawn of Fear (Cooper)   **4**:43
Dawn Rider (Hudson)   **40**:97
Dawn Wind (Sutcliff)   **1**:184; **37**:155
The Day Adam Got Mad (Lindgren)   **39**:164
Day and Night (Duvoisin)   **23**:101
The Day Chiro Was Lost (Nakatani)   **30**:157
The Day Martin Luther King, Jr., was Shot: A Photo History of the Civil Rights Movement (Haskins)   **39**:67
A Day No Pigs Would Die (Peck)   **45**:95
Day of Earthlings (Bunting)   **28**:48
A Day of Pleasure: Stories of a Boy Growing Up in Warsaw (Singer)   **1**:173
The Day of the Dinosaurs (Bunting)   **28**:44
The Day the Gang Got Rich (Kotzwinkle)   **6**:181
The Day the Numbers Disappeared (Bendick)   **5**:40
The Day the Teacher Went Bananas (Howe)   **9**:59
The Day the Tide Went Out...and Out...and Out...and Out...and Out...and Out (McKee)   **38**:164
A Day with Daddy (Tresselt)   **30**:204
A Day with Wilbur Robinson (Joyce)   **26**:85
The Daybreakers (Curry)   **31**:74
Daydreamers (Greenfield)   **4**:103
Daylight Robbery (Williams)   **8**:235
Days of Fear (Nixon)   **24**:144
Days of Terror (Smucker)   **10**:190
The Days of the Dragon's Seed (St. John)   **46**:110
Days with Frog and Toad (Lobel)   **5**:173
Dazzle the Dinosaur (Pfister)   **42**:137
The Dead Bird (Brown)   **10**:66
The Dead Letter Box (Mark)   **11**:154
Dead Man's Light (Corbett)   **1**:44

The Dead Moon and Other Tales from East Anglia and the Fen Country (Crossley-Holland)   **47**:40
The Dead Tree (Tresselt)   **30**:214
Deadly Ants (Simon)   **9**:214
A Deadly Game of Magic (Nixon)   **24**:144
Deadly Music (Hamley)   **47**:66
The Deadman Tapes (Rosen)   **45**:141
Deadmen's Cave (Wibberley)   **3**:225
Dealing with the Devil (Cohen)   **43**:38
Dear Bill, Remember Me? and Other Stories (Mazer)   **23**:224
Dear God, Help!!! Love, Earl (Park)   **34**:163
Dear Lola: Or, How to Build Your Own Family (Gaberman)   **33**:7
Dear Lovey Hart: I Am Desperate (Conford)   **10**:93
Dear Mr. Henshaw (Cleary)   **8**:59
Dear Prosper (Fox)   **44**:61
Dear Readers and Riders (Henry)   **4**:115
Dear Robin: Letters to Robin Klein (Klein)   **21**:165
Dear Shrink (Cresswell)   **18**:110
Dear Snowman (Janosch)   **26**:76
Death Is Natural (Pringle)   **4**:181
Death of a Dinosaur (Bunting)   **28**:44
The Death of Evening Star: The Diary of a Young New England Whaler (Fisher)   **18**:124
Death of the Iron Horse (Goble)   **21**:135
Death Penalty (Hamley)   **47**:65
Deathwatch (White)   **3**:221
Debbie and Her Dolls (Lenski)   **26**:124
Debbie and Her Family (Lenski)   **26**:124
Debbie and Her Grandma (Lenski)   **26**:123
Debbie Goes to Nursery School (Lenski)   **26**:124
Debbie Herself (Lenski)   **26**:124
Debby and Her Pets (Lenski)   **26**:124
Debutante Hill (Duncan)   **29**:65
The December (Garfield)   **21**:120
December Decorations: A Holiday How-To Book (Parish)   **22**:162
The December Rose (Garfield)   **21**:120
Deenie (Blume)   **2**:16
Deer at the Brook (Arnosky)   **15**:9
Deer in the Snow (Schlein)   **41**:179
Deer Valley Girl (Lenski)   **26**:123
Deezle Boy (Spence)   **26**:199
Delbert, the Plainclothes Detective (Nixon)   **24**:135
Del-Del (Kelleher)   **36**:129
Delilah and the Dishwater Dogs (Nimmo)   **44**:151
Delilah and the Dogspell (Nimmo)   **44**:148
The Deliverers of Their Country (Zwerger)   **46**:196
Delivery Van: Words for Town and Country (Betsy and Giulio Maestro)   **45**:82
Delpha Green and Company (Cleaver and Cleaver)   **6**:108
The Delphic Choice (St. John)   **46**:121
The Demon Headmaster (Cross)   **28**:88
Der Denker Greift Ein (Noestlinger)   **12**:188
Department Store (Gibbons)   **8**:98
Depend on Katie John (Calhoun)   **42**:7
Desert Dan (Coatsworth)   **2**:55
Desert Hunter: The Spider Wasp (Williams)   **48**:191
The Desert Is Theirs (Baylor)   **3**:14
The Desert People (Clark)   **16**:81
A Desert Year (Lerner)   **34**:136
Desperate Search (Christopher)   **33**:47
The Devil Hole (Spence)   **26**:197
The Devil in Vienna (Orgel)   **48**:84
Devil on My Back (Hughes)   **9**:78

The Devil on the Road (Westall) **13**:253
Devil Pony (Christopher) **33**:51
The Devil Rides with Me and Other Fantastic Stories (Slote) **4**:203
Devil-in-the-Fog (Garfield) **21**:97
Devils and Demons (Blumberg) **21**:28
The Devil's Arithmetic (Yolen) **44**:184
The Devil's Children (Dickinson) **29**:39
Devil's Hill (Chauncy) **6**:90
Devil's Race (Avi) **24**:11
The Devil's Storybook (Babbitt) **2**:5
The Diamond Champs (Christopher) **33**:52
The Diamond in the Window (Langton) **33**:107
Diana Ross: Star Supreme (Haskins) **39**:49
Dicey's Song (Voigt) **13**:230
Dick Bruna's Animal Book (Bruna) **7**:51
Dick Bruna's Word Book (Bruna) **7**:53
Dick Foote and the Shark (Babbitt) **2**:5
Dick Whittington and His Cat (Brown) **12**:95
Did Adam Name the Vinegarroon? (Kennedy) **27**:98
Did I Ever Tell You How Lucky You Are? (Geisel) **1**:85
The Diddakoi (Godden) **20**:133
Dido and Pa (Aiken) **19**:17
Died on a Rainy Sunday (Aiken) **1**:3
Dierenboek (Bruna) **7**:51
Dietrich of Berne and the Dwarf-King Laurin: Hero Tales of the Austrian Tirol (Sawyer) **36**:164
Dig, Drill, Dump, Fill (Hoban) **13**:103
The Diggers (Brown) **10**:67
Digging Up Dinosaurs (Aliki) **9**:28
Dimitri and the False Tsars (Baumann) **35**:53
Din Dan Don, It's Christmas (Domanska) **40**:45
Dinah's Mad, Bad Wishes (McCully) **46**:63
Dinky Hocker Shoots Smack! (Kerr) **29**:143
Dinner Ladies Don't Count (Ashley) **4**:18
Dinner Time (Pienkowski) **6**:231
Dinosaur Bob and His Adventures with the Family Lazardo (Joyce) **26**:84
Dinosaur Dances (Yolen) **44**:189
Dinosaur Days (Knight) **38**:121
The Dinosaur Is the Biggest Animal That Ever Lived and Other Wrong Ideas You Thought Were True (Simon) **9**:220
Dinosaur Story (Cole) **5**:63
Dinosaur Time (Parish) **22**:161
The Dinosaur Trap (Bunting) **28**:44
Dinosaurs (Cohen) **43**:49
Dinosaurs (Zim) **2**:227
Dinosaurs Alive and Well! A Guide to Good Health (Brown) **29**:19
Dinosaurs and All That Rubbish (Foreman) **32**:87
Dinosaurs and People: Fossils, Facts, and Fantasies (Pringle) **4**:184
Dinosaurs and Their World (Pringle) **4**:174
Dinosaurs and Their Young (Freedman) **20**:84
Dinosaurs, Asteroids, and Superstars: Why the Dinosaurs Disappeared (Branley) **13**:47
Dinosaurs Beware! A Safety Guide (Brown) **29**:9
Dinosaurs Divorce: A Guide to Changing Families (Brown) **29**:14
Dinosaur's Housewarming Party (Klein) **19**:89
Dinosaurs of North America (Sattler) **24**:216
"Dinosaurs" That Swam and Flew (Knight) **38**:130
Dinosaurs to the Rescue: A Guide to Protecting Our Planet (Brown) **29**:20
Dinosaurs Travel: A Guide for Families on the Go (Brown) **29**:17
Dinosaurs Walked Here and Other Stories Fossils Tell (Lauber) **16**:123

Diogenes: The Story of the Greek Philosopher (Aliki) **9**:21
A Dip of the Antlers (McBratney) **44**:117
Directions and Angles (Adler) **27**:23
Dirk Lives in Holland (Lindgren) **39**:151
Dirt Bike Racer (Christopher) **33**:53
Dirt Bike Runaway (Christopher) **33**:56
Dirty Beasts (Dahl) **41**:32
Dirty Dave (Hilton) **25**:60
Dirty Dave, the Bushranger (Hilton) **25**:60
The Disappearance (Guy) **13**:83
The Disappearing Dog Trick (Corbett) **1**:44
Disaster (Sobol) **4**:211
Disastrous Floods and Tidal Waves; Disastrous Volcanoes (Berger) **32**:25
Discontinued (Thompson) **24**:229
Discovering Rocks and Minerals: A Nature and Science Guide to Their Collection and Identification (Gallant) **30**:88
Discovering the American Stork (Scott) **20**:195
Discovering the Mysterious Egret (Scott) **20**:197
Discovering the Royal Tombs at Ur (Glubok) **1**:100
Discovering What Earthworms Do (Simon) **9**:202
Discovering What Frogs Do (Simon) **9**:202
Discovering What Gerbils Do (Simon) **9**:204
Discovering What Goldfish Do (Simon) **9**:202
The Discovery of the Americas (Betsy and Giulio Maestro) **45**:83
Disease Detectives (Berger) **32**:19
Disney's James and the Giant Peach (Smith) **47**:207
The Ditch Picnic (Unnerstad) **36**:197
The Diverting History of John Gilpin (Caldecott) **14**:73
Divide and Rule (Mark) **11**:148
The Divorce Express (Danziger) **20**:54
Do Like Kyla (Johnson) **33**:94
Do Lord Remember Me (Lester) **41**:102
Do Tigers Ever Bite Kings? (Wersba) **3**:216
Do You Have the Time, Lydia? (Ness) **6**:207
Do You Want to Be My Friend? (Carle) **10**:74
Doctor Change (Cole) **40**:11
Doctor De Soto (Steig) **15**:197
Doctor Dolittle (Lofting) **19**:120
Doctor Dolittle: A Treasury (Lofting) **19**:131
Doctor Dolittle and the Green Canary (Lofting) **19**:129
Doctor Dolittle and the Secret Lake (Lofting) **19**:129
Doctor Dolittle in the Moon (Lofting) **19**:126
Doctor Dolittle's Caravan (Lofting) **19**:124
Doctor Dolittle's Circus (Lofting) **19**:124
Doctor Dolittle's Garden (Lofting) **19**:125
Doctor Dolittle's Puddleby Adventures (Lofting) **19**:130
Doctor Dolittle's Return (Lofting) **19**:128
Doctor Dolittle's Zoo (Lofting) **19**:124
Doctor Sean (Breinburg) **31**:67
Doctor Shawn (Breinburg)
  See *Doctor Sean*
The Doctors (Fisher) **18**:123
Dodos Are Forever (King-Smith) **40**:156
The Dog (Burningham) **9**:47
A Dog and a Half (Willard) **2**:217
Dog Breath: The Horrible Trouble with Hally Tosis (Pilkey) **48**:109
Dog Days and Cat Naps (Kemp) **29**:116
The Dog Days of Arthur Cane (Bethancourt) **3**:18
Dog In, Cat Out (Rubinstein) **35**:213
Dog People: Native Dog Stories (Bruchac) **46**:21
A Dog So Small (Pearce) **9**:149
The Dog That Called the Signals (Christopher) **33**:56

The Dog That Could Swim under Water: Memoirs of a Springer Spaniel (Selden) **8**:196
The Dog That Pitched a No-Hitter (Christopher) **33**:59
The Dog That Stole Football Plays (Christopher) **33**:54
The Dog Who Insisted He Wasn't (Singer) **48**:120
The Dog Who Wouldn't Be (Mowat) **20**:170
The Dog Writes on the Window with His Nose and Other Poems (Kherdian) **24**:108
Dogger (Hughes) **15**:124
Dogs and Dragons, Trees and Dreams: A Collection of Poems (Kuskin) **4**:144
A Dog's Body (Cole) **40**:12
Dogs Don't Tell Jokes (Sacher) **28**:204
Dogsbody (Jones) **23**:185
Dogsong (Paulsen) **19**:175
Dogzilla (Pilkey) **48**:106
The Do-It-Yourself House That Jack Built (Yeoman) **46**:186
Dollar a Share (Epstein and Epstein) **26**:43
The Dollar Man (Mazer) **16**:128
Dollars and Cents for Harriet (Betsy and Giulio Maestro) **45**:80
Dollars from Dandelions: 101 Ways to Earn Money (Sattler) **24**:215
Dollmaker: The Eyelight and the Shadow (Lasky) **11**:116
The Dolls' Christmas (Tudor) **13**:193
The Dolls' House (Godden) **20**:125
The Dolphin Crossing (Walsh) **2**:197
Dolphins and Porpoises (Patent) **19**:165
Dom and Va (Christopher) **2**:39
Domestic Arrangements (Klein) **19**:93
Dominic (Steig) **2**:159
Donald and the . . . (Gorey) **36**:93
The Dong with a Luminous Nose (Gorey) **36**:93
The Dong with the Luminous Nose (Lear) **1**:127
The Donkey That Sneezed (Biro) **28**:39
Donkey-Donkey, the Troubles of a Silly Little Donkey (Duvoisin) **23**:90
Donna Jean's Disaster (Williams) **48**:204
Donna Summer: An Unauthorized Biography (Haskins) **39**:43
Don't Call Me Slob-o (Orgel) **48**:98
Don't Care High (Korman) **25**:108
Don't Count Your Chicks (d'Aulaire and d'Aulaire) **21**:48
Don't Forget the Bacon (Hutchins) **20**:148
Don't Forget to Fly: A Cycle of Modern Poems (Janeczko) **47**:100
Don't Look and It Won't Hurt (Peck) **15**:151
Don't Look behind You (Duncan) **29**:79
Don't Make Me Smile (Park) **34**:153
Don't Play Dead before You Have To (Wojciechowska) **1**:196
Don't Put Mustard in the Custard (Rosen) **45**:134
Don't Rent My Room! (Gaberman) **33**:16
Don't Sit under the Apple Tree (Brancato) **32**:69
Don't Spill It Again, James (Wells) **16**:208
Don't Stand in the Soup: The World's Funniest Guide to Manners (Stine) **37**:105
Don't Tell the Whole World! (Cole) **40**:28
Don't You Remember? (Clifton) **5**:55
Don't You Turn Back (Grifalconi) **35**:71
Don't You Turn Back (Hughes) **17**:47
Don't You Turn Back: Poems by Langston Hughes (Hopkins) **44**:85
Doodle Soup (Ciardi) **19**:81
The Doom Stone (Zindel) **45**:202
The Door in the Hedge (McKinley) **10**:122
The Door in the Wall (de Angeli) **1**:53
Door to the North (Coatsworth) **2**:55

The Doorbell Rang (Hutchins) **20**:153
Dorcas Porkus (Tudor) **13**:191
Dorothea Lange: Life through the Camera (Meltzer) **13**:148
Dorrie's Book (Sachs) **2**:132
A Double Discovery (Ness) **6**:203
The Double Life of Pocahontas (Fritz) **14**:118
The Double Planet (Asimov) **12**:34
The Double Quest (Sobol) **4**:206
Double Spell (Lunn) **18**:158
Double Trouble (DeClements) **23**:36
Douglas the Drummer (Owen) **31**:147
Down a Dark Hall (Duncan) **29**:70
Down from the Lonely Mountain: California Indian Tales (Curry) **31**:70
Down Half the World (Coatsworth) **2**:55
Down to Earth (Wrightson) **4**:242
Downtown (Mazer) **23**:229
Dr. Anno's Magical Midnight Circus (Anno) **2**:2
Dr. Beaumont and the Man with the Hole in His Stomach (Epstein and Epstein) **26**:67
Dr. Merlin's Magic Shop (Corbett) **1**:45
Dr. Seuss's ABC (Seuss) **1**:85; **9**:187
Dr. Seuss's Sleep Book (Seuss) **1**:85; **9**:187
Dr. Smith's Safari (Say) **22**:208
The Drackenberg Adventure (Alexander) **48**:19
Dracula: A Toy Theatre for All Ages (Gorey) **36**:99
Draft Horses (Patent) **19**:163
Dragon Boy (King-Smith) **40**:168
Dragon Gets By (Pilkey) **48**:101
The Dragon in the Ghetto Caper (Konigsburg) **47**:132
Dragon Night and Other Lullabies (Yolen) **4**:266
The Dragon of an Ordinary Family (Mahy) **7**:179
The Dragon of an Ordinary Family (Oxenbury) **22**:137
The Dragon of Og (Godden) **20**:136
Dragon of the Lost Sea (Yep) **17**:205
Dragon Steel (Yep) **17**:207
The Dragon Takes a Wife (Myers) **4**:156
Dragonflies (Simon) **39**:189
Dragonfly Summer (Farmer) **8**:79
The Dragonfly Years (Hunter) **25**:88
Dragon's Blood: A Fantasy (Yolen) **44**:175
The Dragon's Eye (St. John) **46**:123
Dragon's Fat Cat (Pilkey) **48**:102
Dragon's Halloween: Dragon's Fifth Tale (Pilkey) **48**:108
Dragons in the Waters (L'Engle) **14**:150
Dragon's Merry Christmas (Pilkey) **48**:102
Dragonwings (Yep) **3**:236
Drag-Strip Racer (Christopher) **33**:56
Drawing from Nature (Arnosky) **15**:6
Drawing Life in Motion (Arnosky) **15**:8
The Dreadful Future of Blossom Culp (Peck) **15**:163
The Dream Book: First Comes the Dream (Brown) **10**:59
Dream Dancer (Bunting) **28**:44
Dream Days (Grahame) **5**:128
The Dream Keeper and Other Poems (Hughes) **17**:37
Dream of Dark Harbor (Kotzwinkle) **6**:183
A Dream of Hunger Moss (Allan) **43**:33
The Dream Time (Treece) **2**:183
The Dream Watcher (Wersba) **3**:216
Dream Weaver (Yolen) **4**:265
The Dream-Eater (Ende) **14**:99
The Dream-House (Crossley-Holland) **47**:35
Dreaming of Larry (Ure) **34**:190
Dreamland Lake (Peck) **15**:153
Dreams (Keats) **1**:114; **35**:138

Dreams of a Perfect Earth (Milne and Milne) **22**:124
Dreams of Victory (Conford) **10**:90
Dreams, Visions, and Drugs: A Search for Other Realities (Cohen) **3**:39
Drei Mal Drei: An Einem Tag (Kruss) **9**:85
Dressing (Oxenbury) **22**:141
The Driftway (Lively) **7**:154
Drina Dances in Italy (Estoril) **43**:8
Drina Dances on Stage (Estoril) **43**:8
The Drinking Gourd (Monjo) **2**:120
The Drive (Oxenbury) **22**:145
A Drop of Blood (Showers) **6**:243
Drowned Ammet (Jones) **23**:188
Drug Abuse A-Z (Berger) **32**:44
Drug Wars (Hyde) **23**:176
The Drugstore Cat (Petry) **12**:210
The Drummer Boy (Garfield) **21**:100
Drummer Hoff (Emberley and Emberley) **5**:94
Dry or Wet? (McMillan) **47**:170
Dry Victories (Jordan) **10**:118
Drylongso (Hamilton) **40**:86
Drylongso (Pinkney) **43**:170
Duck Boy (Mattingley) **24**:126
Duck Dutch (Haar) **15**:114
Duck on a Pond (Willard) **2**:217
Ducks and Dragons: Poems for Children (Kemp) **29**:116
The Dueling Machine (Bova) **3**:32
Dukes (Peck) **45**:118
The Dumb Bunnies (Pilkey) **48**:108
The Dumb Bunnies' Easter (Pilkey) **48**:110
The Dumb Cake (Garfield) **21**:109
Dumb Cane and Daffodils: Poisonous Plants in the House and Garden (Lerner) **34**:135
Dump Days (Spinelli) **26**:204
The Dunkard (Selden) **8**:199
The Duplicate (Sleator) **29**:206
Dust (Adler) **27**:10
Dust Bowl: The Story of Man on the Great Plains (Lauber) **16**:112
Dust of the Earth (Cleaver and Cleaver) **6**:110
Dustland (Hamilton) **11**:80
Dusty and Smudge and the Bride (Schmidt) **22**:222
Dusty and Smudge Keep Cool (Schmidt) **22**:222
Dusty and Smudge Spill the Paint (Schmidt) **22**:211
Dwarf Long-Nose (Orgel) **48**:71
Dwarf Nose (Zwerger) **46**:200
The Dwarfs of Nosegay (Biegel) **27**:32
The Dwindling Party (Gorey) **36**:102
Dynamite's Funny Book of the Sad Facts of Life (Stine) **37**:104
Dynamo Farm (Epstein and Epstein) **26**:42
Each Peach Pear Plum (Ahlberg and Ahlberg) **18**:5
Each Peach Pear Plum: An I Spy Story (Ahlberg and Ahlberg) **18**:5
Eagle and Dove (Kruss) **9**:86
Eagle Fur (Peck) **45**:112
The Eagle Kite (Fox) **44**:77
Eagle Mask: A West Coast Indian Tale (Houston) **3**:85
The Eagle of the Ninth (Sutcliff) **1**:185; **37**:151
Eagle Song (Bruchac) **46**:23
Eagle's Egg (Sutcliff) **37**:174
An Early American Christmas (dePaola) **24**:99
Early Humans: A Prehistoric World (Berger) **32**:39
Early in the Morning: A Collection of New Poems (Causley) **30**:42
Early in the Morning: A Collection of New Poems (Foreman) **32**:100

Early Thunder (Fritz) **2**:80
Early Words: Color Book (Scarry) **41**:167
Ears Are for Hearing (Keller) **45**:54
The Earth in Action (Hyde) **23**:158
Earth: Our Planet in Space (Simon) **9**:220
The Earth: Planet Number Three (Branley) **13**:32
Earth Songs (Fisher) **18**:136
The Earth under Sky Bear's Feet (Bruchac) **46**:20
Earthdark (Hughes) **9**:69
The Earth-Father (Crossley-Holland) **47**:34
Earthquake (Christopher) **33**:50
Earthquakes: Nature in Motion (Nixon) **24**:142
Earthquakes: New Scientific Ideas about How and Why the Earth Shakes (Lauber) **16**:117
Earth's Changing Climate (Gallant) **30**:94
Earth's Enigmas: A Book of Animal and Nature Life (Roberts) **33**:191
Earth's Vanishing Forests (Gallant) **30**:106
"*The Earthsea Quartet*" (Le Guin) **28**:144-88
Earthsea Trilogy (Le Guin) **3**:118
East End at Your Feet (Dhondy) **41**:72
East of the Sun and West of the Moon (Mayer) **11**:174
East of the Sun and West of the Moon: Old Tales from the North (Nielsen) **16**:155
The Easter Cat (DeJong) **1**:56
The Easter Mystery (Nixon) **24**:142
Easter Treat (Duvoisin) **23**:99
Easy Avenue (Doyle) **22**:33
An Easy Introduction to the Slide Rule (Asimov) **12**:39
Eating Fractions (McMillan) **47**:178
Eating Out (Oxenbury) **22**:144
Eating the Alphabet: Fruits and Vegetables from A to Z (Ehlert) **28**:112
Eats: Poems (Adoff) **7**:35
Eavesdropping on Space: The Quest of Radio Astronomy (Knight) **38**:116
Der Ebereschenhof (Benary-Isbert) **12**:72
Echo in the Wilderness (Brinsmead) **47**:13
The Echoing Green (Rayner) **41**:128
The Eclectic Abecedarium (Gorey) **36**:105
Eclipse: Darkness in Daytime (Branley) **13**:39
Ecology (Bendick) **5**:48
Ecology: Science of Survival (Pringle) **4**:175
Ed Emberley's A B C (Emberley) **5**:100
Ed Emberley's Amazing Look Through Book (Emberley) **5**:101
Ed Emberley's Big Green Drawing Book (Emberley) **5**:102
Ed Emberley's Big Orange Drawing Book (Emberley) **5**:102
Ed Emberley's Big Purple Drawing Book (Emberley) **5**:103
Ed Emberley's Crazy Mixed-Up Face Game (Emberley) **5**:103
Ed Emberley's Drawing Book: Make a World (Emberley) **5**:98
Ed Emberley's Drawing Book of Animals (Emberley) **5**:97
Ed Emberley's Drawing Book of Faces (Emberley) **5**:99
Ed Emberley's Great Thumbprint Drawing Book (Emberley) **5**:100
Eddie and Gardenia (Haywood) **22**:95
Eddie and His Big Deals (Haywood) **22**:96
Eddie and Louella (Haywood) **22**:97
Eddie and the Fire Engine (Haywood) **22**:94
Eddie, Incorporated (Naylor) **17**:55
Eddie Makes Music (Haywood) **22**:97
Eddie the Dog Holder (Haywood) **22**:100
Eddie's Green Thumb (Haywood) **22**:99
Eddie's Happenings (Haywood) **22**:101

Eddie's Menagerie (Haywood) **22**:104
Eddie's Pay Dirt (Haywood) **22**:95
Eddie's Valuable Property (Haywood) **22**:102
Edgar Allan Crow (Tudor) **13**:194
The Edge of the Cloud (Peyton) **3**:172
Edie on the Warpath (Spykman) **35**:221
Edith Jackson (Guy) **13**:81
Edith Wilson: The Woman Who Ran the United States (Giblin) **29**:94
An Edwardian Christmas (Goodall) **25**:48
Edwardian Entertainments (Goodall) **25**:53
An Edwardian Holiday (Goodall) **25**:49
An Edwardian Season (Goodall) **25**:50
An Edwardian Summer (Goodall) **25**:47
Egg Thoughts and Other Frances Songs (Hoban) **3**:76
Egg to Chick (Selsam) **1**:161
The Eggs: A Greek Folk Tale (Aliki) **9**:20
Ego-Tripping and Other Poems for Young People (Giovanni) **6**:116
The Egypt Game (Snyder) **31**:154
The Egyptians (Asimov) **12**:41
Eight Days of Luke (Jones) **23**:184
Eight for a Secret (Willard) **2**:217
Eight Plus One: Stories (Cormier) **12**:148
The Eighteenth Emergency (Byars) **1**:35
Einstein Anderson Goes to Bat (Simon) **9**:218
Einstein Anderson Lights Up the Sky (Simon) **9**:219
Einstein Anderson Makes Up for Lost Time (Simon) **9**:216
Einstein Anderson, Science Sleuth (Simon) **9**:216
Einstein Anderson Sees Through the Invisible Man (Simon) **9**:219
Einstein Anderson Shocks His Friends (Simon) **9**:216
Einstein Anderson Tells a Comet's Tale (Simon) **9**:217
The El Dorado Adventure (Alexander) **48**:17
Elbert's Bad Word (Wood and Wood) **26**:224
Electricity in Your Life (Adler) **27**:19
The Electromagnetic Spectrum: Key to the Universe (Branley) **13**:44
Electromagnetic Waves (Adler) **27**:13
Electronics (Adler) **27**:14
Electronics for Boys and Girls (Bendick) **5**:34
Elegy on the Death of a Mad Dog (Caldecott) **14**:74
The Elementary Mathematics of the Atom (Adler) **27**:19
Elena (Stanley) **46**:156
Elephant Boy: A Story of the Stone Age (Kotzwinkle) **6**:180
Elephant Families (Dorros) **42**:73
Elephant in a Well (Ets) **33**:91
Elephant Road (Guillot) **22**:61
The Elephants of Sargabal (Guillot) **22**:58
The Elephant's Wish (Munari) **9**:125
Eleven Kids, One Summer (Martin) **32**:206
The Eleventh Hour (Base) **22**:5
Elf Children of the Woods (Beskow) **17**:16
Eli (Peet) **12**:204
Elidor (Garner) **20**:101
Elidor and the Golden Ball (McHargue) **2**:117
Elijah the Slave (Singer) **1**:174
Elisabeth the Cow Ghost (Pene du Bois) **1**:63
Eliza and the Elves (Field) **21**:69
Elizabite: The Adventures of a Carnivorous Plant (Rey) **5**:194
Eliza's Daddy (Thomas) **8**:213
Ellen Dellen (Gripe) **5**:148
Ellen Grae (Cleaver and Cleaver) **6**:101
Ellen Tebbits (Cleary) **2**:45; **8**:45

Ellie and the Hagwitch (Cresswell) **18**:111
Ellis Island: Gateway to the New World (Fisher) **18**:136
The Elm Street Lot (Pearce) **9**:153
Elmer Again (McKee) **38**:180
Elmer: The Story of a Patchwork Elephant (McKee) **38**:159
Elmer's Colours; Elmer's Day; Elmer's Friends; Elmer's Weather (McKee) **38**:181
Eloise: A Book for Precocious Grown-Ups (Thompson) **22**:226
Eloise at Christmastime (Thompson) **22**:226
Eloise in Moscow (Thompson) **22**:227
Eloise in Paris (Thompson) **22**:226
Eloquent Crusader: Ernestine Rose (Suhl) **2**:165
The Elves and the Shoemaker (Galdone) **16**:105
Elvis and His Friends (Gripe) **5**:148
Elvis and His Secret (Gripe) **5**:148
Elvis! Elvis! (Gripe) **5**:148
Elvis Karlsson (Gripe) **5**:148
The Emergency Book (Bendick) **5**:41
Emer's Ghost (Waddell) **31**:178
Emil and Piggy Beast (Lindgren) **1**:136
Emil and the Detectives (Kaestner) **4**:121
Emil's Pranks (Lindgren) **1**:136
Emily (Bedard) **35**:65
Emily of New Moon (Montgomery) **8**:138
Emily Upham's Revenge: Or, How Deadwood Dick Saved the Banker's Niece: A Massachusetts Adventure (Avi) **24**:5
Emily's Runaway Imagination (Cleary) **2**:45; **8**:50
Emlyn's Moon (Nimmo) **44**:141
Emma (Stevenson) **17**:163
The Emma Dilemma (Waddell) **31**:180
Emma in Love (Arundel) **35**:17
Emma in Winter (Farmer) **8**:78
Emma Tupper's Diary (Dickinson) **29**:41
Emma's Island (Arundel) **35**:12
Emmet (Politi) **29**:193
Emmet Otter's Jug-Band Christmas (Hoban) **3**:76
The Emperor and the Kite (Yolen) **4**:257
The Emperor and the Kite (Young) **27**:216
The Emperor's New Clothes (Burton) **11**:50
The Emperor's Winding Sheet (Walsh) **2**:197
The Empty Sleeve (Garfield) **21**:121
The Empty Window (Bunting) **28**:51
The Enchanted: An Incredible Tale (Coatsworth) **2**:56
The Enchanted Caribou (Cleaver) **13**:73
The Enchanted Castle (Nesbit) **3**:162
The Enchanted Drum (Orgel) **48**:77
The Enchanted Horse (Harris) **30**:122
The Enchanted Island: Stories from Shakespeare (Serraillier) **2**:137
The Enchanted Schoolhouse (Sawyer) **36**:162
The Enchanted Tapestry: A Chinese Folktale (San Souci) **43**:182
Enchantress from the Stars (Engdahl) **2**:69
Encore for Eleanor (Peet) **12**:205
Encounter (Yolen) **44**:195
Encounter at Easton (Avi) **24**:6
Encounter Near Venus (Wibberley) **3**:225
Encyclopedia Brown and the Case of the Dead Eagles (Sobol) **4**:210
Encyclopedia Brown and the Case of the Midnight Visitor (Sobol) **4**:211
Encyclopedia Brown and the Case of the Secret Pitch (Sobol) **4**:207
Encyclopedia Brown, Boy Detective (Sobol) **4**:207
Encyclopedia Brown Carries On (Sobol) **4**:212
Encyclopedia Brown Finds the Clues (Sobol) **4**:208

Encyclopedia Brown Gets His Man (Sobol) **4**:208
Encyclopedia Brown Lends a Hand (Sobol) **4**:210
Encyclopedia Brown Saves the Day (Sobol) **4**:209
Encyclopedia Brown Shows the Way (Sobol) **4**:209
Encyclopedia Brown Solves Them All (Sobol) **4**:208
Encyclopedia Brown Takes the Case (Sobol) **4**:209
Encyclopedia Brown's Record Book of Weird and Wonderful Facts (Sobol) **4**:211
The Encyclopedia of Ghosts (Cohen) **43**:45
The Encyclopedia of Monsters (Cohen) **43**:41
End of Exile (Bova) **3**:32
The End of the Tale (Corbett) **19**:83
The End of the World (Branley) **13**:40
The Endless Steppe: Growing Up in Siberia (Hautzig) **22**:77
The Endocrine System: Hormones in the Living World (Silverstein and Silverstein) **25**:205
The Ends of the Earth: The Polar Regions of the World (Asimov) **12**:52
The Enemies (Klein) **21**:162
The Enemy (Garfield) **21**:109
An Enemy at Green Knowe (Boston) **3**:27
Energy (Adler) **27**:23
Energy (Berger) **32**:31
Energy and Power (Adler) **27**:9
Energy for the 21st Century (Branley) **13**:42
Energy from the Sun (Berger) **32**:17
Energy: Power for People (Pringle) **4**:179
Energy: The New Look (Hyde) **23**:166
Enjoying Opera (Streatfeild) **17**:196
The Ennead (Mark) **11**:147
The Enormous Crocodile (Dahl) **7**:77
Enrico Fermi: Father of Atomic Power (Epstein and Epstein) **26**:62
The Environment (Adler) **27**:26
Environments Out There (Asimov) **12**:42
Enzymes in Action (Berger) **32**:6
Epaminondas (Merriam) **14**:195
The Epics of Everest (Wibberley) **3**:226
Epilepsy (Silverstein and Silverstein) **25**:212
Eric Carle's Storybook: Seven Tales by the Brothers Grimm (Carle) **10**:80
The Erie Canal (Spier) **5**:220
Ernest and Celestine (Vincent) **13**:216
Ernest and Celestine's Patchwork Quilt (Vincent) **13**:219
Ernest and Celestine's Picnic (Vincent) **13**:217
Ernest et Célestine au Musée (Vincent) **13**:221
Ernest et Célestine Chez le Photographe (Vincent) **13**:217
Ernest et Célestine, Musiciens des Rues (Vincent) **13**:216
Ernest et Célestine Ont Perdu Siméon (Vincent) **13**:216
Ernest et Célestine Vont Pique-Niquer (Vincent) **13**:217
Ernstjan en Snabbeltje (Haar) **15**:114
Escapade (Goodall) **25**:50
Escape from Tyrannosaurus (Bunting) **28**:44
Esio Trot (Dahl) **41**:45
ESP (Aylesworth) **6**:50
ESP: The New Technology (Cohen) **43**:46
Estuaries: Where Rivers Meet the Sea (Pringle) **4**:178
E.T.! The Extra-Terrestrial (Kotzwinkle) **6**:184
E.T.! The Extra-Terrestrial Storybook (Kotzwinkle) **6**:185
Eugene the Brave (Conford) **10**:95
Euphonia and the Flood (Calhoun) **42**:22
Eva (Dickinson) **29**:58

Evangeline Booth: Daughter of Salvation (Lavine) **35**:151

Eva's Ice Adventure (Wallace) **37**:213

Even Stevens F.C. (Rosen) **45**:150

An Evening at Alfie's (Hughes) **15**:131

Ever Ride a Dinosaur? (Corbett) **1**:45

Everett Anderson's 1-2-3 (Clifton) **5**:58

Everett Anderson's Christmas Coming (Clifton) **5**:54

Everett Anderson's Friend (Clifton) **5**:57

Everett Anderson's Friend (Grifalconi) **35**:72

Everett Anderson's Goodbye (Grifalconi) **35**:73

Everett Anderson's Nine Month Long (Clifton) **5**:59

Everett Anderson's Nine Month Long (Grifalconi) **35**:73

Everett Anderson's Year (Clifton) **5**:55

Everglades Country: A Question of Life or Death (Lauber) **16**:117

Ever-Ready Eddie (Haywood) **22**:100

Every Living Thing (Rylant) **15**:171

Every Man Heart Lay Down (Graham) **10**:108

Every Time I Climb a Tree (McCord) **9**:100

Everybody Needs a Rock (Baylor) **3**:15

Everyone Knows What a Dragon Looks Like (Williams) **8**:235

Everyone's Trash Problem: Nuclear Wastes (Hyde) **23**:165

Everything Grows (McMillan) **47**:174

Everything Happens to Stuey (Moore) **15**:140

Everything I Know about Writing (Marsden) **34**:150

Everything Moves (Simon) **9**:210

Everything under a Mushroom (Krauss) **42**:129

Everything You Need to Survive: Brothers and Sisters; Everything You Need to Survive: First Dates; Everything You Need to Survive: Homework; Everything You Need to Survive: Money Problems (Stine) **37**:106

Everywhere (Brooks) **25**:35

The Evil Spell (McCully) **46**:65

Evolution (Adler) **27**:19

Evolution (Cole) **40**:18

Evolution Goes On Every Day (Patent) **19**:150

Exactly Alike (Ness) **6**:201

The Excretory System: How Living Creatures Get Rid of Wastes (Silverstein and Silverstein) **25**:208

Exiled from Earth (Bova) **3**:33

Exit Barney McGee (Mackay) **43**:106

Exotic Birds (Singer) **48**:138

The Expeditions of Willis Partridge (Weiss) **4**:222

Experiments in Chemistry (Branley) **13**:24

Experiments in Optical Illusion (Branley) **13**:24

Experiments in Science (Branley) **13**:23

Experiments in Sky Watching (Branley) **13**:28

Experiments in the Principles of Space Travel (Branley) **13**:25

Experiments with a Microscope (Branley) **13**:26

Experiments with Airplane Instruments (Branley) **13**:24

Experiments with Atomics (Branley) **13**:25

Experiments with Electricity (Branley) **13**:23

Experiments with Light (Branley) **13**:26

The Exploits of Moominpappa (Jansson) **2**:93

Exploration and Conquest: The Americas after Columbus: 1500-1620 (Betsy and Giulio Maestro) **45**:88

Exploration of the Moon (Branley) **13**:31

Explorers of the Atom (Gallant) **30**:91

Explorers on the Moon (Herge) **6**:148

Exploring by Astronaut: The Story of Project Mercury (Branley) **13**:30

Exploring by Satellite: The Story of Project Vanguard (Branley) **13**:26

Exploring Chemistry (Gallant) **30**:86

Exploring Fields and Lots: Easy Science Projects (Simon) **9**:212

Exploring Mars (Gallant) **30**:84

Exploring the Brain (Silverstein and Silverstein) **25**:210

Exploring the Mind and Brain (Berger) **32**:29

Exploring the Moon (Gallant) **30**:83

Exploring the Moon: A Revised Edition of the Science Classic (Gallant) **30**:83

Exploring the Planets (Gallant) **30**:86

Exploring the Sun (Gallant) **30**:86

Exploring the Universe (Gallant) **30**:84

Exploring the Weather (Gallant) **30**:85

Exploring the World of Social Insects (Simon) **39**:182

Exploring under the Earth: The Story of Geology and Geophysics (Gallant) **30**:87

Extraterrestrial Civilizations (Asimov) **12**:57

The Eye of Conscience: Photographers and Social Change, with 100 Photographs by Noted Photographers, Past and Present (Meltzer) **13**:131

Eyes in the Fishbowl (Snyder) **31**:156

Eyes of Darkness (Highwater) **17**:31

The Eyes of Karen Connors (Duncan)
   See *The Third Eye*

The Eyes of the Killer Robot (Bellairs) **37**:20

Eyes of the Wilderness (Roberts) **33**:207

The Faber Book of Northern Folk-Tales (Crossley-Holland) **47**:37

The Faber Book of Northern Legends (Crossley-Holland) **47**:35

Fables (Lobel) **5**:174

Fables (Scarry) **41**:161

Fables (Scarry) **41**:161

Fables from Aesop (Biro) **28**:35

A Fabulous Creature (Snyder) **31**:164

Face at the Edge of the World (Bunting) **28**:59

The Face in the Frost (Bellairs) **37**:5

Face-Off (Christopher) **33**:46

Faces in the Water (Naylor) **17**:56

Facing It (Brancato) **32**:74

Facing It (Thompson) **24**:227

The Factories (Fisher) **18**:128

Facts, Frauds, and Phantasms: A Survey of the Spiritualist Movement (McHargue) **2**:118

Fair Play (Leaf) **25**:125

Fair's Fair (Garfield) **21**:116

Fair-Weather Friends (Gantos) **18**:141

The Fairy Doll (Godden) **20**:127

The Fairy Rebel (Reid Banks) **24**:196

Fairy Tales of the Brothers Grimm (Nielsen) **16**:157

The Faithful Friend (San Souci) **43**:193

A Fall from the Sky: The Story of Daedalus (Serraillier) **2**:138

Fall Is Here! (Sterling) **1**:178

Fallen Angels (Myers) **35**:191

Falling in Love: Romantic Stories for Young Adults (Duder) **43**:69

False Face (Katz) **45**:33

Family (Donovan) **3**:51

Family (Oxenbury) **22**:141

The Family Album (Yeoman) **46**:184

A Family Apart (Nixon) **24**:149

The Family at Caldicott Place (Streatfeild) **17**:197

The Family at Caldicott Place (Streatfeild)
   See *Caldicott Place*

The Family Book of Mary-Claire (Spence) **26**:199

The Family Christmas Tree Book (dePaola) **4**:65

The Family Conspiracy (Phipson) **5**:179

A Family Failing (Arundel) **35**:20

Family Grandstand (Brink) **30**:13

A Family of Foxes (Dillon) **26**:24

A Family Project (Ellis) **42**:81

Family Reunion (Singer) **48**:144

Family Sabbatical (Brink) **30**:14

Family Secrets (Klein) **19**:97

Family Shoes (Streatfeild) **17**:192

Family Shoes (Streatfeild)
   See *The Bell Family*

The Family Tower (Willard) **2**:217

Famine (Blumberg) **21**:25

Famous American Architects (Lavine) **35**:150

Famous American Negroes (Hughes) **17**:39

Famous Industrialists (Lavine) **35**:148

Famous Men of Modern Biology (Berger) **32**:3

Famous Merchants (Lavine) **35**:149

Famous Naturalists (Milne and Milne) **22**:118

Famous Negro Athletes (Bontemps) **6**:84

Famous Negro Heroes of America (Hughes) **17**:43

Famous Negro Music Makers (Hughes) **17**:41

The Famous Stanley Kidnapping Case (Snyder) **31**:164

the Fanatic's Ecstatic, Aromatic Guide to Onions, Garlic, Shallots, and Leeks (Singer) **48**:123

Fancy That! (Allen) **44**:11

Fannie Lou Hamer (Jordan) **10**:119

Fanny and the Battle of Potter's Piece (Lively) **7**:163

Fanny's Sister (Lively) **7**:161

The Fantastic Brother (Guillot) **22**:64

Fantastic Mr. Fox (Dahl) **1**:51; **7**:73

Fantasy Summer (Pfeffer) **11**:204

Far and Few: Rhymes of the Never Was and Always Is (McCord) **9**:98

Far Away from Anywhere Else (Le Guin)
   See *Very Far Away from Anywhere Else*

Far Beyond and Back Again (Biegel) **27**:32

The Far Forests: Tales of Romance, Fantasy, and Suspense (Aiken) **19**:10

Far from Home (Sebestyen) **17**:91

Far from Shore (Major) **11**:130

Far Out the Long Canal (DeJong) **1**:57

The Far Side of Evil (Engdahl) **2**:70

Far to Go (Streatfeild) **17**:200

Farewell to Shady Glade (Peet) **12**:196

Farm Animals (Patent) **19**:160

Farm Babies (Freedman) **20**:82

Farmer Duck (Waddell) **31**:200

The Farmer in the Dell (Stanley) **46**:128

Farmer Palmer's Wagon Ride (Steig) **2**:160

Farmer Pelz's Pumpkins (Thiele) **27**:212

Farmer Schulz's Ducks (Thiele) **27**:210

The Farthest Shore (Le Guin) **28**:144-88; **3**:123

The Farthest-Away Mountain (Reid Banks) **24**:191

Fashion Is Our Business (Epstein and Epstein) **26**:44

Fast and Slow: Poems for Advanced Children and Beginning Parents (Ciardi) **19**:80

Fast Friends: Two Stories (Stevenson) **17**:156

Fast Is Not a Ladybug (Schlein) **41**:175

Fast Sam, Cool Clyde, and Stuff (Myers) **4**:156

The Fast Sooner Hound (Bontemps) **6**:79

Fast Talk on a Slow Track (Williams-Garcia) **36**:205

Fast-Slow, High-Low: A Book of Opposites (Spier) **5**:222

Fat Chance, Claude (Nixon) **24**:149

Fat Charlie's Circus (Gay) **27**:88

Fat Elliot and the Gorilla (Pinkwater) 4:162
Fat Lollipop (Ure) 34:189
Fat Men from Space (Pinkwater) 4:168
Fat Polka-Dot Cat and Other Haiku (Betsy and Giulio Maestro) 45:66
Father Bear Comes Home (Minarik) 33:124
Father Christmas (Briggs) 10:24
Father Christmas Goes on Holiday (Briggs) 10:25
Father Figure (Peck) 15:160
Father Fox's Pennyrhymes (Watson) 3:211
A Father Like That (Zolotow) 2:233
Fathom Five (Westall) 13:254
The Fattest Dwarf of Nosegay (Biegel) 27:34
The Favershams (Gerrard) 23:119
Favor for a Ghost (Christopher) 33:57
Fawn (Peck) 45:104
FBI (Berger) 32:18
The Fearless Treasure: A Story of England from Then to Now (Streatfeild) 17:192
Fears and Phobias (Hyde) 23:163
The Fearsome Inn (Singer) 1:174
The Feast of Lanterns (Say) 22:209
Feast or Famine? The Energy Future (Branley) 13:45
The Feather Star (Wrightson) 4:241
Featherbrains (Yeoman) 46:183
The Feathered Serpent (O'Dell) 16:176
Feathers and Fools (Fox) 23:117
Feathers for Lunch (Ehlert) 28:114
Feathers, Plain and Fancy (Simon) 39:184
Feathertop: Based on the Tale by Nathaniel Hawthorne (San Souci) 43:189
February Dragon (Thiele) 27:203
Feeding Babies (Nakatani) 30:161
Feel the Wind (Dorros) 42:66
Feelings (Aliki) 9:32
Feet and Other Stories (Mark) 11:154
The Feet of the Furtive (Roberts) 33:203-04
Felice (Brown) 12:100
Felicia the Critic (Conford) 10:91
Felita (Mohr) 22:133
Fell (Kerr) 29:156
Fell Back (Kerr) 29:157
Fell Down (Kerr) 29:158
Femi and Old Grandaddie (Pinkney) 43:155
Fenny, The Desert Fox (Baumann) 35:52
The Ferlie (Hunter) 25:77
Ferryboat (Betsy and Giulio Maestro) 45:78
A Few Fair Days (Gardam) 12:161
Fiddle-i-fee: A Traditional American Chant (Stanley) 46:129
Fiddlestrings (de Angeli) 1:53
The Fido Frame-Up (Singer) 48:125
Fierce: The Lion (Ness) 6:209
Fierce-Face, the Story of a Tiger (Mukerji) 10:135
Fifteen (Bunting) 28:47
Fifteen (Cleary) 2:46; 8:48
The Fifth of March: The Story of the Boston Massacre (Rinaldi) 46:87
Fifty Below Zero (Munsch) 19:145
Figgie Hobbin: Poems for Children (Causley) 30:34
Figgs and Phantoms (Raskin) 12:218
Fight against Albatross Two (Thiele) 27:207
The Fighting Ground (Avi) 24:11
Fighting Men: How Men Have Fought through the Ages (Treece) 2:184
Fighting Shirley Chisholm (Haskins) 3:64
Figleafing through History: The Dynamics of Dress (Harris) 47:82

The Figure in the Shadows (Bellairs) 37:9
Figure of 8: Narrative Poems (Causley) 30:33
A Figure of Speech (Mazer) 23:222
The Filthy Beast (Garfield) 21:109
Fin M'Coul: The Giant of Knockmany Hill (dePaola) 4:66
The Final Correction (McBratney) 44:118
The Final Test (Owen) 31:142
Find a Stranger, Say Goodbye (Lowry) 6:193
Find Out by Touching (Showers) 6:241
Find the Constellations (Rey) 5:196
Find the Hidden Insect (Cole) 5:66
Find the White Horse (King-Smith) 40:169
Find Waldo Now (Handford) 22:74
Find Your ABC's (Scarry) 41:166
Finders Keepers (Rodda) 32:212
Finding a Poem (Merriam) 14:196
Finding Home (Kherdian) 24:111
Finding Out about Jobs: TV Reporting (Bendick) 5:48
A Fine Boy for Killing (Needle) 43:133
A Fine White Dust (Rylant) 15:172
Finestkind O'Day: Lobstering in Maine (McMillan) 47:159
Finger Rhymes (Brown) 29:7
Fingers (Sleator) 29:203
Finishing Becca: The Story of Peggy Shippen and Benedict Arnold (Rinaldi) 46:89
Finn Family Moomintroll (Jansson) 2:93
The Finn Gang (Waddell) 31:179
Finn MacCool and the Small Men of Deeds (O'Shea) 18:169
Finn's Folly (Southall) 2:150
Finzel the Farsighted (Fleischman) 20:66
Fiona on the Fourteenth Floor (Allan) 43:12
Fire and Hemlock (Jones) 23:194
Fire Engine Shapes (McMillan) 47:170
Fire Fighters (Blumberg) 21:24
Fire! Fire! (Gibbons) 8:98
The Fire Game (Stine) 37:116
A Fire in My Hands: A Book of Poems (Soto) 38:195
The Fire in the Stone (Thiele) 27:205
Fire in Your Life (Adler) 27:5
The Fire Station (Munsch) 19:143
The Fire Station (Spier) 5:228
The Fire Stealer (Cleaver) 13:70
The Fire-Brother (Crossley-Holland) 47:31
Fireflies (Ryder) 37:85
The Firehouse (Spier) 5:228
The Firemen (Kotzwinkle) 6:180
Fires in the Sky: The Birth and Death of Stars (Gallant) 30:93
The Firetail Cat (McBratney) 44:130
Fireweed (Walsh) 2:198
Fireworks, Picnics, and Flags: The Story of the Fourth of July Symbols (Giblin) 29:88
The First ABC (Lear) 1:127
First Adventure (Coatsworth) 2:56
The First Book of Africa (Hughes) 17:43
The First Book of Airplanes (Bendick) 5:37
The First Book of Berlin: A Tale of a Divided City (Knight) 38:105
The First Book of Codes and Ciphers (Epstein and Epstein) 26:54
The First Book of Deserts: An Introduction to the Earth's Arid Lands (Knight) 38:100
The First Book of Electricity (Epstein and Epstein) 26:49
The First Book of England (Streatfeild) 17:194
The First Book of Fishes (Bendick) 5:41
The First Book of Glass (Epstein and Epstein) 26:52

The First Book of Hawaii (Epstein and Epstein) 26:51
The First Book of How to Fix It (Bendick) 5:39
The First Book of Italy (Epstein and Epstein) 26:55
The First Book of Jazz (Hughes) 17:40
The First Book of Maps and Globes (Epstein and Epstein) 26:56
The First Book of Mars: An Introduction to the Red Planet (Knight) 38:102
The First Book of Measurement (Epstein and Epstein) 26:57
The First Book of Medieval Man (Sobol) 4:206
The First Book of Mexico (Epstein and Epstein) 26:53
The First Book of Negroes (Hughes) 17:38
The First Book of News (Epstein and Epstein) 26:60
The First Book of Printing (Epstein and Epstein) 26:52
The First Book of Rhythms (Hughes) 17:40
The First Book of Ships (Bendick) 5:38
The First Book of Sound: A Basic Guide to the Science of Acoustics (Knight) 38:98
The First Book of Space Travel (Bendick) 5:37
The First Book of Supermarkets (Bendick) 5:37
The First Book of Teaching Machines (Epstein and Epstein) 26:58
The First Book of the Ballet (Streatfeild) 17:192
The First Book of the Caribbean (Hughes) 17:42
The First Book of the Ocean (Epstein and Epstein) 26:57
The First Book of the Opera (Streatfeild) 17:196
The First Book of the Sun (Knight) 38:106
The First Book of the West Indies (Hughes) 17:42
The First Book of the World Health Organization (Epstein and Epstein) 26:59
The First Book of Time (Bendick) 5:40
The First Book of Washington, D. C.: The Nation's Capital (Epstein and Epstein) 26:57
The First Book of Words: Their Family Histories (Epstein and Epstein) 26:50
The First Child (Wells) 16:203
The First Christmas (dePaola) 24:95
First Dates (Stine) 37:106
First Day of School (Oxenbury) 22:145
The First Days of Life (Freedman) 20:77
The First Dog (Brett) 27:41
The First Few Friends (Singer) 48:122
The First Four Years (Wilder) 2:205
First Graces (Tudor) 13:195
First Ladies (Blumberg) 21:25
First Ladybugs; First Grade Valentines; Hello, First Grade (Ryder) 37:99
A First Look at Birds (Selsam) 1:162
A First Look at Leaves (Selsam) 1:162
A First Look at Mammals (Selsam) 1:162
The First Margaret Mahy Story Book: Stories and Poems (Mahy) 7:181
The First Noel (Domanska) 40:53
The First Peko-Neko Bird (Krahn) 3:103
First Pink Light (Greenfield) 4:99; 38:82
First Prayers (Tudor) 13:193
The First Seven Days: The Story of the Creation from Genesis (Galdone) 16:91
First Snow (McCully) 46:60
The First Story (Brown) 10:55
The First Strawberries: A Cherokee Story (Bruchac) 46:13
First the Good News (Gaberman) 33:12
First There Was Frances (Graham) 31:95
The First Time I Saw Paris (Pilgrim) 43:9
The First Travel Guide to the Bottom of the Sea (Blumberg) 21:28

The First Travel Guide to the Moon: What to Pack, How to Go, and What to See When You Get There (Blumberg) **21**:26

The First Travel Guide to the Moon: What to Pack, How to Go, and What You Do When You Get There (Blumberg) **21**:26

The First Two Lives of Lukas-Kasha (Alexander) **5**:24

First Words (Burningham) **9**:51

The Fish (Bruna) **7**:49

Fish and How They Reproduce (Patent) **19**:149

Fish Eyes: A Book You Can Count On (Ehlert) **28**:112

Fish Facts and Bird Brains: Animal Intelligence (Sattler) **24**:220

Fish for Supper (Goffstein) **3**:58

A Fish Hatches (Cole) **5**:65

Fish Head (Fritz) **2**:80

Fish Is Fish (Lionni) **7**:133

The Fish with the Deep Sea Smile (Brown) **10**:48

The Fisherman under the Sea (Tresselt) **30**:212

The Fisherman's Son: Adapted from a Georgian Folktale (Ginsburg) **45**:13

"Fitting In": Animals in Their Habitats (Berger) **32**:15

Five Children and It (Nesbit) **3**:163

Five Dolls and the Duke (Clarke) **28**:80

Five Dolls and the Monkey (Clarke) **28**:75

Five Dolls and Their Friends (Clarke) **28**:80

Five Dolls in a House (Clarke) **28**:74

Five Dolls in the Snow (Clarke) **28**:76

Five Down: Numbers as Signs (Burningham) **9**:50

Five Finger Discount (DeClements) **23**:38

The Five Hundred (Dillon) **26**:31

Five Minutes' Peace (Murphy) **39**:173

Flambards (Peyton) **3**:172

Flambards in Summer (Peyton) **3**:173

The Flambards Trilogy (Peyton) **3**:173

Flame-Coloured Taffeta (Sutcliff) **37**:179

The Flash Children (Allan) **43**:27

Flash, Crash, Rumble, and Roll (Branley) **13**:32

Flash Eddie and the Big Bad Wolf (McBratney) **44**:129

Flash Flood (Thiele) **27**:205

Flash the Dash (Freeman) **30**:78

Fleas (Cole) **5**:62

The Fledgling (Langton) **33**:115

Fletcher and Zenobia Save the Circus (Gorey) **36**:94

Flicks (dePaola) **4**:63

Flies in the Water, Fish in the Air: A Personal Introduction to Fly Fishing (Arnosky) **15**:9

Flight 714 (Herge) **6**:149

The Flight of Dragons (Dickinson) **29**:49

Flight of Exiles (Bova) **3**:33

Flight to the Forest (Willard) **2**:218

Flight Today and Tomorrow (Hyde) **23**:153

Flint's Island (Wibberley) **3**:226

Flip-Flop and Tiger Snake (Thiele) **27**:205

Flipsville, Squaresville (Berenstain and Berenstain) **19**:25

Floating and Sinking (Branley) **13**:34

Flock of Watchbirds (Leaf) **25**:128

Flocks of Birds (Zolotow) **2**:234

The Flood at Reedsmere (Burton) **1**:31

Florina and the Wild Bird (Carigiet) **38**:70

Flossie and the Fox (McKissack) **23**:237

The Flower Mother (Calhoun) **42**:18

The Flower of Sheba (Orgel) **48**:94

A Flower with Love (Munari) **9**:130

Flowers of a Woodland Spring (Lerner) **34**:123

The Flowers of Adonis (Sutcliff) **37**:161

The Flute (Achebe) **20**:8

The Flute Book (Berger) **32**:9

Fly Away Home (Bunting) **28**:65

Fly Away Home (Noestlinger) **12**:185

Fly by Night (Jarrell) **6**:165

Fly High, Fly Low (Freeman) **30**:70

Fly Homer Fly (Peet) **12**:199

Fly into Danger (Phipson) **5**:184

Flyaway Girl (Grifalconi) **35**:78

Fly-by-Night (Peyton) **3**:176

The Flying Carpet (Brown) **12**:98

The Flying Fox Warriors (Roughsey and Trezise) **41**:141

Flying Jake (Smith) **47**:198

A Flying Saucer Full of Spaghetti (Krahn) **3**:104

The Flying Ship (Harris) **30**:117

Flying with the Eagle, Racing the Great Bear: Stories from Native North America (Bruchac) **46**:13

Fofana (Guillot) **22**:64

The Fog Comes on Little Pig Feet (Wells) **16**:204

Fog Hounds, Wind Cat, Sea Mice (Aiken) **19**:15

Fog in the Meadow (Ryder) **37**:85

Follow a Fisher (Pringle) **4**:178

Follow My Black Plume (Trease) **42**:186

Follow That Bus! (Hutchins) **20**:148

Follow the Dream: The Story of Christopher Columbus (Sis) **45**:165

Follow the Road (Tresselt) **30**:205

Follow the Water from Brook to Ocean (Dorros) **42**:68

Follow the Wind (Tresselt) **30**:204

The Followers (Bunting) **28**:48

Fonabio and the Lion (Guillot) **22**:69

Fondai and the Leopard-Men (Guillot) **22**:71

Food (Adler) **27**:26

The Food Market (Spier) **5**:228

The Fool (Garfield) **21**:109

The Fool of the World and the Flying Ship: A Russian Tale (Ransome) **8**:184

The Fools of Chelm and Their History (Singer) **1**:174

Football Fugitive (Christopher) **33**:51

Footprints at the Window (Naylor) **17**:56

For Always (Bunting) **28**:47

For Good Measure: The Story of Modern Measurement (Berger) **32**:3

For Me to Say: Rhymes of the Never Was and Always Is (McCord) **9**:101

For Pollution Fighters Only (Hyde) **23**:159

A for the Ark (Duvoisin) **23**:97

Forbidden Frontier (Harris) **47**:80

Forbidden Paths of Thual (Kelleher) **36**:115

Forest of the Night (Townsend) **2**:169

A Forest Year (Lerner) **34**:131

Forever (Blume) **2**:17; **15**:72

The Forever Christmas Tree (Uchida) **6**:253

Forever Free: The Story of the Emancipation Proclamation (Sterling) **1**:178

Forever Laughter (Freeman) **30**:77

The Forge in the Forest (Colum) **36**:35

Forgetful Fred (Williams) **8**:233

The Forgetful Wishing Well: Poems for Young People (Kennedy) **27**:100

A Formal Feeling (Oneal) **13**:157

A Formidable Enemy (Allan) **43**:23

The Fort of Gold (Dillon) **26**:22

Fortunately (Charlip) **8**:27

Fortune (Stanley) **46**:141

A Fortune for the Brave (Chauncy) **6**:89

The Fortune-Tellers (Alexander) **48**:23

Forward, Commandos! (Bianco) **19**:58

Fossils Tell of Long Ago (Aliki) **9**:21

Fossils: The Ice Ages (Gallant) **30**:100

Foster Care and Adoption (Hyde) **23**:168

The Foundling and Other Tales of Prydain (Alexander) **1**:13; **5**:22

The Fountain of Youth: Stories to Be Told (Colum) **36**:36

Four Ancestors (Bruchac) **46**:22

Four Brave Sailors (Ginsburg) **45**:18

The Four Corners of the World (Duvoisin) **23**:96

Four Days in the Life of Lisa (Noestlinger) **12**:187

Four Dolls (Godden) **20**:136

The Four Donkeys (Alexander) **1**:14

Four Fur Feet (Brown) **10**:67

The Four Grannies (Jones) **23**:190

Four Little Troubles (Marshall) **21**:171

Four on the Shore (Marshall) **21**:180

Four Rooms from the Metropolitan Museum of Art (Ness) **6**:208

The Four Seasons of Brambly Hedge (Barklem) **31**:6

Four Stories for Four Seasons (dePaola) **4**:59

The Four-Story Mistake (Enright) **4**:74

The Fourteenth Cadillac (Jackson) **28**:141

The Fourth Grade Wizards (DeClements) **23**:37

The Fourth Plane at the Flypast (Hamley) **47**:58

Fox All Week (Marshall) **21**:179

Fox and His Friends (Marshall) **21**:177

The Fox and the Cat: Animal Tales from Grimm (Crossley-Holland) **47**:44

The Fox and the Hare (Ginsburg) **45**:2

Fox at School (Marshall) **21**:177

The Fox Busters (King-Smith) **40**:139

Fox Eyes (Brown) **10**:61

The Fox Friend (Coatsworth) **2**:57

Fox Hill (Worth) **21**:223

The Fox Hole (Southall) **2**:151

Fox in Love (Marshall) **21**:177

Fox in Socks (Seuss) **1**:85; **9**:188

The Fox Jumps over the Parson's Gate (Caldecott) **14**:81

Fox on Wheels (Marshall) **21**:178

Fox Song (Bruchac) **46**:14

The Fox Steals Home (Christopher) **33**:52

The Fox Went Out on a Chilly Night: An Old Song (Spier) **5**:217

The Foxman (Paulsen) **19**:171

Fox's Dream (Tejima) **20**:203

Fractures, Dislocations, and Sprains (Nourse) **33**:142

Fragile Flag (Langton) **33**:116

Francis Fry, Private Eye (McBratney) **44**:129

Francis: The Poor Man of Assisi (dePaola) **24**:90

Frank and Ernest (Day) **22**:24

Frank and Ernest Play Ball (Day) **22**:26

Frank and Zelda (Kovalski) **34**:117

Frankie's Dad (Ure) **34**:184

Frankie's Hat (Mark) **11**:157

Frankie's Story (Waddell) **31**:189

Franklin and the Messy Pigs (Wilhelm) **46**:164

Franklin Stein (Raskin) **1**:155

Franzi and Gizi (Bianco) **19**:56

Freaky Friday (Rodgers) **20**:190

Freckle Juice (Blume) **15**:72

Freckly Feet and Itchy Knees (Rosen) **45**:140

Fred (Simmonds) **23**:243

Fred the Angel (Waddell) **31**:195

Frederick (Lionni) **7**:131

Frederick Douglass: Slave-Fighter-Freeman (Bontemps) **6**:83

Frederick Douglass: The Black Lion (McKissack) **23**:239

Frederick Sanger: The Man Who Mapped Out a Chemical of Life (Silverstein and Silverstein) **25**:202

Fred's Dream (Ahlberg and Ahlberg) **18**:3

Fred's First Day (Cummings) **48**:46

Free As I Know (Naidoo) **29**:165

Free Fall (Wiesner) **43**:205

Free to Be Muhammad Ali (Lipsyte) **23**:207

Freedom Comes to Mississippi: The Story of Reconstruction (Meltzer) **13**:127

Freedom Train: The Story of Harriet Tubman (Sterling) **1**:179

Freight Train (Crews) **7**:56

Das fremde Kind (Zwerger) **46**:194

French Postcards (Klein) **19**:91

The Frenzied Prince, Being Heroic Stories of Ancient Ireland (Colum) **36**:45

Fresh Brats (Kennedy) **27**:102

Fresh Paint: New Poems (Merriam) **14**:203

Freshwater Fish and Fishing (Arnosky) **15**:5

Freunde (Heine) **18**:147

Fried Feathers for Thanksgiving (Stevenson) **17**:165

Friedrich (Richter) **21**:187

The Friend (Burningham) **9**:47

Friend Dog (Adoff) **7**:36

A Friend for Dragon (Pilkey) **48**:101

A Friend Is Someone Who Likes You (Anglund) **1**:20

Friend Monkey (Travers) **2**:177

Friend: The Story of George Fox and the Quakers (Yolen) **4**:259

The Friendly Beasts: An Old English Christmas Carol (dePaola) **24**:89

The Friendly Wolf (Goble) **21**:131

The Friends (Guy) **13**:78

Friends (Heine) **18**:147

Friends (Oxenbury) **22**:141

The Friends Have a Visitor (Heine) **18**:149

The Friends' Racing Cart (Heine) **18**:149

Friends till the End: A Novel (Strasser) **11**:247

The Fright: Who's Talking? (Ure) **34**:184

Fritz and the Beautiful Horses (Brett) **27**:38

Frog and Toad All Year (Lobel) **5**:170

Frog and Toad Are Friends (Lobel) **5**:165

Frog and Toad Together (Lobel) **5**:167

Frog Goes to Dinner (Mayer) **11**:168

A Frog He Would A-Wooing Go (Caldecott) **14**:81

The Frog in the Well (Tresselt) **30**:207

The Frog Prince (Galdone) **16**:100

The Frog Prince, Continued (Scieszka) **27**:154

Frog Went A-Courtin' (Langstaff) **3**:109

Frog, Where Are You? (Mayer) **11**:165

The Frogmen (White) **3**:221

Frogs and Toads of the World (Simon) **39**:192

A Frog's Body (Cole) **5**:66

Frogs, Toads, Salamanders, and How They Reproduce (Patent) **19**:148

From a Child's Heart (Grimes) **42**:90

From Afar It Is an Island (Munari) **9**:129

From Anna (Little) **4**:151

From Flower to Flower: Animals and Pollination (Lauber) **16**:122

From Hand to Mouth: Or, How We Invented Knives, Forks, Spoons, and Chopsticks and the Table Manners to Go with Them (Giblin) **29**:90

From Lew Alcindor to Kareem Abdul Jabbar (Haskins) **3**:64

From Living Cells to Dinosaurs: Our Restless Earth (Gallant) **30**:101

From Log Roller to Lunar Rover: The Story of Wheels (Knight) **38**:115

From Pond to Prairie: The Changing World of a Pond and Its Life (Pringle) **4**:176

From Shore to Ocean Floor: How Life Survives in the Sea (Simon) **9**:207

From Spring to Spring: Poems and Photographs (Duncan) **29**:76

From Sputnik to Space Shuttles: Into the New Space Age (Branley) **13**:52

From the Mixed-Up Files of Mrs. Basil E. Frankweiler (Konigsburg) **1**:120

From the Thorenson Dykes (McBratney) **44**:119

Front Court Hex (Christopher) **33**:48

Front Porch Stories at the One-Room School (Tate) **37**:192

Frontier Living (Tunis) **2**:192

Frontier Wolf (Sutcliff) **37**:171

Fumio and the Dolphins (Nakatani) **30**:158

Fungus the Bogeyman (Briggs) **10**:26

Fungus the Bogeyman Plop-Up Book (Briggs) **10**:33

The Funniest Dinosaur Book Ever (Wilhelm) **46**:163

Funniest Storybook Ever (Scarry) **3**:183

Funny Bananas (McHargue) **2**:118

Funny, How the Magic Starts (McBratney) **44**:123

The Funny Side of Science (Berger) **32**:9

The Funny Thing (Gag) **4**:89

Funnybones (Ahlberg and Ahlberg) **18**:8

The Fur Seals of Pribilof (Scott) **20**:200

Furry (Keller) **45**:56

The Further Adventures of Nils (Lagerlof) **7**:110

The Further Adventures of Robinson Crusoe (Treece) **2**:184

Further Tales of Uncle Remus: The Misadventures of Brer Rabbit, Brer Fox, Brer Wolf, the Doodang and Other Creatures (Lester) **41**:108

Further Tales of Uncle Remus: The Misadventures of Brer Rabbit, Brer Fox, Brer Wolf, the Doodang and Other Creatures (Pinkney) **43**:165

Future Story (French) **37**:46

FutureLife: The Biotechnology Revolution (Silverstein and Silverstein) **25**:220

Futuretrack 5 (Westall) **13**:258

Gabriel's Girl (St. John) **46**:113

Gaby and the New Money Fraud (Berna) **19**:40

Gadabouts and Stick-at-Homes: Wild Animals and Their Habitats (Milne and Milne) **22**:123

The Gadget Book (Weiss) **4**:226

A Gaggle of Geese (Merriam) **14**:192

Galax-Arena (Rubinstein) **35**:213

Galaxies: Islands in Space (Knight) **38**:122

The Gales of Spring: Thomas Jefferson, the Years 1789-1801 (Wibberley) **3**:226

The Galloping Goat and Other Stories (Naylor) **17**:49

Gambling—Who Really Wins? (Haskins) **39**:36

The Game of Baseball (Epstein and Epstein) **26**:60

A Game of Catch (Cresswell) **18**:102

Game of Danger (Duncan) **29**:66

A Game of Soldiers (Needle) **43**:141

Games (Klein) **21**:162

Games and Puzzles You Can Make Yourself (Weiss) **4**:228

The Games the Indians Played (Lavine) **35**:153

The Garden of Abdul Gasazi (Van Allsburg) **5**:238

The Garden Shed (Keeping) **34**:97

The Garden under the Sea (Selden) **8**:196

The Gardens of Dorr (Biegel) **27**:31

"Garfield's Apprentices" (Garfield) **21**:109

A Garland of Games and Other Diversions: An Alphabet Book (Cooney) **23**:27

Garth Pig and the Ice Cream Lady (Rayner) **41**:122

Garth Pig Steals the Show (Rayner) **41**:129

Gary and the Very Terrible Monster (Williams) **48**:189

Gases (Cobb) **2**:65

Gatalop the Wonderful Ball (Baumann) **35**:52

The Gathering (Hamilton) **11**:82

The Gathering of Darkness (Fox) **44**:77

A Gathering of Days: A New England Girl's Journal 1830-32 (Blos) **18**:14

A Gathering of Gargoyles (Pierce) **20**:183

The Gats! (Goffstein) **3**:59

Gaudenzia, Pride of the Palio (Henry) **4**:113

Gavriel and Jemal: Two Boys of Jerusalem (Ashabranner) **28**:8

Gay-Neck, the Story of a Pigeon (Mukerji) **10**:131

General Store (Field) **21**:81

The Genetics Explosion (Silverstein and Silverstein) **25**:219

Gengoroh and the Thunder God (Tresselt) **30**:212

The Genie of Sutton Place (Selden) **8**:200

The Gentle Desert: Exploring an Ecosystem (Pringle) **4**:183

Gentlehands (Kerr) **29**:148

The Gentleman and the Kitchen Maid (Stanley) **46**:151

Gentleman Jim (Briggs) **10**:30

Geoffrey Strangeways (Murphy) **39**:177

Geography Can Be Fun (Leaf) **25**:132

Geological Disasters: Earthquakes and Volcanoes (Aylesworth) **6**:55

(George) (Konigsburg) **1**:120

George and Martha (Marshall) **21**:168

George and Martha Encore (Marshall) **21**:169

George and Martha, One Fine Day (Marshall) **21**:173

George and Martha Rise and Shine (Marshall) **21**:171

George and Martha, Tons of Fun (Marshall) **21**:175

George and Red (Coatsworth) **2**:57

George and the Cherry Tree (Aliki) **9**:18

George Shrinks (Joyce) **26**:83

George, the Babysitter (Hughes) **15**:122

George Washington (d'Aulaire and d'Aulaire) **21**:43

George Washington (Foster) **7**:93

George Washington and the Birth of Our Nation (Meltzer) **13**:151

George Washington's Breakfast (Fritz) **2**:81

George Washington's World (Foster) **7**:91

George's Marvelous Medicine (Dahl) **7**:80

Georgie Has Lost His Cap (Munari) **9**:125

Geraldine First (Keller) **45**:61

Geraldine, the Music Mouse (Lionni) **7**:138

Geraldine's Baby Brother (Keller) **45**:59

Geraldine's Big Snow (Keller) **45**:51

Geraldine's Blanket (Keller) **45**:46

Gerbils: All about Them (Silverstein and Silverstein) **25**:213

Germfree Life: A New Field in Biological Research (Silverstein and Silverstein) **25**:203

Germs! (Patent) **19**:159

Germs Make Me Sick! (Berger) **32**:33

Gertrude the Goose Who Forgot (Galdone) **16**:101

De geschiedenis van Noord-America (Haar) **15**:114

Get On Board: The Story of the Underground Railroad (Haskins) **39**:70

Get Ready for Robots! (Lauber) **16**:123

Get Set! Go! Overcoming Obstacles (Watanabe) **8**:216

Get Well, Clown-Arounds! (Cole) **40**:3

Get-a-Way and Hary Janos (Petersham and Petersham) **24**:164

Getting Along in Your Family (Naylor) **17**:52

Getting Along with Your Friends (Naylor) **17**:54

Getting Along with Your Teachers (Naylor) **17**:55

Getting Born (Freedman) **20**:79

Ghastlies, Goops and Pincushions: Nonsense Verse (Kennedy) **27**:102

The Ghastly Gertie Swindle, With the Ghosts of Hungryhouse Lane (McBratney) **44**:128

Ghond, the Hunter (Mukerji) **10**:132

The Ghost and Bertie Boggin (Waddell) **31**:177

The Ghost Belonged to Me (Peck) **15**:154

The Ghost Children (Bunting) **28**:63

The Ghost Dance Caper (Hughes) **9**:70

Ghost Doll (McMillan) **47**:164

The Ghost Downstairs (Garfield) **21**:105

The Ghost Girl (Waddell) **31**:183

Ghost Host (Singer) **48**:132

Ghost in a Four-Room Apartment (Raskin) **1**:156

Ghost in the House (Cohen) **43**:57

The Ghost in the Mirror (Bellairs) **37**:26

The Ghost in the Noonday Sun (Fleischman) **1**:74

Ghost Lane (Curry) **31**:83

The Ghost of Skinny Jack (Lindgren) **39**:162

Ghost of Summer (Bunting) **28**:46

The Ghost of Thomas Kempe (Lively) **7**:154

The Ghost on Saturday Night (Fleischman) **15**:107

Ghost Paddle: A Northwest Coast Indian Tale (Houston) **3**:85

Ghost Sitter (Mattingley) **24**:127

Ghostly Companions (Alcock) **26**:4

Ghostly Companions: A Feast of Chilling Tales (Alcock) **26**:4

Ghostly Tales of Love and Revenge (Cohen) **43**:55

Ghost's Hour, Spook's Hour (Bunting) **28**:61

Ghosts I Have Been (Peck) **15**:159

The Ghosts of Cougar Island (Parish) **22**:168

The Ghosts of Departure Point (Bunting) **28**:54

The Ghosts of Glencoe (Hunter) **25**:76

The Ghosts of Hungryhouse Lane (McBratney) **44**:122

The Ghosts of Now (Nixon) **24**:145

The Ghosts of Stone Hollow (Snyder)
  See *The Truth about Stone Hollow*

Ghosts of the Deep (Cohen) **43**:56

The Ghosts of War (Cohen) **43**:52

The Ghosts The Indians Feared (Lavine) **35**:156

The Giant (Pene du Bois) **1**:63

Giant Cold (Dickinson) **29**:55

The Giant Colour Book of Mathematics: Exploring the World of Numbers and Space (Adler) **27**:15

The Giant Devil-Dingo (Roughsey) **41**:140

The Giant Golden Book of Cat Stories (Coatsworth) **2**:57

The Giant Golden Book of Mathematics: Exploring the World of Numbers and Space (Adler) **27**:14

Giant John (Lobel) **5**:163

The Giant Panda at Home (Rau) **8**:188

The Giant Planets (Nourse) **33**:138

The Giant Squid (Bunting) **28**:52

The Giants' Farm (Yolen) **4**:263

The Giants Go Camping (Yolen) **4**:265

The Giant's Toe (Cole) **18**:83

Gidja the Moon (Roughsey and Trezise) **41**:141

The Gift (Dickinson) **29**:43

The Gift (Nixon) **24**:143

A Gift for Mama (Hautzig) **22**:85

A Gift for Sula Sula (Ness) **6**:201

A Gift from St. Francis: The First Crèche (Cole) **40**:25

Gift from the Sky (Milne and Milne) **22**:119

The Gift of a Lamb: A Shepherd's Tale of the First Christmas Told as a Verse-Play (Causley) **30**:40

A Gift of Magic (Duncan) **29**:69

The Gift of Sarah Barker (Yolen) **4**:267

The Gift of the Magi (Zwerger) **46**:190

The Gift of the Sacred Dog (Goble) **21**:133

The Gift of the Tree (Tresselt) **30**:214

The Gift-Giver (Hansen) **21**:150

Gigi cerca il suo berretto (Munari) **9**:125

Gilberto and the Wind (Ets) **33**:88

Gimme a Kiss (Pike) **29**:172

Ginger Pye (Estes) **2**:73

The Gingerbread Boy (Galdone) **16**:100

The Gingerbread Rabbit (Jarrell) **6**:158

Giorgio's Village (dePaola) **24**:91

Gip in the Television Set (Rodari) **24**:207

A Giraffe and a Half (Silverstein) **5**:209

The Giraffe and the Pelly and Me (Dahl) **31**:25; **41**:35

The Giraffe in Pepperell Street (Klein) **21**:158

Giraffe: The Silent Giant (Schlein) **41**:187

Giraffes, the Sentinels of the Savannas (Sattler) **24**:224

The Girl and the Goatherd; or, This and That and Thus and So (Ness) **6**:205

A Girl Called Boy (Hurmence) **25**:93

The Girl Called Moses: The Story of Harriet Tubman (Petry) **12**:210

The Girl in the Golden Bower (Yolen) **44**:202

The Girl in the Opposite Bed (Arundel) **35**:15

The Girl in the Painting (Bunting) **28**:47

A Girl like Abby (Irwin) **40**:111

Girl Missing: A Novel (Noestlinger) **12**:186

The Girl of His Dreams (Mazer) **16**:133

The Girl of the Golden Gate (Garner) **20**:116

The Girl on the Outside (Walter) **15**:205

The Girl Who Cried Flowers and Other Tales (Yolen) **4**:260

The Girl Who Loved the Wind (Yolen) **4**:260

The Girl Who Loved Wild Horses (Goble) **21**:131

The Girl Who Married the Moon: Stories from Native North America (Bruchac) **46**:16

The Girl Who Sat By the Ashes (Colum) **36**:24

The Girl Who Wanted a Boy (Zindel) **45**:194

The Girl Who Would Rather Climb Trees (Schlein) **41**:186

The Girl without a Name (Beckman) **25**:12

The Girlfriend (Stine) **37**:116

The Girls and Yanga Marshall (Berry) **22**:8

Girls Can Be Anything (Klein) **2**:98

Giselle (Ottley) **16**:184

Give and Take (Klein) **19**:96

Give Dad My Best (Collier) **3**:45

The Giver (Lowry) **46**:43

Giving Away Suzanne (Duncan) **29**:66

The Giving Tree (Silverstein) **5**:209

The Gizmo (Jennings) **40**:128

Glaciers: Nature's Frozen Rivers (Nixon) **24**:140

Glasblasarns Barn (Gripe) **5**:144

The Glassblower's Children (Gripe) **5**:144

Glasses and Contact Lenses: Your Guide to Eyes, Eyewear, and Eye Care (Silverstein and Silverstein) **25**:226

Glasses—Who Needs 'Em? (Smith) **47**:201

The Glassmakers (Fisher) **18**:121

Glimpses of Louisa (Alcott) **1**:9

Gloria Chipmunk, Star! (Nixon) **24**:140

The Glorious Flight: Across the Channel with Louis Blériot July 25, 1909 (Provensen and Provensen) **11**:215

The Glory Girl (Byars) **16**:59

Glory in the Flower (St. John) **46**:100

Die Glücklichen Inseln Hinter dem Winde (Kruss) **9**:83

Die Glücklichen Inseln Hinter dem Winde Bd. 2 (Kruss) **9**:84

Glue Fingers (Christopher) **33**:49

Gluskabe and the Four Wishes (Bruchac) **46**:18

Gnasty Gnomes (Stine) **37**:105

The Gnats of Knotty Pine (Peet) **12**:203

Go and Hush the Baby (Byars) **1**:35

Go Away, Stay Away! (Haley) **21**:145

Go Fish (Cummings) **48**:51

Go Jump in the Pool! (Korman) **25**:105

Go Saddle the Sea (Aiken) **19**:11

The Goats (Cole) **18**:84

Gobble, Growl, Grunt (Spier) **5**:220

The Goblin under the Stairs (Calhoun) **42**:13

The Goblins Giggle and Other Stories (Bang) **8**:17

The God beneath the Sea (Garfield) **21**:102

The God Beneath the Sea (Keeping) **34**:94

God Bless the Gargoyles (Pilkey) **48**:114

God is in the Mountain (Keats) **35**:131

God Wash the World and Start Again (Graham) **10**:109

Godfather Cat and Mousie (Orgel) **48**:88

God's Radar (Gaberman) **33**:11

God's Trombones: Seven Negro Sermons in Verse (Johnson) **32**:165

Goggle-Eyes (Fine) **25**:23

Goggles! (Keats) **1**:114; **35**:135

Going Back (Lively) **7**:159

Going Backwards (Klein) **19**:98

Going Home (Mohr) **22**:134

Going on a Whale Watch (McMillan) **47**:181

Going Over to Your Place: Poems for Each Other (Janeczko) **47**:105

Going Solo (Dahl) **41**:37

Going Up!: A Color Counting Book (Sis) **45**:162

Going West (Waddell) **31**:181

Gold and Gods of Peru (Baumann) **35**:46

Gold Dust (McCaughrean) **38**:150

Gold: The Fascinating Story of the Noble Metal through the Ages (Cohen) **3**:40

The Golden Age (Grahame) **5**:126

The Golden Basket (Bemelmans) **6**:64

The Golden Brothers (Garner) **20**:116

The Golden Bunny and 17 Other Stories and Poems (Brown) **10**:63

The Golden Collar (Clarke) **28**:75

The Golden Door: The United States from 1865 to 1918 (Asimov) **12**:54

The Golden Egg Book (Brown) **10**:55

The Golden Fleece and the Heroes Who Lived Before Achilles (Colum) **36**:25

The Golden Heart of Winter (Singer) **48**:139

The Golden One (Treece) **2**:185

The Golden Pasture (Thomas) **19**:221

The Golden Road (Montgomery) **8**:136

The Golden Serpent (Myers) **4**:160

The Golden Shadow (Garfield) **21**:106

The Golden Stick (Paulsen) **19**:171

The Golden Sword of Dragonwalk (Stine) **37**:107

Goldengrove (Walsh) **2**:199

Gold-Fever Trail: A Klondike Adventure (Hughes) **9**:68

Goldie, the Dollmaker (Goffstein) **3**:59

Goldilocks and the Three Bears (Brett) **27**:41

Goldilocks and the Three Bears (Marshall) **21**:184

Golly Gump Swallowed a Fly (Cole) **5**:68

The Golly Sisters Go West (Byars) **16**:63

A Gondola for Fun (Weiss) **4**:220

Gone Is Gone; or, The Story of a Man Who Wanted to Do Housework (Gag) **4**:90

Gone-Away Lake (Enright) **4**:75

Gonna Sing My Head Off! American Folk Songs for Children (Krull) **44**:102

Good Dog, Carl (Day) **22**:24

Good Ethan (Fox) **1**:77

The Good Friends (Bianco) **19**:54

The Good Giants and the Bad Pukwudgies (Fritz) **14**:117

Good Griselle (Yolen) **44**:203

Good Hunting, Blue Sky (Parish) **22**:154

Good Hunting, Little Indian (Parish) **22**:154

The Good Knight Ghost (Bendick) **5**:38

Good Luck Duck (DeJong) **1**:57

Good Luck to the Rider (Phipson) **5**:177

The Good Master (Seredy) **10**:171

Good Morning (Bruna) **7**:53

Good Morning (Oxenbury) **22**:143

Good Morning, Baby Bear (Hill) **13**:95

Good News (Cummings) **48**:43

Good News (Greenfield) **4**:96

Good Night (Oxenbury) **22**;143

Good Night, Fred (Wells) **16**:211

Good Night, Owl! (Hutchins) **20**:146

Good Night, Prof, Dear (Townsend) **2**:170

Good Night to Annie (Merriam) **14**:200

Good Old James (Donovan) **3**:51

Good Queen Bess: The Story of Elizabeth I of England (Stanley) **46**:143

Good Rhymes, Good Times (Hopkins) **44**:98

Good, Says Jerome (Clifton) **5**:55

The Good Side of My Heart (Rinaldi) **46**:80

The Good, the Bad, and the Goofy (Smith) **47**:202

Good Work, Amelia Bedelia (Parish) **22**:162

Goodbye, Charlie (Bunting) **28**:44

Good-bye, Chicken Little (Byars) **16**:56

Goodbye Max (Keller) **45**:49

Good-bye to the Jungle (Townsend) **2**:171

The Goodbye Walk (Ryder) **37**:100

The Good-Byes of Magnus Marmalade (Orgel) **48**:75

The Good-for-Nothing Prince (Williams) **8**:230

The Good-Luck Pencil (Stanley) **46**:136

Goodnight (Hoban) **3**:77

Goodnight Kiss (Stine) **37**:118

Goodnight Moon (Brown) **10**:55

Goody Hall (Babbitt) **2**:6

Goofbang Value Daze (Thompson) **24**:232

A Goose on Your Grave (Aiken) **19**:18

A Gopher in the Garden, and Other Animal Poems (Prelutsky) **13**:163

Gordon the Goat (Leaf) **25**:127

Gorey Posters (Gorey) **36**:99

The Gorgon's Head: The Story of Perseus (Serraillier) **2**:138

Gorilla (Browne) **19**:67

Gorilla (McClung) **11**:194

Gorky Rises (Steig) **15**:197

Gowie Corby Plays Chicken (Kemp) **29**:115

Graham Oakley's Magical Changes (Oakley) **7**:219

Grammar Can Be Fun (Leaf) **25**:115

Gran and Grandpa (Oxenbury) **22**:145

Un gran pequeño (Sanchez-Silva) **12**:232

Grand Constructions (Ventura) **16**:195

Grand Papa and Ellen Aroon (Monjo) **2**:121

Grandad's Magic (Graham) **31**:99

Grandfather (Baker) **28**:19

Grandfather Learns to Drive (Kruss) **9**:88

Grandfather's Dream (Keller) **45**:58

Grandfather's Trolley (McMillan) **47**:189

Le grandi costruzioni (Ventura) **16**:195

Grandma and Grandpa (Oxenbury) **22**:145

The Grandma in the Apple Tree 80 (Orgel) **48**:80

The Grandma Mixup (McCully) **46**:62

Grandma Moses: Painter of Rural America (Oneal) **13**:160

Grandmama's Joy (Greenfield) **38**:83

Grandmas at Bat (McCully) **46**:68

Grandmas at the Lake (McCully) **46**:65

Grandma's Bill (Waddell) **31**:198

Grandmother (Baker) **28**:19

Grandmother Cat and the Hermit (Coatsworth) **2**:58

Grandmother's Journey (Unnerstad) **36**:192

Grandpa and Bo (Henkes) **23**:127

Grandpa's Face (Greenfield) **38**:87

Grandpa's Great City Tour: An Alphabet Book (Stevenson) **17**:160

Grandpa's Wonderful Glass (Epstein and Epstein) **26**:58

Granny and the Desperadoes (Parish) **22**:159

Granny and the Indians (Parish) **22**:157

The Granny Project (Fine) **25**:20

Granny Reardun (Garner) **20**:113

Granny, the Baby, and the Big Gray Thing (Parish) **22**:161

Granny Was a Buffer Girl (Doherty) **21**:57

Granpa (Burningham) **9**:52

Graphology: A Guide to Handwriting Analysis (Aylesworth) **6**:53

The Grass-Eaters (Paulsen) **19**:170

Grasshopper on the Road (Lobel) **5**:172

A Grateful Nation: The Story of Arlington National Cemetery (Ashabranner) **28**:15

Graven Images: 3 Stories (Fleischman) **20**:64

Gravity Is a Mystery (Branley) **13**:36

The Gray Kangaroo at Home (Rau) **8**:189

The Great Airship Mystery: A UFO of the 1890s (Cohen) **43**:39

The Great American Crazies (Haskins) **39**:34

The Great American Gold Rush (Blumberg) **21**:30

The Great Ball Game: A Muskogee Story (Bruchac) **46**:15

The Great Ballagundi Damper Bake (Mattingley) **24**:124

Great Big Air Book (Scarry) **41**:164

The Great Big Car and Truck Book (Scarry) **41**:160

The Great Big Especially Beautiful Easter Egg (Stevenson) **17**:159

Great Big Schoolhouse (Scarry) **41**:163

The Great Blueness and Other Predicaments (Lobel) **5**:165

The Great Brain (Fitzgerald) **1**:69

The Great Brain at the Academy (Fitzgerald) **1**:69

The Great Brain Reforms (Fitzgerald) **1**:69

The Great Duffy (Krauss) **42**:110

The Great Flood (Spier) **5**:224

The Great Flood Mystery (Curry) **31**:84

The Great Gatenby (Marsden) **34**:149

Great Ghosts (Cohen) **43**:53

The Great Gilly Hopkins (Paterson) **7**:235

Great Gran Gorilla and the Robbers (Waddell) **31**:192

The Great Green Mouse Disaster (Waddell) **31**:179

The Great Heritage (Shippen) **36**:169

The Great Houdini: Magician Extraordinary (Epstein and Epstein) **26**:46

Great Ideas of Science: The Men and the Thinking behind Them (Asimov) **12**:45

The Great Land of the Elephants (Guillot) **22**:71

The Great Marathon Football Match (Ahlberg and Ahlberg) **18**:3

The Great Millionaire Kidnap (Mahy) **7**:184

Great Northern? (Ransome) **8**:182

Great Painters (Ventura) **16**:197

The Great Pie Robbery (Scarry) **41**:164

The Great Piratical Rumbustification & The Librarian and the Robbers (Mahy) **7**:185

The Great Quarterback Switch (Christopher) **33**:57

The Great Race of the Birds and Animals (Goble) **21**:134

The Great Rip-off (St. John) **46**:116

The Great Sleigh Robbery (Foreman) **32**:86

Great Steamboat Mystery (Scarry) **41**:167

The Great Waldo Search (Handford) **22**:75

The Great Wall of China (Fisher) **18**:134

The Great Watermelon Birthday (Williams) **9**:231

The Great Wheel (Lawson) **2**:109

The Great White Shark (Bunting) **28**:53

Greedy Greeny (Gantos) **18**:142

Greek Myths (McCaughrean) **38**:148

The Greeks (Asimov) **12**:38

Green Blades Rising: The Anglo-Saxons (Crossley-Holland) **47**:32

The Green Children (Crossley-Holland) **47**:24

The Green Coat (Gripe) **5**:148

Green Darner: The Story of a Dragonfly (Lerner) **34**:124

Green Darner: The Story of a Dragonfly (McClung) **11**:180

Green Eggs and Ham (Seuss) **1**:86; **9**:185

Green Finger House (Harris) **30**:120

The Green Flash and Other Tales of Horror, Suspense, and Fantasy (Aiken) **1**:4

The Green Futures of Tycho (Sleator) **29**:202

Green Grass and White Milk (Aliki) **9**:23

Green Grows the Garden (Bianco) **19**:55

The Green Kids (McBratney) **44**:125

The Green Laurel (Spence) **26**:192

The Green Man (Haley) **21**:146

The Green Piper (Kelleher) **36**:121

Green Says Go (Emberley) **5**:96

Green Street (Arundel) **35**:9

The Greengage Summer (Godden) **20**:128

The Greentail Mouse (Lionni) **7**:135

Greenwitch (Cooper) **4**:45

Greetings from Sandy Beach (Graham) **31**:100

Gregory Griggs and Other Nursery Rhyme People (Lobel) **5**:172

The Gremlins (Dahl) **7**:68

Greta the Strong (Sobol) **4**:209

The Grey Gentlemen (Ende) **14**:97

The Grey King (Cooper) **4**:47

The Grey Lady and the Strawberry Snatcher (Bang) **8**:20

Greyling: A Picture Story from the Islands of Shetland (Yolen) **4**:257

Griffin's Castle (Nimmo) **44**:153

Grishka and the Bear (Guillot) **22**:61

The Groober (Byars) **1**:36

Grossvater Lerner auf Fahren (Kruss) **9**:88

The Grouchy Ladybug (Carle) **10**:81

The Grounding of Group 6 (Thompson) **24**:227

The Grove of Green Holly (Willard) **2**:218

Grover (Cleaver and Cleaver) **6**:104

Growin' (Grimes) **42**:89

Growing Colors (McMillan) **47**:171

Growing Pains: Diaries and Drawings for the Years 1908-1917 (Gag) **4**:91

Growing Season (Carter) **22**:17

The Growing Story (Krauss) **42**:110

The Growing Summer (Streatfeild)
See *The Magic Summer*

The Growing Summer (Streatfeild) **17**:196

Growing Up Wild: How Young Animals Survive (Freedman) **20**:77

Growing Vegetable Soup (Ehlert) **28**:110

The Guard Mouse (Freeman) **30**:75

The Guardian Angels (Haskins) **39**:44

The Guardian Circle (Buffie) **39**:25

The Guardian of Isis (Hughes) **9**:73

The Guardians (Christopher) **2**:39

Guarneri: Story of a Genius (Wibberley) **3**:227

Guess How Much I Love You (McBratney) **44**:126

The Guest (Marshall) **21**:171

Guests in the Promised Land (Hunter) **3**:98

Guillot's African Folk Tales (Guillot) **22**:68

Guilt and Gingerbread (Garfield) **21**:117

Guinea Pigs: All about Them (Silverstein and Silverstein) **25**:206

The Guizer: A Book of Fools (Garner) **20**:112

Gull Number 737 (George) **1**:89

The Gulls of Smuttynose Island (Scott) **20**:196

Gumdrop and the Dinosaur (Biro) **28**:39

Gumdrop and the Farmer's Friend (Biro) **28**:30

Gumdrop and the Monster (Biro) **28**:38

Gumdrop and the Pirates (Biro) **28**:40

Gumdrop and the Secret Switches (Biro) **28**:34

Gumdrop and the Steamroller (Biro) **28**:33

Gumdrop at Sea (Biro) **28**:36

Gumdrop Finds a Friend (Biro) **28**:32

Gumdrop Finds a Ghost (Biro) **28**:33

Gumdrop Gets His Wings (Biro) **28**:33

Gumdrop Goes Fishing (Biro) **28**:36

Gumdrop Goes to London (Biro) **28**:32

Gumdrop Has a Birthday (Biro) **28**:33

Gumdrop Has a Tummy Ache (Biro) **28**:36

Gumdrop Is the Best Car (Biro) **28**:36

Gumdrop on the Brighton Run (Biro) **28**:33

Gumdrop on the Farm (Biro) **28**:36

Gumdrop on the Move (Biro) **28**:31

Gumdrop Posts a Letter (Biro) **28**:33

Gumdrop: The Story of a Vintage Car (Biro) **28**:30

Gumdrop's Magic Journey (Biro) **28**:36

Guy Lenny (Mazer) **16**:128

Gyo Fujikawa's A to Z Picture Book (Fujikawa) **25**:38

Gyo Fujikawa's Come Follow Me...to the Secret World of Elves and Fairies and Gnomes and Trolls (Fujikawa) **25**:40

Gyo Fujikawa's Oh, What a Busy Day! (Fujikawa) **25**:38

Gypsy (Seredy) **10**:179

Gypsy Gold (Worth) **21**:223

Gypsy Moth: Its History in America (McClung) **11**:188

H. M. S. Hood vs. Bismarck: The Battleship Battle (Taylor) **30**:191

The Ha Ha Bonk Book (Ahlberg and Ahlberg) **18**:8

Hadassah: Esther the Orphan Queen (Armstrong) **1**:22

Haircuts for the Woolseys (dePaola) **24**:102

Hairs in the Palm of the Hand (Mark) **11**:151

Hairy Tales and Nursery Crimes (Rosen) **45**:133

Hakon of Rogen's Saga (Haugaard) **11**:102

Hakon's Saga (Haugaard) **11**:102

Half a Moon and One Whole Star (Pinkney) **43**:159

Half a World Away (Chauncy) **6**:91

Half Magic (Eager) **43**:80

Half-a-Ball-of-Kenki: An Ashanti Tale Retold (Aardema) **17**:6

The Half-a-Moon Inn (Fleischman) **20**:63

Halfway Across the Galaxy and Turn Left (Klein) **21**:161

Hallapoosa (Peck) **45**:121

Halley: Comet 1986 (Branley) **13**:48

Halloween (Gibbons) **8**:99

Halloween ABC (Smith) **47**:197

Halloween Howls: Riddles That Are a Scream (Betsy and Giulio Maestro) **45**:72

Halloween Night (Stine) **37**:122

Halloween Party (Stine) **37**:114

Halloween Treats (Haywood) **22**:104

The Hallo-Wiener (Pilkey) **48**:112

Hamilton (Peck) **45**:109

The Hamish Hamilton Book of Goblins (Garner) **20**:108

The Hammerhead Light (Thiele) **27**:207

The Hand of Apollo (Coatsworth) **2**:58

Hand Rhymes (Brown) **29**:13

A Handful of Thieves (Bawden) **2**:11

A Handful of Time (Pearson) **26**:176

Handles (Mark) **11**:155

Handmade in America: The Heritage of Colonial Craftsman (Lavine) **35**:149

The Hand-Me-Down Kid (Pascal) **25**:184

Handtalk: An ABC of Finger Spelling and Sign Language (Charlip) **8**:31

Hang a Thousand Trees with Ribbons: The Story of Phillis Wheatley (Rinaldi) **46**:92

Hang for Treason (Peck) **45**:107

Hang on, Hopper! (Pfister) **42**:139

Hang Tough, Paul Mather (Slote) **4**:200

Hangin' Out with Cici (Pascal) **25**:183

Hangin' Out with Cici; or, My Mother Was Never a Kid (Pascal) **25**:183

Hanging On: How Animals Carry Their Young (Freedman) **20**:78

Hansel and Gretel (Browne) **19**:64

Hansel and Gretel (Galdone) **16**:104

Hansel and Gretel (Jeffers) **30**:134

Hansel and Gretel (Zwerger) **46**:188

Hansel and Gretel and Other Stories (Nielsen) **16**:157

Hansi (Bemelmans) **6**:63

Happy Birthday, Baabee (Khalsa) **30**:144

The Happy Birthday Letter (Flack) **28**:130

The Happy Birthday Mystery (Nixon) **24**:139

Happy Birthday, Sam (Hutchins) **20**:149

Happy Birthday to You! (Seuss) **9**:185

Happy Birthday with Ant and Bee (Banner) **24**:19

The Happy Day (Krauss) **42**:112

Happy Days at Bullerby (Lindgren) **39**:150

The Happy Funeral (Bunting) **28**:53

The Happy Hedgehog Band (Waddell) **31**:200

The Happy Hocky Family! (Smith) **47**:204

The Happy Hunter (Duvoisin) **23**:102

The Happy Islands behind the Winds (Kruss) **9**:83

The Happy Lion (Duvoisin) **23**:99

The Happy Place (Bemelmans) **6**:69

Happy Times in Noisy Village (Lindgren) **1**:137; **39**:150

Happy Valentine's Day, Emma! (Stevenson) **17**:167

Happy's Christmas (Gramatky) **22**:45

Harbor (Crews) **7**:60

Harbour (Crews) **7**:60

Hard Drive to Short (Christopher) **33**:43

The Hard Life of the Teenager (Collier) **3**:45

The Hare and the Bear and Other Stories (Tresselt) **30**:214

The Hare and the Tortoise (Galdone) **16**:92

The Hare and the Tortoise (Wildsmith) **2**:212

The Hare and the Tortoise & The Tortoise and the Hare / La Liebre y la Tortuga & La Tortuga y la Liebre (Pene du Bois) **1**:63

Hare's Choice (Hamley) **47**:60

The Hare's Race (Baumann) **35**:56

Hari, the Jungle Lad (Mukerji) **10**:131

Harlequin and the Gift of Many Colors (Charlip) **8**:29

Harlequinade (Streatfeild) **17**:189

Harnessing the Sun: The Story of Solar Energy (Knight) **38**:118

Harold Urey: The Man Who Explored from Earth to Moon (Silverstein and Silverstein) **25**:204

Harpoon of the Hunter (Markoosie) **23**:211-13

Harquin: The Fox Who Went Down to the Valley (Burningham) **9**:41

Harriet and the Crocodiles (Waddell) **31**:180

Harriet and the Flying Teachers (Waddell) **31**:189

Harriet and the Haunted School (Waddell) **31**:182

Harriet and the Robot (Waddell) **31**:185

Harriet at Play (Betsy and Giulio Maestro) **45**:74

Harriet at School (Betsy and Giulio Maestro) **45**:74

Harriet at Work (Betsy and Giulio Maestro) **45**:74

Harriet Goes to the Circus: A Number Concept Book (Betsy and Giulio Maestro) **45**:67

Harriet Reads Signs and More Signs: A Word Concept Book (Betsy and Giulio Maestro) **45**:70

Harriet: The Life and World of Harriet Beecher Stowe (St. John) **46**:125

Harriet the Spy (Fitzhugh) **1**:71

Harriet Tubman, Conductor on the Underground Railroad (Petry) **12**:210

Harriet Tubman: Guide to Freedom (Epstein and Epstein) **26**:61

Harriet's Hare (King-Smith) **40**:172

Harry and Hortense at Hormone High (Zindel) **45**:195

Harry and Tuck (Keller) **45**:57

Harry Cat's Pet Puppy (Selden) **8**:200

Harry's Mad (King-Smith) **40**:146

Harum Scarum: The Little Hare Book (Janosch) **26**:81

Has Anyone Here Seen William? (Graham) **31**:99

The Hat (Ungerer) **3**:200

Hatchet (Paulsen) **19**:177

Hating Alison Ashley (Klein) **21**:161

The Hating Book (Zolotow) **2**:234

The Hatters (Fisher) **18**:122

Hattie and the Fox (Fox) **23**:114

Hattie the Backstage Bat (Freeman) **30**:77

Haunted House (Hughes) **15**:123

Haunted House (Parish) **22**:159

Haunted House (Pienkowski) **6**:230

Haunted Island (Nixon) **24**:149

The Haunted Mountain (Hunter) **25**:80

The Haunted Souvenir Warehouse: Eleven Tales of Unusual Hauntings (Knight) **38**:121

Haunted United (Hamley) **47**:59

The Haunters of the Silences: A Book of Animal Life (Roberts) **33**:199

The Haunting (Mahy) **7**:187

The Haunting of Cassie Palmer (Alcock) **26**:2

The Haunting of Chas McGill and Other Stories (Westall) **13**:257

The Haunting of Ellen: A Story of Suspense (Waddell)
See *The Back House Ghosts*

The Haunting of Frances Rain (Buffie) **39**:15

The Haunting of Kildoran Abbey (Bunting) **28**:47
The Haunting of SafeKeep (Bunting) **28**:58
Have a Happy Measle, a Merry Mumps, and a Cheery Chickenpox (Bendick) **5**:38
Have You Seen Josephine? (Poulin) **28**:193
Have You Seen My Cat? (Carle) **10**:77
Havelok the Dane (Crossley-Holland) **47**:22
Havelok the Dane (Serraillier) **2**:139
Hawk, I'm Your Brother (Baylor) **3**:15
The Hawk that Dare Not Hunt by Day (O'Dell) **16**:171
Hawk's Vision (Hamley) **47**:65
The Hawkstone (Williams) **8**:231
Hazardous Substances: A Reference (Berger) **32**:37
Hazel Rye (Cleaver and Cleaver) **6**:114
Hazel's Amazing Mother (Wells) **16**:213
He Bear, She Bear (Berenstain and Berenstain) **19**:29
A Head Full of Hats (Fisher) **18**:121
Head in the Clouds (Southall) **2**:152
Headaches: All about Them (Silverstein and Silverstein) **25**:222
The Headless Cupid (Snyder) **31**:158
The Headless Horseman Rides Tonight: More Poems to Trouble Your Sleep (Prelutsky) **13**:168
Healer (Dickinson) **29**:54
Health Can Be Fun (Leaf) **25**:127
Hear Your Heart (Showers) **6**:243
Heart Disease (Silverstein and Silverstein) **25**:214
Heart Disease: America's <crs>1 Killer (Silverstein and Silverstein) **25**:214
The Heart of Stone (Orgel) **48**:74
Heartbeat (Mazer and Mazer) **23**:233
Heartbeats: Your Body, Your Heart (Silverstein and Silverstein) **25**:220
Heart's Blood (Yolen) **44**:178
Heartsease (Dickinson) **29**:38
Heat (Adler) **27**:18
Heat (Cobb) **2**:65
Heat (Graham) **31**:95
Heat and Temperature (Bendick) **5**:47
Heather, Oak, and Olive: Three Stories (Sutcliff) **1**:185; **37**:164
The Heavenly Host (Asimov) **12**:51
Heavy Equipment (Adkins) **7**:26
Heavy Is a Hippopotamus (Schlein) **41**:176
Heb jij een hobbie? (Bruna) **7**:52
Heckedy Peg (Wood and Wood) **26**:223
Hector Protector and As I Went over the Water (Sendak) **1**:167
The Hedgehog Boy: A Latvian Folktale (Langton) **33**:118
Heidi (Harris) **30**:123
Heidi (Spyri) **13**:174
Heiligenwald (Benary-Isbert) **12**:73
Heimkehr aus dem Kriege (Kruss) **9**:87
Heinrich Schliemann, Discoverer of Buried Treasure (Selden) **8**:198
The Helen Oxenbury Nursery Story Book (Oxenbury) **22**:146
The Helen Oxenbury Rhyme Book (Oxenbury) **22**:148
Helen Oxenbury's ABC of Things (Oxenbury) **22**:138
Helga's Dowry: A Troll Love Story (dePaola) **4**:59
H-E-L-L-L-P! The Crazy Gang Is Back! (Williams) **48**:207
Hello and Good-by (Hoberman) **22**:109
Hello, Dandelions (Williams) **48**:197
Hello, Little Pig (Janosch) **26**:81

Hello, Star (Haywood) **22**:106
Hello, Tree! (Ryder) **37**:98
Hell's Edge (Townsend) **2**:172
"Help!" Yelled Maxwell (Stevenson) **17**:153
Helpers (Hughes) **15**:122
Helpful Mr. Bear (Kuratomi) **32**:187
Helping Horse (Phipson) **5**:183
The Henchmans at Home (Burton) **1**:31
Hengest's Tale (Walsh) **2**:200
Henny Penny (Galdone) **16**:93
Henry Aaron: Home-Run King (Epstein and Epstein) **26**:65
Henry and Beezus (Cleary) **8**:46
Henry and Mudge in Puddle Trouble: The Second Book of Their Adventures (Rylant) **15**:173
Henry and Mudge: The First Book of Their Adventures (Rylant) **15**:173
Henry and Ribsy (Cleary) **2**:46; **8**:47
Henry and the Clubhouse (Cleary) **8**:50
Henry and the Paper Route (Cleary) **2**:47; **8**:48
Henry Huggins (Cleary) **2**:47; **8**:44
Henry the Sailor Cat (Calhoun) **42**:34
Henry-Fisherman: A Story of the Virgin Islands (Brown) **12**:94
Henry's Fourth of July (Keller) **45**:47
Henry's Happy Birthday (Keller) **45**:55
Henry's Picnic (Keller) **45**:47
Henry's Red Sea (Smucker) **10**:188
Hepatica Hawks (Field) **21**:77
Hepzibah (Dickinson) **29**:47
Her Majesty, Aunt Essie (Schwartz) **25**:191
Her Majesty, Grace Jones (Langton) **33**:106
Her Seven Brothers (Goble) **21**:135
Her Stories: African American Folktales, Fairy Tales and True Tales (Hamilton) **40**:91
Her Stories: African American Folktales, Fairy Tales, and True Tales (Leo and Diane Dillon) **44**:48
Heracles the Strong (Serraillier) **2**:139
Herb Seasoning (Thompson) **24**:232
Herbert Hated Being Small (Kuskin) **4**:143
Hercules: The Story of an Old-Fashioned Fire Engine (Gramatky) **22**:40
A Herd of Deer (Dillon) **26**:30
Here a Chick, Therea Chick (McMillan) **47**:163
Here Are the Brick Street Boys (Ahlberg and Ahlberg) **18**:3
Here Comes Charlie Moon (Hughes) **15**:127
Here Comes Herb's Hurricane! (Stevenson) **17**:152
Here Comes John (Graham) **31**:92
Here Comes McBroom (Fleischman) **15**:108
Here Comes the Bus! (Haywood) **22**:98
Here Comes Theo (Graham) **31**:92
Here Comes Thursday! (Bond) **1**:27
Here I Stay (Coatsworth) **2**:58
Here There Be Dragons (Yolen) **44**:201
Here There Be Unicorns (Yolen) **44**:203
Here There Be Witches (Yolen) **44**:207
Here We Go Round: A Career Story for Girls (Allan) **43**:3
Hereafterthis (Galdone) **16**:98
Here's a Penny (Haywood) **22**:92
Here's Baabee, Baabee's Things, Baabee Gets Dressed, Baabee's Home (Khalsa) **30**:144
The Heritage of Music (Shippen) **36**:181
Heritage of the Star (Engdahl) **2**:70
Herman the Loser (Hoban) **3**:77
The Hermit and Harry and Me (Hogrogian) **2**:88
The Hermit and the Bear (Yeoman) **46**:180
Hermit Dan (Parish) **22**:163
A Hero Ain't Nothin but a Sandwich (Childress) **14**:88

The Hero and the Crown (McKinley) **10**:125
The Hero from Otherwhere (Williams) **8**:232
Hero Legends of the World (Baumann) **35**:54
Hero of Lesser Causes (Johnston) **41**:85
Heroes and History (Sutcliff) **1**:186; **37**:160
Herpes (Nourse) **33**:144
Hetty (Willard) **2**:218
Hetty and Harriet (Oakley) **7**:221
Hey, Al (Yorinks) **20**:217
Hey, Dad! (Doyle) **22**:29
Hey Diddle Diddle (Caldecott) **14**:78
The Hey Hey Man (Fleischman) **15**:110
Hey, Kid! Does She Love Me? (Mazer) **16**:132
Hey, Lover Boy (Rockwell) **6**:240
Hey Preso! You're a Bear (Janosch) **26**:78
"Hey, What's Wrong with This One?" (Wojciechowska) **1**:196
Hey Willy, See the Pyramids (Kalman) **32**:180
Hezekiah Horton (Tarry) **26**:212
Hi, Cat! (Keats) **1**:114; **35**:136
Hi! Ho! The Rattlin' Bog and Other Folk Songs for Group Singing (Langstaff) **3**:109
Hi Johnny (Hunter) **25**:74
"Hi, Mr. Robin!" (Tresselt) **30**:203
Hi, Mrs. Mallory! (Thomas) **8**:214
Hi There, Supermouse! (Ure) **34**:175
Hiawatha (Jeffers) **30**:135
Hiccup (Mayer) **11**:172
Hickory Stick Rag (Watson) **3**:212
Hidden Gold (Clarke) **28**:75
The Hidden House (Brown) **10**:63
The Hidden House (Waddell) **31**:197
The Hidden Shrine (Myers) **16**:142
Hidden Treasure (Allen) **44**:9
The Hidden World: Life under a Rock (Pringle) **4**:181
Hidden Worlds: Pictures of the Invisible (Simon) **9**:220
Hide and Seek (Coatsworth) **2**:59
Hide and Seek Fog (Duvoisin) **23**:103
Hide and Seek Fog (Tresselt) **30**:208
The Hideout (Bunting) **28**:66
Hiding (Klein) **19**:89
Hiding Out (Rockwell) **6**:238
Higbee's Halloween (Peck) **45**:123
Higglety Pigglety Pop! or, There Must Be More to Life (Sendak) **1**:168
Higgle-wiggle: Happy Rhymes (Wilhelm) **46**:170
High and Haunted Island (Chauncy) **6**:92
The High Deeds of Finn MacCool (Sutcliff) **1**:186; **37**:160
High Elk's Treasure (Sneve) **2**:144
The High Hills (Barklem) **31**:6
The High House (Arundel) **35**:10
The High King (Alexander) **1**:14; **5**:21
High on a Hill: A Book of Chinese Riddles (Young) **27**:218
High Sounds, Low Sounds (Branley) **13**:34
High Tide for Labrador (Bunting) **28**:44
High Wind for Kansas (Calhoun) **42**:10
The High World (Bemelmans) **6**:72
Higher on the Door (Stevenson) **17**:166
The Highest Hit (Willard) **5**:248
The Highly Trained Dogs of Professor Petit (Brink) **30**:14
High-Rise Secret (Lenski) **26**:122
Highway to Adventure: The River Rhone of France (Lauber) **16**:112
The Highwayman (Keeping) **34**:106
High-Wire Henry (Calhoun) **42**:32
Hiking and Backpacking (Paulsen) **19**:172
Hilary's Summer on Her Own (Allan) **43**:8
Hildegarde and Maximilian (Krahn) **3**:104

Hilding's Summer (Lindgren) **20**:155
The Hill and the Rock (McKee) **38**:173
The Hill of th Fairy Calf: The Legend of Knockshogowna (Causley) **30**:39
Hills End (Southall) **2**:152
The Hills of Varna (Trease) **42**:180
"Him" She Loves? (Kerr) **29**:153
Hindu Fables, for Little Children (Mukerji) **10**:133
The Hippo Boat (Nakatani) **30**:157
Hiram Bingham and the Dream of Gold (Cohen) **43**:45
His Own Where (Jordan) **10**:116
Hisako's Mysteries (Uchida) **6**:255
The Hispanic Americans (Meltzer) **13**:142
History Can Be Fun (Leaf) **25**:131
The History of Helpless Harry: To Which Is Added a Variety of Amusing and Entertaining Adventures (Avi) **24**:8
The History of Little Tom Tucker (Galdone) **16**:96
The History of Mother Twaddle and the Marvelous Achievements of Her Son Jack (Galdone) **16**:99
The History of Simple Simon (Galdone) **16**:92
Hit and Run (Stine) **37**:120
The Hit-Away Kid (Christopher) **33**:59
The Hitchhiker (Stine) **37**:121
Hitting, Pitching, and Running—Maybe (Paulsen) **19**:170
Hitty, Her First Hundred Years (Field) **21**:72
The Hoax on You (Singer) **48**:134
Hobby (Yolen) **44**:210
Hobo Toad and the Motorcycle Gang (Yolen) **4**:259
The Hoboken Chicken Emergency (Pinkwater) **4**:167
The Hobyahs (Biro) **28**:39
The Hobyahs (San Souci) **43**:191
The Hockey Machine (Christopher) **33**:58
Hoists, Cranes, and Derricks (Zim) **2**:227
Hold Everything (Epstein and Epstein) **26**:64
Hold Fast (Major) **11**:127
Hold on to Love (Hunter) **25**:88
Hold Zero! (George) **1**:90
Holding Me Here (Conrad) **18**:87
Holding Up the Sky: Young People in China (Rau) **8**:194
A Hole Is to Dig: A First Book of First Definitions (Krauss) **42**:116
Holes and Peeks (Jonas) **12**:174
Holiday Gifts, Favors and Decorations That You Can Make (Sattler) **24**:213
The Hollow Land (Gardam) **12**:169
Holly from the Bongs: A Nativity Play (Garner) **20**:102
The Hollywood Kid (Wojciechowska) **1**:197
Home at Last! A Young Cat's Tale (Lauber) **16**:119
Home Before Dark (Bridgers) **18**:23
Home for a Bunny (Brown) **10**:66
Home Free (Lasky) **11**:121
Home from Far (Little) **4**:147
Home in the Sky (Baker) **28**:20
Home Is the Sailor (Godden) **20**:132
A Home Is to Share...and Share...and Share... (Gaberman) **33**:12
Home on the Range: Cowboy Poetry (Janeczko) **47**:119
Home Place (Pinkney) **43**:166
The Home Run Trick (Corbett) **1**:45
Home to the Island (Allan) **43**:10
Homeboy (Hansen) **21**:150
Homecoming (Voigt) **13**:226

The Homeless: Profiling the Problem (Hyde) **23**:175
Homer and the Circus Train (Gramatky) **22**:43
Homer Price (McCloskey) **7**:203
Homesick: My Own Story (Fritz) **14**:117
The Homeward Bounders (Jones) **23**:190
The Homework Machine (Williams and Abrashkin) **8**:223
Hominids: A Look Back at Our Ancestors (Sattler) **24**:222
The Honest Thief: A Hungarian Folktale (Biro) **28**:32
Honestly, Katie John! (Calhoun) **42**:9
Honey, I Love and Other Love Poems (Leo and Diane Dillon) **44**:34
A Honey of a Chimp (Klein) **19**:92
The Honeybee and the Robber: A Moving / Picture Book (Carle) **10**:84
Hongry Catch the Foolish Boy (Graham) **10**:110
Honker: The Story of a Wild Goose (McClung) **11**:183
Honkers (Yolen) **44**:201
Hoof and Claw (Roberts) **33**:204
Hoofprint on the Wind (Clark) **16**:83
Hoops (Myers) **16**:139
Hooray for Me! (Charlip) **8**:31; **15**:143
Hop Aboard, Here We Go! (Scarry) **41**:165
Hop on Pop (Seuss) **1**:86; **9**:187
Hopper (Pfister) **42**:135
Hopper Hunts for Spring (Pfister) **42**:135
Horace (Keller) **45**:55
Horatio (Foreman) **32**:86
Hormones (Nourse) **33**:142
The Horn of Roland (Williams) **8**:229
Horned Helmet (Treece) **2**:185
The Horns of Danger (Allan) **43**:33
Horror, Fright, and Panic: Emotions that Affect Our Lives (Hyde) **23**:163
Horse (Gardam) **12**:170
A Horse and a Hound, a Goat and a Gander (Provensen and Provensen) **11**:213
The Horse and His Boy (Lewis) **3**:134; **27**:104-51
A Horse Came Running (DeJong) **1**:57
The Horse Comes First (Calhoun) **42**:20
The Horse Hunters (Peck) **45**:121
The Horse in the Camel Suit (Pene du Bois) **1**:64
The Horse, the Fox, and the Lion (Galdone) **16**:92
Horse with Eight Hands (Phipson) **5**:183
The Horse Without a Head (Berna) **19**:33
Horsemaster (Singer) **48**:128
Horses (Brown) **10**:53
Horses and Their Wild Relatives (Patent) **19**:156
A Horse's Body (Cole) **5**:66
Horses of America (Patent) **19**:157
Horses of Dreamland (Duncan) **29**:78
The Horses The Indians Rode (Lavine) **35**:155
Horseshoe Crab (McClung) **11**:184
Horton Hatches the Egg (Seuss) **9**:174
Horton Hears a Who! (Seuss) **1**:86; **9**:179
The Hospital Book (Howe) **9**:57
The Hospitals (Fisher) **18**:129
The Hostage (Taylor) **30**:194
Hot and Cold (Adler) **27**:13
Hot-Air Henry (Calhoun) **42**:28
Hotel for Dogs (Duncan) **29**:69
Hotline (Hyde) **23**:161
The Hotshot (Slote) **4**:202
Houn' Dog (Calhoun) **42**:6
The Hound of Ulster (Sutcliff) **1**:186; **37**:158
The Hounds of the Morrigan (O'Shea) **18**:167
The House at Pooh Corner (Milne) **26**:126
A House by the Sea (Ryder) **37**:100

A House for Spinner's Grandmother (Unnerstad) **36**:200
The House Gobbaleen (Alexander) **48**:27
The House in Cornwall (Streatfeild) See *The Secret of the Lodge*
The House in Norham Gardens (Lively) **7**:158
The House in the Water: A Book of Animal Life (Roberts) **33**:201
A House Is a House for Me (Hoberman) **22**:113
A House like a Lotus (L'Engle) **14**:154
The House of a Hundred Windows (Brown) **10**:53
The House of Cornwall (Streatfeild) See *The Secret of the Lodge*
The House of Dies Drear (Hamilton) **1**:103
The House of Four Seasons (Duvoisin) **23**:100
The House of Hanover: England in the Eighteenth Century (Garfield) **21**:111
The House of Secrets (Bawden) **2**:12
The House of Sixty Fathers (DeJong) **1**:58
House of Stairs (Sleator) **29**:200
The House of Thirty Cats (Calhoun) **42**:10
The House of Wings (Byars) **1**:36
The House on Hackman's Hill (Nixon) **24**:147
The House on the Shore (Dillon) **26**:21
The House that Jack Built (Caldecott) **14**:73
The House that Jack Built (Galdone) **16**:90
The House that Sailed Away (Hutchins) **20**:148
The House with a Clock in its Walls (Bellairs) **37**:7
The House with Roots (Willard) **2**:218
Houseboat Girl (Lenski) **26**:120
The Housenapper (Curry) See *Mindy's Mysterious Miniature*
Houses (Adler) **27**:18
The Houses The Indians Built (Lavine) **35**:155
How a House Happens (Adkins) **7**:19
The How and Why of Growing (Milne and Milne) **22**:122
How Animals Behave (Bendick) **5**:48
How Animals Defend Their Young (Freedman) **20**:80
How Animals Learn (Freedman) **20**:75
How Animals Live Together (Selsam) **1**:162
How Animals Tell Time (Selsam) **1**:163
How Beastly! (Yolen) **4**:266
How Birds Fly (Freedman) **20**:79
How Did We Find Out about Atoms? (Asimov) **12**:53
How Did We Find Out about Black Holes? (Asimov) **12**:56
How Did We Find Out about Coal? (Asimov) **12**:58
How Did We Find Out about Comets? (Asimov) **12**:52
How Did We Find Out about Computers? (Asimov) **12**:63
How Did We Find Out about Dinosaurs? (Asimov) **12**:50
How Did We Find Out about DNA? (Asimov) **12**:64
How Did We Find Out about Earthquakes? (Asimov) **12**:56
How Did We Find Out about Electricity? (Asimov) **12**:49
How Did We Find Out about Energy? (Asimov) **12**:52
How Did We Find Out about Genes? (Asimov) **12**:62
How Did We Find Out about Life in the Deep Sea? (Asimov) **12**:60
How Did We Find Out about Nuclear Power? (Asimov) **12**:53
How Did We Find Out about Numbers? (Asimov) **12**:50

How Did We Find Out about Oil? (Asimov) **12**:58

How Did We Find Out about Our Human Roots? (Asimov) **12**:58

How Did We Find Out about Outer Space? (Asimov) **12**:55

How Did We Find Out about Solar Power? (Asimov) **12**:59

How Did We Find Out about the Atmosphere? (Asimov) **12**:64

How Did We Find Out about the Beginning of Life? (Asimov) **12**:60

How Did We Find Out about the Universe? (Asimov) **12**:61

How Did We Find Out about Vitamins? (Asimov) **12**:51

How Did We Find Out the Earth Is Round? (Asimov) **12**:48

How Do Apples Grow? (Betsy and Giulio Maestro) **45**:85

How Do I Eat It? (Watanabe) **8**:216

How Do I Go? (Hoberman) **22**:108

How Do I Put It On? Getting Dressed (Watanabe) **8**:216

How Do You Lose Those Ninth Grade Blues? (DeClements) **23**:35

How Do You Make an Elephant Float? and Other Delicious Riddles (Hopkins) **44**:93

How Droofus the Dragon Lost His Head (Peet) **12**:201

How Giraffe Got Such a Long Neck—And Why Rhino Is So Grumpy (Rosen) **45**:147

How God Fix Jonah (Graham) **10**:104

How Green You Are! (Doherty) **21**:55

How Heredity Works: Why Living Things Are as They Are (Bendick) **5**:47

How, Hippo! (Brown) **12**:104

How I Broke Up With Ernie (Stine) **37**:112

How I Came to Be a Writer (Naylor) **17**:53

How Insects Communicate (Patent) **19**:149

How It Feels When a Parent Dies (Krementz) **5**:155

How Lazy Can You Get? (Naylor) **17**:54

How Life Began (Adler) **27**:8

How Life Began (Berger) **32**:45

How Life Began: Creation versus Evolution (Gallant) **30**:92

How Many Days to America? A Thanksgiving Story (Bunting) **28**:62

How Many Miles to Babylon? (Fox) **1**:77

How Many Spots Does a Leopard Have? And Other Tales (Lester) **41**:107

How Many Teeth? (Showers) **6**:242

How Much and How Many: The Story of Weights and Measures (Bendick) **5**:35

How Pizza Came to Queens (Khalsa) **30**:149

How Pizza Come to Our Town (Khalsa) **30**:149

How Puppies Grow (Selsam) **1**:163

How Rabbit Tricked His Friends (Tresselt) **30**:211

How Santa Claus Had a Long and Difficult Journey Delivering His Presents (Krahn) **3**:104

How Summer Came to Canada (Cleaver) **13**:65

How the Animals Got Their Colours: Animal Myths from Around the World (Rosen) **45**:144

How the Doctor Knows You're Fine (Cobb) **2**:65

How the Grinch Stole Christmas (Seuss) **1**:86; **9**:184

How the Leopard Got His Skin (Achebe) **20**:8

How the Reindeer Saved Santa (Haywood) **22**:105

How the Sun Was Brought Back to the Sky: Adapted from a Slovenian Folk Tale (Ginsburg) **45**:8

How the Whale Became (Hughes) **3**:92

How to Be a Hero (Weiss) **4**:225

How to Be a Space Scientist in Your Own Home (Simon) **9**:218

How to Be an Inventor (Weiss) **4**:230

How to be Funny: An Extremely Silly Guidebook (Stine) **37**:103

How to Behave and Why (Leaf) **25**:129

How to Eat Fried Worms (Rockwell) **6**:236

How to Eat Fried Worms and Other Plays (Rockwell) **6**:239

How to Get Out of the Bath and Other Problems (Rosen) **45**:133

How to Make a Cloud (Bendick) **5**:44

How to Make an Earthquake (Krauss) **42**:118

How to Make Your Own Books (Weiss) **4**:227

How to Make Your Own Movies: An Introduction to Filmmaking (Weiss) **4**:227

How to Read a Rabbit (Fritz) **14**:112

How to Run a Railroad: Everything You Need to Know about Model Trains (Weiss) **4**:228

How Tom Beat Captain Najork and His Hired Sportsmen (Blake) **31**:19

How Tom Beat Captain Najork and His Hired Sportsmen (Hoban) **3**:78

How We Found Out about Vitamins (Asimov) **12**:51

How We Got Our First Cat (Tobias) **4**:218

How Wilka Went to Sea: And Other Tales from West of the Urals (Ginsburg) **45**:8

How You Talk (Showers) **242**

How You Were Born (Cole) **40**:7

How Your Mother and Father Met, and What Happened After (Tobias) **4**:217

Howard (Stevenson) **17**:156

Howliday Inn (Howe) **9**:58

Howl's Moving Castle (Jones) **23**:195

Hubert's Hair-Raising Adventure (Peet) **12**:193

Hug Me (Stren) **5**:230

Huge Harold (Peet) **12**:194

Hugo (Gripe) **5**:142

Hugo and Josephine (Gripe) **5**:143

Hugo och Josefin (Gripe) **5**:143

The Hullabaloo ABC (Cleary) **2**:47

The Human Body: How We Evolved (Cole) **40**:16

The Human Body: Its Structure and Operation (Asimov) **12**:37

Human Nature-Animal Nature: The Biology of Human Behavior (Cohen) **3**:40

The Human Rights Book (Meltzer) **13**:140

Humbert, Mister Firkin, and the Lord Mayor of London (Burningham) **9**:40

Humbug Mountain (Fleischman) **15**:109

Humphrey: One Hundred Years along the Wayside with a Box Turtle (Flack) **28**:123

Hunches in Bunches (Seuss) **9**:194

Der Hund Herr Müller (Heine) **18**:145

The Hundred Islands (Clark) **30**:61

A Hundred Million Francs (Berna) **19**:33

The Hundred Penny Box (Leo and Diane Dillon) **44**:24

The Hundred Penny Box (Mathis) **3**:149

The Hundredth Dove and Other Tales (Yolen) **4**:264

Hungarian Folk-Tales (Biro) **28**:34

Hungry Fred (Fox) **44**:61

Hungry, Hungry Sharks (Cole) **40**:13

The Hungry Leprechaun (Calhoun) **42**:9

Huni (French) **37**:34

Hunt the Thimble (French) **37**:43

Hunted in Their Own Land (Chauncy) **6**:92

Hunted Like a Wolf: The Story of the Seminole War (Meltzer) **13**:129

Hunted Mammals of the Sea (McClung) **11**:191

The Hunter and the Animals: A Wordless Picture Book (dePaola) **24**:89

Hunter in the Dark (Hughes) **9**:74

Hunters and the Hunted: Surviving in the Animal World (Patent) **19**:156

The Hunting of Shadroth (Kelleher) **36**:116

The Hunting of the Snark: An Agony in Eight Fits (Carroll) **2**:34

The Hurdy-Gurdy Man (Bianco) **19**:53

Hurrah, We're Outward Bound! (Spier) **5**:219

Hurray for Monty Ray! (McBratney) **44**:128

Hurricane (Wiesner) **43**:207

Hurricane Guest (Epstein and Epstein) **26**:59

Hurricane Watch (Betsy and Giulio Maestro) **45**:76

Hurricane Watch (Branley) **13**:51

Hurricanes and Twisters (Adler) **27**:6

Hurry Home, Candy (DeJong) **1**:58

The Hypnotiser (Rosen) **45**:137

I, Adam (Fritz) **2**:81

I Am a Clown (Bruna) **7**:52

I Am a Hunter (Mayer) **11**:165

I Am a Man: Ode to Martin Luther King, Jr. (Merriam) **14**:197

I Am Papa Snap and These Are My Favorite No Such Stories (Ungerer) **3**:201

I Am Phoenix: Poems for Two Voices (Fleischman) **20**:67

I Am Somebody! A Biography of Jesse Jackson (Haskins) **39**:67

I Am the Cheese (Cormier) **12**:139

I Am the Running Girl (Adoff) **7**:35

I Be Somebody (Irwin) **40**:110

I Can (Oxenbury) **22**:147

I Can Build a House! (Watanabe) **8**:217

I Can Count More (Bruna) **7**:51

I Can Do It! (Watanabe) **8**:217

I Can Fly (Krauss) **42**:115

I Can Read (Bruna) **7**:50

I Can Ride It! Setting Goals (Watanabe) **8**:217

I Can Take a Walk! (Watanabe) **8**:217

I Can—Can You? (Parish) **22**:165

I Can't Stand Losing You (Kemp) **29**:123

I Don't Live Here! (Conrad) **18**:86

I Don't Want to Go to Bed (Lindgren) **39**:163

I Feel a Little Jumpy around You: A Book of Her Poems and His Poems (Janeczko) **47**:117

I Feel the Same Way (Moore) **15**:141

I Go by Sea, I Go by Land (Travers) **2**:178

I grandi pittori (Ventura) **16**:197

I Had Trouble in Getting to Solla Sollew (Seuss) **9**:189

I Hate My Teddy Bear (McKee) **38**:171

I Hate You, I Hate You (Leaf) **25**:135

I Have a Dream: The Life and Words of Martin Luther King, Jr. (Haskins) **39**:71

I Have Four Names for My Grandfather (Lasky) **11**:114

I Have to Go! (Munsch) **19**:145

I Hear (Oxenbury) **22**:147

I, Houdini: The Autobiography of a Self-Educated Hamster (Reid Banks) **24**:193

I Klockornas Tid (Gripe) **5**:145

I Know a City: The Story of New York's Growth (Shippen) **36**:174

I Know a Policeman (Williams) **48**:188

I Know What You Did Last Summer (Duncan) **29**:70

I Like Old Clothes (Hoberman) **22**:112

I Like Winter (Lenski) **26**:115

I Love Guinea Pigs (King-Smith) **40**:173

I Love My Mother (Zindel) **3**:248

I Love You, Stupid! (Mazer) **16**:131
I Loved Rose Ann (Hopkins) **44**:88
I Marched with Hannibal (Baumann) **35**:44
I Met a Man (Ciardi) **19**:76
I, Momolu (Graham) **10**:106
I Need a Lunch Box (Caines) **24**:64
I Need a Lunch Box (Cummings) **48**:49
I Never Asked You to Understand Me (DeClements) **23**:36
I Never Loved Your Mind (Zindel) **3**:248
I Own the Racecourse! (Wrightson) **4**:242
I Read Signs (Hoban) **13**:107
I Read Symbols (Hoban) **13**:107
I Sailed with Columbus (Schlein) **41**:197
I Saw a Ship A-Sailing (Domanska) **40**:43
I Saw the Sea Come In (Tresselt) **30**:205
I See (Oxenbury) **22**:147
I See a Song (Carle) **10**:76
I See a Voice (Rosen) **45**:131
I See the Moon: Good-Night Poems and Lullabies (Pfister) **42**:135
I See What I See! (Selden) **8**:197
I Sing the Song of Myself: An Anthology of Autobiographical Poems (Kherdian) **24**:109
I Stay Near You: One Story in Three (Kerr) **29**:155
I Thought I Heard the City (Moore) **15**:142
I Touch (Oxenbury) **22**:147
I, Trissy (Mazer) **23**:221
I, Tut: The Boy Who Became Pharaoh (Schlein) **41**:188
I Walk and Read (Hoban) **13**:108
I Want a Brother or Sister (Lindgren) **39**:159
I Want a Dog (Khalsa) **30**:146
I Want to Go Home! (Korman) **25**:106
I Want to Go to School Too (Lindgren) **39**:159
I Want to Paint My Bathroom Blue (Krauss) **42**:121
I Want to Stay Here! I Want to Go There! A Flea Story (Lionni) **7**:137
I Was Born in a Tree and Raised by Bees (Arnosky) **15**:2
I Was There (Richter) **21**:189
I Wear the Morning Star (Highwater) **17**:32
I Went for a Walk (Lenski) **26**:120
I Wish I Had a Pirate Suit (Allen) **44**:11
I Wish I Had an Afro (Shearer) **34**:166
I Wish That I Had Duck Feet (Seuss) **1**:87; **9**:189
I Would Rather Be a Turnip (Cleaver and Cleaver) **6**:106
I Write It (Krauss) **42**:128
The Ice Ghosts Mystery (Curry) **31**:77
The Ice Is Coming (Wrightson) **4**:245
Ice Magic (Christopher) **33**:47
If All the Seas Were One Sea (Domanska) **40**:41
If All the Swords in England (Willard) **2**:219
If Dragon Flies Made Honey: Poems (Kherdian) **24**:108
If He's My Brother (Williams) **48**:193
If I Asked You, Would You Stay? (Bunting) **28**:56
If I Had... (Mayer) **11**:164
If I Had My Way (Klein) **2**:98
If I Love You, Am I Trapped Forever? (Kerr) **29**:144
If I Owned a Candy Factory (Stevenson) **17**:152
If I Ran the Circus (Seuss) **1**:87; **9**:181
If I Ran the Zoo (Seuss) **1**:87; **9**:178
If It Weren't for Sebastian (Ure) **34**:174
If It Weren't for You (Zolotow) **2**:234
If Only I Could Tell You: Poems for Young Lovers and Dreamers (Merriam) **14**:201
If the Earth Falls In (Clark) **30**:61
If This Is Love, I'll Take Spaghetti (Conford) **10**:98

If Wishes Were Horses and Other Rhymes from Mother Goose (Jeffers) **30**:133
If You Lived on Mars (Berger) **32**:43
If You Love Me, Let Me Go (St. John) **46**:107
If You Say So, Claude (Nixon) **24**:141
If You Were a Writer (Nixon) **24**:151
Iggie's House (Blume) **2**:17
Ik ben een clown (Bruna) **7**:52
Ik kan lezen (Bruna) **7**:50
Iktomi and the Boulder: A Plains Indian Story (Goble) **21**:137
Il venditore di animali (Munari) **9**:124
Il viaggio di Colombo (Ventura) **16**:193
Il viaggio di Marco Polo (Ventura) **16**:194
I'll Always Love You (Wilhelm) **46**:161
I'll Be You and You Be Me (Krauss) **42**:119
I'll Get There; It Better Be Worth the Trip (Donovan) **3**:52
I'll Go My Own Way (Hunter) **25**:90
I'll Love You When You're More Like Me (Kerr) **29**:147
I'll Make You Small (Wynne-Jones) **21**:230
Illinois (Carter) **22**:22
The Illustrated Dinosaur Dictionary (Sattler) **24**:218
The Illustrated Marguerite Henry (Henry) **4**:116
The Illyrian Adventure (Alexander) **48**:15
Ilse Janda, 14 (Noestlinger) **12**:186
I'm Going to Sing: Black American Spirituals, Volume 2 (Bryan) **18**:35
I'm Gonna Make You Love Me: The Story of Diana Ross (Haskins) **39**:39
I'm Hiding (Livingston) **7**:168
I'm in the Zoo, Too! (Ashabranner) **28**:13
I'm Only Afraid of the Dark (At Night!) (Stren) **5**:235
I'm Really Dragged but Nothing Gets Me Down (Hentoff) **1**:107
I'm the King of the Castle! Playing Alone (Watanabe) **8**:217
I'm Trying to Tell You (Ashley) **4**:18
I'm Waiting (Livingston) **7**:169
The Image Game (St. John) **46**:126
Imagine If (Heine) **18**:146
Immigrant Kids (Freedman) **20**:81
The Importance of Crocus (Duvoisin) **23**:107
The Important Book (Brown) **10**:57
Important Dates in Afro-American History (Hopkins) **44**:86
The Important Visitor (Oxenbury) **22**:145
The Impossible People: A History Natural and Unnatural of Beings Terrible and Wonderful (McHargue) **2**:118
Impossible, Possum (Conford) **10**:90
The Improbable Adventures of Marvelous O'Hara Soapstone (Oneal) **13**:155
The Improbable Book of Records (Blake) See *The Puffin Book of Improbable Records*
The Improbable Book of Records (Yeoman) **46**:178
Impunity Jane: The Story of a Pocket Doll (Freedman) **20**:127
In a Beaver Valley: How Beavers Change the Land (Pringle) **4**:175
In a Blue Velvet Dress: Almost a Ghost Story (Waddell) **31**:176
In a Forgotten Place (Orgel) **48**:76
In a People House (Seuss) **9**:192
In a Place of Danger (Fox) **44**:69
In Crack Willow Wood (McBratney) **44**:131
In for Winter, Out for Spring (Pinkney) **43**:167
In Lane Three, Alex Archer (Duder) **43**:64
In My Boat (Betsy and Giulio Maestro) **45**:67

In My Father's House (Rinaldi) **46**:85
In My Garden (Zolotow) **2**:235
In My Mother's House (Clark) **16**:75
In My Tent (Singer) **48**:140
In Nueva York (Mohr) **22**:132
In Powder and Crinoline: Old Fairy Tales (Nielsen) **16**:155
In School: Learning in Four Languages (Hautzig) **22**:83
In Search of Ancient Crete (Ventura) **16**:196
In Search of Ghosts (Cohen) **3**:40
In Search of Pompeii (Ventura) **16**:196
In Search of Troy (Ventura) **16**:196
In Search of Tutankhamun (Ventura) **16**:196
In Spite of All Terror (Burton) **1**:32
In Summer Light (Oneal) **13**:158
In Summertime It's Tuffy (Gaberman) **33**:2
In the Beginning: Creation Stories from Around the World (Hamilton) **40**:79
In the Company of Clowns: A Commedia (Bacon) **3**:11
In the Country of Ourselves (Hentoff) **1**:108
In the Face of Danger (Nixon) **24**:153
In the Flaky Frosty Morning (Kuskin) **4**:140
In the Forest (Ets) **33**:75
In the Land of Small Dragon (Clark) **16**:85
In the Land of Ur: The Discovery of Ancient Mesopotamia (Baumann) **35**:50
In the Middle of the Trees (Kuskin) **4**:135
In the Middle of the World (Korinetz) **4**:130
In the Night Kitchen (Sendak) **1**:168; **17**:118
In the Palace of the Ocean King (Singer) **48**:146
In the Park: An Excursion in Four Languages (Hautzig) **22**:82
In the Rabbitgarden (Lionni) **7**:136
In the Time of the Bells (Gripe) **5**:145
In Their Own Words: A History of the American Negro, Vol. I: 1619-1865, Vol. II: 1865-1916; Vol. III: 1916-1966 (Meltzer) **13**:121
In Your Own Words: A Beginner's Guide to Writing (Cassedy) **26**:13
In-Between Miya (Uchida) **6**:255
The Inca (McKissack) **23**:237
Inch by Inch (Lionni) **7**:128
The Incredible Journey (Burnford) **2**:19
The Incredible Journey of Lewis and Clark (Blumberg) **21**:30
The Incredible Television Machine (LeShan) **6**:189
Independent Voices (Merriam) **14**:195
India Under Indira and Rajiv Gandhi (Haskins) **39**:59
Indian Captive: The Story of Mary Jemison (Lenski) **26**:105
Indian Chiefs (Freedman) **20**:86
Indian Corn and Other Gifts (Lavine) **35**:153
Indian Encounters: An Anthology of Stories and Poems (Coatsworth) **2**:59
Indian Festivals (Showers) **6**:245
The Indian in the Cupboard (Reid Banks) **24**:194
Indian Mound Farm (Coatsworth) **2**:59
Indian Summer (Monjo) **2**:121
Indians (Tunis) **2**:193
Ingri and Edgar Parin d'Aulaire's Book of Greek Myths (d'Aulaire and d'Aulaire) **21**:52
Inky Pinky Ponky: Children's Playground Rhymes (Rosen) **45**:132
The Inn-Keepers Apprentice (Say) **22**:209
Insect Masquerades (Simon) **39**:184
Insect Worlds: A Guide for Man on the Making of the Environment (Milne and Milne) **22**:123
An Insect's Body (Cole) **40**:6
Inside Jazz (Collier) **3**:45

Inside Out (Martin) **32**:200

Inside, Outside, Upside Down (Berenstain and Berenstain) **19**:26

Inside: Seeing Beneath the Surface (Adkins) **7**:21

Inside the Atom (Asimov) **12**:31

Inside Turtle's Shell, and Other Poems of the Field (Ryder) **37**:87

Inspector Peckit (Freeman) **30**:78

Integers: Positive and Negative (Adler) **27**:25

Intelligence: What Is It? (Cohen) **3**:41

Inter-City (Keeping) **34**:103

Interstellar Pig (Sleator) **29**:203

Into a Strange Land: Unaccompanied Refugee Youth in America (Ashabranner and Ashabranner) **28**:10

Into the Dream (Sleator) **29**:210

Into the Woods: Exploring the Forest Ecosystem (Pringle) **4**:178

The Intruder (Townsend) **2**:172

The Invaders: Three Stories (Treece) **2**:185

The Invisible Dog (King-Smith) **40**:166

The Inway Investigators; or, The Mystery at McCracken's Place (Yolen) **4**:258

IOU's (Sebestyen) **17**:91

Irma and Jerry (Selden) **8**:201

The Iron Giant: A Story in Five Nights (Hughes) **3**:92

The Iron Lily (Willard) **2**:220

The Iron Lion (Dickinson) **29**:42

Iron Mountain (Clark) **30**:59

The Iron Ring (Alexander) **48**:29

The Iron Way (Cross) **28**:85

Irrigations: Changing Deserts into Gardens (Adler) **27**:17

Is Anybody There? (Bunting) **28**:63

Is It Larger? Is It Smaller? (Hoban) **13**:110

Is It Red? Is It Yellow? Is It Blue? An Adventure in Color (Hoban) **13**:104

Is It Rough? Is It Smooth? Is It Shiny? (Hoban) **13**:109

Is That You, Miss Blue? (Kerr) **29**:146

Is There Life in Outer Space? (Branley) **13**:50

Is This a Baby Dinosaur? (Selsam) **1**:163

Is This Kid "Crazy"? Understanding Unusual Behavior (Hyde) **23**:169

Is This You? (Krauss) **42**:120

Isaac Campion (Howker) **14**:130

Isaac Newton: Mastermind of Modern Science (Knight) **38**:98

Isabel's Noel (Yolen) **4**:257

Isamu Noguchi: The Life of a Sculptor (Tobias) **4**:214

The Isis Pedlar (Hughes) **9**:75

Isla (Dorros) **42**:73

The Island (Paulsen) **19**:177

Island Baby (Keller) **45**:57

Island Boy (Cooney) **23**:32

An Island in a Green Sea (Allan) **43**:22

The Island Keeper (Mazer) **16**:130

The Island of Ghosts (Dillon) **26**:33

The Island of Horses (Dillon) **26**:22

The Island of Nose (Schmidt) **22**:222

Island of Ogres (Namioka) **48**:64

The Island of One (Bunting) **28**:48

Island of the Blue Dolphins (O'Dell) **1**:146; **16**:163

The Island of the Grass King: The Further Adventures of Anatole (Willard) **5**:248

The Island of the Skog (Kellogg) **6**:172

Island of the Strangers (Waddell) **31**:181

Island of Wild Horses (Scott) **20**:198

The Island on Bird Street (Orlev) **30**:164

L'Isle noire (Herge) **6**:148

Isle of the Sea Horse (Brinsmead) **47**:10

It Ain't All for Nothin' (Myers) **4**:158

It Can't Hurt Forever (Singer) **48**:121

It Doesn't Always Have to Rhyme (Merriam) **14**:193

It Figures!: Fun Figures of Speech (Betsy and Giulio Maestro) **45**:87

It Happened in Arles (Allan) **43**:13

It Happened in Pinsk (Yorinks) **20**:216

It Happened One Summer (Phipson) **5**:178

It Looks Like Snow: A Picture Book (Charlip) **8**:26

It Started in Madeira (Allan) **43**:16

It Started with Old Man Bean (Kherdian) **24**:110

It's a Gingerbread House: Bake It! Build It! Eat It! (Williams) **9**:230

It's a New Day: Poems for Young Brothas and Sistuhs (Sanchez) **18**:200

It's about Time (Schlein) **41**:178

It's an Aardvark-Eat-Turtle World (Danziger) **20**:55

It's Christmas (Prelutsky) **13**:169

It's Getting Beautiful Now (Calhoun) **42**:17

It's Halloween (Prelutsky) **13**:166

It's Hard to Read a Map with a Beagle on Your Lap (Singer) **48**:142

It's My Earth, Too: How I Can Help the Earth Stay Alive (Krull) **44**:103

It's Not the End of the World (Blume) **2**:17

It's Not What You Expect (Klein) **2**:98

It's OK If You Don't Love Me (Klein) **19**:89

It's Snowing! It's Snowing! (Prelutsky) **13**:171

It's Spring! (Minarik) **33**:127

It's Spring, She Said (Blos) **18**:14

It's Thanksgiving (Prelutsky) **13**:170

It's Time Now! (Tresselt) **30**:211

It's Too Frightening for Me! (Hughes) **15**:123

It's Valentine's Day (Prelutsky) **13**:171

Itsy-Bitsy Beasties: Poems from Around the World (Rosen) **45**:146

Izzy, Willy-Nilly (Voigt) **13**:238

Jack and Nancy (Blake) **31**:18

Jack and the Beanstalk (Biro) **28**:39

Jack and the Fire Dragon (Haley) **21**:148

Jack and the Whoopee Wind (Calhoun) **42**:30

Jack Holborn (Garfield) **21**:95

Jack Horner's Pie: A Book of Nursery Rhymes (Lenski) **26**:98

Jack Jouett's Ride (Haley) **21**:143

Jack of Hearts (French) **37**:33

Jack the Treacle Eater (Causley) **30**:43

Jack the Treacle Eater (Keeping) **34**:110

Jack the Wise and the Cornish Cuckoos (Calhoun) **42**:24

Jackanapes (Caldecott) **14**:79

Jackaroo (Voigt) **13**:237

Jackie Robinson: Baseball's Gallant Fighter (Epstein and Epstein) **26**:65

Jackie, the Pit Pony (Baumann) **35**:41

Jackknife for a Penny (Epstein and Epstein) **26**:56

Jacko (Goodall) **25**:44

Jackpot of the Beagle Brigade (Epstein and Epstein) **26**:70

Jackrabbit Goalie (Christopher) **33**:53

Jack's Fantastic Voyage (Foreman) **32**:107

Jacob Have I Loved (Paterson) **7**:238

Jacob Two-Two and the Dinosaur (Richler) **17**:80

Jacob Two-Two Meets the Hooded Fang (Richler) **17**:73

Jafta (Lewin) **9**:90

Jafta—My Father (Lewin) **9**:90

Jafta—My Mother (Lewin) **9**:90

Jafta—The Journey (Lewin) **9**:92

Jafta—The Town (Lewin) **9**:92

Jafta—The Wedding (Lewin) **9**:90

Jaguarundi (Hamilton) **40**:90

Jahdu (Hamilton) **11**:82

Jahdu (Pinkney) **43**:157

Jake (Slote) **4**:199

Jamberoo Road (Spence) **26**:193

Jambo Means Hello: Swahili Alphabet Book (Feelings and Feelings) **5**:107

James and the Giant Peach (Dahl) **1**:51; **7**:68

James and the Rain (Kuskin) **4**:134

James Bond in Win, Place, or Die (Stine) **37**:107

James Van Derzee: The Picture-Takin' Man (Haskins) **39**:36

Janaky and the Giant and Other Stories (Dhondy) **41**:80

Jane Martin, Dog Detective (Bunting) **28**:57

Jane, Wishing (Tobias) **4**:216

Jane Yolen's Mother Goose Songbook (Yolen) **44**:197

Janet Hamm Needs a Date for the Dance (Bunting) **28**:59

Janey (Zolotow) **2**:235

Jangle Twang (Burningham) **9**:51

Janie's Private Eyes (Snyder) **31**:168

Janni's Stork (Harris) **30**:123

Jar and Bottle Craft (Sattler) **24**:214

A Jar of Dreams (Uchida) **6**:259

Jasmine (Duvoisin) **23**:105

Jason and Marceline (Spinelli) **26**:203

Jason Bodger and the Priory Ghost (Kemp) **29**:120

Jay Bird (Ets) **33**:91

Jazz Country (Hentoff) **1**:108

The Jazz Man (Grifalconi) **35**:70

Jean and Johnny (Cleary) **2**:48; **8**:49

The Jedera Adventure (Alexander) **48**:20

Jeeter, Mason and the Magic Headset (Gaberman) **33**:14

Jeffrey Bear Cleans Up His Act (Steptoe) **12**:241

Jeffrey Strangeways (Murphy) **39**:177

Jellybean (Duder) **43**:63

Jem's Island (Lasky) **11**:117

The Jenius (King-Smith) **40**:155

Jennie's Hat (Keats) **1**:115; **35**:130

Jennifer and Josephine (Peet) **12**:199

Jennifer, Hecate, Macbeth, William McKinley, and Me, Elizabeth (Konigsburg) **1**:121

Jennifer Jean, the Cross-Eyed Queen (Naylor) **17**:49

Jenny and Jupie to the Rescue (Fujikawa) **25**:40

Jeremiah in the Dark Woods (Ahlberg and Ahlberg) **18**:4

Jeremy Isn't Hungry (Williams) **48**:196

Jesse (Soto) **38**:206

Jesse and Abe (Isadora) **7**:108

Jesse Jackson: A Biography (McKissack) **23**:241

Jessica (Henkes) **23**:130

Jethro and the Jumbie (Cooper) **4**:49

The Jetty (Mattingley) **24**:125

Jewelry from Junk (Sattler) **24**:213

The Jewish Americans: A History in Their Own Words, 1650-1950 (Meltzer) **13**:143

The Jews in America: A Picture Album (Meltzer) **13**:150

The Jezebel Wolf (Monjo) **2**:122

Jigsaw Continents (Berger) **32**:18

Jim Along, Josie: A Collection of Folk Songs and Singing Games for Young Children (Langstaff) **3**:110

Jim and the Beanstalk (Briggs) **10**:23

Jim Bridger's Alarm Clock and Other Tall Tales (Fleischman) **15**:110

Jim Button and Luke the Engine-Driver (Ende) **14**:97

Jim Grey of Moonbah (Ottley) **16**:187

Jim Knopf und Lukas der Lokomotivführer (Ende) **14**:97

Jim: The Story of a Backwoods Police Dog (Roberts) **33**:205

Jim-Dandy (Irwin) **40**:115

Jimmy Has Lost His Cap: Where Can It Be? (Munari) **9**:125

Jimmy Lee Did It (Cummings) **48**:46

Jimmy of Cherry Valley (Rau) **8**:186

Jimmy Yellow Hawk (Sneve) **2**:145

Jimmy Zest (McBratney) **44**:119

The Jimmy Zest All-Stars (McBratney) **44**:121

Jingle Bells (Kovalski) **34**:116

Jingo Django (Fleischman) **1**:74

Ji-Nongo-Nongo Means Riddles (Aardema) **17**:5

Ji-Nongo-Nongo Means Riddles (Pinkney) **43**:156

Jinx Glove (Christopher) **33**:48

Jo in the Middle (Ure) **34**:187

Joan of Arc (Williams) **8**:225

Jobs in Fine Arts and Humanities (Berger) **32**:12

Jobs That Save Our Environment (Berger) **32**:11

Jock and Jill (Lipsyte) **23**:208

Jock's Island (Coatsworth) **2**:59

Jodie's Journey (Thiele) **27**:211

Joe and the Snow (dePaola) **4**:54

Johannes Kepler and Planetary Motion (Knight) **38**:99

John and the Rarey (Wells) **16**:203

John Barleycorn (French) **37**:45

John Brown: A Cry for Freedom (Graham) **10**:111

John Burningham's ABC (Burningham) **9**:39

John Diamond (Garfield) **21**:115

John Henry (Lester) **41**:110

John Henry (Pinkney) **43**:172

John Henry: An American Legend (Keats) **1**:115; **35**:130

John Henry Davis (Leaf) **25**:126

John J. Plenty and Fiddler Dan: A New Fable of the Grasshopper and the Ant (Ciardi) **19**:78

John S. Goodall's Theatre: The Sleeping Beauty (Goodall) **25**:50

Johnny Long Legs (Christopher) **33**:44

Johnny Maple-Leaf (Tresselt) **30**:202

Johnny No Hit (Christopher) **33**:52

Johnny the Clockmaker (Ardizzone) **3**:4

Johnny Tremain: A Novel for Old and Young (Forbes) **27**:57-74

Johnny's in the Basement (Sacher) **28**:201

Jokes from Black Folks (Haskins) **3**:65

The Jolly Postman or Other People's Letters (Ahlberg and Ahlberg) **18**:10

Jonah, the Fisherman (Zimnik) **3**:243

Jonathan Cleaned Up, Then He Heard a Sound: Or, Blackberry Subway Jam (Munsch) **19**:142

Josefin (Gripe) **5**:142

Josefina February (Ness) **6**:200

Joseph and His Brothers: From the Story Told in the Book of Genesis (Petersham and Petersham) **24**:169

Josephine (Gripe) **5**:142

Joseph's Other Red Sock (Daly) **41**:54

Joseph's Yard (Keeping) **34**:91

Josh (Southall) **2**:153

The Journey (Marsden) **34**:148

Journey (Thomas) **19**:22

The Journey Back (Reiss) **19**:218

Journey behind the Wind (Wrightson) **4**:247

Journey between Worlds (Engdahl) **2**:70

Journey by First Camel (Konigsburg)
See *Journey to an 800 Number*

Journey Cake, Ho! (Sawyer) **36**:161

Journey from Peppermint Street (DeJong) **1**:58

Journey Home (Uchida) **6**:258

Journey into a Black Hole (Branley) **13**:52

Journey to an 800 Number (Konigsburg) **47**:139

A Journey to England (Unnerstad) **36**:194

Journey to Jericho (O'Dell) **1**:147

Journey to Jo'burg (Naidoo) **29**:162

Journey to the Planets (Lauber) **16**:120

Journey to Topaz: A Story of the Japanese-American Evacuation (Uchida) **6**:256

Journey to Untor (Wibberley) **3**:228

The Journey with Grandmother (Unnerstad) **36**:192

The Journey with Jonah (L'Engle) **1**:130

Journeys of Sebastian (Krahn) **3**:105

Joy to the World: Christmas Legends (Sawyer) **36**:165

Joyful Noise: Poems or Two Voices (Fleischman) **20**:68

Juan and the Asuangs (Aruego) **5**:28

Juanita (Politi) **29**:186

Judith Teaches (Allan) **43**:4

Judy and the Baby Elephant (Haar) **15**:116

Judy the Bad Fairy (Waddell) **31**:195

Judy's Journey (Lenski) **26**:111

Jules Verne: Portrait of a Prophet (Freedman) **20**:74

Julian (Khalsa) **30**:150

Julia's House (Gripe) **5**:147

Julias Hus och Nattpappan (Gripe) **5**:147

Julie of the Wolves (George) **1**:90

Julie's Tree (Calhoun) **42**:31

Julius (Pilkey) **48**:105

Jumanji (Van Allsburg) **5**:239

The Jumblies (Gorey) **36**:92

Jumbo Spencer (Cresswell) **18**:98

Jumper Goes to School (Parish) **22**:158

Jumping the Nail (Bunting) **28**:67

June 7! (Aliki) **9**:23

June 29, 1999 (Wiesner) **43**:213

June Anne June Spoon and Her Very Adventurous Search for the Moon (Kuskin) **4**:139

Jungle Beasts and Men (Mukerji) **10**:130

The Jungle Book (Kipling) **39**:74-118

Jungle Jingles (King-Smith) **40**:161

Junie B. Jones and a Little Monkey Business (Park) **34**:163

Junie B. Jones and Her Big Fat Mouth (Park) **34**:164

Junie B. Jones and the Stupid Smelly Bus (Park) **34**:162

Junior Intern (Nourse) **33**:130

Juniper: A Mystery (Kemp) **29**:122

The Juniper Tree and Other Tales from Grimm (Sendak) **1**:169

Junius Over Far (Hamilton) **11**:92

Junk Castle (Klein) **21**:159

Junk Day on Juniper Street and Other Easy-to-Read Stories (Moore) **15**:142

Jupiter Boots (Nimmo) **44**:145

Jupiter: King of the Gods, Giant of the Planets (Branley) **13**:46

Jupiter: The Largest Planet (Asimov) **12**:49

Just a Summer Romance (Martin) **32**:203

Just Across the Street (Field) **21**:78

Just An Overnight Guest (Tate) **37**:187

Just as Long as We're Together (Blume) **15**:82

Just between Us (Pfeffer) **11**:200

Just Cats: Learning Groups (Burningham) **9**:50

Just Ferret (Kemp) **29**:125

Just Like Archie (Daly) **41**:58

Just Like Everyone Else (Bunting) **28**:47

Just Like Everyone Else (Kuskin) **4**:135

Just Like Me (Ormerod) **20**:179

Just Like Me (Schlein) **41**:180

Just Me (Ets) **33**:89

Just Me and My Dad (Mayer) **11**:172

Just Morgan (Pfeffer) **11**:196

Just One Apple (Janosch) **26**:74

Just Plain Fancy (Polacco) **40**:189

Just Right (Moore) **15**:142

Just the Thing for Geraldine (Conford) **10**:92

Just Us Women (Caines) **24**:63

Just Us Women (Cummings) **48**:45

Justice and Her Brothers (Hamilton) **11**:79

Justice Lion (Peck) **45**:114

Justin and the Best Biscuits in the World (Walter) **15**:208

Justin Morgan Had a Horse (Henry) **4**:109

Juvenile Justice and Injustice (Hyde) **23**:162

The Kaha Bird: Folk Tales from the Steppes of Central Asia (Ginsburg) **45**:4

Karen Kepplewhite Is the World's Best Kisser (Bunting) **28**:55

Karen's Curiosity (Provensen and Provensen) **11**:209

Karen's Opposites (Provensen and Provensen) **11**:209

Karen's Witch (Martin) **32**:204

Karlson Flies Again (Lindgren) **39**:157

Karlsson-on-the-Roof (Lindgren) **39**:153

Kasho and the Twin Flutes (Pinkney) **43**:156

Kat Kong (Pilkey) **48**:106

Kate (Little) **4**:150

The Kate Greenaway Treasury: An Anthology of the Illustrations and Writings of Kate Greenaway (Greenaway) **6**:135

Kate Greenaway's Book of Games (Greenaway) **6**:135

Kate Greenaway's Language of Flowers (Greenaway) **6**:133

Kate Rider (Burton) **1**:32

Kate Shelley: Bound for Legend (San Souci) **43**:194

Katherine Dunham (Haskins) **39**:41

Kathleen, Please Come Home (O'Dell) **16**:173

Kati in America (Lindgren) **39**:151

Kati in Paris (Lindgren) **39**:148

Katie and Kit at the Beach (dePaola) **24**:98

Katie John (Calhoun) **42**:6

Katie John and Heathcliff (Calhoun) **42**:26

Katie, Kit, and Cousin Tom (dePaola) **24**:98

Katie's Good Idea (dePaola) **24**:98

Katy and the Big Snow (Burton) **11**:49

Kazoete Miyo (Anno) **14**:32

Keep Calm (Phipson) **5**:185

Keep Smiling Through (Rinaldi) **46**:91

Keep the Pot Boiling (Clarke) **28**:77

Keep Your Mouth Closed, Dear (Aliki) **9**:19

The Keeper (Naylor) **17**:60

The Keeper of the Isis Light (Hughes) **9**:72

Keepers of Life: Discovering Plants through Native American Stories and Earth Activities for Children (Bruchac) **46**:17

Keepers of the Animals: Native American Stories and Wildlife Activities for Children (Bruchac) **46**:7

Keepers of the Earth: Native American Stories and Environmental Activities for Children (Bruchac) **46**:7

Keepers of the Night: Native American Stories and Nocturnal Activities for Children (Bruchac) **46**:17

The Keeping Days (St. John) **46**:99

The Keeping Quilt (Polacco) **40**:182

Title Index

Kelly, Dot, and Esmeralda (Goodall) **25**:45
The Kellyhorns (Cooney) **23**:22
The Kelpie's Pearls (Hunter) **25**:75
Kenny's Window (Sendak) **1**:170
Kermit the Hermit (Peet) **12**:196
Kermit's Garden of Verses (Prelutsky) **13**:170
Kerstmis (Bruna) **7**:49
The Kestrel (Alexander) **5**:25
Kettering: Master Inventor (Lavine) **35**:147
A Kettle of Hawks and Other Wildlife Groups (Arnosky) **15**:4
Kevin's Grandma (Williams) **48**:191
The Key (Cresswell) **18**:107
The Key (Dillon) **26**:28
Key to the Treasure (Parish) **22**:156
The Key Word, and Other Mysteries (Asimov) **12**:55
The Kid in the Red Jacket (Park) **34**:157
Kid Power (Pfeffer) **11**:199
Kid Power Strikes Back (Pfeffer) **11**:205
The Kid Who Only Hit Homers (Christopher) **33**:46
Kidnapped on Astarr (Nixon) **24**:142
The Kidnapping of Christina Lattimore (Nixon) **24**:137
The Kids' Cat Book (dePaola) **4**:63
Kids in Court: The ACLU Defends Their Rights (Epstein and Epstein) **26**:69
Killer Fish (Freedman) **20**:83
Killer Snakes (Freedman) **20**:83
Killer Whales (Simon) **9**:212
Killing Mr. Griffin (Duncan) **29**:71
Kilmeny of the Orchard (Montgomery) **8**:135
Kim/Kimi (Irwin) **40**:112
Kimako's Story (Jordan) **10**:120
Kim's Place and Other Poems (Hopkins) **44**:85
Kind Hearts and Gentle Monsters (Yep) **17**:205
A Kind of Wild Justice (Ashley) **4**:16
Kinda Blue (Grifalconi) **35**:79
A Kindle of Kittens (Godden) **20**:136
The Kindred of the Wild: A Book of Animal Life (Roberts) **33**:191
The King and His Friends (Aruego) **5**:27
King Arthur (Haar) **15**:115
The King at the Door (Cole) **18**:81
King Bidgood's in the Bathtub (Wood and Wood) **26**:222
King George's Head Was Made of Lead (Monjo) **2**:122
King Grisly-Beard (Sendak) **1**:171
King Henry's Palace (Hutchins) **20**:152
King Horn (Crossley-Holland) **47**:23
The King in the Garden (Garfield) **21**:118
King Krakus and the Dragon (Domanska) **40**:48
King Nimrod's Tower (Garfield) **21**:117
King of Another Country (French) **37**:54
The King of Ireland's Son (Colum) **36**:22
King of Kazoo (Peck) **45**:109
King of Spuds; Who's for the Zoo? (Ure) **34**:186
The King of the Cats (Guillot) **22**:66
King of the Cats: A Ghost Story (Galdone) **16**:103
The King of the Copper Mountains (Biegel) **27**:28
King of the Reindeer and Other Animal Stories (Guillot) **22**:70
King of the Wind (Henry) **4**:111
King of Wreck Island (Cooney) **23**:21
King Rollo and the Birthday; King Rollo and the Bread; King Rollo and the New Shoes (McKee) **38**:167
King Rollo's Autumn; King Rollo's Spring; King Rollo's Summer; King Rollo's Winter (McKee) **38**:175
King Rollo's Letter and Other Stories (McKee) **38**:174

King Rollo's Playroom and Other Stories (McKee) **38**:173
King Tree (French) **37**:37
The King Who Saved Himself from Being Saved (Ciardi) **19**:79
The King Who Tried to Fry an Egg on His Head (Ginsburg) **45**:20
The Kingdom and the Cave (Aiken) **1**:4
A Kingdom in a Horse (Wojciechowska) **1**:197
The Kingdom of the Sun (Asimov) **12**:34
The Kingdom Under the Sea and Other Stories (Aiken) **19**:9
The Kingfisher Book of Children's Poetry (Rosen) **45**:135
The King's Beard (Wibberley) **3**:228
The King's Corsair (Guillot) **22**:56
The King's Falcon (Fox) **1**:78
The King's Fifth (O'Dell) **1**:148
The King's Flower (Anno) **14**:33
The King's Fountain (Alexander) **1**:15; **5**:22
Kings in Exile (Roberts) **33**:202
The King's Monster (Haywood) **22**:104
The King's New Clothes (McKissack) **23**:239
The King's Room (Dillon) **26**:30
The King's Stilts (Seuss) **9**:174
The King's White Elephant (Harris) **30**:115
Kintu: A Congo Adventure (Enright) **4**:71
Kirk's Law (Peck) **45**:116
The Kissimmee Kid (Cleaver and Cleaver) **6**:113
Kit (Gardam) **12**:171
Kitchen Carton Crafts (Sattler) **24**:212
The Kitchen Madonna (Godden) **20**:132
The Kite That Braved Old Orchard Beach: Year-Round Poems for Young People (Kennedy) **27**:103
The Kite That Won the Revolution (Asimov) **12**:37
Kitten Can (McMillan) **47**:165
Kitten for a Day (Keats) **35**:139
Kitten from One to Ten (Ginsburg) **45**:15
Kiviok's Magic Journey: An Eskimo Legend (Houston) **3**:86
Klippity Klop (Emberley) **5**:98
The Knee-High Man and Other Tales (Lester) **2**:112
Kneeknock Rise (Babbitt) **2**:6
The Knife (Stine) **37**:117
The Knight and the Dragon (dePaola) **4**:64
The Knight of the Golden Plain (Hunter) **25**:89
The Knight of the Lion (McDermott) **9**:117
Knight's Castle (Eager) **43**:83
Knight's Fee (Sutcliff) **1**:187; **37**:154
Knights in Armor (Glubok) **1**:100
The Knights of King Midas (Berna) **19**:37
Knights of the Crusades (Williams) **8**:225
Knights of the Kitchen Table (Scieszka) **27**:156
Knights of the Kitchen Table (Smith) **47**:200
Knock at a Star: A Child's Introduction to Poetry (Kennedy) **27**:99
Know about AIDS (Hyde) **23**:174
Know about Alcohol (Hyde) **23**:165
Know about Drugs (Hyde) **23**:159
Know about Smoking (Hyde) **23**:169
Know Your Feelings (Hyde) **23**:161
Koala Lou (Fox) **23**:115
Komodo! (Sis) **45**:169
König Hupf der 1 (Heine) **18**:147
Koning Arthur (Haar) **15**:115
Konrad: Oder, das Kind aus der Konservenbüchs (Noestlinger) **12**:187
Konta stis ragies (Zei) **6**:262
Koya Delaney and the Good Girl Blues (Greenfield) **38**:93

Kpo, the Leopard (Guillot) **22**:57
The Kraymer Mystery (Allan) **43**:19
Kristy and the Snobs (Martin) **32**:205
Kristy's Great Idea (Martin) **32**:202
The Kweeks of Kookatumdee (Peet) **12**:207
Labour in Vain (Garfield) **21**:109
The Labours of Herakles (Crossley-Holland) **47**:49
The Lace Snail (Byars) **16**:54
The Lad of the Gad (Garner) **20**:117
Lad With a Whistle (Brink) **30**:12
Ladder of Angels: Scenes from the Bible (L'Engle) **14**:152
Ladies of the Gothics: Tales of Romance and Terror by the Gentle Sex (Manley) **3**:145
Ladis and the Ant (Sanchez-Silva) **12**:232
Lady Daisy (King-Smith) **40**:164
Lady Ellen Grae (Cleaver and Cleaver) **6**:102
The Lady of Guadalupe (dePaola) **4**:63
The Lady Who Put Salt in Her Coffee (Schwartz) **25**:195
Ladybug (McClung) **11**:184
Lady's Girl (Bunting) **28**:44
Lafcadio, the Lion Who Shot Back (Silverstein) **5**:208
Lambs for Dinner (Betsy and Giulio Maestro) **45**:69
The Lamp From the Warlock's Tomb (Bellairs) **37**:21
The Lamplighter's Funeral (Garfield) **21**:109
The Land Beyond (Gripe) **5**:145
Land in the Sun: The Story of West Africa (Ashabranner and Davis) **28**:5
The Land of Black Gold (Herge) **6**:148
The Land of Canaan (Asimov) **12**:46
Land of Dreams (Foreman) **32**:95
The Land of Forgotten Beasts (Wersba) **3**:217
Land under the Sea (Nixon) **24**:146
Landet Utanfor (Gripe) **5**:145
Landings (Hamley) **47**:56
Langston Hughes: A Biography (Meltzer) **13**:125
Language and Man (Adler) **27**:24
The Language of Goldfish (Oneal) **13**:156
The Lantern Bearers (Sutcliff) **1**:187; **37**:154
Larger than Life (Lunn) **18**:158
The Lark and the Laurel (Willard) **2**:220
Larry Makes Music (Unnerstad) **36**:198
Lasca and Her Pups (Trezise) **41**:142
Last Act; Spellbound (Pike) **29**:171
The Last Battle (Lewis) **3**:135; **27**:104-51
The Last Battle (Wibberley) **3**:228
The Last Guru (Pinkwater) **4**:168
The Last Hundred Years: Household Technology (Cohen) **43**:42
The Last Hundred Years: Medicine (Cohen) **43**:40
The Last King of Cornwall (Causley) **30**:40
The Last Little Cat (DeJong) **1**:59
The Last Mission (Mazer) **16**:130
The Last Noo-Noo (Murphy) **39**:180
The Last Princess: The Story of Princess Ka'iulani of Hawai'i (Stanley) **46**:145
The Last Silk Dress (Rinaldi) **46**:81
The Last Slice of Rainbow and Other Stories (Aiken) **19**:16
Last Sunday (Peck) **45**:110
The Last Tales Of Uncle Remus (Lester) **41**:109
The Last Tales Of Uncle Remus (Pinkney) **43**:171
The Last Two Elves in Denmark (Calhoun) **42**:13
The Last Viking (Treece) **2**:186
The Late Spring (Fritz) **14**:110
Laura's Luck (Sachs) **2**:132
Laurie Loved Me Best (Klein) **21**:164
Laurie's New Brother (Schlein) **41**:184

Lavinia's Cottage (Goodall) **25**:53
The Lazies: Tales of the Peoples of Russia (Ginsburg) **45**:6
The Lazy Bear (Wildsmith) **2**:213
Lazy Blackbird, and Other Verses (Prelutsky) **13**:164
Lazy Tinka (Seredy) **10**:182
Lazy Tommy Pumpkinhead (Pene du Bois) **1**:64
Leaders of the Middle East (Haskins) **39**:49
Leaper: The Story of an Atlantic Salmon (McClung) **11**:181
Learning to Say Good-By: When a Parent Dies (LeShan) **6**:188
The Least One (Politi) **29**:184
The Least One (Sawyer) **36**:156
Leave the Cooking to Me (Gaberman) **33**:15
Leave Well Enough Alone (Wells) **16**:208
The Leaving Morning (Johnson) **33**:96
The Left Overs (Spence) **26**:199
The Left-Hander's World (Silverstein and Silverstein) **25**:216
The Legacy of Lucian Van Zandt (St. John) **46**:115
Legend Days (Highwater) **17**:30
The Legend of New Amsterdam (Spier) **5**:226
The Legend of Old Befana: An Italian Christmas Story (dePaola) **4**:65
The Legend of Rosepetal (Zwerger) **46**:195
The Legend of Scarface: A Blackfeet Indian Tale (San Souci) **43**:179
The Legend of Sleepy Hollow: Retold from Washington Irving (San Souci) **43**:182
The Legend of St. Columba (Colum) **36**:44
The Legend of Tarik (Myers) **16**:138
The Legend of the Bluebonnet: An Old Tale of Texas (dePaola) **24**:91
The Legend of the Indian Paintbrush (dePaola) **24**:100
The Legend of the Willow Plate (Tresselt) **30**:210
Legends of Hawaii (Colum) **36**:27
Legends of the Saints (Petry) **12**:212
Leif Eriksson: First Voyage to America (Shippen) **36**:172
Leif the Lucky (d'Aulaire and d'Aulaire) **21**:47
Leif the Unlucky (Haugaard) **11**:109
A Lemon and a Star (Spykman) **35**:216
The Lemonade Trick (Corbett) **1**:46
Lena Horne (Haskins) **39**:45
Lenny and Lola (Brown) **29**:4
Lenny Kandell, Smart Aleck (Conford) **10**:99
Lens and Shutter: An Introduction to Photography (Weiss) **4**:226
Lentil (McCloskey) **7**:200
Leonard Everett Fisher's Liberty Book (Fisher) **18**:126
Leonardo Da Vinci (Stanley) **46**:156
Leonardo da Vinci (Williams) **8**:226
Leonardo da Vinci: The Artist, Inventor, Scientist in Three-Dimensional, Movable Pictures (Provensen and Provensen) **11**:218
The Leopard (Bodker) **23**:11
Leopard's Prey (Wibberley) **3**:229
The Leopard's Tooth (Kotzwinkle) **6**:182
Leo's Christmas Surprise (Daly) **41**:55
Leroy Is Missing (Singer) **48**:126
Lester and the Unusual Pet (Blake) **31**:20
Lester at the Seaside (Blake) **31**:20
Let Me Fall before I Fly (Wersba) **3**:218
Let the Balloon Go (Southall) **2**:153
Let the Circle Be Unbroken (Taylor) **9**:228
Let There Be Light: A Book about Windows (Giblin) **29**:91
Let X Be Excitement (Harris) **47**:81

Let's Be Early Settlers with Daniel Boone (Parish) **22**:156
Let's Be Friends Again! (Wilhelm) **46**:163
Let's Be Indians (Parish) **22**:154
Let's Celebrate: Holiday Decorations You Can Make (Parish) **22**:162
Let's Cook without Cooking (Hautzig) **22**:76
Let's Do Better (Leaf) **25**:128
Let's Find Out about Earth (Knight) **38**:105
Let's Find Out about Insects (Knight) **38**:105
Let's Find Out about Magnets (Knight) **38**:103
Let's Find Out about Mars (Knight) **38**:103
Let's Find Out about Rocks and Minerals (Knight) **38**:109
Let's Find Out about Sound (Knight) **38**:118
Let's Find Out about Telephones (Knight) **38**:104
Let's Find Out about the Ocean (Knight) **38**:109
Let's Find Out about Weather (Knight) **38**:104
Let's Go Dinosaur Tracking! (Schlein) **41**:196
Let's Go Home, Little Bear (Waddell) **31**:199
Let's Grow a Garden (Fujikawa) **25**:39
Let's Hear It for the Queen (Childress) **14**:92
Let's Make More Presents: Easy and Inexpensive Gifts for Every Occasion (Hautzig) **22**:84
Let's Make Presents: 100 Gifts for Less than $1.00 (Hautzig) **22**:77
Let's Make Rabbits: A Fable (Lionni) **7**:139
Let's Paint a Rainbow (Carle) **10**:85
Let's Play! (Fujikawa) **25**:38
Let's Try It Out: Hot and Cold (Simon) **9**:206
A Letter for Tiger (Janosch) **26**:79
The Letter, The Witch, and the Ring (Bellairs) **37**:9
A Letter to Amy (Keats) **1**:115; **35**:135
Letterbox: The Art and History of Letters (Adkins) **7**:27
Letters from Italy (Fisher) **18**:127
Letters from the General (Biegel) **27**:33
Letters from the Inside (Marsden) **34**:150
Letters to Horseface: Being the Story of Wolfgang Amadeus Mozart's Journey to Italy, 1769-1770, When He Was a Boy of Fourteen (Monjo) **2**:123
Letters to Judy: What Your Kids Wish They Could Tell You (Blume) **15**:80
Letters to Pauline (Kruss) **9**:87
Letting Swift River Go (Yolen) **44**:198
Der Leuchtturm auf den Hummer-Klippen (Kruss) **9**:82
Liar, Liar (Yep) **17**:206
Libby on Wednesday (Snyder) **31**:169
Libby, Oscar and Me (Graham) **31**:94
La Liebre y la Tortuga & La Tortuga y la Liebre / The Hare and the Tortoise & The Tortoise and the Hare (Pene du Bois) **1**:63
Life and Death (Zim) **2**:228
Life and Death in Nature (Simon) **9**:211
The Life and Death of a Brave Bull (Wojciechowska) **1**:198
The Life and Death of Martin Luther King, Jr. (Haskins) **3**:65
The Life I Live: Collected Poems (Lenski) **26**:122
Life in Colonial America (Speare) **8**:210
Life in the Dark: How Animals Survive at Night (Simon) **9**:208
Life in the Middle Ages (Williams) **8**:227
Life in the Universe (Silverstein and Silverstein) **25**:200
The Life of Jack Sprat, His Wife, and His Cat (Galdone) **16**:94
The Life of Winston Churchill (Wibberley) **3**:229
Life on Ice: How Animals Survive in the Arctic (Simon) **9**:210

Life Story (Burton) **11**:51
Life with Working Parents: Practical Hints for Everyday Situations (Hautzig) **22**:84
Lift Every Voice (Sterling and Quarles) **1**:179
Lift Every Voice and Sing: Words and Music (Johnson) **32**:173
Light (Crews) **7**:58
Light and Darkness (Branley) **13**:41
The Light Beyond the Forest: The Quest for the Holy Grail (Sutcliff) **37**:170
A Light in the Attic (Silverstein) **5**:212
A Light in the Dark: The Life of Samuel Gridley Howe (Meltzer) **13**:120
The Lightey Club (Singer) **48**:131
Lightfoot: The Story of an Indian Boy (Shippen) **36**:172
Lighthouse Island (Coatsworth) **2**:60
The Lighthouse Keeper's Son (Chauncy) **6**:94
The Lighthouse on the Lobster Cliffs (Kruss) **9**:82
Lightning (Bendick) **5**:39
Lightning and Thunder (Zim) **2**:228
The Lightning Bolt (Bedard) **35**:61
Lights, Lenses, and Lasers (Berger) **32**:39
Lights Out (Stine) **37**:117
A Likely Place (Fox) **1**:78
The Lilith Summer (Irwin) **40**:105
Lillian Wald: Angel of Henry Street (Epstein and Epstein) **26**:46
Lillie of Watts: A Birthday Discovery (Walter) **15**:203
Lillie of Watts Takes a Giant Step (Walter) **15**:204
Lillypilly Hill (Spence) **26**:192
Lily and the Lost Boy (Fox) **44**:68
Limericks (Ehlert) **28**:109
Limericks by Lear (Lear) **1**:127
Lincoln: A Photobiography (Freedman) **20**:87
Lines Scribbled on an Envelope and Other Poems (L'Engle) **1**:131
Linnea in Monet's Garden (Bjork) **22**:12
Linnea's Almanac (Bjork) **22**:15
Linnea's Windowsill Garden (Bjork) **22**:15
Linsey Woolsey (Tudor) **13**:192
The Lion and the Bird's Nest (Nakatani) **30**:158
The Lion and the Mouse: An Aesop Fable (Young) **27**:218
Lion and the Ostrich Chicks and Other African Folk Tales (Bryan) **18**:36
The Lion and the Unicorn (Baumann) **35**:42
The Lion Cub (Dillon) **26**:27
A Lion for Lewis (Wells) **16**:212
Lion Gate and Labyrinth (Baumann) **35**:48
A Lion in the Meadow (Mahy) **7**:178
A Lion in the Night (Allen) **44**:7
The Lion, the Witch, and the Wardrobe (Lewis) **3**:135 **27**:104-51
The Lion's Whiskers: Tales of High Africa (Ashabranner and Davis) **28**:3
Lisa and Lottie (Kaestner) **4**:124
Listen for the Fig Tree (Mathis) **3**:149
Listen for the Singing (Little) **4**:152
Listen, Little Girl, Before You Come to New York (Leaf) **25**:123
Listen to a Shape (Brown) **12**:107
Listen to the Crows (Pringle) **4**:180
Listen to the Wind (Brinsmead) **47**:10
Listening (Seredy) **10**:172
The Listening Walk (Showers) **6**:242
Lito and the Clown (Politi) **29**:192
The Little Auto (Lenski) **26**:100
Little Babar Books (Brunhoff) **4**:37, 38
Little Bear (Minarik) **33**:122
Little Bear's Friend (Minarik) **33**:125
Little Bear's Visit (Minarik) **33**:125

Little Blue and Little Yellow: A Story for Pippo and Ann and Other Children (Lionni) 7:127
Little Boat Lighter Than a Cork (Krauss) 42:130
A Little Book of Little Beasts (Hoberman) 22:110
Little Books (Burningham) 9:46, 47
A Little Boy Was Drawing (Duvoisin) 23:90
The Little Brass Band (Brown) 10:65
Little Brother and Little Sister (Cooney) 23:31
The Little Brute Family (Hoban) 3:78
The Little Captain (Biegel) 27:29
The Little Captain and the Pirate Treasure (Biegel) 27:34
The Little Captain and the Seven Towers (Biegel) 27:30
The Little Carousel (Brown) 12:93
Little Chameleon (Cassedy) 26:11
Little Chicken (Brown) 10:52
The Little Cow and the Turtle (DeJong) 1:59
The Little Cowboy (Brown) 10:56
A Little Destiny (Cleaver and Cleaver) 6:112
Little Dog Lost (Guillot) 22:71
The Little Dog of Fo (Harris) 30:118
Little Dog Toby (Field) 21:72
Little Dogs of the Prarie (Scott) 20:196
Little Dracula at the Seashore (Waddell)
  See *Little Dracula at the Seaside*
Little Dracula at the Seaside (Waddell) 31:189
Little Dracula Goes to School (Waddell) 31:189
Little Dracula's Christmas (Waddell) 31:186
Little Dracula's First Bite (Waddell) 31:186
The Little Drummer Boy (Keats) 1:116; 35:134
Little Eddie (Haywood) 22:93
The Little Farmer (Brown) 10:56
A Little Fear (Wrightson) 14:214
The Little Fir Tree (Brown) 10:64
The Little Fisherman, a Fish Story (Brown) 10:53
The Little Fishes (Haugaard) 11:105
Little Frightened Tiger (Brown) 10:63
Little Fur Family (Brown) 10:53
The Little Giant Girl and the Elf Boy (Minarik) 33:125
Little Giants (Simon) 9:219
The Little Girl and the Dragon (Minarik) 33:128
A Little Girl of Nineteen Hundred (Lenski) 26:99
The Little Girl Who Lived Down the Road (Daly) 41:52
Little Grunt and the Big Egg: A Prehistoric Fairy Tale (dePaola) 24:103
Little Hobbin (Zwerger) 46:202
The Little House (Burton) 11:47
Little House in the Big Woods (Wilder) 2:205
Little House on the Prairie (Wilder) 2:206
Little Indian (Parish) 22:157
The Little Indian Basket Maker (Clark) 16:80
The Little Island (Brown) 10:54
Little John (Orgel) 48:81
The Little Juggler (Cooney) 23:26
The Little King, the Little Queen, the Little Monster and Other Stories You Can Make up Yourself (Krauss) 42:128
Little Kit: Or, the Industrious Flea Circus (McCully) 46:71
Little Leo (Politi) 29:188
Little Little (Kerr) 29:150
Little Little Sister (Curry) 31:87
Little Lost Lamb (Brown) 10:53
A Little Love (Hamilton) 11:91
A Little Lower than the Angels (McCaughrean) 38:139
The Little Man (Kaestner) 4:127
The Little Man and the Big Thief (Kaestner) 4:127
The Little Man and the Little Miss (Kaestner) 4:127

Little Man in the Family (Shearer) 34:166
Little Monster at Home (Mayer) 11:173
Little Monster at School (Mayer) 11:173
Little Monster at Work (Mayer) 11:173
Little Monster's Alphabet Book (Mayer) 11:173
Little Monster's Bedtime Book (Mayer) 11:173
Little Monster's Counting Book (Mayer) 11:173
Little Monster's Mother Goose (Mayer) 11:173
Little Monster's Neighborhood (Mayer) 11:173
Little Monster's Word Book (Mayer) 11:172
Little Navajo Bluebird (Clark) 16:76
Little O (Unnerstad) 36:191
Little Obie and the Flood (Waddell) 31:198
Little Obie and the Kidnap (Waddell) 31:201
Little Old Automobile (Ets) 33:79
Little Old Mrs. Pepperpot and Other Stories (Proysen) 24:181
A Little Oven (Estes) 2:74
Little Plum (Godden) 20:131
A Little Prayer (Cooney) 23:27
The Little Prince (Saint-Exupery) 10:137-61
The Little Prince (Saint-Exupery)
  See *Le petit prince*
Little Rabbit Foo Foo (Rosen) 45:141
Little Rabbit, the High Jumper (Schlein) 41:180
Little Raccoon and No Trouble at All (Moore) 15:142
Little Raccoon and Poems from the Woods (Moore) 15:144
Little Raccoon and the Outside World (Moore) 15:140
Little Raccoon and the Thing in the Pool (Moore) 15:140
Little Red Cap (Zwerger) 46:191
Little Red Hen (Domanska) 40:44
The Little Red Hen (Galdone) 16:99
The Little Red Hen (McKissack) 23:237
The Little Red Horse (Sawyer) 36:160
Little Red Nose (Schlein) 41:177
Little Red Riding Hood (Galdone) 16:99
Little Red Riding Hood (Goodall) 25:56
The Little Roaring Tiger (Zimnik) 3:243
Little Rystu (Ginsburg) 45:11
A Little Schubert (Goffstein) 3:59
Little Spot Board Books (Hill) 13:96
The Little Spotted Fish (Yolen) 4:261
The Little Swineherd and Other Tales (Fox) 44:61
Little Tiger, Get Well Soon! (Janosch) 26:81
Little Tim and the Brave Sea Captain (Ardizzone) 3:5
Little Toot (Gramatky) 22:39
Little Toot and the Loch Ness Monster (Gramatky) 22:46
Little Toot on the Grand Canal (Gramatky) 22:45
Little Toot on the Mississippi (Gramatky) 22:45
Little Toot on the Thames (Gramatky) 22:44
Little Toot through the Golden Gate (Gramatky) 22:46
Little Town on the Prairie (Wilder) 2:206
The Little Train (Lenski) 26:105
The Little Witch (Mahy) 7:180
Little Women; or, Meg, Jo, Beth, and Amy (Alcott) 1:10; 38:1-63
The Little Wood Duck (Wildsmith) 2:213
The Little Worm Book (Ahlberg and Ahlberg) 18:7
The Littlest One in the Family (Duncan) 29:66
Liverwurst Is Missing (Mayer) 11:175
Lives at Stake: The Science and Politics of Environmental Health (Pringle) 4:185
The Lives of Christopher Chant (Jones) 23:197
Lives of Musicians: Good Times, Bad Times (And What the Neighbors Thought) (Krull) 44:102

The Lives of Spiders (Patent) 19:155
Lives of the Artists: Masterpieces, Messes (And What the Neighbors Thought) (Krull) 44:112
Lives of the Writers: Comedies, Tragedies (And What the Neighbors Thought) (Krull) 44:105
Living in Imperial Rome (Dillon) 26:31
Living Lanterns: Luminescence in Animals (Simon) 39:186
Living Things (Bendick) 5:42
Living Up the Street: Narrative Recollections (Soto) 38:186
Liza Lou and the Yeller Belly Swamp (Mayer) 11:170
Lizard in the Sun (Ryder) 37:96
Lizard Music (Pinkwater) 4:164
Lizzie Dripping (Cresswell) 18:105
Lizzie Lights (Chauncy) 6:93
Lizzie Silver of Sherwood Forest (Singer) 48:129
Lizzie's Invitation (Keller) 45:50
Lizzy's Lion (Gay) 27:84
Loads of Codes and Secret Ciphers (Janeczko) 47:103
The Loathsome Couple (Gorey) 36:99
The Loathsome Dragon (Wiesner) 43:203
Lob Lie-by-the-Fire; or, The Luck of Lingborough (Caldecott) 14:83
Local News (Soto) 38:200
Loch (Zindel) 45:201
Lock, Stock, and Barrel (Sobol) 4:207
Locked in Time (Duncan) 29:77
Locks and Keys (Gibbons) 8:91
Lodestar, Rocket Ship to Mars: The Record of the First Operation Sponsored by the Federal Commission for Interplanetary Exploration, June 1, 1971 (Branley) 13:24
Loggerhead Turtle: Survivor From the Sea (Scott) 20:194
Logic for Beginners: Through Games, Jokes, and Puzzles (Adler) 27:18
Lois Lenski's Big Book of Mr. Small (Lenski) 26:125
Lollipop: Kinderroman (Noestlinger) 12:188
The Lollipop Princess: A Play for Paper Dolls in One Act (Estes) 2:74
A Lollygag of Limericks (Livingston) 7:173
Lon Po Po: A Red-Riding Hood Story from China (Young) 27:222
London Bridge Is Falling Down (Emberley) 5:96
London Bridge Is Falling Down! (Spier) 5:217
Lone Bull's Horse Raid (Goble) 21:130
The Loneliness of Mia (Beckman) 25:15
The Lonely Hearts Club (Klein) 21:163
Lonely Veronica (Duvoisin) 23:103
Lonesome Boy (Bontemps) 6:83
Long Ago When I Was Young (Nesbit) 3:164
The Long and Short of Measurement (Cobb) 2:66
Long, Broad, and Quickeye (Ness) 6:205
The Long Christmas (Sawyer) 36:157
A Long Hard Journey: The Story of the Pullman Porter (McKissack) 23:240
The Long Journey from Space (Simon) 9:219
Long Journey Home: Stories from Black History (Lester) 2:113
The Long Lost Coelacanth and Other Living Fossils (Aliki) 9:23
Long Neck and Thunder Foot (Foreman) 32:96
The Long Red Scarf (Hilton) 25:59
Long River (Bruchac) 46:19
The Long Secret (Fitzhugh) 1:72
Long Shot for Paul (Christopher) 33:41
Long Stretch at First Base (Christopher) 33:38

Long Tom and the Dead Hand (Crossley-Holland) **47**:49

The Long View into Space (Simon) **9**:214

The Long Voyage: The Life Cycle of a Green Turtle (Silverstein and Silverstein) **25**:207

The Long Walk (Mattingley) **24**:124

A Long Way from Verona (Gardam) **12**:162

The Long Way Home (Benary-Isbert) **12**:76

The Long Winter (Wilder) **2**:206

Longbeard the Wizard (Fleischman) **15**:107

The Longest Weekend (Arundel) **35**:13

Longtime Passing (Brinsmead) **47**:12

Look Again! (Hoban) **13**:101

Look Around! A Book About Shapes (Fisher) **18**:137

Look at Me! (Daly) **41**:58

Look at Your Eyes (Showers) **6**:242

Look in the Mirror (Epstein and Epstein) **26**:64

Look, There Is a Turtle Flying (Domanska) **40**:39

Look Through My Window (Little) **4**:149

Look to the Night Sky: An Introduction to Star Watching (Simon) **9**:212

Look What I Can Do (Aruego) **5**:29

Look What I've Got! (Browne) **19**:63

Look Who's Playing First Base (Christopher) **33**:45

Look-Alikes (Drescher) **20**:60

The Looking Book (Hoberman) **22**:110

Looking for Santa Claus (Drescher) **20**:60

Looking for Your Name: A Collection of Contempory Poems (Janeczko) **47**:113

Looking-for-Something: The Story of a Stray Burro of Ecuador (Clark) **16**:79

The Looking-Glass Castle (Biegel) **27**:33

The Look-It-Up Book of Mammals (Lauber) **16**:114

The Look-It-Up Book of Stars and Planets (Lauber) **16**:115

The Loon's Necklace (Cleaver) **13**:68

Loopy (Gramatky) **22**:41

The Lorax (Seuss) **1**:87; **9**:192

The Lord Is My Shepherd: The Twenty-Third Psalm (Tudor) **13**:202

Lord Rex: The Lion Who Wished (McKee) **38**:163

The Lord's Prayer (d'Aulaire and d'Aulaire) **21**:41

Lordy, Aunt Hattie (Thomas) **8**:212

Lorry Driver (Munari) **9**:125

Losers Weepers (Needle) **43**:138

Losing Joe's Place (Korman) **25**:112

Lost at the Fair (Sharp) **27**:163

The Lost Boy (Fox) **44**:68

Lost Cities (Gallant) **30**:101

The Lost Diamonds of Killiecrankie (Crew) **42**:60

The Lost Dispatch: A Story of Antietam (Sobol) **4**:206

The Lost Farm (Curry) **31**:78

Lost in the Barrens (Mowat) **20**:168

The Lost Island (Dillon) **26**:20

The Lost Lake (Say) **22**:211

Lost Wild America: The Story of Our Extinct and Vanishing Wildlife (McClung) **11**:185

Lost Wild Worlds: The Story of Extinct and Vanishing Wildlife of the Eastern Hemisphere (McClung) **11**:190

The Lothian Run (Hunter) **25**:78

Lotje, de kleine olifant (Haar) **15**:116

Lotta on Troublemaker Street (Lindgren) **1**:137

Lotta's Bike (Lindgren) **39**:154

Lotta's Christmas Surprise (Lindgren) **39**:157

Lotta's Easter Surprise (Lindgren) **39**:163

Lotta's Progress (St. John) **46**:126

Lottie and Lisa (Kaestner) **4**:124

The Lotus and the Grail: Legends from East to West (Harris) **30**:116

The Lotus Caves (Christopher) **2**:40

The Lotus Cup (Curry) **31**:84

Louie (Keats) **35**:139

Louie's Search (Keats) **35**:141

Louis the Fish (Yorinks) **20**:216

Louisa May: The World and Works of Louisa May Alcott (St. John) **46**:124

Louly (Brink) **30**:17

Love and Betrayal and Hold the Mayo! (Pascal) **25**:185

Love and Tennis (Slote) **4**:202

Love and the Merry-Go-Round (Harris) **30**:125

Love Is a Special Way of Feeling (Anglund) **1**:20

Love Is One of the Choices (Klein) **19**:90

Love You Forever (Munsch) **19**:145

A Lovely Tomorrow (Allan) **43**:29

The Loyal Cat (Namioka) **48**:68

Lucie Babbidge's House (Cassedy) **26**:15

Lucifer Wilkins (Garfield) **21**:107

Lucinda's Year of Jubilo (Sawyer) **36**:155

The Luck of Pokey Bloom (Conford) **10**:93

The Luckiest Girl (Cleary) **2**:48

The Luckiest One of All (Peet) **12**:206

The Lucky Baseball Bat (Christopher) **33**:36

Lucky Chuck (Cleary) **8**:61

Lucky Little Lena (Flack) **28**:126

Lucky, Lucky White Horse (Epstein and Epstein) **26**:59

Lucky Porcupine! (Schlein) **41**:191

Lucky Seven: Sports Stories (Christopher) **33**:45

Lucky Starr and the Big Sun of Mercury (Asimov) **12**:31

Lucky Starr and the Moons of Jupiter (Asimov) **12**:32

Lucky Starr and the Oceans of Venus (Asimov) **12**:31

Lucky Starr and the Pirates of the Asteroids (Asimov) **12**:30

Lucky Starr and the Rings of Saturn (Asimov) **12**:32

The Lucky Stone (Clifton) **5**:59

Lucky You (Leaf) **25**:133

Lucretia Mott, Gentle Warrior (Sterling) **1**:179

Lucy and Tom at the Seaside (Hughes) **15**:123

Lucy and Tom Go to School (Hughes) **15**:122

Lucy and Tom's 1,2,3 (Hughes) **15**:134

Lucy and Tom's A.B.C. (Hughes) **15**:130

Lucy and Tom's Christmas (Hughes) **15**:127

Lucy and Tom's Day (Hughes) **15**:120

Lucy Brown and Mr. Grimes (Ardizzone) **3**:5

Lucy's Bay (Crew) **42**:57

Ludell (Wilkinson) **20**:207

Ludell and Willie (Wilkinson) **20**:210

Ludell's New York Time (Wilkinson) **20**:210

Luke and Angela (Noestlinger) **12**:188

Luki-Live (Noestlinger) **12**:188

Lulu and the Flying Babies (Simmonds) **23**:244

Lum Fu and the Golden Mountains (Tresselt) **30**:214

Lumberjack (Kurelek) **2**:101

Lumps, Bumps, and Rashes: A Look at Kids' Diseases (Nourse) **33**:140

Luna: The Story of a Moth (McClung) **11**:181

The Lure of the Wild: The Last Three Animal Stories (Roberts) **33**:209

Luther Tarbox (Adkins) **7**:22

Lyme Disease: The Great Imitator (Silverstein, Silverstein, and Silverstein) **25**:226

M. C. Higgins, the Great (Hamilton) **1**:104; **11**:71

M. E. and Morton (Cassedy) **26**:14

Ma and Pa Dracula (Martin) **32**:205

MA nDA LA (Adoff) **7**:31

MA Nda La (McCully) **46**:58

Machine Tools (Zim) **2**:229

The Machine-Gunners (Westall) **13**:249

Macho Nacho and Other Rhyming Riddles (Betsy and Giulio Maestro) **45**:89

The MacLeod Place (Armstrong) **1**:22

The Macmillan Book of Astronomy (Gallant) **30**:102

Madame Doubtfire (Fine) **25**:21

Madeline (Bemelmans) **6**:66

Madeline and Ermadello (Wynne-Jones) **21**:229

Madeline and the Bad Hat (Bemelmans) **6**:73

Madeline and the Gypsies (Bemelmans) **6**:74

Madeline in London (Bemelmans) **6**:76

Madeline's Rescue (Bemelmans) **6**:69

Mademoiselle Misfortune (Brink) **30**:10

Madicken (Lindgren) **39**:149

Das Maerchen von Rosenblaettchen (Zwerger) **46**:195

Maggie: A Sheep Dog (Patent) **19**:163

Maggie and the Pirate (Keats) **35**:141

Maggie Forevermore (Nixon) **24**:149

Maggie Rose, Her Birthday Christmas (Sawyer) **36**:160

Maggie the Freak (Bunting) **28**:47

Maggie, Too (Nixon) **24**:146

"Magic": A Biography of Earvin Johnson (Haskins) **39**:40

Magic and the Night River (Bunting) **28**:46

The Magic Auto (Janosch) **26**:76

The Magic Bed-knob; or, How to Become a Witch in Ten Easy Lessons (Norton) **6**:219

Magic by the Lake (Eager) **43**:84

Magic Camera (Pinkwater) **4**:162

The Magic Change: Metamorphosis (Silverstein and Silverstein) **25**:204

The Magic City (Nesbit) **3**:164

The Magic Doctor (Biro) **28**:35

The Magic Finger (Dahl) **1**:52; **7**:72

Magic for Marigold (Montgomery) **8**:139

The Magic Gate (Williams) **8**:222

The Magic Grandfather (Williams) **8**:237

Magic House of Numbers (Adler) **27**:8

Magic in the Alley (Calhoun) **42**:15

The Magic Listening Cap: More Folk Tales from Japan (Uchida) **6**:251

The Magic Meadow (d'Aulaire and d'Aulaire) **21**:51

Magic Money (Clark) **16**:77

The Magic Moscow (Pinkwater) **4**:171

The Magic of Color (Simon) **39**:198

Magic or Not? (Eager) **43**:86

The Magic Pawnshop: A New Year's Eve Fantasy (Field) **21**:71

The Magic Pictures: More about the Wonderful Farm (Ayme) **25**:1

The Magic Porridge Pot (Galdone) **16**:101

The Magic Pudding: Being the Adventures of Bunyip Bluegum and His Friends Bill Barnacle and Sam Sawnoff (Lindsay) **8**:101

The Magic Rug (d'Aulaire and d'Aulaire) **21**:38

The Magic Saddle (Mattingley) **24**:127

The Magic School Bus at the Waterworks (Cole) **40**:14

The Magic School Bus in the Time of the Dinosaurs (Cole) **40**:32

The Magic School Bus inside a Hurricane (Cole) **40**:34

The Magic School Bus inside the Earth (Cole) **40**:20

The Magic School Bus inside the Human Body (Cole) **40**:24

Title Index

The Magic School Bus Lost in the Solar System (Cole) **40**:28
The Magic School Bus on the Ocean Floor (Cole) **40**:30
The Magic Spectacles and Other Easy to Read Stories (Moore) **15**:141
The Magic Stone (Farmer) **8**:77
The Magic Stove (Ginsburg) **45**:17
The Magic Summer (Streatfeild) **17**:196
Magic to Burn (Fritz) **14**:112
The Magic Tree: A Tale from the Congo (McDermott) **9**:110
The Magic Vase (French) **37**:50
The Magic Well (Ventura) **16**:193
The Magical Adventures of Pretty Pearl (Hamilton) **11**:86
The Magical Cockatoo (Sharp) **27**:165
Magical Melons (Brink) **30**:12
The Magician (Shulevitz) **5**:205
The Magician and Double Trouble (McKee) **38**:171
The Magician and the Balloon (McKee) **38**:166
The Magician and the Dragon (McKee) **38**:168
The Magician and the Petnapping (McKee) **38**:165
The Magician and the Sorcerer (McKee) **38**:163
The Magician Who Lost His Magic (McKee) **38**:161
The Magician's Apprentice (McKee) **38**:177
The Magician's Nephew (Lewis) **3**:135; **27**:104-51
The Magicians of Caprona (Jones) **23**:189
Magnets (Adler) **27**:21
The Magnificent Morris Mouse Clubhouse (Gibbons) **8**:92
Magnolia's Mixed-Up Magic (Nixon) **24**:143
Magnus Powermouse (King-Smith) **40**:143
Magpie Island (Thiele) **27**:206
Maho Tsukai No ABC (Anno) **14**:39
Mai contenti (Munari) **9**:125
Maid of the Wood (French) **37**:46
The Maiden on the Moor (Singer) **48**:146
Maikäfer Flieg!: Mein Vater, das Kriegsende, Cohn und Ich (Noestlinger) **12**:185
The Majesty of Grace (Langton) **33**:106
Major André, Brave Enemy (Duncan) **29**:68
Major: The Story of a Black Bear (McClung) **11**:180
Make a Circle, Keep Us In: Poems for a Good Day (Adoff) **7**:32
Make a Joyful Noise! (Haywood) **22**:105
Make a Joyful Noise unto the Lord! The Life of Mahalia Jackson, Queen of Gospel Singers (Jackson) **28**:142
Make It Special: Cards, Decorations, and Party Favors for Holidays and Other Celebrations (Hautzig) **22**:86
Make Way for Ducklings (McCloskey) **7**:200
Make Way for Dumb Bunnies (Pilkey) **48**:113
Make Way for Sam Houston (Fritz) **14**:121
Making Friends (Ormerod) **20**:180
Making Music for Money (Collier) **3**:46
The Making of an Afro-American: Martin Robison Delaney, 1812-1885 (Sterling) **1**:180
The Making of Fingers Finnigan (Doherty) **21**:56
The Making of Man: The Story of Our Ancient Ancestors (Collier) **3**:46
Making Sense of Money (Cobb) **3**:66
Making Sneakers (McMillan) **47**:162
Making the Mississippi Shout (Calhoun) **42**:4
Making the Movies (Bendick) **5**:34
Makoto, the Smallest Boy: A Story of Japan (Uchida) **6**:256

Malcolm X (Adoff) **7**:31
Malcolm X: A Force for Change (Grimes) **42**:91
Malcolm X: By Any Means Necessary (Myers) **35**:200
The Maldonado Miracle (Taylor) **30**:187
The Malibu and Other Poems (Livingston) **7**:170
Mama (Hopkins) **44**:88
Mama and Her Boys (Hopkins) **44**:91
Mama Hattie's Girl (Lenski) **26**:117
Mama, I Wish I Was Snow—Child, You'd Be Very Cold (Krauss) **42**:126
Mama One, Mama Two (MacLachlan) **14**:181
Mama, Papa and Baby Joe (Daly) **41**:58
Mammals and How They Live (McClung) **11**:182
Mammals of the Sea (Silverstein and Silverstein) **25**:205
Man and the Horse (Ventura) **16**:195
Man Changes the Weather (Bova) **3**:34
The Man from the Other Side (Orlev) **30**:165
Man from the Sky (Avi) **24**:8
Man in Space to the Moon (Branley) **13**:37
The Man in the Manhole and the Fix-It Men (Brown) **10**:54
The Man in the Woods (Wells) **16**:212
Man Mountain (Waddell) **31**:200
Man Must Speak: The Story of Language and How We Use It (Gallant) **30**:89
Man the Measurer: Our Units of Measure and How They Grew (Gallant) **30**:91
The Man Who Could Call Down Owls (Bunting) **28**:55
The Man Who Kept His Heart in a Bucket (Pinkney) **43**:168
The Man Who Knew Too Much: A Moral Tale from the Baila of Zambia (Lester) **41**:113
The Man Who Loved Books (Fritz) **14**:115
The Man Who Played Accordion Music (Tobias) **4**:218
The Man Who Sang the Sillies (Ciardi) **19**:77
The Man Who Sang the Sillies (Gorey) **36**:89
The Man Who Talked to a Tree (Baylor) **3**:15
The Man Who Took the Indoors Out (Lobel) **5**:168
The Man Who Was Going to Mind the House: A Norwegian Folk-Tale (McKee) **38**:161
The Man Who Was Poe (Avi) **24**:14
The Man Whose Mother Was a Pirate (Mahy) **7**:180
The Man Whose Name Was Not Thomas (Stanley) **46**:129
Man with a Sword (Treece) **2**:186
The Man with Eyes like Windows (Owen) **31**:146
The Man with the Purple Eyes (Zolotow) **2**:235
Maniac Magee (Spinelli) **26**:205
Man-Made Moons: The Earth Satellites and What They Will Tell Us (Adler) **27**:9
Ein Mann für Mama (Noestlinger) **12**:185
Manners Can Be Fun (Leaf) **25**:116
Man's Reach for the Stars (Gallant) **30**:89
Man's Reach into Space (Gallant) **30**:87
The Mansion in the Mist (Bellairs) **37**:25
The Many Lives of Benjamin Franklin (Aliki) **9**:25
The Many Mice of Mr. Brice (Seuss) **9**:193
Many Smokes, Many Moons: A Chronology of American Indian History through Indian Art (Highwater) **17**:28
Many Thousand Gone: African Americans from Slavery to Freedom (Hamilton) **40**:88
Many Thousand Gone: African Americans from Slavery to Freedom (Leo and Diane Dillon) **44**:46
Many Waters (L'Engle) **14**:155

A Map of Nowhere (Cross) **28**:94
The Maplin Bird (Peyton) **3**:177
Marathon and Steve (Rayner) **41**:128
Marc Brown's Full House (Brown) **29**:4
Marcella's Guardian Angel (Ness) **6**:208
The March on Washington (Haskins) **39**:72
Marcia (Steptoe) **12**:238
Marco Polo (Ventura) **16**:194
Marconi: Pioneer of Radio (Epstein and Epstein) **26**:43
Mardie to the Rescue (Lindgren) **39**:160
The Mare on the Hill (Locker) **14**:158
Marek, the Little Fool (Domanska) **40**:50
Margaret and Taylor (Henkes) **23**:125
Margaret Sanger: Pioneer of Birth Control (Meltzer) **13**:127
Margaret Wise Brown's Wonderful Story Book (Brown) **10**:56
Maria: A Christmas Story (Taylor) **30**:196
Maria Molina and the Days of the Dead (Krull) **44**:109
Maria Tallchief (Tobias) **4**:213
Marian Anderson (Tobias) **4**:213
Marianna May and Nursey (dePaola) **24**:93
Marilka (Domanska) **40**:41
Mark and the Monocycle (McKee) **38**:158
The Mark of the Horse Lord (Sutcliff) **1**:188; **37**:158
Mark Time (McBratney) **44**:116
Mark Twain: A Writer's Life (Meltzer) **13**:149
The Mark Twain Murders (Yep) **17**:205
Marked by Fire (Thomas) **19**:219
Marly the Kid (Pfeffer) **11**:198
Marra's World (Coatsworth) **2**:60
Marrying Off Mother (Noestlinger) **12**:185
Mars (Branley) **13**:25
Mars: Planet Number Four (Branley) **13**:25
Mars, the Red Planet (Asimov) **12**:55
Martha, the Movie Mouse (Lobel) **5**:164
Martha's Birthday (Wells) **16**:203
Martin de Porres: Saint of the New World (Tarry) **26**:215
Martin Luther King, Jr.: A Man to Remember (McKissack) **23**:235
Martin Luther King: The Man Who Climbed the Mountain (Paulsen) **19**:170
Martin's Hats (Blos) **18**:18
Martin's Mice (King-Smith) **40**:153
The Marvellous Adventures of Pinocchio (Collodi) See *Le Avventure di Pinocchio*
The Marvelous Misadventures of Sebastian (Alexander) **1**:16; **5**:21
Marvin K. Mooney Will You Please Go Now (Geisel) **1**:88
Mary Had a Little Lamb (McMillan) **47**:175
Mary Jane (Sterling) **1**:180
Mary Malloy and the Baby Who Wouldn't Sleep (Daly) **41**:62
Mary McLeod Bethune (Greenfield) **4**:99
Mary McLeod Bethune: A Great American Educator (McKissack) **23**:236
Mary of Mile 18 (Blades) **15**:52
Mary of Nazareth (Bodker) **23**:14
Mary Poppins (Travers) **2**:178
Mary Poppins from A to Z (Travers) **2**:179
Mary Poppins in the Park (Travers) **2**:179
The Marzipan Moon (Willard) **5**:249
The Mask (Bunting) **28**:48
Mask for My Heart (St. John) **46**:111
Masquerade (Williams) **4**:231
The Master Monkey (Mukerji) **10**:135
Master of the Elephants (Guillot) **22**:64
Master of the Grove (Kelleher) **36**:118

The Master of the Winds: And Other Tales from Siberia (Ginsburg) **45**:3
The Master Puppeteer (Paterson) **7**:231
Masters of Modern Music (Berger) **32**:5
Math Curse (Smith) **47**:206
Mathematics (Adler) **27**:26
Mathematics: The Story of Numbers, Symbols, and Space (Adler) **27**:12
Mathinna's People (Chauncy) **6**:92
Matilda (Dahl) **41**:40
Matilda Jane (Gerrard) **23**:119
De matroos (Bruna) **7**:50
Matt and Jo (Southall) **2**:155
Matt Gargan's Boy (Slote) **4**:201
Matteo (French) **37**:42
A Matter of Principle: A Novel (Pfeffer) **11**:202
The Matter with Lucy (Grifalconi) **35**:72
Matty's Midnight Monster (Kemp) **29**:126
Maude and Walter (Oneal) **13**:160
Maudie in the Middle (Naylor) **17**:62
Maura's Angel (Reid Banks) **24**:195
Maurice Sendak's Really Rosie: Starring the Nutshell Kids (Sendak) **17**:121
Maurice's Room (Fox) **1**:79
Max (Isadora) **7**:102
Max in Hollywood, Baby (Kalman) **32**:185
Max Makes a Million (Kalman) **32**:182
Maxie, Rosie, and Earl—Partners in Grime (Park) **34**:161
Maxine in the Middle (Keller) **45**:53
Max's Bath (Wells) **16**:213
Max's Bedtime (Wells) **16**:213
Max's Birthday (Wells) **16**:213
Max's Breakfast (Wells) **16**:213
Max's Christmas (Wells) **16**:213
Max's First Word (Wells) **16**:209
Max's New Suit (Wells) **16**:209
Max's Ride (Wells) **16**:209
Max's Toys: A Counting Book (Wells) **16**:209
The May Day Mystery (Allan) **43**:21
The Maya (McKissack) **23**:237
Maybe You Should Fly a Jet! Maybe You Should Be a Vet! (Seuss) **9**:194
Maybelle, the Cable Car (Burton) **11**:51
The Mayday Rampage (Bess) **39**:7
Mazel and Shlimazel; or, The Milk of the Lioness (Singer) **1**:175
McBroom and the Beanstalk (Fleischman) **15**:109
McBroom and the Big Wind (Fleischman) **15**:107
McBroom and the Great Race (Fleischman) **15**:110
McBroom Tells a Lie (Fleischman) **15**:108
McBroom Tells the Truth (Fleischman) **1**:75
McBroom the Rainmaker (Fleischman) **15**:107
McBroom's Almanac (Fleischman) **15**:112
McBroom's Ear (Fleischman) **15**:107
McBroom's Ghost (Fleischman) **1**:75
McBroom's Zoo (Fleischman) **1**:75
McElligot's Pool (Seuss) **9**:175
McGruer and the Goat (Mattingley) **24**:129
Me and Jeshua (Spence) **26**:199
Me and Katie (the Pest) (Martin) **32**:201
Me and My Bones (Gallant) **30**:90
Me and My Captain (Goffstein) **3**:60
Me and My Family Tree (Showers) **6**:247
Me and My Little Brain (Fleischman) **1**:70
Me and My Shadow (Dorros) **42**:66
Me and Neesie (Greenfield) **4**:99
Me and the Man on the Moon-Eyed Horse (Fleischman) **15**:109
Me and the Terrible Two (Conford) **10**:92
Me and Willie and Pa: The Story of Abraham Lincoln and His Son Tad (Monjo) **2**:124

Me Me Me Me Me: Not a Novel (Kerr) **29**:153
Me, Mop, and the Moondance Kid (Myers) **35**:193
Me, Myself, and I: A Tale of Time Travel (Curry) **31**:86
Me Too (Cleaver and Cleaver) **6**:109
The Mean Old Mean Hyena (Prelutsky) **13**:167
The Measure of the Universe (Asimov) **12**:61
Measure with Metric (Branley) **13**:41
Measuring (Bendick) **5**:45
Meatball (McCully) **46**:66
Medical Center Lab (Berger) **32**:16
Medicine (Zim) **2**:229
Medicine from Microbes: The Story of Antibiotics (Epstein and Epstein) **26**:60
Medicine in Action: Today and Tomorrow (Hyde) **23**:154
Medicine Man's Daughter (Clark) **16**:82
Medicine Show: Conning People and Making Them Like It (Calhoun) **42**:23
A Medieval Feast (Aliki) **9**:30
Meet Danitra Brown (Grimes) **42**:92
Meet Murdock (Naylor) **17**:50
Meet My Folks! (Hughes) **3**:93
Meet the Austins (L'Engle) **1**:131
Meet the Giant Snakes (Simon) **9**:214
Meet the Monsters (Yolen) **44**:210
Meeting Death (Hyde) **23**:176
Ho megalos peripatos tou Petrou (Zei) **6**:261
Megastar (Ure) **34**:178
Mein Urgrossvater, die Helden und Ich (Kruss) **9**:87
Mein Urgrossvater und Ich (Kruss) **9**:83
The Mellops' Go Spelunking (Ungerer) **3**:202
Melric and the Balloon (McKee) **38**:166
Melric and the Dragon (McKee) **38**:168
Melusine: A Mystery (Reid Banks) **24**:199
Memory: How It Works and How to Improve It (Gallant) **30**:95
Men from the Village Deep in the Mountains and Other Japanese Folk Tales (Bang) **8**:18
Men, Microscopes, and Living Things (Shippen) **36**:176
Men of Archaeology (Shippen) **36**:182
Men of Medicine (Shippen) **36**:177
Men of the Hills (Treece) **2**:187
Menstruation: Just Plain Talk (Nourse) **33**:142
The Mercy Man (Nourse) **33**:135
Merle the High Flying Squirrel (Peet) **12**:202
Merlin and the Dragons (Yolen) **44**:208
Merlin Dreams (Dickinson) **29**:59
Merlin's Magic (Clarke) **28**:74
The Mermaid and the Whale (McHargue) **2**:119
Mermaid of Storms (Calhoun) **42**:16
The Mermaid Summer (Hunter) **25**:91
Merry Christmas (Marshall) **21**:181
Merry Christmas, Amelia Bedelia (Parish) **22**:167
Merry Christmas, Baabee (Khalsa) **30**:144
Merry Christmas, Ernest and Celestine (Vincent) **13**:220
Merry Christmas from Betsy (Haywood) **22**:101
Merry Christmas from Eddie (Haywood) **22**:106
Merry Christmas, Space Case (Marshall) **21**:181
Merry Christmas, Strega Nona (dePaola) **24**:96
Merry Merry FIBruary (Orgel) **48**:83
The Merry Pranks of Till Eulenspiegel (Zwerger) **46**:199
Merry, Rose, and Christmas-Tree June (Orgel) **48**:78
Merry-Go-Round (Heine) **18**:147
The Merrymaker (Suhl) **2**:165
Message to Hadrian (Trease) **42**:183
A Messenger for Parliament (Haugaard) **11**:107

Messy Baby (Ormerod) **20**:177
Metamorphosis: The Magic Change (Silverstein and Silverstein) **25**:204
Meteor! (Polacco) **40**:179
Meteors and Meteorites: An Introduction to Meteoritics (Knight) **38**:108
Metric Can Be Fun! (Leaf) **25**:135
Mexico (Epstein and Epstein) **26**:53
Mia (Beckman) **25**:14
Mia Alone (Beckman)
    See *Mia*
Mia Alone (Beckman) **25**:14
Mice and Mendelson (Aiken) **19**:12
Mice, Moose, and Men: How Their Populations Rise and Fall (McClung) **11**:188
Michael and the Mitten Test (Wells) **16**:203
Michael Bird-Boy (dePaola) **4**:57
Michael Faraday: Apprentice to Science (Epstein and Epstein) **26**:63
Michael Foreman's Mother Goose (Foreman) **32**:106
Michael Foreman's World of Fairy Tales (Foreman) **32**:105
Michael Jackson, Superstar! (McKissack) **23**:236
Michael Rosen's ABC (Rosen) **45**:151
Mickey's Magnet (Branley) **13**:25
Mickie (Unnerstad) **36**:200
Microbes at Work (Selsam) **1**:163
Microscopic Animals and Plants (Patent) **19**:148
The Middle Moffat (Estes) **2**:74
The Middle of Somewhere: A Story of South Africa (Gordon) **27**:94
The Middle Sister (Duncan) **29**:66
Midnight Adventure (Briggs) **10**:23
The Midnight Adventures of Kelly, Dot, and Esmeralda (Goodall) **25**:45
The Midnight Farm (Jeffers) **30**:136
The Midnight Fox (Byars) **1**:36
The Midnight Horse (Sis) **45**:163
Midnight Hour Encores (Brooks) **25**:32
Midnight Is a Place (Aiken) **1**:4
Midnight Soup and a Witch's Hat (Orgel) **48**:90
Midsummer Magic (Dillon) **26**:20
Mieko (Politi) **29**:193
Miffy in the Hospital (Bruna) **7**:52
Miffy's Dream (Bruna) **7**:52
The Mighty Ones (DeJong) **1**:59
Mik and the Prowler (Uchida) **6**:253
Mike Mulligan and His Steam Shovel (Burton) **11**:44
Miki (Petersham and Petersham) **24**:161
Miki and Mary: Their Search for Treasures (Petersham and Petersham) **24**:166
Milk and Honey: A Year of Jewish Holidays (Yolen) **44**:210
Milk: The Fight for Purity (Giblin) **29**:90
The Milkmaid (Caldecott) **14**:78
Milkweed (Selsam) **1**:164
Milkweed Butterflies: Monarchs, Models, and Mimics (Simon) **39**:185
The Milky Way Galaxy: Man's Exploration of the Stars (Bova) **3**:34
The Milky Way: Galaxy Number One (Branley) **13**:34
Mill (Macaulay) **14**:173
Millicent (Baker) **28**:19
Millicent and the Wind (Munsch) **19**:144
Millie's Boy (Peck) **45**:101
Millie's Secret (Fujikawa) **25**:40
Millions of Cats (Gag) **4**:87
The Mills Down Below (Allan) **43**:31
The Mills of God (Armstrong) **1**:23
The Mimosa Tree (Cleaver and Cleaver) **6**:105

Mind Control (Berger) **32**:34
Mind Drugs (Hyde) **23**:156
Mind the Gap (Rosen) **45**:145
Mind Your Manners! (Parish) **22**:161
Mind Your Own Business (Rosen) **45**:128
Mindy's Mysterious Miniature (Curry) **31**:75
Mine (Mayer) **11**:166
Mine for Keeps (Little) **4**:147
The Minerva Program (Mackay) **43**:108
Minestrone: A Ruth Krauss Selection (Krauss) **42**:131
Ming Lo Moves the Mountain (Lobel) **5**:176
Mini Beasties (Rosen) **45**:144
Mini-Bike Hero (Mackay) **43**:104
Mini-Bike Racer (Mackay) **43**:104
Mini-Bike Rescue (Mackay) **43**:107
The Min-Min (Clark) **30**:56
Minnie's Yom Kippur Birthday (Singer) **48**:133
The Minnow Family—Chubs, Dace, Minnows, and Shiners (Pringle) **4**:180
The Minnow Leads to Treasure (Pearce) **9**:143
The Minnow Leads to Treasure (Pearce)
    See *Minnow on the Say*
Minnow on the Say (Pearce) **9**:143
The Minority Peoples of China (Rau) **8**:193
The Minpins (Dahl) **41**:46
The Minstrel and the Dragon Pup (Sutcliff) **37**:182
The Minstrel and the Mountain (Yolen) **4**:257
Minty: A Story of Young Harriet Tubman (Pinkney) **43**:174
The Mintyglo Kid (Cross) **28**:89
Mio, My Son (Lindgren) **39**:146
Miracle in Motion: The Story of America's Industry (Shippen) **36**:177
Miracle on the Plate (Christopher) **33**:42
The Miracle Tree (Mattingley) **24**:129
The Miracles of Jesus (dePaola) **24**:99
The Miraculous Hind: A Hungarian Legend (Cleaver) **13**:66
Miranda the Great (Estes) **2**:74
Miranda's Pilgrims (Wells) **16**:204
Miranda's Umbrella (Biro) **28**:40
Mirandy and Brother Wind (McKissack) **23**:239
Mirandy and Brother Wind (Pinkney) **43**:162
Mirette on the High Wire (McCully) **46**:67
Mirror Magic (Simon) **9**:215
Mirror, Mirror (Garfield) **21**:109
Mirror of Her Own (Guy) **13**:84
The Mirror Planet (Bunting) **28**:48
Mischief City (Wynne-Jones) **21**:230
The Mischievous Martens (Lindgren) **39**:151
Mischievous Meg (Lindgren) **39**:149
Miss Bianca (Sharp) **27**:162
Miss Bianca and the Bridesmaid (Sharp) **27**:165
Miss Bianca in the Antarctic (Sharp) **27**:164
Miss Bianca in the Orient (Sharp) **27**:164
Miss Bianca in the Salt Mines (Sharp) **27**:163
Miss Dog's Christmas Treat (Marshall) **21**:169
Miss Emily and the Bird of Make-Believe (Keeping) **34**:105
Miss Happiness and Miss Flower (Godden) **20**:131
Miss Maggie (Rylant) **15**:169
Miss Nelson Has a Field Day (Marshall) **21**:180
Miss Nelson Is Back (Marshall) **21**:177
Miss Nelson Is Missing (Marshall) **21**:172
Miss Rumphius (Cooney) **23**:31
Missee Lee (Ransome) **8**:180
Missing Children (Hyde) **23**:171
Missing in Manhattan (Allan) **43**:17
The Missing Lollipop (McBratney) **44**:121
The Missing Maple Syrup Sap Mystery; or, How Maple Syrup Is Made (Gibbons) **8**:90

The Missing Milkman (Duvoisin) **23**:104
The Missing Piece (Silverstein) **5**:211
The Missing Piece Meets the Big O (Silverstein) **5**:212
Missing Since Monday (Martin) **32**:202
The Mission Bell (Politi) **29**:189
Mister Magnolia (Blake) **31**:23
Mister Peale's Mammoth (Epstein and Epstein) **26**:65
Mister Penny (Ets) **33**:74
Mister Penny's Circus (Ets) **33**:88
Mister Penny's Race Horse (Ets) **33**:84
Mistresses of Mystery: Two Centuries of Suspense Stories by the Gentle Sex (Manley) **3**:145
Misty of Chincoteague (Henry) **4**:110
Mitch and Amy (Cleary) **2**:48; **8**:52
The Mitten: A Ukrainian Folktale (Brett) **27**:42
The Mitten: An Old Ukrainian Folktale (Tresselt) **30**:208
Mitzi and Frederick the Great (Williams) **48**:203
Mitzi and the Terrible Tyrannosaurus Rex (Williams) **48**:201
The Mixed-Up Chameleon (Carle) **10**:79
Mixed-Up Magic (Cole) **40**:22
The Mixed-Up Twins (Haywood) **22**:95
The Mock Revolt (Cleaver and Cleaver) **6**:107
Mockingbird Morning (Ryder) **37**:90
Model Buildings and How to Make Them (Weiss) **4**:229
Model Cars and Trucks and How to Build Them (Weiss) **4**:227
Modern Ballads and Story Poems (Causley) **30**:32
Modern China (Carter) **22**:20
Modern Electronics (Carter) **22**:20
Moe Q. McGlutch, He Smoked Too Much (Raskin) **1**:156
Moe the Dog in Tropical Paradise (Stanley) **46**:148
The Moffats (Estes) **2**:75
Mog at the Zoo (Pienkowski) **6**:233
Mog's Mumps (Pienkowski) **6**:230
Moira's Birthday (Munsch) **19**:146
Moja Means One: Swahili Counting Book (Feelings and Feelings) **5**:105
Mojo and the Russians (Myers) **4**:157
Mokokambo, the Lost Land (Guillot) **22**:63
Mole Hole (Dickinson) **29**:58
Molly o' the Moors: The Story of a Pony (Keeping) **34**:88
Mom, the Wolf Man, and Me (Klein) **2**:99
Mommies at Work (Merriam) **14**:192
Momo: Oder, die Seltsame Geschichte von D. Zeitdieben U. von D. Kind, das D. Menschen D. Gestohlene Zeit Zurückbrachte; Ein Märchenroman (Ende) **14**:97
Momoko and the Pretty Bird (Iwasaki) **18**:154
Momoko's Birthday (Iwasaki) **18**:154
Momoko's Lovely Day (Iwasaki) **18**:153
Momo's Kitten (Yashima) **4**:253
Mom's Home (Ormerod) **20**:180
The Mona Lisa Mystery (Hutchins) **20**:151
The Monkey and the Crocodile: A Jataka Tale from India (Galdone) **16**:94
Monkey and the Three Wizards (Foreman) **32**:89
Monkey Business: Hoaxes in the Name of Science (Adler) **27**:9
Monkey Day (Krauss) **42**:123
Monkey in the Middle (Bunting) **28**:56
Monkey Island (Fox) **44**:72
Monkey See, Monkey Do (Oxenbury) **22**:143
Monkey-Monkey's Trick: Based on an African Folk Tale (McKissack) **23**:240
Monkeys (Zim) **2**:229

The Monster and the Tailor: A Ghost Story (Galdone) **16**:104
The Monster and the Teddy Bear (McKee) **38**:179
The Monster Den: Or Look What Happened at My House—And to It (Ciardi) **19**:79
The Monster Den; or, Look What Happened at My House—and to It (Gorey) **36**:91
Monster Dinosaur (Cohen) **43**:44
The Monster from Underground (Cross) **28**:95
The Monster Garden (Alcock) **26**:6
A Monster in the Mailbox (Gordon) **27**:91
Monster Night at Grandma's House (Peck) **15**:159
Monsters (Blumberg) **21**:28
Monsters Are Like That (Daly) **41**:55
The Monsters' Ball (dePaola) **4**:54
Monsters from the Movies (Aylesworth) **6**:49
A Monstrous Story (Hilton) **25**:60
The Month Brothers: A Slavic Tale (Stanley) **46**:132
Monticello (Fisher) **18**:138
Monty (Stevenson) **17**:155
Moominpappa at Sea (Jansson) **2**:94
Moominsummer Madness (Jansson) **2**:94
Moominvalley in November (Jansson) **2**:94
The Moon (Asimov) **12**:40
The Moon and a Star and Other Poems (Livingston) **7**:168
Moon and Me (Irwin) **40**:109
The Moon by Night (L'Engle) **1**:132
The Moon: Earth's Natural Satellite (Branley) **13**:29
The Moon in Fact and Fancy (Slote) **4**:198
The Moon in the Cloud (Harris) **30**:111
Moon Man (Ungerer) **3**:202
The Moon of Gomrath (Garner) **20**:101
A Moon or a Button: A Collection of First Picture Ideas (Krauss) **42**:124
The Moon Ribbon and Other Tales (Yolen) **4**:262
Moon, Stars, Frogs, and Friends (MacLachlan) **14**:181
The Moon Walker (Showers) **6**:247
Moonbeam on a Cat's Ear (Gay) **27**:85
Moon-Bells and Other Poems (Hughes) **3**:93
The Mooncusser's Daughter (Aiken) **1**:5
Moondial (Cresswell) **18**:112
Moonflute (Wood and Wood) **26**:221
The Moonglow Roll-O-Rama (Pilkey) **48**:110
Moonlight (Ormerod) **20**:175
The Moonlight Man (Fox) **44**:66
The Moons of Our Solar System (Knight) **38**:113
The Moon's Revenge (Aiken) **19**:18
Moonseed and Mistletoe: A Book of Poisonous Wild Plants (Lerner) **34**:132
Moonsong Lullaby (Highwater) **17**:29
Moon-Uncle, Moon-Uncle: Rhymes from India (Cassedy) **26**:12
Moon-Whales and Other Moon Poems (Hughes)
    See *Moon-Bells and Other Poems*
Moose (Foreman) **32**:87
Moose (Scott) **20**:200
Moose and Goose (Brown) **29**:4
Moose, Goose, and Little Nobody (Raskin) **12**:223
Mop, Moondance, and the Nagasaki Knights (Myers) **35**:198
Mop Top (Freeman) **30**:70
More About Animals (Bianco) **19**:53
More Adventures of the Great Brain (Fitzgerald) **1**:70
More and More Ant and Bee: Another Alphabetical Story (Banner) **24**:18
More Bunny Trouble (Wilhelm) **46**:165

More Experiments in Science (Branley) **13**:23
More Mr. Small (Lenski) **26**:125
More of Brer Rabbit's Tricks (Gorey) **36**:93
A More Perfect Union: The Story of Our Constitution (Betsy and Giulio Maestro) **45**:79
More Short and Shivery: Thirty Terrifying Tales (San Souci) **43**:192
More Small Poems (Worth) **21**:221
More Stories of Baseball Champions: In the Hall of Fame (Epstein and Epstein) **26**:65
More Stories to Solve: Fifteen Folktales from Around the World (Sis) **45**:164
More Surprises: An I Can Read Book (Hopkins) **44**:94
More Tales from Grimm (Gag) **4**:94
More Tales of Uncle Remus: The Further Adventures of Brer Rabbit, His Friends, Enemies, and Others (Lester) **41**:107
More Tales of Uncle Remus: The Further Adventures of Brer Rabbit, His Friends, Enemies, and Others (Pinkney) **43**:161
More Than One (Hoban) **13**:105
More Words of Science (Asimov) **12**:48
Morgan the Magnificent (Wallace) **37**:216
Morgan's Zoo (Howe) **9**:60
Mori No Ehon (Anno) **14**:34
Morning Is a Little Child (Anglund) **1**:21
Morning Star, Black Sun: The Northern Cheyenne Indians and America's Energy Crisis (Ashabranner) **28**:5
Morris's Disappearing Bag: A Christmas Story (Wells) **16**:207
The Mortal Instruments (Bethancourt) **3**:18
Mortimer (Munsch) **19**:143
Mortimer Says Nothing (Aiken) **19**:16
Mortimer's Cross (Aiken) **19**:14
Moses (Shippen) **36**:171
Moses' Ark: Stories from the Bible (Leo and Diane Dillon) **44**:39
Moses: From the Story Told in the Old Testament (Petersham and Petersham) **24**:169
Moss and Blister (Garfield) **21**:109
Mossflower (Jacques) **21**:154
The Most Important Thing (Ure) **34**:178
The Most Wonderful Egg in the World (Heine) **18**:148
Motel of the Mysteries (Macaulay) **14**:171
Mother Crocodile (Guy) **13**:85
Mother Goose; or, The Old Nursery Rhymes (Greenaway) **6**:132
Mother Goose: Seventy-Seven Verses (Tudor) **13**:192
Mother Goose's Little Misfortunes (Schwartz) **25**:196
Mother, Mother, I Feel Sick, Send for the Doctor Quick, Quick, Quick: A Picture Book and Shadow Play (Charlip) **8**:27
The Mother's Day Mice (Bunting) **28**:59
Mother's Helper (Oxenbury) **22**:143
Moths and Butterflies and How They Live (McClung) **11**:184
Motion and Gravity (Bendick) **5**:45
Motors and Engines and How They Work (Weiss) **4**:225
Motown and Didi: A Love Story (Myers) **16**:141
The Mountain Goats of Temlaham (Cleaver) **13**:65
Mountain Light (Yep) **17**:208
Mountain Rose (Stren) **5**:234
Mountain with a Secret (Guillot) **22**:67
The Mouse and His Child (Hoban) **3**:78
The Mouse and the Motorcycle (Cleary) **2**:48; **8**:51

The Mouse Butcher (King-Smith) **40**:142
Mouse Days: A Book of Seasons (Lionni) **7**:139
Mouse House (Godden) **20**:128
Mouse Manor (Eager) **43**:79
Mouse Numbers and Letters (Arnosky) **15**:6
The Mouse Rap (Myers) **35**:194
The Mouse Sheriff (Janosch) **26**:77
Mouse Soup (Lobel) **5**:171
Mouse Tales (Lobel) **5**:168
Mouse Trouble (Yeoman) **46**:176
Mouse Views: What the Class Pet Saw (McMillan) **47**:182
Mouse Woman and the Mischief-Makers (Harris) **47**:87
Mouse Woman and the Muddleheads (Harris) **47**:88
Mouse Woman and the Vanished Princesses (Harris) **47**:84
Mouse Writing (Arnosky) **15**:6
The Mousewife (Freedman) **20**:126
The Moves Make the Man (Brooks) **25**:30
Movie Monsters (Aylesworth) **6**:51
Movie Shoes (Streatfeild) **17**:190
Moving (Graham) **31**:95
Moving (Rosen) **45**:148
The Moving Adventures of Old Dame Trot and Her Comical Cat (Galdone) **16**:98
The Moving Coffins: Ghosts and Hauntings Around the World (Knight) **38**:128
Moving Day (Tobias) **4**:215
Moving Heavy Things (Adkins) **7**:25
Moving Molly (Hughes) **15**:124
Moy Moy (Politi) **29**:191
Mr. Adams's Mistake (Parish) **22**:166
Mr. and Mrs. Muddle (Hoberman) **22**:114
Mr. and Mrs. Noah (Lenski) **26**:113
Mr. and Mrs. Pig's Evening Out (Rayner) **41**:121
Mr. Archimedes' Bath (Allen) **44**:5
Mr. Bass' Planetoid (Cameron) **1**:40
Mr. Bat's Great Invention (Noestlinger) **12**:184
Mr. Bats Meisterstück; oder, die Total Verjüngte Oma (Noestlinger) **12**:184
Mr. Bear and Apple Jam (Kuratomi) **32**:190
Mr. Bear and the Robbers (Kuratomi) **32**:189
Mr. Bear Goes to Sea (Kuratomi) **32**:188
Mr. Bear in the Air (Kuratomi) **32**:189
Mr. Bear, Postman (Kuratomi) **32**:191
Mr. Bear, Station-Master (Kuratomi) **32**:190
Mr. Bear's Christmas (Kuratomi) **32**:190
Mr. Bear's Drawing (Kuratomi) **32**:190
Mr. Bear's Meal (Kuratomi) **32**:191
Mr. Bear's Trumpet (Kuratomi) **32**:189
Mr. Bear's Winter Sleep (Kuratomi) **32**:191
Mr. Bell Invents the Telephone (Shippen) **36**:174
Mr. Benn, Red Knight (McKee) **38**:157
Mr Bidery's Spidery Garden (McCord) **9**:101
Mr. Bojangles: The Biography of Bill Robinson (Haskins) **39**:54
Mr. Cat in Business (Rodari) **24**:210
Mr. Corbett's Ghost and Other Stories (Garfield) **21**:99
Mr. Fong's Toy Shop (Politi) **29**:195
Mr. Frumble's Worst Day Ever! (Scarry) **41**:171
Mr Gumpy's Motor Car (Burningham) **9**:45
Mr Gumpy's Outing (Burningham) **9**:43
Mr. Kelso's Lion (Bontemps) **6**:84
Mr. Kneebone's New Digs (Wallace) **37**:219
Mr. Little (Peck) **45**:114
Mr. Magus Is Waiting for You (Kemp) **29**:121
Mr. McFadden's Hallowe'en (Godden) **20**:134
Mr. McGee (Allen) **44**:10
Mr. McGee and the Blackberry Jam (Allen) **44**:15
Mr. Miller the Dog (Heine) **18**:145

Mr. Monkey and the Gotcha Bird: An Original Tale (Myers) **16**:142
Mr. Mysterious and Company (Fleischman) **1**:75
Mr. Mysterious's Secrets of Magic (Fleischman) **15**:108
Mr. Noah and the Second Flood (Burnford) **2**:20
Mr. Plunkett's Pool (Rubinstein) **35**:213
Mr. Revere and I (Lawson) **2**:110
Mr. T. Anthony Woo: The Story of a Cat, a Dog, and a Mouse (Ets) **33**:79
Mr. Tuckett (Paulsen) **19**:169
Mr. Wuzzel (Janosch) **26**:75
Mrs. Armitage on Wheels (Blake) **31**:27
Mrs. Beggs and the Wizard (Mayer) **11**:167
Mrs. Cockle's Cat (Pearce) **9**:149
Mrs Discombobulous (Mahy) **7**:179
Mrs. Dog's Own House (Calhoun) **42**:19
Mrs. Fish, Ape, and Me, the Dump Queen (Mazer) **23**:226
Mrs. Frisby and the Rats of NIMH (O'Brien) **2**:127
Mrs. Katz and Tush (Polacco) **40**:193
Mrs. Moskowitz and the Sabbath Candlesticks (Schwartz) **25**:191
Mrs. Pepperpot Again and Other Stories (Proysen) **24**:182
Mrs. Pepperpot in the Magic Wood (Proysen) **24**:183
Mrs. Pepperpot to the Rescue (Proysen) **24**:182
Mrs. Pepperpot's Busy Day (Proysen) **24**:183
Mrs. Pepperpot's Christmas (Proysen) **24**:184
Mrs. Pepperpot's Outing and Other Stories (Proysen) **24**:183
Mrs. Pepperpot's Year (Proysen) **24**:185
Mrs. Pig Gets Cross and Other Stories (Rayner) **41**:125
Mrs. Pig's Bulk Buy (Rayner) **41**:123
Much Bigger than Martin (Kellogg) **6**:174
Mud Puddle (Munsch) **19**:141
Mud Time and More: Nathaniel Stories (Arnosky) **15**:3
Muffie Mouse and the Busy Birthday (Nixon) **24**:137
The Mulberry Music (Orgel) **48**:80
The Mule on the Motorway (Berna) **19**:39
Muley-Ears, Nobody's Dog (Henry) **4**:113
Mummies (McHargue) **2**:119
Mummies Made in Egypt (Aliki) **9**:27
The Mummy, The Will, and The Crypt (Bellairs) **37**:15
Mum's Place (Ottley) **16**:188
Mungoon-Gali the Giant Goanna (Trezise) **41**:144
The Muppet Guide to Magnificent Manners: Featuring Jim Henson's Muppets (Howe) **9**:60
Murmel, Murmel, Murmel (Munsch) **19**:143
The Muscular System: How Living Creatures Move (Silverstein and Silverstein) **25**:207
Museum: The Story of America's Treasure Houses (Schwartz) **3**:189
Mushroom in the Rain (Ginsburg) **45**:6
Music, Music for Everyone (Williams) **9**:235
The Music of What Happens: Poems That Tell Stories (Janeczko) **47**:108
Musk Oxen: Bearded Ones of the Arctic (Rau) **8**:188
Mustang, Wild Spirit of the West (Henry) **4**:115
A Mustard Seed of Magic (St. John) **46**:105
My Ballet Class (Isadora) **7**:105
My Book about Me: By Me, Myself. I Wrote It! I Drew It! With a Little Help from My Friends Dr. Seuss and Roy McKie (Seuss) **9**:191
My Brother Fine with Me (Clifton) **5**:56

Title Index

My Brother Sam Is Dead (Collier and Collier) **3**:47

My Brother Sean (Breinburg) **31**:66

My Cat Maisie (Allen) **44**:12

My Crazy Sister (Goffstein) **3**:60

My Darling, My Hamburger (Zindel) **3**:249

My Darling Villain (Reid Banks) **24**:192

My Day on the Farm (Nakatani) **30**:160

My Dog is Lost (Keats) **35**:121

My Dog Rinty (Ets) **33**:77

My Dog Rinty (Tarry) **26**:213

My Family Vacation (Khalsa) **30**:148

My Father, the Coach (Slote) **4**:200

My Father's Hands (Ryder) **37**:100

My Favorite Thing (Fujikawa) **25**:40

My First Chanukah (dePaola) **24**:103

My First Love and Other Disasters (Pascal) **25**:183

My First Word Book (Scarry) **41**:171

My Folks Don't Want Me to Talk about Slavery: Twenty-One Oral Histories of Former North Carolina Slaves (Hurmence) **25**:94

My Friend Has Four Parents (Hyde) **23**:167

My Friend Jacob (Clifton) **5**:60

My Friend John (Zolotow) **3**:236

My Friend Wants to Run Away (Hyde) **23**:166

My Gang (Waddell) **31**:182

My Grandma Lived in Gooligulch (Base) **22**:3

My Great Grandpa (Waddell) **31**:195

My Great-Grandfather and I: Useful and Amusing Occurrences and Inspirations from the Lobster Shack on Helgoland Told to the "Leathery Lisbeth" and Embellished with Verses from My Great-Grandfather and Me (Kruss) **9**:83

My Great-Grandfather, the Heroes, and I: A Brief Study of Heroes in Verse and Prose, Made Up and Told in Several Attic Rooms by My Great-Grandfather and Myself (Kruss) **9**:87

My Heart's in Greenwich Village (Manley) **3**:146

My Heart's in the Heather (Manley) **3**:146

My Island Grandma (Lasky) **11**:115

My Life as a Body (Klein) **19**:100

My Little Hen (Provensen and Provensen) **11**:211

My Love, My Love; or, the Peasant Girl (Guy) **13**:88

My Mama Needs Me (Cummings) **48**:45

My Mama Needs Me (Walter) **15**:206

My Mama Says There Aren't Any Zombies, Ghosts, Vampires, Creatures, Demons, Monsters, Fiends, Goblins, or Things (Viorst) **3**:208

My Mate Shofiq (Needle) **43**:131

My Mother Got Married (And Other Disasters) (Park) **34**:159

My Mother's Ghost (Buffie) **39**:27

My Mother's Loves: Stories and Lies from My Childhood (Poulin) **28**:197

My Name Is Paula Popowich! (Hughes) **9**:77

My New Kitten (Cole) **40**:33

My Nightingale is Singing (Lindgren) **39**:162

My Parents Think I'm Sleeping (Prelutsky) **13**:173

My Pets (Hill) **13**:93

My Puppy Is Born (Cole) **5**:63

My Real Family (McCully) **46**:70

My Robot Buddy (Slote) **4**:201

My Rotten Redheaded Older Brother (Polacco) **40**:198

My School (Spier) **5**:228

My Shalom, My Peace: Paintings and Poems by Jewish and Arab Children (Ofek) **28**:190

My Side of the Mountain (George) **1**:91

My Spain: A Storyteller's Year of Collecting (Sawyer) **36**:165

My Special Best Words (Steptoe) **2**:163

My Street's a Morning Cool Street (Thomas) **8**:213

My Teddy Bear (Nakatani) **30**:160

My Treasures (Nakatani) **30**:161

My Trip to Alpha I (Slote) **4**:202

My Very First Book (Petersham and Petersham) **24**:177

My Very First Book of Colors (Carle) **10**:77

My Very First Book of Numbers (Carle) **10**:77

My Very First Book of Shapes (Carle) **10**:77

My Very First Book of Words (Carle) **10**:77

My Very First Library (Carle) **10**:77

My Visit to the Dinosaurs (Aliki) **9**:21

My War with Goggle-Eyes (Fine) **25**:23

My War With Mrs. Galloway (Orgel) **48**:87

My World (Brown) **10**:58

My Year (Dahl) **41**:49

Myna Bird Mystery (Berna) **19**:40

Myself and I (St. John) **46**:110

The Mysteries of Harris Burdick (Van Allsburg) **13**:209

Mysteries of Migration (McClung) **11**:194

Mysteries of Outer Space (Branley) **13**:50

Mysteries of the Satellites (Branley) **13**:53

Mysteries of the Universe (Branley) **13**:50

The Mysterious Disappearance of Leon (I Mean Noel) (Raskin) **1**:156

The Mysterious Giant of Barletta: An Italian Folktale (dePaola) **24**:95

The Mysterious Mr. Ross (Alcock) **26**:5

The Mysterious Prowler (Nixon) **24**:136

Mysterious Queen of Magic (Nixon) **24**:142

The Mysterious Red Tape Gang (Nixon) **24**:135

The Mysterious Tadpole (Kellogg) **6**:175

The Mystery at Monkey Run (Christopher) **33**:42

Mystery at the Edge of Two Worlds (Harris) **47**:88

The Mystery Beast of Ostergeest (Kellogg) **6**:170

The Mystery Began in Madeira (Allan) **43**:16

Mystery Coach (Christopher) **33**:46

Mystery in Arles (Allan) **43**:13

Mystery in Rome (Allan) **43**:25

Mystery in Wales (Allan) **43**:19

Mystery Monsters of Loch Ness (Lauber) **16**:118

The Mystery Of Drear House: The Conclusion of the Dies Drear Chronicle (Hamilton) **40**:73

Mystery of Hurricane Castle (Nixon) **24**:133

The Mystery of Saint-Salgue (Berna) **19**:38

The Mystery of Sleep (Silverstein and Silverstein) **25**:224

The Mystery of Stonehenge (Branley) **13**:35

The Mystery of the Bog Forest (Milne and Milne) **22**:125

The Mystery of the Diamond in the Wood (Kherdian) **24**:113

The Mystery of the Flying Orange Pumpkin (Kellogg) **6**:177

The Mystery of the Giant Footsteps (Krahn) **3**:105

Mystery of the Grinning Idol (Nixon) **24**:134

Mystery of the Haunted Woods (Nixon) **24**:134

Mystery of the Hidden Cockatoo (Nixon) **24**:134

The Mystery of the Loch Ness Monster (Bendick) **5**:49

The Mystery of the Magic Green Ball (Kellogg) **6**:175

The Mystery of the Missing Red Mitten (Kellogg) **6**:172

Mystery of the Secret Square (Hagon) **43**:20

Mystery of the Secret Stowaway (Nixon) **24**:134

Mystery of the Ski Slopes (Allan) **43**:14

The Mystery of the Stolen Blue Paint (Kellogg) **6**:178

The Mystery on Crabapple Hill (Christopher) **33**:40

Mystery on the Fourteenth Floor (Allan) **43**:12

Myths of the World (Colum) **36**:37

The Na of Wa (Aardema) **17**:3

The Name of The Tree: A Bantu Folktale (Wallace) **37**:218

Names, Sets, and Numbers (Bendick) **5**:43

Nana Upstairs and Nana Downstairs (dePaola) **4**:54

The Nanny Goat and the Fierce Dog (Keeping) **34**:98

Naomi in the Middle (Klein) **2**:100

The Nap Master (Kotzwinkle) **6**:183

Napper Goes for Goal (Waddell) **31**:178

Napper Strikes Again (Waddell) **31**:180

Napper's Golden Goals (Waddell) **31**:183

The Napping House (Wood and Wood) **26**:221

The Nargun and the Stars (Wrightson) **4**:244

Nasty! (Rosen) **45**:131

Nat King Cole (Haskins) **39**:48

Nathaniel (Arnosky) **15**:2

Nathaniel Hawthorne: Captain of the Imagination (Manley) **3**:147

Nathaniel Talking (Greenfield) **38**:89

National Geographic Picture Atlas of Our Universe (Gallant) **30**:96

The National Weather Service (Berger) **32**:7

Native American Animal Stories Told by Joseph Bruchac (Bruchac) **46**:9

Native American Stories (Bruchac) **46**:7

Nattpappan (Gripe) **5**:146

Natural Fire: Its Ecology in Forests (Pringle) **4**:184

The Nature of Animals (Milne and Milne) **22**:120

The Nature of Plants (Milne and Milne) **22**:121

The Nature of the Beast (Howker) **14**:128

Nature's Champions: The Biggest, the Fastest, the Best (Silverstein and Silverstein) **25**:219

Nature's Clean-Up Crew: The Burying Beetles (Milne and Milne) **22**:124

Nature's Great Carbon Cycle (Milne and Milne) **22**:125

Nature's Living Lights: Fireflies and Other Bioluminescent Creatures (Silverstein and Silverstein) **25**:225

Nature's Weather Forecasters (Sattler) **24**:215

Naughty Nancy (Goodall) **25**:46

Naughty Nancy Goes to School (Goodall) **25**:55

Naughty Nancy, The Bad Bridesmaid (Goodall) **25**:46

The Near East (Asimov) **12**:42

Near the Window Tree: Poems and Notes (Kuskin) **4**:142

A Near Thing for Captain Najork (Hoban) **3**:81

A Necklace of Raindrops (Aiken) **1**:6

Neighborhood Odes (Soto) **38**:196

The Neighbors (Brown) **12**:103

Neighbors Unknown (Roberts) **33**:203

Nella nebbia di Milano (Munari) **9**:128

The Neon Motorcycle (Rockwell) **6**:237

Nessie the Monster (Hughes) **3**:94

Nettie Jo's Friends (McKissack) **23**:240

Never Born a Hero (Naylor) **17**:58

Never Hit a Porcupine (Williams) **48**:193

Never to Forget: The Jews of the Holocaust (Meltzer) **13**:134

The Neverending Story (Ende) **14**:99

The New Air Book (Berger) **32**:12

The New Americans: Changing Patterns in U. S. Immigration (Ashabranner) **28**:6

The New Americans: Cuban Boat People (Haskins) **39**:43

New Baby (McCully) **46**:61

The New Baby at Your House (Cole) **40**:10

A New Baby Is Coming to My House (Iwasaki) **18**:153

The New Boy (Keller) **45**:56

New Broome Experiment (Epstein and Epstein) **26**:44

The New Earth Book: Our Changing Planet (Berger) **32**:23

The New Food Book: Nutrition Diet, Consumer Tips, and Foods of theFuture (Berger) **32**:20

New Found World (Shippen) **36**:168

New Friends for Susan (Uchida) **6**:251

The New Girl (Stine) **37**:110

New Guys around the Block (Guy) **13**:85

A New Home, A New Friend (Wilhelm) **46**:161

The New Kid on the Block (Prelutsky) **13**:172

New Life: New Room (Jordan) **10**:119

New Patches for Old (Mattingley) **24**:125

The New Pet (Flack) **28**:128

A New Promise (Pascal) **25**:186

New Road! (Gibbons) **8**:96

New Shoes (Streatfeild) **17**:195

New Town: A Story about the Bell Family (Streatfeild) **17**:195

The New Water Book (Berger) **32**:10

The New Wizard of Oz (Baum) **15**:42

New Year's Day (Aliki) **9**:20

The New Year's Mystery (Nixon) **24**:138

New York City Too Far from Tampa Blues (Bethancourt) **3**:19

New York for Nicola (Allan) **43**:11

New Zealand: Yesterday and Today (Mahy) **7**:184

The Newspapers (Fisher) **18**:130

Next Door To Xandau (Orgel) **48**:79

Next Time I Will: An Old English Tale (Orgel) **48**:93

Next-Door Neighbors (Ellis) **42**:82

Next-Door Neighbours (Ellis) **42**:82

Nibble, Nibble: Poems for Children (Brown) **10**:67

Nice Girl from Good Home (Gaberman) **33**:13

A Nice Girl Like You (St. John) **46**:109

The Nicest Gift (Politi) **29**:194

Nicholas and the Fast Moving Diesel (Ardizzone) **3**:6

The Nicholas Factor (Myers) **16**:140

Nicholas Knock and Other People (Lee) **3**:116

Nicky Goes to the Doctor (Scarry) **3**:184

Nicola Mimosa (Ure) **34**:178

Nicolette and the Mill (Guillot) **22**:63

Night (Keats) **35**:136

The Night After Christmas (Stevenson) **17**:158

Night Again (Kuskin) **4**:144

Night and Day (Brown) **10**:50

Night Birds on Nantucket (Aiken) **1**:6

Night Cry (Naylor) **17**:58

The Night Daddy (Gripe) **5**:146

Night Fall (Aiken) **1**:6

The Night Flight (Ryder) **37**:89

Night in the Country (Rylant) **15**:172

The Night It Rained Pancakes: Adapted from a Russian Folktale (Ginsburg) **45**:14

The Night Journey (Lasky) **11**:116

Night Journeys (Avi) **24**:6

Night Kites (Kerr) **29**:155

Night Noises (Fox) **23**:117

Night of the Gargoyles (Wiesner) **43**:216

Night of the Whale (Spinelli) **26**:203

The Night of the White Deer (Paulsen) **19**:172

Night on Neighborhood Street (Greenfield) **38**:90

Night Outside (Wrightson) **14**:216

Night Race to Kawau (Duder) **43**:62

The Night Swimmers (Byars) **16**:56

The Night the Lights Went Out (Freeman) **30**:71

The Night the Monster Came (Calhoun) **42**:29

Night Tree (Bunting) **28**:66

The Night Wind (Allan) **43**:24

A Night without Stars (Howe) **9**:58

The Nightingale (Bedard) **35**:64

The Nightingale (Zwerger) **46**:194

Nightmares: Poems to Trouble Your Sleep (Prelutsky) **13**:165

Night's Nice (Emberley and Emberley) **5**:92

Nights of the Pufflings (McMillan) **47**:187

The Nightwalker (Hurmence) **25**:96

The Night-Watchmen (Cresswell) **18**:100

Nijntje in het ziekenhuis (Bruna) **7**:52

Nijntje's droom (Bruna) **7**:52

Nikos and the Sea God (Gramatky) **22**:43

Nilda (Mohr) **22**:130

Nils (d'Aulaire and d'Aulaire) **21**:50

Nils Holgerssons underbara resa genom Sverige (Lagerlof) **7**:110

Nine Days to Christmas (Ets) **33**:85

Nine Lives (Alexander) **5**:18

The Nine Lives of Homer C. Cat (Calhoun) **42**:8

Nine O'Clock Lullaby (Singer) **48**:139

The Nine Planets (Branley) **13**:27

No, Agatha! (Isadora) **7**:106

No Applause, Please (Singer) **48**:120

No Arm in Left Field (Christopher) **33**:47

No Bath Tonight (Yolen) **4**:265

No Beat of Drum (Burton) **1**:32

No Boats on Bannermere (Trease) **42**:183

No Coins, Please (Korman) **25**:107

No Easy Circle (Naylor) **17**:50

No Fighting, No Biting! (Minarik) **33**:124

No Friends (Stevenson) **17**:165

No Kidding (Brooks) **25**:34

No Kiss for Mother (Ungerer) **3**:202

No Measles, No Mumps for Me (Showers) **6**:248

No More Baths (Cole) **18**:82

No More Magic (Avi) **24**:4

No More Monsters for Me! (Parish) **22**:166

No More Tomorrow (Ottley) **16**:188

No Need for Monty (Stevenson) **17**:168

No Pattern for Love (Epstein and Epstein) **26**:47

No Place for a Goat (Sattler) **24**:217

No Place for Me (DeClements) **23**:37

No Place Like (Kemp) **29**:117

No Promises in the Wind (Hunt) **1**:109

No Such Country (Crew) **42**:56

No Such Things (Peet) **12**:206

No Way of Knowing: Dallas Poems (Livingston) **7**:174

Noah and the Ark (dePaola) **24**:94

Noah's Ark (Haley) **21**:143

Noah's Ark (Spier) **5**:224

Noah's Brother (King-Smith) **40**:149

The Noble Doll (Coatsworth) **2**:60

Nobodies and Somebodies (Orgel) **48**:92

Nobody Knows but Me (Bunting) **28**:47

Nobody Plays with a Cabbage (DeJong) **1**:60

Nobody's Family Is Going to Change (Fitzhugh) **1**:73

Noël Chez Ernest et Célestine (Vincent) **13**:220

Noisy (Hughes) **15**:131

The Noisy Bird Book (Brown) **10**:51

Noisy Book (Brown) **10**:48

Noisy Nora (Lofting) **19**:127

Noisy Nora (Wells) **16**:205

Noisy Words (Burningham) **9**:51

Nomi No Ichi (Anno) **14**:43

None of the Above (Wells) **16**:205

Nonsense Book (Lear) **1**:127

Nonstop Nonsense (Mahy) **7**:184

Noodle (Leaf) **25**:122

Noodweer op de Weisshorn (Haar) **15**:114

The Noon Balloon (Brown) **10**:62

Noonan: A Novel About Baseball, ESP, and Time Warps (Fisher) **18**:127

Norby and the Invaders (Asimov) **12**:64

Norby and the Lost Princess (Asimov) **12**:63

Norby, the Mixed-Up Robot (Asimov) **12**:62

Norby's Other Secret (Asimov) **12**:62

Norma and the Washing Machine (Rosen) **45**:138

Norma Jean, Jumping Bean (Cole) **40**:15

Norman the Doorman (Freeman) **30**:71

Norse Gods and Giants (d'Aulaire and d'Aulaire) **21**:53

The Norse Myths: A Retelling (Crossley-Holland) **47**:36

North, South, East, and West (Branley) **13**:32

North Town (Graham) **10**:105

Northern Lullaby (Leo and Diane Dillon) **44**:45

A Nose for Trouble (Singer) **48**:127

Noses Are Special (Sattler) **24**:218

Not Enough Beds for the Babies (Hoberman) **22**:109

Not Now, Bernard (McKee) **38**:170

Not Quite as Grimm (Janosch) **26**:77

Not Separate, Not Equal (Wilkinson) **20**:211

Not So Fast, Songololo (Daly) **41**:56

Not What You Expected (Aiken) **1**:7

Notes for Another Life (Bridgers) **18**:25

Notes to a Science Fiction Writer (Bova) **3**:35

Nothing at All (Gag) **4**:92

Nothing but a Pig (Cole) **18**:82

Nothing Ever Happens on My Block (Raskin) **1**:157

Nothing Like a Fresh Coat of Paint (Spier) **5**:225

Nothing to Be Afraid Of (Mark) **11**:150

The Nothing-Place (Spence) **26**:194

Nothing's Fair in Fifth Grade (DeClements) **23**:34

The Not-Just-Anybody Family (Byars) **16**:63

The Not-So-Jolly Roger (Scieszka) **27**:156

The Not-So-Jolly Roger (Smith) **47**:200

Now is Your Time! The African-American Struggle for Freedom (Myers) **35**:195

Now It's Fall (Lenski) **26**:114

Now One Foot, Now the Other (dePaola) **4**:65

Now That I Know (Klein) **19**:100

Now We Are Six (Milne) **26**:126

Now We Can Go (Jonas) **12**:177

Noy Lives in Thailand (Lindgren) **39**:152

Nuclear Power: From Physics to Politics (Pringle) **4**:185

Number 24 (Billout) **33**:21

Number Art: Thirteen 123s from Around the World (Fisher) **18**:132

Number Play (Burningham) **9**:50

Number the Stars (Lowry) **46**:37

Numbers of Things (Oxenbury) **22**:137

Numbers Old and New (Adler) **27**:14

Numerals: New Dresses for Old Numbers (Adler) **27**:18

Nungadin and Willijen (Trezise) **41**:143

The Nursery "Alice" (Carroll) **2**:35

Nussknacker und Mausekoenig (Zwerger) **46**:191

The Nutcracker and the Mouse King (Zwerger) **46**:191

Nuts about Nuts (Rosen) **45**:147

Nuts to You and Nuts to Me: An Alphabet Book of Poems (Hoberman) **22**:111

Nutshell Library (Sendak) **1**:171

O Jerusalem (Yolen) **44**:208

O Sliver of Liver: Together with Other Triolets, Cinquains, Haiku, Verses, and a Dash of Poems (Livingston) **7**:173

O Zebron Falls! (Ferry) **34**:52
Obedient Jack: An Old Tale (Galdone) **16**:97
Observation (Bendick) **5**:45
An Ocean World (Sis) **45**:168
Ocean-Born Mary (Lenski) **26**:104
Oceanography Lab (Berger) **32**:9
The October Child (Spence) **26**:197
An Octopus Is Amazing (Keller) **45**:54
The Odyssey (McCaughrean) **38**:151
The Odyssey of Ben O'Neal (Taylor) **30**:189
Odyssey of Courage: The Story of Alvar Nunez Cabeza de Vaca (Wojciechowska) **1**:198
Of Course Polly Can Do Almost Everything (Lindgren) **39**:157
Of Course Polly Can Ride a Bike (Lindgren) **1**:137; **39**:154
Of Dikes and Windmills (Spier) **5**:219
Of Man and Mouse: How House Mice Became Laboratory Mice (Lauber) **16**:116
Of Nightingales That Weep (Paterson) **7**:230
Of Time and of Seasons (St. John) **46**:102
Off into Space! Science for Young Space Travelers (Hyde) **23**:154
Off to Bed: Seven Stories for Wide-Awakes (Petersham and Petersham) **24**:178
The Ogre and His Bride (Tresselt) **30**:213
The Ogre Downstairs (Jones) **23**:183
Oh, A-Hunting We Will Go (Langstaff) **3**:110
Oh, Kojo! How Could You! An Ashanti Tale (Aardema) **17**:7
Oh, Rick! (Bunting) **28**:47
Oh, Say Can You Say? (Seuss) **9**:193
Oh, Were They Ever Happy! (Spier) **5**:225
Oh, What A Mess (Wilhelm) **46**:164
Oh What a Noise! (Shulevitz) **5**:204
Oil and Gas: From Fossils to Fuels (Nixon) **24**:136
Okina Mono No Sukina Osama (Anno) **14**:33
Ol' Dan Tucker (Langstaff) **3**:110
Ola (d'Aulaire and d'Aulaire) **21**:39
Ola and Blakken and Line, Sine, Trine (d'Aulaire and d'Aulaire) **21**:40
Old Con and Patrick (Sawyer) **36**:160
Old Hat, New Hat (Berenstain and Berenstain) **19**:26
Old Henry (Blos) **18**:19
Old John (Hartling) **29**:102
The Old Joke Book (Ahlberg and Ahlberg) **18**:3
The Old Man and His Birds (Ginsburg) **45**:21
The Old Man and the Bear (Janosch) **26**:81
The Old Man of Mow (Garner) **20**:103
Old Man Whickutt's Donkey (Calhoun) **42**:22
Old Mother Hubbard and Her Dog (Galdone) **16**:90
Old Mother Hubbard's Dog Dresses Up (Yeoman) **46**:182
Old Mother Hubbard's Dog Learns To Play (Yeoman) **46**:182
Old Mother Hubbard's Dog Needs a Doctor (Yeoman) **46**:182
Old Mother Hubbard's Dog Takes up Sport (Yeoman) **46**:182
Old Mrs. Twindlytart and Other Rhymes (Livingston) **7**:169
Old Peter's Russian Tales (Ransome) **8**:170
Old Possum's Book of Practical Cats (Gorey) **36**:101
Old Rosie, the Horse Nobody Understood (Moore) **15**:139
Old Sadie and the Christmas Bear (Naylor) **17**:58
The Old Testament (de Angeli) **1**:53
The Old Woman and Her Pig (Galdone) **16**:90

The Old Woman Who Lived in a Vinegar Bottle (Godden) **20**:133
An Older Kind of Magic (Wrightson) **4**:244
Older Men (Klein) **19**:98
The Oldest Man, and Other Timeless Stories (Kotzwinkle) **6**:181
An Old-Fashioned Thanksgiving (Alcott) **1**:11
Oley, the Sea Monster (Ets) **33**:78
Oliver Button Is a Sissy (dePaola) **4**:62
Oliver, Clarence, and Violet (Stevenson) **17**:158
Oliver Sundew, Tooth Fairy (McBratney) **44**:131
Olle's Ski Trip (Beskow) **17**:16
Olles Skidfärd (Beskow) **17**:16
Ollie's Ski Trip (Beskow) **17**:16
The Olympians: Great Gods and Goddesses of Ancient Greece (Fisher) **18**:134
Oma (Hartling) **29**:99
Oma and Bobo (Schwartz) **25**:194
Omelette: A Chicken in Peril! (Owen) **31**:147
On a marche sur la lune (Herge) **6**:148
On a Summer Day (Lenski) **26**:117
On Beyond Zebra (Seuss) **1**:88; **9**:180
On Christmas Day in the Morning! (Langstaff) **3**:110
On Christmas Eve (Brown) **10**:68
On Fire (Sebestyen) **17**:92
On Fortune's Wheel (Voigt) **48**:173
On My Horse (Greenfield) **38**:96
"On Stage, Flory!" (Allan) **43**:8
On the Day Peter Stuyvesant Sailed into Town (Lobel) **5**:166
On the Edge (Cross) **28**:90
On the Farm (Hopkins) **44**:98
On the Forest Edge (Lerner) 122
On the Go: A Book of Adjectives (Betsy and Giulio Maestro) **45**:69
On the Other Side of the Gate (Suhl) **2**:165
On the Sand Dune (Orgel) **48**:77
On the Town: A Book of Clothing Words (Betsy and Giulio Maestro) **45**:72
On the Way Home (Murphy) **39**:171
On the Way Home (Wilder) **2**:206
On the Wing: The Life of Birds from Feathers to Flight (Brooks) **25**:35
Once a Mouse...A Fable Cut in Wood (Brown) **12**:101
Once Around the Block (Henkes) **23**:128
Once Around the Galaxy (Gallant) **30**:98
Once More upon a Totem (Harris) **47**:84
Once on a Time (Milne) **1**:142
Once, Said Darlene (Sleator) **29**:201
Once There Was a Swagman (Brinsmead) **47**:14
Once There Were Giants (Waddell) **31**:195
Once Under the Cherry Blossom Tree: An Old Japanese Tale (Say) **22**:209
Once upon a Holiday (Moore) **15**:139
Once upon a Time in a Pigpen and Three Other Margaret Wise Brown Books (Brown) **10**:68
Once upon a Totem (Harris) **47**:76
The Once-a-Year Day (Bunting) **28**:43
The One and Only Two Heads (Ahlberg and Ahlberg) **18**:8
One at a Time: His Collected Poems for the Young (McCord) **9**:103
The One Bad Thing about Father (Monjo) **2**:124
One Big Wish (Williams) **8**:237
One by One: Garth Pig's Rain Song (Rayner) **41**:131
One by Sea (Corbett) **1**:46
One Day in Paradise (Heine) **18**:150
One Earth, Many People: The Challenge of Human Population Growth (Pringle) **4**:175
One Fat Summer (Lipsyte) **23**:205

One Fine Day (Hogrogian) **2**:88
One Fish, Two Fish, Red Fish, Blue Fish (Seuss) **1**:88; **9**:185
One Frog Too Many (Mayer) **11**:169
One Green Leaf (Ure) **34**:182
The One Hundredth Thing about Caroline (Lowry) **46**:28
One Hungry Spider (Baker) **28**:20
1 Hunter (Hutchins) **20**:151
One I Love, Two I Love, and Other Loving Mother Goose Rhymes (Hogrogian) **2**:88
The One in the Middle is the Green Kangaroo (Blume) **15**:72
One Monday Morning (Shulevitz) **5**:202
One Monster after Another (Mayer) **11**:168
One More Flight (Bunting) **28**:45
One More River (Reid Banks) **24**:190
One More River to Cross: The Stories of Twelve Black Americans (Haskins) **39**:64
One More Time! (Ferry) **34**:54
One Morning in Maine (McCloskey) **7**:207
One Nation, Many Tribes: How Kids Live in Milwaukee's Indian Community (Krull) **44**:109
One of Three (Johnson) **33**:95
The One Pig with Horns (Brunhoff) **4**:40
One Proud Summer (Mackay) **43**:107
One Small Blue Bead (Baylor) **3**:16
One Small Fish (Ryder) **37**:99
One Sun: A Book of Terse Verse (McMillan) **47**:174
One Thousand and One Arabian Nights (McCaughrean) **38**:133
One Thousand Christmas Beards (Duvoisin) **23**:100
One to Grow On (Little) **4**:149
One Trick Too Many: Fox Stories from Russia (Ginsburg) **45**:5
One, Two, Buckle My Shoe: A Book of Counting Rhymes (Haley) **21**:141
One, Two, One Pair! (McMillan) **47**:176
One, Two, Three: An Animal Counting Book (Brown) **29**:3
One, Two, Three with Ant and Bee: A Counting Story (Banner) **24**:18
One Was Johnny: A Counting Book (Sendak) **1**:172
One Way to Ansonia (Gaberman) **33**:14
One Wide River to Cross (Emberley and Emberley) **5**:93
One Winter Night in August and Other Nonsense Jingles (Kennedy) **27**:97
One World (Foreman) **32**:103
One-Eyed Cat (Fox) **44**:64
One-Eyed Jake (Hutchins) **20**:150
101 Questions and Answers about the Universe (Gallant) **30**:99
101 Things to Do With a Baby (Ormerod) **20**:177
The Only Earth We Have (Pringle) **4**:174
Ooh-La-La (Max in Love) (Kalman) **32**:183
Ookie-Spooky (Ginsburg) **45**:14
Ootah's Lucky Day (Parish) **22**:158
The Open Gate (Seredy) **10**:178
Open House for Butterflies (Krauss) **42**:125
Operation: Dump the Chump (Park) **34**:154
Operation Sippacik (Godden) **20**:133
The Optical Illusion Book (Simon) **9**:210
The Orchard Book of Greek Myths (McCaughrean) **38**:148
The Orchard Cat (Kellogg) **6**:171
Orchard of the Crescent (Nimmo) **44**:141
Ordinary Jack: Being the First Part of the Bagthorpe Saga (Cresswell) **18**:108

Orfe (Voigt) **48**:177
The Origin of Life (Silverstein and Silverstein)
    25:201
The Original Freddie Ackerman (Irwin) **40**:115
Orlando, the Brave Vulture (Ungerer) **3**:203
Orphans from the Sea (Scott) **20**:200
Orphans of the Wind (Haugaard) **11**:103
Orpheus: Myths of the World (Colum) **36**:37
Osa's Pride (Grifalconi) **35**:77
Oscar Lobster's Fair Exchange (Selden) **8**:196
Oscar Wilde's The Happy Prince (Young) **27**:223
Othello (Lester) **41**:113
The Other Bone (Young) **27**:220
The Other, Darker Ned (Fine) **25**:18
Other People's Houses (Bianco) **19**:56
*The Other Side: How Kids Live in a California
    Latino Neighborhood* (Krull) **44**:106
The Other Side of Dark (Nixon) **24**:148
The Other Side of the Fence (Ure) **34**:179
Otherwise Known as Sheila the Great (Blume)
    2:17
Otis Spofford (Cleary) **8**:46
Otto and the Magic Potatoes (Pene du Bois) **1**:64
Otto at Sea (Pene du Bois) **1**:65
Otto in Texas (Pene du Bois) **1**:65
Otus: The Story of a Screech Owl (McClung)
    11:182
Otwe (Aardema) **17**:3
Ouch! A Book about Cuts, Scratches, and Scrapes
    (Berger) **32**:45
Our Animal Friends at Maple Hill Farm
    (Provensen and Provensen) **11**:211
Our Atomic World (Berger) **32**:44
Our Colourful World and Its Peoples (Guillot)
    22:67
Our Dog (Oxenbury) **22**:145
*Our Federal Union: The United States from 1816-
    1865* (Asimov) **12**:51
Our Hungry Earth: The World Food Crisis
    (Pringle) **4**:181
Our Man Weston (Korman) **25**:106
Our Ollie (Ormerod) **20**:179
*Our Patchwork Planet: The Story of Plate Tec-
    tonics* (Betsy and Giulio Maestro) **45**:91
*Our Six-Legged Friends and Allies: Ecology in
    Your Backyard* (Simon) **39**:189
Our Sixth-Grade Sugar Babies (Bunting) **28**:65
Our Veronica Goes to Petunia's Farm (Duvoisin)
    23:102
Our Village: Poems (Yeoman) **46**:181
Our Wild Weekend (Waddell) **31**:187
Our World: The People's Republic of China (Rau)
    8:187
Out from This Place (Hansen) **21**:152
Out Loud (Merriam) **14**:198
Out of the Blue (Ellis) **42**:86
Out of the Dark (Katz) **45**:40
Out of Time (Marsden) **34**:149
Outcast (Sutcliff) **1**:189; **37**:151
Outdoors on Foot (Arnosky) **15**:2
The Outlanders (Cresswell) **18**:102
OUTside INside Poems (Adoff) **7**:36
Outside Over There (Sendak) **17**:123
The Outside Shot (Myers) **16**:141
The Outsiders (Hinton) **3**:70; **23**:146
*Outward Dreams: Black Inventors and Their In-
    ventions* (Haskins) **39**:63
Over in the Meadow (Keats) **35**:137
*Over in the Meadow: An Old Nursery Counting
    Rhyme* (Galdone) **16**:107
Over Sea, Under Stone (Cooper) **4**:42
Over the Moon: A Book of Sayings (Hughes)
    15:126

Over the Sea's Edge (Curry) **31**:75
*Over, Under, and Through, and Other Spatial
    Concepts* (Hoban) **13**:102
*Overcoming Acne: The How and Why of Healthy
    Skin Care* (Silverstein, Silverstein, and
    Silverstein) **25**:226
The Overnight (Stine) **37**:111
Overnight Sensation (Nixon) **24**:154
Owl and Billy (Waddell) **31**:186
Owl and Billy and the Space Days (Waddell)
    31:192
"The Owl and the Pussycat" (Lear) **1**:127
The Owl and the Woodpecker (Wildsmith) **2**:213
An Owl and Three Pussycats (Provensen and
    Provensen) **11**:214
Owl at Home (Lobel) **5**:169
Owl Babies (Waddell) **31**:202
Owl Lake (Tejima) **20**:202
Owl Moon (Yolen) **44**:183
The Owl Service (Garner) **20**:103
Owls in the Family (Mowat) **20**:170
The Owlstone Crown (Kennedy) **27**:100
Ownself (Calhoun) **42**:21
Oworo (Guillot) **22**:56
*The Ox of the Wonderful Horns and Other Afri-
    can Folktales* (Bryan) **18**:32
Ox-Cart Man (Cooney) **23**:28
Oxygen Keeps You Alive (Branley) **13**:37
*Pacala and Tandala, and Other Rumanian Folk
    Tales* (Ure) **34**:171
Pacific Crossing (Soto) **38**:199
A Pack of Liars (Fine) **25**:22
A Pack of Lies: Twelve Stories in One
    (McCaughrean) **38**:142
The Pack Rat's Day and Other Poems (Prelutsky)
    13:165
Paco's Miracle (Clark) **16**:81
Paddington Abroad (Bond) **1**:28
Paddington at Large (Bond) **1**:28
Paddington at Work (Bond) **1**:28
Paddington Bear (Bond) **1**:28
Paddington Helps Out (Bond) **1**:29
Paddington Marches On (Bond) **1**:29
Paddington Takes the Air (Bond) **1**:29
Paddiwak and Cosy (Doherty) **21**:60
Paddy Finds a Job (Goodall) **25**:51
Paddy Goes Traveling (Goodall) **25**:53
Paddy Pork to the Rescue (Goodall) **25**:54
Paddy Pork—Odd Jobs (Goodall) **25**:54
Paddy Pork's Holiday (Goodall) **25**:47
Paddy the Penguin (Galdone) **16**:89
Paddy to the Rescue (Goodall) **25**:54
Paddy Under Water (Goodall) **25**:54
Paddy's Evening Out (Goodall) **25**:45
Paddy's New Hat (Goodall) **25**:50
Paddy's Payday (Day) **22**:25
Paddy's Pot of Gold (King-Smith) **40**:159
Pageants of Despair (Hamley) **47**:54
The Pain and the Great One (Blume) **15**:80
Paint, Brush, and Palette (Weiss) **4**:223
Painted Devil (Bedard) **35**:67
The Painted Fan (Singer) **48**:144
The Painted Garden (Streatfeild)
    See *Movie Shoes*
*The Painted Garden: A Story of a Holiday in Hol-
    lywood* (Streatfeild) **17**:190
The Painter's Trick (Ventura) **16**:193
Pajamas for Kit (dePaola) **24**:98
Palmiero and the Ogre (Domanska) **40**:38
Palmistry (Aylesworth) **6**:53
Pamela Camel (Peet) **12**:206
Pampalche of the Silver Teeth (Ginsburg) **45**:9
Pancakes for Breakfast (dePaola) **4**:60

Pancakes, Pancakes! (Carle) **10**:74
Panda and the Bunyips (Foreman) **32**:97
Panda and the Bushfire (Foreman) **32**:100
Panda and the Odd Lion (Foreman) **32**:94
Panda's Puzzle, and His Voyage of Discovery
    (Foreman) **32**:90
Papa Albert (Moore) **15**:140
Papa Lucky's Shadow (Daly) **41**:59
Papa Small (Lenski) **26**:116
Papagayo, the Mischief Maker (McDermott)
    9:119
The Paper Airplane Book (Simon) **9**:204
The Paper Bag Princess (Munsch) **19**:142
Paper Chains (Langton) **33**:114
Paper Dolls (Pfeffer) **11**:204
*Paper, Ink, and Roller: Print-Making for Begin-
    ners* (Weiss) **4**:220
Paper, Paper Everywhere (Gibbons) **8**:95
The Paper Party (Freeman) **30**:79
The Paperboy (Pilkey) **48**:113
The Papermakers (Fisher) **18**:122
Papio: A Novel of Adventure (Kelleher) **36**:119
Pappa Pellerin's Daughter (Gripe) **5**:143
Pappa Pellerins Dotter (Gripe) **5**:143
The Parables of Jesus (dePaola) **24**:99
Parade (Crews) **7**:62
The Parade Book (Emberley) **5**:91
Pardon Me, You're Stepping on My Eyeball!
    (Zindel) **3**:250
Paris, Pee Wee, and Big Dog (Guy) **13**:87
The Park (Hill) **13**:93
The Park in the Dark (Waddell) **31**:192
Parker Pig, Esquire (dePaola) **4**:54
Parrakeets (Zim) **2**:229
Parsley (Bemelmans) **6**:72
Parsley Sage, Rosemary and Time (Curry) **31**:78
A Part of the Dream (Bunting) **28**:47
A Part of the Sky (Peck) **45**:125
*Partners, Guests, and Parasites: Coexistence in
    Nature* (Simon) **39**:186
The Party (Pike) **29**:172
Party Frock (Streatfeild) **17**:190
Party Rhymes (Brown) **29**:17
Party Shoes (Streatfeild) **17**:190
Pascal and the Lioness (Guillot) **22**:68
*Passage to America: The Story of the Great Mi-
    grations* (Shippen) **36**:171
Passager (Yolen) **44**:209
Past Eight O'Clock (Aiken) **19**:17
Pastures of the Blue Crane (Brinsmead) **47**:6
Le Patchwork (Vincent) **13**:219
Patchwork Plays (Field) **21**:75
The Patchwork Quilt (Pinkney) **43**:158
Path of Hunters: Animal Struggle in a Meadow
    (Peck) **45**:100
Path of the Pale Horse (Fleischman) **20**:65
Patrick (Blake) **31**:18
Patrick Kentigern Keenan (Hunter) **25**:74
Patrick Kentigern Keenan (Hunter)
    See *The Smartest Man in Ireland*
A Pattern of Roses (Peyton) **3**:177
Patterson's Track (Spence) **26**:191
Paul Laurence Dunbar: A Poet to Remember
    (McKissack) **23**:236
Paul Robeson (Greenfield) **4**:98
*Paul Robeson: The Life and Times of a Free Black
    Man* (Hamilton) **1**:104
Pauline and the Prince of the Wind (Kruss) **9**:86
Pauline und der Prinz im Wind (Kruss) **9**:86
Paul's Horse, Herman (Weiss) **4**:221
Pavo and the Princess (Ness) **6**:202
*Pay Cheques and Picket Lines: All about Unions
    in Canada* (Mackay) **43**:109

Title Index

Peabody (Wells) **16**:212
Peace at Last (Murphy) **39**:169
The Peaceable Kingdom (Coatsworth) **2**:60
The Peacock Spring (Godden) **20**:134
Peanuts for Billy Ben (Lenski) **26**:116
The Pear Tree, The Birch Tree, and The Barberry Bush (Carigiet) **38**:74
The Pearl (Heine) **18**:148
Pearl's Place (Graham) **31**:92
Peasant Pig and the Terrible Dragon (Scarry) **41**:169
The Pedaling Man and Other Poems (Hoban) **3**:81
The Peddlers (Fisher) **18**:123
The Pedlar of Swaffham (Crossley-Holland) **47**:28
Pedro (Flack and Larsson) **28**:127
Pedro, the Angel of Olvera Street (Politi) **29**:185
Peek-a-Boo! (Ahlberg and Ahlberg) **18**:8
Peeper, First Voice of Spring (Lerner) **34**:122
Peeper: First Voice of Spring (McClung) **11**:190
The Peep-Larssons Go Sailing (Unnerstad) **36**:195
Peggy (Duncan) **29**:68
The Pekinese Princess (Clarke) **28**:73
Pelle's New Suit (Beskow) **17**:16
Pelles Nya Kläder (Beskow) **17**:16
Pencil, Pen, and Brush Drawing for Beginners (Weiss) **4**:222
The Penguin Book (Rau) **8**:186
Penguin Pete (Pfister) **42**:135
Penguin Pete, Ahoy! (Pfister) **42**:137
Penguin Pete and Little Tim (Pfister) **42**:138
Penguin Pete and Pat (Pfister) **42**:134
Penguin Pete's New Friends (Pfister) **42**:134
Penguins at Home: Gentoos of Antarctica (McMillan) **47**:184
Penguins, of All People! (Freeman) **30**:77
Penguins on Parade (Lauber) **16**:112
Pennington's Heir (Peyton) **3**:178
Pennington's Last Term (Peyton) **3**:178
Penny and Peter (Haywood) **22**:93
Penny and the White Horse (Bianco) **19**:57
Penny Goes to Camp (Haywood) **22**:94
Penny Pollard in Print (Klein) **21**:163
Penny Pollard's Diary (Klein) **21**:160
Pentecost and the Chosen One (Corbett) **19**:83
Pentecost of Lickey Top (Corbett) **19**:84
People (Spier) **5**:227
People Are Our Business (Epstein and Epstein) **26**:46
The People Could Fly: American Black Folk Tales (Hamilton) **11**:93
The People Could Fly: American Black Folk Tales (Leo and Diane Dillon) **44**:37
People Might Hear You (Klein) **21**:159
The People of New China (Rau) **8**:189
The People of the Ax (Williams) **8**:234
People Who Make a Difference (Ashabranner) **28**:13
People Who Make Movies (Taylor) **30**:175
The People's Choice: The Story of Candidates, Campaigns, and Elections (Schwartz) **3**:190
The People's Republic of China (Rau) **8**:187
The Peopling of Planet Earth: Human Population Growth through the Ages (Gallant) **30**:105
The Peppermint Family (Brown) **10**:60
The Peppermint Pig (Bawden) **2**:12
The Peppernuts (Petersham and Petersham) **24**:179
Percy and the Five Houses (Minarik) **33**:127
A Perfect Father's Day (Bunting) **28**:66
The Perfect Pal (Gantos) **18**:141

Perfect Pigs: An Introduction to Manners (Brown) **29**:11
The Perfect Present (Foreman) **32**:85
Perilous Pilgrimage (Treece) **2**:187
Periwinkle (Duvoisin) **23**:106
Permanent Connections (Bridgers) **18**:27
Pet of the Met (Freeman) **30**:69
Pet Show! (Keats) **1**:116; **35**:138
The Pet Store (Spier) **5**:228
Pete and Roland (Graham) **31**:92
Peter and Butch (Phipson) **5**:181
Peter and Lotta's Christmas (Beskow) **17**:18
Peter and the Wolf: A Musical Fairy Tale (Mueller) **43**:121
Peter and Veronica (Sachs) **2**:132
Peter Duck (Ransome) **8**:174
Peter Graves (Pene du Bois) **1**:65
Peter in Blueberryland (Beskow) **17**:15
Peter Pan; or, The Boy Who Would Not Grow Up (Barrie) **16**:2-40
Peter Piper's Alphabet: Peter Piper's Practical Principles of Plain and Perfect Pronunciation (Brown) **12**:100
Peter the Great (Stanley) **46**:136
Peter Treegate's War (Wibberley) **3**:229
Peter's Adventures in Blueberry Land (Beskow) **17**:15
Peter's Chair (Keats) **1**:116; **35**:132
Petey (Tobias) **4**:217
Petey Moroni's Camp Runamok Diary (Cummings) **48**:54
Le petit prince (Saint-Exupery) **10**:137-61
Petroleum: Gas, Oil, and Asphalt (Adler) **27**:25
Petronella (Williams) **8**:233
Petros' War (Zei) **6**:261
Petrosinella, A Neapolitan Rapunzel (Stanley) **46**:130
Petrouchka (Cleaver) **13**:70
Pets for Keeps (King-Smith) **40**:148
Pets in a Jar: Collecting and Caring for Small Wild Animals (Simon) **9**:209
Petter och Lotta på Äventyr: Bilderbok (Beskow) **17**:18
Petters och Lottas Jul (Beskow) **17**:18
Petunia (Duvoisin) **23**:96
Petunia and the Song (Duvoisin) **23**:96
Petunia, Beware! (Duvoisin) **23**:101
Petunia, I Love You (Duvoisin) **23**:104
Petunia Takes a Trip (Duvoisin) **23**:98
Petunia the Silly Goose Stories (Duvoisin) **23**:107
Petunia's Christmas (Duvoisin) **23**:96
Petunia's Treasure (Duvoisin) **23**:106
Pezzettino (Lionni) **7**:137
Phantom Animals (Cohen) **43**:53
The Phantom Ice Cream Man: More Nonsense Verse (Kennedy) **27**:97
Phebe Fairchild: Her Book (Lenski) **26**:101
The Philadelphia Adventure (Alexander) **48**:21
Philbert the Fearful (Williams) **8**:227
Philip Hall Likes Me. I Reckon Maybe (Greene) **2**:85
Philomena (Seredy) **10**:180
Phoebe and the Prince (Orgel) **48**:78
Phoebe Danger, Detective, In the Case of the Two-Minute Cough (Fleischman) **20**:66
Phoebe's Revolt (Babbitt) **2**:6
The Phoenix and the Flame: D. H. Lawrence, a Biography (Trease) **42**:189
The Phoenix Forest (Milne and Milne) **22**:119
Phone Calls (Stine) **37**:111
The Photo Dictionary of Football (Berger) **32**:23
The Photo Dictionary of the Orchestra (Berger) **32**:24

Piccolo's Prank (Politi) **29**:193
Pick It Up (Epstein and Epstein) **26**:63
Pickle Creature (Pinkwater) **4**:169
A Pickle for a Nickel (Moore) **15**:140
Pick-Up Sticks (Ellis) **42**:84
Picnic (McCully) **46**:59
The Picnic (Unnerstad) **36**:197
Picnic at Babar's (Brunhoff) **4**:34
Picnic at Mudsock Meadow (Polacco) **40**:194
The Picnic Dog (Mattingley) **24**:122
A Picnic for Ernest and Celestine (Vincent) **13**:217
A Pictorial History of the Negro in America (Hughes and Meltzer) **17**:42
The Picts and the Martyrs; or, Not Welcome at All (Ransome) **8**:181
A Picture Book of Cows (Patent) **19**:158
Picture Book of Revolutionary War Heroes (Fisher) **18**:124
The Picture Life of Franklin Delano Roosevelt (Epstein and Epstein) **26**:61
The Picture Story of Britain (Streatfeild) **17**:192
Picture Tales from Spain (Sawyer) **36**:150
A Pie in the Sky (Rodari) **24**:208
A Piece of Cake (Murphy) **39**:176
A Piece of the Power: Four Black Mayors (Haskins) **3**:65
Pieces of Another World: The Story of Moon Rocks (Branley) **13**:39
Pieces of Land: Journeys to Eight Islands (Crossley-Holland) **47**:29
The Pied Piper of Hamelin (Biro) **28**:36
The Piemakers (Cresswell) **18**:98
Pierino and the Bell (Cassedy) **26**:11
Piero Ventura's Book of Cities (Ventura) **16**:191
Pierre: A Cautionary Tale (Sendak) **1**:172
Pig Tale (Oxenbury) **22**:139
Pigeon Post (Ransome) **8**:177
The Pigeon with the Tennis Elbow (Christopher) **33**:49
Pigeons (Schlein) **41**:194
Piggins (Yolen) **44**:179
Piggy in the Middle (Needle) **43**:138
Piggybook (Browne) **19**:70
The Pigman (Zindel) **3**:251
The Pigman and Me (Zindel) **45**:198
The Pigman's Legacy (Zindel) **45**:193
Pigs Ahoy! (Wilhelm) **46**:163
The Pigs' Book of World Records (Stine) **37**:103
Pigs Might Fly (King-Smith) **40**:140
Pigs Might Fly (Rodda) **32**:210
Pigs Plus: Learning Addition (Burningham) **9**:50
The Pigs' Wedding (Heine) **18**:145
The Pig-Tale (Carroll) **2**:35
The Pile of Junk (Schlein) **41**:184
Pilly Seems (Rosen) **45**:150
Pilyo the Piranha (Aruego) **5**:29
The Pinballs (Byars) **16**:54
Pink and Say (Polacco) **40**:198
Pink Lemonade: Poems for Children (Schmidt) **22**:223
The Pink Motel (Brink) **30**:15
Pinkerton, Behave! (Kellogg) **6**:176
Pinky Pye (Estes) **2**:75
Pinocchio (Collodi)
  See *Le Avventure di Pinocchio*
Pinquo (Thiele) **27**:209
Pioneer Oceanographer: Alexander Agassiz (Epstein and Epstein) **26**:58
Pipes & Pearls: A Gathering of Tales (Bedard) **35**:59
Pipes and Plumbing Systems (Zim) **2**:230
The Pip-Larssons Go Sailing (Unnerstad) **36**:195

Pippa Passes (Corbett) **1**:46

Pippi Goes on Board (Lindgren) **1**:138; **39**:147

Pippi in the South Seas (Lindgren) **1**:138; **39**:147

Pippi Longstocking (Lindgren) **1**:138; **39**:133

Pippi on the Run (Lindgren) **39**:156

Pippo Gets Lost (Oxenbury) **22**:151

Pirate Island Adventure (Parish) **22**:161

The Pirate Queen (McCully) **46**:72

The Pirate Uncle (Mahy) **7**:185

Pirates Ahoy! (Wilhelm) **46**:163

Pirate's Island (Townsend) **2**:173

Pish, Posh, Said Hieronymus Bosch (Leo and Diane Dillon) **44**:44

The Pistachio Prescription (Danziger) **20**:52

A Pistol in Greenyards (Hunter) **25**:76

Pitcher Plants: The Elegant Insect Traps (Lerner) **34**:128

A Pitiful Place (Needle) **43**:139

The Pixy and the Lazy Housewife (Calhoun) **42**:14

Pizza for Breakfast (Kovalski) **34**:117

The Place (Coatsworth) **2**:61

A Place Apart (Fox) **44**:62

A Place Called Heartbreak: A Story of Vietnam (Myers) **35**:204

A Place Called Ugly (Avi) **24**:8

The Place My Words Are Looking For: What Poets Say about and through Their Work (Janeczko) **47**:110

A Place to Come Back To (Bond) **11**:30

A Place to Live (Bendick) **5**:43

A Place to Play (Ahlberg and Ahlberg) **18**:3

A Place to Scream (Ure) **34**:193

Plague (Ure) **34**:185

Plague 99 (Ure) **34**:185

Plain City (Hamilton) **40**:89

The Plan for Birdsmarsh (Peyton) **3**:180

The Planet of Junior Brown (Hamilton) **1**:104

The Planet-Girded Suns: Man's View of Other Solar Systems (Engdahl) **2**:71

The Planets: Exploring the Solar System (Gallant) **30**:97

The Planets in Our Solar System (Branley) **13**:46

Planets, Stars, and Galaxies (Berger) **32**:22

Plant Explorer: David Fairchild (Epstein and Epstein) **26**:58

Plant Families (Lerner) **34**:134

Planting a Rainbow (Ehlert) **28**:110

Plants and Insects Together (Patent) **19**:149

Plants in Winter (Cole) **5**:63

Plants That Make You Sniffle and Sneeze (Lerner) **34**:138

Play Ball, Amelia Bedelia (Parish) **22**:160

Play Day: A Book of Terse Verse (McMillan) **47**:178

Play Nimrod for Him (Ure) **34**:187

Play on Words (Provensen and Provensen) **11**:210

Play Rhymes (Brown) **29**:15

A Play to the Festival (Allan) **43**:8

Play with Me (Ets) **33**:81

Play with Spot (Hill) **13**:96

Playing (Oxenbury) **22**:141

Playing Possum (Eager) **43**:83

Playmates (Ahlberg and Ahlberg) **18**:9

Playschool (Oxenbury) **22**:145

Please Don't Squeeze Your Boa, Noah (Singer) **48**:145

The Pleasure Garden (Garfield) **21**:112

Plenty of Fish (Selsam) **1**:164

Plink, Plink, Plink (Baylor) **3**:16

Pocahontas (d'Aulaire and d'Aulaire) **21**:49

A Pocket for Corduroy (Freeman) **30**:81

A Pocket Full of Seeds (Sachs) **2**:133

The Pocket Mouse (Willard) **2**:221

Pocket Poems: Selected for a Journey (Janeczko) **47**:103

Pocket-Handkerchief Park (Field) **21**:75

Poems (Field) **21**:80

Poems for Children (Field) **21**:81

Poems for the Very Young (Rosen) **45**:148

Poems Here and Now (Kherdian) **24**:107

Poems in My Luggage (Thiele) **27**:212

Poems of Lewis Carroll (Carroll) **2**:35

Poetry from A to Z: A Guide for Young Writers (Janeczko) **47**:115

Poetry Is (Hughes) **3**:94

Poetspeak: In Their Work, about Their Work (Janeczko) **47**:101

Poisonous Snakes (Simon) **9**:216

The Polar Express (Van Allsburg) **13**:211

Police Lab (Berger) **32**:15

Policeman Small (Lenski) **26**:122

The Polite Penguin (Brown) **10**:50

Pollution Lab (Berger) **32**:11

Polly Patchwork (Field) **21**:72

Polly's Tiger (Phipson) **5**:183

Poltergeists: Hauntings and the Haunted (Knight) **38**:111

Pompei (Ventura) **16**:196

A Pony and a Trap (Dillon) **26**:23

Pony from Tarella (Clark) **30**:56

The Pooh Story Book (Milne) **1**:142

The Pool of Fire (Christopher) **2**:41

The Pool of Knowledge: How the United Nations Share Their Skills (Shippen) **36**:175

The Pool Party (Soto) **38**:202

Poona Company (Dhondy) **41**:75

Poor Cecco: The Wonderful Story of a Wonderful Wooden Dog Who Was the Jolliest Toy in the House Until He Went Out to Explore the World (Bianco) **19**:51

Poor Richard in France (Monjo) **2**:129

Poor Stainless: A New Story about the Borrowers (Norton) **6**:224

Poor Tom's Ghost (Curry) **31**:81

The Popcorn Book (dePaola) **4**:60

Popcorn Days and Buttermilk Nights (Paulsen) **19**:174

Popinjay Stairs: A Historical Adventure about Samuel Pepys (Trease) **42**:191

Popo and Fifina, Children of Haiti (Bontemps) **6**:78; **17**:38

Popol et Virginie au pays des lapinos (Herge) **6**:149

Popol Out West (Herge) **6**:149

Poppy Pig Goes to Market (Bruna) **7**:52

The Porcelain Cat (Leo and Diane Dillon) **44**:38

Pork and Beans: Play Date (Stine) **37**:109

Porko Von Popbutton (Pene du Bois) **1**:65

Porridge Poetry: Cooked, Ornamented, and Served by Hugh Lofting (Lofting) **19**:124

Portals to the Past: The Story of Archaeology (Shippen) **36**:180

Portfolio of Horse Paintings (Henry) **4**:112

Portfolio of Horses (Henry) **4**:112

Portly McSwine (Marshall) **21**:174

The Portmanteau Book (Rockwell) **6**:237

Portrait of Ivan (Fox) **1**:79

Portrait of Mary (Grimes) **42**:94

Possum Magic (Fox) **23**:113

The Post Office Book: Mail and How It Moves (Gibbons) **8**:93

The Post Office Cat (Haley) **21**:144

Postcard Poems: A Collection of Poetry for Sharing (Janeczko) **47**:99

Potatoes: All about Them (Silverstein and Silverstein) **25**:214

The Potters' Kitchen (Isadora) **7**:103

The Potter's Wheel (St. John) **46**:119

Poverty in America (Meltzer) **13**:150

Power of Three (Jones) **23**:186

Power Play (Christopher) **33**:51

Power Play (Pascal) **25**:184

Practical Music Theory: How Music Is Put Together from Bach to Rock (Collier) **3**:48

The Practical Princess (Williams) **8**:230

The Practical Princess and Other Liberating Fairy Tales (Williams) **8**:236

A Prairie Boy's Summer (Kurelek) **2**:103

A Prairie Boy's Winter (Kurelek) **2**:103

Prairie School (Lenski) **26**:115

Prairie Songs (Conrad) **18**:86

Prank (Lasky) **11**:120

Prayer for a Child (Field) **21**:80

Prehistoric Animals (Cohen) **43**:49

Prehistoric Animals (Epstein and Epstein) **26**:54

Prehistoric Mammals: A New World (Berger) **32**:36

Preposterous: Poems of Youth (Janeczko) **47**:112

Pretend You're a Cat (Pinkney) **43**:166

Pretty Polly (King-Smith) **40**:165

Pretty Pretty Peggy Moffitt (Pene du Bois) **1**:66

Pretzel (Rey and Rey) **5**:195

Pretzel and the Puppies (Rey and Rey) **5**:195

Pretzels (Dorros) **42**:64

Pride of Lions: The Story of the House of Atreus (St. John) **46**:108

The Prime Minister's Brain (Cross) **28**:90

The Prime of Tamworth Pig (Kemp) **29**:112

Prime Time (Pfeffer) **11**:205

Primrose Day (Haywood) **22**:91

Prince Bertram the Bad (Lobel) **5**:163

Prince Caspian: The Return to Narnia (Lewis) **3**:136; **27**:104-51

The Prince in Waiting (Christopher) **2**:41

Prince Lachlan (Hilton) **25**:60

The Prince of the Dolomites: An Old Italian Tale (dePaola) **4**:64

Prince of the Jungle (Guillot) **22**:60

Prince Rabbit and the Princess Who Could Not Laugh (Milne) **1**:143

The Princess and the Clown (Mahy) **7**:180

The Princess and the Giants (Snyder) **31**:160

The Princess and the God (Orgel) **48**:96

The Princess and the Musician (French) **37**:44

Princess Ashley (Peck) **15**:166

Princess Gorilla and a New Kind of Water (Aardema) **17**:8

The Princess of the Golden Mane (Garner) **20**:116

The Printers (Fisher) **18**:122

Printer's Devil (Epstein and Epstein) **26**:42

The Prisoners of September (Garfield) **21**:108

The Private Lives of Orchids (Simon) **39**:192

Private Lives of the Stars (Gallant) **30**:101

The Procession (Mahy) **7**:179

Professor Wormbog in Search for the Zipperump-a-Zoo (Mayer) **11**:172

Profiles in Black Power (Haskins) **3**:66

Project 1-2-3 (Merriam) **14**:197

Project Boy (Lenski) **26**:118

Project Panda Watch (Schlein) **41**:192

Projects with Air (Simon) **9**:209

Projects with Plants (Simon) **9**:207

The Prom Queen (Stine) **37**:117

A Promise for Joyce (Duncan) **29**:66

A Promise Is a Promise (Munsch) **19**:146

The Promised Year (Uchida) **6**:252

Promises Are for Keeping (Rinaldi) **46**:77

A Proper Little Lady (Hilton) **25**:61

A Proper Little Nooryeff (Ure) **34**:172

Prophets of Doom (Cohen) **43**:54

The Protectors: The Petrova Twist (Stine) **37**:109

The Proud Circus Horse (Zimnik) **3**:244

The Proud Maiden: Tungak, and the Sun: A Russian Eskimo Tale (Ginsburg) **45**:7

A Proud Taste for Scarlet and Miniver (Konigsburg) **1**:122

The Proud Wooden Drummer (Kruss) **9**:88

The Prydain Chronicles (Alexander) **1**:16

Psi High and Others (Nourse) **33**:135

Psst! Doggie— (Keats) **1**:117; **35**:138

Psychology in Action (Hyde) **23**:156

Pterosaurs, the Flying Reptiles (Sattler) **24**:220

Puddin' Poems: Being the Best of the Verse from "The Magic Pudding" (Lindsay) **8**:106

The Puffin Book of Improbable Records (Blake) **31**:21

The Puffin Book of Improbable Records (Yeoman) **46**:178

The Puffin Book of Magic Verse (Causley) **30**:37

The Puffin Book of Salt-Sea Verse (Causley) **30**:39

Puffins Climb, Penguins Rhyme (McMillan) **47**:186

Pumpers, Boilers, Hooks, and Ladders: A Book of Fire Engines (Fisher) **18**:121

Pumpkin Moonshine (Tudor) **13**:189

Punch and Judy (Emberley) **5**:92

Puniddles (McMillan) **47**:163

Punography Too (McMillan) **47**:163

Puppeteer (Lasky) **11**:121

Puppy Love (Hill) **13**:93

Puppy Summer (DeJong) **1**:60

Puritan Adventure (Lenski) **26**:107

The Purple Coat (Schwartz) **25**:192

Push (Graham) **31**:95

Push, Pull, Empty, Full: A Book of Opposites (Hoban) **13**:102

Puss in Boots (Brown) **12**:96

Puss in Boots (Galdone) **16**:101

Pussy Willow (Brown) **10**:61

A Pussycat's Christmas (Brown) **10**:59

Put a Saddle on the Pig (McBratney) **44**:124

Puttes Aventyr i Blåbärsskogen (Beskow) **17**:15

Putting on a Show (Berger) **32**:22

Putting the Sun to Work (Bendick) **5**:49

Putting up with Mitchell: My Vancouver Scrapbook (Ellis) **42**:84

Pyramid (Macaulay) **3**:143

Pysen (Unnerstad) **36**:190

Python's Party (Wildsmith) **2**:214

The Quangle Wangle's Hat (Lear) **1**:127

The Quangle Wangle's Hat (Oxenbury) **22**:138

The Quarreling Book (Zolotow) **2**:236

Quarter Horses (Patent) **19**:161

Quasars, Pulsars, and Black Holes in Space (Berger) **32**:17

The Queen Always Wanted to Dance (Mayer) **11**:166

The Queen and Rosie Randall (Oxenbury) **22**:140

The Queen Elizabeth Story (Sutcliff) **1**:189; **37**:148

The Queen Elizabeth Story (Sutcliff) **37**:148

The Queen of Eene (Prelutsky) **13**:167

Queen of Hearts (Cleaver and Cleaver) **6**:111

The Queen of the What Ifs (Klein) **19**:93

Queen of the Wheat Castles (Mattingley) **24**:123

Queen Victoria (Streatfeild) **17**:194

The Queen's Nose (King-Smith) **40**:144

Quentin Blake's ABC (Blake) **31**:27

Quentin Blake's Nursery Rhyme Book (Blake) **31**:24

The Quest for Artificial Intelligence (Patent) **19**:162

A Quest for Orion (Harris) **30**:119

The Quest of Captain Cook (Selsam) **1**:164

The Quest of Galileo (Lauber) **16**:113

The Question Box (Williams) **8**:226

A Question of Survival (Thompson) **24**:228

Questions and Answers about Ants (Selsam) **1**:165

Questions and Answers about Horses (Selsam) **1**:165

Quick, Let's Get Out of Here (Rosen) **45**:132

The Quicksand Book (dePaola) **4**:59

A Quiet Night In (Murphy) **39**:179

The Quiet Noisy Book (Brown) **10**:60

The Quiet Revolution: The Struggle for the Rights of Disabled Americans (Haskins) **39**:37

Quiet! There's a Canary in the Library (Freeman) **30**:76

The Quilt (Jonas) **12**:175

The Quinkins (Roughsey and Trezise) **41**:140

Quips and Quirks (Watson) **3**:213

Quito Express (Bemelmans) **6**:66

The Quitting Deal (Tobias) **4**:215

The Rabbit (Burningham) **9**:46

Rabbit Hill (Lawson) **2**:110

Rabbit Island (Mueller) **43**:119

Rabbit Makes a Monkey of Lion (Pinkney) **43**:163

The Rabbit Story (Tresselt) **30**:206

Rabbits: All about Them (Silverstein and Silverstein) **25**:210

Rabbits and Redcoats (Peck) **45**:108

Rabble Starkey (Lowry) **46**:34

Raccoons and Ripe Corn (Arnosky) **15**:11

Raccoons, Coatimundis, and Their Family (Patent) **19**:154

The Race of the Golden Apples (Leo and Diane Dillon) **44**:43

A Racecourse for Andy (Wrightson) **4**:242

The Racers: Speed in the Animal World (Simon) **39**:196

The Rachel Field Story Book (Field) **21**:80

Rachel Parker, Kindergarten Show-Off (Martin) **32**:206

The Racing Cart (Heine) **18**:149

Rackety-Bang and Other Verses (Rockwell) **6**:235

Radio Astronomy (Nourse) **33**:149

Radio Fifth Grade (Korman) **25**:111

Radio: From Marconi to the Space Age (Carter) **22**;21

Radio Man/Don Radio (Dorros) **42**:72

Raffy and the Nine Monkeys (Rey) **5**:192

The Raggle-Taggle Fellow (Schlein) **41**:182

Raging Robots and Unruly Uncles (Mahy) **7**:186

Raiders from the Rings (Nourse) **33**:133

The Railroads (Fisher) **18**:128

The Railway Children (Nesbit) **3**:164

The Railway Engine and the Hairy Brigands (Mahy) **7**:181

Railway Ghosts and Highway Horrors (Cohen) **43**:54

Railway Passage (Keeping) **34**:99

The Railway Phantoms (Hamley) **47**:65

"Railway Series" (Awdry) **23**:1-7

Rain (Spier) **5**:228

Rain and Hail (Branley) **13**:31

The Rain Car (Janosch) **26**:76

The Rain Cloud (Rayner) **41**:123

Rain Comes to Yamboorah (Ottley) **16**:184

The Rain Door (Blake) **31**:26

Rain Drop Splash (Tresselt) **30**:201

Rain Forest Secrets (Dorros) **42**:67

Rain Rain Rivers (Shulevitz) **5**:203

Rainbow and Mr. Zed (Nimmo) **44**:148

The Rainbow Fish (Pfister) **42**:136

Rainbow Fish to the Rescue! (Pfister) **42**:139

Rainbow Jordan (Childress) **14**:93

A Rainbow of My Own (Freeman) **30**:74

Rainbow Pavement (Cresswell) **18**:103

Rainbow Rhino (Sis) **45**:159

Rainbow Valley (Montgomery) **8**:137

Rainbow Writing (Merriam) **14**:199

Rainbows and Fireworks (Pfeffer) **11**:197

Rainbows Are Made: Poems by Carl Sandburg (Hopkins) **44**:91

Rainbows, Mirages, and Sundogs: The Sky as a Source of Wonder (Gallant) **30**:103

The Rain-Giver (Crossley-Holland) **47**:29

Raining Cats and Dogs (Yolen) **44**:200

Rainy Day Magic (Gay) **27**:86

Rainy Rainy Saturday (Prelutsky) **13**:168

Rajpur: Last of the Bengal Tigers (McClung) **11**:193

Ralph Bunche: A Most Reluctant Hero (Haskins) **3**:66

Ralph S. Mouse (Cleary) **8**:58

Rama, the Gypsy Cat (Byars) **16**:53

Rama, the Hero of India: Valmiki's "Ramayana" Done into a Short English Version for Boys and Girls (Mukerji) **10**:134

Ramona and Her Father (Cleary) **8**:55

Ramona and Her Mother (Cleary) **8**:56

Ramona Forever (Cleary) **8**:62

Ramona Quimby, Age 8 (Cleary) **8**:57

Ramona the Brave (Cleary) **2**:49; **8**:55

Ramona the Pest (Cleary) **2**:49; **8**:52

The Randolph Caldecott Picture Book (Caldecott) **14**:83

Randolph Caldecott's John Gilpin and Other Stories (Caldecott) **14**:84

Randy's Dandy Lions (Peet) **12**:195

Ransom (Duncan) **29**:67

Rapscallion Jones (Marshall) **21**:179

Rasmus and the Tramp (Lindgren) **39**:148

Rasmus and the Vagabond (Lindgren) **1**:139; **39**:148

Raspberry One (Ferry) **34**:54

Ratbags and Rascals: Funny Stories (Klein) **21**:160

Rats and Mice: Friends and Foes of Man (Silverstein and Silverstein) **25**:200

Rattlesnakes (Freedman) **20**:84

The Raucous Auk: A Menangerie of Poems (Hoberman) **22**:110

Raven's Cry (Harris) **47**:78

Ray Charles (Mathis) **3**:151

Razzle-Dazzle Riddles (Betsy and Giulio Maestro) **45**:76

Read One: Numbers as Words (Burningham) **9**:50

Reading (Ormerod) **20**:177

Reading Can Be Fun (Leaf) **25**:132

Ready or Not (St. John) **46**:98

Ready, Steady, Go! (Watanabe) **8**:216

The Real Book about Alaska (Epstein and Epstein) **26**:47

The Real Book about Amazing Birds (Merriam) **14**:191

The Real Book about Benjamin Franklin (Epstein and Epstein) **26**:48

The Real Book about Franklin D. Roosevelt (Merriam) **14**:191

The Real Book about Inventions (Epstein and Epstein) **26**:47

The Real Book about Pirates (Epstein and Epstein) **26**:48

The Real Book about Spies (Epstein and Epstein) **26**:48

The Real Book about Submarines (Epstein and Epstein) **26**:50

The Real Book about the Sea (Epstein and Epstein) 26:51
The Real Hole (Cleary) 2:50; 8:49
The Real Thief (Steig) 2:160
Realm of Algebra (Asimov) 12:36
Realm of Measure (Asimov) 12:34
Realm of Numbers (Asimov) 12:33
Rear-View Mirrors (Fleischman) 20:68
The Reason for the Pelican (Ciardi) 19:75
The Rebel (Burton) 1:33
Rebellion Town: Williamsburg, 1776 (Taylor) 30:187
Rebels of the Heavenly Kingdom (Paterson) 7:242
Rechenka's Eggs (Polacco) 40:180
Recipes for Art and Craft Materials (Sattler) 24:214
Recycling Resources (Pringle) 4:179
Red, Blue, Yellow Shoe (Hoban) 13:112
The Red Bus and the Green Car (Beskow) 17:18
Red Earth, Blue Sky: The Australian Outback (Rau) 8:191
Red Fox: The Story of His Adventurous Career in the Ringwaak Wilds, and of His Final Triumph over the Enemies of His Kind (Roberts) 33:195
Red Hawk's Account of Custer's Last Battle: The Battle of Little Bighorn, 25 June 1876 (Goble) 21:128
Red Head (Eager) 43:79
Red Hot Hightops (Christopher) 33:58
The Red King (Kelleher) 36:125
Red Leaf, Yellow Leaf (Ehlert) 28:115
Red Light, Green Light (Brown) 10:52
Red Magic: A Collection of the World's Best Fairy Tales from All Countries (Nielsen) 16:158
Red Pawns (Wibberley) 3:229
Red Riding Hood (Marshall) 21:182
Red Riding Hood: Retold in Verse for Boys and Girls to Read Themselves (Gorey) 36:97
The Red Room Riddle (Corbett) 1:46
The Red Secret (Nimmo) 44:142
Red Shift (Garner) 20:109
The Red Towers of Granada (Trease) 42:188
The Red Woolen Blanket (Graham)
  See *The Red Woollen Blanket*
The Red Woollen Blanket (Graham) 31:98
Redbird: The Story of a Cardinal (McClung) 11:185
Redecorating Your Room for Practically Nothing (Hautzig) 22:77
Redwall (Jacques) 21:153
Redwork (Bedard) 35:62
Regards to the Man in the Moon (Keats) 35:142
Reilly (Rayner) 41:127
The Relatives Came (Rylant) 15:171
Religions (Haskins) 3:66
The Reluctant Dragon (Grahame) 5:135
The Reluctant Pitcher (Christopher) 33:42
The Remarkable Journey of Prince Jen (Alexander) 48:22
The Remarkable Plant in Apartment 4 (Betsy and Giulio Maestro) 45:64
The Remarkable Plant in Flat No. 4 (Betsy and Giulio Maestro) 45:64
The Remarkable Riderless Runaway Tricycle (McMillan) 47:160
Remember Me (Pike) 29:173
Remember Me to Harold Square (Danziger) 20:56
Remember the Days: A Short History of the Jewish American (Meltzer) 13:134
Remember the Ladies: The First Women's Rights Convention (St. John) 46:126
Remembering the Good Times (Peck) 15:164

Remove Protective Coating a Little at a Time (Donovan) 3:53
Der Rennwagen (Heine) 18:149
The Renowned History of Little Red Riding-Hood (Hogrogian) 2:89
Representing Super Doll (Peck) 15:154
The Reproductive System: How Living Creatures Multiply (Silverstein and Silverstein) 25:206
Reptiles and How They Reproduce (Patent) 19:150
Rescue! An African Adventure (Kelleher) 36:119
The Rescuers (Sharp) 27:161
Rescuing Gloria (Cross) 28:95
The Restless Dead: Ghostly Tales from around the World (Cohen) 43:44
The Restless Robin (Flack) 28:126
Return of the Buffalo (Scott) 20:196
The Return of the Great Brain (Fitzgerald) 1:70
The Return of the Headless Horseman (Christopher) 33:55
Return of the Home Run Kid (Christopher) 33:63
Return of the Indian (Reid Banks) 24:197
Return of the Moose (Pinkwater) 4:169
The Return of the Twelves (Clarke) 28:77
Return to Gone-Away (Enright) 4:76
Return to Morocco (St. John) 46:120
Return to Sender (Henkes) 23:126
Return to South Town (Graham) 10:111
Return to the Happy Islands (Kruss) 9:84
The Revenge of Samuel Stokes (Lively) 7:163
The Revenge of the Incredible Dr. Rancid and His Youthful Assistant, Jeffrey (Conford) 10:97
The Revenge of the Wizard's Ghost (Bellairs) 37:19
Revolt at Ratcliffe's Rags (Cross) 28:86
Revolutionaries: Agents of Change (Haskins) 3:67
The Reward Worth Having (Williams) 8:235
Rhyme Stew (Dahl) 41:43
Rhymes Around the Day (Ormerod) 20:176
Ribsy (Cleary) 2:50; 8:51
Rice without Rain (Ho) 28:133
Rich and Famous: The Future Adventures of George Stable (Collier) 3:48
Richard (Keeping) 34:99
Richard Pryor: A Man and His Madness (Haskins) 39:46
Richard Scarry's Color Book (Scarry) 3:185
The Richleighs of Tantamount (Cleary) 3:221
The Riddle Book (Crossley-Holland) 47:38
Riddle City, USA: A Book of Geography Riddles (Betsy and Giulio Maestro) 45:88
The Riddle of the Drum: A Tale from Tizapán, Mexico (Aardema) 17:5
The Riddle of the Rosetta Stone: Key to Ancient Egypt (Giblin) 29:93
Ride a Purple Pelican (Prelutsky) 13:173
Ride into Danger (Treece) 2:188
A Ride into Morning: The Story of Tempe Wick (Rinaldi) 46:84
Ride Off: Learning Subtraction (Burningham) 9:50
Ride When You're Ready (Bunting) 28:44
The Rider and His Horse (Haugaard) 11:106
Riders of the Storm (Burton) 1:34
Riders of the Wind (Guillot) 22:62
Riding Home (Sanders) 46:120
Right Now (Kherdian) 24:113
The Right to Remain Silent (Meltzer) 13:129
The Righteous Revenge of Artemis Bonner (Myers) 35:199
The Rights of the Victim (Hyde) 23:168

Rilla of Ingleside (Montgomery) 8:138
A Ring of Endless Light (L'Engle) 14:152
Ring Out! A Book of Bells (Yolen) 4:261
Ring-Rise, Ring-Set (Hughes) 9:75
Rise & Shine (French) 37:49
The Rise of Mammals (Gallant) 30:103
Rising Early: Story Poems and Ballads of the Twentieth Century (Causley) 30:32
The Rising Tide (Allan) 43:28
Risking Love (Orgel) 48:86
River (Keeping) 34:103
The River and the Forest (Korinetz) 4:131
A River Dream (Say) 22:211
River Winding (Zolotow) 2:236
The River-Minded Boy (Calhoun) 42:5
The Road Ahead (Lowry) 46:34
A Road Down in the Sea (Graham) 10:109
The Road from Home: The Story of an Armenian Girl (Kherdian) 24:109
Road to Alaska: The Story of the Alaska Highway (Epstein and Epstein) 26:44
The Road to Camlann: The Death of King Arthur (Sutcliff) 37:175
The Road to Damietta (O'Dell) 16:179
The Road to Dunmore (Dillon) 26:27
The Road to Miklagard (Treece) 2:188
Roald Dahl's Revolting Rhymes (Dahl) 7:81
The Roan Colt (Ottley) 16:183
The Roan Colt of Yamboorah (Ottley) 16:183
Roar and More (Kuskin) 4:134
The "Roaring 40" (Chauncy) 6:92
Robber Hopsika (Biegel) 27:32
Robbie and the Leap Year Blues (Klein) 19:93
Robert Francis Weatherbee (Leaf) 25:116
Robert Fulton, Boy Craftsman (Henry) 4:109
Robert Koch: Father of Bacteriology (Knight) 38:98
Robert Rows the River (Haywood) 22:99
Robin and His Merry Men (Serraillier) 2:139
The Robin Hooders (Clarke) 28:77
Robin in the Greenwood: Ballads of Robin Hood (Serraillier) 2:140
Robot (Pienkowski) 6:232
The Robot and Rebecca and the Missing Owser (Yolen) 4:268
The Robot and Rebecca: The Mystery of the Code-Carrying Kids (Yolen) 4:266
The Robot Birthday (Bunting) 28:51
The Robot People (Bunting) 28:48
Robotics: Past, Present, and Future (Knight) 38:126
The Robots Are Here (Silverstein and Silverstein) 25:221
Robots in Fact and Fiction (Berger) 32:23
Rock Collecting (Keller) 45:47
Rock 'n' Roll Nights: A Novel (Strasser) 11:249
Rock Star (Collier) 3:48
Rocket Island (Taylor) 30:193
The Rocket Pioneers: On the Road to Space (Epstein and Epstein) 26:51
Rocket to Limbo (Nourse) 33:130
Rockets and Satellites (Branley) 13:30
The Rocking Horse Secret (Godden) 20:135
Rocks and Minerals and the Stories They Tell (Adler) 27:7
The Rocks of Honey (Wrightson) 4:241
Röda Bussen och Gröna Bilen (Beskow) 17:18
Roland the Minstrel Pig (Steig) 2:161
Roll of Thunder, Hear My Cry (Taylor) 9:226
Roller Skates (Sawyer) 36:150
Rolling Harvey down the Hill (Prelutsky) 13:167
The Rolling Rice Ball (Tresselt) 30:212
The Roman Empire (Asimov) 12:40

The Roman Moon Mystery (Williams) **8**:221
The Roman Republic (Asimov) **12**:39
Romance in Italy (Allan) **43**:7
Romansgrove (Allan) **43**:26
Rome under the Emperors (Dillon) **26**:31
Romeo and Juliet—Together (and Alive!) at Last (Avi) **24**:13
Rondo in C (Fleischman) **20**:70
Ronia, The Robber's Daughter (Lindgren) **39**:160
Ronnie and Rosie (Gaberman) **33**:2
Ronnie and the Giant Millipede (Nimmo) **44**:154
Roof Fall! (Cresswell) **18**:104
Roofs of Gold: Poems to Read Aloud (Colum) **36**:46
Room for Randy (Jackson) **28**:139
A Room Made of Windows (Cameron) **1**:40
A Room of His Own (Beckman) **25**:13
Room with No Windows (Kemp) **29**:124
Roomrimes: Poems (Cassedy) **26**:15
Rooster Brother (Hogrogian) **2**:89
The Rooster Crows: A Book of American Rhymes and Jingles (Petersham and Petersham) **24**:171
Rooster Sets Out to See the World (Carle) **10**:76
The Rooster Who Set Out to See the World (Carle) **10**:76
The Rooster Who Understood Japanese (Uchida) **6**:258
The Rooster's Horns: A Chinese Puppet Play to Make and Perform (Young) **27**:217
The Root Cellar (Lunn) **18**:160
Root River Run (Kherdian) **24**:114
Roots Are Food Finders (Branley) **13**:41
Rosa (Politi) **29**:192
Rosa Parks (Greenfield) **4**:97
Rosata (Keller) **45**:60
Roscoe's Leap (Cross) **28**:92
A Rose for Pinkerton (Kellogg) **6**:177
Rose Meets Mr. Wintergarten (Graham) **31**:101
The Rose on My Cake (Kuskin) **4**:138
Rosebud (Bemelmans) **6**:67
Rosebud (Emberley) **5**:93
Roses Sing on New Snow: A Delicious Tale (Yee) **44**:164
Rosie and Michael (Viorst) **3**:208
Rosie and the Rustlers (Gerrard) **23**:122
Rosie Swanson—Fourth-Grade Geek for President (Park) **34**:161
Rosie's Babies (Waddell) **31**:197
Rosie's Walk (Hutchins) **20**:142
Rosy Starling (Garfield) **21**:109
The Rotten Book (Rodgers) **20**:190
Rotten Island (Steig) **15**:199
Rotten Ralph (Gantos) **18**:140
Rotten Ralph's Rotten Christmas (Gantos) **18**:143
Rotten Ralph's Trick or Treat (Gantos) **18**:143
The Rotten Years (Wojciechowska) **1**:198
Round and Round and Round (Hoban) **13**:106
Round behind the Ice-House (Fine) **25**:19
Round the Twist (Jennings) **40**:127
Round Trip (Jonas) **12**:173
The Roundabout on the Roof (Baumann) **35**:46
Rowan Farm (Benary-Isbert) **12**:72
The Royal Raven (Wilhelm) **46**:171
Rub-a-Dub-Dub: Val Biro's 77 Favorite Nursery Rhymes (Biro) **28**:40
Ruby (Guy) **13**:79
Ruby and the Dragon (Owen) **31**:147
The Ruby in the Smoke (Pullman) **20**:187
Ruby Throat: The Story of a Humming Bird (McClung) **11**:178
Rudi and the Distelfink (Monjo) **2**:125

Rudyard Kipling: Creative Adventurer (Manley) **3**:147
Ruffles Is Lost (Wilhelm) **46**:168
Rufus M. (Estes) **2**:75
Rufus, the Fox: Adapted from the French of Samivel (Bianco) **19**:56
Rufus, the Red-Necked Hornbill (Lauber) **16**:1?:
Rumanian Folk Tales (Ure) **34**:171
Rumbelow's Dance (Blake) **31**:23
Rumbelow's Dance (Yeoman) **46**:180
Rumble Fish (Hinton) **3**:71; **23**:148
Rummage (Mattingley) **24**:126
Rumpelstiltskin's Daughter (Stanley) **46**:158
Rumplestiltskin (Galdone) **16**:106
Run (Sleator) **29**:199
Run, Billy, Run (Christopher) **33**:54
Run for the Money (Corbett) **1**:47
Run Softly, Go Fast (Wersba) **3**:218
The Runaway (Cross) **28**:85
The Runaway Brownie (Calhoun) **42**:12
The Runaway Bunny (Brown) **10**:50
The Runaway Elephant (Tarry) **26**:214
Runaway James and the Night Owl (Kuratomi) **32**:188
Runaway Ralph (Cleary) **8**:54
The Runaway Sleigh Ride (Lindgren) **39**:161
Runaway Sugar: All about Diabetes (Silverstein and Silverstein) **25**:220
Runaway to Freedom: A Story of the Underground Railway (Smucker) **10**:189
The Runaway Train (Farmer) **8**:87
The Runner (Voigt) **13**:236
Running Loose (Crutcher) **28**:103
A Russian Farewell (Fisher) **18**:129
Rusty Rings a Bell (Branley) **13**:26
Ruth: From the Story Told in the Book of Ruth (Petersham and Petersham) **24**:169
Rx for Tomorrow: Tales of Science Fiction, Fantasy, and Medicine (Nourse) **33**:136
Saber-Toothed Tiger and Other Ice Age Mammals (Cole) **5**:65
The Sacramento: Golden River of California (Epstein and Epstein) **26**:61
Sacred Places (Yolen) **44**:209
The Sad Story of Veronica Who Played the Violin (McKee) **38**:175
Saddlebottom (King-Smith) **40**:147
Sad-Faced Boy (Bontemps) **6**:79
Safety Can Be Fun (Leaf) **25**:124
The Saga of Erik the Viking (Foreman) **32**:96
Sailing: From Jibs to Jibing (Paulsen) **19**:173
The Sailing Hatrack (Coatsworth) **2**:61
Sailing Small Boats (Weiss) **4**:224
Sailing to Cythera and Other Anatole Stories (Willard) **5**:245
Sailing with the Wind (Locker) **14**:160
The Sailor (Bruna) **7**:50
Sailor Bear (Waddell) **31**:202
The Sailor Dog (Brown) **10**:63
Sailor Jack and the 20 Orphans (Mahy) **7**:179
Saint Francis and the Animals (Politi) **29**:191
Saint George and the Dragon (McCaughrean) **38**:144
Saint George and the Dragon: A Mummer's Play (Langstaff) **3**:111
Salford Road (Owen) **31**:141
Salford Road and Other Poems (Owen) **31**:142
Sally-Ann in the Snow (Breinburg) **31**:68
Sally-Ann's Skateboard (Breinburg) **31**:68
Sally-Ann's Umbrella (Breinburg) **31**:67
Sally's Secret (Hughes) **15**:121
A Salmon for Simon (Blades) **15**:55
Salt: A Russian Folktale (Langton) **33**:119

Saltwater City: An Illustrated History of the Chinese in Vancouver (Yee) **44**:162
Salvador and Mister Sam: A Guide to Parakeet Care (Gibbons) **8**:88
ㆍam and the Superdroop (Leaf) **25**:129
ㆍm and the Tigers (Pinkney) **43**:174
ㆍm, Bangs, and Moonshine (Ness) **6**:203
ㆍam Patch: The High, Wide, and Handsome Jumper (Bontemps) **6**:81
Sam the Referee (Ahlberg and Ahlberg) **18**:3
Sam Vole and His Brothers (Waddell) **31**:203
Sama (Guillot) **22**:55
Sammy Streetsinger (Keeping) **34**:106
Sam's All-Wrong Day (Fujikawa) **25**:41
Sam's Ball (Lindgren) **20**:157
Sam's Biscuit (Lindgren) **20**:156
Sam's Car (Lindgren) **20**:156
Sam's Cookie (Lindgren) **20**:156
Sam's Lamp (Lindgren) **20**:157
Sam's Place: Poems from the Country (Moore) **15**:143
Sam's Potty (Lindgren) **20**:158
Sam's Teddy (Lindgren) **20**:156
Sam's Teddy Bear (Lindgren) **20**:156
Sam's Wagon (Lindgren) **20**:158
Samson: Last of the California Grizzlies (McClung) **11**:188
Samstag im Paradies (Heine) **18**:150
Samuel Todd's Book of Great Colors (Konigsburg) **47**:143
Samuel Todd's Book of Great Inventions (Konigsburg) **47**:144
The Samurai and the Long-Nosed Devils (Namioka) **48**:62
Samurai of Gold Hill (Uchida) **6**:257
The Samurai's Daughter: A Japanese Legend (San Souci) **43**:188
The Samurai's Tale (Haugaard) **11**:110
San Domingo: The Medicine Hat Stallion (Henry) **4**:116
San Francisco (Fritz) **2**:81
San Francisco Boy (Lenski) **26**:118
The San Sebastian (Dillon) **26**:21
The Sanctuary Tree (St. John) **46**:104
Sand and Snow (Kuskin) **4**:139
The Sand Forest (Brinsmead) **47**:15
The Sandwich (Wallace) **37**:208
Sandy the Sailor (Clarke) **28**:76
Santa Claus Forever! (Haywood) **22**:105
Santiago (Clark) **16**:80
A Santo for Pasqualita (Clark) **16**:80
A Sapphire for September (Brinsmead) **47**:9
Sara Will (Bridgers) **18**:26
Sarah and After: The Matriarchs (Reid Banks) **24**:190
Sarah Bishop (O'Dell) **16**:175
Sarah, Plain and Tall (MacLachlan) **14**:184
Sarah's Room (Orgel) **48**:74
Satellites in Outer Space (Asimov) **12**:35
Saturday in Paradise (Heine) **18**:150
Saturday, the Twelfth of October (Mazer) **23**:223
The Saturdays (Enright) **4**:73
Saturn and Beyond (Asimov) **12**:57
Saturn: The Spectacular Planet (Branley) **13**:48
The Saucepan Journey (Unnerstad) **36**:188
Save Our School (Cross) **28**:87
Saving Electricity (Epstein and Epstein) **26**:66
Saving Grace (Owen) **31**:146
Saving Sweetness (Stanley) **46**:157
Say Goodnight (Oxenbury) **22**:148
Sayonara, Mrs. Kackleman (Kalman) **32**:181
The Scarebird (Sis) **45**:161
The Scarecrow Book (Giblin) **29**:85

Title Index

The Scarecrows (Westall) **13**:255
Scaredy-Cat (Fine) **25**:21
Scary, Scary Halloween (Bunting) **28**:60
Scavenger Hunt (Pike) **29**:173
Scavengers in Space (Nourse) **33**:131
Schloss an der Grenze (Benary-Isbert) **12**:75
Schnitzel Is Lost (Wilhelm) **46**:168
Schnitzel's First Christmas (Wilhelm) **46**:166
Das Schönste Ei der Welt (Heine) **18**:148
The School (Burningham) **9**:46
School (McCully) **46**:60
School for Sillies (Williams) **8**:230
The School Mouse (King-Smith) **40**:170
The Schoolbus Comes at Eight O'Clock (McKee) **38**:181
Schoolmaster Whackwell's Wonderful Sons (Orgel) **48**:73
The Schoolmasters (Fisher) **18**:122
The Schoolmouse (King-Smith) **40**:170
The Schools (Fisher) **18**:132
Science ABC (Knight) **38**:99
Science and Music: From Tom-Tom to Hi-Fi (Berger) **32**:2
Science at the Ball Game (Aylesworth) **6**:53
Science at Work: Projects in Oceanography (Simon) **9**:206
Science at Work: Projects in Space Science (Simon) **9**:204
The Science Book of Meteorology (Knight) **38**:100
Science Can Be Fun (Leaf) **25**:134
"*Science Early Learners*" (Graham) **31**:95
Science Experiments You Can Eat (Cobb) **2**:66
Science in a Vacant Lot (Simon) **9**:203
Science Looks at Mysterious Monsters (Aylesworth) **6**:56
The Science of Music (Berger) **32**:41
Science Projects in Ecology (Simon) **9**:204
Science Projects in Pollution (Simon) **9**:206
Scoop: Last of the Brown Pelicans (McClung) **11**:187
Scorpions (Myers) **35**:190
Scouting with Baden-Powell (Freedman) **20**:74
Scrambled Eggs Super! (Seuss) **9**:178
Scrappy, the Pup (Ciardi) **19**:76
Scruffy (Parish) **22**:168
A Scythe, a Rooster, and a Cat (Domanska) **40**:49
The Sea Egg (Boston) **3**:28
Sea Elf (Ryder) **37**:99
A Sea Full of Sharks (Betsy and Giulio Maestro) **45**:83
Sea Glass (Yep) **17**:204
Sea Gull (Farmer) **8**:77
The Sea Is All Around (Enright) **4**:72
The Sea Lion and the Slick (Freeman) **30**:79
Sea Magic and Other Stories of Enchantment (Harris) **30**:116
The Sea of Gold and Other Tales from Japan (Uchida) **6**:254
Sea Otters and Seaweed (Lauber) **16**:118
Sea People (Mueller) **43**:121
The Sea Rover (Guillot) **22**:58
Sea So Big, Ship So Small (Bendick) **5**:40
Sea Songs (Fisher) **18**:135
Sea Star (McClung) **11**:189
Sea Star, Orphan of Chincoteague (Henry) **4**:111
The Sea Stranger (Crossley-Holland) **47**:31
The Sea View Hotel (Stevenson) **17**:155
The Sea Wall (Dillon) **26**:26
The Sea World Book of Sharks (Bunting) **28**:49
The Sea World Book of Whales (Bunting) **28**:51
The Sea-Beggar's Son (Monjo) **2**:125
Seacrow Island (Lindgren) **1**:139; **39**:153

The Seagull (Farmer) **8**:77
The Seal and the Slick (Freeman) **30**:79
A Seal upon My Heart (Conrad) **18**:88
The Seals (Dillon) **26**:28
The Seal-Singing (Harris) **30**:113
The Seance (Nixon) **24**:140
Sean's Red Bike (Breinburg) **31**:67
Search for a Stone (Munari) **9**:129
The Search for Delicious (Babbitt) **2**:7
The Search for Life (Aylesworth) **6**:52
Seashore Story (Yashima) **4**:254
Seashores and Shadows (Thiele) **27**:209
Season of Ponies (Snyder) **31**:153
Season of the Briar (Brinsmead) **47**:7
Season of the Two-Heart (Duncan) **29**:67
Season Songs (Hughes) **3**:95
Seasons (Berger) **32**:44
Seasons (Burningham) **9**:43
The Seasons for Singing: American Christmas Songs and Carols (Langstaff) **3**:111
Seasons of Splendour: Tales, Myths, and Legends of India (Foreman) **32**:99
Seasons of the Tallgrass Prairie (Lerner) **34**:125
The Sea-Thing Child (Hoban) **3**:82
The Second Bend in the River (Rinaldi) **46**:93
The Second Books of American Negro Spirituals (Johnson) **32**:163
The Second Jungle Book (Kipling) **39**:74-118
The Second Margaret Mahy Story Book: Stories and Poems (Mahy) **7**:181
The Second Mrs. Giaconda (Konigsburg) **47**:133
Second Summer with Ladis (Sanchez-Silva) **12**:232
The Secret (Coatsworth) **2**:61
Secret Agents Four (Sobol) **4**:208
The Secret Bedroom (Stine) **37**:115
The Secret Birthday Message (Carle) **10**:75
The Secret Box (Cole) **5**:61
The Secret Box Mystery (Nixon) **24**:135
The Secret Clocks: Time Senses of Living Things (Simon) **9**:213
The Secret Friends (Chauncy) **6**:91
The Secret Garden (Burnett) **24**:21-60
Secret in a Sealed Bottle: Lazarro Spallanzani's Work with Microbes (Epstein and Epstein) **26**:67
Secret in the Stlalakum Wild (Harris) **47**:83
The Secret Name (Wilkinson) **48**:188
The Secret of Bone Island (McBratney) **44**:123
The Secret of Gumbo Grove (Tate) **37**:188
The Secret of Light (Adler) **27**:4
The Secret of Sarah Revere (Rinaldi) **46**:90
Secret of the Andes (Clark) **16**:77
Secret of the Hawk (Wibberley) **3**:230
The Secret of the Indian (Reid Banks) **24**:200
The Secret of the Lodge (Streatfeild) **17**:188
The Secret of the Lodge (Streatfeild) **17**:188
The Secret of the Missing Boat (Berna) **19**:38
The Secret of the Royal Mounds: Henry Layard and the First Cities of Assyria (Cummings) **48**:44
The Secret of the Sachem's Tree (Monjo) **2**:125
The Secret of the Singing Strings (St. John) **46**:114
Secret Sea (White) **3**:222
Secret Selves (Gaberman) **33**:5
Secret, Silent Screams (Nixon) **24**:151
The Secret Staircase (Barklem) **31**:5
The Secret Trails (Roberts) **33**:204
Secret Water (Ransome) **8**:179
The Secret World of Polly Flint (Cresswell) **18**:111
Secrets of a Wildlife Watcher (Arnosky) **15**:7

Secrets of the Shopping Mall (Peck) **15**:162
Secrets of the Underground Room (Bellairs) **37**:24
The Secrets on Beacon Hill (St. John) **46**:115
See My Lovely Poison Ivy and Other Verses about Witches, Ghosts, and Things (Moore) **15**:143
See the Circus (Rey) **5**:198
See through the Sea (Selsam) **1**:165
See What I Am (Duvoisin) **23**:105
See What I Found (Livingston) **7**:168
See You Around, Sam! (Lowry) **46**:50
See You Later (Pike) **29**:173
See You Thursday (Ure) **34**:171
Seeds: Pop, Stick, Glide (Lauber) **16**:119
The Seeing Stick (Yolen) **4**:264
Seeing the Earth from Space: What the Man-Made Moons Tell Us (Adler) **27**:13
The Seekers (Dillon) **26**:33
El segundo verano de Ladis (Sanchez-Silva) **12**:232
The Selfish Giant (Zwerger) **46**:193
The Self-Made Snowman (Krahn) **3**:105
Selina's New Family (Pilgrim) **43**:17
A Semester in the Life of a Garbage Bag (Korman) **25**:109
A Sending of Dragons (Yolen) **44**:181
Sense of Direction: Up and Down and All Around (Cobb) **2**:67
A Sense of Shame and Other Stories (Needle) **43**:134
The Sense Organs: Our Link with the World (Silverstein and Silverstein) **25**:205
Sense Suspense: A Guessing Game for the Five Senses (McMillan) **47**:185
Senses (Graham) **31**:95
Sentries (Paulsen) **19**:175
Serafina the Giraffe (Brunhoff) **4**:35
The Serpent Never Sleeps: A Novel of Jamestown and Pocahontas (O'Dell) **16**:180
The Serpent's Children (Yep) **17**:206
The Serpent's Teeth: The Story of Cadmus (Farmer) **8**:80
Servants of the Devil (Aylesworth) **6**:49
Sets (Adler) **27**:22
Sets and Numbers for the Very Young (Adler) **27**:23
Settling America: The Ethnic Expression of Fourteen Contemporary Poets (Kherdian) **24**:106
The Seven Days of Creation (Fisher) **18**:130
Seven Days to a Brand-New Me (Conford) **10**:97
Seven Kisses in a Row (MacLachlan) **14**:183
Seven Little Monsters (Sendak) **17**:123
The Seven Ravens (Zwerger) **46**:189
Seven Silly Circles (Conrad) **18**:88
Seven Stories about a Cat Named Sneakers (Brown) **10**:65
Seven Stories by Hans Christian Andersen (Carle) **10**:82
Seven White Pebbles (Clarke) **28**:77
Seven Wild Pigs: Eleven Picture Book Fantasies (Heine) **18**:150
Seven-Day Magic (Eager) **43**:88
Seventeen against the Dealer (Voigt) **48**:172
Seventeen and In-Between (DeClements) **23**:35
Seventeen Kings and Forty-Two Elephants (Mahy) **7**:181
Seventeen Seconds (Southall) **2**:155
The Seventh Mandarin (Yolen) **4**:259
The Seventh Pebble (Spence) **26**:198
The Seventh Raven (Dickinson) **29**:52
The Seven-Times Search (Biegel) **27**:29

Several Kinds of Silence (Singer) **48**:132

Sexual Abuse: Let's Talk about It (Hyde) **23**:169

Sexually Transmitted Diseases (Nourse) **33**:150

Shadow (Brown) **12**:107

The Shadow Cage and Other Tales of the Supernatural (Pearce) **9**:155

Shadow Dancers (Curry) **31**:84

The Shadow Guests (Aiken) **19**:12

Shadow in Hawthorn Bay (Lunn) **18**:165

Shadow in the North (Lindgren) **20**:188

The Shadow in the Plate (Pullman) **20**:188

Shadow Lord (Yep) **17**:207

Shadow of a Bull (Wojciechowska) **1**:199

Shadow of a Unicorn (St. John) **46**:118

Shadow of the Hawk (Trease) **42**:180

The Shadow of Vesuvius (Dillon) **26**:32

The Shadow on the Hills (Thiele) **27**:207

The Shadow on the Sun (Harris) **30**:112

Shadow over the Back Court (Christopher) **33**:38

Shadow Shark (Thiele) **27**:209

Shadows (Adler) **27**:15

Shadows and Light: Nine Stories by Anton Chekhov (Grifalconi) **35**:70

Shadows on the Lake (Waddell) **31**:188

Shadows on the Wall (Naylor) **17**:55

Shadrach (DeJong) **1**:60

Shadrach, Meshach and Abednego: From the Book of Daniel (Galdone) **16**:92

Shadrach's Crossing (Avi) **24**:10

Shag: Last of the Plains Buffalo (McClung) **11**:182

Shaggy (Pfister) **42**:135

Shags Finds a Kitten (Fujikawa) **25**:41

Shaka: King of the Zulus (Stanley) **46**:139

Shaka, King of the Zulus: A Biography (Cohen) **3**:42

Shaker Paper House: To Cut Out and Color (Ness) **6**:209

Shakes, Quakes, and Shifts: Earth Tectonics (Branley) **13**:40

Shakespeare Stories (Foreman) **32**:97

Shakespeare Stories (Garfield) **21**:118

Shapes (Bendick) **5**:42

Shapes (Schlein) **41**:175

Shapes and Things (Hoban) **13**:100

Shapes, Shapes, Shapes (Hoban) **13**:111

The Shaping of England (Asimov) **12**:43

The Shaping of North America from Earliest Times to 1763 (Asimov) **12**:48

Sharing Susan (Bunting) **28**:67

Sharks (Blumberg) **21**:24

Sharks (Freedman) **20**:86

Sharks (Zim) **2**:230

Sharks in the Shadows (Thiele) **27**:209

Sharks, the Super Fish (Sattler) **24**:221

Shatterbelt (Thiele) **27**:211

Shaun and the Cart-Horse (Keeping) **34**:88

Shawn Goes to School (Breinburg)
See *My Brother Sean*

Shawn's Red Bike (Breinburg)
See *Sean's Red Bike*

Shaw's Fortune: The Picture Story of a Colonial Plantation (Tunis) **2**:194

She Come Bringing Me That Little Baby Girl (Greenfield) **4**:97

She Never Looked Back: Margaret Mead in Samoa (Epstein and Epstein) **26**:68

The Sheep Book (Patent) **19**:161

The Sheep-Pig (King-Smith) **40**:144; **41**:124

Sheet Magic: Games, Toys and Gifts from Old Sheets (Parish) **22**:159

Sheila Rae, the Brave (Henkes) **23**:129

Sheila's Dying (Carter) **22**:21

She'll Be Coming Around the Mountain (Orgel) **48**:95

A Shepherd Watches, A Shepherd Sings (Taylor) **30**:190

The Sheriff of Rottenshot (Prelutsky) **13**:169

Shh! We're Writing the Constitution (Fritz) **14**:122

Shhhh (Henkes) **23**:131

SHHhhhh......Bang, a Whispering Book (Brown) **10**:51

The Shield Ring (Sutcliff) **1**:189; **37**:152

Shifting Sands (Sutcliff) **37**:167

The Shimmershine Queens (Yarbrough) **29**:210

Shimmy Shimmy Coke-Ca-Pop! A Collection of City Children's Street Games and Rhymes (Langstaff) **3**:112

The Shining Company (Sutcliff) **37**:181

Ship Models and How to Build Them (Weiss) **4**:227

Ship of Danger (Allan) **43**:25

The Ship That Came Down the Gutter (Kotzwinkle) **6**:181

Shirley Temple Black: Actress to Ambassador (Haskins) **39**:58

Shirlick Holmes and the Case of the Wandering Wardrobe (Yolen) **4**:267

The Shirt off a Hanged Man's Back (Hamley) **47**:57

Shivers and Goose Bumps: How We Keep Warm (Branley) **13**:49

Shoebag (Kerr) **29**:158

Shoes from Grandpa (Fox) **23**:117

The Shooting Star (Benary-Isbert) **12**:74

Shooting Stars (Keller) **45**:53

The Shopping Basket (Burningham) **9**:49

Shopping Trip (Oxenbury) **22**:143

Short and Shivery: Thirty Chilling Tales (San Souci) **43**:183

Short and Tall (Scarry) **41**:167

The Short Voyage of the 'Albert Ross' (Mark) **11**:150

Shortstop from Tokyo (Christopher) **33**:44

A Shovelful of Earth (Milne and Milne) **22**:125

The Show Must Go On (McCully) **46**:60

Showdown (Pascal) **25**:185

Shrewbettina Goes to Work (Goodall) **25**:51

Shrewbettina's Birthday (Goodall) **25**:44

The Shrinking of Treehorn (Gorey) **36**:94

Sia Lives on Kilimanjaro (Lindgren) **1**:140

The Sick Day (MacLachlan) **14**:180

The Sick of Being Sick Book (Stine) **37**:104

The Sickest Don't Always Die the Quickest (Jackson) **28**:140

Sid and Sol (Yorinks) **20**:214

Side by Side: Poems to Read Together (Hopkins) **44**:95

Sidewalk Story (Mathis) **3**:151

Sideways Arithmetic from Wayside School (Sacher) **28**:204

Sideways Stories from Wayside School (Sacher) **28**:200

The Siege of Babylon (Dhondy) **41**:73

Siegfried (Stanley) **46**:146

Sight and Seeing: A World of Light and Color (Simon) **39**:157

The Sign of the Beaver (Speare) **8**:210

The Sign of the Chrysanthemum (Paterson) **7**:230

The Sign of the Unicorn: A Thriller for Young People (Allan) **43**:11

The Sign on Rosie's Door (Sendak) **17**:111

The Signposters (Cresswell) **18**:99

Silas and Ben-Godik (Bodker) **23**:13

Silas and the Black Mare (Bodker) **23**:12

Silas and the Runaway Coach (Bodker) **23**:13

Silent Night (Jeffers) **30**:136

Silent Night (Stine) **37**:116

Silent Ship, Silent Sea (White) **3**:222

Silent Sound: The World of Ultrasonics (Knight) **38**:124

Silky: An Incredible Tale (Coatsworth) **2**:61

Silly Goose (Ormerod) **20**:179

Silly Mother (Duncan) **29**:66

The Silly Tail Book (Brown) **29**:10

Silver (Mazer) **23**:233

Silver Bells and Cockle Shells (Clarke) **28**:79

The Silver Branch (Sutcliff) **1**:190; **37**:153

The Silver Chair (Lewis) **3**:136; **27**:104-51

The Silver Christmas Tree (Hutchins) **20**:147

The Silver Crown (O'Brien) **2**:128

The Silver Mace: A Story of Williamsburg (Petersham and Petersham) **24**:179

Silver on the Tree (Cooper) **4**:47

The Silver Sword (Serraillier) **2**:141

The Silver Train to Midnight (Brinsmead) **47**:16

The Silver Whistle (Williams) **8**:231

Simon (Sutcliff) **1**:190; **37**:150

The Simon and Schuster Book of Fact and Fallacies (Blumberg) **21**:28

Simon Boom Gives a Wedding (Suhl) **2**:166

Simon Pure (Thompson) **24**:230

Simon Underground (Ryder) **37**:84

Simon's Book (Drescher) **20**:59

Simon's Song (Emberley and Emberley) **5**:97

Simple Gifts: The Story of the Shakers (Yolen) **4**:263

Simple Pictures Are Best (Willard) **5**:247

The Simple Prince (Yolen) **4**:264

Sing a Song for Sixpence (Caldecott) **14**:75

Sing Down the Moon (O'Dell) **1**:148

Sing, Pierrot, Sing: A Picture Book in Mime (dePaola) **24**:94

Sing to the Dawn (Ho) **28**:132

The Singing Cave (Dillon) **26**:22

The Singing Hill (DeJong) **1**:61

The Singing Tortoise and Other Animal Folk Tales (Yeoman) **46**:184

The Singing Tree (Seredy) **10**:176

A Single Light (Wojciechowska) **1**:199

Singularity (Sleator) **29**:205

Sink It, Rusty (Christopher) **33**:39

Sir Arthur Evans, Discoverer of Knossos (Selden) **8**:198

Sir Cedric (Gerrard) **23**:120

Sir Cedric Rides Again (Gerrard) **23**:120

Sir Francis Drake: His Daring Deeds (Gerrard) **23**:121

Sirga, Queen of the African Bush (Guillot) **22**:55

Sister (Greenfield) **4**:97

Sister of the Bride (Cleary) **8**:50

Six and Silver (Phipson) **5**:178

Six Men (McKee) **38**:163

The Six Swans (San Souci) **43**:183

Sixes and Sevens (Yeoman) **46**:175

A Six-Pack and a Fake I.D.: Teens Look at the Drinking Question (Cohen) **43**:47

Sixth Grade Can Really Kill You (DeClements) **23**:36

Sixth Grade Secrets (Sacher) **28**:203

Sixth-Grade Sleepover (Bunting) **28**:60

The Size Spies (Needle) **43**:133

Sizes and Shapes in Nature—What They Mean (Patent) **19**:153

The Skate Patrol (Bunting) **28**:52

The Skate Patrol and the Mystery Writer (Bunting) **28**:54

Skateboard Tough (Christopher) **33**:62

Skates! (Keats) **1**:117; **35**:138

Skating Shoes (Streatfeild) **17**:191

The Skeletal System: Frameworks for Life (Silverstein and Silverstein) **25**:208

Sketching Outdoors in Spring (Arnosky) **15**:10

Ski Pup (Freeman) **30**:73

Ski Weekend (Stine) **37**:115

Skiing to Danger (Allan) **43**:14

The Skin: Coverings and Linings of Living Things (Silverstein and Silverstein) **25**:209

The Skin Horse (Bianco) **19**:52

The Skin Spinners (Aiken) **19**:9

Skinnybones (Park) **34**:155

Skip Trip (Burningham) **9**:51

Skipper John's Cook (Brown) **12**:96

Skipping Village (Lenski) **26**:98

The Skirt (Soto) **38**:197

The Sknuks (Thiele) **27**:208

Skrallan and the Pirates (Lindgren) **39**:153

Sky Dogs (Yolen) **44**:190

A Sky Full of Poems (Merriam) **14**:203

The Sky Is Falling (Pearson) **26**:178

The Sky is Free (Clark) **30**:60

Sky Man on the Totem Pole? (Harris) **47**:84

Sky Songs (Fisher) **18**:133

The Sky Was Blue (Zolotow) **2**:236

Sky Words (Singer) **48**:143

The Sky-God Stories (Aardema) **17**:3

Skymaze (Rubinstein) **35**:212

The Skyscraper Book (Giblin) **29**:86

Slam Bang (Burningham) **9**:51

Slam Book (Martin) **32**:203

Slappy Hooper, the Wonderful Sign Painter (Bontemps) **6**:80

Slater's Mill (Monjo) **2**:126

The Slave Dancer (Fox) **1**:79

Slavery: From the Rise of Western Civilization to the Renaissance (Meltzer) **13**:128

Slavery, Volume II: From the Renaissance to Today (Meltzer) **13**:128

A Slave's Tale (Haugaard) **11**:103

Sledges to the Rescue (Briggs) **10**:23

Sleep and Dreams (Silverstein and Silverstein) **25**:210

Sleep Is for Everyone (Showers) **6**:246

The Sleepers (Curry) **31**:71

Sleepers (Khalsa) **30**:148

The Sleepers on the Hill (Waddell) **31**:176

Sleeping (Ormerod) **20**:177

The Sleeping Beauty (Mayer) **11**:175

Sleeping Beauty and Other Favourite Fairy Tales (Foreman) **32**:94

Sleeping Ugly (Stanley) **46**:132

The Sleepwalker (Stine) **37**:113

Sleepy ABC (Brown) **10**:62

The Sleepy Owl (Pfister) **42**:133

Sleepy People (Goffstein) **3**:61

Sleepy Ronald (Gantos) **18**:140

Sloan and Philamina; or, How to Make Friends with Your Lunch (Stren) **5**:231

Slumber Party (Pike) **29**:170

The Sly Old Cat (Potter) **1**:153

Small Faces (Soto) **38**:187

Small Fry (Merriam) **14**:194

The Small Ones (Paulsen) **19**:171

Small Pig (Lobel) **5**:164

Small Poems (Worth) **21**:220

Small Poems Again (Worth) **21**:224

A Small Tall Tale from the Far Far North (Sis) **45**:171

The Smallest Dinosaurs (Simon) **9**:218

The Smallest Elephant in the World (Tresselt) **30**:207

The Smallest Witch (Sattler) **24**:218

The Smartest Man in Ireland (Hunter) **25**:74

Smeller Martin (Lawson) **2**:111

Smile, Ernest and Celestine (Vincent) **13**:217

Smile Please, Ernest and Celestine (Vincent) **13**:217

Smith (Garfield) **21**:97

Smith's Hoard (Clarke) **28**:75

Smoke from Cromwell's Time (Aiken) **1**:7

Smoke over Golan (Ofek) **28**:190

Smokey (Peet) **12**:195

Snail in the Woods (Ryder) **37**:86

Snail Tale: The Adventures of a Rather Small Snail (Avi) **24**:4

Snail, Where Are You? (Ungerer) **3**:203

Snails (Zim) **2**:230

Snails of Land and Sea (Simon) **39**:193

The Snail's Spell (Ryder) **37**:87

Snake Fights, Rabbit Fights & More: A Book about Animal Fighting (Schlein) **41**:189

The Snake That Went to School (Moore) **15**:139

Snakes and Ladders: Poems about the Ups and Downs of Life (Klein) **21**:162

Snakes Are Hunters (Lauber) **16**:124

A Snake's Body (Cole) **5**:67

Snakes: The Facts and the Folklore (Simon) **39**:190

Snakes: Their Place in the Sun (McClung) **11**:192

Snapshots (Klein) **19**:96

Sneakers: Seven Stories about a Cat (Brown) **10**:65

The Sneetches and Other Stories (Seuss) **9**:186

Sniff Shout (Burningham) **9**:51

Sniper (Taylor) **30**:195

Snippy and Snappy (Gág) **4**:89

The Snopp on the Sidewalk, and Other Poems (Prelutsky) **13**:166

The Snow (Burningham) **9**:46

Snow before Christmas (Tudor) **13**:190

Snow Day (Betsy and Giulio Maestro) **45**:81

Snow Is Falling (Branley) **13**:31

The Snow Monkey at Home (Rau) **8**:190

The Snow Spider (Nimmo) **44**:140

Snow Tracks (George) **1**:92

Snow White in New York (French) **37**:47

The Snow Wife (San Souci) **43**:190

Snow Woman (McKee) **38**:178

Snowbound (Mazer) **16**:128

Snowbound with Betsy (Haywood) **22**:98

Snow-Cat (Calhoun) **42**:25

The Snowman (Briggs) **10**:29

The Snowman (Stine) **37**:115

The Snowstorm (Carigiet) **38**:71

Snow-White and Rose-Red (Cooney) **23**:27

Snowy and Woody (Duvoisin) **23**:106

The Snowy Day (Keats) **1**:117; **35**:122

Snuff (Blake) **31**:19

Snuffie (Bruna) **7**:51

Snuffy (Bruna) **7**:51

So Long at the Fair (Irwin) **40**:113

So Many Marvels (Shippen) **36**:176

So Much to Tell You . . . (Marsden) **34**:146

So What If I'm a Sore Loser? (Williams) **48**:200

So You Want to Be a Chemist (Nourse) **33**:134

So You Want to Be a Chemist (Nourse) **33**:134

So You Want to Be a Doctor (Nourse) **33**:131

So You Want to Be a Lawyer (Nourse) **33**:131

So You Want to Be a Scientist (Nourse) **33**:132

So You Want to Be a Surgeon (Nourse) **33**:135

So You Want to Be an Engineer (Nourse) **33**:133

So, You're Getting Braces: A Guide to Orthodontics (Silverstein and Silverstein) **25**:216

Social Welfare (Myers) **4**:157

Sock Craft: Toys, Gifts, and Other Things to Make (Sattler) **24**:213

Socks (Cleary) **2**:51; **8**:54

Socrates and the Three Little Pigs (Anno) **14**:44

Die Softly (Pike) **29**:174

Solägget (Beskow) **17**:18

Solar Energy (Branley) **13**:26

The Solar System (Asimov) **12**:53

The Soldier and Death: A Russian Folk Tale Told in English (Ransome) **8**:171

Soldier and Tsar in the Forest: A Russian Tale (Shulevitz) **5**:205

Soldier, Soldier, Won't You Marry Me? (Langstaff) **3**:112

The Solid Gold Kid (Mazer and Mazer) **16**:129; **23**:225

Solids, Liquids, and Gases (Bendick) **5**:47

Solids, Liquids, and Gases: From Superconductors to the Ozone Layer (Berger) **32**:42

A Solitary Blue (Voigt) **13**:233

The Solomon System (Naylor) **17**:58

Solomon the Rusty Nail (Steig) **15**:200

Solomon's Child (Clark) **30**:62

Some Birthday! (Polacco) **40**:191

Some of Aesop's Fables, with Modern Instances (Caldecott) **14**:79

Some of the Days of Everett Anderson (Clifton) **5**:53

Some Swell Pup; or, Are You Sure You Want a Dog? (Sendak) **17**:122

Somebody Else's Nut Tree: And Other Tales from Children (Krauss) **42**:123

Somebody Spilled the Sky (Krauss) **42**:130

Someday Angeline (Sachar) **28**:201

Someday, Said Mitchell (Williams) **48**:192

Someone Could Win a Polar Bear (Ciardi) **19**:80

Someone Else's Ghost (Buffie) **39**:27

Someone Is Hiding On Alcatraz Island (Bunting) **28**:57

Someone to Love (Mazer) **23**:229

someplace Beautiful (Brinsmead) **47**:15

The Something (Babbitt) **2**:8

Something for Now, Something for Later (Schlein) **41**:179

Something Left to Lose (Brancato) **32**:70

Something New Begins: New and Selected Poems (Moore) **15**:144

Something on my Mind (Grimes) **42**:90

Something Special (Rodda) **32**:209

Something Special for Me (Williams) **9**:234

Something Upstairs: A Tale of Ghosts (Avi) **24**:13

Something Weird Is Going On (Harris) **47**:91

Sometimes I Dance Mountains (Baylor) **3**:16

Sometimes I Think I Hear My Name (Avi) **24**:9

Sometimes My Mom Drinks Too Much (Krull) **44**:102

Somewhere in the Darkness (Myers) **35**:197

"Son No. 6" (Guillen)
　　See *Karen's Opposites*

Son of a Gun (Ahlberg and Ahlberg) **18**:6

Son of Columbus (Baumann) **35**:35

Son of Interflux (Korman) **25**:109

The Son of Someone Famous (Kerr) **29**:145

Song for a Dark Queen (Sutcliff) **37**:169

Song for a Tattered Flag (Trease) **42**:192

A Song for Uncle Harry (Kherdian) **24**:115

The Song in My Drum (Hoban) **3**:82

A Song in Stone: City Poems (Hopkins) **44**:92

The Song in the Walnut Grove (Kherdian) **24**:112

The Song of Pentecost (Corbett) **19**:82

Song of Sedna (San Souci) **43**:180

Song of the Boat (Graham) **10**:110

Song of the Boat (Leo and Diane Dillon) **44**:28

Song of the City (Owen) **31**:143
Song of the Gargoyle (Snyder) **31**:169
Song of the Swallows (Politi) **29**:187
Song of the Trees (Taylor) **9**:225
Songbird Story (Rosen) **45**:147
Songs for Alex (Duder) **43**:67
Songs for Mr. Small (Lenski) **26**:118
Songs from Dreamland: Original Lullabies (Duncan) **29**:80
Songs of the Dream People: Chants and Images from the Indians and Eskimos of North America (Houston) **3**:86
Songs of the Fog Maiden (dePaola) **4**:62
Sonora Beautiful (Clifton) **5**:60
Sons from Afar (Voigt) **48**:168
Sons of the Steppe: The Story of How the Conqueror Genghis Khan was Overcome (Baumann) **35**:38
Sonsense Nongs (Rosen) **45**:146
Sootface: An Ojibwa Cinderella Story (San Souci) **43**:193
Sophia Scrooby Preserved (Bacon) **3**:11
Sophie Hits Six (King-Smith) **40**:164
Sophie in the Saddle (King-Smith) **40**:170
Sophie Is Seven (King-Smith) **40**:174
Sophie's Snail (King-Smith) **40**:155
Sophie's Tom (King-Smith) **40**:163
S.O.R. Losers (Avi) **24**:12
The Sorcerer's Apprentice (Leo and Diane Dillon) **44**:46
The Sorely Trying Day (Hoban) **3**:82
The Soul Brothers and Sister Lou (Hunter) **3**:99
Sound (Owen) **31**:95
Sound and Ultrasonics (Adler) **27**:12
A Sound of Chariots (Hunter) **25**:81
The Sound of Coaches (Garfield) **21**:107
The Sound of the Dragon's Feet (Zei) **6**:262
Sounder (Armstrong) **1**:23
Soup (Peck) **45**:103
Soup 1776 (Peck) **45**:126
Soup and Me (Peck) **45**:106
Soup for President (Peck) **45**:111
Soup in the Saddle (Peck) **45**:117
Soup on Fire (Peck) **45**:120
Soup on Ice (Peck) **45**:120
Soup on Wheels (Peck) **45**:115
Soup's Goat (Peck) **45**:119
Sour Land (Armstrong) **1**:24
South Pole Station (Berger) **32**:7
South Swell (Wibberley) **3**:230
South Town (Graham) **10**:105
Southerly Buster (Mattingley) **24**:127
Southern Africa: South Africa, Namibia, Swaziland, Lesotho, and Botswana (Blumberg) **21**:27
Southern Fried Rat and Other Gruesome Tales (Cohen) **43**:43
Space and Time (Bendick) **5**:42
Space Case (Marshall) **21**:175
Space Challenger: The Story of Guion Bluford (Haskins) **39**:47
Space Colony: Frontier of the 21st Century (Branley) **13**:47
Space Demons (Rubinstein) **35**:211
The Space People (Bunting) **28**:48
Space Shots, Shuttles, and Satellites (Berger) **32**:31
Space Songs (Fisher) **18**:138
Space Station Seventh Grade (Spinelli) **26**:201
A Space Story (Kuskin) **4**:143
Space Talk (Berger) **32**:32
Space Telescope (Branley) **13**:51
Space Telescope: A Voyage into Space Book (Betsy and Giulio Maestro) **45**:76

Space Trap (Hughes) **9**:77
Space Witch (Freeman) **30**:72
The Spaghetti Party (Orgel) **48**:96
The Spanish Armada (Williams) **8**:228
Spanish Hoof (Peck) **45**:119
The Spanish Letters (Hunter) **25**:75
The Spanish Smile (O'Dell) **16**:177
Spark of Opal (Clark) **30**:58
Sparky: The Story of a Little Trolley Car (Gramatky) **22**:42
Sparrow Alone (Colum) **36**:40
The Sparrow Bush (Coatsworth) **2**:62
Sparrow Socks (Selden) **8**:198
The Sparrow's Song (Wallace) **37**:214
Speak Out in Thunder Tones: Letters and Other Writings by Black Northerners, 1787-1865 (Sterling) **1**:181
Speak Out on Rape! (Hyde) **23**:161
Speak Up, Blanche! (McCully) **46**:66
Speak Up: More Rhymes of the Never Was and Always Is (McCord) **9**:104
The Special Present (Mattingley) **24**:124
A Special Trick (Mayer) **11**:165
The Specter (Nixon) **24**:143
Speedboat (Marshall) **21**:171
A Spell Is Cast (Cameron) **1**:41
The Spell of the Sorcerer's Skull (Bellairs) **37**:18
The Spellcoats (Jones) **23**:189
The Spettecake Holiday (Unnerstad) **36**:192
Sphinx: The Story of a Caterpillar (Lerner) **34**:126
Sphinx: The Story of a Caterpillar (McClung) **11**:178
A Spider Bought a Bicycle and Other Poems (Rosen) **45**:136
Spider Magic (Patent) **19**:158
Spiderman-Anancy (Berry) **22**:9
The Spiders Dance (Ryder) **37**:86
The Spider's Web (Keeping) **34**:98
Spiderweb for Two: A Melendy Maze (Enright) **4**:75
Spike: The Story of a Whitetail Deer (McClung) **11**:179
Spin a Soft Black Song: Poems for Children (Giovanni) **6**:115
The Spirit House (Sleator) **29**:207
The Spirit of the Lord: Revivalism in America (Cohen) **3**:42
Spirit of the Place (Hamley) **47**:66
The Spitball Gang (Paulsen) **19**:173
Splash, Splash (Dorros) **42**:66
The Splendor of Iridescence: Structural Colors in the Animal World (Simon) **39**:187
The Splintered Sword (Serraillier) **2**:188
The Spook Birds (Bunting) **28**:52
The Spooky Tail of Prewitt Peacock (Peet) **12**:202
Sports (Berger) **32**:29
The Sports (Fisher) **18**:129
Sports Great Magic Johnson (Haskins) **39**:60
Sports Medicine (Berger) **32**:26
Spot at Play (Hill) **13**:96
Spot at the Fair (Hill) **13**:96
Spot at the Farm (Hill) **13**:96
Spot Goes to School (Hill) **13**:95
Spot Goes to the Beach (Hill) **13**:96
Spot Goes to the Circus (Hill) **13**:97
Spot Looks at Colors (Hill) **13**:96
Spot Looks at Shapes (Hill) **13**:96
Spot on the Farm (Hill) **13**:96
Spot's Birthday Party (Hill) **13**:94
Spot's First Christmas (Hill) **13**:94
Spot's First Walk (Hill) **13**:92
Spot's First Words (Hill) **13**:96

Spotted Salamander (McClung) **11**:182
Spotty (Rey and Rey) **5**:195
Die Sprechmachine (Kruss) **9**:86
The Sprig of Broom (Willard) **2**:222
Spring Begins in March (Little) **4**:148
Spring Comes to the Ocean (George) **1**:92
Spring Holidays (Epstein and Epstein) **26**:59
Spring Is (Domanska) **40**:45
Spring Is a New Beginning (Anglund) **1**:21
Spring Is Here (Lenski) **26**:107
Spring Is Here! (Sterling) **1**:181
Spring Snow (Duvoisin) **23**:102
Spring Story (Barklem) **31**:2
The Springs of Joy (Tudor) **13**:202
Springtime in Noisy Village (Lindgren) **39**:152
The Spy on Third Base (Christopher) **33**:60
The Spy Who Never Was and Other True Spy Stories (Knight) **38**:122
Square as a House (Kuskin) **4**:136
Squawwk! (Rockwell) **6**:236
Squeak Saves the Day and Other Tooley Tales (Snyder) **31**:168
Squeak-a-Lot (Waddell) **31**:199
Squib (Bawden) **2**:13
Squid and Spider: A Look at the Animal Kingdom (Billout) **33**:23
Squirrel Watching (Schlein) **41**:198
The Squirrel Wife (Pearce) **9**:153
Squirrels (Wildsmith) **2**:214
St. Jerome and the Lion (Godden) **20**:131
St. Patrick's Day in the Morning (Bunting) **28**:50
Stable of Fear (Bunting) **28**:44
Stage Fright (Martin) **32**:201
The Stained Glass Window (Lively) **7**:161
The Stalker (Nixon) **24**:146
Stand in the Wind (Little) **4**:151
Stanley and Rhoda (Wells) **16**:209
Star Baby (Nixon) **24**:153
Star Boy (Goble) **21**:133
A Star for the Latecomer (Zindel) **45**:192
Star Gazing, Comet Tracking, and Sky Mapping (Berger) **32**:36
The Star in the Pail (McCord) **9**:102
A Star in the Sea (Silverstein and Silverstein) **25**:202
Star of Night: Stories for Christmas (Paterson) **7**:237
Star Signs (Fisher) **18**:133
The Star Spangled Banner (d'Aulaire and d'Aulaire) **21**:47
Star Surgeon (Nourse) **33**:132
Stardust otel (Janeczko) **47**:114
The Starlight Cloak (Nimmo) **44**:152
A Starlit Somersault Downhill (Pinkney) **43**:170
Starring Peter and Leigh: A Novel (Pfeffer) **11**:199
Starring Sally J. Freedman as Herself (Blume) **15**:76
Starrring Becky Suslow (Orgel) **48**:91
Starry Messenger: Galileo Galilei (Sis) **45**:176
Starry Night (Waddell) **31**:185
Stars (Berger) **32**:6
The Stars: Decoding Their Messages (Adler) **27**:7
The Stars: Steppingstones into Space (Adler) **27**:7
The Star-Spangled Banner (Spier) **5**:222
Starting with Melodie (Pfeffer) **11**:203
The Statue of Liberty (Fisher) **18**:134
The Statue of Liberty: America's Proud Lady (Haskins) **39**:51
Stay Up Late (Kalman) **32**:179
Staying Alive in Year 5 (Marsden) **34**:149
Staying Home Alone on a Rainy Day (Iwasaki) **18**:152

The Steadfast Tin Soldier (Brown) **12**:97
The Steamroller: A Fantasy (Brown) **10**:68
Steffie Can't Come Out to Play (Gaberman) **33**:4
Steinmetz: Maker of Lightning (Lavine) **35**:146
Step by Step: All by Myself (McMillan) **47**:169
Step into the Night (Ryder) **37**:90
Stepmother (Mahy) **7**:182
The Stereo Hi-Fi Handbook (Berger) **32**:22
Steven Kellogg's Yankee Doodle (Kellogg) **6**:174
Stevie (Steptoe) **2**:163
Sticks, Spools, and Feathers (Weiss) **4**:223
Still More Small Poems (Worth) **21**:222
The Stinky Cheese Man: And Other Fairly Stupid Tales (Smith) **47**:202
A Stitch in Time (Lively) **7**:160
A Stitch In Time (Rinaldi) **46**:88
The Stolen Fire: Legends of Heroes and Rebels from Around the World (Baumann) **35**:54
The Stolen Lake (Aiken) **19**:13
The Stolen Oracle (Williams) **8**:221
Stone and Steel: A Look at Engineering (Billout) **33**:22
The Stone Book (Garner) **20**:113
The Stone Doll of Sister Brute (Hoban) **3**:83
Stone Giants and Flying Heads (Bruchac) **46**:6
Stone Giants and Flying Heads: More Iroquois Folk Tales (Bruchac) **46**:6
The Stone Menagerie (Fine) **25**:18
The Stone Mouse (Nimmo) **44**:151
The Stone of Victory and Other Tales (Colum) **36**:47
The Stone Silenus (Yolen) **44**:179
Stone Soup: An Old Tale (Brown) **12**:94
The Stonecutter: A Japanese Folk Tale (McDermott) **9**:115
The Stone-Faced Boy (Fox) **1**:81
Stoneflight (McHargue) **2**:120
The Stones of Green Knowe (Boston) **3**:28
The Stonewalkers (Alcock) **26**:2
Stonewall (Fritz) **14**:114
Stopping by Woods on a Snowy Evening (Jeffers) **30**:132
Storie di tre uccellini (Munari) **9**:124
Stories about Rosie (Voigt) **13**:240
Stories for Summer (Proysen) **24**:185
Stories for the Bible (Tresselt) **30**:214
Stories from Shakespeare (McCaughrean) **38**:151
Stories from the Old Testament: Joseph, Moses, Ruth, David (Petersham and Petersham) **24**:169
Stories to Solve: Folktales from Around the World (Sis) **45**:158
Storm (Crossley-Holland) **47**:43
Storm Alert: Understanding Weather Disasters (Aylesworth) **6**:55
Storm and Other Old English Riddles (Crossley-Holland) **47**:26
Storm at the Jetty (Fisher) **18**:130
Storm Boy (Thiele) **27**:202
Storm from the West (Willard) **2**:222
Storm in the Night (Cummings) **48**:48
Storm Rising (Singer) **48**:135
A Storm without Rain (Adkins) **7**:28
Storms (Adler) **27**:17
Storms (Berger) **32**:5
Stormy, Misty's Foal (Henry) **4**:114
A Story, A Story: An African Tale (Haley) **21**:141
The Story about Ping (Flack) **28**:121
The Story Book of Aircraft (Petersham and Petersham) **24**:167
The Story Book of Clothes (Petersham and Petersham) **24**:165

The Story Book of Corn (Petersham and Petersham) **24**:168
The Story Book of Cotton (Petersham and Petersham) **24**:170
The Story Book of Food (Petersham and Petersham) **24**:165
The Story Book of Foods from the Field (Petersham and Petersham) **24**:168
The Story Book of Houses (Petersham and Petersham) **24**:165
The Story Book of Rayon (Petersham and Petersham) **24**:170
The Story Book of Rice (Petersham and Petersham) **24**:168
The Story Book of Ships (Petersham and Petersham) **24**:167
The Story Book of Silk (Petersham and Petersham) **24**:170
The Story Book of Sugar (Petersham and Petersham) **24**:168
The Story Book of Things We Use (Petersham and Petersham) **24**:165
The Story Book of Things We Wear (Petersham and Petersham) **24**:170
The Story Book of Trains (Petersham and Petersham) **24**:167
The Story Book of Transportation (Petersham and Petersham) **24**:165
The Story Book of Wheat (Petersham and Petersham) **24**:168
The Story Book of Wheels (Petersham and Petersham) **24**:167
The Story Book of Wheels, Ships, Trains, Aircraft (Petersham and Petersham) **24**:167
The Story Book of Wool (Petersham and Petersham) **24**:170
Story for a Black Night (Bess) **39**:2
The Story Girl (Montgomery) **8**:135
The Story of a Baby (Ets) **33**:75
The Story of a Castle (Goodall) **25**:55
The Story of a Farm (Goodall) **25**:57
The Story of a High Street (Goodall) **25**:55
The Story of a Main Street (Goodall) **25**:55
The Story of a Nail (Adler) **27**:15
The Story of a Puppet (Collodi)
  See *Le Avventure di Pinocchio*
The Story of America (Haar) **15**:114
The Story of an English Village (Goodall) **25**:48
The Story of Babar, the Little Elephant (Brunhoff) **4**:30
The Story of Chicken Licken (Ormerod) **20**:178
The Story of Doctor Dolittle, Being the History of His Peculiar Life at Home and Astonishing Adventures in Foreign Parts (Lofting) **19**:120
The Story of Dogs (Lauber) **16**:114
The Story of Ferdinand (Leaf) **25**:116
The Story of Folk Music (Berger) **32**:16
The Story of George Washington Carver (Bontemps) **6**:82
The Story of Grains: Wheat, Corn, and Rice (Parish) **22**:155
The Story of Holly and Ivy (Godden) **20**:130
The Story of Johnny Appleseed (Aliki) **9**:17
The Story of Jumping Mouse: A Native American Legend (Steptoe) **12**:241
The Story of Light (Adler) **27**:25
The Story of Money (Betsy and Giulio Maestro) **45**:87
The Story of Mrs. Tubbs (Lofting) **19**:123
The Story of Numbers (Lauber) **16**:114
The Story of Paul Bunyan (Emberley and Emberley) **5**:92

The Story of Persephone (Farmer) **8**:85
The Story of Religion (Betsy and Giulio Maestro) **45**:90
The Story of Ruth (Asimov) **12**:47
The Story of Stevie Wonder (Haskins) **3**:67
The Story of the Amulet (Nesbit) **3**:165
The Story of the Dancing Frog (Blake) **31**:25
The Story of the International Red Cross (Epstein and Epstein) **26**:58
The Story of the Milky Way: A Cherokee Tale (Bruchac) **46**:20
Story of the Negro (Bontemps) **6**:80
The Story of the Presidents of the United States of America (Petersham and Petersham) **24**:178
The Story of the Seashore (Goodall) **25**:57
The Story of the Seaside (Goodall) **25**:57
The Story of the Statue of Liberty (Betsy and Giulio Maestro) **45**:77
The Story of the Three Wise Kings (dePaola) **24**:92
The Story of Vampires (Aylesworth) **6**:53
The Story of Werewolves (Aylesworth) **6**:54
The Story of William Penn (Aliki) **9**:18
The Story of William Tell (Aliki) **9**:17
The Story of Witches (Aylesworth) **6**:54
The Story of Your Foot (Silverstein and Silverstein) **25**:223
The Story of Your Mouth (Silverstein and Silverstein) **25**:221
A Story to Tell (Bruna) **7**:51
Storybook Dictionary (Scarry) **41**:162
A Storybook from Tomi Ungerer (Ungerer) **3**:203
Stotan! (Crutcher) **28**:104
The Stowaway to the Mushroom Planet (Cameron) **1**:41
Stranded (Christopher) **33**:48
The Strange Affair of Adelaide Harris (Garfield) **21**:104
The Strange Appearance of Howard Cranebill, Jr. (Drescher) **20**:58
Strange Attractors (Sleator) **29**:207
The Strange Child (Zwerger) **46**:194
Strange Creatures (Simon) **9**:217
A Strange Enchantment (Allan) **43**:32
Strange Mysteries from Around the World (Simon) **9**:215
Strange Objects (Crew) **42**:53
Strange Partners (Lavine) **35**:147
Strange Travelers (Lavine) **35**:148
The Stranger (Van Allsburg) **13**:213
A Stranger at Green Knowe (Boston) **3**:29
Stranger at the Inlet (Epstein and Epstein) **26**:45
A Stranger Came Ashore (Hunter) **25**:85
Stranger Danger? (Fine) **25**:23
The Stranger from Somewhere in Time (McBratney) **44**:129
The Stranger from the Sea (Guillot) **22**:70
The Stranger in Primrose Lane (Streatfeild) **17**:189
Stranger on the Ball Club (Slote) **4**:199
Stranger with My Face (Duncan) **29**:75
Strangers' Bread (Willard) **5**:247
Strangers Dark and Gold (St. John) **46**:101
Strangers in Africa (Ashabranner and Davis) **28**:5
Strangers in New York (Pilgrim) **43**:12
Strangers in Skye (Allan) **43**:4
Strangers in Wood Street (Allan) **43**:32
Strawberry Girl (Lenski) **26**:108
The Streamlined Pig (Brown) **10**:48
Streams to the River, River to the Sea: A Novel of Sacagawea (O'Dell) **16**:179
Street Gangs: Yesterday and Today (Haskins) **3**:68

A Street of Little Shops (Bianco) **19**:53
Strega Nona: An Old Tale (dePaola) **4**:57
Strega Nona's Magic Lessons (dePaola) **24**:91
Strictly for Laughs (Conford) **10**:100
Striding Slippers (Ginsburg) **45**:12
A String in the Harp (Bond) **11**:26
A String of Chances (Naylor) **17**:57
Strings: A Gathering of Family Poems (Janeczko) **47**:102
Stripe: The Story of a Chipmunk (McClung) **11**:179
A Striving after Wind (St. John) **46**:103
The Strongest One of All: A Caucasian Folktale (Ginsburg) **45**:11
The Stronghold (Hunter) **25**:84
Stuart Little (White) **1**:195
Studenplan: Roman (Noestlinger) **12**:187
The Stupids Die (Marshall) **21**:175
The Stupids Have a Ball (Marshall) **21**:172
The Stupids Step Out (Marshall) **21**:170
The Submarine Bird (Scott) **20**:198
The Submarine Pitch (Christopher) **33**:51
Such Nice Kids (Bunting) **28**:64
A Sudden Puff of Glittering Smoke (Fine) **25**:24
A Sudden Silence (Bunting) **28**:62
A Sudden Swirl of Icy Wind (Fine) **25**:25
Suds: A New Daytime Drama (Gaberman) **33**:10
The Sugar Disease: Diabetes (Silverstein and Silverstein) **25**:218
Sugar Ray Leonard (Haskins) **39**:41
Sugaring Time (Lasky) **11**:117
Suicide: The Hidden Epidemic (Hyde) **23**:164
Sukey and the Mermaid (San Souci) **43**:186
The Sultan's Perfect Tree (Yolen) **4**:263
Sumi and the Goat and the Tokyo Express (Uchida) **6**:256
Sumi's Prize (Uchida) **6**:253
Sumi's Special Happening (Uchida) **6**:254
The Summer after the Funeral (Gardam) **12**:166
A Summer at Sea (Allan) **43**:13
The Summer Birds (Farmer) **8**:76
The Summer Book (Jansson) **2**:95
Summer Fun (Haywood) **22**:105
Summer Girls, Love Boys, and Other Short Stories (Mazer) **23**:228
Summer Ice: Life Along the Antarctic Peninsula (McMillan) **47**:188
The Summer In Between (Spence) **26**:191
A Summer in Brittany (Estoril) **43**:8
A Summer in Provence (Pilgrim) **43**:10
A Summer in the South (Marshall) **21**:172
Summer Is for Growing (Clark) **16**:82
A Summer Life (Soto) **38**:192
The Summer Night (Zolotow) **2**:237
The Summer Noisy Book (Brown) **10**:60
Summer of Decision (Allan) **43**:6
Summer of Fear (Duncan) **29**:70
The Summer of My German Soldier (Greene) **2**:86
The Summer of the Falcon (George) **1**:93
The Summer of the Swans (Byars) **1**:37
Summer on Wheels (Soto) **38**:207
The Summer People (Townsend) **2**:174
Summer Rules (Lipsyte) **23**:208
Summer Story (Barklem) **31**:2
Summer Switch (Rodgers) **20**:191
A Summer to Die (Lowry) **6**:192
The Summer with Spike (Willard) **2**:223
The Summerboy (Lipsyte) **23**:209
The Summer-House Loon (Fine) **25**:17
Summers of the Wild Rose (Harris) **30**:124
The Sun (Zim) **2**:231
The Sun and Its Family (Adler) **27**:9
Sun and Moon (Pfister) **42**:134

The Sun, Dancing: Christian Verse (Causley) **30**:41
Sun Dogs and Shooting Stars: A Skywatcher's Calendar (Branley) **13**:45
Sun Flight (McDermott) **9**:118
Sun God, Moon Witch (Katz) **45**:32
The Sun He Dies: A Novel about the End of the Aztec World (Highwater) **17**:29
Sun Horse, Moon Horse (Sutcliff) **37**:167
The Sun Looks Down (Schlein) **41**:177
The Sun: Our Nearest Star (Branley) **13**:30
The Sun: Star Number One (Branley) **13**:31
The Sun, the Wind, the Sea and the Rain (Schlein) **41**:183
Sun Up (Tresselt) **30**:203
Sun Up, Sun Down (Gibbons) **8**:97
Sunburn (Stine) **37**:122
Sunday Morning (Viorst) **3**:209
The Sunday Outing (Pinkney) **43**:172
The Sun-Egg (Beskow) **17**:18
The Sun's Asleep Behind the Hill (Ginsburg) **45**:16
Sunshine (Bemelmans) **6**:68
Sunshine (Klein) **19**:88
Sunshine (Ormerod) **20**:174
Sunshine Makes the Seasons (Branley) **13**:40
The Sunshine Years (Klein) **19**:89
Super People: Who Will They Be? (Bendick) **5**:50
Super, Super, Superwords (McMillan) **47**:172
Superbowl Upset (Gaberman) **33**:17
Supercharged Infield (Christopher) **33**:57
Supercomputers (Carter) **22**:18
Superfudge (Blume) **15**:77
Supergirl (Mazer) **23**:230
Superhare (Heine) **18**:146
The Supermarket Mystery (Scarry) **41**:164
Supermouse (Ure) **34**:175
The Supernatural: From ESP to UFOs (Berger) **32**:18
Superpuppy: How to Choose, Raise, and Train the Best Possible Dog for You (Pinkwater) **4**:167
Supersuits (Cobb) **2**:67
Suppose You Met a Witch (Serraillier) **2**:142
The Supreme, Superb, Exalted and Delightful, One and Only Magic Building (Kotzwinkle) **6**:182
Surprise for Davy (Lenski) **26**:113
The Surprise Mouse (Mattingley) **24**:124
The Surprise Party (Hutchins) **20**:144
The Surprise Picnic (Goodall) **25**:48
Surprises: An I Can Read Book of Poems (Hopkins) **44**:93
Surrender (White) **3**:222
Surrogate Sister (Bunting) **28**:58
Survival Camp! (Bunting) **28**:47
The Survivor (White) **3**:223
The Survivors (Hunter) **3**:101
The Survivors: Enduring Animals of North America (Scott) **20**:194
Susan (Smucker) **10**:189
Susanna B. and William C. (Field) **21**:78
Suzuki Goodbye (McBratney) **44**:130
Swallowdale (Ransome) **8**:174
Swallows and Amazons (Ransome) **8**:171
The Swallow's Song (St. John) **46**:106
Swampy Alligator (Gantos) **18**:142
Swan Sky (Tejima) **20**:205
Swans (Scott) **20**:201
Sweeney's Ghost (Fisher) **18**:125
Sweet Baby Coming (Greenfield) **38**:96
Sweet Bells Jangled out of Tune (Brancato) **32**:73
Sweet Dreams, Spot (Hill) **13**:95

Sweet Friday Island (Taylor) **30**:193
Sweet Illusions (Myers) **16**:143
The Sweet Patootie Doll (Calhoun) **42**:5
Sweet Pea: A Black Girl Growing Up in the Rural South (Krementz) **5**:150
Sweet Whispers, Brother Rush (Hamilton) **11**:84
Sweetgrass (Hudson) **40**:94
Sweetwater (Yep) **3**:238
The Swift Deer (McClung) **11**:184
A Swiftly Tilting Planet (L'Engle) **14**:150
Swimathon! (Cross) **28**:91
Swimmy (Lionni) **7**:129
The Swineherd (Zwerger) **46**:190
The Swing in the Summerhouse (Langton) **33**:109
Swings and Roundabouts (Ure) **34**:181
Swiss Holiday (Allan) **43**:5
Switch On, Switch Off (Berger) **32**:41
Switcharound (Lowry) **46**:32
The Switherby Pilgrims (Spence) **26**:193
The Swoose (King-Smith) **40**:168
The Sword and the Circle: King Arthur and the Knights of the Round Table (Sutcliff) **37**:173
The Sword and the Scythe (Williams) **8**:221
Sword at Sunset (Sutcliff) **37**:156
The Sword of Esau (Southall) **2**:156
The Sword of King Arthur (Williams) **8**:229
The Sword of the Spirits (Christopher) **2**:42
Sword of the Wilderness (Coatsworth) **2**:62
Swords from the North (Treece) **2**:189
Sylvester and the Magic Pebble (Steig) **2**:161
The Sylvia Game (Alcock) **26**:3
Sylvie and Bruno (Carroll) **2**:36
Symbiosis: A Book of Unusual Friendships (Aruego) **5**:28
Symbol Art: Thirteen Squares, Circles, Triangles from Around the World (Fisher) **18**:136
Symbols: A Silent Language (Adkins) **7**:24
Tabi No Ehon (Anno) **14**:33
Tabi No Ehon II (Anno) **14**:37
Tabi No Ehon III (Anno) **14**:39
Tabi No Ehon IV (Anno) **14**:41
The Table, the Donkey, and the Stick: Adapted from a Retelling by the Brothers Grimm (Galdone) **16**:102
Tackle without a Team (Christopher) **33**:60
Taffy and Melissa Molasses (Haywood) **22**:100
The Tail of the Trinosaur (Causley) **30**:35
The Tailor and the Giant (Kruss) **9**:88
The Tailor of Gloucester (Potter) **1**:153
Takao and Grandfather's Sword (Uchida) **6**:252
Take a Look at Snakes (Betsy and Giulio Maestro) **45**:86
Take a Number (Bendick) **5**:39
Take Another Look (Hoban) **13**:105
Take Joy! The Tasha Tudor Christmas Book (Tudor) **13**:198
Take Me Out to the Ballgame (Kovalski) **34**:119
Take My Word For It (Marsden) **34**:150
Take Sky: More Rhymes of the Never Was and Always Is (McCord) **9**:99
Take This Hammer (Epstein and Epstein) **26**:62
Take Two and...Rolling! (Pfeffer) **11**:205
Take Wing (Little) **4**:148
The Take-along Dog (McCully) **46**:64
Takedown (Christopher) **33**:61
Taking a Stand Against Racism and Racial Discrimination (McKissack) **23**:242
Taking Care of Carruthers (Marshall) **21**:176
Taking Care of Terrific (Lowry) **6**:197
The Taking of Mariasburg (Thompson) **24**:231
Taking Root: Jewish Immigrants in America (Meltzer) **13**:138

Taking Sides (Klein)   **2**:100
Taking Sides (Soto)   **38**:194
Taking Terri Mueller (Mazer)   **23**:227
Taking the Ferry Home (Conrad)   **18**:89
Taktuk, an Arctic Boy (Flack and Lomen)   **28**:119
A Tale for Easter (Tudor)   **13**:190
Tale of a One-Way Street and Other Stories (Aiken)   **19**:12
The Tale of Dan de Lion (Disch)   **18**:115
The Tale of Gockel, Hinkel and Gackeliah (Orgel)   **48**:73
The Tale of the Faithful Dove (Potter)   **1**:153
The Tale of the Mandarin Ducks (Leo and Diane Dillon)   **44**:39
The Tale of Thomas Mead (Hutchins)   **20**:150
The Tale of Three Landlubbers (Serraillier)   **2**:143
A Tale of Time City (Jones)   **23**:196
The Tale of Tuppenny (Potter)   **1**:154
Tales and Legends of Hawaii: At the Gateways of the Day (Colum)   **36**:27
Tales and Legends of Hawaii: The Bright Islands (Colum)   **36**:27
Tales for the Third Ear, from Equatorial Africa (Aardema)   **17**:3
Tales from a Finnish Fireside (Bianco)   **19**:54
Tales from a Finnish Tupa (Bianco)   **19**:54
Tales from Gold Mountain: Stories of the Chinese in the New World (Yee)   **44**:162
Tales from Grimm (Gag)   **4**:91
Tales from The Jungle Book (McKinley)   **10**:126
Tales from the Land Under My Table (Wilhelm)   **46**:160
Tales from the Mabinogion (Crossley-Holland)   **47**:41
Tales from the Shop That Never Shuts (Waddell)   **31**:191
Tales from the Story Hat (Aardema)   **17**:3
Tales Mummies Tell (Lauber)   **16**:121
Tales of a Dead King (Myers)   **16**:140
Tales of a Fourth Grade Nothing (Blume)   **2**:18
Tales of a Gambling Grandma (Khalsa)   **30**:145
Tales of Momolu (Graham)   **10**:104
The Tales of Olga da Polga (Bond)   **1**:29
The Tales of Uncle Remus: The Adventures of Brer Rabbit (Lester)   **41**:104
The Tales of Uncle Remus: The Adventures of Brer Rabbit (Pinkney)   **43**:160
Tales Told by a Machine (Rodari)   **24**:210
Talk about a Family (Greenfield)   **4**:101; **38**:83
The Talking Eggs: A Folktale from the American South (Pinkney)   **43**:163
The Talking Eggs: A Folktale from the American South (San Souci)   **43**:184
The Talking Machine: An Extraordinary Story (Kruss)   **9**:86
Talking with Artists (Cummings)   **48**:52
Talking with Artists, Volume Two (Cummings)   **48**:55
Talking with the Animals (Cohen)   **3**:42
Talking Without Words (Ets)   **33**:91
Tall Man in the Pivot (Christopher)   **33**:39
Tall Ships (Lasky)   **11**:114
Tallyho, Pinkerton! (Kellogg)   **6**:178
Tamarindo! (Brown)   **12**:101
Tamar's Wager (Coatsworth)   **2**:62
Taming the Star Runner (Hinton)   **23**:149
Tamworth Pig and the Litter (Kemp)   **29**:113
Tamworth Pig Stories (Kemp)   **29**:122
Tancy (Hurmence)   **25**:93
Tangara: "Let Us Set Off Again" (Chauncy)   **6**:91
Tant Grön, Tant Brun och Tant Gredelin (Beskow)   **17**:16

Tapping Earth's Heat (Lauber)   **16**:119
Tar Beach (Ringgold)   **30**:168-71
Taran Wanderer (Alexander)   **1**:17; **5**:20
Tarantulas on the Brain (Singer)   **48**:123
Taronga (Kelleher)   **36**:123
The Tasha Tudor Book of Fairy Tales (Tudor)   **13**:198
Tasha Tudor's Bedtime Book (Tudor)   **13**:201
Tasha Tudor's Old Fashioned Gifts: Presents and Favors for All Occasions (Tudor)   **13**:202
Tasha Tudor's Sampler (Tudor)   **13**:199
La Tasse Cassée (Vincent)   **13**:219
Taste, Touch, and Smell (Adler)   **27**:21
Tatsinda (Enright)   **4**:76
The Tattooed Potato and Other Clues (Raskin)   **12**:223
Tatty Apple (Nimmo)   **44**:139
The Tavern at the Ferry (Tunis)   **2**:194
Taxi: A Book of City Words (Betsy and Giulio Maestro)   **45**:81
Taxis and Toadstools: Verses and Decorations (Field)   **21**:69
T-Backs, T-Shirts, Coat, and Suit (Konigsburg)   **47**:147
Teach Me to Fly, Skyfighter! (Yee)   **44**:160
Teach Us, Amelia Bedelia (Parish)   **22**:163
Teacup Full of Roses (Mathis)   **3**:151
Tea-Leaf on the Roof (Ure)   **34**:183
The Team That Couldn't Lose (Christopher)   **33**:42
The Team That Stopped Moving (Christopher)   **33**:51
Tear Down the Walls! (Sterling)   **1**:181
The Tears of the Dragon (Tresselt)   **30**:210
The Teddy Bear Habit; or, How I Became a Winner (Collier)   **3**:49
Teddy Bear's Scrapbook (Howe)   **9**:57
Teddy's Ear (Daly)   **41**:55
Teen Guide to AIDS Prevention (Nourse)   **33**:149
Teen Guide to Birth Control: The Guide to Safe Sex (Nourse)   **33**:147
Teen Guide to Survival (Nourse)   **33**:150
Teen Sex (Hyde)   **23**:175
Teen-Age Treasury of Good Humor (Manley)   **3**:148
Teen-Age Treasury of Our Science World (Manley)   **3**:148
Teen-Age Treasury of the Arts (Manley)   **3**:148
Teenagers Who Made History (Freedman)   **20**:73
Teeny Tiny Tales (Scarry)   **41**:162
The Teeny-Tiny Woman: A Ghost Story (Galdone)   **16**:105
TEEP and BEEP Go to Sleep (Mayer)   **11**:176
The Teeth of the Gale (Aiken)   **19**:19
Teetoncey (Taylor)   **30**:188
Teetoncey and Ben O'Neal (Taylor)   **30**:188
Tehanu: The Last Book of Earthsea (Le Guin)   **28**:144-88
Telboek no. 2 (Bruna)   **7**:51
Telephone Systems (Zim)   **2**:231
Telephone Tales (Rodari)   **24**:208
Television Works Like This (Bendick)   **5**:36
Tell Me a Story, Mama (Johnson)   **33**:94
Tell Me a Tale: A Book about Storytelling (Bruchac)   **46**:23
Tell Me If the Lovers Are Losers (Voigt)   **13**:229
Tell Tales (Rosen)   **45**:139
Tell the Truth, Marly Dee (Williams)   **48**:202
Temperature and You (Betsy and Giulio Maestro)   **45**:82
Ten Apples Up on Top! (Seuss)   **9**:187
Ten Black Dots (Crews)   **7**:56
Ten Kids, No Pets (Martin)   **32**:204
Ten, Nine, Eight (Bang)   **8**:22

Ten Pink Piglets: Garth Pig's Wall Song (Rayner)   **41**:131
Ten Sleepy Sheep (Keller)   **45**:45
Tendo Setsu No Hon (Anno)   **14**:37
The Tenement Tree (Seredy)   **10**:180
Tennis Shoes (Streatfeild)   **17**:186
The Tenth Good Thing about Barney (Viorst)   **3**:209
Term Paper (Rinaldi)   **46**:76
The Terrible Churnadryne (Cameron)   **1**:41
Terrible, Horrible Edie (Spykman)   **35**:219
The Terrible Nung Gwama: A Chinese Folktale (Young)   **27**:218
The Terrible Roar (Pinkwater)   **4**:161
The Terrible Tales of Happy Days School (Duncan)   **29**:76
The Terrible Temptation (Arundel)   **35**:19
Terrible Things (Bunting)   **28**:50
The Terrible Tiger (Prelutsky)   **13**:164
Terrible Troll (Mayer)   **11**:165
The Terrible Troll-Bird (d'Aulaire and d'Aulaire)   **21**:54
Terrorism: A Special Kind of Violence (Hyde)   **23**:173
The Terrorists (Meltzer)   **13**:144
Terry and the Caterpillars (Selsam)   **1**:166
Terry on the Fence (Ashley)   **4**:15
Tessie (Jackson)   **28**:139
Tex (Hinton)   **23**:148
Texas Tomboy (Lenski)   **26**:115
Thaddeus Stevens and the Fight for Negro Rights (Meltzer)   **13**:123
Thank You, Amelia Bedelia (Parish)   **22**:155
Thank You, Dr. Martin Luther King, Jr.! (Tate)   **37**:191
Thank You, Henrietta (Daly)   **41**:58
Thanksgiving Day (Gibbons)   **8**:97
The Thanksgiving Mystery (Nixon)   **24**:141
That Dreadful Day (Stevenson)   **17**:163
That Early Spring (Beckman)   **25**:15
That Early Spring (Beckman)
    See *The Loneliness of Mia*
That Terrible Halloween Night (Stevenson)   **17**:156
That Was Then, This Is Now (Hinton)   **3**:72; **23**:147
That Wonderful Pelican (Scott)   **20**:194
That'd Be Telling (Rosen)   **45**:135
That's My Baby (Lindgren)   **39**:158
That's Not Fair! (Fujikawa)   **25**:41
That's Silly (Sleator)   **29**:202
Theater Shoes; or, Other People's Shoes (Streatfeild)   **17**:190
Then Again, Maybe I Won't (Blume)   **2**:18
Then There Were Five (Enright)   **4**:75
Theo Runs Away (Hartling)   **29**:101
Theodore and the Talking Mushroom (Lionni)   **7**:135
Theodore Roosevelt, an Initial Biography (Foster)   **7**:97
There, Far Beyond the River (Korinetz)   **4**:129
There Is No Rhyme for Silver (Merriam)   **14**:193
There Once Was a Time (Ventura)   **16**:197
There Was an Old Woman (Kellogg)   **6**:173
There's a Bat in Bunk Five (Danziger)   **20**:53
There's a Boy in the Girl's Bathroom (Sacher)   **28**:202
There's a Nightmare in My Closet (Mayer)   **11**:160
There's a Nightmare in My Cupboard (Mayer)   **11**:160
There's a Rainbow in My Closet (Stren)   **5**:232
There's Always Danny (Ure)   **34**:185

Title Index

There's No Place like Home (Brown) **29**:12
There's Nothing to Do! (Stevenson) **17**:164
These Happy Golden Years (Wilder) **2**:207
They Didn't Come Back (Berna) **19**:39
They Found a Cave (Chauncy) **6**:89
They Lived with the Dinosaurs (Freedman) **20**:81
They Never Came Home (Duncan) **29**:67
They Put on Masks (Baylor) **3**:17
They Put Out to Sea: The Story of the Map (Duvoisin) **23**:91
They Walk in the Night (Coatsworth) **2**:63
They Who Walk in the Wild (Roberts) **33**:206
Thidwick, the Big-Hearted Moose (Seuss) **9**:176
The Thief (Rockwell) **6**:239
A Thief in the Village and Other Stories (Berry) **22**:7
The Thieves and the Raven (Janosch) **26**:75
The Thieving Dwarfs (Calhoun) **42**:11
Thimble Summer (Enright) **4**:71
Thing (Klein) **21**:158
The Thing in the Woods (Alcock) **26**:7
Thingnapped! (Klein) **21**:161
Things That Go Bump in the Night: A Collection of Original Stories (Yolen) **44**:189
Things That Sometimes Happen: Very Short Stories for Very Young Readers (Avi) **24**:4
Things That Spin: From Tops to Atoms (Adler) **27**:13
Things to Make and Do for Columbus Day (Gibbons) **8**:89
Things to Make and Do for Halloween (Gibbons) **8**:89
Things to Make and Do for Valentine's Day (dePaola) **4**:58
Things to Make and Do for Your Birthday (Gibbons) **8**:89
Think Metric (Branley) **13**:38
Think of Shadows (Moore) **15**:144
The Third Eye (Duncan) **29**:77
The Third Eye (Hunter) **25**:86
The Third Magic (Katz) **45**:35
The Third Margaret Mahy Story Book: Stories and Poems (Mahy) **7**:183
The Third Road (Bacon) **3**:12
Thirteen (Charlip) **8**:32
The Thirteen Days of Yule (Hogrogian) **2**:89
The Thirteen Moons (George) **1**:93
Thirteen Moons on Turtle's Back (Bruchac) **46**:10
The Thirteenth Member: A Story of Suspense (Hunter) **25**:79
Thirty-Six Exposures (Major) **11**:132
Thirty-Two Moons: The Natural Satellites of Our Solar System (Knight) **38**:113
This Can't Be Happening at Macdonald Hall! (Korman) **25**:105
This Crowded Planet (Hyde) **23**:155
This Delicious Day: 65 Poems (Janeczko) **47**:107
This Is a River: Exploring an Ecosystem (Pringle) **4**:176
This Is Australia (Sasek) **4**:196
This Is Cape Kennedy (Sasek) **4**:193
This Is Edinburgh (Sasek) **4**:190
This Is Greece (Sasek) **4**:194
This Is Historic Britain (Sasek) **4**:196
This Is Hong Kong (Sasek) **4**:194
This Is Ireland (Sasek) **4**:193
This Is Israel (Sasek) **4**:192
This Is London (Sasek) **4**:188
This Is Munich (Sasek) **4**:191
This Is My House (Dorros) **42**:70
This Is New York (Sasek) **4**:189
This Is Paris (Sasek) **4**:187
This Is Rome (Sasek) **4**:189

This Is San Francisco (Sasek) **4**:192
This Is Texas (Sasek) **4**:194
This Is the United Nations (Sasek) **4**:195
This Is Venice (Sasek) **4**:192
This Is Washington, D.C. (Sasek) **4**:195
This Is Your Century (Trease) **42**:187
This Little Nose (Ormerod) **20**:180
This Place Has No Atmosphere (Danziger) **20**:55
This Restless Earth (Lauber) **16**:116
This Star Shall Abide (Engdahl) **2**:71
This Strange New Feeling (Lester) **41**:100
This Street's for Me! (Hopkins) **44**:86
This Thumbprint (Krauss) **42**:128
This Union Cause: The Growth of Organized Labor in America (Shippen) **36**:178
This Year's Garden (Rylant) **15**:170
Thistly B. (Tudor) **13**:192
Thomas and the Warlock (Hunter) **25**:77
Thomas' Snowsuit (Munsch) **19**:144
Thor: Last of the Sperm Whales (McClung) **11**:187
Thoroughbred Horses (Patent) **19**:161
Those Amazing Computers! Uses of Modern Thinking Machines (Berger) **32**:10
Those Mysterious UFOs: The Story of Unidentified Flying Objects (Knight) **38**:117
A Thousand Lights and Fireflies (Tresselt) **30**:209
Threat to the Barkers (Phipson) **5**:179
Three Aesop Fox Fables (Galdone) **16**:96
Three and One to Carry (Willard) **2**:223
The Three Bears (Galdone) **16**:97
The Three Bears Rhyme Book (Yolen) **44**:181
Three Big Hogs (Pinkwater) **4**:164
The Three Billy Goats Gruff (Brown) **12**:99
The Three Billy Goats Gruff (Galdone) **16**:97
Three Billy Goats Gruff (McKissack) **23**:239
Three by the Sea (Marshall) **21**:176
Three by Three: A Picture Book for All Children Who Can Count to Three (Kruss) **9**:85
Three Days on a River in a Red Canoe (Williams) **9**:231
Three Gay Tales from Grimm (Gag) **4**:93
Three Girls and a Secret (Guillot) **22**:65
Three Gold Pieces: A Greek Folk Tale (Aliki) **9**:20
The Three Golden Heads of the Well (Garner) **20**:116
The Three Golden Keys (Sis) **45**:172
Three Heads Made of Gold (Causley) **30**:40
The Three Jovial Huntsmen (Caldecott) **14**:75
Three Jovial Huntsmen (Jeffers) **30**:128
Three Kinds of Stubborn (Calhoun) **42**:19
Three Little Kittens (Galdone) **16**:107
The Three Little Pigs (Biro) **28**:40
The Three Little Pigs (Galdone) **16**:95
Three on the Run (Bawden) **2**:14
Three Promises to You (Leaf) **25**:133
The Three Robbers (Ungerer) **3**:204
Three Rolls and One Doughnut: Fables from Russia (Ginsburg) **45**:3
The Three Sillies (Galdone) **16**:103
Three Sisters (Mazer) **23**:230
The Three Sneezes and Other Swiss Tales (Duvoisin) **23**:91
Three Stalks of Corn (Politi) **29**:194
Three Terrible Trins (King-Smith) **40**:171
Three Up a Tree (Marshall) **21**:182
Three Wishes (Clifton) **5**:58
The Three Wishes (Galdone) **16**:90
The Three-Day Enchantment (Hunter) **25**:90
Threshold of the Stars (Berna) **19**:36

Through a Brief Darkness (Peck) **15**:153
Through Grandpa's Eyes (MacLachlan) **14**:180
Through the Broken Mirror with Alice (Wojciechowska) **1**:200
Through the Eyes of Wonder: Science Fiction and Science (Bova) **3**:35
Through the Hidden Door (Wells) **16**:214
Through the Looking-Glass and What Alice Found There (Carroll) **2**:36; **18**:38-80
Through the Looking-Glass, and What Alice Found There (Tenniel) **18**:201-28
Through the Magic Mirror (Browne) **19**:62
Through the Window (Keeping) **34**:93
Through the Year with Harriet (Betsy and Giulio Maestro) **45**:75
Throwing Shadows (Konigsburg) **47**:138
Thumbeline (Zwerger) **46**:196
Thunder and Lightnings (Mark) **11**:145
Thunder Cake (Polacco) **40**:186
Thunder in the Sky (Peyton) **3**:180
Thunder of Valmy (Trease) **42**:184
Thunderbolt and Rainbow: A Look at Greek Mythology (Billout) **33**:22
Thurgood Marshall: A Life for Justice (Haskins) **39**:68
Thursday's Child (Streatfeild) **17**:197
Tia Maria's Garden (Clark) **16**:82
Tic, Tac, and Toc (Munari) **9**:124
Ticket to Freedom (Harris) **30**:126
Tickle, Tickle (Oxenbury) **22**:148
Tico and the Golden Wings (Lionni) **7**:130
A Tide Flowing (Phipson) **5**:186
Tiffky Doofky (Steig) **15**:196
Tiger by the Tail: And Other Science Fiction Stories (Nourse) **33**:133
A Tiger Called Thomas (Zolotow) **2**:237
Tiger Eyes (Blume) **15**:78
Tiger in the Bush (Chauncy) **6**:89
Tiger: The Story of a Swallowtail Butterfly (McClung) **11**:179
The Tiger Who Wore White Gloves; or, What You Are You Are (Brooks) **27**:44-56
The Tiger's Bones and Other Plays for Children (Hughes) **3**:96
Tiger's Milk (Mattingley) **24**:124
Tigger and Friends (Hamley) **47**:61
Tight End (Christopher) **33**:55
Tikta'liktak: An Eskimo Legend (Houston) **3**:86
Tikvah Means Hope (Polacco) **40**:200
Till the Break of Day (Wojciechowska) **1**:200
Tilly Mint and the Dodo (Doherty) **21**:60
Tilly Mint Tales (Doherty) **21**:56
Tilly Witch (Freeman) **30**:77
Tiltawhirl John (Paulsen) **19**:171
Tim All Alone (Ardizzone) **3**:6
Tim and Charlotte (Ardizzone) **3**:6
Tim and Ginger (Ardizzone) **3**:7
Tim in Danger (Ardizzone) **3**:7
Tim Tadpole and the Great Bullfrog (Flack) **28**:123
Tim to the Lighthouse (Ardizzone) **3**:7
Tim to the Rescue (Ardizzone) **3**:8
Time after Time (Berger) **32**:14
Time and Mr. Bass: A Mushroom Planet Book (Cameron) **1**:42
Time Cat: The Remarkable Journey of Jason and Gareth (Alexander) **5**:18
Time Enough for Drums (Rinaldi) **46**:79
The Time Garden (Eager) **43**:85
Time Ghost (Katz) **45**:40
Time in Your Life (Adler) **27**:5
The Time of the Cranes (St. John) **46**:122
The Time of the Ghost (Jones) **23**:191

Time of the Harvest: Thomas Jefferson, the Years 1801-1826 (Wibberley) **3**:230
The Time of the Kraken (Williams) **8**:235
The Time of the Young Soldiers (Richter) **21**:189
Time of Trial (Burton) **1**:34
Time of Trial, Time of Hope: The Negro in America, 1919-1941 (Meltzer) **13**:123
Time of Wonder (McCloskey) **7**:209
Time To. . . (McMillan) **47**:173
Time to Get Out of the Bath, Shirley (Burningham) **9**:48
Time to Go Back (Allan) **43**:23
Time to Go Home (Spence) **26**:196
A Time to Keep: The Tasha Tudor Book of Holidays (Tudor) **13**:200
A Time to Love (Benary-Isbert) **12**:73
Time-Ago Lost: More Tales of Jahdu (Hamilton) **1**:105
Time-Ago Tales of Jahdu (Hamilton) **1**:106
The Times of My Life: A Memoir (Ashabranner) **28**:15
The Times They Used to Be (Clifton) **5**:56
Timewarp Summer (St. John) **46**:112
Timm Thaler (Kruss) **9**:85
Timmy and the Tin-Can Telephone (Branley) **13**:28
Timothy Goes to School (Wells) **16**:211
Timothy Robbins Climbs the Mountain (Tresselt) **30**:208
Tim's Last Voyage (Ardizzone) **3**:8
The Tin Can Beast and Other Stories (Biegel) **27**:34
Tin Cans (Rockwell) **6**:238
Tin Lizzie (Spier) **5**:223
Tin Lizzy, and How She Ran (Epstein and Epstein) **26**:41
Tina and Nina (Baumann) **35**:48
Tina Gogo (Gaberman) **33**:3
The Tinder Box (Bedard) **35**:62
TINK Goes Fishing (Mayer) **11**:176
TINKA Bakes a Cake (Mayer) **11**:176
Tinker and Tanker (Scarry) **41**:160
Tinker and Tanker and Their Space Ship (Scarry) **41**:160
Tinker and Tanker in Africa (Scarry) **41**:160
Tinker and Tanker: Knights of the Round Table (Scarry) **41**:160
Tinker Tailor: Folk Song Tales (Keeping) **34**:90
Tinker Tailor: Folk Songs (Keeping) **34**:90
The Tin-Pot Foreign General and the Old Iron Woman (Briggs) **10**:33
Tintin au pays de l'or noir (Herge) **6**:148
Tintin au Tibet (Herge) **6**:148
Tintin en Amérique (Herge) **6**:147
Tintin in America (Herge) **6**:147
Tintin in Tibet (Herge) **6**:148
The Tiny Planets: Asteroids of Our Solar System (Knight) **38**:112
The Tiny Seed (Carle) **10**:73
The Tiny Seed and the Giant Flower (Carle) **10**:73
Tiny TINK! TONK! Tales (Mayer) **11**:176
Titanic Crossing (Williams) **48**:206
Titch (Hutchins) **20**:145
Tituba of Salem Village (Petry) **12**:211
To All My Fans, with Love, from Sylvie (Conford) **10**:98
To Be a Logger (Lenski) **26**:123
To Be a Slave (Lester) **2**:114
"*To Damon. To inquire of him if he cou'd tell me by the Style, who writ me a Copy of Verses that came to me in an unknown Hand*"
 See *The Grey Gentlemen*
To kaplani tis Vitrinas (Zei) **6**:260

To Live in Two Worlds: American Indian Youth Today (Ashabranner) **28**:7
To Look at Any Thing (Hopkins) **44**:89
To Make a Wee Moon (Naylor) **17**:50
To Market! To Market! (Spier) **5**:218
To Shake a Shadow (Naylor) **17**:49
To Stand against the Wind (Clark) **16**:85
To the Dark Tower (Kelleher) **36**:132
To the Ends of the Universe (Asimov) **12**:41
To the Wild Sky (Southall) **2**:156
To Walk the Sky Path (Naylor) **17**:50
Toad of Toad Hall (Milne) **1**:143
The Toby Man (King-Smith) **40**:157
Toc, toc, chi è? Apri la porta (Munari) **9**:124
Today is Saturday (Snyder) **31**:157
Today We Are Brother and Sister (Adoff) **7**:36
Tom and Pippo and the Dog (Oxenbury) **22**:151
Tom and Pippo and the Washing Machine (Oxenbury) **22**:149
Tom and Pippo Go for a Walk (Oxenbury) **22**:149
Tom and Pippo Go Shopping (Oxenbury) **22**:150
Tom and Pippo in the Garden (Oxenbury) **22**:150
Tom and Pippo in the Snow (Oxenbury) **22**:151
Tom and Pippo Make a Friend (Oxenbury) **22**:151
Tom and Pippo Make a Mess (Oxenbury) **22**:149
Tom and Pippo Read a Story (Oxenbury) **22**:149
Tom and Pippo See the Moon (Oxenbury) **22**:150
Tom and Pippo's Day (Oxenbury) **22**:150
Tom and Sam (Hutchins) **20**:144
Tom and the Two Handles (Hoban) **3**:83
Tom Fobble's Day (Garner) **20**:115
Tom Fox and the Apple Pie (Watson) **3**:213
The Tom Sawyer Fires (Yep) **17**:207
Tom Titmarsh's Devil (Garfield) **21**:109
Tom, Tom, the Piper's Son (Galdone) **16**:92
Tomboy (Klein) **19**:90
The Tombs of Atuan (Le Guin) **3**:123; **28**:144-88
Tomfoolery: Trickery and Foolery with Words (Schwartz) **3**:190
Tomie dePaola's Book of Christmas Carols (dePaola) **24**:100
Tomie dePaola's Book of Poems (dePaola) **24**:101
Tomie dePaola's Favorite Nursery Tales (dePaola) **24**:97
Tomie dePaola's Kitten Kids and the Big Camp-Out (dePaola) **24**:100
Tomie dePaola's Kitten Kids and the Haunted House (dePaola) **24**:100
Tomie dePaola's Kitten Kids and the Missing Dinosaur (dePaola) **24**:100
Tomie dePaola's Kitten Kids and the Treasure Hunt (dePaola) **24**:100
Tomie dePaola's Mother Goose (dePaola) **24**:95
Tommy Helps, Too (Rey) **5**:194
Tommy, Tilly, and Mrs. Tubbs (Lofting) **19**:128
The Tomorrow City (Hughes) **9**:70
Tomorrow Is a Lovely Day (Allan) **43**:29
Tomorrow Is Also a Day (Ure) **34**:186
Tomorrow's Wizard (MacLachlan) **14**:182
Tom's Midnight Garden (Pearce) **9**:144
Tomtebobarnen (Beskow) **17**:16
The Tomten (Lindgren) **39**:149
Tom-Toms in Kotokro (Guillot) **22**:59
Tongue of Flame: The Life of Lydia Maria Child (Meltzer) **13**:122
Tonight at Nine (Janosch) **26**:74
Tonight Is Carnaval (Dorros) **42**:68
Tono Antonio (Sawyer) **36**:150
Tonweya and the Eagles, and Other Lakota Indian Tales (Pinkney) **43**:156
Tony and Me (Slote) **4**:200
Tony the Pony (Moore) **15**:140

Tony's Bread: An Italian Folktale (dePaola) **24**:103
Too Big (d'Aulaire and d'Aulaire) **21**:49
Too Big (Keller) **45**:45
Too Hot to Handle (Christopher) **33**:41
Too Many Hopkins (dePaola) **24**:102
Too Many Rabbits (Parish) **22**:161
Too Many Tamales (Soto) **38**:203
Too Much Garbage (Lauber) **16**:118
The Too-Great Bread Bake Book (Gibbons) **8**:91
Tool Book (Gibbons) **8**:92
Toolchest: A Primer of Woodcraft (Adkins) **7**:21
Toolmaker (Walsh) **2**:201
Tools in Your Life (Adler) **27**:6
Tools of Modern Biology (Berger) **32**:4
The Tools of Science: From Yardstick to Cyclotron (Adler) **27**:10
Tooth and Claw: A Look at Animal Weapons (Freedman) **20**:80
The Tooth Book (Nourse) **33**:141
The Tooth Book (Seuss) **9**:194
Tooth-Gnasher Superflash (Pinkwater) **4**:171
Toppen and I at the Croft (Unnerstad) **36**:197
The Toppling Towers (Willard) **2**:223
Topsy (Flack) **28**:123
Topsy-Turvies: Pictures to Stretch the Imagination (Anno) **2**:2
The Topsy-Turvy Emperor of China (Singer) **1**:175
The Topsy-Turvy Storybook (King-Smith) **40**:167
Tornado Alert! (Betsy and Giulio Maestro) **45**:80
Tornado! Poems (Adoff) **7**:33
Torolv the Fatherless (Clarke) **28**:76
The Toronto Story (Mackay) **43**:110
The Tortoise and the Tree (Domanska) **40**:47
The Tortoise's Tug of War (Betsy and Giulio Maestro) **45**:63
Toucans Two, and Other Poems (Prelutsky) **13**:164
Touch Will Tell (Brown) **12**:107
Touchdown for Tommy (Christopher) **33**:38
Touching All the Bases: Baseball for Kids of All Ages (Mackay) **43**:111
Tough Luck (Doherty) **21**:59
The Tough Princess (Waddell) **31**:187
Tough Tiffany (Hurmence) **25**:92
Tough to Tackle (Christopher) **33**:45
The Tough Winter (Lawson) **2**:111
The Tournament of the Lions (Williams) **8**:224
The Tower of London (Fisher) **18**:138
Tower of the Stars (Harris) **30**:121
Town and Country (Provensen and Provensen) **11**:219
The Town Cats, and Other Tales (Alexander) **5**:23
The Town Mouse and the Country Mouse (Galdone) **16**:96
The Town That Forgot It Was Christmas (Proysen) **24**:183
Town Watch (King-Smith) **40**:152
The Toy Shop (Spier) **5**:228
The Toy Trumpet (Grifalconi) **35**:71
The Toymaker (Waddell) **31**:199
Tracker (Paulsen) **19**:174
Tracks (Bess) **39**:5
Tracks (Crew) **42**:58
Tractors (Zim) **2**:231
Traffic: A Book of Opposites (Betsy and Giulio Maestro) **45**:71
Trail of Apple Blossoms (Hunt) **1**:110
Train Ride (Steptoe) **2**:164
Train Whistles: A Language in Code (Betsy and Giulio Maestro) **45**:75

Train Whistles: A Language in Code (Sattler) 24:214

Traitor: The Case of Benedict Arnold (Fritz) 14:116

The Transfigured Hart (Yolen) 4:261

The Trap (Cresswell) 18:107

The Trapp Family Book (Wilhelm) 46:160

Das Traumfresserchen (Ende) 14:99

Traveling America with Today's Poets (Kherdian) 24:107

The Traveling Ball of String (Calhoun) 42:14

Traveling Shoes (Streatfeild) 17:195

Traveling Shoes (Streatfeild) 17:195

Travellers by Night (Alcock) 26:3

Travels for Two: Stories and Lies from My Childhood (Poulin) 28:199

The Travels of Babar (Brunhoff) 4:31

The Travels of Columbus (Ventura) 16:193

Travels of Marco Polo (Ventura) 16:194

The Treasure (Shulevitz) 5:206

Treasure Island (Stevenson) 10:193-235

The Treasure of Alpheus Winterborn (Bellairs) 37:11

The Treasure of the Long Sault (Hughes) 9:77

The Treasure of Topo-El-Bampo (O'Dell) 1:148

The Treasure-Hunting Trip (Janosch) 26:78

The Tree Angel: A Story and Play (Charlip) 8:26

Tree by Leaf (Singer) 48:170

Tree Flowers (Lerner) 34:130

A Tree for Peter (Seredy) 10:177

Tree House Island (Corbett) 1:47

A Tree on Your Street (Simon) 9:208

Tree Products (Adler) 27:22

A Treeful of Pigs (Lobel) 5:173

The Treegate Series (Wibberley) 3:231

Treegate's Raiders (Wibberley) 3:231

Treehorn's Treasure (Gorey) 36:99

Treehorn's Wish (Gorey) 36:104

The Trek (Jonas) 12:176

The Trial of Anna Cotman (Alcock) 26:8

Trial Valley (Cleaver and Cleaver) 6:111

Trick a Tracker (Foreman) 32:93

Trig (Peck) 45:110

The Trip (Keats) 35:140

The Trip to Panama (Janosch) 26:78

Trip Trap (Dhondy) 41:77

Tristan and Iseult (Sutcliff) 1:190; 37:163

Triumphs of Modern Science (Berger) 32:2

Troia (Ventura) 16:196

Troll Country (Marshall) 21:174

A Troll in a Hole (McKissack) 23:241

The Trolley to Yesterday (Bellairs) 37:22

Der Trommler und die Puppe (Kruss) 9:88

The Troubadour (Guillot) 22:69

Trouble Half-Way (Mark) 11:156

Trouble in the Jungle (Townsend) 2:175

Trouble on Titan (Nourse) 33:130

Trouble River (Byars) 16:53

The Trouble with Adventurers (Harris) 47:90

The Trouble with Charlie (Nixon) 24:142

The Trouble with Donovan Croft (Ashley) 4:14

The Trouble with Jack (Hughes) 15:121

The Trouble with Princesses (Harris) 47:89

The Trouble with Tuck (Taylor) 30:191

Trouble with Vanessa (Ure) 34:185

Trouble's Child (Walter) 15:207

Trubloff: The Mouse Who Wanted to Play the Balalaika (Burningham) 9:39

The Truce of the Games (Sutcliff) 37:163

Truck (Crews) 7:57

A Truckload of Rice (Berna) 19:39

Trucks (Gibbons) 8:92

Trucks (Zim) 2:232

The True Adventure of Daniel Hall (Stanley) 46:154

The True Adventures of Grizzly Adams (McClung) 11:194

The True Confessions of Charlotte Doyle (Avi) 24:15

The True Francine (Brown) 29:7

True Sea Adventures (Sobol) 4:210

The True Story of the Three Little Pigs (Smith) 47:199

The True Story of the Three Little Pigs: by A. Wolf; as Told to JonScieszka (Scieszka) 27:154

The Trumpet Book (Berger) 32:19

The Trumpet of the Swan (White) 1:195

Trumpets in the West (Trease) 42:179

Trust a City Kid (Yolen) 4:256

The Truth about Dragons (Blumberg) 21:26

The Truth about Mary Rose (Sachs) 2:133

The Truth about Santa Claus (Giblin) 29:89

The Truth about Stone Hollow (Snyder) 31:161

The Truth about the Ku Klux Klan (Meltzer) 13:144

The Truth About the Moon (Bess) 39:3

The Truth about Unicorns (Giblin) 29:93

Truth or Dare (Pfeffer) 11:204

The Truthful Harp (Alexander) 1:18; 5:20

Try It Again, Sam: Safety When You Walk (Viorst) 3:210

The Tsar's Promise: A Russian Tale (San Souci) 43:187

Tsubo No Naka (Anno) 14:41

Tuck Everlasting (Babbitt) 2:8

Tuck Triumphant (Taylor) 30:195

Tucker's Countryside (Selden) 8:199

Tuesday (Wiesner) 43:209

Tugboats Never Sleep (Lasky) 11:114

TUK Takes a Trip (Mayer) 11:176

Tulku (Dickinson) 29:48

Tumbleweed (King-Smith) 40:150

Tuned Out (Wojciechowska) 1:200

Tunes for a Small Harmonica (Wersba) 3:220

The Tunnel of Hugsy Goode (Estes) 2:75

Tunnel Vision (Gaberman) 33:6

Tunnels (Epstein and Epstein) 26:70

Tunnels (Gibbons) 8:98

The Turbulent Term of Tyke Tiler (Kemp) 29:114

Turkey Brother, and Other Tales (Bruchac) 46:6

Turkey for Christmas (de Angeli) 1:54

Turn It Up! A Novel (Strasser) 11:250

Turnabout (Leaf) 25:134

The Turnabout Trick (Corbett) 1:47

The Turnip (Domanska) 40:40

Turramulli the Giant Quinkin (Roughsey and Trezise) 41:141

The Turret (Sharp) 27:163

Turtle and Snail (Oneal) 13:155

The Turtle and the Dove (Freeman) 30:74

The Turtle and the Monkey: A Philippine Tale (Galdone) 16:105

Turtle in July (Pinkney) 43:164

Turtle in July (Singer) 48:135

Turtle Meat, and Other Stories (Bruchac) 46:10

Tusk Tusk (McKee) 38:165

Tut, Tut (Smith) 47:208

Tutankhamon (Ventura) 16:196

TV and Movie Animals (Paulsen) 19:173

The TV Kid (Byars) 16:54

'Twas the Night Before Thanksgiving (Pilkey) 48:100

The Twelve and the Genii (Clarke) 28:77

The Twelve Clever Brothers and Other Fools: Folktales from Russia (Ginsburg) 45:13

Twelve Dancing Princesses (Nielsen) 16:155

The Twelve Dancing Princesses: A Fairy Story (Lunn) 18:159

The Twelve Days of Christmas (Brett) 27:39

The Twelve Months: A Greek Folktale (Aliki) 9:26

The Twelve Robbers (Biegel) 27:30

Twelve Tales from Aesop (Carle) 10:83

The Twelve Tasks of Asterix (Goscinny and Uderzo) 37:82

Twentieth Century Discovery (Asimov) 12:44

Twenty Ways To Lose Your Best Friend (Singer) 48:136

Twenty-Four and Stanley (Weiss) 4:219

The Twenty-Four Days Before Christmas (L'Engle) 1:132

The Twenty-One Balloons (Pene du Bois) 1:66

The Twenty-one Mile Swim (Christopher) 33:53

Twenty-Two, Twenty-Three (Raskin) 12:225

The Twilight of Magic (Lofting) 19:127

Twilight Tales (Unnerstad) 36:198

Twin and Super-Twin (Cross) 28:95

Twin Spell (Lunn) 18:158

Twins: The Story of Multiple Births (Cole) 5:62

Twist, Wiggle, and Squirm: A Book about Earthworms (Pringle) 4:177

Twisted (Stine) 37:109

The Twisted Window (Duncan) 29:78

A Twister of Twists, a Tangler of Tongues (Schwartz) 3:190

The Twits (Dahl) 7:78

Two Admirals (McKee) 38:165

Two and Too Much (Cummings) 48:50

Two and Two Are Four (Haywood) 22:91

Two are Better than One (Brink) 30:15

Two Bear Cubs (Jonas) 12:173

Two Boys of Jerusalem (Ashabranner) 28:8

Two Can Toucan (McKee) 38:157

The Two Cars (d'Aulaire and d'Aulaire) 21:51

Two Crows Counting (Orgel) 48:96

Two Different Girls (Bunting) 28:47

Two Dog Biscuits (Cleary) 8:49

Two Fables (Dahl) 41:39

The Two Faces of Silenus (Clarke) 28:81

The Two Giants (Foreman) 32:86

Two Greedy Bears (Ginsburg) 45:10

Two Hoots (Cresswell) 18:107

Two Hoots and the Big Bad Bird (Cresswell) 18:107

Two Hoots and the King (Cresswell) 18:108

Two Hoots Go to the Sea (Cresswell) 18:107

Two Hoots in the Snow (Cresswell) 18:108

Two Hoots Play Hide-and-Seek (Cresswell) 18:107

The 290 (O'Dell) 16:172

Two If By Sea (Fisher) 18:123

Two Laughable Lyrics (Lear) 1:128

Two Little Gigglers (Unnerstad) 36:199

Two Little Trains (Brown) 10:58

Two Lonely Ducks, a Counting Book (Duvoisin) 23:99

Two Love Stories (Lester) 2:115

Two Monsters (McKee) 38:174

Two Moral Tales (Mayer) 11:168

Two More Moral Tales (Mayer) 11:168

The Two of Them (Aliki) 9:26

The Two Old Bachelors (Lear) 1:128

Two Pairs of Shoes (Leo and Diane Dillon) 44:35

Two Piano Tuners (Goffstein) 3:61

Two Shoes, New Shoes (Hughes) 15:132

The Two Sisters (Arundel) 35:11

Two Sisters and Some Hornets (Epstein) 26:64

Two Stories: "The Road to Dunmore" and "The Key" (Dillon) 26:28

Two Strikes on Johnny (Christopher) **33**:37

Two Thousand Years of Space Travel (Freedman) **20**:73

Two Under Par (Henkes) **23**:128

Two Wheels, Two Heads (Ahlberg and Ahlberg) **18**:8

The Two-Thousand-Pound Goldfish (Byars) **16**:58

Tye May and the Magic Brush (Bang) **8**:21

Tyrannosaurus Rex and Its Kin: The Mesozoic Monsters (Sattler) **24**:223

Tyrone the Dirty Rotten Cheat (Wilhelm) **46**:167

Tyrone, the Double Dirty Rotten Cheater (Wilhelm) **46**:167

Tyrone, the Horrible (Wilhelm) **46**:165

Ty's One-Man Band (Walter) **15**:205

UFO (Blumberg) **21**:24

UFOs: A Pictorial History from Antiquity to the Present (Knight) **38**:123

UFOs, ETs, and Visitors from Space (Berger) **32**:40

The Ugly Duckling (Moore) **15**:145

Ultramarine (Nimmo) **44**:145

The Ultra-Violet Catastrophe! or, The Unexpected Walk with Great-Uncle Magnus Pringle (Mahy) **7**:183

Umbrella (Yashima) **4**:253

Unbuilding (Macaulay) **14**:172

Uncanny! Even More Surprising Stories (Jennings) **40**:126

Unclaimed Treasures (MacLachlan) **14**:183

Uncle Charlie Weasel and the Cuckoo Bird (McBratney) **44**:121

Uncle Charlie Weasel's Winter (McBratney) **44**:122

Uncle Elephant (Lobel) **5**:175

Uncle Lemon's Spring (Yolen) **4**:267

Uncle Misha's Partisans (Suhl) **2**:166

Uncle Vova's Tree (Polacco) **40**:185

Under a Changing Moon (Benary-Isbert) **12**:78

Under the Autumn Garden (Mark) **11**:147

Under the Early Morning Trees: Poems (Adoff) **7**:35

Under the Green Willow (Coatsworth) **2**:63

Under the Moon (Ryder) **37**:92

Under the Orange Grove (Dillon) **26**:29

Under the Sun and over the Moon (Crossley-Holland) **47**:48

Under the Sunday Tree (Greenfield) **38**:86

Under the Trees and through the Grass (Tresselt) **30**:208

Under the Window: Pictures and Rhymes for Children (Greenaway) **6**:131

Under Your Feet (Ryder) **37**:95

Underground (Macaulay) **3**:144

Underground Man (Meltzer) **13**:130

Underground to Canada (Smucker) **10**:189

The Undersea People (Bunting) **28**:48

The Underside of the Leaf (Goffstein) **3**:61

Understanding Body Talk (Aylesworth) **6**:54

Understanding Radioactivity (Milne and Milne) **22**:126

The Undertaker's Gone Bananas (Zindel) **45**:192

Undone! More Mad Endings (Jennings) **40**:128

Uneasy Money (Brancato) **32**:75

Die Unendliche Geschichte (Ende) **14**:99

Unfortunately Harriet (Wells) **16**:204

The Unfriendly Book (Zolotow) **2**:237

Unhurry Harry (Merriam) **14**:200

The Unions (Fisher) **18**:131

The Unique World of Mitsumasa Anno: Selected Works (1968-1977) (Anno) **14**:35

The Universe (Zim) **2**:232

The Universe Between (Nourse) **33**:134

The Universe: From Flat Earth to Black Holes—and Beyond (Asimov) **12**:39

The Universe: From Flat Earth to Quasar (Asimov) **12**:39

University: The Students, Faculty, and Campus Life at One University (Schwartz) **3**:191

The Unknown Paintings of Kay Nielsen (Nielsen) **16**:158

Unreal! Eight Surprising Stories (Jennings) **40**:126

Until the Celebration (Snyder) **31**:163

The Untold Tale (Haugaard) **11**:107

Unusual Partners: Symbiosis in the Living World (Silverstein and Silverstein) **25**:201

L'uomo a cavallo (Ventura) **16**:195

L'uomo del camion (Munari) **9**:125

Up a Road Slowly (Hunt) **1**:110

Up a Tree (Young) **27**:220

Up and Up (Hughes) **15**:125

Up Country (Carter) **22**;23

Up from Jericho Tel (Konigsburg) **47**:141

Up in Seth's Room: A Love Story (Mazer) **23**:226

Up in Sister Bay (Ferry) **34**:51

Up in the Air (Flack) **28**:124

Up Periscope (White) **3**:223

Up the Alley with Jack and Joe (Kotzwinkle) **6**:182

Up the Chimney Down and Other Stories (Aiken) **19**:15

Up the Pier (Cresswell) **18**:104

Up There (Hill) **13**:93

Up to Low (Doyle) **22**:30

The Uproar (Orgel) **48**:79

Upside-Downers: More Pictures to Stretch the Imagination (Anno) **2**:2

The Upstairs Room (Reiss) **19**:217

Uptown (Steptoe) **2**:164

The Urchin (Unnerstad) **36**:190

Us and Uncle Fraud (Lowry) **46**:30

Us Boys of Westcroft (Breinburg) **31**:67

Use Your Brain (Showers) **6**:245

Use Your Head, Dear (Aliki) **9**:31

The Uses of Space (Bova) **3**:36

V Is for Victory: America Remembers World War II (Krull) **44**:110

Vacation Time: Poems for Children (Giovanni) **6**:117

Vaccination and You (Cohen) **3**:43

The Vagabonds Ashore (Berna) **19**:41

Vagabonds of the Pacific (Berna) **19**:41

The Valentine (Garfield) **21**:109

The Valentine Bears (Bunting) **28**:55

A Valentine Fantasy (Haywood) **22**:103

A Valentine for Cousin Archie (Williams) **48**:200

Valentine Frankenstein (Gaberman) **33**:18

The Valentine Mystery (Nixon) **24**:139

The Valiant Chatti-Maker (Godden) **20**:137

Valiant Scots: People of the Highlands Today (Lauber) **16**:112

The Valley Between (Thiele) **27**:209

Valley of the Broken Cherry Trees (Namioka) **48**:62

Vampires and Other Ghosts (Aylesworth) **6**:49

The Vandemark Mummy (Voigt) **48**:174

The Vanishing Border: A Photographic Journey along Our Frontier with Mexico (Ashabranner) **28**:10

Vanishing Wildlife of Latin America (McClung) **11**:192

The Vanishment of Thomas Tull (Ahlberg and Ahlberg) **18**:5

VD: The Silent Epidemic (Hyde) **23**:159

VD-STD: The Silent Epidemic (Hyde) **23**:159

Vegetables from Stems and Leaves (Selsam) **1**:166

The Velvet Room (Snyder) **31**:154

The Velveteen Rabbit; Or, How Toys Become Real (Bianco) **19**:50

The Vengeance of the Witch Finder (Bellairs) **37**:27

Venus and Mercury (Nourse) **33**:136

Venus, Near Neighbor of the Sun (Asimov) **12**:59

Veronica (Duvoisin) **23**:101

Veronica and the Birthday Present (Duvoisin) **23**:104

Veronica Ganz (Sachs) **2**:134

Veronica's Smile (Duvoisin) **23**:103

The Very Busy Spider (Carle) **10**:85

Very Far Away from Anywhere Else (Le Guin) **3**:123

Very Far from Here (Hamley) **47**:55

Very First Books (Wells) **16**:209, 213

The Very Hungry Caterpillar (Carle) **10**:72

Very Last First Time (Wallace) **37**:213

A Very Long Tail: A Folding Book (Carle) **10**:76

The Very Long Train: A Folding Book (Carle) **10**:76

A Very Long Way from Anywhere Else (Le Guin) See *Very Far Away from Anywhere Else*

A Very Special House (Krauss) **42**:117

A Very Touchy Subject (Strasser) **11**:251

The Very Worst Monster (Hutchins) **20**:153

A Very Young Circus Flyer (Krementz) **5**:154

A Very Young Dancer (Krementz) **5**:151

A Very Young Gymnast (Krementz) **5**:153

Very Young Poets (Brooks) **27**:44-56

A Very Young Rider (Krementz) **5**:152

A Very Young Skater (Krementz) **5**:154

The Vicar of Nibbleswicke (Dahl) **41**:49

The Vicksburg Veteran (Monjo) **2**:126

Victorians Abroad (Goodall) **25**:51

Victory at Valmy (Trease) **42**:184

The View beyond My Father (Allan) **43**:29

The View from Saturday (Konigsburg) **47**:148

Viking's Dawn (Treece) **2**:189

Viking's Sunset (Treece) **2**:189

Village Books (Spier) **5**:228

The Village by the Sea (Fox) **44**:69

The Village of Round and Square Houses (Grifalconi) **35**:74

Village of the Vampire Cat (Namioka) **48**:63

The Village Tree (Yashima) **4**:250

Vim the Rag Mouse (Daly) **41**:53

Vine Clad Hill (Allan) **43**:5

The Vinegar Works: Three Volumes on Moral Instruction (Gorey) **36**:91

The Vinganee and the Tree Toad: A Liberian Tale (Aardema) **17**:7

The Violin Book (Berger) **32**:8

Violins and Shovels: The WPA Arts Projects (Meltzer) **13**:138

Virgil Nosegay and the Cake Hunt (Biegel) **27**:35

Virgil Nosegay and the Hupmobile (Biegel) **27**:36

Virgil Nosegay and the Wellington Boots (Biegel) **27**:36

The Virus Invaders (Nourse) **33**:151

Viruses (Nourse) **33**:139

Viruses: Life's Smallest Enemies (Knight) **38**:125

De vis (Bruna) **7**:49

Visions of America, by the Poets of Our Time (Kherdian) **24**:106

A Visit to William Blake's Inn: Poems for Innocent and Experienced Travelers (Willard) **5**:250

Visiting Pamela (Klein) **19**:91

Visiting the Art Museum (Brown) **29**:13

The Visitor (Heine) **18**:149

The Visitor (Oxenbury) **22**:145

Vitamins (Nourse) **33**:141

The Voice of Liberty: The Story of Emma Lazarus (Merriam) **14**:192

The Voice of the People: American Democracy in Action (Betsy and Giulio Maestro) **45**:90

Vol 714 pour Sydney (Hergé) **6**:149

Volcano: The Eruption and Healing of Mount St. Helens (Lauber) **16**:121

Volcanoes (Branley) **13**:51

Volcanoes and Earthquakes (Adler) **27**:16

Volcanoes: Nature's Fireworks (Nixon) **24**:137

The Voyage Begun (Bond) **11**:29

The Voyage of Mael Duin (Dillon) **26**:29

The Voyage of Osiris: A Myth of Ancient Egypt (McDermott) **9**:116

The Voyage of QV 66 (Lively) **7**:162

The Voyage of the Dawn Treader (Lewis) **3**:137; **27**:104-51

The Voyagers, Being Legends and Romances of Atlantic Discovery (Colum) **36**:35

The Voyages of Doctor Dolittle (Lofting) **19**:122

Voyages: Poems by Walt Whitman (Hopkins) **44**:96

Vulcan: The Story of a Bald Eagle (McClung) **11**:180

W. E. B. DuBois: A Biography (Hamilton) **1**:106; **26**:149

Wagging Tails: An Album of Dogs (Henry) **4**:112

The Wagon Race (Heine) **18**:149

Wagstaffe the Wind-Up Boy (Needle) **43**:142

Wag-Tail Bess (Flack) **28**:122

Wait for William (Flack) **28**:124

Wait till the Moon Is Full (Brown) **10**:57

Waiting for the Rain: A Novel of South Africa (Gordon) **27**:91

The Waiting Game (Bunting) **28**:52

Waiting to Waltz: A Childhood (Rylant) **15**:169

Wake Up and Goodnight (Zolotow) **2**:237

Wake Up, City! (Tresselt) **30**:206

Wake Up, Farm! (Tresselt) **30**:205

Walk a Mile and Get Nowhere (Southall) **2**:157

Walk Home Tired, Billy Jenkins (Thomas) **8**:213

A Walk in the Park (Browne) **19**:62

Walk Together Children: Black American Spirituals (Bryan) **18**:33

Walk Two Moons (Creech) **42**:41

Walk with Your Eyes (Brown) **12**:107

Walker, the Witch, and the Striped Flying Saucer (Stevenson) **17**:152

The Walking Stones (Hunter) **25**:78

The Walking Stones (Hunter)
See *The Bodach*

Walking through the Dark (Naylor) **17**:51

Walking Up a Rainbow: Being the True Version of the Long and Hazardous Journey of Susan D. Carlisle, Mrs Myrtle Dessery, Drover Bert Pettit, and Cowboy Clay Carmer and Others (Taylor) **30**:193

The Wall (Bunting) **28**:64

Wall Street: The Story of the Stock Exchange (Sterling) **1**:182

Walls: Defenses throughout History (Giblin) **29**:88

Walter, the Lazy Mouse (Flack) **28**:126

The Wanderers (Coatsworth) **2**:63

Wandering Minstrels We: The Story of Gilbert and Sullivan (Lavine) **35**:145

The War and Freddy (Hamley) **47**:63

War and Peas (Foreman) **32**:88

The War and the Protest: Viet Nam (Haskins) **3**:68

War Boy: A Country Childhood (Foreman) **32**:102

War Dog (Treece) **2**:190

The War on Villa Street (Mazer) **16**:130

The War on William Street (Ottley) **16**:187

The War with Mr. Wizzle (Korman) **25**:107

War with Old Mouldy! (Ure) **34**:184

Warlock at the Wheel and Other Stories (Jones) **23**:195

The Warlock of Westfall (Fisher) **18**:125

The Warnings (Buffie) **39**:25

Warrior Scarlet (Sutcliff) **1**:191; **37**:153

Wart, Son of Toad (Carter) **22**:18

A War-Time Handbook for Young Americans (Leaf) **25**:126

Washington, D. C.: The Nation's Capital (Epstein and Epstein) **26**:57

The Washington Picture Book (Lenski) **26**:100

Wasteground Circus (Keeping) **34**:101

The Watch House (Westall) **13**:252

Watch Out! A Giant! (Carle) **10**:82

Watch Out for the Chicken Feet in Your Soup (dePaola) **4**:56

The Watchbirds (Leaf) **25**:125

The Watcher in the Garden (Phipson) **5**:186

The Watcher in the Mist (St. John) **46**:117

The Watchers (Curry) **31**:79

Watchers in the Wild: The New Science of Ethology (Cohen) **3**:43

The Watchers of the Trails: A Book of Animal Life (Roberts) **33**:193

Watching Foxes (Arnosky) **15**:8

Water (Graham) **31**:95

The Water Flowers (Gorey) **36**:103

Water for the World (Branley) **13**:47

Water Girl (Thomas) **19**:221

The Water Horse (King-Smith) **40**:161

Water Music: Poems for Children (Yolen) **44**:208

The Water of Life (Williams) **8**:238

Water on Your Street (Simon) **9**:209

Water Plants (Pringle) **4**:179

Water since the World Began (Lavine) **35**:149

Water to Burn (Epstein and Epstein) **26**:44

Watership Down (Adams) **20**:10-32

Waterslain and Other Poems (Crossley-Holland) **47**:45

The Watertower (Crew) **42**:59

Watson, the Smartest Dog in the U.S.A. (Kuskin) **4**:139

The Wave (Strasser) **11**:248

Waves (Zim) **2**:232

Waving: A Counting Book (Sis) **45**:160

The Way Home (Phipson) **5**:182

The Way Mothers Are (Schlein) **41**:185

The Way of Danger: The Story of Theseus (Serraillier) **2**:143

The Way of the Grizzly (Patent) **19**:164

The Way of the Storyteller (Sawyer) **36**:157

The Way over Windle (Allan) **43**:14

The Way Things Are and Other Poems (Livingston) **7**:171

The Way to Sattin Shore (Pearce) **9**:158

Wayside School Is Falling Down (Sacher) **28**:203

We Are Best Friends (Aliki) **9**:29

We Are Mesquakie, We Are One (Irwin) **40**:108

We Can't Sleep (Stevenson) **17**:159

We Danced in Bloomsbury Square (Estoril) **43**:16

We Didn't Mean to Go to Sea (Ransome) **8**:178

We Have Tomorrow (Bontemps) **6**:80

We Hide, You Seek (Aruego) **5**:30

We Interrupt This Semester for an Important Bulletin (Conford) **10**:96

We Live by the River (Lenski) **26**:119

We Live in the Country (Lenski) **26**:121

We Live in the North (Lenski) **26**:122

We Live in the South (Lenski) **26**:116

We Lived in Drumfyvie (Sutcliff) **37**:165

We Love Them (Waddell) **31**:196

We Read: A to Z (Crews) **7**:55

Weasels, Otters, Skunks, and Their Families (Patent) **19**:147

Weather (Pienkowski) **6**:230

The Weather Changes Man (Bova) **3**:36

The Weather Sky (McMillan) **47**:177

The Weathermonger (Dickinson) **29**:37

The Weaver's Gift (Lasky) **11**:115

Web of Traitors: An Adventure Story of Ancient Athens (Trease) **42**:182

Der Wecker (Heine) **18**:149

The Wedding Ghost (Garfield) **21**:120

The Wedding Ghost (Keeping) **34**:107

The Wednesday Surprise (Bunting) **28**:63

Wee Gillis (Leaf) **25**:124

A Weed Is a Flower: The Life of George Washington Carver (Aliki) **9**:18

Weekend (Pike) **29**:171

A Weekend with Wendell (Henkes) **23**:127

Weetzie Bat (Block) **33**:30

Weight and Weightlessness (Branley) **13**:38

The Weird Disappearance of Jordan Hall (Gaberman) **33**:15

The Weirdo (Taylor) **30**:196

The Weirdstone: A Tale of Aderley (Garner) **20**:100

The Weirdstone of Brisingamen: A Tale of Aderley (Garner) **20**:100

Welcome Home! (Bemelmans) **6**:75

Welcome Is a Wonderful Word (Fujikawa) **25**:40

Welcome to the Green House (Yolen) **44**:199

Welcome, Twins (Khalsa) **30**:144

The Well (Kemp) **29**:119

The Well-Mannered Balloon (Willard) **5**:246

The Well-Wishers (Eager) **43**:88

We're Going on a Bear Hunt (Rosen) **45**:138

Het wereldje van Beer Ligthart (Haar) **15**:116

The Werewolf Family (Gantos) **18**:142

West with the White Chiefs (Harris) **43**:78

Western Wind (Fox) **44**:76

The Westing Game (Raskin) **12**:225

Westmark (Alexander) **5**:24

Westward to Vinland (Treece) **2**:190

A Wet and Sandy Day (Ryder) **37**:85

Whales: Giants of the Deep (Patent) **19**:160

Whales, the Nomads of the Sea (Sattler) **24**:221

Whalesinger (Katz) **45**:36

What a Fine Day For... (Krauss) **42**:128

What a Good Lunch! Eating (Watanabe) **8**:216

What about Grandma? (Irwin) **40**:110

What Alvin Wanted (Keller) **45**:53

What Am I? Looking Through Shapes at Apples and Grapes (Leo and Diane Dillon) **44**:48

What Can You Do with a Pocket? (Merriam) **14**:194

What Can You Do with a Word? (Williams) **8**:227

What Color Is Love? (Anglund) **1**:21

What Did You Bring Me? (Kuskin) **4**:141

What Did You Leave Behind? (Tresselt) **30**:215

What Do People Do All Day? (Scarry) **41**:162

What Do You Call a Dumb Bunny? And Other Rabbit Riddles, Games, Jokes, and Cartoons (Brown) **29**:10

What Do You Do When Your Mouth Won't Open? (Pfeffer) **11**:201

What Do You See? (Domanska) **40**:44

What Do You Think? An Introduction to Public Opinion: How It Forms, Functions, and Affects Our Lives (Schwartz) **3**:191

What Do You Want to Know about Guppies? (Simon) **9**:211

What Does It Do and How Does It Work? (Hoban) **3**:83

What Happened at Rita's Party (Breinburg) **31**:68

What Happens Next? (Domanska) **40**:51

What Happens to a Hamburger (Showers) **6**:245

What Holds It Together (Weiss) **4**:228

What I Did for Roman (Conrad) **18**:88

What I Did Last Summer (Prelutsky) **13**:172

What I Really Think of You (Kerr) **29**:152

What I'd Like to Be (Munari) **9**:125

What If? (Minarik) **33**:127

What If They Saw Me Now? (Ure) **34**:172

What Is a Color? (Provensen and Provensen) **11**:209

What Is a Man? (Krahn) **3**:106

What Is It? (Hoban) **13**:109

What Is Right for Tulip (Duvoisin) **23**:104

What It's All About (Klein) **2**:101

What Jim Knew (Hoberman) **22**:109

What Made You You? (Bendick) **5**:44

What Makes a Boat Float? (Corbett) **1**:47

What Makes a Light Go On? (Corbett) **1**:48

What Makes a Plane Fly? (Corbett) **1**:48

What Makes Day and Night (Branley) **13**:29

What Makes Me Feel This Way? Growing Up with Human Emotions (LeShan) **6**:188

What Makes the Sun Shine? (Asimov) **12**:46

What Next, Baby Bear! (Murphy) **39**:172

What Shall We Do with the Land? (Pringle) **4**:186

What the Dickens! (Curry) **31**:88

What the Gulls Were Singing (Naylor) **17**:49

What the Moon Is Like (Branley) **13**:31

What the Neighbours Did and Other Stories (Pearce) **9**:154

What Time is it Around the World (Baumann) **35**:55

What to Do about Molly (Flack) **28**:125

What to Do: Everyday Guides for Everyone (Bendick) **5**:41

What You Don't Know Can Kill You (Gaberman) **33**:18

Whatever Happened to Beverly Bigler's Brithday? (Williams) **48**:197

Whatever Next! (Murphy) **39**:172

Whatever Words You Want to Hear (Pfeffer) **11**:198

What's Behind the Word (Epstein and Epstein) **26**:67

What's Best for You (Gaberman) **33**:9

What's for Lunch? (Carle) **10**:85

What's for Lunch? The Eating Habits of Seashore Creatures (Epstein and Epstein) **26**:70

What's Fun Without a Friend (Iwasaki) **18**:155

What's Going to Happen to Me? When Parents Separate or Divorce (LeShan) **6**:190

What's Happening to our Weather? (Cohen) **43**:39

What's Hatching Out of That Egg? (Lauber) **16**:119

What's in Fox's Sack? (Galdone) **16**:104

What's So Funny, Ketu? A Nuer Tale (Aardema) **17**:6

What's the Big Idea, Ben Franklin? (Fritz) **14**:113

What's the Matter with Carruthers? A Bedtime Story (Marshall) **21**:168

What's Under My Bed? (Stevenson) **17**:160

What's Wrong with Being a Skunk? (Schlein) **41**:185

Wheat: The Golden Harvest (Patent) **19**:165

Wheel on the Chimney (Brown) **10**:64

The Wheel on the School (DeJong) **1**:61

Wheels (Graham) **31**:95

Wheels: A Pictorial History (Tunis) **2**:194

The Wheels on the Bus (Kovalski) **34**:115

When Cats Dream (Pilkey) **48**:103

When Clay Sings (Baylor) **3**:17

When Dad Felt Bad (Causley) **30**:39

When Did You Last Wash Your Feet? (Rosen) **45**:135

When Everyone Was Fast Asleep (dePaola) **4**:57

When Francie Was Sick (Keller) **45**:48

When I Am Old with You (Johnson) **33**:95

When I Dance: Poems (Berry) **22**:10

When I Grow Up (Lenski) **26**:122

When I Have a Little Girl (Zolotow) **2**:238

When I Have a Son (Zolotow) **2**:238

When I Walk I Change the Earth (Krauss) **42**:130

When I Was a Boy (Kaestner) **4**:126

When I Was a Little Boy (Kaestner) **4**:126

When I Was Nine (Stevenson) **17**:165

When I Was Young in the Mountains (Rylant) **15**:168

When I'm Big (Bruna) **7**:52

When No One Was Looking (Wells) **16**:211

When She Hollers (Bone) **48**:181

When Shlemiel Went to Warsaw, and Other Stories (Singer) **1**:176

When Someone You Know Is Gay (Cohen) **43**:51

When the City Stopped (Phipson) **5**:185

When the Phone Rang (Mazer) **16**:132

When the Pie Was Opened (Little) **4**:148

When the Rattlesnake Sounds (Childress) **14**:92

When the Siren Wailed (Streatfeild) **17**:199

When the Sirens Wailed (Streatfeild) **17**:199

When the Tide Goes Far Out (Milne and Milne) **22**:121

When the Wind Blew (Brown) **10**:47

When the Wind Blows (Briggs) **10**:30

When the Wind Stops (Zolotow) **2**:238

When the Woods Hum (Ryder) **37**:96

When Thunders Spoke (Sneve) **2**:145

When We First Met (Mazer) **23**:228

When We Went to the Park (Hughes) **15**:131

When We Were Very Young (Milne) **26**:126

When Will the World Be Mine? (Schlein) **41**:176

When Winter Comes (Freedman) **20**:81

When You Were a Baby (Jonas) **12**:172

Where Are You, Ernest and Celestine? (Vincent) **13**:221

Where Butterflies Grow (Ryder) **37**:94

Where Can It Be? (Jonas) **12**:178

Where Do You Think You're Going, Christopher Columbus? (Fritz) **14**:115

Where Does the Day Go? (Myers) **4**:155

Where Does the Garbage Go? (Showers) **6**:245

Where Does the Sun Go at Night? (Ginsburg) **45**:15

Where Have You Been? (Brown) **10**:61

Where Is Everybody? (Charlip) **8**:26

Where Is It? (Hoban) **13**:103

Where Is My Friend? (Pfister) **42**:133

Where Is My Friend? A Word Concept Book (Betsy and Giulio Maestro) **45**:66

Where is Sarah? (Graham) **31**:92

Where the Bald Eagles Gather (Patent) **19**:159

Where the Forest Meets the Sea (Baker) **28**:21

Where the Lilies Bloom (Cleaver and Cleaver) **6**:103

Where the River Begins (Locker) **14**:157

Where the Sidewalk Ends (Silverstein) **5**:210

Where the Wild Geese Go (Pierce) **20**:184

Where the Wild Things Are (Sendak) **1**:172; **17**:112

Where the Winds Never Blew and the Cocks Never Crew (Colum) **36**:44

Where There's a Will, There's a Wag (Singer) **48**:130

Where Was Patrick Henry on the 29th of May? (Fritz) **2**:81

Where Wild Willie (Adoff) **7**:34

Where'd You Get the Gun, Bill? (Gaberman) **33**:17

Where's My Baby? (Rey) **5**:195

Where's My Daddy? (Watanabe) **8**:217

Where's Spot? (Hill) **13**:91

Where's the Baby? (Hutchins) **20**:154

Where's Waldo? (Handford) **22**:73

Where's Wally (Handford) **22**:73

Where's Wally Now? (Handford) **22**:74

Wherever Home Begins: 100 Contemporary Poems (Janeczko) **47**:116

Which Horse Is William? (Kuskin) **4**:136

Which Way Freedom? (Hansen) **21**:151

While I Sleep (Calhoun) **42**:33

The Whingdingdilly (Peet) **12**:199

The Whipping Boy (Fleischman) **15**:112

The Whipping Boy (Sis) **45**:159

Whiskers, Once and Always (Orgel) **48**:89

The Whisky Rebellion, 1794: Revolt in Western Pennsylvania Threatens American Unity (Knight) **38**:108

A Whisper of Lace (Clarke) **28**:87

Whisper of the Cat (St. John) **46**:121

The Whispering Knights (Lively) **7**:152

The Whispering Mountain (Aiken) **1**:8

Whispers and Other Poems (Livingston) **7**:167

Whispers from the Dead (Nixon) **24**:153

Whistle for the Train (Brown) **10**:66

Whistle for Willie (Keats) **1**:118; **35**:130

The White Archer: An Eskimo Legend (Houston) **3**:87

White Bear, Ice Bear (Ryder) **37**:91

White Boots (Streatfeild) **17**:191

White Boots (Streatfeild)
  See *Skating Shoes*

The White Cat: An Old French Fairy Tale (San Souci) **43**:185

The White Elephant (Clarke) **28**:73

The White Goose (Tudor) **13**:192

The White Horse Gang (Bawden) **2**:14

The White Marble (Zolotow) **2**:239

The White Mountains (Christopher) **2**:43

The White Mountains Trilogy (Christopher) **2**:43

White Peak Farm (Doherty) **21**:56

A White Romance (Hamilton) **40**:74

The White Room (Coatsworth) **2**:64

The White Sea Horse (Cresswell) **18**:98

White Serpent Castle (Namioka) **48**:62

The White Shadow (Guillot) **22**:62

White Snow, Bright Snow (Duvoisin) **23**:92

White Snow, Bright Snow (Tresselt) **30**:201

The White Sparrow (Colum) **36**:40

The White Stag (Seredy) **10**:173

White Stallion of Lipizza (Henry) **4**:114

White Witch of Kynance (Calhoun) **42**:16

Whizz! (Domanska) **40**:44

Whizz! (Lear) **1**:128

Who are the Handicapped? (Haskins) **39**:34

Who Calls from Afar? (Brinsmead) **47**:11

Who Cares? I Do (Leaf) **25**:135

Who Discovered America? Settlers and Explorers of the New World Before the Time of Columbus (Lauber) **16**:115

Who Drew on the Baby's Head (Rosen) **45**:143

Who Got Rid of Angus Flint? (Jones) **23**:188

Who Has the Lucky-Duck in Class 4-B? (Gaberman) **33**:12

Who I Am (Lester) **2**:115

Who Is Bugs Potter? (Korman) **25**:105

Who is Frances Rain? (Buffie) **39**:15

Who Look at Me (Jordan) **10**:115

Who Needs Holes? (Epstein and Epstein) **26**:62

Who Put That Hair in My Toothbrush? (Spinelli) **26**:202

Who Really Killed Cock Robin? (George) **1**:94

Who, Said Sue, Said Whoo? (Raskin) **1**:157

Who Sank the Boat? (Allen) **44**:6

Who Says You Can't? (Epstein and Epstein) **26**:61

Who Stole the Wizard of Oz? (Avi) **24**:9

Who Will Comfort Toffle? (Jansson) **2**:95

Whodunnit? (Cresswell) **18**:112

The Whole World of Hands (Berger) **32**:27

Whooping Crane (McClung) **11**:181

Whoppers: Tall Tales and Other Lies (Schwartz) **3**:192

Who's a Clever Baby Then? (McKee) **38**:178

Who's Hu? (Namioka) **48**:64

Who's in Rabbit's House? A Masai Tale (Aardema) **17**:5

Who's in Rabbit's House? A Masai Tale (Leo and Diane Dillon) **44**:32

Who's in the Egg? (Provensen and Provensen) **11**:210

Who's Out There? The Search for Extraterrestrial Life (Aylesworth) **6**:51

Who's Seen the Scissors? (Krahn) **3**:106

Who's That Stepping on Plymouth Rock (Fritz) **2**:82

Who's There? Open the Door! (Munari) **9**:124

Whose Furry Nose? Australian Animals You'd Like to Meet (Drescher) **20**:60

Whose Scaly Tail? African Animals You'd Like to Meet (Drescher) **20**:60

Whose Town? (Graham) **10**:107

Whose Turtle? (Orgel) **48**:77

Why? A Books of Reasons (Adler) **27**:15

Why Can't I? (Bendick) **5**:43

Why Can't I Be William? (Conford) **10**:90

Why Don't You Get a Horse, Sam Adams? (Fritz) **2**:82

Why I Cough, Sneeze, Shiver, Hiccup, and Yawn (Berger) **32**:29

Why Me? (Conford) **10**:100

Why Mosquitoes Buzz in People's Ears: A West African Tale (Aardema) **17**:4

Why Mosquitoes Buzz in People's Ears: A West African Tale (Leo and Diane Dillon) **44**:25

Why Noah Chose the Dove (Singer) **1**:176

Why So Much Noise? (Domanska) **40**:37

Why the Sun and Moon Live in the Sky (Daly) **41**:63

Why the Tides Ebb and Flow (Brown) **29**:6

Why Things Change: The Story of Evolution (Bendick) **5**:46

The Whys and Wherefores of Littabelle Lee (Cleaver and Cleaver) **6**:108

The Wicked City (Singer) **1**:176

The Wicked Enchantment (Benary-Isbert) **12**:74

The Wicked One (Hunter) **25**:86

The Wicked Tricks of Till Owlyglass (Rosen) **45**:139

The Wicked Tricks of Tyl Uilenspiegel (Williams) **8**:236

Wide Awake and Other Poems (Livingston) **7**:167

The Wider Heart (St. John) **46**:98

Wiggle to the Laundromat (Lee) **3**:116

The Wigmakers (Fisher) **18**:122

Wigwam in the City (Smucker) **10**:189

The Wild (Graham) **31**:96

Wild and Woolly Mammoths (Aliki) **9**:25

The Wild Angel (Spykman) **35**:218

The Wild Baby (Lindgren) **20**:156

The Wild Baby Gets a Puppy (Lindgren) **20**:158

Wild Baby Goes to Sea (Lindgren) **20**:157

The Wild Baby's Boat Trip (Lindgren) **20**:157

The Wild Baby's Dog (Lindgren) **20**:158

Wild Cat (Peck) **45**:105

The Wild Christmas Reindeer (Brett) **27**:43

Wild Foods: A Beginner's Guide to Identifying, Harvesting, and Cooking Safe and Tasty Plants from the Outdoors (Pringle) **4**:183

The Wild Horses (Bunting) **28**:44

The Wild Hunt (Yolen) **44**:206

The Wild Hunt of Hagworthy (Lively) **7**:153

The Wild Hunt of the Ghost Hounds (Lively) **7**:153

Wild in the World (Donovan) **3**:54

Wild Jack (Christopher) **2**:43

The Wild Little House (Dillon) **26**:21

Wild Pitch (Christopher) **33**:55

Wild Robin (Jeffers) **30**:131

The Wild Swans (Jeffers) **30**:135

The Wild Washerwomen: A New Folk Tale (Blake) **31**:22

The Wild Washerwomen: A New Folk Tale (Yeoman) **46**:179

The Wild White Stallion (Guillot) **22**:65

Wild Wild Sunflower Child Anna (Pinkney) **43**:161

Wild Wood (Needle) **43**:135

Wildcat under Glass (Zei) **6**:260

The Wildest Horse Race in the World (Henry) **4**:113

Wildfire (Clark) **30**:59

The Wildman (Crossley-Holland) **47**:34

The Wildman (Keeping) **34**:102

Wiley and the Hairy Man: Adapted from an American Folktale (Bang) **8**:19

Wilfred the Rat (Stevenson) **17**:153

Wilfred's Wolf (Nimmo) **44**:154

Wilfrid Gordon McDonald Partridge (Fox) **23**:114

Wilkin's Tooth (Jones) **23**:182

Will It Rain? (Keller) **45**:47

Will You Be My Friend (Iwasaki) **18**:154

Will You Be My Posslq? (Bunting) **28**:61

Will You Please Feed Our Cat? (Stevenson) **17**:167

Will You Sign Here, John Hancock? (Fritz) **14**:112

Will You Take Me to Town on Strawberry Day? (Singer) **48**:122

Willaby (Isadora) **7**:103

William and His Kitten (Flack) **28**:127

William and Mary: A Story (Farmer) **8**:85

William and the Good Old Days (Greenfield) **38**:95

William Crawford Gorgas: Tropic Fever Fighter (Epstein and Epstein) **26**:49

William in Love (Ure) **34**:190

William's Doll (Zolotow) **2**:239

Willie Bea and the Time the Martians Landed (Hamilton) **11**:90

Willie Blows a Mean Horn (Thomas) **8**:214

Willie's Adventures: Three Stories (Brown) **10**:63

Willie's Fire-Engine (Keeping) **34**:105

Willie's Not the Hugging Kind (Cummings) **48**:50

Willie's Walk to Grandmama (Brown) **10**:52

Will's Quill (Freeman) **30**:79

Willy and His Wheel Wagon (Gibbons) **8**:88

Willy Is My Brother (Parish) **22**:155

Willy Nilly (Gay) **27**:89

Willy Nilly: A Children's Story for Narrator and Orchestra (Flack) **28**:125

Willy the Champ (Browne) **19**:69

Willy the Wimp (Browne) **19**:68

Willy's Raiders (Gantos) **18**:142

Wilma Unlimited: How Wilma Rudolph Became the World's Fastest Woman (Krull) **44**:112

The Wind and Peter (Tresselt) **30**:202

The Wind between the Stars (Mahy) **7**:184

The Wind Blew (Hutchins) **20**:147

The Wind Eye (Westall) **13**:252

The Wind Has Wings: Poems from Canada (Cleaver) **13**:64

A Wind in the Door (L'Engle) **1**:132; **14**:149

The Wind in the Willows (Grahame) **5**:128

The Wind of Chance (Guillot) **22**:57

The Windmill at Magpie Creek (Mattingley) **24**:122

Window (Baker) **28**:22

Window on the Wind (Scott) **20**:199

Window Wishing (Caines) **24**:63

The Winds That Come from Far Away, and Other Poems (Minarik) **33**:126

The Windswept City: A Novel of the Trojan War (Treece) **2**:191

The Wing on a Flea: A Book about Shapes (Emberley) **5**:90

Wing T Fullback (Christopher) **33**:38

The Winged Colt of Casa Mia (Byars) **1**:37

Wingman (Pinkwater) **4**:163

Wingman on Ice (Christopher) **33**:40

Wings: A Tale of Two Chickens (Marshall) **21**:181

Wings for Icarus (Baumann) **35**:56

Wings for Per (d'Aulaire and d'Aulaire) **21**:48

Wings in the Woods (McClung) **11**:178

The Wings of a Falcon (Voigt) **48**:179

Winnie Mandela: Life of Struggle (Haskins) **39**:55

Winnie Mandela: The Soul of South Africa (Meltzer) **13**:151

Winnie-the-Pooh (Milne) **26**:126

Winning (Brancato) **32**:70

Winston Churchill: Lion of Britain (Epstein and Epstein) **26**:63

Winston, Newton, Elton, and Ed (Stevenson) **17**:155

Winter Cottage (Brink) **30**:16

Winter Holiday (Ransome) **8**:175

The Winter Noisy Book (Brown) **10**:56

The Winter of the Birds (Cresswell) **18**:107

Winter Story (Barklem) **31**:2

Winter Tales from Poland (Wojciechowska) **1**:200

Winter Whale (Ryder) **37**:98

The Winter Wren (Cole) **18**:82

Winterbound (Bianco) **19**:55

Winterkill (Paulsen) **19**:169

Winter's Coming (Bunting) **28**:46

Winter's Tales (Foreman) **32**:91

Winterthing (Aiken) **1**:8

Wintle's Wonders (Streatfeild) **17**:193

Wiplala (Schmidt) **22**:221

Wir Pfeifen auf den Gurkenkönig (Noestlinger) **12**:184

The Wise Fool (Galdone) **16**:93

The Wise Men on the Mountain (Dillon) **26**:29

A Wise Monkey Tale (Betsy and Giulio Maestro) **45**:65

The Wish Card Ran Out! (Stevenson) **17**:157

The Wish Workers (Aliki) **9**:17

The Wishing Pool (Leaf) **25**:134

The Wishing Star (St. John) **46**:98

Witch (Pike) **29**:174
Witch Baby (Block) **33**:31
The Witch Family (Estes) **2**:76
The Witch Herself (Naylor) **17**:54
The Witch in the Cherry Tree (Mahy) **7**:182
The Witch of Blackbird Pond (Speare) **8**:205
The Witch of Hissing Hill (Calhoun) **42**:9
Witch Water (Naylor) **17**:52
Witch Week (Jones) **23**:192
The Witch Who Lost Her Shadow (Calhoun) **42**:26
The Witch Who Wasn't (Yolen) **4**:256
Witchcraft, Mysticism, and Magic in the Black World (Haskins) **3**:69
Witchery Hill (Katz) **45**:32
Witches (Blumberg) **21**:25
The Witches (Dahl) **7**:83
The Witches and the Singing Mice: A Celtic Tale (Nimmo) **44**:150
Witches Four (Brown) **29**:6
The Witches of Worm (Snyder) **31**:159
The Witch-Finder (Rayner) **41**:120
The Witch's Brat (Sutcliff) **1**:191; **37**:162
Witch's Business (Jones) **23**:182
Witch's Business (Jones)
   See *Wilkin's Tooth*
The Witch's Daughter (Bawden) **2**:15
The Witch's Pig: A Cornish Folktale (Calhoun) **42**:23
Witch's Sister (Naylor) **17**:51
The Witch's Tears (Nimmo) **44**:155
Witcracks: Jokes and Jests from American Folklore (Schwartz) **3**:192
With Love, at Christmas (Fox) **23**:116
With You and Without You (Martin) **32**:201
Wizard Crystal (Pinkwater) **4**:162
The Wizard in the Tree (Alexander) **1**:18; **5**:23
The Wizard in the Woods (Ure) **34**:189
Wizard in Wonderland (Ure) **34**:192
The Wizard Islands (Yolen) **4**:260
A Wizard of Earthsea (Le Guin) **3**:124; **28**:144-88
The Wizard of Op (Emberley) **5**:99
The Wizard of Oz (Baum) **15**:42
The Wizard of Washington Square (Yolen) **4**:258
Wizard's Hall (Yolen) **44**:193
Wobble Pop (Burningham) **9**:51
Wobble, the Witch Cat (Calhoun) **42**:6
Woe Is Moe (Stanley) **46**:154
Wolf (Cross) **28**:96
Wolf by the Ears (Rinaldi) **46**:82
Wolf Rider: A Tale of Terror (Avi) **24**:12
Wolf Run: A Caribou Eskimo Tale (Houston) **3**:88
The Wolves of Aam (Curry) **31**:83
The Wolves of Willoughby Chase (Aiken) **1**:8
The Woman Who Loved Reindeer (Pierce) **20**:184
The Wonder City: A Picture Book of New York (Lenski) **26**:99
Wonder Kid Meets the Evil Lunch Snatcher (Duncan) **29**:79
Wonder Wheels (Hopkins) **44**:90
Wonder-Fish from the Sea (Tresselt) **30**:213
The Wonderful Adventures of Nils (Lagerlof) **7**:110
The Wonderful Dragon of Timlin (dePaola) **4**:53
The Wonderful Farm (Ayme) **25**:1
The Wonderful Flight to the Mushroom Planet (Cameron) **1**:42
Wonderful Story Book (Brown) **10**:56
The Wonderful Story of Henry Sugar and Six More (Dahl) **7**:75
The Wonderful Wizard of Oz (Baum) **15**:42
The Wonderful Wizard of Oz (Denslow) **15**:100
Wonders of Badgers (Lavine) **35**:169

Wonders of Camels (Lavine) **35**:159
Wonders of Coyotes (Lavine) **35**:168
Wonders of Donkeys (Lavine) **35**:158
Wonders of Draft Horses (Lavine) **35**:165
Wonders of Flightless Birds (Lavine) **35**:162
Wonders of Foxes (Lavine) **35**:170
Wonders of Giraffes (Lavine) **35**:170
Wonders of Goats (Lavine) **35**:160
Wonders of Herbs (Lavine) **35**:157
Wonders of Hippos (Lavine) **35**:166
Wonders of Hummingbirds (Simon) **39**:183
Wonders of Marsupials (Lavine) **35**:159
Wonders of Mice (Lavine) **35**:161
Wonders of Mules (Lavine) **35**:164
Wonders of Peacocks (Lavine) **35**:163
The Wonders of Physics: An Introduction to the Physical World (Adler) **27**:20
Wonders of Pigs (Lavine) **35**:162
Wonders of Ponies (Lavine) **35**:161
Wonders of Rhinos (Lavine) **35**:164
Wonders of Sheep (Lavine) **35**:165
Wonders of Speech (Silverstein and Silverstein) **25**:224
Wonders of Terrariums (Lavine) **35**:158
Wonders of the Ant Hill (Lavine) **35**:147
Wonders of the Aquarium (Lavine) **35**:146
Wonders of the Bat World (Lavine) **35**:151
Wonders of the Beetle World (Lavine) **35**:148
Wonders of the Bison World (Lavine) **35**:156
Wonders of the Butterfly World (Simon) **39**:183
Wonders of the Cactus World (Lavine) **35**:154
Wonders of the Eagle World (Lavine) **35**:154
Wonders of the Fly World (Lavine) **35**:151
Wonders of the Hawk World (Lavine) **35**:152
Wonders of the Hive (Lavine) **35**:147
Wonders of the Owl World (Lavine) **35**:152
Wonders of the Spider World (Lavine) **35**:150
Wonders of the World of Horses (Lavine) **35**:152
Wonders of Tigers (Lavine) **35**:172
Wonders of Turkeys (Lavine) **35**:167
Wonders of Woodchucks (Lavine) **35**:166
Won't Know Till I Get There (Myers) **16**:139
Won't Somebody Play with Me? (Kellogg) **6**:171
The Wood Street Group (Allan) **43**:18
The Wood Street Rivals (Allan) **43**:21
The Wood Street Secret (Allan) **43**:18
Wooden Ship (Adkins) **7**:23
Woodsedge and Other Tales (Bedard) **35**:59
A Word about Horses (Ottley) **16**:188
A Word from Our Sponsor: Or, My Friend Alfred (Gaberman) **33**:4
A Word or Two with You: New Rhymes for Young Readers (Merriam) **14**:201
Word to Caesar (Trease) **42**:183
Wordhoard: Anglo-Saxon Stories (Crossley-Holland) **47**:26
Wordhoard: Anglo-Saxon Stories (Walsh) **2**:201
Words by Heart (Sebestyen) **17**:86
Words from History (Asimov) **12**:43
Words from the Exodus (Asimov) **12**:37
Words from the Myths (Asimov) **12**:35
Words in Genesis (Asimov) **12**:36
Words of Science, and the History behind Them (Asimov) **12**:33
Words on the Map (Asimov) **12**:36
Workin' for Peanuts (Strasser) **11**:250
Working (Oxenbury) **22**:141
Working with Cardboard and Paper (Weiss) **4**:229
A World in a Drop of Water (Silverstein and Silverstein) **25**:201
The World in the Candy Egg (Tresselt) **30**:209
The World of Ben Lighthart (Haar) **15**:116

The World of Bionics (Silverstein and Silverstein) **25**:218
The World of Captain John Smith, 1580-1631 (Foster) **7**:98
The World of Christopher Robin (Milne) **1**:143
The World of Columbus and Sons (Foster) **7**:98
The World of Dance (Berger) **32**:22
World of Our Fathers: The Jews of Eastern Europe (Meltzer) **13**:133
A World of Poetry (Rosen) **45**:142
The World of Pooh (Milne) **1**:143
World of the Brain (Silverstein and Silverstein) **25**:210
The World of the Pharaohs (Baumann) **35**:43
The World of UFOs (Cohen) **43**:37
The World of William Penn (Foster) **7**:100
The World of Worms (Patent) **19**:153
World on a String: The Story of Kites (Yolen) **4**:258
World Problems (Gordon) **27**:90
World Song (Clark) **16**:81
World War Won (Pilkey) **48**:100
Worlds Apart (Murphy) **39**:174
The World's Best Karlson (Lindgren) **39**:159
World's End Was Home (Chauncy) **6**:89
The World's Greatest Freak Show (Raskin) **1**:157
The World's Most Famous Ghosts (Cohen) **43**:38
Worm Weather (Mattingley) **24**:123
The Worms of Kukumlina (Pinkwater) **4**:171
A Worm's Tale (Lindgren) **20**:158
Worse than Rotten, Ralph (Gantos) **18**:141
Worse than Willy! (Stevenson) **17**:161
The Worst Person in the World (Stevenson) **17**:154
The Worst Person in the World at Crab Beach (Stevenson) **17**:168
The Worst Witch (Murphy) **39**:168
The Worst Witch All at Sea (Murphy) **39**:179
The Worst Witch Strikes Again (Murphy) **39**:168
Would You Rather... (Burningham) **9**:49
Wouldn't You Like to Know (Rosen) **45**:129
The Wreck of the Zephyr (Van Allsburg) **13**:207
A Wrinkle in Time (L'Engle) **1**:133; **14**:142
The Writing Bug (Hopkins) **44**:98
The Writing on the Wall (Reid Banks) **24**:195
The Wrong Number (Stine) **37**:112
The Wuggie Norple Story (Pinkwater) **4**:170
Wulf (Crossley-Holland) **47**:47
The Wump World (Peet) **12**:200
Yang the Third and Her Impossible Family (Namioka) **48**:67
Yang the Youngest and His Terrible Ear (Namioka) **48**:65
The Yangtze River (Rau) **8**:186
The Year at Maple Hill Farm (Provensen and Provensen) **11**:213
The Year Mom Won the Pennant (Christopher) **33**:43
Year of Columbus, 1492 (Foster) **7**:99
Year of Independence, 1776 (Foster) **7**:99
A Year of Japanese Festivals (Epstein and Epstein) **26**:65
The Year of Jubilo (Sawyer) **36**:155
Year of Lincoln, 1861 (Foster) **7**:100
The Year of the Christmas Dragon (Sawyer) **36**:163
The Year of the Currawong (Spence) **26**:192
The Year of the Gopher (Naylor) **17**:61
The Year of the Horseless Carriage, 1801 (Foster) **7**:101
The Year of the Panda (Schlein) **41**:195
Year of the Pilgrims, 1620 (Foster) **7**:99
Year Walk (Clark) **16**:84

Yeck Eck (Ness) 6:208

Yeh-Shen: A Cinderella Story from China (Young) 27:219

Yellow and Pink (Steig) 15:198

The Yellow Auto Named Ferdinand (Janosch) 26:76

Yellow Bird and Me (Hansen) 21:151

Yellow Butter, Purple Jelly, Red Jam, Black Bread: Poems (Hoberman) 22:113

The Yellow Shop (Field) 21:75

The Yellow Umbrella (Drescher) 20:62

Yertle the Turtle and Other Stories (Geisel) 1:88

Yesterday's Island (Bunting) 28:49

Yobgorgle: Mystery Monster of Lake Ontario (Pinkwater) 4:170

Yossel Zissel and the Wisdom of Chelm (Schwartz) 25:193

You Bet Your Britches, Claude (Nixon) 24:154

You Can Pick Me Up at Peggy's Cove (Doyle) 22:30

You Can't Catch Me! (Rosen) 45:130

You Can't Make a Move without Your Muscles (Showers) 6:248

You Can't Pet a Possum (Bontemps) 6:79

You Have to Draw the Line Somewhere (Harris) 24:77

You Just Don't Listen! (McBratney) 44:124

You Know Who (Ciardi) 19:78

You Lucky Duck! (McCully) 46:62

You Never Can Tell (Conford) 10:100

You Never Knew Her as I Did! (Hunter) 25:87

You Read to Me, I'll Read to You (Ciardi) 19:77

You Tell Me (Rosen) 45:130

You Two (Ure) 34:176

You Win Some, You Lose Some (Ure) 34:176

You'll Soon Grow into Them, Titch (Hutchins) 20:152

The Young Ardizzone: An Autobiographical Fragment (Ardizzone) 3:8

Young Booker: Booker T. Washington's Early Days (Bontemps) 6:84

Young Faces in Fashion (Epstein and Epstein) 26:53

Young Ghosts (Cohen) 43:38

Young Jim: The Early Years of James Weldon Johnson (Tarry) 26:215

Young Joe (Ormerod) 20:179

Young Kangaroo (Brown) 10:65

The Young Landlords (Myers) 4:159

Young Man from the Piedmont: The Youth of Thomas Jefferson (Wibberley) 3:232

The Young Man of Cury and Other Poems (Causley) 30:44

Young Martin's Promise (Myers) 35:203

Young Paul Revere's Boston (Epstein and Epstein) 26:61

The Young Performing Horse (Yeoman) 46:178

A Young Person's Guide to Ballet (Streatfeild) 17:199

Young Poet's Primer (Brooks) 27:44-56

The Young Unicorns (L'Engle) 1:134

The Young United States: 1783 to 1830 (Tunis) 2:195

Your Body and How It Works (Lauber) 16:114

Your Body's Defenses (Knight) 38:116

Your Brain and How It Works (Zim) 2:232

Your First Garden Book (Brown) 29:7

Your Heart and How It Works (Zim) 2:233

Your Immune System (Nourse) 33:143

Your Insides (Cole) 40:31

Your Mother Was a Neanderthal (Smith) 47:206

Your Move, J.P.! (Lowry) 46:41

Your New Potty (Cole) 40:27

Your Skin and Mine (Showers) 6:242

Your Stomach and Digestive Tract (Zim) 2:233

You're the Scaredy-Cat (Mayer) 11:169

You're Thinking about Doughnuts (Rosen) 45:137

Yours Turly, Shirley (Martin) 32:204

The You-Two (Ure) 34:176

Yuck! (Stevenson) 17:162

Yum Yum (Ahlberg and Ahlberg) 18:9

Yum, Yum (Dorros) 42:66

Yummers (Marshall) 21:68

Yummers Too: The Second Course (Marshall) 21:181

Z for Zachariah (O'Brien) 2:129

Zamani Goes to Market (Feelings and Feelings) 5:105

Zampano's Performing Bear (Janosch) 26:77

Zaza's Big Break (McCully) 46:64

The Zebra Wall (Henkes) 23:129

Zebra's Hiccups (McKee) 38:180

Zebulon Pike, Soldier and Explorer (Wibberley) 3:233

Zed (Harris) 30:122

Zed and the Monsters (Parish) 22:164

Zeee (Enright) 4:77

Zeely (Hamilton) 1:106

Zella, Zack, and Zodiac (Peet) 12:208

Zeralda's Ogre (Ungerer) 3:204

Zesty (McBratney) 44:120

Zia (O'Dell) 16:171

Zlateh the Goat and Other Stories (Singer) 1:177

Zoo Doings: Animal Poems (Prelutsky) 13:171

A Zoo for Mister Muster (Lobel) 5:163

The Zoo in My Garden (Nakatani) 30:159

Zoom at Sea (Wynne-Jones) 21:229

Zoom Away (Wynne-Jones) 21:229

Zozo (Rey) 5:193

Zozo Flies a Kite (Rey and Rey) 5:198

Zozo Gets a Medal (Rey) 5:198

Zozo Goes to the Hospital (Rey and Rey) 5:199

Zozo Learns the Alphabet (Rey) 5:199

Zozo Rides a Bike (Rey) 5:196

Zozo Takes a Job (Rey) 5:196

The Zucchini Warriors (Korman) 25:111

ISBN 0-7876-2025-4

90000